W9-BVJ-086

THEORIES OF PSYCHOTHERAPY & COUNSELING
Concepts and Cases

Second Edition

Richard S. Sharf

University of Delaware

Australia • Canada • Denmark • Japan • Mexico • New Zealand • Philippines
Puerto Rico • Singapore • South Africa • Spain • United Kingdom • United States

Publisher: *Craig Barth*
Counseling Editor: *Eileen Murphy*
Assistant Editor: *Julie Martinez*
Editorial Assistant: *Annie Berterretche*
Marketing Manager: *Jennie Burger*
Project Editor: *John Walker*
Print Buyer: *Karen Hunt*
Permissions Editor: *Lillian Campobasso*
Production Service: *Graphic World Publishing Services*

Cover Designer: *John Walker*
Cover Image: *The Langlois Bridge, Vincent van Gogh. Wood River Gallery/PNI*
Cover Printer: *R.R. Donnelley & Sons*
Signing Representative: *Ron Shelly*
Compositor: *Graphic World, Inc.*
Printer/Binder: *R.R. Donnelley & Sons*

This book is printed on acid-free recycled paper.

For more information, contact
Wadsworth/Thomson Learning
10 Davis Drive
Belmont, CA 94002-3098
USA
www.wadsworth.com

International Headquarters
Thomson Learning
290 Harbor Drive, 2nd Floor
Stamford, CT 06902-7477
USA

UK/Europe/Middle East
Thomson Learning
Berkshire House
168-173 High Holborn
London WC1V 7AA
United Kingdom

Asia
Thomson Learning
60 Albert Street #15-01
Albert Complex
Singapore 189969

Canada
Nelson/Thomson Learning
1120 Birchmount Road
Scarborough, Ontario M1K 5G4
Canada

Library of Congress Cataloging-in-Publication Data
Sharf, Richard S.
    Theories of psychotherapy and counseling : concepts and cases / Richard S. Sharf.—2nd ed.
        p. cm.
    Includes bibliographical references and indexes.
    ISBN 0-534-36485-3
    1. Psychotherapy. 2. Counseling 3. Psychotherapy Case studies.
4. Counseling Case studies.   I. Title.
RC480.S355   1999
616.89'14—dc21   99-23686

For Jane, Jennie, and Alex

123459

Brief Contents

Contents

2   Psychoanalysis: Drive, Ego, Object Relations, and Self Psychology   25

3 *Jungian Analysis and Therapy   86*

6 *Person-Centered Therapy   211*

7 *Gestalt Therapy   245*

8 *Behavior Therapy*   *287*

9 Rational Emotive Behavior Therapy   332

10 *Cognitive Therapy*   *371*

11 *Reality Therapy*   *416*

12 *Feminist Therapy*   454

13 Family Systems Therapy   499

14 *Other Psychotherapies*   *554*

Preface

I am pleased to offer a second edition of this text that explains psychotherapy and counseling theories and illustrates each using several case examples.

Learning how to help people with psychological problems has been a challenge for thousands of mental health professionals for almost 100 years. I present significant theories that provide a systematic approach to the helping professions. Although I am responsible for writing this book, the chapters represent the expertise of over 50 experts in a wide variety of theoretical approaches to psychotherapy and counseling. This is in essence a book with input by many experts on specific theories who have provided suggestions for inclusion of specific content as well as reading chapters at various stages of development of this book. However, I am responsible for the organization and presentation of these theories.

To provide a comprehensive overview of theories of psychotherapy and counseling, I have presented an explanation of concepts, as well as examples of their application by using case summaries and therapist-client dialogue to illustrate techniques and treatment. I believe that the blending of concepts and examples makes psychotherapy and counseling clearer and more real for the student wanting to learn about the therapeutic process. For each theory, I have shown how it can be applied to individual therapy or counseling for common psychological disorders, such as depression and generalized anxiety disorders. Because many therapists work with couples, families, and groups, I have also shown how each theory can be applied to these modes of treatment.

Although I have placed theories in the general chronological order in which they were developed, I have written the chapters so that they may be read in almost any order, with some exceptions. The chapter on Jungian analysis should follow the chapter on psychoanalysis because of the close relationship between the development of the two theories. Also, Chapter 12, Feminist Therapy, and Chapter 13, Family Systems Therapy, should follow other chapters on major theories because they make use of knowledge about these theories.

Chapter 2, Psychoanalysis: Drive, Ego, Object Relations, and Self Psychology, is the longest and most difficult chapter. To present the modern-day practice of psychoanalysis, it is necessary to explain contributions to psychoanalysis that have taken place since Freud's death, including important ideas of Winnicott, Kohut, and intersubjectivity theory. Instructors may wish to allow more time for reading this chapter than others and may find it helpful to assign this chapter after students have read a few other chapters, especially if members of the class have little familiarity with personality theory.

Flexibility is incorporated into this text so that instructors do not need to assign all chapters. Comparison and critique of theories is provided in Chapter 15, making it easier for each chapter to stand alone. Another reason for critiquing each theory in the last chapter is so that students can learn and understand each theory before criticizing it. Also, because knowledge of theories serves as a basis for making judgments about other theories, it is helpful to have an overview of theories of psychotherapy before describing each theory's strengths and limitations. Knowledge of several theories is important to the understanding of integrative theories, such as Lazarus's multimodal approach, which is discussed in Chapter 15.

For the major theories presented in the text, basic information about background, personality theory, and theory of psychotherapy provides a means for understanding the application of psychotherapy theory. Understanding the personal life and philosophical influences of a theorist helps to explain how the theorist views human behavior. Knowing a theorist's view of personality provides insight into the theorist's approach to changes in behavior, thoughts, or feelings—his or her theory of psychotherapy.

In presenting theories of psychotherapy, I have discussed goals, assessment, therapeutic relationships, and techniques. Goals show the aspects of human behavior that theorists see as most important. Assessment includes inventories and interviewing approaches as they relate to the theorists' goals. The therapeutic relationship provides the context for the techniques of change, which are illustrated through examples of therapy.

I have also included information on topics relevant to theories of psychotherapy. Research on the effectiveness of each theory of psychotherapy, as well as evidence for significant concepts, is discussed in each chapter. An important issue in the practice of psychotherapy is treatment length, which is described for each theory, as it relates to different methods and psychological disorders. I also discuss current issues that each theory is facing, as well as ways in which each theory can be incorporated into or make use of ideas from other theories.

Cultural and gender differences are issues that theories approach differently. An understanding of clients' background is of varying importance to theorists yet is of profound significance in actual psychotherapy. Each chapter addresses these issues, and Chapter 12, Feminist Therapy, focuses on them in considerable detail, so that the student can learn about the interaction of cultural and gender influences and methods of therapeutic change.

Each area of application is presented in a self-contained manner, allowing instructors to emphasize some and deemphasize others. For example, instructors could choose not to assign the research or couples counseling sections to suit their teaching purposes. However, I have included application topics that I feel are most relevant for teaching theories of psychotherapy and counseling.

I have written an instructor's manual that includes multiple-choice and essay questions. Also, I have provided suggestions for topics for discussion. An alphabetical glossary is included in the textbook.

NEW TO THE SECOND EDITION

Several changes and additions have been made that can be found in most chapters. Over 300 new references, most quite recent, have been added. Many of these references are new research studies added to the research sections. Two new topics are addressed in the Current Trends or other sections. The use of treatment manuals to further specify the theoretical approach of several theories is presented to the student. A very different trend, that of constructivism and postmodernism, has had an impact on many theories. These terms are described in the first chapter and then illustrated as they apply to specific theories in the Current Trends sections of each chapter. Other new information is also presented in this section. Additionally, new case material replaces older cases to provide the student with interesting brief examples of therapy as they relate to common psychological disorders. Specific changes have been made within each chapter.

- Chapter 2: Psychoanalysis. The brief core conflictual theme psychotherapy of Luborsky and his colleagues replaces Mann's time-limited psychotherapy. Information about intersubjectivity theory shows students how some psychoanalysts have changed the way they view the patient-therapist relationship.
- Chapter 5: Existential Therapy. New information on a brief approach to existential therapy is described. Several new perspectives on existential couples counseling are illustrated.
- Chapter 6: Person-Centered Therapy. A person-centered approach to grief and loss is illustrated with the case of a 7-year-old boy. New trends in the training of person-centered therapists show the consistency of the approach of person-centered therapists to both students and clients.
- Chapter 7: Gestalt Therapy. Gestalt therapists increasingly have been concerned with the client-therapist relationship as reflected in the changes in this chapter.
- Chapter 8: Behavior Therapy. Seen in this chapter is the continued productiveness of behavior therapists in research. The section on Eye Movement Desensitization has been expanded due to the current interest in the topic.
- Chapter 10: Cognitive Therapy. More diagrams help make this chapter clearer for the student.
- Chapter 11: Reality Therapy. Glasser uses choice theory rather than control theory as an explanation of reality theory. This is a change in emphasis rather than substance.
- Chapter 12: Feminist Therapy. A multicultural approach provides a context for feminist therapy.
- Chapter 13: Family Systems Therapy. Two social constructionist therapies (solution-focused and narrative) have been given full descriptions. The role of medicine in family therapy is also explained.
- Chapter 14: Other Psychotherapies. Klerman's interpersonal psychotherapy, a good example of a therapy developed as the result of research, replaces the section on hypnosis.

STUDENT MANUAL

This text provides a thorough overview of theories of therapy and counseling. To make this material as interesting as possible for students and to help them learn it, I have written a student manual. Case examples with multiple-choice questions put students in the role of a therapist using the particular theory under discussion.

Chapters of the student manual start with a preinventory to help students compare their views of therapy to the theory. The history of the theory is presented in outline form so that students can summarize the most important influences on the theory or theorist. Significant terms used in the theory of personality and the theory of psychotherapy sections are defined. A portion of a case is presented along with multiple-choice questions on assessment, goals, and techniques. Questions and information are also presented for other sections in the text. Each chapter concludes with a 25-item quiz about the theory.

ACKNOWLEDGMENTS

In writing this book, I have received help from over 50 people in various aspects of the review and preparation for both editions of this book. I would like to thank Emery Cummins, San Diego State University; Christopher Faiver, John Carroll University; and David Lane, Mercer University, who reviewed the entire manuscript and made useful suggestions for both editions of the book. I would also like to thank Ruthellen Josselson, Towson State University, and Sara Miller, University of Delaware, for reviewing the first edition and Ellyn Kaschak, San Jose State University; David Dillon, Trinity International University; Beverly B. Palmer, California State University–Dominquez Hills; and James R. Mahalik, Boston College, who reviewed the entire second edition. I am also very appreciative of those individuals who provided suggestions for chapter contents, reviewed the chapter, or did both, for the first and/or second editions of this textbook.

Constructivism: Robert Neimeyer, University of Memphis.

Chapter 1: Introduction. E. N. Simons, University of Delaware.

Chapter 2: Psychoanalysis. Cynthia Allen, private practice; Ann Byrnes, State University of New York at Stony Brook; Lawrence Hedges, private practice; Jonathan Lewis, University of Delaware; Steven Robbins, Virginia Commonwealth University; Judith Mishne, New York University.

Chapter 3: Jungian Analysis and Therapy. Amelio D'Onofrio, Fordham University; Anne Harris, California School of Professional Psychology; Stephen Martin, private practice; Seth Rubin, private practice.

Chapter 4: Adlerian Therapy. Michael Maniacci and Harold Mosak, Adler School of Professional Psychology.

Chapter 5: Existential Therapy. Stephen Golston, Arizona State University; William Gould, University of Dubuque; Emmy van Deurzen, Regent's College.

Chapter 6: Person-Centered Therapy. Douglas Bower, private practice; Jerold Bozarth, University of Georgia; David Cain, private practice.

Chapter 7: Gestalt Therapy. Stephen Golston, Arizona State University; Rich Hycner, Institute for Dialogical Psychotherapy; Joseph Wysong, Editor, *Gestalt Journal*; Gary Yontef, private practice.

Chapter 8: Behavior Therapy. Alan Kazdin, Yale University; Michael Spiegler, Providence College.

Chapter 9: Rational Emotive Behavior Therapy. Albert Ellis, Director, Albert Ellis Institute for Rational Emotive Behavior Therapy.

Chapter 10: Cognitive Therapy. Aaron and Judith Beck, Beck Institute; Denise Davis, Vanderbilt University Medical Center; Bruce Liese, University of Kansas Medical Center.

Chapter 11: Reality Therapy. Laurence Litwack, Northeastern University; Robert Wubbolding, Center for Reality Therapy.

Chapter 12: Feminist Therapy. Amy Alfred and Cyndy Boyd, University of Delaware; Carolyn Enns, Cornell College; Ellyn Kaschak, San Jose State University; Pam Remer, University of Kentucky.

Chapter 13: Family Systems Therapy. Dorothy Becvar, private practice; Herbert Goldenberg, California State University.

Chapter 14: Other Psychotherapies. Charles Beale, University of Delaware; Ron Hays, Hahnemann University; David K. Reynolds, Constructive Living; Edward W. L. Smith, Georgia Southern University.

Chapter 15: Comparison, Critique, and Integration. Arnold Lazarus, Rutgers University.

I additionally want to thank Lisa Sweder, who typed the manuscript. Her patience and helpfulness is very much appreciated. Cynthia Carroll, Elizabeth Parisan, and Gwen RoBison also provided further secretarial support and help. Throughout the process of writing this book, I have been fortunate to have the support of John B. Bishop, Assistant Vice President for Student Life, University of Delaware. Finally, I wish to thank my family, Jane, Jennie, and Alex, to whom this book is dedicated.

Richard S. Sharf

1

Introduction

Helping another person in distress can be one of the most ennobling human activities. The theories that are represented in this book all have in common their desire to help others with psychological problems. Through research and the practice of psychotherapy with patients and clients, many different approaches have been developed to alleviate personal misery. In this book, I describe major theories of psychotherapy, their background or history, theories of personality from which they are derived, and applications to practice. To help the reader understand the practice of psychotherapy and counseling, I give many examples of how theories are used with a variety of clients and patients. An overview of the theories and the many ways that they can be applied is also described in this chapter. Before doing so, however, I define the words that make up the title of this book: *theory, psychotherapy* and *counseling*.

THEORY

To understand theories of psychotherapy and counseling, which are based on theories of individual personality, it is helpful to understand the role and purpose of theory in science and, more specifically, in psychology. Particularly important in the development of physical and biological science, theory has also been of great value in psychology. Briefly, theory can be described as "a group of logically organized laws or relationships that constitute explanation in a discipline" (Heinen, 1985, p. 414). Included in a theory are assumptions related to the topic of the theory and definitions that can relate assumptions to observations (Earman, 1992; Hall, Lindzey, & Campbell, 1998). In this section, criteria by which theories of psychotherapy can be evaluated are briefly described (Fawcett & Downs, 1986; Marx, 1951; Snow, 1973).

Precision and Clarity

Theories are based on rules that need to be clear. The terms used to describe these rules must also be specific. For example, the psychoanalytic term *ego* should have a definition on which practitioners and researchers can agree. If possible, theories should use

1

operational definitions, which specify operations or procedures that are used to measure a variable. However, operational definitions for a concept such as ego can be difficult to reach agreement on, and definitions may provide a meaning that is more restricted than desired. A common definition of the Freudian concept *ego,* "the reality aspect of personality, also mediates the demands of other aspects of personality (id and super-ego)" (Liebert & Liebert, 1998, p. 522), may be clear to some but not provide a definition that is sufficiently specific to be used for research purposes. Along with clear concepts and rules, a theory should be parsimonious or as straightforward as possible. Constructs, such as id, ego, and superego (terms to be described in Chapter 2, "Psychoanalysis"), must be related to each other and should be related to rules of human behavior. Theories should explain an area of study (personality or psychotherapy) with as few assumptions as possible.

Comprehensiveness

Theories differ in events that they attempt to predict. In general, the more comprehensive a theory, the more widely it can be applied, but also the more vulnerable it may be to error. For example, all of the theories of psychotherapy and counseling in this book are comprehensive in that they are directed to men and women without specifying age or cultural background. A theory of psychotherapy directed only at helping men change their psychological functioning would be limited in its comprehensiveness.

Testability

To be of use, a theory must be tested and confirmed. With regard to theories of psychotherapy, not only must experience show that a theory is valid or effective but also research must show that it is effective in bringing about change in individual behavior. When concepts can be clearly defined, hypotheses (predictions derived from theories) can be stated precisely and tested. Sometimes, when hypotheses or the entire theory cannot be confirmed, this failure can lead to development of other hypotheses.

Usefulness

Not only should a good theory lead to new hypotheses that can be tested but also it should be helpful to practitioners in their work. For psychotherapy and counseling, a good theory suggests ways to understand clients and techniques to help them function better. Without theory, the practitioner would be left to unsystematic techniques or to "reinventing the wheel" by trying new techniques on new patients until something seemed to help. When theories are used, proven concepts and techniques can be organized in ways to help individuals improve their lives.

Neither theories of personality nor theories of psychotherapy and counseling meet all of these criteria. The theories in this book are not described in a formal way but rather in a way to help one understand changes in behavior, thoughts, and feelings. Even the term *theory* is used loosely, as human behavior is far too complex to have clearly articulated theories, such as those found in physics. Each chapter includes examples of research or systematic investigations that relate to a specific theory of personality and/or theory of psychotherapy and counseling. The type of research presented depends on the precision, explicitness, clarity, comprehensiveness, and testability of the theory.

PSYCHOTHERAPY AND COUNSELING

Defining *psychotherapy* and *counseling* is quite difficult, as there is little agreement on definitions and on whether there is any difference between the two. The brief definition given here covers both psychotherapy and counseling.

> Psychotherapy and counseling are interactions between a therapist/counselor and one or more clients/patients. The purpose is to help the patient/client with problems that may have aspects that are related to disorders of thinking, emotional suffering, or problems of behavior. Therapists may use their knowledge of theory of personality and psychotherapy or counseling to help the patient/client improve functioning. The therapist's approach to helping must be legally and ethically approved.

Although this definition can be criticized because not all theories or techniques would be included, it should suffice to provide an overview of the main components in helping individuals with psychological problems.

There have been many attempts to differentiate psychotherapy from counseling. Some writers have suggested that counseling is used with normal individuals and psychotherapy with those who are severely disturbed (Tyler, 1958). The problem with this distinction is that it is difficult to differentiate severity of disturbance, and often practitioners use the same set of techniques for clients of varying severity levels. Another distinction is that counseling is educational in nature, and psychotherapy is personal in nature. Differentiation between educational, vocational, and personal counseling is not clear; furthermore, many counselors (pastoral, school, and mental health) work with personal problems. Another attempt at separating counseling and psychotherapy suggests that psychotherapists work in hospitals, whereas counselors work in situations such as schools or guidance clinics. Because the overlap of patient problems is great regardless of work setting, such a distinction is not helpful. As Patterson (1986) notes, there are no strong differences between psychotherapy and counseling as to process, techniques, goals, or clients. Gelso and Fretz (1992) describe a continuum from relatively brief work that is situational or educational on one end (counseling) and long-term, in-depth, and seeking to reconstruct personality on the other end (psychotherapy). In between these extremes, counseling and psychotherapy overlap. In this book, the terms *counseling* and *psychotherapy* are used interchangeably, except where they have special meanings as defined by the theorist.

Traditionally, the term *psychotherapy* has been associated with psychiatrists and medical settings, whereas the term *counseling* has been associated with educational and, to some extent, social work settings. Although there is much overlap, theories developed by psychiatrists often use the word *psychotherapy*, or in its briefer form, *therapy*, more frequently than they do *counseling*. In the chapters in this book, I tend to use the term that is used most frequently by practitioners of that theory. In a few theoretical approaches (Adlerian and feminist), some distinctions are made between psychotherapy and counseling, and I describe them. Two theories, psychoanalysis and Jungian analysis, employ the term *analyst,* and in those two chapters I explain the role of analyst as it differs from that of the psychotherapist or counselor.

A related issue is that of the terms *patient* and *client. Patient* is used most often in a medical setting, with *client* applied more frequently to educational and social service settings. In this book, the two terms are used interchangeably, both referring to the recipient of psychotherapy or counseling.

THEORIES OF PSYCHOTHERAPY AND COUNSELING

How many theories of psychotherapy are there? Before the 1950s there were relatively few, and most were derived from Freud's theory of psychoanalysis. Since that time there has been a marked increase in the number of theories that therapists have developed to help people with psychological dysfunctions. Corsini (1981) lists 241 different systems of psychotherapy and describes 65; now there may be over 400 (Corsini & Wedding, 1995). Although most of these theories have relatively few proponents and little research to support their effectiveness, they do represent the creativity of psychotherapists in finding ways to alleviate individual psychological discomfort.

At the same time that there has been a proliferation in the development of theoretical approaches, there has been a move toward integrating theories, as well as a move toward eclecticism. Broadly, eclecticism refers to the use of techniques and/or concepts from two or more theories. In a review of seven studies reporting the percentage of therapists who identify themselves as eclectics, Garfield and Bergin (1994) found that between 29 and 68% of psychiatrists, clinical or counseling psychologists, social workers, and marriage and family therapists identified themselves as eclectics. In each of these studies, more therapists identified themselves as eclectics than with any single theory of psychotherapy.

Several researchers have asked therapists about their theoretical orientations (Table 1.1). For example, Prochaska and Norcross (1999) combined two studies published in 1986 and 1988 in which a total of 818 psychologists, counselors, psychiatrists, and social workers were asked to identify their primary theoretical orientations with a study of clinical psychologists (Norcross, Karg & Prochaska, 1997; Norcross, Strausser, & Missar, 1988). Their findings are summarized here, listing major theoretical orientations and the percentage of all therapists identifying with a specific orientation. Clearly, those therapists identifying themselves as eclectic exceed the number identifying with a specific theoretical orientation. Also, there is great variation of preference depending on the category of mental health professional.

Psychoanalytic theories (those closely related to the work of Freud and his contemporaries) and dynamic theories (those having some resemblance to psychoanalytic theories) continue to be the most popular single theoretical orientation subscribed to by therapists from a variety of fields. Jensen et al. (1990) found that psychodynamic theories were particularly popular with psychiatrists and social workers, a finding also supported by Prochaska and Norcross (1999). There is some disagreement among studies of therapist preference for theory, due in part to ways in which questions are asked and to changing trends in theoretical preference, with

TABLE 1.1

Primary Theoretical Orientations of American Psychotherapists

Orientation	Clinical Psychologists	Counseling Psychologists	Psychiatrists	Social Workers	Counselors
Adlerian	1%	2%	1%	1%	2%
Behavioral	13%	8%	1%	4%	6%
Cognitive	24%	11%	1%	4%	10%
Eclectic/ Integrative	27%	40%	53%	34%	37%
Existential/ Humanistic	3%	6%	1%	3%	13%
Gestalt	1%	2%	1%	1%	2%
Interpersonal	5%	2%	3%	1%	1%
Psychanalytic/ Psychodynamic	18%	12%	35%	33%	11%
Rogerian/ Person-Centered	1%	8%	0%	2%	8%
Systems	4%	5%	1%	13%	7%
Other	3%	4%	3%	4%	3%

SOURCE: From *Systems of Psychotherapy, fourth edition,* by J. O. Prochaska and J. C. Norcross. Copyright © 1999. Reprinted with permission of Wadsworth Publishing, a division of International Thompson Publishing. Fax 800 730-2215.

specific mental health professions showing some movement toward cognitive and behavioral approaches.

Because eclectic or integrative approaches are so popular, it is helpful to ask eclectic psychotherapists about the various orientations they use. In a study of 423 clinical psychologists, marriage and family therapists, social workers, and psychiatrists, Jensen, Bergin, and Greaves (1990) found that 68% identified themselves as eclectics. When these practitioners were asked to identify the theories that made up their approach, therapists listed an average of 4.4 theories. The percentage for each theory that appeared on the lists of the 283 eclectic therapists is reported here.

Adlerian	12%
Behavioral	49%
Cognitive	54%
Communications	32%
Dynamic	72%
Existential	26%
Gestalt	23%
Humanistic	42%
Religious/transpersonal	17%
Rogerian/person-centered	23%
Sullivanian	16%
Systems (family systems)	48%

In selecting the major theories to be presented in this book, I have used several criteria. I have consulted surveys such as those summarized here to see which are being used most frequently. Also, I have included theories that have demonstrated that they have a following of interested practitioners by having an organization, one or more journals, national or international meetings, and a developing literature of books, articles, and chapters. Additionally, I have consulted with many therapists and professors to determine which theories appear to be most influential. Ultimately, I tried to decide which theories would be most important for those wishing to become psychotherapists or to learn more about psychotherapy.

The remaining 14 chapters in this book discuss 27 different theoretical approaches. Some theories, such as psychoanalysis, have subtheories that have been derived from the original theory. I have also kept in mind that there is a strong movement toward the integration of theories (using concepts or techniques of more than one theory) and that including a number of significant theories provides a background from which students can develop or select their own theoretical approach. The following paragraphs present a brief, nontechnical summary of the chapters (and theories) in this book to give an overview of the many different and creative methods for helping individuals who are suffering because of psychological problems or difficulties.

Psychoanalysis: Drive, Ego, Object Relations, and Self Psychology

Sigmund Freud stressed the importance of inborn drives (particularly sexual) in determining later personality development. Others who followed him emphasized the importance of the adaptation to the environment, early relationships between child and mother, and developmental changes in being absorbed with oneself at the expense of meaningful relationships with others. All of these views of development make use of Freud's concepts of unconscious processes (portions of mental functioning that we are not aware of) and, in general, his structure of personality (ego, id, superego). Traditional psychoanalytic methods require several years of treatment. Because of this, moderate length and brief therapy methods that use more direct, rather than indirect, techniques have been developed. New writings continue to explore the importance of childhood development on later personality as well as the use of new techniques in brief therapy.

Jungian Analysis and Therapy

More than any other theorist, Jung placed great emphasis on the role of unconscious processes in human behavior. Jungians are particularly interested in dreams, fantasies, and other material that reflects unconscious processes. They are also interested in symbols of universal patterns that are reflected in the unconscious processes of all people. Therapy focuses on the analysis of unconscious processes so that patients can better integrate unconscious processes into conscious awareness.

Adlerian Therapy

Alfred Adler believed that the personality of individuals was formed in their early years as a result of relationships within the family. He emphasized the importance of individuals' contributions to their community and to society. Adlerians are interested in the ways that individuals approach living and family relationships. The Adlerian approach to therapy is practical, helping individuals to change dysfunctional beliefs and encouraging them to take new steps to change their lives. An emphasis on teaching and educating individuals and families about dealing with interpersonal problems is another characteristic of Adlerian therapy.

Existential Therapy

A philosophical approach to people and problems relating to being human or existing, existential psychotherapy deals with life themes rather than techniques. Such themes include living and dying, freedom, responsibility to self and others, finding meaning in life, and dealing with a sense of meaninglessness. Becoming aware of oneself and developing the ability to look beyond immediate problems and daily events to deal with existential themes are goals of therapy, along with developing honest and intimate relationships with others. Although some techniques have been developed, the emphasis is on issues and themes, not method.

Person-Centered Therapy

In his therapeutic work, Carl Rogers emphasized understanding and caring for the client, as opposed to diagnosis, advice, or persuasion. Characteristic of Rogers's approach to therapy are therapeutic genuineness, through verbal and nonverbal behavior, and unconditionally accepting clients for who they are. Person-centered therapists are concerned about understanding the client's experience and communicating their understanding to the client so that an atmosphere of trust can be developed that fosters change on the part of the client. Clients are given responsibility for making positive changes in their lives.

Gestalt Therapy

Developed by Fritz Perls, Gestalt therapy helps the individual to become more aware of self and others. Emphasis is on both bodily and psychological awareness. Therapeutic approaches deal with being responsible for oneself and attuned to one's language, nonverbal behaviors, emotional feelings, and conflicts within oneself and with others. Therapeutic techniques include the development of creative experiments and exercises to facilitate self-awareness.

Behavior Therapy

Based on scientific principles of behavior, such as classical and operant conditioning, as well as observational learning, behavior therapy applies principles of learning such as reinforcement, extinction, shaping of behavior, and modeling to help a wide variety of clients with different problems. Emphasis is on precision and detail in evaluating psychological concerns and then assigning treatment methods that may include relaxation, exposure to a feared object, copying a behavior, or role-playing. Its many techniques include those that change observable behavior as well as those that deal with thought processes.

Rational Emotive Behavior Therapy

Developed by Albert Ellis, rational emotive behavior therapy (REBT) focuses on irrational beliefs that individuals develop that lead to problems related to emotions (for example, fears and anxieties) and to behaviors (such as avoiding social interactions or giving speeches). Although REBT uses a wide variety of techniques, the most common method is to dispute irrational beliefs and to teach clients to challenge their own irrational beliefs so that they can reduce anxiety and develop a full range of ways to interact with others.

Cognitive Therapy

Belief systems and thinking are seen as important in determining and affecting behavior and feelings. Aaron Beck developed an approach that helps individuals understand their own maladaptive thinking and how it may affect their feelings and actions. Cognitive therapists use a structured method to help their clients understand their own belief systems. By asking clients to record dysfunctional thoughts and using questionnaires to determine maladaptive thinking, cognitive therapists are then able to make use of a wide variety of techniques to change beliefs that interfere with successful functioning. They also make use of affective and behavioral strategies.

Reality Therapy

Reality therapists assume that individuals are responsible for their own lives and for taking control over what they do, feel, and think. Developed by William Glasser, reality therapy uses a specific process to change behavior. A relationship is developed with clients so that they will commit to the therapeutic process. Emphasis is on changing behaviors that will lead to modifications in thinking and feeling. Making plans and sticking to them to bring about change while taking responsibility for oneself are important aspects of reality therapy.

Feminist Therapy

Rather than focusing only on the individual's psychological problems, feminist therapists emphasize the role of society in creating problems for individuals. Particularly, they are concerned about gender roles and power differences between men and women from diverse cultural backgrounds. They have examined different ways that men and women develop throughout the life span (including social and sexual development, child-raising practices, and work roles). Differences in moral decision making, relating to others, and roles in abuse and violence are issues of feminist therapists. By combining feminist therapy with other theories, feminist therapists take a sociological as well as a psychological view that focuses not only on gender but also on multicultural issues. Among the techniques they use are those that help individuals address gender and power inequalities not only by changing client behavior but also by changing societal groups or institutions.

Family Systems Therapy

Whereas other theories focus on the problems of individuals, family systems therapists attend to interactions between family members and view the entire family as a single unit or system. Treatment is designed to bring about change in the functioning and relationships within the family rather than within a single individual. Several different approaches to family systems therapy have been developed. Some focus on the impact of the parents' own families, others on how family members relate to each other in the therapy hour, and yet others on changing symptoms. Some family systems therapists request that all the family members be available for therapy, whereas others may deal with parents or certain members only.

Other Psychotherapies

Five different psychotherapies are treated briefly in this chapter. *Asian therapies* often emphasize quiet reflection and personal responsibility to others. *Body therapies* work with the interaction between psychological and physiological functioning. *Interpersonal therapy* is a very specific treatment for depression based on a review of research. *Psychodrama* is an active system in which clients, along with group and audience members, play out roles related to their problems while therapists take responsibility for directing the activities. *Creative arts therapies* include art, dance movement, drama, and music to encourage expressive action and therapeutic change. Any of these therapies may be used with other therapeutic approaches.

Although each theory is treated as a distinct approach, different from others, this presentation disguises the movement toward integration that is found in many, but not all, theories. I have tried to emphasize the concepts and techniques that are associated with each theory. When a theory borrows from other theories, such as when cognitive therapy borrows from behavior therapy, I have tended to focus mainly on the techniques that are associated with the original theory. In Chapter 15, "Comparison, Critique, and Integration," I describe different approaches for integrating theories of psychotherapy in actual practice. In each chapter, I explain important concepts and techniques that characterize a theory as well as ways to apply the theory to a variety of psychological problems, issues, and situations.

ORGANIZATION OF THE CHAPTERS

For all of the remaining chapters except the last three, I follow the same organizational format. The first two sections, on history and personality theory, provide a background for the major section that describes that theory of psychotherapy, in which goals, assessment methods, and techniques are described. Sections that follow describe a variety of areas of application. Case examples are used to show the many ways that theories can be applied. Additionally, important issues such as brief psychotherapy, current trends, using a theory with other theories, and research into the theory are explained. Also, application to couples, families, and group therapy is given, along with information about how the theory deals with gender and cultural issues.

History or Background

To understand a theory of helping others, it is useful to know how the theory developed and which factors were significant in its development. Often the discussion of background focuses on the theorist's life and philosophy, as well as literature and other intellectual forces that contributed to the theorist's ideas about helping others with psychological problems. For example, Freud's ideas about the Oedipus complex (sexual attraction for the opposite-sex parent and hostility toward the same-sex parent) derive, in a limited way, from Freud's reflections on his own childhood and his intellectual pursuits. However, Freud's work with patients was the most important factor in developing the Oedipus complex. Theorists have grown up in different countries, eras, and family backgrounds. All of these factors, as well as theorists' exposure to prominent philosophers, physicians, psychiatrists, or psychologists in their early professional development, have an impact on their theories of psychotherapy.

Personality Theories

Each theory of psychotherapy is based on a theory of personality, or how theorists understand human behavior. Personality theories are important because they represent the ways that therapists conceptualize their clients' past, present, or future behavior, feelings, and thoughts. Methods of changing these behaviors or thoughts all derive from those factors that theorists see as most important in understanding their patients. The presentations on personality theory in this book differ from those in personality theory textbooks in that the explanations given here are briefer and designed to explain and illustrate concepts that are related to the practice of psychotherapy. In each chapter, the goals, assessment, and treatment methods of a theory of psychotherapy are directly related to its theory of personality.

Theories of Psychotherapy

For most chapters, this section is the longest and most important. First, I describe the important goals or purposes of therapy. What do therapists want to achieve with their clients? What will the clients be like when they get better? What kind of psychological functioning is most important in the theory? All of these questions are implicit in the explanation of a theory's view of goals.

From goals follows an approach to assessment. Some theorists want to assess the relationship of unconscious to conscious processes; others focus on assessing distorted thinking. Some theories attend to feelings (sadness, rage, happiness, and so forth), whereas others specify behaviors of an individual (refusal to leave the house to go outside or sweating before talking to someone of the opposite sex). Many theorists and their colleagues have developed their own methods of assessment, such as interview techniques or questions to ask the client, but they also include inventories, rating forms, and questionnaires. All relate to making judgments that influence the selection of therapeutic techniques.

Theorists vary widely in their use of techniques. Those theories that focus on the unconscious (psychoanalysis and Jungian analysis) use techniques that are likely to bring unconscious factors into conscious awareness (for example, dream analysis). Other techniques focus on changing beliefs (cognitions), accessing and reflecting feelings (emotions), and having clients take actions (behavior). Because techniques of therapy can be difficult to understand, I have used examples to show the therapeutic relevance of methods for changing behavior, emotions, thoughts, or other aspects of oneself. As most theorists have found, helping individuals change aspects of themselves can be difficult and complex. To explain this process further, I have described several psychological disorders to which theories can be applied.

Psychological Disorders

Increasingly, therapists no longer ask, "Which is the best therapy?" but "What is the best therapy for a specific type of client?" To provide an answer to the latter question, I have selected three, four, or five case examples of individual therapy that illustrate how the theory can be applied to some of the more common diagnostic classifications of psychological disorders listed in the *Diagnostic and Statistical Manual of Mental Disorders*, Fourth Edition (DSM-IV) (American Psychiatric Association, 1994). For individual therapy, there are both advantages and problems in describing how different theories can be applied to common categories of psychological disorders.

The advantage of describing ways in which theories help individuals with a variety of psychological problems is to provide a broader and deeper view of the theory than if no reference to diagnostic classification was made. By examining several brief case studies or descriptions of treatment, the breadth of theoretical application can be seen by applying it to different situations. Also, some theoretical approaches have devoted particular attention to certain types of disorders, describing specific methods and techniques. The depth of the theories can be assessed by comparing one type of client (for example, a depressed client) with another, across several theories.

Although it would be extremely helpful if I could say for each therapy, "For this type of disorder you use this type of treatment from theory A, but for another type of disorder, you use a different treatment from theory A," this is not possible. Perhaps most important, clients do not fit easily into specific categories such as depression, anxiety disorder, and obsessive-compulsive disorder. Individuals often have problems that overlap several areas or diagnostic criteria. Furthermore, problems differ in severity within a particular category, and clients differ due to cultural background, gender, age, motivation to solve their problem, marital situation, the problem that they present to the therapist, and the history of the problem. All of these factors make it difficult for therapists of a given theoretical orientation to say, "I will use this technique when treating these types of patients."

Additionally, practitioners of many theories do not find the DSM-IV classification system (or any other general system) a useful way of understanding clients. Practitioners of some theories see classification systems as a nuisance, required for agency or insurance reimbursement purposes but having little other value. The theories of psychotherapy that make the most use of assessment of diagnostic classification are psychoanalysis, Adlerian therapy, and cognitive therapy, with cognitive therapy probably making the most extensive use of diagnostic classification information. Although many practitioners of other theories do not use conceptualizations and techniques that warrant use of diagnostic classification systems, they do not treat everyone in the same manner. Instead, they respond to clients based on their own theory of personality and assessment, rather than using a classification system.

In general, the main reason for using examples of several psychological disorders for each theory is to enable the reader to develop a greater understanding of the theory through comparison with other theories and through the presentation of diverse applications. To provide a background for understanding common disorders, I give a general description of the major disorders that are discussed in this book. For every major theory, except psychoanalysis, I present an example of how that theory can be applied to depression; for each theory, except person-centered and feminist therapy, I give an example of how that theory is applied to anxiety disorders. (The reasons that some theories are omitted from these two comparisons are that there either appear to be no appropriate cases for demonstration purposes, or that it was important to focus on other disorders.) In the next section, depression and anxiety disorders are described broadly, along with other disorders that are used as examples in this text.

Depression.   Signs of depression include sadness, feelings of worthlessness, guilt, social withdrawal, and loss of sleep, appetite, sexual desire, or interest in activities. With severe depression may come slow speech, difficulty in sitting still, inattention to personal appearance, and pervasive feelings of hopelessness and anxiety, as well as suicidal thoughts and feelings. Depression is one of the most common psychological disorders and may affect between 4 and 5% of the population at some time during their lifetimes (Weissman, Leaf, Tischler, & Blazer, 1988).

Two types of depression are usually distinguished: unipolar and bipolar. In bipolar depression, a manic mood in which the individual becomes extremely talkative, distractible, and active occurs along with episodes of extreme depression. In unipolar depression, a manic phase is not present. Some differences in the depression phase have been found between unipolar and bipolar depression. Generally in unipolar depression, individuals' activity is agitated and they have difficulty sleeping, whereas in bipolar depression, activity tends to be depressed and people sleep more than usual.

In discussions on treating depression in this book, distinctions between unipolar and bipolar depression are not frequently made. The psychotherapeutic treatments described here generally apply both to unipolar depression and the depressive phase of bipolar depression.

Generalized anxiety disorder.   Excessive worry and apprehension are associated with general anxiety disorders. Individuals may experience restlessness, irritability, problems in concentration, muscular tension, and problems in sleeping. Excessive worry about a variety of aspects of life is common, with anxiety being diffuse rather than related to a specific fear (phobia), rituals or obsessions (obsessive-compulsive disorder), or physical complaints (somatoform disorder). These disorders have been characterized as neuroses, as they all are associated with anxiety of one type or another. The term neurosis is a broad one and, because of its general nature, is used infrequently in this text; it has been used most frequently by early theorists such as Freud, Jung, and Adler. In general, the term *anxiety disorder* can be said to represent nonspecific neuroses or anxiety.

Borderline disorders.   More accurately described as *borderline personality disorder*, borderline disorders are one of a number of different personality disorders (such as narcissistic). Personality disorders are characterized by being inflexible, of long duration, and including traits that make social or vocational functioning difficult. They have earned a reputation as being particularly difficult to treat psychotherapeutically.

Individuals with borderline disorders are characterized by having unstable interpersonal relationships. Their view of themselves and their moods can change very rapidly and inexplicably in a short period of time. Behavior tends to be erratic, unpredictable, and impulsive in areas such as spending, eating, sex, or gambling. Emotional relationships are often intense, with individuals with borderline disorders becoming angry and disappointed in a relationship quite quickly. Such individuals have fears of being abandoned and often feel let down by others who do not meet their expectations. Suicide attempts are not unusual.

Obsessive-compulsive disorder.   When individuals experience persistent and uncontrollable thoughts or feel compelled to repeat behaviors again and again, they are likely to be suffering from an obsessive-compulsive disorder. *Obsessions* are recurring thoughts that cannot be controlled and are so pervasive as to interfere with day-to-day functioning. Some obsessions may appear as extreme worrying or indecision in which the individual debates over and over again, "Should I do this or should I do that?" *Compulsions* are behaviors that are repeated continually to reduce distress or prevent something terrible from happening. For example, individuals with a compulsion to wash their hands for 20 minutes at a time may believe that this prevents germs and deadly disease. The fear is exaggerated, and the compulsion interferes with day-to-day activity. Individuals with an obsessive-compulsive disorder differ as to whether their symptoms are primarily obsessions, compulsions, or a mixture of the two.

Obsessive-compulsive disorder should be distinguished from obsessive-compulsive personality disorder, which refers, in general, to being preoccupied with rules, details, and schedules. Such individuals often are inflexible about moral issues and the behavior of others. Because they insist that others do things their way, their interpersonal relationships tend to be poor. Normally, they do not experience obsessions and compulsions. Although an important disorder, obsessive-compulsive personality disorder is not used as an example in this book.

Phobias.   Being afraid of a situation or object out of proportion to the danger of the situation or object describes a phobic reaction. For example, experiencing extreme tension, sweating, and other anxiety when seeing a rat or being at the top of a tall building are reactions that can be debilitating. Phobic individuals go beyond the cautious behavior that most people would experience when seeing a rat or being at the top of a building.

Somatoform disorders.   When there is a physical symptom but no known physiological cause, and a psychological cause is suspected, then a diagnosis of somatoform disorder is given.

Posttraumatic stress disorder.   Extreme reactions to a highly stressful event constitute posttraumatic stress disorder (PTSD). Examples of a stressful event would be being raped, robbed, or assaulted; escaping from a flash flood; or being in military combat. Stress reactions last for months or years and often include physiological symptoms such as difficulty in sleeping or concentrating. Individuals with PTSD may reexperience the event through nightmares or images that remind them of the event. Another aspect of PTSD is attempting to avoid feeling or thinking about the trauma or event.

Eating disorders.   Two types of eating disorders are discussed: anorexia and bulimia. *Anorexia* is diagnosed when individuals do not maintain a minimally normal body weight. Such individuals are very afraid of gaining weight and view parts of their body as too big (such as buttocks and thighs), whereas others may see themselves as emaciated. *Bulimia* refers to binge eating and inappropriate methods of preventing weight gain. Binge eating includes excessive consumption of food at meals or other times, such as eating a box of cookies or a half gallon of ice cream. Inappropriate methods of controlling weight gain include self-induced vomiting, misuse of laxatives or enemas, or excessive fasting or exercise. Individuals with bulimia often are of normal weight. Some individuals have experienced both anorexia and bulimia at various times in their lives.

Substance abuse.   When individuals use drugs to such an extent that they have difficulty meeting social and occupational obligations, substance abuse has occurred. Relying on a drug because it makes difficult situations less stressful is called *psychological dependency*. Developing withdrawal symptoms, such as cramps, is called *physiological dependency*. When physiological dependence exists, individuals are said to be *substance-dependent* or *addicted*. In this text, the term *substance abuse* is used broadly and includes psychological and/or physiological dependence on a variety of drugs such as alcohol, cocaine, marijuana, sedatives, stimulants, and hallucinogens. Because substance abuse is so widespread, many practitioners of theories have devoted significant attention to this area. Examples of treating alcoholism or other drug abuse are found in chapters on existentialism, REBT, reality therapy, and cognitive therapy.

Hysteria.   This disorder refers to psychological disturbances that take a physical form, such as paralysis of the legs, when there is no physiological explanation. The term hysteria has been replaced by *conversion reaction*, and the disorder is infrequently seen. However, patients with hysteria made up a large portion of Freud's clientele, and observations about these patients were important in the development of psychoanalysis. In Chapter 2, an example of Freud's treatment of a patient with hysteria is explained.

Narcissistic personality disorder.   Showing a pattern of self-importance, the need for admiration from others, and a lack of empathy are characteristics of individuals with a narcissistic personality disorder. They may be boastful or pretentious, inflate their accomplishments and abilities, and feel that they are superior to others or special and should be recognized and admired. Believing that others should treat them favorably, they become angry when this is not done. Also, they have difficulty being truly concerned for others except when their own welfare is involved. Heinz Kohut's self psychology, discussed in Chapter 2, focuses on the development of narcissism in individuals.

Schizophrenia.   Severe disturbances of thought, emotions, and behaviors characterize schizophrenia. Individuals may think and speak in illogical fragments that are very disorganized. They may also have delusions, beliefs that exist despite evidence to the contrary, such as the belief (a paranoid delusion) that one is being followed by the director of the Central Intelligence Agency. Hallucinations are prevalent among individuals with schizophrenia and refer to seeing, hearing, feeling, tasting, or smelling things that are not there, such as hearing the voice of Abraham Lincoln. Other symptoms include unusual motions or immobility, extreme lack of energy or emotional response, and inappropriate affect, such as laughing when hearing about the death of a friend. The term *psychosis* is a broader term including schizophrenia and other disorders in which individuals have lost contact with reality.

Although schizophrenia appears somewhat frequently in the general population, between 0.5 and 1% (American Psychiatric Association, 1994), I have not focused on psychotherapeutic treatment of schizophrenia, as many researchers believe that this disorder is resistant to most psychotherapeutic techniques and responds better to medication. However, cognitive and behavioral treatments are used in the treatment of schizophrenia.

The 12 categories of psychological disorders that I have just explained may seem complex. In later chapters, as treatment approaches are presented for various disorders, characteristics of these disorders should become clearer. Because the disorders themselves are described only in this section of the book, it may be helpful, when reading about a particular case, to return to this section or consult the glossary for a specific explanation of a disorder.

In this chapter, information about these disorders is presented in summary form. A more in-depth description of these and many other disorders can be found in the *Diagnostic and Statistical Manual of Mental Disorders* (American Psychiatric Association, 1994), Durand and Barlow (1997), and textbooks on abnormal psychology. In general, practitioners of theoretical approaches use diagnostic categories more superficially and crudely than do investigators of abnormal psychology or psychologists who specialize in the diagnosis or classification of disorders. However, the information provided in this section should help readers understand the different types of problems to which various theoretical approaches can be applied.

Brief Psychotherapy

Length of therapy has become an issue of increasing importance to practicing psychotherapists. Because of client demand for services, many agencies such as community mental health services and college counseling centers set limits on the number of sessions that they can provide for clients. Session limits may range broadly from 3 to more than 40, depending on the agency's resources and philosophy. Additionally, health maintenance organizations (HMOs) and insurance companies that reimburse mental health benefits put limits on the number of sessions for which they will pay. Furthermore, clients often seek treatment that will take several weeks or months rather than several years. All of these forces have had an impact on treatment length and the development of brief psychotherapeutic approaches.

Several terms have been used to refer to brief approaches to psychotherapy: *brief psychotherapy*, *short-term psychotherapy*, and *time-limited therapy*. In general, brief and short-term therapy refer to limits placed on the number of sessions, for example, no more than 20 sessions. Time-limited therapy represents a theoretical approach to therapy that takes a certain number of sessions for completion, such as 12, with specific issues being addressed in each phase of the 12-session limit. The approach that most thoroughly addresses the issue of both long-term and brief therapeutic treatments is psychoanalysis. In that chapter, two brief approaches to psychoanalysis are discussed, along with traditional long-term methods.

Most of the other theoretical approaches acknowledge the importance of brief psychotherapy and demonstrate under what circumstances their therapies can be applied briefly. For the most part, Jungian, existential, person-centered, and Gestalt therapy do not have methodologies that result in treatment length being less than 6 months or a year. Other approaches, such as REBT and behavior, cognitive, and reality therapies, demonstrate how certain types of problems require less therapeutic time than others. Additionally, some varieties of family systems therapy are designed to be completed in 5 to 10 meetings. For each chapter, the issue of brief psychotherapy is explained from the point of view of the theory.

Current Trends

Theories are in a continual state of change and growth. Although they may start with the original ideas of a particular theorist, theories are, to varying degrees, influenced by new writings based on psychotherapeutic practice and/or research. Some of the innovations deal with applications to areas such as social problems, education, families, or groups. Other trends reflect challenges to existing theoretical concepts and the development of new ones. Two very different trends will be discussed in several chapters: the growth and development of treatment manuals and the influence of constructivism on the theory and practice of psychotherapy.

Treatment manuals are guidelines for therapists as to how to treat patients with particular disorders or problems. Typically, they describe skills and the sequence of using these skills that therapists should use. Suggestions are given for dealing with frequently encountered questions or problems. A major advantage of treatment manuals is that they specify procedures in a clear manner. Essentially, instructions are given so that therapists know how to conduct therapy with a specific problem. Additionally, treatment manuals provide an opportunity for researchers to investigate the effectiveness of a particular method, because all therapists who use the method in research can be checked to see if they comply with directions. A goal of treatment manuals is to have a specific approach that has been proven to be effective that therapists can use to help clients (Wilson, 1997). However, treatment manuals have also been the subject of criticism.

Because psychotherapy is a very complex process, some therapists have been concerned that treatment manuals oversimplify therapy (Silverman, 1996). Treatment manuals may focus on technique but not help therapists develop an important working relationship with clients. Also, treatment manuals may be aimed at a few specific problems. What happens when the client has several problems? Individuals are unique, and the way they experience some problems may be different than the way others do. Will a treatment manual work for all clients with a particular problem? I will discuss the use of treatment manuals in the "Current Trends" section, when appropriate. The theories that are most frequently recognized as having treatment manuals are psychoanalytically oriented theories and cognitive and behavioral theories.

A very different influence is that of postmodernism (Neimeyer & Stewart, 1998). A philosophical position, *postmodernism* does not assume that there is a fixed truth, rather individuals have constructs or perceptions of reality or truth. This is in reaction to *modernism*, which takes a *rationalist* approach that emphasizes scientific truth and is a reflection of advances in technology and science. Postmodernism reflects a multiculturally diverse world in which psychologists, philosophers, and others have recognized that different individuals can have their own construct or view of what is real for them.

Related to postmodernism is *constructivism*. Constructivists view individuals as creating their own views of events and relationships in their lives. Constructivist therapists attend not only to the meanings that their patients give to their own problems, but also help them see problems as meaningful options that have outlived their usefulness. Constructivist therapists deal with the ways in which their clients impose their own order on their problems and how they derive meanings from their experiences with others. There are several constructivist points of view. One that is discussed in this text is *social constructionism*, which focuses on the shared meanings that people in a culture or society develop (Neimeyer, 1998). These social constructions are a way that individuals relate to each other. Two specific social constructionist approaches, solution-focused therapy and narrative therapy, will be described in Chapter 13, "Family Systems Therapy."

To make this explanation less abstract, I will use the example of 10-year-old Molly, who was suffering from nightmares and an inability to sleep in her own room (Duncan, Hubble, & Miller, 1997). Molly and her divorced mother had seen two therapists. One had the goal of exploring for sexual abuse and investigating Molly's feelings about her father. This approach had not worked. Rather than take a detailed history and make hypotheses about Molly's problem, the current therapist asked Molly for her solution to the problem. Molly suggested that she could sleep in her own bed and her nightmares may disappear if she could "barricade herself in her bed with pillows and stuffed animals" (Duncan et al., p. 24). Molly tried this and during the course of the third session made the following comment:

> Psychiatrists [therapists] just don't understand you. . . [the client] also have the solutions, for yourself, but they say, "Let's try this and let's try that" and they're not helping. You know, you're like, "I don't really want to do that." Your asking me what I wanted to do with my room, got me back in my room. So, *what I am saying to all psychiatrists is we have the answers, we just need someone to help us bring them to the front of our head.* It's like they're [the solutions] locked in an attic or something. It's a lot better when you ask a person what they want to do and they usually tell you what they think would help, but didn't know if it was going to help and didn't want to try. (p. 25)[1]

Molly's situation is very unusual, as she had a solution in mind. Very few clients have explicit answers to their problems clearly in mind when they seek psychotherapy. However, constructivists frequently assume that careful exploration of the meaning of the problems, combined with respectful negotiation of possible solutions, will yield answers that neither the client nor the therapist could have envisioned at the outset of therapy. Molly's example illustrates the postmodern or constructivist approach to understanding the client's view of reality and valuing it. The constructivist philosophy has had an impact on many theories discussed in this book. When relevant, the constructivist influence on a theory will be discussed in the "Current Trends" section.

Using a Theory with Other Theories

Although 30 or 40 years ago practitioners of various theoretical points of view were often isolated from each other, communicating at conventions and through journals with only those who shared their own theoretical persuasion, increasingly this is no longer the case. Practitioners (as shown previously) have become much more eclectic and integrative in their work, making use of research and theoretical writings outside their own specific point of view. This section provides some information as to the openness of theories to the ideas of others and the similarity of various theoretical perspectives.

Research

Theories of psychotherapy differ dramatically in terms of their attitude toward research, type of research done, and the accessibility of the theory for research. Although attitudes are changing, traditionally a number of psychoanalysts and Jungian analysts, as well as Glasser (the developer of reality therapy), questioned the value of research in determining the effectiveness of psychotherapy. In general, the more specific the concepts to be measured and the briefer the therapeutic approach, the easier it is to conduct research. However, as is shown shortly, there is little that is easy about research on psychotherapy. Because behavior, cognitive, and REBT therapies use relatively brief and specific methods and goals, there is far more research on the effectiveness of psychotherapy for these theories than for others. It is not possible to conclude on the basis of research that theory x is superior to theory y either in general or for a specific disorder. However, it is possible to show some trends in directions of effectiveness and to highlight the types of research that are currently being done to assess therapeutic benefits.

Evaluation of the effectiveness of theories is a very sophisticated and complex skill that cannot be covered in an introductory text but requires comprehensive coverage (Bergin & Garfield, 1994). A brief overview of important points in conducting psychotherapeutic research can provide some understanding of the factors that need to be considered in trying to determine the advantages of a particular theory of psychotherapy (Kazdin, 1994).

A major goal of psychotherapy research is to understand how different forms of treatment operate. Another goal is to develop and evaluate new and traditional approaches that can be used by therapists. To do this, researchers try to design experiments that control sources of bias within the study so that comparisons can be made. A common method is to compare a group receiving a treatment to one that does not or to another group receiving a different treatment. Measurement of important variables to be studied should take place before and after the treatment, a *pretest-posttest control group design*. Other designs, called *factorial* designs, provide ways of studying more than one important variable at a time. When research on the effectiveness of psychotherapy has accumulated either generally or in a specific area, such as depression, it is sometimes helpful to conduct a *meta-analysis*, which is a way of statistically summarizing the results of a large number of studies. In this book, reference is made to meta-analyses as well as to specific studies that are examples of research on the therapeutic effectiveness of a particular theory.

In designing research, attention needs to be given to the type of treatment used, assignment of subjects, therapist characteristics, and measures of therapeutic outcome. Researchers must determine the problem that they are going to study, such as depression, and make sure that treatment is focused on this variable. Participants in the study must be assigned to the control and treatment groups using an unbiased system. The treatment provided the participants must represent the treatment to be studied. For example, if behavior therapy is the treatment to be studied, it may be inappropriate to have graduate students administer the treatment. The question would arise, Is their treatment as effective as that of experienced behavior therapists, and did they carry out the training the way they were supposed to, even if they did receive training? Also, personal characteristics of the therapist should be controlled for, so that investigators can feel confident that it was the treatment that brought about change rather than therapist charisma. Not only must therapeutic variables be controlled, but also effective measures of outcome must be used.

A number of measures of therapeutic outcome that assess areas such as social and marital adjustment and emotional, cognitive, and behavioral functioning have been developed. Appropriate measures must be used before and immediately following treatment, as well as at a later time. For example, some treatments have been found to be effective 1 year after therapy but not 2 years after the therapeutic experience. In general, the longer the follow-up period, the greater the chance that participants in the study will no longer be available for follow-up because of factors such as change of address or death. When evaluating the effectiveness of therapeutic techniques, a variety of statistical methods can be used. Decisions about whether to compare clients with untreated individuals, those who would be expected to be normal, or to look at changes within individuals are all decisions that research investigators must make. In presenting examples of research, I have tried to use those that are representative of research that is related to the theory that is being studied.

Gender Issues

Virtually all theories of psychotherapy that are discussed in this book have been developed by men (feminist therapy being the major exception). Does this mean that the theories have different assumptions about men and women and their treatment? Furthermore, are there issues that affect women differently than men or specific problems that theories should address, such as rape or eating disorders? Perhaps the theory that has been most frequently criticized for negative values regarding women is psychoanalysis. This theory, as well as others, is discussed in relationship to its assumptions and values about men and women. Not surprisingly, the chapter that most completely addresses the issue of gender is that of feminist therapy, in which the effect of societal values on individuals as they are reflected in therapy is discussed. Another issue regarding gender that is not frequently addressed by theories is that of attitudes and values toward homosexuality. Where there seems to be a clear point of view regarding this issue I have tried to address it within the appropriate chapter. In general, an assumption that I make in this book is that the more one knows about one's own values about gender and those of theories of psychotherapy, the more effective one can be as a therapist with both men and women.

Multicultural Issues

Just as assumptions about the values of theories and therapists about gender are important, so are assumptions about cultural values. Increasingly, therapists deal with clients whose cultural backgrounds are very different from their own. Knowledge of theories of psychotherapy and values about cultural issues that are implicit within them assists therapists in their work with a variety of clients. When examining theories, it is helpful to ask if the values implicit in that theory fit with values of a particular culture. For example, if a culture emphasizes not divulging feelings to others, what implications are there for applying a theory that focuses primarily on understanding feelings?

Theories may reflect the culture and background of the theorist. For example, Sigmund Freud lived in Vienna in the late 19th and early 20th centuries. It is reasonable to ask to what extent the values that are implicit in psychoanalysis are a reflection of his culture and to what extent they can be applied to a current multicultural society. The fact that Freud lived in a society somewhat different from our own does not invalidate his theory but does raise questions about the role of cultural values in theories of psychotherapy. Theorists differ in the attention that they pay to cultural issues. For example, Carl Jung and Erik Erikson are noted for their interest in many different societies and cultures. Currently, the theory of psychotherapy that appears most concerned with multicultural issues is that of feminist therapy. In each chapter, I describe writings or research that pertain to the study of multicultural issues for that specific theory of psychotherapy.

Couples and Family Therapy

Most therapists and counselors who work with individual clients also work with couples, and many treat families. Problems of individuals do not exist in isolation and often involve members of the family or others who are very close to clients. Couples and family therapy receive attention in this text because this work represents a large amount of actual therapy done by therapists and counselors. Each theoretical approach is consistent in applying the same concepts and techniques to couples and families as to individuals. However, there are some differences in application, and I have described treatment of couples separately from treatment of families except for existential, person-centered, and feminist therapies, where the two treatments are combined. One theoretical point of view, family systems therapy, focuses on relationships, interactions, and problems only within couples and families and does not specifically address individual dysfunctions.

In this text, I use the term *couples counseling* rather than *marriage counseling* to reflect that couples, although often married, may be unmarried or may be of the same sex. The diversity of family structures is even greater than that of couples. Some families may be led by a single parent, an aunt or uncle, grandparents, or some other combination of adults. Also, in some families older brothers or sisters may play an important role in child raising. Thus, a broad view of what constitutes a couple or family is assumed in this text.

Group Therapy

Group therapy has the advantage of being more efficient than individual therapy because it serves more people at the same time. Also, it offers some benefits that individual therapy does not. Although groups vary in size, they frequently have between 6 and 10 members and 1 or 2 leaders. An advantage of group therapy, when compared with individual therapy, is that participants can learn effective social skills and try out new styles of relating with other members of the group (Corey, 2000). Also, group members are often peers and provide, in some ways, a microcosm of the society that clients deal with daily. Because groups exist to help members with a variety of problems, group members can offer support to each other to explore and work on important problems. Also, groups help individuals become more caring and sensitive to the needs and problems of others. Although most groups are therapeutic in nature, focusing on the development of interpersonal skills or psychological problems, others are more educational in function, teaching clients skills that may be useful in their lives.

Theorists differ as to the value they place on group therapy. Some practitioners of theories view groups primarily as an adjunct to individual therapy (for example, Jungian therapists), whereas other practitioners of theories give central importance to group therapy, often suggesting it as a treatment of choice (as do Adlerian, person-centered, Gestalt, and feminist therapists). For each major theory presented, some specific applications to group therapy are described and illustrated.

ETHICS

The basic purpose of psychotherapy and counseling is to help the client with psychological problems. To do this effectively, therapists must behave in an ethical and legal way. Professional organizations for mental health practitioners such as psychiatrists, psychologists, social workers, mental health counselors, pastoral counselors, and psychiatric nurses have all developed codes of ethics that describe appropriate behavior for therapists. These ethical codes are in substantial agreement as to actions that constitute ethical and unethical behavior on the part of the therapist. All practitioners of theories should accept their profession's ethical codes. It is implicit in theories of psychotherapy and counseling that therapists are ethical as they seek approaches to benefit the life situation of their clients.

Although a full discussion of ethics is outside the scope of this book, therapists must be familiar with such issues. For example, an important ethical issue is the prohibition against erotic or sexual contact with clients. A related issue is the appropriateness of touching or holding clients. Ethical codes also discuss limitations on social and personal relationships with clients such as dual relationships with clients outside of therapy. Confidentiality and the issue of releasing information about clients are also major issues addressed in ethical codes. Other issues include concerns about referrals and record keeping. Competency to practice and to help clients with many different issues can raise ethical dilemmas. Several books have been written describing ethical issues (for example, Corey, Corey, & Callanan, 1998; Welfel, 1998) and deal with them in depth. I discuss ethics only in relation to specific issues that affect certain theories. For example, body therapists (Chapter 14) make significant use of touch, and behavior therapists (Chapter 8) deal with severely psychologically disabled clients who are unable to make decisions for themselves. Although not discussed frequently in this book, legal and ethical behavior on the part of all therapists is essential to the effective practice of all forms of psychotherapy.

MY THEORY OF PSYCHOTHERAPY AND COUNSELING

For the past 25 years I have seen, on average, about 20 adult and older adolescent clients per week, primarily for individual therapy but also for couples counseling. In my own work, I have incorporated concepts and techniques from most of the approaches that are discussed in this book. I have come to have a profound respect for the theorists, practitioners of the theories, and researchers because of their contribution to helping people in distress. I have found that many of the theories that are discussed in this book have guided me in helping individuals alleviate their distress. Although I have biases and preferences for theoretical concepts and techniques, I believe that my profound respect for theories of psychotherapy has kept these biases to a minimum.

After 25 years as a therapist and counselor, I find that I am continually touched by the distress of my clients, concerned about their problems, and excited by the opportunity to help them. Helping others continues to be a value that is exceedingly important to me and does not waiver.

YOUR THEORY OF PSYCHOTHERAPY AND COUNSELING

For readers who are considering this field or planning to become therapists or counselors, this book is an opportunity to become familiar with some of the most influential theories of psychotherapy and counseling. Also, it can be the start of developing your own approach to therapy. I encourage you to be open to different points of view and gradually choose approaches that fit you personally as well as the clientele that you plan to work with. To foster this openness, I have described the theories as thoroughly as possible and have reserved a critique of the theories for the last chapter of the book. For most therapists, the choice of theory is a slowly evolving process, the result of study and, most important, supervised psychotherapy or counseling experience.

Suggested Readings

For each chapter, I have provided a brief list of readings that I think will be most helpful in learning more about the theory. Many readings are at an intermediate rather than an advanced level of complexity, providing more detail on a number of issues that are discussed in each chapter. The following readings are suggestions related to important topics covered in this introductory chapter.

BERGIN, A. E., & GARFIELD, S. L. (EDS.). (1994). *Handbook of psychotherapy and behavior change* (4th ed.). New York: Wiley. • This is a comprehensive volume that describes methods and procedures for research on psychotherapy. Included are evaluations of psychotherapeutic treatment for major theories. Also, research on group, brief psychotherapy, and children and adolescents is presented.

COREY, G., COREY, M., & CALLANAN, P. (1998). *Issues and ethics in the helping professions* (5th ed.). Pacific Grove, CA: Brooks/Cole. • Chapters in this book cover values in the client-counselor relationship, responsibilities of the therapist, therapeutic competency, and therapist-client relationship issues. Case examples of ethical issues are provided.

AMERICAN PSYCHIATRIC ASSOCIATION. (1994). *Diagnostic and statistical manual of mental disorders* (4th ed.). Washington, DC: American Psychiatric Association. • Known as DSM-IV, this manual describes the widely accepted classification of psychological and/or psychiatric disorders. Specific criteria for each disorder are listed and explained, along with a thorough explanation of the psychological disorders discussed in this chapter (as well as many other disorders).

MADDI, S. R. (1996). *Personality theories: A comparative analysis* (6th ed.). Pacific Grove, CA: Brooks/Cole. • This text is a comprehensive review of personality theories. It provides detailed information on many personality theories as well as an extensive review of research related to each theory.

References

AMERICAN PSYCHIATRIC ASSOCIATION. (1994). *Diagnostic and statistical manual of mental disorders* (4th ed.). Washington, DC: American Psychiatric Association.

BERGIN, A. E., & GARFIELD, S. L. (EDS.). (1994). *Handbook of psychotherapy and behavior change* (4th ed.). New York: Wiley.

COREY, G. (2000). *Theory and practice of group counseling* (5th ed.). Pacific Grove, CA: Brooks/Cole.

COREY, G., COREY, M., & CALLANAN, P. (1998). *Issues and ethics in the helping professions* (5th ed.). Pacific Grove, CA: Brooks/Cole.

CORSINI, R. J. (ED.). (1981). *Handbook of innovative psychotherapies.* New York: Wiley.

CORSINI, R. J., & WEDDING, D. (1995). *Current psychotherapies* (5th ed.). Itasca, IL: Peacock.

DUNCAN, B. L., HUBBLE, M. A., & MILLER, S. D. (1997). *Psychotherapy with "impossible" cases: The efficient treatment of therapy veterans.* New York: Norton.

DURAND, V. M., & BARLOW, D. H. (1997). *Abnormal psychology: An introduction.* Pacific Grove, CA: Brooks/Cole.

EARMAN, J. (1992). *Inference, explanation, and other philosophical frustrations: Essays in the philosophy of science.* Berkeley: University of California Press.

FAWCETT, J., & DOWNS, E. S. (1986). *The relationship of theory and research.* Norwalk, CT: Appleton-Century-Crofts.

GARFIELD, S. L., & BERGIN, A. E. (1994). Introduction and historical overview. In A. E. Bergin & S. L. Garfield (Eds.), *Handbook of psychotherapy and behavior change* (4th ed., pp. 3–18). New York: Wiley.

GELSO, C. J., & FRETZ, B. R. (1992). *Counseling psychology.* Fort Worth, TX: Harcourt Brace.

HALL, C. S., LINDZEY, G., & CAMPBELL, J. B. (1998). *Theories of personality* (4th ed.). New York: Wiley.

HEINEN, J. R. (1985). A primer on psychological theory. *Journal of Psychology, 119,* 413–421.

JENSEN, J. P., BERGIN, A. E., & GREAVES, D. W. (1990). The meaning of eclecticism: New survey and analysis of components. *Professional Psychology: Research and Practice, 21,* 124–130.

KAZDIN, A. E. (1994). Methodology, design, and evaluation in psychotherapy research. In A. E. Bergin & S. L. Garfield (Eds.), *Handbook of psychotherapy and behavior change* (4th ed., pp. 19–71). New York: Wiley.

LIEBERT, R. M., & LIEBERT, L. L. (1998). *Liebert and Spiegler's personality: Strategies and issues* (8th ed.). Pacific Grove, CA: Brooks/Cole.

MARX, M. H. (1951). The general nature of theory construction. In M. H. Marx (Ed.), *Psychological theory* (pp. 4–19). New York: Macmillan.

NEIMEYER, R. A. (1998). Social constructionism in the counselling context. *Counselling Psychology Quarterly, 11,* 135–149.

NEIMEYER, R. A., & STEWART, A. E. (1998). Constructivist psychotherapies. *Encyclopedia of mental health.* (Vol. 1, pp. 547–559). New York: Academic Press.

NORCROSS, J. C., KARG, R. S., & PROCHASKA, J. O. (1997). Clinical psychologists in the 1990s. *The Clinical Psychologist, 50*(2), 4–9.

NORCROSS, J. C., STRAUSSER, D. J., & MISSAR, C. D. (1988). The process and outcomes of psychotherapists' personal treatment experiences. *Psychotherapy, 25,* 36–43.

PATTERSON, C. H. (1986). *Theories of counseling and psychotherapy* (4th ed.). New York: Harper-Collins.

PROCHASKA, J. O., & NORCROSS, J. C. (1999). *Systems of psychotherapy: A transtheoretical analysis* (4th ed.). Pacific Grove, CA: Brooks/Cole.

SILVERMAN, W. H. (1996). Cookbooks, manuals, and paint-by-numbers: Psychotherapy in the 90's. *Psychotherapy, 33,* 207–215.

SNOW, R. E. (1973). Theory construction for research and testing. In R. W. Travers (Ed.), *Second handbook of research on teaching* (pp. 77–112). Chicago: Rand McNally.

TYLER, L. E. (1958). Theoretical principles underlying the counseling process. *Journal of Counseling Psychology, 5,* 3–10.

WATKINS, C. E., LOPEZ, F. G., CAMPBELL, V. L., & HIMMELL, C. N. (1986). Contemporary counseling psychology: Results of a national survey. *Journal of Counseling Psychology, 33,* 301–309.

WEISSMAN, M. M., LEAF, P. J., Tischler, G. L., & Blazer, D. G. (1988). Affective disorders in five United States communities. *Psychological Medicine, 18,* 141–153.

WELFEL, E. R. (1998). *Ethics in counseling and psychotherapy: Standards, research, and emerging issues.* Pacific Grove, CA: Brooks/Cole.

WILSON, T. (1997). Treatment manuals in clinical practice. *Behaviour Research and Therapy, 35,* 205–210.

2

Psychoanalysis: Drive, Ego, Object Relations, and Self Psychology

Sigmund Freud's contribution to the current practice of psychoanalysis, psychotherapy, and counseling is enormous. Because psychoanalysis was the most influential theory of therapy during the 1930s, 1940s, and 1950s, virtually every major theorist discussed in this book was originally trained in Freudian psychoanalysis. Some theorists totally rejected his ideas, and many developed their own ideas based, in part, on their knowledge of Freud's views of human development and the structure of personality. As new theories were created, it was Freud's theory of psychoanalysis to which they were compared.

For more than 100 years, Freud's views have gathered adherents who have both practiced his theory of psychoanalysis and contributed to the expansion of psychoanalytic theory. From the start, changes in psychoanalytic theory have brought about controversy and disagreement. As a result, psychoanalysis has evolved considerably since Freud's death in 1939. Many of Freud's contributions have been a mainstay of psychoanalytic thought, such as his emphasis on the importance of unconscious processes in human motivation and his concepts of personality (id, ego, and superego). Psychoanalytic writers also accept the importance of early childhood development in determining later psychological functioning. However, they disagree about which aspects of childhood development should be emphasized.

To understand contemporary psychoanalytic thought, it is important to be aware of four different theoretical directions: Freudian drive theory, ego psychology, object relations, and self psychology. Freud, through the psychosexual stages (oral, anal, and phallic) that occur in the first 5 years of life, stressed the importance of inborn drives in determining later personality development. Ego psychologists attended to the need for individuals to adapt to their environment, as exemplified by Erik Erikson's stages of development that encompass the entire life span. Object relations theorists were particularly concerned with the relationship between the infant and others. They, like Freud, used the term *object* to refer to persons in the child's life who can fulfill needs or to whom the young child can become attached. A different view has been that of self psychologists, who focused on developmental changes in self-preoccupation. Most psychoanalytic practitioners are aware of these ways of viewing development but differ as to which of them they incorporate in their work. In this chapter I describe each of these four views of childhood development and show their impact on the practice of psychoanalysis and psychoanalytic therapy.

HISTORY OF PSYCHOANALYSIS

To understand psychoanalysis and Freud's ideas, it is helpful to consider personal and intellectual influences in his own life. Born on May 6, 1856, in the village of Freiburg, Moravia, a small town then in Austria and now a part of the Czech Republic, Sigmund Freud was the first of seven children of Amalia and Jacob Freud. Freud's father had two sons by a former marriage and was 42 when Sigmund was born. When Freud was 4 years old, his father, a wool merchant, moved the family to Vienna to seek more favorable business conditions. In their crowded apartment in Vienna, Freud was given the special privilege of his own bedroom and study. His young mother had high hopes for her son and encouraged his study and schoolwork. He was well versed in languages, learning not only the classical languages—Greek, Latin, and Hebrew—but also English, French, Italian, and Spanish, and he read Shakespeare at the age of 8. In his early schoolwork, he was often first in his class. Later he attended the *Sperlgymnasium* (a secondary school) from 1866 to 1873, graduating summa cum laude (Ellenberger, 1970).

In the winter of 1873, Freud began his medical studies at the University of Vienna and finished his degree 8 years later. Ordinarily, a medical degree was a 5-year program, but his completion was delayed because he spent 6 years working under the supervision of a well-known physiologist, Ernst Brucke, and spent a year (1879–1880) of military service in the Austrian army. During his time with Brucke, he became acquainted with Josef Breuer, 40 years his senior, who introduced him to the complexities of hysterical illness. Because of poor prospects for promotion and financial remuneration, Freud left Brucke's Institute of Physiology and began a residency in surgery. A short time later, in 1883, Freud studied neurology and psychiatry in the large Viennese General Hospital. During that time he worked with patients with neurological disorders; in studying the medical aspects of cocaine, he tried the drug himself, before he was aware of its addictive properties. In 1885, Freud had the opportunity to travel to Paris and spend 4 months with Jean Charcot, a famous French neurologist and hypnotist. At the time, Charcot was studying the conversion reactions of hysterical patients who showed bodily symptoms such as blindness, deafness, and paralysis of arms or legs as a result of psychological disturbance. During that time, Freud observed Charcot using hypnotic suggestion as a way to remove hysterical symptoms. Although Freud was later to question the value of hypnosis as a treatment strategy, his experience in Paris helped him to consider the importance of the unconscious mind and the way in which feelings and behaviors can be influenced to create psychopathological symptoms.

Returning to Vienna, Freud married Martha Bernays in 1886. During their 53 years of marriage, they had six children, the youngest of whom, Anna, was to become a well-known child analyst, making significant contributions to the development of psychoanalysis. During the years immediately following his marriage, Freud began work at a children's hospital and also built a private practice that was slow to develop. At the

SIGMUND FREUD

same time, he continued to read the works of authors in many varied fields.

Information from physics, chemistry, biology, philosophy, psychology, and other disciplines influenced his later thinking. His interest in unconscious processes came not only from his work with Charcot but also from philosophers such as Nietzsche (1937) and Spinoza (1952). The science of psychology was emerging, and Freud had read the works of Wilhelm Wundt and Gustav Fechner. His knowledge of the work of Ludwig Borne, a writer who suggested that would-be writers put everything that occurs to them on paper for 3 days, disregarding coherence or relevance (Jones, 1953), influenced his development of the psychoanalytic technique of free association. Other scientific influences included Darwin's theory of evolution and the biological and physiological research of Ernst Brucke. Throughout many of his writings, Freud made use of scientific models derived from physics, chemistry, and biology (Jones, 1953). His knowledge of science and neurology and his familiarity with the psychiatric work of Pierre Janet and Hippolyte Bernheim were to affect his development of psychoanalysis.

Although Freud was influenced by other writers and psychiatrists in the development of psychoanalysis, its creation is very much his own. Initially, Freud used hypnosis and Breuer's cathartic method as a means of helping patients with psychoneuroses. However, he found that patients resisted suggestions, hypnosis, and asking questions. He used a "concentration" technique in which he asked patients to lie on a couch with their eyes closed, to concentrate on the symptom, and to recall all memories of the symptom without censoring their thoughts. When Freud sensed resistance, he pressed his hand on the client's forehead and questioned the patient about memory and recall. Later, Freud became less active and encouraged his patients to report whatever came to their mind— *free association.* Related to the development of this technique was his discussion with Josef Breuer, his older colleague, who was working with a patient, Anna O., who seemed to be recovering from hysteria by reporting emotional material to Breuer while under hypnosis. Freud used this procedure with other patients, and together Breuer and Freud published *Studies on Hysteria* (1895), in which they hypothesized that symptoms of hysteria resulted from very painful memories combined with unexpressed emotions. The therapeutic task, then, became to bring about a recollection of forgotten events, along with emotional expression. It was Freud's belief, but not Breuer's, that the traumatic events that caused hysteria were sexual and occurred in the patient's childhood.

In part, these beliefs led Freud to undertake a self-analysis of his own childhood and his dreams. As Freud explored his own unconscious mind, he became aware of the importance of biological and particularly sexual drives that were related to suppression of emotion. This realization made him aware of the conflict between the conscious and unconscious aspects of personality. His observations based on his own and patients' dreams were published in *The Interpretation of Dreams* (Freud, 1900).

Although *The Interpretation of Dreams* received relatively little attention from physicians or others, Freud began to attract individuals who were interested in his ideas. Meeting at his home, the Wednesday Psychological Society, started in 1902, gradually grew until in 1908 it became the Vienna Psychoanalytic Society. During these years, Freud published *The Psychopathology of Everyday Life* (1901), *Three Essays on Sexuality*

(1905b), and *Jokes and Their Relation to the Unconscious* (1905a). His writings on sexuality drew condemnation, as they were out of step with the times, and Freud was seen as perverted and obscene by both physicians and nonacademic writers. The event that brought Freud and psychoanalysis American recognition was the invitation from G. Stanley Hall to lecture at Clark University in Worcester, Massachusetts, in 1909. This led to a larger audience for books such as *Introductory Lectures on Psycho-Analysis* (1917) and *The Ego and the Id* (1923), which described his approach to personality.

Freud also wrote about the importance of infant relationships with parents. In his books *Three Essays on Sexuality* (1905b) and *On Narcissism: An Introduction* (1914) Freud refined his views on *libido*, the driving force of personality that includes sexual energy. He wrote about autoeroticism, which precedes the infant's relationship to the first object, the mother (Ellenberger, 1970). He found it helpful to differentiate between libidinal (sexual) energies that were directed toward the self and those directed toward the representation of objects in the external world. When an individual withdraws energy from others and directs it toward himself or herself then narcissism occurs, which, if extreme, can cause severe psychopathology. Freud's writings on early infant relationships and narcissism were the foundation of the work of object relations and self psychology theorists.

Freud (1920) revised his theory of drives that had focused on the importance of sexuality as a basic drive affecting human functioning. Later, he observed the importance of self-directed aggression that occurs in self-mutilation or masochism. Wanting to explain why people continually find ways to punish themselves, Freud (1920) added to the instinct of love or sexuality (*Eros*) an instinct for death or self-destruction (*thanatos*). Freud's emphasis on aggressive and sexual drives has not been shared as readily by many of his followers. Others of his concepts (the unconscious, ego, id, and the superego) are shared by many psychoanalytic theorists. These aspects of personality (Freud, 1923) are described in detail in the next section.

Important in the development of psychoanalysis were not only Freud's writings but also his interactions with other psychoanalysts who were drawn to him. Many of them argued with him, disagreed with him, or broke away from him. Early disciples and important writers were Karl Abraham, Max Eitingon, Sandor Ferenczi, Ernest Jones, and Hans Sachs. Although these disciples stayed relatively loyal to Freud, Alfred Adler (Chapter 4), Carl Jung (Chapter 3), and Otto Rank developed their own theories of psychotherapy and broke their ties with Freud. Later writers who broke with Freud, often referred to as neo-Freudians, focused more on social and cultural factors and less on biological determinants. Objecting to Freud's view of female sexuality, Karen Horney (1937) was concerned with cultural factors and interpersonal relations rather than early childhood traumas. Erich Fromm (1955) differed significantly from Freud by focusing on groups in societies and cultural changes. The neo-Freudian who attracts the most current interest is Harry Stack Sullivan (1953), whose emphasis on interpersonal factors and peer relationships in childhood created added dimensions to psychoanalytic theory. Although these writers present interesting additions and alternatives to psychoanalysis, their thinking is sufficiently different from psychoanalytic theorists presented in this chapter to be beyond its scope.

Freud continued to be productive until his death in 1939 from cancer of the throat and jaw, from which he had suffered for 16 years. At the age of 82, Freud was forced to flee Vienna to escape the Nazi invasion of Austria. Despite his illness and 33 operations on his jaw and palate, Freud was incredibly productive. He made major revisions in his theory of the structure and functioning of the mind, *The Ego and the Id* (1923), highlighting relationships among id, ego, and superego. His prolific work is published in the 24-volume *Standard Edition of the Complete Works of Sigmund Freud*. His life has been described in detail by many writers, most completely by Ernest Jones (1953, 1955, 1957). Jones's work and books by Ellenberger (1970) and Gay (1988) served as resources for this section and are recommended to the interested reader.

Just as Freud continued to refine and develop psychoanalysis, so did the psychoanalysts who followed him. A major contribution has been that of his youngest daughter, Anna, who focused on the development of the ego, that part of the Freudian system that deals with the external world of reality. Her student Erik Erikson also examined the individual's interaction with the real world and described stages of development that incorporate the entire life span. Their work, along with that of Heinz Hartmann, who emphasized adaptation to the environment, is known as *ego psychology*.

Another significant development is that of the object relations school. These theorists focused on the relationship of early childhood development, specifically that of the mother and child. The developmental theory of Margaret Mahler provides a different view of child development than does Freud's drive theory. Additional observations about the relationship between mother and child have been made by Donald Winnicott. The application of their work to severe disorders, such as borderline personality, has been made by Otto Kernberg. Heinz Kohut, the originator of self psychology, drew on object relations theory as well as his own ideas about the childhood development of narcissism. Although many writers have contributed to the development of psychoanalysis, these are among the most important, and their work is described in this chapter after Freud's theory of personality is explained.

FREUD'S DRIVE THEORY

The concepts of Freudian psychoanalytical theory provide a basic frame of reference for understanding not only his work but that of other psychoanalytic theorists. Perhaps his most controversial views (both in his own time and now) concern the importance of innate drives, especially sexuality. These drives often express themselves through unconscious processes, a pervasive concept in psychoanalysis, and in sexual stages. Freud postulated stages of childhood development—oral, anal, phallic, and latency—that, depending on a person's experience, can have an impact on later psychopathological or normal development. To describe the structure of personality, Freud used three concepts—id, ego, and superego—that are avenues for the expression of psychological energy. Conflicts between them result in neurotic, moral, or objective anxiety and may be expressed through unconscious processes such as verbal slips and dreams. To deal with the emergence of strong biological (id) forces, individuals develop ego defense mechanisms to prevent the individual from being overwhelmed. These concepts are necessary in understanding the application of psychoanalytical therapeutic techniques and are explained in the next paragraphs.

Drive and Instincts

In psychoanalysis, the terms *instincts* and *drives* are often used interchangeably, but the term *drive* is more common. Originally, Freud distinguished between self-preservative drives (including breathing, eating, drinking, and excreting) and species-preservative drives (sexuality). The psychic energy that emanates from sexual drives is known as *libido*. In his early work, Freud believed that human motivation was sexual in the broad sense that individuals were motivated to bring themselves pleasure. However, *libido* later came to be associated with all life instincts and included the general goal of seeking to gain pleasure and avoid pain.

When he was in his sixties, Freud put forth the idea of a *death instinct* that accounted for aggressive drives (Mishne, 1993). These include unconscious desires to hurt others or oneself. Often conflict arises between the life instincts (Eros) and the death instincts (thanatos). Examples of conflict include the love and hate that marriage partners may have for each other. When the hate comes out in destructive anger, then the aggressive drive (thanatos) is stronger. Often the two instincts work together, such as in eating, which maintains life but includes the aggressive activities of chewing and biting. Soldiers may express their aggressive drives through socially condoned fighting. Sports provide a more acceptable outlet for physical aggressive expression. Often, libido and aggressive drives are expressed without an individual's awareness or consciousness.

Levels of Consciousness

Freud specified three levels of consciousness: the conscious, the preconscious, and the unconscious. The *conscious* includes sensations and experiences that the person is aware of at any point in time. Examples include awareness of being warm or cold and awareness of this book or of a pencil. Conscious awareness is a very small part of a person's mental life. The *preconscious* includes memories of events and experiences that can easily be retrieved with little effort. Examples might include a previous examination taken, a phone call to a friend, or a favorite dessert that was eaten yesterday. The preconscious forms a bridge from the conscious mind to the much larger *unconscious*, which is the container for memories and emotions that are threatening to the conscious mind and must be pushed away. Examples include hostile or sexual feelings toward a parent and forgotten childhood trauma or abuse. Also included are needs and motivations of which individuals are unaware. Although unconscious motivations are out of awareness, they may still be exhibited in an individual's thoughts or behaviors.

Bringing unconscious material into conscious awareness is a major therapeutic task. It can be done through dream interpretation in which images within the dream may represent various unconscious needs, wishes, or conflicts (Freud, 1900). Slips of the tongue and forgetting are other examples of unconscious expression. When a man calls his wife by the name of a former girlfriend, the name that is uttered may represent a variety of wishes or conflicts. Freud also believed that humor and jokes were an expression of disguised wishes and conflicts (Freud, 1905a). Additionally, when patients repeat destructive patterns of behavior, unconscious needs or conflicts may be represented. For Freud, the concept of the unconscious was not a hypothetical abstraction; it could be demonstrated to be real. In his talks to physicians and scientists, Freud (1917) gave many instances of unconscious material that he had gleaned from his patients' dreams and other behavior. The following is a brief example of unconscious material, symbolizing death, as it was expressed in a patient's dream.

The dreamer was crossing a very high, steep, iron bridge, with two people whose names he knew, but forgot on waking. Suddenly both of them had vanished and he saw a ghostly man in a cap and an overall. He asked him whether he were the telegraph messenger . . . "No." Or the coachman? . . . "No." He then went on and in the dream had a feeling of great dread; on waking, he followed it up with a fantasy that the iron bridge suddenly broke and that he fell into the abyss. (Freud, 1917, p. 196)[1]

Attending to unconscious material was crucial for Freud and is central for all psychoanalysts. The techniques that are presented in the section on psychotherapy are generally designed to bring unconscious material into conscious awareness.

Structure of Personality

Freud hypothesized three basic systems that are contained within the structure of personality: the id, the ego, and the superego. Briefly, the id represents unchecked biological forces, the superego is the voice of social conscience, and the ego is the rational thinking that mediates between the two and deals with reality. These are not three separate systems; they function together as a whole.

Id.   At birth, the infant is all id. Inherited and physiological forces, such as hunger, thirst, and elimination, drive the infant. There is no conscious awareness, only unconscious behavior. The means of operation for the id is the pleasure principle. When only the id is operating, for an infant or an adult, individuals try to find pleasure and avoid or reduce pain. Thus an infant who is hungry, operating under the pleasure principle, seeks the mother's nipple.

The newborn child invests all energy in gratifying its needs (the pleasure principle). The infant then is said to *cathect* (invest energy) in objects that will gratify its needs. Investment of energy in an object such as a blanket or nipple—object cathexis—is designed to reduce needs. The primary process is a means for forming an image of something that can reduce the thwarted drive. The infant's image of the mother's nipple, as it exists to satiate hunger and thirst, is an example of *primary process*. In adults, the primary process can be seen in the wishful fantasies that appear in dreams or other unconscious material. To distinguish wish or image from reality is the task of the ego.

Ego.   The ego must mediate between the world around the infant and the instincts or drives within the infant. By waiting or suspending the pleasure principle, the ego follows the reality principle. For example, the young child learns to ask for food rather than to cry immediately when her needs are not met. This realistic thinking is referred to as the *secondary process*, which is in marked contrast to the fantasizing of the primary process. It is the function of the ego to test reality, to plan, to think logically, and to develop plans for satisfying needs. Its control or restraint over the id is referred to as *anticathexis*. In this way the ego serves to keep us from crying or acting angrily whenever we do not get our way.

Superego.   Whereas the id and ego are aspects of the individual, the superego represents parental values and, more broadly, society's standards. As the child incorporates the parents' values, the ego ideal is formed. It represents behaviors that parents approve of, whereas the conscience refers to behaviors disapproved of by parents. Thus the individual develops a moral code or sense of values to determine whether actions are good or bad. The superego is nonrational, seeking perfection and adherence to an ideal, inhibiting both the id and the ego, and controlling both physiological drives (id) and realistic striving for perfection (ego).

When conflicts among the id, ego, and superego develop, anxiety is likely to arise. It is the purpose of the ego and superego to channel instinctual energy through driving forces (cathexes) and restraining forces (anticathexes). The id consists only of driving forces. When the id has too much control, individuals may become impulsive, self-indulgent, or destructive. When the superego is too strong, individuals may set unrealistically high moral or perfectionistic standards (superego) for themselves and thus develop a sense of incompetence or failure. Anxiety develops out of this conflict among id, ego, and superego. When the ego senses anxiety, it is a sign that danger is imminent and something must be done.

In conceptualizing anxiety, Freud (1926) described three types of anxiety: neurotic, moral, and reality. Having an unfriendly person chase after us is an example of reality anxiety; the fear is from the external world, and the anxiety is appropriate to the situation. In contrast, neurotic and moral anxiety are threats within the individual. Neurotic anxiety occurs when individuals are afraid that they will not be able to control their feelings or instincts (id) and will do something for which they will be punished by parents or other authority figures. When people are afraid that they will violate parental or societal standards (superego), moral anxiety is experienced. In order for the ego to cope with anxiety, defense mechanisms are necessary.

Defense Mechanisms

To cope with anxiety, the ego must have a means of dealing with situations. Ego defense mechanisms deny or distort reality, while operating on an unconscious level. When ego defense mechanisms are used infrequently, they serve an adaptive value in reducing stress. However, if they are used frequently, this use becomes pathological, and individuals develop a style of avoiding reality. Some of the more common ego defense mechanisms are described in the following paragraphs.

Repression.   An important defense mechanism, repression is often the source of anxiety and is the basis of other defenses. Repression serves to remove painful thoughts, memories, or feelings from conscious awareness by excluding painful experiences or unacceptable impulses. Traumatic events that occur in the first 5 years of life are likely to be repressed and to be unconscious. Freud (1894) in his work with patients with hysterical disorders believed that they had repressed traumatic sexual or other experiences and responded through conversion reactions, such as paralysis of the hand.

Denial.   Somewhat similar to repression, denial is a way of distorting or not acknowledging what an individual thinks, feels, or sees. For example, when an individual hears that a loved one has died in an automobile accident, she may deny that it really happened or that the person is really dead. Another form of denial occurs when individuals distort their body images. Someone who suffers from anorexia and is underweight may see himself as fat.

Reaction formation.   A way of avoiding an unacceptable impulse is to act in the opposite extreme. By acting in a way that is opposite to disturbing desires, individuals do not have to deal with the resulting anxiety. For example, a woman who hates her husband may act with excessive love and devotion so that she will not have to deal with a possible threat to her marriage that could come from dislike of her husband.

Projection.   Attributing one's own unacceptable feelings or thoughts to others is the basis of projection. When a person is threatened by strong sexual or destructive drives or moral imperatives, rather than accept the anxiety, individuals may project their feelings onto others. For example, a man who is unhappily married may believe that all of his friends are unhappily married and share his fate. In this way, he does not need to deal with the discomfort of his own marriage.

Displacement.   When anxious, individuals can place their feelings not on an object or person who may be dangerous, but on those who may be safe. For example, if a child is attacked by a larger child, she may not feel safe in attacking that child and will not reduce her anxiety by doing so. Instead, she may pick a fight with a smaller child.

Sublimation.   Somewhat similar to displacement, sublimation is the modification of a drive (usually sexual or aggressive) into acceptable social behavior. A common form of sublimation is participating in athletic activities or being an active spectator. Running, blocking, or yelling may be appropriate in some sports but not in most other situations.

Rationalization.   To explain away a poor performance, a failure, or a loss, people may make excuses to lessen their anxiety and soften the disappointment. An individual who does poorly on an examination may say that he is not smart enough, that there is not time enough to study, or that the examination was unfair. Sometimes it is difficult to determine what is a real and logical reason and what is a rationalization.

Regression.   To revert to a previous stage of development is to regress. Faced with stress, individuals may use previously appropriate but now immature behaviors. It is not uncommon for a child starting school for the first time to cling to his parents, suck his thumb, and cry, trying to return to a more secure time. If a college student has two tests the next day, rather than studying, she may fantasize about pleasant days back in high school and regress to a more comfortable and more secure time.

Identification.   By taking on the characteristics of others, people can reduce their anxiety as well as other negative feelings. By identifying with a winning team, an individual can feel successful, even though he had nothing to do with the victory. Identifying with a teacher, musician, or athlete may help individuals believe that they have characteristics that they do not. Rather than feel inferior, the individual can feel self-satisfied and worthwhile.

Intellectualization.   Emotional issues are not dealt with directly but rather are handled indirectly through abstract thought. For example, a person whose spouse has just asked for a divorce may wish to dwell on issues related to the purpose of life rather than deal with hurt and pain.

These ego defense mechanisms are ways of dealing with unconscious material that arises in childhood. How and when these defense mechanisms arise depend on events occurring in the psychosexual stages discussed next.

Psychosexual Stages of Development

Freud believed that the development of personality and the formation of the id, ego, and superego, as well as ego defense mechanisms, depend on the course of psychosexual development in the first 5 years of life. The psychosexual oral, anal, and phallic stages occur before the age of 5 or 6; then there is a relatively calm period for 6 years (the latency period), followed by the genital stage in adolescence, which starts at the beginning of puberty. Freud's theory is based on biological drives and the importance of the pleasure principle; thus, certain parts of the body are thought to be a significant focus of pleasure during different periods of development (Freud, 1923). Freud believed that infants receive a general sexual gratification in various parts of the body that gradually become more localized to the genital area. The oral, anal, and phallic stages described in the following paragraphs show the narrowing of the sexual instinct in the development of the child.

Oral stage.   Lasting from birth to approximately 18 months, the oral stage focuses on eating and sucking and involves the lips, mouth, and throat. Dependency on the mother for gratification—and therefore the relationship with the mother—is extremely significant in the oral stage. The mouth has not only the function of taking in and eating but also holding on to, biting, spitting, and closing. The functions of eating and holding can be related to the development of later character traits referred to as *oral incorporation*, which might include the acquiring of knowledge or things. The functions of biting and spitting can be related to oral aggressive characteristics that might include sarcasm, cynicism, or argumentativeness. On one hand, if, during the oral stage, a child learns to depend too often on the mother, the child may fixate at this stage and become too dependent in adult life. On the other hand, if the child experiences anxiety through inattentive or irregular feeding, the child may feel insecure not only at this early stage but also in adult life.

Anal stage.   Between the ages of about 18 months and 3 years, the anal area becomes the main source of pleasure. Exploration of bodily processes such as touching and playing with feces is important. If adults respond to children with disgust toward these activities, children may develop a low sense of self-esteem. During this period, the child develops bowel control, and conflicts around toilet training with parents can develop into personality characteristics in later life, such as an overconcern with cleanliness and orderliness (anal retentive) or disorderliness and destructiveness (anal expulsive). Not only do children establish control over their own body but also they are attempting to achieve control over others.

Phallic stage.   Lasting from the age of about 3 until 5 or 6, the source of sexual gratification shifts from the anal region to the genital area. At this age, stroking and manipulation of the penis or clitoris produces sensual pleasure. The concept of castration anxiety comes from the boy's fear that his penis may be cut off or removed. Particularly during the Victorian era, when masturbation was believed to be destructive, parental attempts to stop masturbation may have led the boy to fear the loss of his penis. If he had observed a nude girl, he might have believed that she had already lost her penis. The concept of penis envy refers to girls who wondered why they lacked penises and thought that perhaps they had done something wrong to lose their penises. Freud believed that later personality problems could be attributed to castration anxiety or penis envy. The sexual desire for the parent can lead to the development of the Oedipus complex in boys or the Electra complex in girls (although this latter idea was dropped in Freud's later writings). Named after the ancient Greek playwright Sophocles' play about a young man who becomes king by marrying his mother and killing his father, the Oedipus complex refers to the boy's sexual love for his mother and hostility for his father. In this traumatic event, the child eventually learns to identify with the same-sex parent and change from sexual to nonsexual love for the opposite-sex parent, eventually developing an erotic preference for the opposite sex. In this way, sexual feelings for the opposite-sex parent are sublimated. Difficulties in this stage of development may result in later sexual identity problems affecting relationships with the same or opposite sex.

Latency.   When the conflicts of the Oedipus complex are resolved, the child enters the latency period. Lasting roughly from the ages of 6 to 12 (or puberty), the latency period is not a psychosexual stage of development because at this point sexual energy (as well as oral and anal impulses) is channeled elsewhere. This force (libido) is repressed, and children apply their energy to school, friends, sports, and hobbies. Although the sexual instinct is latent, the repressed memories from previous stages are intact and will influence later personal development.

Genital stage.   Beginning in early adolescence, about the age of 12, the genital stage continues throughout life. Freud concerned himself with childhood development rather than adult development. In the genital stage, the focus of sexual energy is toward members of the opposite sex rather than toward self-pleasure (masturbation). In contrast to the genital stage, which focuses on others as the sexual object, the three earlier stages (oral, anal, and phallic) focus on self-love.

Freud's theory of psychosexual development has been challenged by other psychoanalytic theorists. Although all psychoanalytic theorists accept the importance of the unconscious and, to a great extent, make use of Freud's concepts of ego, id, and superego, their greatest area of difference concerns his emphasis on drives and psychosexual stages. Other theorists' focus on ego rather than id functioning and on the importance of infant-mother interactions provides the subjects of the next sections.

EGO PSYCHOLOGY

Freud had said, "Where there is id, ego shall be." Those who followed Freud found ways to incorporate psychosexual drives (id) with social and nondrive motives (ego). Among the best-known ego psychologists who added to the theoretical model of psychoanalysis were Anna Freud, Heinz Hartmann, and Erik Erikson. Anna Freud applied psychoanaly-

ANNA FREUD

sis to the treatment of children and extended the concept of ego defense mechanisms. Heinz Hartmann addressed the function of the ego in psychoanalytic theory by stressing its adaptive functions. Bringing ego psychology into Freudian developmental theory, Erik Erikson widened the concept of life stages into adulthood and introduced social and nonpsychosexual motives to the stages.

Anna Freud

Anna Freud (1895–1982) studied nursery school children and provided psychoanalytic treatment at her Hampstead Clinic in London. Her writings reflect her work with both normal and disturbed children. When evaluating child development, she attended not only to sexual and aggressive drives of children but also to other measures of maturation, such as moving from dependence to self-mastery. The gradual development of various behaviors has been referred to as *developmental lines*. For example, she shows how individuals go from a gradual egocentric focus on the world, in which they do not notice other children, to a more other-centered attitude toward their schoolmates to whom they can relate as real people (A. Freud, 1965). These developmental lines show an increasing emphasis on the ego.

Anna Freud believed that the ego as well as the id should be the focus of treatment in psychoanalysis (Blanck & Blanck, 1986). In *The Ego and the Mechanisms of Defense* (A. Freud, 1936), she describes 10 defense mechanisms that had been identified by analysts at that time, most of which have been discussed in this chapter. To this list she added the defenses "identification with the aggressor" and "altruism." In the former, the person actively assumes a role that he or she has been passively traumatized by, and in altruism one becomes "helpful to avoid feeling helpless." She wrote also of "defense against reality situations," a recognition that motivation can come not only from internal drives but also from the external world (Greenberg & Mitchell, 1983). With her experience in understanding child development, she was able to articulate how a variety of defenses developed and recognize not only the abnormal and maladaptive functions of defense mechanisms but also adaptive and normal means of dealing with the external world.

Heinz Hartmann

Following Anna Freud, Heinz Hartmann (1894–1970) elaborated the theory of ego psychology, emphasizing the autonomous and adaptive functions of the ego. Hartmann (1958, 1964) believed that the id and ego came out of an early amorphous phase, with both having their own courses of development. Hartmann (1958) emphasized the importance of the ego in broad-based interactions with the external world. Not only did the ego exist in a conflictual stance with the id, with resulting ego-defense mechanisms, but also the ego existed in a "conflict-free" ego sphere. Different from the conflict implied in Freud's drive theory, the ego could operate without being at odds with the id, superego, or external reality.

In focusing on the ego's adaptive functions, Hartmann (1958) discussed various conscious and coping functions of the ego such as perceiving, thinking, and remem-

ERIK ERIKSON

bering. These ego functions could solve a variety of problems for the individual, as they were responsive to the external world and able to function independently of the id. Like Anna Freud, Hartmann focused on the nonpathological functioning of the ego, as well as its pathological role in defense mechanisms.

Erik Erikson

A student of Anna Freud, Erik Erikson (1902–1994) has made a number of contributions to ego psychology, but perhaps most important is his explanation of psychosocial life stages that include adult as well as child development. Starting with Freud's psychosexual stages, he shows their implications for growth and development as the individual relates to the external world. Erikson's eight stages focus on crises that must be negotiated at significant points in life. If these crises or developmental tasks are not mastered, this failure can provide difficulty when other developmental crises are encountered. Unlike Freud's stages, a stage is not completed but remains throughout life. For example, the first stage—trust versus mistrust—begins in infancy; if not encountered successfully, it can affect relationships at any time during the life cycle.

Erikson's eight psychosocial stages are briefly described below. So that comparisons can be made with Freud's psychosexual stages, Freud's stages are listed in parentheses next to Erikson's.

Infancy: Trust Versus Mistrust (Oral).   An infant must develop trust in his mother to provide food and comfort, so that when his mother is not available he does not experience anxiety or rage. If these basic needs are not met, nontrusting interpersonal relationships may result.

Early Childhood: Autonomy Versus Shame and Doubt (Anal).   Being able to develop bladder and bowel control with confidence and without criticism from parents is the crucial event in this stage (Erikson, 1950, 1968). If parents promote dependency or are critical of the child, the development of independence may be thwarted.

Preschool Age: Initiative Versus Guilt (Phallic).   At this stage, children must overcome feelings of rivalry for the opposite-sex parent and anger toward the same-sex parent. Their energy is directed toward competence and initiative. Rather than indulge in fantasies, they learn to be involved in social and creative play activities. Children who are not allowed to participate in such activities may develop guilt about taking the initiative for their own lives.

School Age: Industry Versus Inferiority (Latency).   At this point the child must learn basic skills required for school and sex role identity. If the child does not develop basic cognitive skills, a sense of inadequacy or inferiority may develop.

Adolescence: Identity Versus Role Confusion (Genital).   A key stage in Erikson's schema, adolescents develop confidence that others see them as they see themselves. At this point, adolescents are able to develop educational and career goals and deal with issues regarding the meaning of life. If this is not done, a sense of role confusion may result, in which it is difficult to set educational or career goals.

Young Adulthood: Intimacy Versus Isolation (Genital).   Cooperative social and work relationships are developed, along with an intimate relationship with another person. If this is not done, a sense of alienation or isolation may develop.

Middle Age: Generativity Versus Stagnation (Genital).   Individuals must go beyond intimacy with others and take responsibility for helping others develop. If individuals do not achieve a sense of productivity and accomplishment, they may experience a sense of apathy.

Later Life: Integrity Versus Despair (Genital).   When individuals reach their sixties (or later) and feel that they have not handled their lives well, they may experience a sense of remorse and regret about not having accomplished what they wanted in life. Having passed successfully through life, individuals contribute their accumulated knowledge to others. In her nineties, Joan Erikson, who was married to Erik for 64 years and was intimately involved in his work, added a ninth stage (Erikson, 1997). She proposed a stage called "Disgust: Wisdom" in which those in their eighties and nineties can move toward gerotranscendence, a shift from a materialistic and rational vision to peace of mind and spirituality.

Although these stages encompass the entire life span, Erikson's major contribution to psychoanalytic practice has been through his work with adolescents and children (Mishne, 1993). He has developed several innovative approaches to play therapy, and his concept of the identity crises of adolescents has been found useful by many counselors and therapists. His work and that of other ego psychologists have provided a conceptual approach that counselors and those who work in a short-term model can apply to their clients by emphasizing ego defenses, current interactions with others, conscious as opposed to unconscious processes, and developmental stages across the life span.

OBJECT RELATIONS PSYCHOLOGY

Object relations refer to the developing relationships between the child and significant others or love objects in the child's life, especially the mother. The focus is not on the outside view of the relationship, but on how the child views, consciously or unconsciously, the relationship-internalization. Of particular interest is how early internalized relationships affect children as they become adults and develop their own personalities. Examining not merely the interaction between mother and child, object relations theorists formulate the psychological or intrapsychic processes of the infant and child. This emphasis on internalized relationships differs markedly from Freud's emphasis on internal drives as they express themselves in psychological stages. Many writers have developed theoretical constructs to explain object relations, described stages of object relations development, and related their work to Freud's drive theory. Among the most influential writers on this subject are Balint (1952, 1968), Bion (1963), Blanck and Blanck (1986), Fairbairn (1954), Guntrip (1968), Jacobson

(1964), Kernberg (1975, 1976), Klein (1957, 1975), Mahler (1968, 1979a, 1979b), and Winnicott (1965, 1971). An explanation of their contributions, similarities, and differences goes beyond the scope of this text, but is available in St. Clair (1996) and Greenberg and Mitchell (1983).

To provide an overview of object relations psychology, I next describe the contributions of Margaret Mahler, Donald Winnicott, and Otto Kernberg. Through her study of normal and psychotic children, Mahler and her associates (Mahler, Bergman, & Pine, 1975) have detailed the stages of object (mother-child) relations. Winnicott explains problems that occur as the child develops in relationship to the mother and others and offers solutions for them. More recently, Kernberg has offered useful insights into the development of object relations as it affects normal behavior and psychological disturbance, especially borderline disorders. A discussion of their contributions provides a broad overview of how early mother-child relationships affect later personality development.

Margaret Mahler

A pediatrician who later became a psychoanalyst, Margaret Mahler (1897–1985) moved from Vienna to New York in 1938. By studying the interactions of mothers and their babies, Mahler and her colleagues made inferences about psychic processes that took place inside the children during the first 3 years of life. The development of the child can be described by three phases: normal autism, normal symbiosis, and separation and individuation. The latter stage is divided into four subphases: differentiation and body image, practicing, rapprochement, and individuality and emotional object constancy. Before describing these stages, it is important to discuss three concepts essential to understanding Mahler's theory of object relations: symbiosis, separation, and individuation.

In making their observations of children and their mothers, Mahler and her colleagues were particularly interested in how children separated from their mothers and developed individuality. *Symbiosis* is a metaphor borrowed from biology used to refer to the very early experience of infants in which they do not differentiate themselves from their mothers (St. Clair, 1996; Mahler, Bergman, & Pine, 1975). Separation takes place as children are able to distinguish themselves from their mothers and others in the world. Individuation is the sense of being an individual, an awareness of *I am*. As individuals separate from their mothers, they have the opportunity to develop a sense of who they are and what they can do. Mahler (St. Clair, 1996) sees the process of separation and individuation as two issues that children deal with throughout the three developmental stages: normal autism, normal symbiosis, and separation and individuation.

Normal autism occurs during the first few weeks of life. In this stage, infants cannot differentiate between their own attempts to reduce tension through urinating or squirming and their mothers' attempts to reduce hunger by feeding or to reduce other tensions (changing a diaper). This stage is objectless; Mahler, Bergman, and Pine (1975) see this early state as one of primitive and hallucinatory disorientation.

Normal symbiosis takes place around the second month, when the infant develops a dim awareness of the mother as an object that satisfies needs. During this time infants live in an undifferentiated state, in that they do not distinguish between themselves and others such as the mother. During this temporary fusion of mother and child, it is essential that this symbiosis be satisfactory, as it sets the stage for the later phases in which the infant separates from the mother and becomes an individual (St. Clair, 1996).

Separation and individuation: differentiation subphase occurs at about 4 or 5 months of age. At this point, the baby moves away from her mother and starts to develop motor skills and to play. Visually, the infant may scan others and start to compare her mother with others. The baby starts to examine what belongs to the mother's body and what does not. *Hatching* is a term Mahler and colleagues (1975) used to describe the alertness and the attention that is directed toward others. If her mother is too intrusive in earlier stages, an infant may push herself away too vigorously from the mother and differentiate herself in too dramatic a fashion.

Separation and individuation: practicing subphase lasts from about 9 months to about 15 to 18 months. As children are able to crawl and walk, they are able to venture further and further from the mother as well as to return to the mother for reassurance. If children are unable to separate from the mother at this stage, they may have a delusional sense of oneness with the mother (symbiosis) and want the mother to serve as an extension of them (Mahler, 1968). Usually the child delights in his new abilities and may enter a period of saying "no" to his mother as a means of separating from his mother.

Separation and individuation: rapprochement subphase begins at about 15 to 18 months and ends at about 2 years. The child begins to become more aware of being separate from the mother and starts to turn back to the mother for comforting. Anxiety at being away from the mother may be greater at this age than at the practicing substage. *Rapprochement* refers to resolving the conflict between needing the mother and desiring autonomy. At this age, children may be more aware of their mother's distance from them and return to the mother if the absence is too long or too far.

Separation and individuation: individuality and emotional object constancy subphase starts at about the third year of life. The child begins the development of her identity and is able to separate from her mother because of the love and approval that have taken place in the earlier stages and phases. In the beginning of this phase, the child may have a sense or an image that the mother would approve of "good" things that the child does. Object constancy evolves when the child develops a stable self-concept and a stable concept of others, especially the mother (Greenberg & Mitchell, 1983). Mahler gives no ending point to this stage, as it continues throughout life.

Stern (1985) compares experimental research on infants with Mahler's clinical observations. He is critical of her age-related stages, as he finds little evidence for stating that an adult problem arose because of a failure in mother-child relationships during a specific time period in early childhood. Rather, he suggests that many of these issues can be important throughout life.

Psychoanalytic therapists and counselors familiar with Mahler's theory of separation and individuation often find it helpful to use this theory as a general background for working with many different separation crises. Separation and individuation occur when the child starts kindergarten or nursery school and leaves the mother for a substantial period of time. Staying overnight at a friend's house and going to an overnight camp are other examples of separation. Increased responsibility for schoolwork requires responsibility for one's performance (individuation). In later life, problems such as dealing with parental divorce, going away to college for the first time, or getting married bring separation and individuation issues to the forefront. As aging parents need to be taken care of in their failing health, or die, separation issues may arise again. Such issues, as well as severe psychopathology arising out of problematic object relations, have been the concern of all prominent object relations theorists.

Donald Winnicott

An English pediatrician, Donald Winnicott (1896–1971) has not offered a systematized theory of object relations. However, "his ideas have likely had more influence on the understanding of the common, significant issues met with by psychoanalysts and psychotherapists in their everyday practice than anyone since Freud" (Bacal & Newman, 1990, p. 185). Like Margaret Mahler, he made many direct observations of the relationship between infant and mother in his work with children and families who had consulted him for assistance with psychological problems (Winnicott, 1965, 1975). His concepts (described later in this chapter) of the good-enough mother, the transitional object, and the true self and false self have been particularly useful in helping therapists work with both children and adults in understanding the importance of early childhood attachment to the mother and its impact on later life.

The importance that Winnicott attached to maternal care cannot be overemphasized. The mother is the facilitating environment on which the infant depends. Increasingly during pregnancy, but particularly during the first month of the infant's life, the mother gives herself over to the needs of the infant (Winnicott, 1965). This very early stage of environmental attention to the infant gives the infant a hallucination of omnipotence in which the baby expects that the breast will be there to feed him (St. Clair, 1996). The infant moves from this state of total dependence toward independence.

In the gradual movement from absolute dependence through relative dependence toward independence, the characteristics of the care that is provided by the mother (and others involved in parenting) change. Particularly in the first month of life, the holding environment, that is, the physical holding of the child, is important to foster a feeling of security (Winnicott, 1965). By touching and gently handling the baby's body, the basis for ego development is initiated (St. Clair, 1996). The holding and handling that the infant receives affect the way the baby relates to objects—the mother, care providers, food, and toys. The mother shapes how the infant deals with feeding (the breast), and the infant hallucinates or imagines the breast when hungry. In this way, the relationship between the infant and objects around her develops. The earlier fusion or lack of separation from the mother ceases, as the mother is differentiated from the child. Frustration with not being fed when hungry helps the child separate herself from other objects (St. Clair, 1996).

Gradually, infants move from a state in which they have a feeling of creating and controlling all aspects of the world that they live in to an awareness of the existence of others. Winnicott (Greenberg & Mitchell, 1983) believes that a transitional object, such as a stuffed animal or baby's blanket, is a way of making that transition. This transitional object is neither fully under the infant's fantasized control of the environment nor outside his control, as the real mother is. Thus the attachment to a stuffed rabbit can help an infant gradually shift from experiencing himself as the center of a totally subjective world to the sense of himself as a person among other persons (Greenberg & Mitchell, 1983, p. 195). In adult life, transitional objects or phenomena can be expressed as a means of playing with one's own ideas and developing creative and new thoughts (Greenberg & Mitchell, 1983).

Crucial to the healthy development from dependence to independence is the parental environment. Winnicott (1965) uses the term *good-enough* to refer to the mother being able to adapt to the infant's gestures and needs, totally meeting needs during early infancy, but gradually helping the infant toward independence when appropriate. However, infants learn to tolerate frustration, so the mother needs to be good-enough, not perfect. If the mother is too self-absorbed or cold to the infant, does not pick her up, and good-enough mothering does not occur, a true self may not develop. The *true self* provides a feeling of spontaneity and realness in which the distinction between the child and the mother is clear. In contrast, the *false self* can occur when there is not good-enough mothering in early stages of object relations (St. Clair, 1996). When reacting with the *false self*, infants are compliant with their mother and, in essence, are acting as they believe they are expected to, not having adequately separated themselves from their mother. In essence, they have adopted their mother's self rather than developed their own. Winnicott believed that the development of the false self arising from insufficient caring from the mother was responsible for many of the problems that he encountered with older patients in psychoanalysis (Bacal & Newman, 1990).

Winnicott held a developmental view of mental illness. He believed that psychosis (severe illness) resulted from early maternal deprivation that interfered with satisfactory relations with other people (objects). Intermediate illness, including borderline disorders, occurred as a result of a maternal environment that was good-enough at first but later failed, preventing an appropriate formation of independence. Winnicott saw psychoneurosis (less severe problems) as occurring because of disruptions related to the Oedipus complex. He saw Freudian analysis, focusing on drive theory, as appropriate to the treatment of psychoneurosis, whereas his own work would help in understanding psychosis (St. Clair, 1996).

Winnicott's view of therapy is consistent with his view of the object relations approach. He saw the goal of therapy as dealing with the false self "by providing a successful experience of early narcissism or omnipotence" (St. Clair, 1996, p. 85). A process of controlled regression is used in which the patient returns to the stage of early dependence. To do so, the therapist must sense what being the client is like and be the subjective object of the client's love or hate. The therapist must deal with the irrationality and strong feelings of the patient without getting angry or upset at the patient, encouraging the development of the true self (Winnicott, 1958).

Otto Kernberg

Born in Austria in 1928, Otto Kernberg is a psychoanalyst, a training and supervising analyst, a teacher, and a prolific writer. A current influential theorist, he has attempted to integrate object relations theory and drive theory. A major focus of his work has been on the treatment of borderline disorders and the helpfulness of object relations theory (more so than Freudian drive theory) in understanding patients' problems. Influenced by Mahler and Edith Jacobson, Kernberg has proposed a five-stage model of object relations that is not described here because of its similarity to Mahler's model (pp. 39–40). Important concepts that are described here are Kernberg's explanation of splitting and his view of internalization, that is, the taking in of relationships from outside the individual. These concepts are then related to Kernberg's view of the borderline disorder.

The structure of the psyche has been a particular focus of Kernberg's work. He believes that individuals internalize relationships by having a view of themselves, a view of others, and a feeling regarding these two (Kernberg, 1976). The three levels of internalization—introjection, identification, and ego identity—take place at increasingly greater levels of developmental maturity. In *introjection*, information from the outside world is not totally differentiated from information about the self, but gradually becomes differentiated. *Identification* can take place near the end of the first year, when the child is able to differentiate social roles into recognized interactions with other people. In *ego identity*, the third stage, children have a clear self-image and clear sense of their external world. In the progression of these three stages, Kernberg integrates the object relations concept of internalization (relationships with self and others) with Freud's (and Erikson's) concept of ego identity. Thus the development of the ego comes from a process of evolving relations with the mother and other objects rather than as a means of managing id drives, as Freud suggested.

Splitting is a process of keeping incompatible feelings separate from each other. This is a normal developmental process, as well as a defensive one, that can occur at any of the three levels of internalization. It is an unconscious means of dealing with unwanted parts of the self or threatening parts of others. For example, the child who sees a baby-sitter as all bad because she will not give him candy is splitting. The baby-sitter is not viewed as a total person, but only as bad. Splitting as a defense is seen frequently in psychoanalysis and psychotherapy, particularly with borderline disorders. Kernberg (1975) gives an example of a patient's use of splitting.

> The patient felt that if she really expressed to the psychotherapist-father how much she needed him and loved him, she would destroy him with the intensity of her anger over having been frustrated so much for so long. The solution was to keep what she felt was the best possible relationship of detached friendliness with the therapist, while splitting off her search for love, her submission to sadistic father representatives in her masochistic submission to unloving men, and her protest against father in alcoholic episodes during which rage and depression were completely dissociated emotionally from both the therapist and her boyfriends. (Kernberg, 1975, p. 95)[2]

In describing the reason for borderline disorders, Kernberg (1975) states that most patients with a borderline disorder have had a history of great frustration and have displayed aggression during their first few years of life. If a child is frustrated in early life, he may become intensely angry and protect himself by acting angrily toward his mother (and/or father). Rather than seen as a nurturing or good-enough mother, the mother is seen as threatening and hostile. Because of this early development, such adults may have difficulty integrating feelings of love and anger in their images of themselves and others. In this way, they are likely to "split," or see others, including the therapist, as all bad or, sometimes, as all good.

In treating borderline patients, Kernberg finds that this early anger and aggression that was never resolved is transferred to the therapist early in the therapeutic process (negative transference). Thus the therapist is likely to be distrusted, feared, and seen as attacking the patient, when in reality the therapist is doing none of these. In working with such people, Kernberg (1975) shows the patient how the negative transference is affecting therapy and structures therapy so that patients are less likely to act out their negative transference feelings. Such therapeutic work requires that the therapist be able to recognize negative feelings toward the patient (counter-transference) as a result of the patient's acting out frustrations that occurred as a result of not establishing good relationships with others during the first 2 years of life (Kernberg, 1997).

It is difficult to convey the complexity and depth of object relations psychology by discussing major concepts of only three of many object relations theorists. Mahler's model of the development of object relations is similar to, but not identical to, many other models of object relations. Because Winnicott's insights into the interaction between infant and mother have been influential in object relations psychology, they are essential in understanding applications to analysis and psychotherapy. The views of Kernberg are particularly useful in linking early childhood experience with later disturbance in childhood, adolescence, or adulthood. The emphasis of these theorists on early relationships with the mother (and others) is closely related to the developmental aspects of Kohut's self psychology.

KOHUT'S SELF PSYCHOLOGY

The newest major development within psychoanalysis has been self psychology, introduced by Heinz Kohut (1913–1981), whose works *The Analysis of the Self* (1971), *The Restoration of the Self* (1977), and *How Does Analysis Cure?* (1984) have elicited a great amount of reaction from critics and followers (St. Clair, 1996). The essence of self psychology is its emphasis on narcissism, not as a pathological condition but as a partial description of human development. Whereas Freud saw narcissism as an inability to love or relate to others due to a self-love or self-absorption, Kohut sees narcissism as a motivating organizer of development in which love for self precedes love for others. Crucial to understanding Kohut's theory are concepts of self, object, and selfobject. Self-absorption (the grandiose self) and the attention of the powerful parent (the idealized selfobject) occur in the course of child development before the age of 4. Difficulty with early developmental stages has an impact on how individuals relate to others and how they view themselves.

The self and related concepts are defined differently by various schools of psychoanalysis. Kohut came to understand the self through an empathic understanding of his patients (described in detail later in this chapter), whereas Mahler described the self based on her systematic observations of young children (St. Clair, 1996). Basically, the self is the core or center of the individual's initiative, motivating and providing a central purpose to the personality, and responsible for patterns of skills and goals (Wolf, 1988, p. 182). As Kohut's work developed, he made more and more use of the concept of the self and less frequent reference to the concepts of ego, id, and superego. In this respect, his work is further removed from Freud's than are the writings of the ego and object relations psychoanalysts. In infancy, the rudimentary self is made up of an *object*, which is an image of the idealized parent, and a *subject*, the grandiose self that is the "aren't I wonderful" part of the child. The *selfobject* is not a person (a whole love object) but patterns or themes of unconscious thoughts, images, or representations of another. For example, the young child, used to his mother's praise, may respond to other children as if he deserves to play with their toys when he wants to. In this case, the mother's praise serves as the child's "selfobject" (Hedges, 1983; St. Clair, 1996), as the child makes no distinction between himself and his mother in his mental representation of events.

Although acknowledging the role of sexual energy and aggressive drives, Kohut focused on the role of narcissism in child development. At the earliest stages, like Mahler, he believed that infants have a sense of omnipotence, as they do not distinguish themselves from the mother (St. Clair, 1996). When the child's needs are frustrated (for example, he is not fed when he wants to be), he establishes a self-important image, the grandiose self. When the child is fed, he attributes perfection to the admired selfobject, the idealized parental image.

Through a series of small, empathic failures, such as not getting what the child wants from the parent, a sense of self is developed. A state of tension exists between the grandiose self ("I deserve to get what I want") and the idealized parental image ("My parents are wonderful"). The tension between these two forms the bipolar self. In other words, the child chooses between doing what she expects her parents want her to do (the idealized selfobject) and doing what she wants to do (the grandiose self) (Kohut, 1977). When young children do not get what they want, they may burst into a tantrum, a narcissistic rage.

As described to this point, narcissism is a motivating organizer of development, and outbursts are normal. These outbursts are due to the removal of the mirroring selfobject. Mirroring occurs when the parent shows the child that she is happy with the child. In this way, the grandiose self is supported and the child sees that her mother understands her (reflects the child's image to the child) and incorporates the mirroring parent into the grandiose self. Thus the parent is viewed, in a sense, as a part of the child, performing the function of mirroring (Patton & Meara, 1992).

When children get stuck at a stage or when the grandiose self or idealized selfobject does not develop normally, problems arise in later life. For example, a child who does not have a responsive (mirroring) mother may be depressed in later life or continually search for love from others that was not supplied at an early age. Some people may never have had a sufficient relationship with parents (idealized selfobject) and may search for the ideal and perfect marriage partner or friend but always experience failure, because no one can meet their standards (St. Clair, 1996).

Psychological disturbances were referred to by Kohut as selfobject disorders or self disorders. Kohut assumed that the problems in developing adequate selfobjects, and thus a strong self, were the rationale for disorders. For example, psychosis is seen as a disorder occurring where there are no stable, narcissistic images or no stable idealized object. Thus individuals may develop delusions to protect themselves against loss of idealized objects (adequate parents) (St. Clair, 1996). For those with borderline disorders, the damage to the self may be severe, but defenses are sufficiently adequate for individuals to function (Wolf, 1988). In the case of narcissistic personality disorders, the grandiose self and the idealized selfobject have not been sufficiently integrated into the rest of personality and self-esteem may be lost (Kohut, 1971).

In his therapeutic approach, Kohut focused particularly on narcissistic and borderline disorders. His approach, in general, was to understand and be empathic with the individual's inadequate or damaged self, which was due to the inability to have experienced successful development of the grandiose self and the idealized selfobject. In his psychoanalytic work, Kohut found that patients expressed their narcissistic deficits through their relationship with him. How he experienced this relationship (transference) is explained in the next section.

Psychoanalysts and psychotherapists differ greatly as to which of these four approaches (drive, ego, object relations, and self psychology) they use to understand their patients. Originally, psychoanalysts used only Freud's drive theory in understanding clients. Those who do so now are usually known as *classical* or *traditional psychoanalysts*. Although some psychoanalysts and psychotherapists use only one of these approaches, more and more analysts are using a combination of two, three, or all four psychoanalytic theories. In a systematic approach to a variety of disorders, Hedges (1983) uses the term *listening perspective* as a means of selecting the appropriate theoretical approach for a specific disorder. For example, for patients with neurotic personality disorders, he recommends attention to Oedipal problems and the use of Freudian drive theory. For those with narcissistic personality disorders, he finds Kohut's approach helpful. With patients with borderline personality disorders, he uses an object relations approach to listen for disturbances in early object relations (parenting problems in early childhood). During the course of therapy, Hedges's listening perspective may change as the patient does. Although not defining the four psychoanalytic theoretical approaches exactly as they have been presented here, Pine (1990) describes how he may switch his approach in understanding patients to any of the four perspectives within a therapy session. How psychoanalysts and psychotherapists understand the early development of their patients has a great impact on how they implement therapeutic techniques.

PSYCHOANALYTICAL APPROACHES TO TREATMENT

Although psychoanalysts make use of different listening perspectives from drive, ego, object relations, and/or self psychology, they tend to use similar approaches to treatment. In their goals for therapy, they stress the value of insights into unconscious motivations. In their use of tests and in their listening to patients' dreams or other material, they concentrate on understanding unconscious material. Depending on whether they do psychoanalysis or psychoanalytic therapy, their stance of neutrality and/or empathy toward the patient may vary. However, both treatments deal with the resistance of the patient in understanding unconscious material. Each of these issues is discussed more extensively later in this chapter, as are therapeutic approaches.

Techniques such as the interpretation of transference or of dreams can be viewed from the four listening perspectives, as can countertransference reactions (the therapist's feelings toward the patient). Applying these perspectives to dream interpretation, to a transference reaction, and to countertransference issues can clarify these different approaches and show several ways that treatment material can be understood.

Therapeutic Goals

Psychoanalysis and psychodynamic psychotherapy are designed to bring about changes in a person's personality and character structure. In this process, patients try to resolve unconscious conflicts within themselves and develop more satisfactory ways of dealing with their problems. Self-understanding is achieved through analysis of childhood experiences that are reconstructed, interpreted, and analyzed. The insight that develops helps bring about changes in feelings and behaviors. By uncovering unconscious material through dream interpretation or other methods, individuals are better able to deal with the problems they face in unproductive, repetitive approaches to themselves and others.

The emphasis in bringing about resolution of problems through exploration of unconscious material is common to all four approaches to psychoanalysis. For Freud, increasing awareness of sexual and aggressive drives (id processes) helps the individuals achieve greater control of themselves in their interaction with others (ego processes). Ego psychoanalysts emphasize the need to understand ego defense mechanisms and to adapt in positive ways to the external world. For object relations therapists, improved relationships with self and others can come about, in part by exploring separation and individuation issues that arise in early childhood. Somewhat similarly, self psychologists focus on the impact of self-absorption or idealized views of parents that may cause severe problems in relating with others in later life, and they seek to heal these early experiences. The differences among these four approaches are oversimplified here; in clinical work, psychoanalysts may have one or more of these goals in their work with patients.

Assessment

Because unconscious material is revealed slowly, the process of assessing patients' family history, dreams, and other content continues through the course of analysis or therapy. Some psychoanalysts may use a rather structured approach in the first few sessions by taking a family and social history, whereas others may start therapy or do a trial analysis, using the first few weeks to assess appropriateness for therapy. By applying their understanding of personality development, as described in the prior section, they listen for unconscious motivations, early childhood relationship issues, defenses, or other material that will help them assess their patients' problems.

A few may make use of projective or other tests in their assessment process. Perhaps the most common test used is the Rorschach, which provides ambiguous material (ink blots) onto which patients can project their feelings and motivations. An instrument that was designed specifically to measure concepts within Freudian drive theory is the Blacky Test, a series of 12 cartoons portraying a male dog named Blacky, his mother, father, and a sibling. Examples of dimensions that are measured are oral eroticism, anal expulsiveness, and Oedipal intensity (Blum, 1949). The Quality of Relations Scale (Azim, Piper, Segal, & Nixon, 1991) assesses different levels of maturity of relationships with others. Although the Quality of Relations Scale has been used primarily for research purposes, some practitioners have found it to be of value in assessment of patients' problems.

Psychoanalysis, Psychotherapy, and Psychoanalytic Counseling

It is easier to differentiate between the structures of psychoanalysis, psychoanalytic therapy, and psychoanalytic counseling than it is to separate the processes of these approaches. Usually, psychoanalysis is conducted with a patient lying on a couch and the analyst sitting in a chair behind him. Most commonly, analysands (patients) meet with the analysts four times per week, although sometimes it may be two, three, or five times a week. Psychoanalytic therapy takes place in a face-to-face situation, with psychoanalytic therapy meetings occurring one to three times a week. In psychoanalytic counseling, meetings are usually once per week. In general, free association in which a patient reports whatever thoughts come to his mind is used less frequently in psychotherapy and counseling than in analysis. In psychoanalysis, analysts are more likely to allow the full exploration of unconscious and early development, which may be counterproductive to those with severe disturbances. In general, when doing psychoanalysis the therapist speaks much less than in a face-to-face psychotherapeutic interaction, offering occasional clarification and interpretation. Most psychoanalysts also do psychotherapy. Although ability to explore unconscious processes and to tolerate less interaction from the therapist is an important consideration in undertaking psychoanalysis, so is cost. A year of four times per week psychoanalysis can exceed $20,000.

Differentiation between psychoanalytic therapy and psychoanalytic counseling is less clear than between these two and psychoanalysis. Furthermore, the overlap between psychoanalytic brief therapy (discussed later) and psychoanalytic counseling is such that distinction between the two is blurred. In their discussion of psychoanalytic counseling, Patton and Meara (1992) emphasize the working alliance between client and counselor as they explore problems. Like psychotherapists, counselors may make use of suggestion, support, empathy, questions, and confrontation of resistance, as well as insight-oriented interventions in the form of clarification and interpretation (Patton & Meara, 1992). Although some of these techniques are used in many types of counseling and therapy, free association, interpretation of dreams, and transference, as well as countertransference issues, are the cornerstones of psychoanalytic treatment and are discussed next.

Free Association

When patients are asked to free-associate, to relate everything of which they are aware, unconscious material arises for the analyst to examine. The content of free association may be bodily sensations, feelings, fantasies, thoughts, memories, recent events, and the analyst. Having the patient lie on the couch rather that sit in a chair is likely to produce more free-flowing associations. The use of free association assumes that unconscious material affects behavior and that it can be brought into meaningful awareness by free expression. Analysts listen for unconscious meanings and for disruptions and associations that may indicate that the material is anxiety provoking. Slips of the tongue and omitted material can be interpreted in the context of the analyst's knowledge of the patient. If the patient experiences difficulty in free-associating, the analyst interprets, where possible, this behavior and, if appropriate, shares it with the patient.

Neutrality and Empathy

In psychoanalysis, neutrality and empathy are compatible. The analyst wants the patient to be able to free-associate to materials that are affected as little as possible by aspects of the analyst that are extraneous to the patient. For example, discussing the analyst's vacation with the patient or having prominent pictures of the analyst's family in the analyst's office may interfere with the analyst's understanding of the patient's unconscious motives, feelings, and behavior. When analysts do disclose about themselves, they think carefully about the impact of this disclosure on the patient. This does not mean that the analyst is cold and uncaring. Rather, the analyst is empathic with the patient's experience and feeling. By understanding the patient's feelings and encouraging free association rather than responding directly to the patient's feelings (anger, hurt, happiness, and so forth), the analyst allows a transference relationship (feelings about the analyst) to develop. Perhaps no analytical theorist stresses the importance of empathy as a means of observing the patient in analysis more than has Kohut. Hedges (1992) gives an example of Kohut's description of empathizing with the patient's very early childhood needs for nurturing, given at a conference shortly before Kohut's death in 1981.

> She lay down on the couch the first time she came, having interrupted a previous analysis abruptly and she said she felt like she was lying in a coffin and that now the top of the coffin would be closed with a sharp click . . . she was deeply depressed and at times I thought I would lose her, that she would finally find a way out of the suffering and kill herself . . . at one time at the very worst moment of her analysis [after] . . . perhaps a year and a half, she was so badly off I suddenly had the feeling—"you know, how would you feel if I let you hold my fingers for awhile now while you are talking, maybe that would help." A doubtful maneuver. I am not recommending it but I was desperate. I was deeply worried. So I moved up a little bit in my chair and gave her two fingers. And now I'll tell you what is so nice about that story. Because an analyst always remains an analyst. I gave her my two fingers. She took hold of them and I immediately made a genetic interpretation—not to her of course, but to myself. It was the toothless gums of a very young child clamping down on an empty nipple. That is the way it felt. I didn't say anything . . . but I reacted to it even there as an analyst to myself. It was never necessary anymore. I wouldn't say that it turned the tide, but it overcame a very, very difficult impasse at a given dangerous moment and, gaining time that way, we went on for many more years with a reasonably substantial success. (Hedges, 1992, pp. 209–210)[3]

This example is a dramatic and unusual instance of empathy. However, it shows Kohut's understanding and response to his client within an object relations and self psychology context.

Resistance

During the course of analysis or therapy, patients may resist the analytical process, usually unconsciously, by a number of different means. They may be late for appointments, forget appointments, or lose interest in therapy. Sometimes they may have difficulty in remembering or free-associating during the therapy hour. At other times resistance is shown outside therapy by acting out other problems through excessive drinking or having extramarital affairs. A frequent source of resistance is known as transference resistance, which is a means of managing the relationship with the therapist so that a wished or feared interaction with the analyst can take place (Horner, 1991). A brief example of a transference resistance and the therapist's openness to the patient's perception follows:

Patient: I sensed you were angry with me last time because I didn't give you what you wanted about the feelings in my dream. I could tell by your voice.

Therapist: (Very sure this was a misperception) I don't know what my voice was like, but what is important is how you interpreted what you perceived.

Patient: I was aware of trying to please you, so I tried harder.

Therapist: I wonder if these concerns have shaped how you've been with me all along.

Patient: Sure. I don't know what to do in this room. I look for messages. (Horner, 1991, p. 97).[4]

Listening for resistances is extremely important. The decision as to when to interpret the resistance depends on the context of the situation.

Interpretation

To be meaningful to the patient, material that arises from free association, dreams, slips of the tongue, symptoms, or transference must be interpreted to the patient. Depending on the nature of the material, the analyst may interpret sexually repressed material, interpret unconscious ways that the individual is defending against repressed memories of traumatic or disturbing situations, or interpret early childhood disturbances relating to unsatisfactory parenting. Analysts need to attend not only to the content of the interpretation but also to the process of conveying it to the patient (Arlow, 1987). The patient's readiness to accept the material and incorporate it into his own view of himself is a significant consideration. If the interpretation is too deep, the patient may not be able to accept it and bring it into conscious awareness. Being attuned to the patient's unconscious material often requires that the analyst be attuned to her own unconscious processes as a way of evaluating the patient's unconscious material (Calder, 1976). In general, the closer the material is to the preconscious, the more likely the patient is to accept it.

Interpretation of Dreams

In psychoanalytic therapy, dreams are an important means of uncovering unconscious material and providing insight for unresolved issues. For Freud, dreams were "the royal road to a knowledge of the unconscious activities of the mind" (Freud, 1900). Through the process of dream interpretation, wishes, needs, and fears can be revealed. Freud believed that some motivations or memories are so unacceptable to the ego that they are expressed in symbolic forms, often in dreams. For Freud, the dream was a compromise between the repressed id impulses and the ego defenses. The content of the dream included the manifest content, which is the dream as the dreamer perceives it, and the latent content, the symbolic and unconscious motives within the dream. In interpreting dreams, the analyst or therapist encourages the patient to free-associate to the various aspects of the dream and to recall feelings that were stimulated by parts of the dream. As patients explore the dream, the therapist processes their associations and helps them become aware of the repressed meaning of the material, thus developing new insights into their problems. Although Freud focused on repressed sexual and aggressive drives, other analysts have used other approaches to dream interpretation and emphasized an ego, object relations, or self psychology approach.

To illustrate drive, object relations, and self psychology approaches to dream interpretation, here is Mitchell's (1988) example of how a dream can be interpreted from these three different points of view. He gives the case of a patient who, after several years of productive analysis, reports a recurring dream. In this example, Mitchell describes the dream and three different perspectives of the dream.

The Dream
I am on a subway somewhere—it is chaotic—I feel overloaded, both mentally and physically, carrying several bags and my briefcase—something catches my attention, and for a few seconds I leave my things to explore it—when I get back, the briefcase is gone—I get very angry at myself for having done this—then I feel a great terror. (p. 36)[5]

A Drive Interpretation
In the drive model the basic units of analysis are desire and fear of punishment. Relations with other people are important, but not as basic constituents of mind or as contributing meaning of their own; they are vehicles for the expression of drive and defenses. In this dream the anal referent in the underground tunnel, the phallic significance of the train, the castration and vaginal imagery in the *briefcase*, the oedipal significance of following ill-fated impulses—all these would be granted motivational priority. Other people are objects of desire; other people are instruments of punishment. But the form of the conflict, the shape of the drama, is inherent in the desire itself, which will inevitably lead to the fear of punishment. Meaning is provided a priori in the inherent nature of desire. (p. 39)

An Object Relations Interpretation
Within a relational-model perspective, the dream would be seen as representing the patient's experience of herself, and herself in relation to others, in different sorts of ways: one mediated by the oppressive, compulsive devotion through which she characteristically binds herself to others, the other more spontaneous and yet also risky and dangerous. Can she go after things she spontaneously desires, or will this isolate her from other people, cut her off with no sense of identity, no way to connect with others? From the vantage point of the relational model this is the central question of the analysis and change entails her slowly tolerating enough anxiety to gradually redefine herself in relation to others, the analyst included. (pp. 36–37)

A Self Psychology Interpretation
Self psychologies call our attention here to the self component of the field—the sense of being overburdened, the fear of her own spontaneity, the terror of depletion. The familiar, oppressive briefcase with its obligations and demands represents the self which is seen and mirrored within her family and which, therefore, although distorted, is the only vehicle for self-recognition; the analysand equates losing her briefcase with disintegration, losing her self. (p. 38)

Depending on the analyst's or therapist's point of view and the nature of the patient's problem and disorder, an analyst or therapist might use any of these means of understanding the unconscious material in a dream. Additionally, an ego psychology approach might reveal a different way of understanding the dream, as would other psychoanalytic approaches that are not covered in this chapter, such as those based on the work of Sullivan or Horney. In interpreting the dream, Mitchell (1988) makes use not only of the dream itself but also of the variations within the recurring dream and, particularly, knowledge of the patient that he has gathered during the several years of analysis.

Interpretation and Analysis of Transference

The relationship between patient and analyst is a crucial aspect of psychoanalytic treatment. In fact, Arlow (1987) believes that the most effective interpretations deal with the analysis of the transference. Patients work through their early relationships, particularly with parents, by responding to the analyst as they may have with a parent. If there was an emotional conflict in which the patient at age 3 or 4 was angry at her mother, then anger may be transferred to the analyst. It is the task of the analyst to help patients work through their early feelings toward parents as they are expressed in the transference.

The four psychological approaches (drive, ego, object relations, and self psychology) base interpretations of transference on early, unconscious material. The way they differ reflects their special listening perspective. Pine (1990) gives a hypothetical example of four differing interpretations of a female patient's flirtatious behavior with her male analyst. In this example, the woman is described as having had "as a child, a flirtatious sexualized relation to her father of a degree that was intensely exciting to her and who suffered a profound sense of rebuff when she felt she lost him when her mother was near" (p. 5). In the following four hypothetical responses that analysts of differing orientations could make, I include Pine's responses and summarize his explanation:

1. "So, now that your mother has left for her vacation you seem to feel safe in being flirtatious here, too, as you say you've been all day with others. I guess you're figuring that this time, finally, I won't turn away to be with her as you felt your father did." (*Drive theory: The sexual drive, the wish to be with the father is interpreted.*)

2. "It's not surprising that you suddenly found yourself retelling that incident of the time when your mother was critical of you. I think you were critical of yourself for flirting with me so freely just now, and you brought her right into the room with us so that nothing more could happen between us." (*Ego psychology: The focus is on the anxiety*

aroused from the flirtation and the guilt for flirting; attention is paid to the patient's defense mechanisms.)

3. "Your hope seems to be that, if you continue to get excitedly flirtatious with me, and I don't respond with excitement, you'll finally be able to tolerate your excitement without fearing that you'll be overwhelmed by it." (*Object relations: The interpretation relates to dealing with high levels of intensity in an early object relation [parental] experience.*)

4. "When those profound feelings of emptiness arise in you, the flirtatiousness helps you feel filled and alive and so it becomes especially precious to you. It was as though when your father turned his attention to your mother, he didn't know that you would wish to be healed by him and not only be sexy with him." (*Self psychology: The emphasis is on a painful subjective experience within the grandiose self, with the father turning from the patient toward the mother.*) (Pine, 1990, p. 6)[6]

Although these different approaches may seem subtle, they illustrate that the listening perspectives of the four psychologies are somewhat different, yet all use the interpretive mode. Both Kernberg (with borderline disorders) and Kohut (with narcissistic disorders) integrate transference into their theoretical approaches, as illustrated in the examples of their therapeutic work later in this chapter.

Countertransference

Psychotherapists approach their reactions to the patient (countertransference) from different viewpoints. Moeller (1977) presents three different positions on countertransference. First, the traditional interpretation of countertransference is the irrational or neurotic reactions of therapists toward the patient. Second, a broader usage of the term refers to the therapist's entire feelings toward the patient, conscious or unconscious. The third view sees countertransference as a counterpart of the patient's transference. In other words, the feelings of the patient affect those of the therapist and vice versa. In this third way of viewing countertransference, the therapist might think, "Am I feeling the way my patient's mother may have felt?" In this way therapists try to understand (or to empathize with) their patient, their own feelings, and the interaction between the two. A great variety of positions have been taken on countertransference issues.

Although psychoanalysis, psychoanalytic psychotherapy, and psychoanalytic counseling differ in terms of the length of treatment, whether a couch is used for the patient, and their emphasis on exploring and interpreting unconscious material, they do have much in common. All examine how relationships and/or motivations before the age of 5 affect current functioning in children, adolescents, and adults. In general, their goals are to help an individual gain insight into current behaviors and issues and thus enable the patient to change behaviors, feelings, and cognitions by becoming aware of unconscious material affecting the current functioning. Although projective and objective tests may be used for assessing concerns, most often the analyst's or therapist's theoretical approach to understanding the patient's childhood development provides a way of assessing analytic material. Much of this material may come from free association toward daily events, feelings, dreams, or other events in the patient's life. As the relationship develops, the analyst or therapist observes a transference—the relationship of the patient to the therapist—and the countertransference—the therapist's reactions to the patient. Observations about the patient-therapist relationship as well as material coming from dreams and other material are interpreted to the patient in ways that will bring about insight into the patient's problems.

PSYCHOLOGICAL DISORDERS

Finding consensus on how to treat patients with psychoanalysis, psychoanalytic therapy, or psychoanalytic counseling is very difficult. Because of the length of therapy, the emphasis on unconscious material, and the many psychoanalytic writers with varying opinions, it is difficult to describe a specific procedure for each disorder. In this section, I try to illustrate further the different treatment and conceptual approaches of the four psychologies by describing cases of each: Drive theory (Freud), ego psychology (Erikson), object relations (Kernberg), and self psychology (Kohut). My emphasis is on presenting the theorists' way of working with disorders that they have written about extensively, rather than presenting an overview of treatment for each disorder. An example of Freud's work with a young woman illustrates his conceptualization of sexuality as it relates to hysteria. Many psychoanalysts, such as Anna Freud, Margaret Mahler, and Erik Erikson, have applied psychoanalytic principles to treatment of children. I show how Erik Erikson makes use of ego psychology perspectives with a 3-year-old girl with nightmares and anxiety. Otto Kernberg is well known for applying object relations perspectives to borderline disorders, and a case of a man presenting a borderline disorder with paranoid aspects illustrates this. Self psychology has been applied to people with many disorders, but its focus has been on the development of narcissism. Kohut's work with a person with a narcissistic disorder provides insight into his conceptualization of transference in the therapeutic relationship. Freud's and Erikson's brief interventions could be called psychoanalytic counseling, whereas Kernberg's and Kohut's are long term and deeper in nature and come close to fitting the definition of psychoanalytic psychotherapy. Finally, I describe a case using psychoanalytic psychotherapy that combines the view of Freudian drive theory with object relations theory in helping a young woman with an eating disorder.

Treatment of Hysteria

Much of Freud's early work was with patients who presented symptoms of hysteria, as is documented in five case histories in *Studies on Hysteria* (Breuer & Freud, 1895). The case of Katharina is unusual in that it is extremely brief, basically one contact with the patient, and it took place when Freud was on vacation in the Alps. However, it illustrates several of Freud's approaches to hysterical disorders. In the vast writings on Freud and his contribution to psychoanalysis, his kind concern for his patients is often lost. It is evident in this case, which illustrates the value of unconscious processes and the defense mechanism of repression in dealing with early traumatic sexual events. Although he was later to believe that many of the "facts" reported by patients with hysteria were fantasy, his experience with Katharina does not fit that description. In fact, he says, writing prior to 1895,

> In every analysis of a case of hysteria based on sexual traumas we find that impressions from the pre-sexual period which produced no effect on the child attained traumatic

power at a later date as memories when the girl or married woman has acquired an understanding of sexual life. (p. 133)[7]

In the summer of 1893, Freud had gone mountain climbing in the eastern Alps and was sitting atop a mountain, when 18-year-old Katharina approached to inquire if he was a doctor; she had seen his name in the visitor's book. Surprised, he listened to her symptoms, which included shortness of breath (not due to climbing the high mountains) and a feeling in her throat as if she was going to choke, as well as hammering in her head. He recorded the dialogue.

"Do you know what your attacks come from?" "No."
   "When did you first have them?"
   "Two years ago, while I was still living on the other mountain with my aunt. (She used to run a refuge hut there, and we moved here eighteen months ago.) But they keep on happening."
   Was I to make an attempt at an analysis? I could not venture to transplant hypnosis to these altitudes, but perhaps I might succeed with a simple talk. I should have to try a lucky guess. I had found often enough that in girls, anxiety was a consequence of the horror by which a virginal mind is overcome when it is faced for the first time with the world of sexuality.
   So I said: "If you don't know, I'll tell you how I think you got your attacks. At that time, two years ago, you must have seen or heard something that very much embarrassed you, and that you'd much rather not have seen."
   "Heavens, yes!" she replied, "that was when I caught my uncle with the girl, with Franziska, my cousin." (pp. 126–127)

At this time in his career, Freud was still using hypnosis in treatment, although he ceased doing so shortly after this. The uncle that Freud makes reference to was actually Katharina's father. Because of Freud's wish to protect Katharina's confidentiality, he changed the father's identity to uncle in his case studies (1895) and did not reveal this change until 30 years later. As Katharina talked with Freud, she revealed occasions on which her father had made sexual advances toward her when she was 14, and later she had to push herself away from her father when he was drunk. In her physical reaction to seeing her father having intercourse with Franziska, Freud realized, "She had not been disgusted by the sight of the two people but by the memory which that sight had stirred up in her. And, taking everything into account, this could only be a memory of the attempt on her at night when she had 'felt her uncle's body'" (p. 131). This leads to his conclusion as to why she unconsciously converted her psychological distress to physical symptoms.

So when she had finished her confession I said to her: "I know now what it was you thought when you looked into the room. You thought: 'Now he's doing with her what he wanted to do with me that night and those other times.' That was what you were disgusted at, because you remembered the feeling when you woke up in the night and felt his body."
   "It may well be," she replied, "that that was what I was disgusted at and that that was what I thought."

"Tell me just one thing more. You're a grown-up girl now and know all sorts of things. . . ."

"Yes, now I am."

"Tell me just one thing. What part of his body was it that you felt that night?"

But she gave me no more definite answer. She smiled in an embarrassed way, as though she had been found out, like someone who is obliged to admit that a fundamental position has been reached where there is not much more to be said. I could imagine what the tactile sensation was which she had later learnt to interpret. Her facial expression seemed to me to be saying that she supposed that I was right in my conjecture. (pp. 131–132)

Although this case occurred at a time very different than ours, conversion hysteria such as this does occur. The other cases of hysteria that Freud presents are far more complex but have in common the repression of unwanted sexual memories or traumas and Freud's work in bringing them into conscious awareness.

Childhood Anxiety

Although psychoanalysis of anxiety disorders with an adult is very different from that of Erikson's work with 3-year-old Mary, many of the conceptual approaches are similar. Mary has just turned 3, is "intelligent, pretty, and quite feminine" (Erikson, 1950, p. 197), has experienced nightmares, and in her play group has had violent anxiety attacks. She has been taken by her mother to see Erikson at the suggestion of her physician and has been told that she was coming to see a man "to discuss her nightmares." Although the case is too long to discuss in its entirety here (pp. 195–207), Erikson's gentle sensitivity to Mary is evident throughout the case description. During the first visit with Erikson, she puts her arms around her mother and gradually looks at Erikson. In a few minutes, the mother leaves and Mary takes a doll, which she uses to touch other toys in the room. Finally, with the doll's head, she pushes a toy train onto the floor "but as the engine overturns she suddenly stops and becomes pale" (p. 199). She then leans back against the sofa and holds the doll over her waist, dropping it to the floor. Then she picks it up again, holds it again over her waist, and drops it again; finally, she yells for her mother. Erikson describes his reactions.

Strangely enough, I too felt that the child had made a successful communication. With children words are not always necessary at the beginning. I had felt that the play was leading up to a conversation. The fact that the mother's anxious interruption was, of course, as significant as the child's play disruption. Together they probably explain the child's babyish anxiety. But what had she communicated with this emotional somersault, the sudden hilarity and flushed aggressiveness and this equally sudden inhibition and pale anxiety? (p. 199)[8]

Erikson goes on to analyze the session.

In this play hour the dropped doll had first been the prolongation of an extremity and a tool of (pushing) aggression, and then something lost in the lower abdominal region under circumstances of extreme anxiety. Does Mary consider a penis such an aggressive weapon, and does she dramatize the fact that she does not have one? From the mother's account it is entirely probable that on entering the nursery school Mary was given her first opportunity to go to the toilet in the presence of boys. (p. 200)

Erikson is here referring to penis envy, the concept put forth by Freud in which the little girl believes that she has been deprived of a penis and wishes to possess one. However, Erikson attends not only to the psychosexual aspect of Mary's development but also to her psychosocial development. He observes her developing autonomy from her mother during the hour, her initiative that she takes in playing with the toys in the playroom, and her aggressiveness in pushing the toys from the shelves with the doll.

In their second meeting, Mary first plays with blocks, making a cradle for her toy cow. Then she pulls her mother out of the room and keeps Erikson in the room. Then Erikson plays a game at Mary's behest and pushes the toy cow through an opening, making it speak. With this, Mary is very pleased and gets her wish to have Erikson play with her. Previously Mary had been pushed away by her father who had been irritated by her. Erikson sees this event as an episode of "father transference" (p. 204) in which Mary is active in directing Erikson in the play situation, in a way in which she had not been able to do at home.

Suggestions were made to Mary's parents about the need to have other children, especially boys, visit at home. She was allowed to experience her nightmares, which disappeared. In a follow-up visit, Mary was relaxed and interested in the color of the train that Erikson had taken on his vacation. Erikson later found that Mary particularly enjoyed her new walks with her father to the railroad yards, where they watched railroad engines. In commenting, Erikson attends not only to the phallic aspect of the locomotive engine but also to the social interaction with her father that leads to diminishment of anxiety.

Borderline Disorders

Because Kernberg's writings have influenced the object relations–based treatment of individuals with borderline disorders, this section focuses on his approach to these difficult psychological disturbances. In brief, Kernberg sees borderline disorders as due to extreme frustration and aggression that children experience before the age of 4 (Kernberg, 1975). When young children are intensely and continuously frustrated by one or both parents, they may protect themselves by projecting their feelings of aggression back to the parents and also by distorting their image of their parents (St. Clair, 1996). When this occurs, the parents are seen as potentially threatening and dangerous rather than loving, thus later love or sexual relationships are likely to be viewed as dangerous rather than nurturing. This results in the development of individuals with borderline disorders who are likely to have difficulty in integrating loving and angry images of themselves and others and thus "split" their reactions into all-good or all-bad views of themselves or others. Much of Kernberg's (1975) approach to treatment revolves around work with the negative transference that the patient directs toward the therapist, structuring therapy so that the patient does not act out negative transference feelings to the therapist. Further, he tries to confront the patient's pathological defenses that reduce the ability to accurately interpret external events.

In understanding Kernberg's approach to personality disorders, it is helpful to be familiar with two terms that are related to the negative transference. The *transference psychosis* refers to acting out of early angry and destructive relationships that the patient, as a child, had with his parents. Kernberg observes that this transference emerges early in therapy and is usually negative and confusing. *Projective identification* is an early form of projection in which patients take negative aspects of their personality, project them or place them onto another, and then identify with and unconsciously try to control that person. In therapy, a projective identification is likely to be experienced by the therapist as feelings that the patient has and that the therapist now feels. Applying projective identification to therapy, Kernberg (1975, p. 80) states that "it is as if the patient's life depended on his keeping the therapist under control."

In the case below, Kernberg's application of negative transference and projective identification is evident in his treatment of a hostile and suspicious patient.

Mr. R., a businessman in his late forties, consulted because he was selectively impotent with women from his own socioeconomic and cultural environment, although he was potent with prostitutes and women from lower socioeconomic backgrounds; he had fears of being a homosexual and problems in his relationships at work. Mr. R. also was drinking excessively, mostly in connection with the anxiety related to his sexual performance with women. He was the son of an extremely sadistic father who regularly beat his children, and a hypochondriacal, chronically complaining and submissive mother whom the patient perceived as ineffectually attempting to protect the children from father. The patient himself, the second of five siblings, experienced himself as the preferred target of both father's aggression and his older brother's teasing and rejecting behavior. His diagnostic assessment revealed a severely paranoid personality, borderline personality organization, and strong, suppressed homosexual urges. The treatment was psychoanalytic psychotherapy, three sessions per week.

At one point in the treatment, Mr. R. commented several times in a vague sort of way that I seemed unfriendly and when greeting him at the start of sessions conveyed the feeling that I was annoyed at having to see him. In contrast to these vague complaints, one day he told me, with intense anger and resentment, that I had spat on the sidewalk when I saw him walking on the other side of the street.

I asked him whether he was really convinced that, upon seeing him, I had spat; he told me, enraged, that he knew it and that I should not pretend it was not true. When I asked why I would behave in such a way toward him, Mr. R. angrily responded that he was not interested in my motivations, just in my behavior, which was totally unfair and cruel. My previous efforts to interpret his sense that I felt displeasure, disapproval, and even disgust with him as the activation, in the transference, of his relationship with his sadistic father had led nowhere. He had only angrily replied that I now felt free to mistreat him in the same way his father had, just as everybody in his office felt free to mistreat him as well. This time, he became extremely enraged when I expressed—in my tone and gesture more than in my words—my total surprise at the assumption that I had spat upon seeing him. He told me that he had difficulty controlling his urge to beat me up, and, indeed, I was afraid that he might even now become physically assaultive. I told him that his impression was totally wrong, that I had not seen him and had no memory of any gesture that might be interpreted as spitting on the street. I added that, in the light of what I was saying, he would have to decide whether I was lying to him or telling him the truth, but I could only insist that this was my absolute, total conviction. (Kernberg, 1992, pp. 235–236)[9]

Kernberg then discusses the patient's behavior and the patient's reaction to his explanation.

His attributing to me the aggression that he did not dare to acknowledge in himself—while attempting to control my behavior and to induce in me the aggressive reaction he was afraid of—and, at the time, his attempting to control me as an expression of fear of his own, now conscious, aggression reflect typical projective identification. But rather than interpret this mechanism, I stressed the incompatibility of our perceptions of reality per se, thus highlighting the existence of a psychotic nucleus, which I described to him as madness clearly present in the session, without locating it in either him or me. Mr. R.'s reaction was dramatic. He suddenly burst into tears, asked me to forgive him, and stated that he felt an intense upsurge of love for me and was afraid of its homosexual implications. I told him I realized that in expressing this feeling he was acknowledging that his perception of reality had been unreal, that he was appreciative of my remaining at his side rather than being drawn into a fight, and that, in this context, he now saw me as the opposite of his real father, as the ideal, warm, and giving father he had longed for. Mr. R. acknowledged these feelings and talked more freely than before about his longings for a good relationship with a powerful man. (pp. 236–237)

This excerpt shows Kernberg's view of the powerful anger that can occur in the transference of negative parental experience in early childhood to the therapist. Kernberg also illustrates two concepts related to early object relations: the transference psychosis and projective identification.

Narcissistic Disorders

For Kohut, narcissistic personality disorders or disturbances are due to problems in not getting sufficient attention from a parent in early childhood (the grandiose self) or having sufficient respect for the parents. The cause of narcissistic disorders is due to the failure to develop positive feelings about the self when the experience of parenting has been disruptive or inadequate. When a child has a perception (usually unconscious) that the parent has been absent, uninterested in the child, or faulty, the child may grow into an adult who sees herself at the center of relationships (Kohut, 1971, 1977).

The inadequate relationships with the mother and/or father are likely to emerge in therapy in two types of transferences: mirroring or idealizing. In the mirroring transference patients see themselves as perfect and assign perfection to others, especially the therapist. Thus, the mirroring transference is an enactment of early childhood issues that feature the grandiose self. The term *mirroring* refers to the degree to which the therapist serves the patient's needs by confirming the patient's need for grandiosity through approval and assurance that the patient is wonderful. In the idealized transference, it is not the patient who is wonderful, but the therapist. Patients project their loss of their perfect mother or father onto the therapist.

In therapy, Kohut was attuned to or empathic with the patient's early difficulties in centering all of her attention on the self or on the parent. Therapeutic growth occurs when the patient's needs for attention and admiration from the therapist are replaced by improved relationships with important people in the patient's life. In a sense, the therapist serves as a link so that the patient can move from self-absorption, to attention to the therapist rather than to just herself, and then later to others. Kohut (1971, 1977, 1984) has developed an extensive set of terms that describe his conceptualization and treatment approach to narcissistic and other disorders.

The case of Mr. J. illustrates Kohut's (1971) approach to narcissistic disorders. A creative writer in his early thirties, Mr. J. was in psychoanalytic psychotherapy with Kohut for several years because of his concern about his productivity and unhappiness. An indication of his grandiosity were his dreams, expressed in Superman terms, in which he was able to fly (p. 169). As treatment progressed, Mr. J. no longer dreamed of flying, but that he was walking. However, in these dreams, he knew that his feet never touched the ground, but no one else did. Thus, his grandiosity had diminished, as evidenced by the dreams, but was still present.

In psychoanalysis, seemingly trivial incidents can provide significant material. During one session, Mr. J. reported to Kohut about how he carefully rinsed his shaving brush, cleaned his razor, and scrubbed the sink before washing his face. By attending to the arrogant manner in which he presented this material, Kohut was able to move into an exploration of the patient's childhood history, with a focus on the grandiosity of the patient and the lack of maternal attention.

> Gradually, and against strong resistances (motivated by deep shame, fear of overstimulation, fear of traumatic disappointment), the narcissistic transference began to center around his need to have his body-mind-self confirmed by the analyst's admiring acceptance. And gradually we began to understand the pivotal dynamic position in the transference of the patient's apprehension that the analyst—like his self-centered mother who could love only what she totally possessed and controlled (her jewelry, furniture, china, silverware)—would prefer his material possessions to the patient and would value the patient only as a vehicle to his own aggrandizement; and that I would not accept him if he claimed his own initiative toward the display of his body and mind, and if he insisted on obtaining his own, independent narcissistic rewards. It was only after he had acquired increased insights into these aspects of his personality that the patient began to experience the deepest yearning for the acceptance of an archaic, unmodified grandiose-exhibitionistic body-self which had for so long been hidden by the open display of narcissistic demands via a split-off sector of the psyche, and that a working-through process was initiated which enabled him ultimately, as he put it jokingly, "to prefer my face to the razor." (pp. 182–183)[10]

Kohut helps Mr. J. in several ways. By recognizing Mr. J.'s need to be mirrored or appreciated, Kohut acknowledges the importance of Mr. J.'s mother's lack of attention. When Kohut discusses his insights with Mr. J., Mr. J. starts to genuinely appreciate Kohut as a person, not just as someone who meets his needs.

Eating Disorders

The following case of a young woman with anorexia is presented to show how drive theory and object relations perspectives can be integrated. In the following case of

Laura, an 18-year-old woman who is 5 feet 7 inches tall and weighs 125 pounds, Scharfman (1992) attends to family issues that have contributed to her anorexia. He examines the transference between Laura and himself and how her desire to please him is a reflection of her desire to please her father. An object relations perspective is seen in his comments about her mother's interaction with Laura when she was an infant. Reference is made to Freudian drive theory through a discussion of Oedipal guilt, which is related to her relationships with men. The following is Scharfman's (1992) description of his therapy with Laura.

> Having agreed to begin analysis, Laura then spent the initial period of time trying to demonstrate that she was really not worth the time and effort. There were other patients who certainly must be more interesting than she was, and I would be far more interested in them. This began to focus on those occasions when she saw a particular male patient whose hours preceded hers several days a week. In her fantasy, he was a young doctor I would like and would help to become successful and happy. She could connect this to her feeling about her parents' having preferred her older brother to her. Eventually, her younger brother also appeared in her thoughts as someone who had a preferred status. She was the disappointment. At the same time, she imagined that I would be more interested in her if she were a young psychiatrist who wanted to become a psychoanalyst. It was pointed out to her how much she wanted to please me, just as she had always sought to please her father, but also how she had carried over the anticipation of being disappointed because of a preference for a son.
>
> Laura went through a variety of material centered on various memories that confirmed for her not only that her father preferred boys, but that her mother also had a strong preference for her sons. Her own competitiveness and resentment of her brothers became clearer to her. Throughout her childhood she had sought to win her father's attention, following her initial disappointment in her mother when her younger brother was born. She had done this by becoming a kind of tomboy, being very active in swimming, tennis, and other sports. Her father admired her performance in all of these, and she enjoyed that. It was only in relation to her father watching her perform when she danced that she became very uncomfortable, particularly following puberty. It was now clear that it was also safer to seek attention from her father through her masculine strivings than it was to have him respond to her as a young woman. Much of this was paralleled in the transference. When this was pointed out to her, there began a subtle change in her manner of relating as well as in her dress, all in the direction of presenting herself more as an attractive young woman. Her fears of acknowledging any sexual wishes of her own became much clearer to her. There was clearly a great deal of oedipal guilt involved, but this was also very much connected to her envy and resentment of men. Underlying this phallic envy, the envy of her brother nursing at the mother's breast appeared as we reconstructed some of her early observations of her mother with the new baby. She had strong wishes to suck at and swallow the breast-penis. One of the first aversions she had had when her weight loss started centered on an intense distaste for milk and milk products and a wish to avoid them. She became aware through a series of memories about visiting a farm that she had observed cows being milked and had also observed animals having intercourse. She was startled when she realized the connection she had made between milk and semen and then found it all very funny. Following this, all of her difficulties with food intake began to change.

Material shifted to her relationship with her mother, and more of maternal transference appeared for a while. She and her mother became friends and were much closer emotionally. As the analysis proceeded, oedipal themes again became dominant. In the transference, as well as in the other material, there was a well-organized transference neurosis that was gradually worked through. (pp. 318–319)[11]

The five case examples give some insight into the complexity of psychoanalysis and psychoanalytic therapy, while illustrating drive, ego, object relations, and self psychology perspectives. Although the disorders presented are different, all cases show the emphasis on unconscious forces and the impact of early childhood development on current functioning. Most of the examples also focus on the transference relationship between patient and therapist. Differences in treatment relate not only to the age and sex of the patient and to the type of psychological disorder but also to the therapist's view of early childhood development that influences interpretations and other approaches to psychoanalytic therapy.

BRIEF THERAPY

Because psychoanalysis may require four or five sessions per week over 3 to 8 years (or longer) and psychoanalytic psychotherapy requires meetings at least once a week for several years, many mental health professionals have felt the need to provide briefer therapy. If successful, this would substantially reduce the cost to the patient, provide quicker resolution of psychological distress, provide better delivery of mental health services through shorter waiting lists, and offer more services for more patients. The popularity of brief psychodynamic therapy is indicated by a variety of approaches (Bloom, 1997; Messer & Warren, 1995). Crits-Christoph and Barber (1991) compare 10 short-term dynamic psychotherapies in terms of length, goals, techniques, selection, and process. The impetus for brief approaches to psychoanalytic psychotherapy has been the work of Malan (1976) in England. In using a short-term approach, Malan had to deal with issues such as how to select patients, what goals to choose for therapy, and how long treatment should last.

In general, most current short-term psychoanalytic psychotherapies are designed for people who are neurotic, motivated, and focused rather than for those with severe personality disorders as described by Kernberg and Kohut. The treatment length is usually about 12 to 40 sessions, with several time-limited approaches specifying limits of 12 to 16 sessions. To work in such a short time frame, it is necessary to have focused goals to address. Although short-term therapists use diagnostic or conceptual approaches that are similar to those of long-term therapists, their techniques are not. Where psychoanalysts and psychoanalytic therapists make use of free association, short-term therapists rarely use this technique; rather, they prefer to ask questions, to restate, to confront, and to deal quickly with transference issues. To further describe approaches to brief therapy, I discuss two of the more established approaches: Lester Luborsky's Core Conflictual Relationship Theme Method, based on understanding the transference relationship, and Peter Sifneos's short-term anxiety-provoking psychotherapy, based on drive and ego psychology.

Core Conflictual Relationship Theme

Since 1975, Lester Luborsky and his colleagues have authored over 50 articles that describe and validate aspects of the Core Conflictual Relationship Theme method. This is a specific method for understanding transference and can be used for both short-term and long-term psychotherapy (Luborsky & Crits-Christoph, 1998). However, it has been applied to brief psychodynamic psychotherapy. Luborsky (1984) and Book (1998) describe this approach to brief psychotherapy in detail. This method has three phases, all of which deal with the therapist's understanding of the Core Conflictual Relationship Theme.

To determine a patient's Core Conflictual Relationship Theme, a therapist must listen to the patient's discussion or story of Relationship Episodes. Often, the therapist writes down the three important components of a Relationships Episode. These include a Wish, a Response from the Other, and the Response from the Self (Luborsky, 1984). A patient's wish refers to a desire that is expressed in a Relationship Episode. This is determined by listening to what the patient's actual response from the Other person will be (or an anticipated response). The therapist also listens to what the response to the relationship situation will be from the individual (Response from the Self). Sometimes the relationship discussed is a daydream, or an actual situation. A Core Conflictual Relationship Theme is communicated to the patient when the therapist has discussed five to seven Relationship Episodes with the patient. In doing so, the therapist may say to the client, "It seems to me that you want to be in a relationship where . . ." (Book, 1998, p. 22).

Book (1998) uses the case of Mrs. Brown to describe the three phases of the Core Conflictual Relationship Theme method. This case is summarized here, focusing on the first phase.

The goal of the first phase, usually the first four sessions, is to help the patient become aware of how the Core Conflictual Relationship Theme plays a role in the patient's relationships. The patient becomes curious about why she may expect others to respond to her in a certain way or why others tend to respond to her in a certain way. For example, Mrs. Brown often kept her accomplishments to herself, believing that others might find them silly or unimportant. Because of this, she tended to distance herself from others in relationships, and often felt overlooked and disappointed in her relationships with others. The following excerpt from the second session of therapy shows how the therapist focuses on the Core Conflictual Relationship Theme. In this dialogue, Mrs. Brown discusses her relationship with a co-worker, Beth.

> **P:** So Beth and I were discussing who should make the presentations. I said that she should.
>
> **T:** Why?
>
> **P:** She had more experience.
>
> **T:** So?
>
> **P:** She would stand a better chance of getting it through.
>
> **T:** If she did the presenting?
>
> **P:** Yeah. Others would be taken by the way she presents.
>
> **T:** And, if *you* presented?

P: What do you mean?

T: If you presented, how might others respond (Exploring the Response from the Other)?

P: I don't think I would do such a good job.

T: In their eyes?

P: Yeah. I figure they would think . . . it was stupid.

T: Do you see what you are saying?

P: What? (Perplexed.)

T: Isn't this exactly what we have been talking about? Isn't it another example of your fear that if you put your best foot forward, that if you attempt to promote yourself and your ideas (her Wish), others will see you and your ideas as stupid and worthless (Response from the Other)?

P: Aha! So I shut up (Response from the Self)? Oh, my goodness. There it is again! I didn't even realize it!

T: Yes. It is interesting how you rule yourself in this way without even realizing it and short change yourself in the process (Book, 1998, pp. 66, 67).[12]

In the first phase of therapy, the therapist focuses on identifying the patient's Core Conflictual Relationship Theme as it relates to her everyday life. Thus the patient becomes consciously aware of relationship themes in her life that she was not aware of previously. She now will be able to have control over previously unconscious behavior.

During the second phase, usually the fifth through the twelfth session, the patient works through the Response from Others. This is the major phase of treatment, and during it, the childhood roots of the transference-driven Response from Others are worked through. Here, the therapist interprets how the patients' expectations of Responses from Others are affected by attitudes, feelings, and behaviors that were learned from others in the past. The patient learns how unconscious attitudes from the past affect relationships in the present. In the case of Mrs. Brown, the therapist helped her to understand how her current relationships were affected by her earlier relationship with her father. She had wanted to be praised by her father but rarely received praise or recognition from him. As she realized this, she more willingly shared her achievements with co-workers and family.

Termination is the focus of the third phase, usually the thirteenth to sixteenth sessions. This phase allows the therapist and patient to discuss universal themes such as fears of abandonment, separation, and loss. The therapist may also discuss the patient's worries that gains that were made in treament will not continue. This phase also gives the therapist an opportunity to work through the Core Conflictual Relationship Theme again. Returning to Mrs. Brown, the therapist observed that she was late for her eleventh and twelfth sessions and was less talkative. After discussing this, the patient and therapist found that Mrs. Brown was acting as if the therapist was losing interest and more interested in the patient who would replace her. This gave the therapist the opportunity to return to the Core Conflictual Relationship Theme that could be related to her father's dismissiveness of her and similar early experiences. In this way, the therapist dealt with transference issues so that Mrs. Brown would be freer to share her achievements with others and be less distant in relationships.

As can be seen from the brief example above, the Core Conflictual Relationship Theme method is time-limited and very specific in approach. The therapist attends to relationships that the client discusses, listening for a Wish, a Response from the Other, and the Response from the Self. Observations and interpretations made to the patient allow the patient to understand previously unconscious feelings, attitudes, or behaviors and make changes. Important in this method is the understanding of the transference issues that reflect attitudes and behaviors of early relationships as they influence later relationships, especially those with the therapist.

Sifneos's Brief Therapy

Sifneos (1997) uses an approach that has confrontive and supportive aspects in a time frame of 12 to 15 sessions. Selection of patients for short-term anxiety-provoking psychotherapy (STAPP) is done carefully, with an emphasis on the patient's ability to interact with others, to be flexible, to be motivated for change, and to explore psychological issues. In the first session, the therapist identifies a psychodynamic issue, usually an unresolved Oedipal conflict, as the focus of therapy. Sifneos (1987) uses anxiety-provoking questions to assist the patient in examining areas of psychological conflict that have previously been avoided. In his approach to therapy, Sifneos first establishes a good working alliance with the patient and then proceeds to discuss transference issues (usually positive) with the patient. Through the use of confrontation, clarification, and interpretation, Sifneos explores Oedipal conflicts.

Nielsen and Barth (1991) give an example of this approach in therapy with a 34-year-old female school counselor who is having difficulty in dealing with her father's death, her mother's living in her house, and her relationship with her husband.

Patient: I remember how nice it was to lie between mum and dad in their bed, mother holding my hand and playing with my foot, and father fondling my hair, which I loved him to do. Somehow I decided very early that I should never be like my mother. She couldn't cope with her children. She started to cry when things became difficult for her. Somehow I consciously decided to become better than her.

Therapist: Better than your mother? How?

Patient: Well, I remember our skiing trips high up in the mountains. We had to climb the hillsides. They were steep, you know. The girls started to cry and refused to go any further. I felt contempt for them: Why couldn't they pull themselves together and go on?

Therapist: You felt contempt for your mother, too?

Patient: It was somehow important to be the best. You know, I picked up sports, sports my father was interested in. But I never was interested in the stuff my mother was good at, cooking and sewing, for example.

Therapist: You were afraid of not being able to knock your mother out in that area, too?

Patient: Um (blushing), I haven't thought of it that way . . . I got the thought the other night that my nice pleasing behavior has something to do with my competition with the other girls. When I compete I can even exceed the limits of what I can cope with. I am using my brothers' measures.

Therapist: What do you mean? Please give an example.

Patient: Well, one week after I had given birth to my first child, I still had stitches and couldn't sit, but I started immediately to see my clients again. Well, it was completely crazy when I think of it today.

Therapist: How do you explain your behavior? Why did you do such a thing, and why was it so terribly important to reach that mountain peak? Why was it important to be the best, better than your mother?

Patient: I don't know.

Therapist: Oh, come on, now you are beating about the bush again.

Patient: I think I wanted the recognition from my father. . . . Yes, that was very important, that he acknowledged me, that he showed his love for me. (She goes on giving examples of what she used to do to please her father.)

The therapist actively urges the patient to be specific and to avoid vagueness. She is continuously asking for examples and encouraging the patient to verbalize her own understanding of the situation. Thus, the therapist is making anxiety-provoking clarifications, confrontations, and questions, relying on the working alliance and on the patient's motivation for change. (pp. 62–63)[13]

The patient's psychological conflicts are dealt with directly and confronted, as are any verbal or nonverbal indications of defenses. When the problem, usually an Oedipal conflict, has been solved, termination can then take place (Nielsen & Barth, 1991). The confrontive and focused approach of Sifneos differs dramatically from long-term psychoanalysis, which relies on unfocused free association and the gradual development of transference. Yet both methods use similar conceptual approaches.

CURRENT TRENDS

The oldest of all major theories of psychotherapy, psychoanalysis continues to flourish and thrive. Due to economic and social reasons, there are changes in the practice of psychoanalysis. Also, two psychoanalytical issues are receiving attention now: treatment manuals and the two-person versus one-person model. All of these issues are explained more fully.

It seems reasonable to assume that there are more books written about psychoanalysis than about all the other theories covered in this book combined. It would not be unusual for large universities to have more than a thousand books on psychoanalysis in their libraries. Many books continue to be published in this area, with a few publishers specializing in books on psychoanalysis. The vast majority of these writings are not on research but on applying psychoanalytic concepts to treatment issues. Implicit in this work are the discussion and disputation of previous psychoanalytic writers. An issue of debate relates to how far a theorist can revise Freud or diverge from him and still be considered to be within the framework of psychoanalysis. For example, some writers would state that Kohut's self psychology has overstepped the boundaries of psychoanalysis. Due in part to the large number of psychoanalytic therapists and to the emphasis on writing about ideas rather than doing research, there are many divergent perspectives. These appear not only in books but in many of the psychoanalytic publications: *American Psychoanalytic Association Journal, International Journal of Psychoanalysis, Psychoanalytic Quarterly, Psychoanalytic Study of the Child, Psychoanalytic Review, Psychiatry, International Psychoanalytic Review, International Journal of Psychoanalytic Psychotherapy, Psychoanalysis and Contemporary Science,* and *Psychological Issues*.

The introduction of treatment manuals provides a way to make psychoanalysis more popular and comprehensible to those not directly familiar with it. Treatment manuals allow psychoanalysts to specify what they do and how they do it. Luborsky (1984) and Book (1998) have specified a 16-session model for brief psychodynamic therapy that is described on page 63. Luborsky and Crits-Christoph (1998) spell out in clear detail to students and therapists how the Core Conflictual Relationship method can be used by describing interview strategies along with case illustrations. As treatment manuals become more available to mental health professionals, access to what many consider to be a complex and sometimes arcane model will become more readily available. Psychoanalytic training of new mental health professionals will become easier when they have treatment manuals such as those describing the Core Conflictual Relationship Theme method. Because treatment manuals specify the procedures the therapist must follow in order to practice a particular method, they provide a way for researchers to be more sure that the therapist variable is being controlled in their research. Psychodynamic treatment manuals also make comparisons between therapies with more easily definable concepts, such as behavioral and cognitive therapies, to be compared directly to psychodynamic therapies.

A very different trend has been the interest in psychoanalysis toward a two-person psychology as contrasted with a one-person psychology. The two-person psychology focuses on how the patient and therapist influence each other. In contrast, the one-person psychology emphasizes the psychology of the patient. The two-patient psychology is based on the work of postmodern and relational writers, such as Mitchell (1997). The two-person approach is a constructivist one in which the analyst pays close attention to his contributions to his patient's reactions. There is an awareness that both patient and therapist have important perceptions of reality. In contrast, objectivists or rationalists who follow a one-person model would believe that they can judge the patient's distortion of reality or of facts. Such psychoanalysts would advocate the use of neutrality, and the therapist as a blank screen. Therapists who use a two-person model are more likely to use empathic techniques in their work. They are likely to look inward at their own perceptions in evaluating their patients.

A brief example of using the two-psychology approach shows how a therapist can look at his own view of reality and compare it to his patient's to better understand the patient's experience.

> I had a patient who was quite challenging to me. She gave up her marriage with a conventional man, according to her, controlling and unloving husband who wanted her back, and began a series of relationships with younger, racially and culturally different, and for a time in my mind, inappropriate men who were rejecting and hurting her deeply. It was hard for me to decenter from what I thought would be best for her. Could it be, by my suggestion of

a practical solution to her life problems, which she didn't want—couples therapy for her and her husband—I was trying to avoid having to hear and also experience with her the depths of her inner suffering and suicidal hopelessness? (Kahn, 1996, pp. 35, 36).

Kahn (1996) tries to move away from his own preconceptions of how his patient should lead her life toward being empathic with her suffering. He recognizes his own preconceptions of reality and attends to his client's. A one-person model might look at the patient's sexual acting out as a transference relationship with the therapist based on early negative reactions to her father.

An important model that falls within the two-person psychology is that of intersubjectivity theory. Stolorow and his colleagues (Orange, Atwood, & Stolorow, 1997) have been influenced by Kohut's self psychology. In their work they emphasize the subjectivity of both the patient and the therapist. They examine how the subjective nature of both patient and therapist influence each other. Just as the patient brings his unique experiences to therapy, so does the therapist. A shared reality is constructed between the two. For example, Orange (1994) suggests that the word *co-transference* would better acknowledge the influence that both patient and therapist have on each other than the term *countertransference*. Both two-person psychology and intersubjectivity are having a powerful impact on the way that psychodynamic therapists approach their work.

USING PSYCHOANALYSIS WITH OTHER THEORIES

Many mental health professionals with a wide variety of theoretical orientations make use of psychoanalytic concepts in understanding their patients. To describe such practitioners, the term *psychodynamic* is used. It generally refers to the idea that feelings, unconscious motives, or drives unconsciously influence people's behavior and that defense mechanisms are used to reduce anxiety (Hall, Lindzey, & Campbell, 1998). The term *psychoanalytic* also includes the belief that there are significant stages of development as well as important mental functions or structures such as ego, id, and superego (Robbins, 1989). Often the distinction between the two terms is not clear, and they are sometimes used interchangeably. Gelso and Fretz (1992) use the term *analytically informed therapy* or *counseling* to describe those practitioners who make use of many of the concepts discussed in the four psychologies presented in this chapter but do not rely on analytic treatment methods such as free association and interpretation. Some practitioners use behavioral, cognitive, and/or person-centered techniques while understanding their patients through the use of a psychoanalytic model. Their approach differs from brief analytic psychotherapy in that they use a broader range of techniques.

Just as nonpsychoanalytic practitioners borrow conceptual approaches from psychoanalysis, psychoanalytic practitioners borrow intervention techniques from other theories. In their writings, psychoanalysts tend to focus more on personality theory issues such as child development, interplay of conscious and unconscious processes, and the psychological constructs of the id, ego, and superego than on specific techniques. In the practice of psychoanalytic therapy or counseling, therapists may make use of existential concepts or Gestalt therapy techniques to the extent that they are consistent with understanding the patient's psychological functioning. Also, person-centered statements that indicate that the therapist understands and empathizes with the patient's experience may be used. In general, the closer the approach to psychoanalysis, where the couch is used, the less likely are psychoanalytic practitioners to use techniques from other theories. Conversely, those who use psychoanalytic brief psychotherapy are likely to borrow from a wide variety of approaches, as do Budman and Hoyt (1993), when they incorporate a symptom-oriented approach into their psychodynamic assessment.

RESEARCH

Because psychoanalysis and psychoanalytic therapy are so lengthy and complex and are based on hard-to-define concepts dealing with the unconscious and early childhood development, it has been very difficult to design experiments to test the effectiveness of psychoanalytic psychotherapy or psychoanalytic concepts. Moreover, Freud believed that research on psychoanalytic concepts was not necessary because of his confidence in the variety of clinical observations that he and his colleagues had made in their work with patients (Liebert & Liebert, 1998). Another objection to research on psychoanalytic concepts is that when they are taken out of the patient-therapist relationship and subject to laboratory experiments, the same phenomena are not being measured, as the artificial experimental situation changes the behavior being measured. Related to this objection is the difficulty in clearly defining theoretical concepts. If psychoanalytic writers cannot agree on the meaning of certain concepts, it is going to be very difficult for researchers to define a concept adequately. Despite these difficulties, many investigators have attempted to measure the effectiveness of psychoanalytic therapy and psychoanalytic constructs. In this section are examples of two long-term, continuing investigations of psychoanalysis and/or psychoanalytic therapy that have assessed their effectiveness in as natural a setting as possible. Also, I describe some research into the development of scales designed to measure progress in psychoanalytic counseling. Additionally, I include a brief overview of the concepts that have been studied as they relate to Freudian drive theory and object relations theory.

In a research study extending over 30 years and yielding more than 70 publications, Wallerstein (1986, 1989, 1996) followed 42 patients over the course of treatment, with half assigned to psychoanalysis and half to psychoanalytic psychotherapy. The purpose of this study, conducted at the Menninger Clinic in Topeka, Kansas, was to ask what changes take place in psychotherapy and what patient and therapist factors account for the changes. An unusual aspect of the sample was that the patients came from all over the United States and abroad to receive treatment at the Menninger Foundation. For each patient, most with severe psychological problems, case history and clinical ratings of patient and therapist behavior and interaction were gathered. Follow-up assessments were made 3 years after treatment and, when possible, 8 years after treatment. The investigators wished to contrast expressive techniques-interpretations designed to produce insight and to analyze resistance and transference—with supportive techniques—designed to strengthen defenses and repress inner conflict. Surprisingly, the investigators found that the distinction between these two approaches became blurred. A major explanation for positive change was the "transference cure," which was the willingness to change to please the therapist. As Wallerstein (1989) states, the patient is, in essence, saying, "I make the agreed upon and desired changes for you, the therapist, in order to earn and maintain your support, your esteem and your love" (p. 200). In general, the investigators found that change resulted from supportive techniques without patients having always resolved internal conflicts or achieved insights into their problems. Changes resulting from psychoanalysis and psychoanalytic therapy were proportionately similar and in both, supportive approaches were particularly effective. In further analysis of data from this study, Blatt (1992) concluded that psychoanalytic psychotherapy was particularly effective with individuals who tended to use avoidance as a means of dealing with their problems and had had difficulties in relating to others, whereas psychoanalysis was particularly effective for those who questioned their own worth and had difficulty in developing independence. The vast amount of clinical data produced by the Menninger study has provided many insights into the process of long-term psychotherapy.

In another series of studies on psychoanalytic psychotherapy, Luborsky and Crits-Christoph and their colleagues had studied variables that predicted treatment success before treatment and then followed up patients for 7 years after treatment had ceased. In this study (Luborsky, Crits-Christoph, Mintz, & Auberach, 1988), 42 different therapists worked with a total of 111 patients. When differentiating between poorer and better therapy hours, Luborsky et al. (1988) found that in the poorer hours therapists tended to be inactive, impatient, or hostile, whereas in better hours therapists were more interested, energetic, and involved in the patient's therapeutic work. In describing curative factors, they highlight the importance of a patient's feeling understood by the therapist, which contributed to patients' increasing their level of self-understanding and decreasing conflicts within themselves. They also noted that an increase in physical health accompanied the positive changes in psychotherapy. Another important factor in achieving therapeutic success was the ability of the therapist to help the patient realize and make use of therapeutic gains.

These researchers have continued to investigate psychodynamic therapy with substance abuse, depression, and general anxiety. In one study, McLellan, Alterman, Metzger, Grisson, Woody, Luborsky, and O'Brien (1997) followed up 649 patients being treated for substance abuse. They found that severity of psychoactive problems, problems at work, and family problems predicted later social adjustment. However, despite these difficulties, psychodynamic treatment was helpful. In another study of substance abusers and depressed patients, Luborsky, McLellan, Diguer, Woody, and Seligman (1997) found that when they compared the effectiveness of 22 therapists, "work sample" record (observations of previous work) was the best predictor of therapist success.

In another study trying to determine what factors make therapists effective in their work, Barber, Crits-Christoph, and Luborsky (1996) studied therapists who worked with 29 depressed patients for 16 sessions. The therapist used supportive-expressive psychodynamic therapy. Following specific supportive expressive techniques predicted improvement more than did general therapeutic skill or the role of the therapeutic alliance.

Another investigation examined the effectiveness of psychodynamic therapy for the treatment of generalized anxiety disorder. Crits-Christoph, Connolly, Azarian, Crits-Christoph, and Shappel (1996) found that brief Supportive-Expressive Psychodynamic Therapy showed different patterns of improvement for 29 patients over 16 weeks. This study is a preliminary investigation as it did not include a no-treatment or other type of treatment control group.

In trying to better understand effective treatment methods in psychoanalytic counseling, Patton and his colleagues (Patton & Meara, 1992, 1996) have used and developed a number of instruments to measure therapeutic change, a few dealing specifically with Kohut's self psychology. Much of their work has studied the psychodyamic working alliance. For example, Patton, Kivlighan, and Multon (1997) have found in a study of 6 counselors with 16 clients that the working alliance increased across sessions whereas therapeutic resistance decreased. They have also found that counselors in training's perception of the working alliance are similar to those of their clients (Patton & Kivlighan, 1997). In these and in numerous other studies they have used the Working Alliances Inventory (Horvath & Greenberg, 1989). They have also developed the Missouri Addressing Resistance Scale (Kivlighan, Multon, & Patton, 1996) and the Missouri Identifying Transference Scale (Multon, Patton, & Kivlighan, 1996) to measure resistance and transference, two significant concepts related to understanding the working alliance. Additionally, Lapan and Patton (1986) have developed two self-report scales that measure Kohut's concepts of grandiosity and idealization that they have used with adolescents. Such instruments as those developed by Patton and his colleagues as well as those developed in the two large-scale studies described previously provide a means for better understanding the reasons for positive change in various types of psychoanalytic treatment.

Just as measuring change in therapeutic treatment is difficult, so are measurement and validation of a variety of concepts that make up Freud's developmental stages and his propositions concerning defense mechanisms. Schultz and Schultz (1998) review studies on defense mechanisms such as reaction formation, projection, and repression. They also summarize research that attempts to validate the importance of the first 5 years of life in determining later personality characteristics. Research on 4- to 6-year-old boys does not support Freud's concept of the Oedipus complex. Still other research has investigated the existence of oral, anal, and phallic personality types with only limited support for these types, especially the phallic type. Over 2,500 studies have been done to investigate a variety of these and other concepts developed by Freud (Fisher & Greenberg, 1996).

Research related to object relations theory, known as attachment theory, has studied the infant-mother bond and has been plentiful, as attested to by the work of Ainsworth (1982) and Bowlby (1969, 1973, 1980). In research in Uganda and in the United States, Ainsworth and others (for example, Main & Solomon, 1986) have observed four patterns of mother-infant attachment: secure, ambivalent, avoidant, and disorganized. Secure attachment occurs when infants protest when their mothers separate from them but then greet them with pleasure upon return. If their mothers attempt to leave the room, ambivalently anxious babies become insecure and tend to cling to their mothers, and they become agitated when separated. Avoidant infants appear to be independent and may avoid their mothers when they return to the room. Disorganized toddlers may fail to respond to their mothers when the mothers return to the room. Ainsworth and others have related these types of attachment to the mother to later childhood and adolescent behavior.

In reviewing research related to attachment theory, Bretherton (1987) has linked Mahler's stages of separation and individuation to attachment studies. Because many of Mahler's observations were based on schizophrenic or on autistic children, her approach is different than attachment theorists who focus more on normal mother-child relationships. In general, Mahler attended more to the mental representations that infants may have of their mother and other objects around them than Ainsworth and Bowlby, who studied both social and psychological aspects of the mother-infant relationship.

Recent psychoanalytic researchers have shown how attachment theory is relevant to psychoanalysis. Schore (1997) describes how studies of brain functioning related to mother-child attachment observations, which are in turn related to psychoanalytic concepts. Feldman and Blatt (1996) studied infants in the first year of life, describing the precursors of how infants relate to their mothers. Eagle (1996) describes attachment theory as a scientific model that informs the practice of psychoanalysis. Taking attachment theory a step further, Lyons and Sperling (1996) show how findings from attachment theory can provide treatment suggestions for psychoanalytic practitioners.

The challenges to researchers in working with psychoanalytic theory are daunting. The research of Wallerstein, Luborsky, Patton, Ainsworth, and Bowlby represents, in most cases, more than 30 years of significant research effort from each investigator. Although the work of Ainsworth and Bowlby is not as directly related to psychoanalytic concepts, it also can provide evidence for understanding issues and concepts that inform the practice of psychoanalysis.

GENDER ISSUES

More than other theories of psychotherapy, Freud's view of the psychological development of women and his view of women in general have been subject to criticism. As early as 1923, Horney (1967) criticized Freud's concept of penis envy as it showed that women were inferior to men because, during the Oedipal stage, they felt inferior to boys because they did not have penises. In reviewing Freud's writings on female sexuality, Chasseguet-Smirgel (1976) sees his view as a series of lacks: the female lacks a penis, lacks complete Oedipal development, and lacks a sufficient superego, due to the lack of castration anxiety, which in boys brings on internalization of society's values. A number of writers (for example, Chodorow, 1978; Sayers, 1986) have criticized Freud for believing that women should be subordinate, in many ways, to men.

Chodorow (1996a, 1996b) expresses concern that psychoanalysts will tend to make broad generalities about women and not pay attention to the individuality of patients. She emphasizes the importance of being open to the varied fantasies and transference and countertransference relationships that exist in client-therapist relationships. This focus on not generalizing and not thinking in universal concepts also reflects the view of Enns (1997) in her critique of Freudian psychoanalysis and object relations psychology.

Object relations theorists have been criticized because of their emphasis on the child-mother rather than the child-parent relationship. Chodorow (1978) argues that early relationships between mother and daughter and mother and son provide different relational experiences for boys and girls. She compares the mother-father-son triangle, in which the boy must assert himself and repress feelings, to the mother-father-daughter triangle, in which daughters can see themselves as substitutes for the mother and not develop a fully individuated sense of self. Describing her view of how parent-child relationships should change, she says:

> Children could be dependent from the outset on people of both genders and establish an individuated sense of self in relation to both. In this way, masculinity would not become tied to denial of dependence and devaluation of women. Feminine personality would be less preoccupied with individuation, and children would not develop fears of *maternal* omnipotence and expectations of *women's* unique self-sacrificing qualities. (p. 218)

Gender issues arise not only in psychoanalytic personality theory but also in the practice of psychoanalytic treatment. Examining why female and male patients may seek therapists of the same or the opposite gender, Deutsch (1992) and Person (1986) present several views. Female patients may be concerned that male therapists are sexist and cannot understand them, they may want female role models, and they previously may have been able to confide in women. Some women may prefer a male therapist because of their interactions with their fathers, societal beliefs in men as more powerful, and negative attitudes toward their mothers. In a similar fashion, male patients may prefer male or female therapists depending on their prior interaction with their mothers or fathers. Some male patients, also, may have a societal expectation that female therapists are more nurturing than male therapists. Sometimes patients may also be afraid of an erotic feeling toward a therapist of the opposite sex.

Because gender issues have been discussed and written about widely and psychoanalytic theory has emphasized attention to countertransference feelings, many psychoanalytic practitioners are attuned to gender issues with their patients. However, some writers continue to be concerned about gender bias that they believe is contained within psychoanalytic theory itself.

MULTICULTURAL ISSUES

The formulations of psychoanalysis began in Vienna in the 1890s. How appropriate are they then, 100 years later, for people in many different societies throughout the world? Clearly, there is disagreement as to whether Freud's view of psychoanalysis can transcend time and geography. In a sense, the developments of ego psychology, object relations, and self psychology may reflect, in a small way, responses to different cultural factors. For example, Freud was most concerned with treating patients with neurosis, especially hysteria. Later theorists such as Kernberg and Kohut structured their theoretical response to the more severe disorders—borderline and narcissistic—that they frequently encountered. Freud's concept of the Oedipal complex may be particularly vulnerable to social and cultural factors. In families where there has never been a father, the father was available for only a brief period of time, or there were multiple fathers, the concept of love for the mother and anger (for boys) toward the father becomes complex. To the extent that object relations psychology deals with early maternal relations, it may be less culture-bound. For example, in the first month of life, it is usually common for the infant to be cared for by the mother. However, shortly thereafter, the major relationship that the infant has can be with the mother or with a grandmother, aunt, older sister, father, nursery school teacher, or foster parent. In general, cultural and social factors have been less important to psychoanalytic theorists than internal psychological functioning.

A notable contribution to cultural concerns has been the early work of the ego psychologist Erik Erikson. Many of Erikson's writings (1950, 1968, 1969, 1982) show his interest in how social and cultural factors affect people of many cultures throughout the life span. Of particular interest are his studies of child-raising practices of Native Americans (the Sioux in South Dakota and the Yurok on the Pacific coast) that gave him a broad vantage point to view cultural aspects of child development. Few other psychoanalytic writers have been as devoted to cross-cultural concerns as Erikson. Although there are cultural differences in ways children separate from their parents in terms of going to school, college, working, and leaving home, object relations theorists (and self psychologists) have concentrated on the similarity of developmental issues rather than on cultural differences.

Reaching out to diverse populations has been a recent thrust of psychoanalytic therapists. For example, Thompson (1996) and Williams (1996) discuss how skin color is an important issue to be dealt with in psychodynamic therapy. With African-American and Hispanic clients, they point out how client perceptions of self are related to issues of not being sufficiently light or dark colored, particularly when related to other family members. They also discuss how skin color can affect the transference relationship with the therapist. Transference and countertransference issues also exist with other cultural differences. For example, Gorkin (1996) describes countertransference issues that developed in cases where Jewish therapists treated Arab patients. Potential countertransference issues confronting Jewish therapists in dealing with Arab patients are guilt, aggressiveness, and differences in cultural values, especially independence versus interdependence. The issues of skin color and traditional cultural animosity are only two of a large variety of cultural issues confronting therapists.

Another area of exploration has been the effect of bilingualism on psychoanalysis. Javier (1996) and Perez Foster (1996) discuss how the age at which a language is acquired can affect the reconstruction of early memories. Also, when the therapist speaks only English and the patient speaks another language as her primary language, a variety of transference or resistance issues can result. Both authors describe how the formation of defense mechanisms can be related to language acquisition and the way language can organize experience.

Another way of viewing psychoanalysis and multicultural issues is to observe how drive theory, ego psychology, object relations, and self psychology explain racial and cultural issues. Mattei (1996) discusses how each of these theories can help psychoanalysts to understand racism in patients (and the therapist). All of these authors, and many others, acknowledge the importance of being aware of the diverse cultural issues and values that patients bring to psychoanalytic therapy.

COUPLES COUNSELING

Early drive and ego approaches to couples counseling are described here, followed by an illustration of an object relations approach. Psychoanalytic couples counseling in the 1930s, 1940s, and 1950s made use of individual psychoanalysis. Sometimes one member of a couple would be seen and, when that member completed analysis, the other would start. Other approaches were to see patients in separate analyses with different analysts or separately by the same analyst (Seagraves, 1982). Later, Fitzgerald (1973) used a method in which both members of the couple would be seen together. First, he worked with a couple on communicating with each other, then on problems that existed between them, and finally on interpreting transference within the couple. Thus, the couple could experience each other as they really were, not through their images of each other. Other marriage therapists with a drive or ego psychoanalytic point of view may focus particularly on unresolved childhood conflicts, particularly Oedipal, as they affect the marriage (Wile, 1981).

The object relations approach of Scharff and Scharff (1987, 1991, 1997) uses some concepts from drive theory in that they bring unconscious material into conscious awareness by interpreting resistance or defenses that the couple present in therapy. Unique to object relations theory, however, they see the marriage as offering a relationship that is somewhat similar to the early child-mother relationship in which the child develops a permanent attachment to a caring figure (Scharff & Scharff, 1987, p. 18). In their work, which draws from the object relations theorists W. R. D. Fairbairn and Melanie Klein, Scharff and Scharff (1997) help the couple learn from transference feelings, which they project toward each other and the therapist, as a result of early childhood experiences in their own family. A particularly important concept is that of "shared holding." Just as the mother holds, cares for, and nurtures her baby, so do members of a couple provide the opportunity to care for and be cared for by the other. In the therapeutic hour, the therapist becomes a member of this "holding environment," caring for the members of the couple but also being aware of transference processes. The therapist attends to the psychological processes of each member of the couple as they affect each other and their relationship in therapy to the therapist.

The following brief excerpt from a case will illustrate how Scharff and Scharff (1987) experience transference and countertransference within a session and its relationship to "shared holding." The couple, Pete and Sarah, have been married for 15 years, both are in their fifties, and they have no children of their own. In response to a recent severe illness, Pete had insisted on controlling his diet and his environment (he worked at home). When he was away in Europe, Sarah moved his books to another room and had the floors and walls of the house redone. When he returned, Pete was furious, and both had temper tantrums. Pete became so angry that he turned over a fully laden dining room table. Pete described how he felt out of control and that nothing in the house belonged to him, and the therapist reacted.

As I moved from feeling shut out and detached to feeling included in their bind, I was beginning to get a sense that the problem they may have with each other is the same as what I was struggling with: they each feel shut out and excluded and feel hopeless to change the situation.

I now turned to Pete and asked, "How does this relate to the current feeling about being controlled by your mother?"

"My father left when I was eight," he said. "My mother was very controlling, as you know—and she was very attached to me. Well, it's like this. On my fiftieth birthday I gave a speech, and she corrected my grammar! Recently, I've been feeling furious about her being so controlling. It's true that Sarah doesn't do what my mother does, but I find myself reacting as though she does. And I would say that today I've been feeling she was just like my mother." (pp. 80–81)[14]

The therapist then goes on to confront Sarah as to why she did the redecorating when Pete was absent. Then they discuss Sarah's family. Later the therapist observes, *"She was still crying. I felt suddenly relieved, in touch with her and then, as if I had really been let into the house"* (p. 81). In analyzing the session, the therapist felt shut out from the couple. The house came to symbolize the shared holding, and when the therapist could feel involved in the discussion of the house, then the therapist could enter the shared holding environment. By being aware of being shut out, the therapist was able to ask Sarah and Pete about their own early relationships, which helped them share their home as a comforting holding environment rather than to fight over it. Examining early caring or holding relationships and how they affect the couple's relationships with each other and with the therapist is the essence of Scharff and Scharff's approach to object relations couple counseling.

FAMILY THERAPY

Often considered to be the grandfather of family therapy, Nathan Ackerman (1966) combined a drive-ego point of view with an active and confrontive approach to families. He attended to both family interactions and individual psychological processes, focused on unconscious as well as conscious material and the repression of sexual and aggressive drives, and stressed openness, expression of feelings, and revealing family secrets. How conflicts within individuals were affecting conflicts with other individuals in the family was important to Ackerman, as were how this process had an impact on members of the family's feelings toward him and his feeling toward them. By attending to family dynamics, Ackerman was alert to how other family members could blame or "scapegoat" another family member as a result of their own pathology. Using this approach, he believed he was able to achieve change by meeting with the family once a week for a period of 6 months to 2 years.

Framo (1982), Scharff and Scharff (1987), and Scharff (1989) have applied object relations theory to family therapy. Although their approaches are different, they have focused on the issues of separation from and attachment to the parents of the children in the family and the parents of the parents in the family. When possible, Framo (1982) tried to include several generations of a single family in therapy, so that separation and attachment issues can be worked through with all family members.

In their approach to family therapy, Scharff and Scharff (1987) use a conceptual view that is similar to their approach to marriage counseling. Just as a baby can provide holding for her mother, by being an object to be cared for and nurtured and thus to feel needed, children provide "holding" for their parents. When a member of the family does not provide holding (nurturing or caring) for others, then the family as an entirety changes to deal with this absence of holding. In the therapeutic situation, the therapist provides a "holding" environment so that the family can interact safely and trust the therapist to help. When comparing family therapy to couples therapy, Scharff and Scharff find that often it is easier to enter a family's holding environment than a couple's because there are more people and thus more occasions and places to intervene. In their work with families, they use a variety of techniques, such as giving support and advice, helping the family communicate better with each other, and interpreting family patterns. Interpretation is a technique associated with psychoanalytic therapy but not with other family therapies. However, it is used frequently by Scharff and Scharff (1987), as illustrated here when parents deny therapeutic comments that are confirmed by the son.

> *Therapist:* I think the family is saying that John is speaking for the shared reluctance to come that everyone feels.
>
> *Father:* I think you're wrong. I want them to come and get this solved. I'm tired of the grief they give me about getting here.
>
> *Mother:* Oh, I think my husband and I are together on this therapy.
>
> *John:* Well, on the way here Mom and Dad were arguing and Dad said, "I wish you didn't speak like that to the kids. That's why we have to go to that goddamned family therapy anyway."
>
> *Therapist:* I think John has been speaking for this feeling on behalf of the whole family. It's safer for the family to let him do it because it seems OK for a child to hate coming. But when it's as though he's the only one who hates having things said about him, he is even more isolated and has even more trouble feeling people understand him. If we think about him as speaking for each of you in part, then everyone can help each other figure out what's tough about being here. (pp. 188–190)[15]

In using interpretation, Scharff and Scharff are careful to be clear and direct so that children in the family can understand what they say. For them, interpretation serves the purpose of commenting on a problem that occurs at the moment but also refers to broader communication issues within the family that are related to their needing, caring for, and "holding" of each other.

Only a very broad overview of the drive-ego psychology and object relations approaches to couples and family therapy has been possible. To use these approaches usually requires participation in psychoanalytic treatment and psychoanalytic training and supervision in individual, marital, and family psychoanalytic therapy.

GROUP THERAPY

In trying to help their patients through group therapy, psychoanalytic practitioners attend to unconscious determinants of behavior that are based on early childhood experience. Most of the conceptual approaches to group therapy have taken a drive-ego psychology approach (Wolf, 1975; Wolf & Kutash, 1986), attending to repressed sexual and aggressive drives as they affect the individual's psychological processes in group behavior. Additionally, group leaders observe the use of ego defenses and ways in which Oedipal conflicts affect the interactions of group members and the group leader. As object relations theory has become more influential, some group leaders have focused on issues of separation and individuation as they affect individuals' psychological processes in group interactions. Such leaders may attend to how group participants deal with dependency issues with the group leader and other participants by examining how they react to group pressures and influences. Using the self psychology view of Kohut, group leaders may focus on the ability of patients to be empathic to other group members and to relate in a way that integrates self-concern with concern about others.

A brief insight into the working of psychoanalytic groups is provided by Wolf and Kutash (1986) in their description of different types of resistance that group leaders may encounter. Some group members may be "in love with" or attach themselves first to the therapist and then to one and then perhaps another group member. Others may take a parental approach to the group, trying to dominate it; yet others may observe the group rather than participate. Still others may analyze other members of the group but evade examination of themselves. All of these examples divert attention away from the patient's awareness of his own mental processes and the issues he struggles with.

As in individual psychoanalytic therapy, techniques such as free association and interpreting observations based on dreams, resistances, and transference (Corey, 2000) are used. Additionally, group leaders encourage members to share insights and interpretations about other group members. In group, members may be asked to free-associate to their own fantasies or feelings, to free-associate to the material of others (Wolf, 1963), or to free-associate to their own or others' dreams. When group leaders interpret this material, they make hypotheses about the underlying meaning of unconscious behavior (Corey, 2000). In a similar way, when members share their insights about the behaviors of others, group members can learn from these interpretations. If the insight is poorly timed or not accurate, it is likely to be rejected by the person to whom it is directed. Providing dream material and free-associating and interpreting are often a very important aspect of group. When members discuss and interpret someone else's dreams, they may also be learning about important aspects of themselves. Although the leader must attend to a multitude of transference reactions among the group members, between the leader and each of the group members, and between the leader and the group as a whole, group therapy can provide a broader opportunity for individuals to understand how their unconscious processes affect themselves and others than does individual therapy.

Brief or time-limited group therapy has also been developed, which tends to require more active participation on the part of the leader than traditional psychodynamic group therapy. Budman, Cooley, Demby, and Koppenaal (1996) describe a time-effective model that lasts about 18 months. In this model, the therapist refers to time limits during the therapy. There is an emphasis on meeting patients' goals and on patients' strengths. The therapist comments on the group interactions that take place within the setting. Budman, Demby, Soldz, and Merry (1996) report growth in self-esteem and a decrease in symptoms with group members diagnosed with personality disorders. Brief group therapy continues to be popular in part due to costs and relocation of group members.

SUMMARY

Since the development of psychoanalysis in the late 1800s, psychoanalytic theory has continued to be a powerful force in psychotherapy. Today many practicing psychoanalysts and psychoanalytic therapists not only make use of Freud's concepts but also incorporate later developments that make use of Freud's constructs of conscious and unconscious, and many incorporate his personality constructs of ego, id, and superego. However, relatively few rely only on his conceptualization of psychosexual stages—oral, anal, phallic, latency, and genital. Other psychoanalytic thinkers, including Anna Freud and Erik Erikson, have stressed the need to adapt to social factors and to assist those with problems throughout stages that encompass the entire life span. Adding to this rich body of theory has been the work of object relations theorists, who have been particularly concerned with childhood development before the age of 3, the way infants relate to people around them, particularly their mothers, and how the disruptions in early relationships affect later psychological disorder. The perspective of self psychology has been on a natural development of narcissism evolving from the self-absorption of infants and on how problems in early child-parent relationships can lead to feelings of grandiosity and self-absorption in later life. In their work, psychoanalytic practitioners may make use of any one or more of these ways of understanding child development.

Although there are a variety of conceptual approaches, most make use of techniques that Freud developed to bring unconscious material into conscious awareness. The technique of free association and the discussion of dreams provide unconscious material that can be interpreted to the patient to give insight into psychological disorders. The relationship between patient and therapist (transference and countertransference concerns) provides important material for therapeutic work. Kernberg (borderline disorders) and Kohut (narcissistic disorders) have discussed different ways that certain types of patients are likely to experience their relationship with the therapist. Because much has been written about psychoanalytic treatment, there are many ideas as well as disagreements about a variety of therapeutic issues and treatment procedures with different disorders.

Because psychoanalysis and psychoanalytic psychotherapy can be very time-consuming, there have been efforts to devise methods other than traditional individual treatment. Couples counseling, family therapy, and group therapy incorporate ideas from drive (Freudian), ego, object relations, and self psychology. A variety of treatment methods have been modified for these forms of therapy. The complex transference issues that occur when more people are involved than just one patient and a therapist have been explored. Brief individual (and group) psychotherapy also makes use of similar conceptual frameworks; however, the techniques that are used are more direct and confrontive, and free association is often not a part of this treatment. The various ways of viewing human development and unconscious processes, combined with the development of new approaches to psychotherapy, are indications of the creativity that continues to be a hallmark of psychoanalysis.

Suggested Readings

As theorists create new psychoanalytic concepts, they often develop their own terms to describe them. For the reader who is not familiar with psychoanalytic concepts, this can be confusing and overwhelming. In these suggestions for further reading, I have tried to include materials that are relatively easy to understand without a broad background in psychoanalysis.

GAY, P. (1988). *Freud: A life for our time.* New York: Anchor Books. • This is a well-documented biography of Freud. His family, the development of psychoanalysis, his work with patients, and his interactions with his colleagues and followers are described.

BERZOFF, J., FLANAGAN, L. M., & HERTZ, P. (1996). *Inside out and outside in.* Northvale, NJ: Aronson. • This edited book provides chapters on drive theory, ego psychology, object relations, and self psychology. Also included is a chapter on interpersonal (Sullivanian) psychology and relational theories. Applications to people of color and women are discussed, as are applications to specific psychological disorders.

FREUD, S. (1917). *A general introduction to psychoanalysis.* New York: Washington Square Press. • These lectures, which comprise volumes 15 and 16 of *The Complete Psychological Works of Sigmund Freud,* were given at the University of Vienna. Because he was addressing an audience that was not familiar with psychoanalysis, he presents a clear and readable presentation of the importance of unconscious factors in understanding slips of the tongue, errors, and dreams. Furthermore, he discusses the role of drives and sexuality in neurotic disorders.

HORNER, A. J. (1991). *Psychoanalytic object relations therapy.* Northvale, NJ: Aronson. • In a clear manner, Horner describes stages of object relations development and object relations therapy. Important therapeutic issues such as transference, countertransference, neutrality, and resistance are explained. Several case examples show the application of object relations therapy.

THORNE, E., & SHAYE, S. H. (1991). *Psychoanalysis today: A casebook.* Springfield, IL: Charles C. Thomas. • A variety of case studies featuring patients with a wide range of disorders illustrate the application of psychoanalysis. Each of the four psychologies described in this chapter is represented in this book. Included in the 19 cases are dialogues between patient and therapist.

PATTON, M. J., & MEARA, N. M. (1992). *Psychoanalytic counseling.* New York: Wiley. • The authors describe their view of psychoanalytic counseling, which includes a perspective from both Freud and Kohut. Issues such as client readiness and principles of interviewing are explained. Additionally, they describe special topics such as counseling women, ethical considerations, and research and methodology.

References

NOTE: References to Sigmund Freud are from the *Complete Works of Sigmund Freud* published by Hogarth Press, London.

ACKERMAN, N. W. (1966). *Treating the troubled family.* New York: Basic Books.

AINSWORTH, M. D. S. (1982). Attachment: Retrospect and prospect. In C. M. Parkes & J. Stevenson-Hinde (Eds.), *The place of attachment in human behavior* (pp. 3–30). New York: Basic Books.

ARLOW, J. A. (1987). The dynamics of interpretation. *Psychoanalytic Quarterly, 20,* 68–87.

AZIM, H. F, PIPER, W. E., SEGAL, P. M., & NIXON, G. W. (1991). The Quality of Object Relations Scale. *Bulletin of the Menninger Clinic, 55,* 323–343.

BACAL, H. A., & NEWMAN, K. M. (EDS.). (1990). *Theories of object relations: Bridges to self psychology.* New York: Columbia University Press.

BALINT, M. (1952). *Primary love and psychoanalytic technique.* London: Hogarth Press.

BALINT, M. (1968). *The basic fault.* London: Tavistock Publications.

BARBER, J. P., CRITS-CHRISTOPH, P., & LUBORSKY, L. (1996). Effects of therapist adherence and competence on patient outcome in brief dynamic therapy. *Journal of Consulting and Clinical Psychology, 64,* 619–622.

BION, W. R. (1963). *Elements of psycho-analysis*. New York: Basic Books.

BLANCK, R., & BLANCK, G. (1986). *Beyond ego psychology: Developmental object relations theory*. New York: Columbia University Press.

BLATT, S. J. (1992). The differential effect of psychotherapy and psychoanalysis with anaclitic and introjective patients. *Journal of the American Psychoanalytic Association, 40,* 691–724.

BLOOM, B. L. (1997). *Planned short-term psychotherapy* (2nd ed.). Boston: Allyn & Bacon.

BLUM, G. S. (1949). A study of the psychoanalytic theory of psychosexual development. *Genetic Psychology Monograph, 39,* 3–99.

BOOK, H. E. (1998). *How to practice brief psychodynamic psychotherapy: The Core Conflictual Relationship Theme method.* Washington, DC: American Psychological Association.

BOWLBY, J. (1969). *Attachment and loss: Vol. 1. Attachment.* New York: Basic Books.

BOWLBY, J. (1973). *Attachment and loss: Vol. 2. Separation.* New York: Basic Books.

BOWLBY, J. (1980). *Attachment and loss: Vol. 3. Loss, sadness and depression.* New York: Basic Books.

BRETHERTON, I. (1987). New perspectives on attachment relations: Security, communication, and internal working models. In J. D. Osofsky (Ed.), *Handbook of infant development* (2nd ed., pp. 1061–1100). New York: Wiley.

BREUER, J., & FREUD, S. (1895). *Studies on hysteria* (Standard Edition, Vol. 2).

BUDMAN, S. H., COOLEY, S., DEMBY, A., & KOPPENAAL, G. (1996). A model of time-effective group psychotherapy for patients with personality disorders: The clinical model. *International Journal of Group Psychotherapy, 46,* 329–355.

BUDMAN, S. H., DEMBY, A., SOLDZ, S., & MERRY, J. (1996). Time-limited group psychotherapy for patients with personality disorders: Outcomes and dropouts. *International Journal of Group Psychotherapy, 46,* 357–377.

BUDMAN, S. H., & HOYT, M. E (1993). Active interventions in brief therapy and control mastery theory: A case study. In R. A. Wells & V. J. Giannetti (Eds.), *Casebook of the brief psychotherapies* (pp. 21–26). New York: Plenum.

CALDER, K. T. (1976). Discussion of the paper by David Liberman on "Changes in the theory and practice of psychoanalysis." *International Journal of Psycho-Analysis, 57,* 109–111.

CHASSEGUET-SMIRGEL, J. (1976). Freud and female sexuality. *International Journal of Psycho-Analysis, 57,* 275–287.

CHODOROW, N. (1978). *The reproduction of mothering.* Berkeley: University of California Press.

CHODOROW, N. J. (1996a). Reflections on the authority of the past in psychoanalytic thinking. *Psychoanalytic Quarterly, 65,* 32–51.

CHODOROW, N. J. (1996b). Theoretical gender and clinical gender: Epistemological reflections of the psychology of woman. *Journal of the American Psychoanalytic Association, 44,* 215–238.

COREY, G. (2000). *Theory and practice of group counseling* (5th ed.). Pacific Grove, CA: Brooks/Cole.

CRITS-CRISTOPH, P., & BARBER, J. P. (EDS.). (1991). *Handbook of short-term psychotherapy.* New York: Basic Books.

CRITS-CRISTOPH, P., CONNOLLY, M. B., AZARIAN, K., CRITS-CRISTOPH, K., & SHAPPELL, S. (1996). An open trial of brief supportive-expressive psychotherapy in the treatment of generalized anxiety disorder. *Psychotherapy, 33,* 418–430.

DEUTSCH, B. G. (1992). Women in psychotherapy. In M. J. Aronson & M. A. Scharfman (Eds.), *Psychotherapy: The analytic approach* (pp. 183–202). Northvale, NJ: Aronson.

EAGLE, M. N. (1996). Attachment research and psychoanalytic theory. In J. M. Masling & R. F. Bornstein (Eds.), *Psychoanalytic perspectives on developmental psychology* (pp. 105–150). Washington, DC: American Psychological Association.

ELLENBERGER, H. F. (1970). *The discovery of the unconscious.* New York: Basic Books.

ENNS, C. Z. (1997). *Feminist theories and feminist psychotherapies: Origins, themes, and variations.* New York: Haworth.

ERIKSON, E. H. (1950). *Childhood and society.* New York: Norton.

ERIKSON, E. H. (1968). *Identity: Youth and crisis*. New York: Norton.

ERIKSON, E. H. (1969). *Gandhi's truth*. New York: Norton.

ERIKSON, E. H. (1982). *The life cycle completed*. New York: Norton.

ERIKSON, E. H. Extended by Erikson, J. M. (1997). *The life cycle completed*. New York: Norton.

FAIRBAIRN, W. R. D. (1954). *An object relations theory of the personality*. New York: Basic Books.

FELDMAN, R., & BLATT, S. J. (1996). Precursors of relatedness and self-definition in mother-infant interaction. In J. M. Masling & R. F. Bornstein (Eds.), *Psychoanalytic perspectives on developmental psychology* (pp. 1–42). Washington, DC: American Psychological Association.

FISHER, S. P., & GREENBERG, R. P. (1996). *Freud scientifically reappraised: Testing the theories and therapy*. New York: Basic Books.

FITZGERALD, R. V. (1973). *Conjoint marital therapy*. New York: Aronson.

FRAMO, J. L. (1982). *Explorations in marital and family therapy: Selected papers of James L. Framo*. New York: Springer.

FREUD, A. (1936). *The ego and mechanisms of defense*. New York: International Universities Press.

FREUD, A. (1965). Normality and pathology in childhood: Assessments of development. In *Writings* (Vol. 6). New York: International Universities Press.

FREUD, S. (1894). *The neuropsychoses of defense* (Standard Edition, Vol. 3).

FREUD, S. (1900). *The interpretation of dreams* (Standard Edition, Vol. 4).

FREUD, S. (1901). *The psychopathology of everyday life* (Standard Edition, Vol. 6).

FREUD, S. (1905a). *Jokes and their relationship to the unconscious* (Standard Edition, Vol. 8).

FREUD, S. (1905b). *Three essays on sexuality* (Standard Edition, Vol. 7).

FREUD, S. (1914). *On narcissism: An introduction* (Standard Edition, Vol. 14).

FREUD, S. (1917). *Introductory lectures on psychoanalysis* (Standard Edition, Vols. 15 and 16).

FREUD, S. (1920). *Beyond the pleasure principle* (Standard Edition, Vol. 18).

FREUD, S. (1923). *The ego and the id* (Standard Edition, Vol. 19).

FREUD, S. (1926). *Inhibitions, symptoms and anxiety* (Standard Edition, Vol. 20).

FROMM, E. (1955). *The sane society*. New York: Holt, Rinehart, and Winston.

GAY, P. (1988). *Freud: A life for our time*. New York: Anchor Books.

GELSO, C. J., & FRETZ, B. R. (1992). *Counseling psychology*. New York: Harcourt Brace Jovanovich.

GORKIN, M. (1996). Countertransference in cross-cultural psychotherapy. In R. M. Pérez Foster, M. Moskowitz, & R. A. Javier (Eds.), *Reaching across boundaries of culture and class* (pp. 159–176). Northvale, NJ: Aronson.

GREENBERG, J. R., & MITCHELL, S. A. (1983). *Object relations in psychoanalytic theory*. Cambridge: Harvard University Press.

GUNTRIP, H. (1968). *Schizoid phenomena, object relations and the self*. New York: International Universities Press.

HALL, C. S., LINDZEY, G., & CAMPBELL, J. B. (1998). *Theories of personality* (4th ed.). New York: Wiley.

HARTMANN, H. (1958). *Ego psychology and the problem of adaptation*. New York: International Universities Press.

HARTMANN, H. (1964). *Essays on ego psychology: Selected problems in psychoanalytic theory*. New York: International Universities Press.

HEDGES, L. E. (1983). *Listening perspectives in psychotherapy*. New York: Aronson.

HEDGES, L. E. (1992). *Interpreting the countertransference*. Northvale, NJ: Aronson.

HORNER, A. J. (1991). *Psychoanalytic object relations theory*. Northvale, NJ: Aronson.

HORNEY, K. (1937). *The neurotic personality of our time*. New York: Norton.

HORNEY, K. (1967). On the genesis of the castration complex in women. In K. Horney, *Feminine psychology* (pp. 37–53). New York: Norton.

HORVATH, A., & GREENBERG, L. (1989). Development and validation of the Working Alliance Inventory. *Journal of Counseling Psychology, 36*, 223–232.

JACOBSON, E. (1964). *The self and object world*. New York: International Universities Press.

JAVIER, R. A. (1996). In search of repressed memories in bilingual individuals. In R. M. Perez Foster, M. Moskowitz, & R. A. Javier (Eds.), *Reaching across boundaries of culture and class* (pp. 225–242). Northvale, NJ: Aronson.

JONES, E. (1953). *The life and work of Sigmund Freud: Vol. 1. The formative years and the great discoveries*. New York: Basic Books.

JONES, E. (1955). *The life and work of Sigmund Freud: Vol. 2. Years of maturity*. New York: Basic Books.

JONES, E. (1957). *The life and work of Sigmund Freud: Vol. 3. The last phase*. New York: Basic Books.

KAHN, E. (1996). The intersubjective perspective and the client-centered approach: Are they one at their core? *Psychotherapy, 33*, 31–42.

KERNBERG, O. F. (1975). *Borderline conditions and pathological narcissism*. New York: Aronson.

KERNBERG, O. F. (1976). *Object-relations theory and clinical psychoanalysis*. New York: Aronson.

KERNBERG, O. F. (1992). *Aggression in personality disorders and perversions*. New Haven: Yale University Press.

KERNBERG, O. F. (1997). Omnipotence in the transference and countertransference. In C. S. Ellman & J. Reppen (Eds.), *Omnipotent fantasies and the vulnerable self* (pp. 79–115). Northvale, NJ: Aronson.

KIVLIGHAN, D. M., Jr., MULTON, K. D., & PATTON, M. J. (1996). Development of the Missouri Addressing Resistance Scale, *Psychotherapy Research, 6*, 291–308.

KLEIN, M. (1957). *Envy and gratitude*. New York: Basic Books.

KLEIN, M. (1975). *Love, guilt and reparation and other works*. London: Hogarth.

KOHUT, H. (1971). *The analysis of the self*. New York: International Universities Press.

KOHUT, H. (1977). *The restoration of the self*. New York: International Universities Press.

KOHUT, H. (1984). *How does analysis cure?* Chicago: University of Chicago Press.

LAPAN, R. T., & PATTON, M. J. (1986). Self-psychology and the adolescent process: Measures of pseudoautonomy and peer group dependence. *Journal of Counseling Psychology, 33*, 136–142.

LIEBERT R. M., & LIEBERT, L. L. (1998). *Liebert and Spiegler's personality: Strategies and issues* (8th ed.). Pacific Grove, CA: Brooks/Cole.

LUBORSKY, L. (1984). *Principles of psychoanalytic psychotherapy: A manual for supportive-expressive treatment*. New York: Basic Books.

LUBORSKY, L., & CRITS-CHRISTOPH, P. (1998). *Understanding transference: The core conflictual relationship theme method* (2nd ed.). Washington, DC: American Psychological Association.

LUBORSKY, L., CRITS-CHRISTOPH, P., MINTZ, J., & AUBERACH, A. (1988). *Who will benefit from psychotherapy? Predicting therapeutic outcomes*. New York: Basic Books.

LUBORSKY, L, McLELLAN, A. T., DIGUER, L., WOODY, G. A., & SELIGMAN, D. A. (1997). The psychotherapist matters: Comparison of outcomes across 22 therapists and 7 patient samples. *Clinical Psychology: Science and Practice, 4*, 53–65.

LYONS, L. S., & SPERLING, M. B. (1996). Clinical applications of attachment theory: Empirical and theoretical perspectives. In J. J. Masling & R. F. Bornstein (Eds.), *Psychoanalytic perspectives on developmental psychology* (pp. 221–256). Washington, DC: American Psychological Association.

MAHLER, M. (1968). *On human symbiosis and the vicissitudes of individuation*. New York: International Universities Press.

MAHLER, M. (1979a). *The selected papers of Margaret S. Mahler: Vol. 1. Infantile psychosis and early contributions*. New York: Aronson.

MAHLER, M. (1979b). *The selected papers of Margaret S. Mahler: Vol. 2. Separation-individuation*. New York: Aronson.

MAHLER, M., BERGMAN, A., & PINE, F. (1975). *The psychological birth of the human infant*. New York: Basic Books.

MAIN, M., & SOLOMON, J. (1986). Discovery of an insecure/disorganized attachment pattern. In T. B. Brazelton & M. W. Yogman (Eds.), *Affective development in infancy*. Norwood, NJ: Ablex.

MALAN, D. (1976). *Frontier of brief psychotherapy*. New York: Plenum.

MATTEI, L. (1996). Coloring development: Race and culture in psychodynamic theories. In J. Berzoff, L. M. Flanagan, & P. Hertz (Eds.), *Inside out and outside in: Psychodynamic clinical theory and practice in contemporary multicultural contexts* (pp. 221–246). Northvale, NJ: Aronson.

MCLELLAN, A. T., ALTERMAN, A. I., METZGER, D. S., GRISSON, G. R., WOODY, G. E., LUBORSKY, L., & O'BRIEN, C. P. (1997). Similarity of outcome predictors across opiate, cocaine and alcohol treatments: Role of treatment services. *Journal of Consulting and Clinical Psychology, 62*, 1141–1158.

MESSER, S. B., & WARREN, C. S. (1995). *Models of brief psychodynamic therapy*. New York: Guilford Press.

MISHNE, J. M. (1993). *The evolution and application of clinical theory: Perspectives from four psychologies*. New York: The Free Press.

MITCHELL, S. A. (1988). *Relational concepts in psychoanalysis: An integration*. Cambridge: Harvard University Press.

MITCHELL, S. A. (1997). *Influence and autonomy in psychoanalysis*. Hillsdale, NJ: Analytic Press.

MOELLER, M. L. (1977). Self and object in countertransference. *International Journal of Psychoanalysis, 58*, 365–374.

MULTON, K. D., Patton, M. J., & KIVLIGHAN, D. M., Jr. (1996). Development of the Missouri Identifying Transference Scale. *Journal of Counseling Psychology, 43*, 243–252.

NIELSEN, G., & BARTH, K. (1991). Short term anxiety-provoking psychotherapy. In P. Crits-Christoph & J. P. Barber (Eds.), *Handbook of short-term psychotherapy* (pp. 45–79). New York: Basic Books.

NIETZSCHE, F. (1937). *The philosophy of Nietzsche* (W. Wright, Ed.). New York: Random House.

ORANGE, D. M. (1994). Countertransference, empathy and the hermeneutical circle. In R. D. Stolorow, G. Atwood, & B. Brandchaft (Eds.), *The intersubjective perspective* (pp. 177–186). Northvale, NJ: Aronson.

ORANGE, D. M., ATWOOD, G. E., & STOLOROW, R. D. (1997). *Working intersubjectively: Contextualism in psychoanalytic practice*. Hillsdale, NJ: Psychoanalytic Press.

PATTON, M. J., & KIVLIGHAN, D. M., Jr. (1997). Relevance of the supervisory alliance to the counseling alliance and to treatment adherence in counselor training. *Journal of Counseling Psychology, 44*, 108–115.

PATTON, M. J., KIVLIGHAN, D. M., Jr., & MULTON, K. D. (1997). The Missouri Psychoanalytic Counseling Research Project: Relation changes in counseling process to client outcomes. *Journal of Counseling Psychology, 44*, 189–208.

PATTON, M. J., & MEARA, N. (1992). *Psychoanalytic counseling*. New York: Wiley.

PATTON, M. J., & MEARA, N. (1996). Kohut and counseling: Application of self psychology. *Psychodynamic Counseling, 2*, 328–355.

PEREZ FOSTER, R. M. (1996). Assessing the psychodynamic function of language in the bilingual patient. In R. M. Perez Foster, M. Moskovitz, & R. J. Javier (Eds.), *Reaching across boundaries of culture and class* (pp. 243–263). Northvale, NJ: Aronson.

PERSON, E. (1986). Women in therapy: Therapist gender as a variable. In H. Meyers (Ed.), *Between analyst and patient* (pp. 193–212). Hillsdale, NJ: Analytic Press.

PINE, F. (1990). *Drive, ego, object, and self. A synthesis for clinical work*. New York: Basic Books.

ROBBINS, S. B. (1989). Role of contemporary psychoanalysis in counseling psychology. *Journal of Counseling Psychology, 36*, 267–278.

SAYERS, J. (1986). *Sexual contradictions: Psychology, psychoanalysis and feminism*. London: Tavistock.

SCHARFF, D. E., & SCHARFF, J. S. (1987). *Object relations family therapy*. Northvale, NJ: Aronson.

SCHARFF, D. E., & SCHARFF, J. S. (1991). *Object relations couples therapy*. Northvale, NJ: Aronson.

SCHARFF, J. S. (Ed.). (1989). *Foundations of object relations family therapy*. Northvale, NJ: Aronson.

SCHARFF, J. S., & SCHARFF, D. E. (1997). Object relations couple therapy. *American Journal of Psychotherapy, 51*, 141–173.

SCHARFMAN, M. A. (1992). The treatment of eating disorders. In M. J. Aronson & M. A. Scharfman (Eds.), *Psychotherapy: The analytic approach* (pp. 327–347). Northvale, NJ: Aronson.

SCHORE, A. N. (1997). Interdisciplinary developmental research as a source of clinical models. In M. Moskowitz, C. Monk, C. Kaye, & S. Ellman (Eds.), *The neurological and developmental basis for psychotherapeutic intervention* (pp. 1–72). Northvale, NJ: Aronson.

SCHULTZ, D., & SCHULTZ, S. E. (1988). *Theories of personality*. (6th ed.). Pacific Grove, CA: Brooks/Cole.

SEAGRAVES, R. T. (1982). *Marital therapy: A combined psychodynamic-behavioral approach*. New York: Plenum.

SIFNEOS, P. E. (1987). *Short-term dynamic psychotherapy: Evaluation and technique* (2nd ed.). New York: Plenum.

SIFNEOS, P. E. (1997). Psychoanalytically oriented short-term dynamic in anxiety-provoking psychotherapy for mild obsessional neuroses. In D. J. Stein & M. H. Stone (Eds.), *Essential papers on obsessive-compulsive disorder* (pp. 113–123). New York: New York University Press.

SPINOZA, B. (1952). *The chief works of Benedict de Spinoza*. New York: Dover Publishing.

ST. CLAIR, M. (1996). *Object relations and self psychology: An introduction* (2nd ed.). Pacific Grove, CA: Brooks/Cole.

STERN, D. N. (1985). *The interpersonal world of the infant: A view from psychoanalysis and developmental psychology*. New York: Basic Books.

SULLIVAN, H. (1953). *Conceptions of modern psychiatry*. New York: Norton.

THOMPSON, C. (1996). The African-American patient in psychodynamic treatment. In R. M. Pérez Foster, M. Moskowitz, & R. A. Javier (Eds.), *Reaching across boundaries of culture and class* (pp. 115–142). Northvale, NJ: Aronson.

WALLERSTEIN, R. S. (1986). *Forty-two lives in treatment: A study of psychoanalysis and psychotherapy*. New York: Guilford Press.

WALLERSTEIN, R. S. (1989). The psychotherapy research project of the Menninger Foundation: An overview. *Journal of Consulting and Clinical Psychology, 57*, 195–205.

WALLERSTEIN, R. S. (1996). Outcomes of psychoanalysis and psychotherapy of termination and follow up. In E. Nesessian & R. G. Kopff, Jr. (Eds.), *Textbook of Psychoanalysis* (pp. 531–573). Washington, DC: American Psychiatric Press.

WILE, D. B. (1981). *Couples therapy: A nontraditional approach*. New York: Wiley.

WILLIAMS, A. C. (1996). Skin color in psychotherapy. In R. M. Pérez Foster, M. Moskowitz, & R. A. Javier (Eds.), *Reaching across boundaries of culture* (pp. 211–224). Northvale, NJ: Aronson.

WINNICOTT, D. W. (1958). *Collected papers: Through pediatrics to psychoanalysis*. New York: Basic Books.

WINNICOTT, D. W. (1965). *The maturational processes and the facilitating environment*. New York: International Universities Press.

WINNICOTT, D. W. (1971). *Playing and reality*. London: Tavistock.

WINNICOTT, D. W. (1975). Fear of breakdown. *International Review of Psycho-Analysis, 1*, 103–107.

WOLF, A. (1963). The psychoanalysis of groups. In M. Rosenbaum & M. Berger (Eds.), *Group psychotherapy and group function* (pp. 321–335). New York: Basic Books.

WOLF, A. (1975). Psychoanalysis in groups. In G. M. Gazda (Ed.), *Basic approaches to group psychotherapy and group counseling* (2nd ed., pp. 101–119). Springfield, IL: Charles C. Thomas.

WOLF, A., & KUTASH, I. L. (1986). Psychoanalysis in groups. In I. L. Kutash & A. Wolf (Eds.), *Psychotherapist's casebook* (pp. 332–352). San Francisco: Jossey-Bass.

WOLF, E. S. (1988). *Treating the self: Elements of clinical self psychology*. New York: Guilford.

3

Jungian Analysis and Therapy

Jung was interested in the spiritual side of individuals, which he felt developed at or after midlife. His writings show a curiosity about patients' conscious and unconscious processes and a caring for the distress of his patients. His therapeutic approach emphasizes ways of helping patients become aware of their unconscious aspects through dreams and fantasy material and thus bring the unconscious into conscious awareness. Such an approach is designed to help individuals realize their unique psychological being. This emphasis on the unconscious can be seen in the explanation of Jung's theory of personality and psychotherapy.

Fascinated by dynamic and unconscious influences on human behavior, Jung believed that the unconscious contained more than repressed sexual and aggressive urges, as Freud had theorized. For Jung, the unconscious was not only personal but also collective. Interpsychic forces and images that come from a shared evolutionary history define the collective unconscious. Jung was particularly interested in symbols of universal patterns called *archetypes*, which all humans have in common. In his study of human personality, Jung was able to develop a typology that identified attitudes and functions of the psyche that operate at all levels of consciousness. The constructs that form the basis of his theory came from observations that he made of his own unconscious processes as well as those of his patients.

HISTORY OF JUNGIAN ANALYSIS AND THERAPY

Theology and medicine, the vocations of Carl Jung's ancestors, are important aspects of Jung's development of analytical psychology and psychotherapy (Ellenberger, 1970; Hannah, 1976; Harris, 1996; Jung, 1961). His paternal grandfather was a well-known physician in Basel, Switzerland, and his maternal grandfather was a distinguished theologian with an important position in the Basel church. Additionally, eight of his uncles were pastors of the Swiss Reformed Church, thus Jung was exposed to funerals and other rituals at an early age. Although his family was not wealthy, his family name was well known in Basel. Like his uncles, his father was a pastor; in later years he questioned his own theological beliefs.

CARL JUNG

Born in Kesswil, Switzerland, a small village, in 1875, Jung had a rather solitary and often unhappy childhood. During his early years, he was exposed to the mountains, woods, lakes, and rivers of Switzerland. Nature was to be important to him throughout his lifetime. After his first few years of school, Jung became an excellent student. During his childhood Jung had dreams, daydreams, and experiences he did not share with anyone. Seeking refuge in his attic, Jung (1961) recalled making up ceremonies and rituals with secret pacts and miniature scrolls.

After he completed secondary school, Jung enrolled in medicine at the University of Basel in 1895, having secured a scholarship. While at medical school, Jung continued to study philosophy and to read widely. He experienced a few parapsychological phenomena, such as a table and a knife breaking for no apparent reason, that fed his interest in the spiritual. His dissertation, *On Psychology and Pathology of So-Called Occult Phenomenon*, published in 1902, dealt in part with the spiritistic experiences of a 15-year-old cousin and readings on spiritism and parapsychology. This interest in parapsychology was to continue throughout his work, being reflected in his theoretical writings.

Throughout his life, Jung read widely in many fields, such as philosophy, theology, anthropology, science, and mythology. He started to learn Latin at the age of 6 and later learned Greek. Philosophically, he was influenced by Immanuel Kant's view of a priori universal forms of perception. This concept develops the idea that individuals never perceive reality for what it is but have perceptual imperatives that affect what they believe they see, a precursor of the collective unconscious. Another influence was Carl Gustav Carus's idea that there were three levels of the unconscious, including a universal one. Somewhat similar to Carus's work was the description of three levels of unconscious functioning, one of which described a universal unconscious, as explained by Eduard von Hartmann. Both von Hartmann's and Carus's concepts of a universal unconscious influenced Jung's development of the collective unconscious. In the 18th century, Gottfried Leibniz had written about the irrationality of the unconscious, ideas that influenced Jung's concept of the unconscious. Later, Arthur Schopenhauer described irrational forces in individuals that were based on sexuality and ways in which sexuality is repressed in individual behaviors. All of these philosophical concepts can be recognized in Jung's theory of personality.

Jung's intellectual interests were broad and varied. The work of early cultural anthropologists had an impact on many of his theoretical constructs. The cultural anthropologist Johann Bachofen was interested in the social evolution of humanity and the role of symbolism across cultures. Also seeking universality across cultures, Adolf Bastian believed that the similarity of the psychology of individuals could be understood by examining the rites, symbols, and mythology of cultures. In attempting to understand the similarity of mythology and folktales throughout the world, George Creuzer saw the importance of symbolism in stories and viewed the thinking underlying the story as analogical rather than primitive or undeveloped thinking. The emphasis that these three writers gave to symbolism in many cultures had a direct impact on Jung's concept of archetypes.

On a more practical level, Jung's training with two psychiatrists, Bleuler and Janet, influenced his approach to psychiatry. Jung received psychiatric training at the Burgholzli Psychiatric Hospital in Zurich under the direction of Eugen Bleuler. While there, he and Franz Riklin used scientific methodology to further develop and study the word association test, in which people respond to specific words with the first word that comes to them. Finding that some people responded much more quickly or slowly than average to some specific words, Jung believed that these words would then carry special meaning for that person. This finding was to lead to the development of the concept of the complex. Jung believed that a complex, a group of emotionally charged words or ideas, represented unconscious memories that influenced a person's life. In 1902, he took a leave of absence from the hospital to study hypnosis in Paris with Pierre Janet. Much of Jung's training was with schizophrenic patients, and he was extremely curious about what "takes place inside the mentally ill" (Jung, 1961, p. 114).

In 1903 he married Emma Rauschenbach, who worked with him in the development of his ideas, was an analyst, and wrote *Animus and Anima* (1957). Although he does not write very much about his family in his autobiography, *Memories, Dreams, Reflections* (1961), he acknowledged the importance of his family (he had four daughters and a son) in providing balance to his study of his own inner world. This was particularly important during a 6-year period when Jung did little writing or research, but devoted time to exploring his unconscious through analyzing his dreams and visions. He says:

> It was most essential for me to have a normal life in the real world as a counterpoise to the strange inner world. My family and my profession remain the base to which I could return, assuring me that I was an actually existing, ordinary person. The unconscious contents could have driven me out of my wits. But my family, and the knowledge: I have a medical diploma from a Swiss university, I must help my patients, I have a wife and five children, I live at 228 Seestrasse in Kusnacht—these were actualities which made demands upon me and proved to me again and again that I really existed, that I was not a blank page whirling about in the winds of the spirit, like Nietzsche. (Jung, 1961, p. 189)[1]

One of the reasons for the 6 years of suffering (1913–1919) that Jung experienced was the severing of his relationship with Sigmund Freud. Both Freud and Jung had been aware of each other's work through their writings. In March 1907, they talked together for almost 13 hours. During their 6-year relationship they corresponded frequently, and their correspondence has been preserved (McGuire, 1974). Before meeting Freud, Jung had defended psychoanalysis against attacks and was extremely interested in it, having sent a copy of *Psychology of Dementia Praecox* (Jung, 1960d) to Freud, who was impressed by it. Jung's involvement in psychoanalysis is indicated by the fact that he was the first president of the International Psychoanalytic Association. However, Jung had reservations about Freud's psychoanalysis from its inception, as he was to write later: "Before Freud nothing was allowed to be sexual, now everything is nothing but sexual" (Jung, 1954a, p. 84). Further, Jung was interested in the occult and parapsychology, ideas that Freud did not approve of. In 1909 they traveled together to lecture at Clark University in Worcester, Massachusetts. On the trip they analyzed each other's dreams. At that time, Jung realized that the theoretical differences between Freud and himself were large, as he found himself interpreting one of his own dreams in a way that Freud would accept, rather than in a way that felt honest and accurate to Jung. Freud saw Jung as his "crown prince," as his successor. In 1910 he wrote to Jung:

> Just rest easy, dear son Alexander, I will leave you more to conquer than I myself have managed, all psychiatry and the approval of the civilized world, which regards me as a savage! That ought to lighten your heart. (McGuire, 1974, p. 300)

The reference to Alexander is a reference to Alexander the Great, with Freud being Philip, Alexander's father.

In 1911, Jung wrote *Symbols of Transformation* (1956), in which Jung described the Oedipus complex not as sexual attraction to an opposite-sex parent and hostile or aggressive feeling toward the same-sex parent (Freud's view), but as an expression of spiritual or psychological needs and bonds. Jung sensed that this would cost him Freud's friendship, and it probably did. In January 1913, Freud wrote Jung stating, "I propose that we abandon our personal relations entirely" (McGuire, 1974, p. 539). Jung then resigned his editorship of the *Psychoanalytic Yearbook* and resigned as president of the International Psychoanalytical Association. Although Jung was to credit Freud for many of his ideas, they never saw each other again. This break was difficult for Jung, as he states: "When I parted from Freud, I knew that I was plunging into the unknown. Beyond Freud, after all, I knew nothing; but I had taken the step into darkness" (Jung, 1961, p. 199). Thus, Jung's 6 years of exploration into his own unconscious started.

Following this turbulent period, Jung was extremely productive in his writing, his teaching, and his devotion to psychotherapy and his patients. Furthermore, he traveled frequently. In order to increase his knowledge of the unconscious, Jung felt it would be valuable for him to meet with people in primitive societies. In 1924 he visited the Pueblo of New Mexico; a year later he stayed with an African tribe in Tanganyika and also traveled to Asia. During these visits he kept diaries of his discussions with people and their shamans. Further exploration of other cultures came about through his friendship with Richard Wilhelm, an expert on Chinese writings and folklore. Jung studied alchemy, astrology, divination, telepathy, clairvoyance, fortune telling, and flying saucers to learn more about the mind, particularly the collective unconscious. In the process of learning more about a variety of myths, symbols, and folklore, Jung developed an excellent collection of books on medieval alchemy. His interest in alchemy stemmed from the symbolism that was used throughout the writings of the medieval alchemists. All of these interests represent collective imagery that is related to unconscious functioning.

Jung used painting and stonework to express himself symbolically. He built a tower at the end of Lake Zurich that was a private retreat for Jung with symbolic meaning for him. Although he added to it in three later renovations, he never installed modern conveniences, as he wanted it to remain a place close to his unconscious.

Jung continued to be productive until his death on June 6, 1961. He had received honorary degrees from Harvard and Oxford and many other honors and awards. Also, he gave many interviews for television, magazines, and visitors. His productivity was enormous, with most of his work published in 20 volumes by Princeton University.

Jungian therapy and ideas related to Jung's theory continue to grow in popularity (McCullough, 1993). Interest in Carl Jung's ideas, as represented by the popularity of Jungian associations, has been developing in the United States and throughout the world. Seminars and educational forums are presented both by local societies and by professional organizations. McCullough suggests that the growth and interest in Jungian ideas is due in part to a search for spirituality.

Jungian training institutes can be found in the United States and throughout the world. Requirements for entry into training institutes vary. There are over 2,000 qualified Jungian analysts who are members of the International Association for Analytic Psychology. In the United States there are 13 training institutes. Training requires usually more than 300 hours of personal analysis and at least 3 years of training beyond prior professional training. Coursework includes subjects such as history of religion, anthropology, mythology, fairy tales, and theories of complexes. In addition, trainees are supervised in the analysis of patients. Working with dreams is emphasized in both coursework and therapy.

International meetings have been held every 3 years since 1958. Some of the periodicals that feature Jungian psychology and psychotherapy are *Anima, The Journal of Analytical Psychology, Psychological Perspectives, Parabola,* and *Spring.*

THEORY OF PERSONALITY

Essential to Jung's conception of personality is the idea of unity or wholeness. For Jung this wholeness is represented by the psyche, which includes all thoughts, feelings, and behaviors, both conscious and unconscious. Throughout their lives, individuals strive to develop their own wholeness. Jung viewed the self as both the center and totality of the whole personality. Another aspect of personality includes attitudes of individuals as well as ways they function psychologically. Jung also described the development of psyche in childhood, adolescence, middle age, and old age. Information for this section is drawn from Jung (1961); Hall, Lindzey, and Campbell (1998); Hall and Nordby (1973); Harris (1996); Mattoon (1981); Whitmont (1991); and Jung's collected works.

Levels of Consciousness

In explaining an individual's personality, Jung identified three levels of consciousness. The concepts of soul, mind, and spirit exist at all levels of consciousness and include cognitions, emotions, and behaviors. The levels of consciousness that are an expression of personality include the conscious, which has as its focus the ego; the personal unconscious, which includes thoughts and memories that can be recalled or brought to a conscious level; and the collective unconscious, derived from themes and material that are universal to the human species. The study of the unconscious and *archetypes,* images or thoughts that represent universal ways of being or perceiving, is the focus of much of Jung's writings, as well as those of Jungian analysts. Thus, in this section and in the rest of the chapter, the collective unconscious receives more attention than the conscious.

The conscious level.   The conscious level is the only level that individuals can know directly. Starting at birth, it continues to grow throughout life. As individuals grow, they become different from others. This process, referred to as individuation by Jung (1959b, p. 275), has as its purpose the goal of knowing oneself as completely as possible. This can be achieved, in part, by bringing unconscious contents into "relationship with consciousness" (Jung, 1961, p. 187). As individuals increase their consciousness, they also develop greater individuation. At the center of the conscious processes is the ego.

The *ego* refers to the means of organizing the conscious mind. The ego selects those perceptions, thoughts, memories, and feelings that will become conscious. The organizational structure of the ego provides a sense of identity and day-to-day continuity so that individuals are not a mass of random conscious and unconscious perceptions, thoughts, and feelings. By screening out great amounts of unconscious material (memories, thoughts, and feelings), the ego attempts to achieve a sense of coherence and consistency, while at the same time being an expression of individuality.

The personal unconscious.   Experiences, thoughts, feelings, and perceptions that are not admitted by the ego are stored in the personal unconscious. Materials stored in the personal unconscious may be experiences that are trivial or unrelated to present functioning. However, personal conflicts, unresolved moral concerns, and emotionally charged thoughts are an important part of the personal unconscious that may be repressed or difficult to access. Often these elements emerge in dreams, as the personal unconscious, and may play an active role in the production of dreams. Sometimes thoughts, memories, and feelings are associated with each other or represent a theme. This related material, when it has an emotional impact on an individual, is called a *complex.*

It is the emotionality of a complex that distinguishes it from groups of related thoughts that have little emotional impact on the individual. Jung's work with Bleuler on word association led to his development of the concept of complexes. Although Adler (inferiority complex) and Freud (Oedipus complex) developed the construct of the complex in their own theories, Jung integrated the complex into his own thinking.

What distinguishes Jung's writing on complexes from other theorists in this book is his emphasis on the archetypal core. Thus, each complex has elements not only from the personal unconscious but also from the collective unconscious. Examples of common complexes with archetypal roots are the mother complex, the father complex, the savior complex, and the martyr complex. Such complexes could be detected from a word association test. An atypical response style was an indication that the individual had an emotional reaction to a word, which, grouped with other thematically related words, may be indicative of a complex. Because individuals are not conscious of complexes, it is the therapist's goal to make complexes conscious. Not all complexes are negative; some may be quite positive. For example, an individual who seeks political office and power may be said to have a Napoleonic complex. Such a complex may lead the individual to accomplish positive social goals for herself and her community. If the search for power cannot be satisfied, the positive complex turns into a negative one or evokes the *transcendent function,* which mediates opposite forces and is expressed through symbols. In a sense, an individual can transcend or rise above a conflict and see it from a different point of view. Clinically, the trancendent function can provide an opportunity for therapeutic growth in dealing with transference (Joseph, 1997; Ulanov, 1997) and other issues. In their therapeutic work, analysts encounter a variety of unconscious complexes that are an important aspect of the therapeutic endeavor. Although attaching importance to complexes, Jungian analysts are particularly interested in the role of the collective unconscious in complexes and in other aspects of an individual's functioning.

The collective unconscious.   The concept that most distinguishes Jung's theory of psychotherapy from other theories is that of the collective unconscious, which is not personal, in contrast to the personal unconscious described previously. Images and concepts that make up the collective unconscious are independent of consciousness (Harris, 1996; Whitmont, 1991). The term *collective* denotes materials that are common to all humans and significant to them. The *collective unconscious* refers to "an inherited tendency of the human mind to form representations of mythological motifs—representations that vary a great deal without losing their basic pattern" (Jung, 1970a, p. 228). Because all human beings have similar physiology (brains, arms, and legs) and share similar aspects of the environment (mothers, the sun, the moon, and water), individuals have the ability to see the world in some universally common ways and to think, feel, and react to the differences and commonalities in their environment. Jung was quite clear in stating that he did not believe that specific memories or conscious images were inherited. Rather, it is the predisposition for certain thoughts and ideas that is inherited. Included in the contents of the collective unconscious are instincts and archetypes (Mattoon, 1981). *Instincts* refer to an impulse to act, for example, to run when threatened. Archetypes are ways of perceiving and structuring experiences (Jung, 1960b, p. 137). The concept of archetypes is basic to understanding Jungian psychology and is the focus of the next section.

Archetypes

Although they do not have content, archetypes have form. They represent the possibility of types of perceptions (Jung, 1959a, 1959c). Archetypes are not experience, but their effects are (Mattoon, 1981). Jung was interested in archetypes that have emotional content and strength and that have endured for thousands of years. For example, the archetype of death carries strong emotions and is a universal experience. There are many archetypes that Jung wrote about, including birth, death, power, the hero, the child, the wise old man, the earth mother, the demon, the god, the snake, and unity. These archetypes are expressed as archetypal images, the content of which is described in the section on symbolism. Those archetypes that Jung considered most important in the composition of the personality are the persona, the anima and the animus, the shadow, and the Self. Of these, the persona is the archetype that is the most related to the everyday functioning of the personality, and the Self archetype is the one that is most crucial to proper functioning of the personality.

Persona, meaning "mask" in Latin, is the way individuals present themselves in public. Individuals play various roles—parent, worker, friend. How individuals play these roles depends on how they want to be seen by others and how they believe others want them to act. People vary their personas depending on the situation, acting kindly with a child and defensively with a telemarketer. The persona is helpful in that individuals learn to control feelings, thoughts, and behaviors in specific situations. However, if the persona is valued too highly, individuals become alienated from themselves and shallow; they have difficulty experiencing genuine emotions.

Anima and *animus* represent qualities of the other sex, such as feelings, attitudes, and values. For men, the anima represents the feminine part of the male psyche, such as feelings and emotionality. Animus is the masculine part of the female psyche, representing characteristics such as logic and rationality. The idea that men and women have a part of the opposite sex within them has a basis in biology. Both sexes produce varying degrees of male and female hormones. Individuals vary as to the extent to which psychological characteristics of the opposite sex are a part of their personality.

An assumption inherent in the concept of the anima and animus is that women are traditionally emotional and nurturing and that men are traditionally logical and powerful. The anima and animus do not need to be viewed so narrowly. Harding (1970) described how the animus can function differently in different types of women. Emma Jung (1957) described four major archetypes that women may experience as their animus develops. Other writers have also sought to develop the concepts of anima and animus further and modify Jung's thinking (Hillman, 1985). Jung believed that men must express their anima and women their animus in order to have balanced personalities. If individuals do not do so, they run the risk of being immature and stereotypically feminine or masculine. In psychotherapy, exploration of the anima and animus may lead not only to expression of unconscious parts of an individual's personality, but also to the exploration of sexuality of the individual and sexuality in the transference relationship with the therapist (Schaverien, 1996).

The *shadow* is potentially the most dangerous and powerful of the archetypes, representing the part of our personalities that is most different from our conscious awareness of ourselves. Contained in the shadow are unacceptable sexual, animalistic, and aggressive impulses. The raw nature of the impulsiveness of the shadow is somewhat similar to Freud's id. Jung believed that men tended to project their own shadow (negative and animalistic feelings) onto other men, causing bad feelings between men. This may explain, in part, the frequency of fights and wars between men. Although they are not manifested physically, Jung believed that women projected shadow impulses onto other women. The persona archetype, expressing itself through social expectations, serves to moderate, or keep in check, the shadow. More broadly, the shadow can be projected on many objects by both sexes.

Although this discussion presents the shadow as a negative archetype, it can have positive aspects. Appropriate expression of the shadow can serve as a source of creativity, vitality, and inspiration. However, if the shadow has been repressed, individuals may feel inhibited, out of touch with themselves, and fearful. For such individuals, the goal of therapy is to help bring their shadow into consciousness.

The *Self* is both the center of the personality as well as the central archetype in the collective unconscious. Whereas the ego is the center of consciousness, the Self is the center of the personality (conscious and unconscious), yet paradoxically also contains the personality. For children and individuals who are relatively unindividuated, the Self may be centered in the unconscious, as they may be relatively unaware of their complexes and manifestations of their archetypes. As individuals become mature and individuated, a stronger relationship between ego and Self develops.

For Jung, the development and knowledge of the Self are the goals of human life. When individuals have fully developed their personality functions, they are in touch with the Self archetype and are able to bring more unconscious material into consciousness. Because knowledge of the Self requires being in touch with both conscious and unconscious thoughts, there is an emphasis in Jungian analysis on dreams as a way of providing understanding of the unconscious processes. Furthermore, spiritual and religious experiences can bring about further understanding of the unconscious, which can then be brought into conscious awareness. To develop one's personality, therapists help patients move unconscious thoughts and feelings to consciousness.

Symbols.   Archetypes are images with form but not content. Symbols are the content and thus the outward expression of archetypes. Archetypes can be expressed only through symbols that occur in dreams, fantasies, visions, myths, fairy tales, art, and so forth. Expressed in a variety of ways, symbols represent the stored wisdom of humanity that can be applied to the future. Jung devoted much effort to understanding the wide variety of symbols that were found as archetypal representations in different cultures.

Jung's broad knowledge of anthropology, archeology, literature, art, mythology, and world religions provided him with an excellent knowledge of symbolic representations of archetypes. For example, Jung's interest in alchemy (Jung, 1954f, 1957) helped him find symbols that represented archetypes in his patients. Alchemists, who were searching for the philosophers' stone or ways to make gold out of base metals, expressed themselves through abundant symbolic material. Jung was also well versed in mythology and fairy tales, which provided him with more material for understanding symbols. Talking to people in a wide variety of African, Asian, and Native American cultures about spirituality and dreams also helped him to increase his knowledge of symbolism. Jung's curiosity was vast. He sought to understand why so many individuals believed that they had seen flying saucers. Through discussion of dreams, myths, and historical references, Jung concluded that the flying saucer represents totality, coming to earth from another planet (the unconscious), and containing strange creatures (archetypes) (Hall & Nordby, 1973, p. 115). In reaching this conclusion, Jung used what he called amplification, what he knew about the history and meaning of symbols, such as flying saucers. Jung applied amplification to his work with his patients' dreams by learning as much as possible about a particular image within a dream.

In his research on myths, alchemy, anthropology, spirituality, and other areas, Jung found that certain symbols tended to represent important archetypes. For example, a common image of the persona is the mask used in drama and in religious ceremonies. The Virgin Mary, Mona Lisa, and other well-known women represent the anima in men. Likewise the symbols of men as Christ or King Arthur symbolize the animus. Evil characters such as the devil, Hitler, and Jack the Ripper may represent the shadow. A particularly important symbol is that of the mandala that represents the Self. The mandala is a circular form and usually has four sections. Symbolically it represents an effort or need to achieve wholeness. Four elements can refer to fire, water, earth, and air, the four directions of the winds, or the Trinity and the Holy Mother. These are just some examples of archetypal representations that Jung and others have described.

MANDALA

Personality Attitudes and Functions

By making observations of himself and his patients, Jung was able to identify dimensions of personality that are referred to as personality types. These dimensions have both conscious and unconscious elements. The first dimensions that Jung developed are the attitudes of extraversion and introversion. Later, he developed the functions, those involved in making value judgments—thinking and feeling—and those used for perceiving oneself and the world—sensing and intuiting. Jung combined the attitudes and functions into psychological types. However, he was careful to talk about these as approximations and tendencies rather than as dogmatic categories. For individuals, one function is usually more developed than others. The least developed of the four functions is likely to be unconscious and expressed in dreams and fantasies, having implications for analytical treatment (Jung, 1971).

Attitudes.   Introversion and extraversion are the two attitudes or orientations in Jung's view of personality. Briefly, extraverted individuals are more concerned with their external world, other people, and other things, whereas introverted people are more concerned with their own thoughts and ideas. Introversion and extraversion are polarities or opposite tendencies. Not only are individuals capable of being both introverted and extraverted, but they use both attitudes in their life. As individuals develop, one of the attitudes becomes more dominant or highly developed. The nondominant attitude is likely to be unconscious and influence the person in subtle or unexpected ways. For example, introverts may find themselves attracted to and drawn to extroverts, as extraversion represents an unconscious aspect of themselves. A similar comparison could be made for extroverts. When people who are normally active and outgoing, with an interest in the world around them, become quiet and thoughtful, their introverted attitude that is unconscious becomes more active. Although Jung found the attitudes of introversion and extraversion to be useful dimensions of personality, he found them too simple and inadequate to explain differences between individuals (Jung, 1971).

Functions.   After about 10 years of struggling with concepts that would add to the personality dimensions of attitudes, Jung designated four functions: thinking, feeling, sensing, and intuition. He explains the conceptualization of the rational functions— thinking and feeling—in this way:

> And so it came about that I simply took the concepts expressed in current speech as designation for the corresponding psychic functions, and used them as my criteria in judging the differences between persons of the same attitude-type. For instance, I took thinking as it is generally understood, because I was struck by the fact that many people habitually do more thinking than others, and accordingly give more weight to thought when making important decisions. They also use their thinking in order to understand the world and adapt to it, and whatever happens to them is subjected to consideration and reflection or at least subordinated to some principle sanction by thought. Other people conspicuously neglect thinking in favor of emotional factors, that is, a feeling. They invariably follow a policy dictated by feeling, and it takes an extraordinary situation to make them reflect. They form an unmistakable contrast to the other type, and the difference is most striking when the two are business partners or are married to each other. It should be noted that a person may give preference to thinking whether he be extraverted or introverted, but he will use it only in the way that is characteristic of his attitude-type, and the same is true of feeling. (Jung, 1971, pp. 537–538)

Thus both thinking and feeling require making judgments. When individuals usually use thinking, they are using their intellectual functioning to connect ideas and to understand the world. When they use the feeling function, they are making decisions on the basis of having positive or negative feelings or values about subjective experiences.

Sensation and intuition can be considered irrational functions because they relate to perceiving or responding to stimuli. These two functions are not related to evaluation and decision making. Like thinking and feeling, sensing and intuiting represent a polarity. Sensing includes seeing, hearing, touching, smelling, tasting, and responding to sensations that are felt within one's body. It is usually physical, most often conscious, and shows an attention to detail. In contrast, intuition refers to having a hunch or a guess about something that is hard to articulate, often looking at the big picture. Frequently vague or unclear, it is usually unconscious, for example, "I have a bad impression of Joan. I don't know why but I do."

Combination of attitudes and functions.   By combining each of the two attitudes with each of the four functions, eight psychological types can be described (Hall, Lindzey, & Campbell, 1998). Jung was concerned that individuals would try to put all people into the eight categories. His intent was to help in classifying information. For Jung, each individual had a unique pattern of attitudes and functions that comprise his or her personality. The eight psychological types are described briefly here, focusing only on the most important characteristics, with the four functions combined with the introverted attitude in the left-hand column and the four functions combined with the extraverted attitude in the right-hand column (Myers & McCaulley, 1985).

Introverted-Thinking: Such individuals like to pursue their own ideas and are not particularly concerned about having these ideas accepted. They may prefer abstract ideas to interaction with others or to making plans.

Introverted-Feeling: Strong feelings may be kept inside, erupting occasionally in forceful expression. Creative artists are likely to express their feelings through their works.

Introverted-Sensation: Such individuals may focus on the perceptions of their world, attending especially to their own psychological sensations. They may prefer artistic and creative expression to verbal communication.

Introverted-Intuition: People of this type may have difficulty communicating their own insights and intuitions because they may themselves have difficulty in understanding their own thoughts and images.

Extraverted-Thinking: Although concerned with the outside world, such individuals may try to impose their own view of the world on others. People who work in science and applied mathematics may use their thinking function to help solve real problems.

Extraverted-Feeling: Interactions with other people can often be emotional at times, but also quite sociable and friendly at other times.

Extraverted-Sensation: Experiencing sensations and participating in exciting activities, such as mountain climbing, are characteristic of this type. They often like to gather data and information and are likely to be practical and realistic.

Extraverted-Intuition: Such people enjoy novelty and promoting new ideas and concepts to others. They may have difficulty sustaining interest in one project.

Although there are many ways of assessing psychological type, the danger of overassessing or pigeonholing people into eight categories remains. These types can best be seen as a way of understanding how Jung combines the attitudes and functions of personality in explaining individuals' characteristics.

Function strength.   Because the four functions represent two polarities, thinking-feeling and sensing-intuition, individuals experience all of the four. However, all are not equally well developed in individuals. The most highly developed function is dominant and conscious, referred to as the *superior* function. The second most developed function is the *auxiliary* function, which takes over when the superior is not operating. The function that is least well developed is referred to as the *inferior* function. Unlike the superior function, which is conscious, the inferior function is repressed and unconscious, appearing in dreams and fantasies. Usually when a rational function (thinking or feeling) is superior, then a nonrational function (sensing-intuiting) will be auxiliary. The reverse is also true.

The concept of function strength or dominance can be an elusive one. Jungian analysts find it helpful to explore the inferior functions of their patients that are expressed in dreams or creative work. The following example illustrates how the inferior function was explored with an individual who was normally an introverted-thinking type. This case not only illustrates the use of Jungian type terminology but also relates it to archetypal material, in this case, the anima.

A case will illustrate such use of inferior functions. A young engineer who had excelled in school and at college, under pressure from a demanding father, was motivated by drug experiences and peers in the counterculture to drop out of his first job after college for the purpose of exploring "varieties of religious experience." He drifted to the West Coast and lived in various communal situations, where he experimented with his sexual as well as his religious feelings. He eventually tried to exchange his dominant heterosexual adaptation for a homosexual one, but he became a most absurd and unsuccessful homosexual, affecting a mincing, false feminine persona and a whorish attitude that were in comic contrast to his normally reserved and masculine presentation of Self. He became silly and disorganized under the pressure of these experiments, and he was hospitalized for what appeared to be a psychosis. When he asked to see a "Jungian," he was referred from a day treatment center to an analyst.

After some exploration, the analyst concluded that the patient, in his attempt to undo his father's excessive demands, had turned his psyche inside out. He had fled to his inferior functions in an attempt to discover parts of himself that his father could not organize for him. Normally an introverted thinking type with reliable auxiliary extraverted sensation, he had turned first to his relatively inferior introverted intuition, which he explored through drugs and through participation in a religious cult. Then communal life had stimulated his inferior extraverted feeling, which was normally carried by his anima. He became anima-identified, enacting the part of an inferior extraverted feeling woman. To be sure, he was taking revenge on his father by enacting an unconscious caricature of the "feminine" role he had felt himself to have occupied in his original relation to his father. But the entire compensation, witty though it was, was ruining his life and psychotically distorting his personality. Sadly enough, he was really very like the compulsive engineer his father had wanted him to be.

The analyst took the tack of gently supporting the patient's return to adaptation through his superior functions and quietly discouraged the patient from further exploration of his inferior functions. He firmly refused the more floridly "Jungian" feeling-intuitive approach the patient had at first demanded. With this approach, the patient's near-hebephrenic silliness disappeared. He resumed heterosexual functioning, recovered his dominant introverted personality, and sought work in a less ambitious field related to engineering. (Sandner & Beebe, 1982, pp. 315–316)[2]

Although complex, this example illustrates how a Jungian analyst might attend to inferior functions in understanding the client, while supporting his introverted attitude and thinking functions.

Personality Development

Because he was more concerned with understanding the unconscious and dimensions of personality than he was with the development of personality, Jung's (1954e) stages of personality are less well developed than those of Freud or Erikson. He divided life into four basic stages: childhood, youth and young adulthood, middle age, and old age. The life stage that he was most interested in and wrote most frequently about is that of middle age.

Childhood.   Jung (1954b) believed that psychic energy of children was primarily instinctual—eating, sleeping, and so forth. The parental role is to direct children's energy so that they do not become chaotic and undisciplined. Jung felt that most of the problems of childhood were due to problems at home. If problems of either or both parents could be resolved, then children's disobedient behavior and other problems would be lessened. Fordham (1957) has drawn upon object relations theory as described by Melanie Klein to develop a Jungian approach to child development.

Adolescence.   Adolescents may develop a variety of problems as they are faced with many life decisions, such as choice of schooling and career. Furthermore, they may experience difficulties arising from the sexual instinct, including insecurity while associating with the opposite sex. As they grow and develop, they may wish that they were children again, with relatively few decisions to make. These conflicts and decision points that adolescents encounter are handled differently, depending on their propensity toward introversion or extraversion. To cope with their problems, adolescents must develop an effective persona to deal with the world based on their own dominant function rather than the one imposed by parental expectations. As they enter the period of young adulthood, individuals discover their own personality and develop an understanding of their own persona.

Middle age.   Jung's interest in middle age is probably explained by the fact that he experienced his own midlife crisis, in which he carefully reexamined his own inner being and explored his unconscious life through his dreams and creative work. Furthermore, many of Jung's patients were of middle age, had been successful, and were dealing with questions regarding the meaning of life. As individuals become established in their careers, their families, and their communities, they may be aware of experiencing the feeling of meaninglessness or loss in their lives (Jung, 1954g). In fact, many individuals who wish to become Jungian analysts often do so at middle age rather than in their twenties, a typical age for those seeking training in other psychotherapies. A variety of issues can be encountered at middle age or in the transition from adolescence to middle age. For example, Jung identifies the *puer aeternus*, the man who has difficulty growing out of adolescence and becoming self-responsible, as he is attached unconsciously to his mother. The term *puella aeterna*, where the attachment is to the father, is used for the woman who has difficulty accepting responsibilities of adulthood. Nevertheless, such individuals may be creative and energetic.

Old age.   Jung believed that in old age individuals spend more and more time in their unconscious. However, Jung felt that older individuals should devote time to understanding their life experiences and deriving meaning from them (Jung, 1960e). For Jung, old age was a time to reflect and to develop wisdom. A number of Jung's patients were of retirement age (Mattoon, 1981), reflecting his belief that psychological development continues regardless of age. Millner (1998) shows how knowledge of an individual's personality type (attitudes and functions) can help people understand developmental issues of old age.

In Jungian analysis, knowledge and understanding of levels of consciousness and dimensions of personality, as well as changes in psychic energy, are significant. In particular, familiarity in dealing with the unconscious through archetypal material that is produced in dreams, fantasies, and by other means is a central focus. The overview of these elements of Jungian personality theory is related to the process of Jungian analysis and psychotherapy in the next section.

JUNGIAN ANALYSIS AND THERAPY

Much of Jungian therapy is concerned with bringing unconscious material into consciousness. To accomplish this, assessment is made through the use of projective techniques, objective instruments that measure type, and assessments of dream and fantasy material. The therapeutic relationship is a flexible one, with analysts using their information about their own psyches to guide analysands in bringing the personal and collective unconscious into awareness. To do this, much use is made of dreams, active imagination, and other methods of exploration. Another area of inquiry is transference and countertransference, which refer to an examination of relationship issues that affect the course of therapy. This treatment provides only a brief discussion of the important aspects of Jungian analysis and psychotherapy.

Therapeutic Goals

From a Jungian point of view, the goal of life is individuation (Hall, 1986). As mentioned, *individuation* refers to a conscious realization of psychological reality that is unique to oneself. As individuals become aware of their strengths and limitations and continually learn about themselves, they integrate conscious and unconscious parts of themselves. In her brief description of the goals of analysis, Mattoon (1986) describes the goal of Jungian analysis as the integration of the conscious and unconscious to achieve a sense of fullness, leading to individuation.

Goals of Jungian therapy can depend on the developmental stage of the patient (Harris, 1996), whether childhood, adolescent, midlife, or old age. For children, the goal may be to help them in problems that interfere with their Self archetype (normal development). In adolescence and early adulthood there is often a focus on identity and understanding more about one's self than one's persona. In midlife, goals can shift from pragmatic ones of earning a living and being responsible for a family to less material and more spiritual aspects of one's life. For people 70 or older, seeing life as a whole process and developing serenity are some of the goals of therapy. Of course, individuals may have other goals as well, but these are common ones that are related to stages in the life span.

Analysis, Therapy, and Counseling

Although writers disagree somewhat in their definitions of Jungian analysis, psychotherapy, and counseling, the term *Jungian analyst* is reserved for those who are officially trained at institutions certified by the International Association for Analytical Psychology. In contrasting psychotherapy with analysis, Henderson (1982) believes analysis is more intensive than psychotherapy, involving several sessions a week over a long period of time. For Henderson, psychotherapy is briefer, allowing therapists to provide crisis intervention and to meet immediate needs for psychological insight. In contrast, Mattoon (1981) sees no clear distinction between psychotherapy and analysis in terms of method or content. However, she acknowledges that many Jungian analysts believe that analysis deals more with unconscious material, especially dreams, than does therapy. With regard to counseling, Mattoon sees counselors as usually working less with unconscious material than therapists or analysts. Perhaps a reason for this variation in opinion is that Jungian analysts themselves have a varied background (psychology, social work, the ministry, or employment not associated with the helping professions). Many become analysts in their thirties or forties as a "second career" (Hall, 1986). In general, the more exposure that counselors and psychotherapists have had to Jungian emphasis on the unconscious through their own analysis and specific training, the more likely they are to be comfortable using unconscious materials in their work.

Assessment

The range of assessment methods used by Jungian analysts varies from objective and projective personality tests to the use of their own dreams. Although Jung had few standardized measures of personality available, he used a broad variety of ways of understanding his patients. As diagnostic classification systems were developed (*Diagnostic and Statistical Manual [DSM] II, III,* and *IV*), there have been some limited attempts to relate Jungian typology to diagnostic categories. When projective tests were being developed, the originator's familiarity with Jungian psychology had an impact on their design. Perhaps the greatest effort in assessment of Jungian concepts has been that of objective tests that purport to measure psychological type. All of these efforts can be traced to Jung's creative approach to assessment.

Jung's description of four methods of understanding patients (word association, symptom analysis, case history, and analysis of the unconscious) can best be put in perspective through understanding his subjective and humane approach to therapy.

> Clinical diagnoses are important, since they give the doctor a certain orientation; but they do not help the patient. The crucial thing is the story. For it alone shows the human background and the human suffering, and only at that point can the doctor's therapy begin to operate. (Jung, 1961, p. 124)

Given this caution, Jung described four methods of learning about patients: First, the word association method that he had developed in his work with Riklin (Jung, 1973) provided a way of locating complexes that might disturb the individual (p. 157) and allowed exploration of the unconscious. Second, hypnosis was used to bring back painful memories. Called *symptom analysis*, Jung felt it to be helpful only for posttrau-

matic stress disorders. Third, the case history was used to trace the historical development of the psychological disorder. Jung found that this method was often helpful to
the patient in bringing about changes of attitude (Jung, 1954a, p. 95). Although this
method can bring certain aspects of the unconscious into consciousness, the fourth
method, analysis of the unconscious, was the most significant for Jung. To be used only
when the conscious contents are exhausted, approaches to its exploration varied, usually including attention to the patient's archetypal material as related in fantasies and
dreams. In the following case, Jung gives an example of how he used his own dream
about a patient (and thus his unconscious) to further the analysis of the patient.

> I once had a patient, a highly intelligent woman, who for various reasons aroused my
> doubts. At first the analysis went very well, but after a while I began to feel that I was
> no longer getting at the correct interpretation of her dreams, and I thought I also no-
> ticed an increasing shallowness in our dialogue. I therefore decided to talk with my pa-
> tient about this, since it had of course not escaped her that something was going wrong.
> The night before I was to speak with her, I had the following dream.
>
> I was walking down a highway through a valley in late-afternoon sunlight. To my
> right was a steep hill. At its top stood a castle, and on the highest tower there was a
> woman sitting on a kind of balustrade. In order to see her properly, I had to bend my
> head far back. I awoke with a crick in the back of my neck. Even in the dream I had rec-
> ognized the woman as my patient.
>
> The interpretation was immediately apparent to me. If in the dream I had to look up
> at the patient in this fashion, in reality I had probably been looking down on her.
> Dreams are, after all, compensations for the conscious attitude. I told her of the dream
> and my interpretation. This produced an immediate change in the situation, and the
> treatment once more began to move forward. (Jung, 1961, p. 133)[3]

Although Jung used a highly personal approach to understanding clients, his theory
of personality has had an impact on the development of two significant projective
techniques: the Rorschach Test and the Thematic Apperception Test (TAT). As
Ellenberger (1970) states, Hermann Rorschach was interested in Jung's typology, particularly the introversion and extraversion functions as they related to his development of the Rorschach Psychodiagnostic Inkblot Test. Of the several methods that
have been used to score the Rorschach, one of the better known ones was developed
by Bruno Klopfer, a Jungian analyst. Other Jungian analysts have contributed to the
development of the Rorschach, especially McCully (1971). The originator of the TAT,
Henry Murray, studied with Jung in Zurich and was involved in starting the first Jungian training institute. With regard to the use of the Rorschach and the TAT, there are
wide variations among Jungian analysts, with some preferring one projective test over
the other, no test, or objective tests of psychological types.

Three objective measures of types have been developed: the Gray-Wheelwright
Jungian Type Survey (GW) (Wheelwright, Wheelwright, & Buehler, 1964), the
Myers-Briggs Type Indicator (MBTI) (Myers & McCaulley, 1985), and the Singer-
Loomis Inventory of Personality (SLIP) (Singer & Loomis, 1984). All instruments give
scores on a variety of combinations of the functions and attitudes described on pages
94–97. The GW has been used for more than 50 years by some Jungian analysts,
whereas the SLIP has been developed within the last 15 years. By far the most widely
known is the MBTI, used by many counselors and helping professionals to assist indi-

viduals in understanding how they make decisions, perceive data, and relate to their inner or outer world. The MBTI is often used without relating its concepts to broader Jungian theory. Both the GW and the MBTI use a bipolar assumption, whereas the SLIP does not. For instance, thinking and feeling are opposite ends of a bipolar scale, whereas in the SLIP each function is paired with each attitude to develop eight separate scales. The data that these instruments have provided are discussed in the research section of this chapter. Although these instruments are objective measures of Jung's typology, his typology does not relate directly to *DSM-IV* categories.

The Therapeutic Relationship

Accepting the patient and his psychological disturbance and unconscious processes were essential for Jung. In fact, he was often fascinated by severely disturbed patients who had been hospitalized with psychoses for many years. His colleagues, including Sigmund Freud, sometimes found this perplexing, as they did not share his interest. Jung saw the role of the analyst as using personal experience to help the patient explore his own unconscious. Previous experience as an analysand gives the analyst a respect for the difficult process of exploring the human psyche. The importance of this can be seen by the following quotation.

> The psychotherapist, however, must understand not only the patient; it is equally important that he must understand himself. For that reason the *sine qua non* is the analysis of the analyst which is called the training analysis. The patient's treatment begins with the doctor. Only if the doctor knows how to cope with himself, and his own problems will he be able to teach the patient to do the same. Only then. In the training analysis the doctor must learn to know his own psyche and to take it seriously. If he cannot do that, the patient will not learn either. (Jung, 1961, p. 132)[4]

Overriding Jung's approach to therapy was his humanness. His selection of the approach to use with a patient varied considerably.

> Naturally, a doctor must be familiar with the so-called "methods." But he must guard against falling into any specific routine approach. In general one must guard against the theoretical assumptions. Today they may be valid, tomorrow it may be the turn of other assumptions. In my analyses they play no part. I am unsystematic very much by intention. To my mind, in dealing with individuals, only individual understanding will do. We need a different language for every patient. In one analysis I can be heard talking the Adlerian dialect, in another the Freudian. (Jung, 1961, p. 131)

Although Jung took what might be called an individualistic and patient-oriented approach to his psychiatric work, he and others have proposed stages of the process of analysis to provide a clearer understanding of analytical work.

Stages of Therapy

To further describe analytic therapy, Jung outlined four stages (Adler, 1967, p. 339; Jung, 1954d). These stages represent different aspects of therapy that are not necessarily sequential and not represented in all analyses. The first stage is that of catharsis, which includes both intellectual and emotional confession of secrets. The second, elucidation, or interpretation, borrows from Freud and relies heavily on interpretation of the transference relationship. The third stage makes use of some of the insights of Alfred Adler, who focused on the social needs of individuals and their striving for superiority or power. At this point, there is a need for social education or relating the patient's issues to society. The fourth stage, "transformation" or "individuation," goes beyond the need to be fulfilled socially to focus on individuals' understanding of their unique patterns and their individual personalities.

Dreams and Analysis

For Jung, dream interpretation was the core of analysis. "Dreams are neither mere reproductions of memories nor abstractions from experience. They are the undisguised manifestation of unconscious creativity" (Jung, 1954a, p. 100). Also dreams are a symbolic representation of the state of the psyche (Hall, 1986, p. 93). Although dreams were important for Jung, not all dreams were of equal value. He distinguished between "little" and "big" dreams. More common than big dreams, little dreams come from the personal unconscious and are often a reflection of day-to-day activity. "Significant dreams, on the other hand, are often remembered for a lifetime, and not infrequently prove to be the richest jewel in the treasure-house of psychic experience" (Jung, 1960c, p. 290). Images within big dreams are symbols of still unknown or unconscious material. Before discussing the interpretation of dreams, practical considerations in recovering dream material, as well as the structure of dreams, are examined.

Dream material. The sources of dream material are varied. They may include memories of past experiences, important events in the past that were repressed, unimportant daily or past events, and memories of deeply disturbing secrets. Sometimes the dream comes from physical stimuli such as a cold room or a need to urinate. Sources of the dream are not important; what is important is the meaning that the images have for the dreamer (Mattoon, 1981).

To remember dreams and their images is not always easy. Most analysts advise patients to record their dreams on a notepad as soon as possible, even if the dreams are remembered during the middle of the night. A tape recorder may also be used instead of a notepad. Although dreams often are forgotten soon after a person wakes, sometimes they may come into memory shortly after one awakens. As much information about the dream as can be remembered, including small details, should be recorded, as details are often symbolically significant and may turn an otherwise little dream into a significant dream (Harris, 1996). When dreams are fully remembered, they usually follow a particular structure.

Structure of dreams. Although reported dream narratives vary widely in their content, many have four basic elements (Jung, 1961, pp. 194–195). Dream narratives begin with an exposition that describes the place of the dream, the major characters in the dream, the relationship of the dreamer to the situation, and sometimes the time: "I was in a barn with my sister, and a farmer was bringing in a load of hay. It was early evening and we were tired." The second part of the dream is the plot development, an indication of the tension and conflicts developing in the dream: "The farmer was angry at us and wanted us to unload the hay quickly into the barn." The third part is the decisive event, in which a change takes place in the dream: "The farmer's face turned wild and menacing. He got off the tractor and came for us." The last phase of the dream is the conclusion or solution: "My sister and I went out two different open barn doors. I ran as fast as I could, but the farmer was close on my heels with a hay fork. I awoke breathing rapidly." By learning the full structure of the dream, analysts can make sure that details are not overlooked and that parts are not missing. Of course, sometimes the dreamer can remember only parts or fragments of a dream. Such fragmentary dreams require more caution in interpretation than fully remembered dreams.

Dream interpretation. Jung's goal in dream interpretation was to relate the symbolic meaning of the dream to the conscious situation of the patient (Jung, 1960c). How he approached dream analysis depended on the nature of the dream. Sometimes the images reflected personal associations and other times archetypal associations. Furthermore, he looked for continuity among dream images or patterns of dreams and attended to the subjective or objective meaning of the images within the dream.

Dreams that reveal personal associations are those that relate to the dreamer's own waking life. Such dreams may need to be interpreted not only in terms of the daily events of an individual but also in terms of information about her family, past, friends, and cultural background. Although dreams with personal associations occur much more frequently than those with archetypal associations, the significance of both can be profound.

The following dream, which was related to Jung by an acquaintance, can help illustrate the great significance that Jung attached to dreams. In this case, the dreamer did not see the associations that Jung (1954b) did:

The dreamer was a man with an academic education, about fifty years of age. I knew him only slightly, and our occasional meetings consisted mostly of humorous gibes on his part at what we called the "game" of dream interpretation. On one of these occasions he asked me laughingly if I was still at it. I replied that he obviously had a very mistaken idea of the nature of dreams. He then remarked that he had just had a dream which I must interpret for him. I said I would do so, and he told me the following dream:

He was alone in the mountains, and wanted to climb a very high, steep mountain which he could see towering in front of him. At first the ascent was laborious but then it seemed to him that the higher he climbed the more he felt himself being drawn towards the summit. Faster and faster he climbed, and gradually a sort of ecstasy came over him. He felt he was actually soaring up on wings, and when he reached the top he seemed to weigh nothing at all, and stepped lightly off into empty space. Here he awoke.

He wanted to know what I thought of his dream. I knew that he was not only an experienced but an ardent mountain climber, so I was not surprised to see yet another vindication of the rule that dreams speak the same language as the dreamer. Knowing that mountaineering was such a passion with him, I got him to talk about it. He seized on this eagerly and told me how he loved to go alone without a guide, because the very danger of it had tremendous fascination for him. He also told me about several dangerous tours, and the daring he displayed made a particular impression on me. I asked myself what it could be that impelled him to seek out such dangerous situations, apparently with an almost morbid enjoyment. Evidently a similar thought occurred to him, for he added, becoming at the same time more serious, that he had no fear of danger, since he thought that death in the mountains would be something very beautiful. This remark threw a significant light on the dream. Obviously he was looking for danger, possibly with the unavowed idea of suicide. But why should he deliberately seek death? There must be some special reason. I therefore threw in the remark that a man in his position ought not to expose himself to such risks. To which he replied very emphatically that he would never "give up his mountains," that he had to go to them in order to get away from the city and his family. "This sticking at home does not suit me," he said. Here was a clue to the deeper reason for his passion. I gathered that his marriage was a failure, and that there was nothing to keep him at home. Also he seemed disgusted with his professional work. It occurred to me that his uncanny passion for the mountains must be an avenue of escape from an existence that had become intolerable to him. I therefore privately interpreted the dream as follows: Since he still clung on to life in spite of himself, the ascent of the mountain was at first laborious. But the more he surrendered himself to his passion, the more it lured him on and lent wings to his feet. Finally it lured him completely out of himself: he lost all sense of bodily weight and climbed even higher than the mountain, out into empty space. Obviously this meant death in the mountains.

After a pause, he said suddenly, "Well, we've talked about all sorts of other things. You were going to interpret my dream. What do you think about it?" I told him quite frankly what I thought, namely that he was seeking death in the mountains, and that with such an attitude he stood a remarkably good chance of finding it.

"But that is absurd," he replied, laughing. "On the contrary, I am seeking my health in the mountains."

Vainly I tried to make him see the gravity of the situation. (Jung, 1954b, pp. 60–63)

Six months later he "stepped off into the air." A mountain guide watched him and a young friend letting themselves down on a rope in a difficult place. The friend had found a temporary foothold on a ledge, and the dreamer was following him down. Suddenly he let go of the rope "as if he were jumping into the air," as the guide reported afterwards. He fell on his friend, and both went down and were killed. (Jung, 1970a, p. 208)[5]

In contrast with dream material that has many personal associations, dreams that show archetypal associations contain material that reflects the collective unconscious rather than the personal unconscious. Because archetypes have form, but not content, analysts must use their knowledge of symbolism that is present in mythology, folklore, and religion. With this knowledge, the analyst can expand on the meaning of the material to the patient, through the process of amplification.

The following brief example of symbolic dream interpretation comes from a theologian who related a reoccurring dream to Jung. Using biblical symbolism, information that Jung knew the dreamer was familiar with, Jung relates the dream to the dreamer, but the dreamer chooses not to accept it.

He had a certain dream which was frequently repeated. He dreamt that he was standing on a slope from which he had a beautiful view of a low valley covered with dense woods. In the dream he knew that in the middle of the woods there was a lake, and he also knew that hitherto something had always prevented him from going there. But this time he wanted to carry out his plan. As he approached the lake, the atmosphere grew uncanny, and suddenly a light gust of wind passed over the surface to the water which rippled darkly. He awoke with a cry of terror.

At first this dream seems incomprehensible. But as a theologian the dreamer should have remembered the "pool" whose waters were stirred by a sudden wind, and in which the sick were bathed—the pool of Bethesda. An angel descended and touched the water, which thereby acquired curative powers. The light wind is the pneuma which bloweth where it listeth. And that terrified the dreamer. An unseen presence is suggested, an omen that lives its own life and in whose presence man shudders. The dreamer was reluctant to accept the association with the pool of Bethesda. He wanted nothing of it, for such things are met with only in the Bible, or at most on Sunday mornings as the subjects of sermons, and have nothing to do with psychology. All very well to speak of the Holy Ghost on occasions—but it is not a phenomenon to be experienced! (Jung, 1959a, pp. 17–18)[6]

Another important feature in interpreting dreams is to determine whether the images in the dream are to be treated objectively or subjectively. In an objective interpretation, the objects and people in the dream represent themselves. In a subjective interpretation, each object or person represents a part of the dreamer. For example, a woman who dreams of being in a restaurant and talking to a strange man can view the man in the dream as representing her animus (Jung, 1960a). In general, Jung felt an objective interpretation was usually appropriate when the people in the dream are important to the dreamer. A subjective interpretation may be appropriate when the individuals are not important to the dreamer. When making an objective interpretation, it is often helpful to see if there is a theme among the elements of the dream. For example, a woman who dreams of being in a park with young children and babies crying in the background may connect the young children and babies to the theme of birth. The Jungian analyst may choose to amplify those symbols that are related to a theme and relate them to the patient's life.

Where possible, Jungian analysts find it helpful to work with a group or series of dreams. When dreams are difficult to understand, relating them to earlier or later dreams can be helpful. Of significance are dreams that recur or have recurring themes with changing details (Mattoon, 1981). In such cases, archetypal association can be very helpful. As analysts interpret dreams, they try to assess the function of the dream for the dreamer.

Compensatory functions of dreams.   Jung believed that most dreams are compensatory and part of the process of regulating the individual's personality (Whitmont, 1991). The question is what the dream does for the dreamer. By bringing unconscious material from the dream into consciousness, the dreamer may be able to determine the purpose of the dream. Dreams may compensate the conscious by confirming, opposing, exaggerating, or in some other way relating to conscious experience. However, not all dreams have a compensatory function. Some dreams may anticipate future events or actions, and others represent traumatic events from the unconscious.

To summarize the Jungian approach to dreams is quite difficult. There is a vast amount of literature describing symbols in dreams, archetypal representations, and methods for dream interpretation. Although dreams are extremely important in the interpretive process in Jungian analysis, sometimes analysts encounter patients with few dreams. Analysts must be able to use a variety of treatment methods.

Active Imagination

Jungian analysts often seek a variety of ways to allow new unconscious contents to emerge into consciousness. Active imagination is a way of helping this process. The major purpose is to let complexes and their emotional components emerge from the unconscious to the conscious (Mattoon, 1981, p. 238). Although active imagination can be done verbally or nonverbally, it is often done by carrying on an imaginary conversation with a human or nonhuman figure that may be suggested by a dream or fantasy. This approach is different than passively fantasizing about experiences or images, as it can deepen over time and cover several patient issues. Active imagination is most often done with symbols that represent archetypes such as one's anima or animus or the "wise old man" archetype. To use this approach, analysands must have had much experience with analytic therapy, and still it may be difficult to learn. This method is described more fully by Dallett (1982) and Hannah (1981). An illustration of active imagination will help show the dramatic and often emotional aspects of this method.

> A patient in his thirties had a recurrent fantasy in which he felt threatened by a completely veiled dark figure. He had never been able to discover its identity. I asked him to try to concentrate on this figure instead of suppressing it. He did so and in the end could imagine how he took off veil after veil until he discovered that it was a feminine figure. He had to summon up all his courage to undo the last veil covering her face and found with a tremendous shock that the face was that of his mother. It is just the courage needed to proceed with the unveiling and the final shock of discovery that testify to the genuineness of the fantasy and to having contacted a psychic reality. (G. Adler, 1967, p. 366)[7]

Gerhard Adler mentions that other ways of dealing with this recurrent fantasy would be to have a conversation with the figure or to ask for its name. Thus, active imagination is a method in which the ego, the center of consciousness, can relate to the collective unconscious.

Other Techniques

Jungian analysts may use a variety of creative techniques to help unconscious processes enter into consciousness. Examples include dance and movement therapy, poetry, and artwork. Patients can use artistic expression without being conscious of what they are creating and provide material with symbolic value. Using the Gestalt technique of talking to an imagined person in an empty chair may be another way of accessing unconscious material. A method that is used with both children and adults is the sandtray, a sandbox with small figures and forms that individuals can assign meaning to. The variety of approaches that Jungian analysts use depends on their training and the needs of their patients.

Up to this point, discussion of treatment has included methods of accessing the unconscious through dream material, active imagination, and other methods. This discussion has not included examination of the relationship of the analyst and analysand. As in psychoanalysis, an important aspect of Jungian analysis is the transference and countertransference. In Jungian analysis, these relationships have specific relevance to Jungian personality theory.

Transference and Countertransference

The source of transference and countertransference is projection, the process in which characteristics of one person are reacted to as if they belong to another object or person. When patients project aspects of themselves or significant others toward the analyst, this is considered transference. When analysts project their unconscious feelings or characteristics onto a patient, it is called countertransference. Both transference and countertransference can be negative, such as when either patient or analyst is frustrated with the course of therapy, and the source of the frustration is characteristic of the individual's experience, such as arguments with parents. Likewise, the transference and countertransference can be positive, such as when a warm relationship with the mother is projected onto the other person. One aspect of transference and countertransference that is unique to Jungian analysis is the emphasis on the projection of not only personal experience but also archetypal material from the collective unconscious.

Jung's view of transference and countertransference changed considerably throughout his more than 50 years of writings. During the time that he was heavily influenced by Freud, he generally agreed with Freud that working with transference issues was an important part of cure in analysis. When Jung devoted his studies to archetypes and their symbols, he began to feel that personal transference was not important in analysis and could be avoided. Later, however, he began to believe that transference had archetypal dimensions and devoted much effort (Jung, 1954f) to describing archetypal material that can be projected onto the therapist.

To illustrate the role of transference and countertransference in Jungian analysis, the following example of a female analyst working with a woman who is experiencing intense anxiety arising from being criticized and belittled by her mother (Ulanov, 1982) demonstrates several important issues. Ulanov describes her patient as lacking self-confidence and having much repressed anger, which is gradually realized as analysis progresses. In the following paragraph, the first sentence summarizes the transference relationship. The rest of the paragraph describes Ulanov's awareness of her own archetypal material and its role in the countertransference process.

> In the transference, she needed now to please me the way she used to try to please mother. The whole mother issue was there with us and I could feel different parts of the mother role in its archetypal form come alive in me at different times. Sometimes I would find myself wanting to react as the good mother the woman never had. Other times her frantic anxiety aroused in me the thought of brusque responses with which to put a swift end to all her dithering. Other times, such as the day the patient greeted me at the door with "I'm sorry" before she even said hello, I wanted to laugh and just get out from under the whole mother constellation. (Ulanov, 1982, p. 71)[8]

Now, Ulanov comments on the patient's separation of the transference from the therapist to better understand her mother's criticism.

> The patient's transference took her back into her actual relationship with her mother in the past. Because the patient perceived me as different from her real mother, she could risk facing her repressed angry reactions to her mother. In addition, she came to see how

her mother's criticism continued to live in her own belittling attitude toward herself. (Ulanov, 1982, pp. 71–72)

Here Ulanov discusses the role of archetypal material in the patient's transference.

The issue of relating to the mother archetype arose in the midst of all of her personal struggles. For around associations and memories of her real mother, and mixed in with transference feelings to me as a mother figure, appeared images and affects, behavior patterns and fantasies, connected to relating to the archetypal mother. The patient reached to feelings of happy dependence, and which she did not experience with her real negative mother, but which can be an authentic response to the mother image. She reached to a deep sadness that her mother was so anxiously distressed herself that she could not be a secure refuge for her child. Thus she went beyond her own bruises to perceive her mother's damaged state and to feel genuine compassion for her parent. The patient could wonder about where all this led, at moments seeing her mother problem as an important thread in her own destiny, setting her specific tasks to solve. She could accept the relationship now, with all its hurts, as an essential part of her own way of life. (Ulanov, 1982, p. 72)

The patient's transference makes the analyst aware of her own issues and countertransference concerns.

On the countertransference side, I found my patient's material touched issues of my own, experienced with my own mother, some finished, and easy to keep from intruding upon the treatment, others needing more work and attention so that they did not interfere. The life issues around "the mother," good and bad, were posed for me as well, to think about, to feel again, to work on. (Ulanov, 1982, p. 72)

This example shows the interrelationship between transference and countertransference on the part of the patient and therapist. Furthermore, the use of archetypal imagery (the mother) is integrated into comments about the transference and countertransference phenomena.

Both transference and countertransference reactions may be found by bringing some unconscious material into consciousness. Dreams can be a rich source of material, not only for transference but also for countertransference issues. An illustration of this can be seen in Singer's (1973) work with Nicholas, who sought analysis after taking an important job for which he did not feel qualified. The thought of undertaking this assignment made him feel depressed and occasionally panicky. Dreams played an important role in Nicholas's progress, but it was Singer's dream that signaled to her that therapy may be over and that it was time to dissolve the transference relationship. The following dream that Singer had resulted from her countertransference projections onto Nicholas. To Singer, this dream meant that she and Nicholas had gone as far together in analysis as they could, and it was time for him to go on by himself:

I have climbed to the top of a snowy mountain with Nicholas. We look down and see some men and machines cutting a hole in the ice, maybe for fishing. It is noisy. But atop the mountain the sun is warm. I lie back in the snow and enjoy the sun. Nicholas remains standing. (Singer, 1973, p. 325)

Taking cues from unconscious or dream materials is a common practice among Jungian psychoanalysts when dealing with transference and countertransference issues. Furthermore, interpretations about archetypal material are frequently used throughout the process of therapy.

PSYCHOLOGICAL DISORDERS

Illustrating a Jungian approach to a variety of diagnostic psychopathological concerns is difficult for many reasons. Much of Jungian psychotherapy and analysis takes place over several years and deals with archetypal representations in the unconscious, rather than behaviors related to diagnostic classification. Furthermore, some Jungian analysts combine object relations theory or Kohut's self psychology with a Jungian approach to the unconscious, making it difficult to separate Jungian analysis from other approaches. Also, it is difficult to understand a Jungian approach to analysis without a knowledge of mythology and folk culture and a familiarity with the wide variety of archetypes referred to by Jungian analysts. Such detailed information is beyond the scope of this text.

Thus the information about four diagnostic categories that is presented here does not show how all Jungian analysts would work with these disorders, but it illustrates a variety of conceptual and therapeutic approaches. The example of anxiety neurosis disorder is used to illustrate how Jung conceptualized patient problems and how he worked therapeutically. Because the case is brief, it is not typical of his approach. An example of work with a depressed client shows the use of a dream series. By examining unconscious archetypal material, the conceptualization and treatment of borderline and psychotic disorders is illustrated.

Anxiety Neurosis

Jungian analysts differ in the role that their unconscious plays in conceptualizing and treating patients. This case shows how Jung's unconscious was an important part of his work with a woman with an anxiety disorder. Before Jung had heard of the attractive young woman he was to see the next day, he had a dream in which an unknown young girl came to him as a patient. He was perplexed by the woman in the dream and did not understand what was behind her problems. Suddenly he realized that she had an unusual complex about her father. Jung's description of the case shows the importance that he attributes to therapists' and patients' spirituality in psychological health.

The girl had been suffering for years from a severe anxiety neurosis. . . . I began with an anamnesis (case history), but could discover nothing special. She was a well-adapted, Westernized Jewess, enlightened down to her bones. At first I could not understand what her trouble was. Suddenly my dream occurred to me, and I thought, "Good Lord, so this is the little girl of my dream." Since, however, I could detect not a trace of a father complex in her, I asked her, as I am in the habit of doing in such cases, about her grandfather. For a brief moment she closed her eyes, and I realized at once that here lay the heart of the problem. I therefore asked her to tell me about this grandfather, and learned that he had been a rabbi and had belonged to a Jewish sect. "Do you mean the Chassidim?" I asked. She said yes. I pursued my questioning. "If he was a rabbi, was he by any chance a zaddik?" "Yes," she replied, "it is said that he was a kind of saint and also possessed second sight. But that is all nonsense. There is no such thing!"

With that I had concluded the anamnesis and understood the history of her neurosis. I explained to her, "Now I am going to tell something that you may not be able to accept. Your grandfather was a zaddik. Your father became an apostate to the Jewish faith. He betrayed the secret and turned his back on God. And you have your neurosis because the fear of God has got into you." That struck her like a bolt of lightning.

The following night I had another dream. A reception was taking place in my house, and behold, this girl was there too. She came up to me and asked, "Haven't you got an umbrella? It is raining so hard." I actually found an umbrella, fumbled around with it to open it, and was on the point of giving it to her. But what happened instead? I handed it to her on my knees, as if she were a goddess.

I told this dream to her, and in a week the neurosis had vanished. The dream had showed me that she was not just a superficial little girl, but that beneath the surface were the makings of a saint. She had no mythological ideas, and therefore the most essential feature of her nature could find no way to express itself. All her conscious activity was directed toward flirtation, clothes, and sex, because she knew of nothing else. She knew only the intellect and lived a meaningless life. In reality she was a child of God whose destiny was to fulfill His secret will. I had to awaken mythological and religious ideas in her, for she belonged to that class of human beings to whom spiritual activity is demanded. Thus her life took on a meaning, and no trace of the neurosis was left. (Jung, 1961, pp. 138–140)[9]

Jung's reliance on his unconscious awareness of the patient's anxiety allowed him to get to the root of the matter. Having a dream about a patient or an event before meeting the patient or before the event occurred was not unusual for Jung. Such events contributed to his interest in parapsychology.

The occurrence of the first dream before Jung saw the patient can be considered a meaningful coincidence. Jung observed many such coincidences that had no causal connection. He used the term *synchronicity* to describe events that were related in their meaning but not in their cause.

Depression

Jungian analysts have looked at depression from several points of view. Samuels (1991) states that "Jung saw depression as a damming up of energy, which, when released, may take on a more positive direction" (p. 17). Jung believed that a depression should be entered into fully, so that patients could clarify their feelings. In the following example of Mattoon's (1986) work with a series of dreams with a depressed individual, one approach to depression is shown.

In describing Beth, a woman in the second half of her life with six children, Mattoon (1986) focuses on Beth's unconscious in their analytical work. Beth is depressed and bored with housework. During the time of the analysis, Beth was reassessing her view of religion, friends, and family. After about a year of analysis, she reported several dreams that show that she is moving out of her depression.

> Often a dream series provides much of the context for an individual dream. The series may comprise all the dreams in a given time period, or several dreams, perhaps experienced over many months, with a common motif (image). Beth had periodic dreams of houses that seemed to augment the message of the initial dream. About a year into analysis she dreamed: "I have a big, beautiful house, but I'm not satisfied. I have a room for everything. The house is on a hillside. I go outside and walk up the hill enjoying the scenery. I can't understand why I'm still feeling restless when I have everything." The dream seems to indicate that much change has occurred (the new house) and all the components are present for a satisfying life, but she still must put the psychic components into proper relation to one another.
>
> After another four months, Beth dreamed: "We had changed houses. It seemed that we were on the same lot but had moved a different house in. I was pleased with more room." In this dream she has gone beyond having everything to having more room—an expansion of her vision and possibilities.
>
> After about a year and a half of analysis, Beth had dealt with enough of her problems that her depression lifted. She thought increasingly of getting a teaching job. She began to have dreams in which she was interviewed for jobs and one in which she was hired. We concluded that her dreams were supporting her inclination to reenter the teaching profession. (Mattoon, 1986, p. 141)[10]

Through dream material, the unconscious aspects of the depression are revealed. Beth's later dreams also show activity and energy. Thus, psychic energy that had been manifest in her depression is now channeled into teaching.

Borderline Disorders

In writing about the borderline process, Schwartz-Salant (1989, 1991) emphasizes the importance of archetypal symbolism. He finds alchemical symbolism to be particularly useful, specifically the notion of *coniunctio*, based on the concept of unity in alchemy. For Schwartz-Salant, borderline patients may be difficult to communicate with, as they may be expressing themselves not through personal feelings, but through archetypal themes. Often, the patient presents very concrete associations to dreams that may yield very difficult unconscious material to bring into conscious awareness.

For example, Schwartz-Salant (1991) presents the case of Ed, a bright 38-year-old man, who could spend hours contemplating why someone had treated him in a particular way. He was often critical of the morality of his own behavior and that of others. In helping Ed, Schwartz-Salant deals with the coniunctio archetype as represented by Ed's inner couple—two aspects of himself in union with each other. The therapist also saw himself and Ed as a transference couple that desired nonunion, and acting at times at cross-purposes. Schwartz-Salant (1991, p. 171) puts it more dramatically: "Whenever I would invoke disharmony by being out of harmony with myself, Ed would become very nasty and have the urge to hit me." Ed improved when patient and therapist could examine the couple within Ed that was at war, but really desired no contact within itself. Ed's individuation increased as he became aware of important archetypal and transference themes.

Psychotic Disorders

In his early training with Bleuler, Jung had the opportunity to work with many psychotic patients. He was particularly interested in the symbolism that was inherent in their incoherent verbiage. He heard the expression of schizophrenic patients as a verbalization of unconscious material. In his book, *The Self in Psychotic Process*, Perry (1987) gives a case history of a schizophrenic patient who, when most disturbed, was most involved in a quest for "a center." Although not familiar with symbolism, the patient described, over a period of time, a fourfold center, a mandala symbol. In her psychotic processes, Perry saw the themes of death and rebirth as they were related to dealing with parental domination in developing individuation. For Perry, the verbalizations of the psychotic come not from exposure to one's culture but from the collective unconscious. He gives as evidence the spontaneous occurrence of the mandala symbol, not only with this patient but with others. For him, this provides support that the Self is the center of the psyche for all people (Perry, 1987).

BRIEF THERAPY

The length of Jungian analysis varies considerably, depending on the needs of the patient and the approach of the analyst. Analysts who use a developmental approach, combining Jungian theory with object relations theory, are likely to meet two or more times per week, whereas those who follow a more classical model of Jungian analysis may meet once or sometimes twice a week. The duration also varies considerably, sometimes less than a year and often many years. It is not unusual for analysands to leave analysis for a period of time and return later. However, there is not a brief or time-limited approach to Jungian analysis. Harris (1996) suggests that a Jungian frame of reference can be used for brief therapy if the problem is limited in scope.

At times, Jungian analysts may have relatively few contacts with their patients but that usually occurs when analysis may not be the appropriate treatment. Jung was quite flexible, sometimes using methods that he associated with Adler or Freud or a method that seemed appropriate and expedient to him. In general, Jungian analysts vary as to their flexibility in using methods that are not usually associated with Jungian exploration of the unconscious. Also, some patient problems may indicate that they are not appropriate for Jungian analysis. For example, Jung (1961, p. 135) gives the case of a doctor with whom he decided to terminate therapy because of the nature of the dream material that revealed to Jung that the patient had the potential of developing a psychosis. In cases such as this, Jungian analysts recognize when exploration of the unconscious will lead not to individuation but to fragmentation of the psyche.

CURRENT TRENDS

Jung's ideas have become increasingly popular with the public. One reason was Joseph Campbell's television series featuring the importance of myth in modern life. In this series and the book published based on this series (Campbell & Moyers, 1988), Jung's collective unconscious and archetypes are discussed. A best-selling book, *Women Who Run with the Wolves* (Estes, 1992) describes the "wild woman" archetype. Bly's (1990) book *Iron John* discusses the importance of male archetypes. While these books have contributed to making Jungian therapy more popular to the public, there have been two significant ongoing issues affecting the development of Jungian therapy: post-Jungian schools and postmodernism.

In describing post-Jungian thought, Samuels (1997) groups analytical writers into three overlapping categories: developmental, classical, and archetypal. The developmental school of Jungian analysis, based in England, combines Jungian thought with that of many of the object relations theorists such as Klein and Winnicott. Fordham's (1957) work best elucidates this theoretical thrust. The classical school makes use of Jung's ideas as he has written them; it balances developmental issues with archetypal emphasis but tends to neglect transference and countertransference issues. The archetypal school, best exemplified by Hillman (1972, 1989), attends to a wide variety of archetypes rather than emphasizing the persona, anima-animus, and the shadow. A recent example of this school is the full discussion of the Trickster Archetype as it affects both men and women (McNeely, 1996). The use of many archetypal images is increasingly common among analysts in the United States, as can be seen in the section on gender issues later in this chapter. Archetypal imagery and symbolism are often a subject of discussion at educational seminars for the public.

Postmodern thinking has been brought to Jungian theory most notably by Young-Eisendrath (1997a, 1997b). Her work helps readers understand that archetypes are not stereotypes into which the patient's thoughts or images must fit. She acknowleges that individuals make up their own reality (constructivism) and that stepping back to understand the relationships between the therapist's and patient's reality is important. Jung believed that he had no preconceptions about interpreting a dream before it was told to him, that he saw it from the patient's point of view. Young-Eisendrath and others (Kugler, 1997) caution Jungian therapists to understand how their own views of the world, such as views of gender roles, can affect their work with patients.

USING JUNGIAN CONCEPTS WITH OTHER THEORIES

Jungian therapists often make use of concepts from other theories. Because of Jung's close association with Freud during the early part of his professional life, many similarities between the two theories exist. Jungian analysts often find it helpful to make use of Freud's concepts of child development. Although Jung wrote on this topic, he devoted more effort to other areas. Many Jungians, often referred to as the *developmental* or *British school* of Jungian analysis, have been attracted to the work of object relations theorists who further examine childhood development. Although psychodynamic theories of therapy are most closely related to Jungian analysis, Jungians have also made use of Gestalt enactment techniques such as the empty chair, which can bring unconscious material into conscious awareness.

Those who are not Jungian analysts but use object relations or other psychoanalytic theories may find Jung's concept of archetypal forms to be useful and to provide new insights into unconscious behavior. Although the Jungian concept of the personal unconscious corresponds to the psychoanalytic concept of the unconscious, there is no corresponding concept to the collective unconscious. Use of this concept does require knowledge of the archetypal formation of the collective unconscious and archetypal symbols. Easier to integrate are Jung's notions of complexes, which are broader and more comprehensive than the Freudian. Additionally, Jung's emphasis on the second half of life may be of much value to psychodynamic therapists working with older patients.

For mental health professionals who do not make use of psychodynamic concepts in their work, the application of Jung's typology of attitudes and functions may be helpful in providing a means of understanding an individual's personality. The attitudes of introversion and extraversion alert the therapist to attend to the patient's inner and outer world. The Jungian typology also provides insight into how individuals view their world (sensing or intuiting) and how they make judgments or decisions (thinking or feeling). These concepts can be measured through several instruments, including the Myers-Briggs Type Indicator (MBTI) and other inventories, but they do not provide in-depth information obtained in therapy sessions. The MBTI and the attitudes and functions of personality are used widely by many helping professionals. These concepts are relatively easy to understand and do not require the specific training and supervision (usually including personal analysis) that is necessary in working with unconscious material.

RESEARCH

Although Jung used word-association tests to study his concept of complexes, he used evidence from myths, folklore, and dreams of patients to confirm his hypotheses about most of his concepts. Perhaps the most thorough review of research on a variety of Jungian concepts and hypotheses was done by Mattoon (1981), who described evidence relevant to many of his constructs. Most of the research related to Jungian thought has been on his typological system—attitudes and functions. There is scattered research but no coherent research efforts on other concepts. An example of research on differences between the dreams of normal and eating-disordered women illustrates research on Jungian concepts. Research on the comparative effectiveness of Jungian analysis and other forms of therapy is not available. Jungian analysis may be the most difficult type of treatment to assess in terms of effectiveness because the therapeutic process is long, outcome and process measures need to deal with concepts related to the personal and collective unconscious, and approaches of Jungian analysts differ widely in terms of style and the integration of other theories. Most of this section concentrates on studies related to Jung's concepts of personality, specifically, attitudes and functions.

Three inventories have been developed to measure not only introversion-extraversion but also the functions of thinking, feeling, sensing, and intuiting: the Gray-Wheelwright Jungian Type Survey (Wheelwright, Wheelwright, & Buehler, 1964), the Myers-Briggs Type Indicator (Myers & McCaulley, 1985), and the Singer-Loomis Inventory of Personality (SLIP) (Singer & Loomis, 1984). In terms of use as a research instrument, the MBTI has received more attention than the other two. For example, the MBTI has sample sizes ranging between 15,000 and 25,000 from which estimates are made about the percentage of women (65%) in the United States who prefer feeling to thinking, and the percentage of men in the United States (60%) who prefer thinking to feeling. Among Native American and African-American high school students there appears to be a preference for extraversion, sensing, and thinking (Nuby & Oxford, 1998). Another study (Power & Lundsten, 1997) found that extraversion, intuition, feeling, and perception were related to right brain thinking, and sensing, thinking, and judging to left brain thinking in a sample of 1,925 MBA students. The MBTI has also been the subject of a study with individual and fraternal twins reared apart (Bouchard, Hur, & Horn, 1998) showing that extraversion, intraversion, and thinking-feeling, in particular, are found to be similar in twins reared apart. Relating MBTI typology to Jungian theory, Cann and Donderi (1986) found a correlation between type and recall of "little" and archetypal dreams, with intuitive types recalling more archetypal dreams and introverts recalling more everyday dreams. Regarding dream experiences, Jacka (1991) found that intuitive students view their dreams as more emotionally intense and disturbing than did students who scored high on sensing. Such studies illustrate the wide variety of physical and psychological characteristics that have been related to MBTI type.

Compared to studies relating type to various factors in normal populations, the research on patients is quite sparse. Studying the dreams of 12 anorectic and bulimic patients, Brink and Allan (1992) compared dream content with 11 normal women using a 91-item scale. They found that eating-disordered women had more dream scenarios depicting doom at the end of the dream, attitudes of not being able to succeed, and images of being attacked and watched. Eating-disordered women scored significantly higher than normal women on psychological traits of feelings of ineffectiveness, self-hate, inability to care for themselves, obsession with weight, and anger. The writers suggest that analysts working with eating-disordered women address the mother-daughter wound as a way of moving toward development of the Self. They warned against blaming the patient's mother while exploring the archetypes of the Good Mother and Good Father.

GENDER ISSUES

Not only for Jung, but for many Jungian writers and analysts, conceptual issues related to gender have been extremely important. The anima-animus archetypes, which represent opposite-sex sides of the individual, have been the basis of further inquiry for Jungian writers. Part of the interest, historically, has been due to the fact that many of the early analysts were women. Their writings have been important, as have those of more recent writers who have dealt with feminist and developmental issues related to the animus. Also, leaders of the men's movement have made use of Jungian archetypes in helping men become more aware of themselves. Many of the writings on gender issues reflect not only the desire to help men and women in their search for individuation but also the tension between men and women.

In reviewing the history of Jungian analysis, Henderson (1982) describes how various female analysts have made contributions through writing and speaking in areas related to Jungian analysis. Henderson believes that one of the attractions that Jung held for female analysts was "the principal of relationship in which neither sex is limited to playing a stereotyped role" (p. 13). The archetypes of the anima and animus spoke to issues important for both men and women that were not addressed in Freudian theory or in other psychological writings of the 1920s and 1930s. In a broad sense, the concepts of anima and animus develop the concept of the "not-I" (Young-Eisendrath, 1992). These archetypal concepts can be viewed as supporting the notion of men and women looking at their feminine and masculine sides, respectively. In a narrower sense, however, the concepts of anima and animus have been criticized as reinforcing sex role stereotypes. In fact, Jung had made statements showing that he viewed men's and women's roles differently: "No one can get around the fact that by taking up a masculine profession, studying and working like a man, woman is doing something not wholly in accord with, if not directly injurious to, her feminine nature" (Jung, 1970b, p. 117). In contrast to this statement was Jung's high regard for female analysts. In describing the need for therapists to have someone to talk to who could give another point of view, Jung says that "women are particularly gifted for playing such a part. They often have excellent intuition and a trenchant clinical insight and can see what men have up their sleeves, at times see also into men's anima intrigues" (Jung, 1961, p. 134). The disparities within his own views and the awareness of discrimination issues affecting women have prompted creative response from Jungian analysts.

In bringing together feminist and archetypal theory, Lauter and Rupprecht (1985) see positive ways in which Jung's ideas can be applied to women. In their Feminist Archetypal Theory (1985), they present essays that bring together ideas about the female psyche and concepts from myth, dreams, the unconscious, and therapy. They feel it is important not only to do consciousness-raising about women's issues, but also unconsciousness-raising to focus on issues related to women's images and dreams, art, literature, religion, and analysis. The concepts of anima and animus continue to be a frequent source of examination by analysts, as illustrated by the collection of essays *Gender and Soul in Psychotherapy* (Schwartz-Salant & Stein, 1992).

Pandora, the first mortal woman, according to Greek legend, is used by Young-Eisendrath (1997a) as a symbol of male-female issues that is a current struggle for North American society. Pandora was created by Zeus as a punishment to men for having stolen fire from Zeus and the other gods. Very beautiful, Pandora is deceitful, manipulating men with her sexual desirability. Young-Eisendrath uses the myth of Pandora to address men's focus on women as sexual objects. She also uses this myth to draw attention to women's focus on beauty that can lead to eating disorders. How to be free of Pandora's curse is the theme of *Gender and Desire: Uncursing Pandora*, which takes a creative approach to understanding gender roles and issues.

Jungian archetypal concepts have also been used to explain men and their issues and development. Bly (1990) and Moore and Gillette (1991, 1992) discuss the needs for ritual and awareness of male archetypes, such as King, Warrior, Magician, and Lover. These writers have led groups to help men get in touch with their own power through myths and stories that present these archetypal forms. As Collins (1993) points out, these writings emphasize male issues at the expense of the feminine side, the anima, that can make men more whole and generally masculine. Collins (1993) feels that male awareness requires appreciation and integration of the Father, Son, and feminine archetypal elements. It is likely that the prolific rate of writing on gender issues within Jungian theory will continue.

MULTICULTURAL ISSUES

During their training, Jungian analysts are often told "when you treat the patient, you treat the culture" (Samuels, 1991, p. 18). By this statement, Samuels is referring to the fact that analysts should have knowledge of the culture of the analysand, including myths and folklore. He is also interpreting the statement to mean that by treating the patient, analysts help the patient in some way to positively influence their culture. Jung was interested in cultures of all types, as evidenced by his interests in anthropology, mythology, alchemy, religion, and folklore. Because of his interest in the universality of archetypal imagery, he traveled to many countries and continents (the United States, Egypt, parts of Asia and Africa, and other areas) to talk to people in nonliterate cultures about their dreams and folklore. However, generalizations that he made about the psychology of various cultures have contributed to criticism of his views as racist.

Jung's interest in religion and spirituality was wide and varied. He learned languages in order to read about religious symbolism as it related to his concept of the collective unconscious. His travels and talk with people of other cultures provided him with material to integrate into his knowledge of mythology, folklore, and religion to relate to his concept of archetypal memory. The type of anthropological investigation that Jung did continues, with analysts and researchers studying dreams and folklore across a wide variety of cultures. For example, Petchkovsky and Cawte (1986) have studied the images in psychosis and dreamwork of Australian aborigines. Molina (1996) described Espiritismo, a healing process used in Puerto Rico to help the suffering person confront the spirit world, an approach that has some similarity to Jungian therapy. Krippner and Thompson (1996) show how 16 different Native American societies do not have a distinct separation between the dreamed world and the waking world that Western societies have. In studies like these, cultural experience, whether conscious or unconscious, has been related to Jungian archetypal material and therapy.

Although Jung's intellectual curiosity was vast, his views of cultures could be narrow. In the 1930s and 1940s Jung often referred to the psychology of races or nations (Martin, 1991). He ascribes psychological characteristics to Protestants, Jews, Swiss, "primitive Africans," and many other groups. During the rise of Nazism, he was attacked by some as being anti-Semitic, partly due to his remarks about the psychology of the Jews. The issues surrounding charges of anti-Semitism are fully explored in a book of essays by Maidenbaum and Martin (1991). Because of the charges against Jung of being racist, Jungian analysts have been careful to point out the full complexity of Jung's thought and not to make generalizations about national or racial characteristics.

The use that Jungian analysts make of knowledge of other cultures can be illustrated by Sullwold's (1971) work with a 6-year-old boy who was often physically destructive with objects and other children and in fact, had just shattered a glass partition in the office of a referring colleague. In her work, Sullwold used a sandtray with a large collection of figures, small buildings, and various other objects. The boy was of Mexican and Native American extraction, but had been adopted by Orthodox Jewish parents. Although not aware of his Indian tradition, he had a Native American name, Eagle Eye, which was a name he had given himself at Indian Guides, a boys' organization. In his initial work with the sandtray he used the cowboy and Native American figures, identifying with the Native Americans. In understanding this boy, Sullwold made use of her knowledge of Hopi and Zuni rituals and religion. In her work with the sandtray, Sullwold made observations about archetypal imagery, such as the Great Mother, which were expressed in his playing with animals in the sandtray. Assessing the future of the boy, Sullwold stated the following:

> The continued health of this boy depends on his ability to maintain the strength of his ego and develop ways of using his energies creatively so that the tremendous spiritual and psychic forces in him do not overwhelm him and throw him back into the dark cage of the monsters. (Sullwold, 1971, p. 252)

Thus, Sullwold emphasizes spiritual forces and the importance of the collective unconscious that contribute to the boy's problems. Creative expression is a positive outlet for forces that are out of reach of his conscious processes.

COUPLES COUNSELING

Although many Jungian analysts do only individual therapy, some analysts have written about approaches to couples therapy. For some analysts, attention to the correspondence between the personality types of each member of the couple is important. Others emphasize the importance of integration of the persona and the relationship between the man's anima and the woman's animus. Yet others may focus on archetypal imagery as it is played out in the couple's relationship.

In emphasizing the importance of typology, Quenk and Quenk (1982) believe that failure to appreciate the difference in type between partners can lead to difficulties in understanding the partner. They give an example of a husband who perceived his wife as disorganized and illogical, and the wife who perceived her husband as organized to the point of rigidity. These perceptions were the grounds for psychological and physical battles. By explaining the husband's type as extraverted thinking (the superior function) with sensation (the auxiliary function) and the wife's as extraverted intuition with feeling and explaining the meaning of these types, Quenk and Quenk were able to help the couple understand and respect their differences.

For Hall (1986), it is the archetypal imagery of the coniunctio that is the basis of the institution of marriage. The reality of marriage is often far different than the archetypal imagery of the coniunctio, which is a "state of perfect union in which the opposites function in the service of the whole without warring between themselves" (Hall, 1986, p. 112). Emphasizing the importance of an archetypal framework, Hall (1986) states that partners must be aware of the impact that their negative anima and animus are having on the relationship. When they are aware, communication can be enhanced. For Jung (1954c), helping individuals bring more of unconsciousness into their conscious process could bring about freer conscious choices and awareness of reasons for conflicts.

An archetypal approach to couples therapy is taken by Young-Eisendrath, who combines a feminist approach with Jungian theory. In her book *Hags and Heroes* (1992), she uses the story of Sir Gawain and the Lady Ragnell as an archetypal tale that is a paradigm of conflicts between couples. She discusses the female role of hag and the

Negative Mother Complex as they interact with the male role of Hero and Bully as they appear in three phases that correspond to the Gawain-Ragnell myth in couples therapy. The first is the desire to dominate and possess. The second phase is understanding the repressed feminine or dealing with the woman's authoritativeness. The third phase is the growth of love and free choice and the acceptance of the woman's authority by the man. In her work, Young-Eisendrath makes use of a variety of therapeutic techniques in addition to the use of legend to help couples rework conscious and unconscious paradigms.

The three methods of conceptualizing couples counseling in this section help illustrate the variety of approaches that can be taken to couples counseling when a Jungian framework is used.

FAMILY THERAPY

From a Jungian point of view, the family is a small society in which the members individuate (Hall, 1986). Most Jungian analysts do not do family therapy but refer to other practitioners. In discussing the impact of family problems on individual therapy, Hogle (1974) believes that analysts should make a careful evaluation of the family and marital relationships of the patient before embarking on individual analysis. Hogle cautions that individual analysis may have a negative impact on family or marital relationships because of the emphasis on individuation rather than on the dynamics of a family relationship. If Jungian analysts do choose to do family therapy, their knowledge of archetypal material can provide a conceptual basis for understanding the family matrix.

> One can readily see archetypal patterns at work in family interaction: the human sacrifice (often willing) of one family member for the "good" of the family (scapegoating), the old king and the princess as "protective" father and compliant daughter, an alliance of married sisters maintaining their unconscious childhood matriarchy against the men they married, etc. (Hall, 1986, p. 114)

Analysts with training in family therapy may be able to use such a conceptual view. Those Jungian analysts who are trained to work with both children and adults may be more inclined to work with families than those whose practice consists of adults.

GROUP THERAPY

Group therapy is practiced by only a relatively few Jungian analysts. Those who do so see it as an adjunct to, not as a replacement for, individual analysis. Because of the importance that he placed on the individual and the pressures on individuals for conformity from a group, Jung was not in favor of group psychotherapy (Hall, 1986). However, some Jungians see positive values in group therapy. Recently, dream groups, with or without a leader, have been started, some of them on-line (Harris, 1996). When a group member brings a dream into a group, that can be a focus of discussion, and group members with similar dreams may relate to the presented dream. Also, a dream can be enacted in the group through the use of psychodrama. Some Jungian analysts may make use of active imagination in therapy groups, having participants focus their attention on the imaginal journey of the group member. Additionally, Jungian analysts may wish to use Gestalt awareness or other group techniques. Because of the emphasis on individuation, group therapy continues to be an adjunct to rather than a substitute for individual analysis.

SUMMARY

Jung paralleled Freud's emphasis on unconscious processes, the use and interpretation of dreams in therapy, and his developmental approach to personality. Perhaps Jung's most original contribution is that of the collective unconscious and archetypal patterns and images that arise from it. Archetypal images are universal; they can be found in the religions, mythologies, and fairy tales of many cultures. Jung, in particular, emphasized the persona (the individual's social role), the anima-animus (the unconscious opposite-sex side of a man or woman's personality), the shadow (unconscious aspects of the personality that are rejected or ignored by the conscious ego), and the Self (regulating center of the personality). Many other archetypes exist, such as the Wise Old Man, the Great Mother, the lion, and so forth.

The contribution of personality types (introversion-extraversion, thinking-feeling, and sensing intuiting) is widely known, although their use in analysis varies greatly from analyst to analyst. Although Jung wrote about developmental issues across the life span, he was particularly interested in midlife issues and the role of spirituality in the life of his patients. He often worked with complexes (emotionally charged ideas that are related to an archetypal image) as they occurred at any time in the person's lifetime, but especially at midlife. Underlying all of Jung's personality constructs and central to his theory is his concern with unconscious processes.

The focus of analysis is that of working with unconscious processes to provide more conscious awareness about them. Although this is done mainly by using dream material, active imagination and fantasy approaches are also used. By recognizing archetypal themes in dreams and other material, analysts help analysands become aware of previously unconscious material. In dealing with issues between the analyst and analysand (transference and countertransference), analysts often use material from the patients' dreams. As therapy progresses, the analysand develops a stronger and more integrated Self.

To be a Jungian analyst, one must receive training at a Jungian institute, which includes information about psychological and psychotherapeutic processes as well as information from the fields of anthropology, mythology, folklore, and other areas of knowledge that would help the analyst work with archetypal symbolism. This training prepares analysts to help their patients individuate and become conscious of their unique psychological reality. Because of the emphasis on individuation, individual treatment is preferred to group, couples, or family therapy. However, recently these modes have been used more frequently. Interest in the concept of unconscious processes continues to grow, as does interest in Jung's approach to psychotherapy.

Suggested Readings

JUNG, C. G. (1956). *Two essays on analytical psychology.* New York: Meridian Books.   •   These essays present core Jungian ideas on the personal and collective unconscious. Included also is information on Jung's view of Freud and Adler and three key archetypes (persona and anima and animus), as well as Jung's approach to psychotherapy.

JUNG, C. G. (1963). *Memories, dreams, reflections.* New York: Pantheon Books. • Written near the end of his life, these autobiographical recollections describe the development of his ideas and his struggles with his unconscious processes. He also discusses his relationship with Freud and his approaches to psychotherapy.

DE LASZLO, V. (1990). *The basic writings of C. G. Jung.* Princeton, NJ: Princeton University. • Originally published by Random House in 1959, this collection of selected works from Jung includes writings on the psyche. the unconscious, typology, therapy, and human development.

HARRIS, A. S. (1996). *Living with paradox: An introduction to Jungian psychology.* Pacific Grove, CA: Brooks/Cole. • This short book describes the major features of Jungian personality theory and treatment techniques. Current issues in Jungian psychology and its practice are discussed.

WHITMONT, E. C. (1991). *The symbolic quest.* New York: Putnam. • In this overview, Jung's major ideas are presented, along with clinical material that illustrates them. This is a good introduction to Jungian thought.

References

ADLER, G. (1967). Methods of treatment in analytical psychology. In B. Wolman (Ed.), *Psychoanalytic techniques* (pp. 338–378). New York: Basic Books.

BLY, R. (1990). *Iron John: A book about men.* Reading, MA: Addison-Wesley.

BOUCHARD, T. J., Jr., HUR, Y. M., & HORN, J. M. (1998). Genetic and environmental influences on the continuous scales of the MBTI. An analysis based on twins reared apart. *Journal of Personality, 66,* 135–149.

BRINK, S. J., & ALLAN, J. A. B. (1992). Dreams of anorexic and bulimic women. *Journal of Analytical Psychology, 37,* 275–297.

CAMPBELL, J., & MOYERS, B. (1988). *The power of myth.* Garden City, NY: Doubleday.

CANN, D. R., & DONDERI, D. C. (1986). Jungian personality typology and recall of everyday and archetypal dreams. *Journal of Personality and Social Psychology, 50,* 1021–1030.

COLLINS, A. (1993). Men within. *The San Francisco Jung Institute Library Journal, 11,* 17–32.

DALLETT, J. (1982). Active imagination in practice. In M. Stein (Ed.), *Jungian analysis* (pp. 173–191). LaSalle, IL: Open Court.

ELLENBERGER, H. E. (1970). *The discovery of the unconscious.* New York: Basic Books.

ESTES, C. P. (1992). *Women who run with the wolves.* New York: Ballentine.

FORDHAM, M. (1957). *New developments in analytical psychology.* London: Routledge & Kegan Paul.

HALL, C. S., LINDZEY, G., & CAMPBELL, J. B. (1998). *Theories of personality* (4th ed.). New York: Wiley.

HALL, C. S., & NORDBY, V. J. (1973). *A primer of Jungian psychology.* New York: New American Library.

HALL, J. A. (1986). *The Jungian experience: Analysis and individuation.* Toronto: Inner City Books.

HANNAH, B. (1976). *Jung: His life work: A biographical memoir.* New York: Putnam.

HANNAH, B. (1981). *Encounters with the soul: Active imagination as developed by C. G. Jung.* Santa Monica: Sigo Press.

HARDING, M. E. (1970). *The way of all women.* New York: Putnam.

HARRIS, A. S. (1996). *Living with paradox: An introduction to Jungian psychology.* Pacific Grove, CA: Brooks/Cole.

HENDERSON, J. L. (1982). Reflections on the history and practice of Jungian analysis. In M. Stein (Ed.), *Jungian analysis* (pp. 3–26). La Salle, IL: Open Court.

HILLMAN, J. (1972). *The myth of analysis: Three essays in archetypal psychology.* Evanston, IL: Northwestern University Press.

HILLMAN, J. (1985). *Anima: An anatomy of a personified notion.* Dallas: Spring.

HILLMAN, J. (1989). *A blue fire: Selected writings by James Hillman.* (Introduced and edited by Thomas Moore). New York: Harper & Row.

HOGLE, G. H. (1974). Family therapy: When analysis fails. In G. Adler (Ed.), *Success and failure in analysis* (pp. 167–177). New York: Putnam.

JACKA, B. (1991). Personality variables and attitudes towards dream experiences. *Journal of Psychology, 125,* 27–31.

JOSEPH, S. M. (1997). Presence and absence through the mirror of transference: A model of the transcendent function. *Journal of analytical psychology, 42,* 139–156.

JUNG, C. (1954a). Analytical psychology and education. In *The development of personality,* Collected works (Vol. 17, pp. 63–132). Princeton, NJ: Princeton University Press. (Original work published 1926.)

JUNG, C. (1954b). Child development and education. In *The development of personality,* Collected works (Vol. 17, pp. 47–62). Princeton, NJ: Princeton University Press. (Original work published 1928.)

JUNG, C. (1954c). Marriage as a psychological relationship. In *The development of personality,* Collected works (Vol. 17, pp. 187–204). Princeton, NJ: Princeton University Press. (Original work published 1925.)

JUNG, C. (1954d). Problems of modern psychotherapy. In *The practice of psychotherapy,* Collected works (Vol. 16, pp. 53–75). Princeton, NJ: Princeton University Press. (Original work published 1946.)

JUNG, C. (1954e). The development of personality. In *The development of personality,* Collected works (Vol. 17, pp. 165–186). Princeton, NJ: Princeton University Press. (Original work published 1934.)

JUNG, C. (1954f). The psychology of the transference. In *The practice of psychotherapy,* Collected works (Vol. 16, pp. 163–322). Princeton, NJ: Princeton University Press. (Original work published 1946.)

JUNG, C. (1954g). Psychotherapy today. In *The practice of psychotherapy,* Collected works (Vol. 16, pp. 94–125). Princeton, NJ: Princeton University Press. (Original work published 1945.)

JUNG, C. (1956). *Symbols of transformation.* Collected works (2nd ed., Vol. 5). Princeton, NJ: Princeton University Press. (Original work published 1911.)

JUNG, C. (1957). On the psychology and pathology of so-called occult phenomena. In *Psychiatric studies,* Collected works (Vol. 1, pp. 1–88). Princeton, NJ: Princeton University Press. (Original work published 1902.)

JUNG, C. (1959a). Archetypes of the collective unconscious. In *The archetypes and the collective unconscious,* Collected works (Vol. 9, Part 1, pp. 3–42). Princeton NJ: Princeton University Press. (Original work published 1954.)

JUNG, C. (1959b). Conscious, unconscious, and individuation. In *The archetypes and the collective unconscious,* Collected works (Vol. 9, Part 1, pp. 275–289). Princeton, NJ: Princeton University Press. (Original work published 1938.)

JUNG, C. (1959c). The concept of the collective unconscious. In *The archetypes and the collective unconscious,* Collected works (Vol. 9, Part 1, pp. 42–53). Princeton, NJ: Princeton University Press. (Original work published 1936.)

JUNG, C. (1960a). General aspects of dream psychology. In *The structure and dynamics of the psyche*, Collected works (Vol. 8, pp. 235–280). Princeton, NJ: Princeton University Press. (Original work published 1916.)

JUNG, C. (1960b). Instinct and the unconscious. In *The structure and dynamics of the psyche*, Collected works (Vol. 8, pp. 129–138). Princeton, NJ: Princeton University Press. (Original work published 1919.)

JUNG, C. (1960c). On the nature of dreams. In *The structure and dynamics of the psyche*, Collected works (Vol. 8, pp. 281–297). Princeton, NJ: Princeton University Press. (Original work published 1945.)

JUNG, C. (1960d). The psychology of dementia praecox. In *The psychogenesis of mental disease*, Collected works (Vol. 3, pp. 1–152). Princeton, NJ: Princeton University Press. (Original work published 1907.)

JUNG, C. (1960e). The stages of life. In *The structure and dynamics of the psyche*, Collected works (Vol. 8, pp. 387–404). Princeton, NJ: Princeton University Press. (Original work published 1930.)

JUNG, C. (1961). *Memories, dreams, reflections*. New York: Random House.

JUNG, C. (1970a). Symbols and the interpretation of dreams. In *The symbolic life*, Collected works (Vol. 18, pp. 185–266). Princeton, NJ: Princeton University Press. (Original work published 1950.)

JUNG, C. (1970b). Women in Europe. In *Civilization in transition*, Collected works (Vol. 10, pp. 113–133). Princeton, NJ: Princeton University Press. (Original work published 1964.)

JUNG, C. (1971). *Psychological types*, Collected works (Vol. 6). Princeton, NJ: Princeton University Press. (Original work published 1921.)

JUNG, C. (1973). Studies in word association. In *Experimental researches*, Collected works (Vol. 2, pp. 3–479). Princeton, NJ: Princeton University Press. (Original work published 1904.)

JUNG, E. (1957). *Animus and anima*. Irving, TX: Spring.

KRIPPNER, S., & THOMPSON, A. (1996). A 10-facet model of dreaming applied to dream practices of sixteen Native American cultural groups. *Dreaming, 6*, 71–96.

KUGLER, P. (1997). Psychic imagery: A bridge between subject and object. In P. Young-Eisendrath & T. Dawson (Eds.), *The Cambridge companion to Jung* (pp. 71–85). Cambridge, UK: Cambridge University Press.

LAUTER, E., & RUPPRECHT, C. S. (1985). *Feminist archetypal theory: Interdisciplinary revisions of Jungian thought*. Knoxville: University of Tennessee Press.

MAIDENBAUM, A., & MARTIN, S. A. (1991). *Lingering shadows: Jungians, Freudians, and anti-Semitism*. Boston: Shambhala.

MARTIN, S. (1991). Introduction. In A. Maidenbaum & S. A. Martin (Eds.), *Lingering shadows: Jungians, Freudians, and anti-Semitism* (pp. 1–15). Boston: Shambhala.

MATTOON, M. A. (1981). *Jungian psychology in perspective*. New York: Free Press.

MATTOON, M. A. (1986). Jungian analysis. In I. L. Kutash & A. Wolf (Eds.), *Psychotherapist's casebook* (pp. 124–143). San Francisco: Jossey-Bass.

McCULLOUGH, L. (1993). Interest in Carl Jung's ideas is growing. *Guidepost, 36*, 12–13.

McCULLY, R. (1971). *Rorschach theory and symbolism: A Jungian approach to clinical material*. Baltimore: Williams & Wilkins.

McGUIRE, W. (Ed.). (1974). *The Freud/Jung letters*. Princeton, NJ: Princeton University Press.

McNEELY, D. A. (1996). *Mercury rising: Women, evil, and the trickster gods*. Woodstock, CN: Spring.

MILNER, N. B. (1998). *Creative aging: Discovering unexpected joys of later life through personality type*. Palo Alto, CA: Davies-Black.

MOLINA, M. A. N. (1996). Archetypes and spirits: A Jungian analysis of Puerto Rican Espiritismo. *Journal of Analytical Psychology, 41*, 227–244.

MOORE, R., & GILLETTE, D. (1991). *King, warrior, magician, lover: Rediscovering the archetypes of the mature masculine*. New York: HarperCollins.

MOORE, R., & GILLETTE, D. (1992). *The king within: Accessing the king in the male psyche*. New York: William Morrow.

MYERS, J. B., & MCCAULLEY, M. H. (1985). *Manual: A guide to the development and use of the Myers-Briggs Type Indicator*. Palo Alto, CA: Consulting Psychologists Press.

NUBY, J. F., & OXFORD, R. L. (1998). Learning style preferences of Native American and African American secondary students. *Journal of Psychological Type, 44*, 5–19.

PERRY, J. W. (1987). *The self in psychotic process* (Rev. ed.). Dallas: Spring.

PETCHKOVSKY, L., & CAWTE, J. (1986). The dreams of the Yolngu aborigines of Australia. *Journal of Analytical Psychology, 31*, 357–375.

POWER, S. J., & LUNDSTEN, L. L. (1997). Studies that compare type theory and left brain/right brain theory. *Journal of Psychological Type, 43*, 22–28.

QUENK, A. T., & QUENK, N. L. (1982). The use of psychological typology in analysis. In M. Stein (Ed.), *Jungian analysis* (pp. 157–172). LaSalle, IL: Open Court.

SAMUELS, A. (1991). *Psychopathology: Contemporary Jungian perspectives*. New York: Guilford Press.

SAMUELS, A. (1997). Introduction: Jung and the post-Jungians. In P. Young-Eisendrath & T. Dawson (Eds.), *The Cambridge Companion to Jung* (pp. 1-13). Cambridge, UK: Cambridge University Press.

SANDNER, D. E., & BEEBE, J. (1982). Psychopathology and analysis. In M. Stein (Ed.), *Jungian analysis* (pp. 294–334). La Salle, IL: Open Court.

SCHAVEREIN, J. (1996). Desire and the female analyst. *Journal of Analytical Psychology, 4*, 261–287.

SCHWARTZ-SALANT, N. (1989). *The borderline personality: Vision and healing*. Wilmette, IL: Chiron.

SCHWARTZ-SALANT, N. (1991). The borderline personality: Vision and healing. In A. Samuels (Ed.), *Psychopathology: Contemporary Jungian perspectives* (pp. 157–204). New York: Guilford Press.

SCHWARTZ-SALANT, N., & STEIN, M. (1992). *Gender and soul in psychotherapy*. Wilmette, IL: Chiron.

SINGER, J. (1973). *Boundaries of the soul: The practice of Jung's psychology*. Garden City, NY: Anchor.

SINGER, J., & Loomis, M. (1984). *The Singer-Loomis Inventory of Personality (SLIP)*. Palo Alto, CA: Consulting Psychologists Press.

SULLWOLD, E. (1971). Eagle eye. In H. Kirsch (Ed.), *The well-tended tree* (pp. 235–253). New York: Plenum.

ULANOV, A. B. (1982). Transference/countertransference: A Jungian perspective. In M. Stein (Ed.), *Jungian analysis*, pp. 68–85. La Salle, IL: Open Court.

ULANOV, A. B. (1997). Transference, the transcendent function, and transcendence. *Journal of Analytical Psychology, 42*, 119–138.

WHEELWRIGHT, J. B., WHEELWRIGHT, J.H., & BUEHLER, H. A. (1964). *Jungian Type Survey: The Gray Wheelwright Test* (18th revision). San Francisco: Society of Jungian Analysts of Northern California.

WHITMONT, E. C. (1991). *The symbolic quest*. Princeton, NJ: Princeton University Press.

YOUNG-EISENDRATH, P. (1992). *Hags and heroes: a feminist approach to Jungian psychotherapy with couples*. Toronto: Inner City Books.

YOUNG-EISENDRATH, P. (1997a). *Gender and desire*. College Station, TX: Texas A & M University Press.

YOUNG-EISENDRATH, P. (1997b). Why it is difficult to be a Jungian analyst in today's world. In M. A. Mattoon (Ed.), *Zurich 95: Open questions in analytical psychology* (pp. 167–174). Einsiedeln, Switzerland: Daimon Verlag.

4

Adlerian Therapy

Although Adler is considered by some to be a neo-Freudian, his views are very different from Freud's. Their similarity is mainly in their belief that the personalities of individuals are formed in their early years, before the age of 6. Beyond that, their views are different in almost every respect. Adler emphasized the social nature of the individual—that psychological health can be measured by the contribution that individuals make to their community and to society. Adler believed that lifestyle, the way individuals approach living, and their long-term goals can be determined by examining the family constellation, early recollections (memories of incidents from childhood), and dreams. Individuals attempt to achieve competence or a place in the world, but in doing so, they may develop mistaken beliefs that give them a false sense of superiority or a sense of inferiority. Adlerians help their patients develop insight into these beliefs and assist them in achieving goals. Creative strategies for meeting therapeutic goals and helping individuals change their cognitions, behaviors, and feelings are a hallmark of Adlerian psychotherapy and counseling.

Education is important to Adlerians as a part of their approach not only to psychotherapy and counseling but also to child raising, school problems, and marriage and family issues. Adlerians have developed clinics and centers to assist individuals with problems of living in their community and society. This educational approach is not a new one, as Adler was involved in child guidance clinics in his early work in Vienna.

HISTORY OF ADLERIAN THEORY

Born on February 7, 1870, Alfred Adler was the second son and third child of six children of middle-class Hungarian-Jewish parents. He was born in Rudolfsheim, Austria, a small village near Vienna. Whereas Freud grew up in a district that was mostly Jewish, Adler's neighborhood was ethnically mixed. He identified more with Viennese than with Jewish culture. He did not concern himself in his writings with anti-Semitism and later as an adult converted to Protestantism (Bottome, 1939; Ellenberger, 1970).

ALFRED ADLER

Adler's early life was marked by some severe illnesses and traumatic events. Developing rickets, a deficiency of vitamin D, may have affected his self-image. He also suffered from spasms of the glottis that affected his breathing and put him in danger of suffocation if he cried. A severe case of pneumonia when he was 5 was almost fatal. In addition to these illnesses, Adler experienced the death of his younger brother, who died in the bed next to him when Adler was 3. Also, he was almost killed twice in two different accidents outside his home. Although the accuracy of this information may be subject to question, it does suggest an early exposure both to feelings of inferiority, in this case mostly physical inferiority, and a view of life that may have influenced the development of Adler's important concept of social interest.

During his early school years Adler was an average student, having to repeat a mathematics course. Adler had a warm relationship with his father, who encouraged him to continue in his studies despite his teacher's suggestion to his father that Adler should leave school and learn a trade. With his father's encouragement, Adler became both an excellent mathematics student and a good student overall. Although he improved his academic abilities, he had always had a love for music and had memorized operettas when he was young.

When Adler completed secondary school, he attended the Faculty of Medicine in Vienna in 1888, left for a year of military service, and graduated in 1895. During this time he continued his interest in music and attended political meetings that dealt with the development of socialism. In 1897 Adler married Raissa Epstein, a student from Russia, who had a strong interest in and dedication to socialism. Adler entered private practice as an ophthalmologist in 1898, later becoming a general practitioner. After a few years in general practice, he became a psychiatrist, believing that he needed to learn about his patients' psychological and social situations, as well as their physical processes. This interest in the whole person was to typify his writings and attitude toward psychiatry in his later years.

In 1902 Sigmund Freud invited Adler to join the psychoanalytic circle that Freud was developing. Adler was one of the first four members to do so, staying a member of the Vienna Psychoanalytic Society until 1911. Starting in 1905, he wrote psychoanalytically oriented articles for medical and educational journals, making a particularly important contribution to psychoanalysis at that time through *Studies of Organ Inferiority and Its Psychical Compensation*, published in 1907 (Adler, 1917). Adler's views became more and more divergent from psychoanalytic theory, as they emphasized the subjectivity of perception and the importance of social factors, as opposed to biological drives. In 1911 Adler was president of the Vienna Psychoanalytic Society but left the society with 9 of the 23 members. Although reconciliation with Freud was attempted, it failed. Adler then formed the Society for Free Psychoanalytic Research or Investigation, which 1 year later was renamed the Society for Individual Psychology. In 1914 Adler, along with Carl Fürtmuller, began the *Zeitschrift für Individual-Psychologie (Journal for Individual Psychology)*.

Adler's work was slowed by the advent of World War I. During a portion of that time, Adler was recalled for military service as a physician in military hospitals. When

Austria-Hungary lost the war, famine, epidemics, and other tragedies wracked Vienna. These events seemed to confirm Adler's socialist views. The defeat of Austria, however, did give Adler an opportunity to implement his educational views, as schools and teacher training institutions were overhauled.

In 1926, Adler was very active in publishing papers and giving lectures in Europe and then in the United States. In October of 1927 he participated in the Wittenburg Symposium held at Wittenburg College in Springfield, Ohio. After that time he spent more and more time in the United States as a lecturer. In 1935, having foreseen the outbreak of Nazism in Europe, Adler and his wife moved to New York City. Having been appointed to the chair of medical psychology at the Long Island College of Medicine in 1932, Adler maintained his association with this institution. He continued his private practice in the United States and his worldwide lectures. While on a lecture tour in Europe, Adler died of a heart attack in Aberdeen, Scotland, in 1937. Two of his children, Kurt and Alexandra, continued his work as practicing psychotherapists. Adler left a theory of personality and psychotherapy that has had an impressive impact on psychology and psychiatry.

Influences on Adlerian Psychology and Therapy

Before examining Adler's theories of personality and psychotherapy, it will be helpful to explore some of the influences on Adler. Ellenberger (1970, p. 608) shows how Adler was influenced by Kant's desire to find ways to help individuals acquire practical knowledge of themselves and of others. Both Adler and Nietzsche made use of the concept of will to power. For Adler, this concept meant attempts to attain competence, but for Nietzsche it referred to power over others, vastly different from Adler's emphasis on equality. As indicated earlier, Adler was influenced by socialism, more specifically by the ideas of Karl Marx. Adler was appreciative and in sympathy with the ideas of social equality but objected vigorously to the "enforcement of socialism by violence" by the Bolsheviks (Ansbacher & Ansbacher, 1956). Although others' philosophical writings had an impact on Adler's work, he was also affected by his immediate contemporaries.

In particular, Hans Vaihinger's The Philosophy of "As If" (1965) influenced several of Adler's theoretical constructions. His concept of "fictionalism" was to have an impact on Adler's concept of the "fictional goal" (Ansbacher & Ansbacher, 1956). "Fictions" are ideas that do not exist in reality, yet they are useful in helping us deal more effectively with reality. Ansbacher and Ansbacher (1956) give the example of "all men are created equal" as a "fiction." Although this is a statement that can provide guidance in everyday life, it is not a reality. It is a useful fiction for interactions with others, although its truth is doubtful. This "philosophy of 'as if'" refers to treating values as if they were true.

Adler's early association with Freud provided him with the opportunity to have a framework from which to specify and develop his own theory. Between 1902, when Adler joined Freud's society, and 1911, when he left the society, his views had become increasingly different from Freud's. They disagreed on many things: the role of the unconscious, the importance of social issues, and the role of drive theory and biology, to name but a few. The differences of opinion between Freud and Adler were never reconciled. Although Adler would often demonstrate differences between his work and that of Freud's, he did give credit to Freud for his emphasis on dreams and on unconscious factors. He also credited Freud with having significantly emphasized the importance of early childhood in the development of neurotic and other conflicts that occurred in later life. However, Freud's dislike for Adler's concepts hindered the development of Adlerian thought both in Europe and in the United States.

When he arrived in New York from Vienna, Rudolf Dreikurs, perhaps the most notable adherent of Adlerian theory, had a great deal of difficulty being accepted by psychologists and psychiatrists whose theoretical orientations were Freudian (Terner & Pew, 1978). Dreikurs and his colleagues were creative in their innovations in the application of Adlerian theory. For example, Dreikurs is responsible for the concept of multiple therapy (Dreikurs, 1950), the use of more than one therapist; systematic analysis of early recollections; and creative approaches to psychotherapy. Many Adlerian therapists have worked on novel approaches to group psychotherapy, systems for teaching elementary and high school students, and programs for dealing with delinquency, criminal behavior, drug and alcohol abuse, and poverty. The emphasis that Adler put on the need to improve society has been carried on by his adherents.

ADLER'S THEORY OF PERSONALITY

Adler's view of personality was broad and open and not only considered the individual as a whole, unified organism but also emphasized the importance of the individual's interaction with the rest of society. This emphasis on the individual as a whole organism was consistent with Adler's view of the individual as a creative and goal-directed individual who was responsible for her own fate. In his writings (Ansbacher & Ansbacher, 1970), Adler examined closely the striving for perfection or superiority of individuals as it conflicted with and complemented the social nature of the individual and society as a whole. This emphasis on the individual and society is in direct contrast to Freud's emphasis on biological needs as a basis for personality theory. By examining the basic concepts underlying Adler's individual psychology, it will be easier to understand the more specific Adlerian concepts such as style of life, social interests, inferiority, and birth order.

Style of Life

The style of life determines how a person adapts to obstacles in his life and ways in which he creates solutions and means of achieving goals. Adler believed that the style of life was developed in early childhood (Ansbacher & Ansbacher, 1956, p. 186), allowing children to strive, in individual ways, for perfection or superiority. For example, the child who had been picked on by other children in the neighborhood may develop a style of verbally manipulating other children. This behavior would then compensate for the inferiority that the child had experienced. Adler believed that lifestyle was based on overcoming a series of inferiorities. Most of these would be established by the age of 4 or 5, so that it would be difficult to change one's lifestyle after that time. For Adler, expressions of lifestyles throughout life were elaborations of earlier lifestyles. Using the previous example, the child who develops a style of manipulating other children to get his way may as an adolescent create excellent excuses for late or poorly done work or reasons for missed meetings with friends. As an adult, this individual may find ways to persuade others to buy products or to excuse him for poorly done work. These adult behaviors are not due to reactions to other adults at a particular point in time, but rather to a lifestyle developed at an early age.

Adler noted that the lifestyle can be understood by observing how individuals approach three major tasks that are interrelated: occupation, society, and love (Grey, 1998). Adler stated, "The person who performs useful work lives in the midst of the developing human society and helps to advance it" (Ansbacher & Ansbacher, 1956, p. 132). Choice of occupation can be seen as a way of expressing one's lifestyle (Sharf, 1997). For example, the individual who felt bullied as a child may express her lifestyle as an insurance salesperson, persuading and convincing others, yet providing a service that helps others in a catastrophe. Lifestyle also has its expression in how individuals deal with friends and acquaintances as well as love. Occupation, society, and love are not discrete categories, but overlap.

Adler categorized some common types of lifestyles, knowing that they are examples of ways of dealing with occupation, friendship, and love that may be oversimplified. These lifestyles are based on two dimensions: social interest and degree of activity. Social interest refers to a feeling of caring for others and has its expression through cooperation with others for social advancement. *Degree of activity* refers to the amount of energy that an individual displays for dealing with his problems. The types that Adler describes (Ansbacher & Ansbacher, 1970, p. 68) differ as to their degree of social interest and activity. The four types—socially useful, ruling, getting, and avoiding—are described next, along with their level of social interest and activity.

The socially useful type.   Such a person has high social interest and high activity. In Adler's system, this is a mature and positive individual. This person is likely to be concerned about family, friends, co-workers, and society in general. Such a person may help others in his family, work for social or political change, and be considerate to customers and colleagues. To be socially useful, it is necessary to have at least a moderate level of activity and preferably a high level of activity. Someone with a high level of social interest but a low activity level would not be expressing his social interest and therefore would not be socially useful.

The ruling type.   People who have little social interest yet are active constitute the ruling type. Their activity may be asocial, such as that of thieves, con artists, substance abusers, or others who take a dominating and antisocial approach to society.

The getting type.   With little social interest or activity, some people who are "the getting type" may wait for others to satisfy their needs through charity, but others, like fund-raisers, may "get" or solicit funds from others (Mosak, 1959; Boldt & Mosak, 1997).

The avoiding type.   Like the getting type, these people have low social interest and low activity levels. They avoid failure by avoiding involvement with occupation, friends, or society. Others may view them as lonely or unsuccessful.

These types illustrate lifestyles and their interaction with social interest and activity. Because of the emphasis that Adlerians put on uniqueness and individual differences, these types would infrequently be used as a source of conceptualization in Adlerian psychotherapy and counseling. Mosak (1977) has provided further information on the development of types.

Social Interest

Social interest was particularly well developed in Adler's later work (Ansbacher & Ansbacher, 1970), occurring in his writings on occupation, society, and love. Social interest evolves in three stages: aptitude, ability, and secondary dynamic characteristics (Ansbacher, 1977). An individual has an innate ability or aptitude for cooperation and social living. After the aptitude has been developed, the individual develops abilities to express social cooperation in various activities. As these abilities are developed, secondary dynamic characteristics express themselves as attitudes and interests in a variety of activities that then become a means of expressing the social interest. Although Adler viewed social interest as an innate concept, he believed that the parent-child relationship was highly instrumental in shaping it.

The first relationship in which social interest arises and is taught is in the mother-child bond. Adler sees the mother's task as developing a sense of cooperation and friendship in her child. By caring deeply for her child, the mother communicates a model of caring to the child. Furthermore, her care for her husband, the child's siblings, and other friends and relatives becomes a model of social interest. If the mother concentrates only on friends and relatives but not her children, or only on her husband but not friends and relatives, then the child's potential for developing social interest has been thwarted. If social interest is truly thwarted, then a child may develop an attitude toward others similar to the ruling type, the getting type, or the avoiding type, described previously. Although the mother-child relationship is the earliest and most significant relationship in the development of social interest, the father-child relationship is also important, and the father should have favorable attitudes toward his family, his occupation, and social institutions. According to Adler, the emotional or social detachment or authoritarianism of a parent can bring about a lack of social interest in the child. The relationship between father and mother is an important model for the child. If the marriage is unhappy and the parents actively disagree, an opportunity to develop social interest in the child is missed. Such a relationship can have an impact on the lifestyle of a child by affecting romantic relationships in later life and overall adaptation.

The concept of social interest is so important that Adler used it as a means of measuring psychological health. If a person has little social interest, then that person is self-centered, tends to put down others, and lacks constructive goals. Adler, more so than other personality theorists and psychotherapists of his time, had an interest in the problematic development of social interest in criminal and antisocial populations, which he hoped to help through development of social interest (Ansbacher, 1977; Ansbacher & Ansbacher, 1956, pp. 411–417).

Inferiority and Superiority

While still a member of the Vienna Psychoanalytic Society, Adler tried to explain why a person develops one illness rather than another. He suggested that within individuals some organs or part of the body are stronger or weaker than others. The weaker ones make an individual susceptible to illness or disease. Such organs or parts of the body were inferior at birth, causing an individual to compensate for this inferiority by participating in activities to overcome this inferiority. A classical example is Demosthenes, a stutterer in his youth who became a great orator by practicing speech with pebbles in his mouth. A more common example would be that of an individual who compensates for childhood illness by developing her intellect. Adler suggested that individuals tried to overcome physical inferiorities by psychological adjustments. Adler developed this concept early in his work and largely ignored it in later years. Instead, he focused on how people perceived their social inferiority rather than on their perceptions of physical inferiority.

In a sense, the infant is exposed to inferiority at birth. The parents and older siblings are bigger, more powerful, and more independent than the child. Throughout life, individuals struggle to achieve their places in life, striving for perfection and completion. As the child moves from inferiority toward superiority or excellence, three factors may threaten the development of self-confidence and social interest (Ansbacher, 1977): physical disabilities, pampering, and neglect. Physical disabilities may include organ inferiority as described previously, as well as childhood diseases. Pampered children may expect to have things given to them and may not develop an urge to be independent and to overcome inferiorities. Neglected children or those who feel unwanted may try to avoid or escape others rather than overcome their inferiorities. Adler believed that the pampered or spoiled child could, in later life, fail to strive for superiority or to develop social interests.

> Extreme discouragement, continuous hesitation, over sensitivity, impatience, exaggerated emotion, and phenomena of retreat, physical and psychological disturbances showing the signs of weakness and need for support as found in the neurotic, are always evidence that a patient has not yet abandoned his early-acquired pampered style of life. (Ansbacher & Ansbacher, 1956, p. 242)

Although the desire to overcome inferiority and achieve superiority is normal in individuals and a major goal of life, some inferiority complexes and superiority complexes are not normal. Although the term *inferiority complex* has had several meanings in the development of Adlerian psychology, Adler in his latest writings stated that it is "the presentation of the person to himself and others that he is not strong enough to solve a given problem in a socially useful way" (Ansbacher & Ansbacher, 1956, p. 258). The pervasive feeling that one's abilities and characteristics are inferior to those of other people can take many forms. Individuals may feel less intelligent than others, less attractive, less athletic, or inferior in many other ways. Adler found that neurotic individuals who came to him for psychotherapy often presented an inferiority complex or superiority complex. For Adler, superiority was a means of inflating one's self-importance in order to overcome inferiority feelings. People may try to present themselves as strong and capable to maintain their mistaken feelings of superiority, when actually they are feeling less capable than others. An arrogant person expresses an inferiority complex when he states, "Other people are apt to overlook me. I must show that I am somebody" (Ansbacher & Ansbacher, 1956, p. 260).

Behind everyone who behaves as if he were superior to others, we can suspect a feeling of inferiority which calls for very special efforts of concealment. It is as if a man feared that he was too small and walked on his toes to make himself seem taller. Sometimes we can see this very behavior if two children are comparing their height. The one who is afraid that he is smaller will stretch up and hold himself very tensely; he will try to seem bigger than he is. If we ask such a child, "Do you think you are too small?" we should hardly expect him to acknowledge the fact. (Ansbacher & Ansbacher, 1956, p. 260).

The superiority complex may be more obvious in children, but neither adults nor children are likely to easily acknowledge their superiority complex. A normal person strives for superiority but does not develop a superiority complex to mask feelings of inferiority. People who demonstrate a superiority complex may often be boastful, self-centered, arrogant, or sarcastic. Such people are likely to feel important by making fun of or demeaning others.

The striving for superiority or competence is a natural and fundamental motivation of individuals, whereas the superiority complex is not. However, in striving for superiority or competence, an individual can do so in a negative or positive direction. Trying to achieve superiority in a negative direction might include trying to achieve wealth or fame through unethical business or political purposes. Seeking the goal of superiority in a positive sense might mean helping others through business, social dealings, education, or similar methods. A positive striving for superiority implies a strong social interest. It also requires considerable energy or activity to achieve these goals. In a sense, it is a healthy striving for perfection (Schultz & Schultz, 1998).

Birth Order

In many ways the family is a microcosm of society. For Adler, birth order could have an impact on how a child relates to society and the development of her style of life (Grey, 1998). Although the birth order in the family was important to Adler, birth order itself did not provide sufficient information from which to draw conclusions, and more recently it has been less important in the practice of Adlerian therapy. Adlerians are often critical of birth order research that looks only at position in the family. For example, in a family of three children in which the oldest child is 1 year older than the middle child and the middle child is 12 years older than the youngest child, Adlerian therapists might view this family constellation as being more like a family with a younger and older sibling (the first two children) and see the youngest child as being more like the only child in a one-child family. More important is the subjective approach of Adler, which emphasizes the context of a family situation.

ADLERIAN THEORY OF THERAPY AND COUNSELING

Adlerians tend to vary widely on how they do therapy and counseling (Mosak & Maniacci, 1998), and Adlerians make use of many concepts and techniques in their treatment of individuals. In this chapter, I first discuss the goals of counseling versus the goals of psychotherapy, which are seen differently by some Adlerians. Then I use

Dreikurs's (1967) four processes of psychotherapy to explain Adlerian psychotherapy and counseling. The first process is the relationship; the maintenance of a cooperative relationship is not only essential but also requires attention from a therapist. Second, assessment and analysis of patient problems include consideration of analysis of early recollections, family constellation, and dreams. Third, interpretation of the comments of patients is an important aspect of Adlerian therapy, particularly as it relates to the goals of therapy. The fourth process, reorientation, takes the insights and interpretations that come from the patient-therapist work and helps individuals find alternatives to previously ineffective beliefs and behaviors. Adlerians make use of a large variety of reorienting techniques, and a large sampling of these techniques is presented. These phases often overlap and may not always be used in the order in which they are presented here, but they provide a way of understanding the Adlerian psychotherapy and counseling process.

Goals of Therapy and Counseling

The conceptualization of differences between psychotherapy and counseling has a direct impact on the goals of treatment for Adlerians. Dreikurs (1967) believed that psychotherapy was required if changes in lifestyle were necessary but that counseling was appropriate if changes could be made within a lifestyle. Dreikurs also felt that significant changes should occur in early recollections that were reported in the beginning and end of psychotherapy, reflecting lifestyle changes (Mosak, 1958). In contrast, Dinkmeyer, Dinkmeyer, and Sperry (1987) view counseling as concerned with helping individuals change self-defeating behaviors and solve problems more efficiently. Generally, if the problem is in only one life task, rather than pervasive throughout the client's life, counseling is sufficient (Manaster & Corsini, 1982). In actual practice, the differentiation between counseling and psychotherapy is rather minor. In general, Adlerians do both counseling and psychotherapy; which they do depends less on their view of this particular issue than on the presenting problem of the client. Implicit in the goals of psychotherapy and counseling are an increase in the client's social interest. Because counseling and psychotherapy overlap and are not clearly distinguished, the following discussion applies to both counseling and psychotherapy.

The Therapeutic Relationship

In trying to achieve a good therapeutic relationship, Adlerians attempt to establish a relationship of respect and mutual trust (Dreikurs, 1967). In order for this relationship to develop, the goals of the patient and the therapist must be similar. If the goals are different, the therapist is likely to experience the patient as resisting progress in therapy. In many cases the therapist educates the patient as to appropriate goals for therapy. For example, if the patient does not feel that he can make progress, the therapist must work to encourage the patient that progress is possible and that symptoms, feelings, and attitudes can change. For Dreikurs (1967), anticipation of success in therapy is particularly important in a therapeutic relationship. The encouragement process is an important one, continuing throughout the entire process of therapy. As the patient is encouraged to develop goals, it is important to make them explicit. In fact, some Adlerians prefer to use a contract that specifies the goals of the counseling process and the responsibilities of the patient and therapist (Dinkmeyer, Dinkmeyer, & Sperry, 1987). In developing the relationship, the therapist must not only plan goals but also listen and observe as patients present themselves and their goals.

Because the individual is unique, most actions can be considered meaningful (Manaster & Corsini, 1982). How the patient enters the office, sits, phrases questions, and moves his eyes can all be important material. As the therapist stores this information, she is able to decide on later strategies. Often the patient may sabotage therapy by playing games or presenting situations that make therapeutic progress difficult (Manaster & Corsini, 1982). Because patients have had concerns or interpersonal difficulties that bring them to therapy, these problems are likely to occur in the therapeutic relationship. The therapist need not confront the patient with sabotaging therapy but may choose to ignore it or to bring it to the patient's attention in an educational way. In doing the latter, the therapist may help the patient develop insight into self-defeating behaviors.

Sabotaging or resisting therapy should not prevent the therapist from being empathic with the patient. Empathy involves attention not only to feelings but also to beliefs. As the patient gradually produces material, the Adlerian develops an understanding of the patient's lifestyle. Empathic responses often reflect the acknowledgment of the lifestyle. For Adlerians, beliefs result in feelings (Dinkmeyer, Dinkmeyer, & Sperry, 1987). Statements such as "I must help others," "I need to be the best," "No one else understands me," and "I try hard, but nothing ever works" are examples of beliefs that are often reflective of lifestyles that indicate discouragement with self or others. In response to clients' statements that express these beliefs, Adlerians may respond not only to the feeling but also to the belief itself. For example, Dinkmeyer, Dinkmeyer, and Sperry (1987, pp. 67–68) describe how they would respond to a client who has the belief "I must please."

> **Michelle:** I do everything I can to please the boss, but he's never satisfied. I can't figure him out.
>
> **Counselor:** Perhaps what you're feeling is that, if you can't please, there's no point in trying.[1]

The counselor is helping the client identify not only the feeling, but the belief—I must please—behind the feeling. To respond only, "You're confused" would be to respond only to the feeling and not help Michelle become aware of how her belief that she must please influences the feeling of confusion. If the counselor believes that she has a clear understanding of the client's feelings and beliefs, then an even stronger response to Michelle's comment may be appropriate.

> **Counselor:** Is it possible that you believe that, if you can't please, there is no point in trying? Your boss's failure to recognize your efforts justifies your becoming less cooperative or even quitting.

The statement helps the client become more aware of her intentions. Also, the counselor shows that the client has the power to change the situation by being less cooperative or by quitting. The tentative nature of the counselor's response "Is it possible . . ." allows the client to determine if the counselor's response seems accurate and appropriate. The counselor does not impose her understanding of the client's belief on the client.

Assessment and Analysis

Assessment starts as the relationship builds. Adlerians are often likely to be making many observations about the patient in the first session. These observations may become material to be used for comparison for later assessment. Some Adlerians may use informal assessment, whereas others may use projective techniques, lifestyle questionnaires, or standardized interviews. Many of the more formal or detailed methods for collecting information about lifestyle originated with Dreikurs. Other Adlerians have developed a variety of protocols and questionnaires (e.g., Kern, 1982; Kopp & Dinkmeyer, 1975; Shulman & Mosak, 1988; Wheeler, 1996). Most of these procedures include information about family dynamics and early recollections. Other information, which may come from less formal assessment, includes data from dreams. Additionally, Adlerians often wish to assess not only the problems that the person may be experiencing but also assets, those things in a patient's life that work well for him and that can be considered strengths.

Family dynamics and constellation.   In assessing the lifestyle of an individual, it is very important to attend to early family relationships—relationships among siblings and parents, as well as with friends or teachers (Sperry, 1996b). The family represents a microcosm of society; thus it is here where social interest is developed, frustrated, or thwarted. Although Adlerians may be known for their emphasis on birth order, they are more interested in the dynamics of the siblings with the patient, the dynamics of child-parent interaction within the family, and changes in the family over time. It is the patients' perceptions of their childhood development that form the basis for therapeutic interpretations and interventions that occur in the process of helping the patients reach their goals.

Regarding birth order, several different types of questions are asked (Manaster & Corsini, 1982). The patients are asked to describe their siblings as they remember them. Then the therapist may learn the view that the client has toward others in the family and how the client's lifestyle developed in the family. If a male patient says that his older brother was both brighter and more athletically inclined, it leads the Adlerian to look for what the client felt were his particular strengths and how he dealt with possible feelings of inferiority.

Information about the siblings as an interactive group is also obtained. Ages of the siblings and the number of years separating the siblings are noted. For example, in a family with four children, many possible interactions could be observed. The oldest may protect the youngest, the oldest and next oldest may gang up on the youngest two, or three children may gang up on a fourth. As children go to school and leave home, these interactions may change. Adlerians (Manaster & Corsini, 1982) have observed that clients, when they describe themselves as children and as adults, do so in similar ways. In collecting this data, Adlerians may proceed from one question to the next, or they may test out hypotheses as they move through the data collection. For some, this process may be an hour, for others, 3 or 4 hours.

Comparative ratings of siblings on a number of characteristics are often useful material. For example, Shulman and Mosak (1988) suggest rating siblings on characteristics such as the hardest worker, the worst temper, the bossiest, the most athletic, the prettiest, the most punished, the most selfish, and the most unselfish. Also, Adlerians may ask about significant events such as serious illness or injury, disciplinary problems in school or in the community, or special accomplishments or achievements. In large families, therapists must decide which siblings or groups of siblings to concentrate on. For example, in a family of nine children, the therapist needs to organize the information so that a lifestyle analysis can be made. Focus may be on relatively few siblings or on groups of siblings.

Parental values, interactions, and relationships with children are important information for Adlerians. Questions about each parent, such as the type of persons the father and mother are or how each separately disciplined the child or other siblings, are asked. Also information about how the parents got along with each other and how this relationship may have changed at various points in time may be valuable information. If parents divorced, or one parent died, or grandparents lived in the home, adjustments need to be made to assimilate this information in developing a sense of the patient's lifestyle. This provides a view of the patient's perception of himself and how interactions with siblings and family affected his perceptions.

Early recollections. Information from early recollections is essential in helping to determine an individual's lifestyle. Early recollections are the memories of the actual incidents that patients recall.

> It is not important whether the incidents did occur in this way; but it is all important that the patient thinks that it did happen. Members of the same family may remember the same incident; but what they remember of it generally differs greatly, in accordance with their basic outlook on life. (Dreikurs, 1967, p. 93)

In gathering information about early recollections, it is important for Adlerians to get as much detail as possible, and they may ask several questions to do this. According to Adler (1958), memories do not occur by chance. People remember those incidents that have a bearing on their lives. It is not a coincidence that the very few memories that we may have out of thousands of incidents in childhood are related to how we will live our lives. They reinforce and reflect our basic life views. Early recollections are different from reports, which are not valid early recollections. A report would be: "My mother always told me that when I was 3 I liked to play with the neighbor's poodle, which was very friendly and would tolerate my abuse." Obtaining early memories is relatively straightforward: "Would you try to recall your earliest memories for me? Start with your earliest specific memory, something that happened to you that you can remember, not something that was told to you." After that memory is recalled and the patient seems to be doing it well, it may be sufficient to say, "Try to recall another specific memory, something that happened when you were very young." Kopp and Dinkmeyer (1975) give longer, more specific directions for obtaining several early memories.

Adlerians vary as to how many early recollections they use. Adler may have used only one or two with a patient; Dreikurs often obtained 10 or more early recollections from his patients. Usually Adlerian therapists ask for early recollections throughout therapy rather than just at the beginning.

Although Adler felt that more recent remembrances could be useful, he felt that older remembrances, such as those occurring at the age of 4 or 5, were most helpful, as they occur near the beginning of the time when the style of life is crystallized. Examining Adler's analysis of one of his patient's earliest memories is instructive. The patient is a 32-year-old man who experiences anxiety attacks when he starts to work. The anxiety that interferes with his keeping a job also had occurred before examinations at school, as he often tried to stay home from school because he felt tired. Adler (Ansbacher & Ansbacher, 1956, p. 355) described him as "the eldest, spoiled son of a widow." The earliest recollection that the man recalled was the following: "When I was about four years old I sat at the window and watched some workmen building a house on the opposite side of the street while my mother knitted stockings." Adler's analysis is as follows: "The pampered child is revealed by the fact that the memory recalls a situation that includes the solicitous mother. But a still more important fact is disclosed: he looks on while people work. His preparation for life is that of an onlooker. He is scarcely anything more than that." Adler concludes by saying, "If he wants to make the best use of his preparation, he should seek some work in which observation chiefly is needed. This patient took up successfully dealing with the objects of arts" (Ansbacher & Ansbacher, 1956, p. 356).

It is helpful when analyzing memories to consider such issues as what are the dominant themes for several memories. Also, the person's situation in the memory can be important. Are individuals participating in the event that they describe, or are they observing it, like the man in the situation just mentioned? Also, being aware of the feelings expressed in the memories and their consistency can be useful.

Dreams. In doing an assessment of lifestyle, Adlerians may respond to childhood dreams and to more recent recurrent dreams. Throughout the course of therapy, clients are encouraged to relate dreams to the therapist. Adler believed that dreams were purposeful and that they were often indications of an individual's lifestyle. Also, they could be useful in determining what the individual may like or fear for his future. In Adlerian therapy, symbols do not have fixed meanings in dreams. To understand a dream, one must know the individual dreamer (Mosak, 1989).

Dreikurs's discussion of dreams, along with examples, is quite helpful in understanding how Adlerians understand dreams and interpret them. In one example, Dreikurs explains how dreams can show the patient's attitude toward psychotherapy.

A patient relates the following dream. He is in a lifeboat with a man looking for rescue. They see a merchant ship and they steer toward it. Then they see a Japanese warship coming from behind the horizon to capture the merchant ship. They decide to steer away from the merchant ship to avoid being captured.

It is obvious that the patient sees some danger in being rescued. The discussion of the dream and the present life situation brings an admission from the patient that he is afraid of getting well. Then he would have to face the danger of life. Losing his symptoms would deprive him of an alibi to withdraw as soon as he felt exposed to situations where his prestige or superiority was threatened. (Dreikurs, 1967, p. 223)[2]

In another example, Dreikurs shows how dreams often can show change or movement in therapy.

> One of my patients had a very peculiar type of dream. All his dreams were rather short and without any action. He did in his dreams what he did in life; he continuously figured out the best way of getting out of a problem, mostly without actually doing anything. He dreamed about difficult situations, figuring out what would happen if he acted in one or the other way, but even in his dreams nothing actually happened. When his dreams started to move and to be active, he started to move in his life, too. (Dreikurs, 1967, p. 226)

Dreikurs's emphasis on the temporal nature of dreams is consistent with that of other Adlerians, such as Shulman (1971). Dreams can be used as an assessment of current change and progress. In terms of an assessment of lifestyle, dreams may be used as an adjunct to family constellation and early memories.

Basic mistakes. Derived from early recollections, basic mistakes refer to the self-defeating aspects of an individual's lifestyle. They often reflect avoidance or withdrawal from others, self-interest, or desire for power. All of these are in opposition to Adler's concept of social interest (Dinkmeyer, Dinkmeyer, & Sperry, 1987).

Although basic mistakes vary for each individual, Mosak (1989, p. 87) provides a useful categorization of mistakes:

1. *Overgeneralizations.* This includes words such as "all," "never," "everyone," and "anything." Examples of overgeneralizations are: "Everyone should like me," "I never can do anything right," or "Everyone is out to hurt me."
2. *False or impossible goals of security.* The individual sees the society as working against him or her, and is likely to experience anxiety. Examples are "People want to take advantage of me" and "I'll never succeed."
3. *Misperceptions of life and life's demands.* Examples are "Life is too hard," and "I never get a break."
4. *Minimization or denial of one's worth.* These include expressions of worthlessness such as "I am stupid," or "No one can ever like me."
5. *Faulty values.* This has to do primarily with behavior. Examples are "You have to cheat to get your way" or "Take advantage of others before they take advantage of you."

Although it is helpful to identify basic mistakes, correcting the mistakes can be quite difficult, as individuals may have many defenses that inhibit their correction of mistakes. Manaster and Corsini (1982) give some examples of patients' basic mistakes that show incorrect views of life:

A man who married four times unsuccessfully
1. He does not trust women.
2. He feels alone in life.
3. He is unsure of his success, but won't admit it; he is a smiling pessimist.

An alcoholic nurse
1. She feels she does not belong to the human race.
2. She rejects people, but thinks they reject her.
3. She trusts things more than she does people. (Manaster & Corsini, 1982, p. 102)[3]

According to Manaster and Corsini (1982), people are completely unaware of having these basic views of themselves. Although people may come to therapy for one basic mistake, they may have several interrelated mistakes. In therapy, the therapist attempts to present basic mistakes clearly so that they may be understood and the patient can become aware in future situations when he is about to make a basic mistake.

Assets.   Because family constellation, early recollections, dreams, and basic mistakes often lead to finding out what is wrong with the person, it is helpful to look at what is right. As an analysis of an individual's lifestyle can take several hours, countering discouragement with discussion of the patient's assets can be useful. In some cases, the assets are obvious; in others, the patient is not aware of his assets. Assets can include a number of characteristics: honesty, academic or vocational skills, relationship skills, or attention to family. For example, the sensitive writer who can write about the social injustices of others may have difficulty in social relationships. Applying the asset of sensitivity to others that is present in his writings may be helpful to the patient.

Insight and Interpretation

During the process of analyzing and assessing an individual's family dynamics, early recollections, dreams, and basic mistakes, the therapist interprets the material so that patients can develop insights into their actions. The timing of the interpretations depends on progress toward the patient's goals. Dreikurs (1967, p. 60) emphasizes that interpretations are made in regard to goals and purposes; therapists do not interpret psychological conditions. For Dreikurs, telling patients that they feel insecure or inferior is not useful because these statements do not help patients change their goals and intentions. Adlerians help their patients develop insights into mistaken goals and behaviors that interfere with achieving these goals. When patients develop insights into their behavior, it is helpful to act on these insights. The therapist often expresses interpretations to patients tentatively, as no one can know the patient's inner world or private logic. Suggestions are often in the form of questions or statements that are made tentative with phrases such as "is it possible that," "it seems to me that," and "I wonder if." Patients are less defensive and less likely to argue with the therapist when interpretations are presented this way, and there are fewer obstacles in making insights from the therapist's interpretations.

Interpretations are made throughout the therapeutic process. To illustrate interpretation, it may be helpful to examine a brief case that Adler presents about a young woman suffering from headaches. The case illustrates Adler's attention to family dynamics and to social interest.

A girl who had been very pretty, spoiled by her mother and ill-used by a drunkard father became an actress and had many love affairs which culminated in her becoming the mis-tress of an elderly man. Such an obvious exploitation of an advantage indicates deep feelings of insecurity and cowardice. This relationship, however, brought her trouble; her mother reproached her, and although the man loved her, he could not get a divorce. During this time her younger sister became engaged. In the face of this competition, she began to suffer from headaches and palpitations and became very irritable towards the man. (Ansbacher & Ansbacher, 1956, p. 310)[4]

Adler goes on to explain that headaches are produced by feelings of anger. He says that tensions are held in for some time, and they may erupt in a variety of physiological responses. Adler shows that children and people like the patient who are unsocial in their nature are likely to display their temper. Adler interprets the girl's behavior in this way:

> The girl's condition was the result of a neurotic method of striving to hasten her marriage, and was not at all ineffective. The married man was greatly worried by her continuous headaches, coming to see me about my patient, and said that he would hurry the divorce and marry her. Treatment of the immediate illness was easy—in fact, it would have cleared up without me, for the girl was powerful enough to succeed with the help of her headaches.
>
> I explained to her the connection between her headaches and the competitive attitude toward her sister: it was the goal of her childhood not to be surpassed by her younger sister. She felt incapable of attaining her goal of superiority by normal means, for she was one of those children whose interest has become absorbed in themselves, and who tremble for fear that they will not succeed. She admitted that she cared only for herself and did not like the man she was about to marry. (Ansbacher & Ansbacher, 1956, pp. 310–311)

Adler's explanation of the patient's behavior demonstrates the consistency of Adler's interpretations and his emphasis on family constellation and social interest (or lack of it). How to make use of interpretations is the subject of the next section.

Reorientation

It is in the reorientation phase that patients make changes in beliefs and behaviors to accomplish goals (Dreikurs, 1967). Insights that are derived from early recollections, family dynamics, and dreams are used to help the patient accomplish therapeutic goals, which may have altered as patient and therapist explore the patient's lifestyle. To do this, patients may have to take risks, making changes in actions that will be unlike any that they have made in earlier times in their lives. Adlerians have been imaginative in developing action-oriented techniques that lead to new patterns of behavior (Dinkmeyer, Dinkmeyer, & Sperry, 1987).

Immediacy. Expressing your experience of what is happening at this very moment in therapy defines immediacy. The patient communicates, either verbally or nonverbally, something related to the goals of therapy. It may be helpful for the therapist to respond to this. Because it may appear abrupt to the patient, or out of nowhere, it is often helpful to be tentative about this communication. The following is an example of immediacy:

Joan: (is looking at her hands in her lap and softly says to the therapist) I want to tell Harry to listen to me, to pay attention to what I have to say, but he never listens.

Therapist: Although you say that you want to have Harry listen to you, your soft voice and downcast glance seem to communicate that you believe you won't be listened to. Is that right?

In this example, the therapist contrasts the verbal and nonverbal behavior, showing that Joan may be preventing herself from improving her relationship with Harry. By adding a question at the end of the therapeutic statement, the therapist allows Joan to respond to the observation.

Encouragement. Encouragement, used throughout the process of Adlerian psychotherapy, is useful in building a relationship and in assessing client lifestyle. In the reorientation stage, it is helpful to bring about action and change. By focusing on beliefs and self-perceptions, the therapist can help the patient overcome feelings of inferiority and a low self-concept. In the reorientation phase, the individual's willingness to take risks and to try new things is supported. For example:

Patient: My work has been frustrating for me. I think I know how I could do it better, but the instructions that my boss gave me make me feel so awkward.

Therapist: You seem to have devised a strategy that will be productive and effective. I'd like to hear about it.

In this example, the patient is discouraged at work; the therapist encourages her by referring to her assets and asking for her ideas.

For Adler, encouragement was much more than "Just try harder. I'm sure you can do it." His creativity and humanity are seen in this dramatic example of being encouraging with a young woman with schizophrenia.

Once I was called in to do what I could for a girl with dementia praecox. She had suffered from this condition for eight years, and for the last two years had been in an asylum. She barked like a dog, spat, tore her clothes, and tried to eat her handkerchief. We can see how far she had turned away from interest in human beings. She wanted to play the role of a dog, and we can understand this. She felt that her mother had treated her as a dog; and perhaps she was saying, "The more I see of human beings, the more I should like to be a dog." When I first spoke to her, on eight successive days, she did not answer a word. I continued to speak to her, and after thirty days she began to talk in a confused and unintelligible way. I was a friend to her and she was encouraged. . . . When I next spoke to this girl, she hit me. I had to consider what I should do. The only answer that would surprise her was to put up no resistance. You can imagine the girl—she was not a girl of great physical strength. I let her hit me and looked friendly. This she did not expect, and it took away every challenge from her. She still did not know what to do with her reawakened courage. She broke my window and cut her hand on the glass. I did not reproach her, but bandaged her hand. The usual way of meeting such violence, to confine her and lock her in a room, was the wrong way. We must act differently if we wish to win this girl. . . . I still see this girl from time to time, and she has remained in good health for ten years. She earns her own living, is reconciled to her fellows, and no one who saw her would believe that she had ever suffered from insanity. (Ansbacher & Ansbacher, 1956, pp. 316–317)[5]

As this example shows, encouragement can take courage and creativity on the part of the therapist.

Acting as if.   This technique helps the patient take an action she may be afraid of, often because the patient believes that the action may fail. The patient is asked to "act as if" the action will work (Mosak, 1989). If patients do not want to try a new behavior, Mosak and Dreikurs (1973, p. 60) suggest that they try on a new role the way they might try on a new suit. An attractive suit does not make a person become a new person, but it may give a person a new feeling, perhaps a confident feeling.

Patient: It's hard for me to talk to professors. I need to talk to my math professor, there was a mistake in grading my last exam, but I'm afraid to.

Therapist: It is hard for you to speak to your professors; but next week I'd like you to talk to your math professor. Act as if you are confident of the discovery of the error and casually explain it to him.

In this situation the patient is given a relatively straightforward task on which to follow through. If the patient is unsuccessful, the therapist will explore what interfered with the "acting as if" experience.

Catching oneself.   As patients try to change and implement their goals, they may need to "catch themselves" doing behaviors they desire to change. Because the behavior has been repeated many times in their lifetime, they may need to make an extra effort to "catch themselves." Although they may be initially unsuccessful and catch themselves after they have completed the behavior they wish to change, with practice they are able to catch themselves before they initiate the behavior. As they do this, they learn to make effective changes and see that they are more easily accomplishing their goals. In doing so, they may have an "Aha" response: "Oh, now I see it; now it's clear!" (Harold Mosak, personal communication, October 17, 1994).

Sylvia: When Alex starts to get angry, I just know that I'm going to walk away into the bedroom and close the door.

Therapist: You're aware that you start to feel scared and that you want to leave.

Sylvia: It seems whenever he gets angry I lock myself in my room.

Therapist: You might want to try this. When you sense Alex is getting angry, you may catch yourself and say something like, "Alex, I sense you starting to get angry and I'm getting scared. Maybe we can talk this out and I won't go into the bedroom."

Later, when Sylvia experiences an urge to leave the room, she "catches herself," having an insight that she is about to leave the room. She stops herself and then talks to Alex, thus using awareness of her belief to change her behavior.

"The question."   Adler originally developed this technique to determine if a person had physiological or psychological problems. If a person complained of a physical symptom, Adler would ask, "What would be different if you were well?" If the answer is something like "I could walk more easily" or "I wouldn't be awakened by pain at night," then the answer indicates a physiological basis. However, if the answer is "I could do a better job at work" or "I could get along better with my wife," then the patient may be having the illness to avoid psychological issues. Dreikurs (1967) has several good examples of how to use this technique.

Spitting in the client's soup.   This phrase comes from the method that children used at boarding schools to get someone else's food by spitting on it. As a technique, the counselor assesses the purpose of a client's behavior and then makes comments that make the behavior less palatable or attractive. For example, if a well-to-do mother describes how much she sacrifices in terms of her time and money for her children, the therapist may point out how unfortunate it is that she has no time for her personal life and her need for self-expression. The therapist does not say that the mother cannot continue with her behavior but makes the behavior seem less attractive to the woman.

Avoiding the tar baby.   Some self-defeating behaviors are very difficult to change and may be particularly important to a patient. Although the pattern may be based on faulty assumptions and may not result in meeting goals, the patient may hang onto old perceptions. Further, the patient may try to get the therapist to behave as others do in order to maintain the patient's self-perceptions. For example, a patient who feels worthless may act in annoying ways so that the therapist may be annoyed and thus confirm her perception that she is worthless. The therapist must avoid falling into this trap and thus avoid touching the tar baby. Rather, therapists should encourage behaviors that will lead to greater psychological health instead of commenting on the patient's ineffective perceptions or behavior.

> *Patient:* When new co-workers arrive at our store I try to help them, but they tend to ignore me. I notice that you ignore me and don't really listen to me when I talk about my problems.
>
> *Therapist:* You might like me to ignore you, but I'm not. I want to hear more about things that are happening to you at work.

The counselor wants to avoid having the patient see that he is ignoring her. He says that he is not and then goes on to work on patient goals.

Push-button technique.   In this technique, developed by Mosak (1985), patients are asked to close their eyes and remember a pleasant incident that they have experienced. They are then instructed to attend to the feelings that accompany the pleasant images. Next they are asked to re-create an unpleasant image—it may be of hurt, anger, or failure—and then are asked to create the pleasant scene. By doing this,

Adlerians show that patients can create whatever feeling they want just by deciding the subject of their thinking. This technique shows the patients that they have the power to change their own feelings.

Paradoxical intention. This strategy has been variously described as "prescribing the symptom" by Adler and as "anti-suggestion" by Dreikurs. In this technique, patients are encouraged to develop their symptoms even more. For example, a young child who sucks his thumb may be told to do it more often. The person who compulsively washes her hands may be told to do it much more frequently. By prescribing the symptom, the therapist makes the patient more aware of the real nature of the situation. Patients then must accept the consequences of their behavior. By accepting the patient's behavior, Adlerians believe that the inappropriate then becomes less attractive to the client. To use this procedure, the therapist should have confidence that when the symptom is prescribed, the patient will have a different perception of the behavior and then choose to change it.

Task setting and commitment.   Sometimes patient and therapist plan to take specific actions about problems. When a choice is made, the therapist and patient then determine the best way to implement the choice. It is best if the task is relatively brief and the likelihood of success is high. This would make it easier for the therapist to provide encouragement to the patient. If the patient is not successful, patient and therapist evaluate what about the plan needs to be changed to be more effective.

For example, a patient who is recovering from a back injury may decide to get a job. If she plans to look into want ads, respond to the ads, and then get a job, the therapist may wish to discuss how she will determine which ads to follow up on, what to do if the ads are not sufficient in producing job leads, and how to develop sources. The therapist is likely to focus on the job search behavior as the task, not the getting of the job. By doing this, the therapist assures that success is more easily obtained by following up on job leads rather than obtaining the actual job, which may take months.

Homework.   To help patients in accomplishing tasks, Adlerians often find it helpful to assign homework. The homework is usually something that is relatively easy to accomplish between therapy sessions. Assigning homework is often done carefully so that the therapist is not directing the patient's life. In the previous example, the therapist may suggest that the patient call her hospital social worker about job leads before Tuesday or make three phone calls to prospective employers before the next session. Some homework may be assigned on a week-to-week basis. A child may be told to make her bed just for a week; try it and see what happens. Then the child and the therapist can discuss what to do next.

Life tasks and therapy.   As mentioned earlier, Adler identified three main tasks in life: love, occupation, and society. Manaster and Corsini (1982) suggest testing clients' satisfaction with each of these three areas. They ask clients to rate their happiness with their family (husband, wife, or children), satisfaction with work, and satisfaction with friends and community (society). This may identify some issues to work on in therapy that the patient has some difficulty in recognizing. This method can be used throughout therapy to measure change and progress in achieving therapeutic goals.

Terminating and summarizing the interview.   Adlerians believe that it is helpful to set clear time limits. With children, sessions may be 30 minutes, and with adults, 45 to 50 minutes. At the end of the session, the therapist does not bring up new material, but, along with the patient, may summarize the interview to provide a clear picture of the counselee's perception of the session. At this point, homework assignments may be discussed, and the client may be encouraged to apply the materials that were discussed in the session to situations as they arise during the week.

These action-oriented approaches are often associated with Adlerian techniques. Although they may be used by other therapists using other theories, they are not often conceptualized in the same way. Adlerians are likely to borrow techniques from other therapies when they feel they will be effective and consistent with Adlerian principles. Like many other therapists, they may clarify, confront, give emotional support, ask questions, or reassure the patient when they feel that the response is effective. Also, they may give advice if they feel a patient is ready to accept it. Often they find humor is an effective way of making goal-directed changes more palatable (Mosak, 1987). In general, these techniques are illustrative of the action-oriented approach that Adlerians take to assist clients in meeting their therapeutic goals.

PSYCHOLOGICAL DISORDERS

Adlerians take a pragmatic approach to psychotherapy and counseling. This can be seen in the five examples described in this section. The use of family constellation and early recollections, along with active interventions, is illustrated in the complex case of a young woman diagnosed with depression. A brief example of an adolescent illustrates an Adlerian approach to general anxiety. An overview of Adlerian conceptualization of borderline, eating, and somatoform disorders is also provided.

Depression

Adlerians view people with depression as trying to "overcome inferiority feelings and gain superiority" (Sperry & Carlson, 1993, p. 141), trying very hard to become more effective, but failing. In doing so, they lose social interest and become self-absorbed. Pancner and Jylland (1996) note how depressed people are "angry and ready for battle (p. 46)." Depressed people do not often use the word angry in describing themselves. They do not wish to acknowledge anger because then they may have to remedy the situation or confront the individual who is making them angry. Depressed individuals also gain a sense of superiority over others through the way their family and loved ones respond to them—with compassion and concern. This puts the depressed person in the center, experiencing the attention of others and showing little social interest.

Adlerians often help depressed patients develop insight into their distorted and pessimistic perceptions, which were formed in childhood. Further, they work toward helping patients become less self-absorbed and develop social interest by changing beliefs and behaviors. As they move into the reorientation phase of therapy, depressed patients learn to *catch themselves* when they are about to repeat a depressed pattern of behavior. When they catch themselves, they then decide whether to do things differently than they have in the past. The therapist *encourages* the patient in new beliefs, behaviors, and perceptions. In doing this, the therapist may show the patient how others have a high regard for the patient and that the patient's negative perceptions were based on misperceptions of childhood experiences. Mosak (1989) uses the *push-button technique* to show depressed patients that to be depressed means one must choose to be depressed. In this way, depressed patients learn to alter their feelings. These examples illustrate a few approaches Adlerians may take to assist depressed patients in understanding and changing their depressed feelings and beliefs.

To describe an Adlerian approach to depression in more detail, I am summarizing a thorough case study of Sheri by Peven and Shulman (1986, pp. 101–123). In this synopsis, I focus particularly on the use of early recollections and family dynamics in Adlerian psychotherapy. Sheri is a 33-year-old single woman who showed symptoms of neurotic depression. Although she had had psychotherapeutic treatment before, she was in treatment with Peven for $2^1/_2$ years. She reported feeling "flawed" by an incestuous relationship that she had had with her father before she was an adolescent. Additional symptoms included feelings of inferiority, difficulty sleeping, diarrhea, and weight loss. Her parents were divorced, and both had remarried. Sheri had an older brother who was married and in business with their father.

The therapist used a number of Adlerian techniques in the first session. For example, she asked *"The Question"*—that is, what Sheri would do with herself if she were symptom-free. Sheri's answers were to "change careers, study something interesting, spend more time with friends, marry, and 'develop myself as a person like taking up painting, reading, and sports'" (p. 102). The therapist listened to Sheri's concern about her incestuous experience with her father and her strong anger for him. Because she was so angry, the therapist suggested a way in which she could get revenge on her father by taking steps to get more money from him. As Peven says, "Sometimes in the initial interview, I seek to impress new patients, saying or suggesting something novel. I would like them to leave the first interview with something to think about" (p. 103).

After 4 months of therapy, Sheri's depression worsened, and she was referred for medication. She had discussed suicide and had reported uncontrollable crying spells, being very concerned about her symptoms but not ready to examine her issues that were causing depression.

Around this time Peven conducted a formal lifestyle analysis. She interpreted Sheri's lifestyle and presented it to her, along with another therapist, Shulman, in the form of the following summary:

> The younger of two and only girl in a family with a dictatorial czar for a father who was not able to relate to the family except as a dictator. Each family member responded to father's exercise of power in different ways: Mother played the role of an inferior female in order to be less threatening to father and used techniques that caricature femininity in order to establish the territory. Brother imitated father and thus came into conflict with him ("junior czar"), but he was supported by Mother, who indulged him. Sheri imitated Mother both in outward compliance and in an inner resentment. Power over others was the highest value and was achieved by hook or by crook, and females were devalued.

Sheri found herself in an inferior position because of her gender, because of her position as the second-born, and because the family dynamics did not automatically grant family members a worthwhile place. One had to fight or finagle for one's place. Being the youngest and weakest, Sheri discovered that if she submitted to Father, she could be his favorite and thereby achieve some vicarious power.

This was a family in which no human being could trust another and all relationships were competitive. (p. 105)[6]

In addition to this analysis of the family dynamics, early recollections were obtained in the first few months of therapy.

> *Age four.* I'm standing up in my crib. Brother's bed is on another wall. I want a doll that I see across the room, and I can't get it. I cry. I feel frustrated. I am alone in the room.
>
> *Age two.* I was crawling around on the floor in the living-room. People are there and the TV is going. I am crawling around, stopping, looking around. Everybody else is watching television. I have a feeling of solitude.
>
> *Age five.* In the house. My parents had gone out of town and were returning. They came in with a dog. I felt real happy. It was exciting and nice to have them back.
>
> *Age six.* First grade. I beat a neighborhood kid, a boy. He pissed me off, so I grabbed him by the arm and was twirling him around; then I let him go and he bumped his head on a pole. Somebody came and helped him. I stood there feeling very bad, like a criminal. I said to myself, "How could you?" (p. 106)

These recollections, according to Peven and Shulman, illustrate Sheri's feelings of alienation from others, along with her frustration in achieving desired goals. She is outside the mainstream of her social network, and her actions lead to little that is useful. In the incident at age 6, she feels bad for hurting someone else. The single happy memory that is reported is one in which she depends on the behaviors of others (when her parents came back with a dog). The therapist presented the following analysis of the early recollections to Sheri:

> I am too small, too hemmed in, to achieve my goals, and there is no one to help me. Surrounded by others, I am still really alone. In my relationship with others, I, at least, want to be the person who acts justly and with consideration so that I can have some positive feelings about myself. I do not get much positive feeling from others. (p. 106)

From the preceding family dynamics and early recollections, Shulman and Peven determine that Sheri's basic mistakes were the following:

She has been trained to feel negative about herself.

She experiences her goals as impossible to attain and herself as impotent to do anything about it.

The only thing she feels able to do is to suffer and rage at heaven. (p. 107)

In receiving the analysis of her lifestyle, Sheri agreed with, or added to, everything that the therapist presented. However, at this time she was not willing to deal with the therapeutic observations.

During much of the first year of therapy, Sheri complained about herself and others. Gradually she began to look at herself. After 2 years of therapy, she began to write to her father and to see him again. At about this time, Sheri decided that she could choose to act and be less depressed.

About a year into therapy, the therapist asked for more early recollections from Sheri. They were different from her earlier recollections. Although they still showed that Sheri found fault with herself, the incidents did not show the rejection that the earlier recollections did.

An example of insight that Sheri developed in the later stages of therapy can be seen in this brief interchange:

Patient: I'm sitting with three other people, we are all on vacation, and I get so insecure that other people are getting around me. You know, it's terrible.

Therapist: It is neurotic if you want to be the center of attention all the time.

Patient: Yes.

Therapist: Well, all right, but it isn't that you want to be the center of attention all the time. What's the smile? [*Apparently Sheri had a recognition reflex; that is, she had an unconscious, uncontrollable grin on her face. Adlerians consider the recognition reflex a sign of sudden, not quite conscious awareness that an interpretation is correct* (Dreikurs, 1967)]

Patient: I don't know.

Therapist: Dr. Dreikurs used to put it this way: "It's a basic mistake if you add the words *only if*" so that it comes out "*Only if* I'm the center of attention do I feel good." If I tell you I like to be the center of attention, that's fine. So what? But I am *only happy if* I'm the center. That's a neurotic shtick. (p. 116; italics in original)

During the latter part of therapy, Sheri is more accepting of the therapist's interpretations, clarifications, and support.

Throughout therapy, Sheri had had several relationships with men, some quite difficult. Toward the end of therapy, she began a longer-lasting relationship. Her depression lifted, and she developed an improved relationship with her father. Although not forgiving him, she no longer dwelled on her feelings of being abused.

Only highlights of this difficult and complex case have been shown. However, they illustrate the application of early recollections and family constellation to making therapeutic insights. In addition, a few Adlerian techniques that bring about action have been illustrated.

Generalized Anxiety

Adlerians view generalized anxiety, tension, sweating, palpitations, and similar bodily symptoms as being indicative of an individual's inability to cope. Often such individuals have experienced failure in their life. Dealing with difficult decisions is done very hesitantly, if at all. Physiological stress symptoms arise out of the need to avoid defeat or to avoid making poor decisions. Inside, the patient feels inferior and unable to make decisions or to be interested in others. On the outside, the individual may make others aware of the anxiety, and may dominate others through the concern that he has for the symptoms of anxiety (Sperry, 1996a).

In treatment, encouraging the client becomes very important. The therapist looks for ways to help the individual develop social interest and increase his self-esteem. For the therapist, the symptoms of anxiety are the underlying tar baby that the therapist must avoid sympathizing with or patronizing. Helping the patient develop effective coping strategies and educating the patient in becoming interested in activities around him are important.

A brief example of an adolescent experiencing anxiety and school phobia can help illustrate Adlerian treatment (Thoma, 1959, pp. 423–434). In treating Robert, who had run away from home and left a suicide note, Thoma describes several Adlerian strategies. Robert reported several physical symptoms, including stomachaches. He tried to avoid school, was a poor student, and rarely talked in class because he felt stupid.

He felt distant from his father and saw both of his parents as sick and weak. Emotional feelings were those of hopeless frustration and a resigned weariness. In treating Robert, a school psychologist saw him weekly, but a team of teachers, a counselor, a nurse, and a consulting psychiatrist worked to formulate an approach that would involve professionals in a very significant part of Robert's society-school. Teachers made efforts to involve him in schoolwork and encourage his learning experience. Members of the team helped him assert himself. The psychologist encouraged Robert to disagree with her and to express his opinions. He identified with and was encouraged by male teachers. With this combined encouragement from the entire team, Robert's social interest grew, as evidenced by improved participation in sports events, better relationships with teachers and peers, and improved school attendance.

Eating Disorders

Adlerians tend to conceptualize eating disorders as situations in which the child is overprotected, overindulged, or overcontrolled by the parents. Usually one and sometimes both of the parents have unrealistic hopes and expectations for the child. This demand for perfection is not challenged by the other parent or by siblings. The young girl develops a compliant attitude, trying to model her parents in order to receive approval: "If I obey you, you should approve of what I do." As the girl gets older, she strives for perfection, yet does not believe that she will be able to be perfect. If the family also emphasizes eating or appearance, an eating disorder is even more likely to develop. Rather than rebelling actively, a woman with an eating disorder is more likely to deny body sensations and functions, hunger, and feelings. She will also develop an inability to see herself as others see her (Carlson, 1996, pp. 529–532).

The following brief case example illustrates an Adlerian approach to bulimia (Carlson, 1996). The middle of three girls, Judy is a 17-year-old whose parents expect much from each of their daughters. Judy's older sister tried to be perfect by being good and being effective in school. Judy tried to please her father by trying to become a champion swimmer, but this did not put her in a strong position with her mother. She tried to please her parents with her swimming and academic accomplishments, but as she became a teenager, she found herself unable to achieve the perfection she wanted. She began to gain considerable weight and to purge and binge.

Her early recollections are summarized as follows:

"Life is a fight and dangerous," "Everyone will give you a hard time unless you can remain perfect," and "People don't treat me the way I should be treated" (p. 531).

Her basic mistakes included not believing that she could develop good relationships with others; being defensive with others, which then gets her into arguments; and feeling like a deprived princess in disguise. Treatment with Judy started with an assessment of her medical condition. The therapist then examined the way that Judy's beliefs of perfectionism and pessimism caused problems for her. Through encouragement, the therapist helped Judy improve her self-concept and feel more powerful.

Somatoform Disorders

When an individual complains of illness that appears to have no physiological basis, Adlerians help him examine the entire context in which the symptom may play a role in his lifestyle and solves problems for him, although ineffectively (Mays, 1996). Adlerians can help patients explore what it can mean to be ill in our culture. For example, if an individual is ill, he may get more attention from friends and family; coworkers may assist with work problems. If an individual develops paralysis of the vocal cords before a singing audition, an Adlerian would explore the individual's lifestyle and the social context of the situation. The Adlerian might wonder if an event occurred because the individual was discouraged and needed a way to deal with the reaction of others if she was turned down at the audition. This is a way of saying, "I would have if I could have" (Mays, 1996, p. 235). Another explanation might be that the singer does not want to overshadow her husband and is therefore unable to sing, or it might be that the singer can be assured of attention for illness from her family when she cannot be sure that she will be successful in her audition. All of these guesses have in common an assessment of the individual's social interaction. The person is trying to develop a creative means of resolving a conflict between her lifestyle and family and/or social demands.

Borderline Disorders

Although psychoanalytic theory views borderline disorder as an arrested level of development, Adlerian theory (Croake, 1989; Shulman, 1982) treats borderline disorder as a style of functioning. From the Adlerian perspective, borderline disorder is found in those who were not only neglected or abused as children but also, at some time, pampered. Due to inappropriate child-raising, these individuals take a self-centered view in their interactions with others and do not show a true sense of social interest. Occasionally they may appear to be interested in others, but only when it is to their own advantage (Croake, 1989). Those individuals who are identified as having a borderline disorder generally feel little or no support from others, as they have felt support from their parents in only a random or inconsistent way. Because of this inconsistent support, they continue to seek attention from others, doing this in a maladaptive or manipulative style. If they do not receive enough attention, they may become angry. However, they also continue to try to please others so that they can be noticed by them. From an Adlerian perspective, "Borderline personality disorder is a product of discouragement, poor self-confidence, and pessimism" (Croake, 1989, p. 475).

In treatment of borderline disorders, Adlerian therapists believe that changing borderline behavior requires many sessions to work on goals over and over again, and from different perspectives. Adlerian therapy with borderline disorders features confronting guiding fictions—beliefs about views of themselves and others (Croake, 1989). These guiding fictions often include unreasonable expectations about how others should behave, requiring continual discussion and education from Adlerian therapists. In their therapeutic work, Adlerians help those with borderline disorders to become more flexible in their view of others and more reasonable in their expectations about themselves. Throughout therapy, Adlerians provide unconditional acceptance, encouraging their patients while at the same time examining inappropriate patient behavior. Adlerians try to promote social interest in patients with borderline disorder by encouraging their cooperation with others. The accepting, encouraging, and educative approach of an Adlerian therapist to a patient with a borderline disorder is illustrated in the following brief example.

Jane is a 26-year-old white woman who met the DSM-III-R criteria for borderline personality disorder. She had been seen for more than 45 sessions by Croake (1989), often twice a week. Many of the later sessions were multiple therapy sessions with a psychiatric resident. Jane reported early recollections that show a history of sexual abuse. Currently she is having brief, unsatisfactory romantic relationships with men. She is enrolled part-time in college and looking for a job. After discussing an early recollection taking place between the ages of 4 and 6, in which her mother is cooking and she is telling her mother that her stepfather has asked her to pull her pants down, Croake (1989, pp. 478–479) has the following dialogue with her.

Therapist: Is it fair to state that you divide people into two groups: those that care about you and those that don't?

Jane: Doesn't everyone?

Therapist: No, but I can better understand why you have stormy relationships, while you are enthralled with someone and then get yourself furiously angry with that person.

Jane: I don't know what you mean.

Therapist: Perhaps you feel that if someone is nice to you, they like you. If they make a comment that you interpret as critical, you believe that they don't like you anymore.

Jane: Well, it certainly isn't nice for a friend to criticize me (angry affect).

Therapist: I'm guessing that you believe I have just criticized you?

Jane: Well, haven't you?

Therapist: I was making a comment about your style. I was not putting you down.

Jane: It felt like you were putting me down.

Therapist: It would be difficult to always be on guard protecting yourself from possible attack. What did you learn this session?

Jane: I think you were telling me that I get my feelings hurt too easily.[7]

Croake is helping Jane to learn from her behavior and her style of functioning, while at the same time dealing with her anger. He helps her to go beyond her over-simplified, dichotomized thinking. It is not sufficient for him to encourage expression of feelings; he also helps Jane understand the beliefs beneath the feelings. This is illustrated by the last interchange between therapist and Jane. This very limited dialogue taken from a very complex case provides a glimpse into an Adlerian therapeutic approach to borderline disorders.

BRIEF THERAPY

Adler believed that he could help the patient within 8 to 10 weeks (Ansbacher & Ansbacher, 1970). Because he saw most of his patients twice a week, his total number of sessions would often be less than 20, considered brief by most definitions of brief therapy. This is still typical for many Adlerians (Shlien, Mosak, & Dreikurs, 1962). In a survey of 50 Adlerian therapists, Kern, Yeakle, and Sperry (1989) found that 86% of their clients were seen for less than a year and 53% for less than 6 months. There was a wide variation in the number of sessions, often depending on the severity of the problem.

Adlerians focus on limiting time rather than limiting goals. As Manaster states, "Adlerian therapists attempt full and complete therapy in whatever time is available and in the shortest time possible" (1989, p. 245). Kurt Adler (1989) describes two cases that he treated, seeing each patient twice. Sperry (1989) states that Adlerian therapy is briefer if the problem is related to only one of the three life tasks (family, work, or society). Manaster does not believe that diagnostic category is related to length of treatment because it is the "reasoning behind the choice of symptoms," not the symptoms themselves, that determine the length of treatment (1989, p. 247). Being action and goal oriented in their focus on the problem helps Adlerians limit the time needed for therapy (Ansbacher, 1989).

The Adlerian approach to assessment can also make therapy briefer. Time taken to learn about family constellation and to obtain information from early recollections does not have to take many sessions and rarely requires more than four to six. In some cases, Adlerians make guesses about lifestyle with only partial information about these areas. Kern and White (1989) describe a 35-item lifestyle inventory with these subscales: control (taking charge and solving problems), perfectionist (a desire to be orderly and to avoid mistakes), need-to-please (feeling good when getting positive feedback from others), victim (feeling misused by others), and martyr (a sense of self-righteousness). This inventory can be used when a brief assessment of lifestyle may be appropriate.

CURRENT TRENDS

Adler always had a broad interest in social and educational issues that went beyond individual psychotherapeutic services. Both in Europe and in the United States, Adlerians have been active in developing programs and educational systems within public schools (Mosak, 1971; Corsini, 1977). Partly because of this, they are better known for their work with children and families than with adults. Adlerians believe that they can have a greater impact on society as a whole by working through the educational system than by doing only individual psychotherapy.

Dreikurs and his students and co-workers were responsible for the development of Adlerian psychotherapy and educational ideas in the United States. Training institutes that provide certificates in child guidance, counseling and psychotherapy, and family counseling are spread throughout the United States and Canada: New York, Chicago, St. Louis, Dayton, Ft. Wayne, Cleveland, Minneapolis, Berkeley, San Francisco, Montreal, Toronto, and Vancouver. These training institutes grew out of local Adlerian societies in a number of large cities throughout the United States. The North American Society of Adlerian Psychology publishes a quarterly journal, the *Journal of Individual Psychology*, formerly *Individual Psychology*, and a newsletter, *Individual Psychology Newsletter*. For doctoral-level training, there is the Adler School of Professional Psychology, which offers a doctoral degree in clinical psychology. The North American Society of Adlerian Psychology has about 1,200 members. Although this number is small, the number of practicing Adlerians is larger. Furthermore, the influence of Adlerian theory is great, influencing many cognitive, existential, and Gestalt therapists.

Adlerians have critiqued their own progress, believing that Adlerian psychology cannot stand still but must move in new directions. Mosak (1991) believes that there is a need for Adlerians to add to their normative approach to child psychology with a more developmental one that would look at such factors as physiological readiness for learning and other tasks. He would like to see Adlerians incorporate several areas of scientific psychology into their work, including learning theory, developmental perceptual theory, information related to career decision making, and other life tasks. Because Adlerians attend to social issues, Mosak (1991) would like to see Adlerians more involved in community outreach, poverty, homelessness, discrimination, and women's issues. Similarly, Jon Carlson, in his interview with Nystul (1991), suggests that Adlerians become more involved in social issues that affect incest victims, AIDS patients, and people involved in family violence. Powers and Griffith (1996) caution Adlerians to continue to attend to social interest as it relates to therapeutic goals. For Adlerian psychology to grow and not disappear into history, such critiques are both helpful and necessary.

USING ADLERIAN THERAPY WITH OTHER THEORIES

Just as theorists of psychotherapy have made broad use of Adlerian principles, so do counselors and psychotherapists make use of the concepts and techniques developed by Alfred Adler. Many find that the action-oriented and goal-directed approach of Adlerian psychotherapy can provide guidance in their work, particularly in brief therapy. Others find that the collaborative nature of the Adlerian relationship and its emphasis on encouraging the client are a helpful guideline for therapeutic intervention.

From a developmental point of view, the focus on family constellation and birth order gives a broad framework from which to view patients and their interactions with their environment (not only parents, but siblings and others). The uniquely important contribution of early recollections can be used by many therapists and counselors to explore a patient's early development. Additionally, Adler's clarity of purpose of therapy provides therapists and counselors a reminder of the purpose of their work. Adler emphasized the importance of assisting individuals in meeting their goals. It is not unusual for therapists to wonder, in the middle of therapy, "What does this have to do with anything?" The focus that Adler put on ascertaining individuals' basic mistakes from their lifestyle helps the therapist focus on the goals of therapy and not be sidetracked by other issues.

Throughout therapy—the development of the relationship, the analysis of lifestyle, interpretation, insight, and reorientation—Adlerians seek to encourage their clients in meeting goals. Somewhat similar to the reinforcement of goals provided by behavior therapists, encouragement helps patients see that there are resolutions to their problems. Encouragement, as conceptualized by Adlerians, can fit with many types of therapy and counseling.

Adlerians have developed creative action-oriented strategies that help bring about client change. In helping clients make changes in social situations, therapists may find it productive to have clients act as if they are not fearful or worried about a situation. The strategy of catching oneself is extremely useful in helping people change old habits. The push-button technique can help patients start to develop confidence in handling their feelings. Whether a therapist or counselor is an "Adlerian" or not, Adler, Dreikurs, and their students have developed concepts and strategies that many therapists can employ in their work.

RESEARCH

Compared to other theories of psychotherapy, relatively little research has been done on Adlerian concepts and the outcome of psychotherapeutic research. One reason that there has been so little research on Adlerian psychotherapy is that in general Adlerians have preferred the use of the case method as contrasted with research on therapeutic change (Harold Mosak, personal communication, April 28, 1998). Because Adlerians emphasize the subjective nature of the individual, some have been concerned that research that compares groups to each other provides relatively little understanding of Adlerian concepts and therapy. Birth order and social interest are the two areas of Adlerian personality theory that have been studied in most detail and are discussed briefly in terms of their general findings.

Studies on the outcome of psychotherapy include those on both Adlerian individual and family therapy. In one study on individual therapy, Shlien, Mosak, and Dreikurs (1962) compared the effects of time-limited Adlerian therapy to both unlimited and time-limited client-centered therapy, as well as to a control group of normal individuals and a control group of patients. The time-limited therapy patients received a maximum of 20 sessions, whereas the unlimited client-centered therapy averaged 37 sessions. Researchers used a Q-sort measure comparing views of self with views of the ideal self before treatment, after seven therapy sessions, immediately after treatment, and at a 1-year follow-up. A Q-sort is a measure that asks people to take a deck of cards with statements on them such as "I often feel humiliated" or "I enjoy being alone" and to sort these cards into a series of categories, usually seven, corresponding to a point on a continuum between "most like me" to "least like me." All three treatment groups showed a significant improvement at the end of the study and a year later. To put it another way, time-limited Adlerian therapy was shown to be as effective as time-unlimited client-centered therapy. Rachman and Wilson (1980) are critical of the study for relying on Q-sort as a means for measuring the outcome of psychotherapy. They are also critical of other aspects of the methodology used and the way the study was reported.

Comparing attitudes of parents who attended Adlerian study groups and those who did not, Croake and Burness (1976) observed no differences after four or six sessions of family counseling. However, Lauver and Schramski (1983), in reviewing other studies of Adlerian parent-study groups, found positive changes on measures of attitudes toward child-rearing and children, and in becoming less authoritarian and more tolerant in their attitude toward children after participating in study groups.

The area of Adlerian psychology that has received the most attention has been that of birth order. The research has focused particularly on first-born, last-born, and only children. A thorough review of this literature may be found in Maddi (1996) and Sulloway (1996).

Adler believed that first-borns would attain higher levels of achievement, both academically and professionally, than their siblings. Maddi (1996) reports several studies showing that first-born individuals were overrepresented in the college population compared with their siblings. In a large study of almost 400,000 young men from the Netherlands, Belmont and Marolla (1973) found a positive relationship between birth order and nonverbal intellectual aptitude. Breland (1974) found a similar relationship in terms of professional achievement. Zweigenhaft (1975) reported that first-borns were overrepresented as members of the U.S. Congress. Among women who hold doctorates, Melillo (1983) found that first-borns were overrepresented in the sample. In a study of 134 children ages 9 to 13 years, coping resources (family support, peer acceptance, and social support) were highest for first-born or only children and lowest for middle children (Pilkington, White, & Matheny, 1997). The general view that first-born children are more dominant, responsible, and achievement oriented tends to be borne out by Sulloway's (1996) review of birth order literature. In general, research tends to have supported the Adlerian view of the responsible nature of first-borns. However, not all studies have been supportive of this thesis, and some have shown results that contradict this concept (Maddi, 1996).

Adler wrote that the last-born child was likely to be spoiled or pampered by other members of the family. He believed this pampering would make the last-born child more dependent on others and create problems in dealing with difficult life issues. In a review of studies, Barry and Blane (1977) found that last-borns were overrepresented among alcoholics. Longstreth (1970) reported that later-born children were more apprehensive about dangerous activities than were first-borns. Also, last-born children appeared to have lower social competence in general than their siblings (Schooler, 1964). However, first-borns were shown to have the highest number of irrational beliefs about romantic relationships, and last-borns the lowest (Sullivan & Schwebel, 1996). The relationship of birth order issues is unclear (Maddi, 1996).

In his *Theory and Measurement of Social Interest*, Crandall (1981) quantifies Adler's concept of social interest, finding a positive relationship between social interest and altruism, optimism about the future, and cooperation and empathy. Worthen and O'Connell (1969) have found a relationship between social interest and humor appreciation. Johnson (1997) has related social interest to Adlerian therapy by studying its role in the training of therapists.

Adlerian research is particularly lacking in studies on psychotherapeutic change. Case studies that focus on the use of early recollections, family constellation, or lifestyle development may be helpful. The documentation of the effectiveness of Adlerian action-oriented techniques would also be helpful.

GENDER ISSUES

Early in the development of his theory Adler was concerned with the role of men and women in society. He saw the relative roles of men and women in early 20th-century Vienna in this way:

> Due to their dominance, men influenced the female position in the division of labor, in the production process, to their own advantage. Men prescribed to women the sphere of life and are in a position to enforce this; they determined forms of life for women that followed primarily the male viewpoint.
>
> As matters stand today, men continuously strive for superiority over women, while women are constantly dissatisfied with the male privileges. (Ansbacher & Ansbacher, 1978, p. 5)

Thus, the male was in a superior role to the female. Both men and women wanted to be superior, or more like the masculine, according to Adler. Neurotic men would focus on "masculinity" rather than their personal development as a way of seeking perfection (Ansbacher & Ansbacher, 1956). He used the term *masculine protest* to refer to a desire to be superior, to strive to be perfect, a striving away from inferiority toward superiority. Adler's view was that all individuals should seek to be superior, to do their best. The sex role expectations of his day were a hindrance to this, and Adler supported the women's rights movement, believing that women should have the right to abortion (Ansbacher & Ansbacher, 1978). Adler wrote extensively on gender issues, and his writings have been compiled by Ansbacher and Ansbacher (1978) under the title *Cooperation Between the Sexes*, with a significant part of the book dealing with the myth of women's inferiority. Bottome (1939) suggests that Adler's attitude toward women may be due, in part, to his interest in Marxism and socialism, which emphasized equality. Also, Adler's wife, Raissa, was interested in these same philosophical and political views, having strong opinions about women's rights. This view of equality has been carried on by Dreikurs and his colleagues.

MULTICULTURAL ISSUES

For Adlerians, to be emotionally healthy means that an individual must develop a social interest extending beyond the immediate family to the individual's broader cultural group. As Newlon and Arciniega (1983) note, many minority groups (Native Americans, Mexican Americans, and African Americans) value social group identity along with individual identity. This emphasis on social interest was the focus of a study by Miranda and White (1993) with a Hispanic population. Using a Spanish version of the Kern lifestyle inventory (1982), they found that those Hispanic individuals who remain loyal to the Hispanic culture showed lower social interest than did those who identified both with the Hispanic and the dominant U.S. culture.

Newlon and Arciniega (1983) and Arciniega and Newlon (1983) discuss several social issues that counselors and therapists should be aware of when working with people of color.

Language.   Within a family, members differ in their fluency and use of their language of origin and English. Paying attention to the individual's use and the role of language for that individual can be helpful in therapy and counseling.

Cultural identity.   How individuals label themselves and see themselves can be significant. For example, does an Asian-American patient identify herself as American, Asian, or Japanese?

Family dynamics.   The issue of birth order often needs to be viewed broadly for minorities. For example, in many Hispanic families, uncles, grandparents, cousins, or friends may play a significant role in child-raising. Also, in Mexican American and Native American cultures, the oldest child may be given more responsibility for raising siblings than in some other cultures.

Geographical location.   The neighborhood or area in which individuals live and develop can differ within cultural groups. For example, African Americans raised in the southern part of the United States are exposed to a very different culture than those living on the West Coast. Newlon and Arciniega state, "A minority family living in a totally ethnic area views itself differently than a family living in an integrated neighborhood" (1983, p. 9). This emphasis on social context provides a means for Adlerians to understand different cultural groups.

COUPLES COUNSELING

The Adlerian approach to couples counseling is quite similar to the Adlerian approach to individual counseling or psychotherapy. It is often educational in nature, and lifestyle assessment and action-oriented techniques are its hallmark.

Dinkmeyer et al. (1987) conduct a full lifestyle assessment, using the lifestyles scale (Kern, 1982) or other inventories. They believe these inventories convey a serious purpose to the individuals, assessing what is right about the relationship and what needs improvement. When the lifestyle analysis is completed, each partner receives a copy of both lifestyles. In examining the two lifestyles, Dinkmeyer et al. (1987) look for areas of agreement, keeping copies of both lifestyles in front of the therapist. The resolution of conflict follows Dreikurs's four principles: "(1) showing mutual respect, (2) pinpointing the issues, (3) reaching a new agreement, and (4) participating in decision-making" (p. 269). Each individual's concern is often revealed through the stress and conflict that come with relationship difficulties. The therapist tries to show that these concerns are understood. When the goals of the couple differ, resistance may develop. Then the therapist must work to realign the goals so that all parties are working on the same issues. Techniques that assist communication include *discuss it* (Hawes, 1989), in which the therapist asks the couple to face each other and to discuss the issue of concern with the therapist listening for communication style and watching for nonverbal communication strategies. Hawes (1989) also describes a "contract of expectations" as a useful way to make previously implicit expectations explicit and clear. Partners then are clearer about what they will expect of each other. Several other techniques may also be used to assist couples in achieving compatible goals.

Because Adlerians are interested in educating and preventing problems from arising, more than 50 marriage education centers have been established throughout the United States. They have three major purposes: to educate a large audience on basic mental health principles that will lead to more effective and cooperative living, to provide help for troubled couples, and to train counselors to work with couples (Dinkmeyer et al., 1989). In marriage education centers, volunteer couples are interviewed before an audience. This format allows the co-counselors to provide encouragement not only to the volunteer couple but also to the members of the audience. In participating by asking questions and giving feedback to the couple, the audience can see that they, too, are not alone, and that other couples have similar problems. Although this method may sound as if it would frighten couples, Dinkmeyer et al. (1989) state that the trust, support, and encouragement that are given by both the co-counselors and audience allow for the discussion of virtually any topic. This method is an efficient one, as more people can be reached through the marriage education centers than could be reached through individual couples counseling. Additionally, marriage study groups that have an educational and topic-related focus, and couples group therapy with five or six married couples working on marriage issues, may be a part of the programs offered by a marriage education center.

FAMILY COUNSELING

Family counseling and education are an important aspect of Adlerian psychology. Before World War II, Alfred Adler had conducted 32 child guidance clinics in Vienna. Similar clinics were established in Germany and Hungary before World War II (Dreikurs, 1957). Dreikurs established a child guidance clinic in Chicago, and since then many others have been established throughout the United States. Quite common in these centers is public family counseling. In this approach, parents visit a center with their children; the parents are interviewed while the children are observed playing by a playroom worker. If an intake worker believes that public counseling is appropriate, the parents are interviewed by a counselor who assesses goals and family information. Parents are then asked to describe a typical day. The counselor assesses the problem, and then the children are interviewed. In the last part of the session, direct advice is given to parents by the counselor (Manaster & Corsini, 1982), often involving the audience in this process.

Manaster and Corsini (1982) distinguish between family counseling and family therapy. Family counseling is a process in which advice is given to parents for relief of immediate problems and to teach parents how to deal with difficulties at home. Often only one or two sessions, perhaps with telephone follow-up, are likely to be necessary.

Family therapy involves the whole family and is likely to take 6 to 12 sessions, possibly more. It is used often with aggressive or withdrawn adolescents and their families.

Adlerians "stress using natural and logical consequences in training children" (Manaster & Corsini, 1982, p. 220). Rather than focusing on reward or punishment, Adlerians focus on the outcome of natural consequences. In this procedure, a parent would give information to the child, observe the child acting appropriately or not, and allow the child to receive the consequences of the behavior. An example of how Adlerians deal with bed-wetting illustrates this concept. Manaster and Corsini (1982) give the example of 4-year-old Gregg who comes all wet to his parents' bed and asks to get in bed with his parents. The Adlerian approach is to tell Gregg that bed-wetting is his problem. Gregg is to put wet things in a separate container and then make up his bed. The parents are not to check on Gregg's room and are to make minimal comments when Gregg reports wetting or not wetting the bed. If there is no commenting, complaining, or complimenting, the bed-wetting should stop.

Goals of Adlerian family therapy (Dinkmeyer et al., 1987) include improving family communications and the behavior of children. Families are taught to resolve conflicts by developing mutual respect for each other, pinpointing the issue that is a problem, reaching agreements on how to handle the problem, and helping family members to participate fully in this process. In therapeutic work, Adlerians use several techniques to approach their goals. They may prescribe the symptom, using paradoxical intention, which may bring about a change in the family situation. Another technique is that of role reversal, in which members of the family are asked to act as if they were the person with whom they are in conflict. When resistance occurs, the usual problem is lack of common goals between the therapist and the family, or within the family. The therapist then proceeds to get all parties working on the same goal. Throughout the therapeutic process, the therapist is positive and encouraging. Because family therapy is a complex and demanding task, Dinkmeyer et al. (1987) recommend that co-therapists work together. A detailed outline of the family counseling process is provided by Christensen and Marchant (1983). Using a flow chart approach to outline the specific therapeutic tasks that are necessary to bring about problem resolution, Sherman and Dinkmeyer (1987) describe Adlerian family therapy and compare it with several other methods of family therapy.

GROUP COUNSELING AND THERAPY

Adlerian approaches to group counseling and psychotherapy are varied, characterized by educational and creative methods in applying Adlerian principles. Dinkmeyer et al. (1987) and Corsini (1988) explain the varied formats that can be the basis for Adlerian group therapy. Typical of Adlerian groups is the lifestyle group. In this group, members would develop a mini-lifestyle that includes family relationships, comparisons with siblings, and early recollections. It is the leader's responsibility to summarize each individual's mistaken perceptions, assets, and goals. The group then can discuss each member's lifestyle in terms of the individual's beliefs and goals. The members help each other develop strategies for change. In such a group, participants may take notes on the lifestyle of each participant.

Dinkmeyer et al. (1987) have developed a "teleoanalytic workshop" that is designed to help individuals have more effective relationships by activating their social interest. This workshop combines lectures on topics such as social interest, life tasks and challenges, and encouragement and courage. For each topic, exercises help individuals improve their communication skills. The exercises start with people communicating in groups of two, then four, then eight, and then to the larger group. Each exercise involves "presenting oneself to the group in terms of one's strengths, priorities, self-esteem, family atmosphere, family constellation, and assets" (p. 231). Somewhat similar is O'Connell's (1975) "encouragement labs," which are designed to improve individuals' self-esteem and social interest.

Adlerians have used and modified Moreno's psychodrama technique. Psychodrama is a means of using acting to help individuals solve their problems (Starr, 1977). A director or trained psychodrama therapist assists patients in acting out situations or relationships that are problems. Other people—and occasionally the actual people who are part of the patient's problem—play roles in the psychodrama. In this process, the patient moves around the stage, acting out episodes that reflect difficult issues in the patient's life. As they act out their problem and see the problem acted out in front of them, patients develop insights and new strategies for dealing with their issues. Shulman (1971) has developed the Midas technique, in which a group member or leader creates the kind of relationships that the individual would ideally like to have. In "action therapy" (O'Connell, 1975), members act out situations in such a way that people in the group support each other and encourage each other in building self-esteem. This type of social interaction stimulates social interest in the group members.

SUMMARY

Adlerian psychotherapy and counseling make the assumptions about individuals that they are part of a larger social system and that they are to be seen subjectively and humanistically. The Adlerian view is developmental in the sense that an individual's lifestyle and views held about the world and about the self are formed before the age of 6. Individuals act on these views and convictions as if they are true. Adlerians emphasize the cognitive nature of individuals, focusing on beliefs that people have about themselves as they interact with their society.

Adlerians understand their patients through the assessment of information about family constellation, early recollections, and dreams. Often conducted through questionnaires and interviews, the lifestyle analysis provides the basis for therapists to help their patients by encouraging them to meet important life goals: love, work, and participation in society.

The therapeutic process is seen (in part) as educational. Adlerians encourage and assist their patients in correcting their faulty perceptions and their basic mistakes. By doing this, patients learn to cooperate with others and to contribute to society in various ways. Adlerians have developed many innovative action techniques, including paradoxical intention, the push-button technique, and acting as if.

The educational emphasis of Adlerians is seen in their involvement with child guidance centers, marriage counseling, and group counseling. More than most systems of psychotherapy, Adlerians focus on preventive goals to assist people in functioning productively within their social setting. Because the Adlerian approach is pragmatic, they use therapeutic and educational strategies from other theoretical approaches that are consistent with Adler's ideas. Also, Adler's ideas have been used, borrowed, or absorbed by many other theorists in the development of their own theoretical perspectives. Adlerians have always been more concerned about the improvement of society than about ownership of Adlerian thought.

Suggested Readings

ANSBACHER, H. L., & ANSBACHER, R. (Eds.). (1956). *The individual psychology of Alfred Adler.* New York: Basic Books. • The editors have compiled many of Adler's writings into this volume. The editorial comments provided by the editors are particularly helpful in understanding how Adler's theory developed.

ANSBACHER, H. L., & ANSBACHER, R. (Eds.). (1970). *Superiority and social interest.* Evanston, IL: Northwestern University Press. • This book is a compilation of Adler's later writings, mainly between 1931 and 1937. Included are Adler's views on psychotherapy, with ideas on conceptualization and treatment of a variety of psychopathological disorders.

ANSBACHER, H. L., & ANSBACHER, R. (Eds.). (1982). *Co-operation between the sexes.* New York: Norton. • This is a compilation of Alfred Adler's writings on women and men, love and marriage, and sexuality. It will be of interest to those who would like to learn more about Adler's view on gender issues.

DINKMEYER, D. C., DINKMEYER, D. C., JR., & SPERRY, L. (1987). *Adlerian counseling and psychotherapy* (2nd ed.). Columbus, OH: Charles E. Merrill. • This is a well-written introduction to counseling and psychotherapy, featuring sections on children, adolescents, and the elderly. Also included are sections on group counseling, health care counseling, family therapy, marriage therapy, and parent education.

MANASTER, G. J., & CORSINI, R. J. (1982). *Individual psychology.* Itasca, IL: F. E. Peacock. • This is another good introduction that describes Adlerian theory of personality and psychotherapy. Details on lifestyle assessment and approaches to therapy and counseling are provided.

MOSAK, H. H. (1995). Adlerian psychotherapy. In R. J. Corsini & D. Wedding (Eds.), *Current psychotherapies* (5th ed., pp. 51–94). Itasca, IL: E. E. Peacock. • This chapter by Harold Mosak, a leading Adlerian scholar, describes historical, theoretical, and applied aspects of Adlerian psychotherapy.

References

ADLER, A. (1917). *Study of organ inferiority and its psychical compensation.* New York: Nervous & Mental Disease Publishing Co.

ADLER, A. (1958). *What life should mean to you.* New York: Capricorn.

ADLER, K. A. (1989). Techniques that shorten psychotherapy. *Individual Psychology, 45,* 62–74.

ANSBACHER, H. L. (1977). Individual psychology. In R. J. Corsini (Ed.), *Current personality theories* (pp. 45–85). Itasca, IL: Peacock.

ANSBACHER, H. L. (1989). Adlerian psychology: The tradition of brief psychotherapy. *Individual Psychology, 45,* 26–33.

ANSBACHER, H. L., & ANSBACHER, R. (Eds.). (1956). *The individual psychology of Alfred Adler.* New York: Basic Books.

ANSBACHER, H. L., & ANSBACHER, R. (Eds.). (1970). *Superiority and social interest by Alfred Adler.* Evanston, IL: Northwestern University Press.

ANSBACHER, H. L., & ANSBACHER, R. R. (Eds.). (1978). *Cooperation between the sexes.* New York: Anchor Books.

ARCINIEGA, M., & NEWLON, B. (1983). Cross-cultural family counseling. In O. C. Christensen & T. Schramski (Eds.), *Adlerian family counseling: A manual for counselor, educator and psychotherapist* (pp. 279–292). Minneapolis: Educational Media.

BARRY, H., III, & BLANE, H. T. (1977). Birth order of alcoholics. *Journal of Individual Psychology, 33,* 62–79.

BELMONT, L., & MAROLLA, E A. (1973). Birth order, family size, and intelligence. *Science, 182,* 1096–1101.

BOLDT, R. M., & MOSAK, H. H. (1997). Characterological resistance in psychotherapy: The getter. *Individual Psychology, 53,* 67–80.

BOTTOME, P. (1939). *Alfred Adler: A biography.* New York: Putnam.

BRELAND, H. M. (1974). Birth order, family configuration, and verbal achievement. *Child Development, 45,* 1011–1019.

CARLSON, J. (1996). Eating disorders (2nd ed.). In L. M. Sperry & J. Carlson (Eds.), *Psychopathology and psychotherapy: From diagnosis to treatment* (pp. 567–596) (2nd ed., pp. 513–537). Washington: Accelerated Development.

CHRISTENSEN, O. C., & MARCHANT, W. C. (1983). The family counseling process. In O. C. Christensen & T. G. Schramski (Eds.), *Adlerian family counseling: A manual for counselor, educator and psychotherapist* (pp. 29–56). Minneapolis: Educational Media.

CORSINI, R. J. (1977). Individual education. *Journal of Individual Psychology, 33,* 295–349.

CORSINI, R. J. (1988). Adlerian groups. In S. Long (Ed.), *Six group therapies* (pp. 1–48). New York: Plenum.

CORSINI, R. J. (1989). Introduction. In R. J. Corsini & D. Wedding (Eds.), *Current psychotherapies* (4th ed., pp. 1–18). Itasca, IL: Peacock.

CRANDALL, J. E. (1981). *Theory and measurement of social interest.* New York: Columbia University Press.

CROAKE, J., & BURNESS, M. R. (1976). Parent study group effectiveness after four and six weeks. *Journal of Individual Psychology, 32,* 108–111.

CROAKE, J. W, (1989). Adlerian treatment of borderline personality disorder. *Individual Psychology, 45,* 473–489.

DINKMEYER, D. C., DINKMEYER, D. C., JR., & SPERRY, L. (1987). *Adlerian counseling and psychotherapy* (2nd ed.). Columbus, OH: Charles E. Merrill.

DREIKURS, R. (1950). Techniques and dynamics of multiple psychotherapy. *Psychiatric Quarterly, 24,* 788–799.

DREIKURS, R. (1957). *Psychology in the classroom.* New York: Harper.

DREIKURS, R. (1967). *Psychodynamics, psychotherapy, and counseling: Collected papers.* Chicago: Alfred Adler Institute.

ELLENBERGER, H. E (1970). *The discovery of the unconscious.* New York: Basic Books.

ERNST, C., & ANGST, J. (1983). *Birth order: Its influence on personality.* Berlin: Springer-Verlag.

FALBO, T, & POLIT, D. E. (1986). Quantitative review of the only child literature: Research evidence and theory development. *Psychological Bulletin, 100,* 176–189.

GREY, L. (1998). *Alfred Adler: The forgotten prophet.* Westport, CT: Praeger.

HAWES, E. C. (1989). Therapeutic interventions in the marital relationships. In K. Kern, E. C. Hawes, & O. C. Christensen (Eds.), *Couples therapy: An Adlerian perspective* (pp. 77–114). Minneapolis: Educational Media.

JOHNSON, E. P. (1997). Novice therapists and social interest. *Individual Psychology, 53,* 105–109.

KERN, R. (1982). *Lifestyle scale.* Coral Gables, FL: CMTI Press.

KERN, R., & WHITE, J. (1989). Brief therapy using the life-style scale. *Individual Psychology, 45,* 186–190.

KERN, R. M., YEAKLE, R., & SPERRY, L. (1989). Survey of contemporary Adlerian clinical practices and therapy issues. *Individual Psychology, 45,* 38–47.

KOPP, R. R., & DINKMEYER, D. (1975). Early recollections in life style assessment and counseling. *School Counselor, 23,* 22–27.

LAUVER, P. J., & SCHRAMSKI, T. G. (1983). Research and evaluation of Adlerian family counseling. In 0. C. Christensen & T. G. Schramski (Eds.), *Adlerian family counseling* (pp. 367–388). Minneapolis: Educational Media.

LONGSTRETH, L. E. (1970). Birth order and avoidance of dangerous activities. *Developmental Psychology, 2,* 154.

MADDI, S. R. (1996). *Personality theories: A comparative analysis* (6th ed.). Pacific Grove, CA: Brooks/Cole.

MANASTER, G. (1989). Clinical issues in brief psychotherapy: A summary and conclusion. *Individual Psychology, 45,* 243–247.

MANASTER, G., & CORSINI, R. J. (1982). *Individual psychology.* Itasca, IL: E. E. Peacock.

MAYS, M. (1996). Somatoform disorders and psychological factors affecting physical condition. In Sperry, L. M., & Carlson, J. (Eds.), *Psychopathology and psychotherapy: From diagnosis to treatment* (2nd ed., pp. 221–243). Washington: Accelerated Development.

MELILLO, D. (1983). Birth order, perceived birth order, and family position of academic women. *Individual Psychology, 39,* 57–62.

MIRANDA, A. O., & WHITE, P. E. (1993). The relationship between acculturation level and social interest among Hispanic adults. *Individual Psychology, 49,* 76–85.

MOSAK, H. H. (1958). Early recollections as a projective technique. *Journal of Projective Techniques, 22,* 302–311.

MOSAK, H. H. (1959). The getting type: A parsimonious social interpretation of the oral character. *Journal of Individual Psychology, 15,* 193–196.

MOSAK, H. H. (1971). Strategies for behavior change in schools: Consultation strategies. *Counseling Psychologist, 3,* 58–62.

MOSAK, H. H. (1977). *On purpose.* Chicago: Alfred Adler Institute of Chicago.

MOSAK, H. H. (1985). Interrupting a depression: The pushbutton technique. *Individual Psychology, 41,* 210-214.

MOSAK, H. H. (1987). *Ha ha and aha: The role of humor in psychotherapy.* Muncie, IN: Accelerated Development.

MOSAK, H. H. (1989). Adlerian psychotherapy. In R. J. Corsini & D. Wedding (Eds.), *Current psychotherapies* (4th ed., pp. 65–116). Itasca, IL: F. E. Peacock.

MOSAK, H. H. (1991). Where have all the normal people gone? *Individual Psychology, 47,* 437–446.

MOSAK, H. H., & DREIKURS, R. (1973). Adlerian psychotherapy. In R. J. Corsini (Ed.), *Current psychotherapies.* Itasca, IL: F. E. Peacock.

MOSAK, H. H., & MANIACCI, M. P. (1998). *Tactics in counseling and psychotherapy.* Itasca, IL: F. E. Peacock.

NEWLON, B. J., & ARCINIEGA, M. (1983). Counseling minority families: An Adlerian perspective. *Counseling and Human Development, 16,* 111.

NYSTUL, M. S. (1991). An interview with Jon Carlson. *Individual Psychology, 47,* 498–503.

O'CONNELL, W. (1975). *Action therapy and Adlerian theory: Selected papers by Walter O'Connell.* Chicago: Alfred Adler Institute.

PANCNER, R. J., & JYLLAND, C. W. (1996). Depressive disorders. In L. Sperry & J. Carlson (Eds.), *Psychopathology and psychotherapy* (2nd ed., pp. 115–157). Washington: Accelerated Development

PEVEN, D. E., & SHULMAN, B. H. (1986). Adlerian psychotherapy. In I. L. Kutash & A. Wolf (Eds.), *Psychotherapist's case book* (pp. 101–123). San Francisco: Jossey-Bass.

PILKINGTON, L. R., WHITE, J. A., & MATHENY, K. B. (1997). Perceived coping resources and psychological birth order in school-aged children. *Individual Psychology, 53,* 42–57.

POWERS, R. L., & GRIFFITH, J. (1996). Enhancing the quality of Adlerian life: An assessment and reorientation. *Individual Psychology, 52,* 3–21.

RACHMAN, S. J., & WILSON, G. T. (1980). *The effects of psychological therapy* (2nd ed.). New York: Pergamon.

SCHOOLER, C. (1964). Birth order and hospitalization for schizophrenia. *Journal of Abnormal and Social Psychology, 69,* 574–579.

SCHULTZ, D., & SCHULTZ, S. E. (1998). *Theories of personality* (6th ed.). Pacific Grove, CA: Brooks/Cole.

SHARF, R. S. (1997). *Applying career development theory to counseling* (2nd ed.). Belmont, CA: Brooks/Cole.

SHERMAN, R., & DINKMEYER, D. (1987). *Systems of family therapy: An Adlerian integration.* New York: Brunner/Mazel.

SHLIEN, J. M., MOSAK, H. H., & DREIKURS, R. (1962). Effect of time limits: A comparison of two psychotherapies. *Journal of Counseling Psychology, 9,* 31–34.

SHULMAN, B. H. (1971). *Contributions to individual psychology.* Chicago: Alfred Adler Institute.

SHULMAN, B. H. (1982). An Adlerian interpretation of borderline personality. *Modern Psychoanalysis, 7,* 137–153.

SHULMAN, B. H., & MOSAK, H. H. (1988). *Manual for life style assessment.* Muncie, IN: Accelerated Development.

SPERRY, L. M. (1989). Contemporary approaches to brief psychotherapy: A comparative analysis. *Individual Psychology, 45,* 3–25.

SPERRY, L. M. (1996a). Anxiety disorders. In L. M. Sperry & J. Carlson (Eds.), *Psychopathology and psychotherapy from diagnosis to treatment* (2nd ed., 163–178). Washington: Accelerated Development.

SPERRY, L. M. (1996b). Psychopathology and the diagnostic and treatment process. In L. Sperry & J. Carlson (EDS.) *Psychopathology and psychotherapy* (2nd ed., pp. 3–17). Washington: Accelerated Development.

SPERRY, L. M., & CARLSON, J. (1993). *Psychopathology and psychotherapy from diagnosis to treatment.* Muncie, IN: Accelerated Development.

STARR, A. (1977). *Psychodrama.* Chicago: Nelson-Hall.

SULLIVAN, B. F., & Schwebel, A. J. (1996). Birth-order position, gender, and irrational relationship beliefs. *Individual Psychology, 52,* 54–64.

SULLOWAY, F. (1996). *Born to rebel.* New York: Pantheon.

TERNER, J., & PEW, W. L. (1978). *The courage to be imperfect: The life and work of Rudolf Dreikurs.* New York: Hawthorn Books.

THOMA, E. (1959). Treatment of an adolescent neurotic in a public school setting. In K. A. Adler & D. Deutsch (Eds.), *Essays in individual psychology* (pp. 423–434). New York: Grove Press.

VAIHINGER, H. (1965). *The philosophy of "as if."* London: Routledge & Kegan Paul.

WHEELER, M. S. (1996). Using the BASIS-A Inventory: Examples from a clinical setting. *Individual Psychology, 52,* 104–118.

WORTHEN, R., & O'CONNELL, W. E. (1969). Social interest and humor. *International Journal of Social Psychiatry, 15,* 179–188.

ZWEIGENHAFT, R. L. (1975). Birth order, approval seeking, and membership in Congress. *Journal of Individual Psychology, 31,* 205–210.

5

Existential Therapy

Based on a philosophical approach to people and their existence, existential psychotherapy deals with important life themes. Rather than prescribing techniques and methods, existential psychotherapy is an attitudinal approach to issues of living. Themes include living and dying, freedom, responsibility to self and others, finding meaning in life, and dealing with a sense of meaninglessness. More than other therapies, existential psychotherapy examines individuals' awareness of themselves and their ability to look beyond their immediate problems and daily events to problems of human existence. Because individuals do not exist in isolation from others, developing honest and intimate relationships with others is a theme throughout existential therapy.

Trained in psychoanalysis, the first existential therapists were European psychiatrists who were dissatisfied with Freud's emphasis on biological drives and unconscious processes. Rather, they were interested in the patients in front of them and what was happening to them, seeing their patients as they really are, not as an extension of a theory. Influenced by 19th century Western European philosophers, they listened to how their patients dealt with anxieties due to difficult responsibilities, loneliness, despair, and fears of death. These existential themes, rather than specific approaches (although a few are described), are the focus of this chapter.

HISTORY OF EXISTENTIAL THOUGHT

Existential psychotherapy developed from the early work of European philosophers. Perhaps the first was Kierkegaard, who wrote of the anxiety and uncertainties in life. Emphasizing subjectivity and the will to power, Nietzsche popularized existential thought in 19th century Europe. Developing existentialism further, Heidegger and Jaspers worked out sophisticated systems of existential philosophy. A more pessimistic view of existentialism was put forth by the French philosopher Sartre. Additionally, theologians have made important statements that combine elements of their particular beliefs and existentialist philosophy. Also, writers such as Dostoyevski, Camus, and Kafka have dealt with existential themes in their plays, novels, and other writings.

Familiarity with the views of these writers, theologians, and philosophers provides a background for understanding existential psychotherapy.

Existential Philosophers

Soren Kierkegaard, the Danish philosopher, has been called the grandfather of existentialism (Lowrie, 1962), in part due to his opposition to Hegel's emphasis on human rationality. Born in 1813 and living only 42 years, Kierkegaard wrote books, including *The Concept of Dread* and *Either/Or,* that dealt with the conflicts and problems of human existence. Kierkegaard viewed individuals as desiring to be eternal, like God, but having to deal with the fact that existence is temporary. When possible, individuals forget their temporal nature and deal with trivial issues of living. In adolescence, an awareness of one's finiteness emerges, and individuals must deal with the torment, angst, and dread that result, issues of philosophical and personal interest to Kierkegaard. Without this experience, individuals merely go through the motions of living and do not directly confront issues of choice and freedom. Dealing with this uncomfortable state is a task of becoming human and a focus of Kierkegaard's work.

The German philosopher Friedrich Nietzsche (1844–1900) emphasized the importance of human subjectivity. He believed that the focus on the rationality of individuals was misleading and that the irrational aspects of human nature played an important role. In particular, he emphasized the dynamics of resentment, guilt, and hostility that individuals attempt to repress (May, 1958a). Nietzsche was concerned that Europeans would express their repressed instincts in self-hatred and aggression rather than in creative means. In his development of the concept of "superman," Nietzsche argued that individuals who allow themselves to develop their "will to power" are creative and dynamic, achieving positions of leadership. By truly realizing their own individual potentialities and courageously living out their own existence, individuals seek to attain Nietzsche's concept of "will to power." Although Kierkegaard's views were based on theology and Nietzsche's on a "life force," both emphasized the subjective and irrational nature of individuals that was to have a direct impact on other existential philosophers and psychotherapists.

Phenomenology, as it was developed by Edmund Husserl (1859–1938), has been part of the evolution of existential psychotherapy. For Husserl, phenomenology was the study of objects as they are experienced in the consciousness of individuals. The methodology of phenomenology includes intuiting or concentrating on a phenomenon or object, analyzing aspects of the phenomenon, and freeing oneself of preconceptions so that the observer can help others understand phenomena that have been intuited and analyzed (Spiegelberg, 1971). This approach is used both in therapy and, as is shown later, in the existential method of psychological experimentation. Related to the concept of phenomenology is intentionality, which refers to the process of bringing objects into the mind to intentionally observe the environment. Phenomenological concepts have been important for many Gestalt and existential writers.

Perhaps the philosopher who had the most direct impact on the development of existential therapy was Martin Heidegger (1889–1976), who succeeded Husserl as the chair of philosophy at the University of Freiburg. Heidegger's *Being and Time* (1962) has been of particular importance in existential therapy as it emphasizes the awareness of existence, which he calls *Dasein* and is translated as "being-in-the-world." *Dasein* refers to attempting to attain high levels of consciousness and uniqueness by examining oneself, others, and the world. This is distinguished by Heidegger from *Das Man*, which refers to conventional thinking or going through the motions. When individuals become aware that their existence is not a consequence of choice, but of having their existence thrown upon them, they may experience dread and anguish in dealing with an incomprehensible and threatening world. If they deal with this world by conforming to conventional ways of acting and thinking, they are being "inauthentic." Individuals start in a state of inauthenticity, but if they accept the inevitability of death and nothingness and become aware of their moods and feelings, they move toward "authentic" existence. The act of being-in-the-world refers not only to conscious and active awareness of one's own life but also to an active caring about the needs and lives of others in one's world.

A practicing psychiatrist who later became a professor of philosophy, Karl Jaspers (1883–1969) sought to develop a philosophy that would encompass all problems related to the existence of humanity. Influenced by Kierkegaard's writings on the human condition and David Hume's work on understanding knowledge, Jaspers saw humanity as being continually confronted with situations involving death, suffering, struggle, and guilt. In dealing with such situations, Jaspers believed that we must find ways to "transcend" them by being-oneself, a state in which we depend on awareness of ourselves and our assertion of ourselves through choices and decisions. This is contrasted with being-there, which refers to knowing the world through observation and experiment. Being-oneself is attained not only through self-awareness but also through communication with others via discussion, education, politics, and other means.

Known widely because of his novels, plays, and articles, Jean-Paul Sartre (1905–1980) dealt with issues concerning the meaning of human existence. Sartre's answer to this problem is that there is no intrinsic reason to explain why the world and humanity should exist; individuals must find a reason. Humanity is freedom, and individuals must choose, within their own and environmental limitations, and decide constantly; they are condemned to be free. Sartre believed that existential psychoanalysis should deal with emotional problems resulting from individuals not acknowledging their original choices. Because one's freedom and nothingness is difficult to face, the psychotherapist must help the patient to confront excuses such as "The reason my life is miserable is because I was born out of wedlock." Sartre emphasizes that, no matter what a person has been, he can choose to be different.

Not only have philosophers contributed to the development of existential thought but also theologians have made important contributions, notably Martin Buber (1878–1965) on existential dialogue, Gabriel Marcel (1889–1973) on trust, and Paul Tillich (1886–1965) on courage. Combining existential philosophy with a Jewish Hasidic perspective, Buber emphasized the betweenness of relationships. There is never just an *I*. There is also a *thou*, if the person is treated as a human individual. If the person is manipulated or treated as an object, the relationship becomes *I-it*. From a Catholic perspective, Marcel described the person-to-person relationship, focusing on the being-by-participation in which individuals know each other through love, hope, and faithfulness, rather than as objects or as an "it." The Protestant theologian Paul Tillich is best known for his emphasis on *courage*, which includes faith in one's ability to make a meaningful life, as well as a knowledge of and a belief in an existential view of life. These philosophers have emphasized relationships with others and with God, in contrast to Sartre's pessimistic view of the meaning of existence.

Other negative views of the existence of humanity have been expressed by a number of well-known novelists and playwrights, among the most famous of whom are Dostoyevski, Camus, and Kafka. The Russian novelist Fyodor Dostoyevski, in *Notes from Underground*, had his protagonist deal with issues of consciousness and awareness of actions. The French novelist and philosopher Albert Camus, like Sartre, emphasized the absurdity of trying to understand a meaningless world. A similar attitude was displayed much earlier in the writings of Franz Kafka, who presented despairing and frustrating situations that question the meaningfulness of existence. Stories, novels, and plays with existential themes have helped to popularize the philosophical ideas of existentialism.

This brief overview of the philosophical antecedents of existential psychotherapy skims only the surface of important philosophical contributions. As can be seen, there are many divergent views within existentialism. For example, contrast the more optimistic views of the theological philosophers with the pessimistic views of the existential writers. Followers of existential philosophy differ widely as to their view of the impact that various philosophers have made to existentialism. For example, Gelven (1989) believes that Heidegger has made a greater contribution to existentialism than any other philosopher, whereas Cannon (1991) believes that Sartre's contribution to existentialism has been more substantial. However, Boss and Binswanger, early existential psychoanalysts, have relied heavily on Heidegger's existential philosophy.

Originators of Existential Psychotherapy

Using ideas from existential philosophy, Ludwig Binswanger, Medard Boss, and Viktor Frankl were early proponents of existential psychiatry. In their writings, they have not put forth a clear and articulate theory of psychotherapy. Rather, their writing is sometimes poetic and metaphorical (Maddi, 1996). Their concern has been the meaning of existence and its ramifications. The contributions that Binswanger, Boss, and Frankl have made to existential psychotherapy are described in more detail next.

The Swiss psychiatrist Ludwig Binswanger (1881–1966) was interested in many of Freud's ideas about individual drives and motives, but he was more influenced by Heidegger's concepts of being-in-the-world. A major contribution of Binswanger, *Being-in-the-World* (1975) was his view of fundamental meaning structure, which refers to the unlearned ability of individuals to perceive meaning in their world and to go beyond specific situations to deal with life issues. This universal ability to perceive meaning, also called *existential a priori*, provides individuals with the opportunity to develop their way of living and the direction of their lives. By focusing on the patients' views of their world and their present experience, Binswanger was able to help them understand the meaning of their behavior and become their own authentic selves through understanding their relationships with their world, their associates, and themselves.

Another Swiss psychiatrist, Medard Boss (1903–1990), was also quite familiar with Freud, having been analyzed by him in Vienna. Although trained by several psychoanalysts, Boss was also influenced strongly by the philosophy of Martin Heidegger. Integrating existentialism with psychoanalysis in *Psychoanalysis and Daseinsanalysis* (1963), Boss outlines universal themes that individuals incorporate to varying degrees in their being-in-the-world. Boss emphasized that individuals must coexist in the same world and share that world with others. In doing so, individuals relate with varying degrees of openness and clarity to others (spatiality of existence) and do so in the context of time (temporality of existence). The mood of individuals determines how they relate to the world. For example, a sad person is aware of misfortunes, and a happy person is attuned to enjoyable events in relationships. Another important existential theme is that of guilt, which occurs when we make choices and, in doing so, must reject a variety of possibilities. Guilt for not following through on those possible choices can never be fully relieved. For example, the person who decides to become a lawyer rather than a minister may never fully come to terms with the decision. Finally, by being mortal, individuals have the responsibility to make the most of existence. These existential themes greatly affected Boss's view of his patients and his psychotherapeutic work.

Although having basic views that are consistent with those of Binswanger and Boss, Viktor Frankl, born in Vienna in 1905, has expressed and developed his approach to psychotherapy differently. Like Boss and Binswanger, Frankl was also influenced by his study of psychoanalysis. However, his experience in German concentration camps was to affect his development of existential psychotherapy by bringing him in constant contact with existential issues such as guilt and mortality. Important concepts for Frankl (Gould, 1993) deal with the individual's freedom and responsibility for oneself and others. *Logotherapy*, a concept based on the idea that the most fundamental drive for individuals is to understand the meaning of their existence, has been developed eloquently in Frankl's popular book *Man's Search for Meaning* (1992) and can be seen in the context of Frankl's life in *Victor Frankl—Recollections: An Autobiography* (1997). Although Frankl has made use of specific techniques, his emphasis is not on techniques but on dealing with existential or spiritual questions that focus on the realization of values, the fulfillment of personal tasks, and the meaning of life for the individual.

Recent Contributors to Existential Psychotherapy

Several contemporary existential psychotherapists have applied existential themes to the practice of psychotherapy. Writing over a period of more than 40 years, Rollo May has expanded on existential themes and existential therapy for both the general reader and the professional. Irvin Yalom and James Bugental have written books that are particularly helpful to psychotherapists in their application of existential themes to the practice of psychotherapy. Other original concepts come from Laing (1961) and van Deurzen-Smith (1988). The work of contemporary existential psychotherapists is used extensively in this chapter.

ROLLO MAY

The best known contemporary writer on existential psychotherapy, Rollo May (1909–1994), has been influenced by the ideas of Binswanger and Boss, but his greatest influence, both personally and professionally, has been Paul Tillich, especially through *The Courage to Be* (1952). Throughout May's articles and books, he deals with important existential issues such as anxiety, dealing with power, accepting freedom and responsibility, and developing individual identity. An example of his early work is *The Meaning of Anxiety* (1950, 1977). May's familiarity with anxiety came not only from his readings but also from a 2-year hospitalization for tuberculosis. In *Man's Search for Himself* (1953), May wrote about the anxiety and loneliness that confront individuals in modern society. Two edited books

(May, 1961; May, Angel, & Ellenberger, 1958) were important in bringing together related approaches to existential psychology and therapy. As can be seen by the titles, many of his books develop salient existential themes: *Love and Will* (1969), *Power and Innocence* (1972), *The Courage to Create* (1975), and *Freedom and Destiny* (1981). More recently, May combined a long-term interest in the classics with his interest in existentialism in *The Cry for Myth* (1992). May's approach to psychotherapy shows an integration of psychoanalytic concepts with existential themes.

Perhaps the most thorough and comprehensive explanation of existential psychotherapy can be found in Yalom's (1980) text. Acknowledging the influence of many of the existential philosophers and psychotherapists mentioned previously in this chapter, Yalom presents an in-depth approach to existential psychotherapy by dealing with the themes of death, freedom, isolation, and meaninglessness. His therapeutic approach can be seen in a book of his published case studies, *Love's Executioner* (1989). The frequent use of case material in his textbook, as well as the material in his casebook, is helpful to psychotherapists who wish to focus their attention on the existential themes of their patients.

Another writer who has brought together approaches to existential therapy is James Bugental. His writings focus on helping patients develop an existential understanding of themselves through a search for authenticity (Bugental, 1978, 1981). In his work, he takes a humanistic focus that stresses the ability of individuals to enhance their awareness and to self-actualize. The existential themes he develops are similar to, but not identical to, those of Yalom, for example, change, contingency, responsibility, and relinquishment. His *The Art of the Psychotherapist* (1987) illustrates his therapeutic approach with patients by using abundant clinical material.

In addition to the American existentialist writers described in this chapter, two English existentialists have been influential. R. D. Laing (1961) established a therapeutic community in England for severely disturbed patients, based on an existential philosophy that reflects respect for patients. Van Deurzen (formerly known as van Deurzen-Smith) has written *Paradox and Passion in Psychotherapy* (1998) and *Everyday Mysteries: Existential Dimensions of Psychotherapy* (1997) along with other books. Her work has helped to create an active interest in existential psychotherapy in England known as the British School of Existential Psychotherapy.

Although there are differences in the existential views of all of these philosophers and therapists, there are many commonalities. The existential approach that is presented in the sections on existential psychology and psychotherapy represents themes that are common to most existential psychotherapists.

EXISTENTIAL PERSONALITY THEORY

Existential psychology deals with the dynamic or ever-changing transitions that individuals encounter as they emerge, evolve, and become. To be truly human, individuals must be aware of their own being-in-the-world, asking, "Who will I be? Who am I? Where do I come from?" Human beings are responsible for their own plans and destinies. Existentialism is concerned with how individuals relate to their objective world, to other human beings, and to their own sense of self. Existential psychology emphasizes the importance of time—past and future, but particularly the present—in understanding oneself and one's world. Anxiety results from having to make choices in a world that may often be perceived as hostile or uncaring. The major existential themes that are described in this chapter follow Yalom's (1980) model and include living and dying; freedom, responsibility, and choice; isolation and loving; and meaning and meaninglessness. How honestly and authentically individuals deal with these themes affects their existential and psychological well-being.

Being-in-the-World

The ability to be consciously aware of themselves and others separates human beings from other species. Boss (1963) and Binswanger (1975) used the term *Dasein* or *being-in-the-world*, which refers to the ability of individuals to be able to think about and reflect on events and to attribute meaning to them. This concept has also been expressed by Binswanger and others (May, 1958b) as being-for-itself, with the implication that people can decide and make choices about many events. Such authors use the phrase "Dasein choosing," which means "the-person-who-is-responsible-for-his-existence choosing" (May, 1958b, p. 41). In describing the full meaning of *human being*, May (1958b) uses the phrase "I-am." To illustrate this experience, May gives an example of a patient in her fourth month of therapy, an illegitimate child of a prostitute, who describes her I-am experience in a dream:

> I remember walking that day under the elevated tracks in a slum area, feeling the thought, "I am an illegitimate child." I recall the sweat pouring forth in my anguish in trying to accept that fact. Then I understood what it must feel like to accept, "I am a Negro in the midst of privileged whites," or "I am blind in the midst of people who see." Later on that night I woke up and it came to me this way, "I accept the fact that I am an illegitimate child." But, "I am not a child anymore." So it is, "I am illegitimate." That is not so either: "I was born illegitimate." Then what is left? What is left is this, "I am." This act of contact and acceptance with "I am," once gotten hold of, gave me (what I think was for me the first time) the experience "since I am, I have the right to be." (May, 1958b, p. 43)[1]

For May, this powerful "I-am" experience is important as a precondition for solving the patient's problems. Furthermore, this is an experience of the self and is not related to relationships with the therapist or to society. For May, the "I-am" experience is not like the ego that is the subject in a subject-object relationship but rather the "I am the being who can, among other things, know himself as the subject of what is occurring" (May 1958b, p. 46). Thus, "being" is an experience that is different than ego development. This experience is an ontological experience that refers to the science of being or existence—ontology.

Four Ways of Being

Existentialists identify four ways of being-in-the-world. Human beings exist in the *Umwelt, Mitwelt, Eigenwelt,* and *Überwelt* simultaneously. The *Umwelt* refers to the biological world or the environment. The *Mitwelt* means "with-world" and concerns the area of human relationships. The *Eigenwelt* is the "own-world" and refers to the relationship that individuals have to themselves. The *Überwelt* refers to one's relationship with spiritual or religious values. The first three were introduced by Binswanger; the last has been recently added by van Deurzen.

Umwelt is what we generally think of as the world, objects, the environment, and living beings. All animals and humans have an *Umwelt* that includes drives, instincts, and natural laws and cycles such as sleeping and waking, living and dying. The *Umwelt* is the "thrown world" that individuals and animals are thrown into. Examples of such uncontrollable factors are storms, floods, disease, and aging. Existentialists do not ignore the *Umwelt*, but neither do they view it as the only way of being.

Mitwelt refers to interrelationships that only human beings may have. The instinctual relationships that animals have in mating or the herd instinct belong to the *Umwelt*. For humans, the meaning of relationships with others depends on how much of oneself goes into the relationship. As May states: "The essence of relationship is that in the encounter both persons are changed" (1958b, p. 63). May is referring to the mutual awareness of the other in a human encounter. When the person is treated as an object (an object of ridicule or a sex object), the person is dehumanized and treated as an instrument (*Umwelt*), a way of meeting the needs of the other.

Überwelt was added by van Deurzen-Smith (1997, 1998) to emphasize the importance of beliefs about the world. Often these beliefs are religious or spiritual in nature. For example, wars are often fought based on conflicts of beliefs, such as conflicts between Catholics and Protestants in Northern Ireland. The *Überwelt* is the ideal world, the way the individual wants the world to be.

Eigenwelt, one's "own world," is more than a subjective, inner experience; it is a self-awareness from which we see the world. Implied in the observation "That is a lovely sunset" is the phrase "for me" or "I believe" or "I perceive" (that is a lovely sunset). As May (1958b) points out, Eastern languages, such as Japanese, include the reference to the self ("for me") that are unstated in Western languages. Clearly, the question of the self knowing itself is a difficult one to grasp, as are the concepts of consciousness and self-awareness.

> Each of these phenomena goes on almost every instant with all of us; they are indeed closer to us than our breathing. Yet, perhaps precisely because they are so near to us, no one knows what is happening in these events (May, 1958b, p. 64).

Binswanger and May are critical of psychoanalysis and behavioral and cognitive therapies because they deal basically with the *Umwelt* and not the *Eigenwelt*.

It is important to emphasize that these four modes of being in the world are always related to each other. At each moment, individuals are in the *Umwelt*, the environment; the *Mitwelt*, human relationships; the *Überwelt*, spiritual values; and the *Eigenwelt*, self-awareness. For example, when a person eats a meal, she is in the biological world in the sense of the physical act of eating, in the realm of human relationships in the sense of relating to others if eating with them or not relating to others if eating alone, possibly saying grace before her meal, and self-aware of her eating activity. Existential analysts are aware that being-in-the-world takes place in the context of time and space. It is time that is of particular interest to existential writers.

Time and Being

Time has attracted the attention of most existentialist writers, many believing that time is at the center of existential issues and can be viewed from several perspectives.

In the *Umwelt*, time can be viewed as "clock time" or in terms of space points on a clock or calendar (May, 1958b). In the *Mitwelt*, time has a less quantitative function. For example, one cannot measure how much a person cares about another by the number of years that they have known each other. In the *Überwelt* time also has a less quantitative function, but individuals vary greatly as to the attention they pay to their religious or belief system. In the *Eigenwelt* time has little to do with "clock time." When one has an insight or moment of self-awareness, the experience is immediate and profound.

In their work, existential therapists focus on the future, past, and present. The future is an immediate rather than a distant future; it does not allow escape from past or present. The individual is always in a process of self-actualization and moving into an immediate future. To focus on the past, exclusively, is to focus on history and development, the area of the *Umwelt*. May relates the past to the future in this way: "*Whether or not a patient can even recall the significant events of the past depends on his decision with regard to the future*" (1958b, p. 70).

Minkowski (1958) gives an interesting case of a 66-year-old psychotic man who can think only in the present, and his inability to be future oriented creates his anxiety and depression. An unusual aspect of the case is that Minkowski lived with the patient for 2 months and was able to observe him very frequently. The man was preoccupied with delusions of persecution and felt that everything around him would lead to his demise. He believed that everything had been designed for him and that all residue that he came in contact with would have to be eaten. For example, he saw a clock as hands, springs, screws, and so forth that he would have to eat. The patient's focus on the present and his inability to grasp the future is illustrated by Minkowski's description.

> From the first day of my life with the patient, my attention was drawn to the following point. When I arrived, he stated that his execution would certainly take place that night; in his terror, unable to sleep, he also kept me awake all that night. I comforted myself with the thought that, in the morning he would see that all his fears would be in vain. However, the same scene was repeated the next day and the next, until after three or four days I had given up hope, whereas his attitude had not budged one iota. What had happened? It was simply that I as a normal human being, had rapidly drawn from the observed facts my conclusion about the future. He on the other hand had let the same facts go by him, totally unable to draw any profit from them for relating himself to the same future. I now knew that he would continue to go on, day after day, swearing that he was to be tortured to death that night, and so he did, giving no thought to the present or the past. (Minkowski, 1958, p. 132)[2]

Minkowski points out that the patient's disorder is one of disoriented attitudes toward the future, with the delusions being only one aspect of this. This is different than the usual psychopathological view that would state that the patient is unable to deal with the future because of his delusions. This focus on the role of time in psychotherapy is a significant aspect of existential psychotherapy.

Related to the notion of time is that of timing in psychotherapy. Ellenberger (1958) describes *kairos*, a Greek word referring to the critical point at which a disease is expected to get better or worse. In psychotherapy, the timing of an intervention can be critical. For example, an alcoholic may benefit from suggestions or confrontations about alcoholism only at certain times. Ellenberger (1958) believes that a "surprisingly rapid cure" (p. 120) can occur when a therapist times an intervention appropriately.

Anxiety

For May (1977) as well as other existentialists, anxiety is viewed more broadly than by most other psychotherapy theorists, and it is separated into two major types (May & Yalom, 1989), normal anxiety and neurotic anxiety. A significant subset of normal anxiety—and the focus of attention by existential psychotherapists—is existential anxiety (Cohn, 1997). Although anxiety has physical manifestations, it arises from the basic nature of being. Individuals must confront the world around them, deal with unforeseen forces ("the thrown condition"), and in general develop a place within their world.

For May and Yalom (1989), normal anxiety has three features that differentiate it from neurotic anxiety. First, it is appropriate to the situation that the individual deals with in her life. Second, normal anxiety is not usually repressed. For example, a severe illness may make us come to terms with our death. Third, normal anxiety can provide an opportunity to confront existential dilemmas, such as dying, responsibility, and choices.

In contrast, neurotic anxiety is a reaction that is blown out of proportion or inappropriate for the particular event. For example, the man who is so afraid of disease that he washes his hands several times before and during a meal is experiencing neurotic anxiety. The anxiety is out of proportion to the situation, destructive, and of little value to the patient. Furthermore, the patient may have repressed fears that may be a source of this anxiety. In this example of neurotic anxiety or obsessional neurosis, there is an existential component. The individual is unable to control his anxiety about disease that may lead to his death. The individual compulsively washes his hands rather than dealing with the uncertainty of life. Existential therapists often help their patients develop awareness of their courage to deal with the existential issues that underlie neurotic anxiety.

Living and Dying

A certainty about living is its termination. We do not know how we will die or how long we will live, but awareness of death is inescapable. Although the awareness of death can create dread in individuals, it can also lead toward the development of a creative life (May, 1981). Yalom's (1980) work with cancer patients illustrates how individuals cope with their imminent death. Yalom does not limit his discussion to adults; he cites many studies that show how children deal with death through denial by believing that children do not die, personifying death ("death catches bad children"), and seeing death as a temporary condition or as sleep.

Frankl's 4 years of experience as a prisoner in a concentration camp during World War II has given him a unique perspective on death (Frankl, 1997). On a daily basis, he was faced with choices that could lead to his imminent death.

> Instinctively, I straightened on approaching the officer, so that he would not notice my heavy load. Then I was face to face with him. He was a tall man who looked slim and fit in his spotless uniform. What a contrast to us, who were untidy and grimy after our

long journey! He had assumed an attitude of careless ease, supporting his right elbow with his left hand. His right hand was lifted, and with the forefinger of that hand he pointed very leisurely to the right or to the left. None of us had the slightest idea of the sinister meaning behind that little movement of a man's finger, pointing now to the right and now to the left, but far more frequently to the left.

It was my turn. Somebody whispered to me that to be sent to the right side would mean work, the way to the left being for the sick and those incapable of work, who would be sent to a special camp. I just waited for things to take their course, the first of many such times to come. My haversack weighed me down a bit to the left, but I made an effort to walk upright. The SS man looked me over, appeared to hesitate, then put both his hands on my shoulders. I tried very hard to look smart, and he turned my shoulders very slowly until I faced right, and I moved over to that side.

The significance of the finger game was explained to us in the evening. It was the first selection, the first verdict made on our existence or non-existence. For the great majority of our transport, about 90 per cent, it meant death. Their sentence was carried out within the next few hours. Those who were sent to the left were marched from the station straight to the crematorium. (Frankl, 1992, p. 25)[3]

Such experiences have added to Frankl's appreciation of the meaningfulness of life. He sees death not as a threat but as an urging for individuals to live their lives fully and to take advantage of each opportunity to do something meaningful (Gould, 1993). Thus the awareness of death can lead to creativity and living fully, rather than to fear and dread.

Freedom, Responsibility, and Choice

Freedom to live our own lives carries with it the responsibility to do so. Existentialists believe that individuals do not enter or leave a structured universe that has a coherent design (May & Yalom, 1989). Rather, in their pursuit of freedom, individuals are responsible for their own world, their life plans, and their choices. Although the terms *freedom, responsibility,* and *choice* may first appear unrelated, they are integrally related, as we are free to choose in what ways we will be responsible for leading our lives and, implicitly, what values are significant to us.

Although freedom appears to be a principle that human beings would value positively, Camus and Sartre see it more negatively. To be truly free, individuals must confront the limits of their destiny. Sartre's position is that individuals are condemned to freedom (1956). They are responsible for creating their own world, which rests not on ground, but on nothingness. In his writings, Sartre gives the feeling that individuals are on their own, like people walking on a thin veneer that could open, leaving a bottomless pit. Sartre believes that our choices make us who we really are.

Responsibility refers to owning one's own choices and dealing honestly with freedom. Sartre uses the term *bad faith* to denote that individuals are finite and limited. For an individual to say, "I can't treat my children well, because I was abused as a child" or "Because I didn't go to a good high school, I can't go to a good college" is to act in bad faith by blaming someone else for the problem and not examining one's own limitedness. The person who compulsively handwashes can, from an existential point of view, be seen as acting in bad faith. Such an individual is choosing a repetitive, compulsive act rather than dealing with the implications of disease and death. Responsibility also includes caring for others and not blaming others for one's problems.

In discussing freedom, May (1969) uses the concept *willing* as the process by which responsibility is turned into action. There are two aspects of willing: wishing and deciding. May (1969) discusses psychological illness as the inability to wish, which connotes emptiness and despair. Part of the therapeutic task for existential therapists is to mobilize individuals' feelings so that they can wish and then act on choices.

When people have expressed their wishes or desires, they must also choose. This process can lead to panic or to the desire to have someone else make the choice. When people make choices, they must also live with the other side of the choice. If Dora decides to marry Fred and be part of a couple, she must live with the decision to stop dating other men. If she decides not to marry Fred, then she must deal with the potential loneliness that may result. The responsibility for choosing can carry great anxiety for individuals, depending both on the situation and on their ability to act in "good faith."

Isolation and Loving

In discussing isolation, Yalom (1980) differentiates three types of isolation: interpersonal, intrapersonal, and existential. Interpersonal isolation refers to distance from others—geographical, psychological, or social. For example, a person with schizophrenia is isolated personally from other individuals due to lack of ability to develop a relationship. Intrapersonal isolation occurs when one separates parts of oneself by using defense mechanisms or other methods to be unaware of one's own wishes. The person who focuses on what she should do may be distrusting of her judgment and unaware of her abilities and internal resources. Existential isolation is even more basic than either personal or intrapersonal isolation. It refers to being separated from the world. There is a sense of aloneness and isolation that is profound.

Yalom (1980) gives an example of a patient's dream that illustrates the incredible loneliness and dread that come with a sense of existential isolation.

> I am awake and in my room. Suddenly I begin to notice that everything is changing. The window frame seems stretched and then wavy, the bookcases squashed, the door knob disappears, and a hole appears in the door which gets larger and larger. Everything loses its shape and begins to melt. There's nothing there anymore and I begin to scream. (Yalom, 1980, p. 356)[4]

Yalom (1980) uses a phrase that conveys responsibility for one's own life: "the loneliness of being one's own parent." Adults are responsible for themselves and supply their own parental guidance to themselves.

When one is confronted with death, the sense of existential isolation is powerful. Being in an automobile and experiencing crashing into a building is a moment of extreme existential isolation and dread. The feeling of being totally alone and helpless can create a panicky feeling of "nothingness."

Loving relationships are a means of bridging a sense of existential isolation. Buber (1970) emphasizes the importance of the "I-thou" relationship in which two people fully experience the other. Yalom (1980) cautions that such a relationship should be need-free. Caring should be reciprocal, active, and a way of fully experiencing the other person. Yalom (1980) speaks of *fusion*, which occurs when the individual loses a sense of self in the relationship. To avoid existential isolation, individuals may desperately rely on another for a sense of self. Yalom gives an example of a woman who had alienated herself because of a poor relationship with a boyfriend. However, she could not leave him because she could not stand being alone. The patient said, "I don't exist when I'm alone" (Yalom 1980, p. 374). An important therapeutic task is to bridge the existential loneliness experienced by the patient without having the patient fuse with or become excessively dependent on the therapist.

Meaning and Meaninglessness

Questions about the meaning of life may haunt people at various times during their lives: Why am I here? What about my life do I find meaningful? What in my life gives me a sense of purpose? Why do I exist? As May and Yalom (1989) point out, human beings need a sense of meaningfulness in their lives. A sense of meaning provides a way of interpreting events that occur to the individual and in the world, and it furnishes a means for the development of values as to how people live and wish to live.

Sartre, Camus, and others have written about the absurdity of life and have dealt fully with the question of meaninglessness. Others, such as Frankl (1997), have focused on the importance of the development and search for meaning in one's life. Frankl has been concerned that individuals do not look at the spiritual meanings in their lives or beyond material values.

Paradoxically, Yalom has found that people who are terminally ill have found meaning in life far beyond what they had prior to their illnesses. The following is an example of one of Yalom's patients who found meaning in the face of death.

> Eva, a patient who died of ovarian cancer in her early fifties, had lived an extraordinarily zestful life in which altruistic activities had always provided her with a powerful sense of life purpose. She faced her death in the same way; and, though I feel uneasy using the phrase, her death can only be characterized as a "good death." Almost everyone who came into contact with Eva during the last two years of her life was enriched by her. When she first learned of her cancer and again when she learned of its spread and its fatal prognosis, she was plunged into despair but quickly extricated herself by plunging into altruistic projects. She did volunteer work on a hospital ward for terminally ill children. She closely examined a number of charitable organizations in order to make a reasoned decision about how to distribute her estate. Many old friends had avoided close contact with her after she developed cancer. Eva systematically approached each one to tell them that she understood their reason for withdrawal, that she bore no grudge, but that still it might be helpful to them when they faced their own death, to talk about their feelings toward her. (Yalom, 1980, p. 432)[5]

Self-Transcendence

It is the existential nature of human beings to transcend their immediate situation, and their self-interest to strive toward something above themselves (May, 1958b; Yalom, 1980). Buber (1961) writes that although human beings begin by asking themselves what they want, what is meaningful for them, they should not end with themselves, but should forget themselves and immerse themselves in the world. Boss (1963) remarks that individuals have the capacity for transcending their immediate situation because they have the ability to understand their own being and to take responsibility for being. By using imagination and creativity, individuals transcend their own needs so that they may be aware of others and act responsibly toward them. Human beings can transcend time and space through their imagination. We can think of ourselves in ancient Rome in 100 B.C. or in a far-off galaxy in the year 3000. We can also transcend ourselves and put ourselves in the position of others and feel the distress or happiness that they may experience. As Kierkegaard (1954) writes, imagination is an individual's most important faculty, helping individuals to go beyond themselves and reflect on their being and the being of others.

There are numerous examples of people transcending themselves. News accounts occasionally detail how individuals gave up their lives so that others may live. Yalom (1980) gives many examples of individuals who, on becoming aware that they were terminally ill, rather than focus inwardly on their own illnesses transcended themselves and cared for and helped others who were in distress. In a poignant personal situation, Frankl (1992) illustrates self-transcendence in the face of imminent death.

> On my fourth day in the sick quarters I had just been detailed to the night shift when the chief doctor rushed in and asked me to volunteer for medical duties in another camp containing typhus patients. Against the urgent advice of my friends (and despite the fact that almost none of my colleagues offered their services), I decided to volunteer. I knew that in a working party I would die in a short time. But if I had to die there might at least be some sense in my death. I thought that it would doubtless be more to the purpose to try and help my comrades as a doctor than to vegetate or finally lose my life as the unproductive laborer that I was then. (Frankl, 1992, pp. 59–60)[6]

Frankl (1969) believes that in order to self-realize, it is necessary first to be able to transcend oneself. For Frankl, the noölogical (spiritual) dimension that human beings can obtain comes through self-transcendence. In this way, people go beyond their biological and psychological selves to develop values and achieve meaning in their lives. Only when individuals transcend their own being can they become their own true selves.

Striving for Authenticity

The journey toward authenticity is the focus of many existential psychotherapists, including Loy (1996) and Bugental (1981). Authenticity refers to a "central genuineness and awareness of being" (Bugental, 1981, p. 102) that includes a willingness to face up to the limitations of human existence. Issues related to being authentic relate to moral choices, the meaning of life, and being human.

By contrasting the values, the experiencing, the social interactions, and the thoughts and feelings of authentic individuals with inauthentic individuals, Kobasa and Maddi (1977) explain the concept of authenticity. The values and goals of authentic individuals are very much their own, whereas inauthentic individuals may have goals based on values of others and be less conscious of what is important to them. In social interactions, authentic individuals are oriented toward intimacy, whereas inauthentic individuals are more concerned with superficial relationships. In a broader sense, authentic individuals are concerned about their society and social institutions such as schools and charities, whereas inauthentic individuals are less concerned with them. Authentic individuals, being aware of themselves, are more flexible and open to change than individuals who are inauthentic. The authentic person experiences existential anxiety over issues related to freedom, responsibility, death, isolation, and meaning. In contrast, the inauthentic individual experiences guilt about having missed opportunities, as well as cowardice because she has not had the courage to change or make risky decisions. Whereas the authentic person may experience existential crises that produce anxiety, the inauthentic individual is more likely to experience psychopathology and maladaptive means of dealing with crises. Thus, the authentic individual has a genuine awareness of herself and copes with existential questions and crises by experiencing them directly and acting on them.

Because the individual's being is a major focus of existentialist writers, they have not devoted much attention to the development of authenticity and values (Baum & Stewart, 1990). However, May (1966) has described four stages in the development of existential awareness: The first stage is the innocence and openness to experience of the infant. Second, at the age of 2 or 3, children react to the values of the world around them, specifically their parents. Children may respond to parental actions by accepting, demanding, defying, or using. The third stage is the consciousness of oneself as an individual. The fourth is transcendent consciousness, in which individuals can stand outside themselves and be aware of their world and how they relate to it. By not pampering, but by encouraging independence and accomplishment, parents help children develop values and rely on themselves. Too much dependence on parents can lead to a type of fusion and difficulty in developing self-transcendence. Similarly, Frankl (1969) sees the need for adolescents to be able to be independent and develop their own sense of values, even ones that may conflict with those of their parents. In doing so, they can develop authenticity—a true genuineness and awareness of their being.

The issues of anxiety, living and dying, freedom and responsibility, isolation and loving, and meaning and meaninglessness are dealt with directly in existential therapy. It is these issues, rather than specific techniques, that are important in helping the patient develop authenticity.

EXISTENTIAL PSYCHOTHERAPY

Because existential psychotherapy deals with attitudes and thematic concerns, goals focus on issues such as finding a purpose or meaning in life and fully experiencing one's existence. Although assessment instruments are occasionally used (described later in the chapter), it is primarily the therapeutic relationship that allows for the assessment of important existential tasks and themes. In helping their clients, existential therapists deal with resistance and transference issues that may interfere with the development of a real relationship with the client. In working with clients, existential therapists may take a variety of approaches to important existential themes, such as dealing with the death of others or with one's own mortality. Also, clients struggle with being responsible for choices and decisions that come from their freedom in leading their lives. The struggle to be appropriately loving and intimate with others in contrast to struggling with loneliness and isolation is a theme that existential therapists approach through their relationship with the client. Finding meaning in one's life and being able to love others authentically are related issues. How existential therapists approach these major existential themes is the subject of this section.

Goals of Existential Psychotherapy

Authenticity is the basic goal of psychotherapy. In therapy, clients learn how their lives are not fully authentic and what they must do to realize the full capability of their being. As Frankl states, "Clients must find a purpose to their existence and pursue it. The therapist must help them achieve the highest possible activation" (1965, p. 54). As an individual develops an awareness of having a task to pursue in life, he will be better able to actualize significant values. Similarly, van Deurzen-Smith (1998) believes that the aim of therapy is to help individuals become authentic and recognize when they are deceiving themselves. Therapy should help clients understand their beliefs and values, have confidence in them, and make choices based on them that can lead to new directions in living. A sense of aliveness comes from therapy as the individual sees life with interest, imagination, creativity, hope, and joy, rather than with dread, boredom, hate, and bigotry.

For May "the aim of therapy is that the patient *experiences his existence as real*" (1958b, p. 85). The focus is not on curing symptoms but on helping individuals fully experience their existence. Another way of viewing this is that neurotic individuals are overconcerned about their *Umwelt* (the biological world) and not sufficiently concerned with their *Eigenwelt* (their own world). In these terms, the goal of psychotherapy is to help the individual develop his *Eigenwelt* without being overwhelmed by the therapist's *Eigenwelt*. The therapist must be with the patient as he experiences *Eigenwelt*. In learning about the patient, May (1958b) does not ask, "*How* are you?" but rather, "*Where* are you?" May wants to know not just how patients feel and how they describe their problems but how detached patients are from themselves. Do patients seem to be confronting their anxiety, or are they running away from their problems? As May (1958b, p. 85) points out, it is often easier to focus on the mechanism of the behavior rather than the experience in order to reduce anxiety. For example, a patient who reports symptoms of agoraphobia (a fear of being out in public places or outside home) may describe his physical anxiety when he leaves the house and how far he is able to go, without attending to the overall dread and anxiety that he experiences because of his limitations. Although the cure of agoraphobia may be a by-product of existential therapy, the goal is to have the individual experience his own existence and become fully alive rather than adjust or fit cultural expectations.

Existential Psychotherapy and Counseling

Existential therapists and counselors do not make a distinction between the two. Although May writes of existential therapy, he also has written about existential counseling (May, 1989). There seems to be an implication in the writings of existential therapists that counseling is briefer in duration and less intense (meeting once a week as opposed to two or three times). Furthermore, counseling may focus on specific issues, such as bereavement or confronting one's own death. However, this may be an artificial distinction. Whether called therapy, counseling, or analysis, the work of existential therapists has as its focus existential themes. The issues of death, freedom, responsibility, isolation, and meaninglessness are important, not the techniques or methods used to deal with them. These are often a reflection of the counselor or therapist's being, which is inclusive of the therapist's personal experience and professional training.

Assessment

Rather than attending to diagnostic categories (DSM-IV) and specific behavioral complaints, existential psychotherapists are attuned to existential themes. In the initial presentation of problems, therapists listen for issues related to responsibility, mortality, isolation, and meaninglessness. Later, they may make similar assessments of existential issues in patients' dream material. Furthermore, some therapists use objective tests specifically designed to assess existential themes.

Initial assessment.   Not all clients are appropriate for existential counseling and therapy. Those individuals wishing advice and suggestions from the therapist are likely to be frustrated by an existential approach. If a client wants assistance in reducing physical stress but does not wish to attend to broader issues that contribute to this stress, existential therapy is inappropriate. By listening for themes of isolation, meaninglessness, responsibility, and mortality, the therapist ascertains which issues require therapeutic work. Furthermore, the therapist assesses the clients' authenticity—how aware of their problems and responsible for them clients are. The therapist must assess the clients' ability to fully engage with the therapist and to face life issues honestly (van Deurzen-Smith, 1995).

Dreams as assessment   For existential therapists, dreaming, like waking, is a mode of existence or being-in-the-world. Whereas events in one's waking life are connected and shared with other people, dreams have events that are not connected and are special for the dreamer, openings to understanding the dreamer's being (Cohn, 1997). Boss (1977) felt that dreams can help in understanding waking experience and waking experience can help in understanding dreams. What is important is the client's experience of the dream, not the therapist's interpretation.

In listening to dreams, existential therapists are alert to themes that go beyond the client's conscious experiences and reveal other aspects of being. In her work with Brenda, van Deurzen-Smith focuses on determining the essential meaning of a dream. In one dream, Brenda is running through knee-deep snow with wolves in pursuit. This is followed by a second dream in which

> she had suddenly found herself on the snow plough, or sledge, which dispersed the wolves but killed the people running through the snow and she felt intense guilt for this when waking up. The guilt was that of her realization that she was trying to escape from her original plight of being a runner through the snow, by joining the public, safe, but ruthless camp. Her guilt reminded her of her aspiration to mean more to others than she had seemed to be able to for the moment. (van Deurzen-Smith, 1988, p. 168)[7]

In her therapeutic work with Brenda, van Deurzen-Smith made frequent use of dream material to assess existential themes that are significant to Brenda.

Yalom (1980) describes research showing how frequently dreams of death occur among individuals in the general population and in those who have recently experienced the death of a friend or loved one. For many individuals, dreams of disease, being chased by someone with a weapon, or encountering a life-threatening storm or fire are not infrequent. For existential therapists, this is often an opportunity to discuss the themes of death and dying.

Use of objective and projective tests. Although most assessment takes place in the interaction between therapist and client, some existential therapists do make use of projective and objective instruments. Some therapists have used the Rorschach and the Thematic Apperception Test (TAT) to assess existential themes. For example, Murray's TAT (1943) assesses the needs of abasement, affiliation, dominance, and play, which have an indirect relationship to existential themes.

More directly related to existential concepts are objective tests that have been developed to measure specific themes. Based on Frankl's concern about meaninglessness in life, the Purpose in Life Test (PIL) (Crumbaugh & Henrion, 1988) is a 20-item scale that surveys individuals' views of life goals, the world, and their death. Measuring the degree to which individuals actively experience their feelings and have an authentic sense of self-awareness, the Experiencing Scale (Gendlin & Tomlinson, 1967) can be used to assess a commitment to the therapeutic process. Assessing powerlessness, adventurousness, nihilism, and vegetativeness, all related to aspects of meaninglessness, the Alienation Test (Maddi, Kobasa, & Hoover, 1979) measures more aspects of meaninglessness than does the PIL. However, the PIL has considerably more validation information than do the other instruments. In general, these instruments, when used, are more applicable to research on existential themes than to psychotherapeutic use.

The Therapeutic Relationship

The focus of existential therapy is that of two individuals being-in-the-world together during the length of the therapy session. This authentic encounter includes the subjective experience of both therapist and client, which takes place during the present. The therapist's attitude toward the patient, referred to by Yalom (1980) as therapeutic love, is central to other therapeutic issues, including transference and resistance. The process of existential therapy, which has the therapist-patient relationship as a major focus, differs among existential therapists. For example, Bugental (1987) describes an approach that features a developing and deepening relationship with the client and an exploration of the inner self. These issues are described in more detail in the following paragraphs.

Therapeutic love. The therapeutic relationship is a special form of the I-thou relationship (Buber, 1970). Yalom writes of the relationship as a "loving friendship" (1980, p. 407) that is nonreciprocal. In other words, the client may experience the therapist in a variety of ways, but the therapist strives to develop a genuine caring encounter that does not encumber the client's growth with the therapist's personal needs. In a sense, the therapist is in two places at once, authentic with herself and authentically open to the client (Buber, 1965; Yalom, 1980).

By truly caring for the client, the therapist helps intimacy between client and therapist to grow. Even though the client may be angry, hostile, untruthful, narcissistic, depressed, or unattractive in other ways, there should be a feeling of authentic love for the client (Sequin, 1965). As the therapeutic relationship develops, clients experience an atmosphere of true openness and sharing with the therapist. Bugental (1987) gives an example of the intimate sharing that can take place with a client when the therapist is truly authentic. In this example, Betty explores the pain in the relationship with her father, which changed when she grew older.

Client: I know I keep coming back to the pendant my father gave me when I had my seventh birthday party, and I don't know just what it means to me, but it's been in my thoughts again today.

Therapist: Uh-huh.

Client: I wore the pendant today. See? (It hung about her neck and she pulls it forward toward therapist.)

Therapist: Yes. It's very nice.

Client: It's just a child's present, I know, but . . . (weeps).

Therapist: But?

Client: But it means so much to me. (Still weeping) It . . . it . . . it's as though . . . .

Therapist: Mmmmm.

Client: . . . as though he . . . (sobs) he loved me then. He loved me then; I know he did (crying strongly).

Therapist: He loved you then.

Client: Yes, he loved me then (crying eases; voice drops, becomes more reflective). But then I . . . but then I . . . what did I do? I did something so that he stopped loving me and was angry all the time. What did I do? (Crying again, a protesting tone)

Therapist: (Tone low, intent) What you did made him stop loving you?

Client: (Crying stopping, eyes unfocused, searching inwardly) Yes . . . (deeply seeking). Yes, what was it? What did I do? Oh!

Therapist: (Silent, waiting)

Client: I think I know (fresh sobs, face miserable). (Pause, hardly aware of anything but inner thoughts and feelings.)

Therapist: (Silent, breathing slowed)

Client: I know (quietly, firmly, resignedly). I know: I became a woman!

In that moment a door opened inside of Betty, and she became aware of so much that she *had known but not let herself know* for so very long. That awareness within her was so much larger than she could ever reduce to words. In that enlarged inner vision is the healing/growth dynamic. In that recognition there was no need for words for several moments. Therapist and client were very close emotionally; their heads and bodies bent toward each other; they do not touch though they might well have. A time of true intimacy. (Bugental, 1987, p. 44)[8]

Resistance.   For Bugental (1981), resistance on the part of the client is natural, the way she deals with life's tasks. Resistance, from an existential point of view, occurs when a client does not take responsibility, is alienated, is not aware of feelings, or otherwise is inauthentic in dealing with life. Resistance is rarely directed at the therapist but is a way of dealing with overwhelming threats, an inaccurate view of the world, or an inaccurate view of self. Expressed in resistance are not only the fears of clients but also their own courageous way of dealing with themselves and their world. Clients display resistance in the therapy hour by whining, complaining, talking about insignificant material, being seductive with the therapist, or otherwise being inauthentic. The therapist attempts to establish a real and intimate relationship with the client, being supportive of the client's struggle with such issues (Frank, 1997).

Transference.   As Cohn (1997) points out, too great a focus on the transference relationship interferes with an authentic relationship with the client. Bugental (1981) recognizes that some resistances "are acted out through the transference" (p. 145). He believes that it is important to recognize when the client's attention implicitly or explicitly focuses on the therapist. For example, if the client continually praises the therapist inordinately for her help, the therapist may explore how this behavior is an acting out of relationship issues with the client's mother or father. Then the client and therapist can make progress in the process of developing a real and authentic relationship.

The therapeutic process.   Throughout the therapeutic process, existential therapists are fully present and involved with their clients. If they become bored, look forward to the end of the hour, or lose their concentration on the client, the therapists are not achieving an authentic encounter with their clients. Although existential therapists would agree on the importance of the authentic therapeutic encounter, the process in which therapists proceed varies, as they encounter issues that inhibit the development of authenticity. In dealing with them, they may disclose their own feelings and experiences, when doing so helps clients fully develop their own sense of authenticity. In the movement toward authenticity, therapists explore important existential themes such as living and dying; freedom, responsibility, and choice; isolation and loving; and meaninglessness.

Living and Dying

As Yalom has observed, "Death anxiety is inversely proportional to life satisfaction" (1980, p. 207). When an individual is living authentically, anxiety and fear of death decrease. Yalom notes two ways that individuals choose to deny or avoid issues of dying: belief in their own specialness and belief in an ultimate rescuer who will save them from death. Recognizing these issues helps the therapist deal directly with issues of mortality. Such issues may confront those who are grieving, those who are dying, and those who have attempted suicide. Ways that existential therapists work with these issues are described in this section.

Yalom (1980) shows the many ways that individuals try to support a view that they are invulnerable, immortal, and will not die. The notion of narcissism emphasizes the specialness of the individual and the belief that he is invulnerable to illness and death. Coming to grips with death may be gradual or sudden.

Jan had breast cancer that had spread to her brain. Her doctors had forewarned her of paralysis. She heard their words but at a deep level felt smugly immune to this possibility. When the inexorable weakness and paralysis ensued, Jan realized in a sudden rush that her "specialness" was a myth. There was, she learned, no "escape clause." (Yalom, 1980, p. 120)[9]

Another defense against our own mortality is a belief in an ultimate rescuer. When patients develop a fatal illness, they must confront the fact that no one will save them. Often, they may become frustrated and angry with physicians who cannot perform magic, and they cannot believe that the doctor will fail them. Other examples of the "ultimate rescuer" are people who live their lives for others: spouse, parent, or sibling. They invest all of their energy in an interpersonal relationship that cannot save them when they are dying.

Dealing with grief is a common therapeutic task of the therapist. The loss may be that of a parent, a spouse, a child, a friend, or a pet. Existential therapists deal openly with grief and emotions such as ambivalence, guilt, and anger. Furthermore, Yalom (1980) shows how individuals confront their own deaths when dealing with the deaths of loved ones. Often dreams show material that deals not only with the death of the loved one but also fear of one's own death. In dealing with death, therapists must be aware of their own belief systems and their own fears and anxieties. If the therapist chooses to deny her own anxieties regarding death, it is likely that she may avoid the issue of death when working with a client.

To deal with suicidal patients is to deal with those who may choose death over life. Van Deurzen-Smith (1988) gives the example of Susan, a 17-year-old who had taken an overdose of sleeping tablets. She felt misunderstood, ridiculed, and hopeless. Van Deurzen-Smith views Susan's suicide attempt in brave and courageous terms rather than cowardly ones. Susan valued her action and was offended by those who discounted the importance of her attempt, felt sorry for her, or lectured her. Van Deurzen-Smith's approach was to help Susan confront her own existence.

Existential work with Susan meant confirming those aspects of her outlook on life that were based on her discovery of hard realism while helping her to reach a more constructive conclusion in her thinking about those facts. It was no good pretending that life could be easy and that people would end up understanding her. Her recognition of life as basically rough and of people as basically unfair was one of her greatest discoveries and personal realities. She needed to get some credit for daring to look at life in such a way. Moreover she needed to be reminded that if she had the courage to brave death, all on her own, then surely she would have the courage to brave life as well. At least she had no illusions left, so she would now be able to move forward without the paralysis of constant disappointments. (1988, p. 35)[10]

The therapist takes a caring yet forthright approach to Susan's life and death. She helps Susan accept full responsibility for taking the right to live and the right to die. In this example, the therapist's and client's attitudes toward life and death are significant, specific techniques are not.

Although there are many group techniques and exercises for helping individuals become aware of their mortality, Yalom (1980) prefers to deal directly with the individual issues rather than use techniques. However, methods such as guided fantasies, in which people imagine their death and their funeral, may be helpful. Other exercises have included talking with people who are elderly or terminally ill or writing one's own obituary or epitaph (May & Yalom, 1989). Whatever approach is used to help individuals deal with their own fears and anxieties about death can help them develop a fuller experience of being-in-the-world.

Freedom, Responsibility, and Choice

Frequent themes in counseling and psychotherapy are choices and decisions that clients must make. The existential therapist sees a client as being thrown into the world with the opportunity to make purposeful and responsible choices. The existential point of view allows clients to experience their freedom of being in the world and its inherent responsibilities.

Freedom.   The existential therapist sees freedom as an opportunity to change, to step away from the client's problems, and to confront oneself (Fabry, 1987). Despite what may have happened in the past—child abuse, traumatic incidents, financial deprivation—clients have the freedom to change their lives. This is why many existential therapists prefer to work in the present rather than dwell on the past. They may talk about the past as it affects the present, but the focus is on the client's freedom to change. Although it can be exhilarating, this freedom to change can be terrifying as well. For example, Yalom describes Bonnie, who is in a restrictive 20-year marriage to a husband who made all of her decisions. She was terrified of being alone.

> Though her husband was unspeakably restrictive, she preferred the prison of her marriage to, as she put it, the freedom of the streets. She would be nothing, she said, but an outcast, a soldier in the army of misfit women searching for the occasional stray single man. Merely asking her, in the therapy hour, to reflect on the separation was sufficient to bring on a severe bout of anxious hyperventilation. (Yalom, 1980, p. 139)[11]

It is not unusual for adolescents to complain about their family and their lack of freedom in not being able to come and go as they please, not being able to smoke, and so forth. Rather than empathize with the restrictiveness that adolescents feel and help them to develop assertiveness, the existential therapist would assist adolescents in discovering their ability to make their own choices (van Deurzen-Smith, 1988).

Responsibility.   Therapists encounter vast differences in their clients' willingness to accept responsibility for themselves and their current situations. Clients may often blame parents, bosses, spouses, or others for their difficulties. In assisting the client in becoming more responsible, the therapist assumes that clients have created their own distress. Therapy progresses as clients identify their own role in their problems and stop blaming their parents, spouses, or others. Such interventions are made at appropriate points, bearing in mind timing or *kairos* (Ellenberger, 1958), the critical point at which to intervene.

In working with Betty (a different client than the Betty described on p. 184), Yalom (1989) found that he was becoming bored and irritated with her. Betty was an obese, lonely woman in her thirties who constantly externalized her problems. She complained about work, the sterile California culture, people's attitudes toward her obesity, and her inability to lose weight because she had inherited obesity. She would come into the therapy hour and complain, tell stories, and try to present objective reasons as to why she was depressed. Yet she presented a joking and falsely gay facade. In the following crucial intervention, Yalom persists in confronting Betty's pretense and refusal to take responsibility for her own condition, even though Betty resists.

"I'm really interested in what you said about being, or rather pretending to be, jolly. I think you are determined, absolutely committed, to be jolly with me."

"Hmmmm, interesting theory, Dr. Watson."

"You've done this since our first meeting. You tell me about a life that is full of despair, but you do it in a bouncy 'aren't-we-having-a-good-time?' way."

"That's the way I am."

"When you stay jolly like that, I lose sight of how much pain you're having."

"That's better than wallowing in it."

"But you come here for help. Why is it so necessary for you to entertain me?"

Betty flushed. She seemed staggered by my confrontation and retreated by sinking into her body. Wiping her brow with a tiny handkerchief, she stalled for time.

"Zee suspect takes zee fifth."

"Betty, I'm going to be persistent today. What would happen if you stopped trying to entertain me?"

"I don't see anything wrong with having some fun. Why take everything so . . . so . . . I don't know—You're always so serious. Besides, this is me, this is the way I am. I'm not sure I know what you're talking about. What do you mean by my entertaining you?"

"Betty, this is important, the most important stuff we've gotten into so far. But you're right. First, you've got to know exactly what I mean. Would it be O.K. with you if, from now on in our future sessions, I interrupt and point out when you're entertaining me—the moment it occurs?"

Betty agreed—she could hardly refuse me; and I now had at my disposal an enormously liberating device. I was now permitted to interrupt her instantaneously (reminding her, of course, of our new agreement) whenever she giggled, adopted a silly accent, or attempted to amuse me or to make light of things in any distracting way.

Within three or four sessions, her "entertaining" behavior disappeared as she, for the first time, began to speak of her life with the seriousness it deserved. She reflected that she had to be entertaining to keep others interested in her. I commented that, in this office, the opposite was true: the more she tried to entertain me, the more distant and less interested I felt.

I was less bored now. I looked at the clock less frequently and once in a while checked the time during Betty's hour. Not, as before, to count the number of minutes I had yet to endure, but to see whether sufficient time remained to open up a new issue. (Yalom, 1989, pp. 97–98, 99)[12]

This was a turning point in therapy for Betty. She began the process of losing a considerable amount of weight, developed relationships with men, and took responsibility for her own life. By making responsible choices, Betty was able to alleviate her depression and to be more open and honest with herself and others.

Choice.   In describing the process of choice, May (1969) delineates the process as wishing, willing, and deciding. Some individuals are so depressed that they have few wishes, and in such a case the therapist must help the individual become more aware of feelings. Other clients may avoid wishing by acting impulsively or compulsively. In other words, they act, but do not think about what they want. By "willing," individuals project themselves onto a point at which they will be able to decide. Willing involves the ability to change and to decide. When the individual decides, action follows. Implicit in this process is the responsibility for one's own wishing, willing, and deciding. This responsibility may be felt strongly by clients, when they find themselves panicked in deciding important issues such as whether to leave an unsatisfactory job or to get married.

When dealing with choices, the existential therapist recognizes the importance of client decision making as opposed to therapist decision making. The following example illustrates succinctly how Bugental deals with a client's indecisiveness.

Thelma's daughter wants to date a boy that Thelma does not like. The daughter, 17, insists that she can handle her own affairs and that Thelma is babying her. Thelma wants to avoid being overprotective and wants to keep her daughter's affection; yet she is frankly concerned about the reputation of the boy with whom her daughter wants to go. She tells me about this at some length, pauses and seems about to change the subject.

Therapist: So what will you do?

Patient: Do? What can I do?

Therapist: That's a good question, what can you do?

Patient: I can't do a thing; she's going to go, and that's it.

Therapist: So you decided to let her go with John?

Patient: I haven't decided. She's the one who has decided.

Therapist: No, you've decided too. You've chosen to let her go with John.

Patient: I don't see how you can say that. She's insisting.

Therapist: That's what she's doing; what you're doing is accepting her insistence.

Patient: Well, then I won't let her go. But she'll be unhappy and make life hell for me for a while.

Therapist: So you've decided to forbid her to go with John.

Patient: Well, isn't that what you wanted? What you said I should do?

Therapist: I didn't say that you should do anything. You have a choice here, but you seem to be insisting that either your daughter is making a choice or that I am.

Patient: Well, I don't know what to do.

Therapist: It is a hard choice.

And so Thelma begins to confront her choice. It should be evident that this same procedure would have been followed whether Thelma had first concluded to deny her daughter permission to go with the boy or had given the permission. (Bugental, 1981, pp. 345–346)[13]

Issues of freedom, responsibility, and choice are intimately related. Experiencing a sense of freedom can cause clients to fear or to welcome the responsibility that falls upon them for the choices that they make in their own lives. As seen in the case of Betty, by taking responsibility for themselves, clients decrease the isolation and loneliness in their own lives.

Isolation and Loving

Individuals enter the world alone and leave the world alone. An awareness of the individual's relationships with others constitutes an integral part of existential treatment. Exploring feelings of loneliness and isolation are an important aspect of a therapeutic relationship. As adults grow away from their families, issues of developing new and loving relationships exist. Those who come to therapy often show an inability to develop intimacy with others. The most severe categories of psychological disturbance— paranoia and schizophrenia—show an extreme isolation in which the patient may be unable to communicate to others on the most basic levels. For the existential therapist, the challenge is to bring intimacy and therapeutic loving into the relationship to affect the loneliness of the client.

Yalom's (1980) concept of therapeutic love, described on page 183, deals directly with the loneliness of the client. Each of the examples in this section shows, to some degree, the intimate interaction with the client. Such intimacy, as in the case of Betty on page 184, can stimulate clients to have the courage to change their lives so that intimacy with others can develop. Bugental (1981), in writing about therapists' love, cautions that dependency can develop and the patient may not establish intimacy with others, only with the therapist. He gives the example of Kathryn, who made frequent phone calls, requested special meetings, and presented several crises. By setting limits, he was, with difficulty, able to stabilize the relationship. The therapeutic relationship is not a reciprocal one, as the client receives love but does not have to give it. In that sense, it can be an inaccurate representation of the relationships that the client seeks, which requires loving and giving from both individuals. Therapists communicate that along with the sense of loving and intimacy that comes with genuine caring, reciprocal giving relationships increase the meaningfulness of life.

Meaning and Meaninglessness

Helping clients—and people in general—find meaningfulness in their lives has long been a concern of Frankl (1969, 1978, 1992, 1997). As Gould (1993) shows, meaning is a central concept throughout Frankl's thoughts on therapy and is the key to the mentally healthy self (p. 136). If an individual searches for the meaning of life, he will not find it.

Meaning emerges as one lives and becomes concerned with others. When individuals focus too much on themselves, they also lose a perspective on life. For Frankl, helping a patient who is self-absorbed by searching for causes of anxiety and disturbance only makes the person more self-centered. Rather, for Frankl (1969), the solution is to look toward events and people in which the client finds meaning.

In concentrating on the importance of values and meaning in life, Frankl has developed an approach called *logotherapy*. Four specific techniques help individuals transcend themselves and put their problems into a constructive perspective: attitude modulation, dereflection, paradoxical intention, and Socratic dialogue. In attitude modulation, neurotic motivations are changed to healthy ones. For example, motivations to take one's life are questioned and replaced by removing obstacles that interfere with living responsibly. In dereflection, clients' concerns with their own problems are focused away from them. For example, clients who experience sexual performance difficulties may be asked to concentrate on the sexual pleasure of the partner and to ignore their own. Similarly, paradoxical intention requires that patients increase their symptoms so that attention is diverted away from them by having them view themselves with less concern and often with humor. (An example of paradoxical intention is shown in the next section.) Guttmann (1996) considers Socratic dialogue to be the main technique in logotherapy. It can be used to guide clients to find meaning in their lives, assess current situations, and become aware of their strengths. Discussed more fully in Chapters 9 and 10, it is a series of questions that help clients arrive at conclusions about beliefs or hypotheses, guided in part by therapist perceptions of the client's misunderstandings. These techniques help patients become less self-absorbed and develop meaning in their lives through concern with other events and people.

Some existential therapists object to Frankl's approach, which appears to them to emphasize techniques over existential themes (Yalom, 1980). They prefer to help individuals become more fully aware of meaning in their lives by looking for issues that interfere with the process of finding meaning. As the therapist and the patient engage in their relationship, and as the therapist works authentically in creating a caring atmosphere, those issues that trouble the client are shared and meaningfulness emerges from their work together.

These themes—living and dying; freedom, responsibility, and choice; isolation and loving; and meaning and meaninglessness—are interrelated. They all deal intimately with issues concerning the client's existence or being-in-the-world. Engaging the client, showing therapeutic love, and involving oneself with the client are all ways of entering the client's world. They show clients that they are not alone and that they can be aided in their struggle with existential themes.

PSYCHOLOGICAL DISORDERS

As may be clear at this point, existential therapists conceptualize and treat psychological disorders by focusing on existential themes, not on psychodiagnostic categories. However, it is helpful to see how existential therapists apply their treatment approach to a variety of different disorders. In working with depressed patients, Bugental (1976, 1987) discusses depression in terms of the "dispirited condition" and suggests three phases for working with such patients. With a patient with a borderline disorder, Yalom focuses on the importance of "engagement" to work with such individuals who feel isolated from others. Often paradoxical intention has been applied to individuals with obsessive-compulsive disorders. Lukas (1984) helps a patient "step outside herself" and be more aware of her own being by changing her approach to compulsive behavior. In the case of a man with extreme anxiety over losing his job, Yalom (1980) helps him grow and alleviate his distress by confronting his death anxiety. With an alcoholic, Bugental (1981) raises the importance of taking responsibility for one's own life and ceasing self-blaming behaviors. Although different existential themes are associated with various disorders in these examples, these themes are not specific to the disorders, as several existential themes may arise in any of the disorders that are discussed here.

Depression

In his work with depressed patients, Bugental (1987) prefers to refer to their condition as *dispirited*. To him, *dispiritedness* refers to blocks to intending or wishing. The depressed or dispirited person feels that there is nothing worth doing or bothering with. There may be a desire to be still, be alone, and not participate in the world.

In dealing with dispiritedness, Bugental suggests three phases that underlie his therapeutic approach. First, when patients casually report inactivity or joke about their depression, the therapist deals directly with this detachment by bringing it to the patient's awareness. Second, as people become less detached, the therapeutic process involves calling attention and reducing the guilt or blame patients feel for their own depression or dispiritedness. Third, clients are helped to accept their own dispiritedness and to sense it. When this happens, they are likely to feel existential anxiety, fears of death, meaninglessness, or aloneness. Therapy then deals with issues of responsibility and choices.

Although not using Bugental's model, van Deurzen-Smith (1988) uses a remarkably similar approach with Catherine, a young woman who had been diagnosed as having a postpartum depression. She had felt hopeless and unable to care for her baby. Her husband and her mother suggested that Catherine go away for a while and rest, in essence, disengage. This is exactly what Catherine did not want to do, and it exacerbated the problem. Catherine felt more alive when she resisted her husband and her mother than when she gave in. First, Catherine was helped to acknowledge her depression and then to deal with her disillusionment about having a baby. The therapist helped Catherine to accept her exhaustion and her disappointment and to rediscover her enjoyment and desire to be with her baby. In essence, the therapist was helping Catherine to recover her lost desire and motivation to fully experience mothering a child. Although not strictly following Bugental's three phases, there is an increased engagement as Catherine "moved from depression to anxiety" (p. 55) while gaining insights about herself and her baby. As van Deurzen-Smith says, "anxiety was a sign of her engagement with life and expressed her readiness for its inevitable crises" (p. 55). As Catherine accepted her responsibilities for her baby, she grew more confident and dealt self-assuredly with her husband and her mother. Having a sense of direction and will helped her to live authentically.

Borderline Disorder

In working with a young woman whom he diagnosed as having a borderline disorder, Yalom (1980) helped her to "bridge the gulf of isolation" (p. 396) that she experienced with others. Anna had been hospitalized after she had tried to kill herself, and she appeared to be very bitter and isolated.

In her treatment, Anna profited from her participation in group therapy. She had been critical of herself for being phony and for not having real feelings. Often she felt she did not belong and that other people had close relationships that she would not be able to have. In group, she was encouraged to enter the world of the other group members, to be open to their experience and to her own. During one group meeting, Anna was able to become involved with several members, "weeping with and for one of them" (p. 396). Yalom points out that it was important not only for her to have this experience but also to examine the experience and comment on what it had been like. Anna said that she had felt alive and involved and unaware of her usual feeling of isolation.

Dealing with individuals with borderline disorder is long and complex work. The point of this example is to show that borderline clients can be helped when they can engage in a meaningful way with others. In this example, Yalom approaches the conceptualization and treatment of a person with a borderline disorder by focusing on the theme of isolation.

Obsessive-Compulsive Disorder

Frankl (1969, 1992, 1997) developed logotherapy as a means of helping clients deal with meaning in their lives. In working with obsessive-compulsive clients, he developed paradoxical intention, which essentially helps clients get outside themselves in order to deal with their problem. Paradoxical intention helps clients find that their fear does not occur when they try to engage in it. When clients have trust in the therapist, a sense of humor about themselves, and an ability to distance themselves from their problems, they are more likely to experience a positive reaction to paradoxical intention. Unlike the approach of many existential therapists, who focus on existential themes in the lives of clients, the approach of logotherapy is brief and active (Guttmann, 1996).

In the following example of her work with a patient who compulsively looked at herself in the mirror many times during the day, Lukas (1984) not only makes paradoxical suggestions but also participates in the paradoxical intervention herself.

> One of my patients had mirror compulsion that prompted her to run to a mirror up to 20 times a day to make sure that her hair was sufficiently well-groomed. She resisted paradoxical intention until I offered to participate with her in a game of "hair rumpling": We would see who could rumple our hair more thoroughly by attacking it with all ten fingers. Afterwards we ran hand in hand around the block, all the while paradoxically intending to show all passers-by just how wildly our hair "stood on end." When someone passed us without paying any attention, we roughed up our hair a bit more because it obviously was not disheveled enough. This game won the cooperation of the patient who up to then had resisted all paradoxical formulations. Of course, no one paid any attention to us. Who nowadays cares whether someone's hair is well-groomed? My patient realized this and was able to overcome her compulsion to go to the mirror by paradoxically wishing, "Let my hair stand on end. Let it be a mess!" After eight weeks her mirror compulsion was gone. (Lukas, 1984, p. 24)[14]

In using paradoxical intention, Lukas feels that it is important to show that she can identify with her clients and that she takes their problems seriously. By participating with them in the practice of paradoxical intention, she finds that they are likely to accept her intervention, even though it may seem ridiculous at first (p. 83).

Anxiety Disorder

In dealing with anxiety, Yalom (1980) attends to anxiety as it is expressed through a variety of existential themes. His conceptualization focuses not on the physical manifestations of anxiety, but on anxiety as it is expressed in the themes of death, responsibility, intimacy, and time. Each of these themes appears in the case of Philip, a 53-year-old business executive who was a workaholic. Philip enjoyed little in life and had a distant relationship with his wife and children. When Philip lost his high executive position, he developed severe anxiety. He would wake early in the morning and think for hours about his department, his anger, and related issues. He became more anxious as his job finally ended. Yalom describes Philip's death anxiety in this way.

> Gradually in therapy we pried loose his anxiety from the work concerns to which it adhered like barnacles to a pier. It became apparent that Philip had considerable death anxiety. Nightly he was tormented by a dream in which he circled the very edge of a "black pit." Another frightening recurrent dream consisted of his walking on the narrow crest of a steep dune on the beach and losing his balance. He repeatedly awoke from the dream mumbling "I'm not going to make it." (His father was a sailor who drowned before Philip was born.) (Yalom, 1980, p. 209)[15]

Philip experienced a frightening incident one morning at 3 A.M. when he went downstairs to read. He saw at a window a large stocking-masked man. After his terror and panic, it later occurred to him that something could have happened to his wife and children. Yalom's reaction was not to comfort him, but to remind him that eventually something will happen to his wife, to his children, and to himself.

Now that Philip had lost his job, his sense of specialness, and his feeling of invulnerability, he began to deal with the reality of his own death. As he did so, he worked hard to develop intimacy in his life and he began to find meaning in his life.

> As he learned to accept his vulnerability, his sense of communion at first with me and then with his family, deepened; he achieved an intimacy with others he had never previously attained. His orientation to time changed dramatically: no longer did he see time as an enemy—to be concealed or killed. Now, with day after day of free time, he began to savor time and to luxuriate in it. He also became acquainted with other long dormant parts of himself and for the first time in decades allowed some of his creative urges expression in both painting and writing. (Yalom, 1980, p. 210)[16]

Later, Philip found a challenging position and moved to another city. He commented to Yalom that he had grown and learned through his frightening experience of anxiety. Yalom states that "what Philip learned was that a life dedicated to the concealment of reality, to the denial of death, restricts experience and will ultimately cave in upon itself" (1980, p. 210).

Although other therapists might approach anxiety related to a job loss in a variety of ways, Yalom's approach is consistent with his view of the importance of existential themes in psychological growth. For Yalom, death anxiety is an important and common therapeutic issue when clients report a lack of satisfaction in their lives. Issues of intimacy and authenticity are also frequent themes.

Alcoholism

A common existential theme among drug and alcohol abusers is their refusal to take responsibility for their own lives. Bugental (1981, p. 340) points out that such individuals may blame themselves rather than take responsibility for their own behaviors. If therapists allow and support the blaming behaviors of clients, they may introduce an *iatrogenic* complication. Iatrogenic refers to making matters worse. In the following example, Bugental (1981) confronts Harry's self-blaming and focuses on the need for him to take responsibility. Recognizing that Harry uses blame to avoid responsibility, Bugental persists in explaining Harry's actions to him.

Harry was very guilty and ashamed this Tuesday morning, as he was from time to time after he had a drinking bout over the weekend. "So, I did it again! Tied one on, swung my weight around the house, had Leah and the kids terrified. Oh, I'm the big man all right. Just let me get a snoot full and. . . ."

I interrupted him, "You really sound pretty enthusiastic when you get going on cussing yourself out."

"Well, hell, I'm just no damned good. I'm to blame for every lousy thing that's wrong with my family. Why Leah puts up with an eight ball like me is. . . ."

"You're just no good, huh?"

"That's right. I never was any count. My father told me I made mother sick with worry. If I was any good, I'd . . . I'd. . . ."

"Well, there's really nothing to feel badly about, is there?"

"What do you mean?"

"Well, you're no good and never have been any good. So plainly it's not your responsibility. Somebody else messed you up: God or your parents, but you don't have to carry the load."

"What? I'm taking the blame, aren't I? What do you want?"

"Sure, you're taking the blame and dodging the responsibility."

"It's the same thing."

"Is it? I don't think so. I've heard you take the blame a dozen times, and all I can see that it does is pay a little emotional bill for your drunk. Then the next time you can't deal with things you can get drunk again and pay the bill with blaming yourself and do it all over. You've never taken responsibility for yourself, only blame."

"Well, what's the difference?"

"Just this: If you took responsibility for the feeling you had before you started to drink, if you took responsibility for starting to drink, if you took responsibility for the way you treat Leah and the kids when you're loaded—instead of blaming it on the alcohol. . . . If you took it on yourself to know what you were doing at each of those points, what do you think would happen?"

"I wouldn't do it. But, hell, I don't think about it that way. I just get kind of wound up, and I figure a drink would relax me and then before I know it. . . ."

"That's the point: 'Before you know it. . . .' You're not taking responsibility. All you do is sing the 'Ain't I bad!' song so you can do it all over again."

Harry did not get a sweeping insight this time, but we did get two points of importance before his awareness so that we could refer to them again and again in the future: (a) he used blame to avoid responsibility; (b) if he accepted responsibility, he would find that he was fully aware of what he was doing and probably could not slide through the dismal sequence again. In dealing with these recognitions, Harry came to make his first really sincere efforts to inquire into the sources of his needs to get drunk periodically. (Bugental, 1981, pp. 339-340)[17]

BRIEF THERAPY

Because existential therapy represents an attitude toward living and toward the client, to speak of brief existential therapy is to imply that existential therapy is far more systematic than it really is. Most existential therapists have a background in psychoanalysis, which, when combined with existential attitudes, is usually practiced in an indepth manner. In contrast, Frankl's logotherapy often requires less than a few months of treatment. Additionally, pastors and counselors who work with crises such as death of a loved one or loss of a job often use a brief existential approach with their clients.

Although existential therapy may appear to resist attempts to structure it, Freddie Strasser and his daughter, Allison Strasser (Strasser & Strasser, 1997) have developed a time-limited existential therapy with a minimal amount of structure. At the core of their system are two wheels (Figure 5.1). Wheel I has 10 segments with each segment representing the limitations and possibilities that individuals encounter in their world. Wheel II shows therapeutic application of treatment to each segment of Wheel I. Thus segment 7 of Wheel I refers to the four dimensions of existence (Umwelt, Mitwelt, Eigenwelt, and Überwelt). Wheel II, segment 7 applies methods and skills to explore the four worlds. In describing cases, Strasser & Strasser use each of the 10 segments to describe aspects of their work. In helping James deal with his romantic relationship with Stewart, they describe his way of coping with the four worlds in this way:

> James' life centered on his private inner and natural world. This made his relation to the world somewhat unbalanced. He neglected his relationship with his social world and left untended his own spirituality. (p. 185)

In contrast, Frankl (1969, 1992) and his colleagues (Fabry, 1987; Lukas, 1984) have developed a different short-term approach. Because logotherapy makes use of techniques of attitude modulation, dereflection, and paradoxical intention (p. 196), an active and challenging approach is used. Furthermore, many logotherapists use a Socratic dialogue in assisting clients in finding meaning in their lives. Although logotherapy is used with traditional psychological disorders, particularly obsessive-compulsive neurosis, it is used specifically for noögenic neuroses, when clients experience little meaning in their lives, such as when they have too much leisure or abuse drugs. Such an approach may take only a few sessions or require several months of meetings.

Counselors, nurses, social workers, and clergy often do short-term crisis counseling. Common crises include dying, the death of a loved one, the loss of a job, sudden illness, a divorce, and similar life milestones. By combining helping skills with a knowledge of existential themes, these mental health professionals may not only be empathic to the pain of their clients but also be able to help them examine their lives from different points of view.

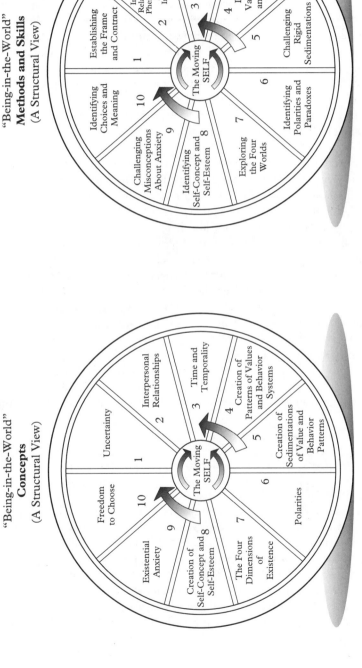

FIGURE 5.1 Strasser's Two Wheels of Existential Concepts and Corresponding Skills
From *Existential Time-Limited Therapy: The Wheel of Existence* by F. Strasser and A. Strasser. Copyright © 1997 John Wiley & Sons Limited. Reproduced with permission.

CURRENT TRENDS

Interest in existential therapy is strongest in Europe. The International Federation for Daseins-analyse has members from many countries. The Society for Existential Analysis, formed in England in 1988, sponsors an annual conference and a journal. Because most existential therapists (and most therapists, in general) had a psychoanalytic orientation in the 1930s and 1940s, much existential writing reflects this background. However, in more recent years, psychotherapists with backgrounds in person-centered psychotherapy, Gestalt therapy, Jungian therapy, feminist therapy, and some cognitive and behavioral approaches have been able to integrate existential attitudes into their work. Such integration is likely to be reflected in actual practice rather than in the writing of academicians. Few psychologists have been attracted to using research to test existential principles (the work of Salvatore Maddi [1996] is a notable exception). Because the dissemination of existentialism takes place through supervision, demonstrations, and reading rather than in systematic research, it is extremely difficult to assess its current impact.

Although the growth of existential therapy is informal, this is not true of Frankl's logotherapy. His writings have been extremely popular, with *Man's Search for Meaning* (1992) selling millions of copies. Also, the Viktor Frankl Institute of Logotherapy publishes a journal, *The International Forum for Logotherapy*. Viktor Frankl not only wrote widely but also spoke throughout the world. There are a number of logotherapy centers, with several active ones in Germany and South America. Because of the emphasis on the spirit in Frankl's writings, many clergy and religious workers find his writings and therapeutic approach consistent with their views that spirit is the key to self.

With its emphasis on phenomenology, the client's subjective experience, existential therapy is consistent with certain aspects of postmodern thought. By emphasizing authenticity, existential therapists help their clients be aware of their own view of reality (such as views on death or responsibility) and not deny their views. Rather than being hindered by techniques that may derive from their own perception of reality, existential therapists concentrate on the client's subjective experience. Some might criticize existentialists, however, for trying to fit client experience into their own notions of universal life themes, finding their approach to be inconsistent with postmodern thought.

USING EXISTENTIAL THERAPY WITH OTHER THEORIES

The value of existential psychotherapy is that it deals with assumptions underlying psychotherapy in general. Because there are no specific techniques (with the exception of a few techniques used by logotherapists), existential psychotherapists must have a background in other psychotherapeutic modalities. With expertise in the use of one or more theoretical approaches to responding to clients' problems, the therapist is then able to attend to existential themes. As May and Yalom (1989) point out, most therapies deal with the client in relationship to the biological or environmental world (*Umwelt*) or relationships with others (*Mitwelt*), but few deal with the individual's relationship to his or her self (*Eigenwelt*), nor with the spiritual self (*Überwelt*) (van Deurzen-Smith, 1997, 1998). It is this emphasis on self-awareness and self-relatedness that distinguishes existential therapy from other therapies. Awareness of self allows both client and therapist to concentrate on existential themes. As the case examples have shown, existential therapists apply a variety of listening skills, confrontative techniques, and other ways of responding while being aware of a variety of existential themes. To do this presupposes that existential psychotherapists have developed counseling skills first, before they integrate their existential philosophy and attitudes.

RESEARCH

Because existential psychotherapy makes use of techniques and practices of other theories, it is very difficult to study its effectiveness. A few studies that have tried to assess whether existential goals were realized in group therapy are discussed here. More common are studies that relate existential themes such as death, anxiety, and meaning to therapeutic issues and individual characteristics. All of these studies use traditional methods of assessment such as interviews and objective tests. In contrast, some existential researchers have focused specifically on the individual's subjective experience and have used a phenomenological approach to understanding psychological disorders and therapeutic change. An overview of the limited research in all of these areas is given in this section.

There seems to be some support for the conclusion that existential themes can be addressed and dealt with successfully in group therapy. Opalic (1989) suggests that an existential approach can be assessed by the Minnesota Multiphasic Personality Inventory (MMPI) and other objective measures. In studying the progress of four groups of bereaved spouses, Yalom and colleagues (Lieberman & Yalom, 1992; Yalom & Lieberman, 1991; Yalom & Vinogradov, 1988) found modest improvement in psychological functioning when they were compared with untreated control bereaved individuals. The investigators implied there was an increasing existential awareness in the experimental group. They suggest that the most helpful roles that leaders could take were in attending to existential issues and themes such as the group members' sense of identity and their responsibility for their future lives. Other studies have examined internal versus external control to assess increasing self-responsibility as a result of group therapy. A recent study (van der Pompe, Duivenvoorden, Antoni, & Visser, 1997) examined the impact of experiential existential group therapy on physiological measures of breast cancer patients. They found positive changes in endocrine and immune functions in a small group of 50- to 70-year-old patients that was not found in a waiting list control group. Although research measuring changes in existential themes in group therapy are few, they are suggestive of the types of exploration of changes in existential themes that can be studied.

Concerns with death as a general issue and, more specifically, the loss of a loved one have been the subject of a variety of investigations. In a large study of dreams of a broad sample of individuals, Kramer, Winget, and Whitman (1971) found that death anxiety was a topic in 29% of reported dreams and that many other themes, such as being chased by someone else, were related to death. In a study of college students who were grieving the death of a family member, Edmonds and Hooker (1992) found that grief can have positive aspects by bringing about growth in existential concerns. Similarly, Kessler (1987) found that positive changes that heighten awareness of existential themes can come about as the result of loss of a loved one. These findings would seem to be consistent with the observations of Yalom and his colleagues in their work with bereaved spouses.

An existential issue of particular concern to Viktor Frankl is that of meaninglessness, or what he refers to as *existential vacuum*. To assess this concept, Crumbaugh (1968) and Crumbaugh & Henrion (1988) have developed the Purpose-in-Life Test (PIL). This instrument has been used both with clients and in research on meaninglessness. Using the PIL with 48 married couples, McCann and Biaggio (1989) found that those individuals who scored high on the PIL also reported higher levels of sexual enjoyment in their marriage than those with low scores on the PIL. Using the Alienation Test, Maddi, Kobasa, and Hoover (1979) and Csikszentmihalyi (1975) found that individuals who scored high on meaninglessness in interpersonal relationships and alienation from family spent more time in solitary activities such as watching television. In their study of college students who had experienced the death of a relative or friend within the past 3 years, Pfost, Stevens, and Wessels (1989) found that those who scored low on the PIL (having little meaning in their lives) reported more anger in response to the death of a friend or relative than did those who scored high on the PIL. Reporting on family members who cared for elderly relatives with Alzheimer's disease, Farren, Keene-Hagerty, Salloway, and Kupferer (1991) concluded that caregivers respond to their experience with their relative by valuing positive aspects of the experience and by searching for meaning in their caregiving. Other studies supporting Frankl's belief that meaning and the search for meaning are a significant issue for many individuals are described in Guttman (1996).

An entirely different approach to research is taken by those who use a phenomenological method. They choose not to use test scores or observations of behavior, but to use individual reports of their own experience (Fischer, 1991, 1996). First, they collect verbatim descriptions from individuals about an actual event, such as being frightened, lonely, or isolated. Then the researchers try to remove their own preconceptions of the subject's experience. Taking each segment of a transcript of a subject's report, they ask questions such as, "What is essential to being fearful?" to assess the subject's relationship with self, others, and the world, using the subject's original language. Then they write a summary of the transcript, including the gradual unfolding of the event. This process is then repeated for each subject in the study. Conclusions are abstracted from the summaries of the subjects.

Fischer (1991) reports that this phenomenological method has been used in more than 135 doctoral dissertations at Duquesne University. The topics of these studies include emotional states such as disappointment, resentment, and anger. Other studies have dealt with disabilities such as brain damage, alcohol addiction, depression, and low back pain. Some topics have included subjects' reaction to psychotherapeutic treatments such as psychodrama, desensitization, the experience of interpretation, and the meaning of psychological change. One qualitative study using two adult men and two adult women showed one approach to using in-depth interviewing methods to understand the importance of spiritual life (*Überwelt*) (Adams, 1996). Although a few academic psychology departments support this method of investigation, such research is relatively rare and tends to be reported in journals such as *Human Studies, Humanistic Psychologist, Journal of Phenomenological Psychology, Review of Existential Psychology and Psychiatry*, and *Journal of the Society for Existential Analysis*.

GENDER ISSUES

Existential therapists tend to see the themes that have been discussed in this chapter as universal, applying to men and women, and may not concentrate on biological and social factors that affect men and women differently. Biological factors affecting women's existential themes are pregnancy, birth, miscarriage, and unwanted pregnancy. The case of Catherine (p. 192), who is suffering from a postpartum depression, is such an example.

Cultures and societies may differ in the sex role expectations that are placed on men and women. However, it is clear that sex role stereotypes do affect the way in which individuals deal with existential themes. In a study of 88 college students, Stevens, Pfost, and Potts (1990) found that masculine-type men and feminine-type women tended to avoid existential issues more than other college students. Because many societies expect women to be subservient to men, women must deal with how to make choices authentically. In contrast, men may feel that they have been given too much responsibility and may hide from it. Being aware of clients' gender role stereotypes can often help the therapist to identify those existential issues the client fears. In addition to genderj204 role concerns, there are societal problems that present great existential challenges. For example, Saynor (1988) and Triggs and McDermott (1991) discuss the impact of confrontation with their own mortality for individuals who test positive for HIV antibodies.

MULTICULTURAL ISSUES

To what extent does existential philosophical thought, which has a Western European history, represent universal values? In contrasting Japanese, Chinese, and Indian theological views as they are represented in Hindu and Buddhist religions, Gould (1993) points out the many similarities between Eastern thought and Frankl's existential psychology. Some differences do exist; for example, many Eastern religions tend to look at the universe as a whole and focus less on the separation between humans and other living and nonliving things than does existential philosophy. Furthermore, as Yalom (1980) points out, Indian philosophers and theologians tend to view life as a mystery to be lived, whereas Western thinkers tend to focus on life as a problem to be solved. Loy (1996) describes the commonalities inherent in Buddhism and existentialism showing how both work toward transcendence of dependence and hostility and deal with somewhat similar topics. In discussing cross-cultural counseling, Vontress (1988) points out that clients and counselors are members of the same universal culture and must deal with a variety of existential themes. In general, existential psychotherapy seems to strike universal chords, as evidenced by the popularity of Frankl's logotherapy throughout the world.

Because existential therapy emphasizes individuals' responsibility and their struggle with mortality and isolation, sociocultural factors may be overlooked. Examining cultural values and existential themes provides a perspective that existential philosophy itself does not. For inner-city African American children in grades 5 through 7, identification with Afrocultural values was related to an altruistic view of human nature, cooperative and competitive academic attitudes, and spirituality (Jagers, Smith, Mock,

& Dill, 1997). The Spirituality Scale has been developed to study spirituality from an Afrocultural perspective (Jagers & Smith, 1996). Studying existential themes as they relate to cultural values of different groups serves to widen the application of existential therapy. Recognizing the external pressures of discrimination and oppression can help therapists increase their understanding of the forces that have an impact on existential themes and crises.

Van Deurzen-Smith (1988) finds that existential counseling is particularly relevant for work with cross-cultural issues and that existential themes can provide guidance for working with crisis situations. She gives the example of Gabriel, a young man from Africa, who came to England to study. At home, he was a prominent member of his society who was treated with respect. In England, he became very confused by the expectations of fellow students, stopped attending classes, and was doubting his decision to come to England. He felt isolated from his country and alone.

> To remain in contact with his homeland and culture he had begun to prolong the daily rituals of cleansing himself of the influence of his new environment. The rituals involved the use of water and one day he unintentionally provoked a minor flood in the residential hall of the college. (pp. 31–32)

Gabriel denied responsibility for the flooding and explained that his ancestors had made the flood happen because they disapproved of his new way of life. Hearing this explanation, administrators and students questioned Gabriel's sanity, as they made judgments about his behavior based on their own cultural experience. Van Deurzen-Smith explained the existential counseling approach to Gabriel.

> What was needed was in the first place that the counselor grasped his isolation and the essential cultural miscommunication that had been taking place. Gabriel had not had a fair chance of fully presenting the situation from his own perspective. In the second place he lacked the plain and simple comprehension of what people were trying to get him to do. An explanation of Western notions of personal responsibility and honour went a long way toward easing the situation for him. He had felt accused, when he was only asked not to deny his part in an event. He had felt offended in his honour when people rejected his mention of his ancestors as the origin of all this. Western dismissal of magical thinking seemed like a personal affront. While he needed to be understood from his perspective he also needed to be told about the perspective that he misunderstood himself. (p. 33)[18]

In essence, what van Deurzen-Smith did was to help Gabriel transcend his immediate situation and look at it from a perspective outside himself. Further, she was able to understand Gabriel's issues from the point of view of the existential theme of isolation and then deal with his crises in the new culture.

COUPLES AND FAMILY COUNSELING

Approaches to existential couples and family counseling deal with not only the relationship between the individuals but also the awareness that individuals have of themselves and their own being-in-the-world. Several approaches to being aware of oneself and the family relationship illustrate an existential approach to family change and an emphasis on the need to create new patterns of living. A particular interest of logotherapists has been family counseling and approaches to it. Relatively little distinction is made between couples and family counseling among many existential therapists, and these two areas are combined in this section.

The importance of being outside oneself to get a new perspective on patterns and problems can be illustrated by several strategies suggested by existential therapists. In helping couples become more aware of their partner's inner world and their own, van Deurzen-Smith (1988, p. 96) suggests that the therapist conduct a counseling session with one partner while the other partner observes and says nothing. Therapy can occur with partners taking turns at being the observer, as well as sessions in which both partners participate. Another approach to accessing the inner world is that of Burton (1967, p. 90) who suggests that each partner keep a secret diary during the course of therapy to make entries about the private world of each. Such an approach allows marital partners to see issues about which they may disagree from a less involved perspective.

Lantz (1996) sees the therapist in couples therapy as a host. It is the hosts' role to help the couple see the potential for meaning in their relationship. Then the host assesses ways in which the couple can join together to bring meaning into their relationship.

The essence of Frankl's logotherapy is that meaning exists in all situations. Applying this to family therapy, logotherapists examine the meaning in the family relationship and use logotherapeutic techniques to bring about change (Lentz, 1986). In helping a family search for meaning, logotherapeutic techniques such as dereflection, attitude modulation, and paradoxical intention can be used with families to develop new strategies and change patterns (Lentz, 1989). Additionally, by taking a family history that emphasizes the role of meaning in life, by using Socratic dialogue, and by making unusual or provocative comments to bring about change, a therapist can help the family develop a sense of meaning.

When used in logotherapy, Socratic dialogue often reflects the philosophical nature of existential therapy. Guttmann (1996) shows how Hiroshi Takashima (1990) uses this with a family issue. A 50-year-old woman who had cared for her sick child for years was grieving over her daughter's death and had become suicidal. Takashima uses questions to help the woman deal with death and the suffering that results.

Q: If your daughter were alive, who amongst you would suffer?

A: My daughter.

Q: Do you still love her?

A: Yes, very much.

Q: Would you be willing to suffer instead of her, if she were alive?

A: Of course, I would suffer willingly.

Q: But she has already died and cannot suffer. And thus you can suffer instead of her—if someone has to suffer. Let me give you an example: Suppose that suffering is like water. You are now drowning in the water, and you try to save yourself, despite your feeling that it can't be done, correct?

A: I simply cannot.

Q: But in the water of suffering you can swim instead of drowning, isn't it so?

A: Yes, I think so.

Q: You can even swim nicely?

A: Yes, I will try to do so.

Takashima adds that this simple, uneducated woman was able to understand that her suffering had a meaning, and she accepted it. She changed her attitude to suffering, from the negative and self-destroying, to a positive and constructive one. She and her husband held hands. She cured herself by her wisdom, orientation to meaning, and free decision (Takashima, 1990, pp. 98–100).

GROUP COUNSELING AND PSYCHOTHERAPY

Group counseling and psychotherapy can be an excellent format to deal with existential issues (May & Yalom, 1989). Corey (2000) sees the purpose of an existential group as helping people make a "commitment to a life long journey of self exploration" (p. 238). The atmosphere of a group helps individuals search inside themselves and attend to their own subjective experience while sharing these experiences with others who have similar goals. In this way, meaningful issues and questions can be dealt with and respected. This section briefly addresses from the point of view of group therapy the four major existential themes discussed in this chapter: living and dying; freedom, responsibility, and choice; isolation and loving; and meaning and meaninglessness.

Living and Dying

A group format provides an excellent opportunity to deal with issues regarding living life fully and purposefully with awareness and authenticity. In his approach to existential group work, Corey asks, How meaningful is your life? How would you answer this if you knew you were about to die? Have you made decisions that you have not acted on? A group is a safe place for people to express sadness about change, difficulties in changing, and fears of death and incompleteness. Additionally, Spira (1997) discusses the value of having patients in the group who are confronting their own deaths cope with their diagnosis, adjust to their illness, and live more fully with it.

Freedom, Responsibility, and Choice

In a group, individuals are responsible for their own existence, actions, and miseries. When existential therapists observe group members viewing themselves as victims and as helpless, they point out that the group members are not taking responsibility for their own lives (Corey, 2000).

Yalom sees clients as "born simultaneously: each starts out in the group on an equal footing" (1980, p. 239). For Yalom, the group is an excellent place for individuals to become aware of their own responsibility through the feedback of the members and the leader. In groups, patients can learn how their behavior is viewed by others, how they make others feel, how their behavior influences others' opinions of them, and how their behavior in group influences their own opinions of themselves. In a group, members have not only responsibility for themselves but also an obligation for the functioning of the group. In this way, a group becomes a small social system (Yalom, 1980). It is the leader's task to be aware of group processes, to encourage members to act appropriately in group, and to discuss the matter of members' participation in group.

Isolation and Loving

A group experience provides the opportunity to develop close and real relationships with others. Individuals can learn to be themselves and to be authentic, and they find that it is a rewarding experience. The ways of relating that are learned in group can be applied to people outside the group so that a sense of intimacy can develop. The development of intimacy is illustrated by the following example of Eve, who had been passive and a peripheral member of a group for 6 months.

> I asked Eve if she could try to engage any of the members. She compliantly went around the group and discussed, in a platitudinous manner, her feelings toward each person. "How would you rank," I asked, "your comments to each member on a one-to-ten risk-taking scale?" "Very low," she ventured, "about two to three." "What would happen," I said, "if you were to move up a rung or two?" She replied that she would tell the group that she was an alcoholic! This was, indeed, a revelation—she had told no one before. I then tried to help her open herself even more by asking her to talk about how she felt coming to the group for so many months and not being able to tell us that. Eve responded by talking about how lonely she felt in the group, how cut off she was from every person in the room. But she was flushed with shame about her drinking. She could not, she insisted, be "with" others or make herself known to others because of her drinking.
>
> I turned Eve's formula around (here the real therapeutic work began): *she did not hide herself because she drank, but she drank because she hid herself!* She drank because she was so unengaged with the world. Eve then talked about coming home, feeling lost and alone, and at that point doing one of two things: either slumping into a reverie where she imagined herself very young and being cared for by the big people, or assuaging the pain of her lostness and loneliness with alcohol. Gradually Eve began to understand that she was relating to others for a specific function—to be protected and taken care of—and that, in the service of this function, she was relating only partially. (Yalom, 1980, p. 394)[19]

Group often serves as a way to engage with others and to develop a sense of intimacy that individual therapy cannot provide.

Meaning and Meaninglessness

The group experience allows individuals to reexamine their values and compare them with the values of others in the group. Often group members challenge the values of another member, forcing that person to deal with his sense of identity and his purpose in life (Corey, 2000). When values are present in a group but unexamined, group members are likely to confront and challenge. In such a way, group members and leaders can be supportive yet confrontative as individuals search for a purpose and meaning in their lives.

Because they deal with important life issues, existential groups tend to meet for a year or more and to be emotionally intense. As the leader fosters sincere relationships among participants, caring and concern are developed for other participants. By being themselves (authentic), leaders encourage members to challenge themselves and others to bring about personal growth.

SUMMARY

Existential therapy is an attitude toward life, a way of being, and a way of interacting with oneself, others, and the environment. Rooted in 19th century Western European philosophy, existential philosophy was applied to psychotherapy by the Swiss psychiatrists Ludwig Binswanger and Medard Boss. Other existential psychotherapists, both in the United States and in Europe, have examined a variety of issues as they affect the human experience.

Existential therapists, in their focus on individuals' relationships with themselves, others, and the environment, are concerned with universal themes. In this chapter, the existential themes provide a means of conceptualizing personality and of helping individuals find meaning in their lives through the psychotherapeutic process. All individuals are "thrown" into the world and ultimately face death. How they face their own deaths and those of others is an important concern of existential therapists. Individuals are seen not as victims, but as responsible for their own lives, with the ability to exercise freedom and make choices. Dealing with the anxiety that can evolve from these concerns is an aspect of existential therapy. Forming relationships with others that are nonmanipulative and intimate is a goal of existential therapy that often arises from a sense of isolation and loneliness. Finding a sense of meaning in the world has been a particular concern of Viktor Frankl and those who use his logotherapeutic techniques. Significant therapeutic issues in existential psychotherapy concern transference, countertransference, and resistance. Most existential psychotherapists take an attitudinal or thematic approach to therapy and do not use techniques, although Frankl does make use of techniques.

Exploring existential themes is done in marriage and family therapy as well as in group therapy. In these modalities, there is an emphasis not only on relationships between members of the group or family but also on individuals' experience of their own sense of themselves. Existential issues transcend culture and gender, although certain biological and social realities are encountered differently, depending upon one's gender or cultural identification.

Suggested Readings

YALOM, I. D. (1980). *Existential psychotherapy*. New York: Basic Books.   •   This excellent book, the source for much of the material in this chapter, deals in depth with existential themes that are covered only briefly here. Yalom uses many clinical examples to illustrate existential themes.

YALOM, I. D. (1989). *Love's executioner*. New York: Basic Books.   •   In this selection of 10 case studies, Yalom demonstrates his existential approach to psychotherapy. The cases are engaging and fully developed.

BUGENTAL, J. F. T. (1987). *The art of the psychotherapist*. New York: Norton. • Bugental describes his own in-depth approach to psychotherapy. The book is clear and well organized.

COHN, H. W. (1997). *Existential thought and therapeutic process*. London: Sage. • This short book contrasts existential therapy with psychoanalysis. Subjects that are discussed include anxiety, guilt, the unconscious, dreams, and sexuality.

DEURZEN-SMITH, VAN E. (1997). *Everyday mysteries: Existential dimensions of psychotherapy*. London: Routledge. • Included are a discussion of philosophical contributions to existential therapy and a discussion of the existential worldview. Major existential psychotherapists' contributions are illustrated.

FRANKL, V. (1992). *Man's search for meaning*. Boston: Washington Square Press. • This very popular book, in its 26th edition, is an autobiographical account of Frankl's own search for meaning during his experience in World War II Nazi concentration camps. Additionally, he describes his development of logotherapy and its basic approaches.

References

ADAMS, W. (1996). Discovering the sacred in everyday life: An empirical phenomenological study. *Humanistic Psychology, 24*, 28–54.

BAUM, S. M., & STEWART, R. B. (1990). Sources of meaning through the lifespan. *Psychological Reports, 67*, 3–14.

BINSWANGER, L. (1975). *Being-in-the-world: Selected papers of Ludwig Binswanger*. London: Souvenir Press.

BOSS, M. (1963). *Psychoanalysis and daseinanalysis*. New York: Basic Books.

BOSS, M. (1977). *Existential foundations of medicine and psychology*. New York: Aronson.

BUBER, M. (1961). The way of man according to the teachings of Hasidism. In W. Kaufman (Ed.), *Religion from Tolstoy to Camus* (pp. 425–441). New York: Harper Torchbooks.

BUBER, M. (1965). *The knowledge of man* (M. Friedman & R. 0. Smith, Trans.). New York: Harper Torchbooks.

BUBER, M. (1970). *I and thou* (W. Kaufman, Trans.). New York: Scribner's.

BUGENTAL, J. F. T. (1976). *The search for existential identity: Patient-therapist dialogues in humanistic psychotherapy*. San Francisco: Jossey-Bass.

BUGENTAL, J. F. T. (1978). *Psychotherapy and process: The fundamentals of an existential-humanistic approach*. Reading, MA: Addison-Wesley.

BUGENTAL, J. F. T. (1981). *The search for authenticity: An existential-analytic approach to psychotherapy* (Rev. ed.). New York: Holt, Rinehart & Winston.

BUGENTAL, J. F. T. (1987). *The art of the psychotherapist*. New York: Norton.

BURTON, A. (1967). *Modern humanistic psychotherapy*. San Francisco: Jossey-Bass.

CANNON, B. (1991). *Sartre and psychoanalysis*. Wichita: University Press of Kansas.

COHN, H. W. (1997). *Existential thought and therapeutic practice: An introduction to existential psychotherapy*. London: Sage.

COREY, G. (2000). *Theory and practice of group counseling* (5th ed.). Pacific Grove, CA: Brooks/Cole.

CRUMBAUGH, J. C. (1968). Cross validation of Purpose-in-Life Test based on Frankl's concept. *Journal of Individual Psychology, 24*, 74–81.

CRUMBAUGH, J. C., & HENRION, R. (1988). PIL Test: Administration, interpretation, uses, theory and critique. *The International Forum for Logotherapy Journal of Search for Meaning, 11*, 76–88.

CSIKSZENTMIHALYI, M. (1975). *Beyond boredom and anxiety*. San Francisco: Jossey-Bass.

DEURZEN-SMITH, E. VAN (1988). *Existential counseling in practice*. Newbury Park, CA: Sage.

DEURZEN-SMITH, E. VAN (1995). *Existential therapy*. London: Society for Existential Analysis.

DEURZEN-SMITH, E. VAN (1997). *Everyday mysteries: Existential dimensions of psychotherapy.* London: Routledge.

DEURZEN-SMITH, E. VAN (1998). *Paradox and passion in psychotherapy: An existential approach to therapy and counselling.* Chichester, UK: Wiley.

EDMONDS, S., & HOOKER, K. (1992). Perceived changes in life meaning following bereavement. *Omega Journal of Death and Dying, 25,* 307–318.

ELLENBERGER, H. E. (1958). A clinical introduction to psychiatric phenomenology and existential analysis. In R. May, E. Angel, & H. F. Ellenberger (Eds.), *Existence: A new dimension in psychiatry and psychology* (pp. 92–124). New York: Basic Books.

FABRY, J. B. (1987). *The pursuit of meaning* (Rev. ed.). Berkeley, CA: Institute of Logotherapy Press.

FARREN, C. J., KEENE-HAGERTY, E., SALLOWAY, S., & KUPFERER, S. (1991). Finding meaning: An alternative paradigm for Alzheimer's disease family caregivers. *Gerontologist, 31,* 483–489.

FISCHER, C. (1991). Phenomenological-existential psychotherapy. In M. Hersen, A. E. Kazdin, & A. S. Bellack (Eds.), *The clinical psychology handbook* (2nd ed., pp. 535–550). New York: Pergamon Press.

FISCHER, C. (1996). A humanistic and human science approach to emotion. In C. Magai & S. H. McFadden (Eds.), *Handbook of emotion, adult development, and aging* (pp. 67–82). San Diego: Academic Press.

FRANK, M. L. B. (1997). Existential theory. In D. Capuzzi & D. R. Gross (Eds.), *Counseling and psychotherapy: Theories and interventions* (2nd ed., pp. 151–178). Upper Saddle River, NJ: Merrill.

FRANKL, V. (1965). *The doctor and the soul.* New York: Bantam Books.

FRANKL, V. (1969). *The will to meaning: Foundations and applications of logotherapy.* New York: New American Library.

FRANKL, V. (1978). *The unheard cry for meaning.* New York: Simon & Schuster.

FRANKL, V. (1992). *Man's search for meaning: An introduction to logotherapy.* Boston: Beacon Press. (Original work published 1963.)

FRANKL, V. (1997). *Viktor Frankl—Recollections: An autobiography.* New York: Plenum.

GELVEN, M. (1989). *A commentary on Heidegger's* Being and Time (Rev. ed.). De Kalb, IL: Northern Illinois University Press.

GENDLIN, E. T., & TOMLINSON, T. M. (1967). The process conception and its measurement. In C. R. Rogers, E. I. Gendlin, D. J. Kiesier, & C. B. Truax (Eds.), *The therapeutic relationship and its impact: A study of psychotherapy with schizophrenics* (pp. 109–131). Madison, WI: University of Wisconsin Press.

GOULD, W. B. (1993). *Viktor E. Frankl: Life with meaning.* Pacific Grove, CA: Brooks/Cole.

GUTTMANN, D. (1996). *Logotherapy for the helping professional: Meaningful social work.* New York: Springer.

HEIDEGGER, M. (1962). *Being and time* (J. Macquarrie & E. Robinson, Trans.). New York: Harper & Row. (Original work published 1927.)

JAGERS, R. J., & SMITH, P. (1996). Further examination of the Spirituality Scale. *Journal of Black Psychology, 22,* 429–442.

JAGERS, R. J., SMITH, P., MOCK, L. O., & DILL, E. (1997). An Afrocultural social ethos: Component orientations and some social implications. *Journal of Black Psychology, 23,* 328–343.

KESSLER, B. G. (1987). Bereavement and personal growth. *Journal of Humanistic Psychology, 27,* 228–247.

KIERKEGAARD, S. (1954). *Fear and trembling and the sickness unto death* (W. Lowrie, Trans.). Garden City, NY: Doubleday. (Original work published 1843.)

KOBASA, S. C., & MADDI, S. R. (1977). Existential personality theory. In R. J. Corsini (Ed.), *Current personality theories* (pp. 243–276). Itasca, IL: Peacock.

KRAMER, M., WINGET, C., & WHITMAN, R. (1971). A city dreams: A survey approach to normative dream content. *American Journal of Psychiatry, 127,* 86–92.

LAING, R. D. (1961). *Self and others*. Harmondsworth, England: Penguin.

LANTZ, J. (1996). The existential psychotherapist as host in couples therapy. In B. J. Brothers (Ed.), *Couples: Building bridges* (pp. 67–78). New York: Haworth.

LENTZ, J. (1986). Family logotherapy. *Contemporary Family Therapy, an International Journal, 8*, 124–135.

LENTZ, J. (1989). Family logotherapy with an overweight family. *Contemporary Family Therapy, an International Journal, 11*, 287–297.

LIEBERMAN, M. A., & YALOM, I. (1992). Brief group psychotherapy for the spousally bereaved: A controlled study. *International Journal of Group Psychotherapy, 42*, 117–132.

LOWRIE, W. (1962). *Kierkegaard* (2 Vols.). New York: Harper. (Original work published 1938.)

LOY, D. (1996). *Lack and transcendence: The problem of death and life in psychotherapy, existentialism, and Buddhism*. Atlantic Highlands, NJ: Humanities Press.

LUKAS, E. (1984). *Meaningful living*. Berkeley, CA: Institute of Logotherapy Press.

MADDI, S. R. (1996). *Personality theories* (6th ed.). Pacific Grove, CA: Brooks/Cole.

MADDI, S. R., KOBASA, S. C., & HOOVER, M. (1979). An alienation test. *Journal of Humanistic Psychology, 19*, 73–76.

MAY, R. (1950). *The meaning of anxiety*. New York: Ronald Press.

MAY, R. (1953). *Man's search for himself*. New York: Dell.

MAY, R. (1958a). The origins and significance of existential movement in psychology. In R. May, E. Angel, & H. E. Ellenberger (Eds.), *Existence: A new dimension in psychiatry and psychology* (pp. 3–36). New York: Basic Books.

MAY, R. (1958b). Contributions of existential psychotherapy. In R. May, E. Angel, & H. E. Ellenberger (Eds.), *Existence: A new dimension in psychiatry and psychology* (pp. 37–92). New York: Basic Books.

MAY, R. (1961). *Existential psychology*. New York: Random House.

MAY, R. (1966). *Psychology and the human dilemma*. New York: Norton.

MAY, R. (1969). *Love and will*. New York: Norton.

MAY, R. (1972). *Power and innocence: A search for the sources of violence*. New York: Norton.

MAY, R. (1975). *The courage to create*. New York: Norton.

MAY, R. (1977). *The meaning of anxiety* (Rev. ed.). New York: Norton.

MAY, R. (1981). *Freedom and destiny*. New York: Norton.

MAY, R. (1989). *The art of counseling*. New York: Gardner.

MAY, R. (1992). *The cry for myth*. New York: Norton.

MAY, R., ANGEL, E., & ELLENBERGER, H. (Eds.). (1958). *Existence: A new dimension in psychiatry and psychology*. New York: Basic Books.

MAY, R., & YALOM, I. (1989). Existential psychotherapy. In R. J. Corsini & D. Wedding (Eds.), *Current psychotherapies* (4th ed., pp. 363–402). Itasca, IL: F. E. Peacock.

MCCANN, J. T., & BIAGGIO, M. K. (1989). Sexual satisfaction in marriage as a function of life meaning. *Archives of Sexual Behavior, 18*, 59–72.

MINKOWSKI, E. (1958). Findings in a case of schizophrenic depression (B. Bliss, Trans.). In R. May, E. Angel, & H. F. Ellenberger (Eds.), *Existence: A new dimension in psychiatry and psychology* (pp. 127–138). New York: Basic Books.

MURRAY, H. H. (1943). *Thematic Apperception Test manual*. Cambridge, MA: Harvard University Press.

OPALIC, P. (1989). Existential and psychopathological evaluation of group psychotherapy of neurotic and psychotic patients. *International Journal of Group Psychotherapy, 39*, 389–411.

PFOST, K. S., STEVENS, M. J., & WESSELS, A. B. (1989). Relationship of purpose in life to grief experience in response to the death of a significant other. *Death Studies, 13*, 371–378.

POMPE, G. VAN DER, DUIVENVOORDEN, H. J., ANTONI, M. H., & VISSER, A. (1997). Effectiveness of a short-term group psychotherapy program on endocrine and immune function in breast cancer patients: An exploratory study, *Journal of Psychosomatic Research, 42*, 453–466.

SARTRE, J. P. (1956). *Being and nothingness* (H. E. Barnes, Trans.). New York: Philosophical Library.

SAYNOR, J. K. (1988). Existential and spiritual concerns of people with AIDS. *Journal of Pallative Care, 4,* 61–65.

SEQUIN, C. (1965). *Love and psychotherapy.* New York: Libra.

SPIEGELBERG, H. (1971). *The phenomenological movement: A historical introduction* (2nd ed., 2 Vols.). The Hague: Nijhoff.

SPIRA, J. L. (1997). Existential group therapy for advanced breast cancer and other life-threatening illnesses. In Spira, J. L. (Ed.), *Group therapy for medically ill patients* (pp. 165–122). New York: Guilford.

STEVENS, M. J., PFOST, K. S., & POTTS, M. W. (1990). Sex-role orientation and the willingness to confront existential issues. *Journal of Counseling and Development, 68,* 414–416.

STRASSER, F., & STRASSER, A. (1997). *Existential time-limited therapy: The wheel of existence.* Chichester, England: Wiley.

TAKASHIMA, H. (1990). *Humanistic psychosomatic medicine.* Tel-Aviv. (In Hebrew.)

TILLICH, P. (1952). *The courage to be.* New Haven, CT: Yale University Press.

TRIGGS, J., & McDERMOTT, D. (1991). Short-term counseling strategies for university students who test HIV-positive: The case of John Doe. *Journal of College Student Development, 32,* 17–23.

VONTRESS, C. E. (1988). An existential approach to cross-cultural counseling. *Journal of Multicultural Counseling and Development, 16,* 73–83.

YALOM, I. D. (1980). *Existential psychotherapy.* New York: Basic Books.

YALOM, I. D. (1989). *Love's executioner.* New York: Basic Books.

YALOM, I. D., & LIEBERMAN, M. A. (1991). Bereavement and heightened existential awareness. *Psychiatry, 54,* 334–345.

YALOM, I. D., & VINOGRADOV, S. C. (1988). Bereavement groups: Techniques and themes. *International Journal of Group Psychotherapy, 38,* 419–446.

6

Person-Centered Therapy

First called *nondirective therapy*, later *client-centered therapy*, and currently *person-centered therapy*, this therapeutic approach, developed by Carl Rogers, takes a positive view of individuals, believing that they tend to move toward becoming fully functioning. Rogers's work represents a way of being rather than a set of techniques for doing therapy. Emphasizing understanding and caring rather than diagnosis, advice, and persuasion, Rogers believed that therapeutic change could take place if only a few conditions were met. The client must be anxious or incongruent and in contact with the therapist. Therapists must be genuine, in that their words, nonverbal behavior, and feelings agree with each other. They must also accept the client and care unconditionally for the client. Furthermore, they must understand the client's thoughts, ideas, experiences, and feelings and communicate this empathic understanding to the client. If clients are able to perceive these conditions as offered by the therapist, Rogers believed that therapeutic change will take place.

Rogers applied the core concepts of genuineness, acceptance, and empathy to a variety of human behaviors. He was committed to the group process as a positive means for bringing about personal change and trusted in the growthful characteristics of group members. Other areas of application included marriage and couples counseling, education, and administration. Especially in his later life, Rogers was committed to applying person-centered concepts to deal with international conflicts and to promote world peace. Person-centered therapy changed and grew, as did Carl Rogers's approach to personality and psychotherapy.

HISTORY OF PERSON-CENTERED THERAPY

Born in a suburb of Chicago (Oak Park) in 1902, Carl Rogers was the fourth of six children (five were boys). Rogers (1961) describes his parents as loving, affectionate, and in control of their children's behavior. Because both parents were religious fundamentalists, the children learned that dancing, alcohol, cards, and theater were off-limits to them. When Carl was 12, his father, a prosperous civil engineer and contractor, moved the family to a farm west of Chicago.

CARL ROGERS

Much of Carl Rogers's adolescent life was spent in solitary pursuits. Because he attended three different high schools and commuted long distances to each one, he did not participate in extracurricular activities. Reading adventure stories and agricultural books occupied much of his time. In the summers, he spent long hours operating farm equipment in the fields (Kirschenbaum, 1979). His interest in agriculture, as shown by raising farm animals and collecting and breeding a specific type of moth, led him to pursue agriculture as a career at the University of Wisconsin. However, because of his participation in religious conferences, particularly one in China, he shifted his career goals to the ministry (Rogers, 1961). In China Rogers questioned the religious views that he had learned as a child and broadened his conception of religion.

Upon graduation from Wisconsin, he married Helen Elliott and went to New York City to study at the Union Theological Seminary. After completing 2 years there, he transferred to Columbia University Teachers College to study clinical and educational psychology; he received his Ph.D. in clinical psychology in 1931. Perhaps one reason for pursuing psychology instead of the ministry was Rogers's reluctance to tell others what they should do. He did not feel he should be in a field where he must profess a certain set of beliefs (Thorne, 1992).

Person-centered therapy can be divided into four stages or phases. The first, a developmental stage, includes Rogers's early professional years. His nondirective stage marked the beginning of his theoretical development and his emphasis on understanding the client and communicating that understanding. The third stage, client-centered, involved more theoretical development of personality and psychotherapeutic change, as well as a continued focus on the person rather than on techniques. The fourth stage, person-centered, goes beyond individual psychotherapy to include marriage counseling, group therapy, and political activism and change. The gradual formation of these stages and Rogers's contribution to psychotherapy is discussed next.

His first position was in the child study department at the Society for the Prevention of Cruelty to Children in Rochester, New York. During the first 8 of his 12 years in Rochester, he was involved in diagnosing and treating delinquent and underprivileged children who were referred by the courts and social agencies (Rogers, 1961). His early work was influenced by psychoanalytic concepts, but gradually his view changed as he realized "that it is the *client* who knows what hurts, what directions to go, what problems are crucial, what experiences have been buried" (Rogers, 1961, pp. 11–12). During his time in Rochester, he wrote *The Clinical Treatment of the Problem Child* (1939) and trained and supervised social workers and psychologists.

In 1940, Rogers moved to Columbus, Ohio, to start an academic career in clinical psychology at Ohio State University. Due mainly to his successful book, he was offered the rank of full professor. While Rogers was at Ohio State University, the second stage (nondirective) of his theoretical approach was articulated (Holdstock & Rogers, 1977). When giving a paper at the University of Minnesota in 1940, he became aware that his views on psychotherapy were a new contribution to the field. His focus was on the client's taking responsibility for himself. Important was the therapist's relationship with clients, which established trust and permission for clients to explore their feelings and themselves and thus take more responsibility for their lives. Reflection of the client's feelings and clarifications that led to an understanding of client feelings were the essence of Rogers's therapy at this point. Questions were used rarely, as they might interfere with the client's personal growth. The Minnesota lecture and his book *Counseling and Psychotherapy* (1942a) were controversial—enthusiastically received by some, criticized vehemently by others (Thorne, 1992).

How did Carl Rogers come to develop this new nondirective approach? During his work with children in Rochester, Rogers was influenced by a seminar led by Otto Rank. Additionally, a social worker at the Rochester clinic, Elizabeth Davis, and a student of Rank's, Jessie Taft, shared their interpretation of Rank's ideas, which were to have considerable impact on Rogers's thinking (Rogers & Haigh, 1983). Rank, who had previously broken away from Freud's psychoanalytic approach, focused not on ego and id, but rather was struck by the creativity of individuals. For Rank, the goal of therapy was to help individuals accept their uniqueness and responsibility for their lives. To achieve this goal of self-empowerment and expression, the therapist needed to take a role as a nonjudgmental helper rather than as an expert or authority (Rank, 1945). Unlike psychoanalysts, Rank did not emphasize techniques or past history but rather the uniqueness of the individual and the need to attend to that individual's experience.

Adler's theoretical views had less direct influence on Rogers's therapy. Rogers and Adler shared an emphasis on the value of the individual and the need for good relationships with others. Both believed that individuals should be viewed holistically and as persons who can develop creatively and responsibly.

A concept that has been important to the development of person-centered therapy has been that of self-actualization. Originated by Kurt Goldstein (1959), self-actualization implies that individuals seek and are capable of healthy development, which leads to full expression of themselves. Goldstein's writings were furthered by Maslow (1968, 1987), who developed humanistic psychology. Not a therapist, Maslow focused on the needs and characteristics of "normal" individuals and wrote about love, creativity, and "peak experiences"—the state in which an individual might feel pure relaxation or, more commonly, intense excitement. Maslow (1987) stressed significant aspects of being human including freedom, rationality, and subjectivity. In writing about human needs, Maslow (1987) wrote not only of the need to satisfy physiological needs, such as hunger and thirst, and security and safety needs, but also the importance of searching for belongingness, love, self-esteem, and self-actualization. For Maslow, self-actualization meant to become all that one can be and thus to live a life that brings meaning and accomplishment. Maslow's positive view of humanity is congruent with Rogers's in that both take a positive and optimistic view of humanity, called *humanism*.

Additionally, Rogers's views of humanity and therapy have been affected by existentialist writers. Both existentialism and person-centered therapy stressed the importance of freedom, choice, individual values, and self-responsibility. Although much existentialist writing deals with anxiety and difficult human experiences such as meaningfulness, responsibility, and death, a more pessimistic view than that of Rogers, writers such as Buber and May have much in common with person-centered therapy. Rogers and May (Kirschenbaum & Henderson, 1989) had an active correspondence that contrasts Rogers's positive humanistic views with May's more negative existentialist ones. Additionally, Rogers valued the views of Martin Buber on the "I-thou" dialogue and the impact of human relationships on individuals (Cissna & Anderson,

1997). The existentialist emphasis on being in the present and understanding the clients' phenomenological world is shared by Rogers.

Although the influences of Rank, Adler, and existential and humanistic thinkers can be seen in Rogers's writings, many of his early writings are quite practical and reflect his therapeutic experience. *Counseling and Psychotherapy* (1942a) describes the nature of the counseling relationship and the application of nondirective approaches. His view of the processes of counseling and extensive excerpts from his therapy with Herbert Bryant illustrate his therapeutic style during his nondirective stage. Rogers fully enters the subjective state of his client, feeling what it is like to be Herbert Bryant.

In 1945, Rogers left Ohio State for the University of Chicago, where he continued to develop his theory and to conduct research into its effectiveness. His client-centered stage began with the publication of *Client-Centered Therapy: Its Current Practice, Implications, and Theory* (1951). In this book, client-centered therapy was extended to include a theory of personality and applications to children, groups, leadership training, and teaching. The concept of reflection of feelings and incongruity between the experiencing self and the ideal self were fully discussed, as were the clients' and counselors' growth in the therapeutic process. In a detailed analysis of Rogers's recorded interviews between 1940 and 1986, Brodley (1994) showed that Rogers was more theoretically consistent in the third phase (client-centered) than in the nondirective phase, as almost all (96%) of his responses to clients were "empathic following responses," whereas earlier he had made more interventions from his own, rather than a client's, frame of reference.

While at the University of Chicago, Carl Rogers was both professor of psychology and director of the university counseling center. During this time he was involved in training and research with graduate students and colleagues. His work was recognized by the American Psychological Association in 1956, with the Distinguished Scientific Contribution Award. Both this award and the publication of *Client-Centered Therapy* brought Rogers considerable recognition from within and beyond the United States.

Rogers's scholarly accomplishments can serve to mask the intensity and earnestness of his approach to therapy. While at the University of Chicago, he was in an intense therapeutic relationship with a young woman (Rogers, 1972). In his work with her, Rogers found it difficult for him to separate his own "self" from the client's. Although he sought help from his colleagues, he felt that the intensity was too much. One morning, after making a referral for the client, he walked out of his office and, with his wife, left Chicago for 6 weeks. Occasionally, Rogers's writings are personally revealing, presenting not only his therapeutic responses but also comments about his internal feelings, thus providing further insight into his work.

In 1957, Rogers took a position at the University of Wisconsin, where he was first affiliated with the department of psychology, and later the department of psychiatry. He found his work at the psychology department to be agonizing, and he was frequently in conflict with his colleagues (Thorne, 1992). While at the University of Wisconsin, he undertook an ambitious research project (Rogers, Gendlin, Kiesler, & Truax, 1967) to study the impact of psychotherapy on hospitalized schizophrenic patients. The study was marked by many difficulties and conflicts and had few significant findings. Dissatisfied with his position at the University of Wisconsin, Rogers left in 1963 for the Western Behavioral Science Institute, which was devoted to the study of interpersonal relationships.

Before leaving Wisconsin, Rogers published *On Becoming a Person* (1961), which brought him even more recognition than his earlier works. Written for both psychologists and nonpsychologists, the book is personal and powerful, describing his philosophy of life and his view of research, teaching, and social issues. Marking the beginning of the person-centered stage, this book went beyond approaches to therapy to consider issues that affected all individuals. While at the Western Behavioral Sciences Institute in La Jolla, California, he devoted energy to encounter groups (Rogers, 1970) and to education (Rogers, 1969).

In 1968, Rogers, along with others, formed the Center for Studies of the Person, where Rogers called himself "resident fellow." The center became a base of operations for Rogers to become involved in worldwide travel and global issues. His *Carl Rogers on Personal Power* (1977) is concerned with how person-centered principles can be applied to people of different cultures and to bring about political change. Often, Rogers led workshops with disputing parties, such as South African blacks and whites and Protestants and Catholics from Northern Ireland. Political change continued to take a considerable amount of Rogers's energy and interest, as indicated in *A Way of Being* (1980). Traveling, writing, and working tirelessly, Rogers continued to show enthusiasm and a desire to learn until his death in February 1987 at the age of 85.

Person-centered therapy continues to attract international interest, as contributors to person-centered work come from many different countries. Beginning in 1986 an international journal, the *Person-Centered Review*, was published for 5 years. Currently, *The Person-Centered Journal*, which is published twice a year, and a quarterly newsletter, *Renaissance*, are sponsored by the Association for the Development of the Person-Centered Approach, an organization with about 200 members worldwide that sponsors training, workshops, and international conferences. Also, the Center for Studies of the Person in La Jolla offers workshops and training seminars and maintains the Carl Rogers Memorial Library. Their other programs include an Institute of Psychotherapy, Training, and Supervision, along with a women's program.

PERSON-CENTERED THEORY OF PERSONALITY

Rogers had a strong personal interest in helping people change and grow. Before setting out to develop a theory of personality, Rogers (1959) devoted his effort to presenting his ideas of therapeutic change in an organized way. His theory of personality can be seen as a way of broadening his theory of therapy to include normal as well as abnormal behavior and of outlining individual growth toward becoming fully functioning. Additionally, Rogers examined forces that interfered with the development of functioning fully and those who promote it. By closely attending to the factors that determine improving relationships between people, Rogers was able to describe a model of relating that went beyond individual therapy. Only a few of Rogers's writings deal primarily with personality theory (Rogers, 1959; Holdstock & Rogers, 1977), as much of his effort was devoted to helping individuals grow and change in individual therapy, groups, and in society.

Psychological Development

From birth onward, individuals experience reality in terms of internal and external experiences. Each person is biologically and psychologically unique, experiencing different social, cultural, and physical aspects of the environment. As infants develop, they monitor their environment in terms of degrees of pleasantness and unpleasantness. Differentiation is made between a variety of bodily senses, such as warmth and hunger. If parents interfere with this process, such as urging children to eat when they are not hungry, children can have a difficult time in developing "organismic sensings" or trusting in their reactions to the environment (Holdstock & Rogers, 1977).

As children develop an awareness of themselves, their need for positive regard from those around them develops. As they grow older, they manage their own physical needs more effectively, and the need for positive regard from others increases. Such needs include being loved by others, being emotionally and/or physically touched, and being valued or cared for (Patterson & Hidore, 1997).

Individuals' perceptions of the positive regard that they receive from others have a direct impact on their own self-regard. If children believe that others (parents, teachers, friends) value them, they are likely to develop a sense of self-worth or self-regard. Additionally, children, in interaction with others, experience satisfaction from meeting the needs of others as well as their own needs. Although needs for positive regard and self-regard are essential, individuals have many experiences that do not foster these conditions.

Development and Conditionality

Throughout their lives, individuals experience conditions of worth, the process of evaluating one's own experience based on the beliefs or values of others that may limit the development of the individual. For Rogers, conditions of worth led to an incongruence between a person's experience of self and experiences and interaction with others. To gain the conditional positive regard of others, individuals may discount their own experience and accept the values or beliefs of others. People who do not listen to their own beliefs and values but act to please others so that they may feel loved are operating under conditions of worth and are likely to experience anxiety as a result.

When there is conditional regard, individuals may lose touch with themselves and feel alienated from themselves. In order to deal with conditional or positive regard, individuals can develop defenses that result in inaccurate and rigid perceptions of the world, for example, "I must be kind to all others, regardless of what they do to me, so that they will care for me." Such an individual is likely to experience anxiety because of the conflict between the need to have a positive self-concept and the need to please others. Additionally, individuals may experience anxiety that exists between the values of one group and values of another, with both being incongruent with the individual's own sense of self.

The greater the incongruence between an individual's experiences and her self-concept, the more disorganized her behavior is likely to be. Thus, when the view of self and the experiences are in extreme conflict, psychosis may result. In general, Rogers classifies behavior along a continuum of severity, depending on the strength of distortion. Some common defenses include rationalization, fantasy, projection, and paranoid thinking (Holdstock & Rogers, 1977). Often defenses such as rationalization are quite common and minor, as in the following example. Alberta believes "I am a competent salesperson," but she experiences "I have been fired from my job." She then rationalizes, "I wouldn't have been fired, if my boss didn't dislike me." Thus, Alberta ignores her rude behavior to customers and rationalizes her behavior. In this case, there is a conflict between view of self and experience.

To counter the conditions of worth that an individual experiences, Rogers believed that there must be unconditional positive regard from some others so that a person's self-regard can be increased. Often, individuals seek out others who appreciate them rather than judge them and who behave in a warm, respectful, and accepting way. Although individuals may not experience unconditional positive regard with their family or friends, it is essential that the therapist provide these conditions.

Self-Regard and Relationships

An important part of Rogers's (1959) personality theory is the nature of personal relationships. In describing the process of an improving relationship, Rogers emphasizes congruence, the process of the therapist or listener in accurately experiencing and being aware of the communication of another person. Relationships improve when the person being listened to feels understood, empathically listened to, and not judged. The individual feels a sense of unconditional positive regard and a feeling of being heard by the other person. This relationship can be called *congruent* because the therapist or listener is able to understand and communicate the psychological experience of the other, being "in tune" with the other person. Sometimes individuals are incongruent within themselves, such as when one's facial expression or voice tone does not match one's words. The listener who perceives incongruence in the behavior of the speaker may choose to communicate this perception by saying, "You say that you are glad that your parents got a divorce, yet you sound sad." Thus, relationships improve to the extent that the listener perceives and communicates the other's present experience.

The Fully Functioning Person

Because Rogers viewed human development as a positive movement or growth, a view of the fully functioning person is consistent with his theory (Rogers, 1969). To become fully functioning, individuals must meet their need for positive regard from others and have positive regard for themselves. With these needs met, an individual can then experience an optimal level of psychological functioning.

Rogers's view of what constitutes congruence and psychological maturity includes openness, creativity, and responsibility. According to Rogers (1969), a fully functioning person is not defensive but open to new experiences without controlling them. This openness to congruent relationships with others and self allows an individual to handle new and old situations creatively. With this adaptability, individuals experience an inner freedom to make decisions and to be responsible for their own lives. As part of being fully functioning, individuals become aware of social responsibilities and the need for fully congruent relationships with others. Rather than being self-absorbed, such individuals have needs to communicate empathically. Their sense of what is right includes an understanding of the needs of others as well as of themselves.

Rogers saw the goal of being a fully functioning person as an ideal to strive toward that was not attainable by any one individual. He believed that, in effective relationships, individuals moved toward this goal. It was his goal as a family member, as a group leader, and as an individual therapist to grow to become a congruent, accepting, and understanding person, and in that way he would be able to help others around him do the same.

A PERSON-CENTERED THEORY OF PSYCHOTHERAPY

The development of Rogers's theory of psychotherapy came about as a result of his experience as a therapist, his interaction with colleagues, and his research on the therapeutic process. He believed that the goals of therapy should be to help individuals become congruent, self-accepting persons by being more aware of their own experiences and their own growth. Assessment was seen as a part of the therapeutic process, appraising the individual's current awareness and experiencing. Psychological change was brought about through a genuine, accepting, and empathic relationship, which was perceived as such by the client. How clients and counselors experience this therapeutic process is a part of Rogers's psychotherapeutic conceptualization of personality change.

Goals

The goals of therapy come from the client, not the therapist. Clients move away from phoniness or superficiality to become more complex in that they more deeply understand various facets of themselves. With this comes an openness to experience and a trusting of self "to be that self which one truly is" (Kierkegaard, 1941), as well as acceptance of others. Goals should be to move in a self-directed manner, being less concerned about pleasing others and meeting the expectations of others. As a consequence of becoming more self-directed, individuals become more realistic in their perceptions, better at problem solving, and less defensive with others. Thus, the therapist does not choose the goals that the client will have for counseling, but rather helps develop a therapeutic atmosphere that can increase positive self-regard so that the client can become more fully functioning.

Assessment

Although there is some disagreement among person-centered therapists as to whether psychodiagnosis is appropriate in therapy, most person-centered writers believe that psychodiagnosis is not necessary (Bozarth, 1991). Boy (1989) considers psychodiagnosis to be inconsistent with understanding the client in a deep and meaningful way. For Seeman (1989), psychodiagnosis is helpful only when there is a need to assess physiological impairment that affects psychological functioning. Interestingly, Rogers (Kirschenbaum, 1979) used diagnostic procedures in his early work but later abandoned them to focus on the functioning of the client. For most person-centered therapists, assessment takes place as the therapist empathically understands the experience and needs of the client.

Although assessment for diagnostic purposes has little or no role in person-centered therapy, there are times when testing may be appropriate. Bozarth (1991) suggests that testing may be used when clients request it, particularly for vocational counseling. Also, there may be times when either client or therapist finds that it is helpful to use a reference that is external to the client to assist in decision making or for other purposes. Basically, Bozarth believes that the test information needs to fit within the context of the client-counselor relationship. For example, it would be inappropriate for a person-centered therapist to rely on a test to make a decision for the client; decision making is the client's responsibility.

Although Rogers questioned the value of diagnostic or assessment instruments, he recognized their value for research. He developed a process scale (Rogers & Rablen, 1958) to measure stages of the therapeutic process. Others (Carkhuff, 1969; Truax & Carkhuff, 1967) have developed scales to measure therapeutic conditions in the client-counselor relationship. Such scales have been important in the development of methods of teaching helping skills (Carkhuff, 1987; Egan, 1998). Most person-centered therapists believe that such scales should be used for research purposes but not when doing therapy.

The Necessary and Sufficient Conditions for Client Change

The core of person-centered therapy is the six necessary and sufficient conditions for bringing about personality or psychotherapeutic change (Rogers, 1957, 1959). Drawing from his clinical experience, Rogers felt that if all six of the following conditions were met, change would occur in the client.

1. Psychological contact.   There must be a relationship in which two people are capable of having some impact on each other.

2. Incongruence.   The client must be in a state of psychological vulnerability, that is, fearful, anxious, or otherwise distressed. Implied in this distress is an incongruence between the person's perception of himself and his actual experience. Sometimes individuals are not aware of this incongruence, but as they become increasingly aware, they become more open to the therapeutic experience.

3. Congruence and genuineness.   In the therapeutic relationship, the therapist must genuinely be herself and not "phony." Rogers (1966) defines genuineness (similar to congruence) as follows.

Genuineness in therapy means that the therapist is his actual self in his encounter with his client. Without facade, he openly has the feelings and attitudes that are flowing in him at the moment. This involves self-awareness; that is, the therapist's feelings are available to him—to his awareness—and he is able to live them, to experience them in the relationship and to communicate them if they persist. The therapist encounters his client directly, meeting him person to person. He is being himself, not denying himself. (p. 185)

As Rogers clarifies, genuineness does not mean that the therapist discloses all of her feelings to the client. Rather, the therapist has access to her feelings and makes them available, where appropriate, to further the therapeutic relationship. Genuineness by itself is not a sufficient condition; a murderer may be genuine but not meet other conditions. The following is an example of a therapist responding genuinely.

Client: I'm lost, totally lost. I've got no direction.

Therapist: You're feeling lost and not sure where to go. I sense your despair, and feel I'm here to be with you, to be here with you in this tough time.

The therapist expresses herself openly. She genuinely feels for the client, is aware of her feelings, and expresses her desire to be there for the client.

4. Unconditional positive regard or acceptance.   The therapist must have no conditions of acceptance but must accept and appreciate the client as is (Rogers, 1957). Hurtful, painful, bizarre, and unusual feelings, as well as good feelings, are to be accepted by the therapist. Acceptance does not mean agreement with the client but rather refers to caring for the person as a separate individual. By accepting but not agreeing with the client, the therapist is not likely to be manipulated by the client. Clearly, therapists do not always feel unconditional positive regard for their clients, but it is a goal toward which they strive.

By appreciating clients for being themselves, the therapist makes no judgment of the person's positive or negative qualities. Conditions of worth that are imposed on the client by others are not fostered by the therapist. As the client values the unconditional positive regard of the therapist, there is an increase of positive self-regard within the client.

An example of Rogers's warmth or unconditional positive regard for a young, depressed patient with schizophrenia is given in the following excerpt. At the conclusion of a session, Rogers asks the patient if he wants to see him next Tuesday. Not getting an answer, Rogers replies with this suggestion.

T: I'm going to give you an appointment at that time because I'd sure like to see you then.
(Writing out appointment slip)
(Silence of 50 seconds)

T: And another thing I would say is that—if things continue to stay so rough for you, don't hesitate to have them call me. And if you should decide to take off, I would very much appreciate it if you would have them call me and—so I could see you first. I wouldn't try to dissuade you. I'd just want to see you.

C: I might go today. Where, I don't know, but I don't care.

T: Just feel that your mind is made up and that you're going to leave. You're not going to anywhere. You're just—just going to leave, hm?
(Silence of 53 seconds)

C: *(muttering in discouraged tone)* That's why I want to go, 'cause I don't care what happens.

T: Huh?

C: That's why I want to go, cause I don't care what happens.

T: M-hm, M-hm. That's why you want to go, because you really don't care about yourself. You just don't care what happens. And I guess I'd just like to say—*I* care about you. And *I* care what happens.
(Silence of 30 seconds) *(Jim bursts into tears and unintelligible sobs.)*

T: (*tenderly*) Somehow that just—makes all the feelings pour out.
(*Silence of 35 seconds*)

T: And you just weep and weep and weep. And feel so badly. (*Jim continues to sob, then blows nose and breathes in great gasps.*)

T: I do get a sense of how awful you feel inside. You just sob and sob. (*He puts his head on desk, bursting out in great gulping, gasping sobs.*)

T: I guess all the pent-up feelings you've been feeling the last few days just—just come rolling out.
(*Silence of 32 seconds, while sobbing continues*)

T: There's some Kleenex there, if you'd like it—Hmmm.
(*sympathetically*) You just feel kind of torn to pieces inside.
(*Silence of 1 minute, 56 seconds*) (Rogers et al., 1967, p. 409)[1]

The caring and warmth for the patient, Jim, are evident. The voice tone and words must be congruent within the therapist to be perceived as caring from the therapist. Statements such as those Rogers makes reduce the isolation that the patient feels by expressing acceptance and stressing caring.

5. Empathy. To be empathic is to enter another's world without being influenced by one's own views and values (Rogers, 1975). To do so, individuals must have sufficient separateness so that they do not get lost in the perceptual world of the other person. Rogers has eloquently described the process of empathy.

> The way of being with another person which is termed empathic has several facets. It means entering the private perceptual world of the other and becoming thoroughly at home in it. It involves being sensitive, moment to moment, to the changing felt meanings which flow in this other person, to the fear or rage or tenderness or confusion or whatever, that he/she is experiencing. It means temporarily living in his/her life, moving about in it delicately without making judgements, sensing meanings of which he/she is scarcely aware, but not trying to uncover feelings of which the person is totally unaware, since this would be too threatening. It includes communicating your sensings of his/her world as you look with fresh and unfrightened eyes at elements of which the individual is fearful. It means frequently checking with him/her as to the accuracy of your sensing, and being guided by the responses you receive. You are a confident companion to the person in his/her inner world. By pointing to the possible meanings in the flow of his/her experience you help the person to focus on this useful type of referent, to experience the meanings more fully, and to move forward in the experiencing. (Rogers, 1975, p. 4)

For Rogers, empathy is a process. Early in his career he ceased using the phrase "reflecting the client's feelings" because it had been misunderstood by a number of practitioners. Some mistook Rogers to mean that the therapist was to repeat what the client has said verbatim or to repeat the last words. Because of this, Rogers preferred to speak about an empathic attitude rather than about reflecting or empathic listening (Rogers, 1975).

The following example is taken from a transcript of a session with Jim, the same client described previously. In this example, Rogers's attitude of empathy toward Jim in his depressed state is clearly evident.

C: No. I just ain't no good to nobody, never was, and never will be.

T: Feeling that *now*, hm? That you're just no good to yourself, no good to anybody. Never will be any good to anybody. Just that you're completely worthless huh?—Those really are lousy feelings. Just feel that you're no good at *all*, hm?

C: Yeah. (*muttering in low, discouraged voice*) That's what this guy I went to town with just the other day told me.

T: This guy that you went to town with really told you that you were no good? Is that what you're saying? Did I get that right?

C: M-hm.

T: I guess the meaning of that if I get it right is that here's somebody that meant something to you and what does he think of you? Why he's told you that he thinks you're no good at all. And that just really knocks the props out from under you. (*Jim weeps quietly.*) It just brings the tears. (*Silence of 20 seconds*)

C: (*rather defiantly*) I don't care though.

T: You tell yourself you don't care at all, but somehow I guess some part of you cares because some part of you weeps over it. (*Silence of 19 seconds*)

T: I guess some part of you just feels, "Here I am hit with another blow, as if I hadn't had enough blows like this during my life when I feel that people don't like me. Here's someone I've begun to feel attached to and now he doesn't like me. And I'll say I don't care. I won't let it make any difference to me— But just the same the tears run down my cheeks." (Rogers et al., 1967, p. 404)

6. Perception of empathy and acceptance.   It is not sufficient for the therapist to unconditionally accept and empathically understand the client. The client must also perceive in some way that she is being understood and accepted. Communication of empathy and acceptance can be verbal or nonverbal, but it needs to be natural and not forced or artificial. By reading aloud any of the therapist comments in the previous examples, the reader can hear the difference between a stilted expression and a genuine expression. When the conditions of genuineness, acceptance, and empathy are communicated and perceived, then, Rogers believed, therapeutic change will take place.

In commenting on the relationships among the concepts of genuineness, acceptance, and empathy, Bozarth (1996) reviews Rogers's writings on these three conditions. Bozarth concludes that "*Genuineness and Empathic Understanding are viewed as two contextual attitudes for the primary conditions of change, i.e., Unconditional Positive Regard*" (p. 44). Ultimately, Bozarth believes that these are one condition and should be viewed as the attitude that the therapist holds in therapy.

Other writers have discussed different aspects of person-centered therapy, but always the six conditions remain as the core. For example, Patterson (Myers & Hyers,

1994), among many other writers, has talked about the need for specificity or concreteness when communicating an empathic attitude to clients. He believes that counselors should encourage their clients to be specific in describing their problems and that counselors themselves should be specific in responding to their clients, avoiding generalizations and labels. Most books that describe methods of helping relationships (such as Egan, 1998) emphasize specificity as well as Rogers's concepts of genuineness, acceptance, and empathy.

The Client's Experience in Therapy

When clients come to therapy, they are usually in a state of distress, feeling powerless, indecisive, or helpless. The therapeutic relationship offers them an opportunity to express the fears, anxieties, guilt, anger, or shame that they have not been able to accept within themselves. When the six necessary and sufficient conditions are met, they will be better able to accept themselves and others and to express themselves creatively. In the process of therapy, they will experience themselves in new ways by taking responsibility for themselves and their process of self-exploration, leading to a deeper understanding of self and to positive change. In the sections that follow, excerpts from the case of Mrs. Oak (Rogers, 1953, 1961) are used to illustrate clients' experiencing in therapy.

Experiencing responsibility.   In therapy, clients learn that they are responsible for themselves both in the therapeutic relationship and more broadly. Although clients may at first be frustrated or puzzled by the therapist's emphasis on the client's experience, person-centered therapists believe that clients soon come to accept and welcome this.

Experiencing the therapist.   Gradually, the client comes to appreciate the empathy and nonconditional positive regard of the therapist. There is a feeling of being cared for and being fully accepted (Rogers, 1953). The experience of being truly cared for assists clients in caring more deeply for themselves and for others and is illustrated by Mrs. Oak at the beginning of her 30th hour with Rogers.

C: Well, I made a very remarkable discovery. I know it's—*(laughs)* I found out that you actually care how this thing goes. *(Both laugh)* It gave me the feeling, it's sort of well—"maybe I'll let you get in the act," sort of thing. It's—again you see, on an examination sheet, I would have had the correct answer, I mean but it suddenly dawned on me that in the—client-counselor kind of thing, you actually care what happens to this thing. And it was a revelation, a—not that. That doesn't describe it. It was a—well, the closest I can come to it is a kind of relaxation, a—not a letting down, but a—*(pause)* more of a straightening out without tension if that means anything. I don't know.

T: Sounds as though it isn't as though this was a new idea, but it was a new experience of really feeling that I did care and if I get the rest of that, sort of a willingness on your part to let me care.

C: Yes. (Rogers, 1961, p. 81)[2]

Although Mrs. Oak finds it difficult to describe the experience of being cared for, she finds ways of doing so. Rogers empathically responds to this new experience and accepts her caring.

Experiencing the process of exploration.   The caring and empathy of the therapist allow the client to explore fearful or anxiety-producing experiences. By exploring feelings that are deeply felt, rather than feelings that *should* be sensed, the client can experience a feeling of total honesty and self-awareness. Contradictions within oneself can be explored, such as, "I love my daughter, but her violent anger toward me makes me really question this." In the following example, Mrs. Oak comments on her exploration process at the close of her 30th session.

C: I'm experiencing a new type, a—probably the only worthwhile kind of learning, a—I know I've—I've often said what I know doesn't help me here. What
I meant is, my acquired knowledge doesn't help me. But it seems to me that
the learning process here has been—so dynamic, I mean, so much a part of
the—of everything, I mean, of me, that if I just get that out of it, it's something, which, I mean—I'm wondering if I'll ever be able to straighten out into
a sort of acquired knowledge what I have experienced here.

T: In other words, the kind of learning that has gone on here has been something
of quite a different sort and quite a different depth; very vital, very real. And
quite worthwhile to you in and of itself, but the question you're asking is:
Will I ever have a clear intellectual picture of what has gone on at this somehow deeper kind of learning level?

C: M-hm. Something like that. (Rogers, 1961, pp. 85–86)

Mrs. Oak struggles to put into words her nonintellectual learning experience, and Rogers helps her clarify her sense of exploration through his empathic response.

Experiencing the self.   With self-exploration comes the realization that the deepest layers of personality are forward-moving and realistic (Rogers, 1953). As individuals deal with their angry and hostile feelings, they gradually encounter positive feelings about themselves and others. They are "getting behind the mask" (Rogers, 1961, p. 108). In essence, they are exploring who they really are and their inner world, as well as dropping pretenses about who they should be. In the following example from the 35th session with Mrs. Oak, there is, in her self-expression, a positive direction.

C: Yeah. Well, I have the feeling now that it's okay, really. . . . Then there's something else—a feeling that's starting to grow; well, to be almost formed, as I
say. This kind of conclusion, that I'm going to stop looking for something terribly wrong. Now I don't know why. But I mean, just—it's this kind of thing.
I'm sort of saying to myself now, well, in view of what I know, what I've
found—I'm pretty sure I've ruled out fear, and I'm positive I'm not afraid of
shock—I mean, I sort of would have welcomed it. But—in view of the places
I've been, what I learned there, then, also kind of, well, taking into consideration what I don't know, sort of, maybe this is one of the things that I'll have
to date, and say, well, now, I've just—I just can't find it. See? And now with-

out any—without, I should say, any sense of apology or covering up, just sort of simple statement that I can't find what at this time, appears to be bad.

T: Does this catch it? That as you've gone more and more deeply into yourself, and as you think about the kind of things that you've discovered and learned and so on, the conviction grows very, very strong that no matter how far you go, the things you're going to find are not dire and awful. They have a very different character.

C: Yes, something like that. (Rogers, 1961, p. 101)

Rogers is empathic with Mrs. Oak's awkwardly worded experience of being herself. His empathic response more clearly articulates her struggle within herself.

Experiencing change.   As the client struggles, as Mrs. Oak does, there is a sense of progress, even when the client may still feel confused (Patterson, 1986). Clients bring up some issues, discuss them and sense them, and move on to others. The therapist's warm presence allows the client to deal with issues that may be upsetting and difficult.

When the client has sufficient positive self-regard, he is likely to bring up the prospect of stopping therapy. Because the therapeutic relationship has been a deep one, the client and counselor may experience a sense of loss. Discussion of the ending process may take a few sessions, and the period between sessions may be lengthened to help the client deal with the loss of a significant therapeutic relationship.

The encounter between client and therapist is deeply felt by the client, although this may occur very gradually. The therapist's genuineness, acceptance, and empathy help facilitate the client's positive self-exploration, while at the same time helping the client deal with disturbing thoughts and feelings. Because of the deep personal involvement of clients—in the relationship and the intense search for an inner self—clients are likely to experience the relationship in different ways than the facilitative and empathic therapist. Clients may experience their own change in a deeply felt manner, including a wide range of emotions, whereas therapists experience caring and empathy for clients.

The Process of Person-Centered Psychotherapy

After participating in and listening to many interviews, Rogers (1961) was able to describe seven stages of therapeutic progress that ranged from being closed, not open to experience, and not self-aware, to the opposite, openness to experience, self-awareness, and positive self-regard. Because the stages are somewhat difficult to differentiate and combine several aspects of therapeutic growth, I describe here some of the changes that Rogers believed took place as a result of therapeutic relationships. In describing the stages, Rogers noted that individuals could be quite far along in dealing openly and congruently with some issues, but less open to others. Important aspects of the therapeutic process include changes in feelings, willingness to communicate them, openness to experience, and intimacy in relating to others.

When individuals are at beginning stages of openness to change, they are not likely to express feelings or take responsibility for them. Gradually, they may come to express their feelings with decreasing fear about doing so. At the higher stages, they will be able to experience and readily communicate feelings to the therapist.

Throughout the therapeutic process, individuals come to be more internally congruent, that is, more aware of their own feelings. Some individuals may be so lacking in awareness that they find it difficult or impossible to initiate the therapeutic process. They may have rigid views of themselves that cut them off from relationships with others, including the therapist. With progress in therapy, individuals come to understand how they have contributed to their own problems and may not blame others for them. Experiencing genuineness, acceptance, and empathy from the therapist leads to changes in how the individual relates to others. There is greater openness to intimacy, including more spontaneous and confident interactions with others.

As clients progress, not evenly or neatly but gradually through stages of therapeutic progress, they come closer to Rogers's description of the fully functioning person. Sharing their fears, anxiety, and shame in the presence of the therapist's genuine caring helps individuals trust their own experience, feel a sense of richness in their lives, become physiologically more relaxed, and experience life more fully (Rogers, 1961).

PSYCHOLOGICAL DISORDERS

Rogers believed that his six necessary and sufficient conditions for change applied to all psychological disorders. Regardless of the client's disorder, if the therapist is genuine, has unconditional positive regard, and is empathic with the client, improvement in psychological disorders takes place. Some critics have remarked that person-centered therapists apply the same approach to all clients. In response, person-centered therapists reply that they use a different approach with each client, reflecting the uniqueness of the client's humanness. Although some person-centered therapists may diagnose a client's disorder, it is usually for the purpose of insurance reimbursement or agency demands.

In this section, illustrations of the application of person-centered therapy are given for depression, grief and loss, and borderline disorders. The example of Rogers's therapy with a depressed client helps illustrate his style. Therapy with a 7-year-old boy whose father was killed in an accident shows the broad range of person-centered therapy. In describing approaches to treating patients with a borderline disorder, a therapist builds upon Rogers's theory of person-centered psychotherapy to suggest new approaches to treating these difficult clients.

Depression

In dealing with all psychological disorders, Rogers was empathic with the deep feelings within his clients. Often he helped them become aware of strong feelings that were below their surface of awareness. With depressed people, feelings of sadness, hopelessness, despair, and discouragement were present. However, Rogers was also empathic with the inner strength that was within an individual and helped clients take responsibility for their own decisions and judgments.

In the following example, Rogers (1961) helps a young female graduate student to become aware that she is responsible for her own life and her own choices. The woman had considered suicide and was concerned with many problems. Part of her concerns were that she wanted others to tell her what to do and was bitter that her professors were not sufficiently guiding or educating her. This segment is drawn from a therapeutic session near the end of therapy and concludes with a commentary by Rogers.

C: Well now, I wonder if I've been going around doing that, getting smatterings of things, and not getting hold, not really getting down to things.

T: Maybe you've been getting just spoonfuls here and there rather than really digging in somewhere rather deeply.

C: M-hm. That's why I say—(*slowly and very thoughtfully*) well, with that sort of a foundation, well, it's really up to me. I mean, it seems to be really apparent to me that I *can't depend on someone else* to give me an education. (*Very softly*) I'll really have to get it myself.

T: It really begins to come home—there's only one person that can educate you— a realization that perhaps nobody else can give you an education.

C: M-hm. (*Long pause—while she sits thinking*) I have all the symptoms of fright. (*Laughs softly*)

T: Fright? That this is a scary thing, is that what you mean?

C: M-hm. (*Very long pause—obviously struggling with feelings in herself*)

T: Do you want to say any more about what you mean by that? That it really does give you the symptoms of fright?

C: (*Laughs*) I, uh—I don't know whether I quite know. I mean—well it really seems like I'm cut loose (*pause*), and it seems that I'm very—I don't know in a vulnerable position, but I, uh, I brought this up and it, uh, somehow it almost came out without my saying it. It seems to be—it's something I let out.

T: Hardly a part of you.

C: Well, I felt surprised.

T: As though, "Well for goodness sake, did I say that?" (*Both chuckle.*)

C: Really, I don't think I've had that feeling before, I've—uh, well, this really feels like I'm saying something that, um is a part of me really. (*Pause*) Or, uh, (*quite perplexed*) it feels like I sort of have, uh, I don't know. I have a feeling of strength, and yet, I have a feeling of—realizing it's so sort of fearful, of fright.

T: That is, do you mean that saying something of that sort gives you at the same time a feeling of, of strength in saying it, and yet at the same time a frightened feeling of what you have said, is that it?

C: M-hm, I am feeling that. For instance, I'm feeling it internally now—a sort of surging up, or force or outlet. As if that's something really big and strong. And yet, uh, well at first it was almost a physical feeling of just being out alone, and sort of cut off from a—a support I had been carrying around.

T: You feel that it's something deep and strong, and surging forth, and at the same time, you just feel as though you'd cut yourself loose from any support when you say it.

C: M-hm. Maybe that's—I don't know—it's a disturbance of a kind of pattern I've been carrying around, I think.

T: It sort of shakes a rather significant pattern, jars it loose.

C: M-hm. *(Pause, then cautiously, but with conviction)*, I think—I don't know, but I have the feeling that then I am going to begin to do more things that I know I should do. . . . There are so many things that I need to do. It seems in so many avenues of my living I have to work out new ways of behavior, but—maybe—I can see myself doing a little better in some things.

I hope that this illustration gives some sense of the strength which is experienced in being a unique person, responsible for oneself, and also the uneasiness that accompanies this assumption of responsibility. To recognize that "I am the one who chooses" and "I am the one who determines the value of an experience for me" is both an invigorating and a frightening realization. (pp. 120–122)[3]

Grief and Loss

Person-centered therapists do not diagnose or suggest, they empathize with the individual experiencing grief. If the person is talking about an issue not related to grief, they stay with the clients' concern and follow the client's change in topic.

In the following example, Donna Rogers (not related to Carl Rogers) is helping 7-year-old Justin, a kindergarten student. Donna is a graduate student working in an elementary school. Justin has been referred by his teacher for counseling because he is acting angrily, fighting with others, and not being willing to change his behavior (Rogers & Bickham, 1995).

His father had been killed in an auto accident about four months before, and had a history of alcohol abuse. Also there had been some violence in the family. Justin has just started to deal with the loss of his father. This is the third counseling session.

In this brief excerpt, Ms. Rogers is empathic with Justin's statements. He moves from feeling hated and being aware of being mean to others to physical problems with his ear, to a feeling of hearing screaming in his head, to his father's death, to his locked-up tears. Ms. Rogers' responses facilitate his expression of his experience (Rogers & Bickham, 1995, pp. 96–97).

Justin: Like everybody on the playground, it seems like they hate me. Because how mean I've been 'cause, how mean I been to everybody.

Donna: You've really been mean to your friends.

Justin: Uh, huh. Like I don't know how rough I play but I play rough with them. And I don't know cause they don't tell me.

Donna: Maybe it would be easier if they told you that you were hurting them, and that might stop you.

Justin: I will stop.

Donna: You will stop.

Justin: Because they're my friends. And now I don't have that many friends because they're not my friends no more because I was playing rough with them, they didn't tell me. And no people, only one person on the bus likes me, that is Christopher.

Donna: It's really hard, hard not having anybody to talk to and to play with. And maybe all this stuff bottled up inside of you maybe could be relieved a little if you had some friends to help you.

Justin: I don't feel good either. And I still ain't going to that hospital thing because I don't want to tell my Mom 'cause I don't want to go that hospital thing. I keep on hurting, we don't have no pills. And my ear is stopped up and I can't even hear out of it. And I went to the doctor about it. And I still cannot hear out of it 'cause gook got clogged up in there. My Mamma, we don't have very much of those things you clean out your ears. My Mom finally bought some but she doesn't use them very much. So, um, things get clogged up in there a lot, behind my ear drum. It like soaks through my ear drum, that's how watery it is, it soaks through my ear drum. Just like inside my ear drum.

Donna: Sounds like you have stuff that's keeping you from hearing very good.

Justin: I can only hear out of this ear. I know I can't hear out of this ear because when I cover this ear, I cannot hear very loud. And when I cover this ear, I can hear loud. Because it seems like it's echoing in there. It echoes in there when I cover this ear.

Donna: You've got this stuff inside of you that, that is all bottled up and won't come out and it's like you have a lot of noise in your head. It's real confusing. A lot of things going on. It hurts.

Justin: I have been having like inside of this ear. It seems like something is in that gook and it's saying, it's screaming in there. It's like screaming inside that gook.

Donna: You have someone screaming inside your head.

Justin: Because it seems like in that gook that someone is screaming because they don't want to be drowned in that gook. And it's screaming, it hurts my head.

Donna: It hurts when someone's screaming inside.

Justin: And it's echoing and only in this ear.

Donna: They're afraid that maybe they can't get out.

Justin: Yea. Like they're trying to get out, out of that ear and they can't.

Donna: Like they're trapped, and they don't know what to do.

Justin: Like I am.

Donna: You feel trapped. Like you don't have anywhere to turn.

Justin: My dad died, and it's been hard for me and my Mom and all them. I felt like, it seems like I cannot cry and because I can make other people cry with my songs about him, see I was on the bus and singing this song and these two girls crying 'cause it was so pretty on that, and I didn't cause it was hard for me to cry, 'cause my tears were up, it felt like my tears were locked up in there, like down here in here, it felt like it was locked up in a cage.

Donna: There's all these things inside of you . . .

Justin: That's locked up.

Donna: Yea. And they can't come out. Even though sometimes you want them to.

Justin: It seems like the key is lost to all of them.

Donna: The key is lost.[4]

Borderline Disorder

In treating patients with borderline symptoms, Swildens (1990) applies the person-centered approach to three phases of therapy. Because Swildens sees the self-concept of a person with a borderline disorder as lacking cohesion, continuity, and adequate defenses, he believes therapy must proceed slowly and carefully. In the first phase of therapy, the therapist tries to develop trust with the client and to prevent acting out, such as destructive behavior toward self or others. The therapist is likely to focus on diffuse feelings of anxiety, and empathic responses are likely to be limited and not penetrate too deeply into the client's sense of self. Empathy is directed at understanding the client's fears, without trying to describe or explain them to the client. Understanding acting-out behavior, rather than getting involved in resulting conflicts, is important.

In the second phase, the therapist tries to understand the unsafe situations that clients find themselves in and works with clients in finding ways to survive stress. In dealing with the client's splitting and all-good or all-bad remarks, Swildens suggests using statements that have an "as well as" pattern, which expands the client's frame of reference. This can best be illustrated in an example.

A 40-year-old woman constantly saw one or the other of her friends in diabolical terms. In a therapeutic session, she once again reported how cunning and mean one of her friends had been and how hard and relentless she had felt in this situation. The therapist responded with "Hard and relentless as well as vulnerable and sensitive . . . like your friend who is not only sly and unreliable but who has also been affectionate and caring toward you." This "as well as" confrontation was accepted with tears in her eyes and resulted in the client correcting her judgment. (Swildens, 1990, p. 630)[4]

In the third phase, the therapist is not as concerned with acting out or fits of rage but more with helping clients accept their own oversensitivity and lack of stability. Attention is paid to helping clients understand their feelings of being vulnerable and defenseless. Also, help in processing day-to-day decisions is important.

Client: It is hard to choose: Should I rent the small house in Alkmaar or should I rather wait until something bigger presents itself in the country?

Therapist: Small in the city or something bigger in the country . . . does the choice have any other consequences for you?

Client: Yes, and I must give it some serious thinking: Anonymity and perhaps loneliness, or many people I can get to know . . . both possibilities have their pros and cons. (Swildens, 1990, pp. 632–633)[4]

In his work, Swildens takes an existential as well as a person-centered approach to help clients with borderline disorders reduce their anxiety and deal with their fears. He highlights the importance of a positive and nonthreatening relationship with the client. Being empathic, congruent, and accepting is approached somewhat differently in the three phases of counseling.

BRIEF THERAPY

In person-centered therapy, the client plays a major role in determining the length of therapy and its termination. Being empathic and accepting of the client's distress means that the therapist understands the client's concerns as deeply as possible and, if possible, avoids artificial limits on therapy. However, genuineness also requires that the therapist speaks to the client, if the client's demands seem unreasonable, such as requesting therapy 5 days a week. Typically, person-centered therapists see their clients weekly for a few weeks to a few years. In general, person-centered therapists do not use a brief therapy model.

CURRENT TRENDS

Of the several issues now facing person-centered therapy, four diverse issues and trends are discussed here. One area of particular importance during the latter part of Rogers's life that is still important for current person-centered therapists is the application of person-centered principles to international concerns of conflict and peace. The issue of eclecticism and the incorporation of other theoretical modes by therapists has been a source of debate among person-centered therapists. Constructivism has also changed the way some person-centered therapists view therapy, focusing on the way the relationship between therapist and client affects both. Training programs, which are mostly in Europe, have developed approaches that deal with these and other issues that are important in person-centered therapy.

Societal Implications

As Rogers's writings (1951, 1961, 1970, 1977, 1980) became known worldwide, he received invitations to discuss his philosophy of life and his views of psychotherapy with large audiences throughout the world. Rogers's (1970) work with groups has been applied to improve cross-cultural communications and to ease political tensions. Even when he was over 80, he led intense workshops in South Africa with black and white participants and facilitated groups that included militant Protestants and Catholics from Northern Ireland. The countries where he led workshops included Brazil, France, Italy, Japan, Poland, Mexico, the Philippines, and the Soviet Union. His impact in these countries has been such that colleges, universities, and clinics throughout the world continue to teach and practice his principles.

Rogers taught and practiced psychotherapy when there was great political tension between the Soviet Union and the United States, as well as many other significant national and international conflicts, terrorism, local wars, and threats of nuclear conflict. In his work with people in political conflict, such as those in Northern Ireland, Rogers applied the principles of genuineness, acceptance, and empathy in large groups. This work was extremely dangerous. In Northern Ireland, factions talking with each other could be seen as traitors to the cause and assassinated. However, Rogers felt that if individuals could extend their powers of understanding to the pain, fears, and anxieties of their political opponents, then tension among enemies should lessen. As an example of the application of person-centered principles to black and white South Africans in exile, Saley and Holdstock (1993) report that person-centered discussions were successful in breaking down barriers toward intimacy and self-disclosure despite fears of political persecution. Such work has continued after Rogers's death, some of it sponsored by the Carl Rogers Institute for Peace in La Jolla, California, which tries to bring local and national leaders together to work through real and potential crisis situations.

Theoretical Purity Versus Eclecticism

Rogers's theoretical constructs can present a dilemma for the person-centered therapist (Hutterer, 1993). On the one hand, person-centered therapy describes six necessary and sufficient conditions for therapeutic change, to which therapists should adhere. On the other hand, Rogers took an antidogmatic approach and said that "he would rather help the psychologist or psychotherapist who prefers a directive and controlling form of therapy to clarify his or her aims and meanings, than convince him or her of the person-centered position" (Hutterer, 1993, p. 276). Rogers was very open to the beliefs of others, yet he was also very committed to his own person-centered views. Those who practice person-centered therapy are often faced with decisions about whether to apply other types or styles of therapy. This can be particularly difficult for some beginning therapists because Rogers's basic principles are often integrated with other techniques (Egan, 1998) into an eclectic approach in graduate training.

Constuctivist Trends

Some person-centered writers have applied a constructivist view to person-centered issues. Lynch (1997) discusses ways in which therapists' own experiences may influence the way they try to help clients change their narratives. Therapists' empathic responding may be influenced by their own view of the good life. Going beyond this observation, a systematic application of a postmodern narrative approach to therapy has been applied to person-centered therapy (McLeod & Balamoutsou, 1996).

Western ways of knowing have been called egocentric and some non-Western ways as sociocentric (O'Hara, 1997). O'Hara (1997) talks of visiting a community workshop in Brazil in 1977 with Carl Rogers. Typically, Carl Rogers would be empathic with a group member, an example of an egocentric approach. Rather, she describes empathy from a sociocentric point of view. An impasse had occurred in the community in which group members could not agree on whether or not Rogers should give a formal presentation. On the third day, three group members reported dreams that dealt with this impasse. That night a representative of the African-Brazilian religion, Macumba, performed rituals that indirectly unlocked the groups impasse. This experience relaxed the group and was seen as richer than a formal talk by Rogers. In this way, empathy emerged from the group with shared perceptions of an experience rather than relying on Rogers's view of the impasse. In this situation, Rogers'. approach was consistent with a postmodern framework, as he did not impose his perception on others but rather let theirs develop.

Training Trends

Training therapists in the person-centered model has been problematic for students wishing to learn this approach. This model has not been as popular in the United States as it has been in Europe. In the United States only the Chicago Counseling Center offers a formal training program (Mearns, 1997a). Mearns (1997a, 1997b) describes a model for training that focuses on individual dynamics that has been developed in Scotland at the University of Strathclyde. Shared responsibility between student and faculty for training is related to the person-centered focus on self-actualization. Self-acceptance is developed through the unconditional positive regard of the faculty. In keeping with a person-centered approach, the curriculum is individualized, as is the evaluation and assessment of participants. Much of the progress in the program is based on self-assessment of participants. Other formal training programs are offered in Holland, Germany, Belgium, Greece, and Britain, as well as other countries (Mearns, 1997a).

USING PERSON-CENTERED THERAPY WITH OTHER THEORIES

All the theorists discussed in this book recognize the importance of the client-counselor relationship and the need for the therapist to want to help the client. However, there is disagreement on the application of genuineness, acceptance, and empathy. For example, theorists such as Frankl and Haley, who apply paradoxical treatments, can be accused of not being genuine with their clients. Others such as Ellis or Kohut may experience empathy for their clients but may not show it the way Rogers does. Cognitive and behavioral therapists may accept their clients but try to change their behavior. However, almost all theorists draw on the principles of genuineness, acceptance, and empathy in their work; they just do not believe that these conditions are necessary and sufficient for change.

Particularly during early stages of therapy, other theorists are likely to listen empathically to the worries and concerns of their patients. They show genuineness and congruence by not being interrupted in their work and by giving the client full attention, both verbally and nonverbally, and do not criticize or ridicule the client. All of these actions are consistent with Rogers's principles.

In their application of person-centered therapy to clients, some person-centered therapists may draw on other theories, especially existential and Gestalt therapies. Existential therapists are concerned with the human condition, being in the present, and experiencing the self, and in that way they share values that were important to Carl Rogers. Gestalt therapy, which also has a strong existential basis, emphasizes experiencing current awareness in a more bodily and active way than does person-centered therapy. O'Leary (1997) demonstrates how the person-centered emphasis on the client-therapist relationship can be integrated with the emphasis that Gestalt therapy gives to self-support and interdependence.

In general, person-centered therapists are more likely to make use of theories that emphasize "knowing" the client rather than cognitive and behavioral therapies that are more directive in nature. However, Tausch (1990) describes situations in which person-centered therapists may wish to make use of behavioral methods such as relaxation strategies. Other writers have addressed the issue of integration with other therapies (Bohart, 1990) and, more specifically, with Jungian concepts (Wingaarden, 1990) and object relations theory (Lindt, 1988). Farber and Brink (1996) have assembled a series of chapters that discuss some of Rogers' cases from client-centered, psychoanalytic, cognitive, behavioral, and other points of view, giving insights as to how other theories may be integrated with the person-centered point of view. In using other theories, most person-centered therapists ask, "To what extent are these other theoretical concepts consistent with the necessary and sufficient conditions of Rogers?"

RESEARCH

At the same time that Rogers was advocating a humanistic and phenomenological approach to helping clients, he also believed that it was necessary to use research methods to validate the effectiveness of psychotherapeutic concepts and the outcome of psychotherapy. Rogers was a pioneer in therapy research, as can be seen in his early advocacy (Rogers, 1942b) of recording sessions of psychotherapy for training and research purposes. Throughout his career, Rogers (1986) believed that research would test person-centered hypotheses, add to theoretical explanations, and provide a deeper understanding of individuals' personality and of psychotherapy. In general, there have been two types of research on person-centered therapy: tests of the importance of genuineness, acceptance, and empathy (the core conditions) for therapeutic change and studies comparing the effectiveness of person-centered therapy with other theories.

Research on the Core Conditions

For more than 30 years, there has been research on the role of empathy, genuineness, and acceptance in therapeutic change. At first, research focused on developing scales for measuring Rogers's core concepts. Later there was criticism of this work. Although recent studies have not been abundant, they have examined the core conditions, particularly empathy, from a variety of perspectives.

Early research on the core conditions concluded that therapists who are genuine, empathize accurately with their clients, and are accepting and open are effective in bringing about therapeutic change (Truax & Carkhuff, 1967; Truax & Mitchell, 1971). In their research review, Truax and Mitchell cite more than 30 studies that use scales to measure accurate empathy, nonpossessive warmth, and genuineness. The typical approach in many of these investigations was for raters to listen to tapes of therapy and rate therapists' responses to clients' statements on previously developed rating scales. In a later review, Beutler, Crago, and Arezmendi (1986) concluded that there was no clear evidence that genuineness, acceptance, and empathy were necessary and sufficient conditions for client change.

In explaining the criticisms of research that used rating scales to measure the effectiveness of the core conditions, Barkham and Shapiro (1986) describe four major problems with the methodological approach of the early studies. First, ratings included the rater's view of the amount of the core condition, not the client's. Second, early studies tended to use a 4-minute segment, rather than the whole session, for the ratings. Third, listening to audiotapes does not account for the nonverbal communication of core conditions. Fourth, the ratings scales were criticized for not being sufficiently specific. Also, there has been criticism for not paying sufficient attention to the occurrence of empathy, genuineness, or acceptance in the early, middle, or late stages of therapy.

As a partial answer to such criticisms, Barkham and Shapiro (1986) studied 24 client-counselor pairs at various phases of therapy. They found that clients felt that counselors were more empathic in later sessions, whereas counselors believed that they were themselves more empathic in the initial sessions of counseling. There were also differences between how clients and counselors defined *empathy*. For some categories, statements that were interpretation, exploration, reflection, advisement, and reassurance were considered to be empathic. This study highlights the complexity of the concept of empathy and suggests that it is not unitary.

Another view of empathy is provided by Bachelor (1988), who studied how clients perceive empathy. Analyzing the descriptions of empathic perceptions of 27 clients who were participating in therapy, she was able to specify four different client perceptions of empathy: cognitive, affective, sharing, and nurturing. Cognitive-style clients perceived empathy when their innermost experience or motivation was understood. Affective-style clients experienced empathy when the therapist was involved in the client's feeling state. Sharing empathy was perceived when the therapist disclosed opinions in her life that were relevant to the client's problem. Less frequent than the others, nurturant empathy was sensed when the therapist was attentive and provided security and support. Bachelor's study suggests that empathy should be seen in a variety of ways rather than as one dimension.

Another investigation has focused on how individuals' belief systems affect their perceptions of empathy, warmth, and genuineness (Withers & Wantz, 1993). The authors interpreted and supported Harvey, Hunt, and Schroder's (1961) Belief System Theory as suggesting that individuals who tend to be positive toward authority and tradition would respond better to person-centered therapy than those who reject social conventions and distrust authority, those who emphasize friendship and harmony, or those who tend to think abstractly and creatively. Although the findings of Withers and Wantz are more complex than this brief summary suggests, there is evidence that belief systems do have an effect on how clients perceive therapeutic empathy, warmth, and genuineness.

Both the therapists' trust in the client and the client's trust in the therapist can have an impact on the experience of empathy (Peschken & Johnson, 1997). Studying 48 clients involved in ongoing therapy, the authors did not find predicted relationships between therapist and client ratings of empathy and the facilitative conditions. Such research suggests the need to study how clients (and therapists) are likely to experience empathy inside the therapeutic relationship.

The Effectiveness of Person-Centered Therapy

Over the last 25 years, outcome research on client-centered therapy has been sporadic. Early research was done by Rogers et al. (1967) on a small group of schizophrenic patients. Since that time there have been other studies on similar hospitalized patients, as well as on a variety of other clinical populations. Reviews of research comparing client-centered therapy with other therapies shows common findings and recent trends in research. Examples of typical outcome studies are illustrated here.

While Rogers was at the University of Wisconsin, he conducted an in-depth study of 28 schizophrenic patients, half of whom were in a control group. The investigators were interested in the effect of Rogers's core conditions on the process of hospitalization and the length of hospital stay, which is described in a lengthy book (Rogers et al., 1967). In brief, the investigators found that those patients who received high degrees of empathy, warmth, and genuineness spent less time in the hospital than those who received lower conditions. This was also found to be true in a follow-up study 9 years later (Truax, 1970). Unfortunately, few differences were found between the patients who received high core conditions and the control group that was not treated. Patients who received lower levels of empathy, warmth, and genuineness spent more days in the hospital than did the control group or those receiving high core conditions. Although there was some support for the importance of the core conditions in several of the analyses, the patients receiving high levels of core conditions made disappointingly small gains relative to the control group.

Reviewing studies that compared client-centered or nondirective therapy to either control groups or other therapies, Greenberg, Elliot, and Litaer (1994) suggest several conclusions. Interestingly, the vast majority of recent research on client-centered therapy has been done in Belgium and Germany, with relatively little taking place in the United States, whereas in the 1960s and 1970s most research was in the United States. Calculating effect sizes for 18 studies, Greenberg et al. (1994) found positive changes between pretreatment and posttreatment for all studies, with most studies using follow-up measures between 3 months and 1 year after treatment completion. When client-centered therapy is compared to a waiting list or no treatment control, all studies showed more powerful effect sizes for client-centered therapy. However, when person-centered therapy was compared to cognitive or behavioral therapy in five studies, there were slightly stronger effect sizes, differences that favored the behavioral and cognitive treatments. Comparing client-centered therapy to two different types of dynamic therapy, client-centered therapy had more positive results in one case, and there were no differences in another.

While Greenberg and his colleagues (1994) studied experiential therapies specifically, other investigations have included the entire range of therapies in their analyses. Weisz, Weiss, Alicke and Klotz (1987) and Weisz, Weiss, Han, Granger, and Morton (1995) have conducted meta-analyses on the effectiveness of treatments with adolescents and children. If both investigations are combined, they examined 26 studies in which person-centered therapy was used. They found a lower effect size (less effectiveness), in general, for person-centered therapy than behavioral, cognitive, parent training, or social skills interventions. Examining the treatment of adults, Grawe, Donati, and Bernauer (1998) found person-centered therapy to be better than a wait-list or no treatment control in most studies, but produced less benefits than cognitive or behavioral treatments. Examining only studies that met stringent criteria for rigorousness, DeRubeis and Crits-Christoph (1998) found relaxation procedures to be more effective than person-centered therapies in the treatment of anxiety in two studies. In two studies comparing cognitive behavioral treatment to person-centered therapy in the treatment of anxiety, one study found no differences between the two approaches and one found cognitive behavioral treatments to be more effective.

Rather than ask which therapy is best, it is helpful to ask who benefits best from which types of therapy. In reviewing several studies, Greenberg et al. (1994) suggest that client-centered therapy may be particularly helpful to clients who are resistant or, more technically, high in reactance, that is, high on a measure of dominance and low on a measure of submissiveness. Greenberg et al. (1994) suggest that those who are low in reactance do better in Gestalt therapy than in client-centered therapy. Other variables besides reactance have been examined to determine who can best benefit from client-centered therapy; however, the results are not clear (Greenberg et al., 1994). There continues to be a need for research that studies client characteristics and therapist performance to learn more about the effective aspects of client-centered therapy.

GENDER ISSUES

Can a therapist of one gender be truly genuine, accepting, and empathic with a client of a different gender? Kaplan and Yasinski (1980) suggest that therapists' values may influence their work and that the gender socialization that occurs in most societies may make it difficult, to some degree, to be empathic with clients of the opposite sex. Implied in Rogers's concepts of genuineness, acceptance, and empathy are knowing oneself, being aware of biases or prejudices, and moving through them to prevent distortions in understanding the client.

When working with homosexual clients, value conflicts may arise because societies often have strong prejudices against homosexuality. Rogers wrote little on this subject, focusing on the quality of the intimacy of relationships rather than the nature of the sexual relationship (Knopf, 1992). Even when therapists are able to prevent their values from interfering with understanding their clients, the independence and freedom of choice that are part of the therapeutic process may not transfer to the real world, where some individuals may experience discrimination.

MULTICULTURAL ISSUES

Especially in the last 20 years of his life, Rogers (1977) was motivated to apply person-centered ways of thinking and being to all cultures, as can be seen in his chapter "The Person-Centered Approach and the Oppressed." In order to promote cross-cultural communication, Rogers conducted large workshops in Northern Ireland, Poland, France, Mexico, the Philippines, Japan, the Soviet Union, and other countries.

Several authors have pointed out similarities between person-centered and Eastern thought, giving perspectives on person-centered therapy. Miller (1996) points out how Taoist philosophy emphasizes that individuals need to be receptive to their own being. Person-centered therapists strive for that in their work and indirectly communicate this to clients. Similarly, Buddhist psychology, like person-centered therapy, emphasizes openness to other experience (Harman, 1997). Both authors see the self as a process rather than a fixed being. In this process individuals learn to accept and trust themselves. Singh and Tudor (1997) take a broader approach in which they define race, culture, and ethnicity as a basis for discussing Rogers's six conditions for change from the viewpoint of culture. They give examples of how person-centered concepts can be applied to Sikh and Moslem clients.

Rogers's belief in the core conditions of genuineness, acceptance, and empathy as a way of relating socially and politically can be seen as a set of cultural values. Some writers have questioned their universality and the appropriateness of the person-centered approach for clients of all cultures. Psychotherapy is either unknown or carries strong negative social stigma in many cultures. When individuals from some Asian cultures seek therapy, it may be as a last resort, and they are likely to seek direction or advice that will be immediate, not gradual (Chu & Sue, 1984). In cultures where individuals learn to respect and take direction from authority, the transition to a less directive person-centered approach may be very difficult. Also, many cultures focus on familial and social decision making rather than on individual empowerment, as does Rogers. Although these comments represent cautions as to the universal application of person-centered therapy, Mokuau (1987) suggests that counselors should not assume that one particular style of counseling is appropriate or inappropriate for members of a culture. Instead, counselors should respect the individual differences that exist within cultures.

COUPLES AND FAMILY COUNSELING

The core conditions that are essential to individual counseling are also the basis of couples and family counseling. The importance of self-actualization in individual development pertains to family growth and development as well (Rogers, 1972, 1977). As Gaylin (1990, 1996) has commented, the power of the family to foster self-actualization is far stronger than that of the therapist. However, as children develop, they are faced with increasing pressure to develop conditions of worth from their own internalization of interaction with others, from family dynamics that affect their view of themselves, and from social forces outside the family. It is the therapist's role to assist family members in their attempts to become more fully functioning (Rogers, 1972, 1977).

The person-centered approach to family therapy (Gaylin, 1990, 1996) is quite similar to methods of treating couples (Esser & Schneider, 1990; Rombauts & Devriendt, 1990). Although person-centered therapists do have different approaches to couples and family counseling, most would agree with Rombauts and Devriendt, who view empathy as the central component in therapy. For them, it is essential that the therapist try to understand, at the deepest possible level, the conflict between the couple or members of the family. In communicating understanding to the family, therapists may not only empathize with the client but also with the relationship issues at hand. Gaylin (1996) refers to reflecting the "interspace." By this, he means responding to a conflict in perception between two or more members of the family. In the following example, the first therapist response is to an individual, the second to the relationship or the "interspace."

Susie: (to husband) You don't understand the pressures that I have at work.

Harvey: I don't understand! You don't understand how my boss is nagging me all day long.

Therapist: Susie, when you talk about your work, you just don't feel that Harvey listens to you.

Therapist: Susie and Harvey, when you both try to talk about your work, it is as if a wall goes up between you, and it's hard to listen to each other.

Not only may the therapist empathize with an individual or a relationship, but also at times it may be appropriate to make other interventions. For example, Gaylin (1993) describes *ghosting* as a way of being empathic with a member of the couple or family who is absent. To use ghosting, a therapist might say, "I understand how you might be disappointed in Martha for not listening to you, but I wonder if she were with us now, if she might feel that she didn't have an opportunity to respond." Thus, ghosting is not a technique, but an extension of empathy to an absent family member. Often it may be important to structure family and couples therapy to a greater degree than is done in individual therapy. For example, Rombauts and Devriendt (1990) believe that members of a family or couple may interrupt each other so frequently that it is necessary to intervene and ask members to stop a variety of destructive behaviors. But as much as possible, person-centered therapists try to empathize with the couple or family members and assist the members to do the same with each other.

GROUP COUNSELING

Rogers had a strong belief in and commitment to the power of groups, both those designed for personal growth and those designed to ease conflicts between people of different ethnic or national groups. Since the 1960s, Rogers believed deeply in the power of individuals to help each other grow through the group process, as indicated in his *Carl Rogers on Encounter Groups* (1970).

The same philosophy that Rogers had toward individual therapy was directed toward the process of *facilitating* (a word he preferred to leading) groups (Rogers, 1970). Like the individual, the group was an organism with its own direction that could be trusted to develop positively. This trust could be extended to the goals of the group, which were to arise from the group members, not from the facilitator. Rather than lead, the facilitator's goal was to facilitate core conditions so that individuals may become more genuine, accepting, and empathic with each other so that leadership, in the sense of direction, became less necessary. Yet at the same time, Rogers (1970) recognized the need for the facilitator to make the atmosphere in a group psychologically safe for each member.

The role of the core conditions of person-centered therapy are evident in Rogers's (1970) writings on group process. Individuals are accepted for themselves regardless of whether they wish to commit to the group, participate, or remain silent. For Rogers, empathic understanding is key: The facilitator tries to understand what is being communicated by an individual at the moment within the group. As a result, Rogers rarely made comments about the group process. He preferred that group members do this themselves. However, some group facilitators feel that process comments reflect an empathic understanding of the group feeling. For Rogers, it was important to be aware of his own feelings, impulses, and fantasies, to trust them, and to choose to react to them through interaction with participants. Having applied his philosophy to many groups, Rogers was able to articulate a process that most groups went through in their development.

When the core conditions were met in the group, trust would develop and a process similar to the one summarized here would take place (Rogers, 1970, pp. 14–37). At first there would be confusion among group members about what to do or who is responsible for movement in the group. Along with this, resistance to exploring personal issues and a sense of being vulnerable might occur. Then group members could disclose past feelings, which were safer to express than current feelings.

As trust developed in the group, members would become more likely to expose their inner selves, which might include discussion of negative feelings about themselves, other members, or the group leader. Gradually the material would become personally more meaningful and reflect immediate reactions to people within the group.

As interpersonal interaction became more meaningful, Rogers observed changes within the group. As honesty developed among members, communication became deeper, with honest positive and negative feedback given to others in the group. As members became closer and more genuinely in contact with each other, they were able to express and experience more positive feelings and closeness within the group. This often resulted in behavior change, less affectation or fewer mannerisms, new insights into problems, and more effective ways of dealing with others. Such changes occurred in interaction with group members and with other people who were significant in their lives.

Recognizing the power of the group process, Rogers also was aware of the risks and dangers. He was concerned that positive changes might not last as long as members would like. Also relationships within the group that could be quite positive and warm might threaten intimate relationships outside the group, such as with a spouse or parents. For some individuals, sharing deep feelings and thoughts with group members could lead to feeling vulnerable and exposed at the end of the group or workshop. Although Rogers discusses these risks, his trust in the positive healing power of the group process was strong, causing him to believe that the risks were minimal and that the prospects of positive personal growth outweighed potential hazards.

SUMMARY

Essential to the person-centered approach of Carl Rogers is the belief that individuals are able to develop an ability for self-understanding, for changing their behaviors and attitudes, and for fully being themselves. Individuals integrate positive self-regard (an attitude of confidence) in part from receiving positive regard (warmth, caring, and affection) from others. When individuals receive conditions of worth (limited caring or conditional affection) from others, they may develop a lack of confidence or lack of self-regard. which can result in anxiety, defensiveness, or disorganized behavior.

To help individuals with relatively low self-regard who are experiencing psychological stress, Rogers believed that providing the core conditions of person-centered therapy would bring about positive change. By being empathic to the individuals' experience (offering a complete and accurate understanding of the client's concern), by accepting and respecting the individuality of the person, and by being genuine (saying what is truly felt), therapists can help the client become a more fully functioning person. To do this, the client must be able to perceive the empathy, acceptance, and genuineness that are offered by the therapist.

Along with this humanistic approach to therapy, Rogers had a deep commitment to research and was involved in several early studies to assess the effectiveness of the core conditions of person-centered therapy. Although Rogers continued to value research, as he grew older his interest turned to issues other than individual psychotherapy and its evaluation.

When Rogers left academic life in 1964, he devoted attention to a variety of issues. One important area for Rogers was encounter groups and his belief in the power of groups of people to work together to bring about positive change for the individual members. Other areas of interest included couples counseling, teaching, and supervision. During the last decade of his life, Rogers applied concepts of person-centered therapy to bring about political change and world peace and to alleviate suffering among individuals who were involved in political conflict. To do this, Rogers traveled to many countries to facilitate small and large groups of individuals in conflict. By communicating empathy, acceptance, and genuineness for others, Rogers believed that group leaders could help group members to experience and incorporate these conditions into their lives. Rogers's caring for others, his warmth, and his continual emphasis on being empathic to the experience of others epitomize his work and are the essence of person-centered therapy.

Suggested Readings

BOHART, A. C., & GREENBERG, L. S. (1997). *Empathy reconsidered: New directions in psychotherapy.* Washington: American Psychological Association. • This volume provides many different views, including person-centered, on Roger's essential concept—empathy. Chapters by J. Shlien and J. D. Bozarth emphasize the person-centered viewpoint.

ROGERS, C. R. (1951). *Client-centered therapy.* Boston: Houghton Mifflin. • Rogers's view of the process of therapy and the conditions under which change takes place is described, along with applications to groups, teaching, and individual therapy.

ROGERS, C. R. (1961). *On becoming a person.* Boston: Houghton Mifflin. • In one of his best-known books, Rogers provides autobiographical comments as well as his view of psychotherapy. He also addresses broader questions such as the place of research and the applications of client-centered principles for education, family life, and interpersonal relations.

ROGERS, C. R. (1980). *A way of being.* Boston: Houghton Mifflin. • Published when Rogers was 78, this book describes changes in events and thoughts over Rogers's life. Of particular interest are his views on the therapist's role in social and political issues.

References

BACHELOR, A. (1988). How clients perceive therapist empathy: A content analysis of "received" empathy. *Psychotherapy, 25,* 227–240.

BARKHAM, M., & SHAPIRO, D. A. (1986). Exploratory therapy in two-plus-one sessions: A research model for studying the process of change. In G. Lietaer, J. Rombauts, & R. Van Balen (Eds.), *Client-centered and experiential psychotherapy in the nineties* (pp. 429–445). Leuven, Belgium: Leuven University Press.

BEUTLER, L. E., CRAGO, M., & AREZMENDI, T. G. (1986). Research on therapist variables in psychotherapy. In S. L. Garfield & A. E. Bergin (Eds.), *Handbook of psychotherapy and behavior change* (3rd ed., pp. 257–310). New York: Wiley.

BOHART, A. C. (1990). Psychotherapy integration from a client-centered perspective. In G. Lietaer, J. Rombauts, & R. Van Balen (Eds.), *Client-centered and experiential psychotherapy in the nineties* (pp. 481–500). Leuven, Belgium: Leuven University Press.

BOY, A. V. (1989). Psychodiagnosis: A person-centered perspective. *Person-Centered Review, 4,* 132–151.

BOZARTH, J. D. (1991). Person-centered assessment. *Journal of Counseling and Development, 69,* 458–461.

BOZARTH, J. D. (1996). A theoretical reconceptualization of the necessary and sufficient conditions for therapeutic change. *The Person-Centered Journal, 3,* 44–51.

BRODLEY, B. T. (1994). Some observations of Carl Rogers's behavior in therapy interviews. *The Person-Centered Journal, 1,* 37–48.

CARKHUFF, R. R. (1969). *Helping and human relations.* New York: Holt, Rinehart & Winston.

CARKHUFF, R. R. (1987). *The art of helping* (6th ed.). Amherst, MA: Human Resource Development Press.

CHU, J., & SUE, S. (1984). Asian/Pacific-Americans and group practice. In L. E. Davis (Ed.), *Ethnicity in social group work practice* (pp. 23–36). New York: Haworth.

CISSNA, K. N., & ANDERSON, R. (1997). Carl Rogers in dialogue with Martin Buber: A new analysis. *The Person-Centered Journal, 4,* 4–13.

DERUBEIS, R. J., & CRITS-CHRISTOPH, P. (1998). Empirically supported individual and group psychological treatments for adult mental disorders. *Journal of Consulting and Clinical Psychology, 66,* 34–52.

EGAN, G. (1998). *The skilled helper* (5th ed.). Pacific Grove, CA: Brooks/Cole.

ESSER, U., & SCHNEIDER, I. (1990). Client-centered partnership therapy as relationship therapy. In G. Lietaer, J. Rombauts, & R. Van Balen (Eds.), *Client-centered and experiential psychotherapy in the nineties* (pp. 813–828). Leuven, Belgium: Leuven University Press.

FARBER, B. A., & BRINK, D. C. (Eds.). (1996). *The psychotherapy of Carl Rogers: Cases and commentary.* New York: Guilford.

GAYLIN, N. L. (1990). Family-centered therapy. In G. Lietaer, J. Rombauts, & R. Van Balen (Eds.), *Client-centered and experiential psychotherapy in the nineties* (pp. 813–828). Leuven, Belgium: Leuven University Press.

GAYLIN, N. L. (1993). Person-centered family therapy. In D. Brazier (Ed.), *Beyond Carl Rogers* (pp. 181–200). London: Constable.

GAYLIN, N. L. (1996). The self, the family, and psychotherapy. *The Person-Centered Journal, 3,* 31–43.

GOLDSTEIN, K. (1959). *The organism: A holistic approach to biology derived from psychological data in man.* New York: American Book. (Original work published 1934.)

GRAWE, K. , DONATI, R., & BERNAUER, F. (1998). *Psychotherapy in transition.* Seattle: Hogrefe & Huber.

GREENBERG, L. S., ELLIOTT, R. K., & LITAER, G. (1994). Research on experiential therapies. In A. E. Bergin & S. L. Garfield (Eds.), *Handbook of psychotherapy change* (4th ed., pp. 509–539). New York: Wiley.

HARMAN, J. L. (1997). Rogers' late conceptualization of the fully functioning individual: Correspondences and contrasts with Buddhist psychology. *The Person-Centered Journal, 4,* 23–31.

HARVEY, O. J., HUNT, D. E., & SCHRODER, H. M. (1961). *Conceptual systems and personality organization.* New York: Wiley.

HOLDSTOCK, L. (1990). Can client-centered therapy transcend its monocultural roots? In G. Lietaer, J. Rombauts, & R. Van Balen (Eds.), *Client-centered and experiential psychotherapy in the nineties* (pp. 109–121). Leuven, Belgium: Leuven University Press.

HOLDSTOCK, T. L., & ROGERS, C. R. (1977). Person-centered theory. In R. J. Corsini (Ed.), *Current personality theories* (pp. 125–152). Itasca, IL: Peacock.

HUTTERER, R. (1993). Eclecticisms: An identity crisis for person-centered therapists. In D. Brazier (Ed.), *Beyond Carl Rogers* (pp. 274–284). London: Constable.

KAPLAN, A. G., & YASINSKI, L. (1980). Psychodynamic perspectives. In A. M. Brodsky & R. T. Hare-Mustin (Eds.), *Women and psychotherapy* (pp. 191–219). New York: Guilford.

KIEKEGAARD, S. (1941). *The sickness unto death.* Princeton, NJ: Princeton University Press.

KIRSCHENBAUM, H. (1979). *On becoming Carl Rogers.* New York: Delacorte Press.

KIRSCHENBAUM, H., & HENDERSON, V. L. (Eds.) (1989). *Carl Rogers: Dialogues.* London: Constable.

KNOPF, N. (1992). On gay couples. *The Person-Centered Journal, 1,* 50–62.

LINDT, M. W. (1988). Holding and the person-centered approach: Experience and reflection. *Person-Centered Review, 3,* 229–240.

LYNCH, G. (1997). The role of community and narrative in the work of the therapist: A postmodern theory of the therapist's engagement in the therapeutic process. *Counselling Psychology Quarterly, 10,* 353–363.

MASLOW, A. H. (1968). *Toward a psychology of being* (Rev. ed.). New York: Van Nostrand Reinhold.

MASLOW, A. H. (1987). *Motivation and personality* (3rd ed.). New York: Harper & Row.

MCLEOD, J., & BALAMOUTSOU, S. (1996). Representing narrative process in therapy: Qualitative analysis of a single case. *Counselling Psychology Quarterly, 9,* 61–76.

MEARNS, D. (1997a). Central dynamics in client-centered therapy training. *The Person-Centered Journal, 4,* 31–43.

MEARNS, D. (1997b). Training in person-centered counselling. London: Sage.

MILLER, M. J. (1996). Some comparisons between Taoism and person-centered therapy. *The Person-Centered Journal, 3,* 12–14.

MOKUAU, N. (1987). Social workers' perceptions of counseling effectiveness for Asian-American clients. *Journal of the National Association of Social Workers, 32,* 331–335.

MYERS, J. E., & HYERS, D. A. (1994). The philosophy and practice of client-centered therapy with older persons: An interview with C. H. Patterson. *The Person-Centered Journal, 1,* 49–54.

O'HARA, M. (1997). Relational empathy: Beyond modernist egocentrism to postmodern contextualism. In A. C. Bohart & L. S. Greenberg (Eds.), *Empathy reconsidered: New directions in psychotherapy* (pp. 295–320). Washington: American Psychological Association.

O'LEARY, E. (1997). Towards integrating person-centered and Gestalt therapies. *The Person-Centered Journal, 4,* 14–22.

PATTERSON, C. H. (1986). *Theories of counseling and psychotherapy* (4th ed.). New York: Harper-Collins.

PATTERSON, C. H. & HIDORE, S. (1997). The primary prevention of psychological disorders. *The Person-Centered Journal, 4,* 8–17.

PESCHKEN, W. E. , & JOHNSON, M. E. (1997). Therapist and client trust in the therapeutic relationship. *Psychotherapy Research, 7,* 439–447.

RANK, O. (1945). *Will therapy, truth and reality.* New York: Knopf.

ROGERS, C. R. (1939). *The clinical treatment of the problem child.* Boston: Houghton Mifflin.

ROGERS, C. R. (1942a). *Counseling and psychotherapy.* Boston: Houghton Mifflin.

ROGERS, C. R. (1942b). The use of electrically recorded interviews in improving psychotherapeutic techniques. *American Journal of Orthopsychiatry, 12,* 429–434.

ROGERS, C. R. (1951). *Client-centered therapy: Its current practice, implications, and theory.* Boston: Houghton Mifflin.

ROGERS, C. R. (1953). Some of the directions evident in therapy. In O. H. Mowrer (Ed.), *Psychotherapy: Theory and research.* New York: Ronald Press.

ROGERS, C. R. (1957). The necessary and sufficient conditions of therapeutic personality change. *Journal of Consulting Psychology, 21,* 95–103.

ROGERS, C. R. (1959). A theory of therapy, personality and interpersonal relationships as developed in the client-centered framework. In S. Koch (Ed.), *Psychology: A study of science: Formulations of the person and the social context* (pp 184–256). New York: McGraw-Hill.

ROGERS, C. R. (1961). *On becoming a person.* Boston: Houghton Mifflin.

ROGERS, C. R. (1966). Client-centered therapy. In S. Arieti (Ed.), *American handbook of psychiatry* (Vol. 3, pp. 183–200). New York: Basic Books.

ROGERS, C. R. (1969). *Freedom to learn: A view of what education might become.* Columbus, OH: Charles E. Merrill.

ROGERS, C. R. (1970). *Carl Rogers on encounter groups.* New York: Harper & Row.

ROGERS, C. R. (1972). *Becoming partners: Marriage and its alternatives.* New York: Delacorte Press.

ROGERS, C. R. (1975). Empathic: An unappreciated way of being. *Counseling Psychologist, 5*, 2–10.

ROGERS, C. R. (1977). *Carl Rogers on personal power.* New York: Delacorte Press.

ROGERS, C. R. (1980). *A way of being.* Boston: Houghton Mifflin.

ROGERS, C. R. (1986). Carl Rogers on the development of the person-centered approach. *Person-Centered Review, 1*, 257–259.

ROGERS C. R., GENDLIN, G. T., KIESLER, D. V., & TRUAX, C. (Eds.). (1967). *The therapeutic relationship and its impact: A study of psychotherapy with schizophrenics.* Madison: University of Wisconsin Press.

ROGERS C. R., & HAIGH, G. (1983). I walk softly through life. *Voices: The Art and Science of Psychotherapy, 18*, 6–14.

ROGERS C. R., & RABLEN, R. A. (1958). *A scale of process in psychotherapy.* Unpublished manuscript.

ROGERS, D., & BICKHAM, P. J. (1995). A child's journey through loss. *The Person-Centered Journal, 2*, 94–103.

ROMBAUTS, J., & DEVRIENDT, M. (1990). Conjoint couple therapy in client-centered practice. In G. Lietaer, J. Rombauts, & R. Van Balen (Eds.), *Client-centered and experiential psychotherapy in the nineties* (pp. 847–863). Leuven, Belgium: Leuven University Press.

SALEY, E., & HOLDSTOCK, L. (1993). Encounter group experiences of black and white South Africans in exile. In D. Brazier (Ed.), *Beyond Carl Rogers* (pp. 201–216). London: Constable.

SEEMAN, J. (1989). A reaction to "Psychodiagnosis: A person-centered perspective." *Person-Centered Review, 4*, 152–156.

SINGH, J., & TUDOR, K. (1997). Cultural conditions of therapy. *The Person-Centered Journal, 4*, 32–46.

SWILDENS, J. C. A. G. (1990). Client-centered psychotherapy for patients with borderline symptoms. In G. Lietaer, J. Rombauts, & R. Van Balen (Eds.), *Client-centered and experiential psychotherapy in the nineties* (pp. 623–635). Leuven, Belgium: Leuven University Press.

TAUSCH, R. (1990). The supplementation of client-centered communication therapy with other valid therapeutic methods: A client-centered necessity. In G. Lietaer, J. Rombauts, & R. Van Balen (Eds.), *Client-centered and experiential psychotherapy in the nineties* (pp. 447–455). Leuven, Belgium: Leuven University Press.

THORNE, B. (1992). *Carl Rogers.* London: Sage.

TRUAX, C. B. (1970). Effects of client-centered psychotherapy with schizophrenic patients: Nine years pre-therapy and nine years post-therapy hospitalization. *Journal of Consulting and Clinical Psychology, 3*, 417–422.

TRUAX, C. B., & CARKHUFF, R. R. (1967). *Toward effective counseling and psychotherapy.* Chicago: Aldine.

TRUAX, C. B., & MITCHELL, K. M. (1971). Research on certain therapist interpersonal skills in relation to process and outcome. In A. E. Bergin & S. L. Garfield (Eds.), *Handbook of psychotherapy and behavior change: An empirical analysis* (pp. 299–344). New York: Wiley.

WEISZ, J. R., WEISS, B., ALICKE, M. D., & KLOTZ, M. L. (1987). Effectiveness of psychotherapy with children and adolescents: A meta-analysis for clinicians. *Journal of Consulting and Clinical Psychology, 55*, 542–549.

WEISZ, J. R., WEISS, B., HAN, S. S., GRANGER, D. A., & MORTON, T. (1995). Effects of psychotherapy with children and adolescents revisited: A meta-analysis of treatment outcome studies. *Psychological Bulletin, 117*, 450–468.

WIINGAARDEN, H. R. (1990). Carl Rogers, Carl Jung and client-centered therapy. In G. Lietaer, J. Rombauts, & R. Van Balen (Eds.), *Client-centered and experiential psychotherapy in the nineties* (pp. 469–480). Leuven, Belgium: Leuven University Press.

WITHERS, L. E., & WANTZ, R. A. (1993). The influences of belief systems on subjects' perceptions of empathy, warmth and genuineness. *Psychotherapy, 30*, 608–615.

7

Gestalt Therapy

The term *Gestalt* refers to the dynamic organization of a whole that comprises two or more related parts. Gestalt therapy is concerned with the whole individual, who is viewed as more than the sum of her behaviors. A phenomenological method that values human experience as the source of data, Gestalt therapy emphasizes the patient's and the therapist's experience of reality. It is an existential approach in that it stresses the responsibility of individuals for themselves and their ability to determine their own present experience. In Gestalt therapy, issues dealing with the past or future are brought into the present. The general goal of Gestalt therapy is awareness of self, others, and the environment that brings about growth and integration of the individual.

Gestalt therapy emphasizes having an appropriate boundary between self and others. The boundary must be flexible enough for meaningful contact with others but firm enough for the individual to experience a sense of autonomy. When an individual is not clear about the boundary between self and others, a disturbance of contact and awareness can occur, resulting in psychopathology. Approaches to therapy focus on being responsible for oneself and being attuned to one's language, nonverbal behaviors, emotional feelings, and conflicts within oneself and with others. Gestalt therapists have developed creative experiments and exercises to facilitate self-awareness that they use in an empathic relationship with the client. Along with individual therapy, group therapy has been an important part of Gestalt treatment. Both modalities assist the individual in resolving conflicts with self and others, as well as dealing with problems from the past that have emerged into the present.

HISTORY OF GESTALT THERAPY

In understanding Gestalt therapy, it is helpful to understand both its developer, Fritz Perls, and the various psychological and psychotherapeutic theories that influenced his thinking (Clarkson & Mackewn, 1993). Although trained in psychoanalysis, other psychological theories and philosophical approaches led to his development of a therapeutic system that is very different from psychoanalysis.

FRITZ PERLS

Frederick S. (Fritz) Perls originated, developed, and popularized Gestalt therapy. He was born in Berlin in 1893, the youngest of three children, to older middle-class German Jewish parents. His family was affected by the rise of Nazism, and his eldest sister was killed in a concentration camp (Shepard, 1975). Both Perls and his younger sister describe him as being a problem child who was in trouble at home and at school, failed the seventh grade twice, and was asked to leave school. For a short time he worked for a merchant before returning to school at the age of 14. Later he studied medicine and, at 23, left school to volunteer to serve in World War I as a medic, first as a private and later as an officer.

After he obtained his medical degree in 1920, he worked as an assistant to Kurt Goldstein at the Institute for Brain Injured Soldiers. Perls was influenced by Goldstein, who viewed the soldiers with brain injuries from a Gestalt psychology perspective, focusing on the perceptions that the soldiers had of themselves and their environment. While he was at the Institute in Frankfurt, Perls met several people who were to have great impact on his later work, including his future wife, Laura, 12 years younger than he.

Perls trained as a psychoanalyst at the Vienna and Berlin Institutes of Psychoanalysis. His training analyst was Wilhelm Reich, who was to become particularly influential in the development of Perls's ideas about Gestalt therapy. Perls was also influenced by analysts Helene Deutsch, Otto Fenichel, and Karen Horney. During this time, he also met Adler, Jung, and Freud. In 1934, due to the rise of Nazism, Perls left Germany for South Africa.

He established the South African Institute for Psychoanalysis in 1935. While in South Africa he met Jan Smuts, author of *Holism and Evolution* (1926), which had an influence on Perls's development of Gestalt psychotherapy. After 12 years in South Africa, he left for New York City. Along with Paul Goodman and Laura Perls, he established the New York Institute for Gestalt Therapy in 1952. After 9 years in New York, Perls moved to or visited a variety of cities and countries and established Gestalt training centers in Miami, San Francisco, Los Angeles, Israel, Japan, and Canada. Between 1964 and 1969 he was an associate psychiatrist in residence at the Esalen Institute. In 1969 he moved to Cowichan Lake on Vancouver Island, British Columbia, where he initiated the establishment of a therapeutic community. He died about 6 months later in 1970.

The development of Gestalt therapy and Perls's movement away from psychoanalysis can be seen in the dramatic contrast between his early and later writings. While in South Africa, Perls wrote *Ego, Hunger, and Aggression* (1969a) (originally published in 1947), which combined his ideas about the whole organism with traditional ideas of psychoanalysis. He also focused on the hunger instinct, which he related to psychological functioning. In eating and in psychological functioning, people bite off what they can chew (food, ideas, or relationships), then chew and digest (think about and receive physiological or psychological nourishment). What Perls called "mental metabolism" represents psychological functioning in Gestalt therapy. In this book he describes "concentration-therapy," which was the early term for Gestalt therapy that had as its goal "waking the organism to a fuller life" (Perls, 1969a). Although she is not given credit in the book, Laura Perls wrote several of the chapters. In 1951 Perls, along with Ralph F. Hefferline and Paul Goodman, wrote *Gestalt Therapy: Excitement and Growth in the Human Personality*, which consists of two parts. The first has exercises designed to develop awareness of the senses and the body; the second describes the theory of Gestalt therapy.

Perls's later works are more informal in style. *Gestalt Therapy Verbatim* (1969b) includes a section on the theory of Gestalt therapy, along with questions from participants in a seminar and Perls's answers. Most of the book is made up of verbatim transcripts of Perls's work with individuals who attended weekend training sessions on dreams, as well as those in a 4-week intensive workshop. Perls's autobiography, *In and out of the Garbage Pail* (1969c), is very informal, interspersed with poetry, humor, and comments about his work. After his death, two books that he was working on were published. The first, *The Gestalt Approach* (1973), included theoretical material about Gestalt therapy as well as transcripts from films. The second book, *Legacy from Fritz* (1975), written by Patricia Baumgardner, includes transcripts from films of Fritz Perls working with individuals in group training seminars. The abundant case material contained in the last four books gives excellent examples of Perls's style of working with individuals in a group training format.

After Perls's death, Gestalt therapy continued to grow. There are more than 60 Gestalt therapy institutes throughout the world, with many in the United States. There are no national or international standards for Gestalt therapists, with each institute establishing its own standards for training and qualifications. Forums for the development of the theory and practice of Gestalt therapy are *The Gestalt Journal*, the *Gestalt Review*, and the *British Gestalt Journal*. Also, an annual meeting as well as numerous conferences have provided the opportunity for presentations on recent developments in Gestalt therapy.

Influences on the Development of Gestalt Therapy

Although trained as a psychoanalyst and influenced by Freud's theoretical work, Perls took advantage of the intellectually rich city of Frankfurt when he was a medical student and practicing psychiatrist. He was influenced by Wilhelm Reich's ideas on verbal and nonverbal behavior, and was attracted to Sigmund Friedlander's work on creative difference. Work with Kurt Goldstein introduced Perls to the application of Gestalt psychology to therapeutic treatment. From a more theoretical and philosophical point of view, his development of Gestalt therapy was influenced by Lewin's field theory, phenomenology, and existentialism. On a more personal level, his wife, Laura, a practicing Gestalt therapist, writer, and teacher, made an invaluable contribution to Gestalt therapy. These various influences are the intellectual underpinnings of Perls's development of Gestalt therapy.

Wilhelm Reich was particularly influential in Perls's development of Gestalt therapy, both as his training analyst and through his writings. Reich paid attention to the linguistic, facial, and body positions of his patients. Rather than view libido as energy inherent in childhood sexuality, Reich saw libido as excitement that was apparent in an individual. The defenses that individuals applied to repress their libido he called *body armor*. For Reich, therapy involved helping individuals become less rigid by attending to tensions in their language and body awareness. In his new introduction for *Ego, Hunger, and Aggression* (1969a), Perls pays a special tribute to Reich's "bringing down to earth the psychology of resistances" (p. 5), which Reich did by attending to bodily awareness within individuals.

The work of the philosopher Sigmund Friedlander had an impact on Perls's concept of polarities. Friedlander believed that every event was related to a zero-point from which opposites can be differentiated. This zero-point was a balance point in which an individual could move creatively in either direction. Perls (1969a, p. 15) states: "By remaining alert in the centre, we can acquire a creative ability of seeing both sides of an occurrence and completing an incomplete half." When an individual is too far on one side or the other of an external or an internal need, there is a tendency to need to balance it or move to the center. In his work, Perls was often involved in helping individuals achieve a sense of balance, centeredness, or control over their needs.

Perls was influenced by Kurt Goldstein, not only through working with him at the Institute for Brain Injured Soldiers, but also through Goldstein's (1939) writings. Goldstein believed that behavior is made up of performances (voluntary activities, attitudes, feelings) and processes (bodily functions). Like Friedlander, Goldstein believed that organisms moved in a direction to balance their needs. In doing so, they came to terms with environmental pressures. In this process, they strived for "self-actualization" (Emerson & Smith, 1974).

Perls (1969a) found Goldstein's view of anxiety as arising from the fear of the possible outcome of future events to be relevant to Gestalt therapy. Also, anxiety could lead to the separation of parts of the personality from the whole person, bringing about a splitting of the personality. Another contribution of Goldstein, as well as of the semanticist Alfred Korzybski, was the emphasis on precision in language in therapy. In his work with brain-damaged soldiers, Goldstein observed their inability to think abstractly and, therefore, their inability to use language fully.

Field theory was developed by Kurt Lewin and several other Gestalt psychologists. Similar to Gestalt psychology, field theory studies an event by looking at the whole field of which an event is a part. The relationship of the parts to each other and to the whole is the object of the study. This is a descriptive approach rather than one of classification. Field theory takes a phenomenological approach in that the field is related to the observer. To understand an event, one must know the observer's way of viewing the event. An example of using field theory to make hypotheses is the Zeigarnik effect in which Zeigarnik hypothesized and found that unfinished tasks could be remembered better than finished tasks because of tension remaining within the field (Woodworth & Schlosberg, 1954).

The phenomenological approach that was inherent in the work of Reich, Friedlander, Lewin, and Goldstein, as well as in that of Gestalt psychologists, has had an impact on the development of Perls's Gestalt therapy. The phenomenological perspective holds that an individual's behavior can be understood only through studying his subjective perceptions of reality. Phenomenologists study both the perceptions and the process of perceiving. The environment is seen only as something that exists as it is experienced by individuals (Watzlawick, 1984). The focus on, and the enhancing of, awareness was an important aspect of Perls's therapeutic approach, which was perhaps most impressed upon him by his work with Wilhelm Reich. From a phenomenological point of view, Perls was interested in not only the patient's awareness but also the entire field—the therapist's awareness of the interaction of the patient and therapist (Watzlawick, 1984).

Perls viewed Gestalt therapy as one of three existential therapies, along with Binswanger's Daseinanalysis and Frankl's logotherapy. Because existentialism is rooted in phenomenology, existentialists focus on the direct experience of existence, joys and suffering, and relationships with others. The existentialist's concept of authenticity has some similarity to the Gestalt concept of awareness in that both include an honest appraisal and an understanding of oneself. The existential emphasis on individual responsibility for actions, feelings, and thoughts is consistent with that of Gestalt therapy. Like Gestalt therapy, existentialism focused on the present rather than the past or future. Although it is difficult to judge the impact of existentialism on Gestalt therapy, there are many similarities between the two.

On a more personal level, Laura Posner Perls made an essential contribution to Gestalt psychotherapy. Yontef and Simkin (1989) consider her to be a cofounder of Gestalt therapy. Born near Frankfurt, Germany, in 1905, she married Fritz Perls in 1930 and received the D.Sc. degree from the University of Frankfurt in 1932. She was influenced by Max Wertheimer and the existentialists Paul Tillich and Martin Buber (Humphrey, 1986). Not only did she contribute to Fritz Perls's first book, *Ego, Hunger, and Aggression*, but she also participated in the discussions leading to his second major book, *Gestalt Therapy*. Laura became involved in the New York Institute for Gestalt Therapy, founded in 1952, in both leading training groups and providing leadership of the institute, until her death at age 85 in 1990. Although they were physically separated for most of the last 15 years of Fritz's life, they kept in contact, discussing issues related to Gestalt therapy. Because she published very little, her contribution to Gestalt therapy is difficult to assess. One contribution of her work was her respect for and maintenance of marital and other relationships, in contrast to the work of her husband, who focused on awareness rather than the development of relationships (Rosenblatt, 1988).

GESTALT THEORY OF PERSONALITY

Awareness and relationships with self and others are the major emphasis of Gestalt personality theory. Many of the concepts that are important in Gestalt psychotherapy have their basis in Gestalt psychology concepts such as figure and ground. Gestalt personality theory attends to the contact between the individual and others or objects that immediately affect the individual. There is a focus on the boundaries between individuals and their environment, as well as the depth of contact with self and others. Gestalt personality theory emphasizes the importance of the individual being-aware of oneself and one's environment in terms of the senses, bodily sensations, and emotional feelings. The attention to being in contact with oneself and others and the awareness of self and others takes place in the present, rather than past or future. These somewhat vague concepts are described in more detail here.

Gestalt Psychology and Gestalt Therapy

Gestalt psychology was first developed by Max Wertheimer and later by Wolfgang Kohler and Kurt Koffka. Essentially, Gestalt psychology is based on the view that psy-

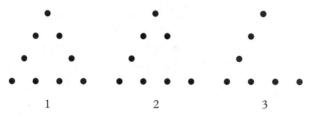

FIGURE 7.1 Stages of completeness in triangles.

chological phenomena are organized wholes rather than specific parts. Gestalt psychologists principally studied visual and auditory perception and viewed learning as a perceptual problem in which individuals attempt to discover a correct response in their perceptual field (Emerson & Smith, 1974). In doing so, individuals experience the "Aha!" response, or "Now I see it" or "Now, I understand it; it's all come together for me!" Some properties of a phenomenon cannot be observed by looking at its parts but occur only when individuals view the entirety. For example, a student learning algebra may know formulas, but only when these formulas are brought together is she able to arrive at the solution to the problem.

In Gestalt psychology the "field" can be viewed in terms of "figure" and "ground." The figure is what stands out, and the ground is the background. For example, when you look at Triangle 1 in Figure 7.1, that is the figure; the rest of the page and your surroundings are the ground. The triangle, page, and surroundings make up the field. Figures differ in their strength and goodness of form. The series of dots in Triangle 1 are perceived as a triangle. The dots in Triangle 2 are an incomplete Gestalt but can also be perceived as a triangle. The third series of dots is a very weak Gestalt that can be viewed as two lines, an angle, or a triangle. Gestalt psychologists have developed Gestalt laws, or laws of perception, to explain how individuals see these series of dots. In fact, Boring (1950) lists more than 114 laws.

Although therapists have applied these concepts to feelings and bodily sensations, Gestalt psychologists did not (Wallen, 1970). In fact, Gestalt psychologists have been quite critical of the loose and inaccurate ways in which Perls applied Gestalt psychology to Gestalt psychotherapy (Arnheim, 1974; Henle, 1978). Sherrill (1986, p. 54) states: "Gestalt therapists see close kinship between the two Gestalt systems; Gestalt psychologists deny any meaningful similarity."

Despite the criticisms of Gestalt psychologists about the applications of Gestalt psychological concepts to Gestalt therapy, concepts of figure and ground are important in understanding the theoretical rationale of Gestalt therapy. When figures are incomplete or unclear, they are forced into a background that may be distracting for the individual (Polster & Polster, 1973, p. 30). For example, a boy who is afraid of snakes is unable to bring the concept of snakes fully into the foreground or to become a complete figure. When the boy can touch snakes and be unafraid, then the figure is complete.

Wallen (1970) cites three kinds of interferences in developing a complete Gestalt, or clear figure against the ground. First, individuals may have poor perceptual contact with others and with themselves. An example would be looking away from a friend when one is talking to her. Second, a complete Gestalt is thwarted when expression of needs is blocked. Wanting to express affection to a friend but refraining from doing so is an illustration. Third, repressing feelings or perceptions can prevent the formation of a complete Gestalt. Inability to express psychological hurt after someone has insulted an individual may interfere with the development of a full Gestalt experience. Such an individual is likely to feel anxious, experience some muscular tension in the stomach, or otherwise be unable to complete the Gestalt.

The therapist then works to assist individuals in unblocking their tensions, thus completing the Gestalt, so that the figure is full and complete. In doing so, the therapist helps the patient develop improved contact with people in his world. Taking risks and removing blocks to experiences help individuals discover their own boundaries.

Contact

"Contact is the lifeblood of growth, means for changing oneself, and one's experience of the world" (Polster & Polster, 1973, p. 101). Contact differs from fusion, as contact exists when there is a sense of separateness that is maintained. In fusion, there is no separateness. Although contact is a quality that occurs with other persons and objects, rarely are people aware of the contact that they have with others. With contact can come a sense of self as well as a sense of impingement on a boundary. For Polster and Polster (1973), the challenge is how to maintain lively, productive contact with people and things, without losing a sense of identity (being fused).

Although much contact is ordinary and occurs frequently during an individual's day, contact episodes in Gestalt therapy can be powerful and meaningful. The following excerpt gives an example of the power of therapeutic contact.

> Witness the experience of a lovely young woman, 20 years old, in the center of a group telling about already having been a drug addict and prostitute and, four years earlier, having had a child who had been given up for adoption. Now she was on a new track in life, helping young addicts and going through college herself. In a peak poignant moment, she turned to one of the men in the group and asked him to hold her. He nodded, and after some hesitation, she went over to him and he held her. At this point she let go and cried. After her crying subsided, she looked up, alarmed about what the other women in the group might feel about her being held and being the center of focus in the room. I said that perhaps she could teach the other women something about how to be held. She was obviously at home being held and showed a fluid grace and welcoming quality which wouldn't hurt anyone to learn. For a while, then, she felt calm, remaining in the man's arms but still tuned in to the reactions of the women in the group, who were actually very moved emotionally and were unjudging. She then asked one of the more attractive and guiding women whether she would hold her. The drama was of such force that it was almost inevitable that the woman would indeed want to hold her. She walked over to where the girl was seated and took her into her arms. At this point the final letting go came, and the girl cried more deeply than before. When she was done, her tension had left, she felt unselfconscious and altogether at one with the group. (Polster & Polster, 1973, pp. 104–105)[1]

Levels of contact have been described by Perls (1969b, 1969c, 1970) as five layers of neuroses. To become psychologically mature, individuals must strip off each of the five layers: phony, phobic, impasse, implosive, and explosive. Each layer's removal reveals increasingly impactful contact with the environment.

1. The *phony* layer refers to reacting to others in unauthentic or patterned ways. Examples are "How are you?" and "Have a nice day." More substantial examples include trying to be nice to someone so they will buy something from you.

2. At the *phobic* layer is an avoidance of psychological pain. For example, we may not want to admit to ourselves that an important relationship is over.

3. *Impasse* is the point at which we are afraid to change or move. We may feel very little, only a sense of stuckness. Perls (1970, p. 25) gives an example of a marriage in which the partners are no longer in love; they have ideas of what the other should be, but no ideas of what the other is really like. They blame each other and are at an impasse. Individuals feel little internal or external support. This is a particularly significant level for making therapeutic change.

4. At the *implosive* level we experience our feelings, start to become aware of the real self, but may do little about the feelings.

5. Contact with the *explosive* layer is authentic and without pretense. For Perls it was necessary to experience the explosive to become truly alive and authentic. The example of the young woman on the previous page illustrates the experiencing of the explosive layer.

Contact Boundaries

I-boundaries are those that distinguish between one person and another, a person and an object, or the person and a quality of the person (Polster & Polster, 1973, pp. 107–108). I-boundaries are formed by an individual's life experiences. Polster and Polster distinguish vantage points from which I-boundaries can be described: body-boundaries, value-boundaries, familiarity-boundaries, and expressive-boundaries.

Body-boundaries are those that may restrict sensations or place them off-limits. Polster and Polster (1973, pp. 115–116) describe a man with a complaint of impotence who was at first aware only of head movements and became more and more aware of a trembling sensation in his legs that led to a sense of peacefulness in his body. Thus, his body-boundary was extended.

Value-boundaries refer to values we hold that we are resistant to changing. When a man who holds anti-abortion values must deal with the unwanted pregnancy of an unmarried 17-year-old daughter, value boundaries may be challenged, possibly changed, or possibly reinforced.

Familiarity-boundaries refer to events that are often repeated but may not be thought about or challenged. Examples include going to the same job every day, taking the same route to work every day, or interacting in a stereotyped way with an associate. If an individual loses a job or experiences the rejection of a marriage partner, the challenge to familiarity-boundaries can be devastating.

Expressive-boundaries are learned at an early age. We learn not to yell, not to whine, not to touch, and so forth. In the United States, men have often been taught not to cry. For a man to be in contact with important others, it may be necessary to extend his expressive-boundary.

Contact Boundary Disturbances

There are occasions when the boundary between self and others becomes vague, disintegrates, or is otherwise disturbed. Sometimes an individual keeps out nourishing and helpful aspects of objects or others. In one sense, the individual is out of balance, and needs are not being met. If the contact with objects or others is resisted, the interaction with the object or other may be observed following one of these five patterns: introjection, projection, retroflection, deflection, and confluence (Polster & Polster, 1973).

Introjection refers to swallowing whole or accepting others' views without reviewing them. For example, children often take their parents' opinions as fact rather than as values. As children grow older, they introject their parents views less frequently. Doing so may be appropriate at some times, but not at others. Introjection can be healthy or pathological, depending on the circumstances.

Projection refers to the dismissing or disowning of aspects of ourselves by assigning them to others. Often feelings of guilt or anger may lead individuals to project blame onto someone else. By doing so, the individual may feel better temporarily, but full contact with others is reduced. In projection, aspects of the self are put onto others, thus extending the boundary between self and others. Blaming a professor for failing an exam for which an individual did not study is an example of projection.

Retroflection consists of doing to ourselves what we want to do to someone else, or it can refer to doing things for ourselves that we want others to do for us. The statement "I can do it myself" when we want others to help us is an example of retroflection. Although this behavior is designed to make us feel self-sufficient, we may feel alone and cut off from others. In retroflection a function that is originally directed from an individual toward others changes directions and returns to the individual. In an extreme example, suicide becomes a substitute for murder. More symbolically, biting one's nails can be a substitute for aggression toward others or biting off their heads. In this way, the nailbiter symbolically treats himself as he wants to treat others.

Deflection refers to indirect avoidance of contact. The person who does not get to the point, who is overly polite, or talks constantly is deflecting—avoiding contact. Other examples include talking about something rather than talking to someone or substituting mild emotions for strong ones. Particularly at the beginning of the therapeutic process, it is common for patients to deflect—to describe their problems abstractly or as if they belong to another person, or to include irrelevant details. Avoiding physical contact is an example of deflecting contact.

Confluence occurs when the boundary between one's self and others becomes muted or lessened. In relationships there may be a perception that both individuals have the same feelings and thoughts, when in fact the individuals have become less aware of their own feelings and values. People who feel a strong need to be accepted may experience confluence; they relinquish their true feelings and opinions for the acceptance of others. Thus, knowing how they truly feel or think is difficult for them.

O'Leary (1997) compares confluence with empathy. In doing so, she draws person-centered and Gestalt therapy closer together. Healthy confluence can be experienced as empathy toward individuals or groups. Unhealthy confluence may serve to isolate individuals from others, as they agree with others without unconditional positive regard or understanding. Healthy expression of confluence by therapists can be experienced by clients as empathic understanding. O'Leary, Purcell, McSweeney, O'Flynn, O'Sullivan, Keane, and Barry (1998) show how person-centered Gestalt groups can be useful by modeling and teaching empathy, confluence, and other Gestalt approaches in training therapists.

Gestalt therapists assume that contact is healthy and necessary for satisfactory psychological functioning. Introjection, projection, retroflection, deflection, and confluence are ways of diminishing, avoiding, or otherwise resisting contact. In judging whether these are used in a healthy or unhealthy way, Frew (1988) uses two major criteria. He wants to know if individuals are aware of what they are doing and how their particular style works for them. Also, he wants to assess whether the style lets individuals meet their current needs. Awareness of what they are doing and how their needs are being met is an indication of the degree of contact that they have with their boundaries with other people and other things. Both in individual and group therapy, Gestalt therapists are attuned to how individuals avoid psychological contact with themselves or with others.

Awareness

Awareness of oneself is an important part of Gestalt personality theory, referring to contact within individuals themselves, as well as with others and objects. Polster and Polster (1973) identify four types of awareness: (1) Awareness of sensations and actions pertains to sensing through seeing, hearing, touching, or other senses and then expressing oneself through movement or vocal expression; (2) awareness of feelings concerns awareness of both emotional feelings and physical feelings such as sweaty palms or shortness of breath; (3) awareness of wants refers to awareness of desires for future events to take place, such as to graduate from college or to win the lottery; and (4) awareness of values and assessments concerns larger units of experience than those mentioned, including how one values others, social and spiritual issues, and other assessments of events related to these. Awareness refers to what is happening now, rather than what is remembered.

To be fully aware is to be in contact with one's boundaries. In the following description of Tom, Polster and Polster (1973) give an example of how a patient is helped to become more aware of sensations and actions, feelings, and wants. It helps illustrate the value that Gestalt therapists place on the development of awareness.

A simple example of following awarenesses from moment to moment is this illustration from a therapy session. The session started with Tom's awareness of his tight jaw and moved through several intermediate steps to a loosening up of his speaking mannerisms and then to the recovery of some childhood memories. Tom, a minister, felt that he could not pronounce words as he would like to. His voice had a metallic tone and he turned out his words like a brittle robot. I noticed an odd angle to his jaw and asked him what he felt there. He said he felt tight. So I asked him to exaggerate the movements of his mouth and jaw. He felt very inhibited about this and described his awareness first of embarrassment, then stubbornness. He remembered that his parents used to nag him about speaking clearly and he would go out of his way *not* to. At this point he became aware of tightness in his throat. He was speaking with muscular strain, forcing out his voice rather than using the support which his breathing could give him. So, I asked Tom to bring more air into his speech, showing him how to coordinate speaking with breathing by using a little more air and by trying to feel the air as a source of support. His coordination was faulty, though so faulty as to border on stuttering. When I asked him whether he had ever stuttered, he looked startled, became aware of his coordination troubles, and then remembered what he had until then forgotten that he had stuttered until he was six or seven. He recalled a scene from a day when he had been three or four years old; his mother was phoning from some distant place and was asking him what he wanted. He tried to say, "ice cream," but his mother misunderstood and thought he said, "I scream" and took it to mean that he was going to scream at his brother and she became infuriated with him. He recalled still another scene. His mother was in the bathroom and he heard what at first he thought was her laughter. He was startled when he realized it was not laughter at all; she was crying hysterically. Tom remembered once again the horrible feeling of incongruity. As he recounted the story he also became aware of his own feelings of confusion both in being misunderstood by his mother and by misunderstanding her. Having recovered the old sensations, his speech became more open and his jaw softened too. He felt relieved and renewed. (Polster & Polster, 1973, pp. 212–213)[2]

The Present

Prior and future events are seen through the present. The present is also important because only here can an individual's bodily and sensory systems be seen. When a patient talks *about* an event, the individual is distanced from the event and is not in the present. Although the present is important, past history and future plans are also considered. Gestalt therapists may assess the way in which the past and future are stated in the present.

An important concept in Gestalt therapy is that of *unfinished business*, which refers to feelings from the past that have been unexpressed but are dealt with in the present. The feelings may be of anger, hatred, guilt, fear, and so forth, or they may be memories or fantasies that are still within the individual. Sometimes unfinished business may take the form of an obsession with money, sex, or some other issue. By working through unfinished business, individuals are completing a Gestalt. When closure has been accomplished, the preoccupation with the past is completed.

In the last case, Tom brings the past into the present. His tight jaw reminds him of being nagged by his parents about speaking clearly. It brings him back to unfinished business about his mother's misinterpretation of his attempt to say "ice cream" and his feeling of incongruity when he realized his mother was not laughing, but crying. Moving the past into the present enabled Tom to feel a sense of relief. The unfinished business was finished. Notice in this example that Tom does not talk *about* his mother, but rather feels the situation in the therapy hour. As Enright (1970) points out, it is important to be in the present where bodily tension and nonverbal behavior can be attended to, so that the past can be brought into the present.

THEORY OF GESTALT PSYCHOTHERAPY

Gestalt therapy has as its basic goal the development of growth and personal integration through awareness. Given this goal, the therapeutic role is different than that in other therapies, with an emphasis on the present and utilization of awareness. In Gestalt therapy, much assessment is through the therapist's moment-to-moment observation of the patient. Many observations provide a useful overview of the problem for both patient and therapist. Resulting from this assessment are procedures to enhance the patient's awareness, both verbal and nonverbal. Integrating approaches to awareness takes creativity and experience.

Goals of Therapy

Perls (1969b, p. 26) has stated that the goal of therapy is to help individuals mature and to grow. Implied in this definition (Passons, 1975) is the emphasis on self-responsibility, helping patients depend on themselves rather than on others (Perls, 1969b). Therapy should assist patients in seeing that they can do much more than they think they can do. Thus, patients become more self-aware and move toward self-actualization.

Implicit in the goal of maturity and growth is that of achieving integration. Perls (1973, p. 26) states, "The man who can live in concernful contact with his society, neither being swallowed up by it nor withdrawing from it completely, is the well integrated man." Integration implies that a person's feelings, perceptions, thoughts, and body processes are part of a larger whole (Gary Yontef, personal communication, September 1, 1998). When a person is not fully integrated, there are voids and the individual is likely to experience contact boundary disturbances. Perls (1948) believed that the integration of previously alienated parts was an extremely important goal of psychotherapy.

Basic to maturity, growth, and integration is the development of awareness. Perls (1969b, p. 16) put it this way: "Awareness per se—by and of itself—can be curative." He believed that with full awareness the organism or individual would regulate itself and function optimally. Fully aware individuals are aware of their environment, are responsible for their choices, and accept themselves.

Zinker (1978, pp. 96–97) outlines in more detail the ways in which Gestalt therapy helps individuals become more fully aware of themselves and their environment.

- Individuals develop fuller awareness of their bodies, feelings, and environment.
- Individuals own their own experiences, rather than projecting them onto others.
- Individuals learn to be aware of their own needs and skills in order to satisfy themselves without violating the rights of others.
- Fuller contact with sensations (smelling, tasting, touching, hearing, and seeing) allows individuals to savor all aspects of themselves.
- Rather than whining, blaming, or guiltmaking, individuals experience their power and ability to support themselves.
- Individuals become sensitive to their surroundings, yet are able to protect themselves from those parts of the environment that may be dangerous.
- Responsibility for actions and consequences are a part of greater awareness.
- Individuals are comfortable with their awareness, of their fantasy in the expression of this life.

As therapy progresses (Zinker, 1978), individuals gradually feel more comfortable in experiencing their own energy and using it in a productive and complete way. These are general goals of Gestalt therapy. By feeding back observations and encouraging the client to become more aware, the therapist helps clients achieve their goals.

Gestalt therapy can be applied to many individuals, including those with severe psychological problems. In her discussion of borderline personality, Greenberg (1989) suggests that many Gestalt techniques that will bring about awareness need to be introduced later in therapy, when the patient's emotionality becomes more stable. For Shepherd (1970), the first step with patients who are severely disturbed is to help them develop contact with reality. Deeper struggles are left until later. With patients who may be sociopathic or delinquent, goals related to awareness may be difficult because of aggressive or manipulative behavior on the part of the client. With severely disturbed and sociopathic clients, the goals of integration and growth may take years of therapy.

Gestalt therapy is particularly appropriate for individuals who are inhibited. Examples are people who are overly socialized or feel restrained or constricted in some way. Those who are perfectionistic, phobic, or feel depressed may be inhibiting their awareness of themselves and others. Shepherd (1970) warns that as individuals get in touch with themselves and experience dissatisfaction with conventional goals or relationships, they may find themselves frustrated with much social interaction and find less in common with others who do not share their growth or awareness.

The Therapeutic Relationship

For Gestalt therapy to be effective, a good therapeutic relationship is important. Gestalt therapists have been influenced by the work of Carl Rogers, Martin Buber, and more recently, the concepts found in intersubjectivity theory, an approach related to self psychology. All of these focus on ways to understand the client and to communicate this understanding to the client. Gestalt interventions (to be described later) are used within the context of the client therapist relationship.

Being attuned to the client's experience was essential for Carl Rogers. Gestalt therapists concur, agreeing with Roger's emphasis on empathy. Being genuine and showing the client that you understand is an important aspect of therapy (Greenberg, Rice, & Elliott, 1993). The empathic responding of the therapist provides continuing support to the client. Additionally, clients support themselves through their own motivation for therapy, their intelligence, and their commitment to therapy (Yontef, 1995).

To bring about growth through awareness a meaningful relationship with the therapist is essential (Yontef, 1995). Buber's (1965) discussion of the I-thou relationship has been important in understanding the Gestalt view of a *dialogic* relationship. The dialogue exists to meet or understand the other person, not to do something to the person. In this dialogue the individual becomes fully aware of the other person while still being aware of his or her own separate existence. The dialogue occurs; it is not directed toward an outcome. In the dialogue the therapist is genuine, yet focused on the patient's needs. The dialogic relationship is fully described by Hycner and Jacobs (1995), who are influenced by the work of Buber and the intersubjectivity theorists. Intersubjectivity theorists have written within the framework of psychoanalysis to emphasize the importance of a two-way relationship between patient and therapist.

Assessment in Gestalt Psychotherapy

Traditionally, Gestalt therapy has not addressed itself in a systematic way to diagnosis or assessment. Because Gestalt therapists are attending to moments in therapy that include patients' bodily movements, feelings, sensations, or other materials, Miller (1985) believes that a diagnostic approach in Gestalt therapy can assist the therapist in more articulately identifying and helping patients become aware of their own reality. Yontef (1988) states that Gestalt therapy by itself does not provide sufficient diagnostic information to help patients with serious problems such as narcissistic or borderline disorders. He believes that developmental insights drawn from object relations and intersubjectivity theory provide a background that can be integrated with the application of Gestalt therapeutic processes. As Miller and Yontef suggest, Gestalt therapists may find a need for making assessments of broad units of patients' awareness and disturbances of contact boundaries.

Fagan (1970) suggests that Gestalt therapists are perceivers and constructors of patterns. For Fagan, diagnosis refers to classification of psychological problems. Fagan prefers *patterning* to *diagnosis* because it relates to the artistic creativity of the therapy, which may involve cognitive, perceptual, and intuitive skills that interact with the material presented by the patient. These therapist skills are based on past experience, both personal and as a therapist, as well as knowledge of psychotherapeutic theory, and are applied to the events and experiences of patients. Thus, the Gestalt therapist may respond to specific moments in the therapeutic process but also be aware of larger patterns that emerge in therapy.

Although Gestalt therapists are making greater and greater use of traditional diagnostic categories and need to do so for administrative and insurance reimbursement purposes, they also are able to use a variety of approaches to conceptualize and assess. Because many Gestalt therapists use other therapeutic systems such as relational forms of psychoanalysis (intersubjective self psychology or object relations), and Jungian theory as part of the assessment process, assessment techniques of Gestalt therapists are likely to be varied.

Therapeutic Change

In Gestalt therapy, both patient and therapist are fully present, allowing for the development of a fully functioning I-Thou relationship. The therapist's nondefensive posture and awareness of self and of the patient provide an atmosphere for change. Change occurs by exploring the patient's wishes rather than by gratifying them (Yontef & Simkin, 1989). If there is frustration, the therapist investigates it. If a patient is reluctant to follow a suggestion for exploration by the therapist, the therapist gently explores the reluctance rather than pushing the patient to follow the therapist's instructions. Beisser (1970) notes that the process of change is a paradoxical one, stating (p. 77): "*Change occurs when one becomes what he is, not when he tries to become what he is not.*"

When patients reach an impasse in therapy and have difficulty changing, Perls (1969b) has suggested that the patient be stuck and stay with the feeling of no progress. Perls believed that people are unable to make progress in therapy because they are afraid of what might happen. A patient might say, "If I really look at my friendship with

Harry, there won't be any friendship, and I won't have any friends." The Gestalt therapist helps the patient to experience the blockage and to experiment with, or fantasize about, what would happen if the patient explores his relationship with Harry. Working through such an impasse is an important part of the change process in Gestalt therapy.

The change process can be further articulated by examining Miriam Polster's (1987) description of a three-stage sequence of integration. In the first stage, *discovery*, patients may get a new view of themselves or of an old problem or situation. In the second stage, *accommodation*, patients learn that they have choices and can try out different behaviors. In this process, therapeutic support is particularly important. In the third stage, *assimilation*, patients progress from choosing and trying out new behaviors to learning how to make changes in their environment. It is at this point that they are apt to act assertively in obtaining what they want from others. Although patients do not move neatly through these three stages, and some may not fully experience each stage, Polster's model for client growth does provide an overview of the change process.

Enhancing Awareness

The purpose of this section is to show the many ways that Gestalt therapists use to bring about changes in client awareness within the context of a therapeutic relationship. However, techniques such as cognitive and behavioral methods may be used by Gestalt therapists, but they are used as an experiment to help the patient learn by doing something different. In focusing on the goal of achieving patient awareness, Gestalt therapists have developed many exercises and experiments to bring about client growth. Exercises are specific techniques that have been developed to be used in group or individual counseling. Experiments are innovations of the therapist that grow out of the struggles that patients have when they encounter an impasse or have difficulty in achieving awareness. When applied in therapy, exercises become experiments as the client learns new ways of learning or of achieving awareness. Some methods are relatively simple, involving commenting on or emphasizing awareness. Others involve enhancing awareness through verbal or nonverbal behaviors. Some exercises and experiments increase awareness of self; others increase awareness of other people. The dialogue with oneself, often using another chair, is a means of becoming aware of different parts of oneself. *Enacting*—that is, playing out parts of oneself or others—can be a dramatic Gestalt experiment to bring about change. Gestalt therapists have been creative in how they deal with dreams as a means of furthering awareness. Gestalt therapists also make use of homework to encourage growing awareness throughout the patient's life, not just in the therapeutic session.

Awareness statements and questions.   Sometimes awareness can be enhanced by relatively straightforward questions (Passons, 1975, p. 61). For example, if a patient is talking about her phone conversation with her mother, the therapist may simply say, "What are you aware of now?" to focus on what is happening to the patient in the present. Sometimes the therapist may focus the awareness a little more closely, as in "Mel, can you be aware of what you are doing when you are sitting in this chair?" or the therapist may go a step further and use a statement that starts with, "I am aware that you" (Passons, 1975, p. 63), thus, "Mel, I'm aware that as you sit in the chair you're looking at your knees." Sometimes it may be appropriate to ask the patient to use a sentence such as "Now I am aware" to bring about more awareness; for example, "Mel, as you sit there looking at your knees, could you use the phrase, 'Now I am aware that' and finish it and go right into another phrase, such as 'Now I'm aware of the dictionary on your desk, now I am aware of the lamp behind you'?" and so forth. Such statements and questions can be used relatively easily in the course of therapeutic work.

Emphasizing awareness.   Sometimes it is helpful simply to ask a client to repeat a behavior, as in "Please wring your hands together again." In Gestalt terms this makes the figure clearer and more separate from the ground. Similarly, requesting that the patient "stay with" the feeling he is experiencing may sharpen awareness by bringing the figure to the foreground. Exaggeration of a behavior also emphasizes the patient's present awareness. For example, it may be appropriate to ask a son who is being critical of his mother to emphasize the critical tone in his voice, thus making him more in touch with the critical quality within his voice. Levitsky and Perls suggest the phrase "May I feed you a sentence?" (1970, p. 148). This remark lets the therapist pick out a particular portion of the present encounter that the therapist would like the patient to increase awareness of. Reversal is a similar but opposite approach from exaggeration in increasing awareness (Levitsky & Perls, 1970, p. 146). In this technique, a patient who is usually soft-spoken might be asked to increase the loudness of her voice and to sound brash. In this manner, awareness of her soft-spokenness is enhanced.

Enhancing awareness through language.   Words that are likely to give the patient responsibility for himself and his growth are to be preferred over indirect and vague words. For example, changing pronouns such as *it* and *you* to *I* brings responsibility for the situation to the individual. Passons gives the following example.

> *Patient:* I didn't have very many dates this year. Next year it will be different.
> *Therapist:* It will be different? Who are you talking about?
> *Patient:* Me, I'll be different.
> *Therapist:* What will you do differently? (1975, p. 78)[3]

In this situation the therapist helps the patient take responsibility for getting dates, rather than waiting for dates to happen.

Some verbs distract from the patient's ability to increase awareness and responsibility. Passons gives three common examples of these (1975, pp. 81–87):

> *"Can't versus won't."* Often the use of can't gives the patient the feeling that he is unable to do something, when it is more accurate to say "I won't," meaning, "I choose not to do this for any of various reasons."
> *"Need versus want."* Usually a list of wants is much longer than a list of needs. It is helpful to use the word *want* as in "I want to be popular," rather than "I need to be popular." The former is more accurate, less urgent, and less anxiety-provoking.
> *"Have to versus choose to."* Like *need*, have to implies an urgency, demand, and anxiety that *choose to* does not. *Choose to* gives the patient responsibility for the choice.

Just as experimenting with different verbs can be helpful, changing questions to statements is often useful in emphasizing the responsibility of the patient. Some questions are really declarations rather than questions. They diminish patient responsibility, thus limiting patient awareness.

> *Patient:* You know me, don't you think I'd be better off if I didn't go to school next year?
>
> *Therapist:* You may have given your own answer. Change that question around to a statement and let's see what you have to say.
>
> *Patient:* Going to school next year is not right for me. Not now, anyhow.
> (Passons, 1975, p. 91)

These are some of the more common examples of language that diminish awareness and responsibility. When appropriate, Gestalt therapists may help patients develop self-awareness by listening carefully to language usage.

Awareness through nonverbal behavior.   Attending to nonverbal behavior can be particularly helpful for the Gestalt therapist. Passons gives four reasons for attending to nonverbal behaviors in therapy (1975, pp. 101–102). First, each behavior is an expression of a person at a given moment. Second, people generally are more attuned to listening to what they are saying, rather than noticing what they are doing with their body. Third, nonverbal behaviors are usually spontaneous, whereas verbal behaviors are often thought out in advance. Fourth, individuals who function in an integrated way will have nonverbal and verbal expressions that match. Parts of the body that therapists may respond to include mouth, jaw, voice, eyes, nose, neck, shoulders, arms, hands, torso, legs, feet, and the entire body.

> *Client:* The pressure is really on for getting into college. It seems like there's nothing I can do without college.
>
> *Therapist:* And how do you respond to all this pressure?
>
> *Client:* I'm not as excited about college as everyone else is, so I'm not doing much about it. (Folds arms across chest.)
>
> *Therapist:* Jo Anne, could you concentrate on your arms and hold them there?
>
> *Client:* O.K.
>
> *Therapist:* What do you feel in them?
>
> *Client:* They're kind of tight . . . sort of like I'm holding on.
>
> *Therapist:* Holding onto what?
>
> *Client:* To me. If I don't, they'll shove me all over the place. They don't know how I can hold on. (Passons, 1975, pp. 117–118)

Passons (1975) comments that Jo Anne is resisting pressures for fear others will point her in a direction that may not be right for her. As she becomes more aware of her investment in her resistance, she may find out why she is objecting to going to college. A clearer decision between going to college and not going to college may result.

Awareness of self and others.   Sometimes individuals can understand themselves and others by "becoming" the other person. This approach is often used in racial relations workshops in which people of different races may be asked to play each other's roles. Asking a patient to be his mother and say what his mother would say if the patient came in at 2 in the morning is often more helpful than asking the patient, "What would your mother think if you came in at 2:00 A.M.?" In this way the patient develops a fuller awareness of the differentiation between himself and others.

Sometimes it is also helpful for patients to be more aware of parts of themselves, such as feelings or nonverbal behavior (Passons, 1975). For example, a patient may say, "Sometimes I can be so cold to Marcie." The therapist may reply, "Be that cold self with coldness in your voice, and talk to Marcie as if she were here." Sometimes a therapist may wish to employ a similar technique with a body part. For example, a client who is pointing his finger at the therapist while he talks to her may hear from the therapist, "Let me hear what that finger has to say. It's pointing at me vigorously. Please put some words to it, if you can." In a vast variety of situations like these, therapists may choose to have clients split off a part of themselves or become someone else in order to become more aware of themselves.

Enhancing awareness of feelings.   Attending to emotions in Gestalt therapy is particularly important because emotions provide energy to mobilize a person and provide an orientation to those aspects of the environment that are important to the person (Passons, 1975). Although Gestalt therapists may respond empathically to expressed feelings, they have also developed exercises they frequently use to further the expression of feelings. Polster and Polster discuss how feelings are sometimes directed against the wrong person or not expressed well (1973, p. 226). They give the example of Phyllis, who was resentful and angry toward her boss, out of proportion to his influence in her life. Phyllis received little satisfaction by expressing her resentment toward her boss in therapy. A more creative approach was needed to help Phyllis overcome her impasse with regard to angry feelings about her boss.

> One day I realized that Phyllis was a person who needed a lot of special attention and I asked her whether she was accustomed to getting it. She remembered two men she had been in love with who had really given her "star" treatment. In both cases, though, she wound up abruptly rejected. After the second time she realized she had never permitted herself to get the special treatment she wanted. And so I asked her, in fantasy, to express herself to these two men. In doing so she was able to get out of the complex of rage, loss, grudge and resolve which she had previously been left with and around which she had organized such a substantial chunk of her life. By talking to these men in her fantasy, Phyllis aired her unfinished feelings. Following this deeply moving experience, she grew calm and no longer felt the sharp resentment towards her boss. She was able, finally, to reduce him to a more appropriate level of importance in her life. Phyllis had moved— out of the neurotic system in which she had made her boss the center and into a system which was more organically suited to her feelings. (Polster & Polster, 1973, p. 227)[4]

Awareness through self-dialogue.   Because integrated functioning is an important goal of Gestalt therapy, Gestalt therapists attend to those aspects of the individual that are not integrated. Polster and Polster see each individual as a "never-ending sequence of polarities" (1973, p. 61). Conflict in polarities often results from introjection. For example, if a person introjects parental religious values that are different from religious values that an individual identifies as her own, it is often useful to project the parental values outward so that they can be dealt with. By having dialogues between opposite tendencies, increased integration results and patient self-criticism is likely to decrease. Corey lists several common polarities: "The parent inside versus the child inside, the responsible one versus the impulsive one, the puritanical side versus the sexual side, the 'good boy' versus the 'bad boy,' the aggressive self versus the passive self, the autonomous side versus the resentful side, and the hard worker versus the goof-off" (1996, p. 250). Perhaps the best-known and most common polarity is "top dog" and "underdog."

The conflict between the top dog and the underdog is that between the righteous, moralistic, and demanding person, often seen as the "critical parent," versus the helpless, weak, and passive side of the individual. These two parts of us struggle constantly for control. The top dog tells us what we should do, and the underdog procrastinates and puts off doing. Such conflicts lend themselves to dialogues within oneself.

Self-dialogues can be done by having individuals take each role of the polarity and express it from his chair. However, it is more common to use the empty chair. Used either in individual or group therapy, the individual takes one role in one chair (for example, the top dog) and plays the other role (for example, the underdog) in another chair. As the individual changes roles, he moves to the other chair. The therapist may call attention to what has been said or how it was said. In this way the therapist helps the patient get in touch with the feeling that he may have been denying. Sides of the patient are experienced rather than talked about. Dialogues can be used in diverse situations such as one part of the body versus the other (one hand versus the other), or a dialogue can be between a patient and another person or between the self and an object such as a building or an accomplishment. For a therapist, working with such dialogues requires experience and training.

Awareness through enactment. Dramatizing some part of the patient's existence is the basis of enactment. A patient who says that he feels like a wimpy little dog might be asked to act like a wimpy little dog, to whine, to paw at the therapist, and to lower his head. Enactment may be of a previous experience or of a characteristic, like wimpy. When done in groups, the enactment may involve several group members. Enactment is a bold approach to awareness and must be done in such a way to help patients become more aware of characteristics or unfinished business, not to embarrass them. In the next example, Miriam Polster describes an enactment concerning trust of women.

> For example, in one workshop, there was a huge bear of a man who looked the modern equivalent of Falstaff, a gigantic frame, a large belly, a ruddy face, and a hearty manner. In spite of his huge bulk and a physical power so grand that he dominated the visual quality of the workshop scene, Hal was silent most of the time. When he did speak, he spoke with darting glances, a great self-protective hunching of his shoulders, and addressing no one in particular. A look of fear was in his face and a sense of vagueness and nondirection in his demeanor. Hal looked as though he feared an attack at any moment. When asked about his silence, he said that he had great difficulty in dealing with bossy women, especially when they are in the role of authority. He said he would not turn his back on one, that he wouldn't trust one to be behind him. Thus, Hal expressed his re-

sistance in his silence, his distrust, and his hunched shoulders. I let him use his hunched shoulders, his silence and his distrust. First, I got up and walked behind Hal and asked him what it was like for him now that I *was* behind his back. He was sitting on the floor. When he turned around to confront me, he put his hands down, as though crouching. So, the resistance moved into a crouch. I walked around again, searching for a way we could use his silent, distrustful crouch. This time I climbed on top of his back, crouching on top of him, and I asked Hal what he could do with me. He was free for a whole range of reactions, including flicking me off like a cigarette ash. If I had sensed that was the direction in which his energized resistance would go, I would not have gotten up on him. But he said, "Well, I could ride you around the room." He had chosen his own medicine. Riding me around the room put *him* in control. Even though it looked like the woman was on top, Hal had flipped the sense of dominance over to himself. He also proceeded to turn a threatening situation into a playful one, using his strength, developing great delight and a sense of union within himself, with me, and with the group, which had become aroused by seeing him ignited. The roars and the fun confirmed his power. For me it was like a jolly ride on an elephant. Hal was the mover, determining much of the speed, direction and playfulness. By the time we got back to our original places and I got off his back, he was able to laugh and say in new freshness that he no longer felt cautious with me and expected he would be heard from during the rest of the workshop, which indeed he was, becoming a central figure in the group. Thus through accentuating and mobilizing his resistance, Hal unharnessed its power, making it unique and timely to our interaction. Instead of being dominated by a woman, *he* could dominate; instead of maintaining a stalemate of inaction, filling it with suspicion and projection, he entered an actual contest which had its own rich detail and unpredictable outcome. (1973, pp. 55–56)[5]

In this example Miriam Polster illustrates confidence in Gestalt awareness techniques, as well as a playful sense of humor. Out of context, such behavior from a therapist seems odd and inappropriate. Within the context of Gestalt therapy, it is therapeutically consistent and helpful to Hal in dealing with issues concerning trusting women, as awareness is enhanced through words, bodily positioning, and movement.

Awareness through dreams.   "As in psychoanalysis, the mainstay in Gestalt therapy is the dream. . . . To me, a dream is an existential message. It can lead to understanding one's life script, one's karma, one's destiny" (Perls in Baumgardner, 1975, p. 117). Much of Perls's work in the last 15 years of his life was spent in working with dreams with individuals within a group setting. For Perls, dream work was one of the best ways to promote personal integration. Perls (1970) saw the dream as possibly the most spontaneous expression of an individual. Perls's method was not to interpret the dream but to have the patient relive the dream in the present and to play various parts of the dream. By playing the various persons and objects in the dream, the patient is identifying with parts of the self that have been alienated. Perls would often use the empty chair technique to have the patient play out parts of the dream that would then have a dialogue with each other.

Enright (1970, p. 121) gives the example of a restless, manipulative woman who dreamed of walking down a crooked path in a forest of straight trees. He asked her to become one of these trees. This made her feel more serene and deeply rooted. She was able to take these feelings back into her current life and experience the lack of them and the possibilities of accomplishing them. When she became the crooked path, she became teary-eyed and experienced the crookedness in her own life and the possibilities of straightening out, if she chose.

Enright gives an example of Perls's work with dreams.

The first time I ever saw him do dream work was in that group. It was very touching, there, this gray-haired fellow, somewhat depressed, 55-year-old psychologist had had a dream about seeing some friends off at a railroad station. Fritz had him go through the dream as himself, as the friends, and as the railroad train. None of it seemed to produce very much. Then Fritz said, "Be the station."

Patient: What do you mean, "Be the station"?

Fritz: Just describe the station, only keep saying, "I."

Patient: Well, I'm old and dilapidated, not very well cared for, and actually out of date. Please come and go and use me and pay no attention to me. (*And he started to cry.*)

I was very touched by that, feeling it as part of me, also, I guess. (Gaines, 1979, p. 135)[6]

Another creative approach to dream work is taken by Zinker (1971, 1978, 1991). Rather than have an individual play objects or people in a dream, he has group members do so. This method has the individual first work through the dream, and then a group experiment is devised so that other members of the group as well as the dreamer can profit from playing parts in the dream. Members of the group act out themes that may be particularly appropriate to them. The dreamer experiences the process and progress of the dream, changing action in the dream when appropriate. The dreamer may serve as a director or coach at times or experiment with different outcomes. In Perls's method, the audience participates mainly through observation (and occasional participation), whereas in Zinker's approach the entire group is active in the dream interpretation.

Awareness outside of therapy: homework. Homework can be assigned that puts individuals in a position of confronting areas that are blocking their emerging awareness. In some cases, individuals are asked to write dialogues between parts of themselves or between parts of their body. Others may be asked to find information or do a specific task that fits congruently with the therapeutic process. As individuals' awareness develops in therapy, they may be ready for more difficult assignments that may help them in becoming more aware of themselves and others, which in turn can provide more material for therapeutic work.

Awareness of avoidance. When feelings are present in a person, yet the person is not aware of them, the individual is in the process of avoiding them. Avoidance is an active process, not a passive one. An individual may be expending energy to avoid feelings such as happiness, loneliness, fear, or sadness. Expression of feelings is often viewed as doing, whereas avoiding may be seen as not doing by non-Gestalt therapists.

From a Gestalt point of view, an individual who is avoiding is working to adjust herself. Helping patients own their feelings and experience awareness regarding a number of issues may help in reintegrating avoided feelings.

Approaches such as emphasizing awareness, enhancing awareness through language or nonverbal behavior, and self-dialogues can be helpful in assisting people to become aware of their avoidance behaviors.

Integration and Creativity

Because the Gestalt focus on the whole person is so broad, all the parts—verbal behavior, nonverbal behavior, emotional feelings—are all attended to and integrated. The approaches to awareness that are described above can be used at any time in the course of therapy.

> Everything the person disowns can be recovered, and the means of this recovery is understanding, playing, becoming these disowned parts, and by letting him play and discover that he already has all this (which he thinks only others can give him), we increase his potential. (Perls, 1969b, p. 37)

Thus, techniques are not done in isolation, they are all directed toward the integration of the whole person. How this is done often depends on the disturbance of the contact boundary. For example, if a person projects anger onto someone or something else, it may be important to attend to the language process. Does the individual use *you* or *it* instead of the more responsible *I*? When a projection is recognized, it then can be accepted, modified, assimilated, and thus integrated. Other boundary disturbances (introjection, retroflection, deflection, and confluence) require different approaches to the integration of the whole person. The creative process by which integration of awarenesses takes place is difficult to describe, and the approaches are boundless in number.

The therapeutic process is doubly unique. The unique creative process of the therapist as a person interacts with the unique creative process of the patient. Erving Polster gives a brief example of the creativity, awe, and aliveness that can take place in therapy.

> This woman came in for a first session. She's separated from her husband and is in great mourning about it. She cries a lot. So, she's crying also in the office, but she looks like she's also a spunky woman. But, she's crying in a way that will *never* give her any kind of satisfaction, or release, or even appreciation of the dimensions of her loss. So, I asked her, instead of trying to stop herself from crying, to see if she could put some words to her crying. A very simple thing that many Gestalt therapists would do. I don't remember exactly what words she wound up saying, but as she said it she burst into *crying*, not just dripping. She then said, "Where am I gonna put all this love that's inside of me?" And I said to her, [speaking in a most reverent tone] "*The whole world is dying for it.*" That just changed the whole tone of her experience. The realization that what she has inside, there's a place for it, all over the world. That it doesn't have to be stuck inside her chest. (Hycner, 1987, p. 55)[7]

Polster's reverence for his client is clear. His statement "The whole world is dying for it" comes from his being, his experience, his interaction, and care for the patient. Not fitting into any of the approaches to awareness described previously, it is a creative, spontaneous, and moving comment that changes the tone of the therapy hour at that point. Such a statement is consistent with Buber's "I-thou" relationship or the importance that Gestalt therapists attach to the therapeutic relationship.

Risks

Just as Gestalt therapy can bring about powerful change through awareness, it also can be misused. George Brown, a prominent Gestalt therapist, has said (1988, p. 37): "Of all the therapies, Gestalt has the most potential for somebody really being cruel and hurting other people." He warns about therapists being enchanted by the techniques of Gestalt therapy without being skeptical of themselves and without having a clear grasp of Gestalt theory. Yontef (1987) worries about the use of "Gestalt therapy and," referring to therapists who use portions of Gestalt therapy with other theories of therapy, without grounding their work in the theory of Gestalt therapy. To avoid misuse of Gestalt therapy, preparation is paramount.

In discussing preparation to be a Gestalt therapist, Resnick (1984) believes therapists should have three parts to their training: personal therapy, academic preparation, and supervision. The therapy should be intensive enough to form a relationship between the beginning therapist (the patient) and the therapist, with self-dialogue an important part of the therapy. The academic preparation should include study of personality theories, theories of psychotherapy, and diagnosis. Supervision should include cognitive and experiential supervision by several Gestalt therapists. Such training helps ensure that the therapist is experienced, well grounded in theory, and ethical.

To give some sense of the complexity of using Gestalt therapy—more specifically, the empty chair technique—here is a small portion of a therapy session between a beginning therapist and a patient, with comments by an experienced supervisor (Fagan et al., 1974). In using the empty chair technique, beginning therapists need to be ready for strong emotional responses and know how to keep the therapeutic process moving while keeping the therapeutic role to a minimum. When confronted with impasses, they should know how to move in small rather than large steps. Backup support from experienced therapists is important also.

Here is the work of a graduate student, with Fagan's comments in parentheses. This excerpt is a second session with a patient who is a divorced woman in her late twenties, uncomfortable at the way her own mother has assumed direction of the patient's 4-year-old daughter following the accidental death of the mother's youngest son. The patient does not know how to deal with her mother except by leaving to move to a new location. Initiating the empty chair technique with a patient who has not used it before is illustrated.

> *Patient:* She won't find it as easy to come to Alabama to mind my business as she does here.
>
> *Therapist:* How would you handle that, do you think, if she did?
>
> *Patient:* Hmm. I guess I'd have to face it really and true, wouldn't I? (pause) Well, I think by my making this break. . . . See, it's—in a way I think I'm going to take some of the responsibility off of her of keeping on trying, when I do this. It's going to be pretty clear to her then that I'm not going to stay right where she tells me to stay.

Therapist: Do you hope she is?

Patient: No! If I could have what I really wanted, she would say to me: "I want you to have the freedom to do what you want to do." But I mean, that would be just beautiful if she said that.

Therapist: Would you like to try that here, sort of in a fantasy way?

(O.K. Patient has set up her own dialogue, even if very idealized and unrealistic. Therapist picks up the opportunity to use the empty chair. However, starting off with a patient who has never done this before can be facilitated by more structure, such as "I'm hearing many things you'd like to be able to say to her that are difficult when she's really there. Let's try saying them to her here, so you can get clearer what your wishes and feelings are. Would you be willing to try that?" Perls's instructions usually included the phrase, "write your own dialogue.")

Patient: Yeah.

Therapist: O.K. Let's put Mother in this chair and let's put you in that chair. And you tell her, first of all, what you'd like her to let you do, what you'd like her to say to you, and how you'd like her to let you live your life.

(Poor. Therapist has gotten patient's consent—an obvious if sometimes overlooked requirement, and sets the stage. But he errs in instructing patient to make requests and demands of Mother, rather than asking her to describe Mother as she sees her, or state what her feelings are. This base of support of self-centering is especially important with a patient who has too little sense of her own position and who feels overwhelmed by the topdog.) (Fagan et al., 1974, pp. 36–37)

There are many Gestalt techniques that require practice and supervision to use effectively. The spontaneity of Gestalt techniques can be deceptive, erroneously implying that whatever the therapist feels or senses is appropriate. The following examples provide a context for approaches to awareness and integrative techniques in therapy.

PSYCHOLOGICAL DISORDERS

In 1983 Tobin (1985) spoke of the absence of literature on ways of working with a variety of diagnostic groups. Since that time there has been some writing on various diagnostic groups, particularly borderline disorders. However, because some Gestalt therapists work moment to moment in the present, taking a social and/or psychological history does not necessarily fit with that approach, and diagnoses may not be made. One way of dealing with depression as it emerges in the therapy hour is presented. A therapeutic response to anxiety and staying with anxious feelings when the client wishes to digress is also shown. A brief example of physical tension interfering with musical performance illustrates how Fritz Perls made use of nonverbal behavior. A Gestalt approach to treating posttraumatic stress disorder by reliving the past and completing unfinished business is illustrative of a type of treatment for this disorder. Attending to an addict, who has been in recovery for 15 years, and having him put words to bodily changes shows an example of a Gestalt approach to addiction treatment. These approaches have much in common, using different ways of enhancing patient awareness.

Depression

Although depression is seen by many non-Gestalt therapists as a diagnostic category, Gestalt therapists are apt to see the degree of depression fluctuate throughout the session. Because behaviors change from moment to moment, there is no set way of responding to depression in Gestalt therapy. In the following case Simkin, Simkin, Brien, and Sheldon (1986, pp. 209–221) explain how James Simkin treats a woman in her early fifties who, during most of this session, seemed depressed and contained. She was described as someone waiting for life to happen to her. The following excerpt is not a prescribed way of dealing with depression; rather, it is one of an infinite number of ways of responding in the present to crying, lack of energy, or generally depressed feelings.

> *Florence:* I would like to be more comfortable.
>
> *Jim:* What would you like me to do as you're getting yourself more comfortable?
>
> *Florence:* I, let's see, what do I want from you? I would like to explore with you inner structure—which procedure or structure or program to use—[Sighs] I'm split. [Sounds teary] *I don't want to do what I am doing.*
>
> *Jim:* Right now?
>
> *Florence:* Right now, which is crying, [Sighs] and that other split part of me, I want to—I will get on and listen.
>
> *Jim:* Uh-huh. If this feels right to you, I want you to say: "I don't want to cry and I am crying."
>
> *Florence:* I don't want to cry and I am crying.
>
> *Jim:* "And I want to get on with living."
>
> *Florence:* And I want to get on with living. I don't want to cry and I *am* crying, and I want to get on with living,
>
> *Jim:* How can I be useful, or how do you want to use me in this process?
>
> *Florence:* When I think of getting on with living, I think of Chet and I start to cry. When I am away from here. That is the only time I cry.
>
> *Jim:* When you think of getting on with living and you think of Chet, you start to cry. Does Chet have anything to do with living, getting on with living?
>
> *Florence:* No. Well, nothing that comes to my head, I guess.
>
> *Jim:* Chet, I am interested in getting on with living, and when I think of you, I start to cry.
>
> *Florence:* "And crying is part of my living," I would say to finish that sentence.
>
> *Jim:* Have you any experience of getting on with your living without Chet?
>
> *Florence:* Yeah.
>
> *Jim:* What's that like?

Florence: Good, I'd be living good. A couple of things, one thing's missing.

Jim: What's missing?

Florence: My sexual drive. [Pause] I'm getting warm.

Jim: Is it true that without Chet your sexual drive is low? Or does that have nothing to do with it?

Florence: He has nothing to do with my sexual drive. To me.

Jim: So one of the ways you keep yourself from being fully alive is dampening your sexual appetite or interest. (Simkin et al., 1986, pp. 211–212)[8]

In the entire session and in this brief excerpt, Simkin never leads or pushes Florence. He stays with her as she becomes clearer about the ways that she restrains her playful, sexy, warm, and tender self. In this segment Simkin explores with her what she wants from herself and from him. In using the sentence, "I don't want to cry, and I am crying," Simkin helps Florence explore the present versus future polarity. When Simkin asks about Chet in the last part of this excerpt, he is bringing the past into the present.

Anxiety

Like treating depression, treating anxiety is done as it occurs in the session. In this example, Naranjo (1970) responds to an expression of anxiety by staying in the moment, despite the patient's attempt to avoid the therapist's requests. Naranjo's comments at the end of the excerpt are instructive in that they deal with the patient's avoiding responsibility for his feeling of gratitude to the therapist.

Patient: My heart is pounding. My hands are sweating. I am scared. I remember the time when I worked with you last time and. . . .

Therapist: What do you want to tell me by going back to last week?

Patient: I was afraid of exposing myself, and then I felt relieved again, but I think that I didn't come out with the real thing.

Therapist: Why do you want to tell me that now?

Patient: I would like to face this fear and bring out whatever it is that I am avoiding.

Therapist: O.K. That is what you want now. Please go on with your experiences in the moment.

Patient: I would like to make a parenthesis to tell you that I have felt much better this week.

Therapist: Could you tell me anything of your experience while making this parenthesis?

Patient: I feel grateful to you, and I want you to know it.

Therapist: I get the message. Now please compare these two statements: "I feel grateful," and the account of your well-being this week. Can you tell me what it is you felt that makes you prefer the story to the direct statement of your feeling?

Patient: If I were to say, "I feel grateful to you," I would feel that I still have to explain. . . . Oh! Now I know. Speaking of my gratefulness strikes me as too direct. I feel more comfortable in letting you guess, or just making you feel good without letting you know my feeling.

Because of his ambivalence, the patient has avoided expressing and taking responsibility for his feeling of gratitude. In an attempt to please the therapist rather than becoming aware of his desire for the therapist to be pleased, the patient has acted out his feelings instead of disclosing them. (Naranjo, 1970, pp. 57–58)[9]

A Pseudo-Psychosomatic Case

Gestalt therapists may occasionally work with individuals who present physiological concerns as a part, or all, of their problem. Although approaches vary, Gestalt therapists pay attention to the physiological processes that they observe. The following case is an anecdote from Perls's autobiography (1969c). In it he describes his treatment of a violinist who was unable to play for a long enough time to become a soloist in an orchestra.

I have seen many cases of psychoanalysis of long duration. Five to ten years are quite frequent. But he was tops. He had had twenty-seven years of it with six different therapists. Needless to say, all aspects of the Oedipus complex, masturbation, exhibitionism, etc., were gone over again and again.

When he came to me and made a dive for the couch, I stopped him and asked him to bring his violin along,

"What for?"

"I want to see how you manage to produce this cramp."

He brought his violin and played beautifully, standing up. I saw that he got his support from his right leg and that he had his left leg crossed over. After about ten minutes he began to wobble slightly. This wobble increased imperceptibly, and within a few more minutes his fingering slowed down and many notes were inaccurately played. He interrupted: "You see. It's getting difficult. If I force myself to go on, I get my cramp and I can't play at all."

And you don't get the cramp in the orchestra?

"Never."

Do you sit?

"Of course, but as soloist I have to stand up."

O.K. Now let me massage your hands. Now stand with your feet apart, slightly bent in at your knees. Now start again.

After twenty minutes of perfect playing, tears came to his eyes. He muttered: "I won't believe it, I won't believe it." (Perls, 1969c, unpaginated)[10]

Perls goes on to discuss physical polarities, right-left dichotomies, and front-rear and upper-under carriage splits. By attending to balance within his body, the patient was able to support himself on both legs, whereas he had primarily been using his right leg. Perls also worked with the patient to relax other parts of his body, such as his jaws.

Posttraumatic Stress Disorder

Traumatic incidents and the behavior resulting from them can be seen in Gestalt therapy terms like unfinished business (Serok, 1985). In this conceptualization, events from the past prevent the individual from developing full awareness in the present. These events from the past demand energy and affect the quality of the person's life. As Perls, Hefferline, and Goodman (1951) point out, a traumatic moment may actually be a series of frustrated or dangerous moments in which the feelings of tension and the dangerous explosiveness are very high. When "unfinished business" is not resolved, an individual may display irrelevant reactions such as compulsive behaviors, weariness, or self-defeating activity that interferes with daily life.

In treating a survivor of the Holocaust, Serok (1985) used re-created and guided fantasy to help a 40-year-old woman, married and the mother of three children. The woman complained of anxiety and depression, with difficulty functioning in most areas of her life, including sexual activity. At the age of about 5, her mother gave her to an aunt to prevent Nazis from taking her. Much of the therapeutic work focused on replaying the separation, at the age of 5, from her mother. The entire situation was explored: the hall where the separation took place, the other captives, the guards with their weapons, and the dogs next to the guards. At times Serok suggested talking to the guards to ask why she was being treated so badly. At other times the patient walked around the therapy room, recalling further details of the scene. Later therapy focused on separation from the aunt and other people in her early experience. As a result of a year and a half of treatment, the patient began to have more control over her energy and to experience full expression in motherhood, personal grooming, education, and sexuality. Dealing with such trauma can be exhausting for both patient and therapist, and it requires considerable commitment to the therapeutic process.

Substance Abuse

Gestalt therapy has been applied to all phases of addiction problems. Since denial is an important defense in addiction, Gestalt techniques can be helpful in helping substance abusers become more aware of themselves and their relationships with others. Clemmens (1997) describes important themes that are dealt with in the recovery process: trust, shame, confidence and boredom. These themes may be dealt with when the individual is first becoming drug free and years later as the individual continues the recovery progress.

In the following example Clemmens (1997) shows how Gestalt therapy can be used with an addict who has been in recovery for 15 years. Mike is dealing with issues related to feeling out of touch with his family and hurting his relationship with them. Clemmen's attends to Mike's bodily awareness.

Mike is a recovering addict of fifteen years who came to therapy complaining of feeling "out of touch with myself." He wondered if he were depressed. I noticed by looking at Mike's chest and stomach that his breathing was shallow and slow. This made him look stiff as he spoke about his life and family. I told Mike the way in which I perceived his breathing. He was surprised (as many clients are when I comment on their physical be-

havior) and asked, "What does that mean?" I answered that I wasn't sure what it meant, but believed he might learn by experimenting with his breathing.

Mike agreed to do this and initially took deeper breaths, eventually filling up his chest and stomach on each inhale and emptying out of each exhalation. As he did so, Mike began to shudder and shake. I asked him if he could stay with this experience. After a few minutes, Mike began to modulate his breathing in a more rhythmic way. The sound that he made was like a moaning. Mike's chin shook and he began to cry. I asked him if there were words for his crying and he said, "I'm not sure." I suggested his words from the beginning of the session, "I feel so out of touch." He tried saying these words three times, each filling his chest and tearing up, and then added, "And in so much pain . . . That's it. I feel so out of touch and so sad about my life." We spent the rest of the session defining what about himself and others Mike was out of touch with. (Clemmens, 1997, p. 148).

BRIEF THERAPY

Typically, there is not a time-limited or brief Gestalt individual psychotherapy, and therapists usually meet with their patients once a week. When sessions are less often than once a week, there is a danger that patients do not make use of material developed in the sessions. Then again, if sessions are held too often, there is the danger that patients become dependent on the therapist and do not have opportunity to incorporate the material covered in therapy into their own lives.

An interesting approach to brief therapy has been applied to Gestalt therapy by Dierks (1996). She focuses on specific contact boundary disturbances of individuals, often using diagrams of people reacting in certain ways to educate clients. Clients learn not to act on regressed or inappropriate interactions with their environment. The goal is to help clients "operate out of a boundaried, contactful, integrated state" (p. 54). Thus, clients become more aware of their feelings and attitudes, and more able to choose and control their behaviors.

CURRENT TRENDS

There is a continuing trend in Gestalt therapy to focus on relationship issues with clients and to use softer rather than abrupt or abrasive methods in helping clients bring issues into the present (Hycner & Jacobs, 1995). Although Perls was known for using creative and strong approaches in his Gestalt demonstrations, current Gestalt therapists are concerned with the impact of techniques on their continuing therapeutic relationships with clients.

Another area of recent interest has been that of shame, particularly among Gestalt therapists with a psychodynamic orientation. Jacobs (1996) demonstrates how shame emerges and can be dealt with in the therapeutic relationship. Yontef (1996) has addressed shame from a theoretical point of view as it relates to Gestalt therapy and also as it relates to the training of Gestalt therapists (1997). Lee (1994) approaches this issue from the point of view of couples therapy. In general, these writers address the importance of therapists being aware of their own feelings of shame and being aware of when shame may be inadvertently introduced into therapeutic or therapist training situations.

USING GESTALT PSYCHOTHERAPY WITH OTHER THEORIES

Gestalt therapists are cautious about using Gestalt approaches to awareness with other theories. Yontef (1987) has been critical of those who combine elements of Gestalt therapy with elements of other theoretical systems and believe that new insights will develop. Because some therapists have gone beyond the constructs of the theory of Gestalt therapy, Yontef worries that Gestalt therapy as a whole will be hurt by those who use a variety of techniques without a clear understanding of boundary disturbances and the need for an integrated approach to the patient.

Several Gestalt therapists see the value of integrating Gestalt therapy with psychodynamically derived therapy. For example, Jacobs (1992) argues that Kohut's self psychology offers important insights for Gestalt therapists in understanding both the contacting process and its development. She believes that perspectives from this theory about the patient's childhood development add to concepts such as contact and Gestalt formation. Likewise, Breshgold and Zahm (1992) see a compatibility between self psychology and Gestalt therapy, in that both have a relational perspective. They find that self psychology can help Gestalt therapists by making them more aware of the developmental needs that they are meeting in their work with their patients. Mullen (1990) offers another view of incorporating developmental psychology into Gestalt theory by making use of Kegan's (1982) stages of development. In her discussion of treating borderline personality, Greenberg (1989) incorporates object relations theory into the Gestalt treatment process. Recognizing the need to work with personality disorders and borderline patients, Yontef (1988) suggests that psychoanalytical concepts have much to offer Gestalt therapists. Writings that combine developmental concepts from psychoanalytically oriented theory with awareness approaches of Gestalt therapy are likely to continue to be important in the future.

RESEARCH

In some ways Gestalt therapy is a highly experimental approach with Gestalt therapists frequently creating experiments for their patients to try. However, these individualistic experiments do not lend themselves to reproducible scientific research. As Perls et al. (1951, p. 8) say, "We must, for instance, face the fact that we blandly commit what to the experimentalist is the most unpardonable of sins: *we include the experimenter in the experiment!*" They assert that many researchers are a part of and affect their experiment, whether they wish to admit it or not. Their own emphasis on individual experimentation can be seen by the fact that the first half of their book, *Gestalt Therapy*, is a series of experiments for individuals to test the validity of principles of Gestalt therapy themselves. These experiments include exercises such as sharpening the sense of one's body, integrating awareness, and focusing on concentrating. These exercises are the precursors of experiments that Gestalt therapists use with their patients in helping them explore previously unknown aspects of themselves.

In terms of published and verifiable research, there is relatively little. *The Gestalt Journal* publishes very little research, and experimental studies are scattered throughout other psychological journals. There are two main reasons for the lack of published research: Treatments cannot be planned, but occur spontaneously, and the therapeutic interaction between patient and therapist is very complex, so that measuring it is very difficult (Fagan & Shepherd, 1970, p. vii). Furthermore, as Harman (1984) points out, many Gestalt therapists are usually not in academic positions, and relatively few academicians are trained in Gestalt therapy. Despite these difficulties, research has been done in a variety of areas. I will examine studies that compare Gestalt therapy with other approaches, specific techniques (especially use of the empty chair), and contact boundary disturbances.

Research comparing Gestalt therapy with other approaches or with a no treatment control group are very sparse. One study compared Gestalt therapy and REBT on issues dealing with anger. Conoley, Conoley, McConnell, and Kimzey (1983) found that both therapies reduced blood pressure and intensity of feelings, when compared to a control condition. Comparing Gestalt empty chair techniques with treatments that encourage affect but did not include dialogue and two other treatments, Tyson and Range (1987) found that all treatments, including a no treatment control, helped individuals who had mild depression, some anxiety, and social introversion. Studying 36 depressed clients, Watson and Greenberg (1996) compared a Gestalt approach including two-chair work for self-critical splits, empty chair work for unfinished business, and other interventions with a person-centered approach. The Gestalt (called process-experiential) approach produced higher levels of experiencing and greater problem resolution than the person-centered approach. In a study comparing treatment of snake phobia with 23 participants, Johnson and Smith (1997) found that participants who received the empty-chair Gestalt dialogue approach did as well as those receiving systematic desensitization. Both groups improved more than nontraditional control participants.

A common complaint about these studies is that the therapists who are administering the treatments are not always experts. Often, but not always, they are graduate students who are just learning a theoretical approach. Brunink and Schroeder (1979) did a content analysis comparing expert psychoanalysts, Gestalt therapists, and behavior therapists. They found that Gestalt therapists were more direct, disclosed more about themselves, took greater initiative in therapy, and gave less emotional support. In a somewhat similar study comparing therapists of the same three orientations, Bouchard, Lecomte, Carbonneau, and Lalonde (1987) found that Gestalt therapists spent about half of their time in awareness-related activities. They found clear differences in the content of the transcripts of the 12 therapists in the three theoretical orientations. It is easier to show differences in style of content than it is to ascertain differences in effectiveness among the therapies.

The empty chair technique has been a focus of a series of research studies by Leslie Greenberg. He and his students and colleagues have assessed the effectiveness of the empty chair technique in conflict resolution. For example, Clarke and Greenberg (1986) compared a cognitive problem-solving group, a Gestalt group that featured use of the empty chair, and a waiting list control group. Clients were seen for two sessions, and pretests and posttests of indecision and stages of decision making were made. Although both counseling approaches were more effective than no treatment in facilitating decision making, the affective (Gestalt) intervention was more effective than the cognitive behavioral approach. Clarke and Greenberg suggest that the Gestalt approach may have been more successful than the cognitive behavioral approach in maintaining a focus on the decision problems. A student of Greenberg, Foerster (1990) has studied the use of the empty chair dialogue in resolving "unfinished business." Much of Greenberg's research has shown that the empty chair technique was helpful to patients by reducing their self-criticism and increasing their self-understanding. The empty chair technique has been particularly appropriate for research because, more than most Gestalt experiments, it can be specified and controlled. For Greenberg and his colleagues to do their work, it was necessary to focus on a specific area such as conflict resolution and to use relatively brief therapeutic interventions.

Several studies have focused on contact boundary disturbance issues. Kepner (1982) developed the Gestalt Contact Style Questionnaire (GCSQ), which included measures of introjection, projection, retroflection, and confluence. Caffaro (1991) has designed a measure of deflection. Studying a group of young women who had been sexually abused as children and a control group, Leininger (1992) found that both groups favored projective and aggressive defenses and retroflection, a bringing back to themselves what they would like to do to someone else, indicating to Leininger a need for self-sufficiency. Kiracofe (1992) also reported that retroflection and confluence were common styles among her 21 subjects, who were patients receiving Gestalt therapy. Applying the contact boundary disturbance to ways people handle interpersonal conflicts, Mills (1997) suggests that deflection, projection, introjection, and retroflection have promise in being applied to understanding conflict resolution styles. Brothers (1986) suggests that this finding supports the Gestalt theory of healthy aggression. With scales available for measuring contact boundary disturbances, more research in this area would appear to be warranted.

GENDER ISSUES

In discussing gender differences in Gestalt therapy, it is useful to note that both men and women have been involved in the leadership and the development of Gestalt therapy. Laura Perls had been active since the inception of Gestalt therapy, writing chapters of early books on Gestalt therapy, until her death in 1990. Her leadership of the New York Institute for Gestalt Therapy had a powerful effect on the many Gestalt therapists she trained. Although difficult to ascertain, the fact that many of those who supervised new therapists and led workshops were women has helped Gestalt therapy maintain an appreciative and balanced approach to gender issues.

In a general sense, men and women are apt to react differently to the Gestalt approach of developing awareness and growth in individuals. For women Gestalt therapy can be empowering, helping them be aware of a sense of powerfulness as well as blocks to powerfulness that create tension, often due to societal restrictions and expectations. When women develop a sense of empowerment and a full awareness of their abilities after participation in Gestalt therapy, they may have to develop new ways to deal with societal expectations that are relatively unchanged. To the extent that men are taught to hide their feelings, not show emotions, and repress rather than deal with difficult experiences, Gestalt therapy can provide an opportunity to become aware of blocks to functioning in roles as lover, father, co-worker, and so forth. However, men who become more aware of their feelings, nonverbal behaviors, and other aspects of themselves may have to explore appropriate social contexts for self-expression.

Miriam Polster has addressed the societal limitations that exist for women because of the lack of female heros. In *Eve's Daughters* (1992), she points out that traditionally heros are men, with women either being heroines in the sense of supporters of men or having negative characteristics, such as Helen of Troy, who was beautiful but deceptive. Polster states that the image of a hero comes from witnessing and telling an act that is so outstanding that people repeat the story from generation to generation. Women's heroism can include involvement in civil rights, child advocacy, and scientific accomplishments. As a part of the heroic quest, Polster believes that women should be helping other women along their way rather than helping the male hero in his quest. As women achieve heroic feats, they display a combination of support, knowledge, and power that enables other women to achieve. Polster urges a new view of heroism, a neoheroism, viewing women's heroic accomplishments on a par with that of men. Polster's work is unusual in Gestalt writings, as it emphasizes societal empowerment and awareness as well as the development of individual awareness.

MULTICULTURAL ISSUES

There are several ways in which Gestalt therapy can be effective in working with culturally diverse populations. The Gestalt therapist can use Gestalt experiments to help individuals deal with and perceive their own culture. Also, because the patient-therapist relationship focuses on the present, there is an opportunity for the therapist to bridge cross-cultural barriers by responding to issues that they perceive are interfering with the patient-therapist relationship and that may have a cultural base. For example, a white therapist perceiving an Asian American client as reticent may say, "Can you put words to your soft voice?" This may enable the patient to verbalize her concerns about being understood by a white therapist. Also, bicultural clients may experience pressures from two cultures as a polarity (Corey, 1996). A dialogue between the patient's perceptions of herself in the two cultures may help bring a cultural conflict to greater awareness. There are times that such dialogues or other Gestalt experiments may be carried out in the patient's native language or vernacular. In general, sensitivity to the patient's immediate experience also includes sensitivity to the patient's culture.

From another perspective, Gestalt therapy can create problems in working with people from different cultures. Because Gestalt therapy can arouse deep emotions, this can be problematic for people whose cultural traditions discourage expression of emotion. In many cultures, displaying emotionality, particularly for men, can be seen as a display of weakness and vulnerability. Some cultures have traditions that make interactions with various family members limited and proscribed. For example, in many Asian cultures, the way one interacts with older family members, particularly parents, is often with respect and authority. To display anger toward them, even in a dialogue, can be disturbing for individuals.

Criticizing Gestalt therapy as practiced in the United States, Saner (1989) feels that American Gestalt therapists tend to overemphasize the individual and deemphasize the social context. As he sees it, the price for freedom in America and for individuality has been high divorce rates, vandalism, educational illiteracy, and profiteering. He is concerned about the lack of supportiveness in American society. For Asian and South American cultures, Saner suggests that psychodrama may be a therapeutic approach appropriate to the emphasis on groups and families in these countries, whereas the "hot seat" approach, which stresses individuality, would be less appropriate. His comments suggest that Gestalt therapists should be sensitive not only to the awareness that individuals have about their own selves but also to how cultural factors can affect awareness of self, family, friends, acquaintances, and people in society as a whole.

COUPLES COUNSELING

Work with couples follows the same principles as work with individuals. As Polster and Polster (1973) point out, it is helpful when working with contact boundary disturbances to have the source of the disturbance in the same room. For example, couples may project their own fears onto the other partner, such as when a wife uncritically accepts her husband's beliefs without being aware of doing so (introjection). Therapists may experience confluence in the session as they observe the couple having difficulty distinguishing each from the other as in a situation where a man's strong need to be loved by his wife may make it difficult for him to express his own feeling and be aware of himself apart from his wife (confluence). With couples, the therapist has the opportunity to promote awareness of each of the individuals. The awareness may focus on sensations, listening, watching, or touching.

Often in marriage counseling the therapist brings the past or unfinished business into the present. The following is a brief, pointed example from Enright (1970, p. 109) that illustrates how responding to the present can help people move out of an unproductive impasse.

Therapist: What are you looking at?

Wife: The tape recorder.

Therapist: Can you describe what you are seeing?

Wife: Yes, it's just going round and round and round.

Therapist: Round and round?

Wife: Yes.

Therapist: Is anything else going round and round?

Husband and wife: (*simultaneously and rather impatiently*) We certainly are.[11]

The husband and wife now are in a better position to examine why their interactions in the past and present have been so fruitless. More examples of Gestalt approaches to couples can be seen in Wheeler and Backman (1994).

FAMILY THERAPY

Much of the writing on Gestalt family therapy has been done by Kempler (1970, 1973, 1974, 1981), who stresses the importance of current interaction as the center for interventions (Kempler, 1970). In general, where families are available, Kempler (1981) prefers working with families to couples or individuals so that individuals causing boundary disturbance for others are available for therapeutic work. For Kempler, the goals of family therapy are negotiated by attention to the interaction that is occurring in the present. Writing about the process of doing Gestalt family therapy, Lawe and Smith (1986) emphasize the importance of individuals in the family becoming aware of their patterns of interactions, as members of dysfunctional families are often unaware of their own needs as well as the needs of others.

When working with a family, Kempler prefers to work with the entire family and calls reluctant members of the family to ask them to participate. The following example shows why that is important and how the therapist attends to interaction occurring in the moment.

On one occasion, a mother called for assistance, identifying her 14-year-old daughter as the problem. There were two younger sisters, ages 12 and 10, in addition to a three-year-old boy in the family. I invited the mother to bring her husband and all four children in for the initial evaluation. The mother reluctantly agreed to bring the other daughters and her husband, but desperately tried to exclude the three-year-old son. I insisted, and short of an ultimatum from her, decided to hold my position. She finally consented. An attractive family of six came to the office, sat down, and looked at me uncertainly. This lasted only a brief moment, as the three-year-old boy got out of his chair and began wandering around the room, knocking down ashtrays and coffee tables. All eyes focused on him, but no one said a word. After a while the three older girls alternately tried whispering to the young lad to sit down. It was all to no avail. He finally moved to the doorway and kept opening and slamming the door. After what seemed like hours, but in reality was about ten minutes, the 14-year-old so-called problem child turned to me and pointing to her parents, angrily burst out, "It's like this all the time at home. They never take over." The mother looked at us, smiling triumphantly, and said, "There is our problem, Doctor. She has a low threshold." I looked at her in astonishment and replied, "It is higher than mine." Therapy had begun. (Kempler, 1981, p. 15)[12]

For family therapy to be successful, the therapist must be active. Kempler's activity is evident in the following example of family therapy, where he is dealing with a father who is unwilling to take responsibility in the family.

Therapist: You sit silently. I'd like to know where you are now.

Father: [*ignoring mother's sadness and criticism of him, he responds on his safest ground*] I tell the kids to listen to her.

Mother: [*angrily to father through her tearfulness*] But you're not effective, they don't listen to you, either, and then you blow up at them. That's not the way to treat kids; you can't be hitting them all the time.

Father: [*whining*] You always stop me. They'd listen to me, but they know you'll come in and stop me.

Therapist: You're whining at your wife.

Father: What else can I do? She stops me at every turn.

And later in the session—

> **Therapist:** [*sarcastically, to provoke him*] You poor thing, overpowered by that terrible lady over there.
>
> **Father:** [*ducking*] She means well.
>
> **Therapist:** You're whimpering at me, and I can't stand to see a grown man whimpering.
>
> **Father:** [*firmer*] I tell you, I don't know what to do.
>
> **Therapist:** Like hell you don't. [*offering and at the same time, pushing*] You know as well as I that if you want her off your back, you just have to tell her to get the hell off your back and mean it. That's one thing you could do instead of that mealy-mouth apology: "She means well."
>
> **Father:** I'm not used to talking that way to people. (Kempler, 1970, pp. 155–157)

The dialogue continues, with the father eventually taking more responsibility by expressing his anger at the therapist and later at his wife. The therapist reinforces the father's strength and then asks the children what they think about their father's being stronger. The family responds positively to Kempler's confrontive style of working with them, which bring about clear changes in family interactions. Many Gestalt therapists may use a style that focuses on the relationships within the family and with the therapist.

GROUP THERAPY

Group therapy has always been a common intervention in Gestalt therapy. In the 1960s and 1970s, Gestalt therapists were better known for their work in groups than for work with individuals. The types of groups can be divided into three kinds: hot seat, where individuals work with a therapist and the audience observes; process groups, where attention is paid to current group processes; and a variation of process groups, process-thematic groups, where in addition to attending to process, themes that involve the entire group may be acted out. In a survey of 251 Gestalt therapists, Frew (1988) found that 70% were currently using groups in their practice. Of these, 4% reported using the hot seat approach primarily or exclusively; the majority (60%) indicated that they use a variety of leadership models with their groups. Group therapy continues to be an important approach to treatment, providing an opportunity for members to improve their interactions with others (Polster, 1997).

The hot seat approach was popularized by Perls and also by James Simkin; it has been used less and less since the 1970s. In this approach, one group member works from a few minutes to as many as 40 minutes with a leader. During this one-to-one work, audience members do not participate. Later they may talk about how they were affected by the observed work. Each member of the group has an opportunity to work one to one before a second round is started. Some Gestalt therapists using the hot seat method have incorporated group dynamics into their approach and use a combination of a group process and a hot seat approach. Perls (1969b) believed that the hot seat approach was superior to individual therapy and that audience members learned through their observation of those on the hot seat.

In explaining Gestalt group process, Kepner (1980) describes personal growth as a boundary phenomenon that results from contact between the individual and others. Gestalt process groups may include experiments and exercises to further group awareness. Kepner describes three developing stages of a Gestalt therapy group. The first, identity and dependence, involves setting limits and boundaries for the group. This includes modeling approaches that will be used in the group and encouraging interpersonal contact among the group members. In the second stage, influence and counterdependence, group members deal with influence, authority, and control of the group. The group leader, as well as individual group members, may be challenged, and open differences of opinions may be expressed. Also, roles in the group are differentiated from the person. For example, if scapegoating appears in the group and a person becomes designated as a "victim," the leader can differentiate the role from the person. In the third stage, intimacy and interdependence, a sense of closeness between group members is developed. Kepner believes that it takes a group a year or two of being together to function consistently at this third stage. At this point the leader is a consultant who makes relatively few interventions. Not all groups reach this third stage, where processing can be fast and respectful, even though issues of grief and pain are dealt with. This structure is not a format for leading a group, but rather a description of processes that Kepner has observed.

Zinker (1978) finds that group members often work on themes that occur in everyday life, such as family conflicts, grief, aspirations, and unfinished life traumas. As in his approach to dream work, Zinker (1978) may have group members act out an issue or theme to bring it into the present. Such experiments may be spontaneous, involving all group members. Whether working with themes or with group processes, Zinker (1980) believes that group awareness develops from here-and-now statements, such as "You're hunched up and your shoulders are near your ears," "Joan, your jaw tightened when John said. . . ." To facilitate the group awareness process further, Zinker (1980) suggests such group behaviors as looking at people when you speak to them and using their names, being aware of your own body and other people's body language, speaking directly to people and not about them, not intruding when other people are in the middle of working on an issue, speaking in the first person, converting questions into statements, and respecting the needs and values of others. These values illustrate the emphasis on the here-and-now approach of Gestalt therapists.

Because of the intensity brought about by the approaches illustrated by Kepner's and Zinker's process and theme work, Gestaltists have attended to issues of therapeutic safety. Feder (1980) believes that the most important variable regarding group safety is the therapist's approach. Being caring, respectful of group members, and flexible helps ensure that group members experience healing of contact boundary disturbances rather than damaging of them. Screening prospective group members also helps ensure that the group process will be effective and that members will not damage or be damaged in the process. Feder has found it helpful to use a "safety index," in which he asks members of the group to assign a number between 0 and 10 to the level of safety that they are experiencing. He often asks the group to review the current safety level and check current experiences of members. Establishing whether members have had prior relationships with each other can also help ensure the safety of the group. Opportunities to participate in and later co-lead a Gestalt therapy group are useful in helping the beginning group therapist experience a sense of safety in group leadership.

SUMMARY

Although the developer of Gestalt therapy, Fritz Perls, was trained as a psychoanalyst, his method of psychotherapy evolved into a very different approach. Perls was influenced by phenomenology and existentialism in his emphasis on the whole person. The theory and research of field theory and Gestalt psychology helped him to develop a terminology for his theory of psychotherapy. He was able to use Gestalt psychology concepts of figure and ground to talk about the awareness that individuals had of themselves, others, and objects in their surroundings. The emphasis on bringing the past or future into the present is an extremely important concept in Gestalt psychotherapy. Gestalt therapy examines the ways in which individuals are in good or poor contact with themselves and others and observes contact boundary disturbances, including introjection, projection, retroflection, deflection, and confluence. They also look for polarities, or opposites, that individuals experience. This view of the individual then influences the practice of psychotherapy.

Gestalt therapists focus on the importance of awareness in the growth and integration of the whole person. They assess individuals' contact boundary disturbances, including their here-and-now verbal and nonverbal behavior. Gestalt therapists assist their patients in enhancing awareness by attending to an individual's nonverbal behaviors and awareness of sensations and feelings in the context of a caring relationship. Methods include dialogues with the self and acting out polarities and contact boundaries. Dreams are an important part of the therapeutic experience for many Gestalt therapists, with objects and people in dreams being representations of the individual. Gestalt experiments and exercises are used in individual therapy, family therapy, and group therapy to bring about a deeper awareness of oneself. Experience with Gestalt techniques, training, and supervision are necessary in order to help therapists become aware, integrate their experiences, and grow and mature as therapists.

Suggested Readings

POLSTER, E., & POLSTER, M. (1973). *Gestalt therapy integrated: Contours of theory and practice*. New York: Brunner/Mazel. • This excellent book covers present awareness, figure and ground, contact-boundary, and Gestalt experiments. The case illustrations are very well written.

PASSONS, W. R. (1975). *Gestalt approaches in counseling*. New York: Holt, Rinehart & Winston. • Gestalt experiments and exercises for both individual and group counseling are described systematically and illustrated with examples.

FAGAN, J., & SHEPHERD, I. L. (Eds.). (1971). *Gestalt therapy now*. Palo Alto, CA: Science and Behavior Books. • This collection of articles by a number of experts on Gestalt therapy explains the theory of Gestalt therapy and its applications to visual problems, art experiences, and working with children.

PERLS, F. (1969). *Gestalt therapy verbatim:* Moab, UT: Real People Press. • The beginning of the book includes lectures by Perls and answers to questions from the audience. The second part includes verbatim transcripts of Perls doing dream work, seminars, and weekend workshops.

References

ARNHEIM, R. (1974). "Gestalt" misapplied [Letter to the editor]. *Contemporary Psychology, 19*, 570.

BAUMGARDNER, P. (1975). *Legacy from Fritz.* Palo Alto, CA: Science and Behavior Books.

BEISSER, A. R. (1970). The paradoxical theory of change. In J. Fagan & I. L. Shepherd (Eds.), *Gestalt therapy now* (pp. 77–80). Palo Alto, CA: Science and Behavior Books.

BORING, E. G. (1950). *A history of experimental psychology.* New York: Appleton-Century-Crofts.

BOUCHARD, M. A., LECOMTE, C., CARBONNEAU, H., & LALONDE, F. (1987). Inferential communications of expert psychoanalytically oriented, Gestalt and behavior therapists. *Canadian Journal of Behavioral Science, 19*, 275–280.

BRESHGOLD, E., & ZAHM, S. (1992). A case for the integration of self psychology developmental theory into the practice of Gestalt therapy. *The Gestalt Journal, 15*, 61–94.

BROTHERS, C. L. (1986). The Gestalt theory of healthy aggression in beyond-control youth. *Psychotherapy, 23*, 578–585.

BROWN, G. (1988). The farther reaches of Gestalt therapy: A conversation with George Brown. *The Gestalt Journal, 11*, 33–50.

BRUNINK, S., & SCHROEDER, H. (1979). Verbal therapeutic behavior of expert psychoanalytically oriented, Gestalt, and behavior therapists. *Journal of Consulting and Clinical Psychology, 47*, 567–574.

BUBER, M. (1965). *Between man and man.* New York: Macmillan.

CAFFARO, J. (1991). A factor analytic study of deflection. *The Gestalt Journal, 14*, 73–96.

CLARKE, K. M., & GREENBERG, L. G. (1986). Differential effects of the Gestalt two-chair intervention and problem solving in resolving differential conflict. *Journal of Counseling Psychology, 33*, 11–15.

CLARKSON, P., & MACKEWN, J. (1993). *Fritz Perls.* London: Sage.

CLEMMENS, M. C. (1997). *Getting beyond sobriety: Clinical approaches to long-term recovery.* San Francisco: Jossey-Bass.

CONOLEY, C., CONOLEY, J., MCCONNELL, J., & KIMZEY, C. (1983). The effects of the ABC's of rational emotive therapy and the empty-chair technique of Gestalt therapy on anger reduction. *Psychotherapy: Theory, Research and Practice, 20*, 112–117.

COREY, G. (1996). *Theory and practice of counseling and psychotherapy* (5th ed.). Pacific Grove, CA: Brooks/Cole.

DIERKS, J. M. (1996). Listening within: A brief therapy model for use with Gestalt theory. *The Gestalt Journal, 19*, 51–100.

EMERSON, P., & SMITH, E. W. L. (1974). Contributions of Gestalt psychology to Gestalt therapy. *The Counseling Psychologist, 4*, 8–12.

ENRIGHT, J. B. (1970). Awareness training in the mental health professions. In J. Fagan & I. L. Shepherd (Eds.), *Gestalt therapy now* (pp. 263–273). Palo Alto, CA: Science and Behavior Books.

FAGAN, J. (1970). Gestalt techniques with a woman with expressive difficulties. In J. Fagan & I. L. Shepherd (Eds.), *Gestalt therapy now* (pp. 169–193). Palo Alto, CA: Science and Behavior Books.

FAGAN, J., with LAUVER, D., SMITH, S., DELOACH, S., KATZ, M., & WOOD, S. (1974). Critical incidents in the empty chair. *The Counseling Psychologist, 4*, 33–41.

FAGAN, J., & SHEPHERD, I. L. (1970). *Gestalt therapy now.* Palo Alto, CA: Science and Behavior Books.

FEDER, B. (1980). Safety and danger in the Gestalt group. In B. Feder & R. Ronall (Eds.), *Beyond the hot seat* (pp. 41–52). New York: Brunner/Mazel.

FOERSTER, F. S. (1990). Refinement and verification of a model of the resolution of unfinished business. Masters Abstracts, V. 30104, p. 1485. York University (Canada).

FREW, J. (1988). The practice of Gestalt therapy in groups. *The Gestalt Journal, 11,* 77–96.

GAINES, J. (1979). *Fritz Perls: Here and now.* Millbrae, CA: Celestial Arts.

GOLDSTEIN, K. (1939). *The organism.* New York: American Book.

GREENBERG, E. (1989). Healing the borderline. *The Gestalt Journal, 12,* 11–56.

GREENBERG, L. S., RICE, L. N., & ELLIOTT, R. (1993). *Facilitating emotional change: The moment-by-moment process.* New York: Gulford.

HARMAN, R. (1984). Gestalt therapy research. *The Gestalt Journal, 7,* 61–69.

HENLE, M. (1978). Gestalt psychology and Gestalt therapy. *Journal of the History of the Behavioral Sciences, 14,* 23–32.

HUMPHREY, K. (1986). Laura Perls: A biographical sketch. *The Gestalt Journal, 7,* 5–11.

HYCNER, R., (1987). An interview with Erving and Miriam Polster. *The Gestalt Journal, 10,* 27–66.

HYCNER, R. & JACOBS L. (1995). *The healing relationship in Gestalt therapy. A dialogic/self psychological approach.* Highland, NY: The Gestalt Journal Press.

JACOBS, L. (1992). Insights from psychoanalytic self-psychology and intersubjectivity theory for Gestalt therapists. *The Gestalt Journal, 15,* 25–60.

JACOBS, L. (1996). Shame in the therapeutic dialogue. In R. Lee & G. Wheeler (Eds.), *The voice of shame: Silence and connection in psychotherapy.* San Francisco: Jossey-Bass.

JOHNSON, W. R., & SMITH, E. W. L. (1997). Gestalt empty-chair dialogue vs. systematic desensitization in the treatment of phobia. *Gestalt Review, 1,* 150–162.

KEGAN, R. (1982). *The evolving self.* Cambridge, MA: Harvard University.

KEMPLER, W. (1970). Experiential psychotherapy with families. In J. Fagan & I. L. Shepherd (Eds.), *Gestalt therapy now* (pp. 150–161). Palo Alto, CA: Science and Behavior Books.

KEMPLER, W. (1973). Gestalt therapy. In. R. J. Corsini (Ed.), *Current psychotherapies* (pp. 251–286). Itasca, IL: F. E. Peacock.

KEMPLER, W. (1974). *Principles of Gestalt family therapy.* Costa Mesa, CA: Kempler Institute.

KEMPLER, W. (1981). *Experiential psychotherapy within families.* New York: Brunner/Mazel.

KEPNER, E. (1980). Gestalt group process. In B. Feder & R. Ronall (Eds.), *Beyond the hot seat* (pp. 5–24). New York: Brunner/Mazel.

KEPNER, J. (1982). Questionnaire measurement of personality styles from the theory of Gestalt therapy. Unpublished doctoral dissertation, Kent State University.

KIRACOFE, N. L. (1992). A process analysis of Gestalt resistances in individual psychotherapy (doctoral dissertation, Temple University, 1992). *Dissertation Abstracts International, 53,* 109–B, 4958.

LAWE, C. F., & SMITH, E. W. (1986). Gestalt processes and family therapy. *Individual Psychology, 42,* 537–544.

LEE, R. (1994). Couples shame: The unaddressed issue. In G. Wheeler & S. Backman (Eds.), *On intimate ground: A Gestalt approach to working with couples.* San Francisco: Jossey-Bass.

LEININGER, E. M. (1992). Ego defense mechanisms and Gestalt resistance styles in a group of female survivors of childhood incest (doctoral dissertation, The Fielding Institute, 1992). *Dissertation Abstracts International, 53,* 10-B, 5448.

LEVITSKY, A., & PERLS, F. (1970). The rules and games of Gestalt therapy. In J. Fagan & I. L. Shepherd (Eds.), *Gestalt therapy now* (pp. 140–149). Palo Alto, CA: Science and Behavior Books.

MILLER, M. V. (1985). Some historical limitations of Gestalt therapy. *The Gestalt Journal, 8,* 51–54.

MILLS, B. (1997). An exploratory examination of relationships between contact boundary styles and conflict resolution. *Organization Development Journal, 15,* 17–25.

MULLEN, P. R. (1990). Gestalt therapy and constructive developmental psychology. *The Gestalt Journal, 13,* 69–90.

NARANJO, C. (1970). Present-centeredness: Technique, perception, and ideal. In J. Fagan and I. L. Shepherd (Eds.), *Gestalt therapy now* (pp. 47–69). Palo Alto, CA: Science and Behavior Books.

O'LEARY, E. (1997). Confluence versus empathy. *The Gestalt Journal, 20,* 137–154.

O'LEARY, E., PURCELL, V., McSWEENEY, E., O'FLYNN, D., O'SULLIVAN, K., KEANE, N., & BARRY, N. (1998). The Cork person-centered Gestalt project: Two outcome studies. *Counselling Psychology Quarterly, 11,* 45–61.

PASSONS, W. R. (1975). *Gestalt approaches in counseling.* New York: Holt, Rinehart & Winston.

PERLS, F. S. (1948). Theory and technique of personality integration. *American Journal of Psychotherapy, 2,* 572–573.

PERLS, F. S. (1969a). *Ego, hunger and aggression.* New York: Vintage. (Original work published 1947.)

PERLS, F. S. (1969b). *Gestalt therapy verbatim.* Moab, UT: Real People Press.

PERLS, F. S. (1969c). *In and out of the garbage pail.* Moab, UT: Real People Press.

PERLS, F. S. (1970). Four lectures. In J. Fagan & I. L. Shepherd (Eds.), *Gestalt therapy now* (pp. 14–38). Palo Alto, CA: Science and Behavior Books.

PERLS, F. S. (1973). *The Gestalt approach.* Palo Alto, CA: Science and Behavior Books.

PERLS, F. S., HEFFERLINE, R. F., & GOODMAN, P. (1951). *Gestalt therapy.* New York: Julian Press.

POLSTER, E., & POLSTER, M. (1973). *Gestalt therapy integrated.* New York: Brunner/Mazel.

POLSTER, M. (1987). Gestalt therapy: Evolution and application. In J. K. Zeig (Ed.), *The evolution of psychotherapy* (pp. 312–325). New York: Brunner/Mazel.

POLSTER, M. (1992). *Eve's daughters: The forbidden heroism of women.* San Francisco: Jossey-Bass.

POLSTER, M. (1997). Beyond one-to-one. In J. K. Zeig (Ed.), *The evolution of psychotherapy: The third conference* (pp. 233–241). New York: Brunner/Mazel.

RESNICK, R. (1984). Gestalt therapy East and West: Bicoastal dialogue, debate or debacle? *The Gestalt Journal, 7,* 13–32.

ROSENBLATT, D. (1988). What has love got to do with it? *The Gestalt Journal, 9,* 63–76.

SANER, R. (1989). Culture bias of Gestalt therapy: Made-in-U.S.A. *The Gestalt Journal, 12,* 57–72.

SEROK, S. (1985). Implications of Gestalt therapy with post traumatic patients. *The Gestalt Journal, 8,* 78–89.

SHEPARD, M. (1975). *Fritz.* Sagaponack, NY: Second Chance Press.

SHEPHERD, I. L. (1970). Limitations and cautions in the Gestalt approach. In J. Fagan & I. L. Shepherd (Eds.), *Gestalt therapy now* (pp. 234–238). Palo Alto, CA: Science and Behavior Books.

SHERRILL, R. E. (1986). Gestalt therapy and Gestalt psychology. *The Gestalt Journal, 9,* 53–66.

SIMKIN, J. S., SIMKIN, A. N., BRIEN, L., & SHELDON, C. (1986). Gestalt therapy. In I. L. Kutash & A. Wolf (Eds.), *Psychotherapist's case book* (pp. 209–221). San Francisco: Jossey-Bass.

SMUTS, J. C. (1926). *Holism and evolution.* New York: Macmillan.

TOBIN, S. (1985). Moderator: A case presentation in Gestalt therapy. *The Gestalt Journal, 8,* 27.

TYSON, G. M., & RANGE, L. M. (1987). Gestalt dialogues as a treatment for mild depression: Time works just as well. *Journal of Clinical Psychology, 43,* 227–231.

WALLEN, R. (1970). Gestalt therapy and Gestalt psychology. In J. Fagan & I. L. Shepherd (Eds.), *Gestalt therapy now* (pp. 8–13). Palo Alto, CA: Science and Behavior Books.

WATSON, J. C., & GREENBERG, L. S. (1996). Pathways to change in the psychotherapy of depression: Relating process to session change and outcome. *Psychotherapy, 33,* 262–274.

WATZLAWICK, P. (1984). *The invented reality.* New York: Norton.

WHEELER, G., & BACKMAN, S. (Eds.). (1994). *On intimate ground: A Gestalt approach to working with couples.* San Francisco: Jossey-Bass.

WOODWORTH, R., & SCHLOSBERG, H. (1954). *Experimental psychology.* New York: Holt, Rinehart, & Winston.

YONTEF, G. M. (1987). Gestalt therapy 1986: A polemic. *The Gestalt Journal, 10,* 41–68.

YONTEF, G. M. (1988). Assimilating diagnostic and psychoanalytic perspectives into Gestalt therapy. *The Gestalt Journal, 11,* 5–32.

YONTEF, G. M. (1995). Gestalt therapy. In A. S. Gurman & S. B. Meisser (Eds.), *Essential psychotherapies: Theory and practice* (pp. 261–303). New York: Guilford.

YONTEF, G. M. (1996). Shame and guilt in Gestalt therapy theory and practice. In R. Lee & G. Wheeler (Eds.), *The voice of shame: Silence and connection in psychotherapy.* San Francisco: Jossey-Bass.

YONTEF, G. M. (1997). Supervision from a Gestalt therapy perspective. In C. E. Watkins (Ed.), *Handbook of psychotherapy supervision* (pp. 147–163). New York: Wiley.

YONTEF, G. M., & SIMKIN, J. S. (1989). Gestalt therapy. In R. J. Corsini & D. Wedding (Eds.), *Current psychotherapies* (4th ed., pp. 323–361). Itasca, IL: F. E. Peacock.

ZINKER, J. (1971). Dream work as theater: An innovation in Gestalt therapy. *Voices, 7,* 2.

ZINKER, J. (1978). *Creative process in Gestalt therapy.* New York: Brunner/Mazel.

ZINKER, J. (1980). The developmental process of a Gestalt therapy group. In B. Feder & R. Ronall (Eds.), *Beyond the hot seat* (pp. 55–77). New York: Brunner/Mazel.

ZINKER, J. (1991). Creative process in Gestalt therapy: The therapist as artist. *The Gestalt Journal, 14,* 71–88.

8

Behavior Therapy

Built on scientific principles of behavior that have been developed over the last 100 years, behavior therapy began in the late 1950s. Many of the first therapeutic approaches were based on Pavlov's concept of classical conditioning and Skinner's work on operant conditioning. This research, along with studies on observational learning, provided a background for the development of psychotherapeutic behavioral techniques. Behavior therapists have been able to apply basic principles such as reinforcement, extinction, shaping of behavior, and modeling to help clients. The application of scientific method can be seen in the detailed assessment that behavior therapists use.

In behavior therapy there has been a general trend from working only with observable events, such as screaming, to working with unobservable events, such as the learning that takes place by watching someone do something. More recently, many therapists have combined behavioral approaches with cognitive ones that attend to the client's thoughts. In this chapter, illustrations that combine behavioral strategies to treat a variety of specific disorders are provided. Because behavior therapy includes so many methods, however, not all can be described here.

HISTORY OF BEHAVIOR THERAPY

Unlike other theories of psychotherapy, behavior therapy has its roots in experimental psychology and the study of the learning process in humans and animals. Although there have been instances of physicians using approaches that are remarkably similar to behavior therapy as it is practiced today, there was no systematic study of behavior that led to principles of behavior change until the work of Ivan Pavlov (Pichot, 1989; Wolpe, 1990). Pavlov's observations about the salivation of dogs before receiving food led to the study and development of classical conditioning (also called respondent conditioning). Influenced by Pavlov's conditioning experiments, John Watson applied these concepts to human behavior. Another important approach to learning is operant conditioning, developed by B. F. Skinner, which examines how environmental influences affect or shape the behavior of individuals. Both classical and operant conditioning study observable behaviors that operate outside the individual. In contrast, so-

Ivan Pavlov

cial learning theory, developed by Albert Bandura, deals with internal or cognitive processes that attempt to explain how individuals learn through observations or perceptions of their environment. These three approaches (operant and classical conditioning and social learning theory) are described in more detail in this chapter, as is the current status of behavior therapy.

Classical Conditioning

While studying the digestive process of dogs, Pavlov observed that dogs would salivate before food was put on their tongues (Hyman, 1964). On closer observation, he concluded that the dogs had learned from environmental events, such as a sound or the sight of food, that they were about to be fed. He was able to present a neutral stimulus, such as a sound or a light (the conditioned stimulus, CS), for a second or two before presenting the food (the unconditioned stimulus, UCS) to the dog. The dog's salivation at the sight of food (the UCS) was the unconditioned response (UCR). After the CS (light or tone) was presented together with the UCS (food), the CS (by itself) would produce salivation, the conditioned response (CR), from the dog. Thus, the learned behavior was the conditioned response (CR) to the presentation of a conditioned stimulus (CS).

Classical conditioning could be applied to a variety of species (including humans) and types of behavior. For example, Pavlov was able to pair a black square with a previously conditioned stimulus, a beat of a metronome, and demonstrate second-order or higher-order conditioning. Other experimentation dealt with how long an animal might respond to the conditioned stimulus (CS) without the presentation of the unconditioned stimulus, before the CS (a light) would fail to evoke a CR (salivation) and the CR would be extinguished. In this way, scientific findings regarding the learning process began to develop. As research into classical conditioning and other behavioral principles has increased, investigators have found that the principles are quite complex. For example, classical conditioning does not always occur with pairings such as those described in this section.

In the early 1900s, John Watson, an experimental psychologist at Johns Hopkins University, was impressed by Pavlov's research. He appreciated the objectivity of the approach, which called for studying directly observable stimuli and responses without resorting to internal mental processes, such as thoughts or imagery (Watson, 1914). In a famous study (Watson & Rayner, 1920), Watson explained how an emotional reaction could be conditioned in a child by using a classical conditioning model. Investigators had noted that Albert, an 11-month-old boy, would show fear and appear startled when he heard a loud noise. Albert also played comfortably with a white rat. However, when the sound was presented immediately before Albert saw the white rat, he became afraid. After seven pairings of the sound and the rat over a 1-week period, Albert cried when the rat was presented alone. Watson's work (1914, 1919) that was based on research, such as the study of Albert, was to have an impact on many other psychologists.

Mowrer and Mowrer (1938) were intrigued by classical conditioning principles and applied them to bed-wetting in their New Haven Children's Center, where they developed a urine alarm system that paired bladder tension with an alarm. When the child would go to sleep and urination began, the urine would seep through the cloth, closing an electric circuit and sounding an alarm. After this had happened for several times, the bladder tension alone would arouse the child before urination could occur. Variations of this method have been used for more than 50 years (Liebert & Liebert, 1998) in a process that takes 6 to 12 weeks to stop bed-wetting.

Operant Conditioning

Whereas classical conditioning focuses on the antecedents of behavior (the presentation of the CS before the UCS), operant conditioning focuses on antecedents and consequences of behaviors. Based on the early work of E. L. Thorndike and B. F. Skinner, operant conditioning (also known as *instrumental conditioning*) laid the groundwork for much of what constitutes behavior therapy today. This work formed the basis for the application of principles of behavior to a wide variety of problems, especially those dealing with severe mental disabilities such as schizophrenia and autism.

Working at about the same time as Pavlov, Edward L. Thorndike (1898, 1911) was using controlled experimental procedures to study learning. Rather than studying reflex behavior, as Pavlov had done, he was interested in the learning of new behaviors. Using cats as subjects, he would place food outside a cage and observe how a cat would try to escape and find the food by releasing a latch. The first escape from a box occurred in a trial-and-error fashion. Later the cat would be able to escape from the box more and more quickly. Recording the time taken to press the latch, Thorndike plotted a learning curve. From his experiments and observations, Thorndike was able to derive the Law of Effect, that "consequences that follow behavior help learning" (Kazdin, 1994, p. 10). In essence, the correct response (for example, touching the lever) was strengthened, and incorrect responses (biting at the bars of the cage) were weakened or lessened. Besides the Law of Effect, Thorndike derived many other principles of behavior from his experiments, emphasizing the importance of the adaptive nature of learning for animals to survive and function well.

The name associated with operant conditioning is B. F. Skinner (1904–1990). Whereas Thorndike had seen classical and operant conditioning as being quite similar, Skinner saw many differences. Basically, *operant* conditioning is a type of learning in which behavior is altered by systematically changing consequences. An example of this is the pigeon in a Skinner box, a small chamber in which a pigeon can peck at a lighted key. The experimenter controls the amount of food the pigeon receives (reinforcement), and the pigeon's "pecks" are automatically recorded. By selectively reinforcing a green light rather than a red light, the pigeon can learn to peck at the green light and not the red light. Although much of Skinner's work was with laboratory animals, he extended his principles of operant conditioning to human behavior as well.

Skinner's (1953) attempt to apply operant conditioning principles to complex human behavior drew much attention. He wrote of the relevance of operant conditioning for

B.F. SKINNER

government, education, business, religion, psychotherapy, and a variety of human interactions. His novel, *Walden Two* (1948), shows how operant conditioning can provide the basis for an ideal community. Much of the controversy over Skinner's views
dealt with critics' objections to the application of limited laboratory findings to prescriptions for living.

Social Learning Theory

Whereas classical and operant conditioning focus on overt behavior, actions that people can directly observe, social learning theories focus on the study of covert behaviors,
those that take place within the individual and cannot be observed (or at least not easily). These include physiological responses (such as blood pressure and muscle tensions), thinking (observing, remembering, imagining), and feeling (emotions such as
sadness and anger). The term *cognitive-behavioral* is often used to describe theorists who
consider both overt and covert behaviors in their research and psychotherapy. One
particularly significant contribution to this field has been the research of Albert
Bandura, which can be traced to earlier investigators such as Mary Cover Jones.

A student of Watson, Jones (1924) described the treatment of a 3-year-old boy,
Peter, who was afraid of rabbits. Jones's treatment of Peter illustrates two important aspects of social learning theory: observation and modeling. Peter's fears were treated by
having him observe children who enjoyed their play with a rabbit and served as models for Peter. In this way, Peter could observe that rabbits did not need to be frightening. Later, Jones put a caged rabbit into a room, at some distance from Peter, while he
was eating his favorite food. Over a period of days, Jones brought the rabbit closer and
closer, always making sure that Peter was comfortable with the rabbit. At the end of
this treatment, Peter was able to play with and pat the rabbit. In this example, Jones
worked with both Peter's overt and covert behavior.

Initiated in the 1960s by Albert Bandura, social learning theory emphasizes the role
of thoughts and images in psychological functioning. Bandura proposed a triadic reciprocal interaction system involving the interactions among the environment; personal
factors including memories, beliefs, preferences, predictions, anticipations, and self-
perceptions; and behavioral actions. These three factors operate interactively, with
each affecting the other two. An important aspect of Bandura's theory is that individ-

uals learn by observing others. At the center of this triad
is the self-system, a set of cognitive structures and perceptions that regulates behavior (Bandura, 1978, 1997).
These cognitive structures include self-awareness, self-
inducements, and self-reinforcement that can influence
thoughts, behaviors, and feelings. Related to these is the
concept of self-efficacy, which deals with how well people
perceive that they are able to deal with difficult tasks in
life (Bandura, 1986). Associated with a strong sense of
self-efficacy is the ability to accomplish significant tasks,
learn from observation, believe that one can succeed, and
have a low level of anxiety.

ALBERT BANDURA

Although classical conditioning and operant conditioning are important components of behavior therapy as

it is practiced today, a blend of cognitive and behavioral approaches is more representative of current practice, particularly for people who are not living in institutions. The flexibility provided by theorists such as Bandura provides many ways for viewing psychological disorders.

Current Status of Behavior Therapy

Before the 1960s, behavior therapy was not well accepted within psychology, social work, education, or psychiatry. Since the 1970s, behavior therapy has been applied to a great number of areas such as business and industry, child-raising, improving athletic performance, and enhancing the lives of people in nursing homes, psychiatric hospitals, and other institutions. Furthermore, behavior therapy has been better understood as a process in which patient and therapist, in many cases, collaborate together for improvement in psychological functioning. In behavior therapy, the relationship with the client is valued, just as it is in other therapies.

Increased acceptance of behavior therapy has come about as a result of the growth in numbers of behavioral practitioners and their publications. The Association for Advancement of Behavior Therapy was founded in 1966 and in 1990 had more than 4,000 members. Although this organization was established in the United States, other behavior therapy societies are found in a number of different countries. With the increased interest in behavior therapies has come the establishment of more than 15 journals devoted to behavior therapy: *Advances in Behaviour Research and Therapy, Behavior Modification, The Behavior Therapist, Behavior Therapy, Behaviour Research and Therapy, Behavioural and Cognitive Psychotherapy, Behavioural Interventions, Child and Family Behavior Therapy, Clinical Behavior Therapy Review, Cognitive and Behavioral Practice, Cognitive Therapy and Research, Corrective and Social Psychiatry and Journal of Behavior Technology Methods and Therapy, Journal of Applied Behavior Analysis, Journal of Behavior Therapy and Experimental Psychiatry, Journal of Behavioral Assessment and Psychopathology, Journal of Rational-Emotive and Cognitive-Behavior Therapy,* and *Mexican Journal of Behavior Analysis.* All but two of the journals have been established since 1970. Virtually all of these journals demonstrate the close relationship between research and the practice of behavior therapy.

BEHAVIOR THEORY OF PERSONALITY

Unlike most theories of psychotherapy described in this book, behavior therapy does not have a comprehensive personality theory from which it is derived (Liebert & Liebert, 1998). Learning theories have been developed to explain personality, but few have been integrated into the practice of behavior therapy. For example, Dollard and Miller (1950) translated psychoanalytic concepts into learning theory terminology, based in part on the work of Hull (1943). Mowrer (1950) suggested two important learning processes to explain psychological disorder: the tendency to find a solution to a problem and learning based on expectations and beliefs. A social learning theory that stresses behavior potential, expectancies, reinforcement value, and situational factors has been developed by Rotter (1954). Eysenck's (1970) theory of traits is based on underlying behaviors that focus on introversion-extraversion and stability-neuroticism.

Believing that people's behaviors are consistent across time but may differ, depending upon the nature of the situation, Mischel (1973) has stressed the importance of competencies, personal constructs, values, and self-regulating systems in personality development. Although these theories have had relatively little impact on the practice of behavior therapy, Bandura's social learning theory (discussed previously) has had an impact on behavior therapy through the practice of modeling and the emphasis on self-observation. The important principles that underlie most of these theories are those developed through research on classical and operant conditioning and on observational learning.

Basic principles of behavior, especially those derived from operant conditioning, describe reinforcement, the process in which the consequences of behavior increase the likelihood that a behavior will be performed again. Lack of reinforcement can bring about extinction of behavior. Through a variety of processes, behavior can be shaped, narrowed (discrimination), broadened (generalized), or otherwise changed. Another key principle to basic learning is that of learning through observation. Implicit in the study of behavior is that behavior has antecedents (events occurring before the behavior is performed) and consequences (events occurring after a behavior is performed) (Spiegler & Guevremont, 1998). An important aspect of behavior therapy is the attention paid to each specific situation. Examples in this chapter show therapeutic and other situations that illustrate these basic principles of behavior.

Positive Reinforcement

An event presented as a consequence of a person's performing a behavior is called *positive reinforcement*. When an event follows a behavior, and that behavior increases in frequency, the event is a positive reinforcer (Spiegler & Guevremont, 1998). If you say "Thank you" to a friend who brings you a sandwich, your expression of thanks is a positive reinforcer for the act of your friend that increases the chance that your friend will do something like this for you or someone else in the future. If the friend does something positive for you again, you have observed positive reinforcement, which is different than a reward—something given to or awarded to someone for doing something. Rewards do not necessarily increase the probability that the frequency of a response following a favorable event will increase, whereas a positive reinforcer does.

Positive reinforcement is considered to be one of the most widely used behavior therapy procedures because of its effectiveness in bringing about changes in behavior and its compatibility with cultural values (Groden & Cautela, 1981). Intermittent positive reinforcement is longer lasting than continuous positive reinforcement. Intermittent reinforcement can be given at time intervals (an interval schedule) or after a certain number of correct responses (ratio reinforcement).

Kazdin (1994) gives a brief example from Kirby and Shields (1972) of the use of social reinforcement with a seventh-grade boy who is doing poorly in school and not doing his work. In this example, praise is used as a secondary reinforcer and is provided on an intermittent schedule of reinforcement in which the ratio of correct responses to praise became greater and greater. (Praise was frequent at first, but tapered off later.)

For example, in one program, praise was used to alter the behavior of a 13-year-old boy named Tom in a seventh-grade classroom (Kirby & Shields, 1972). Tom was of average intelligence but was doing poorly on his class assignments, particularly the arithmetic assignments. Also, he rarely paid attention to the lesson and constantly had to be reminded to work. Praise was used to improve his performance on arithmetic assignments. Each day in class, after he completed the arithmetic assignment, he was praised for correct answers on his arithmetic worksheet. At first, every couple of responses were praised, but the number of correct problems required for praise was gradually increased. The praise consisted merely of saying, "Good work," "Excellent job," and similar things. (pp. 133–134)

Extinction

When reinforcers are withdrawn or not available, individuals stop performing a behavior. *Extinction* is the process of no longer presenting a reinforcer. Examples of extinction include ignoring a crying child, working without being paid, or not responding to someone who is talking to you. Parents may use the basic principle of extinction when dealing with a child. On the one hand, for example, if a child grabs her mother's pants and pulls, the mother may choose to ignore the behavior and let it extinguish. If she responds to the child warmly, she runs the risk of positively reinforcing the pants-grabbing behavior. On the other hand, appropriate behavior can be extinguished when it is desirable to reinforce the behavior. For example, if a father reads a magazine while his son is playing productively and quietly and does not attend to the son, there is a danger of extinguishing the child's appropriate play.

Generalization

When behavior is reinforced, it may generalize to other behavior. Reinforcement increases the chances that ways of responding to one type of stimulus will transfer to similar stimuli. Thus, when one encounters a difficult problem in dealing with someone, if the solution had been effective, that way of interacting with people will generalize to other situations. By learning how to deal with one angry person, individuals learn how to deal with that same person in different situations and with different individuals who are angry. To use another example, if a child is praised for doing well on an arithmetic test, then she may not only work harder on her arithmetic problems but also generalize this behavior to other subjects. Just as it is important to be able to generalize from one experience to others, it is important to be able to discriminate among different situations.

Discrimination

The ability to be able to react differently, depending upon the stimulus condition that is presented, is extremely important for individuals. To use an example, drivers must be able to discriminate between red and green traffic lights. If they are color-blind, they must learn to discriminate based upon the position of the light. In social interactions, children soon learn how to act differently around bullies as opposed to friends and may act differently with a substitute teacher than with their regular teacher. Individuals may also make subtle distinctions, responding differently to the statement "You look very nice today," depending on who has said it and in what tone of voice. In brief, discrimination comes about as certain responses are reinforced and others are ignored and thus extinguished.

Shaping

When a therapist shapes a client's behavior, reinforcement, extinction, generalization, and discrimination are involved. In shaping, there is a gradual movement from the original behavior to the desired behavior by reinforcing approximations of the desired behavior. For example, shaping occurs when parents reinforce their toddler's attempt to walk. First, the child is praised for walking while holding onto a parent's hand, later for walking while holding onto the furniture, later for taking a few steps without holding onto anything, and later for walking from one end of the living room to the other. As each new target is reached, the child is no longer praised for reaching the previous target.

Observational Learning

In describing social learning theory, Bandura (1977; 1997) states that reinforcement is not sufficient to explain learning and personality development. He believes that much learning takes place through observing and modeling the actions of others. For example, children may learn by watching parents, friends, television, or movies; by reading; or by working on puzzles. In the process of learning, behavioral processes are important, as are cognitive processes that symbolically code observations and memories (Bandura, 1986, 1989a). Bandura describes the processes that explain observational learning as having four basic functions: attention, retention, motor reproduction, and motivation.

Attentional processes.   Important in the observational process is the attending process itself, as well as the persons and/or situations that are being observed. It is not enough to see something; to observe, one must perceive it accurately. For example, if a student watches a professor who is lecturing, he may attend to what is being presented in varying degrees.

Additionally, the pattern of associations (Bandura, 1989a) that an individual has with the model or situation being observed greatly influences attention. Strong associational patterns with parents make them important models for children to observe. Models vary in terms of their interpersonal attractiveness and interest. Advertisers take advantage of this fact by using athletes or other celebrities who attract the attention of a large proportion of the audience of potential customers. In doing so, advertisers want the star to draw attention to the product, not to himself.

Retention processes.   For observation to be successful, a model's behavior must be remembered. In proposing a cognitive system for recalling the observed model, Bandura describes imaginal coding and verbal coding. *Imaginal coding* refers to mental images of events, such as picturing two friends having talked to each other yesterday. *Verbal coding*, sometimes called *self-talk*, refers to subvocal descriptions of events. For example, a person who is trying to master golf may say to herself, "I grip the putter with my hands in an interlocking grip." Bandura believes that verbal coding is particularly effective in retaining observed events because it can be easily stored. For observation to be effective, the memories of the situation must be directed toward performing behaviors.

Motor reproduction processes.   It is one thing to observe and remember the behaviors of a model and quite another to translate what is observed into action. Imitating the way a baseball player puts on a hat is relatively simple, requiring little rehearsal to perform the action correctly. Hitting a baseball the way a star athlete does is another matter. Extremely quick and accurate perceptual and motor skills are needed to imitate highly skilled behavior. Even if someone has a degree of success in imitating modeled behavior, there is no guarantee that the modeled behavior will be maintained for a significant period of time.

Motivational processes.   If an individual observes and puts into action modeled behavior, it is likely to be continued only if it is reinforced. A person is likely to use a particular hitter's stance only if the behavior leads to success at the plate. Incentives can be important in modeling. For example, if a math teacher's presentation of fractions reinforces the student's success with fractions, the student is likely to model the behavior of the math teacher.

Bandura argues that reinforcement does not have to be external but can be internal—that is, come from individuals themselves. He describes two types of internal reinforcement: vicarious and self-reinforcement. *Vicarious* reinforcement refers to observing someone getting reinforced for performing an action and concluding that performing the same behavior will bring about a reinforcement. Self-reinforcement occurs when people set standards for themselves and reinforce themselves for meeting their expectations, as an athlete may on accomplishing a particular goal.

Self-efficacy.   According to Bandura (1989b, 1997), *self-efficacy* is the individual's perception of her ability to deal with different types of situations. People with high self-efficacy expect success, which often leads to success itself, whereas those with low self-efficacy have self-doubts about their abilities to accomplish tasks, the chance of successful outcome may be lower, and self-esteem will be lowered. Those who have high self-efficacy are likely to have imaginal coding and verbal coding that reflect success. In other words, a student with a high sense of self-efficacy can visualize herself doing well on an exam and can think confidently about her upcoming exam.

In describing the acquisition of self-efficacy, Bandura (1989b, 1997) believes that four major sources can bring about self-efficacy: performance accomplishments, vicarious experiences, verbal persuasion, and lowering emotional arousal. *Performance accomplishments* refer to the fact that past successes are likely to create high expectations and a resulting high sense of efficacy. *Vicarious experiences* mean opportunities to observe someone else and say, "I can do that" or, for those with low self-efficacy, "I don't think I can do that." *Verbal persuasion* refers to the impact that encouragement or praise from parents, friends, or others can have on expectations of performance. Lowering powerful anxiety (*emotional arousal*) will allow individuals to perform more accurately and calmly, leading to a stronger sense of self-efficacy. Of these four sources of self-efficacy, Bandura believes that the strongest factor is an individual's performance accomplishments.

Despite the many theories of behavior and its impact on personality, basic for most behavior therapists are the principles of reinforcement and observational learning. They have been used in a variety of ways to develop techniques to help individuals change covert and overt behavior.

THEORIES OF BEHAVIOR THERAPY

There are no overriding theories of behavior therapy; rather, techniques have been developed that are consistent with basic principles of behavior. Goals of behavior therapy are situationally specific, depending on the desired behavior change. Similarly, assessment focuses on reports and observations of client behaviors in real and simulated situations. With this information, behavior therapists use a variety of techniques, such as systematic desensitization, which can reduce fears and anxieties. Sometimes behavior therapists work with the actual situation in which an event has occurred; other times, they may have the client imagine an event. Additionally, behavior therapists have developed a variety of strategies to model and teach new behaviors. By combining behavioral approaches with self-instruction and other cognitive techniques, some therapists have developed additional creative approaches to help clients cope more effectively with their problems.

Goals of Behavior Therapy

A distinguishing feature of behavior therapy is its emphasis on the specificity of goals. Early in their work with patients, behavior therapists focus on changing target behaviors—that is, behaviors that can be defined clearly and accurately. They identify the actions or events that explain why an individual persists in a certain behavior. Often clients have several problems, and the therapist and client decide together which problem needs to be treated first. Examples of target behaviors include ceasing smoking, decreasing fighting behavior among children, increasing class attendance, and decreasing checking to see if outside doors in a home are all locked. Behavior therapists work with a variety of goals and target behaviors.

Selecting appropriate goals is done as part of a thorough assessment. As behavior therapists learn more about the antecedents and consequences of the behavior, they are more able to help the client identify specific goals. As assessment continues, clients are able to explore, with the help of the therapist, possible advantages and disadvantages of goals, how the goals can be achieved, and the likelihood of doing so. Assessment is a process that continues throughout behavior therapy and after it ends. Measurement of change as it relates to achieving goals is a continuing part of behavior therapy. The detailed approach to assessment as it relates to progress toward goals is described in the next section.

Behavioral Assessment

Assessing specific behaviors rather than broader characteristics or traits is the hallmark of behavioral assessment. There is an emphasis on determining the unique details of a client's problem and situation. Thus, diagnostic categories (DSM-IV) are not a part of behavioral treatment, although they may be used for insurance or reporting purposes. The emphasis on behavioral assessment is current rather than past behavior and on sampling specific discrete behaviors. For example, if a college student is having difficulty in scheduling his homework, he might be asked to keep a list of his activities during the day and the evening. Behavior therapists gather information from clients with behavioral interviews, reports and ratings, and observations of client behavior, among other ways. They are likely to use several of these methods, not one or two.

Behavioral interviews.   The initial behavioral interview is an essential part of the assessment process. Understanding the problem in behavioral terms is essential. For example, if the client says he has difficulty in schoolwork, the therapist may want to know what his grades are, in which courses he is experiencing difficulty, and the nature of that difficulty. By asking about the antecedents and consequences of specific behavior, the therapist assesses information about the target behavior. For example, when and in which course does the client procrastinate on his work? In the process of doing this, the behavior therapist will also tell the client what other information has to be gathered.

Many of the questions that behavioral therapists ask have to do with finding details about the target behavior. They make good use of *what, when, where, how,* and *how often* (Spiegler & Guevremont, 1998). An abbreviated example follows:

T: *What* brings you here today?

P: I feel depressed.

T: *When* did you first start to feel depressed?

P: About three months ago. I just felt down. It was hard to get up out of bed.

T: *How often* has it occurred since then?

P: Well it happened three months ago and then twice more.

T: *When* does your depression occur?

P: I feel it in the mornings; it's worse then.

In this way, the behavior therapist finds out more about the problem. As she does so, the therapist shows concern about the patient's upset about the problem.

Behavioral reports and ratings.   An efficient way of assessing the changes the client wishes to make is to use written instruments that have been developed to assess problem behaviors. Self-report inventories, often quite brief, ask clients to rate themselves on a 5- or 7-point scale or answer "yes" or "no" to items. One of the most widely known self-report inventories is the Beck Depression Inventory, which has been designed to assess fear, anxiety, social skills, health-related disorders, sexual dysfunction, and marital problems (Spiegler & Guevremont, 1998).

Also valuable are checklists and rating scales that parents, teachers, peers, or others complete to describe the client's behavior. When checklists and rating scales are used, it is important that there be *interrater reliability*—that is, close agreement among raters about their observations of the individual.

Behavioral observations.   Besides self-reports and others' ratings, direct observational procedures can be used. By having clients record the number of times they perform a target behavior, immediate records can be kept. Also, diaries that indicate the date, time, place, and activity during which related behaviors occur can be useful. One problem with having clients record their own behavior is that reactivity can result. *Reactivity* refers to change in clients' behavior caused by knowing that behavior is being recorded or observed.

To prevent reactivity, therapists may use naturalistic or simulated observation. *Naturalistic observation* means that observers record the frequency, duration, and/or strength of target behaviors; for example, observers may record the social interactions of 3-year-old children in a nursery school. *Simulated observation* means a situation is set up for monitoring behavior, for example, with microphones and one-way mirrors, so that more accurate data can be obtained than in a natural situation. Because both natural and simulated observation can be time-consuming, therapists sometimes use role playing by requesting that the client enact the behavior, such as a problematic relationship with a parent.

Physiological measurements.   As a measure of stress or fear, therapists may use a variety of measures of physical functioning. Common measures include blood pressure, heart rate, respiration, and skin electrical conductivity. Occasionally, behavior therapies are used specifically to change physiological symptoms, such as when the goal of therapy is to lower high blood pressure.

Although assessment is done particularly at the beginning of therapy, interviewing to assess maintaining conditions of the target behavior continues throughout the therapeutic process. Additionally, self-report measures and natural, simulated, or role-playing observation can be used at any time in the therapeutic process. By gathering this information, assessment of maintaining conditions is made and changes in target behaviors can be measured.

General Treatment Approach

Behavioral therapists have developed a variety of methods based on behavioral principles to reduce fear and anxiety and to change other behaviors. Perhaps the best known approach is Wolpe's desensitization method that makes use of relaxation and gradual imaginal strategies. Some approaches use intense imaginal strategies; others work in the actual environment that causes anxiety. Yet other techniques include modeling the behavior of others. By combining behavioral and cognitive approaches, Donald Meichenbaum has created stress management approaches. Each of these is described more fully here.

Systematic Desensitization

Developed by Joseph Wolpe (1958), systematic desensitization was designed to treat patients who presented with extreme anxiety or fear toward specific events, people, or objects, or had generalized fears. The basic approach is to have clients replace their anxious feelings with relaxation. The first step is to teach the client relaxation re-

JOSEPH WOLPE

sponses that compete with and replace anxiety. Second, the events that make the client anxious are assessed and arranged by degrees of anxiety. The third step is to have the client imagine anxiety-evoking situations while being relaxed. Repeated in a gradual manner, so that relaxation is paired with thoughts of events that had previously evoked anxiety, the client is systematically desensitized to situations that had previously created anxiety.

Excerpts from the case of Miss C. illustrate the three major procedures of systematic desensitization: relaxation, hierarchy construction, and desensitization (Wolpe, 1990).

Relaxation.   The process of progressive relaxation was first developed by Jacobson (1938). Basically it involves tensing and relaxing muscle groups, including arms, face, neck, shoulders, chest, stomach, and legs, to achieve deeper and deeper levels of relaxation. In work with his patients, Wolpe (1990) would ask them to devote 10 to 15 minutes twice a day to relaxation. Wolpe often used five or six sessions to teach relaxation. In introducing this technique to Miss C., he probably started in the following way.

> I am now going to show you the essential activity that is involved in obtaining deep relaxation. I will again ask you to resist my pull at your wrist so as to tighten your biceps. I want you to notice very carefully the sensations in that muscle. Then I will ask you to let go gradually as I diminish the amount of force exerted against you. Notice, as your forearm descends, that there is decreasing sensation in the biceps muscle. Notice also that the letting go is an activity, but of a negative kind—it is an "uncontracting" of the muscle. In due course, your forearm will come to rest on the arm of the chair, and you may then think that you have gone as far as possible—that relaxation is complete. But although the biceps will indeed be partly and perhaps largely relaxed, a certain number of its fibers will still, in fact, be contracted. I will then say to you, "Go on letting go. Try to extend the activity that went on in the biceps while your forearm was coming down." It is the act of relaxing these additional fibers that will bring about most of the emotional effects we want. Let's try it and see what happens. (p. 157)[1]

Relaxation proceeded in this way, with different sessions addressing different parts of the body. Continued relaxation practice throughout the course of therapy was important so that a state of relaxation could be paired with imagined anxious situations.

Anxiety hierarchies.   Obtaining detailed and highly specific information about events that cause a client to become anxious is the essence of constructing an anxiety hierarchy. Often several hierarchies representing different fears are constructed. After describing the events that elicit anxiety, clients then list them in order from least anxiety evoking to most anxiety evoking. This is often done by assigning a number from 0 to 100 to each event. In this way a *subjective units of discomfort scale* (SUDs) is developed, with 0 representing total relaxation and 100 representing extremely high anxiety. These units are subjective and apply only to the individual. As systematic desensitization progresses, events that originally had high SUDs ratings have lower SUDs ratings.

Wolpe (1990, p. 166) describes Miss C. as a 24-year-old art student seeking treatment primarily because she had failed exams due to her extreme anxiety. Further interviewing revealed that Miss C. was anxious not only about examinations but also about being watched or scrutinized by others, being criticized or devalued by others, and seeing others disagreeing or arguing. A brief hierarchy based on the latter concern that was developed by Miss C. with Wolpe's help is listed below along with the SUDs. (Many lists are longer, with more than 10 items.)

Discord between other people
1. Her mother shouts at a servant (50)
2. Her younger sister whines to her sister (40)
3. Her sister engages in a dispute with her father (30)
4. Her mother shouts at her sister (20)
5. She sees two strangers quarrel (10)

Having established a hierarchy like this one, Wolpe is ready to start the process of desensitization.

Desensitization.   Although the relaxation process may not be fully mastered, the desensitization procedures can start (Wolpe, 1990). During the first desensitization session, the therapist asks clients, after they are relaxed, how many SUDs they are experiencing. If the level is too high, above 25, relaxation is continued. The first scene presented is a neutral one, such as a flower against a background. This provides an opportunity for the therapist to gauge how well the client is able to imagine or visualize. Then the therapist proceeds in a way similar to that of Wolpe in his work with Miss C. as shown next. First he has her imagine a neutral scene, then one from her hierarchy of her fear of examinations, and then number 5, from the discord hierarchy.

> ***Therapist:*** I am now going to ask you to imagine a number of scenes. You will imagine them clearly and they will interfere little, if at all, with your state of relaxation. If, however, at any time you feel disturbed or worried and want to draw my attention, you can tell me so. As soon as a scene is clear in your mind, indicate that by raising your left index finger about 1 inch. First, I want you to imagine that you are standing at a familiar street corner on a pleasant morning watching the traffic go by. You see cars, motorcycles, trucks, bicycles, people, and traffic lights, and you hear the sounds associated with all these things. (After a few seconds the patient raises her left index finger. The therapist pauses for 5 seconds.)
>
> ***Therapist:*** Stop imagining that scene. By how much did it raise your anxiety level while you imagined it?
>
> ***Miss C.:*** Not at all.
>
> ***Therapist:*** Now give your attention once again to relaxing. (There is again a pause of 20-30 seconds, with renewed relaxation instructions.)

Therapist: Now imagine that you are home studying in the evening. It is May 20, exactly a month before your examination. (After about 15 seconds Miss C. raises her finger. Again she is left with the scene for 5 seconds.)

Therapist: Stop that scene. By how much did it raise your anxiety?

Miss C.: About 15 units.

Therapist: Now imagine the same scene again—a month before your examination.

At this second presentation the rise in anxiety was five SUDs and at the third it was zero. The numbers given vary with the individual and with the scene. When the initial figure is over 30, repetition is unlikely to lower it. But there are exceptions. There are also occasional patients in whom an initial rise of 10 is too great to be diminished by repetition.

Having disposed of the first scene of the examination hierarchy, I could have moved on to the second. Alternatively, I could have tested Miss C.'s responses in another area, such as the discord hierarchy, which I did.

Therapist: Imagine you are sitting on a bench at a bus stop and across the road are two strange men whose voices are raised in argument. (This scene was given twice. After the patient reported on her response to the last presentation, I terminated the desensitization session.)

Therapist: Relax again. Now I am going to count up to five and you will open your eyes, feeling calm and refreshed. (Wolpe, 1990, pp. 173–174)[2]

After the end of 17 desensitization sessions, Wolpe reports that Miss C. was able to be relaxed while imagining any items from each of the four hierarchies and to be relaxed in the actual situations themselves. Four months later Miss C. took her examinations without being anxious and passed them.

Although Wolpe's approach to desensitization is typical, there are variations. Some therapists have used pleasant thoughts as a substitute for deep muscle relaxation. Although commonly used with anxiety, desensitization has also been used in working with anger, asthmatic attacks, insomnia, nightmares, problem drinking, speech disorders, and other problems (Spiegler & Guevremont, 1998). The application of systematic desensitization, regardless of the type of response used to compete with different emotions, has been explained by Wolpe as counterconditioning, drawing a parallel between desensitization and classical conditioning. However, other principles of behavior can be used to describe this process as well. Note that both physical behaviors (tensing parts of the body) and covert behaviors (imagination of scenes) are used to bring about change. In systematic desensitization, a gradual exposure to anxiety-producing situations is produced through use of imagined scenes. Other techniques make use of dramatic scenes of anxiety-producing situations.

Imaginal Flooding Therapies

Whereas the process of systematic desensitization is a gradual one, flooding is not. In imaginal flooding, the client is exposed to the mental image of a frightening or anxiety-producing object or event and continues to experience the image of the event until the anxiety gradually diminishes. The exposure is not to the actual situation but to an image of a frightening situation such as being mugged, raped, or in an airplane.

The basic procedure in imaginal flooding is to develop scenes that frighten or induce anxiety in the client and then have the client imagine the scene fully and indicate the SUDs. Then the client is asked to imagine the scene again in the same session and in future sessions, indicating the SUDs. With continual exposure, the SUDs should be reduced to a point where discomfort is no longer experienced. For illustration purposes, a simplified example of treating Al, who is afraid of riding on elevators, is described below. Al is asked to imagine these scenes:

1. The client rides on an elevator with his mother from the fourth floor of a four-story building to the first floor.
2. The client rides an elevator from the top floor of a four-story building to the first floor, with no one else in the elevator.
3. The client rides in an elevator alone from the 30th floor of a 30-story building to the basement.

After Al indicates his SUDs ratings to each of these situations, the therapist has the client imagine the situations until they no longer create anxiety. Then the therapist would have Al imagine another scene. In an actual therapeutic situation, more scenes may be used and elevators that were familiar to Al would be imagined. Often relaxation exercises are practiced before flooding to make the imagery more real and, after the flooding, to return to a low level of anxiety (Keane, Fairbank, Kaddell, & Zimering, 1989).

Another imaginal flooding approach is implosive therapy, developed by Thomas Stampfl (1966). In implosive therapy, the scenes are exaggerated rather than realistic, and hypotheses are made about stimuli in the scene that may cause the fear or anxiety. Stampfl (1970) makes use of the client's description of the scene as well as a psychoanalytic interpretation of the scene. If Al reports fears of riding with his mother in the elevator in his mother's apartment building, the implosive therapist would describe a scene using the client's description but perhaps also add to the scene, based on a psychodynamic interpretation of events. Exaggerating the scene, the implosive therapist might say the following:

You're taking the elevator from your mother's apartment on the 30th floor to the ground floor. You and she are alone in the elevator. The dark green walls are vividly clear to you. As you lean on the handrail on the wall of the elevator, the screws pull out and it falls on the floor. As the elevator continues, you press a button so that the elevator will stop at the 25th floor. It doesn't. The elevator picks up speed, going faster and faster. Your mother yells at you to stop the elevator, yet it continues faster and faster, hurtling you and your mother against the walls of the elevator. Finally it comes to a stop in the basement with a resounding thud and crash.

In this example, the fear of riding in the elevator is exaggerated. Additionally, the therapist might include a description of Al's mother calling to Al and being thrown around the elevator based on an interpretation of unresolved Oedipal feelings toward his father that might include desire for his mother. Scenes similar to this would be presented again and again, with the expectation that fear and anxiety will diminish. Hogan (1968, 1969) has shown that implosive therapy can be used successfully without using psychoanalytic hypotheses to add to the images within the scene.

There are several reasons why imaginal flooding and implosive therapy are not widely used. There is a possibility that the high level of anxiety that the client is exposed to will not be reduced. Also, flooding and implosive therapies can be quite unpleasant for clients, who must reexperience anxiety. Because clients are given the option of participating in either of these therapies, they are able to decide if the approach would be too unpleasant or uncomfortable (Spiegler & Guevremont, 1998). Although desensitization, flooding, and implosive therapies involve imaginal presentation of anxiety-producing events, there are times when behavior therapists prefer to use actual situations.

In Vivo Therapies

The term *in vivo* refers to procedures that occur in the client's actual environment. Basically, there are two types of in vivo therapy: those in which the client approaches the feared stimuli gradually (similar to systematic desensitization) and those in which the client works directly with the feared situation (similar to imaginal flooding). With the graduated approach, clients often learn and practice relaxation techniques that will compete with the exposure to anxious situations. In some cases, other competing responses, such as pleasant images, are also used to compete with the anxiety that is experienced in the actual situation. A client choosing a graduated approach to reducing fears and anxiety would discuss with therapists which situations are likely to arouse varying degrees of anxiety, establishing a hierarchy or list of events. For example, given Al's fear of elevators, a list such as the following may be produced.

1. Walk to an elevator door in the presence of the therapist.
2. Watch as the therapist presses the button to open the elevator door.
3. The client presses the elevator button while the therapist watches.
4. Therapist and client walk into the elevator and back out again on the same floor.
5. The therapist holds the elevator door while the client walks around inside the elevator.
6. The therapist and client take the elevator one flight and exit.
7. The client and therapist ride up and ride down one flight in the elevator.
8. The client and therapist go up two flights together and back again, and so forth.
9. The client rides up one flight by himself, to be met by the therapist.
10. The client rides up two flights, three flights, and so forth by himself.

If, at any time, the client is tense, the therapist has the client perform relaxation procedures. Advancement from one step to the next occurs only when the client is comfortable. When the client is able to perform these activities in the presence of the therapist, he is asked to do similar work on his own, riding in elevators daily. The length of therapy will depend on the severity of the anxiety.

In intense in vivo exposure therapy, the exposure is to a strongly feared situation. Before starting the exposure, the therapist assures the client that the therapy is effective, that the therapist will be there with the client, and that some emotional distress will be experienced. To return to the elevator example, the therapist would ride up and down an elevator with Al for half an hour or more at a time. Sessions with the therapist would continue until reported anxiety is low. At that point, the therapist would wait at a floor while Al rides up and down an elevator. Additionally, Al would be asked to ride on elevators several times during each day. In this way, the anxious response to elevators is extinguished, and a nonanxious response to elevators is reinforced.

Whether behavior therapists use imaginal or in vivo approaches or graduated or intense approaches to behavior therapy depends on both the therapist's assessment of target behaviors and the patient's preference. If the anxiety is very great and the patient is fearful, the patient may elect a more graduated approach. In some cases, patients may prefer an intense approach to reduce their discomfort more quickly. Usually, in vivo approaches often provide quicker relief than imaginal approaches, as they are direct and do not rely on the client's ability to imagine events. However, some fears, such as fears of war, lightning, or earthquakes, lend themselves to only imaginal procedures.

Modeling Techniques

The therapeutic use of modeling is based chiefly on the work of Bandura (1969, 1971, 1976, 1977, 1986, 1997). Basically, modeling as a therapeutic technique occurs when a client observes the behavior of another person and makes use of that observation. Learning how the model performs the behavior and what happens to the model as a consequence of learning the behavior are both a part of the modeling technique.

In behavior therapy, there are five basic functions of modeling (Spiegler & Guevremont, 1998): teaching, prompting, motivating, reducing anxiety, and discouraging. Modeling can occur by teaching through demonstration, for example, watching someone throw a baseball or peel an apple. Modeling can serve as a prompt, such as when a child struts like a drum major, imitating his behavior. By reinforcing modeling behavior, people can motivate others to perform that behavior, such as when a parent makes a game of cleaning a room, so that the child can see how the task can be enjoyable. Anxiety reduction can occur as a result of modeling, such as when a child goes into the water after having watched another child do so, thus reducing a fear of the water. Last, an individual can be discouraged from continuing behavior such as when a smoker watches a graphic film of a patient smoking and gradually dying from lung cancer. In this section, these five functions are combined to varying degrees in live, symbolic, participant, and covert modeling, as well as in role playing.

Live modeling.   Basically, live modeling refers to watching a model, sometimes the therapist, perform a specific behavior. Often the modeling is repeated a number of times, and then, after having observed the modeling, the client repeats the observed behavior several times. In Jones's (1924) study cited earlier, Peter's fear was reduced by observing other children modeling nonanxious behavior as they played with a rabbit.

Symbolic modeling.   Often a live model is not available or would be inconvenient, and symbolic modeling is used. Common examples of symbolic modeling are films or videotapes of appropriate behavior; individuals are observed indirectly, rather than in person. Other examples include photographs, picture books, and plays. For example, children's books about a child going to a hospital for an operation serve as symbolic modeling and can reduce a child's anxiety about surgery.

A variation of symbolic modeling is self-modeling. Often it is helpful to videotape a client performing the target behavior in a desired way (Dowrick, 1991). By filming a child interacting in a socially appropriate way with other children and then showing that film to the child, the child can observe himself modeling socially appropriate behavior and replace inappropriate behavior with the newly learned social skills.

Role playing.   One of the most convenient methods of modeling is for therapists to role play certain situations with clients. Therapists may play the role of the client or someone in the client's life. Often this approach is used in helping clients interact more skillfully with others and assert themselves successfully as well. Role playing in therapy can consist of several different interactions that simulate conversations between the client and another person. Having the client practice the newly observed behavior (behavior rehearsal) strengthens the new observation.

Participant modeling.   Sometimes it is helpful for the therapist to model a behavior for the client, and then guide the client in using the behavior–participant modeling. If a client is afraid of climbing ladders, the therapist can model the behavior by first climbing the ladder. Then, using an adjoining ladder, the therapist can help the client climb a ladder, while offering encouragement and physical support when necessary.

Covert modeling.   Sometimes, when a model cannot be observed, it may be helpful to have a client visualize a model's behavior. In this process, covert modeling, the therapist describes a situation for the patient to imagine. Krop and Burgess (1993) give an example of covert modeling with a 7-year-old deaf girl who was sexually abused by her stepfather. As a result of the abuse, the girl was inappropriately touching males (in the crotch area), engaging in other inappropriate sexual behavior, and having tantrums. In using covert modeling, Krop and Burgess had the girl imagine another little girl named Sara who felt good about making decisions not to throw tantrums and instead to interact appropriately with other children. Several scenes involved taking constructive action rather than acting out in a negative way.

Modeling, whether symbolic or live, is often used with other behavioral strategies to bring about change. In particular, modeling is frequently used in situations that involve interpersonal communication. Wolpe (1990), as well as many other behavior therapists, has modeled appropriate assertive behavior with clients who are overly polite, have difficulty expressing negative feelings, or feel they do not have a right to express feelings. Because assertiveness skills are different, depending on the situation, behavior therapists often model and have their clients practice a variety of situations. Although assertiveness is perhaps the most common social skill to which behavior therapists have applied modeling, other social skills such as playing, negotiating, and dating are appropriate for modeling techniques. Such modeling behavior can also be used in cognitive-behavioral approaches that require individuals to observe events and then tell themselves how to perform appropriately.

DONALD MEICHENBAUM

Self-Instructional Training: A Cognitive-Behavioral Approach

Developed by Donald Meichenbaum (Meichenbaum, 1974; Meichenbaum & Goodman, 1971), self-instructional training is a way for people to teach themselves how to deal effectively in situations that had previously caused difficulty. The basic process is that the therapist models appropriate behavior, the client practices the behavior (as in participant modeling), and then the client repeats the instructions to himself. Self-instructional training can be applied to a great variety of behaviors, such as anxiety, anger, eating problems, and creative difficulties.

In applying self-instructional training to assertive behavior, the therapist would first model appropriate behavior, such as how to confront a roommate who borrows shirts. After modeling the behavior, the client would role play appropriate responses to the roommate with the therapist. Then the client would develop and repeat instructions to himself. "He has borrowed my shirt again. I will say to him now: 'Please do not wear my clothing without asking me. There are times when I will be glad to let you wear my shirts, but ask me first, please.'" In this simple example, the client could repeat this self-instruction several times to himself and then use it, or variations of it, at appropriate times with his roommate. Often used with children, self-instructional training can include the use of taped instructions, either by the client or the therapist, that the client listens to and practices. Additionally, the client may wish to keep records using a worksheet or practice the behavior in a variety of situations or with different people.

Stress Inoculation: A Cognitive-Behavioral Approach

Another method developed by Meichenbaum (1985, 1993) is stress inoculation training (SIT). Just as an inoculation to prevent measles puts a little stress on a person's biological system to prevent the development of measles, so giving individuals an opportunity to cope with relatively mild stress stimuli successfully allows them to tolerate stronger fears or anxieties. Underlying the SIT program is Meichenbaum's view that individuals deal with stressful behaviors by changing their beliefs about the behaviors and the statements that they make to themselves about their way of dealing with stress. The SIT program is a broad-ranging one, including information giving, relaxation training, cognitive restructuring, problem solving, behavioral rehearsals, and other cognitive and behavioral techniques. To illustrate Meichenbaum's three-stage model for stress inoculation training, I use the example of Ben, who has been robbed and badly beaten when walking home from work, and outline how SIT would be used with him in the conceptual phase, the skills-acquisition phase, and the application phase.

The conceptual phase.   In the first phase, information is gathered and the client is educated about how to think about the problem. As Ben presents the situations and concerns that cause stress, the therapist points out how cognition and emotions create, maintain, and increase stress and that it is not the events themselves that cause stress. Attention is paid to observing self-statements about the stressful or fearful situation and monitoring stressful behaviors that result. Using a log or diary throughout the therapeutic process is often recommended.

Ben would learn that his fear of walking to work is based on self-statements such as "I am going to be robbed again," "I know there is someone out there who is going to get me again," and "If I am attacked, I will be helpless." The therapist and Ben would go over his inner dialogue, and he would be asked to keep a record of stressful thoughts, feelings, and behaviors. This sets the stage for developing ways to cope with his fears.

Skills acquisition.   To cope with the fear and stress, a variety of cognitive and behavioral skills are taught, including relaxation training, cognitive restructuring, problem-solving skills, and self-reinforcement instructions. To cope with stress, relaxation techniques such as those developed by Wolpe (1990) and Jacobson (1938) are taught, so that relaxation responses compete with fearful and anxious responses. Cognitive restructuring refers to changing negative thoughts to coping thoughts. Ben might replace "I'm afraid and can't do anything" with "When I am afraid, I will pause a moment" and "I can't handle this" with "Take this one step at a time and breathe slowly and comfortably." Problem solving includes rehearsing mentally how one is going to handle a situation. Ben might say to himself, "I will change the situation by gathering information about it; I can plan alternate routes; I can walk with people; I can manage my fear." Self-reinforcement is used by giving positive self-statements such as "I am walking to work, and I am doing well" and "I am almost at work, and I feel comfortable; I'm doing better than I did yesterday." Depending on the situation, therapists using SIT would teach their clients a variety of coping skills to deal with stressful situations.

Application.   When clients have learned coping skills, they are then ready to put them into use in actual situations. First, Ben would mentally rehearse going to work while using the statements that have been developed. The more accurately Ben can visualize the scenes that take place while he is walking to work, the better he will be able to use previously developed coping strategies. When these skills have been mastered, Ben would be given homework assignments regarding what to do while walking to work. These would be gradual, such as practicing the coping statements while walking with a group of people, later practicing them while walking 30 feet behind the people, and so forth.

Like most other therapeutic methods, SIT does not always proceed smoothly, and relapse prevention (dealing with setbacks in treatment) should be a part of SIT (Meichenbaum, 1985). For example, Marlatt and Gordon (1985) have suggested that treatment can include planned failure experiences so that coping responses can be developed. Although stress inoculation training can focus on a few specific target behaviors, it is designed to generalize to other client behaviors as well. In this way, a client develops a feeling of self-efficacy as he is better able to cope with a variety of stressful events as they occur. This is possible because relaxation, cognitive restructuring, problem-solving skills, and self-reinforcement skills have been developed, practiced, and proven to be successful. Ben can apply these skills in situations as diverse as dealing with client pressures for delivery of merchandise at work, his father's insistence that Ben be a more conscientious son, and his brother's late-night alcoholic tirades. Meichenbaum (1993) describes many different applications of SIT, including dealing with general stress, anger, anxiety, and pain with psychiatric patients, athletes, medical patients, machine operators, and alcoholics.

In both behavioral and cognitive behavioral therapy, goals are very specific. Treatment can focus on changing behavior through imagining fearful or anxious scenes or through confronting them in a natural situation. The approach can be graduated or sudden, depending on the client's preference. Often modeling appropriate behavior can bring about therapeutic change, as can combining behavioral techniques with cognitive approaches, such as instructing oneself as to how to cope with a given situation. In the actual practice of therapy, these techniques are rarely used alone but can be combined into various treatment packages, depending on the behavioral assessment.

PSYCHOLOGICAL DISORDERS

Behavioral approaches to therapy depend on a number of factors, such as assessment, research, and client preference. A thorough assessment including observation, where possible, and rating instruments often influences techniques that are to be used. Furthermore, in the treatment of some disorders, research has shown some behavioral methods to be more effective than others. When several methods are likely to be equally effective, therapists give their clients a choice, such as to use graduated or intense exposure. In employing these behavioral techniques, these therapists are able to provide positive change in the lives of their patients.

The following vignettes represent a diverse set of approaches to behavioral treatment. For example, in the treatment of a case of depression, relaxation techniques, time management, assertiveness, and cognitive behavioral approaches are used. For obsessive-compulsive disorders, a behavioral treatment called exposure and response prevention, requiring intense treatment, is explained and illustrated. A variety of techniques of managing general anxiety disorders as well as specific situational anxieties or phobias show different perspectives on assessing and treating psychological disorders. Underlying all of these approaches is an emphasis on assessment, specificity of target behaviors, changing behaviors, and creative and adaptive methodology.

Depression

In general, behavioral therapists seek to reinforce patients' activities and social interactions. Because depressed patients are usually passive, behavioral interventions try to give them a sense of control and options for positive change. To bring about these changes, therapists start with an assessment of moods by asking patients to rate their moods and record pleasant and aversive events. Additionally, a large number of scales such as the Hamilton Rating Scale for Depression and the Beck Depression Inventory assess feelings of guilt, sadness, and failure and changes in appetite, sleeping, health, sex, and other behaviors. With this information, therapists can then set and plan realistic goals with their patients. A general assumption in behavior therapy is that changes in behavior bring about changes in thoughts and feelings.

With this emphasis on behavior, therapists help their patients increase daily activities, which may include more social contact or work productivity. They may develop a contract that provides for rewards such as meals, magazines, or time to do pleasurable things. Additionally, they may include social skills training such as modeling appropriate behavior, role playing, and behavioral rehearsal and generally finding ways to increase pleasant social interactions, while decreasing unpleasant ones.

Many of these techniques are illustrated below in therapy with Jane, a 29-year-old divorced mother with children aged 7 and 5 (Hoberman & Clarke, 1993). Jane complained of crying spells and frequent absences from work. She was worried about her older child's school performance and was upset about her ex-husband's failure to provide child support. The therapist's observation of depression was supported by a score indicating severe depression on the Beck Depression Inventory.

Assessment and treatment for Jane's depression began simultaneously. She was asked to write her sad and anxious feelings daily. Also, she filled out a 320-item Unpleasant Events Schedule to identify reasonable goals. The first target behavior that was attacked was that of lateness. By making a self-change plan, she was better able to estimate the time she needed to get herself and her children ready to leave for school and work and thus to diminish those times that she was late. Additionally, she learned relaxation techniques and used them to relax in a variety of situations, such as dealing with difficulties with her children.

Because problems with her children were creating tension, therapy changed from a focus on Jane's self-management to participating in a child management program. By being better able to manage her children, Jane experienced a feeling of increased self-control. Following from this was the development of time-management skills and an increase in participation in pleasant events. As a part of this work, Jane agreed to participate in two pleasant events per day for a week. To develop her sense of self-esteem and to help her to become more assertive, the therapist assigned exercises from books on self-esteem and assertion.

As a result of these activities, Jane's mood and work performance improved substantially. Her score on the Beck Depression Inventory dropped dramatically. Additionally, she role played a variety of ways of dealing with her son's disruptive behavior. Her sense of self-efficacy developed as she increased her control over her children and began to take courses at a local community college.

Obsessive-Compulsive Disorder

As noted earlier, behavior therapy is characterized by a dedication to measurement of the effectiveness of outcomes of therapeutic procedures. As a result of research, investigators such as Pinto and Francis (1993) and Riggs and Foa (1993) have concluded that exposure and response prevention (E/RP) is effective in approximately 70% of patients diagnosed with obsessive-compulsive disorders, and E/RP is used with both those who may have obsessive thoughts (such as the thought that they will get AIDS from touching a public toilet seat) and compulsions (such as washing one's hands many times per day). Basically, E/RP consists of exposure for an hour or two at a time to situations that provoke discomfort. Also, individuals are asked to refrain from following through on rituals, like hand washing. Usually, situations that produce distress are graded from moderate to severe, with the moderate ones presented earlier in treatment.

When using E/RP, therapists need 4 to 6 hours of appointments to identify cues that cause distress, rituals, and avoidance. Detailed information about the symptoms is important, including a history of the more important ones. Often rating schedules, daily logs, and brief assessment instruments are also used. When, logs of daily activities are kept, SUDs are recorded for the activities, thoughts, and rituals that evoke anxiety. Treatment is intense; where possible, meetings are 5 days a week for a period of 3 weeks, and less frequently thereafter. Home visits or out-side work may also be required. Additionally, assistance from friends and relatives is extremely helpful.

A few excerpts from the case of June, a 26-year-old married woman with obsessions and compulsions regarding cleanliness, are presented (Riggs & Foa, 1993). June re-quires 45 minutes in the shower and washes her hands about 20 times a day. In treat-ment planning, the therapist makes use of both imaginal and in vivo exposure, as in-dicated by the following example.

> *Therapist:* OK, now. I want to discuss our plan for each day during the first week of therapy. We need to expose you both in imagination and in reality to the things that bother you, which we talked about in our first sessions. As I said already we'll also limit your washing. The scenes you will imagine will focus on the harm that you fear will happen if you do not wash. The actual expo-sures will focus on confronting the things that contaminate you. Restricting your washing will teach you how to live without rituals. In imagination you will picture yourself touching something you're afraid of, like toilet seats, and not washing and then becoming ill. We can have you imagine going to a doc-tor who can't figure out what's wrong and can't fix it. That's the sort of fear that you have, right?
>
> *June:* Yes, that and Kenny getting sick and it being my fault.
>
> *Therapist:* OK, so in some scenes you'll be sick and in others Kenny will get sick. Should I add that other people blame you for not being careful? Is this what you're afraid of?
>
> *June:* Yes, especially my mother.
>
> *Therapist:* OK. We'll have her criticize you for not being careful enough. Can you think of anything else we should add to the image?
>
> *June:* No, that's about it.
>
> *Therapist:* We can compose the scenes in detail after we plan the actual expo-sure. Let's review the list of things you avoid or are afraid to touch to make sure that we have listed them in the right order. Then we'll decide what to work on each day. OK?
>
> *June:* OK. [June went over the list, which included such items as trash cans, kitchen floor, bathroom floor, public hallway carpet, plant dirt, puddles, car tires, dried dog "dirt," and bird "doo." Changes were made as needed.]
>
> *Therapist:* Good. Now let's plan the treatment. On the first day we should start with things that you rated below a 60. That would include touching this car-pet, doorknobs that are not inside bathrooms, books on my shelves, light switches, and stair railings. On the second day, we'll do the 60- to 70-level items, like faucets, bare floors, dirty laundry, and the things on Ken's desk. [The therapist continued to detail Sessions 3 to 5 as above, increasing the level of difficulty each day.] In the second week we will repeat the worst situa-tions like gutters, tires, public toilets, bird doo, and dog dirt, and we'll also find a dead animal to walk near and touch the street next to it. (Riggs & Foa, 1993, pp. 225–226)[3]

In vivo exposure often requires time and creativity from the therapist. The following example shows how the therapist uses humor and persuasion to get the patient to participate in an unattractive activity.

> **Therapist:** It's time to do the real thing now. I looked for a dead animal by the side of the road yesterday and I found one about a mile away. I think we should go there.
>
> **June:** Yuck, that's terrific. Just for me you had to find it.
>
> **Therapist:** Today's our lucky day. You knew we were going to have to find one today anyhow. At least it's close.
>
> **June:** Great.

Humor is encouraged and can be quite helpful if the patient is capable of responding to it. It is important that the therapist not laugh at but rather with the patient.

> **Therapist:** [Outside the office]. There it is, behind the car. Let's go and touch the curb and street next to it. I won't insist that you touch it directly because it's a bit smelly, but I want you to step next to it and touch the sole of your shoe.
>
> **June:** Yuck! It's really dead. It's gross!
>
> **Therapist:** Yeah, it is a bit gross, but it's also just a dead cat if you think about it plainly. What harm can it cause?
>
> **June:** I don't know. Suppose I got germs on my hand?
>
> **Therapist:** What sort of germs?
>
> **June:** Dead cat germs.
>
> **Therapist:** What kind are they?
>
> **June:** I don't know. Just germs.
>
> **Therapist:** Like the bathroom germs that we've already handled? (Riggs & Foa, 1993, p. 228)

General Anxiety Disorder

Traditionally, behavioral approaches have focused on replacing an anxiety response with a relaxation response to a variety of stimuli. Borkovec, Crnic, and Costello (1993) recommend a four-step approach in using relaxation training for individuals with a generalized anxiety disorder. First, they suggest teaching clients to identify when they have first experienced becoming anxious. Second, clients learn which aspects of situations make them anxious, so that the general anxiety disorder becomes less generalized. Third, a variety of anxiety relaxation techniques are taught, including muscle relaxation, diaphragmatic breathing, meditation, and imagery. Fourth, clients are taught to apply these relaxation methods throughout the day, especially in anticipation of potentially stressful events.

Borkovec et al. describe the case of Laura, a 20-year-old college junior who worries about grades, getting into graduate school, what sorority sisters think of her, and getting all of her work done. When stressed, Laura reported accelerated heart rate, sweating, pressure in her chest, and headaches. To help her, Laura was trained in progressive relaxation and taught to monitor early anxiety cues. Furthermore, she imagined peaceful scenery so that she could relax during the day.

To help Laura deal with stressful events, the therapist used coping desensitization. A hierarchy of three areas that Laura worried about was developed: academic, social, and family. In the coping desensitization process, Laura practiced adaptive imagery in the presence of relaxation.

Scene: Laura is at a fraternity party, dressed differently from her peers and feeling awkward. She is blushing, her heart is racing, and she has a stomach-ache. She is thinking, "I don't fit in."

Technique: The scene with its situational, physiological, and cognitive components was presented to Laura and she raised her finger to indicate anxiety. The therapist responded by saying, "Relax; all muscles loosening up as you let go. Anxious thoughts are melting away, your heart beat is slowing down through slow, rhythmic breathing. Nothing at all for you to do but just focus on the pleasant feelings of relaxation as you continue to visualize yourself at the party. Muscles of your stomach relaxing more and more deeply as warm pleasant sensations develop. Thinking to yourself, When I reach out to people, they respond to me. You relax and let go, calm and peaceful." (Borkovec et al., 1993, pp. 213–214)[4]

At the end of 12 sessions, Laura had considerable control over her anxiety. Using cognitive strategies, she was able to stop worrying about schoolwork, felt more confident with friends, and had no more physiological complaints. This emphasis on implementing relaxation procedures in a variety of ways to inhibit anxiety is characteristic of a behavioral approach.

Phobic Disorder

Many behavior therapists believe that behavior therapeutic techniques are ideal for the treatment of phobic disorders, whether fears of earthquakes, animals, closed spaces, blood, or medical procedures. The general treatment approach is to reduce the anxiety that is paired with a specific phobic object. A variety of behavioral techniques can be used, such as systematic desensitization, in which a hierarchy of feared situations is developed and gradually paired with relaxation responses, so that anxiety is diminished. Additionally, intense imaginal exposure techniques, such as implosive therapy, have been used to reduce anxiety to the feared object or event. Furthermore, when practical, in vivo exposure and modeling can be used to decrease fear of phobic stimuli.

The treatment of a 6-year-old girl who had a phobia of balloons illustrates the application of modeling techniques (Johnson & McGlynn, 1988). The child's mother had noticed that her daughter avoided situations in which there might be or were balloons. Not only did she avoid activities where there were balloons, but she had nightmares about balloons. The therapist used a model of a girl playing with balloons. Gradually, the patient became less fearful. Then the young girl who was the model in the videotape helped the patient become less fearful of balloons by playing with them in the room. She asked the patient to imitate her behaviors. Later, the therapist served as the model, playing with the balloons. Before treatment was to be stopped, the mother reported that the little girl could come in contact with balloons and not be anxious. A follow-up 2 years later showed that the little girl was no longer phobic of balloons.

BRIEF THERAPY

Because of its emphasis on changing actions, many behavior therapy approaches tend to be relatively brief. However, many factors influence length of therapy. In general, the more difficult target behaviors are to specify and the more there are of them, the longer treatment will take. Also, if a fear or anxiety is very strong and there are ways to avoid an object of fear—for example, by not flying on airplanes—then more sessions may be required. Resources, such as financial backing, supportive friends and family members, and intelligence, can help increase the opportunity of achieving various target behaviors. Some types of treatment strategies take longer than others: imaginal approaches may require more sessions than in vivo techniques, and gradual desensitization may take more sessions than intensive desensitization. Each individual's problem has unique features that may vary over time, making treatment length difficult to predict.

However, there are some general guidelines as to the length of the process for different types of disorders. Treatment of obsessive-compulsive disorders may require five appointments a week of a therapist's time for 3 weeks or so and then weekly follow-up for several more months. Depression and general anxiety may take several months of weekly meetings, but length may depend on ability to assess, define, and treat target behaviors. Additionally, if in vivo work is done outside the therapist's office, more than an hour a week is often needed. More so than many other therapists, behavior therapists are likely not to meet on a weekly basis but rather to have several sessions a week during the beginning of therapy for assessment and in vivo treatments, followed by weekly, biweekly, or monthly follow-up sessions.

CURRENT TRENDS

Because behavior therapy can be applied across the full age spectrum from infants through the elderly, many varied problems have been addressed. Advances in research and application bring new ideas. Many have been documented and illustrated in treatment manuals. New applications such as eye movement desensitization are being developed, as are applications that go beyond psychotherapy, such as work with patients with a variety of medical disorders that follow behavioral principles. Ethical issues regarding involuntary patients have evoked concern on the part of behavior therapists and others. Because much has been written about each of these areas, they are briefly summarized in this section.

Treatment Manuals

As behavior therapists treat problems and assess their client's progress, they collect data to develop treatment manuals. These manuals are often aimed at typical target behaviors rather than diagnostic categories. Types of problems would include anxiety, bed-wetting, chronic pain, insomnia, tic disorders, and bulimia.

Treatment manuals have several benefits in helping therapists approach specific target behaviors (Spiegler & Guevremont, 1998). They show which assessment and treatment methods have been effective in the past. Explaining the process of what will happen to clients in therapy becomes easier. Training therapists in specific procedures becomes much clearer, and training manuals specify procedures, making techniques easier for researchers to learn and apply correctly.

Eye Movement Desensitization and Reprocessing

Relatively new, eye movement desensitization and reprocessing (EMDR) was developed by Francine Shapiro in 1987 (1995, 1997). It was first designed for individuals with posttraumatic stress disorder, but has been applied more broadly since then. This method uses a combination of cognitive and behavioral techniques. First a behavioral assessment is done, imaginal flooding is used, and cognitive restructuring, somewhat similar to that of Meichenbaum, follows.

In explaining EMDR, Shapiro (1995) describes eight phases. The first three phases are an introduction to behavioral assessment. In the first phase, the therapist takes a client history and tries to determine if the client will be able to tolerate the stress that EMDR may bring about. In the second phase, the therapist explains how EMDR works and how the client may feel between sessions as a result of EMDR. In the third phase, the therapist gathers baseline data before desensitizing the client. Typically, the client is asked to select a memory and to assign a SUD in which 10 is the highest distress possible and 0 is the lowest.

With this preparation done, the therapist moves to the desensitization phase, which is the longest one. At this point, the therapist asks the client to think of the traumatic image and to notice feelings attached to it as the therapist moves her hand. The client concentrates on the image and feelings as the therapist moves her hand as rapidly as possible back and forth. Usually the therapist holds two fingers up with her palm facing the client about 12 inches from the client's face. About 15 to 30 bilateral eye movements make a set. After the set, the therapist tells the client to let go and take a breath. Then the client describes his feelings, images, sensations, or thoughts. The therapist may ask, "What are you experiencing now?" Although the most common approach, eye movements are not the only way of activating this information processing system. Therapists may use hand taps or repeat verbal cues. This desensitization process continues until near the end of the session or when the SUD rating drops to 0 or 1.

After the client has been desensitized, the fifth phase is to increase the positive cognition. This stage is called *installation* because a new positive thought is installed. In this phase, the positive cognition is linked to the original memory asking the individual to focus on the positive cognition and the desired target behavior. At this point eye movements are done to enhance the connection.

When the positive cognition is installed, the client moves to the sixth phase and performs a *body scan*. Here, he scans his body from head to toe trying to find any tension or discomfort. If discomfort is located, it is targeted with successive sets of eye movements until the tension is diminished.

In the last two phases, the client returns to an emotional equilibrium. Between sessions, the client is asked to maintain a log of distressing thoughts, images, or dreams. If they occur, the client is told to apply the self-soothing or relaxation exercises that he has learned. Then the entire process is reevaluated and reviewed. Typically EMDR takes four to six sessions for a single target to be reached, but the sessions usually run 90 to 120 minutes.

As EMDR has grown in popularity, over 25,000 mental health professionals have been trained in the system. However, evidence for it has been questioned. Although 30 studies have been done, several researchers question the quality of these investigations (Acierno, Hersen, van Hasselt, Tremont, & Meuser, 1994). Other reviewers (Boudewyns & Hyer, 1996; Foa & Meadows, 1997) find the research to be somewhat mixed, but feel that the techniques may be promising. Lohr, Tolin, and Lilienfeld (1998) reviewed 17 recent studies on EMDR. They concluded that EMDR, like other methods that expose clients to images of the traumatic event, is effective in helping clients improve. However, they question whether the eye movements themselves are necessary for improvement. Clinicians continue to report good results with their clients, which contributes to the popularity of EMDR among therapists.

Behavioral Medicine

A variety of behavioral techniques have been used to help in the treatment and prevention of medical disorders, as well as to help people follow medical advice. In treating high blood pressure, both muscle relaxation and biofeedback (providing information to clients about their physiological processes) have been useful in lowering blood pressure, but not as much as medication (McGrady, Olson, & Kroon, 1995). In working with patients with chronic pain, approaches such as teaching cognitive behavioral coping skills, relaxation training, and biofeedback have been helpful, depending in part on the source of the pain (Spiegler & Guevremont, 1998). Wagner and Winett (1988) have suggested approaches to promote healthy eating.

Also, behavioral techniques have been used to help children and individuals with schizophrenia take medication, follow physicians' instructions, and keep medical appointments. In the process of educating and motivating people to engage in healthy behaviors to prevent heart disease, stress, and AIDS, several techniques have been used. For example, education, assertiveness training, and social skills training were used with gay men who engaged in high-risk sexual practices (St. Lawrence, Jefferson, Alleyne, & Brasfield, 1995). More and more, behavior therapy techniques have been accepted as ways of helping patients with medical problems (Spiegler & Guevremont, 1998).

Ethical Issues

Although ethical issues are important for all mental health practitioners, regardless of their profession or theoretical orientation, behavior therapists have been particularly concerned about ethical issues. First, there is a general public misperception of behavior modification, with some people thinking that behavior therapy is something that people do to others against their will. Second, behavior therapy can be applied to a broader group of patients than any other theory of psychotherapy discussed in this book. For populations such as infants, severely retarded, autistic, and severely psychotic patients, behavior therapy is often the only appropriate approach. For many of these people or their families, behavior therapy can help promote independent decision making by giving them choices about goals and ways to attain them

(Corrigan, 1997). However, behavior therapists may often work with clients who cannot or will not give their permission for therapeutic change. To meet these concerns, a committee of the Association for Advancement of Behavior Therapy developed "Ethical Issues for Human Services" (1977), a guideline for providing ethical behavior therapy that deals with many issues including therapy for voluntary and involuntary clients.

With young children, severely retarded individuals, and psychotic patients, informed consent is usually not possible. However, there are times when partial consent can be obtained, such as a patient with schizophrenia who, during a period of lucidity, agrees to treatment. When possible, individuals participate in treatment selection, even though consent of a legal guardian is often necessary. In institutions, an ethics committee is used to approve involuntary treatment. Sensitivity to both legal and ethical issues has characterized the practice of behavior therapy for more than 30 years.

USING BEHAVIOR THERAPY WITH OTHER THEORIES

For some problems, behavior therapists may draw on other theories, but for others their approach may be strictly behavioral. With young children and nonverbal institutionalized adults, behavior therapists use techniques that are almost entirely behavioral. Also, with patients who have a single phobic reaction, for example, to snakes, behavioral treatments are likely to be used in entirety. With many other problems such as conduct disorders, depression, anxiety, and eating disorders, however, behavior therapists often make use of cognitive strategies as well. If they can conceptualize a technique, such as the Gestalt empty chair technique, from a behavioral point of view, they may use it. Because behavior therapists usually do not apply only one technique to a patient, but rather use treatment packages, they may make use of cognitive or other strategies in their treatment approach.

Other therapists may draw techniques from behavior therapy either knowingly or unknowingly. An early influential book by Dollard and Miller (1950), *Personality and Psychotherapy*, explains psychoanalysis from a reinforcement learning theory point of view that saw neurosis as behavior learned in childhood. In their approach to therapy, Adlerian psychotherapists have often incorporated behavioral techniques. Recently, Albert Ellis changed the name of Rational-Emotive Therapy to Rational Emotive Behavior Therapy, acknowledging the important role of behavioral techniques in his work. In his approach to cognitive therapy, Aaron Beck makes selective use of behavioral techniques.

When a client and therapist are talking to each other, certain behavioral principles are likely to be at work. The therapist may reinforce the client's verbal behavior by smiling, showing interest, nodding, and verbally responding. In many therapeutic approaches, when the client talks of having made therapeutic progress, the therapist is likely to comment on the client's statement and praise it, thus providing positive reinforcement. Furthermore, when the therapist appears calm in the face of the patient's anxiety, the therapist is modeling nonanxious behavior. Although many theorists do not conceptualize the role of the therapist as model and reinforcer, behavioral therapists are well aware of that role.

RESEARCH

More than any other therapy, behavior therapy's effectiveness has been studied with many different populations and a variety of disorders. It is not possible to review the results of several hundred studies here, so I give a broad view of research findings and discuss an early important study comparing psychodynamic and behavior therapy, as well as studies (meta-analyses) that compare the findings of many studies. Discussion of therapeutic effectiveness follows from DeRubeis and Crits-Christoph's (1998) review of empirically supported treatments for adults.

A Comprehensive Study

A comparison of the effectiveness of behavior therapy, brief psychoanalytic therapy, and a no treatment control group was undertaken at Temple University by Sloane, Staples, Cristol, Yorkston, and Whipple (1975). Using a variety of assessment inventories and questionnaires, as well as ratings by the client, the therapist, and observers, 94 clients were studied for 4 months. After 4 months, all three groups had made significant gains, but both behavior and psychoanalytic therapy were shown to be more effective than the waiting list nontreatment. This finding held up over a 1-year follow-up period, but assessment was difficult in the second-year follow-up because some patients were no longer available.

The authors concluded that both behavior and psychoanalytic therapy were effective with moderately severe disorders, but that behavior therapy was more effective with severe disorders. Incidentally, patients saw behavior therapists as more genuine than they did the psychoanalytic therapists, but felt that the behavior therapists encouraged less independence. Also, successful patients, regardless of treatment, rated their personal interaction with the therapist as the most important aspect of their therapy.

Review of the Evidence

By comparing the results of many studies, meta-analyses provide a means of drawing inferences about therapeutic effectiveness from a wide range of research. In some cases, meta-analyses are limited to certain age groups or disorders; in other cases, all studies are included. In a study that examined almost 400 evaluations of psychotherapy, Smith and Glass (1977) concluded, after they had statistically integrated and analyzed the research, that "the typical therapy client is better off than 75% of untreated individuals" (p. 752). No differences were found between the effectiveness of behavioral therapies and that of other therapies. In a more restrictive meta-analysis with an improved design, Shapiro and Shapiro (1982) examined 143 studies that were completed in a 5-year period. Most of the studies were of behavioral treatments, some were of cognitive therapy, and a few were psychodynamic. In general, they found more improvement for behavioral and cognitive therapies than for psychodynamic. However, they also found more improvement with cognitive therapies than with desensitization, the most common of the behavioral methods studied. In a meta-analysis of 74 studies that include over 3,400 patients, Grawe, Donati, and Bernauer (1998) found behavioral and cognitive behavioral treatments were superior to client-centered, psychodynamic, and control groups. In treatments featuring social skills training, stress inoculation, and problem solving, this was true in at least 75% of the comparisons.

Some meta-analytical studies have examined the effectiveness of therapies with children and adolescents. Analyzing the results of 108 outcome studies with 4- to 18-year-old children and adolescents, Weisz, Weiss, Alicke, and Klotz (1987) found that therapy, in general, was more effective for children than for adolescents. Also, behavioral treatments were more effective than nonbehavioral treatments, regardless of type of problem, client age, or therapist experience. Of the treatment groups that were studied, 106 were behavioral, including operant reinforcement, systematic desensitization, relaxation, modeling, social skills training, a combination of behavioral treatments, and cognitive behavioral treatments, whereas only 27 treatment groups were nonbehavioral, person-centered, psychodynamic, or discussion groups.

Later, Weisz, Weiss, Han, Granger, and Morton (1995) analyzed 150 studies published between 1983 and 1993 and found more positive effects for behavioral therapies than nonbehavioral therapies for both children and adolescents. In the 1995 investigation there were more desensitization/relaxation, cognitive, behavioral, and multiple behavioral treatments than in the 1987 study. Studies of social skills training were much more frequent, whereas studies of reinforcement and modeling treatments were less represented. However, Weiss & Weisz (1995) point out that research evaluations of therapy of children and adolescents may not represent the way therapy is practiced in real life.

In an analysis of 4- to 13-year-old children, Durlak, Fuhrman, and Lampman (1991) examined 64 studies using cognitive behavior therapy and found that the average child who received treatment was significantly better than 71% of the control group children. Another meta-analysis (Dush, Hirt, & Schroeder, 1989) examined 48 studies that used relaxation techniques with children being treated for medical conditions and found that almost all relaxation methods were significantly more helpful than a control or a placebo condition, especially for those with headaches, insomnia, and high blood pressure. A few meta-analyses have been done on specific disorders, some of which are described next to point out which types of behavioral treatments are most helpful with certain disorders.

Behavioral Research on Depression

Studies, meta-analyses, and reviews have investigated the effectiveness of behavioral and other treatments on depression. Analyzing the results from 28 studies, Nietzel, Russell, Hemmings, and Gretter (1987) contrasted behavioral (45%) with cognitive (28%) and other treatments (27%) and found that all treatments produced significant change after follow-up, regardless of type of therapy. However, individual approaches were found to be more effective than group therapy. Robinson, Berman, and Neimeyer (1990) compared 12 behavioral, 8 cognitive, 13 cognitive behavioral, and 6 other studies for effectiveness of treatment. Although they initially found some support for the superiority of cognitive therapy over other methods, they found, upon further analysis, that differences may be due to the theoretical allegiance of the researcher. In other words, if a researcher preferred one type of therapy to another, he tended to find results that supported that treatment rather than the other treatments. Thus, no clear evidence is given to support the superiority of behavioral therapies over other therapies.

One investigation (Addis & Jacobson, 1996) studied the impact of a person's reasons for being depressed on responsiveness to treatment. They compared the effectiveness of Beck's cognitive therapy (48 patients) with behavioral activation treatments (50 patients). The latter approach helped patients find reinforcement in their environment by having them monitor their own activities, schedule and structure activities, learn social skills or assertiveness, and increase pleasure and mastery of activities. They found that the more reasons clients give for depression, the more likely the outcome of therapy will be worse than if there were fewer reasons. Patients who believed their depression was caused by existential reasons responded better to cognitive than to behavioral activation therapy. However, those who gave reasons for depression that had to do with problematic relationships with others did not do as well with cognitive as contrasted with behavioral activation therapy. For those who attributed their depression to problems in childhood there was no consistent pattern of response to either treatment.

Obsessive-Compulsive Disorder

Most investigations of behavioral treatment of obsessive-compulsive disorders have studied the effectiveness of exposure and response prevention approaches. Qualitative reviews by DeRubeis and Crits-Christoph (1998) and Emmelkamp (1994) find that both exposure and prevention are helpful in treating this disorder. Both group and individual treatments are reported to be superior to relaxation procedures. Using a meta-analysis, Abramowitz (1996) studied 38 trials from 24 investigations. He concluded that therapist-supervised exposure was more effective than if patients controlled the exposure on their own. He also reported that complete response prevention was more effective than partial or no response prevention when added to exposure treatment. Abramowitz (1997) also finds that cognitive therapies can be as effective as exposure procedures in reducing obsessive compulsive disorder symptoms.

A follow-up study $3\frac{1}{2}$ years after treatment was done with 49 patients who were treated by exposure in vivo and by response prevention (Visser, Hoekstra, & Emmelkamp, 1992). Researchers found that 84% of the patients who received E/RP treatment were rated as "improved" or "much improved" $3\frac{1}{2}$ years after treatment. Predictors of successful therapy were low initial obsessive-compulsive anxiety and depression, younger age at onset of the disorder, and more negative child-rearing practices. Research by Paul Emmelkamp, Edna Foa, and their colleagues has been instrumental in establishing E/RP as an effective treatment method.

Generalized Anxiety Disorder

The typical behavioral approach to helping patients with generalized anxiety disorder is decreasing physiological stress by relaxation or by biofeedback (Emmelkamp, 1990, 1994). Emmelkamp (1990) has made several observations regarding relaxation or biofeedback. In general, progressive relaxation has been found to be superior to meditation for individuals with moderate to severe anxiety. Also, biofeedback does not seem to be superior to other methods of anxiety reduction. Emmelkamp suggests that relaxation techniques taught directly are more effective than those listened to on a tape recorder. A related finding is that patients often do not follow instructions to relax on a daily basis.

In addition to these behavioral approaches, Brown, O'Leary, and Barlow (1993) suggest cognitive strategies based on their review of outcome studies of patients with generalized anxiety disorder. They suggest that worry exposure, identifying basic worries, and practicing imagining them vividly for 25 to 30 minutes, after which clients generate alternatives as to the worst possible outcome, can be effective treatment. Additionally, time management (which includes delegating responsibility, being assertive, and adhering to agendas) and problem solving are effective treatments for generalized anxiety. This approach of Brown et al. has come about both through careful attention to research literature and through research on various aspects of treatment with a few patients with generalized anxiety disorders.

Research on Phobias

In treatment of phobias, there are several approaches, depending on what the phobia is—to open places (agoraphobia), avoidance of social situations (social phobia), or specific fears, such as to spiders (simple phobia). Reviewing research on exposure or flooding therapy for agoraphobia, DeRubeis and Crits-Christoph (1998) report that exposure has been generally more effective than relaxation, supportive therapy, or problem solving in four studies. For extreme shyness or social phobia, Feske and Chambless (1995) in their meta-analysis found that cognitive-behavioral treatment when combined with exposure therapy is not more effective than social phobia alone. Another meta-analysis of social phobia (Taylor, 1996) showed that cognitive restructuring combined with exposure showed slightly larger effects than exposure alone. Even if the patient had one or more personality disorders, exposure in vivo therapy was effective in helping patients recover (Van Velzen, Emmelkamp, & Scholing, 1997). In this study, patients were given specific structured tasks that required interaction with family, friends, and individuals at work.

Several recent investigations have concerned the alleviation of spider phobias. Öst and colleagues have studied the effectiveness of exposure treatment, individually or in group, to videotapes or manuals. In one study, patients were first given a self-help manual to deal with spiders; if that worked, they were considered finished with the study (Öst, Stridh, & Wolf, 1998). If that was not sufficient, they watched a video on dealing with spiders. If that was not sufficient, group therapy and, finally, individual therapy were offered. Although it was clear that group and individual therapy were more effective than the manual or video treatment, the stepwise approach to phobia represents an efficient use of therapeutic resources. Another study (Öst, Ferebee, & Furmark, 1997) examined a one-session group in which the therapist handed group members spiders, in plastic cases, of increasingly larger size. After 1-year follow-up 75% of participants had clinically improved. Of those who observed the group, 14% improved, and of those who watched a videotape of the group, 44% improved. Similar approaches have been applied to phobias of mice, snakes, and bats.

In this section I have been able to give only a brief overview of research on depression, obsessive-compulsive disorders, generalized anxiety disorders, and phobias. Considerable research also exists on behavioral treatment of alcoholism, schizophrenia, panic disorder, sexual dysfunction, and other disorders. As behavior therapists refine their approaches, they use research studies to determine which treatment works best for patients who demonstrate certain characteristics. As this research has become more sophisticated, care in planning precise and accurate studies has become even more important.

GENDER ISSUES

Although value issues enter into behavior therapy, as they do in all therapies, the terms and techniques are free of reference to gender. In terms of the relationship between therapist and client, the behavior therapist is an expert on change who works with the client to develop and achieve behavioral goals. Allowing the client to choose among several treatments emphasizes the equality between therapist and client. Two important principles of behavior therapy—operant conditioning and observational learning—provide a way of viewing the impact of external factors related to gender on individuals.

Operant conditioning provides a means of looking at external factors that affect individuals' behavior (Worell & Remer, 1992). For example, in treating a woman who reports being depressed, a therapist may observe that her husband and parents reinforce only her housekeeping skills, not her intellectual ones. The therapist may help the woman identify events or activities that are potential reinforcers, such as newspaper writing. As her writing develops, active behavior increases and depressive behavior decreases. By writing articles, other aspects of her behavior also increase in frequency, thus reinforcement for writing may generalize to increased social behavior with friends or activity relating to social issues. Therapists may note how certain external events that others may consider reinforcing (praise for housework) are not reinforcing for the client but instead attempt to reinforce gender-stereotyped behavior.

Bandura's (1977, 1997) description of observational learning offers a way of assessing gender issues as they affect individual lives. People may not recognize who the models are in their lives. For example, adolescents may try to shape their bodies and appearances by observing actors. They may purge food to keep thin or do excessive weight lifting to develop a muscular body. Improved social behavior may come from observing the behavior of individuals who are friendly and humorous rather than those who are physically attractive. Behavior therapists may attend to the appropriateness of models for bringing about behavior change as it relates to traditional and nontraditional gender role behavior.

MULTICULTURAL ISSUES

Because behavior therapy is an active approach, designed to implement change, many therapists have seen it as being consistent with meeting the needs of clients with diverse cultural backgrounds. When selecting target behaviors to change, client and therapist consider environmental factors. In Bandura's (1986) triadic model, environmental factors, as well as personal variables and behaviors, are seen as important in personality development. Included in environmental factors are political and social influences (such as discrimination) that have an impact on people's lives.

The emphasis that behavior therapy places on empiricism leading to a functional analysis has been seen by Tanaka-Matsumi and Higgenbotham (1996) as an asset for helping people from many cultures. Cross-cultural therapists take vague expressions of distress that may be commonly used in a culture and specify them in behavioral terms. In doing this the therapist may ask the client to express his problem; then the therapist gives his model of the problem. Following this, the two models can be compared for discrepancies and jointly agreed outcome criteria can be set forth (Kleinman, 1980).

Next the therapist and client identify variables that are antecedents and consequences of the behavior. Cross-cultural knowledge is helpful in understanding behavior. For example, in Balinese and Hawaiian cultures, speaking with entities from the spirit world may be a part of a person's life and should not be confused with symptoms of schizophrenia (Tanaka-Matsumi & Higgenbotham, 1996). Knowing how individuals cope within a particular cultural norm can be helpful. In some cultures the expressions of anger in public is considered inappropriate. Knowing this can help a therapist identify appropriate antecedents and consequences of behavior.

When developing treatment strategies, knowledge of cultural norms can be very helpful. Collaborating with a client from a different culture in choosing strategies becomes very important. For example, Higgenbotham and Streiner (1991) developed a model for preventing misuse of prescription medication by attending to cultural beliefs regarding drug efficacy and related issues. In some cases, the behavioral emphasis on self-control can be compared to the emphasis that Eastern religions put on self-control.

As a general approach to the use of behavior therapy in individuals from different cultures, Tanaka-Matsumi and Higgenbotham (1996) make several suggestions. The therapist should be aware of culture-specific definitions of what constitutes deviant behavior. Similarly knowledge of what roles individuals can play in their culture that are considered acceptable is important. In some cultures, certain individuals, such as a priest, may be considered the only ones to give assistance to psychological disturbance, and the type of assistance may be limited by cultural norms. To put this in behavioral terms, cultural groups differ on what activities are reinforced and when group or individual behavior is reinforced. For example, in some cultures, teachers may reinforce the performance of their entire class as a group, in others it may be more appropriate to reinforce individual performance.

COUPLES THERAPY

Several significant behavioral approaches to couples counseling have been based on behavioral principles such as extinction, reinforcement, and shaping. Additionally, behavioral couples counseling usually includes contingency contracting, in which, in the case of marriage counseling, a husband and wife agree to the circumstances under which one will do something for the other. Thus, the consequences of certain behaviors are defined. One of the earliest couples counseling approaches was that of Liberman (1970), who used an operant conditioning framework in which he determined the specific behavioral changes that partners would like to see, set up behavioral goals, and outlined procedures to follow. Also, Stuart (1976, 1980), describing his operant interpersonal therapy, developed a precise approach that featured a contingency contract, intervention strategies, decision-making approaches, and a way to renegotiate agreements. A method that makes use of elements from Liberman and Stuart is that described by Hahlweg, Baucom, and Markman (1988), which is explained in more detail next.

In their approach to behavioral marital therapy, Hahlweg et al. describe four basic phases: behavioral assessment, establishment of positive reciprocity, communication skills training, and problem-solving training. Assessment might include self-report instruments such as the Locke-Wallace Marital Status Inventory and the Dyadic Adjustment Scale. Questions may also be asked about the strength and skill of the relationship, such as how spouses are currently able to reinforce each other. Questions about presenting problems and the behaviors that spouses complain about are included. Other questions deal with the future prospects of the relationship, the satisfactoriness of the sexual relationship, the impact of dissolution of the relationship, and specific behavioral problems of each spouse. Several interviews may be needed to gather data that describe aspects of the marital relationship.

Once data are gathered and the relationship established with the partners, there is an effort to establish positive reciprocity. A popular technique is that of Stuart's (1976) "caring days," in which each partner chooses a day of the week to do caring behaviors for the other. Examples include paying a compliment, doing chores for the partner, or doing particular activities with the children. Records are kept of the caring behaviors that are planned and that are received. A similar approach is to have partners positively reinforce each other with praise for doing something nice.

Another important aspect of behavioral marital therapy is that of communication skills training, which includes the development of speaking and listening skills. Speaking skills include owning feelings by using the word "I." Also, partners are taught to describe specific situations and behaviors rather than make generalizations about them, saying, "I don't like it when you leave your underwear on the floor" rather than "You're so lazy, you never pick up your stuff." Basic listening skills that are taught include nonverbal attentive behavior, paraphrasing the partner's statements, and asking open questions. By giving positive feedback and accepting the comments of the partner, couples avoid interrupting, blaming, giving ultimatums, and many other unhelpful verbal behaviors.

Another approach, integrative behavior couple therapy (Jacobson, 1992; Cordova & Jacobson, 1997), makes use of many techniques described previously, while emphasizing acceptance and behavior change. Acceptance of each other is promoted through the development of communication programs based on each person's behaviors. This approach has also been viewed from a cross-cultural perspective and found to be valuable (Waller & Spiegler, 1997). Change in couples is brought about by strengthening one behavior, which can then be generalized to other behaviors. Although there are other features and approaches to behavioral couples counseling, the methods described here highlight some of the most significant procedures.

FAMILY THERAPY

Approaches to behavioral family therapy are quite similar to those used in couples therapy. For example, Holder (1993) uses many of the same strategies in working with adolescents. One goal of family therapy is to help the parents cope with problems of the "identified patient"—the child with the problem. Thus, some of the work of behavioral family therapy is directed at training parents to succeed in using behavioral methods to change the child's behavior. A popular behavioral approach, behavioral parent training (BPT), has been described by Patterson, Reid, Jones, and Conger (1975); it includes components that assess and analyze behaviors of the child, as well as strategies for the parents to teach new behaviors.

Patterson (1971) describes ways that parents can establish a baseline for specific behavior that they wish to change. By observing and graphing their child's behavior, they can develop data on which to attempt an intervention, called *baseline* data. For example, if a child screams frequently in the house, parents can record times that this behavior occurs and its duration. In some cases, the parent may need assistance from the therapist, and the therapist can make a home visit to observe the child's behavior and interactions with the family so that interventions can be suggested. Even in children as young as 2 years old, BPT can be effective in bringing about better parent-child interactions (Tucker, Gross, Fogg, Delaney, & Lapporte, 1998).

When parents have observed and measured the child's behavior, techniques can then be applied to increase desirable behavior, decrease undesirable behavior, or both. In doing so, a contingency contract between the parents and the child can be designed. Such a contract is specific; for example, the child can be given privileges, such as watching a television program after the usual bedtime, if screaming behavior decreases. Furthermore, the child can also be positively reinforced, given money toward a desired toy, if helpful behaviors toward her sister are increased. The contract can be negotiated and progress on it can be recorded.

Parents can be trained through behavioral therapy, training programs, books, or other instructions. Parents can be helpful in carrying out procedures to work with therapists in developing child management training strategies (Spiegler & Guevremont, 1998). They may help their children in dealing with pain and in habit reversal. If physically aversive consequences are required, as in the case of a 6-year-old girl with brain damage and no verbal communication skills, parents may be taught how to administer shock or other aversive treatments at home. In general, the therapist's role is to help the parents analyze the child's behaviors and to develop specific strategies for dealing with the child.

GROUP THERAPY

A variety of group programs have been used for most psychological disorders. Sometimes groups are supplementary to individual therapy: at other times they are the only treatment. Some procedures have been developed to be used in involuntary situations, such as a classroom or ward of a psychiatric hospital (Kazdin, 1994), but many have been developed for clients who choose treatment. Important in any type of behavioral group therapy is that the clients share, to some degree, compatible target behaviors. For example, a behavioral group could focus on anxiety reduction. Even though the specific target behaviors of individual members varied, techniques used to bring about change would be similar. In this section, two specific types of behavioral group therapy are explained: social skills groups and assertiveness groups.

Social Skills Training

Different social skills training programs have been applied to a wide variety of populations, such as children, psychiatric patients, and spouse abusers. Rose and LeCroy

(1991) present a general approach to social skills training that incorporates features that many behavioral therapists use: orienting group members to social skills and training them by teaching role-playing skills. Next, group members develop the specifics of problem situations that they will role play, such as dealing with a co-worker who tries to get the client to do her work. When the group has developed and discussed their problem situations, each person is asked to keep a diary of what happens when the situation occurs during the week. In group, members develop goals for dealing with their situation, and they and other members propose how they can meet these goals.

When specific behavioral goals are developed for group members, they then begin to implement change. Modeling is an important step in change, with either a therapist or another group member role playing how to deal effectively with the problem situation. After observing others model how to behave in the situation, the client then practices the situation and receives feedback from other group members as to what might be done differently, as well as feedback about what was done well. If the client has difficulty in practicing the situation, the therapist or another group member may coach a client by giving suggestions during the role play itself. Homework is given so that the individual can apply what has been learned and practice it in a real situation. For example, a client might practice newly learned ways of dealing with colleagues' impositions in the work setting itself. A record can be kept of this activity, and the consequences of the client's new behavior can be discussed in the group. By providing feedback to each other, group members give positive reinforcement to each other and are likely to develop a sense of camaraderie and support. Through their interactions with other group members, even though the focus is on behavior outside the group, group members are likely to increase their social skills.

Assertiveness Training

Similar to social skills training groups, assertiveness training groups are designed for those who have difficulty in asking for what they want or who have difficulty in expressing negative feelings, such as anger and disagreement. In designing an approach to assertiveness, Alberti and Emmons (1995) have suggested important goals of assertiveness training. One of the first goals, learning how to identify and discriminate among assertive, aggressive, and passive behaviors, is addressed through teaching the differences between these behaviors through demonstration or role play. Another goal is to teach individuals that they have the right to express themselves, while at the same time respecting the rights of others. A key goal is to learn assertiveness skills, which are demonstrated, practiced, and tried out in real situations. Meeting the goal of applying assertiveness skills successfully is accomplished through homework that is practiced between sessions, with feedback provided by members and group leaders.

Because teaching, demonstrating, and modeling are behavior strategies that can be applied as easily to a group as to an individual, the use of group therapy with social skills 'and assertiveness is particularly appropriate. Groups provide members an opportunity to practice situations with different group members and to get feedback from several people, rather than just one. Reinforcement from peers as well as from the leader can often be quite powerful. As described by Rose and LeCroy (1991), group approaches to behavior therapy can often be as effective as individual approaches to behavior and cognitive-behavioral therapies.

SUMMARY

Behavior therapy has developed from a strong scientific base, starting with Pavlov's early work on classical conditioning. Other major psychological research thrusts influencing the development of behavior therapy have been Skinner's operant conditioning and Bandura's work on observational learning. From their research, basic behavioral principles have been developed that have broad application for therapeutic practice. These include reinforcement, especially positive reinforcement, extinction of unwanted behavior, shaping of desired behavior, and modeling. Attention to precision and detail is evident in the specific behaviors used in assessing individuals' behavior through such measures as self-report, role playing, observation, interviewing, and behavior ratings.

Basic principles of behavior derived from classical conditioning, operant conditioning, and modeling directly affect the development of behavioral therapeutic approaches. One of the first methods used to help individuals was Wolpe's systematic desensitization procedure, a gradual process of introducing relaxation to reduce fear and anxiety. Other methods use intense and prolonged exposure to the feared stimulus and may use in vivo procedures, in which the client deals with anxiety in the natural environment. Modeling techniques using role playing and other methods have been derived from observational learning. Recently, therapists have combined methods from behavior therapy with those from cognitive therapy to produce comprehensive procedures, such as Meichenbaum's stress inoculation training. The application of a particular method depends on careful assessment and often includes several treatments (a treatment package) rather than the application of just one method.

As a result of a number of research studies, specific procedures have been tested for a variety of disorders, as shown in the research section. Examples of differential behavior treatment are given for depression, obsessive-compulsive disorder, anxiety, and phobias. Unlike other therapies, behavior therapy can also be applied to those with severe mental retardation or severe psychiatric disorders and to very young children. The versatility of behavior therapy and its emphasis on the creative application of scientific methodology to a wide variety of psychological disturbances are its hallmarks.

Suggested Readings

SPIEGLER, M. D., & GUEVREMONT, D. C. (1998). *Contemporary behavior therapy* (3rd ed.). Pacific Grove, CA: Brooks/Cole. • This highly readable text gives examples and exercises to explain important behavioral principles and treatment strategies. Included are chapters on cognitive behavioral therapy and applications to medicine and community psychology, as well as approaches for working with a wide variety of clients.

KAZDIN, A. E. (1994). *Behavior modification in applied settings* (5th ed.). Pacific Grove, CA: Brooks/Cole. • Although this book focuses on the application of operant-conditioning principles to applied settings such as schools and institutions for psychiatric and mentally retarded patients, it also has much information on behavior therapy in outpatient settings. Behavioral principles and research are closely related to behavioral treatments.

KANFER, K. F. H., & GOLDSTEIN, A. P. (Eds.). (1991). *Helping people change: A textbook of methods* (4th ed.). New York: Pergamon. • A well-integrated book of readings, this text takes a primarily behavioral view of helping. Also included are chapters on cognitive and cognitive behavioral methods as well as applications to community psychology.

LAST, C. G., & HERSEN, M. (Eds.). (1994). *Adult behavior therapy casebook*. New York: Plenum. • Case studies are presented for 18 different psychological disorders. These cases show how behavior therapists conceptualize cases and use scientific method in their work.

BARLOW, D. H. (Ed.). (1993). *Clinical handbook of psychological disorders: A step-by-step treatment manual* (2nd ed.). New York: Guilford. • Each of the 12 chapters describes research and practical approaches to dealing with different disorders and includes a case example.

References

ABRAMOWITZ, J. S. (1996). Variants of exposure and response prevention in the treatment of obsessive-compulsive disorder: A meta-analysis. *Behavior Therapy, 27,* 583–560.

ABRAMOWITZ, J. S. (1997). Effectiveness of psychological and pharmacological treatment of obsessive-compulsive disorder: A quantitative review. *Journal of Consulting and Clinical Psychology, 65,* 44–52.

ACIERNO, R., HERSEN, M., HASSELT, V. B. VAN, TREMONT, G., & MEUSER, K. T. (1994). Review of the validation and dissemination of eye-movement desensitization and reprocessing: A scientific and ethical dilemma. *Clinical Psychology Review, 14,* 287–299.

ADDIS, M. E., & JACOBSON, N. S. (1996). Reasons for depression and the process and outcome of cognitive-behavioral psychotherapies. *Journal of Consulting and Clinical Psychology, 65,* 1417–1424.

ALBERTI, R. E., & EMMONS, M. L. (1990). *Your perfect right: A guide to assertive living* (8th ed.) San Luis Obispo, CA: Impact.

BANDURA, A. (1969). *Principles of behavior modification.* New York: Holt, Rinehart & Winston.

BANDURA, A. (Ed.). (1971). *Psychological modeling: Conflicting theories.* Chicago: Aldine Atherton.

BANDURA, A. (1976). Effecting change through participant modeling. In J. D. Krumboltz & C. E. Thoresen (Eds.), *Counseling methods* (pp. 248–265). New York: Holt, Rinehart & Winston.

BANDURA, A. (1977). *Social learning theory.* Englewood Cliffs, NJ: Prentice-Hall.

BANDURA, A. (1978). Reflections on self-efficacy. In S. Rachman (Ed.), *Advances in behaviour research and therapy* (Vol. 1, pp. 237–269). Oxford: Pergamon.

BANDURA, A. (1986). *Social foundations of thought and action: A social cognitive theory.* Englewood Cliffs, NJ: Prentice-Hall.

BANDURA, A. (1989a). Social cognitive theory. In R. Vasta (Ed.), *Annals of child development* (Vol. 6, pp. 1–60). Greenwich, CA: JAI Press.

BANDURA, A. (1989b). Regulation of cognitive processes through perceived self-efficacy. *Developmental Psychology, 25,* 729–735.

BANDURA, A. (1997). *Self-efficacy: The exercise of control.* San Francisco: W. H. Freeman.

BORKOVEC, T. D., CRNIC, K. A., & COSTELLO, E. (1993). Generalized anxiety disorder. In R. Ammerman & M. Hersen (Eds.), *Handbook of behavior therapy with children and adults* (pp. 202–216). Boston: Allyn & Bacon.

BOUDEWYNS, P. A., & HYER, L. A. (1996). Eye movement desensitization and reprocessing as treatment for posttraumatic stress disorder. *Clinical Psychology and Psychotherapy, 3,* 185–195.

BROWN, T. A., O'LEARY, T. A., & BARLOW, D. H. (1993). Generalized anxiety disorder. In D. H. Barlow, *Clinical handbook of psychological disorders* (2nd ed., pp. 137–189). New York: Guilford.

CORDOVA, J. V., & JACOBSON, N. S. (1997). Acceptance in couple therapy and its implication for the treatment of depression. In R. J. Sternberg & M. Hojjar (Eds.), *Satisfaction in close relationships* (pp. 307–334). New York: Guilford.

CORRIGAN, P. W. (1997). Behavior therapy empowers persons with severe mental illness. *Behavior Modification, 21,* 45–61.

DeRUBELIS, R. J., & CRITS-CHRISTOPH, P. (1998). Empirically supported individual and group psychological treatments for adult mental disorders. *Journal of Consulting and Clinical Psychology, 66*, 37–52.

DOLLARD, J., & MILLER, N. E. (1950). *Personality and psychotherapy.* New York: McGraw-Hill.

DOWRICK, P. W. (1991). *Practical guide to using video in the behavioral sciences.* New York: Wiley.

DURLAK, J. A., FUHRMAN, T., & LAMPMAN, C. (1991). Effectiveness of cognitive-behavior therapy for maladapting children: A meta-analysis. *Psychological Bulletin, 110*, 204–214.

DUSH, D. M., HIRT, M. L., & SCHROEDER, H. E. (1989). Self statement modification in the treatment of child behavior disorders: A meta-analysis. *Psychological Bulletin, 106*, 97–106.

EMMELKAMP, P. M. G. (1990). Anxiety and fear. In A. S. Bellack, M. Hersen, & A. E. Kazdin (Eds.), *International handbook of behavior modification and therapy* (2nd ed., pp. 283–306). New York: Plenum.

EMMELKAMP, P. M. G. (1994). Behavior therapy with adults. In A. E. Bergin & S. L. Garfield, *Handbook of psychotherapy and behavior change* (4th ed., pp. 379–427). New York: Wiley.

Ethical issues for human services. (1977). *Behavior Therapy, 8*, v–vi.

EYSENK, H. J. (1970). *The structure of human personality* (3rd ed.). London: Methuen.

FESKE, U., & CHAMBLESS, D. L. (1995). Cognitive behavioral versus exposure only treatment for social phobia: A meta-analysis. *Behavior Therapy, 26*, 695–720.

FOA, E. B., & MEADOWS, E. A. (1997). Psychosocial treatments for posttraumatic stress disorder: A critical review. In J. Spence (Ed.), *Annual Review of Psychology* (pp. 449–480). Palo Alto, CA: Annual Review.

GRAWE, K., DONATI, R., & BERNAUER, F. (1998). *Psychotherapy in transition.* Seattle: Hogrefe & Huber.

GRODEN, G., & CAUTELA, J. R. (1981). Behavior therapy: A survey of procedures for counselors. *Personnel and Guidance Journal, 60*, 175–179.

HAHLWEG, K., BAUCOM, D. H., & MARKMAN, H. (1988). Recent advances in therapy and prevention. In I. R. H. Falloon (Ed.), *Handbook of behavioral family therapy* (pp. 413–448). New York: Guilford.

HIGGENBOTHAM, H. N., & STREINER, D. (1991). Social science contribution to pharmacoepidemiology. *Journal of Clinical Epidemiology, 44* (suppl. 2), 73S–82S.

HOBERMAN, H. M., & CLARKE, G. N. (1993). Major depression in adults. In R. T. Ammerman & M. Hersen (Eds.), *Handbook of behavior therapy with children and adults* (pp. 73–90). Boston: Allyn & Bacon.

HOGAN, R. A. (1968). The implosive technique. *Behaviour Research and Therapy, 6*, 423–432.

HOGAN, R. A. (1969). Implosively oriented behavior modification: Therapy considerations. *Behaviour Research and Therapy, 7*, 177–184.

HOLDER, D. (1993). Family therapy with adolescents. In A. S. Bellack & M. Hersen (Eds.), *Handbook of behavior therapy in the psychiatric setting* (pp. 613–628). New York: Plenum.

HULL, C. L. (1943). *Principles of behavior.* New York: Appleton-Century-Crofts.

HYMAN, R. (1964). *The nature of psychological inquiry.* Englewood Cliffs, NJ: Prentice-Hall.

JACOBSON, E. (1938). *Progressive relaxation.* Chicago: University of Chicago Press.

JACOBSON, N. S. (1992). Behavioral couple therapy: A new beginning. *Behavior Therapy, 23*, 493–506.

JOHNSON, J. H., & McGLYNN, F. D. (1988). Simple phobia. In M. Hersen & C. G. Last (Eds.), *Child behavior therapy case book* (pp. 43–53). New York: Plenum.

JONES, M. C. (1924). A laboratory study of fear: The case of Peter. *Pedagogical Seminary, 31*, 308–315.

KAZDIN, A. E. (1994). *Behavior modification in applied settings* (5th ed.). Pacific Grove, CA: Brooks/Cole.

KEANE, T. M., FAIRBANK, J. A., KADDELL, J. M., & ZIMERING, R. T. (1989). Implosive (flooding) therapy reduces symptoms of PTSD in Vietnam combat veterans. *Behavior Therapy, 20*, 245–260.

KIRBY, F. D., & SHIELDS, F. (1972). Modification of arithmetic response rate and attending behavior in a seventh-grade student. *Journal of Applied Behavior Analysis, 5,* 79–84.

KLEINMAN, A. (1980). *Patients and healers in the context of culture.* Berkeley: University of California Press.

KROP, H., & BURGESS, D. (1993). The use of covert modeling in the treatment of a sexual abuse victim. In J. R. Cautela & A. J. Kearney (Eds.), *Covert conditioning casebook* (pp. 153–158). Pacific Grove, CA: Brooks/Cole.

LIBERMAN, R. R. (1970). Behavioral approaches to family and couple therapy. *American Journal of Orthopsychiatry, 40,* 106–118.

LIEBERT, R. M., & LIEBERT, L. L. (1998). *Liebert and Spiegler's Personality: Strategies and issues* (7th ed.). Pacific Grove, CA: Brooks/Cole.

LOHR, J. M., TOLIN, D. F., & LILIENFELD, S. O. (1998). Efficacy of eye movement desensitization and reprocessing: Implications for behavior therapy. *Behavior Therapy, 29,* 123–156.

MARLATT, G., & GORDON, J. (Eds.). (1985). *Relapse prevention: Maintenance strategies in the treatment of addictive behavior.* New York: Guilford.

McGRADY, A., OLSON, R. P., & KROON, J. S. (1995). Biobehavioral treatment of essential hypertension. In M. S. Schwarz (Ed.), *Biofeedback: A practitioner's guide* (pp. 445–467). New York: Guilford.

MEICHENBAUM, D. (1974). Self-instructional training: A cognitive prosthesis for the aged. *Human Development, 17,* 273–280.

MEICHENBAUM, D. (1985). *Stress inoculation training.* New York: Pergamon.

MEICHENBAUM, D. (1993). Stress inoculation training: A 20-year update. In P. M. Lehrer & R. L. Woolfolk (Eds.), *Principles and practice of stress management* (2nd ed., pp. 373–406). New York: Guilford.

MEICHENBAUM, D., & GOODMAN, J. (1971). Training impulsive children to talk to themselves: A means of developing self-control. *Journal of Abnormal Psychology, 77,* 115–126.

MISCHEL, W. (1973). Toward a cognitive social learning reconceptualization of personality. *Psychology Review, 80,* 730–755.

MOWRER, O. H. (1950). *Learning theory and personality dynamics.* New York: Ronald Press.

MOWRER, O. H., & MOWRER, W. M. (1938). Enuresis: A method for its study and treatment. *American Journal of Orthopsychiatry, 8,* 436–459.

NIETZEL, M. T., RUSSELL, R. L., HEMMINGS, K. A., & GRETTER, M. L. (1987). Clinical significance of psychotherapy for unipolar depression: A meta-analytic approach to social comparison. *Journal of Consulting and Clinical Psychology, 55,* 156–161.

ÖST, L. G., FEREBEE, I., & FURMARK, T. (1997). One-session group therapy of spider phobia: Direct versus indirect treatments. *Behavior Research and Therapy, 35,* 721–732.

ÖST, L. G., STRIDH, B. M., & WOLF, M. (1998). A clinical study of spider phobia: Prediction of outcome after self-help and therapist directed treatments. *Behavior Research and Therapy, 36,* 17–35.

PATTERSON, G. R. (1971). *Families: Application of social learning to family life.* Champaign, IL: Research Press.

PATTERSON, G. R., REID, R. B., JONES, R. R., & CONGER, R. E. (1975). *A social learning approach to family intervention: Vol. 1. Families with aggressive children.* Eugene, OR: Castalia.

PICHOT, P. (1989). The historical roots of behavior therapy. *Journal of Behavior Therapy and Experimental Psychiatry, 20,* 107–115.

PINTO, A., & FRANCIS, G. (1993). Obsessive-compulsive disorder in children. In R. Ammerman & M. Hersen (Eds.), *Handbook of behavior therapy with children and adults* (pp. 155–166). Boston: Allyn & Bacon.

RIGGS, D. S., & FOA, E. B. (1993). Obsessive compulsive disorder. In D. H. Barlow (Ed.), *Clinical handbook of psychological disorders* (pp. 189–239). New York: Guilford.

ROBINSON, L., BERMAN, J., & NEIMEYER, R. (1990). Psychotherapy for treatment of depression: A comprehensive review of controlled outcome research. *Psychological Bulletin, 108,* 30–49.

ROSE, S. D., & LECROY, C. W. (1991). Group methods. In F. H. Kanfer & A. P. Goldstein (Eds.), *Helping people change* (4th ed., pp. 422–454). New York: Pergamon.

ROTTER, J. B. (1954). *Social learning and clinical psychology*. Englewood Cliffs, NJ: Prentice-Hall.

ST.LAWRENCE, J. S., JEFFERSON, K. W., ALLEYNE, E., & BRASFIELD, T. L. (1995). Comparison of education versus behavioral skills training interventions in lowering sexual HIV-risk behavior of substance-dependent adolescents. *Journal of Consulting and Clinical Psychology, 63*, 154–157.

SHAPIRO, D. A., & SHAPIRO, D. (1982). Meta-analysis of comparative therapy outcome studies: A replication and refinement. *Psychological Bulletin, 92*, 581–604.

SHAPIRO, F. (1995). *Eye movement desensitization and reprocessing: Basic principles, protocols, and procedures*. New York: Guilford.

SHAPIRO, F. (1997). *EMDR in the treatment of trauma*. Pacific Grove, CA: EMDR.

SKINNER, B. F. (1948). *Walden Two*. New York: Macmillan.

SKINNER, B. F. (1953). *Science and human behavior*. New York: Free Press.

SLOANE, R. B., STAPLES, F. R., CRISTOL, A. H., YORKSTON, N. J., & WHIPPLE, K. (1975). *Psychotherapy versus behavior therapy*. Cambridge, MA: Harvard University Press.

SMITH, M. L., & GLASS, G. V. (1977). Meta-analysis of psychotherapy outcome studies. *American Psychologist, 32*, 752–760.

SPIEGLER, M. D., GUEVREMONT, D. C. (1998) *Contemporary behavior therapy* (3rd ed.). Pacific Grove, CA: Brooks/Cole.

STAMPFL, T. G. (1966). Implosive therapy. Part 1: The theory. In S. G. Armitage (Ed.), *Behavioral modification techniques in the treatment of emotional disorder* (pp. 12–21). Battle Creek, MI: VA Hospital Publications.

STAMPFL, T. G. (1970). Implosive therapy: An emphasis on covert stimulation. In D. J. Levis (Ed.), *Learning approaches to therapeutic behavior change* (pp. 182–204). Chicago: Aldine.

STUART, R. B. (1976). An operant-interpersonal program for couples. In D. H. L. Olson (Ed.), *Treating relationships* (pp. 119–132). Lake Mills, IA: Graphic.

STUART, R. B. (1980). *Helping couples change: A social learning approach to marital therapy*. Champaign, IL: Research Press.

TANAKA-MATSUMI, J., & HIGGENBOTHAM, H. N. (1996). Behavioral approaches to counseling across cultures. In P. B. Pedersen, J. G. Dragerns, W. J. Lonner, & J. E. Trimble (Eds.), *Counseling across cultures* (4th ed., pp. 266–292). Thousand Oaks, CA: Sage.

TAYLOR, S. (1996). Meta-analysis of cognitive-behavioral treatment for social phobia. *Journal of Behavior Therapy and Experimental Psychiatry, 27*, 1–9.

THORNDIKE, E. L. (1898). Animal intelligence: An experimental study of the associative process in animals. *Psychological Review: Monograph Supplement* (No. 8).

THORNDIKE, E. L. (1911). *Animal intelligence: Experimental studies*. New York: Macmillan.

TUCKER, S., GROSS, D., FOGG, L., DELANEY, K., LAPPORTE, R. (1998). The long term efficacy of a behavioral parent training intervention for families with two-year-olds. *Research in Nursing and Health, 21*, 199–210.

VAN VELZEN, C. J. M., EMMELKAMP, P. M. G., & SCHOLING, A. (1997). The impact of personality disorders on behavioral treatment of social phobia. *Behavior Research and Therapy, 35*, 889–900.

VISSER, S., HOEKSTRA, R. J., & EMMELKAMP, P. M. G. (1992). Follow-up study on behavioural treatment of obsessive-compulsive disorders. In A. Ehlers, W. Fiegenbaum, I. Florin, & J. Margraf (Eds.), *Perspectives and promises of clinical psychology* (pp. 157–170). New York: Plenum.

WAGNER, J. L., & WINETT, R. A. (1988). Prompting one low-fat, high-fiber selection in a fast-food restaurant. *Journal of Applied Behavior Analysis, 21*, 179–185.

WALLER, M. A., & SPIEGLER, M. D. (1997). A cross-cultural perspective on couples differences. *Journal of Couples Therapy, 7*, 83–98.

WATSON, J. B. (1914). *Behavior: An introduction to comparative psychology.* New York: H. Holt.

WATSON, J. B. (1919). *Psychology from the standpoint of a behaviorist.* Philadelphia: Lippincott.

WATSON, J. B., & RAYNER, R. (1920). Conditioned emotional reactions. *Journal of Experimental Psychology, 3,* 1–14.

WEISS, B., & WEISZ, J. R. (1995). Relative effectivenness of behavioral versus non-behavioral child psychotherapy. *Journal of Consulting and Clinical Psychology, 63,* 317–320.

WEISZ, J. R., WEISS, B., ALICKE, M. D., & KLOTZ, M. L. (1987). Effectiveness of psychotherapy with children and adolescents: A meta-analysis for clinicians. *Journal of Consulting and Clinical Psychology, 55,* 542–549.

WEISZ, J. R., WEISS, B., HAN, S. S., GRANGER, D. A., & MORTON, T. (1995). Effects of psychotherapy with children and adolescents revisited: A meta-analysis of treatment outcome studies. *Psychological Bulletin, 117,* 450–468.

WOLPE, J. (1958). *Psychotherapy by reciprocal inhibition.* Stanford: Stanford University Press.

WOLPE, J. (1990). *The practice of behavior therapy* (4th ed.). New York: Pergamon.

WORELL, J. H., & REMER, P. (1992). *Feminist perspectives in therapy: An empowerment model.* New York: Wiley.

9

Rational Emotive Behavior Therapy

Rational emotive behavior therapy (REBT) was developed in the 1950s by Albert Ellis, a clinical psychologist, as a result of his dissatisfaction with his practice of psychoanalysis. He originated an approach that he believed would be more effective and efficient in bringing about psychotherapeutic change. His approach is primarily a cognitive one, with significant behavioral and emotive aspects.

Essential to his theory is his A-B-C model, which is applied to understanding personality and to effecting personality change. Basically this model holds that individuals respond to an activating event (A) with emotional and behavioral consequences (C). The emotional and behavioral consequences are not caused by (A), the activating event, but largely by the individual's belief system (B). When the activating event (A) is a pleasant one, the resulting beliefs are likely to be innocuous. However, when the activating events are not pleasant, irrational beliefs may develop. These irrational beliefs (B) often cause difficult emotional and behavioral consequences (C).

A major role of the therapist is to dispute (D) these irrational beliefs (B) by challenging them through a variety of disputational techniques. Also, a number of other cognitive, emotive, and behavioral techniques are used to bring about therapeutic change. Although the above outline of REBT is relatively simple, the practice of REBT is not. Assessing, disputing, and changing irrational beliefs require familiarity with assessment of implicit irrational beliefs and knowledge of a wide variety of cognitive, emotive, and behavioral techniques for individuals, couples, families, and groups.

HISTORY OF RATIONAL EMOTIVE BEHAVIOR THERAPY

Albert Ellis, the founder and developer of REBT, was born in Pittsburgh in 1913 and moved to New York City 4 years later. He grew up in New York, did all his schooling there, and has maintained a training institute there, where he actively practices individual and group REBT at its psychological clinic. During his childhood, Albert, the oldest of three children, was often sick and was hospitalized nine times, mainly for problems related to kidney disease. As a result, Ellis developed a pattern of taking care of himself and being self-responsible. Making his breakfast

ALBERT ELLIS

and lunch and getting to school by himself are early indicators of the self-sufficiency that was to be a trademark of Ellis's approach to education and professional life. His father, a businessman, was often away from home, and Ellis describes his mother as neglectful of her family (Weiner, 1988, p. 41). In looking back at his childhood, Ellis stated: "I invented rational emotive behavior therapy naturally, beginning even back then, because it was my tendency" (Weiner, 1988, p. 42). But during his adolescence, Ellis was quite shy with girls. Using a method that foreshadows REBT, he made himself talk to 100 girls at the Bronx Botanical Gardens during a 1-month period. Although he was not successful in getting a date, this method helped Ellis decrease his fear of rejection. Also shy about speaking in front of groups, Ellis used a similar approach to overcome this fear, so much so that he later came to enjoy public speaking.

Ellis received his undergraduate degree at the City College of New York in 1934. Between graduation from college and entering graduate school at the age of 28, Ellis wrote novels and worked as a personnel manager in a small business. After obtaining his Ph.D. in 1947 at Columbia University, Ellis started work at a New Jersey mental hygiene clinic, while receiving analysis from Richard Hulbeck, who was later to supervise Ellis in his early psychoanalytic work. In the 1940s Ellis published several articles on personality assessment questionnaires. Later he was to publish and speak frequently on sex, love, and marital relationships (Ellis, 1986a). His books, *Sex Without Guilt* (1958), *The Art and Science of Love* (1965), and *The Encyclopedia of Sexual Behavior* (1961) were popular and sold well, with an influence on marriage and family therapy, as well as on many individual Americans.

While practicing psychoanalysis and psychoanalytic therapy between 1947 and 1953, Ellis became increasingly dissatisfied with it. He felt that although some clients felt better, they rarely improved in a way that would help them be symptom-free and more in control of their lives. Having always been interested in philosophy since the age of 16, Ellis returned to philosophy to try to determine ways to help individuals change their philosophical point of view and develop ways of combating self-defeating behavior. In 1956, at the American Psychological Association annual convention, Ellis gave his first paper on rational therapy, the term he gave then for REBT (Ellis, 1992c). He later regretted using the term *rational therapy*, as many psychologists misinterpreted it as meaning therapy without emotion. That was not Ellis's intention, and he spent time trying to clarify and explain his position. Although other psychologists were developing other direct methods of dealing with clients at about the same time, none made such consistent and pronounced efforts in explicating their point of view as did Ellis.

Although Ellis has been adjunct professor of psychology at three universities, his energy has gone into his practice of individual and group REBT and the training of therapists at the Albert Ellis Institute for Rational Emotive Behavior Therapy in New York. Established in 1959, the institute provides workshops, therapist training, and individual and group psychotherapy. Ellis also initiated the *Journal of Rational-Emotive Behavior and Cognitive-Behavior Therapy*.

Ellis has been extremely productive in professional organizations and in the publication of books and articles. He is a fellow of many divisions of the American Psychological Association, as well as many other professional therapy and sex education organizations, and he has received a number of awards from these organizations for his leadership and contributions to the field. Not only has he served as a consulting or associate editor of more than a dozen professional journals, but he has also written more than 725 articles and 60 books, the more recent ones on REBT. Particularly significant is *Reason and Emotion in Psychotherapy* (1962), which presented the theory and practice of REBT. His *Humanistic Psychotherapy: The Rational-Emotive Approach* (1973) shows the humanistic aspect of REBT. Ellis has also written a significant number of books for the public, most notably *A New Guide to Rational Living* (1997), written with Robert Harper. It is now in its third edition and shows how individuals can apply the concepts of REBT to their own lives. He continues to coauthor and edit important books for rational emotive behavior therapists. Some of these describe changing developments in the theory as well as a variety of clinical applications.

Ellis, in his eighties, is unusually active, working 7 days a week from about 9:00 A.M. to 11:00 P.M. Seeing many clients in half-hour sessions, he conducts more than 70 individual sessions per week, leads six group therapy sessions, supervises therapists in REBT, and lectures. In addition, he writes several articles, chapters of books, or books each year. Ellis supervises the dissemination of information about REBT at the Albert Ellis Institute for Rational Emotive Behavior Therapy (Ellis, 1992c; Weiner, 1988).

RATIONAL EMOTIVE BEHAVIOR THEORY OF PERSONALITY

Ellis's theory of personality is based not only on psychological, biological, and sociological data but also on philosophy. His philosophical approach features responsible hedonism and humanism, which, combined with a belief in rationality, influence his personality theory. Ellis is interested in biological, social, and psychological factors that make individuals vulnerable to psychological disturbances that are cognitive, behavioral, and emotional in nature. It is particularly the cognitive factors that Ellis emphasizes, attending to the irrational beliefs that individuals hold that create disturbances in their lives. By understanding how Ellis views irrational beliefs, it is easier to understand his therapeutic interventions.

Philosophical Viewpoints

From the time he was a high school student, Ellis enjoyed the study of philosophy. He was interested particularly in the Stoic philosophers and was influenced by Epictetus, a Roman philosopher who said, "People are disturbed not by things, but by their view of things" (Dryden, 1990, p. 1). He was also affected by European philosophers who dealt with the issues of happiness and rationality, such as Baruch Spinoza, Friedrich Nietzsche, and Immanuel Kant, as well as Arthur Schopenhauer's concept of "the world as will and idea" (Ellis, 1987b, p. 160). The writings of more modern philosophers, including John Dewey, Bertrand Russell, and Karl Popper (a philosopher of science), influenced Ellis to emphasize cognition in his development of REBT (Ellis, 1973, 1987a, 1991b, 1994a, 1996b, 1996c; Ellis & Whiteley, 1979). The philosophical underpinnings of REBT include responsible hedonism, his basic humanistic beliefs, and his view of the rationality of individuals.

Responsible hedonism.   Although hedonism refers to the concept of seeking pleasure and avoiding pain, responsible hedonism concerns maintaining pleasure over the long term by avoiding short-term pleasures that lead to pain, such as drug abuse and alcohol addiction. Ellis believes that people are often extremely hedonistic, but need to focus on long-range rather than short-range hedonism (Ellis, 1985a, 1985b, 1987a, 1988; Ellis & Dryden, 1997; Walen, DiGiuseppe, & Wessler, 1980). Although REBT does not tell people what to enjoy, its practitioners believe that enjoyment is a major goal in life. This point of view does not lead to irresponsible behavior because individuals with a responsible attitude toward hedonism think through the consequences of their behavior on others as well as on themselves. Manipulating and exploiting others is not in the long-range interest of individuals. An example of Ellis's attention to hedonism is his work directed at irrational beliefs that people have regarding sexuality that interfere with their experience of sexual pleasure. His many books on the subject are a way of promoting responsible hedonism.

Humanism.   Practitioners of REBT view human beings as holistic, goal-directed organisms who are important because they are alive (Dryden, 1990, p. 4). This position is consistent with that of ethical humanism, which emphasizes human interests over the interests of a deity, leading to misinterpretations of Ellis as being against religion. He has stated, "It is not religion, but religiosity, that is a cause of psychopathology. Religiosity is an absolutistic faith that is not based on fact" (Ellis, 1986a, p. 3). Ellis (1986b, 1996a) believes that accepting absolute notions of right and wrong, without thinking them through, leads to guilt, anxiety, depression, and other psychological dysfunctions.

Ellis (Ellis & Dryden, 1997, p. 203) believes that individuals should have Unconditional Self Acceptance (USA). They should accept that they make mistakes, that they have worth, and that some of their own assets and qualities are stronger than other assets that they or others possess. "Thus, Adolf Hitler may be equal in humanity to Mother Teresa, but in terms of their compassion toward human beings, the latter far outscores the former" (Ellis & Dryden, p. 205). To achieve USA, individuals need to work at this, otherwise they may blame themselves for being "worthless" or "no good."

An extension of this view is that people can be perceived as good in themselves, because they exist (Ellis, 1991a). Abhorring discrimination against anyone based on traits such as race, sex, or intellect, Ellis believes that individuals should be accepted for themselves, a concept similar to Carl Rogers's "unconditional positive regard" (Ellis, 1962, 1973, 1988, 1991c, 1993, Ellis & Dryden, 1997). Thus, Ellis believes that both the therapist and the client should rate or criticize their deeds, acts, or performances, but not their essence or themselves. Acceptance of the client, while not liking aspects of his behaviors, is consistent with the philosophy of REBT.

Rationality.   Rationality refers to people using efficient, flexible, logical, and scientific ways of attempting to achieve their values and goals (Ellis, 1962, 1973, 1988, 1991c, 1996a; Ellis & Whiteley, 1979), not to absence of feelings or emotions. Therapy with REBT shows individuals how they can get more of what they want from life by being rational (efficient, logical, and flexible). This means that they may reexamine early parental or religious teachings or beliefs that they had previously accepted. As this is done, an individual develops a new philosophy of life that leads to increased long-range happiness (responsible hedonism).

These philosophies, which have been abbreviated here, are communicated to clients to help them not only in alleviating current problems but also in developing a philosophy of life that will help them deal with problems as they present themselves.

Factors Basic to the Rational Emotive Behavior Theory of Personality

Ellis has recognized a number of factors that contribute to an individual's personality development and personality disturbances, including strong biological and social aspects that present a challenge to the therapist to help change. Depending on biological and social factors, individuals are varyingly vulnerable to emotional disturbance, which is explained by Ellis's A-B-C theory of personality, described in the next section.

Biological factors.   Impressed by the power of biological factors in determining human personality, Ellis has said, "I am still haunted by the reality, however, that humans . . . have a strong biological tendency to needlessly and severely disturb themselves, and that, to make matters much worse, they also are powerfully predisposed to unconsciously and habitually prolong their mental disfunctioning and to fight like hell against giving it up" (Ellis, 1987a, p. 365). Writing that individuals have powerful innate tendencies to hurt themselves or to think in irrational ways, Ellis (1976) believes that individuals have inborn tendencies to react to events in certain patterns, regardless of environmental factors that may affect events, by damning themselves and others when they do not get what they want. Additionally, Ellis (1962) believes that certain severe mental disturbances are partly inherited and have strong biological components. For example, schizophrenia is illustrative of biological limitations that inhibit thinking clearly and logically.

Social factors.   Interpersonal relationships in families, peer groups, schools, and other social groups have an impact on the expectations that individuals have of themselves and others. They are likely to define themselves as good or worthwhile, depending on how they see others reacting to them. If they feel accepted by others, they are likely to feel good about themselves. Individuals receiving criticism from parents, teachers, or peers are likely to view themselves as bad or worthless or in other negative ways.

From a rational emotive behavior perspective, individuals who feel worthless or bad about themselves often are caring too much about the views and values of others. According to Ellis, social institutions such as schools and religions are likely to promote values that suggest the proper ways of relating to others in terms of manners, customs, sexuality, and family relationships (Ellis, 1962, 1985a; Ellis & Dryden, 1997; Ellis & Harper, 1997). Individuals often are faced with dealing with the "musts" and "shoulds" that they have incorporated from their interactions with others. For example, if an individual believes that she *absolutely must* pray twice a day, that is a belief that has been partly learned through religious training. Ellis does not say that this value of praying is inappropriate, only that individuals should be able to question their absolutist "musts" and "shoulds."

Vulnerability to disturbance.   Depending on social and biological factors, individuals vary as to how vulnerable they are to psychological disturbance. Individuals often have goals to enjoy themselves when alone, to enjoy themselves in social groups, to enjoy intimate sexual relationships with another individual, to enjoy productive work, and to enjoy a variety of recreational activities (Ellis, 1991e). Opposing these desires are dysfunctional beliefs that thwart individuals' ability to meet or enjoy these goals. Ellis (1987a, pp. 371–373) gives several examples of irrational beliefs that are indicators of individuals who are disturbed or disrupted in meeting their goals:

> *Irrational Beliefs About Competence and Success*—"Because I strongly desire to get A's in all subjects, I absolutely 'must' get all A's at all times, and do perfectly well."
> *Irrational Beliefs About Love and Approval*—"Because I strongly desire to be loved by Sarah, I absolutely 'must' always have her approval."
> *Irrational Beliefs About Being Treated Unfairly*—"Because I strongly desire Eric to treat me considerately and fairly, he absolutely 'must' do so at all times and under all conditions, because I am always considerate and fair to him."
> *Irrational Beliefs About Safety and Comfort*—"Because I strongly desire to have a safe, comfortable, and satisfying life, I 'must' find life easy, convenient, and gratifying at all times."

These represent just a few examples of irrational beliefs. According to Ellis, the more frequently these beliefs occur, the more likely an individual is vulnerable to psychological disturbance. Whether these beliefs come from biological or social factors is immaterial; they are disruptive to the individual who would lead a happy life. How such beliefs are established within an individual's system of thinking is the subject of the next section.

The Rational Emotive Behavior A-B-C Theory of Personality

The focus of rational emotive behavior personality theory is the A-B-C model of personality. Individuals have goals that may be supported or thwarted by activating events (A's). They then react, consciously or unconsciously, with their belief system (B), by which they respond to the activating event with something such as "This is nice." They also experience the emotional or behavioral consequence of the activating event. This system works well for individuals when the activating events are pleasant and support their goals. When the activating events no longer support their goals, there is potential for disturbance in this system. The potential exists for the belief system to be irrational or dysfunctional, which can lead to further disturbances.

When individuals believe they must have something happen as they wish, emotional disturbance occurs. This is particularly true when tolerance for frustration is low. Although these concepts appear simple, they can, when fully developed, become quite complex (Ellis, 1962, 1991e, 1991f; Ellis & Dryden, 1997). To illustrate these principles, here is Kelly, who has a goal to become a psychologist and a subgoal to do well on her psychology examination.

Rational belief: pleasant activating event.   The A-B-C theory of personality functions well and, for most people, goes unnoticed when the activating events are pleasant. When Kelly receives an A— on her psychology exam (activating event), her belief (B) in her ability to do well on the psychology exam and to become a psychologist is supported. The consequence is an emotional experience of pleasure and a behavioral anticipation of the next psychology examination, an activating event.

Rational belief: unpleasant activating event.   When the activating event is unpleasant, many different beliefs and consequences can result. If Kelly fails her psychology exam, the activating event (A), she may experience a belief (B) such as "This is too bad; I don't like to fail a test." She may experience an emotional consequence of feeling frustrated by her performance on the test. She may also choose to study hard for the next test (an upcoming activating event) so that she will not experience this behavioral consequence again.

Irrational belief: unpleasant activating event.   When individuals do not experience activating events in a way that is congruent with their belief systems (B), they may react with irrational beliefs (IB's). Rather than saying, "It is unfortunate, it is too bad," they may say, "I ought to have, I should, I must, I have to, have my goals fulfilled." Furthermore, they may say, "If my goals are not fulfilled, it is awful," "I can't stand it," "I'm a terrible person," and so forth. It is these irrational beliefs that contribute to emotional disturbance. They are usually followed by emotional consequences such as "I feel hopeless" or "I am extremely angry." Behavioral consequences may be avoidance, attack, or a whole range of inappropriate reactions. When Kelly fails her psychology exam (A), she may react by believing, "I have to have an A on the exam" or "I am a worthless person because I didn't get an A." She may experience an unhealthy emotional consequence, such as deep despair, a sense of worthlessness, and a choice not to study other courses—a behavioral consequence.

Disturbances about disturbances.   Ellis believes that individuals largely upset themselves through their belief systems. They can become disturbed about the consequences resulting from an unfortunate activating event. People may disturb themselves by turning a disturbed consequence into a new activating event. Kelly may continue by saying, "I feel depressed and worthless!"—a new activating event. The new belief that follows is "That is really awful!" This leaves her with a new consequence in which her feelings of worthlessness and upset are even greater. This new upset (new C) can become a third activating event, such as "I am the most worthless person in the world," and the cycle can continue ad infinitum. Thus, Kelly was depressed about her examination performance but became depressed and upset about being depressed. She criticized herself for doing poorly on the exam, felt depressed because she criticized herself, then criticized herself for being overly critical, and then criticized herself for not seeing that she is being critical, and then for not stopping being critical. She can further say, "I am more critical than others, and I'm more depressed than others, and nothing can be done about how hopeless I am." In such a way, individuals can be overwhelmed by their irrational belief systems.

Interrelationship between A, B, and C.   Although the A-B-C personality theory may appear rather simple, Ellis has explained the variety of interactions among A, B, and C. Activating events, beliefs, and consequences can each have components that are emotional, behavioral, or cognitive. Furthermore, each of these (A, B, and C) can influence and interact with each other. Ellis (1991e) describes how cognition, emotions, and behaviors affect one another and combine into a set of dysfunctional philosophical assumptions leading to emotional disturbance.

Musts.   Implicit in individuals' consequences are musts, such as "I must do well on the exam," "I must get an A in the course," "I must become a psychologist," and so forth. Ellis (1991e) states that musts not only are intellectual and cognitive but also have elements that are highly emotional and others that are behavioral. Musts are a part of goals, activating events, beliefs, and ineffective consequences. Ellis (1962) lists 12 musts that he believes are common to many individuals, examples of which follow:

I must be loved by everyone I know.
I must be competent, adequate, and achieving in all respects to be worthwhile. Some people are wicked and must be severely blamed and punished for what they have done.
It is awful when things don't go the way I want them to.
Things must go the way I want them to.
I must worry about dangerous things that I cannot control.
I must rely on someone stronger than myself.
I must become worried about other people's problems.
I must find the right solution to my problems.

Dryden (1990) and Ellis (1985a, 1991b, 1991e, 1991g) divide these irrational beliefs into three categories: demands about self, demands about others, and demands about the world and/or life conditions. Ellis has developed the term *musturbation* for all types of must statements. Musturbating develops irrational beliefs and leads to emotional disturbance. For Kelly to say, "I must get an A on my exam, or I will be a worthless person, and no one will ever respect me" is an example of an irrational belief that can lead to her becoming anxious, fearful, panicky about exams, and physically tense.

Low frustration tolerance.   Individuals who cannot tolerate frustration easily are more likely to be disturbed than those who can. Such statements as "That's too difficult," "I can't take the pressure," and "I'm too frightened to do it" are examples of low frustration tolerance. A personal philosophy maintaining that one should not have to do anything unpleasant or uncomfortable can lead to frustration in obtaining goals. If Kelly is frustrated easily by her poor performance on one exam, she may give up on her goal to become a psychologist and develop anxiety, depression, and so forth.

The A-B-C theory of personality is also the central focus for personality change. The next section describes therapeutic approaches to activating events, beliefs, and emotional and behavioral consequences.

RATIONAL EMOTIVE BEHAVIOR THEORY OF PSYCHOTHERAPY

A characteristic of REBT is its combination of philosophical change with cognitive, behavioral, and emotive strategies to bring about both short-range and long-range change. The emphasis on cognition has its antecedents in Adlerian psychotherapy, which has a strong focus on individuals' beliefs. The goals of REBT stress the use and adoption of the A-B-C theory of personality. Although assessment instruments are used, the A-B-C theory is the core of assessment as well as of psychotherapy. Rational emotive behavior therapists vary their approach to the development of the relationship with a client, but all acknowledge the importance of acceptance of the client as an individual. The core approach to REBT is that of disputing irrational thoughts; however, many other cognitive, emotive, and behavioral approaches are used to bring about change and meet clients' goals.

Goals of Therapy

The general goals of REBT are to assist people in minimizing emotional disturbances, decreasing self-defeating self-behaviors, and becoming more self-actualized so that they can lead a happier existence (Ellis & Bernard, 1985). Major subgoals are to help individuals think more clearly and rationally, feel more appropriately, and act more efficiently and effectively in achieving goals of living happily. Individuals learn to deal effectively with negative feelings such as sorrow, regret, frustration, and annoyance. They deal with inappropriate negative feelings such as depression, anxiety, and worthlessness by using an effective rational emotive behavior philosophy.

For Ellis (1990b), the philosophy of REBT distinguishes it from other cognitive therapies and makes it more efficient and elegant. Although REBT helps individuals minimize or remove emotional disturbances, it is the teaching of philosophical change that prevents individuals from redisturbing themselves with overwhelming irrational thoughts. The A-B-C philosophy can help clients see when they are creating new symptoms or recreating previous ones. The global goals of REBT can be applied to specific client goals through the use of A-B-C personality theory (Ellis & Bernard, 1985; Ellis & Dryden, 1997; Ellis & Grieger, 1986).

Assessment

In REBT assessment is of two overlapping types. The first is assessment of cognition and behaviors that are sources for the problems, as well as themes of cognition, emotions, and behaviors. The second is the use of the A-B-C theory of personality to identify client problems. Both of these methods, but especially the latter, continue throughout the therapeutic process. This assessment is driven by hypotheses that therapists make as they listen to their clients.

A wide variety of scales and tests can be used to assess client concerns. DiGiuseppe (1991, pp. 152–153) lists several instruments such as the Millon Clinical Multiaxial Inventory II and the Beck Depression Inventory that are used at the Albert Ellis Institute for Rational Emotive Behavior Therapy in New York City. Also, rating forms such as the REBT Self-Help Form, Figure 9.1, (Dryden & Walker, 1996), on which clients enter their activating events and consequences, help determine important irrational beliefs. Clients then dispute the irrational beliefs that apply and replace them with effective rational beliefs. Such a form can have both diagnostic and therapeutic purposes. By using a wide variety of assessment procedures, rational emotive behavior therapists not only assess activating events, emotions, and irrational beliefs but also assess cognitive flexibility, social problem-solving skills, and reasons that the client has for maintaining symptoms.

The A-B-C assessment usually starts from the beginning of the first session and continues throughout therapy. Therapists listen while clients describe their feelings and behaviors (consequences) that they feel are caused by specific experiences (activating events). As the client describes problems, therapists listen to the beliefs that the clients have about the activating event. Rational emotive behavior therapists differ as to how long they will listen to descriptions of emotional and behavioral problems before determining irrational beliefs. As the therapeutic process continues, rational emotive behavior therapists may revise or hear new irrational beliefs (Bernard & Joyce, 1984).

The Therapeutic Relationship

The process of assessment and the development of a therapeutic relationship are often closely related in REBT. Ellis believes that the best way to develop a therapeutic relationship is to solve the client's immediate problem (Ellis & Dryden, 1997; DiGiuseppe, 1991). After asking the client what he wishes to discuss, Ellis then identifies the activating events, irrational beliefs, and emotional and behavioral consequences. He may do this for two or three sessions and then possibly work on larger, or other, issues. Clients see and hear that they are being listened to and responded to. Ellis suggests that this is a type of advanced empathy in which the therapist understands the basic philosophies that underlie client communications. Not only do clients feel understood but also they sense that therapists understand their feelings better than they do.

Although students hearing or watching the films of Ellis for the first time are sometimes put off by his direct and assertive style, clients often experience his style differently.

> Group members frequently reported feelings of warmth and respect toward Al. When questioned by us, group members reported that he demonstrated his caring by his many questions, his complete attention to their problems, advocating an accepting and tolerant philosophy and teaching them something immediate that they could do to reduce their pain. (Walen et al., 1980, p. 32)

The relationship between client and therapist is important in REBT. Those rational emotive behavior therapists who have outlined stages of psychotherapy (DiGiuseppe & Bernard, 1983; Dawson, 1991) have rapport-building and relationship issues as their first stage. With patients who are unfamiliar with REBT or psychotherapy, rational emotive behavior therapists often introduce the purpose of therapy before working on problems. When working with children, rational emotive behavior therapists may proceed slowly and cautiously in developing a relationship before teaching REBT methods (Ellis & Bernard, 1983; Bernard & Joyce, 1984).

REBT Self-Help Form

A (ACTIVATING EVENT)

```
┌────────────────────────────────────────────────────────┐
│                                                        │
│                                                        │
│                                                        │
│                                                        │
│                                                        │
└────────────────────────────────────────────────────────┘
```

- Briefly summarize the situation you are disturbed about (what would a camera see?).
- An *A* can be *internal* or *external, real,* or *imagined.*
- An *A* can be an event in the *past, present,* or *future.*

IBs (IRRATIONAL BELIEFS)   **D** (DISPUTING IBs)

```
┌──────────────────────┐   ┌──────────────────────┐
│                      │   │                      │
│                      │   │                      │
│                      │   │                      │
│                      │   │                      │
│                      │   │                      │
│                      │   │                      │
│                      │   │                      │
│                      │   │                      │
│                      │   │                      │
│                      │   │                      │
└──────────────────────┘   └──────────────────────┘
```

To identify IBs, look for:

- DOGMATIC DEMANDS
  (musts, absolutes, shoulds)
- AWFULIZING
  (It's awful, terrible, horrible)
- LOW FRUSTRATION TOLERANCE
  (I can't stand it)
- SELF/OTHER RATING
  (I'm/he/she is bad, worthless)

To dispute ask yourself:

- Where is holding this belief getting me? Is it *helpful* or *self-defeating?*
- Where is the evidence to support the existence of my irrational belief? Is it *consistent with reality?*
- Is my belief *logical?* Does it follow from my preferences?
- Is it really *awful* (as bad as it could be)?
- Can I really not *stand* it?

FIGURE 9.1 REBT Self-Help Form

Reprinted with permission from Windy Dryden and Jane Walker. Copyright © 1996 by The Albert Ellis Institute.

C (CONSEQUENCES)

Major unhealthy negative emotions:

Major self-defeating behaviors:

Unhealthy negative emotions include:
- Anxiety   • Depression   • Rage   • Low Frustration Tolerance
- Shame/Embarassment   • Hurt   • Jealousy   • Guilt

RBs (RATIONAL BELIEFS)

E (NEW EFFECT)

New healthy
negative emotions:

New constructive
behaviors:

To think more rationally, strive for:

- NONDOGMATIC PREFERENCES
  (wishes, wants, desires)
- EVALUATING BADNESS
  (it's bad, unfortunate)
- HIGH FRUSTRATION TOLERANCE
  (I don't like it, but I can stand it)
- NOT GLOBALLY RATING SELF OR
  OTHERS (I—and others—are fallible
  human beings)

Healthy negative emotions include:

- Disappointment

- Concern

- Annoyance

- Sadness

- Regret

- Frustration

FIGURE 9.1 — Cont'd

The A-B-C-D-E Therapeutic Approach

The core of REBT is the application of the A-B-C philosophy to client problems. Often this approach is used in the first and subsequent sessions. Where possible, therapists prefer to explain and make explicit each of the three aspects. In addition, the therapeutic interventions require the use of D and E. There are three basic types of Disputation (D): detecting irrational beliefs, discriminating irrational from rational beliefs, and debating irrational beliefs. When beliefs have been actively and successfully disputed, clients will experience E, a new effect—a logical philosophy and a new level of affect appropriate to the problem. In working with the A-B-C-D-E model, therapists can experience issues and difficulties in application to their clients. Next I provide some examples of the issues involved in applying each of the five parts of the model. Most of the material in this section comes from Walen et al. (1980).

A (activating event).   The activating event can be divided into two parts: what happened, and what the patient perceived happened. Often it is helpful to ask for specifics to confirm an activating event. For example, the activating event "My grade in geology is terrible" combines an event with a perception and an evaluation. To ascertain the activating event, the therapist might ask, "What are your grades on your geology exams at this point?" Getting a clear and active picture of the activating event, while avoiding unnecessary detail and vagueness, is quite helpful. Occasionally, clients present too many activating events, and therapists need to focus on only a few. Therapists also need to be alert as to when a previous consequence becomes an activating event. Sometimes it is possible to change an activating event, such as avoiding a possible confrontation, but doing so may not help clients deal with their irrational behavior or make more than temporary changes.

C (consequences).   Often clients will start the first therapy session with their consequences—"I feel very depressed." Sometimes beginning rational emotive behavior therapists can have difficulty in discriminating between beliefs and consequences. One difference is that feelings cannot be disputed, they are experiences, whereas beliefs can be disputed. When dealing with feelings, clients may be unclear about their emotions, mislabel them, or exaggerate them. Often, but not always, consequences can be changed by altering beliefs. However, clients must be willing for those consequences to occur. For example, if a woman wishes to feel better about herself in her work, she should be willing to change angry feelings about her boss that are debilitating.

B (beliefs).   As discussed earlier, there are two types of beliefs—rational and irrational. Irrational beliefs are exaggerated and absolutistic, lead to disturbed feelings, and do not help individuals attain their goals. Being familiar with typical irrational beliefs (Ellis, 1962) can be helpful in learning to identify beliefs so that they can be disputed.

D (disputing).   A common and important approach in rational emotive behavior therapy is to teach the A-B-C philosophy to clients and then to dispute irrational beliefs. There are three parts to disputing: detecting, discriminating, and debating irrational beliefs. The therapist first detects irrational beliefs in the client and helps the client detect irrational beliefs in his perceptions. Irrational beliefs may underlie several activating events; for example, a client may experience stress on the job because he feels that everyone should be impressed by his abilities. Detecting the irrational belief "Others must find me intelligent and witty" is the first part of disputing. Discriminating irrational from rational beliefs is the next step. Being aware of *musts, shoulds, oughts,* and other unrealistic demands helps the client learn which beliefs are rational and which are not. A major emphasis in REBT is debating irrational beliefs. The therapist questions the client, "Why must you do everything better than everyone else at work?" "Why must you know everything that is going on in the office?" Debating irrational beliefs helps clients change their beliefs to rational ones, which diminishes their emotional discomfort.

Several strategies of disputing or debating irrational beliefs can be used: the lecture, the Socratic debate, humor, creativity, and self-disclosure (Dryden, 1990, pp. 52–54). Using the lecture approach (or, better, minilecture), the therapist gives the client an explanation of why her irrational belief is self-defeating. Obtaining feedback from the client that she understands what has been explained is important. A simple "yes" or "no" from the client is insufficient. In the Socratic style, the therapist points out the lack of logic and the inconsistencies in the client's belief, encouraging argument from the client, so that the client does not just accept the therapist's point of view and instead thinks for herself. Individuals should understand that humor is directed at their irrationality, not at them. By using humor and creative approaches, such as stories and metaphors, the therapist can maintain a relationship in which the client is open to change and not argumentative. Therapists' self-disclosure about how they themselves have used the A-B-C method to deal with their own irrational beliefs can also be helpful. Increased familiarity with disputing the irrational beliefs of clients can lead to the development of new strategies.

E (effect). When clients have disputed their irrational beliefs, they are then in a position to develop an effective philosophy. This philosophy, following the A-B-C model, helps individuals develop rational thoughts to replace inappropriate irrational thoughts. This new effective philosophy can bring about more productive behaviors and minimize feelings of depression and self-hatred, while bringing about satisfying and enjoyable feelings.

The A-B-C-D-E model illustrated. The following transcript features a therapist using disputation techniques within the A-B-C-D-E model. In his work with an older Australian adolescent boy, Bernard provides some guiding comments to illustrate which aspects of the A-B-C-D-E model are being used.

Assessment of feeling and activating event:

Client: Boy, am I down.

Therapist: What are you feeling?

Client: Don't know . . . sorta rotten . . . sick, like someone kicked me in the stomach.

Therapist: Did someone?

Client: Well, I did what we said last week. I went to the disco at my school last night. I went over my little speech that we did last week about how to ask Jane for a dance. I didn't feel as uptight 'cause I had something to say. And so I finally went over to Jane and before I could even ask her she walked away to dance with someone else. And she ignored me for the rest of the night.

Empathic reflection of feelings by practitioner:

Therapist: Sounds like you feel depressed because Jane didn't dance with you and you really want her to like you. Is that about it?

Client: Yeah.

Assessment of the ABC relationship:

Therapist: Well, can you explain using the ABC method why you are still fairly upset?

Client: Starting with C, I guess I am sorta depressed. And A was Jane dancing with this other guy.

Assessment of behavioral consequence:

Therapist: Good, how did you react then?

Client: That was it! I just gave up. Didn't dance, didn't talk to her. I just waited around outside until my dad picked me up.

Assessment of cognition:

Therapist: Okay, what about B? What is B again?

Client: B are my thoughts . . . especially those . . . I can't remember . . .

Therapist: Irrational?

Client: Right. Rational and irrational thoughts about A.

Therapist: Okay, now what are you thinking about A? See if you can focus on some of the nutty things you might be saying.

(reflective pause)

Client: Well, I sorta feel embarrassed. You know, she must not like me at all. She probably thinks I'm a jerk. I hate it when she did it. Makes me feel like a dill.

Therapist: See if you can start your sentences with I'm thinking.

Client: I'm thinking what a dill I am . . . and I'm thinking how much I want her.

Therapist: How much?

Client: More than anything.

Practitioner summarizes ABC assessment data:

Therapist: Okay, that's great, Mark. You've done some good thought detection. You are feeling down and depressed not because you were rejected, but because you keep saying to yourself that you can't stand being rejected. You also are probably saying not only how much you want her, but that you'll die if you don't get her. And finally, as is your way, you are putting yourself down, down, down, down, down, lower and lower, to square zero, and even lower, because of what happened.

Client: U-huh.

Practitioner guides client toward solving problem—the D E link:

Therapist: Well, how does the good book say we can think our way out of misery?

Client: I can see on your wall . . . that's right . . . D. I can challenge my thoughts.

Therapist: Where shall you start?

Client: Huh?

Therapist: It seems to me that you can start to feel better by challenging and changing any one of three thoughts. That you are a dill because you have been rejected. That you need Jane to be happy. That you can't stand it when you are rejected. Shall I pick one?

Client: Okay.

Therapist: How about, and we've discussed this before, your tendency to put yourself down and rate yourself zero because of some personal failure?

Client: I know I shouldn't do it. I know it's stupid to say I'm a dill because I do other things well.

Therapist: Like?

Client: I work well with my Dad's horses, and I'm pretty good at working with machines.

Therapist: Good. So you can never be a dill. Ever! And when you catch yourself saying you're a dill or some other lousy thing, say to yourself something like "While I don't like it when I fail, it doesn't matter all that much; I do other things well."

Client: It's nutty to put myself down for what I do wrong.

Therapist: That's the message! Now how about nutty thought number two: That you must have the lovely, glamorous and scintillating Jane. Come on Tarzan, why must you have her? (Bernard & Joyce, 1984, pp. 89–91)[1]

In this example Bernard uses Socratic dialogue to dispute Mark's irrational beliefs. He also uses brief lectures with analogies to explain concepts to Mark. A reference is made in the dialogue to a wall chart the therapist uses to help the client understand the A-B-C model. The disputational method represents the major cognitive approach used in REBT. However, there are several others. Some are described here; more are explained in *Better, Deeper, and More Enduring Brief Therapy* (Ellis, 1996a).

Other Cognitive Approaches

Rational emotive behavior therapists apply a number of cognitive techniques that help individuals develop new rational beliefs. Many of these are used as an adjunct to, and in support of, disputing techniques. Their variety speaks to the creativity of rational emotive behavior therapists and invalidates a misunderstanding that some have had that rational emotive behavior therapists employ only disputing techniques.

Coping self-statements. By developing coping statements, rational beliefs can be strengthened. For example, an individual who is afraid of public speaking may write down and repeat to himself several times a day statements such as "I want to speak flawlessly, but it is all right if I don't," "No one is killed for giving a poor speech," and "I am an articulate person."

Referenting. This method is particularly helpful for individuals who have addictions and/or low frustration tolerance. Individuals who are addicted to smoking may be asked to make lists of the advantages of stopping smoking and the disadvantages of continuing smoking. They are then instructed to think seriously about these advantages and disadvantages 10 or 20 times a day. This activity gives them good reasons for overcoming the addiction (Ellis, 1991g; Ellis & Velten, 1992).

Psychoeducational methods.   When the session is over, REBT does not stop. Ellis and his colleagues have published a variety of self-help books that they recommend to their clients. Listening to audiotapes that teach the principles of REBT is often recommended, as is listening to audiotapes of the client's therapy session. By doing so, the client is able to better remember points made by the therapist during the session (Ellis, 1991; Ellis & Harper, 1997).

Teaching others.   Ellis recommends that clients teach their friends and associates, when appropriate, the principles of REBT. When others present irrational beliefs to the clients, Ellis suggests that clients try to point out rational beliefs to their friends. Trying to persuade others not to use irrational beliefs can help the persuader to learn more effective ways of disputing her own irrational beliefs (Bard, 1980; Ellis, 1991g).

Problem solving.   By helping people expand their choices of what they want to do and be, REBT helps them choose rational thoughts, feelings, and actions rather than be guided by their dogmatic irrational beliefs. Rational emotive behavior therapists help their clients figure out and arrive at viable options by dealing with both practical problems (finding a job) and emotional problems—problems about having practical problems (fretting and worrying about getting a job). In working with problems about practical problems, rational emotive behavior therapists often make use of the specifics of the A-B-C theory of personality (Ellis, 1986c; Ellis, 1991g).

A common thread that runs throughout most of these cognitive strategies is assigning homework activities that are learned in the session and are to be practiced throughout the client's week. Many of the techniques such as coping self-statements may take only a few minutes a day. The repeated use of such methods is consistent with Ellis's view that irrational beliefs are quite entrenched in individuals (Ellis, 1987a, 1996a).

Emotive Techniques

Like other strategies, emotive techniques are both used in the session and assigned as homework. Some techniques such as imagery and visualization can be viewed as cognitive, emotive, or behavioral. When the emphasis is on emotional aspects, imagery becomes an emotive method of treatment. Role playing also has cognitive, emotional, and behavioral components and is used to get at the strong consequences that accompany irrational beliefs. Ellis believes that strong or powerful approaches are necessary to change irrational beliefs. Examples include shame-attacking exercises, forceful self-statements, and forceful self-dialogue. All of these techniques are used with the full acceptance of the therapist. Not only does the therapist accept the client but also the therapist tries to communicate this acceptance to clients so that they accept themselves.

Imagery.   Imagery is often used in REBT to help clients change their inappropriate feelings to appropriate ones. For example, a man may vividly imagine that, if he is rejected by a woman he wishes to date, he will be terribly depressed afterwards, be unable to think about anything else, and be very angry at himself. The therapist then would have him keep the same negative image and work on feeling disappointed and regretful about the woman's wish not to go out with him, without feeling depressed and angry at himself. Imagining asking the woman for a date, being turned down, and working on experiencing appropriate, rather than inappropriate, emotions can help reduce depression and feelings of inadequacy. Preferably, such techniques should be practiced once a day for several weeks (Ellis, 1986c; Maultsby & Ellis, 1974).

Role playing. Rehearsing certain behaviors to elicit client feelings often can bring out emotions that the client was not previously aware of. For example, by role playing a situation in which a woman asks a man for a date, the woman can be aware of strong fears that she did not know she had. Repeated role playing of the situation gives the individual a chance to feel better about her social skills and change inappropriate emotional self-statements (Ellis, 1986c).

Shame-attacking exercises. The purpose of these exercises is to help clients feel unashamed when others may disapprove of them. Although the exercise can be practiced in a therapy session, it is done outside therapy. Examples include minor infractions of social conventions, such as talking loudly to a store clerk or engaging strangers in conversations. Asking silly questions to receptionists or teachers is another example. Such exercises are continued until one works on feeling sorry and disappointed about others' disapproval instead of feeling ashamed and self-downing. Such exercises must be legal and not harmful for others. Inappropriate examples would be calling a 911 emergency number and leaving a false message or directing traffic in the middle of a street while playing the role of a police officer (Ellis & Grieger, 1977).

Forceful self-statements. Statements that combat "musturbating" beliefs in a strong and forceful manner can be helpful in replacing irrational beliefs with rational beliefs. If a client has told himself that it is awful and terrible to get a C on an examination, this self-statement can be replaced by a forceful and more suitable statement such as "I want to get an A, but I don't have to!" Ellis often uses obscenities as a way of providing more force to a statement (Dryden, 1990).

Forceful self-dialogue. In addition to single self-statements, a dialogue with oneself, somewhat similar to the Socratic dialogue illustrated on page 347, can be quite helpful. Arguing strongly and vigorously against an irrational belief has an advantage over therapist-client dialogue in that all of the material comes from the client. Taping such dialogues, listening to them over and over again, and letting listeners determine if one's disputing is really powerful can help clients impress themselves with their own power (Ellis, 1986c; Ellis, Gordon, Neeman, & Palmer, 1997).

Behavioral Methods

Rational emotive behavior therapists make use of a wide variety of behavioral therapeutic approaches such as those described in Chapter 8. These would include systematic desensitization, relaxation techniques, modeling, operant conditioning, and principles of self-management. Most behavioral techniques are carried out as homework. Three behavioral methods that are frequently used by rational emotive behavior therapists are activity homework, reinforcements and penalties, and skill training (Ellis, 1985a, 1986c; Ellis & Dryden, 1997).

Activity homework.   To combat client demands and musts, therapists may make assignments that reduce irrational beliefs. When clients are in a situation where they feel others should treat them fairly, the rational emotive behavior therapist may suggest that they stay in the uncomfortable situation and teach themselves to deal with hard or uncomfortable tasks. For example, rather than quitting a job, a client may work with an unreasonable boss and listen to unfair criticism, but mentally dispute the criticism and not accept the boss's beliefs as their own irrational beliefs. Other situations might include asking someone for a date or making an attempt to fail at a task, such as writing a report poorly (Ellis, 1962). Clients often observe that when they do such tasks they are anxious or self-conscious at first but are able to comprehend the irrational beliefs underlying their emotions.

Reinforcements and penalties.   When people accomplish a task, it is useful for them to reward themselves. For example, a shy person who has an extended conversation with three sales clerks may reward himself by reading a favorite magazine.

Individuals who fail to attempt a task may penalize themselves. Ellis (1986c) gives the example of burning a $20 bill. Such a self-penalty can quickly encourage clients to complete agreed-upon assignments.

Skill training.   Workshops and groups often teach important social skills. For example, assertiveness training workshops can be helpful for those who are shy and find it difficult to have their needs met by other people (Ellis, 1991d). Workshops on communication skills, job interviewing skills, and other social and work-related skills can supplement individual REBT.

Although these techniques are divided into cognitive, emotive, and behavioral techniques, in actual practice some techniques fall into two or three of those categories. For example, Ellis (1987c) makes frequent use of humor in his application of a variety of methods and asks patients to learn songs he has written that challenge irrational beliefs in a whimsical, nonthreatening way. Decisions as to which techniques to employ come with experience in listening to clients discuss their irrational beliefs. Often the techniques previously described follow disputational techniques. As therapists evaluate how well clients handle various assignments and suggestions, they then revise and reassign other techniques or methods. As therapy progresses, clients often develop insight into their problems.

Insight

Not only does REBT stress cognitive insight, but also it emphasizes emotional insight that can lead to behavioral change. Ellis and Bernard (1985) state that to change inappropriate feelings and behaviors usually requires three types of insight. The first level of insight is acknowledging that disturbances come not from the past but from irrational beliefs that individuals bring to activating events. Thus, individuals upset themselves by their irrational beliefs about past occurrences. The second level of insight has to do with how individuals continually reindoctrinate themselves with the same kind of irrational beliefs that originated in the past. Thus, irrational beliefs can take on lives of their own and continue, even though the original activating event has been forgotten. The third level of insight refers to accepting the first two levels of insight with the realization that knowledge of these insights does not automatically change people. Awareness of irrational beliefs is not sufficient; active challenging of irrational beliefs and development of rational beliefs is essential, using knowledge of the A-B-C theory of personality. For Ellis, changes that occur through the acquisition of all three insights represent elegant change. Thus, individuals not only have changed feelings, thoughts, and beliefs but also know how they have done so and why.

PSYCHOLOGICAL DISORDERS

In REBT, treatment is based on assessment of goals, activating events, beliefs, and consequences rather than on diagnostic categories. For those individuals who are severely disturbed (psychotic, borderline, or obsessive-compulsive), Ellis (1991g) believes that the cause is most likely to include a biochemical disorder as well as environmental stress. He finds that medication, along with REBT and much patience, helps improve the emotional disturbances of individuals with these diagnoses. In this section I discuss the treatment of obsessive-compulsive disorder and drug and alcohol abuse. Examples of the treatment of anxiety with adults and of depression with a 14-year-old girl demonstrate disputing, cognitive, behavioral, and emotive approaches to treatment.

Anxiety Disorder

Ellis often applies disputational strategies along with other cognitive, behavioral, and emotive approaches to individuals with anxiety disorders that may include panic or physical symptoms. He believes that significant improvement can be obtained in a few weeks and that therapy can be completed in 10 to 20 sessions (Ellis, 1992a).

How Ellis uses REBT with an individual with an anxiety disorder can be illustrated by the case of Ted, a 38-year-old African American man who has been married for 10 years and has two young children. Referred by his physician because of pseudo–heart attacks (really panic attacks), Ted has complained of chest pains, particularly when riding a train from Jersey City to Manhattan or vice versa. Ellis's approach was to obtain a brief family history and to administer several tests, including the Millon Clinical Multiaxial Inventory II. Ted's only high score on this instrument was on the anxiety scale. In the first session, after determining Ted's symptoms and obtaining family background, Ellis deals with Ted's "shoulds, oughts, and musts." In the following brief segment from the first session, Ellis challenges Ted's "musts" and explains his irrational beliefs.

> *Therapist:* Well, if we can help you to change your ideas and attitudes about taking trains and about having a heart attack, that will really help you and you won't need medication. You see, you said you were a perfectionist. So you're first making yourself anxious about doing things perfectly well. "I *must* do well! I must do well!" Instead of telling yourself, "*I'd like* to do well, but if I don't, F . . . it! It's not the end of the world." You see, you're rarely saying

that. You're saying, "I've *got* to! I've got to!" And that will *make* you anxious—about your work, about sex, about having a heart attack, or about almost anything else. Then, once you make yourself anxious, you often tell yourself, "I *must* not be anxious! I must not be anxious!" That will make you *more* anxious—anxious about your anxiety. Now, if I can help you to accept *yourself* with your anxiety, first, and stop horrifying yourself about it; if we can help you, second, to give up your perfectionism—your demandingness—then you would not keep making yourself anxious. But you're in the habit of demanding that things *have* to go well and that, when they don't, you *must* not be anxious about them. "I must not be anxious! I must be sensible and sane!" That's exactly how people make themselves anxious—with rigid, forceful shoulds, oughts, and musts.

Client: Like yesterday. Yesterday was my worst day in a long time.

Therapist: Yes, because?

Client: What I did is when I was going to the train, I said: "I need to put something in my mind."

Therapist: To distract yourself from your anxiety that you expected to have when you got on the train?

Client: Yes. I said, "I am going to buy some sports things for the children." So I went to one of the stores and I bought some things, and as soon as I got on the train I started deliberately reading. Ten minutes after I was on the train, I still didn't have any anxiety. I was okay. But then I remembered and I said, "Jesus, I feel okay." At that moment, I started feeling panicked again.

Therapist: That's right. What you probably said to yourself was, "Jesus, I feel okay. But maybe I'll have another attack! Maybe I'll get an attack!" You will if you think that way! For you're really thinking, again, "I must not get another attack! What an idiot I am if I get another attack!" Right?

Client: Yes. (Ellis, 1992a, pp. 39–40)[2]

Later in the first session, Ellis continues to dispute Ted's irrational beliefs of having an attack on the train. He also suggests self-statements that will be useful when riding the train.

Therapist: So suppose you do have an attack on the train? What's going to happen to you then?

Client: Something will happen to me.

Therapist: What?

Client: Most of the time I've said to myself, "Okay, nothing will happen. Because I know that whatever I have is not a heart problem—it's a mental problem, and I create it myself." So I then relax. But what's getting to me is that I have to deal with the same thing every day. Everyday I have to deal with it.

Therapist: I know. Because you're saying, "I *must* not be anxious! I must not be anxious!" Instead of, "I don't *like* being anxious, but if I am, I am!" You see, you're terrified of your own anxiety.

Client: That's exactly what it is!

Therapist: Okay. But anxiety is only a pain in the ass. That's all it is. It doesn't kill you. It's only a pain. Everybody gets anxious, including you. And they live with it!

Client: It's a big pain in the ass!

Therapist: I know. But that's all it is. Just like—well, suppose you lost all the money you had with you. That would be a real pain, but you wouldn't worry about it too much, because you know you'd get some more money. But you're making yourself terrified. "Something awful will happen. Suppose people see I'm so anxious! How terrible!" Well, suppose they do.

Client: I don't care about that.

Therapist: Well, that's good. Most people are afraid of that and it's good that you're not.

Client: When I walk to the train, I know that I am going to start feeling anxious.

Therapist: You know it because you're afraid of it happening. If you said to yourself strongly and really believed, "F--- it! If it happens, it happens!" Then it won't even happen. Every time you say, "I must not be anxious! I must not be anxious!"—then you'll be anxious. (Ellis, 1992a, p. 45)

In the remainder of the first session and in the second session, Ellis continued to go over and over the essentials of REBT, pointing out ways in which the client upset himself. He gets quickly to the central problem for Ted and helps him to do something about attacks on the train. The following comments are taken from the third therapy session and indicate that Ted has been working hard and successfully to apply the principles of REBT.

"I'm feeling better. Whatever I'm feeling, like anxiety, is not it. I'm creating it. Whatever I'm feeling I can make it go away in a couple of minutes and if I get upset about my anxiety, I can talk to myself about that."

"When I get to the train I'm not that anxious. . . . Like this morning, I completely forgot about it until I was on the train. Then I remembered and started saying to myself, 'It's nice to be feeling the way I'm feeling now.' It doesn't bother me anymore. . . . And last week, a couple of days, I'm going home, I fall asleep on the train, and I wake up at my station and I said to myself, 'Whatever happened a couple of months ago is gone.'"

"And even in my work I don't feel anxious. I am working better than before without getting that, uh, anxiety to make everything fast and quick. I can pace myself better than before. . . . Another thing I learned to do: not to upset myself about the others in my office who act badly. If I got upset, they're going to act the same way."

"Before I thought my anxiety meant something was physically wrong. Now I see that I'm creating that sick feeling. Two or three minutes later, I am okay. Two weeks ago it would have taken me fifteen minutes to be less anxious. Now it takes me two or three minutes and there are days when I don't feel panic."

"The other day I got to the train when it was almost full, and I couldn't sit down and read and distract myself. But it didn't bother me and I didn't wait for another train as I used to have to do. . . . I can talk to myself and say, 'Look, whatever anxiety you feel, you created it. And you can uncreate it.'" (Ellis, 1992a, p. 51)

This was Ted's third and last individual session with Ellis. After this he attended Friday night workshops at the Albert Ellis Institute for Rational Emotive Behavior Therapy. He also participated in several 4-hour workshops. Both Ted and his wife reported that he has held the gains that he has made, has lost his panic about trains, was rarely anxious or angry at the office, and was functioning very well sexually.

Depression

In working with depressed clients, rational emotive behavior therapists apply as many of the cognitive, emotive, and behavioral techniques as seem appropriate. In the example below, the emphasis is on cognitive techniques applied with Penny, a 14-year-old student with a hearing loss. She felt hopeless, not as good as her brothers, and nervous when they were not around. Feeling her childhood had been ruined because she had not done the risky things that her brothers had done, Penny's schoolwork was suffering and she felt ineffective. The following excerpt shows how Joyce used REBT to challenge and change Penny's irrational beliefs.

> The main focus of therapy was in teaching her rational emotive behavior ways of challenging her irrational beliefs, and altering her causal attributions regarding her unhappiness. She acquired a new causal attribution belief: "It is possible to do something about my unhappy feelings and I am the one who can do something about them." In addition, she learned that factors under her control, namely the learning of disputational skills and encouraging herself to make an effort, were major influences over what would happen to her in the future and how she would feel. The main irrational beliefs she learned to dispute were "I must have my brothers' love and approval at all times" and "I must perform well in my schoolwork at all times or I am a failure."
>
> Penny was taught to distinguish between herself and her performance and learned to stop rating herself globally. Homework exercises helped her to rehearse exactly what she would say to people when asked to do something she did not want to try (e.g., riding a surfboard in heavy surf). Other in-session rehearsals of rational self-talk, for dealing with schoolwork "catastrophes" worse than she had feared or imagined, reduced her exaggerated evaluations of events such as getting poor marks. Humorous exaggerations by the practitioner helped her to put her perceptions into a new perspective.

After eight sessions she was feeling happier and doing her schoolwork without rating herself globally on her performance level. Changes in Penny reported by her mother included improved self-acceptance, new positive perceptions of her teachers, and improvements in the independence and organization of her schoolwork (Bernard & Joyce, 1984, pp. 310–311).

Obsessive-Compulsive Disorder

Ellis (1991g, 1994b) believes there is a strong biological component to obsessive-compulsive disorders. He attributes this disorder to deficient neurotransmitters (especially serotonin). Although Ellis suggests medication, he also works with individuals who demand absolute and perfect certainty. His approach to those with obsessive-compulsive disorders is to show them that perfect certainty does not exist and to challenge their belief systems. The following is a brief description of a woman with an obsessive-compulsive disorder to whom Ellis has applied REBT.

> I see one now who has both the need for certainty and also awfulizes about her child being switched for another child right after she gave birth. She demands a 100% guarantee that her child wasn't switched, which, of course, she can't have. Although I show her that there's no evidence that the child was switched and only a one-in-a-billion chance that it was, and although the child looks just like her, she still insists that it may have been switched and is panicked about the "horror" of such a possibility.
>
> I then try elegant REBT and show her that, even if the child had been switched, it would not be so bad, because she has OCD (obsessive-compulsive disorder), her mother is schizophrenic, and several of her other close relatives are borderline personalities. So if she got the wrong baby, it might well turn out to be less disturbed than if she got the right one! Finally, after weeks of strongly using REBT with her, I am getting her to accept uncertainty, and she is becoming much less obsessed about the highly unlikely baby switching. (Ellis, 1991g, pp. 21–22)[3]

Alcohol and Substance Abuse

Ellis and his colleagues have devoted considerable attention to the treatment of alcohol and substance abuse. In their book *Rational-Emotive Treatment of Alcoholism and Substance Abuse*, Ellis, McInerney, DiGiuseppe, and Yeager (1988) explain an REBT theory of addiction and specific REBT cognitive, emotive, and behavioral techniques to assist addicts. Their approach to treatment of alcohol or drug abusers starts by establishing a persuasive therapeutic relationship with the client and setting achievable goals. Clients are taught how to dispute their dysfunctional thoughts about drinking or abusing drugs. An example of how abusers can dispute irrational beliefs about inevitability and hopelessness regarding drinking is shown here.

> **Irrational Belief:** "Because I *must* not drink again and I did what I must not do, it's hopeless. I'll *always* be a drunk and *never* be able to stop drinking."
>
> **Disputing:** "How can you prove that anything *always* will exist and *never* will be changeable?"
>
> **IB:** "But look how many times I tried to abstain and didn't. Doesn't that prove that I *can't* do so?"
>
> **Disputing:** "No, it merely proves that you haven't done it yet and that it is *very difficult* to do so. But *very difficult* doesn't mean *impossible*. Unless you *think* it is and thereby *make* it practically impossible."
>
> **Answer:** "Maybe you're right. I'll think about that." (Ellis et al., 1988, p. 74)[4]

When clients have been able to demonstrate some control over addictive behavior, later phases of REBT shift to "self-management of cognitive, emotional, behavioral, and situational triggers for substance abuse" (Ellis et al., 1988, p. 107). Final treatment stages are devoted to helping clients use practical problem solving to continue their abstinence (a common goal but not the only goal of therapy) and to understand underlying irrational beliefs that are major contributors to alcohol and drug abuse.

Ellis and other rational emotive behavior therapists have studied reasons for addiction. A common explanation for addiction, according to Ellis (1992d), is that of low frustration tolerance, a concept suggesting that addicts cannot bear much discomfort over the short term. Ellis has suggested a six-step model to explain addiction that is related to emotional disturbance. According to Ellis (1992d), when the REBT theory of addictive drinking is understood, therapists and abusers can use it to undo thoughts, feelings, and behaviors involved in addiction. This can be done in individual therapy or in self-help groups.

An alternative self-help organization to Alcoholics Anonymous (AA), Rational Recovery Systems, started in 1976 by Jack Trimpey, differs in several ways from AA. Most notably, it does not rely on a higher power or require religious or spiritual beliefs from members (Ellis, 1992e; Ellis & Velten, 1992). Also, it uses a model based on REBT to help alcoholics recover from addiction. Ellis does not deny that Alcoholics Anonymous is helpful. On the contrary, he believes that it has been helpful to many people and that a number of its approaches are consistent with REBT.

BRIEF THERAPY

In general, REBT is a brief therapeutic intervention with many individuals being helped in 5 to 12 sessions (Ellis, 1992b). Providing more data, DiGiuseppe (1991) reported a study at the Albert Ellis Institute for Rational Emotive Behavior Therapy of 731 clients that found that the mean number of sessions was 16.5 and the median was 11 sessions. About 25% had 23 sessions or more. For Ellis himself, most sessions are only half an hour in length. This is not necessarily typical of other rational emotive behavior therapists.

In *Better, Deeper, and More Enduring Brief Therapy* (1996a), Ellis addresses how REBT can be applied in less than 20 sessions. He describes methods that he believes are appropriate to brief but less deep and intensive therapy as well as deeper and more intensive methods of brief therapy. Included in the latter are three of Ellis's favorite methods: disputing, accepting the worst possibilities, and anti-whining philosophies. Ellis, however, also includes a wider variety of other techniques than he has in his previous work, incorporating work of other theorists.

Ellis's approach to therapy is to bring about change as soon as possible. As he says, "I have a gene for efficiency whereas Sigmund Freud had a gene for inefficiency, as most analysts do" (Palmer, 1994, p. 7). He works with out-of-town clients when they visit New York or talks to them over the phone. He has had hundreds of clients who have seen him for only one session (Ellis, 1996a). Most of his sessions are for half an hour. Also, Ellis offers the Friday Night Workshop in which he demonstrates REBT with individuals with problems. He is in the process of compiling data on those who have been a part of this workshop.

CURRENT TRENDS

From its inception in the early 1950s, the A-B-C theory of REBT has grown and developed, becoming more complex and thorough yet maintaining its strong cognitive focus. Ellis has emphasized emotive and behavioral aspects of the model, as well as the humanistic and existential elements of REBT. However, Ellis has been very open to incorporating new techniques and applying them to help clients change their irrational beliefs. For example, he has applied deShazer's (1990) solution-focused approach (see Chapter 13) to help clients change behavior. Ellis (1996c) also uses Gestalt experiential techniques to act out and change irrational beliefs.

Ellis (1997) has incorporated constructivism into his theory. Because Ellis takes a determined and focused point of view, exploring irrational beliefs, his approach would appear to be rationalist (Guterman, 1996). He listens to clients and understands their problems as they relate to A-B-C theory. The "Rational" in Rational Emotive Behavior Therapy would imply that he uses reasoning from his own point of view to understand his clients.

However, Ellis (1997) argues that his position is more constructivist than it is rationalist. Clients react differently to REBT techniques and he observes individual ways that clients perceive their problems. He is also aware that his approach may have flaws and he seeks them out. As mentioned, Ellis is often seeking new ways and techniques for helping clients. He believes his openness to seeing clients in different ways contributes to the creativity of his interventions. For Ellis, this openness is consistent with the constructivist point of view of seeing the world through the clients' constructs.

USING RATIONAL EMOTIVE BEHAVIOR THERAPY WITH OTHER THEORIES

As long as techniques from other theories fit into the consistent A-B-C model of personality, REBT makes use of them. Most frequently, they use a wide variety of techniques that are described in Chapters 8 and 10. Other techniques, such as the Gestalt empty chair approach, have been adopted as an emotive technique in REBT. The models of Meichenbaum (Chapter 8) and Beck (Chapter 10) are most consistent with REBT. However, these approaches do not offer the philosophical model that is inherent in REBT. Because of its emphasis on a philosophical model, REBT is not as easily combined with other theoretical models as are its specific techniques.

The technique most central to REBT is that of disputation. When disputation is used, it can change the therapeutic relationship. For example, disputing a client's irrational beliefs and responding only to a client's feelings or experience (Carl Rogers) are not consistent. Furthermore, disputational techniques require training and confidence on the part of the therapist; some other cognitive techniques are learned more quickly. Therapists who combine REBT with other theoretical approaches must contend with the forcefulness inherent in REBT.

RESEARCH

Rational emotive behavior therapy has been the subject of about 250 studies. Many studies have compared REBT with other therapeutic systems or with a variety of control or treatment groups. In addition, research on REBT concepts and instruments has measured irrational beliefs. In this section, I provide an overview of outcome studies and their findings, along with issues related to doing research on

REBT. Also, I give an example of research that is typical of an outcome study examining REBT and present some typical studies examining irrational beliefs and other important concepts in REBT.

Three related reviews have examined 158 outcome studies comparing REBT with other treatments or control groups. In the first study, DiGiuseppe and Miller (1977) examined 22 published articles. In reviewing 47 later studies, McGovern and Silverman (1984) found that REBT was significantly more effective than other therapies or control groups in 31 of 47 studies. In the studies where REBT was not superior, there were usually no significant differences. Reviewing 89 studies between 1982 and 1989, Silverman, McCarthy, and McGovern (1992) found that REBT was significantly more effective than other therapies or control groups in 49 of the studies. In most of the other 40 studies, differences between groups were not significant. In some cases, REBT was used in combination with other therapy techniques, and in those cases the combination was the most effective.

In a meta-analysis of 70 REBT outcome studies, Lyons and Woods (1991) compared REBT to control groups, cognitive behavior modification, behavior therapy, and other psychotherapies. They found that REBT showed a significant improvement over control groups and initial measures of dysfunction. Improvement was also related to therapists' experience and the length of therapy. However, they note a system problem in this type of research: It is very difficult to assess how much of REBT as developed by Ellis is actually being used. In some cases, therapists may use a combination of REBT with other methods or use a different version of REBT. Furthermore, REBT makes use of many cognitive and behavioral strategies. Separating the effectiveness of REBT and cognitive therapy is quite difficult. However, Lyons and Woods (1991) note that the most stringently conducted studies comparing REBT to other treatment modes demonstrated the effectiveness of REBT procedures. This occurred when the measures of change were relatively unrelated to the treatment being used. For example, changes were found in physiological measures of stress, as well as changes in irrational beliefs. The latter would be expected as it is taught as a part of REBT.

In critiquing outcome research, Haaga, Dryden, and Dancey (1991) are concerned with how well therapists in research studies actually represent REBT. They examine four criteria: adherence to the theory (how well the therapist performs behaviors prescribed by the treatment); purity (the portion of therapists' behaviors that would be considered positive adherence to the theory); differentiability (how well uninformed observers can tell what theory they are observing); and quality (how well the therapist performed the therapy). Although these constructs can be measured, they are difficult to measure, and many studies have not attended to them. However, without doing so, it is difficult to know whether one is really comparing REBT to another theory. Haaga and Davison (1991) also expressed concern about ignoring differences between REBT and other cognitive therapies in research.

In addition to studies of therapeutic outcome, several investigations have examined concepts within REBT. For example, Woods, Silverman, and Bentilini (1991) found a strong relationship between suicidal contemplation and irrational beliefs in 800 college and high school students. A significant relationship between irrational beliefs and problems with drinking was found in a sample of 203 college students (Hutchinson, Patock-Peckham, Cheong, & Nagoshi, 1998). Studying 240 undergraduates, Harran and Ziegler (1991) found a strong relationship between irrational beliefs and reports of hassles and problems in the lives of the undergraduates. This is consistent with Ellis's view that those with high irrational beliefs tend to "awfulize" or "catastrophize." Also focusing on irrational beliefs, Master and Miller (1991) divided 84 female undergraduate students into four groups: those who were exposed to irrational self-statements, those exposed to self-statements about objective observations of problem areas, those who were exposed to rational self-statements, and those exposed to neutral statements. Students who were exposed to rational self-statements were the only ones to decrease levels of physiological arousal of anxiety over time. These studies help relate irrational beliefs to measures of physiological stress and psychological concepts.

GENDER ISSUES

Regardless of client gender, rational emotive behavior therapists examine the irrational beliefs of their clients and work with cognitive, behavioral, and emotive methods to bring about healthy psychological functioning. The nature of the irrational beliefs is often different for males and females, as individuals accept a number of societal expectations as irrational beliefs that they *must* accommodate. Several rational emotive behavior writers have identified societal and other issues that therapists often address when working with women.

Rational emotive behavior therapy can help women examine their beliefs and philosophies and work through emotional and practical problems (Wolfe, 1985). It teaches women how to define their problems, identify factors affecting feelings and actions, alter their behavior, and move toward greater self-acceptance (Wolfe & Russianoff, 1997). Wolfe and Naimark (1991) believe that therapists should encourage their female clients to challenge sex-role stereotypes in their relationships with men, with family, and in community activities. Wolfe and Fodor (1996) discuss these issues, the development of greater self-acceptance, and others as they pertain to "upper" class women. Also, Zachary (1980) described therapeutic approaches to rape, unwanted pregnancy and/or abortion, motherhood and career issues, and homosexuality. Wolfe (1985) lists several types of groups that have been developed at the Albert Ellis Institute for Rational Emotive Behavior Therapy in New York City to help women with these issues, including women's assertiveness, effectiveness, sexuality, life-cycle change, career entry, weight and stress management, mother-daughter communications, and all-women therapy groups.

Women are subject to a number of gender-role socialization messages that promote irrational beliefs (Wolfe & Naimark, 1991). For example, women may receive a gender-role message such as "Nice, sweet girls get husbands." An associated irrational belief is "I must not act assertively, in front of men. I must not put my desires first" (Wolfe & Naimark, 1991, p. 270). Another example is "For women, work is nice, but love is better." The irrational belief behind that socialization message is "I must not take my work too seriously" (p. 270). Wolfe and Naimark list several gender-role socialization messages and irrational beliefs along with common emotional and behavioral consequences, as well as ways in which both men and women may react when women do not behave according to gender-role expectations.

The following example illustrates how an REBT therapist deals with irrational beliefs regarding guilt over being raped (Zachary, 1980, pp. 251–252). Particularly in the last two statements of the therapeutic dialogue, irrational beliefs are dealt with. Conceptually, the therapist has applied the A-B-C-D-E theory to the woman's discussion of the traumatic event in this first session of therapy.

Client: So I'm finding myself feeling really awkward at parties and in groups of people, and I just don't like sex as much as I used to. I think it has to do with the rape a year and a half ago, but I'm not sure of the connection.

Therapist: You're feeling that your current problems are related to being raped.

Client: Uh huh. It was a guy I accepted a date with, but I barely knew him. He drives me out to a really deserted place, raped me, and left me out there. I hitched back into town, went to the police station, and had a medical exam. I even got myself a lawyer, but he told me that since I had accepted a date with the guy I wouldn't have a snowball's chance in hell of proving rape, so I dropped the whole thing.

Therapist: And what do you think about all of that now?

Client: Well, I go back and forth about it. Sometimes I think I should have prosecuted and other times I think it was better to drop it. I mean, the police, the lawyer, they acted like I was asking for it by going out with the guy, and it would have been more humiliating to pursue it.

Therapist: So you're continuing to go over and over it in your mind and you're vacillating back and forth about what would have been the best thing to do.

Client: Yes, I think about it a lot. It's really pretty distracting.

Therapist: So you're thinking that there must have been a perfectly right thing to do and you continue to torture yourself with that thought.

Client: Uh-huh. I even think that maybe I could have avoided being raped.

Therapist: How could you have done that?

Client: I don't know exactly. He said he had a knife, but I never actually saw it. Maybe he didn't. Maybe I could have screamed or fought harder or tried to run away, but I was afraid he might stab me.

Therapist: So at the time, you believed that he had a knife and would really hurt you or even kill you if you didn't give in.

Client: Yes, but I don't know now if he would have. And it was just my word against his. He told the police that I had seduced him and they seemed to believe him. Even my lawyer seemed to question my story.

Therapist: And how do you feel?

Client: This sounds crazy, but I feel guilty and ashamed of myself, like less of a person. He raped me and I feel guilty!

Therapist: So you're feeling guilty, ashamed and devalued as a person. And you're telling yourself that you should have fought him away at the time and you should have stuck by your story. Mostly you seem to be telling yourself that it's all your fault and that you're less of a person because you were raped and didn't do the right thing.

Client: Yes, that's all true, but what do we do with that?

Therapist: We begin by examining the beliefs you have, disputing them, and, hopefully eventually allowing you to put the incident to rest. Let's begin right now by looking at your belief that there is a perfectly right thing that you could have done at the time. (Zachary, 1980, pp. 251–252)[5]

In this session and in ensuing ones, Zachary helped the client gain insight into her irrational belief that she should have done something other than what she did when raped. The focus of therapy then turned to the current rumination about the rape rather than the rape itself. Zachary dealt with the irrational belief that individuals (specifically the client) can be devalued by what other people do to them (the rapist, police officers, and lawyers). After 4 months of therapy, the client was able to let go of the rape incident and to respond satisfactorily socially and sexually.

MULTICULTURAL ISSUES

Rational emotive behavior therapists listen carefully for the cultural values and issues of their clients. They do not plunge into Socratic disputation of irrational beliefs before establishing an understanding of cultural issues. For example, Ellis (1991g) describes his work with a Mormon woman who was pregnant and undecided as to whether she would marry her non-Mormon lover. She had considered having an abortion. If she did, she faced excommunication from her religion. Knowledge of the client's culture often determines the actions of the rational emotive behavior therapist. Ellis (1991g) has treated a number of Chinese, Japanese, and other Asian clients. Although he attends to their family values, he finds that he uses an approach that is similar to his work with clients from the United States.

Rational emotive behavior therapy emphasizes self-sufficiency as opposed to dependency on the support of others. Many Asian and African cultures, for example, promote interdependence rather than independence, stressing reliance on the family and the individual's community, rather than self-reliance (Sapp,1996). Such issues may cause rational emotive behavior therapists to modify their assessment of clients' irrational beliefs. This, then affects their decision as to which beliefs are irrational and warrant disputation. For clients who are used to being told what to do—because of cultural customs or other reasons—therapists need to be certain that clients participate actively rather than passively when Socratic dialogue or other disputational techniques are used. However, REBT has been compared to Zen Buddhism, showing the similarities of their approaches to living and suggesting that the techniques of Zen are similar to those of REBT (Kwee & Ellis, 1998). Because rational emotive behavior therapists function in many ways like teachers (such as Zen masters do), their style may be more congruent with the expectations of clients coming from authoritarian cultures than would a more egalitarian therapeutic approach.

COUPLES COUNSELING

In REBT, the partners are the clients, and the relationship is secondary. Sometimes what is good for an individual may not be good for the relationship and vice versa

(Ellis, Sichel, Yeager, DiMattia, & DiGiuseppe, 1989; Ellis & Dryden, 1997). Given this approach, rational emotive behavior therapists see clients together as a couple some of the time and in individual sessions some of the time. Harper (1981) sees some disadvantages in seeing couples at the same time together (conjointly), believing that to focus on the relationship in a marriage is to focus on an abstraction. A more trusting relationship with a client can occur when there is a one-to-one relationship. Also, seeing partners conjointly risks favoring one partner over another.

The techniques that rational emotive behavior therapists use in couples counseling are very similar to those used in individual therapy. However, rational emotive behavior therapists deal first with emotive disturbances, such as anger or jealousy, that interfere with communications between the two people. After emotional outbursts have been reduced, therapists can use cognitive and behavioral homework and strategies to bring about change. Also, eliciting feelings toward each other and toward the therapist, while ascertaining whether these feelings are helpful or interfering, can provide progress in the session. Expressing good feelings for each other during the session is practice for doing so at home (Ellis et al., 1989, p. 65). Other couples counseling strategies include "10 rounds," which parallels a boxing match. Individuals argue for 3 minutes and then spend 1 minute "between rounds" reminding themselves to use constructive rather than destructive communication skills. In some cases, it is helpful for one partner to take the role of the therapist and to help the other, so that both will be reminding themselves to correct irrational thinking. A behavioral strategy is to have clients comment on and reinforce each other for successfully managing their disturbed emotions. As couples counseling develops, therapists sometimes devise their own creative strategies consistent with REBT principles.

The following example shows how a rational emotive behavior couples counselor focuses on the *musts* and *dire needs* held by a couple who are both jealous and angry.

Therapist: I don't think that you really "don't care."

Husband: Then I shouldn't care either.

Therapist: You are both misunderstanding the point. You can give up your "need" for something without going to the extreme of trying to believe you "don't care." Saying you "don't care" is just not true. Saying you "need" the relationship to have certain features is similarly not true. I want you to both see that you can still really care about something without thinking you *need*, or *absolutely must have* it.

Husband: I understand. But it is important *to me* to have a wife who takes care of me and the things around the house.

Therapist: Fine. But can you give up your dire *need* for something that you really *want*?

Husband: [laughing] Of course.

Wife: I see the point. But I have one problem with that.

Therapist: What's that?

Wife: I accept that I don't *need* the relationship to be a certain way just because I *want* it. But if I don't have a caring and sharing and loving mate, I will be incomplete.

Therapist: Incomplete? Meaning what?

Wife: It would prove that I am not an adequate person. I wouldn't be complete.

Therapist: Because your *marriage* wouldn't be complete or because your *life* may lack some preferred feature? How does that mean that *you* are not adequate? Although your life may have less than you prefer, how does that equate to *you* being *less* than okay?

Wife: [stammers] Uh. . . .

Therapist: You don't have an answer?

Wife: No.

Therapist: What does that tell us?

Wife: There is no answer?

Therapist: Take away the question mark.

Wife: There is no answer!

Therapist: Which means. . . .

Wife: [weakly] I am *not* incomplete just because my marriage might be?

Therapist: Is that a statement or a question?

Wife: A statement!

Therapist: Then, explain it to me more fully.

Wife: Well, I don't need anyone to fulfill my life. I would like to have a different kind of relationship, but I'm not going to die without it. And my worth is not, and I repeat, is not contingent upon the quality of my relationships.

Therapist: How do you feel now that you have given up your *neediness* and self-berating? (Ellis et al., 1989, pp. 94–95)[6]

FAMILY THERAPY

The goals of REBT for families are to help members see that they disturb themselves by their irrational beliefs (Ellis, 1991c; Ellis & Dryden, 1997). By learning about their irrational beliefs and giving them up, family members find that they can still have their wishes, preferences, and desires. Family members are taught techniques similar to those used with individual clients and couples (to assist them in changing beliefs). They learn not only how to deal with family crises but also ways to deal with family situations that may occur in the future. Ellis (1991c) takes the position that each family member is responsible for his own actions and should assume that responsibility. Therapists often see families together but see couples or individual family members where appropriate. Unlike couples counseling, where separating partners may often be the best solution, separating children permanently from parents is a solution of last resort. Thus, seeing families together is often a treatment of choice.

By listening to their clients and pointing out irrational behaviors, therapists model for family members ways to be involved, but not overinvolved or overwhelmed by each other. Therapists teach family members skills and principles of nondisturbance and self-help that can be applied to themselves and other family members. When appropriate, therapists confront their clients with their defensiveness and reluctance, explaining the irrational beliefs behind their behavior. Their therapeutic techniques include expressing their own feelings, taking risks, modeling appropriate ways to behave, and teaching family members, when appropriate, to use and recognize the A-B-C's of REBT.

Acceptance of themselves and each other is a key factor in REBT approaches to family therapy. Family members are encouraged to stay in unpleasant family situations until they have made themselves "unupset" about the situations. Parents are instructed how to accept each other and their children. Also, children, when old enough, are shown how to accept inappropriate behavior, such as alcoholism and borderline disturbance, from their parents. The following example of two adolescent boys dealing with irresponsible parental behavior illustrates how REBT can be applied to dealing with irresponsible family members.

> Thus, in the case of the 14- and 12-year-old sons who are extremely incensed about their alcoholic father's irresponsibility, their mother's neglecting them for a lover who is only a few years older than themselves, they were able to see after only a few sessions of REBT family therapy, both that the parents were acting in a highly irresponsible manner—since they had some choice about drinking and about neglecting their children, and were choosing to act in irresponsible ways and also that they, like all humans, had a *right to be wrong*. They were fallible, disturbed individuals who decided to act the way they did, but who could be accepted and forgiven in spite of their anti-family behaviors. Once these two youngsters learned, in family therapy, to accept their parents *with* their irresponsible behaviors, they were able to maintain reasonably good and loving relationships with these parents and to focus on what they, the children, were going to do to get along better in this poor family environment. Their schoolwork and their relations with their own friends then considerably improved, and they were even, to some degree, able to help their parents face their problems and to act somewhat more responsibly. (Ellis, 1991c, p. 418)[7]

Individual feelings and pathology, as well as family problems, are addressed in REBT with families. The therapist tends to show clients how to dispute absolutist *shoulds* and *musts* more than those family therapists who attend only to dynamics within the family.

GROUP THERAPY

Although REBT can be applied in 2-day rational encounter marathons, 9-hour intensive groups with 10 to 20 participants, public demonstrations of real therapy with audiences as large as 100, and Rational Recovery groups for alcoholics, only traditional group therapy is described here (Ellis, 1992b). These groups usually have between 6 and 10 members, meeting once a week for 2 to 3 hours. The goal of the REBT group is to show clients how they are assessing, blaming, and damning themselves for their behavior. The group also endeavors to help them stop devaluing other people and evaluate only their behaviors, not their self or personhood. They are instructed to try to change or avoid difficulties that they encounter within themselves and with others.

The process of doing this combines a directive educational function on the part of the therapist as well as a discussion of group processes.

Therapists purposefully lead the group in "healthy" rather than "unhealthy" directions (Ellis, 1992b). By organizing the group in a structured way, they see that no one is neglected or monopolizes the group. Therapists discuss the progress and lack of progress of individual group members as well as the results of their previously assigned homework or their failure to complete their homework. Also, they may make statements in the group that refer to both inside and outside behaviors. For example, they may say, "Johanna, you speak so low here that we can hardly hear what you say. Do you act the same way in social groups? If so, what are you telling yourself to make yourself speak so low?" (Ellis, 1992b, p. 69). Often the leaders agree with the group member on cognitive or emotive or behavioral exercises to be done in the group as well as exercises to be done outside the group. Where appropriate, they give brief lectures on important aspects of REBT. Most of the group time is spent on individual problems that group members bring to the group, but some time is spent examining how group members relate to each other.

For groups to be successful, group members need to work together to help each other apply REBT principles (Ellis, 1992b; Ellis & Dryden, 1997). Ellis wants group members to participate appropriately, neither to monopolize the group nor to be too passive. If an individual does not speak up in the group, the group therapist may give an assignment to speak at least three times about other people's issues in the group meeting. If a group member consistently comes late to the group or is absent, Ellis or group members may raise this issue and discuss it in terms of A-B-C theory and examine self-defeating behavior that results from being late. If group members give only practical advice to other members instead of disputing their irrational beliefs, Ellis and the group members will point this out. If a group member rarely completes homework assignments, irrational beliefs such as "It's too hard" and "It should be much easier" are disputed. Thus, REBT techniques are used for both group process and individual problems that are issues in the group.

SUMMARY

Rational emotive behavior therapy asserts that it is not events themselves that disturb people but their beliefs about the events. This view leads to an approach to psychotherapy that stresses cognitive aspects of personality theory and therapeutic intervention yet also makes use of emotive and behavioral components. The philosophical assumptions are humanistic, hedonistic, and rational (self-helping). The focus is on individuals and their potential to overcome irrational (self-defeating) beliefs and to be responsible for their own lives. Rationality does not refer to an absence of emotion; rather, it refers to individuals' ability to use reason to guide their lives and to diminish the impact of irrational (dysfunctional) beliefs on their lives. Responsible hedonism refers to the concept of individuals seeking happiness over the long term, rather than short-term hedonism, which, in the case of alcoholism, for example, can lead to long-term difficulties. The notable contribution that Ellis has made to the treatment of sexual problems as well as his commitment to sex education through his writings is an example of his emphasis on increasing human happiness.

Rational emotive behavior therapy applies cognitive, emotive, and behavioral approaches to changing irrational beliefs. A major method for working with irrational beliefs is disputing, which involves detecting, discriminating, and debating irrational beliefs. The emphasis on understanding the A-B-Cs of the development of one's irrational beliefs separates REBT from other cognitive and behavioral therapies. However, REBT also uses other cognitive strategies, such as using repeated constructive statements about oneself, listening to tapes, and using psychoeducational materials. Methods that employ imagery along with emotions, exercises that attack beliefs that are shameful, and forceful self-dialogue are some of the emotive methods REBT uses. Behavioral methods include homework outside the session, skill training, and reinforcement of desired behavior. Rational emotive behavior therapists make use of a large number of techniques, primarily from other cognitive and behavioral therapies, as well as creative ones that they devise on their own, to help clients deal with strongly entrenched irrational beliefs.

Rational emotive behavior therapists are tolerant of their clients and fully accept them. It is their behavior that they dispute by challenging, confronting, and convincing the clients to practice activities in and out of therapy that will lead to constructive changes in thinking, feeling, and behaving. An active therapy, REBT includes insights about irrational beliefs and about becoming aware of how individuals harm themselves through absolutistic beliefs and then uses these insights to make constructive changes in their lives.

Suggested Readings

ELLIS, A. (1973). *Humanistic psychotherapy: The rational-emotive approach*. New York: McGraw-Hill. • Written for the public and the profession, this book shows both the humanistic and the active approach typical of REBT. It shows how the A-B-C model can be applied to therapy.

ELLIS, A., & HARPER, R. A. (1997). *A new guide to rational living* (3rd ed.). North Hollywood: Wilshire Books. • Written for the public, this self-help book helps individuals recognize their irrational beliefs and overcome emotional disturbances. Suggestions for changing beliefs and homework to bring about change are given.

ELLIS, A., & DRYDEN, W. (1997). *The practice of rational-emotive therapy* (2nd ed.). New York: Springer. • The authors show how REBT can be used with individuals, couples, families, and groups to bring about psychotherapeutic change.

ELLIS, A. (1996). *Better, deeper, enduring brief therapy: The rational emotive behavior therapy approach*. New York: Brunner/Mazel. • This book gives a good perspective on how to apply REBT to a variety of client problems. These include anger, low frustration tolerance, and irrational beliefs. Since REBT is a brief approach, many of the concepts can be applied to REBT in general, but Ellis does address specific issues dealing with brief therapy.

ELLIS, A. (1988). *How to stubbornly refuse to make yourself miserable about anything—yes, anything!* New York: Carol Publishing. • One of Ellis's clearest and most popular self-help books.

References

BARD, J. (1980). *Rational-emotive therapy in practice*. Champaign, IL: Research Press.

BERNARD, M. E., & JOYCE, M. R. (1984). *Rational-emotive therapy with children and adolescents*. New York: Wiley.

DAWSON, R. (1991). REGIME: A counseling and educational model for using RET effectively. In M. E. Bernard (Ed.), *Using rational-emotive therapy effectively: A practitioner's guide* (pp. 111–132). New York: Plenum.

deSHAZER (1990). Brief therapy. In J. K. Zeig & W. M. Munion (Eds.), *What is psychotherapy?* (pp. 278–282). San Francisco: Jossey-Bass.

DIGIUSEPPE, R. (1991). A rational-emotive model of assessment. In M. E. Bernard (Ed.), *Using rational-emotive therapy effectively: A practitioner's guide* (pp. 151–172). New York: Plenum.

DIGIUSEPPE, R., & BERNARD, M. E. (1983). Principles of assessment and methods of treatment with children: Special considerations. In A. Ellis & M. E. Bernard (Eds.), *Rational-emotive approaches to the problems of childhood* (pp. 45–86). New York: Plenum.

DIGIUSEPPE, R., & MILLER, N. J. (1977). A review of outcome studies on rational-emotive therapy. In A. Ellis & R. Grieger (Eds.), *Handbook of rational-emotive therapy* (pp. 72–95). New York: Springer.

DRYDEN, W. (1990). *Rational-emotive counseling in action.* London: Sage.

ELLIS, A. (1958). *Sex without guilt.* New York: Lyle Stuart.

ELLIS, A. (1961). *The encyclopedia of sexual behavior.* New York: Hawthorn.

ELLIS A. (1962). *Reason and emotion in psychotherapy.* Secaucus, NJ: Lyle Stuart,

ELLIS, A. (1965). *The art and science of love.* New York: Lyle Stuart.

ELLIS, A. (1973). *Humanistic psychotherapy: The rational-emotive approach.* New York: McGraw-Hill.

ELLIS, A. (1976). The biological basis of human irrationality. *Journal of Individual Psychology, 32,* 145–168.

ELLIS, A. (1985a). *Overcoming resistance: Rational-emotive therapy with difficult clients.* New York: Springer.

ELLIS, A. (1985b). What is rational-emotive therapy (RET)? In A. Ellis & M. E. Bernard (Eds.), *Clinical applications of rational-emotive therapy* (pp. 1–30). New York: Plenum.

ELLIS, A. (1986a). Awards for distinguished professional contributions. *American Psychologist, 41,* 380–397.

Ellis, A. (1986b). Do some religious beliefs help create emotional disturbance? *Psychotherapy in Private Practice, 4,* 101–106.

ELLIS, A. (1986c). Rational-emotive therapy. In I. L. Kutash & A. Wolf (Eds.), *Psychotherapist's casebook* (pp. 277–287). San Francisco: Jossey-Bass.

ELLIS, A. (1987a). The impossibility of achieving consistently good mental health. *American Psychologist, 42,* 364–375.

ELLIS, A. (1987b). On the origin and development of rational-emotive therapy. In W. Dryden (Ed.), *Key cases in psychotherapy* (pp. 148–175). New York: New York University Press.

ELLIS, A. (1987c). The use of rational humorous songs in psychotherapy. In W. E. Fry, Jr., & W. A. Salameh (Eds.), *Handbook of humor and psychotherapy* (pp. 265–286). Sarasota, FL: Professional Resource Exchange.

ELLIS, A. (1988). *How to stubbornly refuse to make yourself miserable about anything—yes, anything!* New York: Carol Publishing.

ELLIS, A. (1991a). *Intellectual fascism* [Pamphlet]. New York: Institute for Rational Emotive Therapy.

ELLIS, A. (1991b). The philosophical basis of rational-emotive therapy (RET). *Psychotherapy in Private Practice, 8,* 97–106.

ELLIS, A. (1991c). Rational-emotive family therapy. In A. M. Horne & J. L. Passmore (Eds.), *Family counseling and therapy* (2nd ed., pp. 403–434). Itasca, IL: F. E. Peacock.

ELLIS, A. (1991d). Rational-emotive treatment of simple phobias. *Psychotherapy, 28,* 452–456.

ELLIS, A. (1991e). The revised ABC's of rational-emotive therapy (RET). *Journal of Rational-Emotive and Cognitive Behavior-Therapy, 9,* 139–172.

ELLIS, A. (1991f). Suggestibility, irrational beliefs, and emotional disturbance. In J. E. Schumaker (Ed.), *Human suggestibility* (pp. 309–325). New York: Routledge.

ELLIS, A. (1991g). Using RET effectively: Reflections and interview. In M. E. Bernard (Ed.), *Using rational-emotive therapy effectively* (pp. 1–33). New York: Plenum.

ELLIS, A. (1992a). Brief therapy: The rational-emotive method. In S. H. Budman, M. F. Hoyt, & S. Friedman (Eds.), *The first session in brief therapy* (pp. 36–58). New York: Guilford.

ELLIS, A. (1992b). Group rational emotive and cognitive-behavioral therapy. *International Journal of Group Psychotherapy, 42,* 63–80.

ELLIS, A. (1992c). My early experiences in developing the practice of psychology. *Professional Psychology: Research and Practice, 23,* 7–10.

ELLIS, A. (1992d). The rational-emotive theory of addiction. In J. Trimpey, L. Trimpey, P. Tate, M. Sullivan, & L. V. Fox (Eds.), *Rational recovery self-help network: Official manual for coordinators and advisors.* Lotus, CA: Rational Recovery Self-Help Network.

ELLIS, A. (1992e). Rational recovery and the addiction to 12-step therapies. *The Humanist, 52,* 33–35.

ELLIS, A. (1993). *Psychotherapy and the value of a human being* (Rev. ed.). New York: Institute for Rational Emotive Therapy.

ELLIS, A. (1994a). General semantics and rational emotive therapy. In P. D. Johnston, D. D. Bourland, Jr., & J. Klein (Eds.), *More E-prime: To be or not II* (pp. 213–240). Concord, CA: International Society of General Semantics.

ELLIS, A. (1994b). Rational emotive behavior therapy approaches to obsessive-compulsive disorder (OCD). *Journal of Rational-Emotive and Cognitive-Behavior Therapy, 12,* 121–141.

ELLIS, A. (1996a). *Better, deeper, and more enduring brief therapy: The rational emotive behavior therapy approach.* New York: Brunner/Mazel.

ELLIS, A. (1996b). *My philosophy of psychotherapy.* New York: Albert Ellis Institute for Rational Emotive Behavior Therapy.

ELLIS, A. (1996c). The humanisms of rational emotive behavior therapy and other cognitive behavior therapies. *Journal of Humanistic Education and Development, 35,* 69–88.

ELLIS, A. (1997). Postmodern ethics for active-directive counseling and psychotherapy. *Journal of Mental Health Counseling, 10,* 211–225.

ELLIS, A., & BERNARD, M. E. (Eds.). (1983). *Rational-emotive approaches to the problems of childhood.* New York: Plenum.

ELLIS, A., & BERNARD, M. E. (1985). What is rational-emotive therapy (RET)? In A. Ellis & M. E. Bernard (Eds.), *Clinical applications of rational-emotive therapy* (pp. 1–30). New York: Plenum.

ELLIS, A., & DRYDEN, W. (1997). *The practice of rational-emotive therapy.* New York: Springer.

ELLIS, A., GORDON, J., NEEMAN, M., & PALMER, S. (1997). *Stress counselling: A rational emotive behavior approach.* London: Cassell.

ELLIS, A., & GRIEGER, R. (1977). *Handbook of rational-emotive therapy: Vol. 1.* New York: Springer.

ELLIS, A., & GRIEGER, R. (1986). *Handbook of rational-emotive therapy: Vol. 2.* New York: Springer.

ELLIS, A., & HARPER, R. A. (1997). *A new guide to rational living* (3rd ed.). North Hollywood, CA: Wilshire Books.

ELLIS, A., McINERNEY, J. E., DiGIUSEPPE, R. A., & YEAGER, R. (1988). *Rational-emotive treatment of alcoholism and substance abuse.* New York: Pergamon.

ELLIS, A., SICHEL, J., YEAGER, R., DiMATTIA, D., & DiGIUSEPPE, R. (1989). *Rational emotive couples therapy.* New York: Pergamon.

ELLIS, A., & VELTEN, E. (1992). *When AA doesn't work for you: A rational guide for quitting alcohol.* New York: Barricade Books.

ELLIS, A., & WHITELEY, J. M. (1979). *Theoretical and empirical foundations of rational-emotive therapy.* Monterey, CA: Brooks/Cole.

GUTERMAN, J. T. (1996). Doing mental health counseling: A social constructivist revision. *Journal of Mental Health Counseling, 18,* 228–252.

HAAGA, D. A. F., & DAVISON, G. C. (1991). Disappearing differences do not always reflect healthy integration: An analysis of cognitive therapy and rational-emotive therapy. *Journal of Psychotherapy Integration, 1,* 287–303.

HAAGA, D. A. F., DRYDEN, W., & DANCEY, C. P. (1991). Measurement of rational-emotive therapy in outcome studies. *Journal of Rational-Emotive and Cognitive-Behavior Therapy, 9,* 73–88.

HARPER, R. A. (1981). Limitations of marriage and family therapy. *Rational Living, 16,* 3–6.

HARRAN, S. M., & ZIEGLER, D. J. (1991). Cognitive appraisal of daily hassles in college students displaying high or low irrational beliefs. *Journal of Rational-Emotive and Cognitive-Behavior Therapy, 9,* 265–271.

HUTCHINSON, G. T., PATOCK-PECKHAM, J. A., CHEONG, J., & NAGOSHI, C. T. (1998). Irrational beliefs and behavioral misregulation in the role of alcohol abuse among college students. *Journal of Rational Emotive and Cognitive Behavior Therapy, 16,* 61–74.

KWEE, M., & ELLIS, A. (1998). The interface between rational emotive behavior therapy (REBT) and Zen. *Journal of Rational-Emotive and Cognitive-Behavior Therapy, 16,* 5-43.

LYONS, L. C., & WOODS, P. J. (1991). The efficacy of rational-emotive therapy: A quantitative review of the outcome research. *Clinical Psychology Review, 11,* 357–369.

MASTER, S. M., & MILLER, S. M. (1991). A test of rational-emotive theory using a mood induction procedure: The rationality of thinking rationally. *Cognitive Therapy and Research, 15,* 491–502.

MAULTSBY, M. C., Jr., & ELLIS, A. (1974). *Technique for using rational-emotive imagery.* New York: Institute for Rational Emotive Therapy.

MCGOVERN, T. E., & SILVERMAN, M. S. (1984). A review of outcome studies of rational-emotive therapy from 1977–1982. *Journal of Rational Emotive Therapy, 2,* 7–18.

PALMER, S. (1994). In the counsellor's chair: Stephen Palmer interviews Dr. Albert Ellis. *The Rational Emotive Behavior Therapist, 2,* 6–15.

SAPP, M. (1996). Irrational beliefs that can lead to academic failure for African American middle school students who are academically at risk. *Journal of Rational-Emotive and Cognitive-Behavior Therapy, 14,* 123–134.

SICHEL, J., & ELLIS, A. (1984). *RET self-help form.* New York: Institute for Rational-Emotive Therapy.

SILVERMAN, M. S., MCCARTHY, M. L., & MCGOVERN, T. (1992). A review of outcome studies of rational emotive therapy from 1982–1989. *Journal of Rational-Emotive and Cognitive-Behavioral Therapy, 10,* 111–186.

WALEN, S., DIGIUSEPPE, R., & WESSLER, R. L. (1980). *A practitioner's guide to rational-emotive therapy.* New York: Oxford University Press.

WEINER, D. N. (1988). *Albert Ellis: Passionate skeptic.* New York: Praeger.

WOLFE, J. L. (1985). Women. In A. Ellis & M. Bernard (Eds.), *Clinical applications of rational-emotive therapy* (pp. 101–127). New York: Plenum.

WOLFE, J. L., & FODOR, I. G. (1996). The poverty of privilege: Therapy with women of the "upper" classes. *Women and Therapy, 18,* 73–89.

WOLFE, J. L., & NAIMARK, H. (1991). Psychological messages and social context: Strategies for increasing RET's effectiveness with women. In M. E. Bernard (Ed.), *Using rational-emotive therapy effectively: A practitioner's guide* (pp. 265–301). New York: Plenum.

WOLFE, J., & RUSSIANOFF, P. (1997). Overcoming self negation in women. *Journal of Rational-Emotive and Cognitive-Behavior Therapy, 15,* 81–92.

WOODS, P. J., SILVERMAN, E. G., & BENTILINI, J. M. (1991). Cognitive variables related to suicidal contemplation in adolescents with implications for long range prevention. *Journal of Rational-Emotive and Cognitive-Behavior Therapy, 9,* 215–245.

ZACHARY, I. (1980). RET with women: Some special issues. In R. Grieger & J. Boyd (Eds.), *Rational-emotive therapy: A skills based approach* (pp. 249–264). New York: Van Nostrand.

10

Cognitive Therapy

Cognitive therapy, a system developed by Aaron Beck, stresses the importance of belief systems and thinking in determining behavior and feelings. The focus of cognitive therapy is on understanding distorted beliefs and using techniques to change maladaptive thinking, while also incorporating affective and behavioral methods. In the therapeutic process, attention is paid to thoughts that individuals may be unaware of and to important belief systems.

Working collaboratively with clients, cognitive therapists take an educational role, helping clients understand distorted beliefs and suggesting methods for changing these beliefs. In doing so, cognitive therapists may give clients assignments to test out new alternatives to their old ways of solving their problems. As the therapist gathers data to determine therapeutic strategies, clients may be asked to record dysfunctional thoughts and to assess their problems through brief questionnaires developed for a variety of different psychological disorders. In their approach to treatment, cognitive therapists have outlined types of maladaptive thinking and specific treatment strategies for many psychological disturbances, including depression and anxiety disorders.

HISTORY OF COGNITIVE THERAPY

Although several theories of psychotherapy emphasize cognitive aspects of treatment, cognitive therapy is associated with the work of Aaron Beck. Born in 1921, Beck received his doctor of medicine degree from Yale University in 1946. Between 1946 and 1948 he served an internship and residency in pathology at the Rhode Island Hospital in Providence. Following that experience, he was a resident in neurology and then later in psychiatry at the Cushing Veterans Administration Hospital in Framingham, Massachusetts. Also, he was a fellow in psychiatry at the Austen Riggs Center in Stockbridge, Massachusetts. In 1953, he was certified in psychiatry by the American Board of Psychiatry and Neurology. In 1958, he graduated from the Philadelphia Psychoanalytic Institute. He joined the faculty of the Department of Psychiatry of the Medical School of the University of Pennsylvania, where he is now Professor Emeritus. His early research on depression (Beck, 1961, 1964) led to publication of *Depres-*

AARON BECK

sion: Clinical, Experimental, and Theoretical Aspects (1967), which discussed the importance of cognition in treating depression. Since then, he has authored or coauthored more than 300 articles and several books related to cognitive therapy and the treatment of a variety of emotional disorders.

Originally a practicing psychoanalyst, Beck (1991) observed the verbalizations and free associations of his patients. Surprised that his patients experienced thoughts that they were barely aware of and did not report as a part of their free associations, he drew his patients' attention to these thoughts. Appearing quickly and automatically, these thoughts or cognitions were not within the patients' control. Often these automatic thoughts that patients were unaware of were followed by unpleasant feelings that they were very much aware of (Beck, 1991). By asking patients about their current thoughts, Beck was able to identify negative themes, such as defeat or inadequacy, that characterized their view of past, present, and future.

Having been trained as a psychoanalyst, Beck compared his observation of automatic thoughts to Freud's concept of the "preconscious." Beck (1976) was interested in what people said to themselves and the way they monitored themselves—their own internal communication system. From the internal communications within themselves, individuals formed sets of beliefs, an observation reported earlier by Ellis (1962). From these important beliefs, individuals formulated rules or standards for themselves, called schemas, thought patterns that determine how experiences will be perceived or interpreted. Beck noticed that his patients, particularly those who were depressed, used internal conversations that communicated self-blame and self-criticism. Such patients often predicted failure or disaster for themselves and made negative interpretations where positive ones would have been more appropriate.

From these observations, Beck formulated the concept of a negative cognitive shift, in which individuals ignore much positive information relevant to themselves and focus instead on negative information about themselves. To do so, patients may distort observations of events by exaggerating negative aspects, looking at things as all black or all white. Comments such as "I never can do anything right," "Life will never treat me well," and "I am hopeless" are examples of statements that are overgeneralized, exaggerated, and abstract. Beck found such thinking, typical of individuals who are depressed, to be automatic and to occur without awareness. Many of these thoughts developed into beliefs about worthlessness, being unlovable, and so forth. Such beliefs, Beck (1967) hypothesized, were formed at earlier stages in life and became significant cognitive schemas. For example, a student who has several exams coming up in the next week may say to herself, "I'll never pass, I can't do anything right." Such an expression is a verbalization of a cognitive schema indicating a lack of self-worth. The student may express such a belief despite the fact that she is well prepared for her exams and has done well previously in her schoolwork. Thus, the beliefs persist despite evidence that contradicts them.

Although Beck's early work focused on depression, he applied his concepts of automatic thoughts, distorted beliefs, and cognitive schemas to other disorders. For example, he explained anxiety disorders as dominated by threat of failure or abandonment.

From observations of patients and going over transcripts of sessions, Beck identified cognitive schemas that were common to people with different types of emotional disorders and developed strategies for treating them.

Theoretical Influences

Although much of Beck's theory of cognitive psychotherapy is based on observations from his clinical work, he and his colleagues have also been somewhat influenced by other theories of psychotherapy, cognitive psychology, and cognitive science. Because of his training as a psychoanalyst, Beck drew some concepts from psychoanalysis into his own work. Furthermore, there are similarities between cognitive therapy and the work of Albert Ellis and Alfred Adler, notably their emphasis on the importance of beliefs. Also, George Kelly's theory of personal constructs and Jean Piaget's work on the development of cognition played a role in understanding cognitions in personality. Attempts to develop computer models of intellectual thinking, an aspect of cognitive science, also contributed to the continuing development of cognitive psychotherapy.

Psychoanalysis and cognitive therapy share the view that behavior can be affected by beliefs that individuals have little or no awareness of. Whereas Freud hypothesized about unconscious thoughts, Beck has focused on automatic thoughts that can lead to distress. It was Freud's theory that anger, when turned inward, becomes depression that started Beck on his path for understanding the process of depression. Thus, Freud's theories of psychological disorders became the starting point from which cognitive therapy developed. This fact is not readily apparent, as the cognitive view of personality and techniques of psychotherapeutic change are very different from those of psychoanalysis.

More similar in theory and practice are the ideas of Adler, who emphasized the cognitive nature of individuals and their beliefs. Although Adlerians have focused on the development of beliefs, more so than Beck, they also have created a number of strategies to bring about changes in perceptions. Both Adler and Beck share an active approach to therapy, using specific and direct dialogue with patients to bring about change.

Similarly, Albert Ellis (1962) has used active and challenging approaches to confront irrational beliefs. Both Beck and Ellis challenge their patients' belief systems through direct interaction. They believe that by changing inaccurate assumptions, clients can make important changes to overcome psychological disorders. Although there are clear differences, which are discussed later, the commonalities between Beck's and Ellis's systems have served to strengthen the impact of cognitive therapies on the field of psychotherapy, both through the writings of the two theorists and the extensive research on the effectiveness of both approaches.

Although not as directly related to cognitive therapy as the work of psychotherapists, Kelly's theory of personal constructs explores the role of cognitions in personality development. Describing his basic construct of personality, Kelly (1955) said, "A person's processes are psychologically channelized by the way in which he anticipates events" (p. 46). Seeing constructs as individual, dichotomous, and covering a finite range of events, Kelly believed that individuals have a system of personal constructs that express their views of the world. For example, "smart-stupid" may be a personal construct, a way in which we view our acquaintances and friends. Not all people would construe events in this way, and some may have other constructs such as "strong-weak" that explain the way they see others. There is a resemblance between Kelly's personal constructs and Beck's schemas, in that both describe ways of characterizing individuals' systems of beliefs. Also, both theorists share the emphasis on the role of beliefs in changing behavior.

A very different approach to studying cognition has been taken by Piaget, who was interested in the way individuals learn. In his studies of children's intellectual skills, Piaget (1977) has described four major periods of cognitive development: sensorimotor, preoperations, concrete operations, and formal operations. The sensorimotor stage occurs from birth to age 2 and describes the learning that takes place when infants learn by touching, seeing, hitting, screaming, and so forth. The preoperations stage (ages 2 to about 7) includes basic intellectual skills like adding and subtracting. In the third stage, concrete operations, ages 7 to 11, children are better able to tell fantasy from reality and do not have to see an object to imagine manipulating it. They can deal with the concept of adding 4 tigers to 3 tigers, but they cannot add $4z$ to $7z$. This ability takes place in the fourth stage, formal operations, and requires abstract learning. In discussing the implication of Piaget's theory for psychotherapy, Ronen (1997) has described how it can be helpful to match psychotherapeutic techniques of cognitive therapy with the individual's stage of cognitive development.

A broad and developing area of research that has the potential of contributing much to the cognitive theory of psychotherapy is cognitive science. Basically, cognitive science is interested in understanding how the mind works and in developing models for intellectual functioning. Involving fields such as cognitive psychology, artificial intelligence, linguistics, neuroscience, anthropology, and philosophy, cognitive science provides many perspectives on human intellectual processing. In cognitive psychology, researchers have studied how individuals make choices, remember facts, learn rules, remember events selectively, and learn differentially.

Using computer simulation, investigators have tried to make models of the human mind and have used artificial intelligence to attempt to have the computer respond as if it were human. One application to psychotherapy has been the work of Colby (Colby, Faught, & Parkinson, 1979), who developed a program, PARRY, that simulated a paranoid patient and would respond to a person's statement or comments. Cognitive psychologists have also extended the concept of schemas to research in problem solving, movement, language, and concept representation. Additionally, neurobiologists have tried to relate cognition to neurological functioning. Other advances in applying cognitive science to a variety of clinical disorders have been explained from several different points of view in Stein and Young (1992).

Current Influences

Research in cognitive psychology and related fields is important in advancing new techniques in cognitive therapy. As is shown later, outcome research is an important part of the development of new methods and the testing of the effectiveness of cognitive therapy. This research is published widely in cognitive therapy journals such as *Cognitive Therapy and Research, Journal of Cognitive Psychotherapy: An International Quarterly,* and *Cognitive and Behavioral Practice.* Additionally, research studies are published in a variety of behavior therapy and other psychological journals. Information from this work is used in teaching individuals at training centers for cognitive therapy in the United States. In particular, the Beck Institute for Cognitive Therapy and Research in Bala Cynwyd, Pennsylvania, has a large program devoted to training therapists and bringing in visiting scholars to participate in research and clinical activities. Although started only about 35 years ago, cognitive therapy has become increasingly popular, perhaps due to the specificity of its techniques and the positive results of outcome research.

COGNITIVE THEORY OF PERSONALITY

Cognitive therapists are particularly concerned with the impact of thinking on individuals' personalities. Although cognitive processes are not considered to be the cause of psychological disorders, they are a significant component. In particular, automatic thoughts that individuals may have little awareness of can be significant in personality development. Such thoughts are an aspect of the individual's beliefs or cognitive schemas, which are important in understanding how individuals make choices and draw inferences about their lives. Of particular interest in understanding psychological disorders are cognitive distortions, inaccurate ways of thinking that contribute to unhappiness and dissatisfaction in the lives of individuals.

Causation and Psychological Disorders

As Beck (1967, 1991) has said, psychological distress can be caused by a combination of biological, environmental, and social factors, interacting in a variety of ways, so that there is rarely a single cause for a disorder. Sometimes early childhood events may lead to later cognitive distortions. Lack of experience or training may lead to ineffective or maladaptive ways of thinking, such as setting unrealistic goals or making inaccurate assumptions (Beck & Weishaar, 1989). At times of stress, when individuals anticipate or perceive a situation as threatening, their thinking may be distorted. It is not the inaccurate thoughts that cause the psychological disorder; rather it is a combination of biological, developmental, and environmental factors (Beck & Weishaar, 1989). Regardless of the cause of the psychological disturbance, automatic thoughts are likely to be a significant part of the processing of the perceived distress.

The Cognitive Model of Development

Cognitive therapists view individual beliefs as beginning in early childhood and developing throughout life (Figure 10.1). Early childhood experiences lead to basic beliefs about oneself and one's world. Normally, individuals experience support and love from parents, which lead to beliefs such as "I am lovable" and "I am competent," which in turn lead to positive views of themselves in adulthood. Persons who develop psychological dysfunctions, in contrast to those with healthy functioning, have negative experiences in their lives that may lead to beliefs such as "I am unlovable" and "I am inadequate." These developmental experiences, along with critical incidents or traumatic experiences, influence individuals' belief systems. Negative experiences, such as being ridiculed by a teacher, may lead to conditional beliefs such as "If others don't like

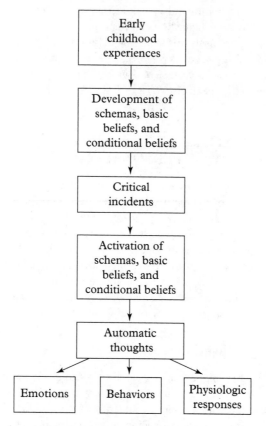

FIGURE 10.1 The Cognitive Developmental Model.
From "Brief Therapy, Crisis Intervention and the Cognitive Therapy of Substance Abuse," by B. S. Liese, 1994, *Crisis Intervention*, 1, 11–29. Copyright © 1994 by Harwood Academic Publishers. Reprinted by permission.

what I do, I am not valuable." Such beliefs may become basic to the individual as negative cognitive schemas.

Automatic Thoughts

As mentioned previously, the automatic thought is a key concept in Beck's cognitive psychotherapy. Such thoughts occur spontaneously, without effort or choice. In psychological disorders, automatic thoughts are often distorted, extreme, or otherwise inaccurate. For example, Nancy put off applying to department stores for a job as an assistant buyer. Unhappy with her job as a sales clerk, she had thoughts such as "I'm too busy now," "When the holiday season is over, I will apply for a job," and "I cannot get time off to go to other stores to get job applications." Recognizing these thoughts as excuses, Nancy, with the help of her therapist, identified automatic thoughts related to job seeking, such as "I won't present myself well" and "Other people will be better than me." By talking with Nancy about her thought processes, the therapist was able to generate several automatic thoughts. By organizing these automatic thoughts, the therapist was able to articulate a set of core beliefs or schemas.

Cognitive Schemas

How individuals think about their world and their important beliefs and assumptions about people, events, and the environment constitute cognitive schemas. There are two basic types of cognitive schemas: positive (adaptive) and negative (maladaptive). What can be an adaptive schema in one situation may be maladaptive in another. Freeman (1993) gives an example of a schema that can be both positive and negative, depending on the circumstance.

> Allen was a 67-year-old male. He had recently retired as chief executive officer of a large international firm. He had worked himself up in the company from the lowest level as a high school student to the chief position over a period of 50 years. In his retirement, he was physically healthy, had a great deal of money, good marital and family relationships, and a circle of friends. When he came for therapy he was, however, moderately to severely depressed. The operative schemas that drove him to success—that is, "I am what I do or produce," "One is judged by others by one's productivity," and "If one isn't working, one is lazy/worthless" were now contributing to his depression. The schemas were the same, but the effect on his life was far different. (p. 60)[1]

In describing schemas, Beck and Weishaar (1989) note that schemas develop early in life from personal experience and interaction with others. Some of the schemas are associated with cognitive vulnerability or a predisposition to psychological distress. For example, individuals who are depressed may have negative schemas such as "I can't do anything right," "I won't amount to anything," and "Other people are much more adept than I." In this way, cognitive vulnerability can be seen in distorted or negative schemas.

When a patient presents a negative schema, the therapist may note a cognitive shift. For each psychological disorder, particular cognitive distortions are likely to be present. By diagnosing the disorder, the therapist can understand how the client integrates data and acts in accordance with the data. Thus, an anxious client may perceive a threat while driving home and take a prescribed route that may include alternates in case traffic jams or accidents are seen ahead. By observing the client describing this situation the therapist may perceive an affective shift that indicates that the client has made a cognitive shift. Signals of such a shift may be facial or bodily expressions of emotion or stress. When such an event takes place in therapy, the cognitive schema may be emotional or "hot." In such a case, the therapist is likely to follow up the "hot" cognition with a question such as "What were you thinking just now?" (Beck, Emery, & Greenberg, 1985).

In further describing schemas, Freeman (1993) discusses five factors, varying in strength, that make up a schema. First, each schema has a strong affective component that is related to the belief system. Second, schemas vary as to how long the individual has held the particular set of beliefs. Third, schemas are usually acquired from other individuals, and the more important the individual, usually the more important the schema. Fourth, the cognitive element accounts for how detailed and pervasive the schema is in the person's thoughts. Fifth, schemas have a behavioral component that determines how the individual acts on the belief system. Thus, cognitive schemas have affective and behavioral components, as well as cognitive ones. In describing schemas, some cognitive therapists have organized them into categories. For example, Bricker, Young, and Flanagan (1993) have described a framework that incorporates 15 schemas, common in personality disorders, into five groupings.

A different approach to schemas that is particularly appropriate with clients with personality disorders has been taken by Freeman (1993), who, like Bricker et al. (1993), emphasizes the developmental aspects of cognitive schemas. Adapting Erikson's (1950) model of psychosocial development, Freeman focuses on the social context of the individual that would include relationships with family, school, friends, and work. By using Erikson's eight stages of development, Freeman is able to conceptualize schemas that develop out of crises at various periods throughout the life span. For example, Erikson's (1950) first stage is that of trust versus mistrust. A schema of trust might arise from thoughts such as "I can rely on others" and "People are here to help me," whereas a schema of mistrust might include automatic thoughts such as "I can't count on anyone" and "People will do what they want despite my wishes." Freeman describes other automatic thoughts that are present in schemas that can be derived from the other seven stages of Erikson's model of psychosocial development.

Cognitive Distortions

An individual's important beliefs or schemas are subject to cognitive distortion. Because schemas often start in childhood, the thought processes that support schemas may reflect early errors in reasoning. Cognitive distortions appear when information processing is inaccurate or ineffective. In his original work with depression, Beck (1967) identified several significant cognitive distortions that can be identified in the thought processes of depressed people. Freeman (1987) has discussed a variety of common cognitive distortions that can be found in different psychological disorders. Eight of these are described here: dichotomous thinking, catastrophizing, overgeneralization, selective abstraction, arbitrary inference, magnification or minimization, labeling and mislabeling, and personalization.

Dichotomous thinking.   By thinking that something has to be either exactly as we want it or it is a failure, we are engaging in all-or-nothing, or dichotomous, thinking. A student who says, "Unless I get an A on the exam, I have failed" is engaging in dichotomous thinking. Grades of A− and B+ then become failures and are seen as unsatisfactory.

Selective abstraction.   Sometimes individuals pick out an idea or fact from an event to support their depressed or negative thinking. For example, a baseball player who has had several hits and successful fielding plays may focus on an error that he has made and dwell on it. Thus, the ballplayer has selectively abstracted one event from a series of events to draw negative conclusions and to feel depressed.

Arbitrary inference.   Referring to coming to a conclusion that contradicts or is not supported by evidence or facts, arbitrary inferences are of two types: mind reading and negative prediction. *Mind reading* refers to the idea that we know what another person is thinking about us. For example, a man may conclude that his friend no longer likes him because he will not go shopping with him. In fact, the friend may have many reasons, such as other commitments, not to go shopping. *Negative prediction* means that an individual believes that something bad is going to happen, although there is no evidence to support this. A person may predict that she may fail an exam, even though she has done well on exams before and is prepared for the upcoming examination. In this case, the inference about failure—the negative prediction—is not supported by the facts. Thus, both mind reading and negative prediction involve making negative inferences based on lack of attention to and/or distortion of available data.

Catastrophizing. In this cognitive distortion, individuals take one event that they are concerned about and exaggerate it so that they become fearful. Thus, "I know when I meet the regional manager, I'm going to say something stupid that will jeopardize my job. I know I will say something that will make her not want to consider me for advancement" turns an important meeting into a possible catastrophe.

Overgeneralization. Making a rule based on a few negative events, individuals distort their thinking through overgeneralization. For example, a high school sophomore may conclude: "Because I did poorly on my first algebra exam I can't do math." Another example would be the person who thinks because "Alfred and Bertha were angry at me, my friends won't like me, and won't want to have anything to do with me." Thus a negative experience with a few events can be generalized into a rule that can affect future behavior.

Labeling and mislabeling. A negative view of oneself is created by self-labeling based on some errors or mistakes. A person who has had some awkward incidents with acquaintances might conclude, "I'm unpopular. I'm a loser" rather than "I felt awkward talking to Harriet." In labeling and mislabeling in this way, individuals can create an inaccurate sense of themselves or their identity. Basically, labeling or mislabeling is an example of overgeneralizing to such a degree that one's view of oneself is affected.

Magnification or minimization. Cognitive distortions can occur when individuals magnify imperfections or minimize good points. They lead to conclusions that support a belief of inferiority and a feeling of depression. An example of magnification is the athlete who suffers a muscle pull and thinks, "I won't be able to play in the game today. My athletic career is probably over." In contrast, an example of minimization would be the athlete who would think, "Even though I had a good day playing today, it's not good enough. It's not up to my standards." In either magnification or minimization, the athlete is likely to feel depressed.

Personalization. Taking an event that is unrelated to the individual and making it meaningful produces the cognitive distortion of personalization. Examples include "It always rains when I am about to go for a picnic" and "Whenever I go to the shopping center, there is always an incredible amount of traffic." People do not cause the rain or the traffic; these events are beyond our control. Furthermore, when people are questioned, they are able to give instances of how it does not always rain when they have planned an outdoor function, and that they do not always encounter the same level of traffic when shopping. For example, traffic is usually heavier at certain times of day than at others, and if one chooses to shop at a particular time, there will be more or less traffic.

If they occur frequently, such cognitive distortions can lead to psychological distress or disorders. Making inferences and drawing conclusions from a behavior are important parts of human functioning. Individuals must monitor what they do and assess the likelihood of outcomes to make plans about their social lives, romantic lives, and careers. When there are frequent cognitive distortions, individuals can no longer do this successfully and may experience depression, anxiety, or other disturbances. Cognitive therapists look for cognitive distortions and help their patients understand their mistakes and make changes in their thinking.

THEORY OF COGNITIVE THERAPY

Characterized as a collaborative relationship, therapists work together with their clients to change thinking patterns, as well as behaviors, that interfere with the clients' goals. The establishment of a caring therapeutic relationship is essential. Cognitive therapy is characterized by its careful approach to detail and the role of the thinking process in behavioral and affective change. In setting goals, cognitive therapists attend to faulty beliefs that interfere with individuals achieving their goals. This is reflected in assessment methods that require individuals to monitor, log, and indicate in a variety of ways their cognitions, as well as their feelings and behaviors. A characteristic of cognitive therapy is that the therapist and client collaborate to reach the patient's goals by using a format that allows for feedback and discussion of client progress. Although therapeutic techniques that are used to bring about change include cognitive, affective, and behavioral elements, only the cognitive approaches to changing automatic thoughts and cognitive schemas are described here.

Goals of Therapy

The basic goal of cognitive therapy is to remove biases or distortions in thinking so that individuals may function more effectively. Attention is paid to the way individuals process information, which may maintain feelings and behaviors that are not adaptive. Patients' cognitive distortions are challenged, tested, and discussed to bring about more positive feelings, behaviors, and thinking.

In establishing goals, cognitive therapists focus on being specific, prioritizing goals, and working collaboratively with clients. The goals may have affective, behavioral, and cognitive components, as seen by this example from Freeman, Pretzer, Fleming, and Simon (1990):

> Frank, a depressed salesman, initially stated his goal for therapy as, "to become the best that I can be." When stated in that way, the goal is quite vague and abstract. It also was clearly unmanageable, considering that Frank was so depressed that he could not manage to revise his resumé or do household chores. After considerable discussion, Frank and his therapist agreed on more specific goals including "feel less depressed and anxious, decrease amount of time spent worrying, and actively hunt for a job (revise resumé, actively search for job openings, complete applications for appropriate openings, etc.)." (pp. 10–11)[2]

The clearer and more concrete the goals, the easier it is for therapists to select methods to use in helping individuals change their belief systems and also their feelings and behaviors.

Assessment in Cognitive Therapy

Careful attention is paid to assessment of client problems and cognitions, both at the beginning of therapy and throughout the entire process in order that the therapist may clearly conceptualize and diagnose the client's problems. As assessment proceeds, it focuses not only on the specific thoughts, feelings, and behaviors of the client but also on the effectiveness of therapeutic techniques as they affect these thoughts, feelings, and behaviors. Specific strategies for assessment have been devised for many different psychological disorders, such as anxiety and depression (J.S. Beck, 1995). In this section, I describe ways cognitive therapists use assessment techniques, including client interviews, self-monitoring, thought sampling, the assessment of beliefs and assumptions, and self-report questionnaires (Freeman et al., 1990).

Interviews. In the initial evaluation, the cognitive therapist may wish to get an overview of a variety of topics, while at the same time creating a good working relationship with the client. The topics covered are similar to those assessed by many other therapists and include the presenting problem, a developmental history (including family, school, career, and social relationships), past traumatic experiences, medical and psychiatric history, and client goals. In making this assessment, Kendall (1981) suggests that specific questions rather than broad, open-ended questions may yield more accurate information. Freeman et al. (1990) emphasize the importance of getting detailed reports of events. They caution against asking biased questions such as "Didn't you want to go to work?" and suggest instead "What happened when you did not get to work?" In assessing thoughts, therapists may need to train their clients to differentiate between thoughts and feelings and to report observations rather than make inferences about the observations. Accuracy of recall is encouraged (although clients are not expected to remember all details) and is preferred to guesses about past events. Sometimes in vivo interviews and observations may be of particular help. For example, if a client suffers from agoraphobia, the therapist may meet the client at home and walk outside with the client, making observations and assessments in the interviewing process.

Keeping notes of patients' experiences, emotions, and behaviors is very helpful. Judith Beck (1995) has developed a Cognitive Conceptualization Diagram (Figure 10.2) to organize patient data. The therapist starts at the bottom half of the diagram, taking each situation one at a time. For example, Fred has been very frightened of presenting at his senior recital at college. He is afraid he will sing off key and embarrass himself in front of the music faculty. Under Situation #1, the therapist would write "Presenting at a recital. Evaluated by 3 music professors." The therapist then helps Fred in determining the automatic thought and writes it in the box below "Situation #1"— "The professors will think I'm terrible." Then they determine the "Meaning of A. T.," which for Fred is "I fold under pressure." The "Emotion" is "anxiety." His "Behavior" is "Singing the song he will present, 5 times." As the therapist and Fred continue, they will discuss at least two more situations in the same way. Each time, the

Pt's Initials: Therapist's Name:

Pt's Diagnosis: Axis I: Axis II:

COGNITIVE CONCEPTUALIZATION DIAGRAM

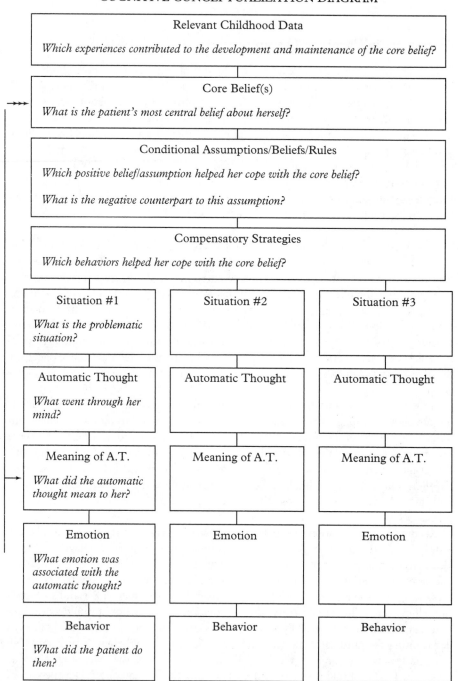

FIGURE 10.2 Cognitive Conceptualization Diagram.
From *Cognitive Therapy: Basics and Beyond,* Guilford Press, 1995. Copyright © 1995 by J. S. Beck. Reprinted by permission.

therapist and Fred determine the automatic thoughts, their meaning, the emotion relevant to the situation, and the behavior.

When the therapist has enough information to assess core beliefs, she will take information that she has about Fred's "Relevant Childhood Data" and integrate this with information from the material she has just gathered to determine Fred's "Core Beliefs." Then she uses "if-then" phrases to determine "Conditional Assumptions/Beliefs/Rules." For Fred, his "Core Belief" may be "I'm not good enough." His "Conditional Assumptions/Beliefs/Rules" may be "If I have to be on my own, I'll screw up." This is a negative assumption. A positive assumption would be "When I'm with others (e.g., singing in a chorus), I'm OK." The final box is "Compensatory Strategies." Fred's are "practice, practice, practice" and "keep telling my girlfriend how nervous I am." This information then becomes material that the therapist uses when developing change strategies. Although the interview is probably the most important way to gather information, cognitive therapists also ask clients to gather specific information on their own.

Self-monitoring.   Another method that is used for assessing client thoughts, emotions, and behaviors outside the therapist's office is self-monitoring. Basically, clients keep a record of events, feelings, and/or thoughts. This could be done in a diary, on an audiotape, or by filling out a questionnaire. One of the most common methods is the Dysfunctional Thought Record (DTR) (Beck, Rush, Shaw, & Emery, 1979) (Figure 10.3). Sometimes called a thought sheet, the DTR has one column in which the client describes the situation, a second in which the client rates and identifies an emotion, and a third column to record her automatic thoughts. Clients may practice using the DTR in therapy, so that they get used to recording automatic thoughts and rating the intensity of feelings. Use of the DTR provides material for discussion in the next session, as well as an opportunity for clients to learn about their automatic thoughts.

Thought sampling.   Another method for obtaining information about cognitions is thought sampling (Hurlburt, Leach, & Saltman, 1984). Having a tone sound at a random interval at home and then recording thoughts is one way to get a sample of cognitive patterns. Clients may then record their thoughts in a tape recorder or notebook. Freeman et al. (1990) give an example of how thought sampling can be productive in therapy.

> A middle-aged factory foreman had made good progress in therapy by using DTRs to identify dysfunctional cognitions related to episodes of anger and depression and then "talking back" to the cognitions. However, he began to experience a vague, depressed mood that seemed not to be related to any clear stimuli. He was unable to identify situations or cognitions related to the depressed mood, and therefore was asked to use a thought sampling procedure to collect additional data. When he returned for his next therapy session, a review of the cognitions he had recorded revealed constant ruminative thoughts centering on the theme of "I'm too tired to . . ." It gradually became clear that these ruminative thoughts were responsible for his decreased motivation to deal with problems actively and for his increased depression. (p. 41)

Thought sampling can be useful in getting data that is related to specific situations, such as work and school. However, thought sampling can interrupt the client's activ-

DYSFUNCTIONAL THOUGHT RECORD (Example)

Directions: When you notice your mood getting worse, ask yourself, "What's going through my mind right now?" and as soon as possible jot down the thought or mental image in the Automatic Thought column.

Date/Time	Situation	Automatic Thought(s)	Emotion(s)	Alternative Response	Outcome
	1. What actual event or stream of thoughts, or daydreams, or recollection led to the unpleasant emotion? 2. What (if any) distressing physical sensations did you have?	1. What thought(s) and/or image(s) went through your mind? 2. How much did you believe each one at the time?	1. What emotion(s) (sad, anxious, angry, etc.) did you feel at the time? 2. How intense (0-100%) was the emotion?	1. (optional) What cognitive distortion did you make? (e.g., all-or-nothing thinking, mind-reading, catastrophizing.) 2. Use questions at bottom to compose a response to the automatic thought(s). 3. How much do you believe each response?	1. How much do you now believe each automatic thought? 2. What emotion(s) do you feel now? How intense (0-100%) is the emotion? 3. What will you do? (or did you do?)
2/2	Thinking about Mark's not calling me.	He must not care. (90%)	Sad (90%)	Jumping to conclusions 1. He didn't call when he said he would but he was affectionate the last time we were together. 2. Maybe he's been busy at work or just forgot. 3. The worst is he'll never call again and I'd survive. Best is he'd call right now. Most realistic is he'll call in a day or two. 4. Believing he must not care makes me feel devastated. Realizing I might be wrong makes me feel more hopeful. 5. I should go ahead and call him myself. 6. If Joan was in this situation I'd tell her to go ahead and call him. (75%)	1. A.T = 70% 2. Sad = 60% 3. I will call him after work tonight.

Questions to help compose an alternative: (1) What is the evidence that the automatic thought is true? Not true? (2) Is there an alternative explanation? (3) What's the worst that could happen? Could I live through it? What's the best that could happen? What's the most realistic outcome? (4) What's the effect of my believing the automatic thought? What could be the effect of changing my thinking? (5) What should I do about it? (6) If _____ was in the situation and had this thought, what would I tell him/her?
(friend's name)

FIGURE 10.3 Dysfunctional Thought Record.

From *Cognitive Therapy: Basics and Beyond*, Guilford Press, 1995. Copyright © 1995 by J. S. Beck. Reprinted by permission.

ity and may become irritating. Also, thoughts irrelevant to the client's problems may be recorded.

Scales and questionnaires.   In addition to these techniques, previously developed self-report questionnaires or rating scales can be used to assess irrational beliefs, self-statements, or cognitive distortions. For example, Kendall and Hollon (1981) have asked their clients to keep a list of thoughts and to write down whatever goes through their minds during a given situation. Structured questionnaires have been developed for specific purposes, such as the Beck Depression Inventory (Beck, Ward, Mendelson, Mock, & Erbaugh, 1961), the Scale for Suicide Ideation (Beck, Kovacs, & Weissman, 1979), and the Dysfunctional Attitude Scale (Weissman, 1979). Questionnaires such as these are usually brief and can be administered at various points in therapy to monitor progress. Additionally, psychological tests such as the Minnesota Multiphasic Personality Inventory may be used for similar purposes.

When gathering data from clients, especially raw data that include automatic thoughts, it is often helpful for the therapist to try to infer themes or cognitive schemas that are represented by the cognitions. As data are reported from session to session, different cognitive schemas, or insights into them, may develop. Schemas can be seen as hypotheses that the client and counselor are continually testing. Progress can be assessed as patients complete homework, fill out questionnaires, and report automatic thoughts. With progress should come a decrease in the number of cognitive distortions, increased challenges to automatic thoughts, and a decrease in negative feelings and behavior.

The Therapeutic Relationship

Beck's (1976) view of the client-therapist relationship is that it is collaborative. The therapist brings an expertise about cognitions, behaviors, and feelings to guide the client in determining goals for therapy and means for reaching these goals. The clients' contributions to therapy are the raw data for change (thoughts and feelings). They participate in the selection of goals and share responsibility for change. The assessment process is a continually evolving one. As new data are gathered, the therapist and client may develop new strategies. In some ways, the therapeutic process can be seen as a joint scientific exploration in which both therapist and client test new assumptions. In this process, the therapist may use listening skills that focus on the client's feelings, somewhat similar to the approach of Carl Rogers, to further understand the client's concerns and to develop the relationship. Although the cognitive therapist is open to the feedback, suggestions, and concerns of the client, the process of therapy is specific and goal oriented.

The Therapeutic Process

More so than many other theories of therapy, cognitive therapy is structured in its approach. The initial session or sessions deals with assessment of the problem, development of a collaborative relationship, and case conceptualization. As therapy progresses, a guided discovery approach is used to help clients learn about their inaccurate thinking. Other important aspects of the therapeutic process are methods to identify automatic thoughts and the assignment of homework, which is done throughout therapy. As clients reach their goals, termination is planned, and clients work on how they will use what they have learned when therapy has stopped. As therapeutic work progresses, clients move from developing insight into their beliefs to moving toward change. Particularly with difficult and complex problems, insight into the development of negative cognitive schemas is important. All of these aspects of the therapeutic process are described more fully here.

Guided discovery.   Sometimes called Socratic dialogue, guided discovery helps clients change maladaptive beliefs and assumptions. The therapist guides the client in discovering new ways of thinking and behaving by asking a series of questions that make use of existing information to challenge beliefs.

Client: I've been afraid that when I report to my new job on Monday, people will think I can't do the work.

Therapist: What does that tell you about the assumptions that you are making?

Client: Like I'm mind-reading, like I know in advance what's going to happen.

Therapist: And what assumptions are you making?

Client: That I know what my new colleagues will think of me.

The three-question technique.   A specific form of the Socratic method, the three-question technique consists of a series of three questions designed to help clients revise negative thinking. Each question presents a way of inquiring further into negative beliefs and bringing about more objective thinking.

1. What is the evidence for the belief?
2. How else can you interpret the situation?
3. If it is true, what are the implications?

A brief example of this technique shows how it is an extension of the Socratic method and how it can help individuals change their beliefs. Liese (1993) gives an example of a physician using the three-question technique with a patient with AIDS.

Dr.: Jim, you told me a few minutes ago that some people will scorn you when they learn about your illness. (reflection) What is your *evidence* for this belief?

Jim: I don't have any evidence. I just feel that way.

Dr.: You "just feel that way." (reflection) How else could you took at the situation?

Jim: I guess my real friends wouldn't abandon me.

Dr.: If some people did, in fact, abandon you, what would the *implications* be?

Jim: I guess it would be tolerable, as long as my real friends didn't abandon me.
(Liese, 1993, p. 83)

Specifying automatic thoughts.   An important early intervention is to ask the client to discuss and to record negative thoughts. Specifying thoughts, using the Dysfunctional Thought Record, and bringing them into the next session can be helpful for work in future sessions. An example of automatic thoughts and helping a patient understand them is given here.

> During the first session, I had asked my client how often he thought that he had negative thoughts. His response was that he had them at times, but only infrequently. Given his Beck Depression Inventory of 38, my thinking was that he would have many, many more. He estimated no more than two to three a day. As a homework assignment I asked him to record as many of his thoughts as possible. I estimated that he probably had several negative thoughts a day, and that by the end of the week he would probably have 50 thoughts recorded. He quickly responded: "I'll never be able to do it. It would be too hard for me. I'll just fail." My response was to indicate that he already had three and only needed 47 more. (Freeman et al., 1990, pp. 12-13)

Homework.   Much work in cognitive therapy takes place between sessions. Specific assignments are given to help the client collect data, test cognitive and behavior changes, and work on material developed in previous sessions (Freeman et al., 1990). If the client does not complete the homework, this fact can be useful in examining problems in the relationship between client and therapist or problems in homework assignments that may indicate lack of clarity or other problems. Generally, homework assignments are discussed and new ones developed in each session.

Session format.   Although therapists may have their own format that they adapt for different client problems, there are certain topics to be dealt with in the therapy session (J. S. Beck, 1995). The therapist checks on the client's mood and how he is feeling. Usually, the therapist and client agree on an agenda for the therapy session based, in part, on a review of events of the past week and on pressing problems that may have emerged. Also, the therapist asks for feedback about the previous session and concerns or problems that the client may have about issues that have occurred since the last meeting. The therapist and client review homework and collaborate to see how the client could get more out of it. Usually, the major focus of the session is on the concerns that the client raised at the beginning of the therapy hour. Having dealt with specific items, new homework is assigned relevant to the client's chief concerns. Feedback from the client about the session is an important element of the collaborative relationship between therapist and client.

Termination.   As early as the first session, termination may be planned. Throughout treatment, therapists encourage patients to monitor their thoughts or behaviors, report them, and measure progress toward their goals. In the termination phase, the therapist and client discuss how this can be done by the client without the therapist. Essentially, clients become their own therapists. Just as clients may have had difficulties in accomplishing tasks and may have relapsed into old thought patterns or behaviors, they work on how to deal with similar issues and events after therapy has ended. Commonly, the frequency of therapy sessions tapers off, and client and therapist may meet every 2 weeks or once a month.

Although issues occur in therapy that may require changes in the therapeutic process described here, the specificity of the therapeutic approach, the emphasis on thoughts, and the use of homework are typical. Throughout the process of therapy, a number of strategies are used to bring about changes in thoughts, behaviors, and feelings. Some of these are discussed next.

Therapeutic Techniques

A wide variety of cognitive techniques are used in helping clients achieve their goals. Some of the techniques focus on eliciting and challenging automatic thoughts, others on maladaptive assumptions or ineffective cognitive schemas. The general approach in cognitive therapy is not to interpret automatic thoughts or irrational beliefs, but to examine them through either experimentation or logical analysis. An example of an experiment would be to ask a client who feels that no one will pay attention to her to initiate a conversation with two acquaintances and observe how they attend or fail to attend to her. An example of questioning a client's logic would be when the client says, "I can never do anything right" to ask, "Have you done anything right today?" Cognitive therapists also use techniques to help clients with feelings and behaviors. Some of the techniques that are used in assisting clients with feelings are described in Chapter 6, and those used to help clients change behaviors are explained in Chapters 8 and 9. About 15 different cognitive therapy techniques are described by Freeman (1987), Dattilio and Freeman (1992), Freeman et al. (1990), and J. S. Beck (1995). In this section, eight common strategies for helping clients change unhelpful thought patterns are explained.

Understanding idiosyncratic meaning.   Different words can have different meanings for people, depending on their automatic thoughts and cognitive schemas. Often it is not enough for therapists to assume that they know what the client means by certain words. For example, depressed people are often likely to use vague words such as upset, loser, depressed, or suicidal. Questioning the client helps both therapist and client to understand the client's thinking process.

> *Client:* I'm a real loser. Everything I do shows that I'm a real loser.
>
> *Therapist:* You say that you're a loser. What does it mean to be a loser?
>
> *Client:* To never get what you want, to lose at everything.
>
> *Therapist:* What is it that you lose at?
>
> *Client:* Well, I don't exactly lose at very much.
>
> *Therapist:* Then perhaps you can tell me what you do lose at, because I'm having difficulty understanding how you are a loser.

Challenging absolutes.   Clients often present their distress through making extreme statements such as "Everyone at work is smarter than I am." Such statements use words like everyone, always, never, no one, and all the time. Often it is helpful for the therapist to question or challenge the absolute statement so that it can be presented more accurately by the client, as in the following example.

> *Client:* Everyone at work is smarter than me.
>
> *Therapist:* Everyone? Every single person at work is smarter than you?

Client: Well, maybe not. There are a lot of people at work I don't know well at all. But my boss seems smarter; she seems to really know what's going on.

Therapist: Notice how we went from everyone at work being smarter than you to just your boss.

Client: I guess it is just my boss. She's had a lot of experience in my field and seems to know just what to do.

Reattribution. Clients may attribute responsibility for situations or events to themselves when they have little responsibility for the event. By placing blame on themselves, clients can feel more guilty or depressed. Using the technique of reattribution, therapists help clients fairly distribute responsibility for an event, as in this example.

Client: If it hadn't been for me, my girlfriend wouldn't have left me.

Therapist: Often when there is a problem in a relationship, both people contribute to it. Let's see if it is all your fault, or if Beatrice may also have played a role in this.

Labeling of distortions. Previously several cognitive distortions such as dichotomous thinking, overgeneralization, and selective abstraction were described. Labeling such distortions can be helpful to clients in categorizing automatic thoughts that interfere with their reasoning. For example, a client who believes that her mother always criticizes her might be asked to question whether this is a distortion and whether she is "overgeneralizing" about her mother's behavior.

Decatastrophizing. Clients may be very afraid of an outcome that is unlikely to happen. A technique that often works with this fear is the "what if" technique. It is particularly appropriate when clients overreact to a possible outcome, as in this case:

Client: If I don't make dean's list this semester, things will be over for me. I'll be a mess; I'll never get into law school.

Therapist: And if you don't make dean's list, what would happen?

Client: Well, it would be terrible, I don't know what I would do.

Therapist: Well, what would happen if you didn't make dean's list?

Client: I guess it would depend on what my grades would be. There's a big difference between getting all B's and not making dean's list and getting all C's.

Therapist: And if you got all B's?

Client: I guess it wouldn't be so bad, I could do better the next semester.

Therapist: And if you got all C's?

Client: That's really not likely, I'm doing much better in my classes. It might hurt my chances for law school, but I might be able to recover.

Challenging dichotomous thinking. Sometimes clients describe things as all or nothing or as all black or all white. In the previous example, the client is not only catastrophizing about grades but also dichotomizing the idea of making or not making the dean's list. Rather than accept the idea of dean's list versus not dean's list, the therapist uses a process called *scaling*, which turns a dichotomy into a continuum. Thus, grades are seen as varying in degree; the client will respond differently to the possibility of getting a 3.0 rather than a 3.25 than to the possibility of dean's list or not dean's list.

Listing advantages and disadvantages.   Sometimes it is helpful for patients to write down the advantages and disadvantages of their particular beliefs or behaviors. For example, a student can write down the advantages of maintaining the belief "I must make dean's list" and the disadvantages of such a belief. This approach is somewhat similar to scaling, as listing the advantages and disadvantages of a belief helps individuals move away from an all-or-none position.

Cognitive rehearsal.   Use of imagination in dealing with upcoming events can be helpful. A woman might have an image of talking to her boss, asking for a raise, and then being told, "How dare you even talk to me about this subject?" This destructive image can be replaced through cognitive rehearsal. The woman can imagine herself talking to her boss and having a successful interview in which the boss listens to her request. The cognitive rehearsal can be done so that the woman presents her request in an appropriate way, with the boss not granting the request in one instance and the boss granting the request in another. The therapist asks her to imagine the interview with the boss and then asks the patient questions about the imagined interview.

Other useful cognitive strategies follow a similar pattern. They question the client's cognitive schemas and automatic thoughts. In addition to cognitive techniques, cognitive therapists may use behavioral techniques such as activity scheduling, behavioral rehearsal, social skills training, bibliotherapy, assertiveness training, and relaxation training (discussed in other chapters). In the practice of psychotherapy, many of these techniques are used at different times in the therapeutic process to bring about change in cognitions, feelings, and behavior.

COGNITIVE TREATMENT OF PSYCHOLOGICAL DISORDERS

Cognitive therapists have probably developed explanations and specific treatments for more psychological disorders than has any other therapeutic approach. Particularly for depression and general anxiety, two disorders described here, they have provided a detailed approach to treatment and have been able to test these approaches through the application of outcome research. Other disorders discussed here include obsessional thinking, and substance abuse. Because the type of cognitive distortions that patients experience can vary within each disorder, and because there are many cognitive techniques, the examples given here are not meant to represent a universal application of cognitive therapy to each of these four disorders. Additionally, the treatment descriptions highlight only major approaches to cognitive therapy with these problems, as a full account goes beyond the scope of this book.

Depression

Beck's (1967) initial application of cognitive therapy was to depression. More writing and research have been devoted to depression in cognitive therapy than to any other disorder. Conceptualizations of depression include the cognitive triad and the downward spiral of depression. These theoretical underpinnings of depression provide a framework for the application of cognitive and other strategies.

The term *cognitive triad* refers to the negative view that depressed people have about themselves, their world, and their futures. In terms of self-perception, depressed people see themselves as worthless, lonely, and inadequate. In a similar way, they view their world as one that makes difficult demands and presents obstacles that keep them from meeting their goals. When they look at the future, depressed people see a dismal view; their problems can get only worse, and they will not be successful. With such perceptions, depressed people are likely to be indecisive, hopeless, tired, and apathetic. Their cognitive distortions may include those that have been discussed earlier: dichotomous thinking, catastrophizing, overgeneralization, selective abstraction, arbitrary inference, personalization, labeling and mislabeling, and magnification or minimization.

Another theoretical view that is helpful to therapists when working with depression is that of the *cognitive spiral*. Related to the cognitive triad is the downward spiral of depression (Freeman et al., 1990), which shows the relationships among schemas, negative automatic thoughts, mood, and negative perceptions. Basic beliefs and schemas about failure can set off a series of reactions. Thus, if Cheryl has lost an ice-skating competition and has a "failure" schema, she can interpret placing fifth of 12 as a failure. The schema may trigger negative automatic thoughts such as "Others are better than I . . .," "I will never get ahead," and "I just can't do it." This may bring about a depressed or sad mood, with Cheryl feeling like giving up skating and feeling lonely and that she does not matter to others. With this depressed mood, Cheryl may have a biased perception of her current and past skating performances, remembering her falls on the ice rather than her successes. This series of beliefs, thoughts, feelings, and perceptions, along with the lack of motivation that comes with depression, tend to perpetuate the depression.

Many of the cognitive distortions that have been described in this chapter, as well as common cognitive therapy techniques, are used in the course of treating depression. In this section, I describe treatment strategies that are suggested by Liese and Larson (1995) in their detailed approach to the treatment of depression with Paul. In their approach, they establish a collaborative therapeutic relationship leading to conceptualization of Paul's problems, which includes assessment of his basic beliefs and cognitive schemas. They then educate Paul by presenting important information that is relevant to his basic beliefs. Additionally, they apply the Socratic method, the three-question technique, and the Daily (Dysfunctional) Thought Record to help Paul make changes in thoughts and behaviors.

Conceptualizing Paul's problems includes a psychiatric diagnosis, determination of his current problems, a history of his childhood development, and a profile of his basic beliefs and automatic thoughts. Paul is a 38-year-old lawyer who recently found out he has AIDS. He had been sad, had difficulties sleeping and concentrating, and had been extremely anxious. According to Liese and Larson (1995), he was experiencing a major depressive episode of moderate severity. An only child, Paul was expected to perform well in school and did so. As a result of relationships with parents and at school, Paul developed two significant beliefs about himself: "I am lovable only when I please others" and "I am adequate only when others love me" (p. 18).

Paul sought love and approval through promiscuous sexual relationships with other men. This behavior reflected his attempts to "avoid feeling lonely" (p. 18). When he entered therapy, his behavior was reflected in certain basic beliefs.

"Now, I'm really unlovable and defective."
"I have disappointed everyone who matters to me."
"I deserve AIDS because of my behavior." (p. 18)

The therapist shared his diagnosis with Paul. Sensitive to Paul's sadness and fear, the therapist was empathic with Paul's feelings. However, Paul was surprised to discover the high degree of structure in cognitive therapy. During his second session Paul commented that the structure made therapy seem "kind of impersonal." With a great deal of encouragement from the therapist, Paul was able to admit (to the therapist): "You seem more concerned about problem solving than you are about me as a person." They discussed this belief and Paul learned from his therapist that such beliefs reflect mind reading. Paul eventually realized from his therapist's spontaneous warmth and empathy that his therapist genuinely cared about him. He further learned that therapeutic structure would contribute substantially to defining problems and resolving them (p. 19).

To help Paul with his depression, the therapist used the Socratic method (guided discovery). In this way Paul could realize that his life was not over.

Ther: How are you feeling today? (open question)

Paul: Pretty depressed.

Ther: You seem depressed. (reflection) What have you been thinking about? (open question)

Paul: My life seems wasted at this point.

Ther: What do you mean by "wasted"? (open question)

Paul: It seems like nothing matters anymore.

Ther: "Nothing." (reflection) . . . (long pause) Can you think of anything that does matter? (open question)

Paul: (long pause) Curt is important, I guess.

Ther: You only "guess"? (reflection/question)

Paul: Okay, Curt really is important.

Ther: What else is important to you? (open question)

Paul: I guess my friends are still important to me.

Ther: What makes your friends important to you? (open question)

Paul: They really seem to care about me.

Ther: When you consider your importance to Curt and your friends, what thoughts do you have? (open question)

Paul: Well, I guess my life isn't completely wasted.

Ther: And how do you feel when you think your life is not wasted? (open question)

Paul: Somewhat less upset.

In this dialogue, the therapist has begun to help Paul feel emotional relief simply by guiding him to think about his important relationships with Curt and his friends. The Socratic method facilitates Paul's ability to discover his *own* positive thoughts, resources, and strengths, rather than having the therapist advise or dispute maladaptive thoughts (pp. 21–22).

To deal further with the issue of feeling that his life is wasted, the therapist uses the three-question technique.

> **Ther:** You told me a few minutes ago that your life was wasted. (reflection) What is your *evidence* for this belief? (question #1)
>
> **Paul:** I don't have any evidence. I just feel that way.
>
> **Ther:** You "just feel that way." (reflection) *How else* could you look at the situation? (question #2)
>
> **Paul:** I guess my life isn't wasted if I'm still important to Curt.
>
> **Ther:** If, in fact, you weren't important to Curt, what would the *implications* be? (question #3)
>
> **Paul:** I guess it might be tolerable if my friends didn't abandon me.

In this very brief interaction, Paul's therapist helps him to become more objective about his own worth. In fact, when Paul realizes that his life has some meaning, he begins to experience emotional relief (p. 23).

> Paul's therapist had him complete at least two DTRs daily when Paul first began therapy. At that time Paul had reported feeling extremely depressed. Hence, "entering counseling" was written in the *situation* column and "depression" was written in the *emotions* column. Paul revealed that his *automatic thoughts* about counseling were: "It's hopeless. I won't benefit from this." These were written in the automatic thoughts column. The therapist helped Paul, using the Socratic method, to identify *rational responses* to his belief "It's hopeless." With prompting, Paul proposed the alternative, more adaptive thoughts: "In fact, I can't say for sure that there is no hope." "Maybe there is some hope for me." (p. 24)[3]

Additionally, Paul's therapist used homework that included filling out a weekly activity schedule. Through this cognitive therapy approach, Paul was able to become less depressed and find more meaning in his life. Implicit in this example is the attention to a detailed assessment of negative automatic thoughts. A great variety of cognitive strategies are used, many more than are presented in this chapter, for changing the depressive thoughts and behaviors of clients (Beck, 1967).

General Anxiety Disorder

In applying the cognitive triad to anxiety, Beck, Emery, and Greenberg (1985) discuss the role of threat. Individuals may view the world as dangerous, where catastrophes may occur or people may hurt them. This threat can be applied to the self, where individuals are afraid to assert themselves or to try to overcome a threat or danger. This outlook carries over into their view of the future, in which they believe that they will be unable to deal with events that they perceive will be dangerous. Anxious people are likely to perceive an event as risky and their abilities as minimal.

Freeman and Simon (1989) identify the significant cognitive schema of anxiety as that of hypervigilance. Individuals with this schema usually have a history of being alert to their surroundings. Some may be very aware of who is sick, the weather, road conditions, or the looks on persons' faces. Less anxious people may perceive such environmental factors but do not have automatic thoughts that indicate that these situations are threats to them. They have an accurate assessment of risk and danger, not a hypervigilant one.

In assessing the cognitive distortions that anxious individuals experience, Freeman et al. (1990) note that catastrophizing, personalization, magnification and minimization, selective abstraction, arbitrary inference, and overgeneralization are common in anxious clients. When anxious clients catastrophize, they dwell on extreme potential negative consequences. They may assume that if something harmful could potentially happen, there is a great likelihood that it will. In the following example, the client's cognitive distortion of catastrophizing is countered by the therapeutic intervention of decatastrophizing. By using the Socratic method, the therapist is able to have the client describe her fears in detail and then counters the fears by asking, "What is the worst that could happen?"

> Amy came into treatment for her fears of eating and drinking in public that were severely limiting her life. As she was planning to go out for coffee with some friends (including Sarah, a woman she did not know well), she had been able to identify the thought, "What if I get upset and really start shaking?" She and the therapist explored the likelihood of that happening and concluded that it was possible (because that had happened before) but not very likely (because she had been quite anxious in a number of situations but had not had a severe shaking episode in a long time). The therapist then moved on to explore the worst possible scenario by asking, "Well, let's just say that you did get so upset that you shook harder than you ever have before. What's the worst that could happen?" Amy replied, "Sarah might notice and ask what's the matter with me." The therapist then asked, "And if she did notice and ask you, what's the worst that would happen next?" This time Amy thought for a second and answered, "Well, I'd be terribly embarrassed, and Sarah would probably think I was weird." Once more, the therapist asked, "And what's the worst that could happen then?" After thinking some more, Amy replied, "Well, Sarah might not want to have any more to do with me, but the other people they are my friends and probably would understand." Finally, the therapist asked, "And if that did happen?" Amy concluded, "I'd feel embarrassed, but I do have plenty of good friends, so I'd live without Sarah as a friend. Besides, if she's that narrow minded, who needs her anyway?" (Freeman et al., 1990, p. 144)[4]

In this example, negative thoughts are identified and modified through questioning. Sometimes therapists may use imagery or actual behavior to challenge fears. Often cognitive therapists use the behavioral technique of relaxation training, together with other cognitive methods, to reduce stress or anxiety that individuals may experience.

Obsessive Disorder

In Chapter 8, a cognitive behavioral approach, response prevention and exposure, is suggested for obsessive-compulsive disorders that combine obsessions with compulsive rituals (such as checking a car door 20 times to see if it is locked). Most individuals with obsessive thoughts (those that clients continually worry about) tend to seek out certainty in situations that others usually believe to be safe. For example, a physically healthy person who obsesses may worry repeatedly about getting cancer, whereas other individuals who do not obsess would not worry continually about a low-risk event but rather address the issue by having a physical examination once every year or two.

In describing automatic thoughts that are typical of individuals with obsessive-compulsive problems, Beck, Freeman, and Associates (1990) list a number of typical automatic thoughts.

1. "What if I forget to pack something?"
2. "I better do this again to be sure I got it right."
3. "I should keep this old lamp because I might need it someday."
4. "I have to do this myself or it won't be done correctly" (p. 314).

Underlying these automatic thoughts are assumptions that Beck et al. (1990) believe that individuals who have obsessive thoughts make about themselves and their world.

"There are right and wrong behaviors, decisions, and emotions" (p. 314). "To make a mistake is to be deserving of criticism" (p. 315).

"I must be perfectly in control of my environment as well as of myself," "Loss of control is intolerable," and "Loss of control is dangerous" (p. 315).

"If something is or may be dangerous, one must be terribly upset by it" (p. 315). "One is powerful enough to initiate or prevent the occurrence of catastrophes by magical rituals or obsessional ruminations" (p. 316).

For people with obsessions, guilt often follows from not doing what one should or must. For such individuals, reassurance is never sufficient and alleviates anxiety only for the moment, not over the long term. Although there are several methods for dealing with obsessive thinking, two specific examples characterize a cognitive approach: habituation training and the thought-action fusion model. Both of these approaches attempt to counter the avoidance that individuals use in trying to deal with obsessional thoughts.

Habituation training elicits obsessional thoughts over and over again in a predictable way to reduce anxiety. Following a detailed assessment of the problem, the client and therapist work on ways to get used to thoughts without feeling that anything needs to be done about them. What emerges is a method that involves having the patient deliberately evoke the thought, write thoughts down repeatedly, and listen to a tape of the thoughts and the patient's voice (Salkovskis & Kirk, 1989; Rush and Beck, in press).

Another approach to helping those with obsessive thoughts is a model that examines the fusion of thoughts and actions. Wells (1997) has continued the work of Rachman

(1993) and Wells and Mathews (1994) that describes how individuals with obsessive thoughts tend to equate them with actions. For example, a person who has a thought about harming a child may think that he is going to harm the child. This fusion of thought and actions can also be applied to past actions. If I think I have done something bad in the past, I probably did it. Thus if I felt that I harmed a child in the past, I may feel that I did it. For example, Wells reports a case of a 27-year-old woman who reported recurrent thoughts that she had mutilated her children or friends. She then ruminated about these thoughts and unsuccessfully tried to tell herself that this was not true. These doubts led to checking trash bins to relieve her anxiety. This monitoring of thought processes is often referred to as heightened *cognitive self-consciousness*.

Wells (1997) makes several suggestions about how to conceptualize and help individuals who fuse their thoughts and feelings. The basic goal of this therapy is to help the patient see the thoughts as irrelevant for further action and to develop a detached acceptance of intrusive thoughts. In gathering data about these thoughts, Wells has developed a modified version of the Dysfunctional Thought Record for obsessive compulsive disorder.

Wells describes several methods for defusing thoughts from actions and events. One of the first steps is to help the patient increase his awareness of when thought-action fusion is taking place. He uses a similar approach in helping patients defuse thoughts and events. In the following, he uses a Socratic dialogue to help a man distinguish between thoughts and events at work.

T: How long have you been checking the power sockets at work?

P: About three years.

T: Have you ever discovered that you forgot to switch them off?

P: No. I go around systematically and switch them off. But that doesn't stop me driving back to work to check.

T: So even though you have many experiences telling you that your doubting thoughts are not true, you still believe that they are. What makes you believe that?

P: I don't know. Perhaps I haven't switched them off properly.

T: When you check is there any evidence of that?

P: No.

T: Yet you continue to check and continue to have a problem. So how helpful is your checking in overcoming your problem?

P: Obviously it's not helping at all.

T: So why don't you stop checking?

P: I'd be too uncomfortable. It would ruin my weekend.

T: What do you mean by uncomfortable?

P: I'd be dwelling on the possibility that I'd not turn things off.

T: So you'd still be responding as if your thoughts were true. What if you responded to your thoughts differently, could that help?

P: Well, I already tell myself that it's stupid to think these things.

T: Does that stop you dwelling on the thought?

P: No. I go through my switching off routine in my head to see if I can remember all of it.

T: So you're still acting as if your thought is true. It sounds as if it might cause its own problems.

P: Sometimes it makes me feel better, but if I can't clearly remember switching off some of the appliances, it means I'll feel worse and I'll end up checking.

T: So how useful is your behavioural or mental checking in the long run?

P: I can see it probably doesn't help. But I'd feel worse if I didn't check.

T: OK. We can explore that possibility in a minute. But I think we should do something about your strategies for dealing with your thoughts. It sounds as if your checking may be generating more doubts and keeping your problem going. (Wells, 1997, pp. 254–255)[5]

Wells uses several other cognitive strategies to help patients defuse their thoughts from actions and events. He also makes use of the exposure and response prevention strategies that have been described on page 309 in Chapter 8. The approaches of Salkovskis and Kirk (1989) and Wells (1997) are not the only models. Two others that are speculative and developing from research and cognitive therapy are described on page 404.

Substance Abuse

The application of cognitive therapy to substance abuse is thorough and complex, described in detail in *Cognitive Therapy of Substance Abuse* (Beck, Wright, Newman, & Liese, 1993). Liese and colleagues (Liese & Franz, 1996; Liese, Vail, & Seaton, 1996) address the issue of substance abuse as it applies to health psychology and advances in the cognitive treatment of substance abuse. Although the treatment of drug-abusing patients follows a cognitive model that is somewhat similar to the treatment of other disorders, there are significant differences. The therapeutic relationship may be difficult because patients may not enter treatment voluntarily, may be involved in criminal activities, may have negative attitudes about therapy, and may be unwilling to be honest about their drug usage. When setting goals, therapists focus not only on being drug-free but also on how this will solve other problems, such as financial and work problems. Particular issues unique to substance abuse are those of dealing with cravings due to withdrawal symptoms and a lack of the pleasure that was previously provided by the drug. Of importance is the focus on the individual's belief system, which is described in more detail here.

Those who abuse drugs tend to hold three basic types of beliefs: anticipatory, relief-oriented, and permissive (Beck et al., 1993). Anticipatory beliefs refer to an expectation of reinforcement, such as "When I see Andy tonight, we'll get high. Great!" Relief-oriented beliefs often refer to the removal of symptoms due to psychological or physiological withdrawal. Permissive beliefs are those that refer to the idea that it is all right to use drugs. Examples include "I can use drugs, I won't get addicted" and "It's OK to use . . . everybody else does." These permissive beliefs are self-deceiving and can be considered rationalizations or excuses. The major focus of cognitive therapy is to challenge and change these beliefs.

To change the belief system of drug abusers, Beck et al. (1993) suggest six methods: assessing beliefs, orienting the patient to the cognitive therapy model, examining and testing addictive beliefs, developing control beliefs, practicing activation of these new beliefs, and assigning homework (p. 171). Assessment of such beliefs comes from questions such as "How do you explain . . .?" and "What are you thinking about?" (p. 171). To further assess beliefs, Beck and his colleagues have developed drug-related questionnaires, such as the Craving Beliefs Questionnaire, Beliefs About Substance Abuse, and Automatic Thoughts About Substance Abuse. After a thorough assessment of beliefs, the patient can then be oriented to the specific cognitive model of addiction.

Belief systems related to drug abuse tend to become firm and entrenched. Such beliefs, including "Marijuana is great," "You can't get off heroin," and "Nothing beats a cocaine high," can be examined and tested by questions such as "What is your evidence for that belief?" "How do you know that your belief is true?" and "Where did you learn that?" (Beck et al., 1993, p. 177). To develop a system of control beliefs, or new beliefs, to replace previous dysfunctional ones, therapists use the Socratic method, as in this example dealing with cocaine use.

Therapist: Bill, you now seem less dead set in believing that nothing is as much fun as getting high.

Bill: I'm not sure what to believe now.

Therapist: What do you mean?

Bill: Well, I still think that getting high with my friends was lots of fun, but maybe it wasn't the perfect high I made it out to be.

Therapist: Bill, what else could you have done with your friends that would have been fun?

Bill: Well, I don't know about these guys, but with other friends in the past I could have gone to a baseball game, or played racquetball, or done something like sports or something.

Therapist: What else?

Bill: I guess there are lots of things . . . but none seems as exciting as doing cocaine.

Therapist: Let's try to think of some more things. What gave you the biggest thrill before you began using cocaine?

Bill: Well, I was an adventurous guy. When I was much younger I would go camping and hiking and rock climbing, but I'm in no shape for that now.

Therapist: What do you mean when you say "I am in no shape for that"?

Bill: I guess I'm just skeptical that I would enjoy that kind of thing anymore. It's just been so long since I last did it.

Therapist: What would it take for you to try doing those things again?

Bill: I guess I'd just have to do them.

Therapist: What were some of the feelings you had in the past when you would go camping or hiking or climbing?

Bill: I felt great . . . really alive!

Therapist: How did that feeling compare to the cocaine high?

Bill: (pause) . . . I guess, in some ways it was better.

Therapist: What do you mean?

Bill: Well, I really earned the high I got from those activities. There were no short cuts then. It was a super feeling.

Therapist: So perhaps you now have a control belief to replace the old addictive belief. "I can experience a super high without using cocaine."

Bill: Yes, I just need to remember that thought. (Beck et al., 1993, pp. 179–180)[6]

After control beliefs have been developed, they then must be practiced. Sometimes therapists use flash cards to reinforce the beliefs, including messages such as "Getting wasted can get me busted" or "When I smoke crack, I have no control of my life." Clients fantasize a craving for the drug and then use control beliefs to counter the craving. Accompanying the practice in using control beliefs within the session is that of assigning homework to be done outside therapy. Control beliefs are practiced in high-risk situations, such as being around friends who use the drug.

Although changing the belief system is essential in cognitive therapy of drug abuse, other issues are also addressed. Therapists help their clients deal with concerns such as reactions of family members or financial issues. Stress from work or from friends who abuse drugs can also add to the patient's problems. Additionally, when working with substance abuse, therapists teach clients methods for preventing relapse. Throughout the process of drug treatment, Socratic methods are used frequently, as are other techniques that help drug abusers change distorted beliefs.

Although this section has focused on disorders of depression, generalized anxiety, obsessive thinking, and substance abuse, cognitive therapy has been applied to many other concerns. Some examples are agoraphobia, posttraumatic stress disorder, grief, bulimia and anorexia, obesity, narcissism, borderline personality disorder, schizophrenia, multiple personality, and chronic pain. For each of these disorders, examples of common cognitive distortions that are likely to be present are given, as well as specific cognitive techniques.

BRIEF COGNITIVE THERAPY

For many disorders, such as depression and anxiety, cognitive therapy tends to be brief, usually between 12 and 20 sessions. Sometimes therapists see patients twice a week for the first month and then weekly for the next several months. A number of factors influence the length of psychotherapy, such as the client's willingness to do homework, the range and depth of problems, and how long the client has had the problem. For narcissistic, borderline, and other personality disorders, treatment often takes between 18 and 30 months, with meetings two or three times a week during the beginning of therapy. Other factors, such as therapists' style and experience, may also affect the length of cognitive therapy.

CURRENT TRENDS

A significant trend that can be seen in cognitive psychotherapy is that of constructivism. Cognitive therapy (Alford & Beck, 1997; Rosen, 1993) shows how clients are helped to look at their problems from many different points of view and think about what has happened to them from different perspectives. The notion of cognitive distortions implies that the therapist has a perception of reality that she shares with clients to help them change their ineffective views of reality. Because cognitive therapy is collaborative, both the client's and therapist's perception of reality is influenced by each other's perceptions. However, the development of very specific treatment manuals for different psychological disorders suggests that cognitive therapists have highly developed views of patients' problems that they bring to therapy, which would be in opposition to the openness of a contructivist point of view.

Recently there have been several books, many of them treatment manuals, that describe how cognitive therapy can be applied to specific populations and to disorders. Recent books have covered the application of cognitive therapy to children and adolescents: *Cognitive Developmental Therapy with Children* (Ronen, 1997) and *Cognitive Therapy with Children and Adolescents* (Reinecke, Dattilio, & Freeman, 1996). Another book describes the application of cognitive therapy to individuals with limited intellectual functioning: *Cognitive-Behavior Therapy with Learning Disabilities* (Kroese, Dagnan, & Loumidis, 1997). Other books cover the application of cognitive therapy to psychological disorders. Because of their specificity, recommending specific interviewing strategies, protocols, and questionnaires, these serve as treatment manuals. *Cognitive-Behavioral Therapy for Bipolar Disorder* (Basco & Rush, 1996) shows specific ways for dealing with the depressive and manic phases of bipolar depression. *Cognitive Therapy of Anxiety Disorders* (Wells, 1997) gives instructions for dealing with anxiety disorders such as panic, hypochondriasis, social phobia, general anxiety disorder, and obsessive-compulsive disorder. Cognitive therapy has also been applied to some of the most severe disorders; Chadwick, Birchwood, and Trower (1996) describe the treatment of psychoses, including schizophrenia and paranoia, in *Cognitive Therapy for Delusions, Voices, and Paranoia*. Other issues and psychological disorders, such as personality disorders, are described more briefly in *Frontiers of Cognitive Therapy* (Salkovskis, 1996). Because of the popularity of cognitive therapy and the number of individuals undertaking research studies, such books are likely to continue to be written in the future.

USING COGNITIVE THERAPY WITH OTHER THEORIES

Because cognitive therapy has both behavioral and affective components, it draws on other theories, especially behavior therapy and REBT. When using cognitive therapy, many behavioral treatments are incorporated, such as in vivo exposure, positive reinforcement, modeling, relaxation techniques, homework, and graded activities. Cognitive therapy shares with behavior therapy the emphasis on a collaborative relationship with the client and the use of experimentation in trying behavioral and cognitive homework. Additionally, cognitive therapists attend to the feelings and moods of the client, incorporating empathic aspects of person-centered therapy. To further integrate experiential and affective experiences of the client into therapy, Fodor (1987) suggests using Gestalt enactment techniques such as the empty chair or awareness exercises. Also, the Gestalt approach to imagery uses emotional responses as a way of accessing cognitions to provide an overview of beliefs and to help clients be aware of painful affect (Edwards, 1989). By using behavioral and Gestalt methods, cognitive therapists make their therapeutic treatments more flexible and more effective in dealing with the noncognitive aspects of individuals' problems.

Cognitive therapy shares with rational emotive behavior therapy (REBT) many techniques and strategies. However, there are some important differences. Whereas REBT challenges irrational beliefs, cognitive therapy helps clients change beliefs into hypotheses that they can contest. Another important difference is that cognitive therapy approaches psychological disorders differentially by identifying cognitive schemas and distortions as well as behaviors and feelings that are appropriate to each disorder, whereas REBT focuses on methods to change irrational beliefs themselves regardless of the nature of the psychological disorder. Although they differ as to the philosophical approach to psychological disturbances, both cognitive and REBT practitioners are likely to make use of Socratic and disputational methods in dealing with clients' belief systems.

Originally developed because of Beck's dissatisfactions with psychoanalytic therapy, cognitive therapy uses some psychoanalytic constructs. Both cognitive and psychoanalytic therapies believe that behavior can be influenced by beliefs. However, psychoanalysis emphasizes the importance of unconscious beliefs, whereas cognitive therapy focuses on the conscious belief system. The concept of automatic thoughts in cognitive therapy bears a similarity to the preconscious of psychoanalysis.

Not only do cognitive therapists draw on a variety of other theories in their work but also other theorists have drawn heavily on cognitive therapy. Behavior therapy and cognitive therapy share an emphasis on detailed assessment and experimenting with methods of change. Additionally, Adlerian therapists and rational emotive behavior therapists emphasize Beck's cognitive methods in their approach and make use of many of the cognitive strategies discussed in this chapter. Also, therapists using other theories may not use detailed cognitive assessment in their work but may examine cognitive distortions of their clients and use cognitive techniques, such as decatastrophizing, to help bring about change. Because cognitive therapy, which was started in the 1960s, has become popular quickly, the integration of it into other therapies is likely to continue.

RESEARCH

In recent years there has been great interest in studying the effectiveness of cognitive therapy, particularly in contrast with behavior, psychodynamic, and psychopharmacological treatments. Without doubt, the greatest amount of effort has been devoted to research on depression. Several meta-analyses on research into effective methods of treating depression are presented here, as are two studies comparing cognitive therapy with other treatments. Additionally, research on the effectiveness of cognitive therapy as treatment for generalized anxiety and obsessional disorders is described. The review of research that is presented in this section is very brief and does not explore the application of cognitive therapy to the many other psychological disorders. An excellent overview of outcome studies for a variety of psychological disorders has been done by Hollon and Beck (1994)and De Rubeis and Crits-Christoph (1998).

Research on Depression

Before discussing outcome studies, it is helpful to discuss a review of research on Beck's personality theory of depression. Haaga, Dyck, and Ernst (1991) analyze a number of studies that have tested Beck's theory of depression. They conclude that it is clear that negative thinking is associated with depression and that depressed people tend to have a negative view of themselves, their ability to cope with their environment, and their future, suggesting support for Beck's concept of the cognitive triad. Also, there is support for a relationship between negative cognitions and depressive behaviors and feelings. Research into the ways that individuals process information has shown that depressed individuals differ from those who are not depressed in the way they recall information. However, Haaga et al. (1991) do not see strong evidence that depressed people think more illogically than those who are not depressed. Regarding research related to determining which factors may cause depression, evidence is unclear.

Much attention has been given to studying the effectiveness of Beck's cognitive therapeutic approach to depression, as can be seen by several meta-analyses that evaluate it. Dobson (1989) identified 28 studies that used the Beck Depression Inventory to assess changes in cognitive therapy. He found that cognitive therapy was superior to behavior therapy or pharmacotherapy in treating clinical depression, regardless of the length of therapy. In his review, Dobson cautions that the research does not suggest that cognitive therapy is superior to pharmacotherapy in all cases, such as with geriatric patients. In a meta-analysis examining 58 investigations, Robinson, Berman, and Neimeyer (1990) found that depressed clients benefitted considerably from psychotherapy, with gains comparable to pharmacotherapy. DeRubeis and Crits-Christoph (1998) review recent meta-analyses and large-scale studies on the effectiveness of cognitive therapy that meet stringent criteria for comparing treatments of depression. They find cognitive therapy to be effective, but not necessarily more so than psychopharmacology or psychodynamic or interpersonal approaches.

One of the largest studies to be undertaken in the study of depression has been the National Institute of Mental Health Treatment of Depression Collaborative Research Program (TDCRP) (Elkin, 1994; Elkin, Gibbons, Shea, & Shaw, 1996). The purpose of this study was to test the comparative effectiveness of cognitive behavior therapy (CBT), interpersonal psychotherapy, pharmacotherapy using imipramine and clinical management, and a pill-placebo and clinical management approach. This study was carried out in three different cities with a random placement of a total of 250 patients into each of the four treatment categories. Each treatment session was videotaped so that the process as well as the outcome of psychotherapy could be measured. Although findings continue to be gathered in this study, some conclusions have been made. Cognitive behavior therapy was not significantly inferior to pharmacotherapy or significantly superior to placebo treatment with minimal support. Also, cognitive therapy seemed to work better for those who were less depressed than for those who were more depressed (pharmacotherapy appeared to be particularly effective for the latter group). In later follow-up there was some support for CBT as being somewhat better than pharmacotherapy in some groups, on certain measures. DeRubeis and Crits-Christoph (1998) point out that the positive effects of cognitive therapy continued beyond a 1-year follow up, whereas the effectiveness of medication sometimes stopped when patients, who had been feeling less depressed, discontinued their medication. Started in 1977 the TDCRP was the first large-scale study to involve clinics in several cities (Parloff & Elkin, 1992). The findings are considerably complex and surprising in that they do not support the superiority of CBT, as do the studies in Dobson's (1989) meta-analyses.

Depression continues to be a topic that is widely investigated in the application of cognitive therapy. Reinecke, Ryan, and Dubois (1998) did a meta-analysis of studies focused on depression in adolescence. They report that cognitive behavioral therapy showed excellent results upon completion of therapy and moderate effects upon follow-up of treatment. Three-year follow-up of bibliotherapy as a treatment for mildly depressed adults showed that treatment gains were maintained (Smith, Floyd, Scogin, & Jamison, 1997). Studying major depression, Gortner, Gollan, Dobson, and Jacobson (1998) found that those in the cognitive therapy treatment group took longer to relapse than those taking medication, but relapse did occur after 12- and 18-month follow-ups.

Research on Generalized Anxiety

In their review of the effectiveness of cognitive therapy with patients who have symptoms of generalized anxiety disorder, Hollon and Beck (1994) conclude that cognitive therapy is successful in reducing individuals' perception of threat and reducing levels of distress. They report that cognitive therapy has been more effective than behavioral or pharmacological therapy, especially in maintaining therapeutic change over time. One reason that cognitive therapy may be superior to behavioral therapy in working with general anxiety disorders is that there are few specific target behaviors for behavioral therapy to focus on, whereas cognitive therapy can focus on distorted cognitions regarding beliefs related to threat. Their conclusions are basically supported by Chambless and Gillis (1993), who found cognitive therapy to be significantly more effective than waiting list or placebo control groups. Although treatment gains held up over time, the evidence that cognitive therapy was more effective than behavioral therapeutic treatments was not clear.

Further insight into differential effectiveness between behavior therapy and cognitive behavior therapy can be seen in a study by Butler, Fennell, Robson, and Gelder (1991). They provided individual treatment lasting between 4 and 12 sessions to 57 patients who met the criteria for generalized anxiety disorder. Those who received behavior therapy were treated with muscle relaxation and, where possible, made a hierarchy of anxious stimuli to which they were exposed in vivo. For the cognitive behavior therapy sample, patients kept records of dysfunctional thoughts and developed skills to examine the thoughts and to formulate alternatives to them that could be tested in subsequent homework. The authors report a clear advantage of cognitive behavioral over behavior therapy, because cognitive techniques, more so than behavioral ones, tend to help individuals by dealing with ways of thinking that promote anxiety as well as the consequences of anxiety (the latter is the focus of behavior therapy). However, as Chambless and Gillis (1993) report, not all studies find such clear differentiation between cognitive behavioral therapy and behavior therapy.

Research on Obsessional Disorders

As described in Chapter 8, response prevention and exposure have been shown to be effective for dealing with obsessive-compulsive disorders. Abramowitz (1997) reviewing studies that compared cognitive techniques to response prevention and exposure found cognitive techniques to be at least as effective as exposure. These approaches overlap somewhat, so it is difficult to separate them. When there are obsessions or ruminations, but no compulsive or ritualistic behavior, the appropriate treatment method is less clear. In comparing cognitive therapy and behavior therapy in the treatments of obsessive disorders, Emmelkamp and Beens (1991) found little difference between exposure therapy, self-statement training (cognitive therapy), or rational emotive behavior therapy. Compared with other psychological disorders, such as depression and generalized anxiety disorder, there is relatively little research into effective methods for changing obsessive thinking. Described next is an exploratory study that uses several single-subject studies to make recommendations for further research and therapy.

In treating obsessive ruminations, Salkovskis and Westbrook (1989) suggest that obsessions can be divided into obsessional thoughts and cognitive rituals. Using a method somewhat similar to exposure and response prevention, they suggest preventing clients from engaging in cognitive rituals, which should increase their exposure to obsessive thoughts. Following up on a preliminary study by Salkovskis and Westbrook, Freeston, Ladouceur, Gagnon, Thibodeau, Rhéaume, Letarte, & Bujold (1997) studied 29 patients with obsessive thoughts but not compulsive rituals. They used procedures similar to Salkovskis and Westbrook, finding that the treatment was effective in patients after a six-month follow-up.

New procedures to deal with obsessions continue to be developed and studied. Rachman (1997) suggests a cognitive approach in which patients modify their catastrophic misinterpretations of the significance of intrusive obsessive thoughts. Jones and Menzies (1997a, 1997b) have done preliminary work using Danger Ideation Reduction Therapy (DIRT), which is designed to help patients change their excessive estimates of the danger of their obsessional thoughts. These somewhat similar approaches are likely to generate more research in the future.

Although I have given examples of research studies evaluating the effectiveness of cognitive therapy with depression, generalized anxiety disorder, and obsessive thinking, cognitive therapy has been evaluated with many other disorders. Particularly, much research has recently been done on the effectiveness of cognitive therapy in treating individuals with panic disorder, agoraphobia, posttraumatic stress, substance abuse, and schizophrenia (DeRubeis & Crits-Christoph, 1998). Another major focus of cognitive therapy has been treatment for drug and alcohol abuse, as well as cigarette smoking. Severe disorders such as schizophrenia and personality disorders have also been the subject of research, but less extensively than other psychological concerns. Other research areas include evaluating the effectiveness of cognitive therapy with children, couples, and families.

GENDER ISSUES

In addressing the application of cognitive therapy to women, Davis and Padesky (1989) and Dunlap (1997) describe how gender issues can be incorporated in dealing with women's concerns. Similarly, Bem's (1981) gender schema theory can be used to comprehend how gender schema interacts with other schemas in understanding psychological problems. In their analysis of cognitive distortions that are common to women, Davis and Padesky (1989) describe issues related to valuing oneself, feeling skilled, and feeling responsible in relationships, concerns that may occur in issues of body image, living alone, relationships with partners, parenting roles, work issues, and victimization. For Davis and Padesky the advantage of cognitive therapy is that it teaches clients to help themselves and to take responsibility for recognizing negative self-schemas that interfere with being autonomous and powerful.

With regard to treating women who are depressed, Piasecki and Hollon (1987) describe the challenge of using cognitive therapy to help women dispute their thoughts and beliefs while at the same time recognizing the value of their own views, as does Dunlap (1997). Because cognitive therapy is active and structured, therapists need to be careful not to take too much power or responsibility in the therapeutic contract. Collaboration is particularly important with clients who may feel that it is the therapist's role to tell them what to do, thus ascribing power to the therapist. When working with depressed female clients, Piasecki and Hollon (1987) caution that the therapist must not only help change distorted cognitions but also support client beliefs and values, thus empowering the client. For example, rather than reading through diaries or Dysfunctional Thought Records, the therapist may have the client discuss her observations about her experience regarding her thoughts and her suggestions about how to proceed. The therapist can then collaborate with the client to make planned changes in thoughts and behaviors.

Cognitive therapy has also been applied to homosexual men (Kuehlwein, 1992) and women (Wolfe, 1992) who are dealing with issues of "coming out" (who to tell about their homosexuality, how to tell, and when to tell). In describing a cognitive therapeutic approach to gay men, Kuehlwein suggests that it is important to help gay men learn more about their sexual orientation and the assumptions they have made about sexuality and sexual roles. Books about sexuality and the coming out process can be particularly helpful to gay men who are dealing with coming out to others to learn about the gay subculture and to integrate their own beliefs about sexuality. Because there is much misinformation about homosexuality and potential shame about being homosexual, the therapeutic process proceeds gradually, with the client taking responsibility for whom, when, and how to tell about his homosexuality. Often the client and therapist role play how the client may "come out" to someone, so the client can have control in important areas in his life. Coming out issues for women can be handled in similar ways (Wolfe, 1992).

MULTICULTURAL ISSUES

Just as gender values and beliefs can be seen in cognitive therapy as gender schemas, so can cultural values and beliefs be viewed as cultural schemas. Because cognitive therapists emphasize a collaborative relationship with their clients, they are likely to be able to ascertain values and beliefs that interfere with effective psychological functioning. Also, cognitive therapy focuses not only on the belief system but also on behaviors and feelings, providing a broad framework to deal with multicultural issues. Such an approach often counteracts the stigma of mental illness that people who are not familiar with the culture of psychotherapy may possess. For many people, the active approach of cognitive therapy in which suggestions can be given during the first session may be quite attractive.

In their writings, cognitive therapists have focused more on treatment of specific psychological disorders and research on the effectiveness of treatment than they have on cultural issues. Little literature exists on psychotherapeutic approaches with different minority groups. Cognitive therapy groups lasting for 32 sessions have been led by probation officers for urban 16- to 20-year-old African American and Latino men who are on probation (Goodman, Getzel, & Ford, 1996). However, cognitive therapy has also been applied to cultures quite different from the United States. In Malaysia, cognitive therapy is reported to be compatible with religions and values of that country and particularly helpful in treating depressed and anxious patients (Varma & Zain-Ashar, 1996). Tehrani and Muhammad (1996) report that it fits with Islamic principles and has been effective in working with a prison population. As cognitive therapy's popularity spreads, so does its application to individuals of different cultures.

COUPLES COUNSELING

Several authors have described, in some detail, cognitive approaches to marriage counseling (Baucom & Epstein, 1990; Dattilio & Padesky, 1990; Epstein & Baucom, 1989). Their approaches mirror the treatment methods used with individuals. Early in therapy, there is an emphasis on assessing distorted cognitions, particularly as they apply to the other person in the relationship. As in individual counseling, the therapeutic process often is structured both in the therapeutic hour and in the course of treatment.

As each member of the couple communicates concerns about problems with the other, the therapist attends to basic beliefs that need to be restructured (Dattilio & Padesky, 1990). Distorted beliefs such as "My husband can't do a thing right with the children" can be changed to an alternate version, such as "My husband doesn't talk to the children when he arrives home." Similarly, members of a couple are likely to have unrealistic expectations of the other, often based on what they have learned in their families of origin. For example, a husband may have grown up in a situation where his mother did not work and expects his wife not to work, either. Another problem in the belief systems of couples is causal attributions or misattributions. By blaming the other person for problems in the relationship, individuals take little responsibility for the disagreements. These problems in the belief systems of couples, along with cognitive distortions, are a major focus of cognitive therapy.

When beginning cognitive therapy, therapists educate their clients as to the process of therapy (Dattilio & Padesky, 1990). In early interviews, the therapist gathers data about the problems and makes an assessment based on cognitive, behavioral, and affective information. Often the next step is to deal with anger between the partners. When that is done, the therapist can start to increase the couple's positive behaviors and encourage a positive outcome of therapy.

Later steps focus on educating and teaching each partner new skills and strategies. One of the first tasks is to identify and record automatic thoughts and to evaluate the accuracy of them. Furthermore, communication skills are taught in the sessions so that each partner can listen and speak to the other more effectively. Emotions such as hurt, anger, and jealousy are discussed, and strategies are developed to resolve them. In working with these and other problems, the therapist teaches the partners new methods to resolve problems and disagreements. As the therapists teach new skills to the partners, they try to change dysfunctional schemas that interfere with the couple's relationship. When therapy nears termination, the therapist and clients anticipate problems that may arise later and try to develop solutions. Often a follow-up appointment is scheduled for a month later.

An example of how a cognitive therapist (Dattilio, 1990) deals with a couple who are arguing gives a brief insight into the style used in cognitive therapy and the importance that is given to automatic thoughts. Zack and Carli have been arguing for a year and a half, as a result of Zack's cocaine usage, which he has recently stopped. They are in their midtwenties and have been married for 3 years. The segment that is presented is taken from the fourth session, after Zack and Carli have been arguing about Carli's concern that Zack will use cocaine again.

> *Therapist:* Okay. Look, we need to hear each other out. It won't be a very productive session if you fall into the pattern of arguing again. So could we establish a ground rule that we will not interrupt each other when speaking?
>
> *Zack:* Yeah, I'll agree to it. But she's the one who can't stop her mouth.
>
> *Therapist:* Well, I'll get to her in a minute, Zack, but I want an agreement from you.
>
> *Zack:* Sure, you have my word.
>
> *Therapist:* Okay. Now, Carli, do you think that you can agree to this?
>
> *Carli:* I don't know. He just lies so damn much. I just have a lot of trouble sitting here listening to some of these statements.
>
> *Therapist:* Well, then let's do this. Would you, Carli, be willing to write down your thoughts, or what we call your automatic thoughts, when you hear these statements that Zack makes?
>
> *Carli:* You mean right now?
>
> *Therapist:* Yes, right now in the session. The same way I had you do when we met individually.
>
> *Carli:* I guess so.
>
> *Therapist:* Now, I'd like you to take your pen and notepad and write down the automatic thoughts that you had when Zack made his last statement. I think the statement was, "I went through rehabilitation and have stayed clean for more than 3 months. She just won't stay off my back."
> (Carli takes a few minutes to write down her automatic thoughts.)
>
> *Carli:* All right, here they are.
>
> *Therapist:* Carli, will you read them out loud.
>
> *Carli:* 1. Yes, big deal, 3 months and he thinks he's kicked the habit.
> 2. As soon as I start to let my guard down, he'll be right back doing the stuff again.
> 3. "What do I want" he says. I just want him to stay clean so that he doesn't ruin our entire marriage.
> 4. Every time that he goes out with those damn friends of his, he takes a step closer to relapse.

Therapist: Okay, good. Now, Carli, I'd like you to weigh the evidence for each one of those statements that you made and balance them with an alternative thought right next to it. I would also like you to label the distortion according to the terms that we discussed earlier. For example, let's take your first thought: "Big deal, 3 months and he thinks that he's kicked the habit." Now what evidence do you have that supports the notion that he believes that he had it made, that he's remained clean for 3 months?

Carli: Well, none really. Just his cocky attitude.

Therapist: Is it cocky? Or is he maintaining a confident attitude?

Carli: Well, confident actually. (Dattilio, 1990, pp. 24–26)[7]

This example illustrates the importance that cognitive therapists give to identifying automatic thoughts, challenging them, developing alternative thoughts, and generally providing evidence for beliefs. Homework assignments are important so that suggestions given in therapy can be tried out and discussed at the next session.

FAMILY THERAPY

Compared to approaches in couples counseling, relatively little has been written about applying cognitive therapy to families. In his discussion of the belief system of families, Bedrosian (1983) identifies three types of cognitions that may require attention from the therapist: mind reading or inferences about the internal states of others, expectations of the other, and rules about relationships. Mind reading, discussed previously, is frequent in families, when members make comments such as, "You're late just because you knew that it would make me angry." (There can be many other reasons for being late.) Often family members have implicit expectations of the other person that are unspoken and unknown by the other person. For example, "I thought that when your mother moved out, you'd pay more attention to the children." (No agreement may have been made that the spouse would pay more attention to the children.) Often families have rules about relationships, which are assumptions about the way members should interact with each other. Bedrosian (1983, p. 103) gives a common example: "If you love someone, you never get angry with him." Although there may be many other cognitive distortions that exist in families, Bedrosian has discussed some common ones.

In general, there has been a much stronger influence of behavior therapy on family treatment than cognitive therapy. However, some therapists have questioned whether a behavioral approach to therapy can be complete without considering the importance of cognitive schemas (Alexander, Jameson, Newell, & Gunderson, 1996). Attending to different negative beliefs of family members can add to the attention given to emotional and behavioral aspects of family dysfunction.

GROUP THERAPY

In cognitive group therapy, therapeutic change comes not as a result of insights that arise from group interaction, but as a result of clients making use of change strategies that are taught by the therapist (Hollon & Evans, 1983). Thus, the cognitive approach to each group session tends to center on specific, structured, and problem-oriented changes. In keeping with this model, it would be appropriate before each session to use a measure of change, such as the Beck Depression Inventory, to monitor alternatives and symptoms. Similarly, cognitive interventions in group tend to be specific and, as is shown next, to emphasize practicing cognitions and behaviors. Some cognitive groups may use a specific type of technique, such as problem solving, whereas others may be designed to help people with the same disorder, such as depression.

To help bring about change, it may be useful first to do cognitive and behavioral rehearsal within a group and then have a client use what is learned outside therapy, a method described by Wessler and Hankin-Wessler (1989). They give an example of a young man who was reluctant to ask women for a date. The therapist's first approach was to use cognitive rehearsal to have the man reevaluate his ideas that he would be rejected. After recognizing cognitive distortions in his ideas about rejection, he role played asking women for dates with two of the female group members. The group members were then able to give him feedback about his approach. Such feedback can be quite reinforcing and increase the chances that individuals will try out the behavior. Following the group exercise, the man invited several women on dates; one agreed to go to a concert with him, while others politely turned down his request. In this situation, the group offers support, alternative beliefs, and useful feedback on various behaviors.

One approach that cognitive therapists may apply as one of several or as the only group technique is problem-solving training (Coché, 1987). In describing a 10- to 12-session problem-solving group with patients in a hospital, Coché lists six steps that are used to develop effective problem-solving skills. In this approach, a log or diary of the group's progress is kept on each of the steps described. The first step is to bring up problems that members have in their lives, such as "My job is boring. What should I do?" The second step is to clarify the problem and get information from the person who presented the problem. "What is the nature of the job? What is boring about the job? What has changed on the job?" In the third step, group members give possible solutions to the problem, with a record kept of the suggestions. At this point, no criticisms are made of the suggestions. However, in the fourth step, the feasibility of possible solutions is given, with group members determining which suggestions should be tried out. In the fifth step, the patient role plays the event in the group. For example, the client may play herself, and another client may play her boss, as she discusses with the "boss" how new duties could be added to the job. Sometimes role playing may not be appropriate, and clients take suggestions and experiment with them outside the group. In the sixth step, clients try out the suggestions that they have decided will be most helpful and then report back to the group the results of the experimental activity. In this method, cognitive distortions are confronted by group members, and effective plans are designed for patients with the help of the group members and therapist.

In the cognitive approaches to group that are described here, several common elements appear. Assessment is specific, with behaviors and cognitions targeted for change. Group members collaborate with the therapist to suggest new ways of thinking about situations and new behaviors to try out. Experimenting with new alternatives to old problems, both within and outside of the group, is an important aspect of group cognitive therapy. Particularly in the beginning of the group meetings, the cognitive therapist takes responsibility for teaching group members new ways to think about their problems. However, cognitive therapy is most often combined with behavioral therapy in group treatment, especially when directed at troubled youth (Feindler & Scalley, 1998; Rose, 1998).

SUMMARY

Developed by Aaron Beck, from his observations about the impact of patients' belief systems on their psychological functioning, cognitive therapy examines the effect of maladaptive thinking on psychological disorders, while at the same time acknowledging the importance of affect and behavior on psychological functioning. As cognitive therapy has developed, it has continued to draw on psychological research into individuals' belief systems, as well as on the study of how people process information from their environment. An important aspect of cognitive therapy is the automatic thoughts—that individuals may not be aware of but that make up their belief systems—called *cognitive schemas*.

In his work with patients, Beck identified cognitive distortions that affect individuals' feelings, thoughts, and beliefs, such as dichotomous thinking, overgeneralization, and catastrophizing. To change these beliefs, a thorough assessment is given by attention to distortions inherent in certain thoughts. To further the process of assessment in therapy, Beck and his colleagues have developed a number of instruments for different psychological disorders that assess relevant cognitions and behaviors.

In their therapeutic approach, cognitive therapists collaborate with their clients to assess and change behaviors. Often in the therapeutic process, the therapist may take an instructional role, using techniques such as guided discovery and Socratic dialogue to identify maladaptive beliefs and help clients develop insights into their beliefs. Within the session, therapists often go over homework, examine current beliefs, and develop alternatives. As well as using behavioral and affective approaches, cognitive therapists make use of techniques such as decatastrophizing, labeling distortions, and cognitive rehearsal.

More than other theories, cognitive therapy has identified particular distorted beliefs that are typical of each of several psychological disorders. Of all the disorders, depression has received the most attention, as it was the focus of Beck's early therapy and research. Just as there has been much emphasis on specific approaches to each psychological disorder, researchers have studied the effectiveness of a variety of cognitive approaches to many common psychological disorders, often comparing cognitive treatments to behavioral and pharmacological approaches.

Suggested Readings

BECK, A. T., RUSH, A. J., SHAW, B. F., & EMERY, G. (1979). *Cognitive therapy of depression.* New York: Guilford. • The cognitive therapy theory of depression is described in detail, along with descriptions of cognitive techniques. Applications to depressed individuals are explained.

BECK, J. S. (1995). *Cognitive therapy: Basics and beyond.* New York: Guilford. Written by Aaron Beck's daughter, Judith, this is an excellent overview of cognitive therapy. Diagrams and case examples add to the clarity of this book.

FREEMAN, A., & DATTILIO, F. M. (1992). *Comprehensive casebook of cognitive therapy.* New York: Plenum. • A brief explanation of treatment strategy along with a case history are given for about 30 different psychological disorders and/or patient populations. The case examples are particularly helpful in understanding a cognitive therapy conceptualization of psychological dysfunction.

KUEHLWEIN, K. T., & ROSEN, H. (Eds.). (1993). *Cognitive therapies in action: Evolving innovative practice.* San Francisco: Jossey-Bass. • This book contains a wide variety of creative applications of cognitive therapy. Examples of topics are constructivist psychotherapy, radical cognitive therapy, and clinical applications of developmental therapy.

References

ABRAMOWITZ, J. S. (1997). Effectiveness of psychological and pharmacological treatment of obsessive compulsive disorder: A quantitative review. *Journal of Consulting and Clinical Psychology, 65,* 44–52.

ALEXANDER, J. F., JAMESON, P. B., NEWELL, R. M., & GUNDERSON, D. (1996). Changing cognitive schemas: A necessary antecedent to changing behaviors in dysfunctional families? In K. S. Dobson, & K. D. Craig (Eds.), *Advances in cognitive therapy* (Vol. 2, pp. 174–192). Thousand Oaks, CA: Sage.

BASCO, M. R., & RUSH, A. J. (1996). *Cognitive-behavioral therapy for bipolar disorder.* New York: Guilford.

BAUCOM, D. H., & EPSTEIN, N. (1990). *Cognitive-behavioral marital therapy.* New York: Brunner/Mazel.

BECK, A. T. (1961). A systematic investigation of depression. *Comprehensive Psychiatry, 2,* 162–170.

BECK, A. T. (1964). Thinking and depression. 2. Theory and therapy. *Archives of General Psychiatry, 10,* 561–571.

BECK, A. T. (1967). *Depression: Clinical, experimental, and theoretical aspects.* New York: Hoeber.

BECK, A. T. (1976). *Cognitive therapy and the emotional disorders.* New York: International Universities Press.

BECK, A. T. (1991). Cognitive therapy: A 30-year retrospective. *American Psychologist, 46,* 368–375.

BECK, A. T., EMERY, G., & GREENBERG, R. L. (1985). *Anxiety disorders and phobias: A cognitive perspective.* New York: Basic Books.

BECK, A. T., FREEMAN, A., & ASSOCIATES. (1990). *Cognitive therapy of the personality disorders.* New York: Guilford.

BECK, A. T., KOVACS, M., & WEISSMAN, A. (1979). Assessment of suicidal intention: The scale for suicidal ideation. *Journal of Consulting and Clinical Psychology, 47,* 343–352.

BECK, A. T., RUSH, A. J., SHAW, B. F., & EMERY, G. (1979). *Cognitive therapy of depression.* New York: Guilford.

BECK, A. T., WARD, C. H., MENDELSON, M., MOCK, J. E., & ERBAUGH, J. K. (1961). An inventory for measuring depression. *Archives of General Psychiatry, 4,* 561–571.

BECK, A. T., & WEISHAAR, M. (1989). Cognitive therapy. In A. Freeman, K. M. Simon, L. E. Beutler, & H. Arkowitz (Eds.), *Comprehensive handbook of cognitive therapy* (pp. 21–36). New York: Plenum.

BECK, A. T., WRIGHT, F. D., NEWMAN, C. E., & LIESE, B. (1993). *Cognitive therapy of substance abuse.* New York: Guilford.

BECK, J. S. (1995). *Cognitive therapy: Basics and beyond*. New York: Guilford.

BEDROSIAN, R. C. (1983). Cognitive therapy in the family system. In A. Freeman (Ed.), *Cognitive therapy with couples and groups* (pp. 95–123). New York: Plenum.

BEM, S. L. (1981). Gender schema theory: A cognitive account of sex typing. *Psychological Review, 88*, 354–364.

BRICKER, D., YOUNG, J. E., & FLANAGAN, C. M. (1993). Schema-focused cognitive therapy: A comprehensive framework for characterological problems. In K. T. Kuehlwein & H. Rosen (Eds.), *Cognitive therapy in action* (pp. 88–125). San Francisco: Jossey-Bass.

BUTLER, G., FENNELL, M., ROBSON, P., & GELDER, M. (1991). Comparison of behavior therapy and cognitive behavior therapy in the treatment of generalized anxiety disorder. *Journal of Consulting and Clinical Psychology, 59*, 167–175.

CHADWICK, P., BIRCHWOOD, M., & TROWER, P. (1996). *Cognitive therapy for delusions, voices, and paranoia*. New York: Wiley.

CHAMBLESS, D. L., & GILLIS, M. M. (1993). Cognitive therapy of anxiety disorders. *Journal of Consulting and Clinical Psychology, 61*, 248–260.

COCHÉ, E. (1987). Problem-solving training: A cognitive group therapy modality. In A. Freeman & V. Greenwood (Eds.), *Cognitive therapy: Applications in psychiatric and medical settings* (pp. 83–102). New York: Human Sciences Press.

COLBY, K. M., FAUGHT, W. S., & PARKINSON, R. C. (1979). Cognitive therapy of paranoid conditions: Heuristic suggestions based on a computer simulation model. *Cognitive Therapy and Research, 3*, 5–60.

DATTILIO, F. M. (1990). Cognitive marital therapy: A case study. *Journal of Family Psychotherapy, 1*, 15–31.

DATTILIO, F. M., & FREEMAN, A. (1992). Introduction to cognitive therapy. In A. Freeman & F. M. Dattilio (Eds.), *Comprehensive casebook of cognitive therapy* (pp. 3–12). New York: Plenum.

DATTILIO, F. M., & PADESKY, C. A. (1990). *Cognitive therapy with couples*. Sarasota, FL: Professional Resource Exchange.

DAVIS, D., & PADESKY, C. (1989). Enhancing cognitive therapy with women. In A. Freeman, D. M. Simon, L. E. Beutler, & H. Arkowitz (Eds.), *Comprehensive handbook of cognitive therapy* (pp. 535–558). New York: Plenum.

DERUBEIS, R. J., & CRITS-CHRISTOPH, P. (1998). Empirically supported individual and group psychological treatments for adult mental disorders. *Journal of Consulting and Clinical Psychology, 66*, 37–52.

DOBSON, K. S. (1989). A meta-analysis of the efficacy of cognitive therapy for depression. *Journal of Consulting and Clinical Psychology, 57*, 414–419.

DUNLAP, S. J. (1997). *Counseling depressed women*. Louisville, KY: Westminster John Knox Press.

EDWARDS, D. J. A. (1989). Cognitive restructuring through guided imagery: Lessons from Gestalt therapy. In A. Freeman, K. M. Simon, L. E. Beutler, & H. Arkowitz (Eds.), *Comprehensive handbook of cognitive therapy* (pp. 283–298). New York: Plenum.

ELKIN, I. (1994). The NIMH treatment of depression, collaborative research program: Where we began and where we are. In A. E. Bergin & S. L. Garfield (Eds.), *Handbook of psychotherapy change* (4th ed., pp. 114–139). New York: Wiley.

ELKIN, I., GIBBINS, R. D., SHEA, M.T., SHAW, B. F. (1996). Science is not a trial (but sometimes it can be a tribulation). *Journal of Consulting and Clinical Psychology, 64*, 92–103.

ELLIS, A. (1962). *Reason and emotion in psychotherapy*. New York: Lyle Stuart.

EMMELKAMP, P. M. G., & BEENS, H. (1991). Cognitive therapy with obsessive-compulsive disorder: A comparative evaluation. *Behaviour Research and Therapy, 29*, 293–300.

EPSTEIN, N., & BAUCOM, D. H. (1989). Cognitive-behavioral marital therapy. In A. Freeman, K. M. Simon, L. E. Beutler, & H. Arkowitz (Eds.), *Comprehensive handbook of cognitive therapy* (pp. 491–513). New York: Plenum.

ERIKSON, E. H. (1950). *Childhood and society*. New York: Norton.

FEINDLER, E. L., & SCALLEY, M. (1998). Adolescent anger management groups for violence reduction. In K. C. Stoiber & T. R. Kratochwill (Eds.), *Handbook of group interventions for children and families* (pp. 100–119). Boston: Allyn & Bacon.

FODOR, I. G. (1987). Moving beyond cognitive-behavior therapy: Integrating Gestalt therapy to facilitate personal and interpersonal awareness. In N. S. Jacobson (Ed.), *Psychotherapists in clinical practice* (pp. 190–231). New York: Guilford.

FREEMAN, A. (1987). Cognitive therapy: An overview. In A. Freeman & V. Greenwood (Eds.), *Cognitive therapy: Applications in psychiatric and medical settings* (pp. 19–35). New York: Human Science Press.

FREEMAN, A. (1993). A psychological approach for conceptualizing schematic development for cognitive therapy. In K. T. Kuehlwein & H. Rosen (Eds.), *Cognitive therapy in action* (pp. 54–87). San Francisco: Jossey-Bass.

FREEMAN, A., PRETZER, J., FLEMING, B., & SIMON, K. M. (1990). *Clinical applications of cognitive therapy*. New York: Plenum.

FREEMAN, A., & SIMON, K. M. (1989). Cognitive therapy of anxiety. In A. Freeman, K. M. Simon, H. Arkowitz, & L. Beutler (Eds.), *Handbook of cognitive therapy* (pp. 347–365). New York: Plenum.

FREESTON, M. H., LADOUCEUR, R., GAGNON, F., THIBODEAU, N., RHÉAUME, J., LETARTE, H., & BUJOLD, A. (1997). Cognitive-behavioral treatment of obsessive thoughts: A controlled study. *Journal of Consulting and Clinical Psychology, 65*, 405–413.

GOODMAN, H., GETZEL, G. S., & FORD, W. C. (1996). Group work with high risk urban youths on probation. *Social Work, 41*, 375–381.

GORTNER, E. T., GOLLAN, J. K., DOBSON, K., & JACOBSON, N. S. (1998). Cognitive-behavioral treatment for depression: Relapse prevention. *Journal of Consulting and Clinical Psychology, 66*, 377–384.

GOULD, R. A., OTTO, M. W., POLLACK, M. H., & YAP, L. (1997). Cognitive behavioral and pharmacological treatment of generalized anxiety disorder: A preliminary meta-analysis. *Behavior Therapy, 28*, 285–305.

HAAGA, D. A., DYCK, M. J., & ERNST, D. (1991). Empirical status of cognitive theory of depression. *Psychological Bulletin, 110*, 215–236.

HOLLON, S. D., & BECK, A. T. (1994). Cognitive and cognitive-behavioral therapies. In A. E. Bergin & S. L. Garfield (Eds.), *Handbook of psychotherapy change* (4th ed., pp. 428–466). New York: Wiley.

HOLLON, S. D., & EVANS, M. D. (1983). Cognitive therapy for depression in a group format. In A. Freeman (Ed.), *Cognitive therapy with couples and groups* (pp. 11–41). New York: Plenum.

HURLBURT, R. T., LEACH, B. C., & SALTMAN, S. (1984). Random sampling of thought and mood. *Cognitive Therapy and Research, 8*, 263–276.

JONES, M. K., & MENZIES, R. G. (1997a). Danger Ideation Reduction Therapy (DIRT): Preliminary findings with three obsessive-compulsive washers. *Behavior Research and Therapy, 35*, 843–850.

JONES, M. K., & MENZIES, R. G. (1997b). The cognitive mediation of obsessive compulsive handwashing. *Behavior Research and Therapy, 35*, 843–850.

KELLY, G. A. (1955). *The psychology of personal constructs*. New York: Norton.

KENDALL, P. C. (1981). Assessment and cognitive-behavioral interventions: Purposes, proposals, and problems. In P. C. Kendall & S. D. Hollon (Eds.), *Assessment strategies for cognitive behavioral interventions* (pp. 1–12). New York: Academic Press.

KENDALL, P. C., & HOLLON, S. D. (1981). Assessing self-referent speech: Methods in the measurement of self-statements. In R. C. Kendall & S. D. Hollon (Eds.), *Assessment strategies for cognitive behavioral interventions* (pp. 85–118). New York: Academic Press.

KROESE, B. S., DAGNAN, D., & LOUMADIS, K. (Eds.). (1997). *Cognitive behaviour therapy for people with learning disabilitie.* London: Routledge.

KUEHLWEIN, K. T. (1992). Working with gay men. In A. Freeman & F. Dattilio (Eds.), *Comprehensive casebook of cognitive therapy* (pp. 249–256). New York: Plenum.

LIESE, B. S. (1993). Coping with AIDS: A cognitive therapy perspective. *Kansas Medicine, 94,* 80–84.

LIESE, B. S., & FRANZ, R. A. (1996). Treating substance-use disorders with cognitive therapy: Lessons learned and implications for the future. In P. M. Salkovskis (Ed.), *Frontiers of cognitive therapy* (pp. 470–508). New York: Guilford.

LIESE, B. S., & LARSON, M. W. (1995). Coping with life threatening illness: A cognitive therapy perspective. *Journal of Cognitive Psychotherapy: An International Quarterly, 9,* 18–24.

LIESE, B. S., VAIL, B. A., & SEATON, A. (1996). Substance use problems in primary care medical settings: Is there a psychologist in the house? In R. J. Resnick & R. H. Rozensky (Eds.), *Health psychology through the life span: Practice and research opportunities.* (pp. 177–194). Washington: American Psychological Association.

PARLOFF, M. B., & ELKIN, I. (1992). Historical development in research centers: NIMH treatment of depression collaborative research program: A sine qua non or a placebo for research problems? *Journal of Consulting and Clinical Psychology, 54,* 79–87.

PIAGET, J. (1977). *The development of thought: Equilibration of cognitive structures.* New York: Viking.

PIASECKI, J., & HOLLON, S. D. (1987). Cognitive therapy for depression: Unexplicated schemata and scripts. In N. Jacobson (Ed.), *Psychotherapists in clinical practice: Cognitive and behavioral perspectives* (pp. 121–152). New York: Guilford.

RACHMAN, S. (1997). A cognitive theory of obsessions. *Behaviour Research and Therapy, 35,* 793– 802.

REINECKE, M. A., RYAN, N. E., & DuBOIS, D. L. (1998). Cognitive-behavior therapy depression and depressive symptoms during adolescence: A review and metanalysis. *Journal of the American Academy of Child and Adolescent Psychiatry, 37.*

REINECKE, M. A., DATTILIO, F. M., & FREEMAN, A. (Eds.). *Cognitive therapy with children and adolescents: A casebook for clinical practice.* New York: Guilford.

ROBINSON, L. A., BERMAN, J. S., & NEIMEYER, R. A. (1990). Psychotherapy for the treatment of depression: A comprehensive review of controlled outcome research. *Psychological Bulletin, 108,* 30–49.

RONEN, T. (1997). *Cognitive developmental therapy with children.* New York: Wiley.

ROSE, S. D. (1998). *Group therapy with troubled youth: A cognitive behavioral interactive approach.* Thousand Oaks, CA: Sage.

ROSEN, H. (1993). Developing themes in the field of cognitive therapy. In K. T. Kuehlwein & H. Rosen (Eds.), *Cognitive therapies in action: Evolving innovative practice* (pp. 403–434). San Francisco: Jossey-Bass.

RUSH, A. J., & BECK, A. T. (in press). Cognitive therapy. In H. I. Kaplan & B. J. Sadock (Eds.), *Comprehensive textbook of psychiatry* (Vol. VII). Baltimore, MD: Williams & Wilkins.

SALKOVSKIS, P. M. (1996). *Frontiers of cognitive therapy.* New York: Guilford.

SALKOVSKIS, P. M., & KIRK, J. (1989). Obsessional disorders. In K. Hawton, P. M. Salkovskis, J. Kirk, & D. M. Clark (Eds.), *Cognitive behaviour therapy for psychiatric problems: A practical guide* (pp. 129–169). Oxford: Oxford University Press.

SALKOVSKIS, P. M., & WESTBROOK, D. (1989). Behaviour therapy and obsessional ruminations: Can failure be turned into success? *Behaviour Research and Therapy, 27,* 149–160.

SMITH, N. M., FLOYD, M. R., JAMISON, C. S., & SCOGIN, F. (1997). Three-year follow-up of bibliotherapy for depression. *Journal of Consulting and Clinical Psychology, 65,* 324–327.

STEIN, D. J., & YOUNG, J. E. (Eds.). (1992). *Cognitive science and clinical disorders.* San Diego: Academic Press.

TEHRANI, S., & MUHAMMAD, M. J. (1996). An application of cognitive therapy in Iran: The Khorasan Prison project. *Journal of Cognitive Psychotherapy, 10,* 219–224.

VARMA, S.L. & ZAIN-ASHAR, M. (1996). Cognitive therapy in Malaysia. *Journal of Cognitive Psychotherapy, 10,* 305–307.

WEISSMAN, A. (1979). The dysfunctional attitudes scale. Philadelphia: Center for Cognitive Therapy.

WELLS, A. (1997). *Cognitive therapy of anxiety disorders: A practice manual and conceptual guide.* New York: Wiley.

WELLS, A., & MATTHEWS, G. (1994). *Attention and emotion. A clinical perspective.* Hove, UK: Erlbaum.

WESSLER, R. L., & HANKIN-WESSLER, S. (1989). Cognitive group therapy. In A. Freeman, K. M. Simon, L. E. Beuller, & H. Arkowitz (Eds.), *Comprehensive handbook of cognitive therapy* (pp. 559–582). New York: Plenum.

WOLFE, J. L. (1992). Working with gay women. In A. Freeman & F. Dattilio (Eds.), *Comprehensive casebook of cognitive therapy* (pp. 257–268). New York: Plenum.

11

Reality Therapy

Reality therapy is designed to help individuals control their behavior and make choices, often new and difficult ones, in their lives. It is based on choice theory, which assumes that people are responsible for their lives and for what they do, feel, and think. Reality therapy was developed by William Glasser, who was disenchanted with psychoanalysis, believing that it did not teach people to be responsible for their behavior, but to look to their past to blame others for it. Reality therapy developed from Glasser's work with difficult and hard-to-reach populations, for example, female adolescent delinquents. He refined the ideas behind reality therapy by using a scientific model called control theory. Glasser's development of reality therapy was based, in some ways, on deficits that he saw in psychoanalysis. He felt that the relationship with the client should be involved and friendly, with appropriate self-disclosure from the therapist, rather than distant, as he perceived the relationship in psychoanalysis. By having clients commit to therapy and explore their behavior, Glasser felt that he could bring about changes in thinking and feeling. Although talking about feelings was acceptable, it was not to be a major focus of therapy. He wanted to help clients plan to make changes in their lives and stick to those plans. In doing so, he would not accept excuses from clients. Rather, he worked hard to help them take control over their lives.

His work has had impact on people in many fields. Teachers, school counselors, and school administrators have found applicable to education the ideas expressed in *Schools Without Failure* (1969), *Control Theory in the Classroom* (1986a), *The Quality School* (1990b), and *Choice Theory: A New Psychology of Personal Freedom* (1998). Drug and alcohol abuse counselors, corrections workers, and others dealing with institutional populations have found reality therapy to be attractive and appropriate in their work with difficult populations. This chapter explains the concepts of choice theory and reality therapy and illustrates how they can be applied to a variety of problems and populations.

HISTORY OF REALITY THERAPY

Born in 1925, William Glasser was educated in Cleveland and earned an undergraduate degree in chemical engineering at 19. At 28 he had completed Case Western Reserve

WILLIAM GLASSER

University medical school. His psychiatric residency was done at the Veterans Administration Center in Los Angeles and the University of California at Los Angeles. He became board certified at 36. Glasser's dissatisfaction with the traditional psychoanalytic training he received became the seeds of the development of reality therapy. Frustrated with these teachings, he expressed his dissatisfactions to G. L. Harrington, who was his clinical supervisor in his third year of residency and was supportive of Glasser. Harrington served as a mentor for Glasser during the next 7 years.

In 1956 Glasser became a consulting psychiatrist at a state institution for delinquent adolescent girls. Although staff members were initially resistant to Glasser's suggestions for changing discipline and teaching practices, they found his approach to be helpful. In *Reality Therapy*, Glasser (1965) showed how a focus on friendliness and responsibility was helpful to the girls, not only while at the school but also after they left. Glasser was able to reach a group of individuals who, at first, were resistant to change. His work included individual and group therapy, as well as staff training. He developed a specific program for girls who abused drugs at the Ventura School.

In 1962 his mentor, Harrington, took charge of a ward of the Veterans Administration Neuropsychiatric Hospital in West Los Angeles. This unit housed chronic and regressed psychotic patients. Until Harrington's arrival, the patients had been taken care of, but no therapy was provided. Patients were discharged at a rate of about two per year. Harrington, who had questioned traditional psychoanalytic principles and had been influential in Glasser's development of reality therapy, used a similar active approach that encouraged patients to take more responsibility for their own behavior. With this approach, a unit that held more than 210 patients, with an average of 17 years of confinement, had a discharge rate of 45 patients the first year, 85 the second, and 90 the third (Glasser & Zunin, 1979).

As Glasser's success at the Ventura School for Girls became known, he began to consult in the California school system. His *Schools Without Failure* (1969) has had an impact on the administration of schools and the training of teachers, not just in the United States but in other countries as well. He had been concerned that schools did not do enough to prevent students from developing a "failure identity." He believed schools could be changed to help students find a sense of control over their lives and have successful learning experiences by developing a success-oriented philosophy that would motivate students to perform well and be involved in their work. Designed to remove failure from the curriculum, this therapy helped students become more responsible in their behavior in a way that would minimize the amount of discipline needed at school.

In 1986 Glasser's *Control Theory in the Classroom* continued and expanded upon Glasser's earlier work on education in the classroom while introducing ideas from choice theory (explained next). More recently, he published *The Quality School* (1990b), which applies ideas from choice theory to the management and administration of schools. It is estimated (Cockrum, 1989) that more than 300,000 teachers have been introduced to the concepts of reality therapy and choice theory through applications that have been developed at Glasser's Education Training Center, an outgrowth of the William Glasser Institute in California.

In 1977 Glasser was introduced to the ideas of William Powers through his book *Behavior: The Control of Perception* (1973). Glasser applied the ideas of Powers to help people make choices as they attempted to control their lives (Glasser, 1985). Powers's work led to Glasser's *Stations of the Mind* (1981), a rather technical application of control theory to human lives. A less technical book that individuals can make use of in their own lives followed, *Control Theory: A New Explanation of How We Control Our Lives* (1985), which was originally published as *Take Effective Control of Your Life* (1984). These books provided information to the reader and/or therapist for applying ideas from control theory to reality therapy.

In his 1998 book, *Choice Theory: A New Psychology of Personal Freedom*, Glasser changed the focus from control theory to choice theory. One reason is that Glasser makes use of only some aspects of Power's control theory and does not want to have readers believe that reality personality theory is the same as Powers's broader ranging theory of control. Another reason is that some people have misunderstood "control" as meaning that people should be controlling of others. That is far from Glasser's intention, which was to promote self-control so that individuals could increase their ability to make and act on responsible choices. In the frequent seminars that Glasser leads, as well as those seminars led by the senior faculty of the Institute, ideas from both control theory and reality therapy are integrated to help people understand how to take control of choices in their lives.

PERSONALITY THEORY: CHOICE THEORY

Although Glasser had developed reality therapy without the benefit of information about control theory, his explication of Powers's (1973) formulation of control theory, as described in *Stations of the Mind* (1981), has made explicit and specific the ideas that were implicit in reality therapy (Glasser, 1961, 1965). In describing control theory, Glasser makes frequent use of metaphors from engineering and physical science. These metaphors are helpful, as the control aspects of the models are relatively easy to understand when contrasted with the complexity of problems in controlling human behavior.

Glasser (1981) uses a model of a thermostat to explain human behavior. A thermostat in a house perceives or senses the actual physical qualities of the temperature of the heat in the house. When the heat reaches a certain temperature, the thermostat "instructs" the heating system to shut off. In this way, a thermostat "controls" the temperature of the home. Human beings operate in a somewhat analogous manner. Like a thermostat, individuals sense the world outside themselves. These perceptions are processed in the brain, and individuals choose how to respond to these perceptions. This is done in "comparing stations" or "comparing places." The brain then organizes or reorganizes this behavior, resulting in thoughts, actions, and feelings. This system is described in more detail in this chapter, with particular emphasis on how individuals behave in adaptive and maladaptive ways.

Pictures of Reality

Glasser (1981, p. 126) makes the point that we do not live "to any extent in the real world." Individuals may have perceptions of reality, but they cannot know reality itself.

For example, that you are reading this book in a chair is a perception of reality that few would argue with. However, it is still a perception. Often people's perceptions of reality differ. As an example, Glasser (1981) cites Marie Antoinette's statement during the French Revolution to peasants who wanted bread, "Let them eat cake" (p. 116). Marie Antoinette perceived the real world as being a place where, if the peasants could not get bread, they could get cake. The peasants' perception of the real world was, of course, that they were starving and there was no food anywhere. If I say to someone "Get real" or "Why don't you face reality?" I am asking them why their perceptions of reality are not the same as my perceptions. We often become interested in others' perceptions of realities in order to satisfy our own needs. This concept of pictures of reality is consistent with the postmodern constructivist position discussed in Chapter 1. For Glasser, perceptions of reality, rather than reality itself, determine behavior—actions, thoughts, and feelings.

Needs

According to Glasser (1985), we develop pictures in our heads to satisfy innate needs. As needs are met, pictures are stored of people, objects, or events that satisfy us. The pictures are stored in what Glasser refers to as the quality world. Glasser (1985, p. 21) estimates that 80% or more of the perceptions that are stored are visual, which is why he refers to them as pictures. The pictures do not have to be rational. For example, an anorectic woman may have a picture of herself as fat, while friends and family see her as emaciated. Alcoholics may view their use of alcohol in pictures in which alcohol satisfies needs. For alcoholics to change, they must change the picture about their drinking from a constructive event to a destructive event. In marriages, couples need to find ways to make their pictures of events compatible. If they cannot, they should be able to tolerate or compromise with the spouse's pictures. The quality world, where the pictures are stored, is the world that we live in where our desires are satisfied. Glasser (1990b) also refers to this as the all-we-want world. It contains our expectations, our core beliefs, and our opportunities to fulfill our needs.

Glasser (1985) describes four basic psychological needs that are essential for human beings: belonging, power, freedom, and fun. The need for belonging includes the need to love, to share, and to cooperate. This need is met by friends, family, pets, plants, or objects such as a stamp collection or antique cars. The need for power and to be better than others often conflicts with our need for belonging. For example, our need to be powerful in a marriage conflicts with the need to be loved by one's spouse. Glasser (1985, 1998) believes that it is not insufficient love that destroys relationships, but the power struggle, the inability of husbands and wives to give up their power and negotiate compromises. The need for freedom refers to how we wish to live our lives, how we wish to express ourselves, whom we wish to associate with, what we wish to read or write, how we wish to worship, and other areas of human experience. In a totalitarian society, the dictator's need for power conflicts with individuals' need for freedom and choice. If an individual has a need for freedom that is so strong that she has no significant relationships with others, then the need for belongingness is not met and the individual is likely to feel lonely. Although the need for fun is not as strong a need as that for power, freedom, or belonging, it is still an important one. Fun may include laughing, joking, sports activities, reading, collecting, and many other areas of one's life. All of these needs (belonging, power, freedom, fun), as well as the need for survival, are met through our perceptions, our pictures in our heads.

Choice

When describing psychological problems, Glasser does not use adjectives such as depressed, angry, anxious, or panicky. Rather, he uses the verb form of these words to emphasize action and the choice implied in taking the action: depressing, angering, anxietying, phobicing, and so forth. People do not become miserable or sad; rather, they choose to be miserable or to be sad. In Glasser's view, a feeling of sadness may occur immediately after an event. For example, if a friend dies, we may feel sad or depressed. After a brief period of time, we choose to depress, that is, to maintain the feeling of depression. Glasser believes that when people say, "I am choosing to depress" rather than "I am depressed," they are less likely to choose to depress and therefore less likely to feel depressed.

Behavior

Glasser defines behavior as "all we know how to do, think, and feel" (Glasser, 1985, p. 88). For Glasser, the behavioral system has two parts: The first contains organized behaviors that we are familiar with. The second part is constantly being reorganized. It is the creative component of behavior. As new pictures and perceptions arise, there is often a need for the reorganization of behaviors. As Glasser (1985, p. 90) states, "Driven by our ever-present needs, we require a large supply of behaviors to deal with ourselves and the world around us." The creativity may range from something very positive, such as a contribution to art or music, to something quite negative, such as suicide or bulimia.

Four components make up "total behavior": doing, thinking, feeling, and physiology. *Doing* refers to active behavior such as walking, talking, or moving in some way. Behaviors may be voluntary or involuntary. For example, when I read a book, I may without thinking about it adjust my sitting position to get more light. *Thinking* includes both voluntary or involuntary thoughts, including daydreams and night dreams. *Feelings* include happiness, satisfaction, dismay, and many others that may be pleasurable or painful. *Physiology* refers to both voluntary and involuntary bodily mechanisms, such as sweating and urinating. These four components are important in understanding Glasser's view of human behavior.

Glasser (1990a) uses a diagram of a car, Figure 11.1, to show how humans behave. In this analogy, the individual's basic needs (belonging, power, freedom, fun, and survival) make up the engine. The vehicle is steered by the individual's wants. The rear wheels are feelings and physiology. These are not steered, and we have less control over feelings and physiology than we do over the front wheels (doing and thinking). Doing and thinking direct our behavior just as the front wheels of a car determine its direction. According to choice theory, it is difficult to directly change our feelings or physiology (the rear wheels) separately from our doing or thinking (the front wheels). However, we are able to change what we do or think in spite of how we feel. For Glasser, the key to changing behavior lies in choosing to change our doing and thinking, which will change our emotional and physiological reactions.

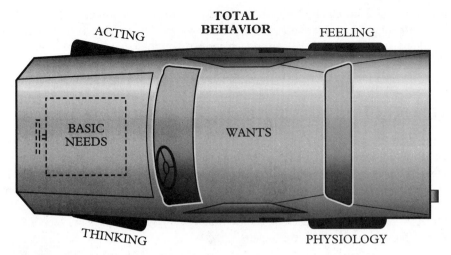

FIGURE 11.1 The Reality Therapy Car.
The Reality Therapy Car is reprinted by permission of The William Glasser Institute, Chatsworth, CA.

Choosing Behavior

If we have control over our behavior, why would we choose behavior that makes us miserable? Glasser (1985) gives four reasons why individuals may choose to depress, to be anxious, or to be otherwise psychologically miserable. First, by choosing to depress or to anxietize, individuals can keep their angering under control. More control and power over others is gained by depressing than by angering. Angering can lead to violence and prison, whereas choosing to depress does not. Second, people may choose to depress or to anxietize in order to get others to help them. This helps meet the need for belonging, and sometimes for power. As Glasser says (1998, p. 81), "Depressing is a way we ask for help without begging. It is probably the most powerful help-me information we can give to another person." Third, individuals may choose pain and misery to excuse their unwillingness to do something more effective. It is often difficult to choose pictures that will lead to effective behavior. If a man has chosen to depress because he has been fired from a job, it is easier to choose to avoid searching for a job and to choose to feel fearful than it is to make the effort to find a new job. Fourth, choosing to depress or to anxietize can help individuals gain powerful control over others. When an individual chooses to depress, others must do things for that person—offer comfort, encourage the person, look after the person, and perhaps provide food and housing. These four reasons explain why it is not an easy task for a therapist to help a client to change from choosing to depress or to anxietize to more effective behaviors.

Just as it would seem difficult at first glance to understand why individuals would choose to depress or to anxietize, it is difficult to understand why they would choose to act "crazy." Glasser (1985, p. 98) views "crazy" behavior as a type of creativity that those of us who are "sane" would not do in a similar situation. For Glasser, hallucinations, delusions, and anorectic behavior are creative. People choose such "crazy" behavior if they are desperate enough because it gives them some control over their lives. Glasser does not view "crazy" behavior as mental illness. For example, if someone chooses to kill a movie star, that is a creative "crazy" idea for which the individual is responsible and for which that person should be punished according to the law. The view of choice theory on the legal question of an insanity defense is that criminals should not be tried until they have enough control over their lives to stand trial. When they have that control, then they should take responsibility for their actions.

THEORY OF REALITY THERAPY

More than many other theories, reality therapy is specific in its goals and procedures. Goals of reality therapy emphasize fulfilling needs by taking control over choices in life. Assessment is integrated into reality therapy and is based on the principles of choice theory. The conduct of reality therapy requires both attention to the relationship and specific procedures to bring about change. In bringing about change, reality therapists utilize strategies such as questioning, being positive, and using humor, confrontation, and paradoxical techniques.

Goals of Reality Therapy

The general goal of reality therapy is to help individuals meet their psychological needs for belonging, power, freedom, and fun in responsible and satisfying ways. The counselor works with the client to assess how well these needs are being met and what changes should take place to meet these needs. For Glasser (1965), the more severe the symptom, the more the client has been unable to fulfill her needs. In helping individuals meet their needs, Glasser (1965, 1985) emphasizes that individuals must behave responsibly and that they must behave in such a way that they do not interfere with other individuals in pursuing their needs. In helping people meet their needs more effectively, reality therapy takes an educational approach. Unconscious processes and dreams play almost no role in reality therapy. The counselor ascertains how realistic the wants of the clients are and whether their behavior (doing, thinking, feeling, and physiology) is helping them realize their wants. The clients determine what they want; counselors do not determine the wants. Rather, clients are helped in assessing their total behaviors and their needs and in developing ways to meet them.

Assessment

An integral part of reality therapy, assessment takes place throughout the therapeutic process. Glasser does not directly address the issue of assessment; rather, he focuses on assessment as a means of producing change in client behavior. Reality therapists do not often use objective and projective tests. Rather, when they do use assessment, they use interview report forms or self-evaluation assessment forms, such as those developed by Hammel (1989) or a goal report form such as that developed by Geronilla (1989). Informal discussion or report forms can be used to assess client needs and wants, client pictures, total behaviors, or choices.

By asking clients what they want, counselors begin to establish goals of therapy and understand the motivation for therapy. Wubbolding (1988) suggests that if counselors continue to pursue client wants—what they "really want"—then counselors are uncovering needs that clients wish to fulfill (p. 33). In this way, counselors assess clients' needs for belonging, power, freedom, and fun. As these needs are met by satisfying wants, pictures will fit into the "picture album." Thus, needs are met by closing the gap between what clients want from the environment and what they perceive or picture that they are getting.

Total behaviors are also assessed by reality therapists. Although this can be done with a report form, the assessment of behaviors often takes place as clients talk about their physical feelings, emotional feelings, their thoughts, and what they are doing. For example, in working with a young man who was assigned to a maximum security unit within a prison, Corry (1989) described the behavioral choices that Everett was making within his correctional unit and how these behaviors were providing him with his wants—release from prison.

- **Doing**—Assaulting inmates over disagreements; attacking child molesters and rapists; confronting correctional officers—verbal defiance; making shanks (prison- made knives)
- **Thinking**—Hate, anger, bitterness, failure, fear
- **Feeling**—Powerless and defeated
- **Physiology**—Tense, agitated, on edge (Corry, 1989, p. 67)

Counseling with Everett included discussion of value judgments and his total behavior. He was able to state that none of his basic needs were being met by these behaviors. Corry continued to ask Everett what he really wanted. Corry and Everett chose to explore the need for fun. Everett was asked which pictures he had in his head to meet his need for fun. He talked about the desire to work out, read, and draw. He was able to make changes in his total behaviors that resulted in his move to a cell block that was less restrictive. After these changes, Corry made the following assessment of Everett's total behavior:

- **Doing**—Reading, drawing, working out, playing basketball
- **Thinking**—More positively, hopefully, skeptically
- **Feeling**—Less angry and defeated, a little successful
- **Physiology**—Less tense (Corry, 1989, p. 69)

In this example, the counselor continues to assess total behavior so that future changes can be planned and accurate evaluation can be achieved. In this difficult case, the counselor continued to integrate an assessment of total behavior into her counseling treatment. This integration of assessment and treatment is typical in reality therapy.

Another aspect of assessment is that of listening for choices. Because choice theory views behavior as a constant attempt to control perceptions, counselors view behavior as volitional, a choice to control. For example, if a client says, "I'm depressed because my girlfriend won't talk to me and doesn't want to see me," the counselor may hear, "I am choosing to depress now because my girlfriend doesn't want to see or talk to me." Depending on appropriateness, the counselor may choose to respond or not respond to the client's statement. However, reality therapists listen for choices and control that are implicit in clients' statements. A full working knowledge of choice theory helps the counselor determine which needs to meet first and which total behaviors to try to help the client change.

The Process of Reality Therapy

Glasser conceptualizes reality therapy as the cycle of counseling that is made up of the counseling environment and specific procedures that lead to change in behavior. Throughout counseling, a friendly relationship is established; in later phases the friendliness is combined with firmness. This relationship helps facilitate change through the application of specific procedures. Wubbolding (1991, 1996a) has taken Glasser's work and developed a more specific model that describes the counseling process. Called WDEP, it refers to W=wants, D=direction and doing, E=evaluation, and P=planning. Each of these refers to a cluster of activities that client and counselor engage in. This well-developed model is used in training reality therapists. To describe WDEP goes beyond the scope of this book. In general, its formulation is similar to Glasser's (1986b), but it gives more specific direction to the counselor.

In the following section, a description of the process of reality therapy provides a brief introduction to reality therapy. Wubbolding's four basic phases are indicated in parentheses.

Establish a friendly environment. The establishment of an environment that shows the concern and helpfulness of the counselor initiates the reality therapy process and continues throughout it.

Client wants, needs, and perceptions are explored. (W=wants)

The client's total behavior, especially the doing aspect of total behavior, is explored. (D=direction and doing) (E=evaluation)

Plans are made to improve the behavior. (P=planning)

A client's commitment to plans is obtained.

Friendly involvement.   Reality therapy begins with a counselor making a sincere effort to build a relationship with a client that will sustain itself through the length of treatment. Glasser (1972) feels that the counselor must show that he cares about the client and is willing to talk about anything that both client and counselor consider worth changing. As Bassin (1993, p. 4) states: "The reality therapist is warm, friendly, personal, optimistic, and honest." This attitude helps the client confide and trust in the counselor. In doing so, the client is able to meet a basic need for belonging (Glasser, 1981) that helps sustain the therapeutic relationship. As a part of this involvement, the counselor should be prepared to disclose information about himself when appropriate. Likewise, using the first-person pronouns *I* and *me* encourages involvement with the client (Bassin, 1993). Even at the beginning of the relationship, the counselor focuses on actions rather than feelings. However, the counselor listens to how clients feel about problems in their lives—that is a part of being involved with the client.

In his explanation of the process of reality therapy, Wubbolding (1988) describes in some detail suggestions for developing a friendly and involved relationship with the client. He speaks first of the importance of attending behaviors: sitting in an open, receptive position, maintaining appropriate eye contact, and occasionally paraphrasing the client. Important conditions for therapeutic relationships include courtesy, enthusiasm, and genuineness. For reality therapy to be successful, these should be coupled with determination that positive change can take place and that rules and responsibilities should be adhered to. Wubbolding does not see a contradiction between courtesy and enthusiasm, on one hand, and firmness and obeying rules and regulations, on the other. When clients break rules, as may often happen in settings such as schools, hospitals, and correctional facilities, the reality therapist does not judge or condemn the behavior, but views it as the clients' way of meeting their needs. At the beginning of the counseling relationship, when there is an appropriate opportunity to share information about the counselor to illustrate that the counselor, too, is vulnerable, then the therapist does so.

Friendly involvement and development of the relationship in counseling can be illustrated by describing Alan's counseling experience. Alan is a 20-year-old Chinese-American college student whose parents were born in Taiwan. He is attending a local university and is in his second semester of his sophomore year. He complains that he does not like his major and has few friends. The friends that he does have are from high school, rather than those he met at the university, as he has been living at home and driving home from school when his classes are over. He would like to date, but does not do so. He reports feeling generally depressed and unhappy.

In the first session of counseling, the therapist listens carefully to Alan. As he listens, the theme of being fearful and inactive arises several times.

Alan: I don't seem to be able to do anything. I'm stuck in the mud. I can't get out.

Counselor: Sounds like you want to get unstuck. Maybe we can get a tow truck to pull you out. I'm not a truck, but I can help you get unstuck.

Alan: You think things can get better?

Counselor: I do. There seem to be a lot of things that you want, and we can work together on how to get them.

The counselor uses some mild humor when talking to Alan. Further, the counselor shows his own involvement through his willingness to help the client get unstuck. The counselor's use of *I* is evident. The counselor mentally retains Alan's use of the metaphor "I'm stuck in the mud" for later work.

Toward the end of the first session, Alan puts his complaints in terms of wants, needs, and perceptions. He wants to find a career path that will be satisfying. He wants to have friends who he feels care for him and do not use him only for rides back and forth to the university. He wants to start dating and to feel more comfortable when he is with women. In terms of needs, he wants to feel a greater sense of belongingness through friendships and dating. He would like to feel more powerful in interactions with others and to initiate and maintain conversations with men and women. The counselor is aware that there seems to be little fun in Alan's life. When the counselor asks, "What would you be doing if you were living the way you wish?" Alan is able to describe his goals for the counselor, which include activities that he finds fun, such as sports. Besides talking about having good friendships and a career choice, he also talks about wanting to play tennis, swim, and work on cars. The counselor helps Alan explore his picture album to see if his wants are being met and then starts the process of helping Alan meet his needs.

Exploring total behavior.   As shown on page 420, total behavior consists of doing, thinking, feeling, and physiology. Reality therapists believe that change in one's life or control over one's life occurs through doing. In fact, this aspect of reality therapy is so important that the first book of case studies illustrating reality therapy was called *What Are You Doing?* (N. Glasser, 1980). Reality therapists want to know what clients are doing now. For example, if a client's parents were alcoholic, it may be helpful to examine how parental alcoholism has affected problems now. However, the focus is on choices that confront the adult children of alcoholics now, rather than blaming parents for past behavior. In determining "what clients are doing," it is helpful to ask specific questions: What happened? Who was there? When did it happen? What happened after you said this? These questions help clarify clients' pictures or perceptions of what they are doing. In future aspects of the reality therapy process, the counselor focuses on planning that involves doing behaviors that meet the needs of the client. This should bring about changes in the clients' pictures or perceptions, as well as feelings.

When Alan talked about what he was doing, his activities during the day followed a pattern. He described a recent day at school in the following way.

Alan: I leave home at about 8:30 and drive to school.

Counselor: Do you drive alone?

Alan: No. Yesterday I came in with Paul. I usually drive with him on Thursday.

Counselor: What do you do in the car?

Alan: We listen to the radio. We usually don't talk.

Counselor: And what do you do next?

Alan: I park the car and then I go to my sociology class, then my English class. Then I have lunch.

Counselor: Where do you eat and who do you have lunch with?

Alan: I usually eat over in the cafeteria near my English class. I always bring a bag lunch from home. I generally eat it in about 15 minutes, then I do some studying for my next class at 1:00.

The counselor hears what Alan is doing, with whom, where, and when. For Alan these are unsatisfactory behaviors because they do not meet his need for belongingness, power, or fun. The counselor continues to talk about other parts of Alan's life and to find out what he is doing. The theme of doing solitary behaviors continues throughout the discussion with the counselor.

Evaluating behavior.   Encapsulated in the word *evaluation* is the word *value*. Clients are asked to make value judgments about their behavior. By skillfully asking questions, counselors can help clients self-evaluate. It is the client who makes the value judgments, not the counselor. Sometimes clients evaluate their behavior casually or with little thought. It is helpful for the client and counselor to evaluate behavior thoroughly and to assess the consequences of the behavior. Wubbolding (1988, pp 50–56) suggests the following questions.[1]

Does your behavior help you or hurt you? For example, a high school student who has been disciplined for leaving class before the teacher has dismissed him might say, "My behavior helps me, I leave class when I want to so that I can smoke." By following this question up, the counselor can help the client assess whether the opportunity to smoke a cigarette is worth the consequences of the discipline involved in leaving class. This question helps clients assess the effectiveness of their actions in a variety of circumstances.

By *doing what you're doing, are you getting what you want?* This question helps clients specifically evaluate their behaviors and see if they are really worthwhile. It clarifies the previous question and makes it easier to evaluate behaviors. For example, by leaving class to smoke, the high school student may be getting only a little bit of what he wants.

Are you breaking the rules? This question helps clients examine their needs and wants in comparison with those of others. For rule breakers, this question makes them aware of what they are doing.

Are your wants realistic and attainable? Assessing the reality of wants can help clients determine whether to persist in a particular behavior. Returning to our example of the smoker, he may determine that it is not realistic for him to leave class whenever he wants to smoke.

How does it help to look at it like that? This gives clients a different way of viewing behavior. In our example, a smoker may view differently leaving class whenever he wants; it may also help him to look at his relationships with the teachers and administrators in the school.

Questions such as these help clients assess the effectiveness of their current behaviors. When asked by a counselor who has a genuine concern about the client, these questions can provoke a thoughtful interchange. They are questions that help clients take responsibility for their choices.

Alan's counselor helped him evaluate his behavior by asking some of these questions. Questions such as "Are you breaking rules?" do not apply to him, but other questions do.

Counselor: Is it helpful to you to eat lunch alone?

Alan: No, it isn't. I feel lonely and I guess I don't really enjoy the time at lunch.

Counselor: What is it that you're doing with your time?

Alan: I'm reading some articles for English. I think I could do something better.

Counselor: You're not getting what you want?

Alan: No. There are people I could talk with. I'd enjoy that more.

Making plans to do better.   When behavior has been evaluated, the next question is what to do about it (Bassin, 1993; Glasser, 1981; Wubbolding, 1988). Plans consist of doing specific behaviors that are often very detailed in nature. For example, if my plan is to get up at 5:30 tomorrow morning, I should know if I have an alarm clock, where I will put it, what time I will set it for, whom I will wake up if I get up that early, and so forth. Plans should fulfill a physiological or psychological need (belonging, power, freedom, and fun). When developing plans, they should be simple and attainable. Reality therapists assist clients in developing plans that are likely to be successful.

The responsibility for the plan should depend on the client, not someone else. A poor plan would be "I'll get up at 5 A.M. tomorrow if my brother wakes me up." I must have control over getting up at 5 A.M. Plans should also be positive in the sense of doing something rather than not doing something. Instead of saying, "I'm not going to smoke tomorrow," it would be better to say, "I will be working on three specific projects that I look forward to doing so that I can control my urge to smoke." Often an individual chooses repetitive plans. For example, the choice to exercise four times a week requires repetitive planning. If the exercise is enjoyable and does not depend on others to participate, the chances for its success are increased. Also, if I plan to exercise tomorrow, rather than in 2 weeks, my chances for successfully completing my exercise plan are improved.

In choosing a plan to meet his need for belongingness, Alan and his counselor developed several plans, one of which was to eat lunch with a friend on Mondays, Wednesdays, and Fridays before class. They discussed which friends to ask, where to meet each of the possible friends, and what to do if a friend was not available. Furthermore, they discussed what to talk about with the friend. When Alan became unsure of what to talk about with certain friends, he and the counselor role played specific examples of conversations that they might have. They talked about which friend to talk to about football, which to talk to about movies, and which to talk to about the election for governor. Plans were made for having lunch with someone in 2 days.

Commitment to plans. When making a commitment to a plan, it is important that the plan be feasible to carry out. Reality therapists may use a verbal or written contract to ensure commitment. An advantage of a written contract is that it makes clear what is going to be done. Also, it is helpful to talk about consequences if the plan is not carried out as agreed.

Alan and his counselor developed a written contract, specifying that Alan would contact Joe and Pedro and make plans for lunch. For many people, a contract sounds like an involved legal document. For the counselor and Alan, the contract was a few sentences on a piece of paper written toward the end of the counseling hour. They discussed consequences if Alan did not follow through on the plan. They decided, as a consequence, that Alan would drive Paul to school each day for a week, rather than share the driving as they had before.

Therapist Attitudes

The following are attitudes that counselors adopt when handling difficulties in exploring total behavior, evaluating the behavior, making plans, and committing to plans. These three aspects of the process reflect the realization of reality therapists that change requires effort and does not come without work.

The following attitudes taken by reality therapists add to the counseling environment:

No excuses for failure to follow through on plans are accepted.
The counselor does not criticize, argue with, or punish the client.
The counselor does not give up on the client, but persists.

Don't accept excuses.   As Wubbolding (1988) points out, to ask "Why?" is to invite excuses. Excuses should be ignored, and the counselor should go on to focus on carrying out other plans. Expressing confidence in clients that they will be able to make future changes is helpful. Discussing why they did not make the change they wanted to make will take the focus away from clients' control over their own lives. There are sometimes legitimate reasons why clients cannot follow through on plans. Most of these have to do with circumstances beyond the client's control. For example, Alan's plans to have lunch with friends does depend somewhat on his friends' behavior. If Joe does not meet Alan as planned, the counselor can comment that Alan followed through with his part of the plan as much as was possible and praise him for doing so. If Alan says, "I forgot to call Joe and make lunch plans," however, the counselor does not ask, "Why didn't you call him?" because that would be asking for excuses. Rather, the counselor talks about new plans for meeting friends for lunch.

No punishment or criticism.   If a client fails to follow through on a plan, the client receives the consequences. If a parolee violates parole, that individual is punished by the legal system. It is not appropriate for the counselor to criticize, punish, or argue with an individual who has not followed through on the procedures of reality therapy as it will damage the therapeutic relationship. In fact, a very important part of Glasser's view of education and therapy is that criticism is destructive to the entire educational and therapeutic process. Sometimes it is necessary to criticize, but it should be done sparingly and with a focus on the person's behavior rather than negative comments about the person. Glasser distinguishes between consequences for misbehavior and punishment that humiliates the person.

If Alan fails to meet with friends for lunch as he planned, it is helpful to examine what the consequences were for not completing his plans. Then the counselor and Alan can start again in reevaluating the plans and making new ones. Perhaps plans that involve meeting friends after class rather than lunch would be better. Later, with more success, Alan could make plans for lunch with friends.

Don't give up.   Change is not an easy process. For clients who have previously made ineffective choices to gain effective control over their choices is difficult. If the client is arrested for drunken driving, has an alcoholic binge, purges food, or otherwise reverts to ineffective behavior, the counselor must not give up on the client. The process of exploring behavior, evaluating it, making plans, and committing to plans is recycled, and the client and counselor reevaluate. When there is success, the reality therapist praises, encourages, or otherwise rewards the client.

The tasks that Alan had set for himself, with the help of his counselor, were reasonable. His problems were quite simple in contrast with those who are incarcerated or have drug or alcohol problems. He was able to develop several plans that led to his developing new friends at the university with whom he could play tennis and work on cars. Furthermore, he was introduced to women through mutual friends. He was able to feel comfortable in a dating situation. As he began to meet his needs for belonging, power, and fun, the necessity for planning dropped away. After 4 months of counseling once a week, he met twice more with the counselor every other week to talk about progress in his academic and social life. Because Alan was making good progress, the tone of the sessions was light. The atmosphere was friendly, sometimes sharing stories, sometimes receiving praise from the counselor for his success in meeting his goals.

The relative simplicity and easy success of Alan's case should not lead to the conclusion that reality therapy is simple or easy to employ. Techniques that reality therapists often use to help individuals to control their own behavior, particularly when the change process is difficult, are described in the next section.

Reality Therapy Strategies

Reality therapy is not a technique-focused psychotherapy system. In fact, Glasser (1965) believes that transcripts, tape recordings, and observing a series of sessions through a one-way mirror would be of relatively little help to new therapists in understanding reality therapy unless they have had previous experience with doing some form of psychotherapy. The relationship and the friendly involvement with the client that are required of reality therapists make it difficult to look at pieces of reality therapy. However, reality therapists do tend to use certain psychotherapeutic techniques more than others (Wubbolding & Brickell, 1998). The ones that are more commonly used are described here: questions, the importance of being positive, metaphors, humor, confrontation, and paradoxical intention.

Questioning. As can be seen from the discussion of the process of counseling on pages 424 to 428, questions play an important role in exploring total behavior, evaluating what people are doing, and making specific plans. Wubbolding (1988) suggests that questions can be useful to reality therapists in four ways: to enter the inner world of clients, to gather information, to give information, and to help clients take more effective control (pp. 162–164). When reality therapists help clients explore their wants, needs, and perceptions, they do so by asking clients what they want and follow the question with more questions to determine what they really want. They also ask clients what they are doing and what their plans are. These questions help the reality therapist understand the inner world (the wants, needs, and perceptions) of clients. Reality therapists often develop different ways of asking questions about the inner world of clients, so that the questions do not become repetitive or mechanical. When gathering information to explore total behavior or to help clients make plans, it is useful to ask specific questions such as "When did you leave the house?" "Where did you go?" "Did you carry out your plan?" and "How many stores did you visit?" Wubbolding (1988, p. 163) also believes that questions can give information in a subtle way.

For instance, in asking a client, "What do you want to do tonight to change your life for the better?" information is provided. There is an implicit message: "You have control over your life and an immediate plan can help you take even better charge of your life."

In this way, a message is delivered that helps clients focus on their own behavior, evaluate that behavior, and make plans. This use of questioning is related to the use of paradox, which is discussed on page 432. Last, questioning helps clients choose which perceptions to focus on, which behaviors to do, and how to evaluate them. Questions give clients choice and, through choice, control over how they are to change their lives. However, Wubbolding (1996b) cautions that therapists should not overuse questions, but integrate them with reflective and active listening, sharing of perceptions, and other statements.

Being positive.   The reality therapist focuses on what the client can do. Opportunities are taken to reinforce positive actions and constructive planning. Positive statements are made to statements of misery and complaint. For example, if a client says, "I am angry about what Mary said to me today," the reality therapist does not respond, "Has this been happening to you for a long time?" or "You're feeling angry that Mary doesn't treat you well." The reality therapist might respond, "What are you going to do so that you will not choose to anger at Mary?" The emphasis of the counselor's questions is on positive actions.

In *Positive Addiction,* Glasser (1976) discusses the potential strength that individuals have. A positive addiction is not easy to obtain but requires practice and repetition. The most common positive addictions are running and meditating. Glasser (1984, p. 229) says, "It [positive addiction] gives you easy access to your creativity. This in turn can provide you with a small, but still significant, amount of additional strength to help deal with any problems you may have in your life." People who have developed negative addictions such as drug, nicotine, or alcohol addiction may find positive addictions such as running, swimming, meditation, zen, yoga, or some combination to contribute to their creative process. Like a negative addiction, positive addictions bring discomfort to the individual if they are withdrawn. To develop a positive addiction, the activity must be noncompetitive; be accomplished with minimal mental effort; be done alone; have physical, mental, or spiritual value; and be done without self-criticism (Glasser, 1976, p. 93). For a small proportion of clients, the choice of a positive addiction may be a part of reality therapy.

Related to being positive are two other qualities (Wubbolding & Brickell, 1998): seeing everything as an advantage and communicating hope. Wubbolding and Brickell show how what could be seen negatively can be reframed positively. An ex-offender who had been fired from 9 jobs in 10 months was told that he was "very skilled at *locating* jobs" (p. 47). Reality therapists often work with ex-offenders, drug abusers, and others. To do so it is important to instill in clients the belief that there is hope for their future. They may do this, in part, by discussing choices and plans.

Metaphors.   Attending to and using the client's language can be helpful in communicating understanding to a client through use of her language (Wubbolding & Brickell, 1998). For example, if a client says, "When he left, it was like the roof fell on me," the therapist might say, "What does it feel like when the roof falls on your body?"

If the client says, "When I got an A on that math exam, the whole world seemed brighter," the therapist may respond, "What is it like in that light and sunshine?" In essence, the therapist is talking in a way that is congruent with the client's personal perceptions.

Humor.   Because of the friendly involvement that reality therapists try to develop with their clients, humor fits in rather naturally. Therapists sometimes have the opportunity to laugh at themselves, which encourages clients to do the same (Glasser & Zunin, 1979). This can take the pressure off client disappointment, if plans are not realized.

Because fun is a basic need, according to reality therapy, it can sometimes be met, to a small degree, in the therapy session itself. When the therapist and client can share a joke, there is an equalizing of power and a sharing of a need (fun). To the extent that humor can create a greater sense of friendly involvement, it also helps to meet the client's need for belongingness. Of course, humor cannot be forced. Some therapists may use humor rarely, others in one type of situation, and yet other therapists in another type.

Confrontation.   Because reality therapists do not accept client excuses and do not give up easily in their work, confrontation is inevitable. Helping clients to make plans and to commit to plans for behaviors that are difficult to change means that often plans are not carried out as desired. In confronting, the therapist can still be positive in dealing with client excuses. Not accepting them is a form of confrontation. The therapist does not criticize or argue with the client but rather continues to work to explore total behavior and to make effective plans.

Confrontation can occur in any aspect of reality therapy. To give an example, let us return to the case of Alan. If Alan were to say, "I didn't get around to meeting anyone after class this week. I guess it really doesn't matter to me," the reality therapist can confront this in several ways. One response would be "You've said before that it really does matter, that you're lonely, and you want to develop friendships. I think it really does matter to you." The counselor could also say, "Yes, I guess it doesn't matter to you. What does matter to you?" The purpose of the latter statement would be to get the client to confront his own excuses and choose to say that making plans to improve friendships is important. How one chooses to confront a client is a matter of personal style.

Paradoxical techniques.   In reality therapy, making plans and getting clients to commit to plans can generally be done directly. However, there are times when clients are resistant to carrying out plans they make. Paradoxical techniques are those that give contradictory instructions to the client (Wubbolding & Brickell, 1998). Positive change can result from following any of the options given by the therapist. For example, clients who are obsessively concerned with not making mistakes at work may be directed to make mistakes. If the client tries to make mistakes, as the therapist suggests, then the client has demonstrated control over the problem. If the client resists the counselor's suggestion, then the behavior is controlled and eliminated. Paradoxical techniques are both unexpected and difficult to use. Reading this section on paradoxical techniques makes it easy to understand why the practice of reality therapy can be complex and why Glasser believes that at least 2 years of training are needed to do reality therapy. In the following paragraphs, paradox within choice theory is explained, types of paradoxical interventions are illustrated, and warnings about the dangers of paradox are given.

By reexamining perceptions, needs, and total behavior in the context of choice theory, paradoxes implicit in choice theory can be illustrated. Individuals want to have control over their perceptions, see themselves as intelligent and successful, and so forth. Wanting a perception does not change it. Wanting to see someone as attractive rather than unattractive does not usually work. Paradoxically, the perception of someone's attractiveness may change if an individual becomes more familiar with and more friendly with that person. The behavior may change the perception more easily than the individual can change one perception to another. Also, there are paradoxes in fulfilling needs. Needs are often in conflict with one another. By supervising a friend who is fixing a car, an individual may sacrifice the need for belongingness for the need for power. Also, our needs (Glasser, 1981, 1990a) cannot be fulfilled directly; needs are met through our perceptions or pictures of our wants. Other paradoxes occur in our total behaviors. Individuals pay more attention to feeling and thinking in their everyday lives, but it is "doing" that brings about change (Wubbolding, 1988, p. 78). Feelings are changed not by talking about feelings but by doing or changing behaviors. If a person who depresses starts becoming active with others, the feeling of depression is likely to change.

Two types of paradox will be described below: reframing and prescriptions (Wubbolding & Brickell, 1998). These paradoxical instructions help clients feel that they are in control and that they choose their behavior. To choose to feel more depressed means that an individual can also choose to feel less depressed.

Reframing helps individuals to change the way they think about a topic. Reframing can help a client see a behavior that was previously undesirable as desirable.

> In counseling a young man whose hand was "frozen" into a fist (with no physiological basis), I suggested that he hold it up for all to see rather than hide it under his arm, as was his habit. We both laughed and were able to see humor in what had been only a "serious" problem for him. I suggested that he try to feel proud of his temporary handicap, and that if he hid it, no one would know when he overcame it. I asked, "Why not use it to show people you can conquer difficulties?" He was able to reframe the problem in a two-fold manner: from seriousness to humor; and from a shameful event to a positive, attention-getting tool. (Wubbolding, 1988, p. 83)

If a young man says that he is upset because a young woman refused his invitation to dinner, this can be reframed by commenting on the young man's strength in asking the woman out for dinner and for weathering rejection. Reframing helps individuals look at their behavior as a choice. This leads to a greater sense of control.

Paradoxical prescriptions refer to instructing the client to choose a symptom. For example, if a person is concerned about blushing, he can tell others how much he blushed and how often. If a person is choosing to depress, she can be told to schedule the depression—to depress at certain times. These instructions give individuals a means of controlling their behavior, an important aspect of control theory.

Paradoxical treatments are complex and can be confusing. Training and familiarity are essential before using them. Weeks and L'Abate (1982) have found that involvement and safety are key concepts in using paradoxical interventions. Such interventions should not be used with individuals who are dangerous (suicidal) or destructive (sociopathic). Confusing paradoxical instructions can make people who have paranoid ideation more suspicious and less trusting. Furthermore, they state that paradox should not be employed in crises, such as loss of a loved one, a job, or similar events. Although powerful and potentially dangerous, paradoxical interventions are illustrative of the creative approaches that reality therapists take to help their clients put more control in their lives.

PSYCHOLOGICAL DISORDERS

More than almost any other theorist, Glasser uses case examples throughout his writing to illustrate control theory and reality therapy. Two books, edited by his first wife, Naomi Glasser, *What Are You Doing?* (1980) and *Control Theory in the Practice of Reality Therapy* (1989), are the sources for most of the examples used in this section. In the latter book, William Glasser provides commentary on each of the case studies. Although the writing styles and personal backgrounds of the contributors are different, their adherence to reality principles is consistent.

These examples deal with eating disorders, drug abuse, depression, and anxiety disorders. For each case, the same systematic process of the aspects of reality therapy is used. However, control theory often offers differential explanation for the disorders.

Eating Disorders: Choosing to Starve and Purge

Glasser's (1989) view of eating disorders is that they are an addiction. For Glasser, "An addiction is a behavior we choose that we can do easily, that does not depend on others, and that consistently gives us immediate pleasure, or we believe will soon give us pleasure" (p. 301). However, those addicted to food (bulimics and anorectics) are unlike other addicts in that they cannot give up their addiction completely; otherwise, they will starve. What they must do, then, is to restrict their eating. By starving themselves, they may find that there is great pleasure in starvation or purging. Such behavior gives them control over their own lives so that they can defy their families and others they see as controlling them. Glasser states: "They do this by saying directly or indirectly 'very thin is right' and 'all you who want me to eat and be fat are wrong'" (p. 301). In the next case, Gloria has given up most of her eating-disordered behaviors and has stopped purging. However, she is still stomach-aching. For Glasser this eating disorder–related behavior, stomach-aching, accomplishes three things. First, the individual restrains the anger against others. Second, stomach-aching is an acceptable way to ask for help. Third, stomach-aching helps Gloria get out of situations she fears. In this conceptualization, Glasser is looking at eating-disordered behavior as a self-destructive and creative choice. In this case, Geronilla (1989) helps Gloria choose more effective behaviors to take control over her life.

Gloria is a 32-year-old single woman who is employed as an assistant to a state senator. She has a bachelor's degree in English and has previously worked as a journalist.

She has been able to stop most, but not all, eating disorder–related behaviors at this point. The focus of reality therapy with Gloria is on interpersonal matters: dating relationships and dealing with her boss, co-workers, and family. Another concern is Gloria's self-image. Gloria was seen for 18 sessions: The first 2 were a week apart, the others were 2 to 4 weeks apart. In the first session, Geronilla works on developing a relationship with Gloria. As soon as possible, she has the client share her wants and perceptions, so that they can discuss the client's needs. The following excerpt shows Geronilla's work with Gloria's perceptions and needs.

At first sessions I am willing to listen to symptoms so that I get a good idea of the function that they play in the client's life, but I try to keep this to a minimum. As soon as I can, I present a notebook entitled, "My Picture Album," which has each of the needs on a separate page in a clear plastic cover. I talk about the needs and I relate them to my own life. I have a picture of my family that I slide into the clear plastic cover to demonstrate how we move pictures into our internal album.

Therapist: Where do you get your loving/belonging need met?

Gloria: My parents are pretty good to me, but I need other relationships. I really don't have a bunch of close friends. I think the one friendship I have at work is destructive.

Therapist: How about anyone else at work?

Gloria: I work with married women who drive Mercedes or BMW's because their husbands make good money, and I drive a Honda. They even pointed it out at lunch the other day. I feel pressure to buy a more expensive car, even though I don't want to do that.

Therapist: Do you feel they are imposing their values on you?

Gloria: Yes. And I don't like it. I don't want to be like them, anyway. I have always been the type to carry my own weight and not count on someone supporting me.

Therapist: Sounds to me as if you don't get much of your love and belonging need met at work.

Gloria: You can say that again.

Therapist: Let's take a look at your other needs. How about power? Do people listen to you, give you approval, and put you in charge of doing things?

Gloria: That's pretty low, too. Not much at work at all.

Therapist: How about fun?

Gloria: Most of the things I do are by myself, like reading.

Therapist: Would you like to be more social in your fun?

Gloria: Yes. (Geronilla, 1989, pp. 260–261)[2]

Geronilla goes on to assess Gloria's needs and perceptions. She does not focus on the eating disorder itself. In the third session, Geronilla helps Gloria evaluate her behaviors. This excerpt illustrates how she does that.

Therapist: So what do you want to be? Get a picture in your head and describe that person to me. Let's go through the four wheels of the behavioral car. [See page 420 for an explanation.]

Gloria: I want to be open and approachable. I want to say "hello" to everyone I meet. I want to be patient and helpful, but know when to draw the line. I don't want to be taken advantage of in professional and business life. Someone people would both like to work around and socialize with. Just a pleasant person.

Therapist: Describe how that person thinks.

Gloria: That person believes that people are basically good. All people are on the same level. People that you deal with are appreciative of what you do for them. If people would take the time to get to know me, they would be appreciative of me.

Therapist: How would that person feel on the inside?

Gloria: Fulfilled and happy all the time. Nothing gnawing away.

Therapist: How would that person's body feel?

Gloria: Like calm water on a lake. No ripples. Smooth.

Therapist: Sounds like you have a good picture of the person you would like to be.

Gloria: Yes, I'm beginning to see what you mean: I can become the person I want to be if I try. (Geronilla, 1989, pp. 268–269)

In the fourth session Gloria and the therapist talk about owning behavior. They discuss ways of planning new behavior that will be more effective. The planning focuses on more effective behavior in dealing with Gloria's boss.

Therapist: Do you want to talk about owning your own behavior?

Gloria: Owning it? What do you mean?

Therapist: Things and/or people don't cause you to be upset. You cause this reaction.

Gloria: That's a lot of responsibility.

Therapist: Yes, that is a biggie! Do you want to be upset?

Gloria: No.

Therapist: Would you like to feel better about your boss?

Gloria: Yes.

Therapist: Let's look at one of the instances in which you upset yourself when he does something incompetent. What are some of the things you say to yourself that keep you upset?

Gloria: When I am listening to his speech, I say things like, "He is taking up all my time if only he weren't such a wimp!"

Therapist: What are you feeling?

Gloria: I'm mad at her [Bessie, a co-worker] for her misbehavior and at him for being incompetent.

Therapist: What are you doing?

Gloria: I am sitting there in a very closed position with my arms folded across my chest, while he is walking back and forth and looking at me instead of at her.

Therapist: How is your body when he is giving this speech?

Gloria: Uptight, and my stomach is slightly upset.

Therapist: What would you like to do to change the way you feel?

Gloria: I'd prefer to handle the whole situation myself. I'd tell Bessie off.

Therapist: Do you want to take over everything he is incompetent in doing?

Gloria: No. He is being paid a big salary. He should do it.

Therapist: What else could you do to get yourself less excited?

Gloria: I could imagine myself in his shoes and not wanting people to be angry with me.

Therapist: So it would be helpful if you could think about how other people feel instead of just about yourself?

Gloria: Yes. (Geronilla, 1989, pp. 271–273)

In this way, the therapist helps Gloria decide on and picture behaviors that will be more effective in dealing with her boss.

In the following dialogue from Session 6, Geronilla (1989) assists Gloria in planning to be more socially active. This excerpt also illustrates the involvement or self-disclosure that is common among reality therapists. Also, at the end of this excerpt Geronilla explicitly deals with the important reality therapy principle of not taking excuses from the client.

Gloria: I don't know, I'm really out of practice. I hate it. Going to my friends' is like going to a cocoon. They eat and vegetate all weekend. I went to a home interior party last week, and I thought going to that was a big deal. Boy, how I have deteriorated! It was a big deal; before, it was easier to stay home than get in my car and go. I'd like to be more social. There are a lot of social opportunities in the next several weeks that I should take advantage of.

Therapist: Do you want to take advantage of them?

Gloria: Yes.

Therapist: How can you make sure you get to them all?

Gloria: I don't know.

Therapist: Do you have a pocket calendar?

Gloria: Yes.

Therapist: Do you write down your social events in it?

Gloria: No, not usually.

Therapist: I don't know about you, but I tend to forget things unless I mark them down. I'm more likely to do it if I mark it down. It is easy to sit and vegetate. But the more things I can schedule, the more things I am likely to do. I remember when I used to force myself to go out for an hour a day.

Gloria: You were the anti-social type? (Shocked.)

Therapist: I wouldn't say I was totally anti-social, but I just wasn't the extrovert that I am today. I was never your cheerleading type in high school. It was in college that I decided that I wasn't going to meet "Mr. Right" in my room in the dorm. That's when I made up my mind to go out for at least an hour a day. It was a lot easier to stay in my room than go out. I found a schedule of social events and marked them down.

Gloria: I was O.K. in college. I always had a lot of friends. Why is this hitting me after 30? I guess I don't have the exposure to people that I used to.

Therapist: Exposure and proximity are important factors, but are we going to let them get in the way and be an excuse?

Gloria: No. That is a good idea. I'll start to mark them down. (Geronilla, 1989, p. 276)

In the 13th session the therapist comments that she wanted to focus on doing, rather than on the behaviors of feeling, thinking, or physiology. In this session the therapist praises Gloria for her commitment to her plans and reinforces the fact that Gloria is making changes for Gloria, not for the therapist.

Gloria: You confronted me last time, and I went home and ate. I upset myself because I wasn't doing the things I needed to do. I've been giving a lot of lip service. I really needed to think about if it was worth working for.

We talked about the two sides, the pleasure and the pain of almost everything. I told Gloria that I did not see her as she saw herself. Coincidentally, we had been at a party together at which she had been socializing well. I encouraged her to try to relax and be herself and not to worry about critical people, because she did not need them. She was making excellent progress, I thought.

Gloria: I had class on the weekend, but I interacted at every break and meal break. Monday I went out to eat with Joe. Tuesday I went to Nautilus and talked to guys there. Wednesday I went out for a drink with two guys from work. I initiated it. Thursday I made two calls and went to exercise. Saturday I took a friend to celebrate her birthday. Sunday I went out to friends' to see their new baby.

Therapist: How did you feel about everything you did?

Gloria: Good, real good.

Therapist: I think you did a fabulous job.

Gloria: I figured I should after the last session.

Therapist: Are you doing it for me or for you? If you're doing it for me, you missed the point. (Geronilla, 1989, p. 290)

At the end of therapy (the 18th session), Gloria brought the therapist a note titled, "WHAT DO I WANT?" In that note she included the following paragraphs that summarize Gloria's progress with her eating disorder.

I feel good about me. I feel like I have something I can grasp now. I don't know how I got to the place where I was when I was anorexic and bulimic. Somewhere I got the idea that thin was the answer to all my problems—it would fill my dance card and make me win friends and influence people. The funny thing was my social life came to a halt when I started doing the dieting thing. I couldn't believe it. I plan on staying out.

I know now that I have a technique to accomplish what I want to do with my life. If I don't do it, it will be my own fault. I never wanted to take responsibility for my own happiness before, but now I feel better that I am responsible for it. It is too important to leave in the hands of others. (Geronilla, 1989, p. 298)

This example illustrates how reality therapy can be used with an eating disorder. Throughout the therapy, the therapist emphasizes a friendly and involved relationship with the client. The therapist explores the wants, needs, and perceptions of the client and evaluates total behavior. An example is given of how specific plans for small situations are made.

The Choice to Abuse Drugs

Reality therapy has been used widely as a treatment for drug abuse. Glasser (1981, 1985) has used choice theory to explain addiction. Briefly, individuals usually are in control of their lives when they feel good. An important exception to this is the use of drugs. Drugs often give a quick burst of pleasure that may make individuals feel ecstatic but are an indication that their lives are very much out of control. In making use of Powers's control theory, Glasser (1985) describes the differential effect of opiates, marijuana, alcohol, and cocaine on individuals. Opiates such as heroin and morphine act on the control system to make individuals feel pleasure. Marijuana (and LSD) seems to act like a pleasure filter, making things that individuals perceive look or sound better. However, LSD does not always make things seem better; in fact, things can often appear quite frightening. Because of its unpredictability, LSD is rarely addictive. By contrast, alcohol gives individuals a powerful sense of control, when in fact they are out of control. Glasser (1985, p. 123) states: "This action is unique; no other drug acts to increase the sense of control that is actually being lost." Cocaine and, to a much lesser extent, caffeine and nicotine give individuals a sense of control in a different way. They energize the behavioral system so that individuals using cocaine can act as if they can do anything. Cigarettes and coffee, in a much milder way, also can give an individual a small feeling of energy. For example, many individuals feel better when they start their day with a cigarette or a cup of coffee. Thus, all of these drugs act in different ways to interfere with individuals' controlling their own lives.

Glasser singles out alcohol as being a particularly insidious drug. His view of how alcohol takes control over people's lives is informative.

I believe that alcohol will always be an integral, accepted, even glorified part of our culture, while other drugs will not, because alcohol is supportive of the cultural ideal—taking control of your life. The fact that alcohol is the single most destructive force in our culture that causes people to lose control is not recognized and will not be recognized, because of how it acts. The culture, or at least the culture presented by the mass media, sees it as a positive force, which it may be if it is used in delicate moderation.

Supported by the media, our culture rarely assumes that "real" men and women will not exceed the very fine line between enhancing and losing control. Alcohol is the get-things-done, take-control drug, and to deal with it well is a sign of strength and maturity. Because it enhances the sense of control, we welcome it instead of fearing it as we should. (Glasser, 1985, p. 132)

In treating alcoholism, Glasser (1981) says that counselors and others must be brutal enough to help the alcoholic see that something is wrong. He believes that Alcoholics Anonymous is particularly helpful, because members make individuals take responsibility for their alcoholism by standing up and admitting that they are alcoholics. Further, individuals must repeat the stupid things that they do while drunk. By doing so they are taking control and responsibility for their behaviors.

In treating Janet, a 16-year-old high school student, who had abused a wide variety of drugs, Abbott (1980) used the principles of reality therapy to help her give up drugs and later become a highly successful college student. He worked very hard to develop a good relationship with her, directly showing his concern and caring for her. The focus of treatment was not on drug use, but on her decision making and the responsibility for dealing with situations in her life that would be more successful. He would continually ask Janet, "Now that this has happened, what are you going to do?" If she was truant from school, he would ask her what she was going to do about graduation requirements. Her behavior was sporadic; she ran away from home on several occasions. Each time Abbott (1980, p. 270) would ask a version of the questions "Are you happy with the way your life is going now?" "What is happening as a result of your behavior?" and "Will it accomplish your goals in life?" Janet's behavior was unpredictable. Throughout, Abbott did not give up on Janet (an important reality therapy principle). Despite her many relapses, he was there to help her to take control of her life, and not to accept excuses from her.

The Choice to Depress

According to Glasser (1985, p. 48), individuals do not feel depressed; rather, they choose to depress, or they display depressing behavior. Getting involved in an active, doing behavior helps individuals change from depressing behaviors and feelings of misery to a feeling of greater control that is accompanied by more positive feelings, more positive thoughts, and greater physical comfort.

A brief example of a case of a depressed physician illustrates the application of choice theory and reality therapy to treating individuals who are choosing to depress. Rob had separated from his wife after 20 years of marriage. In all relationships except his medical practice, he was passive. In talking, he said very little. He was upset about the development of a physiological disease that might threaten his medical practice. Using the medical model, he wanted a prescription—to be told what to do to feel better.

In initiating the relationship with him, Hofhine (1989, p. 226) observed that Rob knew how to depress. She shared her interest in a variety of activities to show how to talk about needs and how to fulfill them. He wanted to marry again. Rob and the therapist made plans to increase and improve his social behaviors that might lead to such a goal. Feeling that their relationship seemed too serious, Hofhine tried to use humor to improve the relationship and help Rob examine his need for fun.

In commenting on Hofhine's work with Rob, Glasser (1989, p. 237) summarizes it as follows.

> She asked him to evaluate the choices that he had been making, and to his surprise, he found out that depressing was a choice, too. He caught on to control theory quickly. He learned about the needs, and he soon learned to evaluate the behaviors he was choosing to meet them and to make plans to change when he saw that what he was doing was not responsible.

> Rob's progress was systematic and quick. He was a capable person who very quickly became able to put control theory to work in his personal life. In about a year, he terminated counseling, his life in much more effective control than when he began.

The Choice to Anxietize

Choice theory provides a conceptualization of anxiety, similar to that of depression, which helps the reality therapist examine those aspects of an individual's life that are not under control. This conceptualization provides a way of examining behaviors and then developing plans to improve upon the behaviors. Glasser (1985) provides a summary of a person experiencing the physical symptoms of anxiety and interprets his symptoms by using choice theory.

> Randy was a highly intelligent college student, who, as an undergraduate made almost straight A's. He continued his success through the first year of the graduate school of business, but in his final year he became suddenly incapacitated with fear and anxietying. He chose to anxious so strongly that he could not sit through an entire class. If he forced himself to stay, he increased his anxietying to the point where he felt total panic, as if he were doomed to die immediately unless he left the room. His stomach became queasy, his hands sweated, heart pounded, his ears buzzed, and his mouth became so dry that he could not speak coherently. Although he was easily able to do "A" work on all assignments, he could not pass the course unless he took the final exam in class, so he was stymied. In his album he had the picture of becoming a highly successful business executive. In the real world he was suddenly a non-successful graduate student. The last thing he thought was that he was choosing what he was doing.

> Randy saw himself as excessively shy and unattractive, and believed that no matter how well he did in school, no one would hire him. If he succeeded in school, he would have to face the real world and possibly find out that he could never be the successful business executive of his album. But he enjoyed his academic success too much to drop out of school, so he took control by failing to go to class and anxietying if he went. Through these behaviors he gained painful control over his anger at not being attractive and gregarious. He was also able to ask for help with the school problems that his behavior was causing. When he learned through counseling to take more effective control, he finished school with honors. Maintaining this control and continuing to work very hard, in a few years he became vice-president of a very successful company. (Glasser, 1985, p. 64)

Using choice theory to conceptualize individuals' problems provides a consistent framework for reality therapists. Although the disorders described are different, the choice theory approach, whether it be to drug abuse or eating disorders, examines ways in which individuals can maintain control over their environment. Methods for bringing about change—be they direct plans or paradoxical techniques—are means of changing thoughts and feelings by developing and following through with a plan of action.

CURRENT TRENDS

Since Glasser coined the term *reality therapy* in 1962 (O'Donnell, 1987), the popularity of reality therapy has grown rapidly. In 1967 the Institute for Reality Therapy was founded in Los Angeles, and in 1968 a special branch for training teachers in the use of reality therapy, the Educators' Training Center, was started. In 1977 the Institute for Reality Therapy (now known as the William Glasser Institute) began to certify reality therapists. Currently, more than 2500 people are certified to use reality therapy. In 1981 the group of certified reality therapists had grown so large that an international organization was created; it has annual conventions in different cities. Nine different regions have been established, with each region represented on the board of directors of the institute. The important functions of the institute are to train and certify practitioners and instructors of reality therapy and to provide continuing education for current reality therapists.

To become certified in reality therapy, individuals must participate in a training program that lasts at least 18 months (Cockrum, 1989). The training includes a week of intensive training, followed by a 6-month supervised practicum. If recommended by the supervisor, the trainee may attend an advanced week of training. This is then followed up by another 6-month practicum period. The supervisor of this practicum may recommend the individual to be invited to certification week, where the trainee is asked to demonstrate and apply an understanding of control theory and reality therapy. Once certified, individuals are referred to as reality therapy certified (RTC) because many who are certified are not counselors or therapists and do not wish to violate state licensure or certification laws.

In 1987 Glasser developed a certification program for certified reality therapists so that they could become qualified as senior faculty. These instructors must have a 3-hour videotape on reality therapy and choice theory approved by Glasser and must pass a test showing their knowledge of these subjects. Certification of reality therapists and instructors allows Glasser to have a means of assuring that those who call themselves certified reality therapists can adequately perform the required skills.

USING REALITY THERAPY WITH OTHER THEORIES

The procedures that make up reality therapy are quite specific. Although there is latitude for using other procedures derived from a variety of theories of psychotherapy, techniques must fit within the reality therapy framework. Because reality therapy focuses on doing, techniques from behavior therapy are likely to be most compatible. Praise is important in reality therapy and comparable to the term *reinforcement* in behavior therapy. Role playing and modeling are other behavior therapy techniques that are consistent with methods used to help clients carry out plans in reality therapy. Although reality therapy is not a problem-solving approach, there are times when it is helpful to use behavioral problem-solving techniques with clients. The strategic therapy of Milton Erickson, which utilizes paradoxical techniques, is consistent with reality therapy (Palmatier, 1990), as is Paul Watzlowick's constructionist approach. The cognitive therapies such as those of Adler (Whitehouse, 1984) and Ellis's rational emotive behavior therapy (Sewall, 1982) have active components that can be used by reality therapists in their work. During the development of a friendly relationship with a client, some reality therapists have found the empathic listening approach of Carl Rogers to be helpful. Knowledge of a variety of theories helps reality therapists to augment their skills while adhering to reality therapy procedures.

Those who are not reality therapists may find the principles of choice theory and reality therapy to be useful. The notion that clients have control over their behavior—that they choose solutions, ineffective though they may be, to problems—can be a useful concept for eclectic therapists. By thinking of clients as having control over their lives, counselors can develop strategies that can provide constructive change. The idea of planning and committing to plans is consistent with a variety of cognitive and behavioral treatments. Although the aspects of reality therapy that include "don't accept excuses," "don't criticize or argue," and "don't give up easily" are particularly appropriate to some of the difficult populations (juvenile and adult offenders and drug and alcohol abusers) that reality therapists encounter, such advice is consistent with many theoretical approaches.

RESEARCH

Research has not been a major focus of Glasser's work with choice theory and reality therapy. Rather, he has focused on doing—implementing reality therapy in human services and educational institutions. He has said, "Evaluations of effectiveness of treatment are generally not considered to be meaningful" (Glasser & Zunin, 1979). Rather, he has pointed to clear changes that have occurred in his work at the Ventura School for Girls that significantly reduced the recidivism rate. He has also pointed to the significant changes that Harrington made in the release rates of hospitalized patients at a veterans hospital in Los Angeles. The case studies edited by his first wife (N. Glasser, 1980, 1989) illustrate, for him, the effectiveness of reality therapy with a large variety of psychological problems.

Typical of the educational studies are those that compare reality therapy with another treatment with elementary, junior high, high school, or college students. In a study in Korea, a small sample (11) of middle school girls responded positively to reality group counseling compared with a control group of 12 students (Kim & Hwang, 1996). Improvements were found in locus of control, motivation for achievement, and discipline. Abbott (1983) found no significant differences on psychological measures when comparing a group of junior high school students who had received counseling based upon reality therapy with students assigned to a study skills unit. Studying the effect of reality therapy on a diverse population of 25 seventh-grade students, Edens and Smyrl (1994) divided the students into groups of three. The authors reported a marked decline in the number of disruptive behavioral incidents. Talbert (1984) studied the effectiveness of reality therapy training of peer counselors on students who participated in a peer counseling program. Results indicate that students' self-concepts improved. However, no comparison was made with another treatment method. In a study in Taiwan, 217 undergraduate students were divided into three groups. One received 8 weeks of group reality therapy, another 8 weeks of classes on choice theory, and a third no treatment (control group). Both the therapy and teaching groups had significant positive effects on the locus of control and self-concept of the students compared with the control group (Peterson, Chang, & Collins, 1997, 1998). These studies show some of the ways that researchers have investigated the effectiveness of reality therapy in an educational setting.

Few studies show the effectiveness of reality therapy itself. One study, Crowley (1974), did attempt to compare the effectiveness of client-centered therapy with reality therapy. No significant differences were found across a variety of psychological and social measures. In a study of 23 females and 22 males who participated in a 21-session program for domestic violence based on reality therapy concepts and reality therapy for the families, there was very little or no reported violence for female offenders (Rachor, 1995). Ingram and Hinkle (1990) used an N of 1, an intensive research design, to study a college student's choice to use depressing behavior less often over the course of eight sessions of therapy. In studying basic needs, Peterson and Woodward (1992) found that reality therapy trainees perceived basic needs as more in competition with each other than complementary to each other. They also saw the basic needs (belonging, power, freedom, and fun) as being more separate from each other than related to each other. Peterson, Woodward, and Kissko (1991) have compared the relative importance of the four basic needs of graduate students versus trainees taking a basic week of reality therapy training. Similar research with emphasis on intensive research designs, even though studies may be limited to one person, and research on aspects of choice theory or reality therapy (such as research on needs) would seem to be a useful direction for the development of research on reality therapy.

Although some research on reality therapy is published in the *Journal of Reality Therapy* and reality therapy is the subject of some doctoral dissertations, the amount of research is quite limited. Because Glasser's approach is pragmatic and oriented toward helping others in the educational and social service systems bring about change, research has not been a priority. Furthermore, the training of certified reality therapists does not include research training.

GENDER ISSUES

In reality therapy, clients present those parts of their lives that are out of control to counselors. Reality therapists help their clients explore how satisfying their current behavior is to others and to themselves. Ideally, this is done irrespective of gender. The counselor does not decide what should be changed. In reality therapy, both men and women learn that they have the power to control their own lives. Historically, it can be argued that this issue has been a greater concern for women than for men.

Depending on one's viewpoint, reality therapy can be seen as enhancing the power of women to control their lives or thwarting them in trying to attain control. In working with battered women, Whipple (1985) states that abused women are not able to meet their needs for belonging, power, freedom, and fun and that their survival needs are threatened. Whipple (1985) shows how the procedures that make up reality therapy can be applied to battered women in helping them meet their basic needs. From a feminist therapy perspective, Ballou (1984) points out that in holding individuals responsible for their behavior, historical and social discrimination is ignored. Furthermore, reality therapy, like other therapies, has neglected the need for social change and for reducing sexism in women's environment. Although the feminist therapy point of view is critical of reality therapy for not focusing on external events, there are areas of agreement between feminist therapy and reality therapy. Both emphasize the therapeutic relationship and the importance of accepting, but not agreeing with, the client's value system. It can also be argued that the fact that Glasser worked to improve school systems across the United States for both boys and girls is an indication of his interest in social change, although changing society is not directly incorporated into reality therapy.

Silverberg (1984) believes that reality therapy is a particularly appropriate treatment for men. He argues that historically men have been more reluctant than women to seek therapy, to explore feelings, and to make insights about their behavior. He believes that the emphasis that reality therapy gives to development of self-control, autonomy, and independence are particularly appealing to men. Further, the emphasis on specific behaviors and on productivity in sessions that have planning as a component would be appropriate for men whose outlook toward life is achievement oriented. Men who have a negative feeling toward examining their feelings and emotions may find reality therapy an attractive approach. Threadgall (1996) believes that reality therapy is appropriate for homosexual men and emphasizes the importance of commitment to therapy and to plans.

MULTICULTURAL ISSUES

Because of its emphasis on individuals' choices and control over their own lives, reality therapy can be seen both positively and negatively from a multicultural point of view. A criticism of reality therapy is that it does not take into account environmental forces such as discrimination and racism that affect people from different cultures. Because of discrimination and racism, individuals' attempts to make certain social and economic choices, such as friendships or employment interviews, can be limited. Nevertheless, reality therapists respect individual cultural differences. The reality therapist does not decide which behaviors the client should change. Thus, clients decide on the changes that they wish to make that are consistent with their own cultural values. Although cultures vary in how they view the basic needs of belonging, power, freedom, and fun, exploring these needs and individuals' wants and perceptions can apply across cultures. Discussing what clients are doing and what they would like to change is also consistent across most cultures. When making plans with clients, reality therapists consider not only the effect of the plan on individual clients but also how the plans will affect the people who are important to them as well as society as a whole. Although use of reality therapy with clients of different cultures can be helpful, it is still important for counselors to have knowledge of the cultures that they are working with.

Several writers have used reality therapy with a wide variety of cultures: African Americans, Mexican Americans, Khmer refugees, Yugoslavians, and students living in Saudi Arabia and Hong Kong. Mickel (1991) states that reality therapy can be used in a manner consistent with an approach that represents traditional African-centered cultural values. Okonji, Osokie, and Pulos (1996) report that a sample of 120 African American Job Corps students preferred reality therapy to person-centered counseling after watching simulated counseling sessions on video. In comparing the effectiveness of class meetings using a reality therapy–based approach versus traditional class meetings, Slowick, Omizo, and Hammett (1984) found that Mexican American adolescents had higher scores than a control group on variables such as academic interest, leadership, and initiative. In her work with Khmer refugees from Cambodia, Rosser (1986) found that a reality therapy approach was consistent with the Cambodian coping style, which emphasized the present rather than the past. Khmer refugees did not find it helpful to discuss the horrors of their past experience in Cambodia. Working with delinquents in a correctional institution in Yugoslavia, Lojk (1986) has found reality therapy to be of value. In Saudi Arabia, Malki (1988) has used reality therapy as a way of motivating underachieving high school students, and in Hong Kong, Yau (1979) used reality therapy as a basis for training high school counselors. For Latino populations cultural beliefs about Fatalism (Fatalismo) and religion can be integrated with choice and reality theory (Sanchez & Garriga, 1996). The variety of uses that reality therapy has had for people of different cultures should be encouraging for those wishing to adapt reality therapy to a specific cultural group.

COUPLES COUNSELING

Choice theory provides a means of conceptualizing a couple's relationship and the changes to be made to bring about a more effective relationship. Glasser (1998) devotes two chapters in *Choice Theory: A New Psychology of Personal Freedom* to couples issues. He emphasizes the importance of relationships to successful living. He discusses the importance of negotiating differences. Assessing one's needs for belonging, power, freedom, and fun and using these assessments to make decisions about varied aspects of married life are a focus consistent with choice and reality theory.

Wubbolding (1988) describes the relationship between couples as being founded on feeling components that include physical and emotional attraction. As the relationship continues, there must be a commonality, not only of feelings but also of doing and thinking. Having shared wants and values is important, as shared feelings cannot sustain a relationship over a long period of time. A satisfactory relationship includes considerable overlap between the perceptions of both members of the couple. Problems exist when couples want to do things that are very different from each other and value different religions, cultures, political parties, leisure activities, and so forth. Related to this, couples should share a commonality of doing and thinking. If they want to purchase a car, both should agree that money should be saved for this purpose, and both should then follow through by actually saving money to purchase the car. Wubbolding (1988) suggests that couples list items that they perceive as being relevant in their lives and indicate the degree to which these perceptions are valued by each member of the couple.

Wubbolding (1988, p. 97) states: "A strong relationship is not only the result of commonality, but also of negotiating the differences, resolving power struggles, and arriving at satisfactory—though often imperfect—solutions." Hallock (1988) describes a way of understanding negotiating styles of couples in conflict by examining five categories of conflict behavior: avoidance, accommodation, competition, compromise, and collaboration. Avoiding puts off a conflict, as does accommodating. In both cases an individual's needs are not likely to be met. Competing means that one person's needs are met, and the other's are not. In compromising, both members of the couple may have some needs met, but both may have other needs unmet. Hallock (1988) discusses the importance of collaborating, so that the pictures of both members of the couple can be reorganized to be more harmonious with each other. In that way, the needs of both partners are more likely to be met. This is consistent with Glasser's (1985) approach to conflict, which states that individuals are trying to control their lives in a way that satisfies their own needs without interfering with others who are trying to meet their own needs. Hallock (1988) believes that learning reflective listening, learning assertiveness, and learning how to collaborate are important reality therapy techniques for couples counseling.

These active approaches to couples counseling often require between 6 and 12 sessions, although sometimes the work is shorter or longer. Although reality therapists approach couples counseling in a variety of ways, most have couples examine the commonality of their perceptions and work to increase their commonality. They may also examine how each member's needs are being met and plan ways that other needs can be met.

FAMILY COUNSELING

Using the principles of choice theory, reality therapists apply a variety of approaches to work with families. Ford (1983) describes a method that he uses in conceptualizing family problems and intervening with family members. Similar to approaches with couples, Ford looks for commonalities in the perceptions of family members. Because criticism can be so destructive to relationships within the family, Ford sees family members separately if they become too critical. To make progress with a family, each member must be able to negotiate with each of the others and be able to make value judgments and plans that each can carry out. While looking for ways to promote family harmony, Ford also tries to assess ways in which individuals can develop their lives separately from other members of the family. When working with children, Ford assesses their wants and areas in which their needs are being met. For example, what activities does the child enjoy? How much of this activity is the child doing? Ford also assesses how family relationships are filling needs of the child. Determining which parent the child is closest to and spends the most time with is valuable. This emphasis on doing is an important aspect of the reality therapy approach to families.

Ford (1983) describes four criteria for assessing what families are doing. First, family members should be aware of the others when they are doing an activity. If two family members are throwing a ball, each should be conscious of the other person's presence, not just that they are throwing a ball. Second, doing an activity should involve effort, whether physical or mental. Thus, walking together is a better activity than watching television together. Third, each member of the family should spend time with each other family member. Children can build confidence by spending time alone with a parent. Fourth, these activities should occur regularly, if possible, every day. Family therapists who practice reality therapy develop commonalities of family members' pictures and wants. They focus on the activities that the family does as a group, as small groups, and separately.

This brief dialogue from a case in which a therapist was working with an adolescent, her parents, and her younger brother illustrates the reality therapy emphasis on doing. In this example, the therapist received a call from the adolescent's mother. Although the argument was over chewing gum that her brother had taken, it was another example of Patti's not getting along with her brother. In this phone conversation the therapist helps Patti take control over this very recent episode in her life.

Therapist: Patti, what are you doing?

Patti: My brother's being a jerk.

Therapist: What are you doing?

Patti: I told my mother I didn't take anything. I just wanted them to leave me alone.

Therapist: It sounds as if you're acting really angry and excited.

Patti: Every time anything happens I get blamed.

Therapist: Are you willing to calm down and do something else?

Patti: I am calm. I'm perfectly fine.

Therapist: Well, you didn't sound calm when I heard you screaming and cursing in the background! First of all, think about your thoughts about your brother and getting jealous of him. Second, tell me what you can do instead of acting crazy.

Patti: I'm going to call [a friend] and meet her at the park.

Therapist: What will you do when you get back home?

Patti: I'll just leave Michael alone.

Therapist: Can you figure out a different way to deal with your anger next time?

Patti: I could ignore the whole thing or talk to them.

Therapist: You could call me, too.

Patti: Yes.

Therapist: Remember, you've been doing just great. You've proved that you can control yourself and choose reasonable ways to settle these things. Think about all our discussions before you decide to blow up. We'll meet together soon.

Patti: O.K. (Zeeman, 1989, pp. 26–27)[3]

The therapist has helped Patti plan ways to deal with her anger, if it happens again. He also tells her to use her thinking process before choosing to anger. Patti is praised for previous times that she has exercised control.

GROUP COUNSELING

Commonly used in junior high and high schools, reality therapy groups have also been used with parent groups, substance abusers, mentally limited adults, and incarcerated adolescents and adults. Although used with a great variety of groups, the same basic model that is applied to individual counseling is appropriate for groups. The emphasis on what group members are doing is key to reality therapy groups. Discussion of past behavior and excuses for current behavior are cut off by the group leader and by other participants. Plans are made by each group member, and the actual carrying out of these plans is followed up by the participants and leaders. Usually each participant takes a certain amount of group time; then the leader moves on to another member.

Bassin (1993) suggests that a group can be an excellent follow-up to individual reality therapy. Having some knowledge of reality therapy, an individual can help other members of the group in understanding principles of choice theory and reality therapy. Likewise, an individual can get suggestions and support from others when bringing in a problem to the group. Corey (2000) describes the use of group reality therapy in more detail, including the role and functions of the group leader, as well as the actual practice of reality therapy in groups.

A description of reality therapy groups with junior high school students (Dalbech, 1981) provides an example of how reality therapy can be used with students having problems in school, at home, or socially. These groups consisted of four students, three of whom were having trouble in their lives and the other who was getting along well in most areas of life. The reality therapy questions of "What are you doing?" "Is it working?" "What do you think you need to do to get things better?" and "Let's make a plan and then will you do it?" (Dalbech, 1981, p. 14) were frequently asked. Each student was given 15 minutes of group time to work on problems and plans. When making plans, other group members participated by asking questions such as "How did you manage to get along with your girlfriend?" or "Did you improve your grade in math?" Dalbech found that having peers ask questions such as these had more impact than if they were asked by the group leader. Although other reality therapy groups are usually run with more participants, this process is typical of procedures followed in reality therapy groups.

SUMMARY

Reality therapists help individuals control their own lives more effectively. Clients are helped to see choices where they thought they had none. For example, a depressed person is taught to understand that she is choosing depressing behavior. An integral part of reality therapy is the personality theory that it is based on—choice theory. Glasser has applied his theories to a wide variety of educational and human services settings.

Choice theory explains how and why people behave. The real world is distinguished from the perceived world, which forms the basis for determining the wants of individuals. Individuals develop pictures of what they want, which will meet, to varying degrees, the basic needs of belonging, power, freedom, and fun. Based on pictures of what they want, individuals behave. This behavior is referred to as total behavior, as it has four components: doing, thinking, feeling, and physiology. Although reality therapy deals with all of these, the focus is on changing doing.

Reality therapy can best be described as a cycle of counseling that intertwines the counseling environment or relationship with procedures that lead to change. Developing a friendly relationship with the client that shows that the therapist is interested starts at the beginning of therapy and continues throughout. The reality therapist uses procedures that will establish the wants, needs, and perceptions of the client. The clients' total behavior, with a focus on what they are doing, is examined in terms of the clients' needs and values. This is done so that the therapist can help clients design plans to change ineffective behavior. It is not enough to make plans; the therapist may contract with clients or otherwise get a commitment for clients to carry out the plans. As a part of the counseling environment or relationship, the therapist is friendly yet firm, not accepting excuses yet not criticizing or arguing with the client. Reality therapists often work with individuals with difficult problems, such as substance abuse, criminal behavior, or psychotic behavior. A precept of reality therapy is that the therapist does not give up on the client.

High school guidance counselors, alcohol and drug abuse counselors, social workers, and others working with juvenile or adult offenders have been attracted to Glasser's emphasis on responsibility and control. Glasser's concern about the educational system, discipline within the school, and school management has had an impact on thousands of teachers, guidance counselors, and school administrators. Workshops for counselors, teachers, and others have been designed to apply principles of choice theory and reality therapy.

Suggested Readings

GLASSER, W. (1998). *Choice theory: A new psychology of personal freedom.* New York: HarperCollins. • Glasser's most recent work replaces control theory with choice theory. He focuses on applications to marriage, family, school, and work.

GLASSER, W. (1965). *Reality therapy: A new approach to psychiatry.* New York: Harper & Row. • Although many of the concepts in this book have been modified, the basic principles of reality therapy still pertain. Glasser's writings include many case examples, making his work easy to read and understand.

GLASSER, N. (1989). *Control theory in the practice of reality therapy: Case studies.* New York: Harper & Row. • This book consists of cases that illustrate how control theory can be applied to reality therapy in helping individuals with a wide variety of problems. At the conclusion of each case study, William Glasser comments on the relevance of the case to control theory and reality therapy.

WUBBOLDING, R. E. (1988). *Using reality therapy.* New York: Harper & Row. • Focusing on the application of reality therapy, Wubbolding explains techniques such as the use of paradox, questioning, and ways to implement reality therapy. Applications to marriage and family counseling are also included.

WUBBOLDING, R. E. (1991). This book fully explains the WDEP system of reality therapy. Metaphors and analogies are used to explain choice theory and reality therapy.

References

ABBOTT, W. J. (1980). Banking on your interests. In N. Glasser (Ed.), *What are you doing?* (pp. 270–280). New York: Harper & Row.

ABBOTT, W. J. (1983). The effect of reality therapy–based group counseling on the self-esteem of learning disabled sixth, seventh, and eighth graders. *Dissertation Abstracts International, 45* (07A), 1989.

BALLOU, M. (1984). Thoughts on reality therapy from a feminist. *Journal of Reality Therapy, 4,* 28–32.

BASSIN, A. (1993). The reality therapy paradigm. *Journal of Reality Therapy, 12,* 3–13.

COCKRUM, J. R. (1989). Reality therapy: Interviews with Dr. William Glasser. *Psychology: A Journal of Human Behavior, 26,* 13–16.

COREY, G. (2000). *Theory and practice of group counseling* (6th ed.). Pacific Grove, CA: Brooks/Cole.

CORRY, M. A. (1989). Value judgments sometimes don't come easily. In N. Glasser (Ed.), *Control theory in the practice of reality therapy* (pp. 64–82). New York: Harper & Row.

CROWLEY, J. J. (1974). Reality versus client-centered group therapy with adolescent males. *Dissertation Abstracts International, 34* (13), 4657.

DALBECH, R. (1981). Reality therapy in school groups. *Journal of Reality Therapy, 1,* 14–15.

EDENS, R., & SMYRL, T. (1994). Reducing disruptive classroom behaviors in physical education. A pilot study. *Journal of Reality Therapy, 13,* 40–44.

FORD, E. E. (1983). Case examples of the application of reality therapy to family therapy. *Journal of Reality Therapy, 2,* 14–20.

GERONILLA, L. S. (1989). Starved for affection. In N. Glasser (Ed.), *Control theory in the practice of reality therapy* (pp. 255–304). New York: Harper & Row.

GLASSER, N. (Ed.). (1980). *What are you doing? How people are helped through reality therapy.* New York: Harper & Row.

GLASSER, N. (Ed.). (1989). *Control theory in the practice of reality therapy: Case studies.* New York: Harper & Row.

GLASSER, W. (1961). *Mental health or mental illness?* New York: Harper & Row.

GLASSER, W. (1965). *Reality therapy: A new approach to psychiatry.* New York: Harper & Row.

GLASSER, W. (1969). *Schools without failure.* New York: Harper & Row.

GLASSER, W. (1972). *The identity society.* New York: Harper & Row.

GLASSER, W. (1976). *Positive addiction.* New York: Harper & Row.

GLASSER, W. (1981). *Stations of the mind.* New York: Harper & Row.

GLASSER, W. (1984). *Take effective control of your life.* New York: Harper & Row.

GLASSER, W. (1985). *Control theory: A new explanation of how we control our lives.* New York: Harper & Row.

GLASSER, W. (1986a). *Control theory in the classroom.* New York: Harper & Row.

GLASSER, W. (1986b). *The control theory–reality therapy workbook.* Canoga Park, CA: Institute for Reality Therapy.

GLASSER, W. (1989). Control theory in the practice of reality therapy. In N. Glasser (Ed.), *Control theory in the practice of reality therapy: Case studies* (pp. 1–15). New York: Harper & Row.

GLASSER, W. (1990a). *The basic concepts of reality therapy* [chart]. Canoga Park, CA: Institute for Reality Therapy.

GLASSER, W. (1990b). *The quality school.* New York: Harper & Row.

GLASSER, W. (1998). *Choice theory: A new psychology of personal freedom.* New York: Harper-Collins.

GLASSER, W., & ZUNIN, L. M. (1979). Reality therapy. In R. Corsini (Ed.), *Current psychotherapies* (2nd ed., pp. 302–339). Itasca, IL: F. E. Peacock.

HALLOCK, S. (1988). An understanding of negotiation styles contributes to effective reality therapy for conflict resolutions with couples. *Journal of Reality Therapy, 8,* 7–12.

HAMMEL, B. (1989). So good at acting bad. In N. Glasser (Ed.), *Control theory in the practice of reality therapy* (pp. 205–223). New York: Harper & Row.

HOFHINE, G. (1989). Father and son learn together. In N. Glasser (Ed.), *Control theory in the practice of reality therapy* (pp. 224–238). New York: Harper & Row.

INGRAM, J. K., & HINKLE, J. S. (1990). Reality therapy and the scientist practitioner approach: A case study. *Journal of Reality Therapy, 10,* 54–58.

KIM, R. J., & HWANG, J. G. (1996). "Making the world I want"—Based on reality therapy. *Journal of Reality Therapy, 16,* 26–35.

LOJK, L. (1986). My experiences using reality therapy. *Journal of Reality Therapy, 5,* 28–35.

MALKI, H. K. (1988). Motivating underachieving high school students in Saudi Arabia. *Dissertation Abstracts International, 50* (07A), 1702.

MICKEL, E. (1991). Integrating the African-centered perspective with reality therapy/control theory. *Journal of Reality Therapy, 11,* 66–71.

O'DONNELL, D. J. (1987). History of the growth of the Institute for Reality Therapy. *Journal of Reality Therapy, 7,* 2–8.

OKONJI, J. M. A., OSOKIE, J. N., & PULOS, S. (1996). Preferred style and ethnicity of counselors by African American males. *Journal of Black Psychology, 22,* 329–339.

PALMATIER, L. L. (1990). Reality therapy and brief strategic interactional therapy. *Journal of Reality Therapy, 9,* 3–17.

PETERSON, A. V., CHANG, C., & COLLINS, P. L. (1997). The effects of reality therapy on locus of control among students in Asian universities. *Journal of Reality Therapy, 16,* 80–87.

PETERSON, A. V., CHANG, C., & COLLINS, P. L. (1998). The effects of reality therapy and choice theory training on self concept among Taiwanese university students. *International Journal for the Advancement of Counselling, 20,* 79–83.

PETERSON, A. V., & WOODWARD, G. D. (1992). Basic needs—competitive or complementary: A statistical study of psychological needs. *Journal of Reality Therapy, 11,* 41–45.

PETERSON, A. V., WOODWARD, G. D., & KISSKO, R. E. (1991). A comparison of basic week students and introduction to counseling graduate students on four basic need factors. *Journal of Reality Therapy, 11,* 31–37.

POWERS, W. M. (1973). *Behavior: The control of perception.* Hawthorne, NY: Aldine.

RACHOR, R. (1995). An evaluation of the First Step passages in domestic violence. *Journal of Reality Therapy, 14,* 29–36.

ROSSER, R. L. (1986). Reality therapy with the Khmer refugee resettled in the U.S. *Journal of Reality Therapy, 6,* 21–29.

SANCHEZ, W., & GARRIGA, O. (1996). Control theory, reality theory and cultural fatalism: Towards an integration. *Journal of Reality Therapy, 15,* 30–38.

SEWALL, K. S. (1982). A comparing and contrasting of reality therapy and rational emotive therapy. *Journal of Reality Therapy, 1,* 18–21.

SILVERBERG, R. A. (1984). Reality therapy with men: An action approach. *Journal of Reality Therapy, 3,* 27–31.

SLOWICK, C. A., OMIZO, M. M., & HAMMETT, V. L. (1984). The effects of reality therapy process on locus of control and self-concepts among Mexican-American adolescents. *Journal of Reality Therapy, 3,* 1–9.

TALBERT, J. A. (1984). The effect of peer counseling on the self-concept of high school students. *Dissertation Abstracts International, 45* (04A), 1043.

THREADGALL, R. A. (1996). Counselling homosexual men. *Journal of Reality Therapy, 15,* 39–43.

WEEKS, G. R., & L'ABATE, L. (1982). *Paradoxical psychotherapy: Theory and practice with individuals, couples, and families.* New York: Brunner/Mazel.

WHIPPLE, V. (1985). The use of reality therapy with battered women in domestic violence shelters. *Journal of Reality Therapy, 5,* 22–27.

WHITEHOUSE, D. G. (1984). Adlerian antecedents to reality therapy and control theory. *Journal of Reality Therapy, 3,* 10–14.

WUBBOLDING, R. E. (1988). *Using reality therapy.* New York: Harper & Row.

WUBBOLDING, R. E. (1991). *Understanding reality therapy.* New York: HarperCollins.

WUBBOLDING, R. E. (1996a). *Reality therapy training* (9th ed.). Cincinnati: Center for Reality Therapy.

WUBBOLDING, R. E. (1996b). Professional issues: The use of questions in reality therapy. *Journal of Reality Therapy, 16,* 122–127.

WUBBOLDING, R. E., & BRICKELL, J. (1998). Qualities of the reality therapist. *Journal of Reality Therapy, 18,* 47–49.

YAU, B. L. (1979). Design of a counselor training program for high school counselors in Hong Kong. *Dissertation Abstracts International, 41* (01A), 112.

ZEEMAN, R. D. (1989). From acting out to joining in. In N. Glasser (Ed.), *Control theory in the practice of reality therapy* (pp. 16–33). New York: Harper & Row.

12

Feminist Therapy

More than other theories of psychotherapy, feminist therapy examines not only psychological factors that lead to individuals' problems but also sociological influences, such as the impact of gender roles and multicultural background on individual development. Feminist therapists recognize the importance of the different ways that men and women develop throughout the life span, including differences in social and sexual adolescent development, child-raising practices, and work roles. Feminist theories of personality examine issues such as how men and women are similar and different in their moral decision making, the way they relate to others, and how they contribute to and confront abuse and violence. An issue of importance to feminist therapists is developing a social and cultural explanation for women's overrepresentation in certain psychological disorders, such as depression and eating problems. Interventions in feminist therapy deal with helping people understand the impact of gender roles and power differences in society and, in some cases, helping them make changes in social institutions that discriminate against or hurt them. Consistent with their emphasis on societal and group issues has been the evolution from the political feminist movement and consciousness-raising groups of the 1960s and 1970s to the current interest in working with people from many cultures and with groups such as families and women's therapy groups.

Before starting this chapter it will be helpful to define the terms *sex* and *gender*. *Sex* is used to distinguish females from males and refers to biological differences, whereas *gender* refers to socially determined thoughts, beliefs, and attitudes about men and women. The term *gender role* is used in this chapter to refer to those behaviors that are generally considered socially appropriate for females or for males. A major focus throughout this chapter is the impact of the social expectations of men's and women's roles on their psychological development and concerns. This focus recognizes the diverse cultural backgrounds of men and women.

GENDER AS A MULTICULTURAL ISSUE

Gender can be viewed broadly as a multicultural issue. Ethnicity and gender can be viewed as cultural issues along with language, religion, sexual orientation, age, and socioeconomic situations (Ivey, Ivey, & Simek-Morgan, 1997). All of these multicultural issues can be viewed from a sociological perspective. A theoretical approach to psychotherapy for one of these issues is likely to have much in common with an approach to another of these issues. Specifically, awareness of cultural values and the need for social action is likely to be a commonality.

Both therapists and clients differ as to their awareness of these issues. Ivey, Ivey, and Simek-Morgan (1997) present a broad five-stage approach to awareness of multicultural issues. These range from being naive or being unaware of the importance of cultural differences to integrating cultural awareness into a positive sense of self. Most work on stages of cultural awareness has been done in the area of racial awareness. Helms (1995) has described models of racial identity for blacks and for whites. Others have expanded this work for people of other racial identities. Typically, this approach has not been used for awareness of gender identity, although it could.

Feminist therapy has been more specific in its development of a personality theory and suggestions for therapeutic techniques than multicultural theories (those based on race or ethnicity). The main reason for this is that there are two sexes but many different cultural heritages. For example, Native Americans may come from a vast array of tribal heritages. Also, there are many differences among the many cultures in Asia. Adding to this, many individuals are multicultural and may speak more than one language. In fact, relatively few individuals in the United States have had all four grandparents who share very similar cultural backgrounds. Because of this complexity, one theory of multicultural psychotherapy that fits all cultures is difficult to develop. In that sense, the task of feminist therapists, focusing on only two sexes, is considerably easier. However, feminist therapists, particularly recently, have been very aware of the importance of racial and ethnic background in their development of approaches to helping clients.

Even though feminist therapists are primarily concerning themselves with two sexes, their approaches to understanding personality theory and suggesting techniques vary widely. However, feminist therapists have emphasized the importance of social action and empowering their clients. Many feminist therapists use techniques of power analysis and intervention, as well as assertiveness training, and other techniques to help their clients. These techniques can be applied to people from diverse ethnic and racial backgrounds. More than other psychotherapy theorists, feminist therapists address the issue of ethnic and racial background. In this chapter, the case examples that I present will illustrate more cultural diversity than in other chapters.

HISTORY OF FEMINIST THERAPY

Unlike other theories of psychotherapy that are discussed in this book, feminist therapy represents the work and effort of not just one or a few theorists but of many women from a variety of academic disciplines who shared the basic belief that women are valuable and that social change to benefit women is needed (Unger & Crawford, 1996). Acting on their observations of the social history of the treatment of women, both currently and in the past, feminists and feminist therapists worked together to bring about change, often in groups called *consciousness-raising (CR) groups*. They were also critical of psychotherapy, particularly psychoanalysis as it was practiced by male therapists on female patients. Feminist therapy developed as women combined their professional training with feminist values. Although all dealt with the impact of social forces on women, feminist therapists differed in the degree and manner in which they dealt with societal as well as personal change (Enns, 1997; Kaschak, 1981).

From a broad historical point of view, two themes can be observed throughout human history: the male as normative and feminine evil (Hyde, 1996). The male-as-normative theme occurs frequently in language. *Mankind, man,* and the pronoun *he* are used to refer to people in general, with women as a subset (Hyde, 1996). Throughout history, men are seen as making the rules that both men and women must follow. In history, women have most frequently achieved recognition as being the "wife of" or "mother of" the general, king, scientist, or world leader. From this vantage point, women follow the "norms;" they do not set them. When women occur in mythology, they often are portrayed as evil or devious (Hays, 1964). In the Bible, Adam and Eve had to leave the Garden of Eden because Eve ate an apple from the tree of knowledge. Because of this act, she became the source of original sin (Hyde, 1996). In Chinese mythology, the yin and yang refer to feminine and masculine characteristics. The yin (the feminine) is portrayed as the dark or evil side of nature (Hyde, 1996). Women were portrayed as evil or destructive not only in literature but also in actual history. Both in the Middle Ages and in early American history, women, much more often than men, were found guilty of witchcraft and viewed as being agents of the devil (Hays, 1964). General cultural stereotypes of women as a subset of men and as potentially destructive are views prevalent enough to have an indirect impact on therapists who treat women.

An early critic of the mental health system, Chesler (1972, 1997) has been, in many ways, responsible for having mental health practitioners reexamine their therapeutic relationships with women. In particular, she has been critical of the relationship between the female patient and the male therapist, which she describes as patriarchal; the therapist is the expert, and the woman submits to his wisdom (Enns, 1993). Chesler argued that women were misdiagnosed because they did not conform to gender role stereotypes of male therapists and thus received higher rates of treatment and hospitalization than were warranted. Furthermore, she pointed out the destructiveness of sexual relations between female patient and male therapist and the severe damage due to this unethical behavior. Her book *Women and Madness* (1972) gives many examples of sexism in psychotherapy and counseling. In an article 25 years later, Chesler (1997) describes gains and problems that still exist within the application of psychotherapy.

Feminist theorists have been particularly critical of gender-biased values and propositions inherent in psychoanalysis. Some female psychoanalysts such as Helen Deutsch (1944) added to orthodox Freudian psychoanalytic theory without challenging many of its basic principles. Others such as Karen Horney (1966) differed with Freud on several significant issues. As described in Chapter 2, she did not subscribe to the belief of penis envy. Rather, she promoted the idea of womb envy in men as representing an overcompensation for feeling inferior to women because of their ability to give birth. Furthermore, she suggested that it was not sexual energy that was the motivating force for women, but envy of men's power, because women lack power in comparison to men. More recent writers (Eichenbaum & Orbach, 1983) have tried to integrate psychoanalysis and feminist psychotherapy by criticizing sexist aspects of psychoanalysis. Chodorow (1989, 1996) has used an object relations perspective to provide insight into the differential development of males and females based on women's primary role in mothering and has also been critical of sexist aspects of Freudian psychoanalysis. Although other feminist writers such as Brown (1994) and Kaschak (1992) have been critical of several psychotherapeutic approaches, it has been psychoanalysis that has been most frequently subject to feminist criticism because of its comparatively more negative treatment of women than of men.

At the same time that female therapists were concerned about sexism in the practice of psychotherapy, women were voicing concerns about social and personal rights. Such organizations as the National Organization for Women provided an opportunity to deal with political issues, such as laws and hiring practices that unfairly discriminated against women. Consciousness-raising groups developed as a means to end isolation among women and to bring about social change (Enns, 1997). These groups served primarily an educational function to develop concern about the connection between personal and political issues and to bring about changes in the society of the United States. In the mid-1970s the focus of consciousness-raising groups started to shift from political and social to personal change, but it never lost sight of the interrelationship between social and personal concerns. Issues such as dealing with gender-role stereotyping in the workplace or in the greater society became topics of discussion (Kravetz, 1987). These groups promoted open discourse and were run without leaders. From the development and use of consciousness-raising groups, it was relatively easy to move into therapy groups in which there was a professional leader who would help women deal with internal and external personal issues. Equality of women within the consciousness-raising groups carried over to the role of the leader, who was expected to be open about her skills, her limitations, and her values, while providing direction and expertise for group members (Kaschak, 1976). A characteristic that all feminist therapy, whether individual or group, had in common was the feminist analysis of discrimination against women (Kaschak, 1981). In this way, women clients became aware of how their problems were similar to those of other women.

In describing characteristics of feminist and nonfeminist therapists, Enns (1997) distinguishes between radical and liberal feminist therapy as well as nonsexist therapy. Nonsexist therapy is distinguished from radical or liberal feminist therapy in that nonsexist therapy does not focus on social change, anger, or power issues but on the therapist's awareness of his or her own values and on an egalitarian approach when working with clients. However, radical and liberal feminist therapy have much in common, such as their emphasis on the political nature of the individual and the importance of changing social institutions. Both recognize the importance of anger as an appropriate response to social pressures and that psychopathology is a result of individual development and societal discrimination. Both support the examination of the difference in power between therapist and client and the use of self-disclosure in therapy.

Distinguishing between radical and liberal feminist therapists, Enns (1997) indicates that the difference is often in the degree to which social issues are participated in and challenged. For example, radical feminist therapists become involved in changing social issues, whereas liberal feminist therapists may or may not opt to do so. Also, therapist self-disclosure is necessary in radical feminist therapy to eliminate exploitation of the patient, but it may be used less often by liberal feminist therapists. In terms of the gender of therapists, radical feminist therapists are more likely to believe that men cannot be feminist therapists because they cannot serve as role models for women or validate their experience as women. However, men can be pro-feminist and can incorporate feminist values in their work. In contrast, liberal feminist therapists believe that men can be trained to work as feminist therapists. The distinction between radical and liberal feminist therapists is not always clear, and some feminist therapists prefer not to use labels for themselves. However, the way in which feminist therapists view the psychological and social development of women has significant impact on each therapist's approach to clients.

FEMINIST THEORIES OF PERSONALITY

Because the study of women's personality is relatively recent (most of it being done after 1970) and is the result of many investigators rather than one specific theorist, theoretical ideas for the most part have not accumulated clear and substantial research support. In this section I summarize some of the major gender differences between men and women in childhood, adolescence, and adulthood to provide a background from which to understand theoretical approaches to personality development. One such approach is gender schema theory, which examines the degree to which individuals use gender-related information to analyze the world around them. Also, many psychologists have studied the relative importance of interpersonal relationships for women and men. Carol Gilligan and Jean Baker Miller take different approaches in describing the development of women's personalities and the role of relationships in this development. These theoretical concepts provide insight as to how feminist therapists approach psychotherapy with their male and female clients.

Gender Differences and Similarities Across the Life Span

Research on gender-related characteristics is extensive, especially for children, but also includes research on many biological, psychological, and sociological or environmental factors. In discussing the study of gender, Hare-Mustin and Marecek (1988) describe two biases in the approach to gender: *Alpha bias* refers to separating women and men into two categories, which has the dangers of treating women as separate and unequal and of furthering male-female stereotypes. *Beta bias* treats men and women as identical and ignores real differences between the lives of women and the lives of men. Hare-Mustin and Marecek caution both researchers and therapists to be sensitive about exaggerating either differences or similarities between men and women. In this section, I focus on differences in the development of men and women, thus running the risk of alpha bias, overgeneralizing about differences. The information in this section is condensed from an extensive discussion of gender differences in Unger and Crawford (1996) and Hyde (1996).

Childhood. Even before birth, there are gender preferences for children. In reviewing the literature on this topic, Unger and Crawford (1996) show that men especially, but also women, from many cultures have a clear preference for a son rather than a daughter. This is particularly true in Asia, where selective abortion of female children is known. If one or both parents have a strong preference for a male child and a daughter is born, it is possible that these preferences may affect parental child-raising attitudes.

Compared with adolescent and adult development, there is generally more gender similarity among young children (Hyde, 1996). The behavior of male and female infants is quite similar. However, adults' treatment of infants shows gender differences. Adults select clothing and toys for young children, often based on gender role expectations. By the way that they and other children are dressed, play, and learn about life through stories and television, children begin to adopt different gender-role expectations.

In elementary school children, sex segregation is common. Boys play with boys and girls with girls, accounting for more separation than racial factors (Schofield, 1982). During these years there is pressure to unlearn behaviors associated with the opposite sex. In other words, girls may be taunted or teased for being a "tomboy" and boys called "sissy." In part, due to the devaluing of opposite-sex stereotype characteristics, friendships between boys and girls that may have been common at the age of 3 become increasingly uncommon at the age of 7 (Gottman & Parker, 1987). Interactions between parents, teachers, and other adults often encourage independence and efficacy in boys and nurturing and helplessness in girls (Unger & Crawford, 1996). Even though some parents may consciously choose not to impart gender-role expectations to their children, children communicate gender-role preferences through their preferences for play, toys, and stereotyped expectations based on gender, which can come from peers, television, movies, and so forth.

Adolescence.   Gender-role pressures tend to be more severe in adolescence than in any other period because of physiological and sociological factors. In general, puberty provides more conflict for girls than for boys because of the ways that society views the female body and the role of female sexuality (Unger & Crawford, 1996). For girls, the onset of menstruation (most commonly between the ages of 11 and 13) is sometimes responded to negatively by girls and/or their parents. Similarly, breast development, because it can be easily observed by others, may be the subject of embarrassment for girls and teasing by boys. Girls often become well aware of the need to be thin and to be seen as physically attractive. Although different peer groups (friends at church or synagogue, female athletes, close friends) may have slightly different expectations, exposure to expectations of women's appearance through magazines and television can have profound effects. Dating becomes an important factor in female personality development, with females being valued for their appearance whereas males are valued for achievements as well as appearance. Females often learn to compete against other girls for the attention of boys, whereas boys may be focused more broadly on academic and athletic accomplishments. Girls, not boys, must learn to regulate sexual activity. Use of contraception and the consequences of teenage pregnancy are usually a much greater problem for the adolescent girl than for the boy. With growing independence, conflicts between parents and teenage adolescents are frequently different for mother-daughter, mother-son, father-daughter, and father-son pairs (Unger & Crawford, 1996), as gender role stereotypes affect parental expectations. Although adolescent-parental relationships are important, it is the emphasis on the need to develop relationships (particularly with men) and thus to be valued for their appearance that carries over into women's experience in adulthood.

Adulthood.   Because there are so many variations in the ways that men and women deal with a complex array of issues, it is difficult to concisely describe women's or men's adult development. However, among the important issues that have a special impact on women, here I address mothering, work, midlife issues, and violence.

Motherhood includes not only biological changes but also changes in social roles. Not only do physiological changes occur due to pregnancy but also decisions about work, marital roles, and issues regarding physical self-image occur differently, depending upon a woman's social class, race, and sexual orientation. Adjustment depends upon a variety of factors, especially the relationship to the child and husband or partner. Married women who decide not to have children are often under considerable social pressure to do so. Controlling the decision to have children requires dealing with sexual issues such as contraception and possibly abortion. Women, more than men, are given the responsibility for raising children in American society and are likely to receive blame if children are not raised properly (Unger & Crawford, 1996).

Work is often quite different for married women than for married men. Although some men share in housework, women usually do most of it (Ferree, 1987). Housework includes not only physical management of the house, meal preparation, and laundry but also relating to others—taking care of a husband, children, and possibly aged parents. In their paid work, women make up 98% of the clerical and secretarial workforce, whereas men account for 92% of the engineers and 57% of managerial and professional positions (U.S. Department of Labor, 1994). Women are also likely to earn considerably less than men (Sharf, 1997). Although traditional women's professions such as teaching, social work, and health occupations have status because they require skill and dedication, their pay is lower than many high-status occupations in which men are predominant (Betz & Fitzgerald, 1987). Furthermore, in applying for a job and in the actual work itself, women are more likely than men to experience discrimination and sexual harassment (Sharf, 1997). Although legislation has brought changes in societal awareness of discrimination, attitudes and behaviors tend to be slower to change.

The aging process can be quite different for women than for men. A part of aging for women is menopause, which is often seen as being a time in which women change negatively in physical and psychological ways. Some women may feel devalued as their children leave home or their role in child care decreases significantly. To the extent that much of society values women in a relational or caring role, this change can be difficult. However, for some women it is an opportunity to achieve and be active. For women, insufficient income can be a particular problem. In summary, aging women are likely to be seen more negatively than men and to experience more financial hardship than men. However, the ability of aging women to develop friendships due to their involvement in nurturing activities is likely to help them deal effectively with children leaving home, the death of husbands, and other losses.

Although most women expect to be able to make decisions about issues of mothering, working, and aging in their lives, violence is very different, being perpetrated against women. Violence to women is much more common than violence to men, and it occurs at all age levels. For children, child abuse and incest can have terrible consequences for their later psychological development. In adolescence and adulthood, women may be victims of date rape, stranger rape, or wife battering (Hyde, 1996; Unger & Crawford, 1996). Statistics tend to underreport acts of violence because victims may fear being further victimized through physical intimidation or being blamed for provoking the incident. As Hyde points out, women can be viewed as strong for surviving and returning to a productive life rather than weak for being victimized.

In discussing women's development, I have mentioned only some major differential impacts of physiological changes and social attitudes on women. In putting forth a theory of personality development for women, feminist theorists have drawn on a variety of these life-span issues. People vary greatly in their response to perceived gender differences. Both men and women differ in terms of the degree to which they apply gender-role stereotyping to themselves and others. This variation in gender-role stereotyping is the essence of gender schema theory.

Gender Schema Theory

To understand gender schema theory, it is important to understand the cognitive psychology term *schema*. A *schema* is an organized set of mental associations used to interpret perceptions. For example, individuals viewing four 5-year-olds playing in the mud may use different schemas to describe the situation. One person may think, "Here are four kids having a great time"; another might think, "The smallest of the children is directing the play of the others." Another might think, "The two girls are getting mud all over their dresses. What will their mothers think?" The first example might be called a "play schema," the second a "leadership schema," and the third a "gender schema."

Gender schema theory tends to examine people in terms of how highly gender typed they are. Some people are more likely to view situations from a gender point of view than are others. Also some situations can be presented to fit into a gender schema. Hyde gives the following brain teaser. See if you can solve it.

> A father and his son were involved in a car accident in which the father was killed and the son was seriously injured. The father was pronounced dead at the scene of the accident and his body was taken to a local mortuary. The son was taken by ambulance to a hospital and was immediately wheeled into an operating room. A surgeon was called. Upon seeing the patient, the attending surgeon exclaimed, "Oh, my God, it's my son!"
>
> Can you explain this? (Keep in mind that the father that was killed in the accident was not a stepfather, nor is the attending physician the boy's stepfather.) (p. 55)[1]

For most of us, our gender schemas may make it difficult to realize that the surgeon is the boy's *mother*.

Sandra Bem (1981, 1987, 1993) has developed gender schema theory based in part on her work with androgyny. More than 100 studies tested the concept of androgyny—that is, having both masculine and feminine psychological traits. Previously, masculinity and femininity had been seen as being at opposite ends of a single scale. The Bem Sex Role Inventory measures whether an individual has highly masculine, highly feminine, or combined (androgynous) gender characteristics. Bem (1983) moved from androgyny to gender schema theory because the concept of androgyny retains the notion of examining individuals as masculine or feminine and may reinforce stereotypes, whereas gender schema does not. Also the concept of androgyny assumes that there is a feminine and masculine within everyone. In contrast, gender schema theory is concerned with the degree to which gender affects our views and social interactions (Bem, 1983).

Gender schema theory can be applied to all levels of development. As Bem (1993) has observed, children not only learn society's views of gender but also learn to apply it to themselves. For example, they learn that girls wear dresses, boys do not; girls may wear lipstick and nail polish, boys do not; and boys are called *handsome* and girls are called *pretty*. Adolescents, in particular, are likely to be highly gender focused as they become concerned about the physical attractiveness of the opposite sex and of themselves. Adults who are gender focused are more likely to view behaviors of associates as "unmanly" or "unfeminine" than those who use other schemas in attributing characteristics to associates. Bem (1983) believes that gender schema theory is one of the strongest schemas, or ways of looking at society. She is concerned that a strong gender schema is a very limiting way to view oneself and others. Differentiating between the necessity for children to learn about physiological sex differences and the stereotyping of gender role behaviors, Bem proposes that parents help their children learn other schemas, such as those focused on individual differences or cultural relativism. An "individual differences" schema emphasizes the variability of individuals within a group. For example, when the young child says, "Harry is a sissy because he likes to paint," a parent might point out that both boys and girls paint and enjoy it. The "cultural relativism" schema refers to the idea that not everyone thinks the same way and that people in different groups or cultures have different beliefs. Fairy tales, which often contain many gender-role stereotypes, can be explained as beliefs that reflect a culture that is different than our current culture (if the child is old enough to understand this concept). Gender schema theory has applications not only for child raising, but also for how clients view themselves and others in therapy. By observing their own gender schemas and those of their clients, therapists can become aware of patterns of thinking that may be hampering progress in therapy.

Gilligan's Ethic of Care

Although Freud and Erikson, as well as other theorists, have written about the importance of human relationships for women in the formation of their identity, Gilligan (1977, 1982) has commented on the values that traditional psychology has placed on

CAROL GILLIGAN

women's concern about relationships. She was concerned that traits such as compassion and care, which define the "goodness" of women, were viewed as a deficit in their moral development and that women's caretaking roles were devalued in favor of the development of individuality and achievement. Working with Lawrence Kohlberg, who had conceived a stage model of moral development that she found less applicable for women than for men, Gilligan undertook a series of studies on women's moral development. Briefly, she viewed Kohlberg's (1981) model as one of morality of justice and her own as one of morality of care and responsibility. This difference can be seen in the comparison of the comments of two 8-year-old children, Jeffrey and Karen, who were both asked to describe a situation where they were not sure what the correct approach should be. Where Jeffrey uses an ordering system to resolve a conflict between desire and duty, Karen uses a relationship system that includes her friends. Jeffrey thinks about what to do first, Karen is concerned about who is left out (Gilligan, 1982, pp. 32–33).

Jeffrey	Karen
When I really want to go to my friends and my mother is cleaning the cellar, I think about my friends, and then I think about my mother, and then I think about the right thing to do. (*But how do you know it's the right thing to do?*) Because some things go before other things.	I have lots of friends and I can't always play with all of them, so everybody's going to have to take a turn, because they're all my friends. Like if someone's all alone, I'll play with them. (*What kinds of things do you think about when you are trying to make that decision?*) Um, someone all alone, loneliness.[2]

Gilligan's and Kohlberg's stages of the development of morality are outlined in Table 12.1.

Gilligan (1982) was critical of Kohlberg (1981) for using hypothetical examples that portrayed males rather than females and for using for his initial work a sample of 84 males. In Kohlberg's studies, women generally reached stage three whereas men reached stage four. Rather than interpret this as a deficiency in women, Gilligan saw it as a deficiency in Kohlberg's theory. Gilligan (1982) wanted not only to use real rather than hypothetical situations but also to present moral dilemmas that women faced. In

TABLE 12.1

Kohlberg's and Gilligan's Levels of Moral Development

Kohlberg's Morality of Justice	Gilligan's Morality of Care
Preconventional Morality	
Stages	Levels
I. Obey rules to avoid being punished. II. Obey rules to get rewards.	I. Be concerned for yourself and your survival. I. (Transition to Level II) Start to be aware of the needs of others.
Conventional Morality	
III. Obey and conform to the rules of others to get approval and avoid disapproval. IV. Follow society's rules and laws rigidly.	II. Be concerned for others following social norms. II. (Transition to Level III). Awareness that morality of care must include care of self as well as others.
Postconventional Morality	
V. An understanding that rules are to be obeyed because they are needed for social order, but can be changed. VI. Society's standards can be violated to meet internal standards of justice.	III. Concern for responsibilities to self and others, and seeing self and others as interdependent.

SOURCE: Reprinted by permission of the publishers from *In a Different Voice: Psychological Theory and Women's Development*, by Carol Gilligan. Cambridge, MA: Harvard University Press. Copyright © 1982, 1993 by Carol Gilligan.

one study, she interviewed women who were considering having an abortion during the first trimester of pregnancy and interviewed them again 1 year later. Their responses contributed to her development of her characterization of three levels of morality. In summarizing the differences between men's and women's morality, Gilligan concluded the following:

> The moral imperative that emerges repeatedly in interviews with women is an injunction to care, a responsibility to discern and alleviate "real and recognizable trouble" of this world. For men, the moral imperative appears rather as an injunction to respect the rights of others and thus to protect from interference the rights to life and self-fulfillment. Women's insistence on care is at first self-critical rather than self-protective, while men initially conceive obligation to others negatively in terms of non-interference. (1982, p. 100)

Gilligan's writings have prompted much attention. More than 100 research studies have been related to her work; Walker (1984) critiques about 70 of them. In general, Walker found little support for Gilligan's observation that women score lower on Kohlberg's scales than men. Books such as Larrabee's (1993) bring together a variety of critiques on Gilligan's work, which has sometimes been misunderstood as saying that men use only reason in approaching moral issues and women use only a care and responsibility approach. She has also been misinterpreted as suggesting that the care and responsibility approach was superior to the morality of justice approach, something that she has denied. Others have criticized her research for not including comparable situations in which both men's and women's moral development can be assessed, for not using well-defined procedures for scoring moral development, and for focusing on sex differences without considering the impact of social class or religion (Unger & Crawford, 1996). Hare-Mustin and Marecek (1988) question whether lack of power rather than gender creates an ethic of care and responsibility. This broad debate on men's and women's moral thinking has provided a forum for viewing gender differences. Perhaps Gilligan's most important contribution is that she helps us look at moral decision making in more flexible ways and pays attention to factors previously ignored that show that both men and women use justice and care orientations. However, women may use care orientations more frequently because of social roles and demands.

The Relational Model

A number of writers based at the Stone Center at Wellesley College have discussed the importance for women of finding a sense of identity through the context of relationships (Jordan, 1997). Miller (1991) has written that women's sense of self is based on their ability to develop and maintain relationships. She believes that women find a sense of effectiveness that comes from experiencing a sense of connection with others. The view of Miller and her colleagues on how women's sense of self depends upon connecting with others (being in relation) is instructive.

Miller (1986) sees women as the subordinate group in society who have developed characteristics that help them cope with this subordination. She sees women (and minorities and poor people) as relegated to providing personal services for the dominant groups (generally white males). When those who are subordinate behave with intelligence or independence, they may be seen as abnormal and criticized for this behavior. To please the dominant group, subordinates develop characteristics that include passivity, dependency, lack of initiative, and inability to act. Those who are subordinate must be able to interpret the verbal and nonverbal behaviors of those who are dominant (men). In this way, women have developed "feminine intuition." As a result of being in a subordinate position, women may feel less important than men and strive to improve their relationships with both men and women by attending to the emotional and physical needs of others and by helping them develop their strength and improve their well-being (mothering or nursing). However, Miller, Jordan, Kaplan, Stiver, and Surrey (1997) show that relatedness is a strength that should be valued and appreciated.

An example of how women may relate differently than men because of their emphasis on responding to emotions rather than deciding or taking charge can help illustrate the relational model.

> **Claire:** When I was walking home, two men came up next to me and started to tease me, making sexual remarks.
>
> **Joan:** Oh, you must have been scared, not knowing what they'd do.
>
> **Claire:** I was frightened. I didn't know whether they would touch me or what they would do. I just kept walking.
>
> **Joan:** I'd be so frightened too. It can feel like there's nothing you can do.

If Claire were to talk to a man, he might respond the way Joan did, but it is more likely that he would focus on taking action or doing something about the situation.

> **Claire:** When I was walking home, two men came up next to me and started to tease me, making sexual remarks.
>
> **Dick:** What did you do? Did you look at them?
>
> **Claire:** No. I just walked faster and looked straight ahead.
>
> **Dick:** Good, because if you looked at them, you probably would have given them the attention that they were looking for.
>
> **Claire:** I just tried to get out of that situation as fast as I could.
>
> **Dick:** Did they stay with you long, or did they leave you alone?

When this brief hypothetical example of a female-female conversation is compared with a female-male conversation, Miller's point about women's emphasis on relating (subordinate) can be compared with men's (dominant) way of relating.

Surrey (1991) believes that women's self develops in the context of relationships, not through the development of autonomy. For Surrey, the core self in women has three basic components. First, there is an interest and ability in forming an emotional connection with others. Second, there is an expectation that a mutually empathic process will lead to a heightened development of the woman and the other. Third, there is an expectation that sensitive relationships will lead to increased empowerment and self-knowledge. In describing how women learn to develop this empathic process, Surrey (1991) describes the significance of the mother-daughter relationship as a model for other relationships. She describes how a girl's interest in being connected with her mother is quite different than a boy's, serving as a model of future connectedness. When a woman gets little emotional response, there is a sense of disconnectedness. The most extreme disconnectedness would be incest or rape, in which a woman's need for relatedness is severely abused. In incestuous situations in which the young girl cannot discuss the experience with anyone, the relational needs are totally thwarted, and psychological disturbances are likely to result (Miller, 1988). This abuse of power leaves the young girl alone, and the value placed on relating is now contradicted.

Although the work of the Stone Center (Jordan, 1997) group has generated little empirical research, their ideas can be helpful to therapists in understanding the frustrations and difficulties of their female clients.

How can gender schema theory, moral development theory, and the relational model be evaluated? Lerman (1986) has proposed a system for evaluating a woman-based theory of personality. Using her criteria, all three theories seem to meet the following propositions: They view women positively and centrally; they encompass, to a large degree, the diversity and complexity of women's lives; they arise from and reflect women's experience; they acknowledge political and social pressures on women; and they are consistent with feminist approaches to psychotherapy. Because they each provide different ways of viewing women's experiences, they are likely to be useful to therapists wishing to conceptualize their clients' issues.

THEORIES OF FEMINIST THERAPY

More than any other theoretical approach discussed in this book, feminist therapy looks at sociological (social) factors that affect human development. The goals of feminist therapy are characterized by an emphasis on appreciating the impact of political and social forces on women, an open and egalitarian relationship between client and therapist, and an appreciation of the female perspective on life. This view has led to criticism of the current psychological classification system, DSM-IV, and suggestions for other approaches to assessment. Almost all feminist therapists combine feminist therapy with other theoretical approaches. However, certain methods associated with feminist therapy recognize the impact of social forces on individuals and provide a way to make individuals more effective in dealing with society. Examples of techniques that help individuals deal with social discrimination are those that focus on gender role, power, and assertiveness. A broad understanding of the purpose of feminist therapy can be gained by examining the therapeutic goals that feminist therapists value.

Goals of Feminist Therapy

Feminist therapists believe that goals of therapy should include not only changes in one's own personal life but also changes in society's institutions (Enns, 1997). A number of feminist writers (Enns, 1997, Gilbert, 1980; Kaschak, 1981; Rawlings & Carter,

1977; Russell, 1984; Worell & Remer, 1992) have expressed considerable agreement in their basic views of the goals of therapy. In this section, I summarize the goals of feminist therapy as described by Klein (1976), Sturdivant (1980), and Enns (1997).

1. *Symptom removal*, a traditional goal of therapy, is appropriate only if it will not interfere with women's development and growth. For example, prescribing medication to a woman who has complained of headaches and depression due to marital conflicts would be inappropriate as it treats only the symptom. Dealing with the marital conflict and helping the woman to express and assert herself would be an appropriate means of helping the headaches go away.

2. *Self-esteem* in feminist therapy requires a move away from being dependent on external sources of self-esteem (what others think) to self-esteem based on one's own feeling about oneself. For women, this may mean liking themselves despite how others (friends, family, and the media) tell them how they should look, act, or think.

3. *Quality of interpersonal relationships* should increase with effective therapy. However, becoming more expressive, facilitative, and caring with friends and family cannot be at the expense of meeting one's own needs. Rather than be dependent or manipulative as a way of influencing others, women can improve their relationships by being more direct and assertive with others (Philpot, Brooks, Lustermen, & Nutt, 1997). Sometimes improving the quality of interpersonal relationships may threaten a marriage if the partner is not willing to change also. A goal of feminist therapy is not just to improve relationships with friends and family but also to pay particular attention to the quality of relationships with women.

4. *Body image and sensuality* are often defined for women by the media and by men, as society puts great importance on physical attractiveness for women. The goal of feminist therapy is to help individuals accept their body and their sexuality and not to use the standards of others to criticize their physicality. Sexual decisions should be made by individuals without coercion from others.

5. *Attention to diversity* refers to valuing cultural differences of clients. Although women share many common issues and goals, there is cultural variation in this. Women's lives are shaped by many different experiences coming from diverse linguistic, religious, economic, and sexual orientation backgrounds. At times, feminist therapists deal with conflicts between feminist values and cultural norms, such as homophobic attitudes that run counter to feminist values.

6. *Political awareness and social action* are key goals in feminist therapy. Often expressed as "the person is political," this goal is dissimilar to those of other therapies. It emphasizes the need for women to be aware of gender-role stereotyping, sexism, and discrimination and then to work toward changing this treatment. This may include being involved in political action groups such as the National Organization for Women that work to change federal and state laws that adversely effect women. Also, working to effect change on a more informal level, such as by confronting a male colleague who has treated a female supervisee in a sexist manner, is also supported. Implicit in this goal is the recognition that society brings about psychopathology through discriminatory practices that affect women.

Underlying assumptions of these goals are that the female point of view is accepted, that relationships between people should be equal (that men should not dominate

women, nor women dominate men), and that people exist in a political and diverse social system that can be discriminatory. These views also influence the diagnosis and
treatment of psychological problems.

Assessment Issues in Feminist Therapy

Because feminist therapists value a sociological and political perspective on psychological problems, cultural diversity, equality with their clients, and the female perspective on life, they have been critical of the major diagnostic system (DSM-IV) and its
earlier versions. They have criticized classification systems because they have been developed primarily by white male psychiatrists, many with a psychoanalytic perspective,
to be used for diagnosing and reporting mental disorders for all people (Brown, 1994).
Also, many feminist therapists have pointed out that classification systems focus on
psychological symptoms and not the social factors that cause them. Rawlings and
Carter (1977) are concerned that a deemphasis on sociological factors that produce
rape and child abuse diminishes the respect that therapists have for clients. Further, diagnostic labeling is criticized because it encourages adjustment to social norms, reinforcing stereotyping rather than questioning social injustices. Laura Brown (1994) succinctly describes the power of naming diagnostic categories in this way: "If you call it
a skunk, you will assume that it smells" (p. 131). Because of their criticism of diagnosis, feminist therapists have been more concerned with exploring strong feelings, such
as anger, and bringing about both individual and societal change (Enns, 1993). Also,
some feminists see behavioral descriptions as allowing for discussion of strengths and
weaknesses, whereas diagnostic labels describe weaknesses (Enns, 1997). Feminist
therapists assess the cultural context of client problems, obtaining information about
the client's power or lack of it, so that clients are not blamed for their problems.

Techniques of Feminist Therapy

Because feminist therapists may combine feminist approaches with any of the theories
that have been discussed in this book, here I describe only some techniques that are either unique to feminist therapy or particularly relevant to the goals of feminist therapy.
In a later section, I explain how feminist therapy and other theoretical approaches may
be integrated. A number of writers have described feminist therapy techniques that can
be applied to women (and men) that recognize the importance of both psychological
and sociological factors.

In describing the approaches of gender-role analysis, power intervention, assertiveness training, reframing and relabeling, and demystifying strategies, the primarily cognitive and behavioral approach of Worell and Remer (1992) is the major source. Although group techniques are used widely in feminist therapy, they are described in a
later section.

Gender-role analysis.   To understand the impact of societal gender-role
expectations on them, clients can participate in a gender-role analysis (Worell &
Remer, 1992). Although this gender-role analysis can be modified, depending on the
needs of the client, the steps provide a way of clearly identifying a sequential approach.

The approach is illustrated by the case of Carla, who is depressed because she is constantly fighting with her parents and as a result is feeling stupid and incompetent.

To use a gender-role analysis with Carla, the therapist would have her first identify various gender-role messages that she had experienced during her life. For example, Carla's father has told her that women should raise children and keep house. Her mother has told her not to argue with her father, to let him be the boss, and to be more understanding of him. Second, the counselor helps the client identify positive and negative consequences of gender-related messages. Carla tells the counselor that she feels she really cannot be effective in her studies or in her job because she believes work is not important for women and she is reluctant to suggest new methods for improving her work to her boss. Third, the counselor and the client identify the statements that clients say to themselves based on these gender-role messages. For example, Carla has said to herself, "I really shouldn't worry about work. It shouldn't be very important to me anyway, so I won't talk to my boss." Fourth, the counselor and client decide which messages they want to change. In Carla's case, after discussing many of the internalized messages about gender roles that she has, she decides to change the message that "work should not be important to me." Last, the client and counselor develop a plan to implement the change and then follow through. Carla writes, "My work is important to me and I want to be able to speak to my clients with more authority, speaking louder and more firmly." Carla then follows through with this change in her behavior. At the next session, she discusses the results of her attempt to change her speaking behavior.

In this hypothetical example, the client learns how assumptions about the way women should behave in society have negatively affected her view of herself and her performance. By identifying her gender-role messages, she is then able to implement a change. In a real counseling situation, there would be many messages to analyze and more complex goals to reach.

Gender-role intervention. Often feminist therapists respond to a client's comments or problems by understanding the impact of societal gender-role expectations on the client. They may not go through the process of gender-role analysis described previously, but do provide the client insights about social issues as they affect the client's psychological problem. Russell (1984, p. 76) describes this as the skill of social analysis, which "provides a rationale, that is a cognitive framework for the skill of positive evaluation of women." Following is an example of a gender-role intervention with a woman who has been separated from her husband and has not worked for 20 years.

Doreen: Now on top of all my other problems, I have to worry about getting a job. I'm not qualified to do any kind of work, and just the thought of looking for work is absolutely petrifying. Offices today are so complicated with computers and new machines. I could never learn to use them.

Counselor B: Well, Doreen, I agree that trying to get a job can be a pretty tough proposition, especially when some employers discriminate against older women. However, that kind of discrimination is not legal, and other employers are aware of the benefits of maturity in their employees. We can work together on looking for all the positive things you can offer an employer and plan how you can best present this.

Comment: Counselor B is using social analysis to indicate that sexist and age-linked discrimination does exist, that the client may need to be prepared for it, and that this is inherently not only unfair but invalid. The counselor is encouraging the client to combat such attitudes by clearly enunciating the positive claims that refute them. Individual action is proposed at this stage, but conceivably social action might be contemplated at a later point in the counseling process. (Russell, 1984, pp. 85–86)[3]

The emphasis on society's discrimination toward women rather than on Doreen's hesitancy toward working is an important aspect of this approach. The counselor helps the client to think positively, so that she can attain her goals.

Power analysis.   Traditionally, white men have had more power than women in making and enforcing decisions about family, work, laws, and social relationships. By increasing clients' awareness of the differences between the power of men and women in society, therapists can then help them to make changes where their lack of power has previously prevented change (Worell & Remer, 1992). To illustrate power analysis, I use the case of Rose, who has been feeling stressed when her husband comes home in the evening. Two weeks ago, after he had been drinking, they had a fight about his going out alone at night without her. Angry at her, he punched her in the stomach and hit her head against the wall.

The first step of power analysis is to have the client choose a definition that fits for her and to apply it to different kinds of power. Rose wants the power to express herself to her husband and to do something about his inappropriate behavior. For her, this may mean investigating legal, physical, or psychological ways to be powerful. Second, because men and women may have different access to legal, financial, physical, or other types of power, this issue is discussed. The counselor and Rose talk about her finances, the value of separate checking accounts, self-defense lessons, and the advantages and disadvantages of consulting a lawyer. Third, different ways that power can be used to bring about change are discussed. Will Rose use indirect and helpless ways of having power by pleading with her husband to stop drinking, or will she consult a lawyer and be clear about what behaviors she will or will not tolerate from her husband? Fourth, clients examine gender-role messages that interfere with their use of power. Because Rose had earlier learned that wives listen to their husbands and help them when they are distressed, she decides to challenge this message. Finally, clients may use a variety of power strategies in appropriate situations. In this case, Rose decides to insist that her husband seek help for his drinking immediately and then move in with a friend if he does not. In this example, the client learns that she can change depressed or anxious feelings in herself by acting in an appropriately powerful way.

Power intervention.   Power analysis is a technique that requires planning and follow-up in counseling. Often, a therapist can strengthen a client's sense of self through reinforcing her statements or through giving information. Empowering a client can occur in the course of therapeutic discussion and does not need to be planned.

In the following example, Bonnie Burstow (1992), using an unusual approach, empowers her client whose father has acted incestuously with her. The client is angry at her father but wondering if she should forgive him.

Client: Bonnie, I really hate his guts. Like I mean, REALLY HATE. I don't know how I'm ever going to be able to forgive him. . . . Do you think I have to?

Bonnie: I want to be clear about this. No, Doris, you don't have to. As far as I am concerned, you don't have to forgive him now. You don't have to forgive him ever. Hating him doesn't make you any less valuable a human being, and it is perfectly natural. Of course you hate him! Why wouldn't you hate someone who crept up on you and molested you night after night!

Client: I feel like spitting every time I think of him.

Bonnie: Feel like spitting now?

(A spitting exercise ensues.)

Bonnie: How do you feel now?

Client: *Funny. Good* funny. Like I really did something, though it's a bit weird. . . .

Bonnie: How do you feel when you think of your father?

Client: Let me see. I am more aware of hating his guts. And I feel a wee bit stronger. I also feel somewhat better about hating his guts. Like it's giving me something. It feels nice to hate.

Bonnie: Of course it does. So, it's okay to hate his guts?

Client: Well, it's okay for now. But what if I continue to hate his guts 20 years from now?

Bonnie: Then you continue to hate his guts.

Client: Oh, I know. But aren't we supposed to forgive?

Bonnie: Sure. We're also supposed to darn men's socks, cook their meals and accept being sexualized.

Client: You mean it's not okay to forgive?

Bonnie: No. I mean it's not mandatory.

Client: I see what you mean. I'm glad you said that. Cause you know, it is more a matter of "should" than "want." I don't actually *want* to forgive him. I want to. . . .

Bonnie: Yeah?

Client: I want to . . . SPIT ON HIM. (laughter) (Burstow, 1992, pp. 140–141)[4]

In this example, Burstow legitimatizes her client's anger and encourages her to express it. The anger and sense of power are important, whereas forgiveness is an optional societal message that does not need to be resolved at the moment.

Assertiveness training.   Because women often do not feel powerful, they may not act in an assertive manner and thus may give up some control over their lives. Laws and gender role expectations are seen by feminist therapists as contributing to the need for women to be assertive because the rules have historically prevented women from being treated with equality.

Assertive skills can be taught to clients so that they feel less depressed, angry, frustrated, or helpless in situations where they give their rights to others. To understand assertiveness, it is helpful to distinguish between assertive behavior and passive or aggressive behavior (Jakubowski, 1977). Assertiveness refers to standing up for one's rights without violating the rights of others. Assertive behavior is a clear and direct (no sarcasm or humor) statement or request. Aggressiveness refers to insisting on one's rights while violating the rights of others. Making fun of, dominating, or belittling another person is aggressive behavior. Passive or nonassertive behavior means giving up one's rights and doing what others may want.

Statement: I borrowed a mirror from your desk drawer. I hope you don't mind.

Assertive: Please don't take things from my desk drawer. If you want to borrow something, I'll probably be able to help you out. Just ask.

Aggressive: Don't go through my drawers and leave my things alone!

Passive: I don't mind.

There are many different ways of acting assertively, and situations vary. For example, being assertive with a parent is often quite different than being assertive with a friend, boss, or teacher. Clients often find it helpful to practice assertiveness by role playing. The counselor and client may take turns playing the roles of the client and the other person. By trying different strategies, including different aggressive, assertive, and passive behaviors, the client can practice a situation that is anticipated.

However, assertiveness can be seen as a male construction (Crawford, 1995). Thus, a man's assertive behavior may be seen as firm or authoritative, a woman's could be seen as pushy or stubborn. Reviewing research on the perception of women's assertive behavior, Enns (1997) suggests that on some occasions, women's assertive behavior may be seen as less acceptable than men's by both men and women.

Reframing and relabeling.   The term *reframing* refers to changing "the frame of reference for looking at an individual's behavior" (Worell & Remer, 1992, p. 102). In feminist therapy, it usually means a shift from blaming oneself to looking at society for an explanation. Reframing often is used to help individuals understand how societal pressures can add to their problem. For example, a woman who is feeling depressed because she believes that she is overweight would be helped to look at the societal pressures in the media and in social values that reinforce thinness as a goal for women. As a result of reframing this situation, she might relabel her problem from being that of depression to that of feeling overwhelmed by and angry at pressures to be thin.

Therapy-demystifying strategies.   Feminist therapists try to have an open and clear relationship with their clients so that inequities of power in society are not recreated in the therapeutic relationship. Therapy should not be a mysterious process or one in which the therapist is more powerful than the client; rather, it should be egalitarian. For example, if therapists call their clients by their first names, then they introduce themselves with a first name. Two important ways of demystifying therapy are by providing information to the client and by using appropriate self-disclosure when working with therapeutic issues.

Therapy is demystified by providing information about the process of therapy and by sharing some of the skills of therapy. At the beginning of therapy, feminist therapists describe their theoretical orientation, relevant personal values, and rights that the client has as a consumer of therapy (Worell & Remer, 1992, p. 103). Also, the therapist is clear about the session fee, session time, length of therapy, and therapeutic goals. Clients must agree to these before counseling can continue. Additionally, feminist therapists may teach relevant counseling skills such as assertiveness, ways to control behaviors, and ways to increase choices. Also, feminist therapists encourage their clients to give information to the therapist regarding the impact that the therapist is having on the client. In these ways, the therapist helps the client understand, as clearly as possible, the process and purpose of therapy.

Another means of demystifying therapy is self-disclosure. Brown and Walker (1990) describe many ways in which self-disclosure can be helpful to the client's growth. In general, self-disclosure is given to help the client in his growth, not for the therapist to share her pain or for the therapist to say, "This is how I became successful, and if you follow my example, you can, too." Self-disclosure that is counselor initiated shows that the counselor is a real person, thus equalizing the relationship. Self-disclosure should feel appropriate to the counselor and educative for the client. Russell (1984) gives the following example of appropriate self-disclosure by the counselor regarding marital issues.

Eileen: I want my husband to be my best friend and favorite companion as well as provider and lover. I am interested in everything that he does, and he should likewise be interested in my activities. If you don't share your life together totally, what is the point of being married?

Counselor B: The kind of marriage you're describing reminds me of my own ideas about marriage when I was first married. I really resented anything my husband did without me, and I remember making some terrible scenes because he wasn't home punctually from a golf game or he planned to attend some sporting events with his friends without consulting me. It still embarrasses me to think about my ranting and raving! I had to learn to give him some more space in our relationship and to enjoy my own space. Now, I wouldn't give up my own activities for the world! And, you know, our marriage is a lot happier than when I was insisting on total sharing.

Comment: Counselor B is disclosing information about herself at a fairly intimate level, information about herself that reveals her own inadequacies and limitations, but as it relates to events in the past that have been subsequently resolved, the riskiness of the disclosure is curtailed. Counselor B is disclosing an experience that she perceives to be parallel to that of the client. She is indicating that she resolved the situation in a particular way and this may also work for the client. Counselor B is therefore indicating that she was in the same situation as the client but managed to move beyond it. In this way, the counselor is addressing both the egalitarian goals and the alternative expansion goals of the self-disclosure. (Russell, 1984, pp. 160–161)

Self-disclosure and giving information about the therapeutic process help make the client more powerful and responsible for her growth. These techniques discourage dependency on the therapist and provide a model for independent behavior with others. Likewise, the other techniques previously discussed—gender role, role and power analysis, assertiveness training, and reframing and relabeling—help clients deal with social forces that interfere with the issues that brought them to therapy. These techniques are not the only ones that feminist therapists use, but they are often used in fostering individuals' growth.

USING FEMINIST THERAPY WITH OTHER THEORIES

As discussed previously, feminist therapy is generally used in conjunction with other theories of psychotherapy. In describing how feminist therapy can be integrated with other theories of psychotherapy, Worell and Remer (1992) mention several steps. First, they look for sources of bias in the theory by examining historical developments of the theory, key theoretical concepts, sexist use of language and labels, and bias in diagnosis and therapeutic techniques. The next step is to eliminate sexist components to see if the theory is still compatible with feminist principles. The major principles, as stated earlier, are that political and social factors influence people's lives and that egalitarian relationships are important, as is valuing the perspective of women. Although feminist therapists who have integrated feminist therapy with other theories have not incorporated Worell and Remer's (1992) principles explicitly, they have done this implicitly, as these themes are important in feminist therapy. In the following sections, I have chosen to describe psychoanalysis, behavioral and cognitive therapy, and Gestalt therapy, as they have been changed to be consistent with the feminist therapy perspective and have received more attention from feminist writers than other theories.

Feminist Psychoanalytic Theory

Complaints about gender bias have taken place within the field of psychoanalysis itself, as discussed in Chapter 2. Broader-based criticisms have also been leveled at psychoanalysis, as documented by the report of the American Psychological Association (1975) task force on sex bias, which found that psychoanalysis was a sexist theoretical orientation for what it says and what it fails to say about women. Feminist psychoanalytic theorists have criticized the Freudian description of women as passive, masochistic, and dependent. They have also criticized the concept of penis envy and have suggested womb envy (Horney, 1966) and breast envy (Eichenbaum & Orbach, 1983), as infants have more contact with breasts than with penises. Critics of psychoanalytic theory have felt that equality between therapist and client can be negatively affected by the need to develop a transference relationship with the patient, thus precluding therapist self-disclosure (Daugherty & Lees, 1988). The focus on mother-child relationships in object relations theory tends to limit emphasis on political and social factors as they affect the individual's development.

However, some feminist therapists have pointed out that psychoanalysis can be a very appropriate technique for helping women. Understanding the influence of gender on conscious and unconscious aspects of men and women can provide insight in the practice of psychoanalysis (Minsky, 1997). As Hayden (1986) has shown, psychoanalytic therapy can free women from symptoms to become more active and independent. By examining Oedipal issues, psychoanalysis explores how people deal with and learn gender identities and how male domination can develop in society (Enns, 1993). Furthermore, by examining the role of the unconscious in repression, psychoanalysis can provide insights on why gender roles are so powerful and difficult to change. Chodorow (1989) has pointed out that psychoanalysis can be helpful in understanding how the role of mother can contribute to women being devalued and being dominated by men. Related to the psychoanalytic object relations approach, the relational model (Jordan, 1997) has been an attempt to revalue the role of the mother. Efforts to extend the integration of psychodynamic and feminist therapies have been made in applications to African American women, taking into account cultural considerations that most psychodynamic therapists do not (Greene, 1997). Even though a psychoanalytic viewpoint does provide some insights into women's issues, some concepts and techniques have been criticized.

Feminist Behavioral and Cognitive Therapy

Some of the criticisms of cognitive behavioral therapies are that they tend to ignore social and political factors that affect clients (Enns, 1997). People who are homeless, battered, or poor may not have the resources or support to use some cognitive and behavioral methods. Also, therapist values about how clients should change may not take into account the client's social or cultural background. Additionally, cognitive behavioral therapies may not attend to clients' cultural assumptions about rationality that are implicit in such therapies.

To make cognitive and behavioral therapies more compatible with feminist therapy, Worell and Remer (1992) have suggested changing labels that stress the pathology of people, focusing on feelings, and integrating ideas about gender-role socialization. Rather than use negative or pathological labels such as distortion, irrationality, or faulty thinking, Worell and Remer (1992) suggest that clients explore ideas based on gender-role generalizations that appear to be distorted or irrational. For example, rather than label the thought that "women's place is in the home" as irrational, the therapist should explore the actual rewards and punishments for living out this stereotyped belief. By focusing on feelings, particularly angry ones, that arise as a result of gender-role limitations or discrimination, women can be helped to feel independence and gain control over their lives. To help women with social role issues, gender-role and power analysis can be useful in exploring ways of dealing with societal pressures that interfere with women's development. Thus, Worell and Remer's ideas broaden and develop cognitive and behavioral therapeutic strategies to incorporate feminist views of therapy.

Feminist Gestalt Therapy

In reviewing the compatibility of Gestalt therapy and feminist therapy, Enns (1997) sees several ways that the two meet similar goals. Both have as goals the increase of awareness of personal power. Gestalt therapists suggest words such as *won't* rather than *can't*, or *want* rather than *need*. By changing "I should do this" to "I choose to do this," therapists encourage independence and build a feeling of power. Feminist therapists also value the expression of anger as a response to discrimination and external limitations. Thus, techniques such as the empty chair encourage clients to say "I'm angry at you" rather than "I am angry at him." Because of the emphasis on awareness of self and choices, women can learn of options that they may not previously have considered. Options develop when one says "I choose to" rather than "I have to." By combining awareness of social and political discrimination with methods of empowerment, Gestalt therapeutic approaches meet many of the goals of feminist therapy.

Enns (1997) also cautions that some aspects of Gestalt therapy do not fit well with feminist therapy. Because Gestalt therapy tends to focus on taking responsibility for one's own behavior, the social, economic, and political factors that interfere with a person's developing independence and choice may be ignored. Such methods as gender-role or power analysis may be viewed as blaming the environment rather than taking responsibility for one's own choices and development. Also, some Gestalt therapists may not recognize the importance of relationships in the lives of many women and focus almost exclusively on the development of self-reliance.

Psychoanalysis, behavioral and cognitive therapies, and Gestalt therapy are not the only therapeutic approaches to individuals that have integrated feminist therapy principles. A number of other theories of therapy, such as object relations and self psychology (Okun, 1992), Jungian therapy (Romaniello, 1992), and person-centered therapy (Enns, 1997), have examined feminist therapeutic value systems as to their compatibility with these approaches. To integrate any theory of psychotherapy with feminist therapy, Worell and Remer's (1992) method of feminist transformation of counseling theories can be helpful.

Feminist Therapy and Counseling

Because of the egalitarian approach of feminist therapists to their work, most do not differentiate between counseling and psychotherapy. However, Russell (1984) sees psychotherapy as "an intensive process of remediation of psychological dysfunction or adjustment to psychic stressors" (p. 14), whereas counseling is more developmental, educational, or preventive. Because feminist therapy is often integrated with another theory of psychotherapy or counseling, the terminology of the other theory, such as psychoanalysis, behavioral or cognitive therapy, or Gestalt therapy, may influence whether *counseling* or *psychotherapy* is the term used.

Brief Therapy

The length of feminist therapy often depends on which other theory or theories it is integrated with. Because much of feminist therapy takes an action-oriented approach in helping clients confront societal and political issues, however, there may be an emphasis on working efficiently and quickly. Adding to the brevity of many feminist therapeutic approaches is the use of therapy and support groups that supplement the work of individual therapy. From the perspective of empowering clients to take more control over their lives, long-term therapy is seen by some feminist therapists as allowing clients to blame themselves or to feel dependent on a therapist. However, certain issues such as incest and rape may require a year or more of therapy.

PSYCHOLOGICAL DISORDERS

In the discussion of the following four cases, the feminist therapeutic approach shows the importance of gender roles and social forces in psychotherapy. As described earlier, feminists often avoid DSM-IV categories, as they feel that classification systems may represent male cultural stereotypes of women and do not emphasize the significance of sociological factors in women's roles. For consistency, the DSM-IV system is used in this chapter as it is in the others. The discussion of four disorders focuses on feminist therapy and features the techniques described earlier in this chapter, recognizing that feminist therapy is often used in combination with other theories. The disorders illustrated have been identified in the DSM-IV as particularly common to women: depression, borderline disorders, posttraumatic stress disorders, and eating disorders.

Depression

From a feminist therapist's perspective, women have many reasons to be twice as likely as men to experience depression. Because women are often taught to be dependent on men, to be helpless, and to please others, they may experience depression because they feel an inability to control their lives and assert themselves. An emphasis on personal appearance and on being valued in terms of how they are perceived by men can contribute to a sense of powerlessness. If a woman experiences personal violence, sexual assault, or discrimination in the workplace, depression can result from a feeling of inability to control one's own environment (Worell & Remer, 1992). Many other factors such as pregnancy, childbirth, and homemaking can affect women in positive and negative ways, depending on their attitudes and those of others close to them. Although depression may be due partly to genetics and hormonal changes, Worell and Remer (1992) believe that gender-role expectations and social discrimination contribute more to depression at varying times during the life span.

In the following case, Turner (1997) describes her work with a young African American woman who has started graduate school. Ms. B is depressed because of her poor performance in school and feeling cut off from her family. Turner uses the relational model of the Stone Center to explain Ms. B's feeling invisible in a white graduate school. Also, Turner attends to Ms. B's feelings of shame and fear of telling her parents about her difficulties at school. Turner helps empower Ms. B by focusing on connections and relations with mentors, study groups, organizations, and family.

> Ms. B is a young Black women in her twenties pursuing an advanced graduate degree. She had not had previous counseling and, until recently, had not experienced any serious setbacks or difficulties. She is one of several siblings, the younger daughter of a low-income intact family. One of her brothers has an advanced professional degree, but she will be the first woman in her family to do so. She presented with issues of deflated self-esteem, low grades and "hot off the press" news from her dean that the school wanted to "counsel her out of the program" by the end of the current semester. She had failed all her tests and didn't seem to be making a good fit at the school, according to most of her teachers. She was shocked in light of her past high achievement in college and her motivation to succeed. She appeared not only defeated but depressed and agitated. She was not suicidal, but very down on herself and very frustrated. She told me that she studied religiously, knew the material, but just couldn't perform when she was expected to.
>
> At a closer look, I discovered that she was cut off from any source of emotional, academic, or social support. She studied alone and *never* conversed with any of her teach-

ers or school staff. She couldn't tell her family because she thought it would destroy them. In short, *no one knew what I knew* about this discrepancy between preparation and performance! She felt shame, embarrassment and a profound sense of failure in letting herself and her family down. There were a handful of Black women and men and a few more white women in her class. She didn't feel she could confide in any of them, and whenever anyone in her class asked how she was doing, she always responded, "OK."

I saw Ms. B for a little over a year. I was able to connect with her around her profound isolation and guilt-laden feelings by helping her to better see *her role and that of significant others* in hiding important parts of herself from people all around her. Basic to this was her inner feeling of not being accepted as a legitimate member of her school environment. This inner feeling caused intense anxiety and somatic symptoms. She fostered a perception of not "belonging" or "being valued" which, as it turned out, *was* shared by a few at the school, but not by everyone. She did have to leave the school for a term; however, she is now re-enrolled there. This time, she has identified and sought out mentors, study groups, an active Black organization, and a greater sense of "entitlement" to study there as a Black woman. I'm happy to say that this activity is also reflected in her grades. She has learned to use a number of stress reduction techniques to move past the anxiety blocks and to relax more. She also knows now that her family loves and respects her, no matter what happens, because she freed herself up to share some of the pressure she felt about being the first woman in her family to achieve professional status. This pressure was tied in with her internal fears about losing her place with them, and in a sense "leaving them behind." On an affective level, this fear contributed to her depressed feelings, while on a cognitive level she wanted to believe that they would still love her as they always had. Because she felt vulnerable to a "perceived loss," her academic pursuits had been conflicted and inhibited (Turner, 1997, pp. 83, 84).[5]

Borderline Personality Disorder

Recent literature (Herman, 1992) notes that "borderline" personality disorder is often connected to childhood abuse, which is due to ways that men learn to treat women. Feminist counselors prefer not to use the label "borderline personality disorder" because of its negative connotations and its tendency to encourage the counselor to view issues as intrapsychic problems rather than as consequences of abuse by others (Brown, 1994). Judith Herman (1992) suggests that many survivors of violence experience symptoms and a disorder that she terms "complex posttraumatic stress disorder" rather than "borderline." The consequences of long-term exposure to violence at home, at school, or elsewhere include (a) alterations in affect regulation (e.g., dysphoria, suicidal preoccupation, self-injury, explosive mood); (b) alterations in consciousness (e.g., amnesia, dissociation, depersonalization, reliving of experiences); (c) alterations in self-perception (e.g., shame, guilt, helplessness); (d) alterations in perceptions of the perpetrator (e.g., idealization, unrealistic attribution of total power); (e) alterations in relationships (e.g., isolation, distrust, search for a rescuer); and (f) alterations in systems of meaning (hopelessness, loss of faith) (Herman, 1992, p. 121). This conceptualization acknowledges the external events that contribute to the client's distress and recognizes the extent and complexity of reactions to abuse. It contains less potential for blaming the client and suggests directions for dealing with the symptoms that are more typically referred to as *borderline personality disorder*. An example of this approach follows.

Jane exhibited many of the qualities that are associated with "borderline" personality disorder. They included involvement in short, intense relationships and a tendency to define in strict categories of good or bad. She experienced mood swings, a diffuse sense of who she was, and periodic suicidal feelings. Jane had also experienced prolonged sexual abuse as a child by her uncle. In working with Jane, her counselor was clear with her about their relationship, explored traumatic memories, and dealt with explosive behaviors in ways that are described in this report.

By establishing a contract that identifies expectations for both Jane and the counselor, the counselor's values and limits are identified. Given the fact that survivors of abuse frequently experience a diffuse sense of self and difficulty in establishing boundaries, the agreement helps the client establish a clearer sense of self and helps the counselor set limits in nonpunitive ways.

Jane's readiness to explore past abuse must be respected to help her maintain control over her inner world, which often seems very fragile. Discussion of intrusive memories and dreams of the client may represent important entry points for discussing these issues. The counselor helps the client "normalize" intrusive memories, dissociation, and frightening dreams by suggesting that these represent ways the client copes and a way in which she is already moving toward healing. The purpose of verbalizing abuse is to help the client gain a new perspective, limit its hold on her, and identify new sources of meaning in the present. It is important for the feminist counselor to frequently acknowledge and explain how profoundly traumatic abuse is in order to help the client understand the long-term process of recovery and to help the client work through a grief process. Identifying concrete goals, behaviors, and self-nurturing activities is important for helping the client identify signs of growing health. A support group for survivors can also help the client deal with current realities, gain support, and receive feedback about behaviors that are unproductive.

Jane's everyday behaviors may often seem explosive, impulsive, or misdirected. The feminist counselor helps her identify the needs underneath the action so that she can find new ways of meeting these needs. The counselor points out healthy components of the client's behavior and helps the client see potential ways to redirect energy into appropriate assertion. The counselor reminds the client of her strength as a survivor and notes that the energy that she has used to survive thus far can be redirected. (Carolyn Enns, personal communication, February 17, 1994)

Posttraumatic Stress Disorder

The term *posttraumatic stress disorder* refers to the fears, anxieties, and stresses that an individual experiences after being victimized. In that sense, the term focuses on the victim rather than the perpetrator. A common cause of women's posttraumatic stress disorder is rape, also called *rape trauma syndrome* (Burgess & Holstrom, 1974).

In dealing with rape victims, Burstow (1992) suggests that feminist therapists must first invite the woman to express the feelings that she has experienced and then to empathize with these feelings from both a personal point of view and from a broader social and political point of view. She suggests that having the client describe the trauma in the present tense can be quite effective. However, the therapist should also empathize with the humiliation and terror that the woman may be feeling but not expressing, as well as her desire to flee from her feelings. The therapist helps the client to be in touch with her feelings and to express them. Burstow also talks about discussing client's rights, such as the right to go out alone at night without being raped.

In the following example, Greenspan (1983) describes counseling with a woman who, before being gang raped, functioned well and had few problems. In her work with Andrea, Greenspan responds to her client in ways similar to those described by Burstow. She empathizes with the client's feelings of rage, hate, and helplessness, but she also helps Andrea to develop a sense of identity and power, to do something positive with her outrage.

> The potentially disastrous consequences of not possessing a healthy fear of men was painfully illustrated by Andrea's story. Andrea was an intelligent and creative woman, fiercely devoted to her independence. She was single and supported herself as a carpenter and artist. She prided herself on her fearlessness, physical strength, and lack of physical intimidation. One evening, her car broke down and had to be towed. She visited with a friend nearby until around midnight. Then, rather than take the subway, she decided that she would try to hitch a ride. She was picked up by two men who took her for a long ride, brought her to a house, threw her on a bed, and called several of their friends. For the next several hours, Andrea was raped at knife point by seven different men. In between rapes, the man with the knife would urge her to tell him how much she enjoyed it. Afterward, she was blindfolded, taken for another ride, and dropped off on the street in an unknown neighborhood.
>
> No woman recovers from an experience like this very easily. The climb back is hazardous and full of pain. For the first few days, Andrea was numb—she could feel nothing at all. Like many rape victims, she told no one what had happened to her. Prior to the rape, Andrea had always kept a firm lid on her feelings. But her instinct for survival now told her that she would have to get to the bottom of what she felt. With just a little encouragement from me, her feelings came gushing out in great torrents; terror, rage, shame, helplessness, and vulnerability overwhelmed her. She saw a rapist in every car. She distrusted men and wanted nothing to do with them—including the male friends she had known before the rape. She was ashamed of her body, which felt numb and dead. She wanted to kill or maim or castrate the men who had raped her. (Greenspan, 1983, pp. 273–274)[6]

Therapy had to help Andrea turn her losses into gains: to offer her a new basis for a sense of identity and power as a woman.

One of the best ways to do this was to work with Andrea's newly found sense of outrage. This burning outrage was like nothing else she had ever experienced. She simply could not understand how any person was capable of doing what these men had done to her. Like all victims, she could not help asking, "Why me?" But beyond this, she wanted to know: "Why any woman? Why do men rape? How will I ever feel strong and free again?" Andrea's fierce outrage was like a bomb exploding in her head. It, more than anything else, motivated her to piece her world back together again. Her consciousness was open in a way that it had not been before. In this lowest point of Andrea's life, therapy could help her make use of this openness, for it was her greatest strength in the task of surviving and recovering with a renewed sense of her power in the world.

Andrea's consciousness of herself after the rape contained the seeds of a very powerful new awareness: that her fate as a woman was inextricably bound to the fate of women as a whole: that she could not be the exceptional free spirit as long as women as a group remained oppressed. This new awareness was the bridge to a new basis for her sense of power as a woman. With her consciousness raised, Andrea came to understand that her post-rape emotions of terror, rage, and powerlessness were supreme exaggerations of the "normal" way that women feel in our society, whether consciously or unconsciously. She saw that her old brand of freedom before the rape was, in part, a denial of these feelings and an escape into a pseudo-haven which did not really exist. At the same time, she saw that none of this meant that she had to feel terrorized or helpless all of her life—that in unity there was strength; that there was a different way to feel powerful in concert with women with whom she now closely identified. (Greenspan, 1983, pp. 278–279)

The emphasis on the social and political activity of the client is part of the feminist therapist's approach to rape. Thus, rape is seen not as a problem of one woman, but of all women.

Eating Disorders

The socialization practices and messages given by society are an important focus of feminist therapists when dealing with anorexia, bulimia, or obesity. As Hyde (1996) shows, several studies reveal that many more American high school girls are dissatis-fied with their bodies than are boys. By applying gender-role analysis, therapists can help their clients examine the messages about body image that come from television, magazines, movies, and advertisements. Using gender-role analysis, therapists can help their clients understand how they accept the many messages about the importance of being thin. Together, therapist and client can work on ways to change these messages. Similarly, power analysis helps women examine their lack of power relative to men, as well as how preoccupation with eating contributes to a lack of power. Because social messages about eating are so strong, it is often helpful for women with eating disorders to work in groups, where they can support each other in fighting societal pressures to look thin.

In dealing with bulimia, anorexia, and obesity, therapists may also make use of a va-riety of other procedures. Behavioral strategies may be useful in monitoring purging, binging, and starving. Psychodynamic approaches look at family relationships and the desire of clients to please parents through appearance. What is important about the feminist approach is that it questions the goal of thinness and helps clients stand up to social pressures.

To give a brief example, Kate, a university junior, was constantly thinking about weight, and was purging three times per week. One of the approaches that her feminist therapist took with her in helping her with her bulimia was to look at messages about thinness that she was getting from sorority sisters, mother, father, boyfriend, television programs, and comparing herself to other female students as she walked to class. Because there were so many pressures on Kate to look thin, it was difficult to question these messages. Being aware of the physical dangers of bulimia and of the problems of two friends who were anorectic helped her to question the validity of thinness as a social value. Al-though Kate's bulimia discontinued after several months of therapy, her dislike of her body (she was of normal weight) was slow to change. She was reluctant to complete a thorough gender-role analysis and found it difficult to challenge the message that it is important to be thin. As she developed friendships with people on the campus newspaper, who were not as concerned with appearance, her constant thinking about eating began to decrease. Having Kate enroll in an eating disorder group helped her to get support for eliminating her purging and reducing her self-anger and disgust with her body.

Because of their diverse backgrounds, feminist therapists use a variety of approaches toward clients with depression, borderline disorders, posttraumatic stress disorder, and eating disorders, as well as other conditions. What distinguishes feminist therapies from other therapies is the emphasis on gender-role issues, power differences between men and women, and the need to look at social and political change in addition to individual psychological change.

CURRENT TRENDS AND ISSUES

Because feminist therapy is relatively recent, starting in the 1970s, and because there are many contributors rather than one leader, it is moving in many different directions. In doing so, feminist postmodern writers have shown how social constructionism can give power to individuals of different genders and cultures. Feminist therapists have also been concerned about determining standards of competency and ethics, as well as how best to train feminist therapists. An issue that was present at the beginning of the development of feminist therapy is that of feminist activism. Each of these issues, described in the next paragraphs, has received the attention of many feminist therapists.

Social constructionism has been an important force within feminist therapy and has been a major focus of postmodern thinking (Enns, 1997). Feminist therapists have questioned the traditional ways that males have perceived reality. Feminist therapy provides a way of examining issues that affect children's rights, minorities, and women from a social constructionist view that gives rather than removes power from these groups (Andrews & Freeman, 1997). Feminist therapists focus on power relationships between groups and seek to help those who are disenfranchised. Social constructionism has helped feminist therapists be more sensitive to cultural diversity, as can be seen in this chapter by the attention given to multicultural issues. Feminist therapist are very careful not to make generalizations about issues related to the race, class, ethnicity, age, and sexual orientation of their clients, but to value the stories and lives of their clients.

Having focused primarily on the lives of white middle-class women, feminist therapists have turned their attention to issues that affect women of color. Since the early 1990s, many books, journals, and comprehensive articles on feminist therapy have included chapters or sections on issues dealing with women from varying cultures and classes (Brown, 1994; Comas-Diaz, 1991; Enns, 1997; Jordan, 1997). These writings have led to the discussion of how social and cultural issues within particular societies interact with gender issues to provide insights into working with women from different groups. Additionally, feminist therapists have shown that feminist therapy is not for women only; it can also be concerned with men (Levant, 1996) and families (Cox, 1997). As feminist therapists reach out to the needs of various populations, the issue of how best to train feminist therapists becomes crucial.

Much of the training of feminist therapists has been informal. However, through their teaching and training, feminist therapists have integrated issues such as sexual exploitation of therapy clients, domestic violence, sexual abuse of children, and sexual harassment into their courses and supervision (Brown & Brodsky, 1992). Additionally, a few institutes or centers, such as the Stone Center at Wellesley College, offer training in feminist therapy. Related to the issue of training for feminist therapists is how to decide when a person is qualified to be called a feminist therapist.

As Brown and Brodsky (1992) point out, there has been a need to regulate the term *feminist therapy,* as nonfeminists may use the term *feminist therapist* in order to attract more clients. Standards for therapy might include minimum requirements in areas such as psychology of women, feminist philosophy, and feminist therapy (Brown & Brodsky, 1992). Related to the issue of standards for practice in training is the development of ethical guidelines (Enns, 1996; Lerman & Porter, 1990) that address therapist abuse of power (for example, through sexual relationships with their clients), overlapping relationships, recovered memories, and a variety of other important ethical concerns. Although most other psychotherapy theories have not examined ethical issues from a theoretical perspective, feminist therapists have done so by examining gender roles and power issues in relationships with clients. Providing help to clients has not been limited to therapeutic services; feminist therapists have also been concerned with broader societal issues.

Although feminist therapists have varied opinions on the importance of social action and the practice of feminist therapy, this issue continues to be an important one (Enns, 1997). In recent years, there has been a trend away from group therapy and dealing with social issues toward concerns about personal changes through individual therapy. However, social change through involvement in local and national groups continues. In her review of the activities of feminist therapists and social change, Enns (1993) describes several ways of taking social action: providing free services to women's shelters and centers, leading community support groups, changing public policy by applying research to women's work roles and sexual harassment policies, and working with organizations to promote day care, antiviolent attitudes toward women, and fair access to medical treatment. When feminist therapists have particular expertise, such as working with battered women, they may often apply their knowledge to issues affecting institutions such as the courts or shelters, rather than limit their activities to individual therapy.

The issues that feminist therapists are concerned with are related to issues of fair and equal treatment of all clients. Because feminist therapy has grown rapidly, the development of theory, standards for training, and ethical concerns continue to present new and problematic issues. These are made more complex as feminist therapists integrate different theories of psychotherapy into their practice.

RESEARCH

Very little research compares the effectiveness of feminist therapies with other approaches to therapy because most feminist therapists integrate other theories of therapy into their approach. Two studies that do discuss feminist therapy versus other therapies are explained. Also, in the 1970s the impact of consciousness-raising groups was studied. A summary of the results of these studies and a comparison of group feminist therapy to nonfeminist individual therapy is also described. Additional information is obtained by surveying feminist therapists about the techniques that they use. Also, new directions in research that will provide more information about feminist therapeutic interventions are discussed.

One study contrasted the therapeutic experiences of 24 women receiving group therapy in a feminist therapy collective with 26 women who participated in individual therapy with male therapists (Johnson, 1976). The average length of therapy for clients in the feminist groups was 4 months compared with 10 months for those receiving individual therapy. Johnson (1976) found that both samples described similar problems and levels of distress at the beginning of therapy and similar degrees of improvement and satisfaction at the end of the therapy experience. Those in feminist group therapy found group cohesiveness, interpersonal learning, and finding the therapist to be a competent woman as the most helpful factors in improvement. Johnson concludes that short-term group therapy in the feminist collective setting was as effective as longer individual therapy.

In another study of women who participated in consciousness-raising groups, Marecek, Kravetz, and Finn (1979) examined the impact of having a feminist therapist versus having a nonfeminist therapist. At the time of entering therapy, there were no differences in the 201 women who were in feminist therapy compared with the 207 women in traditional therapy as to demographic characteristics, degree of disturbance, and stress in marriage, work, or other life issues. Marecek et al. found that those who participated in feminist therapy were more likely to have radical political views and identify themselves as members of the women's movement than were those in traditional therapy. Of those who participated in feminist therapy, 67% found their experiences very helpful in contrast to 38% of women in traditional therapy. Also, those involved in the women's movement viewed traditional therapy much less favorably than did other women, whereas politically moderate and conservative women perceived both feminist and traditional therapy to be helpful.

Although consciousness-raising groups were popular in the 1970s, interest in them dropped significantly in later years. In reviewing six studies that showed the impact of consciousness-raising groups on women, Enns (1993) found that one major outcome was an increase in pro-feminist attitudes and behaviors in comparison with control group subjects who did not participate in consciousness-raising groups. Some of the changes found in consciousness-raising groups included increased assertiveness, more awareness of women's issues, and increased ability to find support from others (Ballou, Reuter, & Dinero, 1979; Ellis & Nichols, 1979; Gulanick, Howard, & Moreland, 1979; Wolfe & Fodor, 1977). Some of these studies made comparisons with control groups, and others used assertiveness groups. In some studies, women participated in both consciousness-raising and assertiveness groups. Generally, greater change was found in consciousness-raising groups than in control groups. Enns (1993) concludes that consciousness-raising experiences had therapeutic elements that, when combined with therapeutic interventions, were useful in helping women reach a variety of goals.

One study compared group feminist treatment with individual therapy in assisting 60 women who had been battered by their spouses (Rinfret-Raynor & Cantin, 1997). Both approaches to helping the women were effective. The researchers found that the women were able to make effective use of social networks and organizations to reduce the domestic violence they encountered. Therapy also helped to empower the women to use their own resources.

Two studies have used different approaches to determine important aspects of feminist therapy. The Feminist Self-Disclosure Inventory (FSDI) was developed to study how different therapists approach this topic (Simi & Mahalik, 1997). Five different factors were measured by the FSDI: Therapist background, promoting liberatory feelings, promoting egalitarianism, therapist availability, and empowering the client. Results from 143 female therapists indicated that the 41 feminist therapists differed from 34 psychoanalytic/dynamic therapists and 68 other therapists on their use of self-disclosure. Feminist therapists were more likely to create an egalitarian relationship in therapy than the other therapists. They also were more likely to encourage the client in choosing a role model in the course of therapy. With regard to their own personal self-disclosure, feminist therapists were more likely to tell their clients of their own sexual orientation than were other therapists.

Another survey was sent only to feminist therapists (Hill & Ballou, 1998). Using only two open-ended questions, the authors wanted to find out how principles of feminist therapy influenced the practice of feminist therapy. A low number of useable responses (28%) makes the results less representative than desirable. There were several commonalities in the responses as to how the therapists practice therapy. Most focused on sociocultural causes of distress and working for social change for clients. Promoting egalitarianism in the therapeutic relationship through self-disclosure or recognizing power differentials was also reported. Additionally, respondents described creative modifications they had made to cognitive, behavioral, and other techniques to be consistent with feminist therapy principles.

For future avenues of feminist therapy research, Enns (1993) recommends that researchers study feminist therapeutic interventions such as gender-role and power analysis, as well as therapist self-disclosure. Enns also suggests that it is important for research on feminist therapy to focus on both client and therapist perceptions of the counseling relationship. Research that links changes within the session to changes outside the session would also be helpful.

GENDER ISSUES

To this point, the discussion of feminist therapy has focused mainly on applications to women. Feminist therapy also has applications for treatment of men. Additionally, because of its focus on gender-role issues, it has probably addressed issues of male and female homosexuality more than other theories.

Feminist Therapy with Men

From a feminist therapy perspective, it is not sufficient to be nonsexist in work with clients; it is also important to help them within the perspective of gender roles (Good, Gilbert, & Scher, 1990). When counselors do not examine gender stereotypes with male clients, they may be supporting traditional views of men and women. For that reason, the assessment and therapeutic intervention of feminist therapy that have been discussed in this chapter can be helpful to men.

Several problems that men have can be treated from a feminist therapy approach. For example, Warren (1983) has discussed men's lack of tolerance in experiencing depression. Also, the societal emphasis on achievement and performance can oppress men to maintain a "masculine" role (Levant, 1996). When dealing with alcohol or drug problems, men may be reluctant to confront their feelings and unacceptable thoughts and choose to express themselves through alcohol or drug abuse (Diamond, 1987). In general, difficulties in developing relationships and being aware of one's own feelings are issues that lend themselves to the application of feminist therapy.

In describing feminist therapy with male clients, Ganley (1988) has identified several issues and techniques for dealing with men that reflect a feminist therapeutic perspective. When men are having difficulty integrating the need for relationships and the need to achieve, Ganley suggests that gender-role analysis can be helpful in understanding the conflict between relationship and achievement aspects of a man's life. With issues of intimacy avoidance, feminist therapists may use gender-role analysis to understand the social rewards of avoiding intimate relationships. In contrast, a nonfeminist therapist might focus on abandonment by the mother or rejection by a spouse. Because feminist therapy encourages self-disclosure in both the client and therapist, the therapist may model self-disclosure and reinforce self-disclosure on the part of the client. Additionally, participation in therapy groups can help men disclose their feelings.

Another issue is that of anger, which may be expressed through inappropriate behaviors such as drugs or fighting rather than constructively through discussion of angry feelings. Related to this issue is dealing with disappointment or rejection. Feminist therapists may help male clients find other feelings besides anger to deal with disappointments that are encountered in relationships or work. Not only is gender-role analysis helpful in dealing with these issues but also power analysis may be useful in helping men understand male-female relationships in terms of the lack of power that society gives to women.

In addition to the use of gender-role analysis and power analysis with emotional issues, Ganley has suggested several skills that feminist therapists can help men learn so that they may deal better with relationships, work issues, and other problems. Because men have often been taught to listen so that they may take action or make suggestions, feminist therapists may teach listening skills to their clients, which will help them understand the feeling behind the message as well as its content. Because men may have been socialized to believe that they are more powerful than women, men may need to learn how to work collaboratively and collegially with women rather than being competitive or dominant. In teaching problem-solving skills, feminist therapists may focus on listening, brainstorming, negotiation, and compromise skills rather than directing or ordering skills. Related to these skills that focus on cooperation are attitudes and beliefs about women that can be confronted and brought to men's attention to help them understand different ways that some men and women use in communicating with each other. By modeling open and collaborative relationships with male clients, feminist therapists can help their male clients improve their relationships with others.

Feminist Therapy with Gay and Lesbian Clients

Because of their emphasis on societal values and sex-role expectations, feminist therapists have paid particular attention to work with lesbians, but they have also applied their approaches to homosexual men. In writing about lesbian women, many writers believe that a common problem for lesbians is coping with a homophobic and hetero-sexist culture. *Homophobia* refers to the dislike, fear, or hatred of homosexual people; *heterosexism* is the concept that being heterosexual is inherently better than being ho-mosexual. Homophobia and heterosexism include societal beliefs that are held by both homosexual and heterosexual people, such as ideas that homosexuals are less psycho-logically healthy than heterosexuals, homosexuality is a developmental disorder, les-bian women hate men, and lesbian women are masculine in appearance (Worell & Remer, 1992). One of the goals of feminist therapy with homosexual clients is to help counter such myths. Thus, feminist therapists focus on social factors such as legal, po-litical, religious, and psychological discrimination rather than psychological factors such as determining the underlying causes of being homosexual or trying to convert homosexuals to heterosexuality. Because societal messages are usually quite antihomo-sexual, it is particularly important for therapists to be aware of their own internal ho-mophobic and heterosexist messages.

In writing about feminist therapy approaches to homosexual people, Brown (1988) addresses the issues of gender role socialization, dealing with homophobia, working with "coming out" issues, and dealing with other social factors that affect homosexu-als. Feminist therapists assess how their clients value or view homosexuality and how that view may have changed over time. A gender-role analysis can be particularly help-ful with lesbians and gay men so that they can understand the impact of social influ-ences on their own development. Analyzing the culture, particularly society's treat-ment of homosexuality, can also be useful. In these ways clients can see how they lower their own self-esteem by criticizing themselves for hurting their families or being fix-ated on homosexuality. Coming out—telling others that one is homosexual—can be viewed as a process rather than an event. Helping individuals deal with criticism or abuse and telling others about their homosexuality can be an important aspect of fem-inist therapy with homosexual clients. In addition to confronting societal discrimina-tion due to homosexuality, feminist therapists may help their lesbian and gay male clients deal with racial or cultural discrimination and biases due to low socioeconomic background. To do this, therapists must have knowledge and appreciation of a variety of cultures and other views of gender role (Brown, 1994).

MULTICULTURAL ISSUES

Feminist therapists have addressed issues affecting women of color (and, to a lesser ex-tent, men of color) in more depth and with more consistency than have other psy-chotherapy theorists. Although feminist therapy was originally based on issues affect-ing middle-class white women, there has been a great concentration of attention in the 1990s to women from a variety of cultures: Native American, Asian American, Hispanic/Latina, and African American women (Enns, 1997). An example of this trend is *Women's Growth in Diversity* (Jordan, 1997), which deals with therapy with women from diverse cultures. Although white feminists have often felt that women from a variety of ethnic groups have more in common with each other than with men from their group, this belief has not been shared by all ethnic minority women, many of whom have felt discrimination along with men (Comas-Diaz, 1987). Because of their awareness of the sociological variable of gender, feminist therapists have extended this awareness to culture.

Many of the techniques of feminist therapy that have been described in this chapter can be applied or extended to cultural issues. When feminist therapists conduct gender-role analyses of their clients, they can also include factors such as ethnic background, class, and relationships with parents and grandparents. When working with women of a different racial group, feminist therapists may share experiences with the client but also acknowledge differences (Enns, 1997). Bibliotherapy with writings by feminists of a particular culture or using examples of women based on myth, legend, or history can also be helpful. Direct help to women, such as referral for social services, health care, and educational assistance, can be helpful in Asian cultures (True, 1990). In working with Native American women, Sears (1990) illustrates the importance of being familiar with the culture and being known in the community, so that potential clients can develop a sense of trust in the therapist. Another effective therapeutic intervention with women of color is support groups or self-help networks of women from a specific culture or community. Using a variety of ways of learning about the culture of one's clients becomes extremely important in the same way that being informed about gender issues of clients is important.

Feminist therapists have also stressed the impact of the attitudes of the therapist on the client (Brown, 1994). In exploring this issue, Greene (1986) lists three major problems that the white therapist must consider: bigotry, color-blindness, and paternalism. *Bigotry* refers to conscious or unconscious views about ethnic deficits that may affect the way the therapist sees the client. *Color-blindness*—meaning attempting to ignore racial differences—may prevent therapists from understanding the client's experience of discrimination. *Paternalism* refers to a therapist who takes responsibility for the discrimination that the client may have received in the past. It is saying, in essence, "I'm not like other white people who have let you down. I won't." This attitude may make it difficult for the client to explore personal issues herself. These three guidelines can be useful for white therapists in understanding the potential impact that they may have upon clients of color.

A more specific approach to African American women by an African American feminist therapist (Childs, 1990) illustrates a sensitivity to both gender and race. In her first contact with African American female clients, Childs conveys the idea that the client does not have to submit to the therapist; rather, the therapist will examine the client's strengths and capabilities and work with them. After discussing the purpose of therapy and estimating its duration, the therapist may encounter the rage, anger, and grief that stem from an African American client's sense of betrayal and depression over being denied her ability, rights, and sense of competence. Childs points out that these strong feelings are a natural response to the client's having repressed her own feelings. This experience of anger or rage can lead to more creative self-expression and does not jeopardize therapy as it is not taken out on the client herself or on the therapist. Discussions in therapy include dealing with the stigma of being African American and being female. Childs helps the client feel independent and creative and not compare herself with others. In this process, the client may find it helpful to read African American feminist literature to understand racial and gender discrimination as it has affected African American women. Additionally, participating in a support group consisting of

African American women can decrease the sense of alienation and increase the sense of belongingness.

Feminist therapists who represent other ethnic groups have described techniques that can be used specifically with that group. Matsuyuki (1998) describes the importance that Japanese feminist therapists put on helping their clients become more independent and less on developing relationships, which Western feminist therapists stress. Alcohol and substance abuse are problems that have been addressed for African American women (Rhodes & Johnson, 1997) and Latinas (Mora, 1998) focusing on cultural and community perspectives as well as feminist ones. Combining sensitivity to gender and sensitivity to racial or cultural societal factors is likely to be a continuing trend of feminist therapy.

FAMILY AND COUPLES THERAPY

Feminist therapists do not separate their approach toward couples counseling from that of family therapy. When considering the term *couple* they include unmarried as well as same-sex couples. Those issues that are important in individual therapy, such as the impact of gender expectations and power differences between men and women, are important issues in family and couples therapy. As Goodrich, Rampage, Ellman, and Halstead (1988) make clear, feminist therapy does not approach couples or family therapy with the idea of helping the unfortunate women who have been mistreated by "bad" men. Rather, they look at political and social factors that provide insight into how people react to each other. Feminist therapy is not concerned with attaching blame or rescuing people; rather, it is attuned to how gender and power issues affect clients and will integrate this knowledge with other approaches to family therapy.

To be a feminist family therapist, it is essential to be aware of one's own gender-role values. Examples include being aware of stereotypes about men and women, about what constitutes a "good" family, and how children and partners should behave in the family.

By being aware of the importance of gender in therapy, a feminist therapist knows that his or her gender has an impact on most families, who are apt to respond to the therapist in a traditionally gender-stereotyped way (Goodrich et al., 1988). For example, a couple may expect a female therapist to be nurturing and ready to rescue the couple from their problems, whereas the same couple might be likely to ask advice and expect direction from a male therapist. Being aware of gender-role–related behavior on the part of the client helps the therapist to have insight into couple or family dynamics.

Feminist therapists can expect to encounter several different gender stereotypes when working with couples or families. Families and couples differ as to how they divide the labor in the household, the decisions that are made, and the benefits that come from the relationship. By examining what the individuals do and how they respond to each other in therapy, feminist therapists can then relate this information to the client's problems and, when appropriate, share it with them. For example, the therapist may observe and comment on the way the husband directly and loudly expresses himself, in contrast with an indirect or no expression of anger from a wife (Goodrich et al., 1988). This discussion may lead to other gender differences that occur in the relationship and then to the influence of societal and family expectations on the development of these traditional gender role behaviors. Providing factual information and statistics about inequalities between men and women may be helpful in this process (Enns, 1997). Also, the counselor may point out the gender role expectations that are inherent in language, such as using the term *mothering* rather than *parenting*, which implies that caring for a child is the mother's role. As these issues are explored, solutions to problems may arise that had previously been unavailable because of an automatic acceptance of traditional gender role values.

One of the important issues that feminist therapists attend to in couples and family therapy is that of power. As has been shown earlier, feminist therapists have demonstrated how men have more power in society than women, which contradicts the belief that men and women have equal opportunity in American society. To make progress in therapy, it is important to be aware of how differences in power affect couples and families (Hare-Mustin, 1991). A discussion of control of financial and emotional resources in the family, as well as how decisions are made, can help toward problem resolution. Examining who makes financial decisions, for example, may lead to questions: How was this decided? What factors influenced the decision as to how financial choices will be made? What would happen if this decision-making power is changed?

Feminists have made use of a postmodern approach to therapy that focuses on the client's view or narration of events (Gottlieb & Gottlieb, 1996). An interesting approach to power in a marriage relationship is reported by Hare-Mustin (1991) based on a case by Smith (1990). A couple had sought counseling because their relationship had deteriorated after the wife reported that she came home from work unexpectedly to find her husband partially dressed and a woman coming out of the bathroom. The sheets were rumpled and stained with semen, and the husband denied that anything improper had taken place. After a few years of therapy, the therapist sought consultation on the case, as the progress had been limited. The consultant's approach was to ask each member of the couple to relate what had happened. The wife's story was detailed and clear whereas the husband's was vague and not persuasive. Pointing this out to the couple, the consultant asked the husband to tell his wife's version. The husband tried to resist doing so, because he said his wife's story was not factual. However, the consultant persisted and said he should tell his wife's story, if he loved his wife. When he did so, the wife went home relieved and reported later that the relationship improved. Hare-Mustin explains the wife's recovery as being due to having her belief validated, while previously it had been denied. In this way, her view of "reality" could be seen as actually existing. Hare-Mustin views the therapeutic encounter from a postmodern or constructionist point of view. Having the wife's construction of reality validated empowers her. Applying this narrative approach to therapy is one method used by feminist couples therapists.

In the following example, Pinderhughes (1986) takes a feminist therapy perspective in working with an African American couple and their 16-year-old daughter. In this case, Pinderhughes examines cultural issues as well as those of gender. In this brief narrative, the focus is on the impact of racial identity and gender roles on Mr. H in his family of origin. Furthermore, the therapist uses relabeling to look at Mr. H.'s mother as hardworking rather than as domineering. Another important intervention that is consistent with a feminist therapy approach is that of taking social action and assisting clients in doing so. All of these issues can be seen in this description.

> Mr. and Mrs. H. initially came to treatment because of marital problems. One day, Mrs. H. came to a session enraged because their daughter Helen, aged 16, had been arrested and taken to Juvenile Court after an altercation with a white salesgirl. Helen had ignored the salesgirl's rude request that she move, and the salesgirl had pushed her. Mrs. H., greatly embarrassed by the incident, was also infuriated by the behavior of the policeman, who had said "niggers again" and had told Helen that she had "better shut up because I don't like you people." Mrs. H. was also angry with Mr. H., who distanced himself from the whole incident. With help from the therapist, Mrs. H. and Helen lodged a complaint against the salesgirl at the store, and Mrs. H. joined a community group that was pressing for the creation of a citizen's review board for police activities. In treatment, Mrs. H. acknowledged her general dissatisfaction with Mr. H.'s passivity, while he expressed his resentment that she "talks too much" and is "always right." Attempts to negotiate these issues were ineffective so the therapist moved to a family-of-origin approach.
>
> Mr. H. had been reared for his first 5 years by a loving grandmother in the South. He then joined his brother, aged 3, and his parents, who had been working in Boston. Ambivalent about both his mother (whom he saw as quarrelsome, angry, and at times unloving) and his father (whom he saw as unable to temper his mother's overassertiveness), he had remained angry at having been pressed into the role of "father substitute" at 13 when his parents separated. Mr. H. had attended an all white high school, often being the only black in his classes. An underachiever, he remembered his teachers' comments that he "would never amount to anything." His subsequent all-out effort to achieve caused him to bury his feelings about his racial identity and to ignore any incident that hinted of racism.
>
> The therapist helped Mr. H. to look at his parents in the context of the family's identity as Afro-Americans and their struggles. He recalled tearfully his father's teachings about "hard work, doing a good job and being a team" when he and his brother worked with their father as a cleaning team. "No one could do a better job." His anger abated as the therapist placed his mother's efforts to work and keep the family together in the context of her struggle as a black for upward mobility. Although Mr. H. called his mother overcontrolling and dominant, the therapist relabeled her as hardworking and organized, adaptive traits in the battle against racism. As Mr. H. recovered the positive feelings related to his father's teaching the value of work, the therapist relabeled his father as strong and patient. After this, both Mr. and Mrs. H. softened in their rigid stance toward one another. As Mr. H. moved toward a more active role in the family, Mrs. H. felt less pressure and relaxed, enjoying the more mutual relationship they had now achieved. (Pinderhughes, 1986, pp. 60–61)[7]

Working with sociological issues such as gender role and racial identity provides a perspective that other theories do not emphasize. When therapists are aware of their own gender roles and cultural values, they are better able to understand how these issues affect their clients. Sometimes the analysis of gender role and power in society can be difficult, at other times straightforward; however, it allows individuals to look at their roles in the social and political context of the environment.

GROUP COUNSELING

Because feminist therapy developed from the consciousness-raising (CR) groups of the 1970s, group treatments have been an important part of feminist therapy. Consciousness-raising groups, usually with 4 to 12 members, dealt with women's roles and experiences in a culture that was often perceived as discriminatory toward women. These groups were leaderless, noncompetitive, and emotionally supportive—characteristics that the participants would like to see in larger society (Kirsch, 1987). Often meeting in people's homes, the groups discussed a variety of topics related to social gender roles. The CR groups were often responsible for services for women such as rape crisis centers, women's counseling centers, shelters for battered women, and women's health centers (Enns, 1997). In this way, social activism and personal awareness of the impact of gender roles on women were combined.

Since the emergence of CR groups, there have been groups designed for women at various life stages and for women with a variety of concerns. Women's groups have sometimes focused on specific issues such as agoraphobia, homelessness, alcoholism, sexual abuse, sexual concerns, battering, work stress, eating disorders, and relationship problems. Additionally, women's groups have been designed for subgroups of women: African Americans, Native Americans, Hispanics, lesbians, pregnant teenagers, working women with families, women raising their children at home, and many other groups. Unlike CR groups, these groups usually have a paid professional leader. Feminist therapists encourage the use of all-female groups, not only because of the need to discuss specific issues such as those listed previously but also to explore their commonalities, affirm each other's strengths, and understand the similar concerns of women (Kravetz, 1978). When men are included in groups, they may do more initiating and directing than women and may be more frequently listened to than women (West & Zimmerman, 1985). Additionally, women may be less likely to discuss topics such as body image and sexuality in mixed groups and less likely to develop trusting and close female relationships within the group (Walker, 1987). Specific issues that women have, as well as their styles of relating, have produced not only groups of all women working on specific topics but also specific techniques for dealing with women's issues.

For individual and group therapy alike, gender role issues are an important aspect of treatment that can be approached in a variety of ways (DeChant, 1996). Group leaders can ask, "What did it mean to you to be female or male growing up?" "What happens when you don't follow general gender role norms?" or "How have you learned about roles of men and women?" (Brown, 1986, 1990). A behavioral approach to gender roles raises issues about the advantages and disadvantages of certain behavior. For example, what are the costs and the benefits of taking care of others at the expense of oneself? What are alternatives so that the individual can give to others but also take care of herself (Enns, 1992)? Women may make lists of the advantages and disadvantages of certain gender-related behaviors and share them in group.

Should group members have contact with each other outside the group? Feminist group therapy supports the growth of women's power in relationships. The relationship is itself highly valued. However, in many approaches to group therapy, members are told not to have contact with other members outside the group. By avoiding contact with other group members no hidden alliances can form and all members are aware of issues affecting other group members. In contrast to this view, Rittenhouse (1997) supported out-of-group contact by members of a female survivors of abuse group. After analyzing group process notes, she concludes that establishment of relationships outside of the group is helpful when issues of isolation, trust, and relationships are so important. Because of its emphasis on empowerment and political change, feminist therapists may take a different view of out-of-group behavior of clients than other group therapists.

SUMMARY

Whereas most theories of psychotherapy focus on individual development, feelings, thoughts, or behaviors, feminist therapy incorporates sociological variables by examining the impact of gender differences on women (and men). Recently, feminist therapists have also examined the interaction of gender and racial and ethnic variables as they affect personal development throughout childhood, adolescence, and adulthood. Feminist theories of personality are new and not complete but offer interesting insights into psychological characteristics of men and women. Gender schema theory provides a means of examining the role of gender in people's behavior. Gilligan's work in moral development gives information as to how men and women differ in their processes of making ethical decisions. The ways in which women and men learn different styles of relating has been the subject of the work of Miller and her colleagues. The theme of unequal power emerges in Gilligan's and Miller's views of how gender roles affect women's development across the life span. These theorists have also addressed, to varying degrees, the impact of violence toward women on personality development.

Feminist therapists have developed techniques that they integrate with other theories that are consistent with their philosophical view of therapy. This view recognizes the importance of political and social factors on individuals, values a female perspective of society and the individual, and works toward egalitarian relationships. Feminist therapy interventions examine gender and power differences with their clients and help them bring about change. Sometimes this is done through assertiveness training, or relabeling or reframing ways of viewing events. Furthermore, many feminist therapists have found diagnostic classification to be unhelpful to their clients and have relabeled client problems in a more positive manner. Disorders, such as depression, borderline diagnoses, eating disorders, and posttraumatic stress, that occur more frequently with females than with males have been discussed in this chapter. Although feminist therapy has focused on women's issues, more recently feminist therapists have also applied their approach, combined with other theoretical perspectives, to men and children.

Suggested Readings

UNGER, R., & CRAWFORD, M. (1996). *Woman and gender: A feminist psychology* (2nd ed.). New York: McGraw-Hill. • A very thorough review of many issues related to the development of women, this textbook on the psychology of women provides an excellent background for understanding feminist psychotherapy.

ENNS, C. Z. (1997). *Feminist theories and feminist psychotherapies: Origins, themes, and variations.* New York: Haworth. • The history of feminist therapy and its principles and variations are summarized. Three of the eight chapters are devoted to feminist therapy and cultural issues and concerns.

WORELL, J., & REMER, P. (1992). *Feminist perspectives in therapy: An empowerment model for women.* New York: Wiley. • Topics such as assessment and therapeutic approaches are explained in some detail. Additionally, ways of integrating other theories of psychotherapy with feminist therapy are explained. Also, approaches to depression, sexual assault, abuse, and working with lesbian and ethnic minority women are described.

BROWN, L. S. (1994). *Subversive dialogues: Theory in feminist therapy.* New York: Basic Books. • Many issues that bring feminist therapy and theory together are discussed, including cultural diversity. The frequent use of case material helps illustrate the applications of feminist therapy.

References

AMERICAN PSYCHOLOGICAL ASSOCIATION. (1975). Report of the task force on sex bias and sex role stereotyping in psychotherapeutic practice. *American Psychologist, 30,* 1169–1175.

ANDREWS, A. B., & FREEMAN, M. L. (1997). The congruence of international children's rights and feminist principles as a foundation for therapy with young people. *Women and Therapy, 20,* 7–27.

BALLOU, M., REUTER, J., & DINERO, T. (1979). An audio-taped consciousness-raising group for women: Evaluation of the process dimensions. *Psychology of Women Quarterly, 4,* 185–193.

BEM, S. L. (1981). Gender schema theory: A cognitive account of sex typing. *Psychological Review, 88,* 354–364.

BEM, S. L. (1983). Gender schema theory and its implications for child development: Raising gender-aschematic children in a gender-schematic society. *Signs, 8,* 598–616.

BEM, S. L. (1987). Gender schema theory and the romantic tradition. In P. Shaver & C. Hendrick (Eds.), *Sex and gender* (pp. 251–271). Newbury Park, CA: Sage.

BEM, S. L. (1993). *The lens of gender: Transforming the debate on sexual inequality.* New Haven, CT: Yale University Press.

BETZ, N. E., & FITZGERALD, L. E. (1987). *The career psychology of women.* New York: Academic Press.

BROWN, L. S. (1986). Gender-role analysis: A neglected component of psychological assessment. *Psychotherapy, 23,* 243–248.

BROWN, L. S. (1988). Feminist therapy with lesbians and gay men. In M. Dutton-Douglas & L. E. Walker (Eds.), *Feminist psychotherapies: Integration of therapeutic and feminist systems* (pp. 206–227). Norwood, NJ: Ablex.

BROWN, L. S. (1990). Taking account of gender in the clinical assessment interview. *Professional Psychology, 21,* 12–17.

BROWN, L. S. (1994). *Subversive dialogues: Theory in feminist therapy.* New York: Basic Books.

BROWN, L. S., & BRODSKY, A. M. (1992). The future of feminist therapy. *Psychotherapy, 29,* 51–57.

BROWN, L. S., & WALKER, L. E. A. (1990). Feminist therapy perspectives on self-disclosure. In G. Stricker & M. Fischer (Eds.), *Self-disclosure in the therapeutic relationship* (pp. 135–154). New York: Plenum.

BURGESS, A. W., & HOLSTROM, L. L. (1974). Rape trauma syndrome. *American Journal of Psychiatry, 131,* 981–986.

BURSTOW, B. (1992). *Radical feminist therapy.* Newbury Park, CA: Sage.

CHESLER, P. (1972). *Women and madness.* New York: Doubleday.

CHESLER, P. (1997, November/December). Women and madness: A feminist diagnosis. *Ms.,* 36–42.

CHILDS, E. K. (1990). Therapy, feminist ethics, and the community of color with particular emphasis on the treatment of black women. In H. Lerman & N. Porter (Eds.), *Feminist ethics in psychotherapy* (pp. 195–203). New York: Springer.

CHODOROW, N. J. (1989). *Feminism and psychoanalytic theory.* New Haven, CT: Yale University Press.

CHODOROW, N. J. (1996). Theoretical gender and clinical gender: Epistemological reflections of the psychology of women. *Journal of the American Psychoanalytic Association, 44,* 215–238.

COMAS-DIAZ, L. (1987). Feminist therapy and Hispanic/Latina women. *Women and Therapy, 6,* 39–62.

COMAS-DIAZ, L. (1991). Feminism and diversity in psychology: The case of women of color. *Psychology of Women Quarterly, 15,* 597–609.

COX, N. (1997). Treating parents and children together: A feminist look at exclusionary child psychotherapy. *Women and Therapy, 20,* 89–100.

CRAWFORD, M. (1995). *Talking difference: On gender and language.* New York: Sage.

DAUGHERTY, C., & LEES, M. (1988). Feminist psychodynamic therapies. In M. A. Dutton Douglas & L. E. Walker (Eds.), *Feminist psychotherapies* (pp. 68–90). Norwood, NJ: Ablex.

DECHANT, B. (Ed.). (1996). *Women and group psychotherapy: Theory and practice.* New York: Guilford.

DEUTSCH, H. (1944). *The psychology of women: A psychoanalytic interpretation.* New York: Grune & Stratton.

DIAMOND, J. (1987). Counseling male substance abusers. In M. Scher, S. Stevens, G. Good, & G. Eichenfield (Eds.), *The handbook of counseling and psychotherapy with men* (pp. 332–342). Newbury Park, CA: Sage.

EICHENBAUM, L., & ORBACH, S. (1983). *Understanding women: A feminist psychoanalytic approach.* New York: Basic Books.

ELLIS, E. M., & NICHOLS, M. P. (1979). A comparative study of feminist and traditional group assertiveness training with women. *Psychotherapy, 16,* 467–474.

ENNS, C. Z. (1992). Self esteem groups: A synthesis of consciousness-raising and assertiveness training. *Journal of Counseling and Development, 71,* 7–13.

ENNS, C. Z. (1993). Twenty years of feminist counseling and therapy: From naming biases to implementing multifaceted practice. *Counseling Psychologist, 21,* 3–87.

ENNS, C. Z. (1996). The Feminist Therapy Institute Code of Ethics: Implications for working with survivors of child sexual abuse. In Contratlo, S., & Gutfreund, M. J. (Eds.), *A feminist clinician's guide to the memory of debate* (pp. 79–91). New York: Haworth.

ENNS, C. Z. (1997). *Feminist theories and feminist psychotherapies: Origins, themes, and variations.* New York: Haworth.

FERREE, M. M. (1987). She works hard for a living: Gender and class on the job. In B. B. Hess & M. M. Ferree (Eds.), *Analyzing gender: A handbook of social science research* (pp. 322–347). Newbury Park, CA: Sage.

GANLEY, A. L. (1988). Feminist therapy with male clients. In M. A. Dutton-Douglas & L. E. Walker (Eds.), *Feminist psychotherapies: Integration of therapeutic and feminist system* (pp. 186–205). Norwood, NJ: Ablex.

GILBERT, L. A. (1980). Feminist therapy. In A. Brodsky & R. T. Hare-Mustin (Eds.), *Women and psychotherapy* (pp. 245–265). New York: Guilford.

GILLIGAN, C. (1977). In a different voice: Women's conception of self and morality. *Harvard Educational Review, 47,* 481–517.

GILLIGAN, C. (1982). *In a different voice.* Cambridge, MA: Harvard University Press.

GOOD, G., GILBERT, L., & SCHER, M. (1990). Gender aware therapy: A synthesis of feminist therapy and knowledge about gender. *Journal of Counseling and Development, 68,* 376–380.

GOODRICH, T. J., RAMPAGE, C., ELLMAN, B., & HALSTEAD, K. (1988). *Feminist family therapy.* New York: Norton.

GOTTLIEB, D. T., & GOTTLIEB, C. D. (1996). The narrative/collaborative process in couples therapy: A postmodern perspective. In M. Hill & E. D. Rothblum (Eds.), *Couples therapy: Feminist perspectives.* New York: Haworth.

GOTTMAN, J. M., & PARKER, J. G. (Eds.). (1987). *Conversations of friends: Speculations on affective development.* New York: Cambridge University Press.

GREENE, B. (1986). When the therapist is white and the patient is black: Considerations for psychotherapy in the feminist heterosexual and lesbian communities. In D. Howard (Ed.), *The dynamics of feminist therapy* (pp. 41–65). Binghamton, NY: Haworth Press.

GREENE, B. (1997). Psychotherapy with African American women: Integrating feminist and psychodynamic models. *Smith College Studies in Social Work, 67,* 299–322.

GREENSPAN, M. (1983). *A new approach to women and therapy.* New York: McGraw-Hill.

GULANICK, N. A., HOWARD, G. S., & MORELAND, J. (1979). Evaluation of a group program designed to increase androgyny in feminine women. *Sex Roles, 5,* 811–827.

HARE-MUSTIN, R. T. (1991). Sex, lies, and headaches: The problem is power. In T. J. Goodrich (Ed.), *Women and power* (pp. 63–85). New York: Norton.

HARE-MUSTIN, R. T., & MARECEK, J. (1988). The meaning of difference: Gender theory, postmodernism, and psychology. *American Psychologist, 43,* 445–464.

HAYDEN, M. (1986). Psychoanalytic resources for the activist feminist therapist. *Women and Therapy, 5,* 89–94.

HAYS, H. R. (1964). *The dangerous sex: The myth of feminine evil.* New York: Putnam.

HELMS, J. E. (1995). An update of Helm's White and People of Color racial identity models. In J. G. Ponterotto, J. M. Casas, L. A. Suzuki, & C. M. Alexander (Eds.), *Handbook of multicultural counseling* (pp. 181–198). Thousand Oaks, CA: Sage.

HERMAN, J. L. (1992). *Trauma and recovery: The aftermath of violence.* New York: Basic Books.

HILL, M., & BALLOU, M. (1998). Making feminist therapy: A practice survey. *Women and Therapy, 21,* 1–16.

HORNEY, K. (1966). *New ways in psychoanalysis.* New York: Norton.

HYDE, J. S. (1996). *Half the human experience: The psychology of women* (5th ed.). Lexington, MA: Heath.

IVEY, A. E., IVEY, M. B., & SIMEK-MORGAN, L. (1997). *Counseling and psychotherapy: A multicultural perspective* (4th ed.). Boston: Allyn & Bacon.

JAKUBOWSKI, P. A. (1977). Assertion training for women. In E. I. Rawlings & D. K. Carter (Eds.), *Psychotherapy for women* (pp. 147–190). Springfield, IL: Charles C. Thomas.

JOHNSON, M. (1976). An approach to feminist therapy. *Psychotherapy: Theory, Research, and Practice, 13,* 72–76.

JORDAN, J. V. (1997). *Women's growth in diversity: More writings from the Stone Center.* New York: Guilford.

KASCHAK, E. (1976). Sociotherapy: An ecological model for psychotherapy with women. *Psychotherapy: Theory, Research, and Practice, 13,* 61–63.

KASCHAK, E. (1981). Feminist psychotherapy: The first decade. In S. Cox (Ed.), *Female psychology: The emerging self* (pp. 387–400). New York: St. Martins.

KASCHAK, E. (1992). *Engendered lives.* New York: Basic Books.

KIRSCH, B. (1987). Evolution of consciousness-raising groups. In C. Brody (Ed.), *Women's therapy groups* (pp. 43–54). New York: Springer.

KLEIN, M. H., (1976). Feminist concepts of therapy outcome. *Psychotherapy: Theory, Research, and Practice, 13,* 89–95.

KOHLBERG, L. (1981). *The philosophy of moral development: Essays on moral development* (Vols. 1–2). San Francisco: Harper & Row.

KRAVETZ, D. (1978). Consciousness-raising groups in the 1970s. *Psychology of Women Quarterly*, 3, 168–186.

KRAVETZ, D. (1987). Benefits of consciousness-raising groups for women. In C. Brody (Ed.), *Women's therapy groups: Paradigms of feminist treatment* (pp. 55–66). New York: Springer.

LARRABEE, M. J. (Ed.). (1993). *An ethic of care: Feminist and interdisciplinary perspectives.* New York: Routledge.

LERMAN, H. (1986). From Freud to feminist personality theory: Getting there from here. *Psychology of Women Quarterly*, 10, 1–18.

LERMAN, H., & PORTER, N. (Eds.). (1990). *Feminist ethics in psychotherapy.* New York: Springer.

LEVANT, R. F. (1996). The new psychology of men. *Professional Psychology: Research and Practice*, 27, 259–265.

MARECEK, J., KRAVETZ, D., & FINN, S. (1979). Comparison of women who enter feminist therapy and women who enter traditional therapy. *Journal of Consulting and Clinical Psychology*, 4, 734–742.

MATSUYUKI, M. (1998). Japanese feminist counseling as a political act. *Women and Therapy*, 21, 65–77.

MILLER, J. B. (1986). *Toward a new psychology of women.* Boston: Beacon Press. (Original work published 1976.)

MILLER, J. B. (1988). *Connections, disconnections, and violations* (No. 33). Wellesley, MA: Stone Center for Developmental Studies.

MILLER, J. B. (1991). The development of women's sense of self. In J. V. Jordan, A. G. Kaplan, J. B. Miller, I. P. Stiver, & J. L. Surrey (Eds.), *Women's growth in connection* (pp. 11–26). New York: Guilford.

MILLER, J. B., JORDAN, J. V., KAPLAN, A. G., STIVER, F. P., & SURREY, J. L. (1997). Some misconceptions and reconceptions of a relational approach. In J. V. Jordan (Ed.), *Women's growth in diversity* (pp. 25–49). New York: Guilford.

MINSKY, R. (1997). *Psychoanalysis and gender: An introductory reader.* London: Routledge.

MORA, J. (1998). The treatment of alcohol dependency among Latinas: A feminist, cultural, and community perspective. *Alcoholism Treatment Quarterly*, 16, 163–177.

OKUN, B. E. (1992). Object relations and self psychology: Overview and feminist perspective. In L. S. Brown & M. Ballou (Eds.), *Personality and psychopathology: Feminist reappraisals* (pp. 20–45). New York: Guilford.

PHILPOTT, L. L., BROOKS, G. R., LUSTERMAN, D. D., & NUTT, R. L. (1997). *Bridging separate gender worlds: Why men and women clash and how therapists can bring them together.* Washington: American Psychological Association.

PINDERHUGHES, E. B. (1986). Minority women: A nodal position in the functioning of the social system. In M. Ault-Riche (Ed.), *Women and family therapy* (pp. 51–63). Rockville, MD: Aspen.

RAWLINGS, E. I., & CARTER, D. K. (1977). Feminist and nonsexist psychotherapy. In E. I. Rawlings & D. K. Carter (Eds.), *Psychotherapy for women* (pp. 49–76). Springfield, IL: Charles C. Thomas.

RHODES, R., & JOHNSON, A. (1997). A feminist approach to treating alcohol and drug addicted African-American women. *Women and Therapy*, 20, 23–37.

RINFRET-RAYNOR, M., & CANTIN, S. (1997). Feminist therapy for battered women: An assessment. In G. K. Kantor & J. L. Jasinski (Eds.), *Out of darkness: Contemporary perspectives on family violence* (pp. 219–234). Thousand Oaks, CA: Sage.

RITTENHOUSE, J. (1997). Feminist principles in survivor's groups: Out of group contact. *Journal for Specialists in Group Work*, 22, 111–119.

ROMANIELLO, J. (1992). Beyond archetypes: A feminist perspective on Jungian therapy. In L. S. Brown & M. Ballou (Eds.), *Personality and psychopathology: Feminist reappraisals* (pp. 46–69). New York: Guilford.

RUSSELL, M. (1984). *Skills in counseling women*. Springfield, IL: Charles C. Thomas.

SCHOFIELD, J. (1982). *Black and white in school*. New York: Praeger.

SEARS, V. L. (1990). Ethics in small minority communities. In H. Lerman & N. Porter (Eds.), *Feminist ethics in psychotherapy* (pp. 204–213). New York: Springer.

SHARF, R. S. (1997). *Applying career development theory to counseling* (2nd ed.). Pacific Grove, CA: Brooks/Cole.

SIMI, N. L., & MAHALIK, J. R. (1997). Comparison of feminist versus psychoanalytic/dynamic and other therapists on self-disclosure. *Psychology of Women Quarterly, 21*, 465–483.

SMITH, T. E. (1990). *Lie to me no more: Believable stories and marital affairs*. Unpublished manuscript.

STURDIVANT, S. (1980). *Therapy with women*. New York: Springer.

SURREY, J. L. (1991). The "self-in-relation:" A theory of women's development. In J. V. Jordan, A. G. Kaplan, J. B. Miller, J. P. Stiver, & J. L. Surrey (Eds.), *Women's growth in connection* (pp. 51–66). New York: Guilford.

TRUE, T. H. (1990). Psychotherapeutic issues with Asian American women. *Sex Roles, 22*, 477–486.

TURNER, C. W. (1997). Clinical applications of the Stone Center theoretical approach to minority women. In J. V. Jordan (Ed.), *Women's growth in diversity: More writings from the Stone Center* (pp. 74–90). New York: Guilford.

UNGER, R., & CRAWFORD, M. (1996). *Women and gender: A feminist psychology* (2nd ed.). New York: McGraw-Hill.

U.S. DEPARTMENT OF LABOR. (1994). *Employment and earnings*. Washington, D.C.: Bureau of Labor Statistics.

WALKER, L. J. (1984). Sex differences in the development of moral reasoning: A critical review. *Child Development, 55*, 667–691.

WALKER, L. J. S. (1987). Women's groups are different. In C. M. Brody (Ed.), *Women's therapy groups* (pp. 3–12). New York: Springer.

WARREN,, L. W. (1983). Male intolerance of depression: A review with implications for psychotherapy. *Clinical Psychology Review, 3*, 147–156.

WEST, C., & ZIMMERMAN, D. H. (1985). Gender, language, and discourse. In T. A. van Dijk (Ed.), *Handbook of discourse analysis in society* (pp. 103–124). London: Academic Press.

WOLFE, J. L., & FODOR, I. G. (1977). Modifying assertive behavior in women: A comparison of three approaches. *Behavior Therapy, 8*, 567–574.

WORELL, J., & REMER, P. (1992). *Feminist perspectives in therapy: An empowerment model for women*. New York: Wiley.

13

Family Systems Therapy

In discussing treatment of family problems, two terms are used throughout this chapter: *family therapy* and *family systems therapy*. Family therapy is psychotherapeutic treatment of the family to bring about better psychological functioning. Each of the preceding chapters illustrates how a particular psychotherapeutic approach can be used with families. Family systems therapy is a type of family therapy that attends to the interactions of family members and views the entire family as a unit or system. Treatment is designed to understand and bring about change within the family structure. This type of family therapy is the topic of this chapter.

Of the many different family systems therapy approaches, this chapter focuses on six: intergenerational, structural, strategic, experiential, solution focused, and narrative. The intergenerational approach of Murray Bowen examines the impact of the parents' interaction with their own family of origin as it affects their interaction with their children. Salvador Minuchin's structural approach is concerned with how family members relate to each other in the therapy hour and at home. Emphasizing the need to bring about change in the family, Jay Haley's strategic approach is directed at bringing about change in symptoms. The experiential family system therapies emphasize the unconscious and affective processes of families and therapists in their work. DeShazer has developed a brief approach that concentrates on new solutions for a problem, rather than focusing on the origin of the problem. Narrative therapy, developed by Epston and White, helps families change problem-saturated stories to ones with more positive outcomes. DeShazer's and Epston and White's models are consistent with a social constructivist view that focuses on the family members' construction of reality. Because most family therapists use several of these six approaches, ways of integrating them are also described. Additionally, other family systems therapists have devoted attention to brief family systems therapy, working with groups of families and integrating educational information and therapy when working with families.

Because family systems therapists address family dynamics and not individual personalities, this chapter requires a different outline than the others. Rather than sections on theories of personality and psychotherapy, six sections describe the family systems approach and the application of technique to each of the following theories:

intergenerational, structural, strategic, experiential, solution focused, and narrative. Each of the six sections describes the way in which the theorists understand the family, their goals for treatment, their treatment approach, and a case example. Later sections describe brief family therapy, current trends and innovations, research, gender issues, cultural issues, applying family therapy to individuals, couples counseling, and group family approaches. First, however, is a brief history of family therapy and general systems theory.

HISTORICAL BACKGROUND

The current practice of family systems therapy has its roots in a variety of theoretical, practical, and research approaches to helping children, married couples, and individuals with family problems. In understanding family therapy as it is now, it will be helpful to learn about the contribution of child guidance clinics and marriage counseling in helping families cope with problems. From both theoretical and in-depth perspectives, Freud and other psychoanalysts have contributed to the understanding of families through their emphasis on early childhood events and their impact on adulthood, as well as their own psychotherapeutic work with children. Also, early research on schizophrenic children and adolescents as part of family systems led to the concepts and ideas that are widely used in the current practice of family therapy. Another important addition to family therapy comes from outside the social sciences: general systems theory. It examines the interactions and processes of parts of a whole in areas such as engineering, biology, economics, politics, sociology, psychology, and psychotherapy. A familiarity with these diverse applied and theoretical approaches is helpful in understanding the development of theoretical approaches to family therapy.

Early Approaches to Family Counseling

Only since the 1930s has formal marriage counseling been available. Before that time, informal counseling was probably provided by friends, doctors, clergy, and lawyers. The first centers for marriage counseling were opened in Los Angeles by Paul Popenoe and in New York City by Abraham and Hannah Stone (Goldenberg & Goldenberg, 2000). In the 1940s, 15 centers devoted to marriage or family issues had been established to help families in the community. These clinics dealt with problems such as infidelity, divorce, child raising, financial problems, communication problems, and sexual incompatibilities. In general, most marital therapy was brief and problem focused, taking into consideration the personality and role expectations of each member of the couple as well as their communicating and decision-making patterns (Cromwell, Olson, & Fournier, 1976). A common practice in the 1930s and 1940s was for different therapists to see individuals separately (Goldenberg & Goldenberg, 2000). In the 1950s, conjoint therapy, in which the couple was seen together by one therapist, became more common. As marriage counseling developed, it focused more and more on attending to and working with the marriage relationship and less on the individual personality issues of each client. During the 1930s and 1940s and into the 1950s, problems with children were often left to child guidance clinics, although they might be discussed in marriage counseling (Mittelman, 1948).

Because of the prevailing psychoanalytic view in the 1930s and 1940s that emotional disorders began in childhood, the treatment of children's problems was seen as an excellent way of preventing mental illness in later life (Goldenberg and Goldenberg, 2000). Usually the parents were treated separately from the children. Often the mothers were seen as the cause of the problem, with little attention given to the fathers. The focus was primarily on treatment of the child and secondarily to help the mother deal with negative feelings that may affect child raising, as well as to help her learn new attitudes or approaches. Levy (1943) wrote about the negative impact of maternal overprotection on children, and Fromm-Reichmann (1948) was concerned about the impact of the schizophrenogenic mother (dominating, rejecting, and insecure) on children.

In the 1950s, there was a shift from blaming parents for children's problems to helping parents and children relate better to each other. For example, Cooper (1974) addressed positive goals of parental involvement so that progress with the child in therapy could develop and so that parents could make changes in the child's environment to help the child's improvement.

Psychoanalytic and Related Influences on Family Therapy

Several early theorists, although focusing mainly on work with individuals, contributed to the development of family therapy treatment. In his individual work, Sigmund Freud treated both children and adolescents and attended to processes related to early childhood development in all of his patients. Another early contribution to family therapy was that of Alfred Adler, who observed the development of social interest within the family and initiated child guidance clinics in Vienna. The work of Harry Stack Sullivan (1953) was concerned with not only intrapsychic factors but also interpersonal relationships within the family and with others. Some of his observations had a direct influence on later family therapists. The person considered to be the initiator of family therapy and work with families as a unit is Nathan Ackerman. The impact of his work on the later development of family therapy is shown here.

A child psychiatrist who was trained in psychoanalysis, Ackerman initially used the traditional model in which the psychiatrist saw the child and the social worker saw the mother. In the mid-1940s, however, he started to see the entire family for both diagnosis and treatment. He was aware of conscious and unconscious issues within the individual and the family, as well as issues that affected the family as a whole. As a result, Ackerman often attended to nonverbal cues such as facial expression, posture, and seating arrangements as a way of assessing family problems. In his therapeutic approach, Ackerman was open, honest, and direct, encouraging families to share their own thoughts and feelings as he did. In his work with families, he also made use of psychoanalytic techniques such as transference and interpretation and observed the countertransference with family members (Becvar & Becvar, 1999). Many family therapists were drawn to his engaging style and his active approach to therapy. However, his writings (Ackerman, 1966a, 1966b) do not provide a clear, systematic approach for therapists who wish to follow his method.

The Study of Communication Patterns in Families with Schizophrenic Members

During the 1950s, several research groups studied communication patterns within families who had a member suffering from schizophrenia. From this work emerged concepts that describe dysfunctional ways of relating within a family: the double bind, marital schism, marital skew, and pseudomutuality.

Double bind.   Working in Palo Alto, Bateson, Jackson, Haley, and Weakland (1956) studied how families with schizophrenic members functioned and maintained stability. They observed the double bind, in which a person receives two related but contradictory messages. One message may be relatively clear, the other message unclear (often nonverbal), creating a "no-win" paradox. Bateson et al. (1956) give a classic example of a mother giving a nonverbal message that says go away, followed by a message that says come closer, you need my love, and then you're interpreting my messages in the wrong way (Goldenberg & Goldenberg, 2000).

> A young man who had fairly well recovered from an acute schizophrenic episode was visited in the hospital by his mother. He was glad to see her and impulsively put his arm around her shoulders, whereupon she stiffened. He withdrew his arm and she asked, "Don't you love me anymore?" He then blushed and she said, "Dear, you must not be so easily embarrassed and afraid of your feelings." (Bateson et al., 1956, p. 259)

Bateson et al. report that, following this interaction, the patient became violent and assaultive upon returning to the ward. No matter how the patient could respond to his mother, he would be wrong. Bateson and his colleagues believed that if individuals were continually exposed to these types of messages, they would eventually lose the ability to understand their own and others' communication patterns and would develop schizophrenic behavior.

Marital schism and marital skew.   In their work with individuals who had been hospitalized with schizophrenia, Lidz and his colleagues found unusual patterns of family communications between parents and their children (Lidz, Cornelison, Fleck, & Terry, 1957). They reported two particular types of marital discord in families with schizophrenic members: marital schism and marital skew. In marital schism, parents preoccupied with their own problems tended to undermine the worth of the other parent by competing for sympathy and support from the children. Because they did not value the other parent, they would be afraid the child would grow up like the other parent, and so the other parent was devalued. In marital skew, the psychological disturbance of one parent tends to dominate the home. The other parent, accepting the situation, implies that the home is normal and that everything is fine and thus distorts reality to the children. This puts imbalance in the marriage and places pressure on the children to try to normalize the family and balance the marriage. In both of these situations, but particularly in marital schism, a child is in a bind; by pleasing one parent, the other parent might be displeased.

Pseudomutuality.   Another early researcher of families with schizophrenic members was Lyman Wynne. He and his colleagues observed that in families of schizophrenic children, there was often a conflict between the child's need to develop a separate identity and also maintain intimate relationships with family members, a concept called *pseudomutuality* (Wynne, Ryckoff, Day, & Hirsch, 1958). There is an appearance of open relationships that serves to conceal distant relationships within the family. Family members develop roles that they use to relate to each other rather than relating openly. Without developing a sense of self, the individual cannot relate well outside the family and relates only superficially within the family. From Wynne's point of view, schizophrenia is in some ways a part of the entire family rather than belonging just to one individual (Singer & Wynne, 1965). Thus the interaction between individuals, not the person's own psychological functioning, is seen as leading to the development of schizophrenia.

The findings of Bateson, Lidz, and Wynne and their colleagues all relate to communication patterns that the participants are unaware of and that create stress in marriages and in child raising. Their observations, although based on parents of schizophrenic children, also applied to other families (Okun & Rappaport, 1980). These findings were to have a significant impact on the development of approaches to family therapy. Complex patterns of communicating and interacting could be clarified, to some degree, by examining general systems theory, which viewed each system as a part of a larger system.

General Systems Theory

Significant contributions to family systems theory came from outside the social sciences. Norbert Wiener (1948), a mathematician who played an important role in the development of computers, wrote of feedback mechanisms that were essential in the processing of information. The work of von Bertalanffy (1968), concerned with biology and medicine, explored the interrelationships of parts to each other and to the whole system. When his general theoretical approach is applied to family therapy, a family cannot be understood without knowing how the family functions as a whole unit. From a systems theory perspective, each family is a part of a larger system, a neighborhood, which is again a part of a larger system, a town, and so forth. Individuals are wholes that comprise smaller systems, organs, tissues, cells, and so forth. If any part of a system changes, the whole system reflects a change. Important concepts in understanding general systems theory are those of feedback and homeostasis, which deal with ways in which systems and their units function.

Feedback.   The term *feedback* refers to the communication pattern within the units of the system. There are two basic patterns of communication: linear and circular. The linear approach is diagrammed in Figure 13.1; it shows that communication occurs in a single direction, moving from A to B to C to D. In a system with circular feedback, each unit may change and thus affect any of the other units. In the example in Figure 13.1, a change in E can trigger a change in F, G, or H, which then can trigger another change, and so forth. To put the concept of circularity into a family context, a mother may feel that her drug dependence is caused by her son's insolent behavior. The son may feel his behavior toward his mother is influenced by her drug abuse. In this way, the feedback of the mother affects the feedback of the son and the feedback of the son affects the feedback of the mother. In family systems theory, the circular interaction is observed, and blame is not placed on either mother or son.

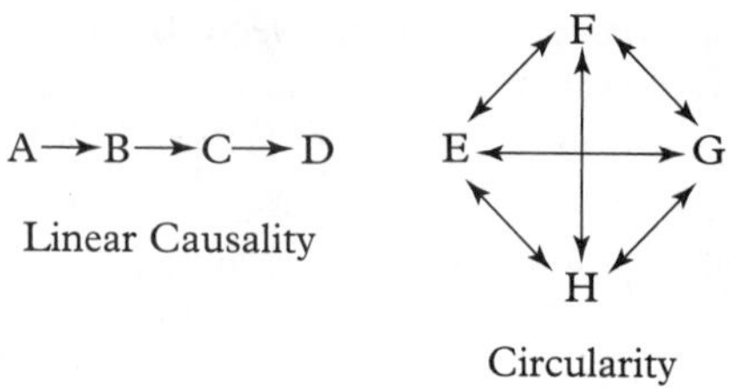

$$A \rightarrow B \rightarrow C \rightarrow D$$

Linear Causality

Circularity

FIGURE 13.1 Linearity and circularity in a system.

Related to circular interaction is the idea in family systems therapy that the emphasis is on process rather than content. Family systems therapists focus on what is happening in the present, rather than what happened or the sequence of events that led up to an event, as in the linear causality sequence diagrammed in Figure 13.1. A husband may describe a family's problem from a linear and content perspective: "When my wife had a stroke, I thought that we all had to pitch in at home in running the house." A process-oriented approach that looks at the interrelationships of the members of the family would focus on circularity in the present: "My wife is in the chair most of the day. Helen comes home from school, leaves her books, goes out, and doesn't come home until after dinner. I am angry at Helen for not helping. I wish that my wife would do more. She seems to think that I don't do enough." In this way, the relationships of each of the three family members are seen to interact from the husband's perspective, and more information is learned by examining the processes of family interactions than from only the content of the interaction.

Related to the idea of complexity in a family system is that of underlying *equifinality*, which implies that there are many different ways to get to the same destination. In Figure 13.1, there are many different paths from E to H. To return to the example of the three-person family, there are many ways that the family can relate to each other and to change the system to create more stability.

Homeostasis. In general, systems have a tendency to seek stability and equilibrium, referred to as *homeostasis* (Goldenberg & Goldenberg, 2000). An example of homeostasis is a thermostat used to regulate temperature so that a house does not become too hot or cold. Likewise, a family system attempts to regulate itself so that stability and equilibrium can be maintained. The process by which this equilibrium is achieved is feedback from units within the system. In a family, new information that is brought into a system affects its stability. In the previous example, if Helen comes home at 2 A.M., this information is likely to affect her relationship with each of her parents, as well as their relationship with each other to some degree.

There are two basic types of feedback: negative and positive. In positive feedback, change occurs in the system; in negative feedback, equilibrium is achieved. For example, if Helen's father talks with Helen about why she is late and works with her to reduce the behavior that causes disequilibrium, negative feedback affects the family system. If instead he gets angry and yells at her, she may stay out late more often, and the system is changed through the use of positive feedback processes. In this brief example, positive feedback is seen as having a destructive impact on a family. Depending on the nature of the change that occurs, positive feedback may also be helpful. (Note that the systems theory use of negative and positive feedback are not related to the common usage of negative and positive feedback. In systems theory, positive and negative feedback are related to changing the system or maintaining stability in the system, respectively.)

Although early psychoanalytic therapy, child guidance, and marriage counseling tended to focus on the individual, family systems therapy has focused on the entire family as the context of the problem. Research with families of schizophrenic children and application of general systems theory to family therapy have been instrumental in the development of family systems therapy. The focus is no longer on the identified patient, the person the parents believe needs help.

In the following sections six approaches to family systems therapy are presented: Bowen's intergenerational approach, Minuchin's structural theory, Haley's strategic approach, Satir and Whittaker's experiential approach, deShazer's solution-focused approach, and Epston and White's narrative therapy. Because family therapists often use several approaches to family systems therapy, as well as individually oriented approaches, integrating family therapy approaches is discussed.

BOWEN'S INTERGENERATIONAL APPROACH

Murray Bowen's (1960) early work with schizophrenic children and their families at the Menninger Clinic was highly influential in his development of a system of family therapy. His approach to systems theory is different than other family therapy theorists, emphasizing the family's emotional system and the history of this system as it may be traced through the family dynamics of the parents' families and even grandparents' families. He is interested in the ways that families project their own emotionality onto a particular family member and that member's reaction to other family members. Preferring to work with parents rather than the whole family, Bowen (1978) sees himself as a coach, helping parents to think through ways that they can behave differently with each other and their children to bring about less destructive emotionality in the family.

Theory of Family Systems

Bowen's theory of family systems is based on the individual's ability to differentiate his own intellectual functioning from feelings. This concept is applied to family processes and the ways that individuals project their own stresses onto other family members. In particular, Bowen examines the triangular relationship between family members such as the parents and a child. How individuals cope with the stress put on them by the way other family members deal with their anxieties is an important issue for Bowen. He is particularly concerned with the ways that children may distance themselves emotionally, and also physically, from their families. One of the most significant aspects of Bowen's theory is how families can transmit over several generations psychological characteristics that affect the interaction of dysfunctional families. Bowen's view of multigenerational transmission and family interactions provides an original way of viewing the family. Eight concepts form the core of his system of family therapy.

MURRAY BOWEN

Differentiation of self. Being able to differentiate one's intellectual processes from one's feeling processes represents a clear differentiation of self. Bowen recognizes the importance of awareness of feelings and thoughts, particularly the ability to distinguish between the two. When thoughts and feelings are not distinguished, fusion occurs. A person who is highly differentiated (Bowen, 1966) is well aware of her opinions and has a sense of self. In a family conflict, people who are able to differentiate their emotions and intellects are able to stand up for themselves and not be dominated by the feelings of others, whereas those whose feelings and thoughts are fused may express a pseudoself rather than their true values or opinions. For example, in a family with 10- and 12-year-old girls, the 10-year-old may have a mind of her own and be clearer about what she will and will not do (differentiated) than the 12-year-old (fused). The 12-year-old who is not able to express herself accurately (pseudoself) may cause problems in relating that affect the whole family. If there is poor differentiation, triangulation is likely to take place.

Triangulation. When there is stress between two people in a family, they may be likely (Bowen, 1978) to bring another member in to dilute the anxiety or tension, which is called *triangulation*. When family members are getting along and are not upset, there is no reason to bring a third person into an interaction. Bowen believes that when there is stress in the family, the least-differentiated person is likely to be drawn into the conflict to reduce tension (Goldenberg & Goldenberg, 2000). Triangulation is not limited to the family, as friends, relatives, or a therapist may be brought into a conflict.

For Bowen (1975) a two-person system is unstable, and when there is stress, joining with a third person reduces the tension in the relationship between the original two people. The larger the family, the greater the possibility for many different interlocking triangles. One problem could involve several triangles, as more and more family members are brought into the conflict. Bringing a third family member into a conflict (triangulation) does not always reduce the stress in the family. Stress reduction depends, in part, on the differentiation level of the members involved. For example, if two children who are arguing bring in a third member of the family (brother, mother, or uncle), the tension between the two children diminishes if the other person does not take sides and helps to solve the problem. If the person becomes excited or acts unfairly, however, stress between the two children may continue (Goldenberg & Goldenberg, 2000). From a therapeutic point of view, it is very important that the therapist triangulates in a clear and differentiated way with a couple while attending to patterns of triangulation in the family.

Nuclear family emotional systems. The family as a system—that is, the nuclear family emotional system—is likely to be unstable unless members of the family are each well differentiated. Because such differentiation is rare, family conflict is likely to exist. Bowen (1978) believes that spouses are likely to select partners with similar levels of differentiation. If two people with low levels of differentiation marry, it is likely that as a couple they will become highly fused, as will their family when they have children.

Family projection process.   When there are relatively low levels of differentiation in the marriage partners, they may project their stress onto one child—the family projection process. In general, the child who is most emotionally attached to the parents may have the least differentiation between feelings and intellect and the most difficulty in separating from the family (Papero, 1983). For example, a child who refuses to go to school and wants to stay home with his parents can be considered to have fused with his parents. How intense the family projection process is depends on how undifferentiated the parents are and on the stress level that the family experiences (Goldenberg & Goldenberg, 2000). The "problem child" can respond to the stress of his undifferentiated parents in a variety of ways.

Emotional cutoff.   When children receive too much stress because of overinvolvement in the family, they may try to separate themselves from the family through emotional cutoff. Adolescents might move away from home, go to college, or run away. For younger children, as well as adolescents, it may mean withdrawing emotionally from the family and going through the motions of being in the family. Their interaction with parents is likely to be brief and superficial. A child experiencing an emotional cutoff may "go to her room" not so much to study but to be free of the family conflict. Such a child may deal with everyday matters, but withdraw when emotionally charged issues develop between parents. In general, the higher the level of anxiety and emotional dependence, the more likely are children to experience an emotional cutoff in a family (Bowen, 1978).

Multigenerational transmission process.   In his approach to work with families, Bowen (1976) looks not just at the immediate family but at previous generations. As mentioned previously, he believes that spouses with similar differentiation levels seek each other out and project their stress and lack of differentiation onto their children. If Bowen's hypothesis is correct, then after six or seven generations of increasingly fused couples, an observer could find highly dysfunctional families who are vulnerable to stress and to lack of differentiation between thoughts and feelings. Such a progressive change could lead to the development of schizophrenia in children. Naturally, Bowen recognizes that spouses do not always marry at their own exact level of differentiation. In the concept of the multigenerational transmission process, the functioning of grandparents, great-grandparents, great-aunts, great-uncles, and other relatives may play an important role in the pathology of the family. To give an example, a great-grandfather who was prone to emotional outbursts and experienced depression may affect the function of the grandmother, who in turn affects the functioning of the father, who may in turn have an impact on the psychological health of the child. Other issues besides differentiation affect family functioning.

Sibling position.   Bowen thought that birth order would have an impact on the functioning of children within the family. Based on the work of Toman (1961), Bowen believed that the sibling position of marriage partners would affect how they perform as parents. Concerned less with actual birth order than with the way a child functioned in the family, Bowen felt that how one behaved with brothers and sisters would have an impact on how one would act as a parent. For example, an oldest brother may have taken care of his younger brother and sister in his family and thus may take on a role of responsibility with his children. This might be particularly true if his wife did not take much responsibility with her siblings, as could be the case if she is the youngest child.

Societal regression. Bowen has extended his model of family systems to societal functioning. Just as families can move toward undifferentiation or toward individuation, so can societies. If there are stresses on societies, they are more likely to move toward undifferentiation. Examples of stresses could be famine, civil uprisings, or population growth. To extend Bowen's model to societies, leaders and policymakers should distinguish between intellect and emotion when making decisions and not act on feelings alone.

Bowen's theory of family structure goes beyond the immediate family system to cross generations. His interest is in how the personality of individuals affects other members in the family. He is particularly interested in the individual's ability to differentiate intellectual processes from feelings and the impact of this individual's ability on other family members. These views bear a direct relationship to his beliefs about the goals of family therapy.

Therapy Goals

In attending to the goals of therapy, Bowen was interested in the impact that past generations have on present family functioning. As he set goals in working with families, he listened to the presenting symptoms and, even more important, to family dynamics as they relate to differentiation of family members and triangulation as it occurs in the family. More specifically, he sought to help families reduce their general stress level and to find ways to help family members become more differentiated and meet their own individual needs as well as family needs (Kerr & Bowen, 1988).

Techniques of Bowen's Family Therapy

In Bowen's system of family therapy, an evaluation period precedes therapeutic intervention. The process of taking a family history is aided by the use of a genogram, a diagram of the family tree usually including the children, parents, grandparents, aunts and uncles, and possibly other relatives. In bringing about family change, Bowen used interpretation of his understanding of intergenerational factors. In his writings, Bowen (1978) saw himself as a coach, helping his patients analyze the family situation and plan strategies for events that are likely to occur. In this work, he often focused on detriangulation, a way of changing patterns of dealing with stress. The effectiveness of coaching, interpreting, and detriangulating depends on effective evaluation of family history.

Evaluation interview. Characteristic of Bowen's therapeutic work are objectivity and neutrality. Even in the initial telephone contact, Bowen (Kerr & Bowen,

1988) warns against being charmed into taking sides in the family or in other ways becoming fused with the nuclear family emotional system. The family evaluation interviews can take place with any combination of family members. Sometimes a single family member can be sufficient if that person is willing to work on differentiating his own feelings and intellectual processes rather than blame other family members.

In taking a family history, Bowen attended to triangles within the family and to the level of differentiation within family members. Because there is usually an identified patient, Bowen family therapists listen for ways in which family members may project their own anxieties onto that patient. How that patient responds to the family is also important. Is he emotionally cut off from other family members? In taking the family history, the therapist attends to relationships within the family, such as sibling position, but also relationships within the parents' families of origin. Because intergenerational patterns can get complex, therapists may use a genogram to describe family relationships.

Genograms.   The genogram is a method of diagramming families and includes significant information about families, such as ages, sex, marriage dates, deaths, and geographical locations. Not only do genograms provide an overview of the extended family but also they may suggest patterns of differentiation that reach back into a family of origin and beyond. A genogram provides the opportunity to look for emotional patterns in each partner's own extended family. As McGoldrick and Gerson (1985) show, genograms can be quite extensive, including many family members and much information about them and their patterns of interaction.

In the accompanying example, a small illustration of one person's family, including parents and children, is shown. In genograms, males are represented by squares and females by circles, and their current ages are noted inside the figures. The person who is the object of the genogram is indicated by a double circle or square. In this oversimplified example, the genogram is of a 45-year-old female whose husband is 46, whose two sons are 10 and 9, and whose daughter is 4 years old.

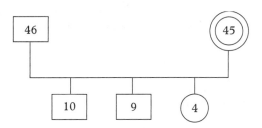

Interpretation.   Information from genograms is often interpreted to family members so that they can understand dynamics within the family. Because of the objectivity that the family therapist maintains, the therapist is able to see patterns within the current family that are reflective of patterns in the family of origin. To do so, it is important that therapists themselves be well differentiated so that they ask thinking questions rather than feeling questions and avoid being drawn into triangles with their patients. One way that Bowen (1978) kept objective enough to make astute interpretations was by having the conversation directed to him rather than from one family member to another.

Detriangulation. When possible, Bowen tried to separate parts of a triangle directly. When dealing with family problems, he often saw the parents or one of the parents. He then worked with them on ways to develop strategies to deal with the impact of their own emotional stress on the identified patient or other family member. In general, Bowen preferred to work with the healthiest member of the family, the person who was most differentiated, so that that person could make changes in various stressful family relationships.

A hallmark of Bowen's work was the calm manner with which he tried to deal with the emotionality that exists between family members. His goal was to reduce anxiety as well as resolve symptoms, which he did by looking not only at self-differentiation within the individual and within the family but within the family of the parents. To do so he used tools such as a genogram and discussed the relationships that went beyond the nuclear family to aunts, uncles, and grandparents. An illustration of his approach will help demonstrate his method.

An Example of Intergenerational Family Systems Therapy

Two very important concepts in Bowen's theory are those of triangulation and multi-generational issues. In this example, Guerin and Guerin (1976) report the case of Catholic parents living in New York City and their three adopted children, two boys and a girl. The identified patient is the daughter, who the parents felt was acting inappropriately. Philip Guerin describes the family as a child-focused family. In his conceptualization of the case, different sets of triangles are important.

> Whenever I see a child-focused family, I automatically assume a set of four potential triangles: the central nuclear triangle of mother, father and symptomatic child; two auxiliary nuclear family triangles, one involving a parent, the symptomatic child, and an asymptomatic sibling, the other an intersibling triangle among three of the children; and finally a triangle over three generations involving a grandparent, a parent, and the symptomatic child. There are many other possibilities, but these are the most frequently encountered clinically. (p. 92)[1]

For this family, not only are the family triangles important but also the fusion that exists within the nuclear family and the families of origin. Guerin and Guerin (1976) see the relationship of fusion within the family and intergenerational issues in this way.

> As the marriage is worked on, and the marital fusion unfolds, the process inevitably involves a tie into the extended family. The interlocking character of the three generations comes into view. Pieces of all three of those generations must be worked on at different times, depending on what's going on in the present time frame with the family. Success and progress don't mean that the symptoms and the dysfunction just disappear; instead symptoms will reappear over time in all three generational levels of the family. (pp. 93–94)

Although the therapist has met with the parents by themselves, with just the daughter, and with the whole family, this excerpt of a session 6 months into therapy is only with the parents. The therapist comments on a three-generational triangulation that revolves around Ann's concern that her mother is playing favorites with her children. Guerin makes comments that encompass Ann, her mother, and each of Ann's children.

Ann: Well, she'll ask how the children are, and I'll start to tell her. Then she gets to talk about things like she tells me how Richie is her favorite, and that she really can't help it, and then I ask her to please try and keep that to herself and not show it to the other two children. I don't think it's a good idea to have a favorite grandchild when you have three, and she knows that I definitely disapprove of something like that.

(Ann begins to develop one aspect of the three-generational triangulation in this family.)

Dr. G: Do you have some kind of principle that your kids should be equal in the eyes of their grandmother?

(Therapist challenges Ann's position.)

Ann: But, you don't realize, it's not practical.

Dr. G: Are you trying to protect your kids from not being the favorite or from being the favorite?

Ann: Well, because I was the favorite in my house over my sister, and then I was faced with the same problem myself with the boys and Susan, and I kind of feel it's not a good thing.

(The generational repeat surfaces.)

Dr. G: How is she going to go around pretending that Richard is not her favorite?

(Therapist continues to challenge).

Ann: Well, she said it Saturday night in front of him. I kind of appreciated it as something she has been feeling for a long time; and usually she sneaks it in without directly saying it. So Saturday night when she said it, I said, "Why?" She wants to take Richie to the ballet for Christmas, and she doesn't want to take the other two anyplace, and I won't let her do that because I don't feel it's fair. She hasn't taken any of them any place in eight years, and I know that they would really be hurt. So I suggested if you take one someplace that you take the other two too, not necessarily to the same thing, but that you follow up with Eddie and Susan some place. Then she takes Eddie into it and completely leaves Susan out. Then I go through the same thing nicely, you know, I really think it's better to take all three, some time at least. It doesn't have to be all the time.

Dr. G: What would happen if she took Richard, the kids would start complaining?

(Therapist moves to concretize the process.)

Ann: Yes.

Dr. G: Eddie and Susan would start complaining that Richard is going on a trip with Grandmother, and she likes Richie better?

Ann: She told Richie that.

Dr. G: If they complain, tell them to go to your mother. Would they like that? (Therapist suggests surfacing the process in the family.) (Guerin & Guerin, 1976, pp. 105–106)

The therapist makes comments that deal with the three-generational triangles that exist in the family. By doing so, Ann is encouraged to think about the impact of her relationship with her mother and children, rather than respond emotionally to her mother. The problem of "playing favorites with the three children" is discussed, and the mother is encouraged to question the triangles and to consider removing herself from the relationship between her mother and each of the children. Although this is only a small sample of dialogue, it illustrates triangulation and multigenerational issues that are important in Bowen's theory of family systems.

STRUCTURAL FAMILY THERAPY

Structural therapy, developed by Salvador Minuchin, helps families by dealing with problems as they affect current interactions of family members. Of particular interest are boundaries between family members. Are members too close or too distant? What is the nature of relationships within the family? Therapeutic approaches emphasize changing the nature and intensity of relationships within the family both inside and outside the therapy session.

Concepts of Structural Family Therapy

How families operate as a system and their structure within the system are the focus of Minuchin's work (1974). By attending to the organization of the family and the rules and guidelines family members use to make decisions, Minuchin forms an impression of the family. Although family members differ in the power that they have in making decisions, the ways in which family members work together is an indication of the degree of flexibility or rigidity that exists within the family structure. Minuchin uses concepts such as boundaries, alignments, and coalitions to explain family systems.

Family structure.   For Minuchin (1974), the structure of the family refers to the rules that have been developed over the years to determine who interacts with whom. Structures may be temporary or long standing. For example, two older brothers may form a coalition against a younger sister for a short period of time or for several years. It is Minuchin's view that there should be a hierarchical structure within the family, with the parents having more power than the children and older children having more responsibilities than younger children. Parents take different roles; for example, one parent may be the disciplinarian, and the other may provide sympathy to the children. Eventually children learn the rules of the family about which parent behaves in what way and to which child. When new circumstances develop, such as one of the children going off to college, the family must be able to change to accommodate this event. Being aware of family rules, and thus the structure, is important for therapists in determining the best way to help dysfunctional families change. Within the family system are subsystems that also have their own rules.

Family subsystems. For a family to function well, members must work together to carry out functions. The most obvious subsystems are those of husband-wife, parents-children, and siblings. The purpose of the husband-wife or marital subsystem is to meet the changing needs of the two partners. The parental subsystem is usually a father-mother team, but may also be a parent and/or another relative who is responsible for raising children. Although the same people may be in the marital subsystem and the parental subsystem, their roles are different, although overlapping. In sibling subsystems, children learn how to relate to their brothers or sisters and, in doing so, learn how to build coalitions and meet their own needs, as well as deal with parents. There may be other subsystems that develop, such as the oldest child learning to make dinner for the family when the mother or father is drunk. Such alliances may develop depending on the roles, skills, and problems of the individual members. Who does what and with whom depend on boundaries that are not always clearly defined.

Boundary permeability. Both systems and subsystems have rules as to who can participate in interactions and how they can participate (Minuchin, 1974). These rules of interaction, or boundaries, vary as to how flexible they are. Permeability of boundaries describes the type of contact that members within family systems and subsystems have with each other. A highly permeable boundary would be found in enmeshed families, whereas nonpermeable or rigid boundaries would be found in disengaged families. For example, if a seventh-grade child who had previously been performing well in school brings a note home from a teacher saying that he is failing English, the child may be told by his father not to let this happen again, to change his behavior, and that there will be no further discussion of this issue. In this case, the boundaries are rigid and the family is relatively disengaged from the child. In an enmeshed family, the father, mother, brother, and sister may inquire about the child's grades. The siblings may tease, the father may be distressed, and the mother may check frequently during the week to see if the child is doing his homework. During dinner the parents may discuss this event with the entire family so that there is little separation between family members. In general, boundaries refer to how a family is organized and follows the rules; they do not address the issue of how family members work together or fail to work together.

Alignments and Coalitions. In responding to crises or dealing with daily events, families may have typical ways that subsystems within the family react. Alignments refer to the ways that family members join with each other or oppose each other in dealing with an activity. Coalitions refer to alliances between family members against another family member. Sometimes they are flexible and sometimes they are fixed, such as when a mother and daughter work together to control a disruptive father. Minuchin uses the term *trial* more specifically than does Bowen to describe a coalition in which "each parent demands that the child side with him against the other parent" (Minuchin, 1974, p. 102). Thus power within the family shifts, depending upon alignments and coalitions.

In the family system, power refers to who makes the decisions and who carries out the decisions. Being able to influence decisions increases one's power. Thus, a child who aligns with the most powerful parent increases her own power. Because certain decisions are made by one parent within a family and other decisions by the other parent, power shifts, depending on the family activity. In an enmeshed family, power is not clear, and children may ask one parent permission to do something, even if the other parent has said "no."

When the family's rules become inoperative, the family becomes dysfunctional. When boundaries become either too rigid or too permeable, families have difficulty operating as a system. If the family does not operate as a hierarchical unit, with parents being the primary decision makers and the older children having more responsibility than younger children, confusion and difficulty may result. Alignments within the family may be dysfunctional, such as parents arguing over money who both ask the oldest child to agree with them (triangulation). Whereas Bowen is particularly interested in family function across generations, Minuchin is more concerned with the current structure of the family, especially as he sees it within the therapeutic transaction.

Goals of Structural Family Therapy

By making hypotheses about the structure of the family and the nature of the problem, structural family therapists can set goals for change (Aponte & Van Deusen, 1981). Working in the present with the current family structure, structural family therapists try to alter coalitions and alliances to bring about change in the family. They also work to establish boundaries within the family that are neither too rigid nor too flexible. By supporting the parental subsystem as the decision-making system that is responsible for the family, therapists work to help the family system use power in a way that functions well. The techniques that family therapists use to bring about these changes are active and highly attuned to family functioning.

Techniques of Structural Family Therapy

The structural approach to family therapy is to join with the family and to focus on current and present happenings. To do this, structural therapists may often use "maps" that provide a shorthand description of boundaries and subsystems as they have an impact on the family. By accommodating to family customs, the therapist

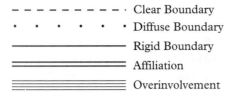

FIGURE 13.2 Minuchin's symbols for family mapping.
Reprinted by permission of the publishers from *Families and Family Therapy,* by Salvador
Minuchin. Cambridge, MA: Harvard University Press. Copyright (c) 1974 by the President
and Fellows of Harvard College.

can act like a member of the family to improve the understanding of family interactions and to gain acceptance. By having a family enact a problem, the therapist can experience the interactions within subsystems in the treatment session.
Suggestions can then be made for changing the power structure and boundaries
within the family. Bringing about change through increasing the intensity of interventions and reframing problems is among the approaches to therapeutic change
that are described.

Family mapping.   Whereas Bowen uses the genogram to show intergenerational
patterns of relating, Minuchin uses diagrams to describe current ways that families relate. For example, the concept of boundaries is extremely important in structural therapy. Figure 13.2 shows lines that represent different types of boundaries within families. These symbols, along with others described by Minuchin (1974), allow the
therapist to use a symbolic way of representing the organization of the family and to
determine which subsystems contribute most actively to a problem (Umbarger, 1983).
Maps of family interaction allow therapists to better understand repeated dysfunctional
behavior within a family so that strategies for modification can be applied.

Accommodating and joining.   To bring about change within a family, Minuchin
(1974) believes that it is important to join a family system and accommodate to its way
of interacting. By using the same type of language, telling amusing stories relevant to
the family, he seeks to fit in. One example of joining the family is mimesis, which refers
to imitating the style and content of a family's communications. For example, if an
adolescent sprawls on his chair, the family therapist may do likewise. Similarly, structural therapists use tracking to follow and to make use of symbols of family life. For example, if an enmeshed family uses the phrase "our life is an open book," a structural
therapist may attend to issues in which family members are too deeply involved in each
others' activities and may later make use of the "open book" metaphor as a way of helping families clarify their boundaries. By joining a family system, a structural therapist
not only has a good understanding of the family's systemic operation but also is in a
good position to make changes in the family's system.

Enactment.   By instructing the family to act out a conflict, the therapist can work
with problems as they appear in the present rather than as they are reported. This al-

lows the therapist to understand the coalitions and alliances within the family and then to make suggestions for changing the family system. For example, the therapist may give specific instructions for the family to enact an argument about not doing homework. Having seen the argument enacted, the therapist is more aware of boundaries and coalitions and thus is prepared to make powerful interventions.

Intensity.   How a suggestion or message is given is extremely important. By repeating the message, by changing the length of time of a particular interaction, or through other means, change can be facilitated (Minuchin & Fishman, 1981). For example, if parents are overprotective, the therapist may suggest that parents not nag the child about his homework, not ask as many questions about school, and not monitor how his allowance is spent. Although these messages differ, they all stress that the child be given more responsibility. Intensity can be achieved in enactment by having the family draw out an interaction or repeat it. As the therapist becomes familiar with the family's style of interacting and its boundaries, more suggestions for change develop.

Changing boundaries.   As the therapist observes the family interacting either in an enactment or in general presentation, the therapist uses boundary marking to note boundaries that exist within the family. To change boundaries, therapists may rearrange the seating of the family members and change the distance between family members. They may also wish to unbalance the structure so that power within a subsystem changes. For example, in an enmeshed family, where children have too much power, the therapist may decide to side with one of the parents to give that person power in dealing with the child. If the husband is indecisive, the therapist may reinforce his suggestions and agree with him. It is the therapist's conscious choice as to which family member to agree with, affiliate with, or exclude from an interaction. In dealing with family systems, the therapist can also interpret events to change the power structure and mode of interaction within the family.

Reframing.   There are several ways to see an event or situation or to reframe it. The therapist may wish to give a different explanation so that a constructive change can occur in a family situation. Writing about anorexia, Minuchin, Rosman, and Baker (1978) suggest a number of ways of reframing an anorectic girl's behavior. By labeling behavior as "stubborn" and not as "sick," the adolescent no longer is the sole source of the problem, as there are several ways a family can deal with stubbornness, whereas sickness emphasizes the problem as being that of the adolescent and one that is out of her control because she is "sick." Because parents are likely to see anorexia as the child's problem, reframing allows the family therapist to present anorexia as a family problem that can be approached by changing subsystems, boundaries, and coalitions.

Example of Structural Family Therapy

Structural family therapists make use of a variety of techniques to challenge their client's perception of reality. Minuchin (1974) describes the "yes, but" or "yes, and" techniques that support the family members while suggesting that there are more things that they can do to change. In the following example, Minuchin describes how he approaches restructuring family subsystems in a family with two boys, whose father is the identified patient. In this example, Minuchin makes alliances with the husband to strengthen his power, while at the same time involving the wife. Identifying a coalition between the mother and sons, Minuchin acts to redefine family boundaries and develop a coalition between the father and younger son.

For example, a wife makes an appointment for therapy because her husband has personal problems and also has great difficulty relating to their two sons. In the first session, the therapist sees the spouses alone. The husband says that he is the member of the family who has the problems. He describes himself as intellectual and logical. Because he is logical, he is sure that he is right; therefore, he tends to be authoritarian.

The therapist interrupts to say that a man who is so concerned with logic and correctness must often be frustrated in life. He criticizes the man for never allowing his wife to perceive the depression he must feel and never allowing her to help him. By this means the therapist is blocking a well-oiled but dysfunctional relationship in terms of an expanded reality. His observation feels right to the man, who acknowledges his depression, and also fits the woman's never-expressed wish for an opportunity to support her husband. Both spouses experience the therapist's challenging, change-requiring input as familiar and welcome, because it recognizes the woman's felt needs and suggests some alternatives that are available to the man. The therapist then assigns a task based on his "yes, but." Under specified circumstances, when the wife feels her husband is wrong, she is nevertheless to side with him against the children.

The parents bring the children to the next session. The adults have performed the assigned task and feel closer. The husband believes that his wife supports him, and she is gratified by the increased sensitivity and decreased authoritarianism he has displayed in response to her support.

When the entire family is seen in therapy, it becomes clear that the children and mother are in a coalition which has isolated the father, making him peripheral and leaving too much of the socialization process to the mother. The children act as a rescue squad. When the father sets rules, he does so in a pompous, ex cathedra manner, which makes the mother feel frustrated and helpless. The children begin to misbehave in ways that deflect their father's wrath to them. The younger child is particularly expert at this, and the relationship between him and his father is particularly tense.

The therapist's tactics are to break up the coalition of mother and children, clarifying the boundary around the spouse subsystem and children. Accordingly, his stratagems must support the father, even though he disagrees with him. He therefore assigns a task that will bring the father and younger son together, excluding the mother. This task also confirms the father in his evident skills of logical thinking and detached observation of behavior, but now directs these skills positively toward a son whom he has always regarded as irritating. The father is to meet with the son at least three times during the week for a period of no longer than one hour. During this period, he is to use his capacity for clear observation and analysis by studying his son, so that during the next session he can describe the son's particular characteristics to the therapist. In this way, the therapist is brought into the contact between father and son as a distant observer. The father, who has always related to this child with impulsive, derogatory, controlling movements, will feel the therapist encouraging him to use his logical skills in relating to his

JAY HALEY

son, inhibiting his impulsiveness. The mother, who has been stressed by her exclusion from this interaction, will nevertheless feel supported in an important area—her wish that her husband become a good father. (Minuchin, 1974, pp. 117–119)[2]

STRATEGIC THERAPY

Concerned with treating symptoms that families present, Haley (1973) takes responsibility for what occurs in treatment and designs approaches for solving family problems. By focusing on the problem, strategic therapists design the best way to reach the goals of the family. In developing his approach, Jay Haley was influenced by Milton Erickson (Haley, 1973), who was known for his use of hypnotic and paradoxical techniques. At the Mental Research Institute in Palo Alto, California, Haley, with Don Jackson and John Weakland, emphasized problem solution rather than insight as a goal of therapy. Additionally, Haley's work with Minuchin was important in developing a theoretical approach to family systems. Although Haley's theory of family systems is not as developed as Minuchin's, his approach to treatment as described in detail in his writings (Haley, 1963, 1971a, 1971b, 1973, 1976, 1979, 1984) is the focus of this section.

Concepts of Strategic Therapy

Like Minuchin, Haley observes the interaction among the family members, attending particularly to power relationships in the family and to the ways that parents deal with power. Viewing relationships as power struggles, Haley (1976) is interested in understanding how relationships are defined. Thus a communication from one person to another is an act that defines the relationship (Haley, 1963). When a mother says to her son, "Your room is messy," she is not only reporting on the state of the room, but also commanding the son to clean it up. If the son does not clean up the room, he is engaging in a power struggle with his mother. Important to Haley, as well as to Minuchin, is the concept of hierarchy, in which the parents are in a superior position to the children in terms of making decisions and adhering to family responsibilities. Like Minuchin, he is concerned with family triangles such as those in which one parent is overinvolved with the child and the other is underinvolved.

What separates structural from strategic approaches is the attention given by strategic family therapists to symptoms. For Haley, symptoms are an unacknowledged way of communicating within the family system, usually when there is no other solution to a problem. For strategic therapists, the symptom is often a metaphor (Madanes, 1981) for a way of feeling or behaving within the family. Contained in a metaphorical message are an explicit element (such as "my stomach hurts") and an implicit element ("I feel neglected") (Brown & Christensen, 1999). For example, the child who says "I have a stomachache" may be communicating pain that his mother feels in an interaction with her husband. In listening to a symptom being described, strategic therapists look for the message that is being communicated as a metaphor of the symptom.

Goals

Consistent with the emphasis on working with the system is the value placed on choosing goals. Although the therapist may ask family members why they have come and what they want to accomplish, the therapist ultimately decides on the goal. Such goals may be intermediate as well as final and must be concrete and not vague. The goal to reduce anxiety must be stated in such a way that the therapist knows which family members are experiencing anxiety, in what way, and in which situations. There must be sufficient information so that therapists can plan strategies to reach goals. For example, if a daughter is anxious because her completion of chores at home is met by criticism from her parents, the therapist might have an intermediate goal of having just the father make requests, and later have another intermediate goal of having the mother and father agree on the chores that they want their daughter to do. For each goal, specific methods for accomplishing them are designed by the therapist.

Techniques of Strategic Family Therapy

Because the presenting problem is the focus of strategic therapy, tasks to alleviate the problem or symptom are the cornerstone of strategic family therapy. Having family members complete tasks is important for three reasons (Haley, 1976). First, tasks change the way that people respond in therapy. Second, because therapists design the task, their role is important, and they are likely to be listened to. Third, whether or not tasks are completed, information about the family is obtained. When working with a task, strategic family therapists must select ones that are appropriate to the family, design the task, and help the family to complete it (Haley, 1976, 1984). Generally, tasks are of two types: straightforward tasks, where the therapist makes directions and suggestions to the family, and paradoxical tasks, for families who may resist change.

Straightforward tasks.   When strategic family therapists judge that the family that they are trying to help is likely to comply with their suggestions, they may assign a straightforward task. By talking with the family and observing family boundaries and subsystems, the therapist will be able to help the family accomplish their goals (Madanes, 1981). Sometimes suggestions can consist of relatively simple advice to families, but more often families require suggestions to change a variety of ways in which members interact with each other (Papp, 1980). Just because tasks are assigned does not mean that each member of the family will be cooperative.

To gain cooperation from family members, Haley (1976) suggests several ways to ensure that family members complete tasks. Before suggesting tasks, therapists should explore what the family has done to solve the problem, so the therapist does not make a suggestion that has been tried and failed. By examining what happens if the problem is not solved, then, family members are more likely to appreciate the importance of doing something about the problem. When tasks are assigned, they should be relatively easy to accomplish, clearly explained, and fit the ability level of the children as well as the adults who will complete the task. In strategic family therapy, the therapist is clearly the expert, and she may make use of her status as the expert to get the family to comply with her instructions. Designing tasks, particularly metaphorical tasks, takes experience and confidence.

Because tasks are designed for each unique situation, general guidelines are insufficient for developing tasks. Some of the unique features of straightforward directives can be seen in these examples from Brown and Christensen (1999).

> A peripheral father and his daughter were asked to do something that the mother would not be interested in, thus reducing the likelihood of the mother's interference.
>
> A conflictual couple was asked to return to a place, such as a restaurant or park, that had been pleasant during their courting period. The focus on positive experiences can change the affect of the relationship.
>
> Parents who had concerns about a local mall frequented by their daughter were asked to visit the mall and see for themselves what it was like. (pp. 93, 94)

Sometimes therapists give a family a task that is a metaphor for the way the therapist believes they need to behave in order to alleviate the symptom. In such cases, family members are not aware of the purpose of the directives given by the therapist.

Sometimes tasks can be given to solve relatively simple problems that are a metaphor for much more difficult and complex problems. In the following example, Brown and Christensen (1999) tell how helping a daughter to stop writing bad checks can be a task that deals with improving the relationship between mother and daughter, while increasing the daughter's independence.

> Take, for example, the case of a depressed 19-year-old brought into treatment because she did nothing but sit around the house and cry. Learning that the girl had been sexually abused by her father several years earlier, the therapist redefined the girl's depression as anger toward her mother. The therapist believed that the anger was there because the mother had allowed (by not stopping it) the abuse of the daughter. The anger (rage) was never expressed because it was so volatile and explosive that the daughter feared losing her mother completely. The daughter and mother were far too overinvolved with each other. The mother admitted that she needed her daughter and did not want her to leave home. The daughter resented her mother's wish but did nothing to change it because she was afraid that any disagreement would end in an explosion of the relationship. Although neither would discuss these issues with the other, the mother complained that her daughter would write bad checks on the mother's account. While the therapist chose not to deal directly with the problems of incest and leaving home, the issue of bad checks could be dealt with as a metaphor for the more serious issues because all the same dynamics were present. The therapist got the mother and daughter to argue about the checks as a metaphor for those other issues. At the end of the discussion, the therapist directed the daughter to get a separate account and directed the mother not to pay the daughter's bills. (Brown & Christensen, 1999, pp. 94, 95)

By assigning metaphorical tasks, the therapist was able to help the daughter develop autonomy through her responsibility for her own checking account and to decrease hostility between mother and daughter by reducing the mother's overinvolvement in the daughter's activities. By successfully completing this task, other tasks involved in separation issues between mother and daughter may be more easily resolved in the future. However, sometimes straightforward tasks, whether they are metaphorical or direct, may not be appropriate to bring about change.

Paradoxical tasks.   Basically, paradoxical suggestions are those that ask the family to continue doing the behavior for which they are requesting help, in such a way that whether they comply or not, positive change will result. In a sense, the therapist is trying to get the family to decide not to do what they have been asked to do. Families are often confused by why the therapist is not asking them to change. Use of paradoxical directives takes experience and confidence on the part of the therapist, and they are used only when there is resistance to straightforward suggestions.

Weeks and L'Abate (1982) discuss several types of family behavior that may be appropriate for paradoxical interventions. When family members fight among themselves, argue, or contradict each others' statements, they may not be providing sufficient support for the use of straightforward tasks, or parents may not be sufficiently responsible to help children carry them out. When children and adolescents challenge or do not listen to their parents, it may be difficult for parents to make use of straightforward suggestions that may be assigned.

In describing the practice of using paradoxical tasks, Papp (1980, 1984) has suggested three steps: redefining, prescribing, and restraining. The first step is to redefine the symptom in terms of the benefits that it provides for the family. As Goldenberg and Goldenberg (2000) suggest, "anger may be relabeled as love, suffering as self sacrifice, distancing as a way of reinforcing closeness." In prescribing the symptom, the family is encouraged to continue what they have been doing, because if they do not there will be a loss of benefits to the family. Thus, an angry child may be asked to continue to be angry and throw tantrums. In prescribing the symptom, the therapist must be clear and sincere in the rationale that is offered. When the family starts to show improvement, the therapist tries to restrain the growth or change in order to keep the paradox working. For example, a couple who argue frequently and have been told to argue over kitchen chores may report that they are fighting less. Rather than reinforce the change, the strategic family therapist may caution the couple to be careful; otherwise, one or the other might lose the powerful position relative to the other. In doing this, the therapist never takes credit for the change or acts sarcastically. Throughout the process of using paradoxical tasks, the therapist shows concern for the family and, when change occurs, may express surprise but also hopes that change can take place.

Because paradoxical tasks are by their very nature confusing, a few examples of tasks that Brown and Christensen (1999) have used in their work will serve as illustrations.

> A fiercely independent single parent who is reluctant to give her son more autonomy was asked to do even more for him, lest she experience the anxiety of being on her own.
>
> A wife who tried to leave her husband but couldn't was urged to stay with her husband because he needed someone to take care of him.
>
> A couple whose only contact occurred when they argued were to increase their bickering so that they would be closer to each other. (pp. 98, 99)

Although these examples describe paradoxical tasks, they do not explain the process of using them in therapy. A more complete example shows how a therapist incorporates paradoxical tasks into therapy.

An Example of Strategic Therapy

In this example of helping a family consisting of a mother and five children, Madanes (1981) makes use of a paradoxical intervention as the mother is concerned because her 10-year-old son is setting fires. As shown in the third paragraph, Madanes sees the boy's behavior metaphorically. By setting fires, he helps his mother by making her feel angry instead of depressed. In prescribing the task, Madanes changes the relationship between mother and son so that the boy can help her, because he is an expert on fires.

A mother consulted because her 10-year-old son was setting fires. He was a twin and the oldest of five children. The family had many other serious problems. The father had just left them and moved to another city. The mother was not receiving any financial support from him. She was Puerto Rican, did not speak English, and did not know how to go about obtaining the help she needed. The mother would not leave the boy alone for a minute for fear that he would set the house on fire.

In the first interview, the therapist gave the boy some matches and told him to light one and asked the mother to do whatever she usually did at home when she caught him lighting a match. The therapist then left the room to observe from behind the one-way mirror. The boy reluctantly lighted a match, and the mother took it and burned him with it.

By providing a focus for her anger, the boy was helping his mother. He was someone whom she could punish and blame. He made her feel angry instead of depressed and in this way helped her to pull herself together in spite of all her troubles.

The therapist told the child that she was going to teach him how to light matches properly. She then showed him how one closes the match box before lighting the match and how, after the match burns, one carefully puts it in the ashtray. She then asked the mother to light a fire with some papers in an ashtray and to pretend to burn herself. The son had to help her by putting out the fire with some water that the therapist had brought into the office for this purpose. The boy had to show his mother that he knew how to put out fires correctly. As all this was going on, the other children were allowed to look but not to participate in any other way. After the fire was put out, the therapist told the boy that he now knew how to light fires and to put them out correctly. She emphasized to the mother that now she could trust him because he knew about fires. The therapist then asked the mother to set aside a time every evening for a week when she would get together with the boy and she would light a fire and pretend to burn herself and he would help her to put it out. The other children were only allowed to participate as spectators.

The interaction between mother and son was changed so that, instead of helping his mother by providing a focus for her anger, the son was helping her in a playful way when she pretended to burn herself. Before, the boy had been helping the mother by threatening her with fires. Now he was helping her because he was an expert on fires. Before the therapy, the child had been special in the family because he was setting fires; after the therapeutic intervention, he was special because he was an expert on fires. When the boy was unpredictably lighting fires, he was in a superior position to the mother. When he set fires under direction, he was beneath her in the hierarchy. (Madanes, 1981, pp. 84–85)[3]

In following up the family, Madanes reports that the boy stopped lighting fires after this session. In later sessions, Madanes discussed different ways of putting out fires with the boy and told his mother that he should be allowed the privilege of lighting fires, a privilege the other children did not have.

Each strategic family therapy intervention is different, depending on the observations of the family structure that the therapist makes. Interventions, whether they are straightforward or paradoxical, are thought out clearly and carefully. When therapists first start to use such interventions, it is suggested that they do so under supervision so that they can discuss their observations of family power struggles and coalitions that exist within the family.

EXPERIENTIAL AND HUMANISTIC FAMILY THERAPIES

Both experiential and humanistic family therapists see dysfunctional behavior as due to interference with personal growth. For families to grow, there needs to be open communication between family members and open self-expression of individuals, while appreciating the uniqueness and differences between family members. In setting goals for therapy, both therapist and the family take responsibility (Goldenberg & Goldenberg, 2000). In this section, the experiential approach of Carl Whitaker and the humanistic approach of Virginia Satir are described briefly. Although both therapists contributed to the development of family systems therapy over a period of more than 40 years, their work is somewhat idiosyncratic and their theoretical approaches are not articulated as well as the other theories presented in this chapter.

The Experiential Therapy of Carl Whitaker

Whitaker (1976) sees theory as a hindrance in clinical work and prefers an intuitive approach, using the therapist's own resources. Characteristic of his approach is the use of countertransference (his own reactions to clients). Not only do clients grow and change in therapy; so do therapists. Because clients and therapists affect each other, each takes on the role of patient and therapist at various moments in therapy. This interaction fosters the goal of interpersonal growth among family members (and therapists).

In his intuitive approach to families, Whitaker (1976) listens for impulses and symbols of unconscious behavior. Sometimes he responds consciously to feelings or family members' ways of relating; at other times he may be unaware of why he is responding the way he is. Relating symbolically, he may suggest clients fantasize about an experience. This may lead to understanding the absurdity of a situation. Situations are viewed in ways that emphasize choice and experience rather than sickness or pathology.

Whitaker's insight into family processes can be seen in a situation where he speaks to a 16-year-old girl who has just concluded an angry and tearful interaction with her father, who has just tried to set limits on her behaviors such as coming home very late at night. In this situation, Whitaker (Napier & Whitaker, 1978) acts spontaneously to address issues that the girl is unaware of.

> **Carl:** "What I thought threw you, pushed you so hard, was your father's *painful reasonableness*. You were mocking him, remember?" Claudia nodded slightly. "And I thought you were doing it to avoid crying or to get your old man to come out of hiding and react to you in some way." Carl shifted slightly in his chair, leaning forward. His unlit pipe was balanced carefully in his hand, and the hand was resting on his knee. "But what your dad did was give you a lecture about how he was your father and how you had to obey the rules of the house. He had lots of very real feelings, but he kept them all covered. I think that was what threw you, that he wouldn't admit what he was feeling, that he kept trying to be reasonable, trying to be a father rather than a person." Then Carl paused, and Claudia waited for him to finish. Finally: "It was the process of Dad's *destroying his own feelings*, his own personhood, that I thought got you so upset. And it was appropriate for you to get upset. I think it's a very serious problem." (pp. 69–70)[4]

Whitaker's response to Claudia reflects his attention to the entire family and the impact of father and daughter on each other. He sees their relationship in ways that Claudia does not. Although Whitaker's approach is spontaneous, it is also structured.

Whitaker and Keith (1981) describe the beginning, middle, and ending phases of therapy. In the beginning phase, there is a battle for taking initiative in developing a structure, such as determining who is going to be present at the therapy sessions. In the middle phase, Whitaker works actively on family issues, bringing in extended family when appropriate. To bring about change, he may use confrontation, exaggeration, or absurdity. When Whitaker picks up an absurdity in the patient, he builds upon it, until the patient recognizes it and can change her approach. The ending phase of therapy deals with separation anxiety on the part of the family (and therapist) and the gradual disentanglement from each others' lives. Throughout the therapeutic process, Whitaker's style is marked by energy, involvement, and creativity.

The Humanistic Approach of Virginia Satir

Known for her creativity and warmth, Satir attended to the feelings of family members and worked with them on day-to-day functioning and their own emotional experiences in the family. With individuals and families, she focused on developing a sense of self-worth and bringing flexibility into family situations to initiate change. Noted for her communication skills, Satir worked on helping family members develop theirs. An example is her outline for effective communication within the family (Satir, 1972): Use the first person and express what you feel; use I statements that indicate the taking of responsibility, such as "I feel angry"; family members must level with each other; and one's facial expression, body position, and voice should match.

One of Satir's contributions to family communications was the identification of five styles of relating within the family (Satir, 1972): the placater, weak and tentative, always agreeing; the blamer, finding fault with others; the superreasonable, detached, calm, and unemotional; the irrelevant, distracting others and not relating to family processes; and the congruent communicator, genuinely expressive, real, and open. Satir's emphasis on communication style influenced her selection of therapeutic interventions.

From the beginning of her work, Satir always met with the entire family, helping them to feel better about themselves and each other. One approach was a family life chronology in which the history of the family's development was recorded. This chronology included how spouses met, how they saw themselves in relationship with their siblings, and their expectations of parenting. The children were also included and asked to contribute by saying how they saw their parents and family activities. This information, as well as her observations about the imbalances within the family system, helped her attend to blockages in the system and intervene in ways that would facilitate growth of each member in the family. One means of accomplishing this was by using family reconstruction, an experiential approach with the family including guided fantasy, hypnosis, psychodrama, and role playing. Additionally, she used family sculpting, in which family members were physically molded into characteristic poses representing a view of family relationships. Using these methods she would have a family enact events in the family's life. Satir (1967) also made use of Gestalt therapy techniques, and her work resembled that of Kempler (Chapter 7) to the extent that both made use of experiencing techniques in family therapy.

A glimpse into Satir's concern and caring about family members can be seen in this interaction with Coby, the middle child and only boy of five children. A brief dialogue with Coby is followed by Satir's explanation of her own experience at the time, illustrating her compassion and her attention to feelings within the family.

> *Virginia:* Let me see now if I hear you. That if your father—if I'm hearing this— some way that he brings out his thoughts. . . . He gets over-angry, you feel, or something like that?
>
> *Coby:* Yes, ma'am.
>
> *Virginia:* Some way—and you're saying if he could find some way to treat that differently—is that what you hope for?
>
> *Coby:* Well, yes, ma'am, but you know, he loses his temper too easy.
>
> *Virginia:* I see.
>
> *Coby:* If he can hold it back and try to talk to us instead of yelling and screaming and everything.
>
> *Virginia:* I see. So sometimes you think your father thinks you do something, and then you don't do it, and then you don't know how to tell him or he doesn't hear you, or something like that? Is that what you're saying? (Satir & Baldwin, 1983, pp. 34, 36)[5]

Satir describes her observations of her response to Coby. She responds to both his verbal and nonverbal messages. Her empathy for the boy and his relationship with his father typifies Satir's sensitive response to families.

Virginia: Here I was aware of the love this child had for his father. And that said to me that if a father could inspire that kind of love, there was also much gentleness underneath and that what must be coming off was his defense against feeling that he didn't count. I saw all of that in this little interchange.

Listening to Coby, I also knew that he would not take the risk of talking the way he did so quickly if there wasn't some leeway for the rule of freedom to comment. And he also told me that his father was not always angry, and that there was a whimsical quality to his anger. This reinforced for me the feeling that the father was struggling for power and that he was often unaware of what he was doing. He wanted to be the head of the family but he wasn't and felt weak. (Satir & Baldwin, 1983, p. 35)

Therapists who trained with Satir were often deeply affected by her humanistic approach that emphasized individual growth and self-worth. Although she died in 1988, her work continues to have an impact on many family therapists.

SOLUTION-FOCUSED THERAPY

A postmodern, social constructivist approach, solution-focused brief therapy is concerned with how the family (or individuals) view the solutions to the problems. Developed by Steve deShazer and his wife Insoo Berg, this therapeutic method is less interested in why or how a problem arose than in possible solutions. De Shazer (1985, 1991, 1994) uses the metaphor of a lock and key to explain his therapeutic approach. Client complaints are like locks on doors that have not been opened. DeShazer and Berg (Berg, 1994; Berg & deShazer, 1993; DeJong & Berg, 1998) do not want to focus on why the lock is the way it is or why the door won't open, rather they want to help the family look for the key to the problem. Thus, they focus on the solution. Although they listen to the client's complaint, they attend particularly to the expectations that family members have of possible changes and solutions. Limiting the number of sessions to about 5 to 10, they create an expectation of change.

Goals

In solution-focused therapy, it is important that goals be clear and concrete (DeJong & Berg, 1998). In the beginning of therapy, questions make the goals clearer. It is also important that these goals be small so that several small goals can be met rather quickly. Information about exceptions and about "miracles" helps develop specific goals. By finding out what would be different in one's life, problems are solved. How well goals are being met is evaluated at several points during therapy. Often the client is asked to rate progress on the goals on a scale from 0 to 10.

One technique that relates directly to feedback about progress on goals is the "end-of-session feedback." Messages, written or oral, are explicit and given to the client at the end of the session. These include compliments to the client about progress or other aspects of the therapy. They may also include suggestions that will help the clients and solve their problems.

Techniques of Solution-Focused Brief Therapy

Questions are the basic tools of solution-focused therapy. Although a number of different kinds of questions may be used at times, there are five types that are basic to solution-focused therapy. These include questions that help the client describe what changes have already been made before therapy. The "miracle question" is one that helps define the client's goal and bring about a possible solution. Exception-finding questions are ones that look at times when things worked, when the problem did not exist. Coping questions are ones that highlight the client's abilities to cope with difficult events. Scaling questions are those that add further precision to the problem by providing a "measure" of the change that may take or has taken place. These concepts are illustrated further here.

In this hypothetical case, Cheryl (the therapist) starts by trying to understand the problem and being empathic with it.

Cheryl: How can I be of assistance?

Rosie: Well, I've got some big problems. First thing—I'm pregnant again. I already have two babies, two little girls who are 3 and 2 (years old), and I have two boys who are in school. I'm going crazy with all I have to do, and I'm afraid that my two boys are gonna be put in a foster home again because I have trouble getting them to school in the morning. They don't wanna get up in the morning. They just wanna lay around and watch TV. They say school won't do them any good, and they can make more delivering goods for their uncles.

Cheryl: "Delivering goods"?

Rosie: Yeah, drugs I think. I tell them that is no good and they're gonna get into trouble, but they don't listen to me. I feel better when they're in school, because at least then they can't be with Lamar and Brian (the uncles). But they won't get up and I'm so tired because I'm pregnant again.

Cheryl: (empathically) Wow, I can see you really have your hands full. Handling four kids by yourself is really tough to start with, but to be pregnant on top of all that . . .

Rosie: Yeah, it is, and I don't want my boys to be taken away again. But they fight me on school, and I'm so tired with everything I have to do and being pregnant. (DeJong & Berg, 1998, pp. 14, 15)[6]

The interview continues, as Cheryl gathers information about Rosie and her involvement with prostitution, child welfare needs, and her pregnancy. Then the therapist moves to a different topic where she is able to introduce the "miracle" question. In the following example, Rosie does not answer the question initially and in a useful way. The therapist is patient and keeps asking. Notice the solutions that start to emerge in the last two client statements.

Cheryl: So you have several big problems—getting your boys to school, getting enough money, being pregnant and very tired. Let me ask you a different kind of question about these; it's called the miracle question. (pause) Suppose that you go to bed as usual tonight and, while you've been sleeping, a miracle happens. The miracle is that the problems you've been telling me about are solved! Only you're sleeping, and so do not know right away that they've been solved. What do you suppose you would notice tomorrow morning that would be *different*—that would tell you, wow, things are really better!

Rosie: (smiling) That's easy; I would have won the lottery—$3 million.

Cheryl: That would be great wouldn't it. What else would you notice?

Rosie: Some nice man would come along who has lots of money and lots of patience with kids, and we get married. Or I wouldn't have so many kids and I would finish high school and I would have a good job.

Cheryl: OK, that sounds like a *big* miracle. What do you imagine would be the first thing that you would notice which would tell you that this day is different, it's better, a miracle must have happened?

Rosie: Well, I would get up in the morning before my kids do, make them breakfast, and sit down with them while we all eat together.

Cheryl: If you were to decide to do that—get up before them and make them breakfast—what would they do?

Rosie: I think maybe they would come and sit down at the table instead of going and turning on the TV.

Cheryl: And how would that be for you?

Rosie: I'd be happier because we could talk about nice things, not argue over TV. And my babies won't start crying over all the fighting about the TV.

Cheryl: What else? What else would be different when the miracle happens? (De Jong & Berg, 1998, p. 15)

In the next section, the therapist asks an implicit exception question. She wants to know what the exceptions are to the problem by asking in the first statement, "Are there times already, say in the last two weeks, which are like the miracle which you have been describing, even a little bit?" In this segment Rosie describes the exceptions to the problems and then how she copes with the problem in answer to Cheryl's question, "How did you manage that, reading to four kids?"

Cheryl: Rosie, I'm impressed. You have a pretty clear picture of how things will be different around your house when things are better. Are there times already, say in the last two weeks, which are like the miracle which you have been describing, even a little bit?

Rosie: Well, I'm not sure. Well, about four days ago it was better.

Cheryl: Tell me about four days ago. *What* was different?

Rosie: Well, I went to bed about ten the night before and had a good night of sleep. I had food in the house, because I had gone to the store and to the food pantry on Saturday. I had even set the alarm for 6:30 and got up when it rang. I made breakfast and called the kids. The boys ate and got ready for school and left on time. (remembering) One even got some homework out of his backpack and did it—real quick—before he went to school.

Cheryl: (impressed) Rosie, that sounds like a big part of the miracle right there. I'm amazed. How did all that happen?

Rosie: I'm not sure. I guess one thing was I had the food in the house and I got to bed on time.

Cheryl: So, how did you make that happen?

Rosie: Ah, I decided not to see any clients that night and I read books to my kids for an hour.

Cheryl: How did you manage that, reading to four kids? That seems like it would be really tough.

Rosie: No that doesn't work—reading to four kids at the same time. I have my oldest boy read to one baby, because that's the only way I can get him to practice his reading; and I read to my other boy and baby.

Cheryl: Rosie, that seems like a great idea —having him read to the baby. It helps you, and it helps him with his reading. How do you get him to do that?

Rosie: Oh, I let him stay up a half hour later than the others because he helps me. He really likes that. (DeJong & Berg, 1998, p. 16)

The following segment uses scaling questions to address the problem and Rosie's view of its level of severity for her.

Cheryl: I'd like you to put some things on a scale for me, on a scale from 0 to 10. First, on a scale from 0 through 10, where 0 equals the worst your problems have been and 10 means the problems we have been talking about are solved, where are you *today* on that scale?

Rosie: If you had asked me that question before we started today, I would have said about a 2. But now I think it's more like a 5.

Cheryl: Great! Now let me ask you about how *confident* you are that you can have another day in the next week like the one four days ago—the one which was a lot like your miracle picture. On a scale of 0 to 10, where 0 equals no confidence and 10 means you have every confidence, how confident are you that you can make it happen again?

Rosie: Oh, . . . about a 5.

Cheryl: Suppose you were at a 6; what would be different?

Rosie: I'd have to be sure that I always had food in the house for breakfast for the kids. (DeJong & Berg, 1998, p. 17)

The use of these techniques is positive and focused on finding the solution. Others have developed similar approaches that use some different techniques, but a similar solution focus (Lipchik, 1993; O'Hanlon, 1993).

NARRATIVE THERAPY

Listening to the stories of their clients and focusing on the importance of the stories and alternative ways of viewing them characterize the work of Michael White and David Epston (Epston & White, 1992; Freeman, Epston, & Lobovits, 1997; White & Epston, 1990, 1994). Michael White is co-director of the Dulwich Centre in Adelaide, South Australia, and David Epston is co-director of the Family Therapy Centre in Auckland, New Zealand. Their work very much reflects the influence of postmodernism and social constructionism. The key to change in families (or individuals) is the reauthoring or retelling of stories. They use techniques such as externalizing, searching for unique outcomes and exploring alternative narratives or stories to help their clients bring about changes in their lives. In their work, they may write letters or give certificates as a way of making their stories more permanent. They may also use stories of other successful clients.

Concepts of Narrative Therapy

White and Epston take a social constructivist view of the world. They are interested in how their clients perceive the events and the world around them. They know that some family members are likely to have different views than other family members, which can lead to conflict and problems. The narratives or stories that are people's lives represent political, cultural, economic, and social influences. When these stories are problem oriented or negative, they often affect the attitude of the clients or family. Influenced by White and Epston (1990), Omer and Alon (1997) are concerned with fully understanding the story of their clients, an approach they refer to as *narrative empathy*. In examining clients' descriptions of their world and their problems, they try to understand the role of the characters and the various plots or narrative lines within a story. Their approach is to look for themes and meanings within the clients' stories. Although their approach is somewhat different than White and Epston, their focus on valuing the client's stories is very similar.

Goals

Narrative therapists try to help their clients see their lives (stories) in ways that will be positive rather than problem saturated. They help their clients shape meaning from the characters and plots in their stories so that they can overcome their problems. They believe in the power of words to affect the way individuals see themselves and others. By phrasing a client's problem in such a way that the client can see alternatives or avenues that are open to him, the client becomes ready to pursue a resolution for his problem.

The following example of 8-year-old Samuel (Freeman, Epston, & Lobovits, 1997, pp. 57, 58) shows different ways of construing Samuel's problem and setting goals for Samuel.

Samuel's parents say that *"Samuel is very self-centered. He has no patience. When he can't have just what he wants, exactly when he wants it, he throws a fit."* (p. 57)

Samuel puts the problem differently. He says: *"I hate school. The stuff they want me to do is boring, I'd rather play my own games. The teacher and the other kids don't like me because I won't pretend to be interested. If they get in my face, I get in theirs."* (p. 57)

A therapist also takes a problem oriented view of Samuel's behavior, *"Samuel has an abbreviated attention span. He should be further evaluated for attention deficit hyperactivity disorder. Samuel cannot contain his anxiety well for his age. Samuel regresses to a narcissistic and grandiose stage of development in social situations that require age-appropriate cooperation."* (pp. 57–58)[7]

Freeman, Epston, and Lobovits (1997) see this issue from a positive point of view. In their positive approach to the problem, they put the problem outside of the individual (externalizing it). They use questions that can have productive answers rather than making statements such as those of Samuel, his parents, and the therapist. They raise the following questions:

"Is Samuel the type of young person who can be very clear about what he wants and expects? Do Temper and Impatience get the better of him when he perceives an injustice, or when events don't follow the lead of his vivid imagination? Has this interfered with his peace of mind? Has it affected his reputation with the teachers and other kids? What do his own games offer that elicit his interest?" (p. 58)

These questions may help the client and his parents view the problem differently and develop goals for Samuel. They offer hope to the family that new solutions can be achieved.

Techniques of Narrative Therapy

The techniques that narrative therapists use have to do with the telling of the story. They may examine the story and look for other ways to tell it differently or to understand it in other ways. In doing so, they find it helpful to put the problem outside of the child or family, thus externalizing it. They look for unique outcomes, positive events, that are in contrast to a problem-saturated story. They often find that it is helpful to explore alternative narratives or stories.

Externalizing the problem. In narrative therapy, the problem becomes the opponent, not the child or the family with which the problem is associated. The family may work together to combat the problem. Thus in the example above, "Temper" and "Impatience" are the oppressors that the family will work against. This places the problem outside of the family and makes it a separate entity, not a characteristic of the individual. Samuel does not have a bad temper, rather Temper is interfering with Samuel. Thus the therapist might ask, "What do you think Temper's purpose is in upsetting Samuel?" This counters the parent's assumption that Samuel is the problem. This paves the way for finding different solutions, rather than blaming Samuel for the problem.

The therapist can then deconstruct a problem or story and then reconstruct or reauthor a preferred story. The therapist (Becvar & Becvar, 1999) can help the family work together to defeat a problem rather than hold onto their own stories of the problem.

To make stories more definitive and significant, Epston (Freeman, et al., 1997) uses letters to clients or certificates to emphasize positive ways of viewing the problem or progress that the client has made.

Unique outcomes.   When narrative therapists listen to a story that is full of problems, they look for exceptions to the stories (Freeman, et al., 1997). They try to find moments in the story where the family worked well together or the problem started to dissolve. These exceptions are seen as sparkling moments or as "unique outcomes." These moments may consist of thoughts, feelings, or actions that are different than those that are found in the problem that family members have. By focusing on these unique outcomes, narrative therapists start to explore the influence that the family may have over the problem. This can begin a new story.

Alternative narratives.   Exploration of strengths, special abilities, and aspirations of the family and the person with the problem is the focus of the alternative narrative or story. Therapists comment on the positive aspects of what the identified patient or family is doing and develop them into a new way of viewing the problem. They may ask questions such as "Can you think of a time when you did not go along with Temper's requests? How were you able to trust your own view? What does this tell you about how you handle yourself?" The therapist might also ask, "How did you accomplish that positive goal? What was different that you said to yourself?" In this way, the narrative therapist helps clients see strengths by telling their stories about themselves in a more powerful and positive way.

Although narrative therapists may make use of a variety of other approaches that are related to understanding the client's story, all focus on ways that the client can look differently at her story to bring about a new sense of hope or accomplishment. The family works with the client to bring about a new narrative that works for all of them and fights the "problem."

An Example of Narrative Therapy

The following example is a description by David Epston of his work with 12-year-old Terry (a Caucasian New Zealander) and his mother Dorothy. David Epston met with Terry and his mother eight times over an 8-month period. In this excerpt describing the first session, David externalizes the problem for Terry by attacking Guilt and Compulsions.

> "He's overloaded with guilt," Dorothy summarized after sharing her concerns about her son, Terry. She had just told David of Terry's handwashing, excessive worrying, daily vomiting on the way to school, and hysterical responses to viewing people kiss on TV and to "dirt" in general.
>
> Dorothy, still undecided about its merit, told of an attempt that she and Terry's older sister had made to disrupt his screaming demands to put cushions over their eyes when people on TV were kissing. They had, with exaggerated good humor and a bit of teasing thrown in, refused to comply with his demands. Their policy behind such a practice was that "it was better to be open with him so he felt okay about it." Terry nicknamed their tactics as "teasing"; when asked by David if he considered "teasing" to be benevolent or malevolent, he assured David that it was "benevolent."

David asked what effect "benevolent teasing" had on the problem. Terry was quick to say, "I'm making headway with the compulsions and it (benevolent teasing) has been helping me along." David speculated, "Your mum and your sister could have thought they were upsetting you rather than strengthening you?"

"Not really," replied Terry.

David asked for further information. "You knew it was for your own good? How?"

"Yeah, they were laughing and they weren't shouting. They didn't have frowns on their faces."

David wondered aloud to Terry, "Do you think that you saw the joke of it all? Do you think Guilt and Compulsions don't like to be made fun of?"

Terry replied sagely, "Yeah, but I like them to be made fun of because then it is a lot easier to talk about them. And you just think, 'They are silly thoughts and I can fight them off.'"

David, thinking that everyone had stumbled onto something outstanding, asked a question to confirm this and to contribute to his on-going process of reviewing his ideas, "When your mother and older sister benevolently tease you—you can fight off the thoughts and be stronger?" Terry answered in the affirmative.

Picking up on Dorothy's initial comment that Terry was "overloaded with guilt," David double-checked with Terry, "Is it okay for me to call it Guilt?" When Terry concurred, David took the liberty of personifying the problem: "Do you mind my saying that Guilt has a voice and kind of speaks to you?"

"No," said Terry.

"I'm asking you this because Chris, who had a run-in with similar sorts of problems— he was sixteen at the time by the way—gave me his consent to tell you what he found out—that Guilt talked to him and told him to do things," David continued. "What does Guilt say to you Terry?"

Terry replied by speaking through the voice of Guilt: "You have to be perfectly clean. Your hands have to be all nice and clean. They're not meant to be dirty."

David couldn't help getting angry hearing Guilt's demands on Terry's hands, and could not stop himself from telling Terry about his feelings: "I get quite angry just thinking about it!"

Terry went on in further detail about the demands, still mimicking the voice of Guilt: "The thoughts you are having at the moment are nasty and malicious. You are not meant to have them. Your are strange and inhuman. You are the only one who has them. You are abnormal!"

Earlier David had promised Terry that he would not get overly excited or angry about things, so he had to control his rising anger at the ludicrous lies that Guilt was telling Terry. (Freeman, et al., 1997, pp. 278, 279.)

In the following section, David Epston continues to externalize the problem, but he also adds a new story. He reads out loud a letter that he had written to a successful client, Chris. In this way, he takes a positive story from someone else and uses it to encourage Terry.

David formed the opinion that Terry was "quite a smart character" and his mother smiled and nodded in agreement. He assumed that Terry was, in fact, a smarter person than Guilt was taking him for. So he asked him, "Why do you think Guilt lies that way? What are its purposes in having you spend all your time obsessed and compelled?"

Terry replied thoughtfully, "Well, it's trying to help me get my mind off things I don't want to think about—that I'm scared of thinking. It's trying to help me not think about things, but it is hurting me really."

This answer confirmed David's opinion about Terry's overall smartness and his knowledgeable relationship with the problem. It reminded him of similarly knowledgeable thoughts of Chris. David read out loud a letter he had written to Chris, which Chris had donated to the "archives" of The Anti-Habit League for just such a purpose.

Dear Chris,

Chris, you told me you aren't worrying so much about your schoolwork. I marveled at this. You told me that "worrying isn't helping" and for that reason you dropped it and yet your effort level has stayed the same. Chris, do you think your compulsions have tricked you and almost betrayed you into their grip? What promises did they make to suck you in? Did they promise you everlasting happiness if you wiped your bum clean, or washed your body spic-and-span? Do you think these are childish ideas or do you think there is any truth in them? Before, you thought, "They were just weird things I did." Now it seems you are seeing through the tricks that Guilt was playing on you. (Freeman, et al., 1997, p. 280)

Epston continues to build an alternative story of Terry's life. For example, he asks Terry's mother about the qualities that Terry has that would have predicted that he could overcome his adversities. At the third meeting, Terry brought a letter to Epston in which he says "After only one visit, the shell of guilt that had covered me crumbled and light and freedom came to me again. I started making new friends and with my old friends started tying the tethers back together which over time had been left to rot and slowly decay" (p. 285). In their eighth and last meeting, Epston presents a "diploma in imperfection" to Terry that reiterates the positive story that is now a part of Terry's life. This example shows one therapist's approach to narrative therapy. Other therapists, such as Tom Andersen, have also contributed creatively to the development of narrative therapy.

The Reflecting Team

Tom Andersen (1991, 1993) makes use of narrative therapy techniques. However, he has developed an additional method called the "reflecting team." It is somewhat similar to the approach of the Milan Associates described on p. 536 who may stop a session with a family in order to consult with professionals who are watching through a one-way mirror. However, Andersen makes this a two-way process. He may ask for comments from the professionals who are watching, but then he allows the family and therapist to watch the professionals have a conversation about the family. When the professionals have finished their reflections, the family members can discuss their view of the reflecting team's comments about their earlier conversations. This allows the family to have different perspectives about the way they interact. From this discussion, a new dialog or story about the family may develop.

INTEGRATIVE APPROACHES TO FAMILY SYSTEMS THERAPY

The current practice of family therapy reflects a creative approach on the part of family therapists who integrate transgenerational, structural, strategic, experiential, solution-focused, and narrative family therapies. As Quinn and Davidson (1984) report, the majority of family therapists make use of more than one theory of family therapy. Although this chapter has covered six approaches to family systems therapy, there are others as well, such as brief family therapy, illustrated in the next section. Additionally, each theory that has been described in this book (with the exception of Jungian psychotherapy) has been adapted to families.

Because many therapists come to family therapy after having been trained as individual therapists, they are likely to combine their training with family systems therapy. Often the approaches that therapists use in working with families are influenced by their own personalities and the patient population that they work with, as well as their prior training. For example, social workers who must do crisis intervention are likely to use briefer techniques such as strategic therapy rather than psychoanalytic or transgenerational approaches. Therapists often find that they cannot always work with the family system or even a family subsystem. At times they may need to work with the patient alone, a view recognized by family structural therapists (Minuchin, et al., 1978), as well as other family therapists.

Integrative approaches to family therapy are becoming increasingly common (Lebow, 1997). Several ways have been described in which family systems therapists incorporate approaches that have been described as well as others. Several reasons for this integrative trend can be identified (Lebow, 1997): Distinctions between individual and family therapy are less definitive. Therapists may mix individual, couple, and family sessions in treatment. There is currently a greater focus on use of concepts rather than theory. Thus "differentiation" (Bowen), "enactment" (Minuchin), and genograms may be used by therapists of many orientations. Also, as integrative approaches emerge, no single integrative approach dominates. As will be shown in the "research" section, research does not support one approach more than others. Integrative approaches that have been developed are theoretically sound in that a rationale is given for using several theories.

BRIEF FAMILY SYSTEMS THERAPY

By attempting to make interventions in a short period of time, innovators of brief family systems therapy have developed approaches that are practical, clear as to method, and related to the presenting problem. However, they desire not just to produce temporary change in the family to solve a pressing problem, first-order change, but a lasting change in the family system, second-order change. Because these approaches use powerful interventions, they often use therapy teams, some members of which observe behind a one-way mirror and may enter the therapy room, on occasion, or confer with the therapist during a break in the session. Two of these brief approaches are described here: the Brief Therapy Project at the Mental Research Institute in Palo Alto involved in training, theory development, and research since 1967 and the long brief therapy approach based in Milan, Italy.

The Mental Research Institute Brief Family Therapy Model

Based in part on the work of Gregory Bateson, Don Jackson, Jay Haley, and Milton Erickson, the Mental Research Institute (MRI) approach to brief therapy emphasizes resolving problems and relieving symptoms (Watzlawick, Weakland, & Fisch, 1974). Lasting less than 10 sessions, MRI brief therapy is a structured approach to problem resolution, similar to Haley's strategic system. However, it differs in that it does not make use of Minuchin's structural concepts of power and hierarchy within the family, which Haley does.

Particularly important to MRI brief family therapists are communication patterns, such as those that are complementary or symmetrical. In complementary relationships, one person is superior, while the other is inferior or submissive. In a symmetrical relationship, there is equality between partners. However, a symmetrical message can be escalated in such a way that one angry remark is met with an angrier remark, which in turn is met with an even angrier remark, so that fighting continues until one partner is ready to concede. The way such an argument continues depends on what is termed each partner's *punctuation*, which is based on the idea that each partner believes what he or she said is caused by the other partner. This is reminiscent of the dialogue between children who are arguing about who started an argument: "You did it!" "No, you did it!" In such circular interaction, there is no reason to look for a starting point, but rather attention is paid to the double binds that exist in family communication (Weakland, 1976).

In their approach to therapy, MRI brief therapists make use of many of the techniques described in the section on Haley's strategic approach: reframing, relabeling, and paradoxical interventions. In approaching their work with families, they try to get a clear view of the problem and devise a way to change the parts of the system that maintain the problem (Segal, 1987). In seeking to make changes, they look for small changes and encourage patients to progress slowly. As therapy progresses, the family's way of viewing its problems and its communication style is gradually restructured. Arguments and disagreements are avoided while working with the family. Each type of problem demands a different approach.

In the following example, based on work with 10 families in which the husband suffered a heart attack but refused to exercise or change his diet, Segal (1982) worked with the wives to change solutions from ineffective ones to productive ones. Staying within a five-session limit, the therapist attempted to change the system so that the husband's behavior would be adaptive. Observing that the wives nagged and argued to change their husband's behavior, instructions were given to the wives. In one case, a wife was told to tell her husband to live out his life in any way he wanted to no matter how short his life might be. She was instructed to take control over her life and to go over life insurance and estate planning with her husband. Furthermore, she was asked to call life insurance agencies and have them call back at a time when she would not be at home, but her husband would. After 2 weeks of dealing with her husband this way, he participated in rehabilitation exercises and watched his diet.

Long Brief Therapy of the Milan Associates

Based on the work of the MRI theorists and Haley's strategic model, an approach has been developed that focuses on differences in the ways that family members behave, relate, and perceive events. This approach is difficult to describe because it has changed over time, and members of the group, based in Milan, Italy, have evolved different views. Their original work was described as "long brief therapy" because they had relatively few sessions, about 10, but met monthly with the family rather than weekly (Tomm, 1984). Of note are two creative approaches to family interventions developed by different members of the Milan group. An intervention developed by Boscolo and Cecchin, termed *circular questioning*, was designed to bring out differences in the way family members saw events and relationships by asking them the same question. For example, they might ask various family members (Boscolo, Cecchin, Hoffman, & Penn, 1987), How bad was the arguing this week? Who is the closest to the other? Who is most upset by Andy's not eating? Such questions help family members expand their perspective on issues and find new ways to understand their problems and find new solutions.

Another innovative technique has been designed by Selvini-Palazzoli to help in situations where parents and children collude in a dysfunctional way. Using the *invariant prescription*, Selvini-Palazzoli gives the parents a written prescription that is to be followed by the family, after the family has been interviewed. This prescription is designed to create clear boundaries between parents and children (Selvini-Palazzoli, Cirillo, Selvini, & Sorrentino, 1989). Developed from research done by Giuliana Prata and Mara Selvini-Palazzoli, the invariant prescription relies on paradoxical intervention.

The following case explains how Selvini-Palazzoli et al. (1989) used the invariant prescription in their work. Helping a married couple with three adolescent daughters, one of whom had attempted suicide, the therapist tried to determine the type of "game" that was going on in the family. After the fifth session, they found a way to keep the adolescent girls from meddling in their parents' concerns. Having separated the children from the parents in the therapist's offices, they gave the parents the following message in writing.

> Keep everything that has been said during this session absolutely secret from everyone. Should your daughters ask questions about it, say that the therapist has ordered everything to be kept only between her and the two of you. On at least two occasions between now and your next scheduled appointment, you are to "disappear" from home before dinner without any forewarning. Leave a note worded as follows: "We shall not be in tonight." Each time you go out, pick some place to meet where you are reasonably sure no one will recognize you. If, when you get back home, your daughters ask you where on earth you've been, simply smile and say: "That concerns only the two of us." Each of you is also to keep a sheet of paper, well out of everyone's sight, on which to jot down personal observations on how each of your daughters has reacted to her parents' unusual behavior. At our next meeting, which will again be with only the two of you, each of you will read your notes out loud. (p. 16)[8]

The therapists reported that at the next meeting, a month later, the parents had carried out their orders, and the identified patient had improved her behavior. After three more sessions with only the parents attending, relationships between the parents improved, as well as those among the three daughters.

The creative approaches of the Milan Group go beyond the techniques that have been described. In general, their work diverges somewhat from the strategic approach of Haley, but it is similar in its emphasis on dealing with interventions within the family system. Their use of sessions spaced at monthly intervals emphasizes the importance of the tasks given to the family and gives them time to make changes.

CURRENT TRENDS IN FAMILY SYSTEMS THERAPY

The field of family therapy, including family systems therapy, is a quickly growing, very diverse area. As can be seen by the fact that family therapy is discussed in almost every chapter in this book, it has become increasingly integrated into many aspects of psychotherapeutic practice. Trends that are discussed in this section include the impact of educational approaches to families on family therapy. As family therapy has grown as a profession, organizational groups and training centers have developed, and family therapists have increasingly become involved in the legal system. Also, advances in medicine have had an impact on family therapy.

Psychoeducational Approaches

Since the beginning of family therapy, therapists have been interested in helping families with a schizophrenic child. Although other family systems therapists have often seen the family as the cause or at least an impediment to good family functioning, the psychoeducational approach of Anderson, Reiss, and Hogarty (1986) takes what would appear to be a more traditional approach to support and empower the family to deal with the schizophrenic patient. They use a 1-day "survival skills workshop" to teach family members about schizophrenia and its prognosis, psychobiology, and treatment. By teaching families information about schizophrenia, they help them learn what they can do to assist the identified patient. Additionally, they schedule regular family sessions, often continuing for more than a year, to help the families deal with a schizophrenic child. Anderson et al. (1986) have also applied their model to depression. Rolland (1987) has used a somewhat similar approach in work with families who have a chronically ill member. These psychoeducational approaches are quite intensive, as they are designed to help families who have members who are severely disabled and distressed.

A number of programs have been developed to teach families coping and communication skills (Levant, 1986). Skills and communication training has three different goals: to teach the family how to deal with the identified patient; to teach the whole family how to communicate, problem solve, or negotiate conflict more effectively; or to enhance already adequate functioning. These programs may be designed for a variety of family issues, such as premarital counseling, marital relationships, parent-adolescent relationships, children of divorce, and families of drug abusers. The theoretical orientation of these programs varies, as they have been offered by psychoanalytic, Adlerian, person-centered, Gestalt, cognitive, behavioral, rational emotive behavioral, reality, and feminist therapists. Although some of the approaches to teaching families how to function more effectively may be more educational than psychoeducational, they are among the many treatment alternatives offered to families.

Professional Training and Organizations

As the field of family therapy has grown, so has the need to set standards for training and practice. Started in 1942, the American Association for Marriage and Family Therapy (AAMFT) serves as a credentialing body for the field of family therapy by setting requirements for membership and working with state and federal governments in the development of licensing laws. With a membership of more than 18,000, AAMFT offers continuing education and training to its members through conferences and the *Journal of Marital and Family Therapy*. Also, the American Family Therapy Association (AFTA), started in 1977, is designed so that researchers, clinicians, and trainers can exchange ideas about family therapy. Increasingly, graduate schools in counseling, social work, and psychology offer course work and supervision in family therapy. Also, the AAMFT credits masters and doctoral programs that specialize in marital and family therapies. Training centers not affiliated with universities offer advanced training in family therapy.

Family Law

Knowledge of the legal system as it relates to families can be extremely important for family therapists (Goldenberg & Goldenberg, 2000). Issues such as confidentiality, child abuse laws, and dealing with dangerous clients are concerns that make family therapists vulnerable to malpractice suits. Occasionally, family therapists may be called upon to give expert testimony in the courts on issues involving custody, disposition of juvenile offenders, and hospitalization or incarceration. Making assessments and writing reports for families involved in custody and divorce cases may be increasingly common, as more and more child custody and visitation disputes are brought to the court system. To perform these activities therapists need to be informed about the law and be willing to work closely with attorneys.

Medicine

As there have been advances in pharmacology or biological psychiatry, there has been an increasing trend for patients and families to see the root of the problem as a "chemical imbalance." This has led to a trend toward a medicalization of social deviance (Combrinck-Graham, 1998; Keith, 1998). When there are problems in a family, such as a child becoming aggressive, a relatively easy solution is to have the child take a prescribed medication. By doing so, the answer to the problem is clear-cut, requiring no behavioral or attitudinal change on the part of the family. Medical advances in treating childhood psychological problems have been remarkable. However, family therapists believe that both psychological and biological approaches need to be considered when working with children.

As family therapy has grown, so have the issues about which it has been concerned. With growth has come the development of professional organizations, training centers, and journals, as well as the need to be prepared to deal with legal situations. The growth of different therapeutic approaches to families, whether through psychoeducation or the application of a variety of therapeutic interventions, has caused therapists to be selective and to integrate family systems therapy as well as other approaches as they continue to be developed.

RESEARCH

Investigations into family therapy have been quite diverse, studying a variety of approaches to family therapy. Several investigators have been concerned with examining the effectiveness of specific theories of family systems therapy. Another avenue of study has been to focus on the effectiveness of different types of family therapy as they are applied to identified patients with varying disorders. Each of these is discussed in some detail.

Evaluation of Family Systems Therapies

A number of reviews of research on family therapy have found family therapy to be useful for a variety of problems and to be at least as effective as other types of therapy (Bednar, Burlingame, & Masters, 1988; Hazelrigg, Cooper, & Borduin, 1987; Henggeler, Borduin, & Mann, 1993; Pinsof, Wynne, & Hambright, 1996). However, most studies of family therapy do not completely define *family therapy* and may not be measuring specific family systems therapeutic approaches. However, there has been some research to support the effectiveness of behavioral, MRI, structural, Milan group, solution-focused, and narrative approaches.

A thorough review of a variety of therapies for family and marital therapy reports that many of the studies have focused on behavioral treatments (Baucom et al., 1998). Behavioral studies are more likely to meet stringent criteria for effectiveness that is used by researchers. The review by Baucom et al. (1998) focused on couples counseling and counseling when one or more members of the couple had mental health problems. Although behavioral treatments were most common, interpersonal, cognitive, and family systems were also used. All demonstrated effectiveness in couples counseling where one or both partners had conditions including anxiety, depression, sexual dysfunction, alcoholism, and schizophrenia. The findings of this review are consistent with those of Pinsof et al. (1996), who find substantial evidence to support the effectiveness of marital and family therapy.

Many studies combine Haley's strategic method or the MRI model with structural or other approaches, making determinations about the effectiveness of strategic therapy difficult. In an early study, Watzlawick et al. (1974) followed up 97 families about 3 months after treatment. After an average length of therapy of seven sessions, 40% reported complete symptom relief, 32% considerable relief, and 28% no change. An advantage of the MRI model is its brevity. In a study that divided 40 couples into an immediate treatment or a waiting list control group, improvement was found in marital adjustment and decrease in complaints using three sessions of couple counseling (Davidson & Horvath, 1997). A treatment manual was used that, among other techniques, used reframing to help couples see that their conflict could be seen as a way of regulating intimacy. In general, strategic therapists have devoted more attention to presenting case material than in doing research.

Evaluation of the Milan model is difficult because the model has been changing and there are different Milan models. In reviewing Milan systemic family therapy, Carr (1991) found that the Milan approach led to symptomatic change in between 66% and 75% of the cases in 10 studies. A relatively large study (not included in Carr's review) of 118 participants who were randomly assigned to a Milan approach or another approach found that both treatments achieved similar changes in symptoms at the end of a 6-month follow-up (Simpson, 1990). However, the Milan approach was briefer, and families of the identified patients reported more positive changes than did families of patients receiving other therapies. These positive results contrast with the more negative findings of Coleman (1987) and Machal, Feldman, and Sigal (1989), who reported lower success rates and negative reactions to the therapist or team of therapists. These mixed findings are not surprising in light of the fact that Milan therapy has been practiced differently by different people at different times.

Perhaps the best evidence for the effectiveness of Minuchin's structural therapy has come from work with diabetic and anorectic children (Minuchin et al., 1978). Using the level of free fatty acids in the blood as a measure of stress, Minuchin et al. were able to reduce stress levels in diabetic children and their families with structural family therapy. With a group of 43 children suffering from anorexia nervosa, Minuchin et al. reported a 90% improvement rate upon completion of therapy. This positive improvement rate continued on follow-up several years later.

Solution-focused therapists at the Brief Family Therapy Center in Milwaukee, Wisconsin, have monitored the efficacy of their work by following up with clients who seek therapy (DeJong & Berg, 1998). During a 10-month period, 275 clients received services at the Center. Of the 275 clients, 57% were African American and 36% were white. In this short-term approach, 26% came for only one session and 80% for four or fewer sessions. Of the 275 clients, 136 were reached by telephone 7 to 9 months after counseling. Of those contacted, 45% said that their goals were met and 32% said some progress was made toward their goals. Although no control group was used in this study, the success rate for such brief therapy compares favorably with other studies (DeJong & Berg, 1998).

Determining how to study narrative therapy is quite difficult because some narrative therapists would see research as problematic, as any research constraints, such as a treatment manual, would affect the outcome and be something researchers "do" to families or couples rather than being a part of the process. One approach to the process that is consistent with a postmodern philosophy is to analyze the type of conversational practices that occur (Kogan & Gale, 1997). An analysis was made of a couples therapy session with a well-respected narrative therapist that described five different conversational practices. Another study examined Sluzki's (1992) narrative approach that seeks to transform an individual construction of the problem to an interpersonal or relational one (Coulehan, Friedlander, & Heatherington, 1998). Studying eight families, four were judged to make the transformations successfully and four were not. The successful and unsuccessful approaches were compared to develop a model of a successful transformation process. New approaches to family therapy often require new research methodology. Sprenkle and Moon (1996) describe both traditional and new approaches to research in family therapy.

Family Therapy Applied to a Variety of Problems

Two studies (Henggeler et al., 1993; Lange, Schaap, & van Widenfelt, 1993) have reviewed the effectiveness of family therapy for children with schizophrenia, mood disorders, anxiety disorders, drug abuse, eating disorders, and conduct disorders. In drawing conclusions about the effectiveness of those approaches to each of these disorders, Lange et al. suggest that individual interventions can often be integrated into the application of family therapy. In working with schizophrenia and bipolar disorder, treatments should include educational information to the family and psychopharmacological treatment, as well as a therapeutic focus on stress reduction. With drug and alcohol addiction, they suggest the importance of individual self-control programs and family involvement in reinforcing change. With agoraphobia and obsessive-compulsive disorders, they recommend the involvement of family members as cotherapists. However, their conclusions are general and do not speak to the effectiveness of specific family systems therapeutic approaches with specific problems of the identified patient.

Interest in psychoeducational approaches to families with schizophrenic or psychotic members continues to be growing. This interest has been strong due in part to the high cost of inpatient or other intensive care and the disruptiveness of severe mental illness. Fadden (1998) reviews over 50 studies that include a diverse set of approaches to psychoeducational interventions. Summarizing these findings she concludes that psychoeducational interventions significantly decrease the rate of relapse and hospitalizations. These effects are sustainable over time and apply to people from many cultures. In order to reduce relapse, the identified patient must be seen with the family, at least part of the time. Effective approaches are educational, focusing on coping skills and dealing with day-to-day problems, rather than psychodynamic issues. Education combined with teaching coping skills is more effective in preventing relapse than education alone. Multiple-family therapy (p. 546), where several families are seen together, can be effective. However, not all families are open to this type of treatment. In terms of the timing of interventions, it is often easiest to choose times of crisis or when the problem gets worse. Some therapists may see the family in their homes. As psychoeducational interventions become more popular, more research is likely to result.

Most current studies have tended to focus on the outcome of family therapy as compared with other methods of therapy. There has been relatively little work on understanding the processes of family systems therapy that contribute to its effectiveness. As new developments in research methodology are created and implemented (Sprenkle & Moon, 1996), a greater variety of research approaches are likely to be reported.

GENDER ISSUES

As shown in Chapter 12, the roles of men and women, in general and in the family, are quite different from each other in the United States, as well as in other cultures. Women are often expected to work and take major responsibility for household chores and child care. Additionally, they are expected to take the major responsibility for relationships with friends and families of origin (Goldenberg & Goldenberg, 2000). On the other hand, men have often taken responsibility for financial support and major family decisions. When children grow and leave the home, women's priorities for themselves may be quite different from those of men, which can lead to marital conflict or divorce (McGoldrick, 1988b). Women, as they age, may react negatively to having taken responsibility for care of their children and later their aging parents. Until the 1980s, these general differences between men and women and the way they relate in the family was often taken for granted by family therapists, and not questioned.

Feminist family therapists have had a significant impact on how family therapists deal with gender issues in their work (Goodrich, Rampage, Ellman, & Halstead, 1988) by making family therapists aware of their own gender values regarding the roles of men and women and stereotypes about them. As feminist therapists have observed, the therapist's role is never gender-neutral. Family members are likely to bring expectations as to how the therapist will respond based on their own gender-role stereotypes. These expectations in combination with therapists' values about how families operate can limit families' abilities to make positive change.

The traditional view of the family has been that of having a distant but dominant father with a mother who is too involved in her children's behavior. Feminist therapists have cautioned family therapists against stereotyped views of families that result in blaming the mother for a child's problems (Wright & Fish, 1997). Rather, feminist therapists have suggested that family therapists need to examine and challenge gender-role beliefs of families. Questioning how decisions are made about parenting, work roles, financial decisions, and doing household chores can produce an atmosphere of change and can help a couple relate differently to each other. The questioning of gender-role assumptions has a direct impact on the ways that feminist therapists have viewed family systems theory and resulting therapeutic interventions.

The major theories of family systems therapy have been thoroughly critiqued as to how they deal with or fail to deal with gender role issues (Ault-Riche, 1986; Luepnitz, 1988). In discussing a variety of approaches, feminist therapists caution against techniques that might bring about change at the expense of reinforcing gender roles. For example, a paradoxical task that might ask a woman to clean and reclean the kitchen several times is reinforcing the role that women belong in the kitchen. Rather, therapists are encouraged to use techniques that help each member of the couple feel more empowered, more likely to share with each other, and more equal in their relationship. By doing so, they can support each other in working with problems related to children. Sharing of responsibility can start at the beginning of therapy. For example, often a wife brings a family to therapy, and a husband may be reluctant to attend. Feminist family therapists encourage the husband to share responsibility for the family, and questions about the family are directed to both husband and wife.

MULTICULTURAL ISSUES

Just as gender issues became important in family therapy in the 1980s, so did the emphasis on the impact of culture on family relationships and values. Books (Falicov, 1983; McGoldrick, Giordano, & Pearce, 1996) have been written that describe values and characteristics of a variety of ethnic groups. Boyd-Franklin (1989) and Watts-Jones (1997) explain both issues and approaches to family therapy with African Americans. McGoldrick, Giordano, and Pearce (1996) have discussed the interaction of ethnicity and gender as it affects family therapy in over 40 different cultures. Increasingly, articles are being written that attend to cultural issues as they affect family therapy. Articles on the interaction between culture and family therapy can provide useful insights for therapists in understanding cultural backgrounds of their clients.

A brief summary of some important issues for families from different cultures is provided by Goldenberg and Goldenberg (2000). They discuss how families, depending on their cultural background, define the family, how family life cycles differ in various cultures, and how child-raising practices can differ across cultures.

Even the definition of "family" differs in different groups. The dominant white Anglo Saxon Protestant (WASP) focus is on the intact nuclear family, extending back over generations. Blacks expand their definition to include a wide informal network of kin and community. Italians think in terms of tightly knit three-or-four generational families, often including godfathers and old friends; all may be involved in family decision making, may live in close proximity to one another, and may share life-cycle transitions together. The Chinese tend to go even further, including all their ancestors and all their descendants in their definition of family membership (McGoldrick, 1988a).

Family life cycle timing is influenced by ethnic considerations. Mexican Americans tend to have longer courtship periods and extended childhoods beyond the dominant American pattern, but shorter adolescent periods and hastened adulthood. Similarly, different groups give different importance to life-cycle transition points. The Irish wake is a ritual that represents a view of death as the most important transition, freeing humans so that they can go on to a happier afterlife. Polish families emphasize weddings, their lengthy celebration reflecting the importance of the family's continuity into the next generation. For Jewish families, the Bar Mitzvah signifies the transition into adulthood, reflecting the high value placed on continued intellectual development (McGoldrick, 1988a).

Child rearing practices may also vary greatly. While the dominant American pattern is for the mother to have primary responsibility, blacks often rely on grandparents and extended family members to care for children, especially if the mother is working outside the home. Greeks and Puerto Ricans tend to indulge young infants, but later become strict with children, particularly girls. Adolescent girls from Italian-American families may find themselves in intergenerational conflicts with parents and grandparents as they rebel against traditional female roles of waiting on fathers, brothers, and later, husbands and sons. (Goldenberg & Goldenberg, 2000)

Although the information that Goldenberg and Goldenberg (2000) present is a useful example of the type of information that is available to those who work with families, both they and many other writers warn against the danger of stereotyping clients based on general observations. As Ho (1987) explains, there are many issues that affect the impact of culture on a family, such as how long families have been established in a new culture, intermarriage, the diversity of neighborhoods, and issues of social class. Family functioning is influenced by cultural traditions, societal expectations such as gender role, and family interactive patterns.

Knowledge of cultural issues can affect the way family therapists work with couples or families. Richeport-Haley (1998) describes Haley's strategic approach, comparing it to culture-focused therapy. Richeport-Haley presents different ways for dealing with an alternative belief system. These include using aspects of the alternative system to accomplish therapeutic goals as well as collaborating with or referring to a local healer. In the example below she describes both a strategic and culture-focused approach to working with a young South American man.

Problem: A young man in his early 20s was court ordered to therapy for repeated possession and dealing of marijuana. He would be imprisoned if this happened one more time. His mother, who spoke only Spanish, and the eldest son, who translated for her, came to therapy. The goal was to get the boy off marijuana. The intervention was to have the family come up with a strong consequence if the youth relapsed. Once the family realized that they could do something, they had a lengthy discussion of what to do if the youth relapsed. They decided that the consequence would be to ostracize the son from the family for 3 months and to shun him if he took drugs again. The son has not gone back to drugs. The therapist did not need to understand the strong bond of a Latin American family and the difficulty it had in banning a member. The goal of therapy, regardless of ethnic group, was for the family to take charge of its member and make a serious consequence rather than have the community do so.

A *Culture-Focused Approach*. In contrast to this directive approach, culturally focused therapy would have explored the importance and positive functions of a close-knit family. It would have emphasized the values of forgiveness based on a religious charity ethic. In keeping the communication style of this ethnic group, the therapist might have been authoritarian and told the family exactly what to do rather than letting them decide. (Richeport-Haley, 1998, p. 86)[9]

A number of other case examples in the family therapy literature not only instruct about different values systems within cultures but also alert therapists to the importance of understanding the interaction of their own cultural value system and that of the family's.

FAMILY SYSTEMS THERAPY APPLIED TO THE INDIVIDUAL

When working in psychotherapy with an individual, therapists can apply concepts from any of the family systems theories discussed in this chapter. The intergenerational approach of Bowen reminds the therapist of the importance of background across several generations. Intergenerational therapists occasionally do work with one individual and help that individual in making appropriate changes in the family. When the structural approach of Minuchin is used in individual therapy, the therapist can listen for ways family members align with each other, are enmeshed in each other's lives, and form coalitions. Hypotheses based on ideas about family subsystems can form interventions that can help the individual deal better with family issues. Using ideas from strategic family systems therapy, therapists can help patients bring about change in their lives, whether related to family issues or not, through the use of straightforward and paradoxical tasks. When experiential family systems therapy is applied to the individual, unconscious reactions to the patient and feelings about the patient can be communicated in much the same way that Whitaker and Satir communicated to the families with whom they worked. As more and more therapists work with both families and individuals, family systems therapy is likely to become better integrated into other therapeutic approaches.

COUPLES COUNSELING

The fact that the American Association of Marriage Counselors changed its name to the American Association of Marriage and Family Counselors in 1970 is indicative of the overlap between marriage and family therapy. Because a marriage is a small system, family systems theory can be applied to it. From the point of view of Bowen's intergenerational approach, awareness of the therapist-partner-partner triangular relationship and the ways that each partner is able to differentiate feeling and intellect within himself or herself can be applied directly to marital therapy, as can the concept of the influence of the family of origin. Regarding Minuchin's structural family therapy, attending to the balance in decision making of the partners and to the degree to which they are disengaged or enmeshed with each other can be used in understanding the interactive processes of the couple. Similarly, in Haley's strategic therapy, the therapist can focus on the power distribution within the couple and suggest direct or indirect interventions that will bring about balance and communication between partners. Ways in which Whitaker and Satir, expressive family therapists, attend to and model communication styles and skills apply as well to couples therapy as to family therapy. Solution-focused and narrative couple therapists attend to the way couples tell their stories and look for exceptions to their problems.

Just as there is relatively little difference between marriage and family therapies in other theories (as described in each chapter), there is little difference in the application of family systems therapy to couples counseling.

GROUP FAMILY SYSTEMS THERAPY

Two distinct types of large group therapy have been developed to work with families: multiple-family therapy and network therapy. The concept of multiple-family therapy refers to working with several families at once on a variety of issues. Network therapy refers to working with one family, but including extended family, friends, neighbors, and/or acquaintances who can contribute to helping the family with their problems. These approaches often combine aspects of group therapy with those of family therapy.

Multiple-Family Therapy

Based on the work of Laqueur (1976) with schizophrenic patients and their families, multiple-family therapy was designed to have families help each other with their problems. Using a family systems approach, Laqueur saw each individual as a subsystem within the family, which was a subsystem within the multiple-family therapy group. Such groups usually included four to six families (screened or unscreened) for the group. In their approach, Gritzer and Okun (1983) often worked with families alone for four or five meetings before bringing them into a larger group, so that families might be more likely to interact more easily with other families than if they had been brought directly into multiple-family therapy. In these large groups, the therapist leads discussions and talks about patterns within families, sometimes having family members sit in different groups, for example, fathers in one group, mothers in another. Sometimes structured exercises would be used with families; at other times family members of one family might confront members of other families and serve as co-therapists to provide a powerful intervention with the family (Laqueur, 1976).

There are several advantages to working in such large groups. Family members can identify and receive support from nonfamily group members (Goldenberg & Goldenberg, 2000). Also, by seeing how other families solve their problems, families can learn new ways of relating. In particular, children sometimes can get support from other children as well as other adults, which may be easier to accept than support from the therapist or from their own parents. Techniques such as role playing can be done with individuals from another family, enabling children, particularly "identified patients," to try out more productive ways of interacting with their own parents. In a study comparing 42 families receiving multiple-family therapy with 39 families receiving traditional family therapy, those children in multiple-family therapy were more assertive and had fewer overall behavior problems than those in traditional family therapy (Meezan & O'Keefe, 1998). The focus of multiple-family therapy is on solving family problems, with input from a variety of sources.

Network Therapy

By assembling an individual's social network, Speck and Attneave (1973) (Speck, 1998) felt they could develop a powerful intervention incorporating the support and effort of a number of people to help a family or individual in distress. Rueveni (1979) likens this to a tribe all working together to help someone in trouble. Although originally developed for work with schizophrenic patients and their families, network therapy has been used internationally (Speck, 1998) with juvenile offenders, substance abusers (Galanter, 1996), and other individuals who may be disruptive in their interactions with their family and community. Meetings are often held for about 4 hours, usually for four to six sessions, at weekly or monthly intervals. To work with a group of 40 to 50 individuals requires a team of therapists, often including professionals and paraprofessionals, numbering two to six or more. One therapist may provide leadership, while others work with subgroups. The goal is to use the power of the large number of assembled people to challenge and support the family in distress.

The process of network therapy has been described by Speck and Attneave (1973) as taking place in six phases. The first phase, retribalization, includes exercises that bond the group together as a network (holding hands, talking loudly, or doing stretching exercises). The group then goes through a phase of polarization, in which conflicts become apparent, usually between generational groups, such as parents and children. During the mobilization phase, the group is organized into smaller groups, often with an inner and outer circle, increasing tension and involvement on the part of the group members. This phase may be followed by a period of depression, during which group members feel frustrated by their inability to solve the problem. Finally, a breakthrough occurs when action is taken to resolve a problem. For example, a group of peers may be assigned to work with a teenager who has been arrested for repeated stealing. Other children or parents might be asked to work with younger brothers or sisters, and perhaps others might provide support for parents who are attempting to discipline the identified patient. At the end of the long meeting comes exhaustion and elation, as members experience a feeling of togetherness and accomplishment. This feeling occurs frequently not only at the end of a meeting but also at the end of a series of interventions as a group of individuals continues to work as a supportive and caring group.

Although multiple-family therapy and network therapy can be powerful interventions, they are not often used. Because of their size, they require a certain amount of scheduling and organizing time, especially network therapy. Because there are so many people, it may be difficult to deal with distractions, particularly with children, and to remain focused on specific issues or family members for any length of time. Also, the talents that are required by therapists include organizational and group process skills that may be different than those used by many family systems therapists. Sometimes smaller networks of 5 to 20 people may be used in confronting a substance abuser, a powerful intervention but easier to organize than the large network. These large-group approaches are an example of the creativity that family therapists have used when confronted with difficult dilemmas within the family.

SUMMARY

Unlike other theories of psychotherapy that are based on assumptions about individual personality, family systems therapy is concerned with interactions among family members. Based in part on early work with families of patients with schizophrenia, family systems therapy has focused not just on the identified patient, but on the entire functioning of the family. Bowen's intergenerational theory deals not only with relationships between two family members and how they involve a third, but also on relationships that go back one or more generations. Less concerned with past relationships, Minuchin's structural approach has addressed the flexibility of boundaries within the family and how members can become too close or too distant, thus inhibiting proper family functioning. The strategic therapy of Jay Haley, while incorporating concepts about family boundaries, concentrates on resolving symptoms within the family through direct or indirect means. The experiential approaches of Satir and Whitaker are based in part on intuitive reactions of the therapist to the family and making therapeutic interventions that lead to healthier family functioning. Recent creative approaches of deShazer (solution-focused therapy) and Epston and White (narrative therapy) concentrate on the stories that families bring to therapy and find new ways to view them to solve the problems within the family. As the field of family therapy has grown, there has been a tendency among family therapists to not only draw from a variety of family systems therapies, but also to incorporate aspects of other theories of psychotherapy in their work.

Although many family therapists see their clients for less than 20 or 30 sessions, there has been an emphasis on brief therapy and innovative approaches to changing family dynamics. A number of feminist therapists and other writers have challenged assumptions about roles within the family based on gender-role and cultural differences. Currently, the development of family therapy and family systems therapy is noted by two divergent trends: incorporating a variety of theoretical and other concepts and developing new creative approaches for dealing with families.

Suggested Readings

GOLDENBERG, I., & GOLDENBERG, H. (2000). *Family therapy: An overview* (5th ed.). Pacific Grove, CA: Brooks/Cole. • Significant theories of family therapy are discussed fully. The background and use of a variety of theoretical approaches are explained in this readable text.

NICHOLS, M. P., & SCHWARTZ, R. C. (1998). *Family therapy: Concepts and methods* (4th ed.). Boston: Allyn & Bacon. • A more extensive text than that of Goldenberg and Goldenberg, this book goes into detail on many systems of family therapy and their development. Discussion of the history as well as the current trends affecting family therapy is extensive.

DEJONG, P., & BERG, I. K. (1998). *Interviewing for solutions.* Pacific Grove, CA: Brooks/Cole. • This book is written for the student wanting to learn how to do solution-focused therapy. Examples illustrate this approach.

MINUCHIN, S. (1974). *Families and family therapy.* Cambridge, MA: Harvard University Press. • This excellent description of Minuchin's theory of structural family therapy is well illustrated with transcripts of therapy sessions. Many techniques are explained, along with their application to different families.

MADANES, C. (1981). *Strategic family therapy.* San Francisco: Jossey-Bass. • Describing her approach and that of her husband, Jay Haley, to strategic family therapy, Madanes explains basic dimensions and elements of their work. Particularly helpful in understanding strategic family therapy is the presentation of 15 case studies that illustrate innovative interventions, including direct and paradoxical suggestions, as well as the use of metaphor.

References

ACKERMAN, N. W. (1966a). Family psychotherapy—theory and practice. *American Journal of Psychotherapy, 20,* 405–414.

ACKERMAN, N. W. (1966b). *Treating the troubled family.* New York: Basic Books.

ANDERSEN, T. (1991). *The reflecting team: Dialogues and dialogues about dialogues.* New York: Norton.

ANDERSEN, T. (1993). See and hear, and be seen and heard. In S. Friedman (Ed.), *The new language of change: Constructive collaboration in psychotherapy* (pp. 303–323). New York: Guilford Press.

ANDERSON, C. M., REISS, D., & HOGARTY, B. (1986). *Schizophrenia and the family.* New York: Guilford.

APONTE, H., & VAN DEUSEN, J. M. (1981). Structural family therapy. In A. S. Gutman & D. P. Kniskern (Eds.), *Handbook of family therapy* (pp. 310–360). New York: Brunner/Mazel.

AULT-RICHE, M. (Ed.). (1986). *Women and family therapy.* Rockville, MD: Aspen.

BATESON, G., JACKSON, D. D., HALEY, J., & WEAKLAND, J. (1956). Towards a theory of schizophrenia. *Behavioral Science, 1,* 251–264.

BAUCOM, D. H., SHOHAM, V., MUESER, K. T., DAIUTO, A. D., & STICKLE, T. R. (1998). Empirically supported couple and family interventions for marital distress and adult mental health problems. *Journal of Counseling and Clinical Psychology, 66,* 53–88.

BECVAR, D. S., & BECVAR, R. J. (1999). *Family therapy: A systemic integration* (4th ed.). Boston: Allyn & Bacon.

BEDNAR, R. L., BURLINGAME, G. M., & MASTERS, K. S. (1988). Systems of family treatment: Substance or semantics? *Annual Review of Psychology, 39,* 401–434.

BERG, I. K. (1994). *Family based services: A solution-focused approach.* New York: Norton.

BERG, I. K., & DESHAZER, S. (1993). Making numbers talk: Language in therapy. In S. Friedman (Ed.), *The new language of change: Constructive collaboration in psychotherapy* (pp. 5–24). New York: Guilford.

BERTALANFFY, C. VON. (1968). *General systems theory: Foundation, development, applications*. New York: Braziller.

BOSCOLO, L., CECCHIN, G., HOFFMAN, L., & PENN, P. (1987). *Milan systemic family therapy: Conversations in theory and practice*. New York: Basic Books.

BOWEN, M. (1960). A family concept of schizophrenia. In D. D. Jackson (Ed.), *The etiology of schizophrenia* (pp. 346–372). New York: Basic Books.

BOWEN, M. (1966). The use of family theory in clinical practice. *Comprehensive Psychiatry, 7,* 345–374.

BOWEN, M. (1975). Family therapy after twenty years. In S. Arieti, D. X. Freedman, & J. E. Dyrud (Eds.), *American handbook of psychiatry V. Treatment* (2nd ed., pp. 367–392). New York: Basic Books.

BOWEN, M. (1976). Theory in the practice of psychotherapy. In P. J. Guerin, Jr. (Ed.), *Family therapy: Theory and practice* (pp. 42–90). New York: Gardner.

BOWEN, M. (1978). *Family therapy in clinical practice*. New York: Aronson.

BOYD-FRANKLIN, N. (1989). *Black families in therapy: A multi-systems approach*. New York: Guilford.

BROWN, J. H., & CHRISTENSEN, D. N. (1999). *Family therapy: Theory and practice* (2nd. ed.). Pacific Grove, CA: Brooks/Cole.

CARR, A. (1991). Milan systemic family therapy: A review of ten empirical investigations. *Journal of Family Therapy, 13,* 237–263.

COLEMAN, S. (1987). Milan in Bucks County. *Family Therapy Networker, 11,* 42–47.

COMBRINCK-GRAHAM, L. (1998). Where have all the family therapists gone? *AFTA Newsletter, 72,* 25–27.

COOPER, S. (1974). Treatment of parents. In S. Arieti & G. Caplan (Eds.), *American handbook of psychiatry II: Child and adolescent psychiatry, sociocultural and community psychiatry* (2nd ed.). New York: Basic Books.

COULEHAN, R., FRIEDLANDER, M. L., & HEATHERINGTON, L. (1998). Transforming narratives: A change event in constructivist family therapy. *Family Process, 37,* 17–33.

CROMWELL, R. E., OLSON, D. H., & FOURNIER, D. G. (1976). Diagnosis and evaluation in marital and family counseling. In D. H. Olson (Ed.), *Treating relationships* (pp. 517–562). Lake Mills, IA: Graphic.

DAVIDSON, G. N. S., & HORVATH, A. O. (1997). Three sessions of brief couples therapy: A clinical trial. *Journal of Family Psychology, 11,* 422–435.

DEJONG, P., & BERG, I. K. (1998). *Interviewing for solutions*. Pacific Grove, CA: Brooks/Cole.

DESHAZER, S. (1985). *Keys to solution in brief therapy*. New York: Norton.

DESHAZER, S. (1991). *Putting differences to work*. New York: Norton.

DESHAZER, S. (1994). *Words were originally magic*. New York: Norton.

EPSTON, D., & WHITE, M. (1992). *Experience, contradiction, narrative, and imagination: Selected papers of David Epston and Michael White, 1989–1991*. Adelaide, South Australia: Dulwich Centre Publications.

FADDEN, G. (1998). Research update: Psychoeducational family interventions. *Journal of Family Therapy, 20,* 293–309.

FALICOV, C. J. (Ed.). (1983). *Cultural perspectives in family practice*. New York: Gardner.

FREEMAN, J., EPSTON, D., & LOBOVITS, D. (1997). *Playful approaches to serious problems: Narrative therapy with children and their families*. New York: Norton.

FROMM-REICHMANN, F. (1948). Notes on the development of treatment of schizophrenics by psychoanalytic psychotherapy. *Psychiatry, 11,* 253–273.

GALANTER, M. (1996). Network therapy. In Washton, A. M. (Ed.), *Psychotherapy and substance abuse: A practioner's handbook* (pp. 357–371). New York: Guilford.

GOLDENBERG, I., & GOLDENBERG, H. (2000). *Family therapy: An overview* (6th ed.). Pacific Grove, CA: Brooks/Cole.

GOODRICH, T. J., RAMPAGE, C., ELLMAN, B., & HALSTEAD, K. (1988). *Feminist family therapy.* New York: Norton.

GRITZER, P. H., & OKUN, H. S. (1983). Multiple family group therapy: A model for all families. In B. B. Wolman & G. Stricker (Eds.), *Handbook of family and marital therapy.* New York: Plenum.

GUERIN, P. J., JR., & GUERIN, K. B. (1976). Theoretical aspects and clinical relevance of the multi-generational model of family therapy. In P. J. Guerin, Jr. (Ed.), *Family therapy: Theory and practice* (pp. 91–110). New York: Gardner.

HALEY, J. (1963). *Strategies of psychotherapy.* New York: Grune & Stratton.

HALEY, J. (1971a). Approaches to family therapy. In J. Haley (Ed.), *Changing families: A family therapy reader* (pp. 227–236). New York: Grune & Stratton.

HALEY, J. (1971b). Family therapy: A radical change. In J. Haley (Ed.), *Changing families: A family therapy reader* (pp. 272–284). New York: Grune & Stratton.

HALEY, J. (1973). *Uncommon therapy: The psychiatric techniques of Milton H. Erickson, M.D.* New York: Norton.

HALEY, J. (1976). *Problem-solving therapy.* San Francisco: Jossey-Bass.

HALEY, J. (1979). *Leaving home: Therapy with disturbed young people.* New York: McGraw-Hill.

HALEY, J. (1984). *Ordeal therapy: Unusual ways to change behavior.* San Fransciso: Jossey-Bass.

HAZELRIGG, M. D., COOPER, H. M., & BORDUIN, C. M. (1987). Evaluating the effectiveness of family therapies: An integrative review and analysis. *Psychological Bulletin, 101,* 428–442.

HENGGELER, S. W., BORDUIN, C. M., & MANN, B. J. (1993). Advances in family therapy: Empirical foundations. *Advances in Clinical Child Psychology, 15,* 207–241.

HO, M. K. (1987). *Family therapy with ethnic minorities.* Newbury Park, CA: Sage.

KEITH, D. V. (1998). Family therapy, chemical imbalance, blasphemy, and working with children. *AFTA Newsletter, 72,* 21–25.

KERR, M. E., BOWEN, M. (1988). *Family evaluation: An approach based on Bowen theory.* New York: W. W. Norton.

KOGAN, S. M., & GALE, J. E. (1997). Decentering therapy: Textual analysis of a narrative therapy session. *Family Process, 36,* 101–124.

LANGE, A., SCHAAP, C., & WIDENFELT, B. VAN (1993). Family therapy and psychopathology: Developments in research and approaches to treatment. *Journal of Family Therapy, 15,* 113–146.

LAQUEUR, H. P. (1976). Multiple family therapy. In P. J. Guerin, Jr. (Ed.), *Family therapy: Theory and practice* (pp. 405–416). New York: Gardner.

LEBOW, J. (1997). The integrative revolution in couple and family therapy. *Family Process, 36,* 1–6.

LEVANT, R. E. (Ed.). (1986). *Psychoeducational approaches to family therapy and counseling.* New York: Springer.

LEVY, D. (1943). *Maternal overprotection.* New York: Columbia University Press.

LIDZ, T., CORNELISON, A., FLECK, S., & TERRY, D. (1957). The intrafamilial environment of schizophrenic patients: II. Marital schism and marital skew. *American Journal of Psychiatry, 114,* 241–248.

LIPCHIK, E. (1993). "Both/and" solutions. In S. Friedman (Ed.), *The new language of change: constructive collaboration in psychotherapy* (pp. 25–49). New York: Guilford.

LUEPNITZ, D. A. (1988). *The family interpreted: Feminist theory in clinical practice.* New York: Basic Books.

MACHAL, M., FELDMAN, R., & SIGAL, J. (1989). The unraveling of a treatment program: A follow-up study of the Milan approach to family therapy. *Family Process, 28,* 457–470.

MADANES, C. (1981). *Strategic family therapy.* San Francisco: Jossey-Bass.

McGoldrick, M. (1988a). Ethnicity and the family life cycle. In B. Carter & M. McGoldrick (Eds.), *The changing family life cycle: A framework for family therapy* (2nd ed., pp. 70–90). New York: Gardner.

McGoldrick, M. (1988b). Women and the family life cycle. In B. Carter & M. McGoldrick (Eds.), *The changing family life cycle: A framework for family therapy* (2nd ed., pp. 31–69). New York: Gardner.

McGoldrick, J., & Gerson, R. (1985). *Genograms in family assessment.* New York: Norton.

McGoldrick, M., Giordano, J., & Pearce, J. K. (1996). *Ethnicity and family therapy* (2nd ed.). New York: Guilford.

Meezan, W., & O'Keefe, M. (1998). Multifamily group therapy: Impact on family functioning and child behavior. *Families in Society, 79,* 32–44.

Minuchin, S. (1974). *Families and family therapy.* Cambridge, MA: Harvard University Press.

Minuchin, S., & Fishman, H. C. (1981). Family therapy techniques. Cambridge, MA: Harvard University Press.

Minuchin, S., Rosman, B. L., & Baker, L. (1978). *Psychosomatic families: Anorexia nervosa in context.* Cambridge, MA: Harvard University Press.

Mittelman, B. (1948). The concurrent analysis of married couples. *Psychoanalytic Quarterly, 17,* 182–197.

Napier, A. Y., & Whitaker, C. A. (1978). *The family crucible.* New York: Harper & Row.

O'Hanlon, W. H. (1993). Take two people and call them in the morning: Brief solution-oriented therapy with depression. In S. Friedman (Ed.), *The new language of change: Constructive collaboration in psychotherapy* (pp. 50–84). New York: Guilford.

Okun, B. E., & Rappaport, L. J. (1980). *Working with families: An introduction to family therapy.* Belmont, CA: Wadsworth.

Omer, H., & Alon, N. (1997). *Constructing therapeutic narrative.* Northvale, NJ: Aronson.

Papero, D. V. (1983). Family systems theory and therapy. In B. B. Wolman & G. Stricker (Eds.), *Handbook of family and marital therapy* (pp. 137–158). New York: Plenum.

Papp, P. (1980). The Greek chorus and other techniques of paradoxical therapy. *Family Process, 19,* 45–57.

Papp, P. (1984). Setting the terms for therapy. *The Family Therapy Networker, 8,* 42–47.

Pinsof, W. M., Wynne, L. C., & Hambright, A. B. (1996). The outcomes of couple and family therapy: Findings, conclusions, and recommendations. *Psychotherapy, 33,* 321–331.

Quinn, W., & Davidson, B. (1984). Prevalence of family therapy models: A research note. *Journal of Marital and Family Therapy, 10,* 393–398.

Richeport-Haley, M. (1998). Ethnicity in family therapy: A comparison of brief strategic therapy and culture-focused therapy. *The American Journal of Family Therapy, 26,* 77–90.

Rolland, J. S. (1987). Chronic illness and the life cycle: A conceptual framework. *Family Process, 26,* 203–221.

Rueveni, Q. (1979). *Networking families in crisis.* New York: Human Sciences Press.

Satir, V. M. (1967). *Conjoint family therapy* (Rev. ed.). Palo Alto, CA: Science and Behavior Books.

Satir, V. M. (1972). *Peoplemaking.* Palo Alto, CA: Science and Behavior Books.

Satir, V. M., & Baldwin, M. (1983). *Satir step by step.* Palo Alto, CA: Science and Behavior Books.

Segal, L. (1982). Brief family therapy. In A. M. Horne & M. M. Ohlsen (Eds.), *Family counseling and therapy* (pp. 279–301). Itasca, IL: F. E. Peacock.

Segal, L. (1987). What is a problem? A brief family therapist's view. *Family Therapy Today, 2,* 1–7.

Selvini-Palazzoli, M., Cirillo, S., Selvini, M., & Sorrentino, A. M. (1989). *Family games: General models of psychotic processes in the family.* New York: Norton.

SIMPSON, L. (1990). The comparative efficacy of Milan family therapy for disturbed children and their families. *Journal of Family Therapy, 13*, 267–284.

SINGER, M. T., & WYNNE, L. C. (1965). Thought disorder and family relations of schizophrenics. III. Methodology of using projective techniques. *Archives of General Psychiatry, 12*, 201–212.

SLUZKI, C. E. (1992). Transformations: A blueprint for narrative changes in therapy. *Family Process, 31*, 217–230.

SPECK, R. V. (1998). Network therapy. *Marriage and Family Review, 27*, 51–69.

SPECK, R. V., & ATTNEAVE, C. L. (1973). *Family networks.* New York: Pantheon.

SPRENKLE, D. H., & MOON, S. M. (Eds.). (1996). *Research methods in family therapy.* New York: Guilford.

SULLIVAN, H. S. (1953). *The interpersonal theory of psychiatry.* New York: Norton.

TOMAN, W. (1961). *Family constellation: Its effects on personality and social behavior.* New York: Springer.

TOMM, K. M. (1984). One perspective on the Milan approach: Part 1. Overview of development, theory, and practice. *Journal of Marital and Family Therapy, 10*, 113–125.

UMBARGER, C. C. (1983). *Structural family therapy.* New York: Grune & Stratton.

WATTS-JONES, D. (1997). Toward an African American genogram. *Family Process, 36*, 375–383.

WATZLAWICK, P., WEAKLAND, J. H., & FISCH, R. (1974). *Change: Principles of problem formation and problem resolution.* New York: Norton.

WEAKLAND, J. (1976). Communication theory and clinical change. In P. J. Guerin, Jr. (Ed.), *Family therapy: Theory and practice.* New York: Gardner.

WEEKS, G. R., & L'ABATE, L. (1982). *Paradoxical psychotherapy: Theory and technique.* New York: Brunner/Mazel.

WHITAKER, C. (1976). The hindrance of theory in clinical work. In P. J. Guerin, Jr. (Ed.), *Family therapy: Theory and practice* (pp. 154–164). New York: Gardner.

WHITAKER, C. A., & KEITH, D. V. (1981). Symbolic-experiential family therapy. In A. S. Gutman & D. P. Kniskern (Eds.), *Handbook of family therapy.* New York: Brunner/Mazel.

WHITE, M., & EPSTON, D. (1990). *Narrative means to therapeutic ends.* New York: Norton.

WHITE, M., & EPSTON, D. (1994). *Experience, contradiction, narrative, and imagination.* Adelaide, South Australia: Dulwich Centre Publications.

WIENER, N. (1948). *Cybernetics, or control and communication in the animal and the machine.* Cambridge, MA: Technology Press.

WRIGHT, C. I., & FISH, L. S. (1997). Feminist family therapy: The battle against sexism. In N. V. Benokraitis (Ed.), *Subtle sexism: Current practice and prospects for change* (pp. 201–215). Thousand Oaks, CA: Sage.

WYNNE, L. C., RYCKOFF, I. M., DAY, J., & HIRSCH, S. I. (1958). Pseudomutuality in the family relationships of schizophrenics. *Psychiatry, 21*, 205–220.

14

Other Psychotherapies

This chapter includes a discussion of five unrelated psychotherapies. They are presented here because they represent innovative approaches to therapy that are different than those in the other chapters. Some reasons that they have not been given a full chapter each are that they are not as widely used as other theories, there is relatively little research, or they are limited in the problems that they treat.

Included in this chapter are Asian therapies, body psychotherapies, interpersonal psychotherapy, psychodrama, and creative arts therapies. A feature of Asian therapies is their emphasis on meditation or quiet reflection and, in some cases, their stress on personal responsibility to others. Both mind and body are important in the body psychotherapies, and assessment is made of movement and physique to make judgments about an individual's personality. Therapeutic techniques include suggestions for movement as well as manipulation of body parts to bring about psychological change. Interpersonal therapy was developed as a treatment for depression. Techniques are based on a review of research and theory and are explained in treatment manuals. Psychodrama is an active system in which clients enact their problems, assisted by the therapist, who directs the psychodrama, and by group or audience members, who may play roles related to the client's concern. Creative arts therapies include art, dance movement, dramatherapy, and music. Often seen as an adjunct to psychotherapy, some therapists combine them with traditional verbal therapy to help bring about more awareness of emotions and improved social interactions with others.

Because five very different therapeutic approaches are described in this chapter, the format is quite different than that of the preceding chapters. For all but the creative arts therapies, I describe the background of the theory, a synopsis of the personality theory, and the theory of psychotherapy. Regarding the creative arts therapies, I describe some of their commonalities and then give a brief overview of art, dance movement, dramatherapy, and music therapy. Additionally, I give examples of applications for all of the therapeutic approaches. Because each of the five approaches is distinct, references are listed after each of the five sections. I have not included recommended readings but rather suggest any of the references following a section of interest.

ASIAN PSYCHOTHERAPIES

The teachings of Asian philosophies, Hindu, Buddhist, and Confucian, have had an impact on the psychological development of millions of people in Asia over thousands of years. More so than most Western therapies, Eastern therapies have focused on self-awareness and have provided individuals the opportunity to receive guidance in practicing self-awareness. Meditation is often viewed as a modern therapy, leading to relaxation and stress reduction, even though it has been practiced in the East for millennia. Also, two Japanese therapies, Morita and Naikan, that trace their origins to Buddhist teachings are explained, along with Western adaptations of these therapies.

Background

Ideas about psychology that are embedded in Asian philosophy date back over 3,000 years. Concepts related to personality theory can be found in the ancient Indian Vedic literature going back to about 750 B.C., which contains some of the teachings of Hinduism. Adding to the abundant literature of Hinduism are the teachings of Gautama Buddha, born in 563 B.C., which have been very influential in Asian philosophy and psychology. Gradually, Buddhist and Hindu teachings spread eastward to China and Japan (Murphy & Murphy, 1968).

Basic to Indian psychology are four concepts that are important in understanding therapeutic techniques that are derived from Hindu and Buddhist philosophy: dharma, karma, maya, and atman. *Dharma* refers to rules that describe goodness and appropriate behavior. *Karma* refers to the movement from past incarnations that affect the present and the future. *Maya* refers to distorted perceptions of reality and experience that can be identified as such only with direct attention to our own processes of awareness that come about through internal concentration or meditation. *Atman* refers to a concept of universality in which the self is not seen as individual, but as part of the entire cosmos. Thus, the individual is a part of God, a part of universal wisdom, and a part of others, past and future. All of these concepts are teachings that emerge from the abundant literature of India.

Of particular interest in current psychotherapy are the Hindu teachings related to yoga, particularly those related to Hatha-yoga, which deals with the physiological discipline required in separating self from thought processes. Hatha-yoga combines meditative and physical exercises; other yoga practices focus mainly on meditative abilities. Research (Walsh, 1996) has shown that the practice of yoga can bring about changes in muscle tension, blood pressure, heart rate, and brain waves. Current approaches to meditation that are derived from yoga and other systems are described more fully later.

Concepts developing from Buddhist teachings include the four noble truths and the eightfold path. Embodied in the four noble truths are the ideas that living is subject to suffering, wanting to live causes repeated existence, giving up desire releases one from suffering, and escape from suffering is achieved through adherence to the eightfold path. Following this path means that individuals should have correct beliefs, thoughts, speech, actions, ways of living, effort, mindfulness, and attention to escaping from desire (Bankart, 1997). These teachings and moral values have influenced thinking in India, China, and Japan for centuries.

BUDDHA

About 2,000 years ago, Buddhism was brought to China, where its ethical teachings made an impact on the Chinese social system. Practical teachings of Buddhism, along with the teachings of Confucius (551–479 B.C.), helped to structure Chinese values and morality that include presenting oneself so that one's moral views can be judged according to the standards of one's community, submitting to the authority of one's elders (family or community leaders), and observing proper conduct in social situations. Confucius's writings describe the way to achieve perfection. These values are often recognized by psychologists writing about cultural differences between Chinese and Western patients, when deciding upon appropriate therapeutic procedures. Around the sixth century, the writings of Confucius and Buddha were brought to Japan. Their influences can be seen later in this section when the relatively recent Morita and Naikan psychotherapies are described.

Asian Theories of Personality

Given the brief amount of space and the vast Hindu, Buddhist, and Confucian literature, as well as other writings, I explain some basic ideas that most Asian philosophies have in common rather than describe an Asian theory of personality. Generally, Asian views of personality emphasize experience rather than logic, focusing on a subjective view. Attention is paid to inner states and watching oneself, as one might watch one's cut finger bleed and feel the pain, but not give in to the feeling of pain. Asian philosophies are somewhat similar to those of existential philosophers, but dissimilar from many other Western philosophies.

One of the most important concepts is that the self is closely related to the universe. According to Asian philosophies, in understanding the self, one has to understand other aspects of the universe as they relate to the self. Understanding where oneself ends and the rest of the universe begins can give a sense of identity and of knowing oneself. Linked to this concept is the emphasis on social relationships, deemphasizing the individual and valuing the whole of humanity. If individuals are seen in the context of those around them, then the family, often including the extended family, is important throughout life. The concept of independence, growing and leaving one's family, is a Western concept, as Asian values emphasize responsibility for the family. Given this concept of interdependence, in many Asian cultures many aunts and cousins, as well as parents, may take responsibility for child raising (Bankart, 1997). The emphasis of interdependence applies not only to one's family but also to one's ancestors and to future generations. The concept of reincarnation is consistent with a close relationship to the entire cosmos, past, present, and future.

Buddhist and Hindu writings have implications for psychopathology and problematic personality development. Whereas many Western psychologists focus on only one state of consciousness, Asian philosophers have described several and believe that fantasies, dreams, and perceptions are often distorted (maya) but can be observed through meditation and other awareness processes that are free of illusions. Ability to achieve other states of consciousness can lead to enlightenment or freedom from psychological pain. Observing one's fantasies and thoughts through the process of meditation can be seen as dehypnosis (Tart, 1986). Whereas hypnosis is the absence of awareness of one's consciousness, meditation provides direct observation of it. However, like hypnosis, higher states of consciousness can lead to changes in brain waves, breathing rate, a feeling of relaxation, changes in body temperature, and many other physiological changes (Walsh, 1996).

Psychological health, from an Asian perspective, can be viewed as enlightenment or a freedom from compulsions, fears, and anxieties. Addictions and aversions are dependencies on things, people, or events. Those with addictions (food, drugs, work, or many other things) believe, "I must have a cigarette, a drink, her love, people's admiration," and so forth. Aversions are the opposite: "I must avoid snakes, food, criticism," and so forth. From an Asian perspective, it is important not to be controlled by fears, dependencies, and feelings. By detaching oneself and reaching other states of consciousness, aversions and addictions no longer have strength. Reynolds (1980) gives an example of two hungry Zen priests walking by a bakery:

> The aroma of baking bread drifted in to the street. "What a lovely smell," the junior priest noted. "It certainly is." A few blocks later the junior monk remarked again, "The odor from that bakery makes me want to eat some bread." "What bakery?" (pp. 93–94)

One can assume that the senior priest, able to move quickly from one state of consciousness to another, could quickly move beyond the tantalizing aroma of the bread. This ability to observe one's own fears, desires, and anxieties is an important principle in the treatment strategies that are discussed next.

Asian Theories of Psychotherapy

In this section, three therapeutic approaches, all dealing with attention to one's own processes, are described. Reynolds (1980) refers to Asian therapies as "quiet" therapies because individuals spend time in isolation dealing with their thoughts and in varied states of awareness. Watts (1961) provided a thorough explanation of the Asian approach to psychotherapy. Meditation trains individuals to control and attend to mental processes, bringing about relaxation and other therapeutic benefits. Naikan therapy has patients focus on past relationships and their mistakes in dealing with others to bring about better relationships with others and greater contributions to society. Morita therapy was designed as an intensive inpatient therapy to help anxious patients redirect tension away from themselves and has been adapted to outpatient therapy. Each is described here, and its application to different psychological disorders is discussed.

Meditation therapies.   Although meditation is practiced by relatively few people in the West, it is used by many millions of people in the East (Walsh, 1981). Generally, meditation is applied in the East by people seeking higher psychological or religious levels of self-development, whereas in the West it is often used for stress management, relaxation, and developing a better sense of well-being. Implicit in views on meditation is that the usual conscious state is not an optimal state because it is subject to distortions, *maya*, and is not under the control of the individual. Walsh (1981) describes higher states of consciousness as follows:

> Without exclusive identification the me/not me dichotomy is transcended and the individual thus perceives him or herself as being no thing and every thing. That is, such people experience themselves as both pure awareness (no thing) and the entire universe (every thing). All defenses drop away since when experiencing oneself as no thing there is nothing to defend; when experiencing oneself as every thing there is nothing to defend against. This experience of unconditioned or pure awareness is apparently very blissful. It is described in the Hindu tradition as comprised of "sat-chit-ananda": awareness, being, and bliss.
>
> To those with no experience of these states, such descriptions sound paradoxical if not bizarre. However, there is a remarkable similarity in such descriptions across cultures and centuries by those who have taken these practices to their limits. (p. 473)

According to some forms of Buddhist psychology, seven qualities arise from the meditative process (Walsh & Shapiro, 1980). By focusing on consciousness, a sense of mindfulness develops so that distorted perceptions can be recognized as such. Stimulating factors are energy, investigation, and rapture. Balancing these factors are calming ones: concentration, tranquillity, and equanimity (Walsh, 1981). Thus meditation brings about a sense of peace and joy coming about through the application of energy to concentrating and understanding one's awareness.

In describing the practice of meditation, Walsh (1981) differentiates between concentration and awareness meditation practices. In concentration meditation, attention is to a stimulus, such as the act of breathing. The purpose is to develop the ability to attend to objects or feelings without distractions, a surprisingly difficult goal to attain for most people. Awareness meditations are designed to examine consciousness and the mind. Most Asian meditators see concentration meditation as a means of achieving awareness and may prefer to let the mind explore experience rather than focus on an object (Walsh, 1981). Gradually, as awareness meditation develops, progress toward the seven qualities of Buddhist psychology is made.

Meditative practices are deceptively simple but take years of devoted practice to master. Reynolds (1981) describes *zazen*, which is the practice of meditating as described by Zen Buddhism. To try out the process of meditation, Reynolds suggests that those who have not meditated try *bonpu zazen*, which is the first level of Zen meditation. He suggests that meditation can be practiced in a straight-backed chair by following these instructions for 10 to 30 minutes, preferably twice a day.

> In bonpu sitting the person concentrates on his breathing, mentally counting each breath. There are various styles of bonpu sitting, and different masters have different preferences. One can count each inhalation and exhalation up to ten, then start over; one can count only exhalations; one can extend the exhalations and the internal count as ooooone, then twooooo, threeeee and so forth. (p. 97)[1]

The purpose of the counting is to help maintain mental concentration and to let extraneous thoughts drop off. Some meditators keep a pad to jot down important ideas that may intrude so that they can consider them at another time. As one becomes more skilled in meditating, a focus other than counting, such as visualizing breathing, may be used. The process becomes integrated into one's being. Herrigel (1971) in *Zen and the Art of Archery* describes his state, not of breathing, but of being breathed.

The process of meditation requires much discipline and practice. Walsh (1981) reports meditating an average of an hour per day for a year, then 2 hours per day for another year, often including meditative retreats in which 18 to 20 hours per day were spent in meditation, walking or sitting, without contact with others or reading or writing. Many Asian meditators invest considerably more of their lifetime to this process.

Meditation, when practiced for about 30 minutes a day, has been seen to have a variety of benefits. Walsh (1996) reports that meditation has been useful in reducing anxiety and fear of enclosed spaces, exams, or being alone. Also, meditation has been effective in reducing drug and alcohol use and in helping patients with insomnia. Additionally, meditation has been useful for those with physiological conditions such as asthma and heart problems. Changes in heart rate, breathing rate, body temperature, and brain waves (Austin, 1998) have been observed for patients participating in meditative therapy. However, Shapiro (1992) warns that meditation practiced by Westerners can have negative effects such as anxiety, confusion, and feelings of incompleteness and social withdrawal in some meditators. Most participants in his study reported more positive than negative effects.

Naikan psychotherapy. Developed by Ishin Yoshimoto in the early 1950s, Naikan therapy is based on principles related to Mishirabe, a practice of a subsect of Buddhist priests. It is designed to be applicable to patients with a wide variety of problems, as it views self-centeredness as a problem that many people need to overcome. Individuals should become more accepting of others and more appreciative of the kindness of family members and friends. Naikan therapy helps individuals to develop and view their relationships as more healthy and satisfying. Reynolds (1980, 1989, 1993) has described Naikan therapy as it is practiced in its highly structured state in Japan and the adaptations that have been made in the United States.

In Japan, the first week of Naikan therapy is spent in a hospital or similar facility, with individuals being assigned to a small room. From 5 A.M. until about 9 P.M., individuals are to spend their hours in self-observation, with only brief time spent for meals and bodily functions. About every hour or two the therapist, or teacher, called *sensei*, enters the room to give instructions and to focus self-observations on past relationships, especially with parents. The patient is to be guided by the following three questions:

1. What did I receive from this person?
2. What did I return to this person?
3. What troubles and worries did I cause this person? (Reynolds, 1993, p. 124)

The sensei serves as a confessor, listening to the patient's reports of past relationships. Resentment and anger toward significant people are recognized but overshadowed by the contributions of others to the patient's life, and gradually the patient becomes more sympathetic and accepting of the viewpoints of others.

After this week of intensive self-observation, patients return home to practice, often for a few hours per day, the self-observation that they learned in the intensive week of inpatient self-observation. Reynolds (1981) gives an example of an interview that Yoshimoto had with a middle-aged woman, Mrs. O, midway through her intensive inpatient week.

Y: What did you reflect upon for the month of August?

O: My husband calls the family together each year in August for a family trip. All the children and grandchildren come. We all go somewhere together. There's nothing so wonderful as that, but I always put on a grumbling face. "Well, since everyone is here, I suppose I'll go too," I'd say and go along with them.

Y: What did you receive from your husband, what did you return to him, and what troubles did you cause him?

O: That he took me along on the trip was something I received from him.

Y: And what did you return to him?

O: Well, the family asked me to make rice balls for everyone, and though I didn't feel like it, there was no way out of doing it. But I made them too salty.

Y: What troubles did you cause him? (Reynolds, 1981, p. 550)

Although this interviewing style may seem severe, it is consistent with the emphasis on responsible behavior and the need to understand and appreciate the behavior of others.

Reynolds (1993) has adapted Naikan therapy to the United States by shortening the lengthy periods of reflection and introducing assignments that lead to recognition of services performed for us by others and of the troubles we cause others. For example, patients may be asked to say "Thank you" while reflecting, to a mental image of a person, in 10 different ways 10 times a day. They may also be asked to write letters of thanks or apology to important people in their lives, to do services for others, and to contribute to the community. Additionally, they are asked to keep a journal or record of past experiences related to the three questions. Reynolds believes that Naikan therapy can help individuals develop a more balanced, less self-centered, and more realistic perspective on life.

Morita therapy.   Originated by Morita Masatake around 1915, Morita therapy was designed as an inpatient therapy for patients suffering from *shinkeishitsu* neuroses, which include obsessive-compulsive disorders, panic disorders, and phobic states. Basically, it is a program of isolation in which patients are taught to accept and reinterpret their symptoms (Sakuta, Shiratsuchi, Kimura, & Abe, 1997). The patient's attention is shifted from symptoms to address the tasks that life puts before a person. Participation in life without waiting for symptoms to dissipate is encouraged (Fujita, 1986).

In traditional Morita therapy that is practiced in Japan, the patient is hospitalized for 4 to 5 weeks and undergoes four stages of treatment. In the first phase, from 4 to 7 days, individuals are completely inactive except for eating or going to the bathroom. They are told to suffer, worry, and accept their experience. This helps the patient experience his symptoms and the need for changing his lifestyle. Also, the patient learns that isolation is unpleasant and uncomfortable, making social interaction and physical activity more desirable than before. During the next three phases, patients take on increasingly difficult but mundane and tiring tasks and increase their social interactions, while at the same time keeping a diary upon which the therapist writes comments. The therapist's comments and periodic group discussions on the fundamental teachings of Morita therapy are an important aspect of treatment. In this process, the patient learns that thinking needs to be practical and specific, not idealistic and perfectionistic, so that actions can be taken despite symptoms.

Reynolds has adapted Morita therapy for application in the United States. One change has been to make Morita therapy apply to a wider range of disorders than *shinkeishitsu* neuroses. Basically, patients need to have sufficient intellectual development to understand the teachings implicit in Morita therapy. The severe isolated bed rest used by Morita is rarely employed in the United States. Rather, clients may, when appropriate, engage in quiet sitting. Also, the work tasks Reynolds and his colleagues use are not necessarily the repetitive tasks used by Morita but more often simple tasks of living. Additionally, Zen teachings are incorporated to help individuals learn basic principles to redirect their lives.

An example of outpatient Morita therapy with a test-anxious 40-year-old divorced woman illustrates the Morita therapy approach. Ishiyama (in Reynolds, 1989) describes the physiological and psychological symptoms of V, who was worried about her college exams. His approach can be seen by his summary of the first half-hour session and his instructions to the client.

> I explained her anxiety in terms of the desire for living fully: "Where there is a desire, there is anxiety about being unable to fulfill it. The intensity of your anxiety is an indication of the strength of your desire for meaningful academic accomplishment. Which would you choose, exhausting your energy trying to conquer anxiety or getting your studying done in spite of it?" She agreed that she would prefer to try the latter.
>
> At the end of our thirty-minute session I gave V the following set of instructions:
>
> 1. Accept fears and other feelings as they come. Continue studying and abandon any attempts to change the feelings.
> 2. Acknowledge the anxiety when it appears and continue studying while experiencing it.
> 3. Notice the fine details of her anxiety. When she cannot get her mind off the anxiety, study it as she would any natural object. (p. 51)[2]

An important part of Morita therapy is the attention to detail and the writing down of the detail in a diary and the therapist's comments. In a follow-up interview, V found that the active acceptance was helpful in relieving self-blame. Attention shifted from self-evaluation to objective self-observation.

Summary

Meditation, Morita, and Naikan therapies all have their roots in Zen Buddhism, which has been influenced by Hindu teachings that originated in India. The Hindu and Buddhist philosophies teach a way of detaching oneself from judgments, events, and blame. Meditation develops higher states of consciousness that can lead to relaxation, less stress, and improved physiological function. Naikan therapy emphasizes isolation as a way of realizing and developing social responsibility. Morita therapy stresses the development of practical and concrete approaches to reality, rather than the search for idealism or perfection. All emphasize self-awareness and social responsibility.

References

AUSTIN, J. H. (1998). *Zen and the brain: Toward an understanding of meditation and consciousness.* Cambridge, MA: The MIT Press.

BANKART, C. P, (1997). *Talking cures: A history of Western and Eastern psychotherapies.* Pacific Grove, CA: Brooks/Cole.

FUJITA, C. (1986). *Morita therapy: Psychotherapeutic system for neurosis.* Tokyo: Igaku-Shoin.

HERRIGEL, E. (1971). *Zen and the art of archery.* New York: Random House.

MURPHY, G., & MURPHY, L. (1968). *Asian psychology.* New York: Basic Books.

REYNOLDS, D. K. (1980). *The quiet therapies.* Honolulu: University Press of Hawaii.

REYNOLDS, D. K. (1981). Naikan psychotherapy. In R. J. Corsini (Ed.), *Handbook of innovative psychotherapies* (pp. 544–553). New York: Wiley.

REYNOLDS, D. K. (1989). *Flowing bridges, quiet waters.* Albany: State University of New York Press.

REYNOLDS, D. K. (1993). *Plunging through the clouds: Constructive living currents.* Albany: State University of New York Press.

SAKUTA, T., SHIRATSUCHI, T., KIMURA, Y., & ABE, Y. (1997). Psychotherapies originated in Japan. *International Medical Journal, 4,* 229–230.

SHAPIRO, D. H. (1992). Adverse effects of meditation: A preliminary investigation of long term meditation. *International Journal of Psychosomatics, 39* (Special Issues Nos. 1–4), 62–67.

TART, C. (1986). *Waking up: Overcoming the obstacles to human potential.* Boston: New Science Library/Shambhata.

WALSH, R. (1981). Meditation. In R. J. Corsini (Ed.), *Handbook of innovative psychotherapies* (pp. 470–488). New York: Wiley.

WALSH, R. (1996). Meditation research: The state of the art. In B. W. Scotton, A. B. Chinena, & T. R. Battista (Eds.), *Textbook of transpersonal psychiatry and psychology* (pp. 167–175). New York: Basic Books.

WALSH, R., & SHAPIRO, D. (Eds.). (1980). *Beyond health and normality: Explorations of extreme psychological well-being.* New York: Van Nostrand.

WATTS, A. (1961). *Psychotherapy east and west.* New York: Pantheon.

BODY PSYCHOTHERAPIES

Body psychotherapies are characterized by their integration of verbal and bodily processes. By viewing the patient's posture, physique, breathing, musculature, and other physical features, the therapist may make comments about inferred emotional issues or about physical manifestations or, guided by such observations, may touch the patient to bring about bodily or psychological change. Body therapy began with Wilhelm Reich, a psychoanalyst and a member of the Vienna Psychoanalytic Society from 1921 to 1934. Reich observed his patients carefully, focusing on their breathing and physical changes, especially when they discussed emotional issues. His work was extended by his student, Alexander Lowen, who originated bioenergetic analysis, integrating psychoanalytic concepts with bodily processes. A number of colleagues and students of Lowen have developed a variety of strategies of integrating physiological

WILHELM REICH

and verbal processes. In this section, Reich and Lowen's views of personality development and psychotherapy are described, along with Smith's integrative approach that includes concepts from Gestalt therapy and those of several body psychotherapists.

Background

Wilhelm Reich (1897–1957) was viewed by Freud (Jones, 1957) as an excellent analyst, but he later came to be known for innovative ideas in psychotherapy, some of which were bizarre. His innovative ideas were the integration of body and mind in psychotherapy. His bizarre ideas dealt with the belief that severe illnesses such as cancer or schizophrenia could be cured by lying in a metal box surrounded by wood (an orgone box) that would pass life-sustaining orgone energy from the universe to the patient. This latter involvement led to Reich's trial and imprisonment for selling orgone accumulators in violation of a federal injunction. This event and some of his ideas in later life have served to divert the focus away from his innovative and influential contributions to body psychotherapy.

One of Reich's (1951, 1972) important contributions is that of muscular armor. Developed in early childhood when the infant's instinctual needs conflict with demands of the parent and others in the environment, the muscular armor is a protective mechanism to deal with punishment for acting on instinctual demands, such as urinating in public. The body armor or muscular rigidities that develop are an expression of the neurotic character that reflects the social need to restrain instinctual impulses (Smith, 1985).

To deal with the body armor that had developed, Reich observed and manipulated a patient's body so that emotional energy could be released and life forces could flow freely through the body. This approach, called *vegetotherapy*, reflects Reich's view that all living things possess vital energy that should flow unblocked. Applying this to patients, Reich would have them disrobe and lie down on a bed so that he could observe and feel the blockage or body armor of his patients. By working on muscle knots and exerting pressure in particular areas, Reich (1972) allowed energy to flow in the patients' bodies and dealt with the emotions that would be unlocked along with the muscles. His process was to start at the top of the head and work down to the pelvic area. For example, in working in the neck area, he might find that the patient may express anger toward a brother who was a pain in the neck. Along with working gradually down the body, Reich also helped his patients to breathe more freely. As a result of this therapeutic process, patients would dissolve some of their body armor and become more spontaneous in and out of therapy. Thus physiological and psychological changes occurred together.

Whereas Freud had viewed libido as an abstract concept representing energy or the driving force of personality, Reich saw energy as a physical force that could be measured, which he first called bioelectrical energy and later orgone (Smith, 1985). When Reich reduced muscular tension, orgone would then flow, and individuals might then experience anxiety, anger, or sexual excitation. Reducing blocks to muscular tension would also reduce neurotic behavior and encourage efficient energy flow. For Reich, full orgiastic potency was not possible in a neurotic personality. Along with full emotional expression, orgiastic potency could be brought about by reducing muscular blockage and allowing energy to flow.

Bioenergetic analysis. A patient and student of Reich, Alexander Lowen (b. 1910), along with John Pierrakos, expanded Reich's work in several ways, including the use of a more varied method of treatment. One of Lowen's (1975, 1997) most important additions is grounding, which emphasized that the individual must, literally, be in strong contact with the ground through feet and legs, as well as, figuratively, grounded in the real world. Individuals who are not well grounded may experience a variety of neurotic disorders (to be described later) and may be unable to take a stand on issues, be a pushover for others, and be afraid of falling, literally or figuratively (for example, falling to the back of the class). One implication of Lowen's (1975, 1980) concept of grounding is his work with patients in a variety of positions, such as standing or bending, rather than lying on a bed. Also, Lowen developed a variety of exercises that could be used both in the therapist's office and at home to make patients less dependent on the therapist.

Another important difference between Reich and Lowen is Lowen's (1975) incorporation of psychoanalytic concepts. In bioenergetic analysis, Lowen (1989) uses analytic concepts of transference and countertransference, as well as dreams, slips of the tongue, and the working through of Oedipal issues. Also, Lowen sees the pleasure principle as an important value for individuals and views it more broadly than did Reich, who focused on sexual fulfillment as an important therapeutic goal. In general, Lowen's approach to working with the body is more flexible than Reich's because he would often work first with concepts related to grounding and then move to other areas of the body, rather than working from the head to the pelvis, as did Reich. Additionally, Lowen has popularized body psychotherapy through his several writings (1958, 1975, 1977, 1980, 1997), his work with therapists in training seminars, and the establishment of the International Institute for Bioenergetic Analysis in New York.

In the following sections, I emphasize Lowen's development of Reich's views of neurotic character types and the physiological characteristics that are associated with them. Additionally, I summarize Smith's (1985) approach to assessment and therapeutic techniques that include gentle and strong physical interventions to bring about psychological change.

Personality Theory and the Body

As can be seen from Reich and Lowen's approach to therapy and psychological health, viewing the human organism as a unified functioning whole is paramount. A problem that affects one part of the body has an impact on other aspects of physical and psychological functioning. When a person develops skin cancer, it is not just the affected part of the body but the whole individual who is ill. When individuals become depressed, their physiological functioning is affected in many ways. The same would be true with obsessions, anxiety, and all other psychological disorders. Also, if an individual is in a sedentary job and rarely uses the lower body, the lower body does not develop fully, and thus neither does the individual as a whole person (Lowen, 1975).

The focus on unity can be seen in the body's pulsations, such as in the beating of the heart or breathing. In breathing, the whole body participates, not just the lungs. When a person is inhaling, there is a wave beginning in the pelvis and moving upward to the mouth, which is reversed when exhaling (Lowen, 1989). Thus it follows from the point of view of body psychotherapists that when individuals suffer from a psychological disorder, their breathing changes also. For example, Lowen (1975) notes that he tries to help depressed individuals increase their oxygen intake to get them to breathe more fully. He has observed that when a patient's respiration is more active, her energy level is likely to rise. Changing breathing does not cure the depressive condition; the change is only momentary. However, analyzing other factors related to being depressed physically and psychologically can bring about a more permanent change in depression level, and breathing becomes easier and deeper.

Not only do physiological and psychological disorders affect each other, but they may be affected by past events. Early traumatic experiences may have an impact on how children breathe, stand, walk, or run. Such changes in physiological development may also influence self-image and confidence in physical expression and interaction with others. Trauma, such as child abuse or absence from the mother for prolonged periods, can affect areas of the body such as the throat and mouth, which could be constricted, as in an attempt to reach out to kiss the absent mother. It may also affect breathing patterns that change due to a child hyperventilating for fear of being abandoned.

Using Reich's typology as a beginning, Lowen (1975) has described five types of character structures that have developed due to trauma at an early age: schizoid, oral, narcissistic, masochistic, and rigid. It is Lowen's belief that the earlier the trauma occurs to produce the disorder, the more severe it is.

Schizoid character.   Traumatized in the uterus or in the first few months of birth, the schizoid personality is characterized by avoiding intimate and affective relationships with others. Thinking tends to be dissociated, and such individuals often are preoccupied with their own fantasy world. Lowen (1975) observed that such individuals may appear to have unexpressive and vacant eyes, a tense body, and arms and legs that are poorly coordinated. When examined, the individual may appear to have upper and lower halves of the body that do not seem to go together. Also, it is not uncommon to notice the head held at an angle to one side and a lack of energy in the face, hands, and feet—the opposite of a vibrant personality.

Oral character.   Arising from a deprivation of nurturing within the first 2 years of life, the oral personality is characterized by depression and dependence. Such individuals are apt to feel tired, have low energy, and may feel abandoned or disappointed in self or others. The lower body, particularly the legs and feet, is likely to be thin and underdeveloped, with tension in the shoulders and legs that symbolize that the person has been left alone or abandoned.

Narcissistic character.   Developing from incidents related to a feeling of being seduced by the parent (usually before the age of 4) or that the patient is special, the narcissistic character develops a sense of being superior to others and a feeling of grandiosity. This superiority can be seen in the overdevelopment of the upper half of the body in comparison to the weakness in the lower half. In posture, the narcissistic personality tends to show tension in the legs and back when standing (Lowen, 1984).

Masochistic character. Developing as a result of the need to be submissive to an overbearing mother or of strict parenting that makes it difficult for the individual to be free and spontaneous (after the second year of life), the masochistic personality is often characterized by whining, complaining, and suppressed anger. In general, such an individual tends to hold in feelings, and the resulting tension can be seen in tight bodily muscles in the arms and legs. Often the eyes have a look of suffering, and the individual has a whining voice.

Rigid character. Developing around the age of 5, the rigid character is different for males and females and is characterized by Oedipal conflicts in both sexes. The traumatic event is often related to a feeling of rejection from the father for both the boy and the girl. Lowen (1975) describes the rigid male as needing to prove himself and to have a tendency toward arrogance, competitiveness, and inflexibility. The female rigid character is described as histrionic, shallow, and sentimental and as having eroticized relationships with men. For both male and female, the posture is erect, with rigidity in the back muscles and stiffness in the neck. Lowen attributes this rigidity to being humiliated by the opposite-sex parent during the Oedipal period.

Lowen (1975) points out that he treats people, not character types, and that individuals usually exhibit a combination of character types. Furthermore, he develops the psychological and physiological factors of each of these types far more fully than is done here (Lowen, 1975). When working with individuals, Lowen integrates information about the body with information about psychological trauma and proceeds in a gradual manner. He compares this process to putting together the pieces of a jigsaw puzzle (Lowen, 1989). Although Lowen's five character types are often used by therapists who subscribe to bioenergetic principles, other body psychotherapists may use other classification systems.

Sheldon's somatotypes. Some body psychotherapists make use of William Sheldon's (1898–1977) system that correlates personality characteristics with body types. Sheldon (explained more fully in Hall and Lindzey, 1985) describes three different types of physiques that, in combination, can be used to illustrate the physique or somatotype of an individual. Each person can be seen as having a combination of characteristics described by endomorphy, mesomorphy, and ectomorphy. The endomorphic person tends to be soft and round, with relatively undeveloped bones and muscle and a physique not suited to physical activity. Mesomorphic physiques tend to be hard and rectangular, suited for physical activity, both strong and resistant to injury. The ectomorphic component is characterized by a thin and lightly muscled body with a large brain and central nervous system. Using these three physical characteristics, as well as others, Sheldon was able to relate body type to psychological temperament. Smith (1985) shows how Sheldon's body types and research on corresponding psychological characteristics can be applied to the assessment of individuals' problems.

Psychotherapeutic Approaches

In this section, I describe Smith's (1985) approach to body psychotherapy, which incorporates many of Lowen's methods used in bioenergetic analysis. The emphasis here is on assessment of the whole person and therapeutic techniques that affect the body in gentle or forceful ways (referred to as *soft* and *hard* techniques by Smith). Additionally, I give an example of soft techniques being applied in body psychotherapy and briefly outline important ethical issues.

Body assessment techniques.   In using assessment in body psychotherapy, Smith describes two different methods: body reading and body awareness. Body reading makes use of systematic observations by the therapist in attempting to understand energy blockages and tensions within the body. In body awareness methods, the patient is more active and develops awareness of his body.

When reading the body, Smith explains the rationale to the patient, and both agree on what the individual will wear during the reading. Smith (1985, p. 71) then helps individuals to relax and informs them that he will observe the client's body. In some cases, he may next run his fingers along the skin to observe temperature differentials. He then writes down his observations. Body psychotherapists often make use of classification systems such as Lowen's or Sheldon's to make hypotheses about the individual's personality. However, body psychotherapists such as Smith also do body reading without a typology. In doing this, Smith looks for tensions and pain within the body that indicate armoring, defensiveness, or areas that are numb or "dead." Additionally, Smith attends to vibrations in the body that indicate an aliveness and energy flow within the body and possible blockages. Hot spots in the body, those that are warm to the therapist's touch, indicate an accumulation of energy that has not been processed. Observations can also be made when the patient is in different body positions, such as standing, lying, or letting the body fall. Although a formal body assessment may be done near the beginning of therapy, the body psychotherapist attends to changes in the body throughout therapy and may make interventions involving the body at any time during therapy.

Soft techniques.   Soft or gentle techniques of body psychotherapy do not bring about strong emotional reactions or body awareness as quickly as do abrupt or hard techniques. However, they are less likely to bring out emotional issues that the patient is not yet ready to deal with than are hard techniques. One soft technique is to ask the patient to assume a particular posture so that she may be able to experience a blocked feeling. Sometimes Smith might observe the patient holding a body part, such as an arm, in an unusual way. The patient may then be asked to move the arm to a different position and to talk about how it feels in both positions.

Touching is an important technique in soft interventions. A hug or a hand on the back can indicate encouragement and caring. Touching the patient where feelings are inhibited, such as on a hot spot, may draw awareness to a particular feeling.

Another important aspect of soft body work is breathing. Smith agrees with Lowen that every emotional problem affects the patient's breathing. As Smith (1985, p. 120) observes, the average individual breathes 14 to 18 times a minute, or as often as 25,000 times a day. One intervention is to call attention to a patient's nonbreathing, if he holds his breath while discussing an issue in therapy. Another intervention is to teach a patient breathing by having him lie on the floor; then he, or the therapist, places a hand on his abdomen to teach and encourage full breathing. By teaching breathing, the therapist can later call attention to changes in breathing that occur in the therapy hour, and the patient may be able to develop increased awareness about breathing and emotional issues, as well as ways to change breathing.

A variety of creative approaches can be used to help patients become more aware of their bodies and their related emotional concerns. One technique is to have patients stretch body parts, such as arms and neck, or to rotate their bodies in one direction or another. Tensing a taut body part may lead to awareness of anxiety or other emotions. Using a mirror can help patients deal with their judgments about their bodies and body parts as bad or ugly. All of these techniques—moving, touching, and breathing—are designed to help patients develop awareness of themselves and of repressed emotions.

Sometimes, when clients are cognitively aware, but are having difficulty accessing their emotions, soft techniques can be a gentle way of facilitating such access. A well-timed and precisely placed touch can convey the therapist's intimate presence and support, as well as help the client focus on the area of the body where the emotion would be experienced, if that experience were allowed. In the following example by Edward Smith (personal communication, April 22, 1998), two soft body techniques, body posturing and touch, are illustrated.

Client: How could she be so cruel? I just don't understand how she could talk to me that way . . . says she wants to break up . . . just doesn't know if she really loves me . . .

Therapist: What are you feeling as you tell me this?

Client: I feel she's cruel.

Therapist: I know. That's what you're thinking. But, what emotion do you feel?

Client: I don't know. Maybe angry . . . or sad maybe.

Therapist: I believe that it may be helpful if you can get in touch with whatever emotions you may have deep down inside.

Client: Yeah, it's helped before. It's hard for me to get out of my head.

Therapist: I have a suggestion. Would you be willing to lie down on your back and let me sit beside you?

Client: I'll give it a try. (He lies down; the therapist sits to his right side.)

Therapist: That's good, Joe. Just breathe and see if you can let go. (A minute passes.) Keep breathing. (Another minute passes.) What is happening now?

Client: I'm starting to feel a little sad.

Therapist: Where in your body do you feel your sadness?

Client: Here . . . and here. (Touching his throat and chest.)

Therapist: Joe, would it be all right if I placed my right hand on your chest, along your sternum, like this? (Therapist demonstrates on himself.)

Client: Yes . . . Go ahead.

Therapist: (Placing his right hand gently on Joe's sternum). Just breathe, feel my touch, and let whatever wants to happen, happen. (Two or three minutes pass.) (A tear appears in the corner of each of Joe's eyes.) Good, Joe. Let that happen. (Another minute passes.) What are you aware of now?

Client: I feel so sad (beginning to sob).

Therapist: Good, Joe. Stay with your sadness. I'm right here. (Therapist wiggling his hand gently on Joe's chest.)

Client: (Sobbing deeply for two or three minutes. Sobbing subsides.)

Therapist: How are you feeling?

Client: Whew! Relieved (sighing).

Therapist: (Slowly removing his hand.) What would you like now?

Client: I wish I could tell Mary how much she has meant to me and how she's hurt me.

Therapist: You can. Let's bring Mary here in fantasy. Sit up as you feel ready and imagine Mary is sitting over here. (Joe sits up.) See Mary as vividly as you can, and when you are ready, speak directly to her.

At this point in the session, having accessed and experienced his hurt and sadness by using body posturing and touch, Joe is ready to clarify his position through a Gestalt empty chair dialogue with Mary (see Chapter 7).

Hard techniques. When using hard techniques, the therapist must use good judgment, as the techniques may be uncomfortable or painful and may bring about intense emotional responses. Uncomfortable postures such as arching the body into a bow, standing on one leg, or lying with legs in the air can bring about vibrating or other bodily responses to which the patient may have an emotional reaction. These postures are related to the concept of grounding, described previously, and may help the individual get in better touch with reality. Smith also discusses deep and heavy massaging of the jaw, neck, and chest that can bring about "energy streamings" and strong emotional reactions. Hard techniques can also be applied to breathing, by pressing hard against different areas of the chest, for instance. Certain techniques are best used in groups. For example, patients can experience the feeling of being safely "contained" by other group members who give them balanced resistance when patients try to strike out with their arms or legs. Thus, the patient can experience rage without any harm or destruction.

Besides direct soft and hard body psychotherapy techniques, Smith uses Gestalt expressive techniques. Several of these methods have been described in Chapter 7, and a few that particularly emphasize bodily awareness are described here. For example, a patient who is angry at his wife may be pounding the arm of his chair while telling about his wife. The therapist may ask the patient to pound a pillow, imagining that it is his wife, and thus express the emotional energy. It is important to explain that this is a way of understanding the emotional energy and is not a rehearsal or permission for doing this to an individual. Other expressive techniques, discussed in Chapter 7, include exaggerating or repeating an action, such as the pounding of the fist, thus expanding the individual's awareness and enhancing the emotional expression. The Gestalt empty chair technique can be used by substituting a large pillow for the chair and allowing the patient to kick, pat, hit, or hug the pillow. Expressive, soft, and hard body psychotherapeutic techniques allow the patient to become more aware of bodily and emotional processes and to experience a safe emotional expression.

Ethics. Because body psychotherapies provide intimate contact between patient and therapist, ethical considerations are of primary importance. Smith (1985) emphasizes that the therapist's function is to help the patient grow, not to show how clever or powerful the therapist is. In ethically guided psychotherapy, it is important that the therapist not have erotic intentions or treat the patient in a way that is not in the patient's best interest. The role of touch in body psychotherapy, and therapy in general, is a complex issue that has received recent attention (Smith, Clance, & Imes, 1997). In workshops that body-oriented psychotherapists give, it is important to be aware that many participants may be in therapy with other therapists and to be respectful of that relationship. Another ethical issue concerns the accurate assessment of patients' abilities and pathology, so that hard techniques are not used that leave the patient unable to cope with strong emotions. Smith (1985) emphasizes that the therapist must be profoundly respectful of the patient and use body-oriented techniques only with the informed consent of the patient.

Summary

Body psychotherapists consider the individual as a whole, believing that bodily and psychological processes are one and the same. Perhaps the best-known approach to body psychotherapy is that of Lowen's bioenergetics, which is based on the earlier work of Reich. In bioenergetics and other body psychotherapies, assessment is made by attending to posture, musculature, and other aspects of physique. Psychotherapeutic interventions may include work on breathing, posture, blockages in muscles, and bodily manipulation. Observations are integrated with psychotherapeutic procedures, such as psychoanalysis (Lowen) and Gestalt therapy (Smith). Because of the power and intimacy of the techniques, ethical issues are of extreme importance.

References

HALL, C. S., & LINDZEY, G. (1985). *Theories of personality*. New York: Wiley.

JONES, E. (1957). *The life and works of Sigmund Freud* (Vol. 3). New York: Basic Books.

LOWEN, A. (1958). *The language of the body*. New York: Macmillan.

LOWEN, A. (1975). *Bioenergetics*. New York: Penguin.

LOWEN, A. (1977). *The way to vibrant health*. New York: Harper & Row.

LOWEN, A. (1980). *Fear of life*. New York: Macmillan.

LOWEN, A. (1984). *Narcissism: Denial of the true self*. New York: Macmillan.

LOWEN, A. (1989). Bioenergetic analysis. In R. J. Corsini & D. Wedding (Eds.), *Current psychotherapies* (4th ed., pp. 573–584). Itasca, IL: Peacock.

LOWEN, A. (1997). My evolution as a body-mind therapist: Healing the split in the modern personality. In J. K. Zeig (Ed.), *The evolution of psychotherapy: The third conference* (pp. 135–145). New York: Brunner-Mazel.

REICH, W. (1951). *Selected writings.* New York: Farrar, Straus & Giroux.

REICH, W. (1972). *Character analysis.* New York: Orgone Institute Press.

SMITH, E. W. L. (1985). *The body in psychotherapy.* Jefferson, NC: McFarland.

SMITH, E. W. L., CLANCE, P. R., & IMES, S. (Eds.). (1997). *Touch in psychotherapy: Theory, research, and practice.* New York: Guilford.

INTERPERSONAL PSYCHOTHERAPY

Interpersonal psychotherapy was developed by Gerald Klerman with contributions by his wife Myrna Weissman and other colleagues. Interpersonal therapy is different than other theories discussed in this book in several respects. First, it was designed to be a brief system (12 to 16 sessions) to be used in research. A psychiatrist, Klerman believed that all methods of treating psychiatric disorders should be tested before being recommended to the public at large. Thus, if medications such as Prozac should be tested, so should psychotherapy. In order to develop a method that can be researched, Klerman felt it was important to specify a specific disorder and to develop a treatment manual for it. His method was developed for the treatment of depression, and although it has been applied to some other disorders, its application has been done carefully and applied to many fewer disorders than other theories, such as cognitive therapy.

The term *interpersonal therapy* is somewhat confusing as it has been used by several approaches. Kiesler (1996) has a very different method that focuses on the transactions between individuals, whereas Klerman's (Klerman, Weissman, Rounsaville, & Chevron, 1984) approach identifies important interpersonal situations and suggests individualistic solutions for clients. Harry Stack Sullivan (1953) also developed a system called interpersonal psychotherapy, which has had some influence on both Kiesler's and Klerman's approaches.

Background

In developing interpersonal psychotherapy, Klerman (Klerman & Weissman, 1993; Klerman et al., 1984) was influenced by both early theorists, as well as research on depression. The writings of Adolf Meyer (1957) emphasized the importance of both psychological and biological forces. According to Meyer, psychiatric disorders developed as individuals tried to adapt to their environment. Early experiences both with the family and various social groups influenced individuals' adaptation to their environment. Also, the work of Harry Stack Sullivan (1953) showed the importance of peer relationships in childhood and adolescence as they had an impact on later interpersonal relationships. Another source of theoretical development was John Bowlby's work (1969) in understanding early attachment and bonding with the mother. Although these three theorists were interested in childhood relationships and experiences, they would be considered as outside of the mainstream of psychoanalytic writers.

In developing a brief therapeutic approach to the treatment of depression, Klerman studied psychological research on depression to determine which factors played a role in the onset of depression. Several important conclusions from the research that helped Klerman (Klerman et al., 1984) determine which aspects of depression to treat are described here. Clearly, certain life events created stress that led to depression. The loss of social relationships also contributed to the onset of depression. When women became depressed, they interacted more poorly socially (for example, were nonassertive). Also, social and interpersonal stress, especially stress in marriage, affected the development of depression. Arguments between spouses were related to the onset of depression. Reviewing this research led Klerman to identify four major problem areas that interpersonal therapy should be able to address and treat: grief, interpersonal disputes, role transitions, and interpersonal deficits. Whereas almost all of the theorists described in this book relied on their clinical experience to develop their theoretical approach to therapy, Klerman made significant use of existing psychological data to develop his.

Not only was research important in the development of interpersonal psychotherapy, but so was the continual testing of interpersonal therapy's effectiveness as it was developed. Several significant research studies are described in Klerman and Weissman (1993) and Markowitz (1998) and summarized here. The most significant and well known of the studies was a comparison with cognitive therapy, psychopharmacological medication, and a placebo in the National Institute of Mental Health Treatment of Depression Collaborative Research Program. The results are complex, but interpersonal therapy proved to be more effective than cognitive therapy and as effective as other approaches in certain situations. However, after 18 months, about one third to one half of all patients in the study, regardless of treatment, showed evidence of relapse. The earliest study was done in Boston and New Haven, Connecticut, which showed that patients who received interpersonal therapy functioned better than patients who received either drugs alone or no treatment. Another study done in New Haven and Boston showed that interpersonal therapy was helpful in enhancing social functioning of patients who had responded well to psychiatric medication. Effects of psychotherapy appeared after 6 to 8 months after the end of treatment. A general conclusion was that combining drugs and psychotherapy was more effective than either alone. Also, research was done in Pittsburgh that examined the effectiveness of interpersonal therapy and psychiatric medication on individuals who had had at least two previous episodes of major depression. Both interpersonal therapy and medication were more effective than no treatment. When combined, there was a tendency for therapy and medication to be more effective than either treatment alone. All of these studies have been carefully designed, and long-term follow-up of treatment has been a part of the design. One part of the clarity and specificity of the research has been the detailed treatment manual and the training of therapists that Klerman and his colleagues have provided. These are discussed in more detail in the next sections.

Personality Theory

Klerman (Klerman et al., 1984) is less concerned with the cause of depression than in helping individuals deal with the kinds of issues that affect their lives. As shown previously, Klerman believed that depression was due to a variety of interpersonal issues. Many of these may have been caused by difficulties in early relationships or problems of attachment within the family. However, to deal with these in a brief treatment approach did not seem to be the most effective way to help individuals deal with their current symptoms of depression. Rather, he believed that there were four interpersonal problem areas that, if they could be alleviated, would help an individual deal with depression: grief, interpersonal disputes, role transitions, and interpersonal deficits.

Grief. Although grief is considered a normal emotion, not a psychiatric disorder, it can provide difficulties for people in mourning, particularly when the reaction is severe and continues over a long period of time. Grief may present a particularly difficult problem when individuals experience the loss of more than one person who is close to them. Furthermore, some individuals are more prone to becoming depressed after losing a close friend or family member than are others. This reaction is often referred to as *complicated bereavement*.

Interpersonal disputes. Often struggles, arguments, or disagreements with others, particularly on a continuing basis, can lead to depression. Sometimes the dispute is with a family member, a spouse, child, parent, or other relative. At other times, the dispute may be with someone at work, a boss, a subordinate, or a co-worker. Other times disputes are with friends or associates, or people in community organizations, such as in church groups. When individuals are depressed, disputes may be with people in many of these groups.

Role transitions. This is a broad category that includes many different types of life changes. Some are planned for and some are not. Examples of developmental changes are going to college, getting engaged or married, separating or divorcing, dealing with difficult children or having a child leave the home. Sometimes role transitions have to do with work, such as trying to find a job, dealing with promotion or demotion, or being fired or laid off. Other role transitions may be accidental or not predictable. An individual may develop a serious illness or disease, may be injured in an accident while at work or somewhere else, or have to deal with losing a house to fire or flood. Individuals who are prone to depression may, when faced with one of these situations, see their situation as hopeless or out of control.

Interpersonal deficits. Some individuals may be socially isolated or have few social skills. Individuals who have few friends, "loners," may have difficulty making or sustaining relationships. This can be a default category for patients who do not fit the other categories (Markowitz, 1998). When individuals do not report recent events that may have caused depression, this category is often used. Individuals falling in this category are more likely to have personality disorders than are those in the others. Because this area implies lack of social skills and continuing interpersonal problems, it can be a more difficult area to treat than the other three (Markowitz, 1998).

As the description of these four problem areas shows, the focus on interpersonal therapy is on current problems that deal with relationships. When assessing patient problems, the therapist finds out which ones of the four categories fit the patient's problems. This will have a direct impact on the therapeutic approach that the therapist takes. Additionally, the therapist may use measures such as the Hamilton Rating Scale for Depression (Hamilton, 1960) to assess severity of depression. The goals of this brief model are directly related to the assessment.

Goals

The goals of interpersonal therapy are directly related to the specific problem areas that the therapist identifies. Table 14.1 summarizes the goals and treatment for each of the four different problem areas. The four goal areas are described here.

> *Grief.* Individuals are helped with the mourning process and to deal with their sadness. They are helped to reestablish interest in relationships and to become involved in both relationships and activities.
>
> *Interpersonal disputes.* Clients are assisted in understanding disputes or arguments as they relate to depression. Clients are helped to develop strategies to resolve the dispute or to bring about a change in an impasse. Sometimes clients may change their expectations of their problems and relationships with others.
>
> *Role transition.* When individuals move from one role to the other, they often need to mourn the loss of the old role. Seeing the new role as more positive is one goal. Another is to develop a sense of mastery, of the new role or roles, and thus increase self-esteem.
>
> *Interpersonal deficits.* By reducing isolation from others, changes in this problem area can be made. Goals are to develop new relationships or improve ones that may be superficial.

Not only do the problem areas determine the goals for therapy, but the goals determine the specific strategies that are to be used. Table 14.1 list the specific strategies that therapists use to reach each of the goals. The following section describes several techniques that are used in the three phases of interpersonal therapy.

Techniques of Interpersonal Therapy

The specificity of interpersonal therapy can be seen by the detailed outline in Table 14.1, which fully describes the procedures that Klerman et al. (1984) explain in their treatment manual. Because the approach is detailed so clearly, it can appear to be mechanical or behavioral (Markowitz, 1998). However, in practice it is quite different. The therapist is an advocate for the patient. Often she may be warm and understanding of the client's difficulty. Clients are encouraged to express their feelings; therapists communicate their understanding of the feelings. In conducting interpersonal therapy, therapists do this in three phases: The initial phase consists of up to three sessions in which an assessment is made and a framework is set for treatment. The intermediate phase is devoted to work on the four problem areas. The termination phase includes discussion of ending therapy and recognition of competence.

Initial phase. In this phase, a diagnosis, when appropriate, of depression is made and shared with the client. Assessment inventories may be used. Additionally, the therapist assesses the patient's current interpersonal problems in each of the four areas. This helps determine the personal area(s) that the patient and therapist will focus on. Rarely, they will focus on more than two areas (Markowitz, 1998). Then an interpersonal formulation is given to the patient that describes the

TABLE 14.1
Outline of Interpersonal Psychotherapy

I. The initial sessions
  A. Dealing with depression
    1. Review depressive symptoms.
    2. Give the syndrome a name.
    3. Explain depression and the treatment.
    4. Give the patient the "sick role."
    5. Evaluate the need for medication.
  B. Relation of depression to interpersonal context
    1. Review current and past interpersonal relationships as they relate to current depressive symptoms. Determine with the patient the following:
      a. Nature of interaction with significant persons
      b. Expectations of patient and significant persons from each other and whether these were fulfilled
      c. Satisfying and unsatisfying aspects of the relationships
      d. Changes in the relationships that the patient wants to make
  C. Identification of major problem areas
    1. Determine the problem area related to current depression and set the treatment goals.
    2. Determine which relationship or aspect of a relationship is related to the depression and what might change in it.
  D. Explanation of the IPT concepts and contract
    1. Outline your understanding of the problem.
    2. Agree on treatment goals (i.e., which problem area will be the focus).
    3. Describe procedures of IPT, including "here and now" focus and the need for patient to discuss important concerns; review of current interpersonal relations; and practical aspects of treatment, such as length, frequency, times, fees, and policy for missed appointments.
II. Intermediate sessions: the problem areas
  A. Grief
    Goals
    1. Facilitate the mourning process.
    2. Help the patient reestablish interest and relationships to substitute for what has been lost.
    Strategies
    1. Review depressive symptoms.
    2. Relate symptom onset to death of significant other.
    3. Reconstruct the patient's relationship with the deceased.
    4. Describe the sequence and consequences of events just prior to, during, and after the death.
    5. Explore associated feelings (negative as well as positive).
    6. Help patient consider possible other ways of becoming involved with others.

Continued

TABLE 14.1 *(Continued)*

Outline of Interpersonal Psychotherapy

B. Interpersonal disputes

Goals

1. Identify dispute.
2. Choose plan of action.
3. Modify expectations or faulty communication to bring about a satisfactory resolution.

Strategies

1. Review depressive symptoms.
2. Relate symptoms' onset to overt or covert dispute with significant other with whom patient is currently involved.
3. Determine stage of dispute:
   a. Renegotiation (Calm down participants to facilitate resolution.)
   b. Impasse (Increase disharmony in order to reopen negotiation.)
   c. Dissolution (Assist mourning.)
4. Understand how nonreciprocal role expectations relate to dispute:
   a. What are the issues in the dispute?
   b. What are the differences in expectations and values?
   c. What are the options?
   d. What is the likelihood of finding alternatives?
   e. What resources are available to bring about change in the relationship?
5. Are there parallels in other relationships?
   a. What is the patient gaining?
   b. What unspoken assumptions lie behind the patient's behavior?
6. How is the dispute perpetuated?

C. Role transitions

Goals

1. Facilitate mourning and acceptance of the loss of the old role.
2. Help the patient to regard the new role as more positive.
3. Help the patient to restore self-esteem by developing a sense of mastery regarding demands of new roles.

Strategies

1. Review depressive symptoms.
2. Relate depressive symptoms to difficulty in coping with some recent life change.
3. Review positive and negative aspects of old and new roles.
4. Explore feelings about what is lost.
5. Explore feelings about the change itself.
6. Explore opportunities in new role.
7. Realistically evaluate what is lost.
8. Encourage appropriate release of affect.
9. Encourage development of social support system and of new skills called for in new role.

TABLE 14.1 *(Continued)*

Outline of Interpersonal Psychotherapy

    D. Interpersonal defecits

       Goals

       1. Reduce the patient's social isolation.

       2. Encourage formation of new relationships.

       Strategies

       1. Review depressive symptoms.

       2. Relate depressive symptoms to problems of social isolation or unfulfillment.

       3. Review past significant relationships including their negative and positive aspects.

       4. Explore repetitive patterns in relationships.

       5. Discuss patient's positive and negative feelings about the therapist and seek parallels in other relationships.

III. Termination

       1. Explicitly discuss termination.

       2. Acknowledge that termination is a time of grieving.

       3. Help patient move toward recognition of independent competence.

IV. Specific techniques

       1. Exploratory

       2. Encouragement of affect

       3. Clarification

       4. Communication analysis

       5. Use of therapeutic relationships

       6. Behavior-change techniques

       7. Adjunctive techniques

V. Therapist's role

       1. Therapist is patient advocate, not neutral.

       2. Therapist is active, not passive.

       3. Therapeutic relationship is not interpreted as transference.

       4. Therapeutic relationship is not a friendship.

From *Interpersonal Psychotherapy for Depression* by G. L. Klerman, M. M. Weissman, and B. J. Rounsville, pp. 73–76. Copyright © 1984 Basic Books.

fact that the person has a medical illness, not a personal weakness. How this is done is shown in the case example on page 579. At this point, the therapist determines if medication, interpersonal therapy, or both should be used. Patients take the sick role in that they are told that being depressed or having an illness is not their fault. By taking the sick role, the patient is encouraged to do something about the illness by coming to therapy to work on it. Since interpersonal therapy follows a medical model, educating the patient about the nature of depression as an illness fits as a part of the initial phase.

    An important aspect of the initial phase is to be supportive of the patient and show him that there is hope. The encouragement and reassurance that the therapist gives helps build a therapeutic alliance with the patient. The therapist offers initial relief to the patient by telling him that depression is treatable and positive change is likely to occur (but not guaranteed). By coming up with a specific formulation of how the treatment is to proceed, the stage is set for the middle phase of therapy.

Middle phase.　Although there are different strategies that the interpersonal therapist uses for each of the four areas (see Table 14.1), there are techniques that are common to most of these. Many of these techniques are similar to others that are described in this book. However, they are discussed in some detail in Klerman et al (1984). All of the techniques deal with interpersonal relationship issues, some more directly than others. Because the role of the therapist is to be supportive and to be on the side of the patient, the therapeutic relationship itself is not typically discussed. However, it may be used as a resource for interpersonal material. The purpose of the therapeutic relationship is to foster relationships outside of therapy. Relationships with others outside of therapy may be long lasting, but the relationship in a 12- to 16-session model will not be. Common techniques used in interpersonal therapy are described here.

Starting the session.　Klerman advocates the use of this question in starting a session: "How have things been since we last met?" (Klerman et al., 1984). The reason for this question is that it asks the patient to bring up recent events, not ones in the distant past. This allows the therapist to discuss events and the moods or feelings that accompany them. By asking for the patient to describe the event in detail, the therapist has significant interpersonal material to work with. Such a question allows the therapist to go into the one or two problem areas that the patient and therapist have decided to work on.

Encouragement of affect.　The therapist encourages expression of painful and other emotions. This provides a way of showing understanding of the patient and an opportunity to offer to help with solutions. For example, the therapist may say "Losing your wife has been so terrible for you," and then may follow it with "We want to work to help you feel better." This then may lead to "What might help you feel less depressed?" The therapist wants to find out the patient's desires so that they can explore ways to accomplish the patient's goals.

Clarification.　The therapist helps the patient clarify interpersonal relationships that he has just discussed. Sometimes the therapist may point out differences between how the patients view their situation and how they actually behave. For example, the therapist may say to the patient, "You say that you are disappointed in your daughter, but I am not clear about how you are disappointed in your daughter in this situation that you described—that time she came home from school late." In this way, the patient can better understand an interpersonal incident that she has just described.

Communication analysis. To analyze an interpersonal situation, the therapist asks the patient to describe exactly what the patient said and what the other person said. Included in this description may be the tone of voice that each used, as well as other details. The more clearly the therapist understands the situation, the more likely the therapist is to be able to effectively come up with new alternatives to different situations.

Other techniques are used by interpersonal therapists as well as the ones described above. For example, role playing is often used following communication analysis. The therapist can play another person so that the patient can develop new ways for dealing with that person. The therapist may give the patient feedback about the words that the patient used, his tone of voice, or his facial expression. Practicing new behaviors to use in interpersonal relationships can be helpful in a variety of situations. In general, the techniques that the therapists use will help individuals improve interpersonal interactions in one or more of the four areas.

Termination.   Typically termination takes place in the last two or three sessions. There is an explicit discussion that treatment is ending. A positive approach to termination is taken by focusing on graduating from therapy and becoming more independent. However, termination can also be a time of sadness, as the therapist's support will not be available. Acknowledging and discussing this sadness or grief can be very helpful. Because of the emphasis on gains and strengths, termination is a time to credit the patient with accomplishments. However, it is also helpful to discuss the potential of reoccurrence of the depression. If the therapy has not been particularly successful, the therapist does not want to blame the client, but may instead put the blame on interpersonal therapy. At this point, other therapeutic options, such as cognitive therapy, or further continuation in interpersonal therapy may be discussed.

As can be seen from the above description of the three phases of interpersonal therapy, the therapy is focused throughout on one of the four basic areas (grief, interpersonal disputes, role transitions, or interpersonal deficits). Each of the three phases is clearly related to the other. The treatment (Klerman et al., 1984) assists the therapist in attending to the goals of the therapy.

An Example of Interpersonal Therapy

The following is a brief example of therapy with a 53-year-old woman with dysthymia. Dysthymia is a condition that is similar to depression. It is a mood disorder in which individuals may have more cognitive concerns such as pessimism and low self-esteem than in typical depression. However, the approach is quite similar. In the following section, Markowitz (1998) describes the beginning of his work with Ms. J. and the interpersonal formulation that he gives to her of her problem. He then goes on to show his approach to dealing with an interpersonal dispute (which he refers to as a role dispute).

Ms. J., a 53-year-old, married saleswoman in an art gallery, reported lifelong dsythymic disorder. "I'm useless," she said, "Just waiting to die." Raised in an emotionally frigid family, she had married unhappily in her late teens in an attempt to escape her family of origin. Her relationship with her husband was distant, asexual, and angry, but she felt too incapable and incompetent to even consider leaving him. She also felt incompetent socially and at work. She could not recall ever feeling happy or capable. Ms. J had had lengthy treatment with psychodynamic psychotherapy, which had provided some fleeting insights but not relief, and with antidepressant medication, which had produced little response even at high doses.

She was dubious about the IPT for dysthymic disorder (IPT-D) definition of her problem as a medical mood disorder but conceded that this was at least a fresh view of things. Her initial Hamilton Depression Rating Scale (Ham-D) (Hamilton 1960) score was 24 on the 24-item version of the scale (significantly depressed). She was passively suicidal but had not made plans or attempts ("I'd only mess it up").

The therapist gave a version of the usual IPT-D formulation:

> I don't think you're useless, you just have a medical illness, dysthymic disorder, that makes you feel that way. You've had it for so long that of course it feels like part of you, but it doesn't have to be that way. I would like to spend the next 16 weeks with you working on a *role transition* in which you move from accepting the depression as part of yourself to distinguishing between depression and your healthy self. If you can do that, you're pretty much bound to feel better and more capable.

Therapy thus focused on the role transition of recognizing her "real" personality in contrast to dysthymic symptoms and on expanding her interpersonal repertoire in her relationship with others. She acknowledged her anger at her husband (a role dispute), felt there was no resolving the chronic role dispute between them, and looked into the possibility of moving out but without much conviction. At the same time, she and the therapist worked on her interactions with co-workers. She had been particularly upset by her interactions with a rude, competitive colleague who interrupted her when she was helping customers.

Ms. J: Rose is rude, interrupts me when I'm dealing with patrons. I don't like her at all.

Therapist: That sounds understandable. What can you do?

J: I'm not good at doing anything. . . . I don't feel very effective. . . . Is there a book I can read on how to be effective?

T: We'll write it right now. Do you feel that it's appropriate for you to be annoyed? I mean, do you feel Rose is genuinely annoying?

J: I never know if it's me or the other person, but I think some other people have been bothered by her too, even though she often comes across as sweet.

T: So if it's reasonable to feel angry, what can you say to Rose?

J: "Excuse me, I'll talk to you later?"

T: Does that get across what you want to say? How do you feel? What do you feel like saying?

J: I feel like telling her to learn some manners!

T: Okay fine! That sounds right, that makes sense to me; but it's a little blunt. Is there another way to put that? Is there a more direct way to tell her *why* you want her to learn some manners?

J: I'd like to tell her that it's rude to interrupt, that if she waits I'll get back to her, but that she shouldn't break in.

T: Fine! Now pretend I'm Rose and say it to me . . .

Note that this interchange tended to normalize anger as an appropriate response for the patient in noxious interpersonal situations. (Markowitz, 1998, pp. 120, 121)

Later in therapy, Markowitz addresses an interpersonal dispute dealing with Rose's marriage after making a transition from the situation with Rose. He then summarizes the case from an interpersonal therapy (IPT) point of view.

Although Ms. J insisted that she was a "slow learner" and unlikely to do anything with her life, in the remaining sessions of the 16-week course of IPT she solidified a shaky sense of social competence at work and began to renegotiate matters with her husband. At the same time, she began looking around for an apartment of her own, with the idea of trying to spend a few months on her own to see whether she could function without her husband. Although she felt "too old to be just starting life at 53," she was taking steps to do so, and her Ham-D score fell to 7, essentially euthymic. In monthly continuation and maintenance sessions she reported that she had neither left her husband nor greatly improved her marriage, but she had a clearer perspective on her role in it, a new appreciation of her husband's failings, and less blame for herself. She put together a resume for new jobs but in the meantime felt new respect from her co-workers and a greater sense of competence in her work.

This case demonstrates how the optimistic, "can-do" approach of IPT can mobilize a doubting patient to action. The therapist supported the patient's feeling of anger, which she had regarded as impotent, and helped her to express it more effectively. For patients whose social skills are shaky, role playing is an important rehearsal of interpersonal skills that can then be used in the world outside the office. (Markowitz, 1998, p. 123)[3]

Other Applications of Interpersonal Therapy

As interpersonal therapy has been tested in several research studies, Klerman and his colleagues developed more confidence in this approach, creating treatment manuals and research procedures for applying interpersonal therapy to disorders that are similar to depression. For example, Klerman and Weissman (1993) have developed treatment manuals similar to the original (Klerman et al., 1984) for depressed patients who have marital disputes, for individuals in distress but not considered to be clinically depressed, and for patients who may require more than brief therapy for the reoccurrence of depression. For these individuals, a once-a-month treatment program has been developed. Additionally, treatment manuals and procedures have been created for patients with a depressive mood disorder or dysthymia and for medically ill patients who are depressed. Other groups include depressed individuals who have been diagnosed as HIV positive and elderly individuals who are diagnosed with depression. Most applications, such as those discussed, have been to conditions that are similar to unipolar depression. However, interpersonal therapy has also been applied to individuals with bulimia and those who abuse drugs. When used with drug-abusing patients, interpersonal psychotherapy has not been as successful as it has been for depressed patients (Rounsaville & Carroll, 1993). When interpersonal therapy is applied to new disorders, a treatment manual is developed or a previous treatment manual is revised, and then the application is, in most cases, tested in a research study.

SUMMARY

The rationale for interpersonal therapy is rather different than that for other theories of psychotherapy. First, it was developed using a medical model, in which a plan was designed to test its effectiveness. Also, interpersonal therapy was created to deal with depression rather than other disorders. A survey of psychological theory and research was made in order to develop a treatment manual that therapists would follow to treat patients. This brief therapy is designed to be completed in 12 to 16 sessions. The initial sessions assess the patient's problems and educate the patient, when appropriate, about depression. The intermediate sessions focus on bringing about change in the four major problem areas: grief, interpersonal disputes, role transitions, and interpersonal deficits. The treatment manuals specify strategies therapists are to use for each of these problem areas, as well as specific techniques that may be used for all problem areas. The third and final phase is termination, in which therapists discuss the ending of therapy and the recognition of being competent and being on one's own. Interpersonal therapy has been applied to other disorders, but most of these have been similar to depression.

References

BOWLBY, J. (1969). *Attachment and loss* (Vol. 1, Attachment). London: Hogarth.

HAMILTON, M. (1960). The rating scale for depression. *Journal of Neurological and Neurosurgical Psychiatry, 25*, 56–62.

KIESLER, B. J. (1996). *Contemporary interpersonal theory and research: Personality, psychopathology, and psychotherapy*. New York: Wiley.

KLERMAN, G. L., & WEISSMAN, M. M. (Eds.). (1993). *New applications of personal therapy*. Washington, DC: American Psychiatric Press.

KLERMAN, G. L., WEISSMAN, M. M., ROUNSAVILLE, B. J., & CHEVRON, E. S. (1984). *Interpersonal psychotherapy of depression*. New York: Basic Books.

MARKOWITZ, J. C. (1998). *Interpersonal psychotherapy for dysthymic disorder*. Washington, DC: American Psychiatric Press.

MEYER, A. (1957). *Psychobiology: A science of man*. Springfield, IL: Charles C. Thomas.

ROUNSAVILLE, B. J., & CARROLL, K. (1993). Interpersonal psychotherapy for patients who have used drugs. In G. L. Klerman & M. M. Weissman (Eds.), *New applications of interpersonal psychotherapy* (pp. 319–352). Washington, DC: American Psychiatric Press.

SULLIVAN, H. S. (1953). *The interpersonal theory of psychiatry*. New York: Norton.

PSYCHODRAMA

Created by Jacob L. Moreno, psychodrama is an approach in which the patient acts out a problem, usually with members of a group or audience who can portray people involved in the problem. The therapist serves as the director of the spontaneous drama, which most frequently takes place before an audience. Attention is paid to the role that the patient has in relationship with other significant people in his life. A variety of techniques are used to help patients examine their roles from different points of view. By acting out the roles, rather than talking about them, patients experience previously unrecognized feelings and attitudes that can lead to changes in behavior.

Background

Born in Bucharest, Romania, Jacob Moreno (1889–1974) was the oldest of six children. At the age of 5, he and his family moved to Vienna (Blatner, 1988). A student of philosophy at the University of Vienna, Moreno became interested in children's play in the Vienna parks when he was about 20 years old. Not only did he observe their play but also he encouraged them to play different roles. Later, Moreno attended medical school at the University of Vienna and became interested in helping disenfranchised social groups, such as prostitutes.

Moreno combined his social interests with his interest in theater and opened the "Theatre of Spontaneity" in 1921. Because he felt theater was dry and studied, he preferred impromptu improvisational dramas. Leaving Vienna for New York in 1925, Moreno applied his ideas to hospitals in the area. He became one of the first group psychotherapists and addressed broader social concerns than could be done in individual therapy. Opening a sanitarium in Beacon, New York, in 1936, Moreno built a theater to be used for psychodrama. In addition to practicing and training therapists in psychodrama, Moreno (1934) carried out research in the area of group relations in prisons, schools, and hospitals. In 1940, he worked with Zerka Toeman, whom he later married and who became an active proponent of psychodrama. She worked as a partner with Moreno and continued her work after his death (Blatner, 1988; Blatner & Blatner, 1988).

When psychodrama was first developed in the 1930s, it represented a marked change in direction from treating the individual in isolation. It was the precursor for many group therapies, including Gestalt and encounter groups. Techniques such as role playing, used in both individual and group therapy, originated from the work of Moreno (1947). In his approach to understanding the personality of individuals, Moreno focused on the variety of roles that they played with others and their ability to examine and change these roles.

Theory of Personality

Moreno's view of the roles that individuals enacted with each other represented his major conceptualization of individual personality. Described by his colleagues as an active, creative, energetic, yet unsystematic man, Moreno lectured throughout the world, wrote widely (see Fox, 1987), and could initiate a psychodrama with a large number of people at a moment's notice. These characteristics can be seen in Moreno's views on interpersonal interaction and are reflected in his development of psychodrama.

Roles and sociometry.   Role theory examines relationships that individuals have with others, such as a woman with her husband, mother, customer, child, or teacher. In particular, Moreno was interested in the changing relationships between individuals and in ways to encourage new changes. In his study of roles, Moreno (Fox, 1987) developed sociometric testing, which measured the nature of relationships between people in a particular group. By interviewing members of the group, a sociogram can be developed that can determine how each person views the other, for example, as a friend, as someone to be relied on, or as someone skilled in a particular area. Not only was Moreno interested in the roles that people played in relationship to others but also he was interested in role distance. By becoming increasingly objective about an event and able to examine one's own role, role distance is increased. In the case of psychodrama, individuals' role distance can be increased as they play different roles that allow them a new perspective on their relationships with others.

Activity in the present.   Although Moreno made use of psychoanalytic concepts in understanding individuals' behavior, he was most interested in current experience. Sociometry provided a way to observe people's relationships to each other in the present. In psychodrama, individuals most often interact with other group members, who play the roles of significant people in their lives. Occasionally, the significant people would be present and act for themselves. For Moreno, psychodrama provided a way to bring past, possible future, or current conflicts or crises into the present. Meaning would be assigned to individuals and events, not as they occurred in the past, but as they were occurring in the present as the individual acted them out in psychodrama.

Encounter.   Of interest to Moreno was the interaction that individuals had when they encountered each other in a relationship. Psychodrama provides a way for individuals to experience a number of meaningful encounters in a short period of time. The energy that takes place between individuals in interpersonal exchange is referred to by Moreno as *tele* (Greenberg, 1986). Moreno also used tele to refer to the feeling of caring that developed between individuals in a psychodrama group. As individuals get to know each other and care for each other, tele is increased and group cohesion develops. Tele includes constructs that other theorists would refer to as empathy, transference, or the relationship.

Spontaneity and creativity.   Noted for his own spontaneity and creativity, Moreno valued these characteristics in others as signs of living healthily and fully. A spontaneous individual should be able to take initiative and risks when faced with a difficult situation. Using thinking and feeling, individuals should react to an external crisis in a constructive manner, in contrast to acting impulsively, which might lead to negative consequences (Blatner & Blatner, 1988).

Creativity was highly valued by Moreno, who observed children in the Vienna parks as entering into creative role playing in fantasy situations more readily than did adults. As a part of his work with groups, Moreno often did spontaneity training, in which individuals were encouraged to respond creatively to an unexpected or stressful problem that was presented by the leader. For example, group members might be presented with situations such as dealing with an angry boss, a tornado, or a stranger with a gun. This emphasis on spontaneous and creative aspects of individual personality, which is found in the writings of humanistic and existential theorists, is clearly apparent in Moreno's writings and in his approach to psychodrama.

Theory of Psychotherapy

Basic to psychodrama is role playing, the process of playing someone else, something else, or oneself in different circumstances. As mentioned previously, individuals play many different roles with different people during the course of their lives. Being aware of how we act toward others in these roles can give individuals the freedom to change their behaviors. By providing many different roles for individuals to play, psychodrama encourages experimentation and learning about new aspects of oneself. Role playing can serve three functions in the course of psychodrama: to assist the leader in assessing how members think and feel, to instruct individuals on new ways to deal with problems, and to train individuals in practicing new skills (Corsini, 1966). Also, the fact that role playing is active helps individuals feel more in control and less passive. Abstract issues, such as frustration about dealing with one's father, become more concrete when they are played out, as the patient must talk to the father, gesture when appropriate, change voice tone and volume, and move physically in relationship to the other players. The specificity and activity of role playing can have several advantages for the participants.

Psychodrama gives individuals an opportunity to test reality, to develop insight into problems, and to express their feelings (catharsis). Reality testing is achieved by playing important situations with real people. Participants may learn that previously held assumptions are no longer valid as they enact various roles and get input from group members. The act of expressing oneself in a role often provides the opportunity to experience strong feelings such as anger, hatred, sadness, joy, or love in ways that thinking or talking about situations does not. By testing reality and experiencing catharsis and insight, individuals are able to learn and try out affective behavior that they previously had not considered.

In the following sections, the details of psychodrama are described more fully. Because assessment is quite different in psychodrama than in other therapies, it deserves special consideration. As in a play, individuals have different roles in a psychodrama, and the basic roles are described. Also, psychodrama refers not only to playing roles but also to helping individuals enter their roles and learn from them. A number of important techniques have been developed to help individuals learn effectively and cognitively from their psychodrama experience.

Assessment.   Unlike other therapies, the psychodrama leader or director must make many assessments about group behavior as the psychodrama unfolds. Although psychodrama is often used in hospital and other institutional settings that have a core of group members, psychodrama is also done in demonstrations or with a group that will not reconvene. The director must assess which problems are appropriate for psychodrama, whether the group member presenting the problem is able to grow from the experience and is not too emotionally vulnerable, and whether other group members are constructively playing their parts. Additionally, leaders must assess when to bring in new members from the group or audience to play parts, when to switch roles, and which roles to initiate. Assessment and the other functions of the director are complicated (Z. T. Moreno, 1987), and individuals need about 2 years of training in psychodrama before they can take the role of director.

Roles in the psychodrama.   There are four basic roles in psychodrama: the director, who produces and leads the interactions; the protagonist, the person who presents the problem; the auxiliaries, who portray different people in the protagonist's life; and the audience, who may participate in the enactment as auxiliaries or make comments or questions. Where possible, the protagonists, auxiliaries, and director act out the psychodrama on a stage large enough to allow freedom of movement. Sometimes, half of a large room may be used for the action and the other half for the audience. Where possible, props are available to be used by the participants.

The director, in addition to assessing the movements and actions of the participants, performs a number of roles (Corey, 2000). The director should establish a tolerant and accepting atmosphere for change in the group, while also providing support and direction for the protagonist. During the course of the psychodrama, the director may describe relationships to be explored, scenes to be enacted, or other experiments. If group members attack other members or make inappropriate suggestions, the director intervenes to maintain a helpful and productive atmosphere in the group. Often the director may stop the action to make comments, invite comments from the audience, or make sure that the roles are being properly played out. To be a director takes creativity and courage to expose one's ideas before a large group of other people (Greenberg, 1986).

The protagonist is the person who presents the problem or event that will be explored. Often this person volunteers but may also be selected by the group or director. Although the protagonist initially describes the problem to be explored, the director encourages the protagonist to act it out. To do this, the protagonist selects group members who will play other roles (auxiliaries) and will instruct them how to play the role of a significant other in the protagonist's life, making suggestions if the portrayal is inaccurate. Often the director suggests that the protagonist play a variety of roles or watch the action while others play the role of the protagonist.

Auxiliaries portray significant others in the protagonist's life, such as a sister. Initially their role is to help the protagonist by playing the perceptions of the significant other (Z. T. Moreno, 1987). The more emotional energy they put into playing this role, the more real it is likely to be for the protagonist. Additionally, when playing such roles, auxiliaries often get insights into their own lives that parallel issues that occur in the psychodrama.

Audience members are not passive participants in a psychodrama. At times, they may be called on to be the protagonist or auxiliaries. Also, they may be asked to share experiences or comment on what they are observing. Often they witness enactments that relate to their own lives and develop new insights into their relationships with others.

The process of psychodrama. There are three basic phases of a psychodrama: the warm-up phase, the action phase, and the discussion and sharing that take place afterward.

A warm-up phase helps participants get ready for the action phase of psychodrama. The basic aim of the warm-up phase is to develop an atmosphere of trust and safety, along with a willingness to play and try out new behavior (Blatner, 1988). Special warm-up procedures are necessary for individuals who are not a part of an ongoing psychodrama group. Describing the purpose of psychodrama and answering questions about what is to take place is helpful in reassuring new participants. Sometimes it is useful to have pairs, small groups, or the entire group share conflicts that they are experiencing that could be material for the psychodrama. As this discussion is going on, the leader assesses appropriate issues to be the focus of the psychodrama and individuals to be protagonists. When a protagonist is selected, the leader listens carefully to his description of the psychodrama scene so that roles can be selected and auxiliaries chosen.

The action phase starts as individuals act out and work through a protagonist's situation. Although protagonists should be encouraged to enact situations and events as soon as possible, traumatic events should be saved for later, rather than dealt with early on in the session (Corey, 2000). The director takes responsibility for having furniture moved and props made available and for helping the protagonist set the scene for the psychodrama. As the action progresses, the director may ask members of the audience to play new roles or for the protagonist to change roles with other group members.

When the action phase is concluded, the sharing and discussion phase begins. First, group members, including auxiliaries, share their observations with the protagonist. A part of the director's responsibility is to help the protagonist who has shared a vulnerable part of his life and to ensure that feedback is helpful and not critical or judgmental. For psychodramas that will last only one session, attention must be paid to having effective closure, and the director may facilitate a winding down of the emotional intensity within the group.

Psychodrama techniques. Essential in psychodrama is the acting out of relationships with others. Participants are encouraged to act as if they are in a situation rather than talk about it. Occasionally, they may dialogue with themselves—which is called monodrama—by using an empty chair to play two roles, but most often they dialogue with auxiliaries. Some of the more common techniques in the action phase of psychodrama include role reversal, the double technique, the mirror technique, act fulfillment, and future projection.

Role reversal is designed to help patients understand the point of view of others and to be more empathic with them. Basically, the protagonist changes roles with an auxiliary to get a different point of view. For example, a man arguing with an auxiliary who is playing his mother may be asked to switch roles, and the auxiliary or another group member then plays the man's role. Moreno (Fox, 1987) gives an example of role reversal when an adolescent boy had told psychiatrists and others that he was worried about turning into or being turned into a girl.

> At a strategic point in his treatment, he was placed in the role of one of the psychiatrists who had heard his disclosure. Acting in the role of the boy, the psychiatrist was to come to the boy—now in the role of the psychiatrist—for advice about his fears. In this way the patient was compelled to act in an advisory capacity toward another person who was exhibiting the same abnormal ideas as those with which he was obsessed. This gave him the opportunity to test for himself the degree of responsibility and stability he had reached in the course of our treatment, and it afforded us a chance to see what degree of maturity he had attained. He seemed to be acting both himself and the psychiatrist at the same time but, by the technique of reversal, he was forced to objectify his real self and his obsession from what he conceived to be a psychiatrist's point of view. (Fox, 1987, p. 75)[4]

The double technique is one in which an auxiliary takes the role of the protagonist and expresses what she perceives to be the protagonist's inner thoughts and feelings. Usually doubles stand close to the protagonist and may speak for her. Additionally, they may enact nonverbal behaviors, such as posture or facial expression. Sometimes multiple doubles are used to express different sides of an individual. Although the role of a double is primarily supportive, it also helps the protagonist in developing further insights about her feelings or attitudes. In the following example, Yablonsky (1976) shows how a double, experienced in psychodrama, was able to provide significant insight for a woman who considered herself to be sexually liberated and was critical of the men in her life.

> In the center of one interaction, her double, for no special reason, based on what the protagonist said but derived from a feeling as her double, exclaimed, "My problem is that I've never had an orgasm." The protagonist wheeled around to her double, broke into tears, and with amazement said, "How did you know?" The double thus propelled the protagonist into a more honest portraiture and broke past the false image the subject was trying to project. She began to reveal that beneath her sexual braggadocio, she was a frightened little girl who was really afraid of men and sex. Often, a double in a role will have an insight that is not apparent to anyone in the group, including the director, and this will open up the protagonist to his deeper, more honest feelings. (Yablonsky, 1976, pp. 120–121)[5]

In the mirror technique, an auxillary plays the role of the protagonist by mirroring postures, expressions, and words, while the protagonist observes his behavior being reflected by another person. Essentially, mirroring is a feedback process in which the patient sees how someone else perceives him. Such a technique must be done carefully so that the protagonist does not feel ridiculed (Blatner & Blatner, 1988).

Psychodrama makes use of real and unreal situations to help an individual. The use of fantasy is sometimes called *surplus reality*, such as when a protagonist has a dialogue with an auxiliary who represents a monster in a dream. Another example of surplus reality is that of act fulfillment. Here, an individual can have a corrective experience that replaces a hurtful experience from the past. For example, if a young woman remembers being ridiculed by a seventh-grade teacher, she can have an auxiliary play the role of the teacher, confront the teacher, and have a dialogue with him.

Another example of incorporating surplus reality into psychodrama is future projection, which is designed to help people clarify concerns about their future. In future projection, a situation is presented, perhaps 4 years from now, where the individual has an interview for graduate school. The protagonist can act out an interview and get feedback from others, or one in which he purposefully botches the interview and experiences the feeling of what would happen in that case.

In part because individuals expose themselves and their innermost fears and feelings to others, psychodrama can be a very powerful technique. It is essential that directors are empathic and protective of group members. Although there are many creative techniques, more than the ones discussed here, the techniques need to be used by a director who can be creative yet take control of the psychodrama so that emotional destructiveness does not take place. Being able to recognize psychopathology as it emerges in participants is important to prevent damage to others. For example, a manipulative or sociopathic individual who plays the role of an auxiliary may take pleasure in making comments that point out the protagonist's inadequacies in a hurtful way. Although spontaneity and creativity are important products of psychodrama, they must be subservient to the positive goals of insight, growth, and understanding of individuals (Blatner, 1988).

Since the pioneering work of Moreno, psychodrama has continued to grow and develop. In the United States there are over 300 certified practioners, and throughout the world there are over 6,000 people trained in psychodrama techniques (Blatner, 1997). Some practitioners have extended Moreno's work and have applied it to individual treatment of children in which they are encouraged to act out imaginative ideas. For example, Hoey (1997) describes a 13-year-old girl whose mother died when she was 6 and who had lived in several foster homes but was about to be adopted. To encourage expression Hoey said, "Shall we make up a story about a girl like you? A girl who's lived in lots of places and now has at last found somewhere where she can be happy?" (p. 109). Creativity charactizes those who use psychodrama, and several have combined it with art therapies and dramatherapy, while others have used it within a psychodynamic framework (Hug, 1997).

Summary

Developed by J. L. Moreno in the 1930s, psychodrama makes use of creativity and spontaneity to help individuals test reality, develop insight, and express feelings. Using a mixture of playfulness and seriousness and techniques such as role reversal and mirroring, psychodrama offers ways to help individuals grow and see themselves in different ways.

References

BLATNER, A. (1988). *Acting in: Practical applications of psychodramatic methods* (2nd ed.). New York: Springer.

BLATNER, A. (1997). Psychodrama: The state of the art. *Arts in Psychotherapy, 24,* 23–30.

BLATNER, A., & BLATNER, A. (1988). *Foundations of psychodrama: History, theory, and practice* (3rd ed.). New York: Springer.

COREY, G. (2000). *Theory and practice of group counseling* (4th ed.) Pacific Grove, CA: Brooks/Cole.

CORSINI, R. J. (1966). *Role playing in psychotherapy.* Chicago: Aldine-Atherton.

FOX, J. (Ed.). (1987). *The essential Moreno: Writings on psychodrama, group method, and spontaneity.* New York: Springer.

GREENBERG, I. A. (1986). Psychodrama. In I. L. Kutash & A. Wolf (Eds.), *Psychotherapist's casebook* (pp. 392–412). San Francisco: Jossey-Bass.

HOEY, B. (1997). *Who calls the tune? A psychodramatic approach to child therapy.* London: Routledge.

HUG, E. (1997). Current trends in psychodrama: Eclectic and analytic dimensions. *Arts in Psychotherapy, 24,* 31–35.

MORENO, J. L. (1934). *Who shall survive? A new approach to the problem of human interrelations.* Washington, DC: Nervous and Mental Disease Publishing Co.

MORENO, J. L. (1947). *Theatre of spontaneity: An introduction to psychodrama.* Beacon, NY: Beacon House.

MORENO, Z. T. (1987). Psychodrama, role theory, and the concept of the social atom. In J. K. Zeig (Ed.), *The evolution of psychotherapy* (pp. 341–366). New York: Brunner/Mazel.

YABLONSKY, L. (1976). *Psychodrama: Resolving emotional problems through role-playing.* New York: Basic Books.

CREATIVE ARTS THERAPIES

Creative arts therapies include art, drama, dance movement, and music therapies, as they all use creative expression to bring about therapeutic change. Some individuals take advantage of the opportunity to express themselves nonverbally through the medium of music, art, movement, dance, or dramatic expression, which leads to increased self-esteem, more productive self-expression, and/or improved social interaction with others.

Creative arts therapies emphasize client use of the artistic medium rather than observation of artistic works. However, music therapists often use recordings in dealing with client affect and moods. The quality of the patient's production is of little importance compared with the meaning that patient and therapist can derive from the work and the ultimate helpfulness for the patient. In this regard, therapists rarely participate in creative expression with clients, so as not to inhibit the client, whose work is often artistically inferior to the therapist's.

In most cases, creative arts therapists work as part of a psychotherapeutic team, although increasingly they may work independently, doing psychotherapy as well as creative arts therapy. Traditionally, they have worked in hospitals and institutions for the mentally disabled, particularly with individuals whose verbal communications are limited. Their qualifications are a combination of knowledge and talent in their own area of artistic endeavor, including knowledge of techniques and forms of artistic production, as well as education in working psychotherapeutically with patient problems. Although certain theories of psychotherapy that emphasize enactment, such as Gestalt therapy, fit well with creative arts therapy, creative arts therapists have varied backgrounds, and they may combine any one or more of the therapies discussed in this book with their creative specialty. Because psychoanalysis was particularly influential in the 1930s to the 1950s, some creative arts therapists, especially art therapists (Simon, 1997), have been educated to take a psychoanalytic approach to their work.

The development of creative arts therapy has been rapid, taking place within the last 40 or 50 years. Each specialty has at least one association: American Art Therapy Association, Association for Dance and Movement Therapy, National Association for Drama Therapy, National Association for Music Therapy, and American Association of Music Therapists. Additionally, each specialty has at least one journal that publishes its contributions: *The Arts in Psychotherapy: An International Journal, The American Journal of Art Therapy, American Dance Therapy Journal, Theatre and Therapy,* and *The Journal of Music Therapy.* Several institutions throughout the world offer master's degree programs in several areas of the creative arts therapies. The variety of approaches to creative arts therapists are seen not only through their journals, but through collections of articles such as that of Bejjani (1993), which includes 144 papers dealing with medicine, psychotherapy, and creative arts therapies. Because these therapies are quite specialized and are usually an adjunct to other psychotherapies, only a brief overview can be given in this chapter.

Art Therapy

The broad purpose of art therapy is to help patients deal with emotional conflicts, become more aware of their feelings, and deal with both internal and external problems.

To reach these goals, art therapists, when appropriate, provide instruction in the use of a variety of art materials. Typically, materials are selected that fit the needs of the client and the issue being addressed. For example, pastels, crayons, or felt-tip pens might be used when patients are free associating or using art to express feelings. Other times, clay, paper, canvas, watercolors, or finger paints may be used, depending on the circumstance (Malchiodi, 1997: Simon, 1997). These materials aid in bringing about the expression of images that are in the human mind before individuals learn to verbally articulate their needs.

Art expression provides the opportunity to depict images that cannot be expressed verbally, to show spatial relationships (such as the patient to his father and mother), and to express oneself without worrying about what one is saying. Unlike verbal expression, art expression is more likely to give a feeling of being creative and to provide the opportunity to increase one's energy level while working physically to develop a product that is tangible. Furthermore, products of artistic creativity can be referred to in later days or weeks, unlike verbal expression, which fades quickly (Malchiodi, 1997). Suggestions for creative expression may come from the patient, therapist, or both. Therapists may suggest exercises such as drawing an image of oneself and then discuss how that image relates to the patient's view of herself. Other exercises might include drawing oneself as one would like to be, drawing one's family, or drawing particular family relationships. In their education and training, art therapists learn the application of a great variety of art media, as well as techniques to help clients express themselves.

As art therapy has developed, so have the variety of means for expression and the populations that therapists work with. With the development of technology has come the use of videotape recording, easy-to-use photographic equipment, computer graphics, and other methods that aid in creative expression (Wadeson, Durkin, & Perach, 1989). As art therapy has changed, some art therapists have combined music, movement, and psychodrama in their work (Wadeson et al., 1989). The types of problems and populations that art therapists work with have also expanded to include bereaved children, battered women, incest survivors, medical patients, prisoners, and war victims (Wadeson et al., 1989).

A brief example of how art therapy might be used can be seen in Wadeson's (1987) work with Craig, a young man hospitalized with a diagnosis of paranoid schizophrenia. Appearing threatening and dangerous to the staff, Craig was able to make gains by expressing secret desires through his love for drawing, and was able to reduce his sense of isolation through his creative expression and discussion with the art therapist. In describing a drawing, Figure 14.1, that was done on notebook paper with pencil and blue ink, Craig said that the picture represented himself.

> The underneath part is "strong and grasping," the sphere is "selfless" and represents his "mind." He explained that the roots are holding the sphere and that basically the underneath shows "control" of the body over the mind. "In order for the mind to exist, the body controls or comforts it," he said. (Wadeson, 1987, p. 309)

In discussing the relevance of Craig's artwork, Wadeson believed that his art expression provided an opportunity to build a bridge from his fear that people would take his secrets away to interaction with others. Through Wadeson's interest in Craig's imagery,

FIGURE 14.1 Craig's drawing

From "An Eclectic Approach to Art Therapy," by H. Wadeson, in *Approaches to Art Therapy: Theory and Technique*, edited by J. A. Rubin. Copyright (c) 1987 by Brunner/Mazel, Inc. Reprinted with permission from the publisher and the author.

he was able to build trust and to describe his strange inner world to someone that he felt understood him. This small example helps show one of many different ways that art therapists may work with patients to help them explore their inner world, to increase communication with others, and to cope more effectively with a variety of problems.

Dance Movement Therapy

The goals of dance movement therapy are to help individuals grow and interrelate psychological and physiological processes by using movement or dance as a means. Individuals can come to understand their own feelings, images, and memories, as well as those of others, by expressing themselves through movement or dance. Although dance movement therapy has its origins in the application of structured dances to individual expression, dance movement therapists rarely teach dances but tend to encourage expression through movement exercises, often making use of music.

Approaches to patients are creative and spontaneous, as dance movement therapists attend to the moods and physical positions of their clients. Implicit in the work of dance therapists is their acknowledgement of the impact that body and mind have on each other as seen in physiological tension, body image, and ordinary movement (Stark, 1982). Dance movement therapy allows clients to experience both emotional and physiological feelings simultaneously, which can lead to a better understanding of self. In groups, reaching toward another person, stretching to touch that person, or holding or being held by group members can help interpersonal relationships, as can the awareness of feelings that are expressed in the bodily movements of others.

Techniques of dance movement therapy are very varied, depending on the nature of the individual or group that the dance movement therapist is working with. One technique is that of exaggeration, in which clients are encouraged to exaggerate a movement, such as a shrug of the shoulder. The client can then be asked to communicate the feeling verbally or to continue moving. Sometimes therapists may find it helpful to copy the actions of a group member to empathically understand what the group member may be experiencing physiologically and affectively. However, this must be done in a way that does not appear to mimic or make fun of the client. Another approach is to translate a client issue into an action. For example, the client wishing to separate from his mother may gradually step backward from the therapist, moving toward the other end of the room, and possibly sharing the experience as he does so. Using rhythm and energy to discharge tension can be very helpful for some clients as they can experience a simultaneous physiological and emotional release (Stark, 1982). A vast variety of approaches can be used with clients ranging from professional dancers to autistic children to those with neurological disabilities. A special issue of Arts in Psychotherapy (1997, Vol. 24, No. 2) has been devoted to multiculturalism in the arts, and several applications to groups such as African Americans are given for dance movement therapy.

An application of dance movement therapy to seven male adults in a therapeutic community shows how creative approaches to movement can help individuals who are resistant and suffering from severe psychological disorders.

It seemed like a sign of growing trust when participants started to express more of the anger stored within. They found ways of venting their frustration in punch-like clapping and stomping movements and sometimes even shouting. An evocative image that emerged was Mike Tyson the boxer. When Jeremy complained of obsessive thoughts, which prevented him from stopping talking, I asked him to translate them into movements. His response was a crescendo of fists, shaking violently, and kicking movements. So he found ways of physical outlet for his nervous mental energy and was eventually able to contact some of the depression which was underneath his anger. Then he could even allow the group to hold him in the middle of the circle and rock him soothingly. (Steiner, 1992, pp. 158–159)[6]

And another exercise:

For what seemed a long time we stayed with small repetitive movements, patting the body, clapping hands, then I introduced my circular band, made of old ties strung together. Everyone held it in one hand and we made some round movements with it. Asked what we were doing, Nigel said "stirring" and Jeremy added "in a cauldron." Encouraged to add ingredients, Nigel put in his sorrow, Jeremy his mother, then me because I had annoyed him by changing "his" music, David added his confrontation, and Billy his anxiety. Thus the group had created a container for the difficult feelings each person experienced. (p. 160)

These brief excerpts suggest how dance movement therapists, using their creativity, can work with individuals to help them integrate psychological and physical processes. Not only do the patients express themselves but they also communicate through bodily energy, rhythm, and touch.

Dramatherapy

The most recently developed of the creative arts therapies, dramatherapy can take many forms. As defined by Jennings (1992), "Dramatherapy is a means of bringing about change in individuals and groups through direct experience of theatre art" (p. 5). For some dramatherapists, psychodrama is a form of dramatherapy. The range of dramatherapeutic approaches runs from Shakespeare to the use of puppets and masks. Jennings (1992) gives an example of how a drama therapist can use lines from Shakespeare's King Lear's relationship with his daughters to explore with middle-aged women their relationships with their aging fathers. In long-term treatment of personality disorders dramatherapy can be an integral part of therapy (Appolinari, 1996). Having wide application, James (1996) gives an example of a man in his early twenties with limited intellectual functioning who felt "the odds are stacked against me" (pp. 30, 31). Jennings became "the odds" and the young man pushed against him. Later, he said that this exercise increased his confidence in his abilities. Although rare, there can be times that it can be helpful to have an audience, such as when a group of patients who were receiving antipsychotic medications acted out Dickens's A Christmas Carol (Andersen-Warren, 1996). Applications of dramatherapy reflect knowledge of and expertise in the theater along with a knowledge of theories of psychotherapy (Jennings, 1987).

In the practice of dramatherapy, both dramatherapists and their clients can take a dramatic role or the traditional client-therapist roles. In the application of drama therapy, the therapist can direct therapy, observe it, lead a group in imagery exercises, and experience a creative exercise, such as a pretend journey, with a group (Johnson, 1992). Dramatherapists may improvise a play, use puppets, or use a sandtray (a tray with different toy figures, toy buildings, trees, and so forth). Because they may play many different roles (including that of psychotherapist) with a client and possibly touch the client, transference and countertransference issues can develop more quickly than they might in other forms of therapy (Johnson, 1992). Although this can be true when working with groups, it is accentuated when working individually with clients.

In individual dramatherapy, Landy (1992) suggests that dramatherapists must attend to the boundaries between client and therapist and to whether clients put too much distance between themselves and the dramatherapist, or not enough. If the client is underdistanced, the therapist needs to have some distance from the client; if the client is too distant from the therapist, the therapist needs to bridge that gap. Landy gives an example of how the therapist might respond with an overdistant client using an elephant and mouse enactment.

> For example, the client in the role of the mouse makes himself very small. His movements are tiny. His voice is barely audible. He avoids any contact with the therapist in-role of elephant. The therapist fills herself up with the role. As the mouse shrinks, she expands. The smaller he becomes, the larger the therapist becomes. She trumpets, flailing her trunk; she swaggers around the room, knocking things off the table, threatening to crush the mouse under her big, round, wrinkled foot. In her fullness being most threatening, challenging, clumsy, provocative, the therapist/elephant acts at being under-distanced. (Landy, 1992, p. 101)[7]

Aware of her role, the therapist may wish to project the image of a large clumsy authority figure to provoke a response from the client. In this role, the therapist is an actor, ready to suggest that the client change roles with her and play the elephant while she plays the mouse. If the client has difficulty playing the mouse, it is the dramatherapist's role to help the client play the mouse. If appropriate, she may play a clever mouse, who can trick the elephant as in a fable, or may encourage the client to play that role. The therapist goes beyond role playing, using acting and directing skills to assist the client in becoming more aware of emotions, developing interpersonal skills, and dealing with a variety of psychological problems.

Music Therapy

Like other creative arts therapies, music therapy can be applied in a myriad of ways. According to Michel (1985), music therapists make use of music both as a basic stimulus and for its social applications. Just as retail stores use background music to make the mood of customers more conducive to buying, music therapists may use rhythmic music to stimulate patients or soothing music to calm them down. The social function of music is seen through choir singing, patriotic songs, and dance music. Music therapists may use music to encourage social behavior, such as special songs to teach mentally disabled individuals toothbrushing, bed making, or personal grooming (Michel, 1985). Although music therapy is used for individuals with diverse problems such as drug abuse, it is used most frequently for individuals with severe disabilities, such as learning disabilities, schizophrenia, autism, speech and language disorders, visual disabilities, and Alzheimer's disease.

The theoretical approaches of music therapists can vary widely, from Michel's (1985) emphasis on behavioral evaluation and change to Austin's (1996) use of psychodynamic theory that sees music as a mediation between concerns and unconcious contents. One example of the creativity of music therapists is Rogers's (1993) work with sexually abused clients. Different musical instruments, particularly percussion instruments, can be assigned to represent different individuals in a child's life.

> Different instruments may be assigned differing roles for personas. A clear example is a child "B" who repeatedly used a large conga drum to symbolize his father, a small xylophone to represent his mother and a smaller handchime to represent himself. These instruments were then physically positioned to indicate the strength of the relationships between family members. In addition, the way the instruments were played had a clear symbolic meaning; "B" associated the large conga drum with his father and on one level perceived his father as being very dominating; "B" then played the conga very gently. A clear distinction between the visual and auditory perceptions of the conga was apparent (the contrast between size of the instrument and the way it was played). This contrast can be subsequently explored. (Rogers, 1993, p. 211)[8]

This exercise can be seen as a type of musical sculpture, with the physical distance between instruments a part of the sculpture. However, therapists may often improvise and encourage clients to spontaneously express themselves in an active way with a variety of instruments to disclose mood or feeling. Sometimes such exercises may be initiated by the client and other times by the music therapist.

In reviewing the current status of music therapy, Bonny (1997) describes new approaches that make use of technology, collaboration with other arts therapies, and a broad application to many different populations. Music therapy can be applied to visually impaired children to help reduce social isolation and to modify behavior associated with loss of sight (Gourgey, 1998). Working with violent, mentally disordered offenders, music can aid in the treatment of psychosis (Sloboda, 1997). For patients in cardiac and pulmonary rehabilitation programs, music therapy has been shown to reduce stress and help patients maintain a healthy lifestyle (Mandel, 1996). Music therapists make use of their knowledge of the physiological and psychological processes of individuals, as well as their knowledge of the aesthetic and physical properties of music.

Summary

The creative arts therapies, which include art, dance movement, drama, and music, use innovative therapeutic techniques to encourage the expressive qualities of their clients. Although often working with severely disturbed patients, creative arts therapists work with all populations, both individually and in groups. Increasingly there is a trend for creative arts therapists to combine modalities, such as art and dramatherapies. Some creative arts therapists work primarily in an adjunctive role with psychotherapists; others may combine psychotherapy with their creative modality.

References

ANDERSEN-WARREN, M. (1996). Therapeutic theatre. In S. Mitchell (Ed.), *Dramatherapy: Clinical studies* (pp. 108–135). London: Kingsley.

APPOLINARI, C. (1996). Dramatherapy and personality disorders: Echoes of abuse. In S. Mitchell (Ed.), *Dramatherapy: Clinical studies* (pp. 1–14). London: Kingsley.

AUSTIN, D. S. (1996). The role of improvised music in psychodynamic music therapy with adults. *Music Therapy, 14*, 29–43.

BEJJANI, F. J. (Ed.). (1993). *Current research in arts medicine.* Pennington, NJ: Cappella.

BONNY, L. L. (1997). The state of the art of music therapy. *Arts in Psychotherapy, 24*, 65–73.

GOURGEY, C. (1998). Music therapy in the treatment of social isolation in visually impaired children. *RE:view, 29*, 157–162.

JAMES, J. (1996). Dramatherapy with people with learning disabilities. In S. Mitchell (Ed.), *Dramatherapy: Clinical studies* (pp. 15–32). London: Kingsley.

JENNINGS, S. (1987). *Dramatherapy: Theory and practice for leaders and clinicians.* London: Routledge.

JENNINGS, S. (1992). "Reason and madness": Therapeutic journeys through King Lear. In S. Jennings (Ed.), *Dramatherapy: Theory and practice 2* (pp. 5–18). London: Routledge.

JOHNSON, D. R. (1992). The dramatherapist's in-role. In S. Jennings (Ed.), *Dramatherapy: Theory and practice 2* (pp. 112–136). London: Routledge.

LANDY, R. (1992). One on one: The role of the dramatherapist working with individuals. In S. Jennings (Ed.), *Dramatherapy: Theory and practice 2* (pp. 97–111). London: Routledge.

MALCHIODI, C. A. (1997). *Breaking the silence: Art therapy with children from violent homes* (2nd ed.). Briston, PA: Brunner/Mazel.

MANDEL, S. E. (1996). Music for wellness: Music therapy for stress management in a rehabilitation program. *Music Therapy Perspectives, 14*, 38–43.

MICHEL, P. E. (1985). *Music therapy* (2nd ed.). Springfield, IL: Charles C. Thomas.

ROGERS, P. (1993). Research in music therapy with sexually abused clients. In H. Payne (Ed.), *Handbook of inquiry in the arts therapies: One river, many currents* (pp. 197–217). London: Kingsley.

SIMON, R. M. (1997). *Symbolic images in art as therapy.* London: Routledge.

SLOBODA, A. (1997). Music therapy and psychotic violence. In E. V. Welldon & C. Van Velsen (Eds.), *A practical guide to forensic psychotherapy. Forensic focus, no. 3* (pp. 121–129). London: Routledge.

STARK, A. (1982). Dance-movement therapy. In L. E. Abt & I. R. Stuart (Eds.), *The newer therapies: A sourcebook* (pp. 308–326). New York: Van Nostrand.

STEINER, M. (1992). Alternatives in psychiatry: Dance movement therapy in the community. In H. Payne (Ed.), *Dance movement therapy: Theory and practice* (pp. 141–162). London: Routledge.

WADESON, H. (1987). An eclectic approach to art therapy. In J. A. Rubin (Ed.), *Approaches to art therapy: Theory and technique* (pp. 299–313). New York: Brunner/Mazel.

WADESON, H., DURKIN, J., & PERACH, D. (Eds.). (1989). *Advances in art therapy.* New York: Wiley.

SUMMARY

Five different therapeutic approaches have been discussed, with each having disparate views on how to produce therapeutic changes. Asian therapies emphasize reflection and contemplation, with some approaches suggesting the importance of responsibility and obligation to others. Body psychotherapies stress attending to posture, movement, and physique to assess psychological problems and then to make interventions that may be physical or psychological. Interpersonal therapy is a research-based approach to treating depression that uses treatment manuals to specify procedures. An established approach, psychodrama is active, is done in groups or in front of an audience, and features the enactment of personal problems. The creative arts therapies use music, artworks, movement, and dramatic expression to help clients express their feelings and become more aware of social interactions.

15

Comparison, Critique, and Integration

In this chapter, I compare theories across each of the areas that have been discussed in this book, which provides some background for a critique of the limitations and strengths of each theory. Then I discuss the contributions of three specific integrative approaches to psychotherapy.

To provide a comparison of theories, I have summarized the basic concepts of personality, goals, essential approaches to assessment, and the most common techniques applied by each theory. Also, I have selected two disorders—depression and anxiety—to compare the treatment indicated for the major theories discussed in this book. I also summarize and compare how each theory deals with brief psychotherapy, current trends that are emerging, how theories make use of other theories, research trends, gender and cultural issues as they affect theories differentially, and applications of theories to couples, families, and groups. The five separate theories discussed in Chapter 14 (Asian therapies, body psychotherapies, interpersonal psychotherapy, psychodrama, and creative arts therapies) are not included in this review.

Following this comparison, I describe what I consider to be the major limitations and strengths of each theory. These views are subjective and reflect opinions formed from contrasting various aspects of theories with each other. Approaches that integrate theories in a variety of different ways have become increasingly popular. For the transtheoretical, theoretical integration, and technical eclecticism integrative approaches, I have selected one example to discuss further. The transtheoretical view—taking concepts from many theories and developing a new or overriding theory—is illustrated by the approach of Prochaska and his colleagues. Theoretical integration consists of combining the concepts of personality and techniques of psychotherapy of two or more theories. It is illustrated by Wachtel's integration of psychoanalysis and behavior theory. Technical eclecticism starts with the personality concepts of one theory and combines techniques of many theories into a systematic method. Lazarus's multimodal approach, which is based on social learning theory, is discussed in sufficient detail to show how a variety of techniques (many described in this book) can be integrated into multimodal therapy. These three integrative approaches provide new ways of viewing psychotherapy. They build upon knowledge that comes from comparing and critiquing the theories described in this book.

COMPARISON OF THEORIES

To compare the various theories in this book, I contrast aspects that I think are important in understanding differences and similarities. Each theory has views of individual personality that influence the goals that theories have for therapy, their approach to assessing or conceptualizing client problems, and the techniques that are used. Comparison between theories can be made, in part, by examining how each approaches the treatment of different psychological disorders. Throughout this chapter, I have shown how each theory deals with the following issues: brief therapy, current trends and innovations, using the theory with other theories, research, gender issues, cultural issues, couples and families counseling, and group therapy. For each of these topics, I describe important directions or views of the various theories.

Basic Concepts of Personality

This section compares the basic concepts of major theories of psychotherapy by grouping theories into three overlapping areas: those that emphasize unconscious processes and/or early development, those dealing with current experience and/or issues related to living, and those dealing with changing actions and/or thoughts. The key concepts that are associated with each theory are listed for comparison purposes in Table 15.1.

Theories that deal with unconscious forces and/or early development are psychoanalysis, Jungian theory, and Adlerian theory. Concepts of conscious and unconscious forces, as well as the structure of personality (id, ego, and superego) are important to varying degrees to each of the four psychoanalytic views: Drive theory emphasizes psychosexual development, ego psychology focuses on defense mechanisms, and object relations theory uses concepts that concern the infant's relationship with the love object (mother). In self psychology, attention is paid to the importance of the development of narcissism in individuals. Whereas psychoanalytic theory focuses on different views of childhood development, Jungian theory is particularly concerned with the unconscious, more specifically, the collective unconscious. To understand Jungian theory, one must have a grasp of the importance of archetypes, a few of which are listed in Table 15.1. Although Adler believed in the importance of unconscious processes, he was particularly interested in individuals' beliefs, their contributions to society, and their interest in others.

Whereas psychoanalysis, Jungian analysis, and Adlerian therapy focus on past issues and development, existential, person-centered, and Gestalt therapy stress present interaction. Existential therapy is distinguished by its attention to issues important to being human: living, death, freedom, isolation, loving, meaning, and meaninglessness. Person-centered therapy is concerned with issues that develop or interfere with experiencing self-worth. Awareness of self and contact with self and others are concepts that are very much related to experiencing the present; they are the essence of Gestalt therapy.

TABLE 15.1

Concepts Basic to Theories of Personality

Psychoanalysis	Jungian Analysis	Adlerian Therapy
Unconscious	Conscious	Style of life
Conscious	Personal unconscious	Social interest
Structure of Personality	Collective unconscious	Inferiority and superiority
Id	Archetypes	Birth order
Ego	Persona	
Superego	Anima, animus	
Defense mechanisms	Shadow	
Drive theory	Self	
Psychosexual stages	Personality attitudes	
Ego Psychology	Introversion	
Defense mechanisms	Extraversion	
Adaptive functions	Personality functions	
Adult development	Thinking and feeling	
Object relations	Sensing and intuition	
Childhood relationship	Personality development	
with mother	Childhood	
Symbiosis	Adolescence	
Separation	Middle age	
Individuation	Old age	
Hatching		
Transitional object		
Good-enough mother		
True and false self		
Splitting		
Self psychology		
Narcissism		
Selfobject		
Grandiosity		
Idealized parent		

Existential Therapy	Person-Centered Therapy	Gestalt Therapy
Being-in-the-world	Development of the need	Figure and ground
Four ways of being	for positive regard	Contact with self and others
Umwelt	Conditionality	Contact boundaries
Mitwelt	Relationships and self-	Disturbances of contact
Eigenwelt	regard	boundaries
Überwelt	Fully functioning person	Introjection
Time and being		Projection
Living and dying		Retrofletion
Freedom, responsibility,		Deflection
and choice		Confluence
Isolation and loving		Awareness
Meaning and meaningless-		Unfinished business
ness		
Self-transcendence		
Striving for authenticity		

Continued

TABLE 15.1 *(Continued)*

Concepts Basic to Theories of Personality

Behavior Therapy	Rational Emotive Behavior Therapy	Cognitive Therapy

Classical and operant principles
  Positive reinforcement
  Extinction
  Generalization
  Discrimination
  Shaping
Observational learning principles
  Self-efficacy
  Attention and retention processes
  Motivational processes
  Motor reproduction processes
	Responsible hedonism
	Humanism
	Rationality
	Unconditional self-acceptance
	Irrational beliefs about
	  Competence and success
	  Love and approval
	  Being treated unfairly
	  Safety and comfort
	A-B-C theory of personality
	  A. Activating event
	  B. Belief
	  C. Consequence
	Disturbances about disturbances
		Automatic thoughts
		Cognitive schemas
		Cognitive distortions
		  Dichotomous thinking
		  Selective abstraction
		  Arbitrary inference
		  Catastrophizing
		  Overgeneralization
		  Labeling and mislabeling
		  Magnification or minimization
		  Personalization
		Cognitive triad
		Cognitive spiral

Reality Therapy	Feminist Therapy	Family Systems Therapy

Responsibility
Choice theory
Psychological needs
  Belonging
  Power
  Freedom
  Fun
Choosing
  Doing
  Thinking
  Feeling
Choosing "crazy" behavior for control
	Developmental gender differences
	Gender schema theory
	Gilligan's ethic of care
	Relational model
		Communication patterns
		Systems theory
		  Feedback
		  Homeostasis
		Bowen's intergenerational approach
		  Differentiation of self
		  Triangulation
		  Family projection process
		  Emotional cutoff
		  Multigenerational transmission process
		Minuchin's structural approach
		  Family structure
		  Boundary permeability
		  Alignments and coalitions
		Haley's strategic approach
		  Power in relationships
		  Communication
		  Symptom focus
		Narrative theory
		  Client stories
		  Narrative empathy

The behavioral and cognitive therapies are concerned with how people act, learn, and think. In particular, behavior therapists focus on classical and operant principles of behavior, as well as observational learning. In rational emotive behavior therapy (REBT), focus is on the irrational belief systems of individuals that create unhappiness for them. Cognitive therapy attends to thinking and distortions in thought processes that lead to ineffective ways of feeling, behaving, or thinking. Also focusing on doing, thinking, and feeling, reality therapy emphasizes the individual's role in being responsible for or taking control of her own behavior.

Whereas the theories that have just been described attend to psychological factors that affect personality development, feminist therapy examines sociological factors—specifically gender differences—as they relate to the development of individuals and their relationships with others. Also going beyond the individual, family systems theorists point out the importance of the relationship of members within a family to each other and how these relationships affect individual personality.

In general, each of these theories provides a distinct way of seeing the world that has an impact on its approach to therapy. However, there are several instances of overlap between theories, particularly cognitive, behavior, and REBT therapies, that integrate cognitive and behavioral principles. Sometimes different terms are used for similar concepts in very different theories. For example, Kernberg uses the term *splitting* to describe the tendency of individuals (particularly those with a borderline disorder) to see things as all good or all bad, whereas Beck uses the cognitive term *dichotomous thinking* to describe a similar process. For most theories, the concepts that are basic to the theories of personality are quite well developed, and only the most important are highlighted in Table 15.1.

Goals of Therapy

Following from basic concepts about human personality, goals of therapy for each theory are a reflection of those concepts that the theorists believe are important aims for clients and therapists. Table 15.2 summarizes, in very brief form, aspects of human experience that are seen as the focus of therapeutic change. In general, the emphasis on specificity and clearly defining change is more important for cognitive and behavior therapies than for others. Because therapeutic goals are all stated differently for each theory, comparisons of the goals of therapy are made somewhat difficult.

Assessment in Therapy

In essence, goals guide therapists as to where they are going; assessment helps them find markers to guide them in bringing about therapeutic change. Although some therapists may make use of personality inventories to learn more about the client, many put the most emphasis on initial interviews, as well as on the therapy sessions, as the assessment process continues throughout therapy. For theories that have cognitive and behavioral goals, the assessment techniques tend to be very specific, with client thoughts and behaviors clearly described. For cognitive therapy, diagnostic classification systems may help guide therapy, along with specific observations and reports. For other therapies such as Jungian, existential, person-centered, Gestalt, and family systems, therapeutic goals are not closely related to the DSM-IV classification system, and assessment

TABLE 15.2

Goals of Therapy

Psychoanalysis	Change in personality and character structure; resolve unconscious conflicts within self; reconstruct and reinterpret childhood experiences.
	Drive Theory—increase awareness of sexual and aggressive drives. *Ego Theory*—understand ego defenses and adapt to external world. *Object Relations*—explore and resolve separation and individuation issues. *Self Psychology*—resolve issues dealing with self-absorption or idealized parents.
Jungian Analysis	Individuation; integration of the conscious and unconscious leading to individuation.
Adlerian Therapy	Increase social interest, change self-defeating behaviors, solve problems.
Existential Therapy	Authenticity; find a meaning for existence and pursue it; fully experience existence.
Person-Centered Therapy	Become more self-directed, increase positive self-regard; the client chooses goals.
Gestalt Therapy	The person's feelings, perceptions, thoughts, and body are in harmony with each other; awareness leads to growth, responsibility, and maturity.
Behavior Therapy	Change specific target behaviors that are clearly and accurately defined.
Rational Emotive Behavior Therapy	Minimize emotional disturbances, decrease self-defeating behaviors, learn a philosophy that will reduce the chances of being disturbed by overwhelming irrational thoughts.
Cognitive Therapy	Remove biases or distortions in thinking to function more effectively and bring about more positive feelings, behavior, and thinking.
Reality Therapy	Help individuals take responsibility for and meet needs for belonging, power, freedom, and fun in satisfying ways.
Feminist Therapy	Should include changes in societal institutions as well as personal issues; also build self-esteem, improve interpersonal relationships, examine gender roles, and accept one's own body.
Family Systems Therapy	*Bowen*—reduce family stress level and help members become more differentiated. *Minuchin*—alter coalitions and alliances in the family to bring about changes. *Haley*—focus on specific goals; strategies planned to reach goals. *Solution-focused*—clear, specific goals; solve problems. *Narrative therapy*—see lives (stories) in positive ways rather than problem saturated.

methods are unique to each therapy. The brief summary of assessment approaches in Table 15.3 describes concepts, tests, and methods that provide a basis for making therapeutic change.

TABLE 15.3	
Assessment Approach	
Psychoanalysis	Family and social history, structured or unstructured Trial analysis Projective techniques—Rorschach, Thematic Apperception Test
Jungian Analysis	Examine archetypal material in dreams and fantasies Projective techniques Measures of attitude and function—Gray-Wheelwright, Myers-Briggs, Singer-Loomis
Adlerian Therapy	Analyze lifestyle, make observations about family dynamics, birth order, and examine early recollections. Assess assets. Questionnaires may be used in addition to interviews.
Existential Therapy	Listen for themes of isolation, meaninglessness, responsibility, and mortality. Also, assess ability to face life honestly. Dreams, objective tests, and projective tests may help.
Person-Centered Therapy	Assessment occurs as therapists empathically understand clients.
Gestalt Therapy	Therapists perceive and construct patterns from patient's words, bodily movements, feelings, and sensations, as they occur.
Behavior Therapy	Inquire about antecedents and consequences of behavior; use behavioral reports, ratings, observations, and physiological measurements; use experimental methods to assess progress.
Rational Emotive Behavior Therapy	Assess thoughts and behaviors using interviews and specific questionnaires; use A-B-C theory to identify problems.
Cognitive Therapy	Techniques include interviews with detailed questioning, self-monitoring, thought sampling, and scales and questionnaires about specific problems or attitudes.
Reality Therapy	Use interviews and self-evaluation questionnaires to find what clients "really want" and to assess needs for belonging, power, freedom, and fun. Also assess doing, thinking, feeling, and physiology.
Feminist Therapy	Caution against traditional psychological assessment; focus on including sociological factors such as violence, discrimination, and gender role.
Family Systems Therapy	In general, make observations about patterns of family interactions.

Therapeutic Techniques

Although the various theories have developed techniques growing out of their views of individuals' personalities, some of the techniques or methods overlap, and practitioners borrow from other theories. For example, most therapists in the course of their work with clients are likely to respond empathically (person-centered therapy) at some point in therapy (particularly during early stages or when clients present emotional issues). The less active techniques of free association and interpretation are usually associated with longer-term therapies such as psychoanalysis and Jungian analysis. More confrontive and direct techniques (confrontations, questions, and directions) are used in brief psychoanalysis and in cognitive, behavioral, REBT, Gestalt, and reality therapies. In psychoanalysis and Jungian analysis techniques emphasize bringing unconscious processes into conscious awareness. In Adlerian, cognitive, and REBT therapy, techniques focus more on cognitive than on behavioral or emotive processes. In behavior and reality therapy, attention is paid first to changing ways of doing, but also to beliefs and feelings. In Gestalt therapy, primary attention is to awareness of verbal and nonverbal processes, often bringing out emotional feelings, whereas person-centered therapists empathize with their client's experience. Although existential therapists may make use of techniques from any of the previous theories, they attend to issues that are of importance in being human. Feminist therapists may make use of a number of these methods but also examine the social context and factors outside the client that influence her problems. Family systems therapists may respond to individuals in a family using some of these approaches but most often are likely to examine the system first and make interventions that may have an impact on two or more members of a family. For convenience, the primary therapeutic techniques that are associated with each theory are listed in Table 15.4 so that further comparison can be made.

Differential Treatment

As has been mentioned previously, theories vary to the degree that they apply different techniques or methods to different disorders. To contrast theoretical approaches, it is more helpful to compare how different theories can be applied to the same disorder than it is to different ones. Table 15.5 gives examples, for most of the theories, as to how a theory can be applied to a particular disorder for a specific client. Because clients differ on so many variables (age, sex, family history, type of problem, temperament, and so forth), it is not possible to say "Use this technique for this disorder." In Table 15.5 a very brief description is given for very complex cases described in this book for the purpose of comparison for depression and anxiety. Returning to the original case in the appropriate chapter can provide much more information about how a particular theoretical orientation might be used to deal with a client.

Because of the particular interests of therapists, certain disorders have come to be associated with different theories. For example, much of Freud's early work was with female patients who presented symptoms of hysteria. Kohut's work with narcissistic clients has linked this disorder with self psychology. Perry (1987) has written extensively on the application of Jungian therapy to schizophrenia. Behavior therapy has been applied to treatment of phobias. Both feminist therapy and Gestalt therapy have been used with people who have experienced traumas due to violence (posttraumatic stress disorder).

TABLE 15.4

Therapeutic Techniques

Psychoanalysis	Jungian Analysis	Adlerian Therapy
Free association	Bring unconscious into	Immediacy
Neutrality and empathy	conscious awareness	Encouragement
Analyzing resistance	Interpretation of dreams,	Acting as if
Interpretation (dreams,	fantasies	Catching oneself
free association, etc.)	Active imagination	"The question"
Analysis of transference	Creative techniques: po-	Spitting in the client's soup
Countertransference	etry, art, sandplay	Avoiding the tar baby
Brief psychoanalysis	Transference	Push-button technique
Questions	Countertransference	Paradoxical intention
Restatements		Task setting and commitment
Confrontations		Homework
Interpretation (limited)		

Existential Therapy	Person-Centered-Therapy	Gestalt Therapy
Techniques are not gener-	Necessary and sufficient	Empathic responding
ally used; rather, con-	conditions for change	Enhancing awareness
ditions are present	Psychological contact	Awareness statements and
and issues are addressed	Psychological vulnerability	questions
Conditions	Congruence and genuine-	Emphasizing and enhancing
Therapeutic love	ness	awareness through
Resistance	Unconditional positive re-	Verbal behavior
Transference	gard or acceptance	Nonverbal behavior
Issues addressed	Empathy	Feelings
Living and dying	Perception of empathy and	Dialogue
Freedom, responsibility,	acceptance	Enactment
and choice		Dreams
Isolation and loving		Awareness of self and others
Meaning and meaning-		Awareness of avoidance
lessness		Taking risks
Frankl's logotherapy tech-		Creativity
niques		
Attitude modulation		
Dereflection		
Paradoxical intention		
Socratic dialogue		

Continued

Some disorders are quite common, and I have tried to give a number of different examples of how theorists approach these problems (alcoholism and drug abuse: existentialism, Gestalt, and cognitive therapy; obsessive-compulsive disorder: existential, cognitive, REBT, behavior, and reality therapy; borderline disorders: object relations, Jung, Adler, existential, person-centered and feminist; eating disorders: psychoanalysis, Adlerian therapy, reality therapy, and feminist therapy).

Examining how different theoretical approaches can be applied to a variety of disorders can increase understanding of the theoretical approach. Due to individual differences in clients, in therapists, and in lack of fit between psychological disorders and theories of psychotherapy prescribing a treatment plan or method for a specific disorder is rarely possible.

TABLE 15.4   *(Continued)*

Therapeutic Techniques

Behavior Therapy	Rational Emotive Behavior Therapy	Cognitive Therapy
Systematic desensitization	Disputing irrational beliefs using A-B-C-D-E model	Structured sessions
Imaginal flooding therapies		Guided discovery
In vivo techniques	Cognitive approaches	Specifying automatic thoughts
Modeling techniques	Coping self-statements	Homework
Live	Teaching others	Cognitive interventions
Symbolic	Problem solving	Understanding idiosyncratic meaning
Role playing	Emotive techniques	Challenging absolutes
Participant	Imagery	Reattribution
Covert	Role playing	Labeling of distortions
Cognitive behavioral techniques	Shame attacking	Decatastrophizing
Self-instructional training	Forceful self statements and dialogue	Challenging dichotomous thinking
Stress inoculation	Behavior methods	Listing advantages and disadvantages
Relaxation techniques	Activity homework	Cognitive rehearsal
Assertiveness	Reinforcement	
Exposure and response prevention	Skill training	
	Insight	

Reality Therapy	Feminist Therapy	Family Systems Therapy
Process	Gender role analysis and intervention	Family systems therapy
Friendly involvement	Power analysis and intervention	Bowen's intergenerational approach
Exploring total behavior	Assertiveness training	Genograms
Evaluating behavior	Bibliotherapy	Coaching
Making plans to do better	Reframing and relabeling	Detriangulation
Commitment to plans	Demystifying therapy	Minuchin's structural approach
Therapist attitudes		Family mapping
Don't accept excuses		Accommodating and joining
No punishment or criticism		Enactment
Don't give up		Changing boundaries
Strategies		Reframing
Questioning		Haley's strategic approach
Being positive		Straightforward tasks
Humor		Paradoxical tasks
Confrontation		Solution-focused
Paradoxical techniques		Miracle question
Metaphor		Exception finding
		Prior change questions
		Coping questions
		Scaling
		Narrative therapy
		Telling the story
		Externalizing the problem
		Unique outcomes
		Alternative narratives

TABLE 15.5

Theoretical Approaches Applied to Two Different Disorders

Chapter and Theory	Depression	Anxiety
2. Psychoanalysis		Mary, 3 years—deals with defense mechanisms and transference.
3. Jungian Analysis	Beth—dream material in a dream series reveals unconscious aspects of depression.	A young woman's dreams reveal that she is running from spiritual issues.
4. Adlerian Therapy	Sheri—early recollections provide insight into distorted perceptions.	Robert builds self-esteem through encouragement, avoids defeat, lessening anxiety.
5. Existential Therapy	Catherine accepts her dispiritedness by bringing detachment to her awareness.	Phillip deals with his death anxiety and develops intimacy and authenticity in his life.
6. Person-Centered Therapy	A female graduate student assumes more responsibility for self as a result of therapeutic empathic listening.	
7. Gestalt Therapy	Florence deals with a lack of energy through therapist's focus on current awareness.	A young man is continually brought to the present to deal with his issues.
8. Behavior Therapy	Jane, 29—behavior is assessed in detail and she learns self-, time-, and child management.	Laura, 20—anxious about grades and sorority sisters. Learns relaxation and coping strategies.
9. Rational Emotive Behavior Therapy	Penny, 14—develops new beliefs and becomes more assertive with brothers.	Ted experiences strong anxiety on a train; therapist disputes irrational beliefs.
10. Cognitive Therapy	Mrs. M. learns distraction and how to deal with negative thoughts; takes action to change behaviors.	Amy—negative thoughts are identified and modified through questions.
11. Reality Therapy	Physician—humor used to increase social behavior; adherence to RT model.	Randy, a college student, takes and maintains control over anxious feelings.
12. Feminist Therapy	Ann reframes and relabels messages from her family; gender analysis leads to more assertive behavior.	

Brief Psychotherapy

In the 1930s and 1940s, much of psychotherapy was psychoanalytically based treatment, which often lasted several years and required three to five sessions per week.

Because of the high cost and time investment from therapist and client, brief methods of psychotherapy have become more and more common. Additionally, many clinics and community services limit the number of sessions per client due to great demands on agency services. Likewise, health maintenance organizations and insurance companies often restrict the number of sessions that they will pay for. Because of these restraints on the length of therapy and because of the large number of practitioners of psychoanalytic therapy, much effort has been directed toward providing a short-term alternative to psychoanalysis that also is consistent with a psychoanalytic view of personality. In Chapter 2, Luborsky's Core Conflictual Relationship Theme method and Sifneos's anxiety-provoking approach requiring less than 20 sessions are explained. Often brief psychoanalytic therapy tends to limit goals, select patients carefully, focus on specific problems, and be more confrontive and directive than traditional psychoanalytic therapy.

Not all theories have been adapted to a brief or short-term model of psychotherapy. Jungian therapists may work for a year or two with patients and may occasionally stop therapy for a few years and then resume it later. Existential therapy is often used with other theories. When applied with a psychoanalytic perspective, it may be as lengthy as psychoanalytic therapy. However, Frankl's logotherapy is a briefer, more focused method as is that of the Strassers. Both person-centered and Gestalt therapy tend to rely on clients to determine the duration of therapy and do not normally use a brief psychotherapeutic method. In contrast, Adlerian therapists often see their clients, on average, for about 20 sessions, with most clients being seen for less than a year. When needed, they do work within a time limit, and prefer to do that rather than limit the goals that they address.

Behavior therapy, REBT, cognitive therapy, and reality therapy tend to be short-term treatments; however, a number of factors may determine length of therapy. For behavior therapists, therapy length can depend on the number of target behaviors addressed, the strength of anxiety, or the type of therapy used. For example, a gradual application of behavioral methods takes longer than does flooding. Likewise, imaginal procedures often require more sessions than in vivo exposure. For behavior, REBT, and cognitive therapy, length of treatment is shorter for phobias, anxiety, and moderate forms of depression than for borderline or obsessive-compulsive disorders. Other factors affecting treatment length are the range and number of problems and the client's willingness to do homework. Many of these comments also apply to reality therapy, in which treatment length varies greatly, with more sessions being needed in the beginning of therapy than toward the end. For feminist therapy, because it may be combined with any of the theories listed previously, treatment length varies widely.

Considerable attention has been paid to brief therapy in family systems therapy. Because it may be logistically difficult to get family members together, because some do not wish to attend therapy sessions, and because many family problems represent crises, there has been an effort on the part of several family systems theorists to develop brief methods. For example, the problem resolution and symptom relief methods described by the Mental Research Institute model, solution-focused, and narrative therapies usually require fewer than 10 meetings. The long brief therapy approach of the Milan Associates typically requires about 10 sessions at monthly intervals. Creative approaches such as these in both family systems therapy and other therapies are likely to continue as demands for cost-effective solutions with minimal delays are sought by patients, therapists, social agencies, health maintenance organizations, insurance companies, and governmental agencies.

Current Trends

Perhaps the most significant trend for the theories discussed in this book is movement toward integration. For example, some Jungian analysts and Gestalt therapists are making use of object relations and self psychology concepts to expand their developmental framework. Adlerian, behavior, REBT, and cognitive therapy already integrate cognitive and behavioral methods and continue to do so. Additionally, theories such as cognitive therapy look for methods from other theories, such as the experiential approach of Gestalt therapy, to expand their treatment methodology. Existential therapy, which has always relied on integration with other methods, continues to provide issues for therapists of all theoretical persuasions to consider.

A trend that is quite different from integration is the development of treatment manuals. Usually designed from one or two theoretical points of view, treatment manuals provide guidelines to therapists as to how to proceed in helping individuals with a specific problem, such as fear of blood. Treatment manuals are also effective for training graduate students as therapists as they provide guidelines about therapeutic procedures. As health maintenance organizations (HMOs) have desired proof of brief, effective therapy, treatment manuals have been useful in replicating a procedure and showing its effectiveness. When research proposals are made to funding agencies, treatment manuals are likely to be attractive because they indicate that the treatment is more likely to be uniformly administered than if a broad training program was undertaken. Those therapies that provide specific techniques for different problems, such as behavioral and cognitive therapies, are most likely to use manuals. Brief psychodynamic therapies such as Luborsky's Conflictual Relationship Theme method also make use of manuals. However, due to the complexity of human problems, treatment manuals often do not provide sufficient specificity for some disorders, especially personality disorders.

Postmodernism, a philosophical movement, that has been applied to psychotherapy has had influences on most theories of therapy. Constructivist ideas remind therapists of the importance of understanding and attending to the client's way of seeing their own lives and not imposing a theory in such a way that preconceived ideas about a client interfere with treatment (Neimeyer & Mahoney, 1995). In essence, therapists are recommended to take a step back to see if they are viewing clients' worlds the way their clients do.

The postmodern movement has also given theorists an opportunity to show how their theory is consistent with a constructivist point of view. The postmodern movement, which values the client's view of reality at least as much as the therapist's, is consistent with an approach that values both genders and all cultures equally. The modern as opposed to postmodern view is rarely defended by theorists, as it can sound like "I know more about my client than he does" or "My view of reality is superior to that of my client." Because of the postmodern influence, almost all theories described in this text have had advocates who describe the theory as flexible and consistent with the postmodern position. They show how they can be open to working with the way their clients construct reality.

Although these trends do not include all of the concerns that each group of practitioners is concerned with, they do represent major issues affecting the practice and theoretical development of various theories.

Using the Theory with Other Theories

As Garfield and Bergin (1994) have noted, there has been a marked trend since the 1950s toward eclecticism and integration of theories. As described later, theories have become increasingly integrative. Some practitioners who subscribe primarily to one theory may find theory A to be helpful, whereas another may find theory B to be useful. For example, one cognitive therapist may find the experiential techniques of Gestalt therapy to be helpful, whereas another may find Erikson's adult developmental model (ego psychology) to be helpful.

Although most therapies are becoming increasingly integrative by incorporating techniques from other theories, two discussed in this book are not moving in this direction. Those person-centered therapists who consider Rogers's six conditions to be necessary and sufficient would restrict their approach to empathy, acceptance, and genuineness. Reality therapists make use of a specific model in helping their clients develop control and responsibility in their lives. Although they may use some behavioral techniques, such as positive reinforcement, the structure of reality therapy may make it difficult to more fully integrate ideas from other therapists. In contrast, existential and feminist therapists must make use of other methods as these approaches do not have a sufficient core of techniques to allow complete reliance on the theory. Thus, there is considerable divergence in the way many theories are practiced.

Research

The approach of theories of psychotherapy toward research are extremely uneven. Relatively little outcome research has been done with theories other than cognitive, behavioral, and rational emotive behavior therapy. The approaches of these three theories to outcome research are discussed, along with research directions germane to specific theories discussed in this book. I then conclude with a few predictions about the future directions of research in psychotherapy.

Outcome research. In recent years, research on cognitive and behavioral therapies (including REBT) has been so abundant that meta-analyses have not only been applied to these therapies but also have been done within diagnostic categories, such as depression and general anxiety. Often research consists of comparing a behavioral technique and a cognitive technique, with both being clearly specified. In Chapter 8, examples of studies using behavior therapy with depression, obsessive-compulsive disorder, anxiety disorder, and phobia are given. Chapter 10 has examples and summaries of treatment findings for depression, general anxiety, and obsessive-compulsive disorders. Some outcome research has also been done on psychoanalytic treatment. However, this research is more difficult than research on cognitive and behavioral therapies because treatment is lengthy, concepts are difficult to define, there is a history of resistance to research, and consistency of application of therapeutic techniques is more difficult to ensure. As described in Chapter 2, a few notable studies have been done with relatively small groups of patients (often about 100 or less), with research efforts in these studies taking place over a period of 30 years or more. General research findings show that almost all therapeutic treatments showed greater improvements among treated groups than among control groups that received no treatment. Comparisons between treatment methods do not show clear patterns and present challenges to the design of studies to show useful differences.

Research procedures and concepts that have been studied by different theories vary widely. Table 15.6 is a synopsis of areas of research related to theorists of psychotherapy.

Future directions.   In their review of psychotherapy research, Bergin and Garfield (1994) see certain trends emerging in research investigations. They note that almost all attention is to studies of psychotherapy that are relatively brief (often 20 sessions or less). With regard to research methodology, they note increased attention to clinical significance (for example, percentage of patients improved) rather than to statistical significance. Also, most research has examined the positive effects of psychotherapy; Bergin and Garfield suggest that it is also important to examine negative effects of therapy. Validation of new and old measures of process and outcome are important in determining the effectiveness of therapeutic approaches. There appears to be an increasing trend toward studying the process of therapy focusing on specific techniques, client behaviors, therapist behaviors, and their interactions.

Gender Issues

For many years, the practice of psychotherapy and, particularly, psychoanalysis appeared to be influenced by the values of male psychotherapists. Chesler (1972) was an early critic of the practice of psychotherapy, claiming that it devalued aspects of women's roles. Although a number of theorists were concerned with gender issues before Chesler's writings, feminist therapists have had an impact on the attention given to gender and cultural issues as they affect the practice of therapy. Gender issues and how they are dealt with in therapy are summarized here.

Although Freud has been criticized for devaluing women and their role, such comments have not generally been applied to his contemporaries, Jung and Adler. In psychoanalysis, notions of castration anxiety and penis envy have been widely criticized, along with implications made from these concepts that women are lacking in qualities that men possess. Furthermore, object relations theory has been criticized because of its emphasis on the mother-child role and lack of attention to the father's responsibility in parenting. Although gender issues are an important current topic in Jungian

TABLE 15.6

Research Directions of Theories of Psychotherapy

Psychoanalysis	Major areas of research exploration have included defense mechanisms and infant-mother bonding. Considerably more outcome research has been done using brief psychodynamic therapies than using long-term psychoanalytic therapy or psychoanalysis.
Jungian Analysis	Most research efforts have examined Jung's attitudes and functions of personality. There have been some cross-cultural studies on archetypes.
Adlerian Therapy	Topics of research include birth order, social interest, early recollections, and lifestyles, with a few studies being done on therapeutic interventions.
Existential Therapy	Some researchers on existentialism have used a subjective or phenomenological approach in which the participant is asked to describe his experience as it relates to the topic of the study. Also, research on group therapy has been done, as well as research on existential issues such as death, anxiety, and responsibility.
Person-Centered Therapy	Carl Rogers's interest in research was partly responsible for a great deal of study on empathy, genuineness, and acceptance in the 1960s and 1970s. Newer research questions the measurement and definitions of these concepts. Some recent therapy research addresses the issue of who will benefit most from different kinds of therapeutic interventions.
Gestalt Therapy	Experimentation is a part of the therapeutic process of Gestalt therapy. Unfortunately, this approach does not lend itself to controlled research conditions. Some areas of controlled research include studies of specific therapeutic techniques such as the empty chair method and research into contact boundary disturbances.
Behavior Therapy	Researchers have carried out many outcome studies and have developed a variety of measures of therapeutic progress, symptoms, and related issues.
Rational Emotive Behavior Therapy	In addition to outcome research, issues relating to the important concept of irrational beliefs have been examined to provide more information about the definition and description of this topic.
Cognitive Therapy	Cognitive therapy researchers have studied concepts that define depression, as well as the treatment of depression itself. Additionally, the effectiveness of therapy with other disorders has been a topic of investigation.
Reality Therapy	Glasser has deemphasized the importance of research, more so than have most other theorists or practitioners of theories. Nevertheless, some research has been done with convicted offenders, high school students, drug abusers, and hospital patients.

TABLE 15.6 *(Continued)*

Research Directions of Theories of Psychotherapy

Feminist Therapy	There have been a few studies comparing feminist therapy to other approaches. Also, some researchers have examined the values and techniques that are important to feminist therapists.
Family Systems Therapy	Although there has been some research on the effectiveness of a variety of family systems approaches, it is relatively limited. New methodologies have been developed for constructivist and other approaches.

analysis, they are not new concepts. Animus and anima archetypes, which represent the opposite-sex aspects of an individual, were thoroughly addressed in Jungian therapy. Additionally, female analysts were prominent in the early development of Jungian therapy. For Adler, gender roles were important throughout his theoretical writings. An early advocate of women's rights, Adler saw how neurotic men used stereotypes of masculinity to mask their feelings of inferiority. Adlerians work to help clients deal with gender-role stereotypes.

For existential, person-centered, and Gestalt therapists, gender roles are often seen as they relate to important theoretical concepts. For existential therapists, major existential themes of living, responsibility, and meaningfulness affect all individuals, although they may affect males and females differently. When clients hold gender-stereotyped views of themselves or others, a blockage in developing authenticity exists. With regard to genuineness, acceptance, and empathy, Rogers saw these concepts as universally important and that therapists should be empathic to gender-related concerns, such as homosexuality. For Gestalt therapists, men and women may respond differently to awareness experiments, but empowerment to deal with problems generally results. Miriam Polster (1992) notes that empowerment and awareness need to be directed not only toward individuals but also toward making society more receptive to women's power.

Cognitive and behavior therapists (including REBT and reality therapy) generally use terms that are not related to gender. These therapies tend to emphasize client responsibility. For clients who are unable to make their own choices, such as severely learning-disabled individuals, behavior therapists are particularly careful in not introducing gender bias. Although rational emotive behavior therapists are aware that irrational beliefs differ for men and women, they attend to the irrational beliefs about gender roles in their therapeutic work and have described issues in their writings that affect women in society. Cognitive therapists are aware of the cognitive schemas or beliefs that individuals have about their gender roles, whether toward the place of women in society or toward homosexuality, and help their clients examine and challenge them. Reality therapists help their clients become more responsible: some men by developing more self-control and some women by not letting others take control of their lives. Each of these therapies approaches gender value issues from its own conceptual perspective.

Naturally, feminist therapy has had the greatest impact on gender issues in therapy. The techniques of gender role and power analysis and intervention specifically examine and attempt to change roles as experienced by the individual and society as a whole. More so than most therapies, feminist therapy has been concerned about gender roles as they affect homosexual clients.

Roles and relationships of males and females within the family have been an area of concern for family systems therapists. Influenced by feminist therapy, family systems therapists have examined power issues within the family structure and ways in which couples share family duties and responsibilities.

Because of the contribution of feminist therapy and the awareness of therapists about gender issues within each of the theories described in this section, beginning therapists are likely to be exposed to ways in which gender roles affect their own value systems and their practice of psychotherapy or counseling.

Multicultural Issues

To some extent, the infusion of cultural issues into theories of psychotherapy has depended on the interest of the theorists and their adherents. As theories have become more widely known, therapists have applied theoretical principles to their work with a variety of clients from different cultures and have written about this experience, informing their colleagues about the interaction between culture and therapy.

For Freud, Jung, and Adler, cultural issues have been prominent, but for very different reasons. Freud's late-19th-century Viennese background influenced his observations about psychological disorders and early childhood development. Erik Erikson's work with Native Americans helped to expand the influence of cultural values on theoretical views of developmental stages. In contrast to Freud, Jung took an active interest in different cultures, traveling widely throughout the world to learn about legends and folklore. Current Jungian analysts are required to have a wide knowledge of myths and folktales in order to understand the collective unconscious of their patients. For Adler, cultural issues are inherent in social interest as it is applied to one's family, neighborhood, and social group. Regarding the practice of psychoanalysis, a continuing issue is the expense of long-term psychotherapy and its availability to individuals who may not have sufficient wealth to afford it, including those from minority groups.

For existential, person-centered, and Gestalt therapy, cultural issues emerge in very different ways. Regarding existential therapy, there are similarities between Eastern thought and existential philosophy, which is based primarily on Western European ideas. The themes of living, responsibility, and meaningfulness tend to be universal, cutting across cultures. For Rogers, bringing his therapeutic approach to promote peace and ease conflict between peoples of different nations was an area that he devoted much attention to during the last 20 years of his life. His emphasis on genuineness, acceptance, and empathy as core conditions for change represent cultural values that many found congruent but that others questioned. In a very different way, cultural issues have emerged in Gestalt therapy. Because a focus on developing awareness can bring emotional relief that helps individuals deal with cultural injunctions, it can also create an experience that may be difficult to integrate with previously learned cultural values. Although existential, person-centered, and Gestalt therapy are related in the sense that existential thought has an impact on their theoretical practice, each theory addresses cultural issues differently.

In general, cognitive and behavioral therapies including REBT and reality therapy have tended to promote self-sufficiency and responsibility in individuals, which can conflict with cultural beliefs and values. However, recent writings in each of these theories have showed the application of the theory to people from a broad range of cultural groups.

In its emphasis on gender and power issues, feminist therapy attends to cultural factors that can affect clients' psychological functioning. Being aware of one's own attitudes and prejudices regarding people from other cultures is a significant aspect of feminist therapy. Techniques of power analysis and intervention lend themselves to application to people from many different cultures.

With regard to the practice of family therapy, a knowledge of cultural traditions and values is particularly helpful. Cultures vary as to child-raising practices, relationships with members of extended and immediate families, and traditions such as wakes and weddings. The behavior and attitudes of family members may be appropriate in some societies but inappropriate in other cultural circumstances.

Being aware of one's own values and biases regarding people of different cultures and having a knowledge of cultural values and customs and an understanding of how theoretical and cultural perspectives interact can help therapists practice their theoretical orientations effectively with clients from diverse cultural backgrounds.

Couples and Family Therapy

Although theories of psychotherapy differ in terms of how much attention is devoted to couples and family therapy as compared with individual therapy, all apply their theory to individual, couples, and family therapy. Relatively few Jungian and existential therapists do couples or family work, preferring individual therapy. Family systems therapy differs from most other couples and family therapy approaches in that the family is viewed as a unit and attention is paid to dysfunctions within the unit rather than to one individual's behavior. Naturally, there are times when family systems therapists attend to individuals and when non–family systems therapists examine the entire system. Table 15.7 describes some distinguishing features of the various theoretical approaches to couples and family therapy. Because relatively little distinction is made between the approach of couples and family therapy by most theorists, they will be combined in this discussion. Any differences in approach to couples and to families are noted.

More and more, therapists are doing all combinations of therapy: individual, couples, and family. As with individual therapy, integration is a growing trend, as therapists combine or make use of aspects of several family systems therapies along with ideas about individual, couples, and family therapy from other theories of psychotherapy.

Group Therapy

Just as approaches to individual therapy vary greatly, depending on theoretical orientation, so do approaches toward group therapy. Some therapies (Adlerian, behavior, REBT, cognitive, and reality therapy) tend to be structured, emphasizing the leader's role in educating and directing group members. Others (psychoanalytic, Jungian, existential, Gestalt, and feminist therapy) tend to be more open and unstructured. For some theoretical orientations (Gestalt, person-centered, and feminist therapy) group approaches are considered as important as individual and are sometimes preferable, whereas for Jungian therapy, group processes are seen as an adjunct to but not a substitute for individual therapy. Major features of each theory's contribution to group therapy are described in Table 15.8.

TABLE 15.7

Summary of Couples and Family Therapy

Psychoanalysis	Psychoanalytic couples therapy tends to focus on unresolved childhood conflicts as they affect the couple. In object relations, couples counseling focuses on shared holding or caring for the other member of the couple as it relates to being cared for as a child. In family therapy, internal conflicts that children are experiencing are examined as they relate to conflict in the family. From an object relations perspective, issues of attachment and separation from the parents are seen as important. Interpreting past behavior and resistance is often a part of the repertoire of psychoanalytic family therapists.
Jungian Analysis	In couples counseling, Jungian therapists may examine the correspondence between the personality types (attitudes and functions) of each member of the couple, or they may attend to archetypal imagery, focusing on the relationship of each member's persona, animus, anima, or other archetypes to those of the other member. Relatively little family therapy is done by Jungians; those who do this work may attend to archetypal patterns that emerge from family interactions.
Adlerian Therapy	More than most therapists, Adlerians take an educational point of view toward couples and family therapy. They may have public sessions to discuss particular issues or demonstrate family and couples therapy, with questions and input solicited from the audience. Their approach to family therapy emphasizes child training and improving family interactions.
Existential Therapy	In couples counseling, existential therapists tend to focus on individuals, looking outside oneself for a new perspective. An example of this approach is to have one partner observe a therapeutic session between the therapist and the other partner. Questioning previously unquestioned patterns of behavior is another method.
Person-Centered Therapy	Empathy is the central component for both couples and family therapy. Therapists may empathize with members of the couple or family, with the relationship, or with members who are not there.
Gestalt Therapy	Gestalt therapists prefer to work with those who are a significant part of an individual's problem, such as the marriage partner or family. There is an emphasis on promoting awareness of the other members, often focusing on sensations, listening, watching, or touching to achieve this awareness of boundaries so that appropriate separation and integration can be obtained.

TABLE 15.7 *(Continued)*	
Summary of Couples and Family Therapy	
Behavior Therapy	Contingency contracting for behavioral goals between members of a couple or between a child and parents is frequent in couples or family behavior therapy. For couples, training may include communications and problem-solving skills. Interventions are based on data gathered and collected by the couple. In behavioral family therapy, the therapist suggests techniques to increase or decrease specific behavior of the identified patient.
Rational Emotive Behavior Therapy	In both couples and family therapy, the focus is on the irrational beliefs of each member and how they interact and affect the irrational beliefs of others. Cognitive and behavioral homework is often used, and members may be asked to rate the behavior of each other.
Cognitive Therapy	Both couples and family therapy feature education as part of therapy. Usually anger and other disruptive emotions are dealt with first, and then distorted beliefs are assessed and challenged. Alternative ways of thinking are suggested, and clients are assigned homework.
Reality Therapy	In couples counseling, reality therapists observe two choice systems that interact and connect with each other. Attention is paid to shared wants and values, not just shared feelings. As with family therapy, suggestions are made to focus on doing things together after an assessment of wants and needs.
Feminist Therapy	In both couples counseling and family therapy, there is an emphasis on political and social factors, with a focus on gender-role behavior. Information may be given about gender role, language usage, and other related activities. Feminist therapy is often combined with family systems therapy or other couples or family therapies.
Family Systems Therapy	Principles that apply to family systems also apply to couples. The intergenerational focus is on how past behavior in one's family of origin can affect relationships in the family system and how members of the family tend to involve other members of the family in conflicts. The structural approach is concerned with boundaries within the family and how members can become too close or too distant, interfering with good family functioning. Strategic family therapy focuses on resolving symptoms through direct or indirect suggestions. Experiential approaches make use of the therapist's intuitive reactions to the family. Solution-focused and narrative therapies are concerned with their clients' views of their problems and finding solutions.

TABLE 15.8

Group Therapy Approaches

Psychoanalysis	Briefly, psychoanalytic group therapy often focuses on free association, dreams, and other material as it relates to underlying unconscious behavior and early childhood development. Drive and ego therapists are likely to focus on repressed and aggressive drives as they affect group members, as well as the use of ego defenses. For object relations therapists, issues of separation and individuation as they affect the psychological processes of group members and group interaction are a major focus. For self psychologists, attention is paid to how group members integrate self-concern with concern about others in the group. In general, psychoanalytic group therapists differ as to how much they interpret group processes and deal with transference and countertransference of members to the group leader and other group members.
Jungian Analysis	Used as an adjunct to individual analysis, Jungian groups may make frequent use of dream analysis and also use active imagination.
Adlerian Therapy	A variety of creative approaches to group therapy characterizes Adlerian work. Lifestyle groups help members analyze their lifestyles, which include family relationships, relationships with siblings, and early recollections. Group leaders summarize results of a brief lifestyle analysis, and they and group members make suggestions for change. Other Adlerian groups may combine lectures on social interests, lifestyle, and courage with exercises to promote change.
Existential Therapy	A variety of existential themes are incorporated, and members deal with questions about how meaningful their lives are, how they deal with freedom and responsibility, how they relate to others, and how they behave authentically. Group members relate to each of these issues and discuss how they affect different group members.
Person-Centered Therapy	Rogers believed strongly in the positive power of groups. For him, the leader's role was to facilitate the group, with the notion that the leader could work toward being a participant. In general, the group was unstructured, but the group leader attended to the need to have safety and growth within the group. Rogers devoted a major part of his later life to using groups to develop trust between social or political groups who opposed each other.
Gestalt Therapy	A frequent treatment of choice of Gestalt therapists, most Gestalt groups use a variety of exercises and experiments to develop awareness among group members. Encouraging open and direct contact between group members, group leaders set limits and work on issues such as family conflicts.

TABLE 15.8 *(Continued)*	
Group Therapy Approaches	
Behavior Therapy	Therapists often function as coaches, giving feedback, teaching, demonstrating, and modeling to individuals who share similar target behaviors. Common types of behavior therapy groups are social skills training, in which clients often role play events in their lives, and assertiveness training, in which individuals learn to discriminate among types of behavior and try out assertiveness skills.
Rational Emotive Behavior Therapy	Therapists function educationally, in a direct manner, showing clients how they blame and damn themselves for their behavior. Clients learn to apply REBT principles to their behavior. The therapist may suggest homework and enlist cooperation from members in helping each other with problems.
Cognitive Therapy	Assessing specific behaviors and cognitions is one of the functions of cognitive therapists. They work collaboratively with group members to suggest changes in behavior inside and outside therapy. Specific change strategies focus on cognitive and behavioral interventions. Some groups are targeted toward specific disorders, others toward specific techniques, such as problem-solving groups.
Reality Therapy	Often used as a follow-up to individual reality therapy, group therapy uses the same process of change applied in individual therapy. Principles of choice theory are followed by asking such questions as, What are you doing? What is working for you? What needs to be done to make things better? Therapists take an active approach in encouraging behavior change.
Feminist Therapy	Consciousness-raising groups were the impetus for the development of feminist therapy. A variety of groups focus now on issues such as homelessness, sexual abuse, battered women, and issues related to different ethnic groups. A major focus in feminist therapy groups are gender role issues, which may be dealt with through a variety of therapeutic approaches, including Gestalt, behavioral, and psychoanalytic theories.
Family Systems Therapy	There are two major types of group family therapy: multiple-family therapy and network therapy. Multiple-family groups consist of several families helping each other with problems; sometimes they may subdivide into groups, such as groups of fathers. Network therapy involves family members, extended family members, neighbors, and other members of the community who focus on problems affecting an individual or family. A powerful approach, this can involve between 20 and more than 80 members, with several therapists.

Continued

Group therapy has several features that individual therapy does not: input from peers, multiple feedback, efficient use of therapists' time, and observational learning. For these reasons, group therapy is likely to continue to be attractive to practitioners of most theories. Organizational problems do present themselves, especially for therapy groups that require a certain type of member, such as incest survivors, or those requiring specific membership, such as network therapy. Advertising or publicity may be used for such groups.

I have tried to summarize the most important aspects of the theories of personality, therapeutic techniques, and important applications of therapies. Not all significant features have been included. The focus to this point has been on describing differences between theories to show their special features. In a later section, I explain their commonalities and discuss integrative therapies. Before doing so, I describe what I believe are the strengths and weaknesses of each of the theories.

CRITIQUE

Basically, when theorists criticize other theories, they find fault with them for not being similar to their own theory. The more dissimilar the two theories, the more numerous and emphatic the criticisms. For example, behavior therapists could criticize psychoanalysis for overemphasizing biology and early childhood development, for not defining concepts clearly, for speculating about unobservable constructs such as the unconscious and ego, for not having testable concepts, for being incredibly inefficient in the frequency and duration of therapy to bring about change, and for having less effective treatment methods than behavior therapy. When criticizing cognitive therapy, behavior therapists have far fewer criticisms. Chiefly, they focus on the emphasis that cognitive therapists may give to unobservable thought processes, but they are less critical of their terms, the testability of procedures, and the effectiveness of therapy. When criticizing cognitive and behavior therapy, psychoanalysts are likely to see the therapies as somewhat similar, in that they are superficial and focus on surface manifestations of inner processes, pay little attention to past development, tend to ignore unconscious processes such as dreams and fantasies, and do not deal with the importance of parent-child relationships or with the development of individual personality. Any theory can be criticized by using the concepts of personality and psychotherapy of another theory as the basis for criticism.

The more dissimilar a critic's values are from those of the theorist's, the greater the chance that the theory will not be respected and not treated seriously. For example, values of faculty in academic departments of psychology *may* favor precise definition, quantitative research, brief therapeutic interventions, and observable behavior, values more compatible with cognitive, behavioral, and REBT therapies than other theories discussed in this book. By contrast, many practicing therapists *may* have values that stress relationships with clients, understanding many different personality constructs, the influence of the past on the present, and spiritual and unconscious processes, all of which are more compatible with therapies other than behavior, cognitive, and REBT theories. In the discussion that follows, I identify common major limitations and strengths of each theory, devoting a paragraph to each. In doing so, my comments are affected by my experience as a therapist and my personal values about human relationships, which I have described in Chapter 1.

Psychoanalysis

Many of the criticisms of psychoanalysis have just been mentioned. Additionally, psychoanalysis can be criticized because it reflects the experiences and values of theorists arising from their own life experiences and observations about patients, which the theorists try to apply to everyone. Just because Freud may have experienced Oedipal feelings and observed Oedipal feelings in his patients does not make it a universal concept. Likewise, Erikson experienced many identity crises in his life and observed them in many others; saying that this is an important construct for most people does not follow logically. Many of the psychoanalytic concepts, such as those just mentioned, are often difficult to define, and psychoanalytic writers may have different definitions in mind when describing a concept, such as the ego or transference neurosis. Some critics complain that psychoanalytic writers describe developmental concepts as if everyone has the same cultural experience without looking at the importance of social interactions in later life. A practical criticism of psychoanalysis is that the treatment is extremely time-consuming and costly. When psychoanalytic concepts are used in brief therapy, the therapists are limited in their goals and in the type of patients that they can work with, whereas behavior and cognitive therapists (including Adlerian, REBT, and reality therapists) do not operate with such restrictions.

The strengths of psychodynamic therapies are that they allow individuals to explore, in depth, their early childhood and past as they affect their current functioning, using a drive, ego, object relations, or self psychology model or a combination. Explanations have been developed to understand resistance, anxiety, and ego defense mechanisms that relate to the individual's psychological functioning. The development of ego, object relations, and self psychology provides a broad framework for understanding many psychological disorders. Additionally, brief therapies make psychoanalytic approaches more available to those who could not afford long-term psychotherapy or psychoanalysis.

Jungian Analysis

From an empirical point of view, Jung's theory is the least scientific of all the major theories described in this book. Other than concepts of attitudes and functions (for example, introversion-extraversion), his constructs are the most difficult to define, the least clear, and more like religion than like science. Jungian analysis is a long, slow process focusing on bringing unconscious processes into conscious awareness. Little research has been done on concepts such as the collective unconscious and archetypes, and there is no published research on the effectiveness of Jungian analysis. It can be argued that Jungian concepts are not useful or definable and that Jungians are more interested in relating their knowledge about folklore and myth to convoluted archetypes than they are to helping alleviate patients' problems.

A strength of Jungian analysis is its emphasis on the spiritual aspects of humanity, something not measurable by scientific experimentation. Jung's ideas help individuals look inside themselves and understand aspects of their personal and collective unconscious that were previously unavailable to them. Moreover, insight and creativity can develop in the process of Jungian psychotherapy. Furthermore, Jungian analysis provides a means of understanding the cultures of others, history, and religion that fosters intellectual development. Individuals wanting greater self-understanding and insight into their self-development rather than alleviation of specific symptoms are likely to find Jungian analysis instructive and helpful.

Adlerian Therapy

Criticisms of Adlerian therapy are that it does a variety of things but none of them in depth. In terms of looking at the past through early recollections and birth order, Adlerian theory is often viewed as simplistic and as fully examining neither conscious nor unconscious processes. Its concepts are difficult to test, and there is little research supporting the effectiveness of its psychotherapeutic approach. Regarding the practice of psychotherapy, too much emphasis may be given to individuals' perceptions of early recollections. Also, many unrelated techniques may be used to bring about change. Focus on the importance of social interest tends to ignore important aspects of individual development. Too much emphasis is placed on changing beliefs and not enough on changing behaviors.

The strength of Adlerian psychotherapy is its diversity. It takes into consideration the importance of familial and social factors and their impact on growth and development. It is a practical approach, goal oriented and emphasizing both social and psychological factors. Techniques are geared to change beliefs and behaviors, often within short amounts of time. More than most therapies, it has an educational emphasis that can be applied to individuals, couples, and families. Perhaps because it is a growth model that acknowledges perceptions of past development and incorporates many therapeutic strategies, it can be applied to a very broad range of client problems.

Existential Therapy

The major criticism of existential psychotherapy is that it is not a system of psychotherapy. Rather, it is a general framework of concepts or issues that some Western European philosophers have seen as being important. Although some of the themes may relate to individual anxieties and problems, not all do. There are no guidelines for therapists, and with the exception of a few unusual techniques offered by Frankl, there are no suggestions for methods for therapists to use. Many of the ideas are intellectual, and clients who are more practical or are not college educated may have difficulty with the philosophical nature of the concepts. Much of the focus in existential psychology is on the negative—death, meaninglessness, and anxiety. Existential psychotherapy offers few specific suggestions for dealing with these issues.

The strength of existential therapy is that it attends to concerns of being human. Other therapies tend to ignore why we are here, why we exist, and our responsibility to ourselves and others. Existential therapy encourages individuals to take a look outside themselves and find meaning in their lives by examining relationships with others as well as confronting major internal life issues. Throughout our lives, people confront many existential crises—marriage, divorce, responsibility for family, death of loved ones, and guilt over past behavior. Existential therapy provides new ways of viewing and understanding such problems.

Person-Centered Therapy

Rogers's view of psychotherapeutic change has been criticized as vague, naive, and limiting. Rogers ignores the unconscious, pays relatively little attention to past development, and follows the client wherever she leads. Empathy is seen as being the cure-all for problems; no consideration of behavioral or cognitive principles is given. Some critics believe that Rogers's view that core conditions are necessary and sufficient for change is simplistic and inaccurate, not reflecting current research. Another criticism is that the importance of the therapist is overvalued; there is more to therapeutic change than being empathically understood for an hour or two a week. Many other theorists believe that empathy is not enough for many clients; many require structure and direction for specific change. Because clients need direction and suggestions that are not provided by the person-centered therapist, other therapies should be used to supplement person-centered therapy.

Then again, Rogers has been widely acknowledged for his enormous contribution to psychotherapy by focusing on the client-therapist relationship and on the importance of acceptance, genuineness, and empathy from the therapist. Many therapists find that these concepts are clear and easy to grasp and that they promote client growth and understanding. Although more research is needed, much research has studied the validity of the concepts and shows them to be valuable. Person-centered therapy is particularly suited to work with couples, family, and group counseling, where the focus is on understanding each other. Many people can profit from the understanding of their experiences, feelings, attitudes, and values that emerges from an empathic relationship with a therapist.

Gestalt Therapy

Criticisms of Gestalt therapy have focused on its powerful emotional effect that can lead an individual to become vulnerable and confused. Also, Gestalt therapy, especially Perls's work, has been characterized as developing the individual while sacrificing or ignoring relationships with others. Although dealing with bodily processes, it does not go as far in integrating the mind and body as do body psychotherapies (Chapter 14). The concepts are rather vague and unsystematic. In the hands of therapists who have difficulty separating their own needs (for example, power or sex) from those of the client, Gestalt therapy has the potential of damaging clients by confusing clients' awareness of self with awareness of the therapist's needs.

When practiced by a competent therapist, Gestalt therapy can help individuals experience feelings and awareness rather than just talk about them. Experimentation in Gestalt therapy can develop self-understanding and willingness to apply this learning to relationships outside therapy. As a result, clients often become more creative and assertive in their work and in relationships. Although it should be used with caution with individuals who are suffering from severe disturbances (such as borderline disorders), Gestalt therapy can be particularly helpful for those people who are anxious or inhibited.

Behavior Therapy

Sometimes criticized as a piecemeal approach, behavior therapy draws from classical and operant conditioning, as well as social learning theory. Attempts to develop an all-encompassing theory of behavior that can be adapted to psychotherapy have failed. Although criticisms that behavior therapy ignores feelings and manipulates its patients no longer apply, behavior therapy can still be criticized for focusing too much on target behaviors and not sufficiently on the whole person or on developmental factors. Changing symptoms may not bring about significant or meaningful change. Furthermore, behavior therapy is seen as focusing too much on changing an individual's behavior; it does not attend sufficiently to a variety of environmental and social conditions. Important existential and social constraints on behavior tend to be ignored.

Behavior therapists have produced a large quantity of research that attests to the effectiveness of their techniques. This research has supported the development of rating and observational techniques, as well as specific therapeutic interventions for many problems. The therapist and client work together, using the therapist's knowledge of techniques to bring about change in a variety of behaviors, including depression, phobia, and sexual disorders. Behavior therapy, often combined with cognitive therapy, is particularly well suited for problems in which a specific target behavior can be identified.

Rational Emotive Behavior Therapy

Criticisms of REBT are both theoretical and practical. Ellis's theory can be seen as a collection of cognitive and behavioral techniques, along with a predilection for convincing clients that their beliefs are wrong. Rather than a coherent theory, REBT tries to convince clients to think more rationally and, if that does not work, tries some other behavioral or cognitive approaches. Unlike cognitive therapies, REBT does not apply different techniques for different disorders. Disputing irrational beliefs, done with all types of problems, can be seen as a way of browbeating clients into changing beliefs, even when they are not convinced to do so. Because REBT focuses so much on cognitive strategies, it tends to ignore behavioral and affective ones.

Ellis pioneered the use of cognitive techniques to bring about therapeutic change in a few sessions or months rather than a few years. His approach is comprehensive and makes use of many different strategies and techniques, but it also helps individuals change irrational beliefs so that future crises and problems can be avoided. The approach is active, featuring homework and role playing as well as record keeping. Ellis's own writings have helped to relieve guilt about sexuality and encouraged individuals to help themselves by no longer blaming themselves. Patients with disorders in which irrational beliefs are an important component, such as anxiety, depression, and phobias, can find REBT to be helpful.

Cognitive Therapy

Like REBT, Beck's cognitive therapy can be criticized as being simplistic and mere common sense. Rather than straightforward, Beck's concepts of automatic thoughts and cognitive schemas may not be easy for clients to grasp, as they are constructs rather than observable behaviors. Although cognitive therapists say that they do attend to clients' feelings, their emphasis on cognitive distortions can be seen as blaming the client and not being empathic with his distress. There is an overemphasis on the client's responsibility for problems and not enough attention to social forces such as violence that cause problems. Convincing clients that their thinking is distorted, even when added to behavioral and affective approaches, is insufficient to deal with complex client problems.

More than any other theoretical approach, Beck and his colleagues have carefully studied specific cognitive techniques to be used for different psychological disorders. In particular, much work has been done to study effective approaches to depression and anxiety. Cognitive therapists take a collaborative approach with clients, working with them to bring about changes in thoughts, feelings, and behaviors. By incorporating behavioral, affective, and experiential strategies in a structured manner to bring about specific changes, cognitive therapy represents a broad approach.

Reality Therapy

Glasser's reality therapy has been criticized for being superficial and simplistic. It is a process that clients must accept. Childhood development, transference, dreams, and unconscious processes are ignored. An artificial mechanistic model, using a car as an analogy, oversimplifies very complex human behavior. Existential issues and deep emotions get short shrift in this problem-solving approach. Guidelines are quite simplistic, whereas the actual practice of reality therapy requires many hours of training to deal with clients' resistance to controlling their own behavior.

Unlike many other therapies, reality therapy can be used with people who are resistant to change. It may be particularly effective for hard-to-reach groups such as delinquents, prisoners, and substance abusers. In its emphasis on taking control of one's own behavior and on the positive results that come with acting in accordance with reality principles, reality therapy can be attractive to many clients. Although the approach is not as easy to use as would first appear, with practice it can be used effectively with clients that other therapists might feel are not motivated to change.

Feminist Therapy

Because feminist therapy focuses so much on political and social change, individual responsibility can be ignored. Rather than having any coherent theory, feminist therapy is a conglomeration of diverse ideas about gender development and issues related to treatment of women. Although feminist therapists claim not to be "male-bashers," elements of this tendency can be found in their writings. The question arises, Do feminist therapists treat women as more equal than men? Another criticism of feminist therapy is that it is not a therapy but a collection of suggestions about how to infuse feminist ideas into other theories, as feminist therapy does not have sufficient techniques to stand alone.

The strengths of feminist therapy are that it has examined sociological factors and gender (and ethnicity) and pointed out how changes can be made in the practice of psychotherapy to provide more effective therapy for both men and women. Already, feminist therapy has helped therapists of all theoretical orientations to be aware of their own attitudes regarding gender, as well as those of their clients. The political thrust of feminist therapy challenges therapists to work on changing political and social conditions that have contributed to the problems of individuals. Whether a therapist is a feminist therapist or informed by feminist therapy, these practitioners can help their clients by examining both psychological dysfunction and its environmental context.

Family Systems Therapy

The most frequent criticism of family systems therapy is that it tends to ignore individual dysfunction and focus on interactions between family members. Rather than concentrate on a person's problem (schizophrenia, for example), family systems therapists look at the family's responsibility for the problem. Although Bowen and psychoanalytic approaches do look at the history of the family, structural, strategic, and experiential theories tend to examine present functioning and ignore family development. Many family systems therapies, especially structural and strategic, may manipulate the family without their knowing it by using paradoxical interventions. Such cases provide a one-down relationship in which clients are unaware of what is being done to them and insight is not valued. Feminist therapy has criticized family systems therapy for not recognizing the wider social context that contributes to role expectations within families. Sometimes family therapists seem more enthralled with new creative approaches to dealing with families than they are with finding a cohesive method of family interventions.

An important contribution of family systems therapy is to recognize that individual problems do not exist in a vacuum and that family members contribute to each other's functioning. By bringing the entire family into treatment, alliances between family members, as well as styles of relating, can be observed. The therapist then is able to help family members help each other resolve problems rather than to blame or focus on the "identified patient." Over the last 25 or more years, there has been a trend not only to integrate various family systems therapies but also to integrate individual therapy into family therapy. The importance of treating families can be seen by the fact that not only are there several approaches to family systems theory but also each theory, except for Jungian analysis, treats family problems.

In characterizing the limitations and strengths of various therapies, a few observations can be made. Evaluations of therapies are subjective, based on the evaluator's values, attitudes, and experience as a therapist, client, or researcher. Clients vary greatly in their cultural background, age, family history, psychological disorder, gender, and many other factors. A therapy that may fit one client may be inappropriate for another. Although most therapies (other than Adlerian, behavioral, cognitive, and psychoanalytic) tend not to have differential treatment for different diagnostic disorders, they recognize psychological dysfunction and bring their perspective on therapy to the problem. By critiquing the limitations and strengths of various therapies, therapists are better able to decide which approaches they want to use or to integrate into their own framework.

THERAPEUTIC INTEGRATION

As shown previously, many practitioners of theoretical points of view are integrating other theoretical perspectives into their work. This can be seen in the relatively recent establishment of three journals: *Integrative Psychiatry, Journal of Integrative and Eclectic Psychotherapy, and Journal of Psychotherapy Integration.* Additionally, two handbooks (Norcross & Goldfried, 1992; Stricker & Gold, 1993) have described a great variety of approaches to integrating concepts and techniques from varied theoretical perspectives. This interest in therapeutic integration is supported by a poll of 75 experts (Norcross, Alford, & DeMichele, 1992) who see an increasing development of theories and techniques, along with a need to integrate emerging and traditional approaches. Consistent with this integrative movement is the notion of "prescriptionism" —suggesting a specific treatment, depending on the disorder and the characteristics of the patient (Norcross, 1991).

In this chapter, I summarize three approaches to integration: transtheoretical, theoretical integration, and technical eclecticism. The transtheoretical approach examines many theories, selecting concepts, techniques, and other factors that effective psychotherapeutic approaches have in common. Theoretical integration combines personality theory concepts and techniques of two or more theories. In technical eclecticism, one theoretical view of personality is selected and influences the use of many treatment techniques, which have been drawn from many theoretical orientations. Before examining the three different approaches to therapeutic integration, commonalities among theories of therapy should be discussed. Up to this point, I have focused on the differences between theories; now it is appropriate to address writings that seek to incorporate aspects of theoretical concepts and techniques that most theories, if not all, have in common. In this section, I draw on Grencavage and Norcross's (1990) review of articles that describe factors common to psychotherapy. The six most commonly agreed-on factors follow.

1. The relationship between client and therapist is important for progress. This factor has received much attention since Fiedler's (1950) early work on this topic. Of particular importance is the patient's perception of the relationship (Orlinsky & Howard, 1986).

2. There is an opportunity for clients to express themselves emotionally, experience catharsis, and discuss problems.

3. Clients learn new behaviors and often have the opportunity to practice these behaviors.

4. Patients expect that therapy will be able to improve their situation and that the therapist will do something to help them.

5. Therapists have qualities that show clients that there is hope for their problem and that the therapist can provide help.

6. Therapists are able to explain client problems and how they will help clients resolve their concerns.

Most of these observations about common factors are based on concepts that therapists think are important, rather than based on research into the therapeutic process. When research on evaluating the reasons why some therapists are more effective than others is done, results are somewhat different. Blatt, Sanislow, Zuroff, & Pilkonis (1996) list several different factors found in their study and others. Few consistent findings cut across studies. Some studies find that more effective therapists are better able to establish a therapeutic relationship, are more psychologically healthy, are more psychologically minded, and have a background in short-term therapy, while other studies do not report these results. All of these factors are very broad and do not give therapists concrete suggestions as to how they should proceed. Transtheoretical approaches to integration, discussed next, are more specific in outlining concepts of change and therapeutic techniques.

Transtheoretical Approach

Despite several other intriguing approaches (Andrews, 1991; Orlinsky & Howard, 1987), I am summarizing the transtheoretical model described by Prochaska and Norcross (1999) because it has been the subject of more research investigations than other similar models. The developers of the transtheoretical model wanted an approach that would transcend or go beyond specific theoretical constructs and would encourage therapists to innovate new techniques by drawing the most effective ones from other therapies. Theirs is a change model, based on client readiness for change, type of problem that needs changing, and processes for techniques to bring about change.

Client's readiness for change has been addressed somewhat by Rogers (Chapter 6) but not by most other theories described in this book. Prochaska and Norcross (1999) describe five levels of readiness for change: precontemplation, contemplation, preparation, action, and maintenance. In precontemplation, the client may have thoughts about changing but is not willing to do so. In contemplation, the client is seriously considering change, but not committed. In preparation, the client intends to change and shows some behavioral changes. In action, the commitment is clear, with the client showing consistent change over a period of time. During the final stage, maintenance, the client works to continue change and to prevent relapse. These five stages would seem to be particularly appropriate to describe levels of commitment to stop smoking, a frequent application of the transtheoretical model for Prochaska and his colleagues (for example, Prochaska & DiClemente, 1992).

These levels of change can be applied to five different types of problems: symptoms; maladaptive thoughts; and interpersonal, family, and intrapersonal conflicts. Symptom problems might include a phobia of snakes. Maladaptive thoughts are negative beliefs such as "I am a terrible person." Interpersonal conflicts include not getting along with individuals in one's life, such as colleagues at work. Family conflicts are often more complex because the relationships are more intimate. Intrapersonal conflicts are indecision and disagreements within oneself and may include intense anger or narcissism. These levels of change are not independent, and clients may experience problems at several levels at any time. Generally, transtheoretical therapists prefer to start dealing with symptoms or maladaptive cognitions and later deal with interpersonal, family, and intrapersonal conflicts. In general, behavioral therapies lend themselves to symptom change; cognitive therapies to maladaptive thoughts; systems therapy to family problems; and Gestalt, psychoanalytic, and existential therapy to interpersonal or intrapersonal conflicts (Prochaska & Norcross, 1999).

In describing 10 processes that bring about change, Prochaska and Norcross draw from all major theories described in this book. There are 10 processes of change (consciousness raising, catharsis/dramatic relief, self-reevaluation, environmental reevaluation, self-liberation, social liberation, counterconditioning, stimulus control, contingency management, and helping relationships) that cover almost all aspects of possible change and draw on different theories of therapy. For example, consciousness raising is a process that all therapies contribute to. In contrast, stimulus control is a process that is drawn from behavior therapy, and dramatic relief, an aspect of catharsis, is taken from Gestalt therapy. Approaches to the therapeutic relationship come mainly from the noncognitive and nonbehavioral therapies.

Prochaska and Norcross discuss how different processes of change can be applied, depending on the patient's level of readiness for change and the level of the problem. For example, consciousness raising and dramatic relief may be most appropriate when clients are in the precontemplation or contemplation stage, but counterconditioning and stimulus control may be more appropriate for the action or maintenance stages. By using this multilevel transtheoretical approach, Prochaska and Norcross wish to integrate contributions from many theories and apply them to clients whose problems can be described differentially by their model.

Theoretical Integration

By combining the theories of personality and the theories of psychotherapy of two or more therapies, a systematic theoretical integration can be developed. Although many therapists do this informally, a number of writers (Stricker & Gold, 1993) have described methods of integrating traditional approaches such as cognitive and Gestalt therapy (Reeve, Inck, & Safran, 1993) and nontraditional approaches such as psychoanalysis and Buddhism (Rubin, 1993). As Prochaska and Norcross (1999) show, there are a wide variety of combinations of theoretical integration. For example, psychoanalytic-behavioral integration was popular in the 1970s, and cognitive therapy in combination with behavioral, humanistic, or psychoanalytic therapies was common in the 1980s. Their conclusions, shown in Table 15.9, are based on asking integrative psychotherapists to label their own style (Garfield & Kurtz, 1977; Norcross & Prochaska, 1988). This research examined only pairs of integrated therapies; it is likely that some therapists combine three or more therapeutic approaches in their work. As Table 15.9 shows, an integrative approach of long-standing interest is that of behavioral and psychoanalytic theories.

The integration of behavioral and psychoanalytic therapy would seem, at first, to combine two approaches that are too theoretically distant to be reconciled. However, this pairing has a long history, with Dollard and Miller (1950) developing a unified theory combining the insights of psychoanalysis with the scientific rigor of behavior therapy. Working in this tradition, Wachtel (1977, 1991, 1993, 1997), with a background in psychoanalysis, has developed a theory that intertwines psychoanalysis and behavior therapy.

This integrative approach combines concepts from the four psychoanalytic psychologies with behavioral, cognitive, and family systems approaches (Wachtel, 1997).

TABLE 15.9

Most Frequent Combinations of Theoretical Orientations

Combination	1986		1976*	
	%	Rank	%	Rank
Cognitive and behavioral	12	1	5	4
Humanistic and cognitive	11	2		
Psychoanalytic and cognitive	10	3		
Behavioral and humanistic	8	4	11	3
Interpersonal and humanistic	8	4	3	6
Humanistic and systems	6	6		
Psychoanalytic and interpersonal	5	7		
Systems and behavioral	5	7		
Behavioral and psychoanalytic	4	9	25	1

*Percentages and ranks were not reported for all combinations in the 1976 study.

SOURCE: From *Systems of Psychotherapy: A Transtheoretical Analysis*, 3rd ed., p. 431, by J. O. Prochaska and J. C. Norcross (adapted from Norcross & Prochaska, 1988). Copyright © 1999, 1994, 1984, 1979 by Brooks/Cole Publishing Company, a division of International Thomson Publishing, Inc., Pacific Grove, CA 93950. Reprinted by permission.

Recognizing that anxiety is common to disorders treated by these methods, Wachtel has developed *cyclical psychodynamics*, a term that comes from his belief that psychological conflicts within oneself create problems in behavior and that problems in behavior create problems within oneself. For example, a person may feel unloved by her parents and be unassertive in her behavior, all the while feeling anger toward her parents. By acting unassertively, she may feel ignored and also feel rage. Thus, the intrapersonal conflict creates behavioral problems, and the behavioral problems create further intrapersonal problems.

In treating patients, Wachtel moves back and forth between helping clients understand their behavior and changing it. Behavioral treatments include relaxation, desensitization, and exposure to anxiety. Psychodynamic treatment includes helping the patient understand past and present unconscious conflicts and how they influence each other. Wachtel deals not only with past issues but also follows how unconscious processes emerge as the end product of anxiety. Thus, unconscious conflicts may cause problems or be the result of problems.

Strategies in understanding the client and treating the client come from both behavioral and psychodynamic perspectives. Wachtel inquires into the unconscious problems of the client as well as the behaviors. Also, he may expose the client to anxiety, not just through behavioral procedures, but also through interpreting and confronting unconscious processes. However, this exposure is done gradually, and change is brought about in small steps rather than in dramatic interventions. As the process proceeds, clients are helped to develop insights into clarifying and interpreting thoughts, fantasies, and behaviors. As psychoanalysis and cognitive therapies have been influenced by constructivist approaches, so has Wachtel (1997). This has caused him to take a sharper view of clients' use of language and the way they view the world and the therapeutic relationship.

The following example of Judy, in her midforties, who complained of chronic depression and severe somatic symptoms, illustrates how therapists using the cyclical psychodynamic approach conceptualize their clients (Gold & Wachtel, 1993). In the beginning of therapy, Judy and the therapist examined the intrapsychic conflict–behavior–intrapsychic conflict–behavior circle (how psychological issues led to behavioral problems and vice versa) and Judy's anxieties and motivations. Gradually, Judy saw how she was being exploited by others, that she was angry at this exploitation, and that she had developed a sense of helplessness about this problem. Exploration of psychodynamic issues, such as parental attachments, helped Judy make a link between past and present behavior. At this juncture, the therapist combined behavioral and psychoanalytic interventions to break the psychodynamic-behavioral cycle.

> The initial period of such interpretive work became the basis for more active interventions aimed at breaking Judy's vicious circle of compliance, self-deprivation, and anger. The first exercise was a blend of dynamic insight and systematic desensitization. Judy was asked if she could imagine scenes in which she pleasurably spoke her mind in an angry or irritable way with her husband and friends. She gradually moved from timid and tiny expressions and imagery to scenes where her expressions of rage were violent and powerful. As Judy became more comfortable with these ideas and images, she spontaneously gained insight into her anxiety about anger, and about some of the unconscious factors which reinforced her compliant behavior. Judy reported imagining herself frightening other people and taking pleasure in the power which that fear represented. She also learned that her caretaking behavior gave her a covert sense of power as well, as it unconsciously provoked fantasies of being better and more capable than the people to whom she acquiesced consciously. (Gold & Wachtel, 1993, pp. 69–70)[1]

This small sample of a description of a cyclical psychodynamic approach shows how behavioral and psychodynarnic concepts can be integrated into an active theoretical approach. Wachtel has developed this approach gradually, adding new concepts where needed to help bridge the gap between psychodynamic and behavioral and cognitive therapies.

Technical Eclecticism

For practitioners to call themselves *eclectics* is to risk criticism for being unsystematic (Garfield, 1980). When eclecticism is unsystematic, practitioners may try to use what they consider to be the best techniques from a variety of theories without basing their selection on a coherent theory of personality. Lazarus and Beutler (1993) warn that such practitioners will not be able to find a consistent rationale for treatment planning, for assessment, for therapeutic intervention, and ultimately for empirical testing of their approach. A theoretical basis for assessing and treating clients keeps therapists from wondering where to go next and what treatment to try next (Lazarus, 1996). Clients may experience unsystematic eclecticism as inconsistency in that the therapist acts one way at one time and differently at another. In contrast to unsystematic eclecticism, technical eclecticism is based on a theory of personality. The goals and means

ARNOLD LAZARUS

of assessing individuals are based on a theory, and treatment methods drawn from many theories are selected to be consistent with that theory. In this section, Lazarus's (1989, 1997) multimodal approach, which is based on a social and cognitive learning theory of personality, is explained, with emphasis on goals of therapy, assessment, and therapeutic techniques.

Multimodal theory of personality. When Lazarus was a student in South Africa in the 1950s, the predominant theories of psychotherapy were psychoanalysis and person-centered therapy. However, he was also exposed to behavior therapy through lectures by Joseph Wolpe and other behaviorists. Impressed by the scientific basis of behavior therapy and the changes that are produced in patients, Lazarus adopted many of its techniques. However, when examining follow-up studies, Lazarus (1971, 1989) recognized that behavioral methods alone were not usually sufficient to bring about lasting change. He also wanted to know which therapy techniques would be best for which types of people and which types of problems. As he investigated these questions, he was able to use social learning theory as a means for understanding the behavior of his clients.

The concepts that were important to Lazarus in understanding and treating human behavior are those that are described in the personality theory section of Chapter 8. Included are the principles of classical and operant conditioning and Bandura's work on observational learning. The latter was particularly influential in Lazarus's work and was combined with cognitive beliefs about personality, as described in Chapter 10. His view of human behavior is that individuals learn what to do from observing and experiencing the positive and negative consequences of interactions with others. However, his conceptualization of social learning went beyond the specific focus of behavior, cognitive, and REBT therapists.

Lazarus's (1997) view is that individuals use seven major modalities to experience themselves and their world, which he refers to as BASIC I.D. Each letter and the modality that it stands for is explained here (Lazarus, 1989, 1997; Lazarus & Lazarus, 1991).

Behavior: Included in this category are habits, responses, and reactions that can be observed and measured. These include problems with eating, drinking, smoking, crying, and self-control. Also covered are problems with working too little or too much and being too aggressive or not assertive enough.

Affect: A variety of emotions and moods are included, such as being depressed, angry, anxious, happy, helpless, tense, and lonely. Important are feelings that are predominant problems for individuals and those that clients feel they may not be able to control. Feelings of fear and the events that may arouse fear fit in this category.

Sensation: Included are the basic senses of seeing, hearing, touching, tasting, and smelling. Emphasis is given to negative sensations that may include headaches, dizziness, numbness, stomach trouble, hallucinations, or sexual disturbances.

Imagery: Fantasies, mental pictures, images, and dreams fit into this category. Included are images that come through auditory or other sensory mechanisms. Body image and self-image are given special attention.

*Cognition:*Included are thoughts, ideas, values, and opinions. Of importance are negative thoughts about oneself, such as being stupid, crazy, unattractive, or worthless, as well as positive thoughts, such as being intelligent and honest.

*Interpersonal relationships:*How one interacts with family, friends, colleagues, teachers, or others fall into this category. Examples include difficulties in relationships with others, including marital and sexual problems.

*Drugs/Biology:*The entire area of health and medical concerns is covered in this category. Physiological functioning and drugs (prescribed or unprescribed) are considered when understanding the individual's personality. (For clarity, the letter D is used instead of the letter B, because the acronym BASIC I.D. has meaning—basic identification—whereas BASIC I.B. does not.) Because this category is broad, it is more accurate to think of it as biology and drugs rather than just drugs. This category is important because all of the other modalities exist in a physiological context.[2]

Lazarus (1997) is interested in how individuals use all of these systems and which are most important to the person. He uses the term *firing order* to describe the sequence of modalities that takes place when a person is confronted with an event. An example of the firing order is that of an impulsive person who

blurts out a stupid remark at a party. A hush descends upon the group, and he understands the air of disapproval. He blushes and begins to perspire and imagines the comments that people will make behind his back. He gets up and walks out of the room. (Lazarus, 1989, p. 16)

The firing order in this situation is behavior-interpersonal-cognition-sensation-imagery-behavior. People react differently to the same situation (with different firing orders), and each individual responds differently to different situations (have different firing orders). In brief, individuals' behaviors, affects, sensations, imageries, cognitions, and interpersonal style of relating are learned through classical and operant conditioning as well as through observational modes. This view of human behavior has a direct impact on the way multimodal therapists conceptualize goals, assessment, and treatment of patient problems.

Goals of therapy.   Client goals for therapy can be seen in a combination of a variety of BASIC I.D. modalities. For example, an individual may seek help to stop smoking (B), seek help to work with fears about being unable to stop (A), be concerned about not having the pleasant sensation of smoking (S), be unable to picture himself as being able to go more than an hour without a cigarette (I), want to change his belief that he is too indecisive to stop smoking (C), be afraid that stopping smoking will make him too irritable with others (I), and be concerned about developing lung cancer through smoking (D). Not all goals are expressed in terms of all modalities, and the strength of each modality varies, depending on the goal. It is important to note that affect can be worked with only through the other modalities, as one cannot directly change emotions, but one can change the behaviors, sensations, imagery, cognition, interpersonal relationships, and biological processes that affect emotions. Thus a person who is depressed feels better when she is doing productive things, having more positive sensations and images, thinking more rationally, interacting more comfortably with others, and feeling physically better. Lazarus (1997) recognizes the importance of clients' hopes and expectations for improvement and early in therapy helps clients feel that there is hope for reaching their goals in a relatively brief time (less than 40 sessions), when he believes that this is possible.

Assessment. Essential to multimodal therapy is a precise and systematic assessment of the BASIC I.D. Assessment is done in three different ways: through interviews with the client, by having clients fill out their own modality profiles, and through assessment instruments such as the Multimodal Life Inventory (Lazarus & Lazarus, 1991). Although assessment predominates in the initial sessions, it continues throughout therapy. The multimodal therapist listens for how problems affect modalities.

> A multimodal elaboration of the statement, "When Mr. Smith has a headache, he worries because he is a hypochondriac," would proceed as follows: When Mr. Smith has a headache, he becomes quiet and withdrawn (behavior), starts feeling anxious (affect), experiences the pain as "an internal hammer with hot spikes driven into the skull" (sensation), and pictures himself dying of a brain tumor (imagery) while convincing himself that the doctors have probably missed something seriously wrong (cognition). During these episodes, he talks monosyllabically while his wife fusses over him (interpersonal) and resorts to aspirins and other painkillers (biological). Multimodal elaboration of any problem not only spells out who or what may be maintaining the ongoing difficulties, but also enables one to pinpoint logical thera-peutic approaches by examining the interactive aspects of the identified problems. (Lazarus, 1989, p. 14)

Additionally, the therapist is likely to draw up a chart rating the predominance or importance of each mode on a scale of 0 to 10. This can be done directly, by asking the client how he or she would rate a given modality, or indirectly, based on the therapist's observations.

Often it is helpful for therapists to ask their clients to construct their own modality profiles after the therapist has given the client a description of the BASIC I.D. Such information gives the therapist insight into clients' views of how their problems fit each modality and familiarizes the client with the seven modalities. The following is an example of a modality profile of a 22-year-old nurse who described his problems as being shy with women, fighting with his mother, and feeling frustrated and depressed (Lazarus, 1989).

B. Stop smoking
   Start exercising
   Start dating
   Shy away from attractive women.
A. Depression
   Anger
   Fear
S. Tension
   Blushing

    I. I imagine women snickering behind my back.
       Many lonely images
       I often imagine my mother saying: "Who do you think you are?"
    C. I am not good enough.
       Attractive women think of me as ugly and dull.
       I'm a loser.
    I. My mother thinks I'm ten years old.
       Awkward and shy with attractive women
       Not enough friends
    D. Smoke $1^{1}/_{2}$–3 packs of cigarettes a day. (Lazarus, 1989, pp. 78–79)

This information is used in addition to that taken from the Multimodal Life History Inventory (Lazarus & Lazarus, 1991). This inventory is more detailed, requesting personal and social history, inquiring about expectations about therapy, requesting descriptions of presenting problems, and having open-ended questions and checklists about each of the seven modalities. Included are a brief medical history and global ratings on each of the seven modalities. With information from the client through the modality profile and the Multimodal Life History Inventory, as well as profiles made by the therapist based on information gathered about each modality, the therapist has an organized and specific method for initiating change with the client.

Sometimes more information is needed from a multimodal assessment, and a "second-order" BASIC I.D. may be necessary, which refers to taking any item on the modality profile and examining it in more detail from each of the seven modalities. For example, in the nurse's modality profile in the previous example, a behavior such as "Start dating," an affect such as "Depression," or a sensation such as "Tension" can each be subject to its own second-order assessment. Thus, one could take the behavior "Start dating" and look at other related behaviors, affect related to it such as fear, sensations such as tingling, images such as being refused a date, cognitions such as "Joan won't want to go out with me," interpersonal relationship issues such as "I don't know what to say on a date," and drug/biology concerns, such as "I sweat profusely before a date." In this way, a second-order assessment could be applied to any of the items on the young man's modality profile or any other modality profile. This detailed assessment approach is used, rather than DSM-IV categories, in multimodal therapy so that the therapist is prepared to implement a variety of therapeutic procedures.

Treatment approach.   By assessing all seven modalities, Lazarus is able to apply a great variety of techniques to bring about therapeutic change. Therapeutic interventions may start in the first session; the multimodal therapist need not wait until a complete assessment is done. Lazarus has applied multimodal therapy to a great variety of outpatients and problems (Lazarus, 1987, 1988, 1997). In the development of the therapeutic relationship and the application of treatment methodology, Lazarus (1993) describes himself as "an authentic chameleon" who changes his style to fit the client's, both to understand the client and to bring about therapeutic change.

To understand the client and intervene effectively, Lazarus (1989) makes use of tracking and bridging. *Tracking* refers to examining the "firing order" of the modalities of different patients. For example, some patients may react to an adverse event with a sensation (S) of flushing, followed by distorted thoughts, "I must have done something wrong" (C), and images (I) of being yelled at. This might result in unassertive behavior (B). Clients do not display the same firing order consistently, and tracking must be done continuously. Therapeutic treatments may be given that follow the tracking sequence, such as using positive imagery of pleasant scenes if imagery is to be addressed first, or relaxation strategies if behavior is primary. Somewhat similar to tracking, *bridging* refers to attending to the client's current modality before moving into another modality that may be more productive to producing change. Thus if an individual uses a cognitive modality to express herself, the therapist stays with that until it seems appropriate to bridge to another modality such as feeling (A). In this way, the therapist tracks the modalities and then moves (or bridges) to another, when appropriate. By doing so, the therapist prevents the client from feeling misunderstood by the therapist, which would occur if the client expressed one modality (such as cognition) and the therapist only reflected feelings (A). In this way, multimodal therapy is very flexible, with the therapist changing modes to make effective therapeutic interventions.

With more than 400 therapies (Corsini & Wedding, 1995) described by various authors and many techniques of therapy available to the therapist, the multimodal therapist has much to choose from. Although other therapists who use Adlerian, REBT, cognitive, or behavioral therapies can draw from a wide variety of affective, behavioral, and cognitive techniques, multimodal therapists draw from an even larger pool as they also include change methods directed at sensations, imagery, and drug/biology in their repertoire. In *The Practice of Multimodal Therapy*, Lazarus (1989) lists 39 commonly used techniques in multimodal therapy. Of these, about half are behavioral, 25% are cognitive, and the rest come from other theoretical orientations. In taking techniques from other theories, Lazarus uses only the technique, not the conceptualization or reason for the technique.

To further understand the range of Lazarus's selective eclecticism, examine Table 15.4 from a multimodal perspective. Like psychoanalysts, Lazarus might use free association, not for its value in revealing unconscious processes, but rather as it reveals the client's sensations and images. Similarly, multimodal therapists may pay attention to the relationship between themselves and the client (transference), but not from the perspective of feelings toward parents being transferred onto the therapist but rather to determine if the therapist is correctly understanding the client's expression of modalities. Some of the techniques of brief psychoanalysis would be shared with multimodal therapy, such as the use of questions, restatements, and confrontations, but brief psychoanalysis aims at understanding childhood dynamics, and multimodal theory uses these techniques to further understand and pursue issues that are related to the seven modalities, as they impede adaptive functioning in the here and now.

Because the conceptual basis of Jungian analysis is so different from that of multimodal therapy, they share few techniques in common. Where the Jungian approach is to explore dream material as it represents the collective unconscious, the multimodal approach is to find out if there are new associations to a dream or to change the course or ending of the dream. Both Jungian analysis and multimodal theory have an interest in exploring imagery and sensations (although from very different points of view), and multimodal therapists could also use a sand tray with small figures to act out images, as do Jungian therapists.

Adlerian psychotherapy uses many techniques, such as "acting as if," spitting in the client's soup, and catching oneself, which are cognitive approaches that multimodal theorists could use in helping clients change beliefs and behavior. These techniques are action oriented, which is consistent with the multimodal view of change.

The philosophy of existential psychotherapy focuses chiefly on important themes or issues, not techniques. Multimodal therapists work on existential issues, such as dealing with a dying relative, being abandoned by a parent, or leaving college to support oneself, but from the perspective of BASIC I.D. The approaches are so different that existential psychotherapy offers very little to multimodal therapists, who would attend to the seven basic modalities. Possibly, Frankl's concepts of attitude modulation and dereflection could be used to change patient cognitions.

Person-centered therapy emphasizes genuineness, acceptance, and empathy. All of these concepts are important to multimodal therapists and are included in the affect modality. However, Rogers's six conditions for change are neither necessary nor sufficient for multimodal therapists, who use many more methods of intervention.

Gestalt therapy offers multimodal therapists many creative ideas that deal with the modalities of affect, sensation, and imagery. Use of the empty chair technique, enacting problems, and awareness exercises tend to develop affect, sensation, and imagery.

Of all the therapies described in this book, behavior therapy has concepts that are most similar to those of multimodal therapy. Therefore, it is not surprising that multimodal therapists would draw heavily on behavior therapy and make use of most of the techniques in Chapter 8.

Both cognitive therapy and REBT offer many strategies that multimodal therapists use to change the cognition and, to a lesser extent, the imagery of the client. Techniques listed for REBT and cognitive therapy in Table 15.4 are all consistent with a multimodal approach.

Because reality therapy is tied to a specific process, there is little that multimodal therapy could draw from this theory. Although techniques such as questioning, being positive, using humor, and confronting are shared by both theories, the strong focus on control and responsibility in reality therapy does not fit well with an emphasis on specific modalities.

Feminist therapy emphasizes gender and power analysis and intervention. Although multimodal therapists acknowledge the importance of gender and cultural issues, they do not incorporate these into the seven modalities. However, both gender-role and power interventions have cognitive and behavioral components that multimodal therapists might use with clients who are dealing with societal and political discrimination.

Multimodal therapists work with both couples and families. Family systems therapy focuses frequently on interpersonal issues, and Minuchin's structural approach does have methods that would be helpful to multimodal therapists in assessing interactions. However, they are more likely to examine how the seven modalities of each member of the couple or family interact with each other than to use a systems theory view.

In addition to drawing from these theories, Lazarus has developed techniques such as time tripping and the deserted island fantasy technique to further develop a client's imagery modality. *Time tripping* refers to having clients picture themselves going backward or forward in time to address particular events or issues. The *deserted island fantasy technique* refers to asking clients what the therapist would learn if he were left alone with the client on a deserted island. This fantasy experience helps the therapist learn more about the cognition, affect, and imagery of the client. Other techniques can be developed by multimodal practitioners, who may make use of ideas from other theories, such as art, drama, dance movement, or music therapies, as well as techniques such as hypnosis. To use multimodal therapy requires empathy for clients, knowledge of social learning theory, ability to assess clients' BASIC I.D., and the application of a variety of strategies to effect changes in the modalities.

An example of a 28-year-old woman who complains of anxiety when going away from home unaccompanied by her husband illustrates a multimodal approach (Lazarus, 1995). The presenting problem is agoraphobia, a disorder that Lazarus would normally treat with in vivo desensitization. He used this method by teaching the client relaxation and deep-breathing techniques and taking walks with the client, gradually increasing the distance between therapist and client. Whereas behavior therapists may stop at this point, Lazarus had information from her Multimodal Life History Inventory showing problems of marital discord, resentment toward parents, and issues related to poor self-esteem. Lazarus's use of switching modalities to meet the client's needs is explained here.

> Initially, a form of role-playing was employed in which Mrs. W attempted to confront her father about certain resentments she had harbored. When she implied that I was not capturing or conveying the essence of her father's tone and demeanor correctly, we switched from role-playing to the two-chair or empty chair technique. Now, while speaking to the empty chair in which she envisioned her father sitting, and then moving to the chair, becoming her father, and talking for him, she achieved a feeling of greater authenticity. This was reflected in considerable emotionality—what she heard herself term "cathartic release." (Lazarus, 1995)[3]

Although using Gestalt techniques, Lazarus was dealing with affective, sensory, and imagery modalities in a social learning framework. In his further treatment of this client, Lazarus goes on to address other modalities through the use of a great variety of therapeutic techniques. Although this approach has the advantage of being flexible and choosing appropriate techniques to meet a variety of client goals, it has the disadvantage of requiring the ability to identify client BASIC I.D. modalities and a wide knowledge of a variety of techniques.

All three integrative approaches—transtheoretical, theoretical integration, and technical eclecticism—share several features in common as well as some dissimilarities. They all require knowledge of many theories of psychotherapy so that judgments can be made about theories of personality to use or techniques to apply. All are systematic; that is, they have a reason or explanation for applying the techniques that they do. They differ in that the transtheoretical approach develops new concepts to explain theoretical constructs that have already been explained by other theorists. Integrative approaches require the melding of concepts and techniques that other practitioners of different theories would see as incompatible with each other. Technical eclecticism, for some practitioners, can drift from a theory of psychotherapy using many techniques to the use of many techniques with very little link to theory. However, when all of these integrative approaches are used correctly, they have the advantage of providing a clear understanding for applying therapeutic techniques that unsystematic eclecticism does not.

CONCLUSION

Helping people with psychological problems gives therapists an opportunity to increase the satisfaction and happiness and improve the interpersonal relationships of other people. Almost all clients try to deal with their psychological suffering on their own or with the help of friends. Only when that has failed do they seek psychotherapy or counseling. The responsibility to help others ethically and competently is a significant one. Theorists pass on to others their views of how to help individuals in distress. Along with the responsibility of using theory accurately are the satisfaction and excitement that come with helping.

Without the theoretical ideas presented in this book, therapists and counselors would have few guidelines of how to proceed. The thousands of books and articles on ways to help and the research into the effectiveness of helping will continue to increase and to provide guidelines and assistance for the therapist. With continued research and increased therapeutic practice, the theories have become deeper and broader. They have become deeper in that new aspects or concepts of theories have been developed, critiqued, and modified further. For some theories, research has played an important role in determining aspects of the theory that are particularly effective or need modification. Theories also have become broader, as practitioners of one theory incorporate other techniques and concepts into their work. As shown in this chapter, many of the theories are moving toward integrating concepts or techniques from other theories. Additionally, some writers have taken an integrative point of view, essentially developing theories that are broadly based on the concepts and/or techniques of other theories.

For the beginning therapist or counselor, this information can seem exciting at some times and overwhelming at others—overwhelming, because there is so much information for beginning therapists, who often feel they need to know their theoretical preference right away. The development of a theoretical style is a gradual one, influenced by readings, by practicum and internship experience, and by supervisors' opinions.

I encourage readers who are choosing to become psychotherapists or counselors to be open to the selection of theoretical points of views. Although the fit between one's own values and personality and those of a theory is important, fit is not the only consideration. Knowledge of the interaction of one's own personality and multicultural values is essential in effective psychotherapy and counseling. The type of client and the work a student anticipates doing often have an impact on the selection of theories. For example, many agencies impose a limit on the number of sessions they can offer their clients, so that longer-term therapies (psychoanalysis and Jungian analysis) would be inappropriate in that setting. Some settings may fit well with certain theories: Therapists and counselors working with juvenile delinquents may find behavior or reality therapy approaches fit their needs, whereas those working with individuals in midlife crises may find existential therapy or Jungian analysis to be appropriate. Some therapists do make small or marked changes in theoretical orientation, depending on changes in their own personal development, the type of clients they work with, and the expectations of a new work setting. Openness to new information and ideas can be seen as a strength rather than as indecisiveness. Developing your own theory of psychotherapy or counseling is a long-term process, subject to change due to one or more of these factors.

At the back of this book is a questionnaire for you to fill out. I would like to hear about your experience with this book, what you like most and what you like least. Helping others learn about psychotherapy and counseling is important to me, and I would appreciate your feedback.

Suggested Readings

STRICKER, G., & GOLD, J. R. (EDS.). (1993). *Comprehensive handbook of psychotherapy integration*. New York: Plenum. • Included in this book is information on the history and research of integrative approaches, as well as more than a dozen different integrative views of therapy. Chapters also address psychotherapy integration with a variety of disorders and populations, such as children, couples, the elderly, and African Americans.

LAZARUS, A. A. (1997). *Brief but comprehensive psychotherapy: The multimodal way*. Baltimore: Johns Hopkins University Press. • Lazarus describes multimodal therapy, its techniques, and its application. Case material is included, along with explanations about the use of multimodal therapy as it relates to efficient treatment.

PROCHASKA, J. O., & NORCROSS, J. C. (1999). *Systems of psychotherapy: A transtheoretical analysis* (4th ed.). Pacific Grove, CA: Brooks/Cole. • Chapter 15 provides a good overview of the transtheoretical model as developed by Prochaska, Norcross, and their colleagues.

WACHTEL, P. L. (1997). *Psychoanalysis, behavior therapy and the relational world*. Washington: American Psychological Association. • The integration of psychoanalysis and behavior analysis is explained, along with an overview of anxiety, learning, and psychoanalysis. The first chapters are a reprint of Wachtel (1977). The last seven chapters update the theory as it relates to modifications in psychoanalysis, cognitive-behavior theory, and constructivism.

References

ANDREWS, J. (1991). *The active self in psychotherapy: An integration of therapeutic styles*. Boston: Allyn & Bacon.

BERGIN, A. E., & GARFIELD, S. L. (1994). Overview, trends, and future issues. In A. E. Bergin & S. L. Garfield (Eds.), *Handbook of psychotherapy and behavior change* (4th ed., pp. 821–830). New York: Wiley.

BLATT, S. J., SANISLOW, C. A., ZUROFF, D. C., & PILKONIS, P. A. (1996). Characteristics of effective therapists: Further analyses of data from the National Institute of Mental Health Treatment of Depression Collaborative Research Program. *Journal of Consulting and Clinical Psychology, 64*, 1276–1284.

CHESLER, P. (1972). *Women and madness*. New York: Doubleday.

CORSINI, R. J., & WEDDING, D. (1995). *Current psychotherapies* (5th ed.). Itasca, IL: Peacock.

DOLLARD, J., & MILLER, N. (1950). *Personality and psychotherapy: An analysis in terms of learning, thinking, and culture*. New York: McGraw-Hill.

FIEDLER, F. E. (1950). A comparison of therapeutic relationships in psychoanalytic, nondirective, and Adlerian therapy. *Journal of Consulting Psychology, 14*, 239–245.

GARFIELD, S. L. (1980). *Psychotherapy: An eclectic approach*. New York: Wiley.

GARFIELD, S. L., & BERGIN, A. E. (1994). Introduction and historical overview. In A. E. Bergin & S. L. Garfield (Eds.), *Handbook of psychotherapy and behavior change* (4th ed., pp. 3–18). New York: Wiley.

GARFIELD, S. L., & KURTZ, R. (1977). A study of eclectic views. *Journal of Clinical and Consulting Psychology, 45*, 78–83.

GOLD, J. R., & WACHTEL, P. L. (1993). Cyclical psychodynamics. In G. Stricker & J. R. Gold (Eds.), *Comprehensive handbook of psychotherapy integration* (pp. 59–72). New York: Plenum.

GRENCAVAGE, L. M., & NORCROSS, J. C. (1990). Where are the commonalities among the therapeutic common factors? *Professional Psychology: Research and Practice, 21,* 372–378.

LAZARUS, A. A. (1971). *Behavior therapy and beyond.* New York: McGraw-Hill.

LAZARUS, A. A. (1987). The multimodal approach with adult outpatients. In M. S. Jacobson (Ed.), *Psychotherapists in clinical practice* (pp. 286–326). New York: Guilford.

LAZARUS, A. A. (1988). A multimodal perspective on problems of sexual desire. In S. R. Leiblum & R. C. Rosen (Eds.), *Sexual desire disorders* (pp. 145–167). New York: Guilford.

LAZARUS, A. A. (1989). *The practice of multimodal therapy.* Baltimore: Johns Hopkins University Press.

LAZARUS, A. A. (1993). Tailoring the therapeutic relationship, or being an authentic chameleon. *Psychotherapy, 30,* 404–407.

LAZARUS, A. A. (1995). Different types of eclecticism and integration: Let's be aware of the dangers. *Journal of Psychotherapy Integration, 5,* 27–39.

LAZARUS, A. A. (1996). The utility and futility of combining treatments in psychotherapy. *Clinical Psychology: Science and Practice, 3,* 59–68.

LAZARUS, A. A. (1997). *Brief but comprehensive therapy: The multimodal way,* New York: Springer.

LAZARUS, A. A., & BEUTLER, L. E. (1993). On technical eclecticism. *Journal of Counseling Development, 71,* 381–385.

LAZARUS, A. A., & LAZARUS, C. N. (1991). *Multimodal life history inventory.* Champaign, IL: Research Press.

NEIMEYER, R. A., & MAHONEY, M. J. (Eds.). (1995). *Constructivism in psychotherapy.* Washington, DC: American Psychological Association.

NORCROSS, J. C. (Ed.). (1991). Prescriptive matching in psychotherapy: Psychoanalysis for simple phobias? *Psychotherapy, 28,* 439–472.

NORCROSS, J. C., ALFORD, B. A., & DEMICHELE, J. T. (1992). The future of psychotherapy: Delphi data and concluding observations. *Psychotherapy, 29,* 150–158.

NORCROSS, J. C., & GOLDFRIED, M. R. (Eds.). (1992). *Handbook of psychotherapy integration.* New York: Basic Books.

NORCROSS, J. C., & PROCHASKA, J. O. (1988). A study of eclectic (and integrative) views revisited. *Professional Psychology: Research and Practice, 19,* 170–174.

ORLINSKY, D. E., & HOWARD, K. I. (1986). Process and outcome in psychotherapy. In S. L. Garfield & A. E. Bergin (Eds.), *Handbook of psychotherapy and behavior change* (3rd ed., pp. 283–330). New York: Wiley.

ORLINSKY, D. E., & HOWARD, K. I. (1987). A generic model of psychotherapy. *Journal of Integrative and Eclectic Psychotherapy, 6,* 6–27.

PERRY, J. W. (1987). *The self in psychotic process* (Rev. ed.). Dallas: Spring.

POLSTER, M. (1992). *Eve's daughters: The forbidden heroism of women.* San Francisco: Jossey-Bass.

PROCHASKA, J. O., & DICLEMENTE, C. C. (1992). Stages of change in the modification of problem behaviors. In M. Hersen, R. M. Eisler, & P. M. Miller (Eds.), *Progress in behavior modification* (Vol. 28, pp. 184–206). Sycamore, IL: Sycamore Publishing.

PROCHASKA, J. O., & NORCROSS, J. C. (1999). *Systems of psychotherapy: A transtheoretical analysis* (4th ed.). Pacific Grove, CA: Brooks/Cole.

REEVE, J., INCK, T. A., & SAFRAN, J. (1993). Toward an integration of cognitive, interpersonal, and experiential approaches to therapy. In G. Stricker & J. R. Gold (Eds.), *Comprehensive handbook of psychotherapy integration* (pp. 113–124). New York: Plenum.

RUBIN, J. B. (1993). Psychoanalysis and Buddhism: Toward an integration. In G. Stricker & J. R. Gold (Eds.), *Comprehensive handbook of psychotherapy integration* (pp. 249–266). New York: Plenum.

STRICKER, G., & GOLD, J. R. (Eds.). (1993). *Comprehensive handbook of psychotherapy integration*. New York: Plenum.

WACHTEL, P. L. (1977). *Psychoanalysis and behavior therapy: Toward an integration*. New York: Basic Books.

WACHTEL, P. L. (1991). From eclecticism to synthesis: Toward a more seamless psychotherapeutic integration. *Journal of Psychotherapy Integration, 1*, 43–54.

WACHTEL, P. L. (1993). *Therapeutic communication: Principles and effective practice*. New York: Guilford.

WACHTEL, P. L. (1997). *Psychoanalysis, behavior therapy, and the relational world*. Washington: American Psychological Association.

Glossary

Many important terms used in the text are defined here. The theory or theorist that is associated with a definition is in parentheses. Words that are italicized in the definitions are defined in the glossary.

A-B-C model (REBT) • The theory that individuals' problems stem not from activating events but from their beliefs about such events. People also experience emotional or behavioral consequences of the activating event.

acceptance (Rogers) • Appreciating clients for who they are without valuing or judging them.

acting as if (Adler) • In this technique, patients are asked to "act as if" a behavior will be effective. Patients are encouraged to try on a new role the way they might try on new clothing.

active imagination (Jung) • A technique of analysis in which individuals actively focus on experiences or images (in dreams or fantasy), reporting changes in these images or experiences as they concentrate on them.

affective shift (cognitive) • A shift in facial or bodily expressions of emotion or stress that indicates that a *cognitive shift* has just taken place, often a *negative* cognitive shift. Often an indication of a *hot cognition*.

Aha response (Adler) • Developing a sudden insight into a solution to a problem, as one becomes aware of one's beliefs and behaviors.

alignment (Minuchin) • The way in which family members join or oppose each other in dealing with events.

alpha bias (feminist) • The bias that occurs by separating women and men into two specific categories, thus running the risk of treating women as unequal to men. See also *beta bias*.

alternative narratives (narrative therapy) • The process of exploring strengths, special abilities, and aspirations of the family to tell a positive story with good outcomes rather than a problem-saturated story.

altruism (Anna Freud) • A defense mechanism in which one learns to become helpful to avoid feeling helpless. Individuals learn that they can satisfy their own egos as well as the demands of society.

amplification (Jung) • A process of using knowledge of the history and meaning of symbols to understand unconscious material, such as that arising from patients' dreams.

anal stage (Freud) • The second stage of psychosexual development occurring between the ages of about 18 months and 3 years. The anal area becomes the main source of pleasure.

androgyny • Possessing both masculine and feminine psychological traits, usually in relatively equal amounts.

anima (Jung) • The *archetype* representing the feminine component of the male personality.

animus (Jung) • The *archetype* that represents the masculine component of the female personality.

anorexia • A disorder in which individuals are unable to eat food, may have a severe decrease in appetite, and have an intense fear of becoming obese even when emaciated. Anorexia is diagnosed when individuals lose at least 25% of their normal weight.

anticathexes (Freud) • The control or restraint exercised by the ego over the *id* to keep *id* impulses out of consciousness.

anxiety • An unpleasant feeling of fear and/or apprehension accompanied by physiological changes such as fast pulse, quick breathing, sweating, flushing, muscle aches, and stomach tension.

arbitrary inference (cognitive) • Coming to a conclusion that is not supported by evidence. Two examples are *mind reading* and *negative prediction*.

archetypes (Jung) • Universal images or symbols that serve as the core of the *collective unconscious*. They predispose an individual to have a certain feeling or thought toward a current object or situation, such as a mother (Earth Mother) or animal instincts (*shadow*).

art therapy • A method of helping patients deal with emotional conflicts and awareness of their feelings by using a variety of art media, such as paints, crayons, paper, or sculpting materials.

assertiveness training (behavior; cognitive; feminist; REBT) • A technique to teach clients to effectively express positive and negative feelings to others so that they may achieve desired purposes.

assets (Adler) • Assessing the strengths of individuals' lifestyle is an important part of lifestyle assessment, as is assessment of *early recollections* and *basic mistakes*.

atman (Asian) • A concept of universality in which the self is not seen as an individual, but as part of the entire universe.

attachment theory (psychoanalysis) • The study of infant-mother relationships and patterns of relating to the mother.

attentional processes (behavior) • The act of perceiving or watching something and learning from it.

attitude modulation (Frankl) • A technique used to change motivations from anxious ones to healthy ones by questioning the client's rationale and by removing obstacles that interfere with being responsible.

attitudes (Jung) • Two ways of interacting with the world: see *introversion* and *extraversion*.

audience (psychodrama) • People present during the enactment who observe the psychodrama. They may be involved at some point as *protagonists* or *auxiliaries*.

authenticity (existential) • Being genuine and real, as well as aware of one's being. Authentic individuals deal with moral choices, the meaning of life, and being human.

automatic thoughts (cognitive) • Notions or ideas that occur without effort or choice, are usually distorted, and lead to emotional responses. Automatic thoughts can be organized into core beliefs or *cognitive schemas*.

auxiliaries (psychodrama) • Members of a group or audience who play significant roles in the life of the *protagonist*.

auxiliary function (Jung) • The function that takes over when the *superior* function is not operating. Functions include *thinking*, *feeling*, *sensing*, and *intuiting*.

avoiding the tar baby (Adler) • By not falling into a trap that the patient sets by using faulty assumptions, the therapist encourages new behavior and "avoids the tar baby."

awareness (Gestalt) • Attending to and observing what is happening in the present. Types of awareness include sensations and actions, feelings, wants, and values or assessments.

BASIC I.D. (multimodal) • An acronym that includes the seven fundamental concepts of multimodal therapy: behavior, affect, sensation, imagery, cognition, interpersonal relationships, drugs/biology.

basic mistakes (Adler) • Self-defeating aspects of individuals' *lifestyles* that may affect their later behavior. Such mistakes often include avoidance of others, seeking power, a desperate need for security, or faulty values.

being-in-the-world (existential) • Derived from the German word *Dasein*, which refers to examining oneself, others, and one's relationship with the world, thus attaining higher levels of consciousness.

beta bias (feminist) • Bias that occurs when treating men and women as identical, thus ignoring important differences between the lives of women and men. See also *alpha bias*.

bibliotherapy • A therapeutic technique in which the therapist chooses readings for the client for purposes such as gaining insight into problems, learning new information, and increasing self-esteem.

bioenergetic analysis (body) • Developed principally by Alexander Lowen, this is a method of understanding personality in terms of the body and its energy flow. Attention is given to physiology, breathing, and bodily movement.

bipolar self (Kohut) • The tension between the *grandiose self* ("I deserve to get what I want") and an idealized view of parents forms the two poles of the bipolar self.

birth order (Adler) • The idea that place in the family constellation (such as being the youngest child) can have an impact on one's later personality and functioning.

body armor (body) • A protective mechanism in the individual to deal with the punishment that comes from acting on instinctual demands, such as defecating in public.

body awareness (body) • Patients may move or change positions and develop more awareness of their body.

body psychotherapy (body) • A means of integrating psychotherapy and attention to and manipulation of bodily processes.

body reading (body) • Systematic observations used to understand energy blockages and tensions within the body.

borderline personality disorder • Characteristics include unstable interpersonal relationships and rapid mood changes in a short period of time. Behavior is often erratic, unpredictable, and impulsive in areas such as spending, eating, sex, or gambling. Emotional relationships tend to be intense, with individuals becoming easily angry or disappointed in the relationship.

boundary marking (Minuchin) • A technique to change boundaries or interactions among individual family members. An example would be to change the seating of family members in therapy.

boundary permeability (Minuchin) • The degree to which boundaries are flexible among family members and the nature of the contact that family members have with each other. See *enmeshed* and *disengaged* families.

bridging (multimodal) • Being aware of and responding to a client's current modality before introducing another modality to the client.

bulimia • Binge eating and inappropriate methods of preventing weight gain, such as vomiting and laxatives, characterize bulimia.

catastrophizing (cognitive; REBT) • Exaggerating the potential or real consequences of an event and becoming fearful of the consequences.

catching oneself (Adler) • In this technique, patients learn to notice that they are performing behaviors they wish to change. When they catch themselves, they may have an *Aha response*.

catharsis (psychoanalysis; psychodrama) • The expression of feelings that have been previously repressed.

cathect (Freud) • Investing psychic energy in a mental representation of a person, behavior, or idea. Infants cathect in objects that gratify their needs.

challenging absolutes (cognitive; REBT) • Statements that include words such as everyone, never, no one, and always are usually exaggerations, which therapists point out to the client.

change questions (solution-focused) • Questions are asked about what positive changes in solving the problem took place prior to therapy.

circular questioning (Milan group) • An interviewing technique designed to elicit differences in perceptions about events or relationships from different family members.

classical conditioning (behavior) • A type of learning in which a neutral stimulus is presented repeatedly with one that reflexively elicits a particular response so the neutral stimulus eventually elicits the response itself (also called respondent conditioning).

coalitions (Minuchin) • Alliances or affiliations between family members against another family member.

cognitive distortions (cognitive) • Systematic errors in reasoning, often stemming from early childhood errors in reasoning; an indication of inaccurate or ineffective information processing.

cognitive rehearsal (cognitive) • A means of using imagination to think about having a positive interaction or experience; for example, to imagine a positive interaction with one's future in-laws.

cognitive schemas (cognitive) • Ways of thinking that comprise a set of core beliefs and assumptions about how the world operates.

cognitive shift (cognitive) • Basically a biased interpretation of life experiences, causing individuals to shift their focus from unbiased to more biased information about themselves or their world.

cognitive spiral (cognitive) • The downward spiral of depression in which basic beliefs and *schemas* can set off a series of negative reactions that may bring about a depressed feeling.

cognitive triad (cognitive) • The negative views that individuals have about themselves, their world, and their future.

collective unconscious (Jung) • That part of the unconscious that contains memories and images that are universal to the human species, in contrast to the *personal unconscious*, which is based upon individual experience. Humans have an inherited tendency to form representations of mythological motives, which may vary greatly but maintain basic patterns. Thus individuals may view the universe in similar ways by thinking, feeling, and reacting to common elements such as the moon or water.

complementary communication (family systems) • A relationship in which there is inequality in two or more members. One is usually submissive to the other.

complex (Jung) • A group of associated feelings, thoughts, and memories that have intense emotional content. Complexes may have elements from the *personal unconscious* and *collective unconscious*.

compulsions • An irresistible impulse to repeat behaviors continually.

conditional positive regard (Rogers) • Receiving praise, attention, or approval from others as a result of behaving in accordance with the expectations of others.

conditionality or conditions of worth (Rogers) • The process of evaluating one's own experience based on values or beliefs that others hold.

conflict-free sphere (Hartmann) • An area of functioning in which the *ego* is not in conflict with either *id* or *superego* but adapts to its own experience.

confluence (Gestalt) • A *contact boundary* disturbance in which the separation between one's self and others becomes muted or unclear. Thus, it can be difficult to distinguish one's own perceptions or values from those of another person.

congruence (Rogers) • The harmony that takes place when there is no disagreement between individuals' experience and their view of themselves. For therapists, congruence refers to matching one's inner experience with external expressions.

conjoint therapy • A type of couples therapy in which one therapist sees both members of the couple at the same time.

conscious or consciousness (Freud) • That portion of the mind or mental functioning that individuals are aware of, including sensations and experiences.

consciousness-raising (CR) groups (feminist) • A creation of the women's movement, in which women met regularly to discuss their lives and issues in them.

constructivism • Believing that individuals create their own views or constructs of events or relationships in their own lives.

contact (Gestalt) • The relationship between "me" and others. Contact involves feeling a connection with others or the world outside oneself while maintaining a separation from it.

contact boundaries (Gestalt) • The boundaries that distinguish between one person (or one aspect of a person) and an object, another person, or another aspect of oneself. Examples include body boundaries, value boundaries, familiarity boundaries, and expressive boundaries.

contingency contract (behavior) • A written agreement between the therapist and the client that specifies the consequence that will follow from performing a *target behavior*.

control theory (reality) • A view that individuals try to control the world and themselves as a part of that world in order to satisfy their psychological needs.

conversion reaction • A disorder in which a psychological disturbance takes a physical form, such as when arms or legs are paralyzed, and there is no physiological explanation.

coping question (solution-focused) • These questions ask about successful experiences that family members have had in dealing with the problem. They highlight the family members' ability to cope with problems.

countertransference (psychoanalysis) • 1. The irrational or neurotic reactions of a therapist toward the patient. 2. The therapist's conscious and unconscious feelings toward the patient. 3. A way of understanding how people in the patient's past may have felt.

covert behavior • Behavior that others cannot directly perceive, such as thinking and feeling.

cyclical psychodynamics • An example of the theoretical integration approach to psychotherapy that was developed by Paul Wachtel. Concepts from psychoanalytic theory are combined with those from behavior therapy (and also cognitive and family systems approaches). The cyclical aspect of this view refers to the belief that psychological problems create problems in behavior, and problems in behavior create psychological conflicts or problems.

dance movement therapy • A method of helping individuals integrate psychological and physiological processes so that they can better understand their own feelings, thoughts, and memories by expressing themselves through movement or dance.

decatastrophizing (cognitive; REBT) • A "what if" technique, in which clients are asked, "What if X happened, what would you do?" It is designed to explore actual rather than feared events.

defense mechanisms (Freud) • A means that the *ego* uses to fight off instinctual outbursts of the *id* or injunctions by the *superego*. Ten common ego defense mechanisms are described in Chapter 2.

deflection (Gestalt) • A *contact boundary* disturbance in which individuals avoid meaningful contact by being indirect or vague rather than by being direct.

delusions • Beliefs that are contrary to reality and that are firmly held despite evidence that they are inaccurate.

denial • A defense mechanism in which individuals may distort or not acknowledge what they think, feel, or see, for example, not believing that a relative has been killed in an auto accident.

depression • An emotional state characterized by deep sadness, feelings of worthlessness, guilt, and withdrawal from others. Other symptoms include difficulty in sleeping, loss of appetite or sexual desire, and loss of interest in normal activities. When not accompanied by *manic episodes,* it is usually referred to as major depression or unipolar depression.

dereflection (Frankl) • A technique in which clients focus away from their problems instead of on them to reduce anxiety.

deserted island fantasy technique (multimodal) • A fantasy experience in which clients are asked what the therapist would learn if he or she were alone with the client on a deserted island. It is designed to help the therapist learn more about the client's seven modalities.

detriangulation (Bowen) • The process of withdrawing from a family member, usually by a therapist, so as not to be drawn into alliances of one person against another.

dharma (Asian) • Rules that describe goodness and appropriate behavior.

dichotomous thinking (cognitive; REBT) • Engaging in all-or-nothing or black-or-white thinking, thus, thinking in extremes, such as all good or all bad, with nothing in the middle.

differentiation (Bowen) • The process of differentiating one's thinking from one's feeling; the opposite of *fusion*.

director (psychodrama) • The person who manages the participants in a psychodrama. The director initiates and organizes a psychodrama and works with the *protagonist, auxiliaries,* and *audience*.

discrimination (behavior) • Responding differently to stimuli that are similar based on different cues or antecedent events.

disengaged (Minuchin) • A reference to families, in which members are isolated or feel unconnected to each other. Boundaries are rigid and nonpermeable.

displacement (Freud) • A defense mechanism in which individuals place their feelings not on a dangerous object or person, but on one who may be safe. For example, it may be safer to express anger at a friend than at a boss who has been angry with you.

double bind (family systems) • A view that when an individual receives an important message with two different meanings and is unable to respond to it, the individual is in an impossible situation. If such messages are repeated over time, some family therapists believe individuals may begin to show signs of schizophrenia.

double technique (psychodrama) • A role in which an *auxiliary* takes the part of the *protagonist* and expresses his perception of the protagonist's thoughts or feelings.

dramatherapy • A means of making psychological change by involving individuals in experiences that are related to theater. Sometimes individuals may enact their own spontaneous drama, play the parts of a play that has been written, or observe a play and discuss it. *Psychodrama* is considered to be one form of dramatherapy.

dreams (Jung) • Arising from unconscious creativity, "big" dreams represent symbolic material from the collective unconscious; "little" dreams reflect day-to-day activity and may come from the personal unconscious.

drive (Freud) • A physiological state of tension, such as hunger, sex, or elimination, that motivates an individual to perform actions to reduce the tension.

drug abuse • Using a drug to the extent that individuals have difficulty meeting social and occupational obligations.

early recollections (Adler) • Memories of actual incidents that patients recall from their childhood. Adlerians use this information to make inferences about current behavior of children or adults.

eclecticism • As applied to psychotherapy, an approach that combines theory or techniques from a wide variety of therapeutic approaches.

ego (Freud) • A means of mediating between one's *instincts* or *drives* and the external world.

ego (Jung) • An expression of personality that includes thoughts, feelings, and behaviors of which we are conscious.

ego ideal (Freud) • In the child a representation of values that are approved of by parents. It is present in the *superego* as a concern with movement toward perfectionistic goals.

Eigenwelt (existential) • A way of relating to one's "own world." It refers to being aware of oneself and how we relate to ourselves.

emotional cutoff (Bowen) • Given too much stress in a family due to overinvolvement of parents, children may withdraw or cut themselves off emotionally from the family.

empathy (Rogers) • To enter the world of another individual without being influenced by one's own views and values is to be empathic with the individual. The therapist, when being empathic, is attuned to the experience, feelings, and sensitivities of the client.

empty chair • A technique developed by Gestalt therapists and adapted by other theorists in which the patient is asked to play different roles in two chairs. Dialogues between different aspects of the client can then take place.

enactment (family systems) • A therapeutic procedure in which families are asked to act out a conflict so that the therapist can work with the actual conflict rather than a report of it.

enactment (Gestalt) • In enactment, the patient may act out a previous experience or a characteristic. If the patient says he feels like a rat for cheating on his wife, the therapist may ask him to act like a rat.

encounter (psychodrama) • The dialogue that takes place between two individuals or two aspects of the same individual upon meeting another individual or another part of themselves.

encounter group (Rogers) • A group designed to promote constructive insight, sensitivity to others, and personal growth among its members. The leader facilitates the interactions of the group members.

encouragement (Adler) • An important therapeutic technique to build a relationship and to foster client change. Supporting clients in changing beliefs and behaviors is a part of encouragement.

enmeshed (Minuchin) • A reference to families in which members are overconcerned and overinvolved in each others' lives. Boundaries are highly permeable.

equifinality (family systems) • The ability of a system to arrive at the same destination from different paths or conditions.

eros (Freud) • The life instinct, derived from libidinal energy, in opposition to the death instinct *(thanatos)*.

exaggeration (dance movement) • Exaggerating a movement so that one can experience feelings related to the movement, such as anger at the shaking of a fist.

exception-finding questions (solution focused) • Therapists ask about exceptions to the problem. When is the problem not there and what is life like when the problem is not there?

exercises (Gestalt) • Specific techniques that have been developed to be used in group or individual therapy.

existentialism • A philosophical view that emphasizes the importance of existence, including one's responsibility for one's own psychological existence. Related themes include living and dying, freedom, responsibility to self and others, meaningfulness in life, and *authenticity*.

experiments (Gestalt) • Creative approaches or techniques used by the therapist to deal with an impasse in therapy brought about by the client's difficulty in achieving awareness.

exposure and response prevention (E/RP) (behavior) • A treatment method used primarily with obsessive-compulsive disorders in which patients are exposed to the feared stimulus for an hour or more at a time. They are then asked to refrain from participating in rituals, such as continually checking the door to see if they have closed it.

externalizing the problem (narrative therapy) • Making the problem the opponent, not the child or family. Thus, removing Guilt becomes the focus of therapy rather than the person's guilty feelings.

extinction (behavior) • The process of no longer presenting a reinforcement. It is used to decrease or eliminate certain behaviors.

extraversion (Jung) • One of the two major *attitudes* or orientations of personality. Extraversion is associated with valuing objective experience and perceiving and responding to the external world, rather than thinking about one's own perceptions or internal world.

eye movement desensitization and reprocessing (EMDR) (behavior) • Designed first for *posttraumatic stress*, EMDR requires that the patient visualize an upsetting memory and accompanying physical sensations. The clients repeat negative self-statements that they associate with the scene. The patient follows the therapist's finger as it moves rapidly back and forth. After completing the eye movements, the client stops thinking about the scene. The procedure is repeated again and again until the client's anxiety is reduced.

factorial designs • A research method that can study more than one variable at a time.

false self (Winnicott) • When *good-enough mothering* is not available in infancy, children may act as they believe they are expected to. Basically, they adopt their mother's self rather than develop their own. It is used in contrast with the *true self*.

family constellation (Adler) • The number and birth order, as well as the personality characteristics of members of a family; important in determining *lifestyle*.

family life chronology (Satir) • A way of recording significant events in a family's development.

family projection process (Bowen) • A means of projecting or transmitting a parental conflict to one or more children.

family sculpting (Satir) • A technique in which family members are physically molded or directed to take characteristic poses to represent a view of family relationships.

family structure (Minuchin) • The rules that have been developed in the course of family life to determine which members interact with which other members and in what way.

family systems therapy • A type of family therapy in which the entire family is seen as a unit or as a system. Focus is often on the interaction of family members.

family therapy • Any psychotherapeutic treatment of the family to improve psychological functioning among its members. Most major theories of psychotherapy have applications to family therapy.

feedback (family systems) • A communication pattern in which information about the consequences of an event is reintroduced into the system. See *negative feedback* and *positive feedback*.

feeling (Jung) • A *function* of personality in which individuals attend to subjective experiences of pleasure, pain, anger, or other feelings. Its polar opposite is *thinking*.

figure (Gestalt) • That part of a field that stands out in good contour clearly from the ground.

firing order (multimodal) • The sequence of modalities that occurs when an individual perceives an event. For example, interpersonal-sensation-imagery.

first-order change (family systems) • A temporary change in the family system to solve a specific problem. Such changes do not alter the basic system of the family. See also *second-order change*.

flooding (behavior) • Prolonged *in vivo* or imagined exposure to stimuli that evoke high levels of anxiety, with no ability to avoid or escape the stimuli. *Implosive therapy* uses flooding.

free association (psychoanalysis) • The patient relates feelings, fantasies, thoughts, memories, and recent events to the analyst spontaneously and without censoring them. These associations give the analyst clues to the *unconscious* processes of the patient.

friendly involvement (reality) • The process of building a relationship with a client that serves as the underpinnings of reality therapy.

fully functioning person (Rogers) • A person who meets his or her own need for *positive regard* rather than relying on the expectations of others. Such individuals are open to new experiences and not defensive.

functions (Jung) • Four ways of perceiving and responding to the world: see *thinking, feeling, sensing,* and *intuiting*.

fusion (family systems) • A merging or meshing of thoughts and feelings in a family member; the opposite of *differentiation*. It is most commonly associated with Bowen's theory.

future projection (psychodrama) • Playing a situation that could occur at some time in the future; for example, playing out an interaction with a future mother-in-law.

gender (feminist) • Socially determined thoughts, beliefs, and attitudes that individuals hold about men and women.

gender role (feminist) • Referring to behaviors that are generally considered socially appropriate for members of one sex.

gender role intervention (feminist) • Such interventions deal with reinforcing or helping clients' interventions or helping them deal with gender role obstacles in their life. Some interventions provide insight into social or political issues that serve as obstacles to clients.

gender-schema (feminist) • A set of mental associations in which individuals are seen from the point of view of their gender, as opposed to other characteristics.

generalization (behavior) • Transferring the response to one type of stimuli to similar stimuli.

generalized anxiety disorder • One of a group of anxiety disorders, it is characterized by a persistent pervasive state of tension. Physical symptoms may include a pounding heart, fast pulse and breathing, sweating, muscle aches, and stomach upset. Individuals may be easily distracted and fearful that something bad is going to happen.

genital stage (Freud) • The final stage of psychosexual development, which usually starts about the age of 12 and continues throughout life. The focus of sexual energy is toward members of the opposite sex rather than toward oneself.

genogram (family systems) • A method of charting a family's relationship system. It is essentially a family tree in which ages, sex, marriage dates, and similar information may be diagrammed.

genuineness (Rogers) • Similar to congruence, genuineness in the therapist refers to being one's actual self with the client, not phony or affected.

Gestalt psychology • A psychological approach that studies the organization of experience into patterns or configurations. Gestalt psychologists believe that the whole is greater than the sum of its parts and study, among other concerns, the relationship of a figure to its background.

good-enough mother (Winnicott) • A mother who adapts to her infant's gestures and needs during early infancy and gradually helps the infant develop independence.

grief (interpersonal therapy) • Although a normal process, grief can contribute to depression. When the loss is severe and lengthy or there is more than one loss, this is particularly true.

ground (Gestalt) • The background that contrasts with the *figure* in the perceptions of a field.

grounding (body) • A concept developed by Alexander Lowen that emphasizes being in contact with the ground literally, through feet and legs, as well as figuratively being grounded in the real world.

guided discovery (cognitive; REBT) • A series of questions designed to help the client arrive at logical answers to and conclusions about a certain hypothesis; also called *Socratic dialogue*.

habituation training (cognitive) • A technique of deliberately evoking a thought, writing the thoughts down, and focusing on an intrusive or obsessional thought.

hallucinations • Perceiving (seeing, hearing, feeling, tasting, or smelling) things or people that are not there.

hard techniques (body) • A method of asking the patient to assume an uncomfortable or painful position or of touching a patient in a somewhat painful way, which may bring about intense emotional responses.

hatching (Mahler) • The alertness and attention of the child that are directed toward others.

Hatha yoga (Asian) • Deals with the physiological discipline required in separating the self from thought processes.

hedonism • A philosophical term referring to the concept of seeking pleasure and avoiding pain. In REBT, responsible hedonism refers to maintaining pleasure over the long term by avoiding short-term pleasures that may lead to pain, such as alcohol or cocaine.

heterosexism • The view that being heterosexual is more normal and better than being homosexual, thus devaluing the lifestyle of homosexual individuals.

holding (Winnicott; Scharff & Scharff) • A feeling of security that develops from the physical holding of the child; also used metaphorically to refer to a caring environment.

homeostasis (family systems) • Balance or equilibrium in a system. Such a balance can bring about a stable environment in the system.

homework • Specific behaviors or activities that clients are asked to do after therapy sessions.

homophobia • The dislike, fear, or hatred of homosexual people.

hot cognitions (cognitive) • A strong or highly charged thought or idea that produces powerful emotional reactions.

hot seat (Gestalt) • A form of group therapy in which individuals work one at a time with the therapist, and the audience observes, occasionally being asked to comment on the therapeutic process.

humanism • A philosophy or value system in which human interests and dignity are valued and that takes an individualist, critical, and secular as opposed to a religious or spiritual perspective.

hysteria • A disorder occurring when psychological disturbances take a physical form and there is no physiological explanation, such as an unexplained paralysis of the arms or legs. This term has been replaced by *conversion reaction* in common usage.

iatrogenic • Refers to a psychological or physical disorder that is induced, aggravated, or made worse by the physician or psychotherapist.

id (Freud) • The biological instincts, including sexual and aggressive impulses that seek pleasure. At birth, the id represents the total personality.

identification (Freud) • A defense mechanism in which individuals take on characteristics of another, often a parent, to reduce their own anxieties and internal conflicts. By identifying with the successful parent, an individual can feel successful, even though she has done little that might make her feel productive.

identification with the aggressor (Anna Freud) • A defense mechanism in which the individual identifies with an opponent that he or she cannot master, taking on characteristics of that person.

identified patient (family systems) • The person whom other members of the family identify as having the problem for which treatment is sought.

immediacy (Adler, Gestalt) • Communicating the experience of the therapist to the patient about what is happening in the moment.

implosive therapy (behavior) • A type of prolonged intense exposure therapy in which the client imagines exaggerated scenes that include hypothesized stimuli.

in vivo • Latin for "in life," referring to therapeutic procedures that take place in the client's natural environment.

incongruence (Rogers) • The disharmony that takes place when there is a disagreement between individuals' experience and their view of themselves.

individuation (Jung) • The process of integrating opposing elements of personality to become whole. It involves, in part, bringing *unconscious* contents into relationship with consciousness.

individuation (object relations) • The process of becoming an individual, becoming aware of oneself.

inferior function (Jung) • The function (*thinking, feeling, sensing, intuiting*) that is least well developed in an individual and may be repressed and unconscious, showing itself in dreams or fantasies.

inferiority (Adler) • Feelings of inadequacy and incompetence that develop during infancy and serve as the basis for striving for *superiority* in order to overcome feelings of inferiority.

inferiority complex (Adler) • A strong and pervasive belief that one is not as good as other people. It is usually an exaggerated sense of feelings of inadequacy and insecurity that may result in being defensive or anxious.

instinct (Freud) • Basic drives such as hunger, thirst, sex, and aggression that must be fulfilled in order to maintain physical or psychological equilibrium.

intellectualization (Freud) • A defense mechanism in which emotional issues are not dealt with directly but rather are handled indirectly by abstract thought.

interpersonal deficits (interpersonal therapy) • Social isolation or lack of social skills may cause loneliness and related problems.

interpersonal disputes (interpersonal therapy) • Ongoing struggles, disagreements, or arguments with others can contribute to depression. The disputes may occur in the family, at school, at work, or in other situations.

interpretation (Adler) • Adlerians express insights to their patients that relate to patients' goals. Interpretations often focus on the *family constellation* and *social interest*.

interpretation (psychoanalysis) • The process by which the psychoanalyst points out the unconscious meanings of a situation to a patient. Analysts assess their patients' ability to accept interpretations and bring them to conscious awareness.

interrater reliability • The degree of agreement between or among raters about their observations of an individual or individuals.

intersubjectivity theory (psychoanalysis) • An approach developed by self psychologists and other psychoanalysts that is influenced by *constructivism*. Emphasis is put on valuing the clients' perceptions and the therapeutic relationship.

intrapsychic processes (psychoanalysis) • Impulses, ideas, conflicts, or other psychological phenomena that occur within the mind.

introjection (Gestalt) • A *contact boundary* disturbance in which individuals accept information or values from others without evaluating them or without assimilating them into one's personality.

introversion (Jung) • One of the two major *attitudes* or orientations of personality. Introversion represents an orientation toward subjective experiencing and focusing on one's own perception of the external world.

intuiting (Jung) • A personality *function* that stresses having a hunch or guess about something, which may arise from the unconscious. Its polar opposite is *sensing*.

invariant prescription (Milan group) • A single directive given to parents, designed to create clear boundaries between parents and children, thus establishing distance between parents and children.

irrational belief (REBT) • Unreasonable views or convictions that produce emotional and behavioral problems.

Jungian analyst • A term used for individuals trained at institutions certified by the International Association for Analytic Psychology.

kairos (existential) • A Greek word that refers to the critical point at which a disease is expected to get better or worse. In psychotherapy, it refers to the appropriate timing of a therapeutic intervention.

karma (Asian) • Movement from past incarnations that affect the present.

labeling (cognitive) • Creating a negative view of oneself based on errors or mistakes that one has made. It is a type of overgeneralizing that affects one's view of oneself.

latency (Freud) • Following the *phallic stage,* there is a relatively calm period before adolescence. When *Oedipal* issues are resolved, the child enters the latency period.

libido (Freud) • The basic driving force of personality, which includes sexual energy but is not limited to it.

life tasks (Adler) • There are three basic obligations and opportunities: love, occupation, and society. These are used to help determine therapeutic goals.

lifestyle (Adler) • A way of seeking to fulfill particular goals that individuals set in their lives. Individuals use their own patterns of beliefs, cognitive styles, and behaviors as a way of expressing their style of life. Often style of life or lifestyle is a means for overcoming feelings of *inferiority*.

logotherapy (Frankl) • A type of existential therapy that focuses on challenging clients to search for meaning in their lives. It is associated with the techniques of *attitude modulation, dereflection, paradoxical intention,* and *socrat dialogue*.

low frustration tolerance (REBT) • Inability or difficulty in dealing with events or situations that do not go as planned, for example, getting very angry because someone does not do as you ask.

magnification (cognitive) • A cognitive distortion in which an imperfection is exaggerated into something greater than it is.

mandala (Jung) • A symbolic representation of the unified wholeness of the *Self*. Usually, it has four sections representing an effort to achieve wholeness in the four sections (such as the four directions of the winds).

mania or **manic episodes** • Individuals may demonstrate unfounded elation as indicated by making grandiose plans, being extremely talkative and easily distracted, and engaging in purposeless activity.

marital schism (family systems) • A situation in which one parent tries to undermine the worth of another by competing for sympathy or support from the children.

marital skew (family systems) • A situation in which the psychological disturbance of one parent dominates the family's interactions. An unreal situation for family members is created so that the family can deal with one member's disturbance.

maya (Asian) • A concept derived from Hindu and Buddhist philosophy referring to the distorted perception of reality and experience. Only by directing attention to one's awareness, through concentration or meditation, can reality and experience be perceived more accurately.

meditation (Asian) • Methods for controlling one's mental processes. In concentration meditation the focus is on a stimulus, such as the act of breathing. In awareness meditation the purpose is to examine consciousness and the mind.

meta-analysis • A method of statistically summarizing the results of a large number of studies.

methodology • A systematic application of procedures used in research investigations.

mimesis (Minuchin) • A process by which a therapist appears similar to family members by imitating body language, styles, or other features. A way of joining a family system and getting cooperation from a family.

mind reading (cognitive) • The belief that we know the thoughts in another person's mind.

minimization (cognitive) • Making a positive event much less important than it really is.

miracle questions (solution-focused) • What would be different if a miracle happened? Questions like this help to further define the goal.

mirror technique (psychodrama) • A process in which the *auxiliary* tries to copy the postures, expressions, and words of the *protagonist* so that the protagonist can view the perceptions of his or her behavior, as held by another person.

mirroring (Kohut) • When the parent shows the child that he or she is happy with the child, the child's *grandiose self* is supported. The parent reflects or mirrors the child's view of herself.

Mitwelt (existential) • A way in which individuals relate to the world by interacting socially with others. The focus is on human relationships rather than relationships that are biological or physical (*Umwelt*).

modeling (behavior) • A technique in which a client observes the behavior of another person (a model) and then uses the results of that observation.

modernism • Modernists take a rationalist view, believing that there is scientific truth, which can be achieved through advances in technology and science.

monodrama (psychodrama) • A dialogue with oneself in which an individual plays both parts in a scene by alternating between them.

Morita (Asian) • A Japanese therapy designed to help patients redirect tension away from themselves.

motivational processes (behavior) • For observations to be put into action and then continued for some time, reinforcement must be present. *Reinforcement* brings about motivation.

motor reproduction processes (behavior) • This refers to translating what one has seen into action using motor skills.

multimodal • A therapeutic approach developed by Arnold Lazarus that uses personality theory concepts from social learning theory and takes techniques from many other theories, which it applies in a manner that is consistent with social learning theory. The seven major modalities are represented in the acronym *BASIC I.D.*

multiple family therapy (family systems) • A type of therapy in which members of several families meet together as a group to address individual and family problems.

muscular armor (body) • A protective mechanism in the individual to deal with the punishment that comes from acting on instinctual demands, such as defecating in public.

music therapy • Patients may listen to or participate in musical experiences through singing or using musical instruments to improve emotional expression, reduce stress, or deal nonverbally with other issues.

musterbation (REBT) • Albert Ellis's phrase to characterize the behavior of clients who are inflexible and absolutistic in their thinking, maintaining that they must not fail or that they must have their way.

Naikan (Asian) • A Japanese therapy in which patients focus on their mistakes in past relationships to improve relationships with others so that they may contribute to society.

narcissistic personality disorder • A pattern of self-importance; need for admiration from others and lack of empathy for others are common characteristics of individuals with this disorder. Boasting or being pretentious and feeling that one is superior to others and deserves recognition are also prominent characteristics.

narrative empathy (narrative therapy) • Fully understanding the story of the family or client.

needs (reality) • Essential to reality therapy, psychological needs include a desire for belonging, power, freedom, and fun.

negative cognitive shift (cognitive) • A state in which individuals ignore positive information relevant to themselves and focus on negative information about themselves. See *cognitive shift*.

negative feedback (family systems) • Information that flows back to a system to reduce behavior that causes disequilibrium.

negative prediction (cognitive) • Believing that something bad is going to happen, even though there is no evidence to support this prediction.

network therapy (family systems) • A type of therapy, usually carried out in the home of a patient, in which family members, friends, neighbors, and others may be involved. It often includes several therapists and 20 to 80 people.

neurosis • A large group of disorders characterized by unrealistic anxiety, fears, or obsessions. They are contrasted with more severe psychotic disorders.

neurotic anxiety (existential) • Anxiety that is out of proportion to a particular event. It is often an indication that an individual is not living *authentically* and may fail to make choices and assume responsibility.

normal anxiety (existential) • Anxiety arising from the nature of being human and dealing with unforeseen forces (the *thrown condition*).

object • A term used in psychoanalytic theory to refer, usually, to an important person in the child's life.

object cathexis (Freud) • The investment of psychic energy or *libido* in objects outside the self, such as a person or activity. Such investment is designed to reduce needs.

object constancy (object relations) • A stable self-concept and a stable concept of others, especially the mother, that arises after successful completion of the early phases of the *separation-individuation* process.

object relations • A study of significant others or love objects in a person's life, focusing on childhood views of the relationship (usually unconsciously).

observational learning (behavior) • A type of learning in which people are influenced by observing the behaviors of another.

obsessions • Pervasive and uncontrollable recurring thoughts that interfere with day-to-day functioning.

obsessive-compulsive disorder • Persistent and uncontrollable thoughts or feelings in which individuals feel compelled to repeat behaviors again and again.

Oedipus complex (Freud) • The unconscious sexual desire of the male child for his mother, along with feelings of hostility or fear toward the father. This conflict occurs in the *phallic stage*.

operant conditioning (behavior) • A type of learning in which behavior is increased or decreased by systematically changing its consequences.

operational definition • An empirical definition that seeks to specify procedures that are used to measure a variable or to distinguish it from others.

oral stage (Freud) • The initial stage of psychosexual development, lasting about 18 months. Focus is on gratification through eating and sucking that involves the lips, mouth, and throat.

orgone (body) • A physical force that is supposed to power all physiological and psychological functions; developed by Wilhelm Reich.

outcome research • A systematic investigation of the effectiveness of a theory of psychotherapy or a technique of psychotherapy or a comparison of techniques or theories of psychotherapy; in contrast to process research.

overgeneralization (cognitive) • An example of distorted thinking that occurs when individuals make a rule based on a few negative or isolated events and then apply it broadly.

overt behavior • Actions that can be directly observed by others.

paradoxical intention • A therapeutic strategy in which clients are instructed to engage in and exaggerate behaviors they seek to change. By prescribing the symptom, therapists make patients more aware of their situation and help them achieve distance from the symptoms. For example, a patient who is afraid of mice may be asked to exaggerate his fear of mice, or a patient who hoards paper may be asked to exaggerate that behavior so that living becomes difficult. In this way individuals can become more aware of and more distant from their symptoms.

penis envy (Freud) • A woman's desire to be like a man, or, more specifically, a little girl's belief that she has been deprived of a penis and wishes to possess one.

persona (Jung) • An *archetype* representing the roles that people play in response to social demands of others. It is the mask or disguise that individuals assume when superficially interacting with their environment. It may often be at variance with their true identities.

personal unconscious (Jung) • Thoughts, feelings, and perceptions that are not accepted by the *ego* are stored here. Included are distant memories, as well as personal or unresolved moral conflicts that may be emotionally charged.

personality disorders • These are characterized by being inflexible, lasting many years or a lifetime, and including traits that make social or occupational functioning difficult.

personality theory • A system or way of describing and understanding human behavior.

personalization (cognitive) • A cognitive distortion in which an individual takes an event and relates it to himself or herself, when there is no relationship. An example would be, "Whenever I want to go skiing, there is no snow." Wanting to go skiing does not cause a lack of snow.

phallic stage (Freud) • The third stage of psychosexual development, lasting from about the age of 3 until 5 or 6. The major source of sexual gratification shifts from the anal to the genital region.

phobia • Fear of a situation or object out of proportion to the danger of the situation or the threatening qualities of the object. Examples include fears of height, rats, or spiders.

pleasure principle (Freud) • The tendency to avoid pain and seek pleasure; the principle by which the *id* operates. It is particularly important in infancy.

political awareness (feminist) • An important goal in feminist therapy, to become aware of biases and discriminations in societal institutions.

positive addiction (reality) • Repeating and practicing positive behaviors such as running or meditating so that individuals develop better access to their creativity and the strength to deal with problems in their lives. Discomfort develops when individuals stop these behaviors.

positive feedback (family systems) • Information that leads to deviation from the system's norm, bringing about change and a loss of stability.

positive reinforcement (behavior) • Process by which the introduction of a stimulus has a consequence of a behavior that increases the likelihood that the behavior will be performed again.

postmodernism • A philosophical position that does not assume that there is a fixed truth, but rather that individuals have their own perception of reality or the truth.

posttraumatic stress disorder (PTSD) • Extreme reactions to a highly stressful or traumatic event, such as being raped, robbed, or assaulted, define PTSD. Resulting behaviors may include being easily startled, having recurrent dreams or nightmares, or feeling estranged from or afraid of others.

power analysis (feminist) • Increasing clients' awareness of the power structure in society and the differences in power between men and women; a five-step set of therapeutic techniques.

power intervention (feminist) • Empowering clients can occur in the course of therapeutic discussion. Often encouragement and *reinforcement* are ways to help clients become more powerful.

preconscious (Freud) • Memories of events and experiences that can be retrieved with relatively little effort, such as remembering what one said to a friend yesterday. Information is available to awareness, but not immediately.

pretest-posttest control group design • Comparing a group given one treatment to another group given another treatment or no treatment, by testing individuals before and after therapy.

primary process (Freud) • An action of the *id* that satisfies a need, thus reducing drive tension, by producing a mental image of an object.

process research • The study of various aspects of psychotherapy. Examples include comparing two or more psychotherapeutic techniques and monitoring a change in personality as a result of the introduction of a technique. It is used in contrast to outcome research.

projection (Freud) • A defense mechanism in which people attribute their own unacceptable desires to others and do not deal with their own strong sexual or destructive drives.

projection (Gestalt) • A *contact boundary* disturbance in which we may ascribe aspects of ourselves to others, such as when we attribute some of our own unacceptable thoughts, feelings, or behaviors to friends.

projective identification (psychoanalysis) • Patients take negative aspects of themselves, project them onto someone else, and then identify with or try unconsciously to control that person. In doing so, a part of oneself is "split" off and attributed to another in order to control that other person.

protagonist (psychodrama) • The individual who presents a problem that will be the focus of a psychodrama.

pseudomutuality (family systems) • Presenting an appearance of open relationships in a family so as to conceal distant or troubled relationships within the family. Members develop roles that they play, rather than relating honestly.

pseudoself (Bowen) • An expression of values or opinions that other family members may find acceptable rather than one's own values or opinions.

psyche (Jung) • Jung's term for personality structure, which includes conscious and unconscious thoughts, feelings, and behaviors.

psychic energy (Jung) • Energy of the personality or psyche developing from desiring, motivating, thinking, looking, and so forth.

psychoanalysis • Based on the work of Freud and others, psychoanalysis includes *free association*, dream analysis, and working through *transference issues*. The patient usually lies on a couch, and sessions are conducted three to five times per week.

psychoanalytic therapy • *Free association* and exploration of *unconscious* processes may not be emphasized as strongly as in psychoanalysis. Meetings are usually one to three times per week, and the patient sits in a chair.

psychodrama • A type of psychotherapy in which patients achieve new insight and alter previously ineffective behaviors by enacting life situations. The therapist serves as *director*, and individuals play out their problems, while other group or *audience* members take the role of important individuals in that person's life (*auxiliaries*).

psychosis • A broad term for severe mental disorders in which thinking and emotion are so impaired that individuals have lost contact with reality.

puella aeterna (Jung) • A woman who may have difficulty accepting the responsibilities of adulthood and is likely to be still attached to her father.

puer aeternus (Jung) • A man who may have difficulty growing out of adolescence and becoming more responsible.

punctuation (family systems) • The concept that each person in a transaction believes what he or she says is caused by what the other person says. Basically the individual holds the other responsible for his or her reactions.

push-button technique (Adler) • Designed to show patients how they can create whatever feeling they want by thinking about it. The push-button technique asks patients to remember a pleasant incident that they have experienced, become aware of feelings connected to it, and then switch to an unpleasant image and those feelings. Thus patients learn that they have the power to change their own feelings.

rapprochement (Mahler) • A subphase of the separation-individuation phase of development (between about 18 and 24 months of age). During this time the child experiences an increase in helplessness and a resurgence of the need to be close to the mother. Rapprochement refers to the eventual resolution of a conflict between needing the mother and desiring autonomy.

rationality (REBT) • Thinking, feeling, and acting in ways that will help individuals attain their goals. This is in contrast with irrationality, in which thinking, feeling, and acting are self-defeating and interfere with goal attainment.

rationalization (Freud) • A defense mechanism in which individuals provide a plausible but inaccurate explanation for their failures. An individual who blames her roommate for her own poor performance on an examination may be making excuses for her lack of study, and thus rationalizing.

reaction formation (Freud) • A defense mechanism in which an acceptable impulse can be avoided by acting in an opposite way. Claiming that you like your occupational choice when you do not can help you avoid dealing with problems that result from not liking your work.

reactivity (behavior) • Occurs when clients change their behaviors because they know that they are being observed.

reality principle (Freud) • A guiding principle of the *ego*. It allows postponement of gratification so that environmental demands can be met or so that greater pleasure can be obtained at a later time.

reattribution (cognitive) • Helping clients distribute responsibility for an event (such as an argument) so as to place equal responsibility for the event.

reconstructing (narrative therapy) • The process of telling a story in a different way to bring about positive change.

reflecting team (narrative therapy) • A team of therapists who observe a family therapy session. The family observes the reflecting team discussing the family's session. Associated with narrative therapy.

reframing (family systems; feminist) • Giving a new or different explanation for an event so that constructive change can occur in the family. In feminist therapy, to help individuals understand how social pressures can affect their problems.

regression (Freud) • A defense mechanism in which an individual retreats to an earlier stage of development that was both more secure and pleasant. A child hurt by a reprimand of the teacher may suck his thumb and cry, returning to a more secure and less mature time.

relabeling (family systems; feminist) • Attaching a new name to a problem so that therapeutic progress can be made. For example, saying that a client is overwhelmed by an issue rather than "depressed" may allow the client to develop methods to deal with the problem.

repression (Freud) • A defense mechanism that excludes threatening or painful thoughts or feelings from awareness.

resistance (existential) • Not taking responsibility for one's own life, not being aware of feelings, or being alienated; in essence, not being *authentic*.

resistance (psychoanalysis) • Patients may resist uncovering repressed material in therapy. Most often, through unconscious processes, patients may show aspects of themselves to the therapist.

responsibility (reality) • The process of satisfying one's own needs without interfering with others' fulfillment of their needs.

retention processes (behavior) • This refers to remembering that which has been observed.

retroflection (Gestalt) • A *contact boundary* disturbance in which we do to ourselves what we want to do to someone else, or doing things for ourselves that we want others to do for us.

role distance (psychodrama) • By playing parts connected to or associated with an event, individuals become more objective (or more distant) from their roles.

role playing • Acting the part of someone, something else, or oneself under different conditions. Used by various therapeutic approaches to have the client try out new or different behavior.

role reversal (psychodrama) • A technique in which individuals play the part of someone else in their life to get a better perspective of their relationships with others.

role transitions (interpersonal therapy) • Life changes such as illness, divorce, marriage, or having children leave home can create stress and contribute to depression.

sand tray (Jung) • This is a sandbox with small figures and forms to which individuals can assign meaning. Jungian therapists may attach archetypal significance to the play or stories that individuals develop as they use the figures and forms.

scaling (cognitive) • A technique of turning a dichotomy into a continuum, so that individuals do not see things as "all or nothing." It is used in challenging *dichotomous thinking*.

scaling questions (solution-focused) • Asking family members to rate their progress on a goal from 0 to 10 is the basic approach in using scaling questions.

schemas (cognitive) • Ways of thinking that comprise a set of core beliefs and assumptions about how the world operates.

schizophrenia • Severe disturbances of thought, emotions, or behaviors may be evident by observing disorganized speech and obtaining reports of *delusions* or *hallucinations*.

second-order change (family systems) • A change that produces a lasting difference in the family, as well as fundamental differences in the family's structure and organization. See also *first-order change*.

secondary process (Freud) • A process of the *ego* that reduces intrapsychic tension by dealing directly with external reality. Logic and problem-solving skills may be used. It is in contrast with the primary process of the *id*.

selective abstraction (cognitive) • Selecting one idea or fact from an event, while ignoring other facts, in order to support negative thinking.

Self (Jung) • An archetype that is the center of personality or *psyche*, in which opposing forces of personality are integrated through a process of individuation.

self-disclosure • A process in which therapists or counselors discuss aspects of their own lives in order to enhance therapeutic progress with the client.

self-efficacy (Bandura) • Individuals' perceptions of their ability to deal with different types of events.

self-esteem • An attitude of self-acceptance and self-respect; a feeling of being worthy and competent; in feminist therapy, moving away from being dependent on others' view of oneself toward valuing one's own positive view of oneself.

self-instructional training (Meichenbaum) • A cognitive-behavioral therapy that teaches patients to instruct themselves verbally so that they may cope with difficult situations.

self-monitoring (behavior; cognitive) • A method of assessing thoughts, emotions, or behaviors outside therapy in which clients are asked to keep records of events, feelings, and/or thoughts.

self-transcendence (existential) • Going beyond one's immediate situation to understand one's being and to take responsibility for that being. Going beyond one's own needs to take responsibility for others, or to see the world in different ways.

selfobject (Kohut) • Patterns or themes of unconscious thoughts, images, or representations of another person in an individual. This representation of the person may affect the individual's self-esteem.

sensing (Jung) • A personality *function* that emphasizes one's perception of oneself and one's world. Its polar opposite is *intuiting*.

separation (object relations) • The process that occurs when children gradually distinguish themselves from their mother and others in their world.

separation-individuation (Mahler) • A phase of development in which the child increasingly disengages from the mother and increasingly gains a sense of autonomy.

sex (feminist) • Biological differences that distinguish females from males, used in contrast to *gender*.

shadow (Jung) • The *archetype* that represents unacceptable sexual, animalistic, or aggressive impulses, usually the opposite of the way we see ourselves.

shame-attacking exercises (REBT) • A strategy to encourage people to do things despite a fear of feeling foolish. This way individuals can learn that they can function well, even though they may be seen as doing something silly or foolish.

shaping (behavior) • Gradually reinforcing certain parts of a *target behavior* to more closely approximate the desired target behavior.

social action (feminist) • An important goal in feminist therapy, to work toward changing gender-role stereotyping, sexism, and discrimination.

social contructionism • A *constructivist* point of view that focuses on the shared meanings that people in a culture or society develop.

social interest (Adler) • The caring and concern for the welfare of others that can serve to guide people's behavior throughout their life. It is a sense of being part of society and taking some responsibility to improve it.

sociometry (psychodrama) • A method of learning the nature of relationships between people in a group by getting feedback from members about their interpersonal preferences.

sociopathy • Also called antisocial personality or psychopathic, this term refers to behavior that shows no regard for others, an inability to form meaningful relationships, and a lack of responsibility for one's own actions.

Socratic dialogue (cognitive; existential; REBT) • A series of questions designed to help the client arrive at logical answers to and conclusions about a certain hypothesis; also called *guided discovery*.

soft techniques (body) • A way of asking the patient to assume a gentle posture or softly touching a patient, so that psychological awareness or change may occur.

somatoform disorders • Physical symptoms are known and present, but there is no physiological cause, and a psychological cause is suspected. Reporting headaches or stomachaches when no physiological cause can be found constitutes an example of somatoform disorders.

somatotype (body) • A method of characterizing the physiology of individuals, relating body type to temperament, behavior, or personality characteristics; developed by William Sheldon.

spitting in the client's soup (Adler) • Making comments to the client to make behaviors less attractive or desirable.

splitting (object relations) • A process of keeping incompatible feelings separate from each other. It is an unconscious way of dealing with unwanted parts of the self or threatening parts of others. Because of problems of early development, adults may have difficulty integrating feelings of love and anger, and "split" their feelings by seeing others as all bad or all good.

straightforward task (Haley) • A task that the family is intended to accept and perform as stated.

stress inoculation training (Meichenbaum) • A cognitive-behavioral therapy in which clients learn coping skills for dealing with stressful situations and then practice the skills, while being exposed to the situation.

style of life (Adler) • A way of seeking to fulfill particular goals that individuals set in their lives. Individuals use their own patterns of beliefs, cognitive styles, and behaviors as a way of expressing their style of life. Often style of life or lifestyle is a means for overcoming feelings of inferiority.

sublimation (Freud) • A defense mechanism in which a sexual or aggressive drive can be modified into an acceptable social behavior. For example, anger at others can be sublimated by expressing anger or frustration while being an active spectator at a sports event.

substance abuse • Using a drug to such extent that individuals have difficulty meeting social and occupational obligations constitutes substance abuse.

superego (Freud) • That portion of the personality that represents parental values and, more broadly, society's standards. It develops from the *ego* and is a reflection of early moral training and parental injunctions.

superior function (Jung) • One of the four functions of personality (*thinking, feeling, sensing, intuiting*), which is most highly developed.

superiority (Adler) • The drive to become superior allows individuals to become skilled, competent, and creative.

superiority complex (Adler) • A means of masking feelings of *inferiority* by displaying boastful, self-centered, or arrogant behavior–inflating one's importance at the expense of others.

surplus reality (psychodrama) • Experiences that are not physical reality but rather refer to fantasies, dreams, *hallucinations*, or relationships with imagined people.

symbiosis (Mahler) • A time, usually before the sixth month of life, when infants do not differentiate themselves from their mother.

symbols (Jung) • The content and outward expression of *archetypes*. Symbols represent the wisdom of humanity that can be applied to future issues and are represented differently in a variety of cultures.

symmetrical communication (family systems) • A type of communication characterized by equality among individuals. Such communication can result in one angry remark following another, leading to an argument.

synchronicity (Jung) • Coincidences that have no causal connection. Dreaming of seeing two snakes and then seeing snakes the next day is an example of synchronicity.

systematic desensitization (Wolpe) • A specific procedure for replacing anxiety with relaxation while gradually increasing the imagined exposure to an anxiety-producing situation.

systems theory • A study of the relationship of parts in their context, emphasizing their unity and their relationship to each other. It is applied to biology, medicine, and other fields and used as a basis for family systems therapy.

target behavior (behavior) • A part of the client's problem that can be clearly defined and easily assessed. It is the focus of treatment in behavior therapy.

technical eclecticism • A psychotherapeutic approach in which the personality concepts of one theory provide the rationale for using psychotherapeutic techniques from many theories.

tele (psychodrama) • The energy that is present in an interaction between two people in an interpersonal exchange. Moreno frequently used tele to refer to a sense of caring that developed in group members in the process of psychodrama.

thanatos (Freud) • An instinct toward self-destruction and death; in opposition to the life instinct (*eros*).

The Question (Adler) • Asking "what would be different if you were well?" was a means Adler used to determine if a person's problem was physiological or psychological.

theoretical integration • A psychotherapeutic approach in which concepts of personality and techniques of psychotherapy from one theory are combined with those of one or more other theories.

theory • A group of related laws or relationships that are used to provide explanations within a discipline.

thinking (Jung) • A function of personality in which individuals attempt to understand the world and to solve problems; in contrast to *feeling*.

thought sampling (cognitive) • A means of obtaining samples of thoughts outside therapy by asking the client to record thoughts on tape or in a notebook at different intervals.

thrown condition (existential) • Unforeseen forces or events in the world that one does not cause.

time-limited therapy • An approach to therapy that takes a certain number of sessions (such as 12) to deal with specific issues.

time tripping (multimodal) • A technique in which clients are asked to picture themselves going backward or forward in time to deal with events or issues.

total behavior (reality) • According to Glasser, total behavior includes doing, thinking, feeling, and physiology. These represent Glasser's view of human behavior.

tracking (Minuchin) • Staying attuned to a family's style of relating and understanding symbols of a family's life.

tracking (multimodal) • Observing and responding to the sequence or *firing order* of the seven modalities (*BASIC I.D.*) of different clients.

transcendent function (Jung) • A process in which opposite forces are mediated and expressed through symbols so that individuals can rise above a conflict and see it from a different vantage point.

transference (psychoanalysis) • The patient's feelings and fantasies, both positive and negative, about the therapist. More specifically, it refers to responses by the patient to the therapist as though the therapist were a significant person in the patient's past, usually the mother or father.

transference psychosis (psychoanalysis) • Patients may act out with the therapist early and destructive relationships that they had with their parents.

transitional object (object relations) • An object such as a teddy bear that serves as a transition for infants to shift from experiencing themselves as the center of the world to a sense of themselves as a person among others.

transmuting internalization (Kohut) • Views or representations of interactions with others that gradually form a personality structure for the child. Children learn that they cannot always get what they want and that their parents are not perfect.

transtheoretical • A psychotherapeutic approach in which concepts common to many theories are used to develop a new theory of psychotherapy.

treatment manuals • Written guidelines for therapists on how to treat patients with a particular disorder. They describe skills to be used and the specific sequencing of these skills.

triangulation (family systems) • A process in which two people who are in conflict involve a third person in order to reduce the tension in the relationship between the original two people.

true self (Winnicott) • A sense of being real, whole, and spontaneous that comes from the caring of a *good-enough mother*; used in contrast to the *false self*.

Überwelt (existential) • Religious or spiritual beliefs about the ideal world, the way an individual wants the world to be.

Umwelt (existential) • Relating to the environment, the objects and living beings within it; attending to the biological and physical aspects of the world.

unconditional positive regard (Rogers) • Accepting and appreciating clients as they are, regardless of whether the therapist agrees with the person. Positive regard is not contingent on acting or thinking in a specific way. It is essentially appreciating clients for being themselves.

Unconditional Self Acceptance (USA) (REBT) • Individuals have worth. They should accept that they make mistakes and that some of their assets and qualities are stronger than others. Individuals' acts or performances should be criticized, not their personal worth.

unconscious (Freud) • The part of the mind of which people have no knowledge. It includes memories and emotions that are threatening to the conscious mind and are pushed away.

unfinished business (Gestalt) • Unexpressed feelings from the past that occur in the present and interfere with psychological functioning. They may include feelings, memories, or fantasies from earlier life (often childhood) that can be dealt with in the present.

unique outcomes (narrative therapy) • Sometimes called sparkling moments, unique outcomes are thoughts, feelings, or actions that occur when the family is working well together or the problem starts to dissolve.

word association (Jung) • A method developed by Jung and Riklin in which individuals are asked to respond to a word with another word or phrase. Delayed reaction or other physiological response may provide a way of locating *complexes* that may be disturbing to the individual.

yoga (Asian) • Hindu teachings dealing with ethics, lifestyle, body postures, breath control, intellectual study, and meditation.

zazen (Asian) • A Zen Buddhist approach to *meditation*.

Notes

Chapter 1

[1]From *Psychotherapy with "Impossible" Cases: The Efficient Treatment of Therapy Veterans*, by B. L. Duncan, M. A. Hubble, and S. D. Miller. Copyright © 1997 W. W. Norton & Company, Inc.

Chapter 2

[1]From Introductory Lectures on Psychoanalysis, by S. Freud, 1917, in *The Standard Edition of the Complete Psychological Works of Sigmund Freud* (Vols. 15 and 16), translated and edited by James Strachey. Copyright © 1976. Reprinted by permission of W. W. Norton & Company, Inc., and Hogarth Press.
[2]From *Borderline Conditions and Pathological Narcissism*, by O. F. Kernberg. Copyright © 1975 by Jason Aronson, Inc. Reprinted by permission.
[3]From *Interpreting the Countertransference*, by L. E. Hedges. Copyright © 1992 by Jason Aronson, Inc. Reprinted by permission.
[4]From *Psychoanalytic Object Relations Theory*, by A. J. Horner. Copyright © 1991 by Jason Aronson, Inc. Reprinted by permission.
[5]Reprinted by permission of the publishers from *Relational Concepts in Psychoanalysis: An Integration* by Stephen A. Mitchell, Cambridge, Mass.: Harvard University Press. Copyright © 1988 by the President and Fellows of Harvard College.
[6]Excerpt from *Drive, Ego, Object and Self* by Fred Pine. Copyright © 1990 by Rachael and Daniel Pine. Reprinted by permission of Basic Books, a division of HarperCollins Publishers, Inc.
[7]From *Studies on Hysteria*, by S. Freud, 1895, in *The Standard Edition of the Complete Psychological Works of Sigmund Freud* (Vol. 2), translated and edited by James Strachey. Copyright © 1976. Reprinted by permission of W. W. Norton & Company, Inc., and Hogarth Press.
[8]*From Childhood and Society*, by E. H. Erikson. Copyright © 1950. Reprinted by permission of W. W. Norton & Company, Inc., and Chatto & Windus.
[9]From *Aggression in Personality Disorders and Perversions*, by O. F. Kernberg. Copyright © 1992 by Yale University Press. Reprinted by permission.

671

[10]From *The Analysis of the Self*, by H. Kohut. Copyright © 1971 by International Universities Press, Inc. Reprinted by permission.

[11]From "The Treatment of Eating Disorders," by M. A. Scharfman, in *Psychotherapy: The Analytic Approach*, edited by M. J. Aronson and M. A. Scharfman. Copyright © 1992 by Jason Aronson, Inc. Reprinted by permission.

[12]From *How to Practice Brief Psychodynamic Psychotherapy: The Core Conflictual Relationship Theme Method*, by H. E. Book. Copyright © 1998 American Psychological Association. Reprinted by permission.

[13]Excerpt from pp. 62–63 of *Handbook of Short-Term Dynamic Psychotherapy*, edited by Paul Crits-Cristoph and Jacques P. Barber. Copyright © 1991 by Basic Books, Inc. Reprinted by permission of Basic Books, a division of HarperCollins Publishers, Inc.

[14]From *Object Relations Family Therapy*, by D. E. Scharff and J. S. Scharff. Copyright © 1987 by Jason Aronson, Inc. Reprinted by permission.

[15]From *Object Relations Family Therapy*, by D. E. Scharff and J. S. Scharff. Copyright © 1987 by Jason Aronson, Inc. Reprinted by permission.

Chapter 3

[1]From *Memories, Dreams, Reflections*, by C. G. Jung, recorded and edited by Aniela Jaffe, translated by R. & C. Winston. Translation copyright © 1961, 1962, 1963 by Random House, Inc. Copyright renewed 1989, 1990, 1991 by Random House, Inc. Reprinted by permission of Pantheon Books, a division of Random House, Inc., and William Collins Sons & Co. Ltd.

[2]Reprinted from "Psychopathology and Analysis," by D. F. Sandner and J. Beebe, in *Jungian Analysis*, edited by M. Stein, by permission of Open Court Publishing Company, La Salle, Illinois. Copyright © 1982 by Open Court Publishing Company.

[3]From *Memories, Dreams, Reflections*, by C. G. Jung, recorded and edited by Aniela Jaffe, translated by R. & C. Winston. Translation copyright © 1961, 1962, 1963 by Random House, Inc. Copyright renewed 1989, 1990, 1991 by Random House, Inc., Reprinted by permission of Pantheon Books, a division of Random House, Inc., and William Collins Sons & Co. Ltd.

[4]From *Memories, Dreams, Reflections*, by C. G. Jung, recorded and edited by Aniela Jaffe, translated by R. & C. Winston. Translation copyright © 1961, 1962, 1963 by Random House, Inc. Copyright renewed 1989, 1990, 1991 by Random House, Inc. Reprinted by permission of Pantheon Books, a division of Random House, Inc., and William Collins Sons & Co. Ltd.

[5]Carl Jung, "The Development of Personality," in *The Collected Works of C. Jung, Volumes 17 and 18*. Copyright © 1954 and 1970 by Princeton University Press. Reprinted by permission of Princeton University Press.

[6]From *The Collected Works of C. Jung, Volume 9*, Part 1. Copyright © 1959 by Princeton University Press.

[7]From "Methods of Treatment in Analytical Psychology," by G. Adler, in *Psychoanalytic Techniques*, edited by B. Wolman. Copyright © 1967 by Basic Books, Inc.

[8]Reprinted from "Transference/Countertransference," by A. B. Ulanov, in *Jungian Analysis*, edited by M. Stein, by permission of Open Court Publishing Company, La Salle, Illinois. Copyright © 1982 by Open Court Publishing Company.

[9]From *Memories, Dreams, Reflections,* by C. G. Jung, recorded and edited by Aniela Jaffe, translated by R. & C. Winston. Translation copyright © 1961, 1962, 1963 by Random House, Inc. Copyright renewed 1989, 1990, 1991 by Random House, Inc. Reprinted by permission of Pantheon Books, a division of Random House, Inc., and William Collins Sons & Co. Ltd.

[10]From "Jungian Analysis," by M. A. Mattoon, in *Psychotherapist's Casebook,* edited by I. L. Kutash and A. Wolf. Copyright © 1986 by Jossey-Bass Inc., Publishers. Reprinted by permission.

Chapter 4

[1]Reprinted with the permission of Simon & Schuster, Inc., from the Macmillan College text *Adlerian Counseling and Psychotherapy, 2nd edition,* by Don C. Dinkmeyer, Don C. Dinkmeyer, Jr., and Len Sperry. Copyright © 1987 by Merrill, an imprint of Macmillan College Publishing Company, Inc.

[2]From *Psychodynamics, Psychotherapy, and Counseling: Collected Papers,* by R. Dreikurs. Copyright © 1967 by the Alfred Adler Institute. Reprinted by permission.

[3]Reproduced by permission of the publisher, F. E. Peacock Publishers Inc., Itasca, Illinois. From C. Manaster and R. Corsini, *Individual Psychology,* copyright 1982, p. 102.

[4]Quotes and examples from selected pages from *The Individual Psychology of Alfred Adler* by Heinz L. Ansbacher and Rowena R. Ansbacher. Copyright © 1956 by Basic Books, Inc. Copyright renewed 1984 by Heinz L. and Rowena R. Ansbacher. Reprinted by permission of Basic Books, a division of HarperCollins Publishers, Inc.

[5]Quotes and examples from selected pages from *The Individual Psychology of Alfred Adler* by Heinz L. Ansbacher and Rowena R. Ansbacher. Copyright © 1956 by Basic Books, Inc. Copyright renewed 1984 by Heinz L. and Rowena R. Ansbacher. Reprinted by permission of Basic Books, a division of HarperCollins Publishers, Inc.

[6]From "Adlerian Psychotherapy," by D. E. Peven and B. H. Shulman, in *Psychotherapist's Casebook,* edited by I. L. Kutash and A. Wolf. Copyright © 1986 by Jossey-Bass Inc., Publishers. Reprinted by permission.

[7]From "Adlerian Treatment of Borderline Personality Disorder," by J. W. Croake, in *Individual Psychology,* Vol. 45:4 (1989), pp. 478–489. By permission of the author and the University of Texas Press.

Chapter 5

[1]Excerpt from *Existence: A New Dimension in Psychiatry and Psychology,* edited by R. May, E. Angel, and H. Ellenberger. Copyright © 1958 by Basic Books, Inc. Reprinted by permission of Basic Books, a division of HarperCollins Publishers, Inc.

[2]Excerpt from *Existence: A New Dimension in Psychiatry and Psychology,* edited by R. May, E. Angel, and H. Ellenberger. Copyright © 1958 by Basic Books, Inc. Reprinted by permission of Basic Books, a division of HarperCollins Publishers, Inc.

[3]From *Man's Search for Meaning: An Introduction to Logotherapy,* by Viktor E. Frankl. Copyright © 1959, 1962, 1984, 1992 by Viktor E. Frankl. Reprinted by permission of Beacon Press.

[4]Excerpt from *Existential Psychotherapy*, by Irvin D. Yalom. Copyright © 1980 by The Yalom Family Trust. Reprinted by permission of Basic Books, a division of HarperCollins Publishers, Inc.

[5]Excerpt from *Existential Psychotherapy*, by Irvin D. Yalom. Copyright © 1980 by The Yalom Family Trust. Reprinted by permission of Basic Books, a division of HarperCollins Publishers, Inc.

[6]From *Man's Search for Meaning: An Introduction to Logotherapy*, by Viktor E. Frankl. Copyright © 1959, 1962, 1984, 1992 by Viktor E. Frankl. Reprinted by permission of Beacon Press.

[7]From *Existential Counseling in Practice*, by E. van Deurzen-Smith, p. 168. Copyright © 1988 by Sage Publications, Inc. Reprinted by permission.

[8]From *The Art of the Psychotherapist*, by J. F. T. Bugental. Copyright © 1987 by W. W. Norton & Company, Inc. Reprinted by permission.

[9]Excerpt from *Existential Psychotherapy*, by Irvin D. Yalom. Copyright © 1980 by The Yalom Family Trust. Reprinted by permission of Basic Books, a division of HarperCollins Publishers, Inc.

[10]From *Existential Counseling in Practice*, by E. van Deurzen-Smith, p. 35. Copyright © 1988 by Sage Publications, Inc. Reprinted by permission.

[11]Excerpt from *Existential Psychotherapy*, by Irvin D. Yalom. Copyright © 1980 by The Yalom Family Trust. Reprinted by permission of Basic Books, a division of HarperCollins Publishers, Inc.

[12]From *Love's Executioner and Other Tales of Psychotherapy*, by Irvin D. Yalom. Copyright © 1989 by Irvin D. Yalom. Reprinted by permission of Basic Books, a division of HarperCollins Publishers, Inc.

[13]From *The Search for Authenticity: An Existential-Analytic Approach to Psychotherapy*, revised edition, by J. F. T. Bugental. Copyright © 1981 by Holt, Rinehart & Winston.

[14]From *Meaningful Living*, by E. Lukas. Copyright © 1984 by the Institute of Logotherapy Press.

[15, 16]Excerpts from *Existential Psychotherapy*, by Irvin D. Yalom. Copyright © 1980 by The Yalom Family Trust. Reprinted by permission of Basic Books, a division of HarperCollins Publishers, Inc.

[17]From *The Search for Authenticity: An Existential-Analytic Approach to Psychotherapy*, revised edition, by J. F. T. Bugental. Copyright © 1981 by Holt, Rinehart & Winston.

[18]From *Existential Counseling in Practice*, by E. van Deurzen-Smith, p. 33. Copyright © 1988 by Sage Publications, Inc. Reprinted by permission.

[19]Excerpt from *Existential Psychotherapy*, by Irvin D. Yalom. Copyright © 1980 by The Yalom Family Trust. Reprinted by permission of Basic Books, a division of HarperCollins Publishers, Inc.

Chapter 6

[1]From *The Therapeutic Relationship and Its Impact: A Study of Psychotherapy with Schizophrenics*, by C. R. Rogers, G. T. Gendlin, D. V. Kiesler, and C. Truax. Copyright © 1967 by The University of Wisconsin Press. Reprinted by permission.

[2]Carl R. Rogers, *On Becoming a Person*. Copyright © 1961 Houghton Mifflin Company. Excerpted with permission.

[3]Carl R. Rogers, *On Becoming a Person*. Copyright © 1961 Houghton Mifflin Company. Excerpted with permission.

[4]From "A Child's Journey Through Loss," by D. Rogers and P. J. Brickman, 1995, *The Person-Centered Review*, 2, 94–103. Copyright © 1995 Sage Publications, Inc.

Chaper 7

[1]From *Gestalt Therapy Integrated*, by E. Polster and M. Polster. Copyright © 1973 by Brunner/Mazel, Inc. Reprinted by permission.

[2]From *Gestalt Therapy Integrated*, by E. Polster and M. Polster. Copyright © 1973 by Brunner/Mazel, Inc. Reprinted by permission.

[3]Excerpts from *Gestalt Approaches in Counseling*, by William R. Passons, copyright © 1975 by Holt, Rinehart & Winston, Inc., reprinted by permission of the publisher.

[4]From *Gestalt Therapy Integrated*, by E. Polster and M. Polster. Copyright © 1973 by Brunner/Mazel, Inc. Reprinted by permission.

[5]From *Gestalt Therapy Integrated*, by E. Polster and M. Polster. Copyright © 1973 by Brunner/Mazel, Inc. Reprinted by permission.

[6]From *Fritz Perls: Here and Now*, by J. Gaines. Copyright © 1979 by Jack Gaines. Reprinted by permission.

[7]From "An Interview with Erving and Miriam Polster," by R. Hycner, 1987, *Gestalt Journal*, 10, 27–66. Copyright © 1987 by the *Gestalt Journal*. Reprinted by permission.

[8]From "Gestalt Therapy," by J. S. Simkin, A. N. Simkin, L. Brien, and C. Sheldon, in *Psychotherapist's Case Book*, edited by I. L. Kutash and A. Wolf. Copyright © 1986 by Jossey-Bass. Reprinted by permission.

[9]From "Present-Centeredness: Techniques, Perception, and Ideal," in *Gestalt Therapy Now*, edited by J. Fagan and I. L. Shepherd. Copyright © 1970 by Science and Behavior Books. Reprinted by permission.

[10]From *In and Out of the Garbage Pail*, by F. S. Perls. Copyright © 1969 by Real People Press. Reprinted by permission.

[11]From *Gestalt Therapy Now*, by J. Fagan and I. L. Shepherd. Copyright © 1970 by Science and Behavior Books. Reprinted by permission.

[12]From *Experiential Psychotherapy Within Families*, by W. Kempler. Copyright © 1981 by Brunner/Mazel, Inc. Reprinted with permission.

Chapter 8

[1]From J. Wolpe, *The Practice of Behavior Therapy*, 4th edition. Copyright © 1990 by Allyn & Bacon. Reprinted by permission.

[2]From J. Wolpe, *The Practice of Behavior Therapy*, 4th edition. Copyright © 1990 by Allyn & Bacon. Reprinted by permission.

[3]From "Obsessive Compulsive Disorder," by D. S. Riggs and E. B. Foa, in *Clinical Handbook of Psychological Disorders*, edited by D. H. Barlow. Copyright © 1993 by Guilford Publications, Inc. Reprinted by permission.

[4]From "Generalized Anxiety Disorder," by T. D. Borkovec, K. A. Crnic, and E. Costello, in *Handbook of Behavior Therapy with Children and Adults*, edited by R. Ammerman and M. Hersen. Copyright © 1993 by Allyn & Bacon. Reprinted by permission.

Chapter 9

[1]From *Rational-Emotive Therapy with Children and Adolescents*, by M. E. Bernard and M. R. Joyce. Copyright © 1984 by John Wiley & Sons, Inc. Reprinted by permission of John Wiley & Sons, Inc.

[2]From "Brief Therapy: The Rational-Emotive Method," by A. Ellis, in *The First Session in Brief Theory*, edited by S. H. Budman, M. F. Hoyt, and S. Friedman. Copyright © 1992 by Guilford Press. Reprinted by permission.

[3]From "Using RET Effectively: Reflections and Interview," by A. Ellis, in *Using Rational-Emotive Therapy Effectively*, edited by M. E. Bernard. Copyright © 1991 by Plenum Publishing Corporation. Reprinted by permission.

[4]From *Rational-Emotive Treatment of Alcoholism and Substance Abuse*, by A. Ellis, J. F McInerney, R. A. DiGiuseppe, and R. Yeager. Copyright © 1988 by Allyn & Bacon. Reprinted by permission.

[5]From "RET with Women: Some Special Issues," by I. Zachary, in *Rational-Emotive Therapy: A Skills Based Approach*, edited by R. Grieger and J. Boyd. Copyright © 1980 by Van Nostrand Reinhold. Reprinted by permission.

[6]From *Rational-Emotive Couples Therapy*, by A. Ellis, J. Sichel, R. Yeager, D. DiMattia, and R. DiGiuseppe. Copyright © 1989 by Allyn & Bacon. Reprinted by permission.

Chapter 10

[1]From "A Psychosocial Approach for Conceptualizing Schematic Development for Cognitive Therapy," by A. Freeman, in *Cognitive Therapies in Action: Evolving Innovative Practice*, edited by K. T. Kuehlwein and H. Rosen. Copyright © 1993 by Jossey-Bass Inc., Publishers. Reprinted by permission.

[2]From *Clinical Applications of Cognitive Therapy*, by A. Freeman, J. Pretzer, B. Fleming, and K. Simon. Copyright © 1990 by Plenum Publishing Corporation. Reprinted by permission.

[3]From "Coping with Life-Threatening Illness: A Cognitive Therapy Perspective," by B. S. Liese and M. W. Larson, 1995, *Journal of Cognitive Psychotherapy*, 9, 18–24. Copyright © 1995 by Springer Publishing Company. Reprinted by permission.

[4]From *Clinical Applications of Cognitive Therapy*, by A. Freeman, J. Pretzer, B. Fleming, and K. Simon. Copyright © 1990 by Plenum Publishing Corporation. Reprinted by permission.

[5]From *Cognitive Therapy of Anxiety Disorders: A Practice Manual and Conceptual Guide*, by A. Wells, pp. 254–255. Copyright © 1997 John Wiley & Sons, Inc. Reprinted by permission.

[6]From *Cognitive Therapy of Substance Abuse*, by A. T. Beck, F. D. Wright, C. F. Newman, and B. Liese. Copyright © 1993 by Guilford Press. Reprinted by permission.

[7]From "Cognitive Marital Therapy: A Case Study," by F. M. Dattilio, 1990, *Journal of Family Psychotherapy*, 1, 15–31. Copyright © 1990 by Haworth Press, Inc. Reprinted by permission.

Chapter 11

[1]Excerpt from *Using Reality Therapy*, by Robert E. Wubbolding. Copyright © 1991 by Robert E. Wubbolding. Reprinted by permission of HarperCollins Publishers, Inc.

[2]Case: Geronilla from *Control Theory in the Practice of Reality Therapy*, by Naomi Glasser. Copyright © 1989 by Naomi Glasser. Reprinted by permission of Harper-Collins Publishers, Inc.

[3]Case: Zeeman from *Control Theory in the Practice of Reality Therapy*, by Naomi Glasser. Copyright © 1989 by Naomi Glasser. Reprinted by permission of HarperCollins Publishers, Inc.

Chapter 12

[1]From *Half the Human Experience: The Psychology of Women*, 4th ed., by J. S. Hyde. Copyright © 1991 by D. C. Heath and Company. Reprinted by permission.

[2]Reprinted by permission of the publishers from *In a Different Voice: Psychological Theory and Women's Development*, by Carol Gilligan. Cambridge, MA: Harvard University Press. Copyright © 1982, 1993 by Carol Gilligan.

[3]From *Skills in Counseling Women*, by M. Russell. Copyright © 1984 by Charles C. Thomas. Courtesy of Charles C. Thomas, Publisher, Springfield, Illinois.

[4]From *Radical Feminist Therapy*, by B. Burstow, pp. 140–141. Copyright © 1992 by Sage Publications, Inc. Reprinted by permission.

[5]From "Clinical Applications of the Stone Center Theoretical Approach to Minority Women," by C. W. Turner, in *Women's Growth in Diversity: More Writings from the Stone Center*, edited by J. V. Jordan, pp. 83–84. Copyright © 1997 Guilford Press. Reprinted by permission.

[6]From *A New Approach to Women and Therapy*, by M. Greenspan. Copyright © 1983 by McGraw-Hill, Inc. Reprinted with permission of the author and McGraw-Hill, Inc.

[7]From "Minority Women: A Nodal Position in the Functioning of the Social System," by E. B. Pinderhughes, in *Women and Family Therapy*, edited by M. Ault-Riche. Copyright © 1986 by Aspen Publishers, Inc. Reprinted by permission of the author.

Chapter 13

[1]From "Theoretical Aspects and Clinical Relevance of the Multi-Generational Model of Family Therapy," by P. J. Guerin, Jr., and K. B. Guerin, in *Family Therapy: Theory and Practice*, edited by P. J. Guerin, Jr. Copyright © 1976 by Gardner Press. Reprinted by permission.

[2]Reprinted by permission of the publishers from *Families and Family Therapy*, by Salvador Minuchin. Cambridge, MA: Harvard University Press. Copyright © 1974 by the President and Fellows of Harvard College.

[3]From Stategic Family Therapy, by C. Madanes. Copyright © 1981 by Jossey-Bass Inc., Publishers. Reprinted by permission.

[4]Excerpt from *The Family Crucible*, by Augustus Y. Napier and Carl Whitaker. Copyright © 1978 by Augustus Y. Napier and Carl A. Whitaker. Reprinted by permission of HarperCollins Publishers, Inc.

[5]From *Satir Step by Step*, by V. M. Satir and M. Baldwin. Copyright © 1983 by Science and Behavior Books. Reprinted by permission.

[6]From *Interviewing for Solutions, 1st edition*, by P. DeJong and I. K. Berg, pp. 14–16. Copyright © 1998. Reprinted with permission of Wadsworth Publishing, a division of International Thompson Publishing. Fax 800 730-2215.

[7]From *Playful Approaches to Serious Problems: Narrative Therapy with Children and Their Families*, by J. Freeman, D. Epston, and D. Lobovits, pp. 57–58, 278–280, 285. Copyright © 1997 W. W. Norton & Company, Inc.

[8]From *Family Games: General Models of Psychotic Processes in the Family*, by M. Selvini-Palazzoli, S. Cirillo, M. Selvini, and A. M. Sorrentino. Copyright © 1989 by W. W. Norton & Company, Inc. Reprinted by permission.

[9]From "Ethnicity in Family Therapy: A Comparison of Brief Strategic Therapy and Culture-Focused Therapy," by M. Richeport-Haley, 1998, *The American Journal of Family Therapy, 26*, 77–90. Copyright © 1998 Brunner/Mazel, Inc.

Chapter 14

[1]From "Naikan Psychotherapy," by D. K. Reynolds, in *Handbook of Innovative Psychotherapies*, edited by R. J. Corsini. Copyright © 1981 by John Wiley & Sons, Inc. Reprinted by permission of John Wiley & Sons, Inc.

[2]From *Flowing Bridges, Quiet Waters*, by D. K. Reynolds. Copyright © 1989 by the State University of New York Press. Reprinted by permission.

[3]From *Interpersonal Psychotherapy for Dysthymic Disorder*, by J. Markowitz, pp. 120–123. Copyright © 1998 American Psychiatric Press, Inc. Reprinted by permission.

[4]From *The Essential Moreno: Writings on Psychodrama, Group Method, and Spontaneity*, edited by J. Fox. Copyright © 1987 by Springer Publishing Company. Used by permission of Springer Publishing Company, Inc., New York.

[5]From *Psychodrama: Resolving Emotional Problems through Role-Playing*, by L. Yablonsky. Copyright © 1976 by Basic Books. Reprinted by permission of the author.

[6]From "Alternatives in Psychiatry: Dance Movement Therapy in the Community," by M. Steiner, in *Dance Movement Therapy: Theory and Practice*, edited by H. Payne. Copyright © 1992 by Routledge. Reprinted by permission.

[7]From "One on One: The Role of the Dramatherapist Working with Individuals," by R. Landy, in Dramatherapy: Theory and Practice 2, edited by S. Jennings. Copyright © 1992 by Routledge. Reprinted by permission.

[8]From "Research in Music Therapy with Sexually Abused Clients," by P. Rogers in *Handbook of Inquiry in the Arts Therapies: One River, Many Currents*, edited by H. Payne. Copyright © 1993 by Kingsley. Reprinted by permission.

Chapter 15

[1]From *Comprehensive Handbook of Psychotherapy Integration*, edited by G. Stricker and I. R. Gold. Copyright © 1993 by Plenum Publishing Corporation. Reprinted by permission.

[2]From *The Practice of Multimodal Therapy*, by A. A. Lazarus. Copyright © 1981 by McGraw-Hill, Inc. Reprinted with permission of McGraw-Hill, Inc.

[3]From "Different Types of Eclecticism and Integration: Let's Be Aware of the Dangers," 1995, *Journal of Psychotherapy Integration, 5*, pp. 27–39. Copyright © 1995 by Plenum Publishing Corporation. Reprinted by permission.

Name Index

Subject Index

This page is an extension of the copyright page.

TO THE OWNER OF THIS BOOK:

I hope that you have found *Theories of Psychotherapy,* Second Edition, useful. So that this book can be improved in a future edition, would you take the time to complete this sheet and return it? Thank you.

School and address: _____

_____

Department: _____

Instructor's name: _____

1. What I like most about this book is: _____

_____

_____

2. What I like least about this book is: _____

_____

_____

3. My general reaction to this book is: _____

_____

_____

4. The name of the course in which I used this book is: _____

_____

5. Were all of the chapters of the book assigned for you to read?_____

   If not, which ones weren't? _____

6. In the space below, or on a separate sheet of paper, please write specific suggestions for improving this book and anything else you'd care to share about your experience in using this book.

_____

_____

_____

_____

OPTIONAL:

Your name: _____ Date:_____

May we quote you, either in promotion for *Theories of Psychotherapy,* Second Edition, or in future publishing ventures?

Yes: _____ No: _____

Sincerely yours,

Richard S. Sharf

COLLECTION FOLIO

Mehdi Charef

Le thé
au harem
d'Archi Ahmed

Mercure de France

Mehdi Charef est né en Algérie en 1952. Au début des années cinquante, son père part travailler en France comme terrassier, puis fait venir sa famille. Mehdi Charef grandit dans les cités de transit et les bidonvilles. Dès sa jeunesse, il travaille en usine. Son premier roman, paru en 1983, *Le thé au harem d'Archi Ahmed* (Folio n° 1958), a été porté à l'écran. Mehdi Charef est également l'auteur du *Harki de Meriem* (Folio n° 2310).

*Pour Mebarka, ma mère,
même si elle ne sait pas lire.*

Madjid, agenouillé devant sa moto, s'essuya les mains, pleines de cambouis, dans un chiffon.

La vieille moto, une Norton, dorénavant s'essoufflait à chaque difficulté. Il fallait presque la pousser pour qu'elle monte une côte comme celle de la Défense, et sur l'autoroute de Pontoise Madjid avait paniqué le soir où il s'était fait doubler par un camion. Elle n'en voulait plus, sa vieille mécanique. Pour la réparer, fallait des sous, et Madjid n'en avait pas.

A la lueur de la lampe baladeuse, il regardait dessus, dessous, dépité de se retrouver en rade d'engin. Résigné, impuissant, il cala la moto bien en place, décrocha la lampe de la prise électrique et sortit de la cave, verrouillant la porte au cadenas.

Dans le couloir humide et mal éclairé qui sentait l'urine et la merde il s'alluma une cigarette et se dirigea vers la sortie.

Arrivé devant l'escalier qui donnait accès au hall, il se ravisa. Il avait grimpé déjà quelques marches quand il fit demi-tour. Il marcha jusqu'au fond du couloir, jusqu'à la dernière cave. Au bout de l'obscurité, il s'arrêta.

Et là, dans ce réduit, dans ce débarras, entre un sommier dont les ressorts ont crevé la toile juste aux endroits où il y a des taches d'urine et un Frigidaire, porte ouverte, malade, descendu certainement en toute hâte une nuit, là, dans une forte odeur d'hôpital, est allongé le petit Farid, dix-neuf ans, et qui en paraît quinze, le visage sec et amaigri sous une barbe juvénile, complètement dans le cirage.

Farid est allongé sur des cartons d'oranges sud-africaines, marque Outspan, et sous sa tête, en guise d'oreiller, une vieille valise cartonnée en faux cuir marron, cabossée dans les coins.

Madjid s'avance doucement vers Farid, le fixe. Farid ne remarque pas. Il tient dans sa main droite un chiffon sale imbibé d'éther, qu'il porte d'un geste lent et lourd sur son nez.

« Salut, Rustine ! » dit Madjid sans élever la voix, comme s'il lui faisait une confidence. Il se penche une nouvelle fois et rappelle Farid.

Rustine bouge un petit peu la tête et ouvre à moitié les yeux vers Madjid. Il n'y a aucune expression sur son visage. Le regard est vague et lointain. Il a un pauvre sourire malade, qui découvre une dentition jaune. Il tend sa main gauche, imprécise, pour serrer la pince de son visiteur et respire un bon coup son chiffon dégueulasse.

Madjid l'observe, sans savoir quoi penser, quoi dire à ce mec qui pèse à peine quarante kilos et qui est certainement en train de crever, et tout le monde s'en fiche. Tout le monde dans la cité sait que Farid se dope. Il s'est dopé à tout, dit-on. En fait, à toutes les drogues qui lui étaient accessibles financièrement, même à l'essence. C'est du temps où il se droguait à la dissolution, cette colle avec laquelle on répare les chambres à air, que lui est venu ce surnom de Rustine.

Madjid ne trouvait pas ça drôle, mais Pat, son pote, lui, ça le faisait rire, Rustine.

Madjid sort une cigarette et la pose à côté du flacon d'éther qui se trouve sur le ventre de Rustine. Un ventre creux. Rustine ne bronche pas, la main sur le pif. Il met quelques gouttes d'éther sur le chiffon dans le creux de sa main squelettique et renifle encore. Madjid s'impatiente. Les toiles d'araignée poussiéreuses pendent du plafond suintant de cette cave dont Farid a fait sa maison. Les murs sont chargés de graffiti, dessins, slogans.

Dans l'obscurité, on peut lire, entrevoir, des mots ou moitiés de mots, « foutre », « cri », « j'irai bien », « marre », à la craie rouge.

Madjid essaie de lire, de piger. Il n'y a rien à comprendre, que dalle ! Rien à dire ! Rien à faire !

Vaut mieux ne plus revenir dans cette putain de cave, se dit-il.

Tout est devant lui, le désespoir, ça fout les jetons, ça fourmille au creux de l'échine, et ça refroidit dans le dos. Faut mettre les santiagos, et pas demander son reste. Madjid quitte Rustine en grillant sa gitane.

Dans le hall, il retrouve la lumière forte et blanche des néons, et c'est mieux comme ça ! il respire. Il retrouve aussi le père Levesque, son voisin de palier, qui attend l'ascenseur. Madjid le salue, Levesque répond de son sourire difficile à sortir, regard flou. Il a sa dose de Ricard dans la gueule, rentre bourré comme chaque soir après le turbin.

Madjid ne se souvient pas de l'avoir vu un seul jour à jeun, ou seulement en état de se conduire. L'ascenseur arrive, ils s'y engouffrent en se faisant des politesses, à toi, à moi.

Dans la caisse ça sent rudement le Ricard, et c'est lourd à supporter, cette haleine, pour Madjid.

Le père Levesque jure quand il s'aperçoit qu'il a mis ses pieds dans une flaque de pisse. Madjid se retourne et dit en regardant par terre :

— C'est les mômes et les clébards qui pissent !

Le père Levesque, le visage bouffi, rougi par l'alcool et le froid qui règne dehors, ne pipe commentaire.

Pour lui c'est les Arabes qui pissent dans l'ascenseur et dégradent le bâtiment. C'est pourquoi Madjid s'est cru obligé de répondre à ses jurons. Les Arabes n'ont pas de chien, ou très rarement.

Pauvres bêtes de chiens, enfermés toute la sainte journée dans un appartement, attendant que Maîmaître rentre du boulot pour les emmener à la pissette : à peine dans l'ascenseur, ils urinent déjà, leur vessie ne tient plus. Et ça sent fort, le pipi de bête. Et ça fait partie de la vie de la cité.

Au troisième étage, ils sortent de l'ascenseur.

12

Madjid entre chez lui sans sonner, la porte toujours ouverte.

Levesque, lui, sonne. Il sonne à plusieurs reprises avant que sa femme vienne lui ouvrir. Il a du mal à passer la lourde.

Madjid ôte ses chaussures et file droit vers sa chambre, le long du couloir. Ses frères et sœurs, famille nombreuse dont il est l'aîné, chahutent en faisant leurs devoirs de classe autour de la table du salon.

Sa mère Malika, robuste femme algérienne, de la cuisine voit passer son fils furtivement dans le couloir.

— Madjid !

Lui, sans se retourner, entre dans sa piaule.

— Ouais !

— Va chercher ton père.

— T'tà l'heure !

Malika pose sa casserole sur l'évier, en colère :

— Tout de suite !

Dans sa chambre, il met les Sex Pistols et leur *Good save the queen* à fond les cuivres, comme ça il n'entend plus sa mère. Il s'allonge sur son plumard, les mains sous la nuque, et ferme les yeux. Il pense être tranquille, peinard, écoutant le rock dur. Mais voilà que sa mère rapplique et lui rappelle, le regard agressif :

15

— Ti la entendi ce quou ji di ?

Elle parle un mauvais français avec un drôle d'accent et les gestes napolitains en plus.

Madjid, comme un qui revient d'une journée de labeur, fatigué, agacé, lui répond, yeux au plafond :

— Fais pas chier le bougnoule !

Là, vexée, comprenant à moitié ce qu'il vient de dire, elle se met en colère, et dans ces cas-là ses origines africaines prennent le dessus, elle tance en arabe.

Elle s'avance jusqu'au pied du lit et secoue son fils qui ne bronche pas. Elle essuie ses mains sur le tablier éternellement autour de ses hanches, stoppe l'électrophone, remonte la mèche de cheveux grisonnants qui lui tombe sur les yeux et repart de plus belle en injuriant son fils de tout ce qu'elle sait de français.

« Finiant, foyou », tout y passe.

Madjid fait semblant de ne pas comprendre.

Calmement, il répond pour la faire enrager encore plus :

— Qu'est-ce tu dis là, j'ai rien compris.

La mère, hors d'elle : « Pas compris, pas compris. Ah ! Rabbi (ah ! mon Dieu) » en se tapant sur les cuisses.

Elle essaie de lui tirer l'oreille. Il esquive. Il se lève de son lit prestement en se grattant la tête.

La mère, en le suivant :

— Oui, finiant, foyou !

Pendant qu'elle continue à crier en implorant tous les saints du Coran, il remet les Sex Pistols dans leur pochette et soupire d'agacement.

— Je vais aller au consulat d'Algérie, elle dit maintenant à son fils, la Malika, en arabe, qu'ils viennent te chercher pour t'emmener au service militaire là-bas ! Tu apprendras ton pays, la langue de tes parents et tu deviendras un homme. Tu veux pas aller au service militaire comme tes copains, ils te feront jamais tes papiers. Tu seras perdu, et moi aussi. Tu n'auras plus le droit d'aller en Algérie, sinon ils te foutront en prison. C'est ce qui va t'arriver ! T'auras plus de pays, t'auras plus de racines. Perdu, tu seras perdu.

Parfois Madjid comprend un mot, une phrase et il répond, abattu, sachant qu'il va faire du mal à sa mère :

— Mais moi j'ai rien demandé ! Tu serais pas venue en France je serais pas ici, je serais pas perdu... Hein ?... Alors fous-moi la paix !

Elle continue sa rengaine, celle qu'elle porte nouée au fond du cœur. Jusqu'à en pleurer souvent.

On frappe à la porte d'entrée.

— Ce qu'il y a ? demande la mère, toujours en colère.

Elle quitte la chambre et Madjid se rallonge sur son lit, convaincu qu'il n'est ni arabe ni français depuis bien longtemps. Il est fils d'immigrés, paumé entre deux cultures, deux histoires, deux langues, deux couleurs de peau, ni blanc ni noir, à s'inventer ses propres racines, ses attaches, se les fabriquer.

Pour l'instant il attend... il attend. Il ne veut pas y penser, il ne supporte pas l'angoisse.

— Malika... faut venir, y a papa il tape maman.

Fabienne Levesque, qui ressemble tellement à Brigitte Fossey dans *Jeux interdits*, laisse passer Malika devant elle. Celle-ci, tel un semi-remorque, fonce dans l'appartement voisin en implorant :

— Ah! Allah, ah Rabbi!

Du palier on entend cris et plaintes de Mme Levesque. Madjid appuie sur le bouton « stop » de l'électrophone et s'en va au salon.

Il n'y a plus personne. Toute la famille jusqu'au plus petit a suivi la mère pour profiter du spectacle chez Levesque.

Madjid allume la télévision et s'assied sur une chaise en bâillant; il sent que ce soir il n'ira pas chez Levesque. Au cirque, comme il dit.

Ce spectacle-là, il connaît. Bien des fois, quand le père Levesque, non content de battre sa femme de ses poings, prenait soit son ceinturon, soit une chaise, Malika devait faire appel à son fils en lui envoyant Fabienne, ou alors le petit Éric, sept ans, qui arrivait, affolé, criant à Madjid :

— Papa, il a le couteau!

Alors Madjid y allait. Dans l'appartement d'à côté, un petit trois pièces, il se frayait passage entre les gosses qui hurlaient et les meubles, puis il essayait de maîtriser Levesque, Bébert pour les intimes du bistrot, sans lui faire du mal.

18

La petite Fabienne, les mains tremblantes sur ses joues :

— Maman... maman...

Le petit Éric, le fiston qui a quelque chose de son père :

— Arrête, papa, arrête !

Quant à Malika, elle raisonne Levesque, bourré comme une vache, les yeux rouges, haineux, pleins de violence, grimaçant de désespoir et de méchanceté, gueulant à Madjid quand il se décidait à venir :

— Barre-toi, bougnoule, va chez toi, sale bicot, je vais me la faire, cette salope !

Malika n'écoute guère les insultes de Levesque, elle le tient, elle ne le lâche plus jusqu'à ce qu'il s'essouffle.

— Je vais la tuer cette pute, cette salope !

La salope, la pute, c'est sa femme Élise, le nez en sang, car le premier coup surprend toujours. Après elle les évite tant bien que mal en tournant autour de la table. Quand Levesque est en forme, las de tourner sans pouvoir mettre la main sur Élise, il retourne la table carrément avec tout ce qu'il y a dessus. Alors, là, c'est grave, et les secours doivent faire vite, car il coince sa pauvre femme et lui en met plein la tronche. De quoi se cloîtrer pendant une bonne quinzaine, en attendant que les bleus disparaissent du visage.

Et même à ses gosses, qu'il fout des trempes pas possibles. Souvent, d'ailleurs, il frappe dans le tas, aveuglé par l'alcool. Spectacle permanent, seule relation et communication avec les voisins de palier. Dehors on se dit à peine bonjour. C'est comme ça.

Quand, épuisé de gesticuler, de menacer, de hurler, tenu par la grosse Malika qui décidément n'a peur de rien, on l'emmène dans sa chambre, il fatigue, le père Levesque. On le fout au plumard et on attend qu'il se calme, qu'il ne jure plus, qu'il somnole, tranquille. Vomissant, et quelquefois des larmes lui mouillent les paupières, étranges pleurs... on ne sait d'où, ni pourquoi.

Les jurons deviennent imperceptibles, on se dit qu'il s'endort.

Il s'éteint comme la flamme d'une bougie en courbant la tête du côté où il a vomi, et il s'endort de cette façon, souvent sans dîner. Après le ménage fait, Malika et sa marmaille retournent chez eux, laissant Élise, jeune femme de trente-six ans — qui en fait facilement quarante! — devant la porte, la peur encore au ventre et une nuit agitée en perspective, les cheveux en bataille, le visage marqué par les coups et les larmes, qui répète, honteuse, maladroite et lasse :

— Merci, Malika, merci.

Malika ne répond pas. Elle remet ses cheveux sous son foulard et recommence à réprimander ses gosses qui s'accrochent à sa robe. Elle demande le silence sinon elle leur fait comme « missiou Livique » :

— Compris ? dit-elle, le doigt levé.

Madjid est toujours dans le salon, face à la téloche, quand sa mère revient. Il n'y a pas de fauteuil dans ce salon, ni de plantes, rien qui fasse luxe ou décoration. Seulement un lit contre le mur, bien recouvert d'un couvre-lit vert bouteille, que chacun des enfants veut s'approprier pour regarder la télévision.

Les chambres, il y en a quatre, sont partagées chacune par deux enfants. Sauf le petit Mehdi qui dort seul dans le lit du salon. Madjid partage sa chambre avec son père. Malika dort avec la plus grande des filles, Amaria, celle qui bosse tellement bien au lycée, même que Malika lui a acheté une machine à écrire à crédit pour qu'elle travaille encore mieux, au lieu de la lui louer comme auparavant. L'enfant le plus jeune est Ounissa, sept ans, et le plus âgé Madjid, dix-huit. Toutes et tous nés en France, sauf Madjid. Tout jeunes mariés, les parents ont émigré. Ils voulaient faire des gosses qui aillent à l'école pour devenir des médecins, ou des avocats, ou des maîtres d'école, comme on dit à la campagne.

Et déjà le chômage pour Madjid et le père...

— Va chercher ton père ! répète Malika.

Madjid ne bouge pas de sa chaise. Pour bien montrer à sa mère qu'il ne l'écoute pas, il fait des grimaces à sa petite sœur, qui en rit. La mère explose, crie en arabe :

— Tu veux quand même pas que ce soit moi qui aille chercher ton père, hein ?

Il fait un pied de nez à sa petite sœur.

La mère, en français :

— Fatigui, moi, malade. Ji travaille li matin, li ménage à l'icole et toi ti dors. Ji fi li ménage dans li bureau li soir et à la maison. Fatigui moi, fatigui. Hein finiant, va. Et ji cours à la mairie, à

21

l'ide sociale, à l'assistance sociale... j'ai mal à mi jambes... et ti promènes... Ah mon Dieu...

Les enfants jouent, ou apprennent leurs leçons. La mère qui se lamente sur son sort, ils ont l'habitude. Elle repart dans sa cuisine, touille son riz et revient engueuler son fils de plus belle. Il craque ce coup-ci, il se lève et s'en va enfiler ses santiagos. Amaria met le couvert, les gosses rangent leurs cahiers, un œil sur la télévision. Madjid prend le couloir et en sortant il entend sa mère qui lui dit :

— T'as pas honte de vivre aux crochets de ta vieille mère ?

Quand il se retrouve en bas dans le hall, en sortant de l'ascenseur il croise le père Pelletier, quinquagénaire bien tassé, tout fier de tenir en laisse son chien, un berger allemand impressionnant, et de surcroît méchant. Le bête lève la tête vers Madjid qui s'écarte.

Ce qui fait sourire Pelletier, content. La peur règne dans la cité. On se la refile, vu qu'on a rien d'autre à se donner et qu'on veut pas. Surtout pas. Il paraît plus facile de se faire peur et de faire peur aux autres, en restant cloîtré chez soi avec un berger allemand à ses pieds, que de sortir au-devant des gens pour se comprendre et les comprendre.

La crainte domine la cité et ses habitants. Avec tous ces jeunes qui se droguent et qui détroussent, qui violent les vieilles, à ce qu'on dit, c'est l'angoisse! C'est du délire : ils veulent tous s'armer. Les serruriers ne sont pas au chômage avec toutes les nouvelles serrures à placer, et les signaux d'alarme qui sonnent, et hurlent, qui balancent du jus, qui explosent... Il y a le choix, les prospectus affluent dans les boîtes.

Il paraîtrait même qu'il y a des viols dans les caves.

Mais quand on possède un berger allemand et en plus la bonne et grosse bébête, on a moins peur... On passe devant un groupe de jeunes qui s'emmerdent à l'entrée d'un bâtiment, on les frôle, on provoque un peu. On chercherait presque la cogne, avec un monstre d'animal comme ça, la gueule sous muselière, qui ne demande qu'une chose : attaquer. La muselière, ça les rend plus méchants, ces ordures.

Le maître du chien, lui, il exulte, il frime, il se sent plus. Il n'a pas peur de ces jeunes cons de branleurs, brûleurs de bagnoles.

Madjid se retourne sur Pelletier et sa bête. Pas confiance. On ne sait jamais, qu'il lâche son monstre dès qu'on a le dos tourné ! Ils se regardent bien dans les yeux. Méchamment. Ils se connaissent. Ils se sont déjà presque battus, à propos de la fille Pelletier, celle qui allume de son beau petit cul bien moulé dans ses jeans tous les mecs de la cité. Madjid aurait bien voulu se la faire, elle aussi, mais le père Pelletier veillait à la graine. Pas de graine d'Arabe, surtout !...

En traversant l'allée, Madjid remonte la fermeture Éclair de son blouson, c'est qu'il fait bien frais et même froid. Il allume une cigarette et quitte l'allée des Azalées, celle de son bâtiment, pour rejoindre celle des Acacias. Toutes les allées ici portent des noms de fleurs.

La Cité des Fleurs, que ça s'appelle !!!

Du béton, des bagnoles en long, en large, en

24

travers, de l'urine et des crottes de chiens. Des bâtiments hauts, longs, sans cœur ni âme. Sans joie ni rires, que des plaintes, que du malheur.

Une cité immense entre Colombes, Asnières, Gennevilliers et l'autoroute de Pontoise et les usines et les flics. Le terrain de jeux, minuscule, ils l'ont grillagé !

Les fleurs ! les fleurs !...

Et sur les murs de béton, des graffiti, des slogans, des appels de détresse, des S.O.S. en forme de poing levé.

Des grosses couilles avec des grosses bites, bien poilues, peintes.

Des prénoms de garçons et des prénoms de filles, sur des cœurs écorchés ou transpercés par une flèche, qui se cherchent ! Ou des conneries.

Genre : « Annie F. prend la pilule », écrit certainement par la famille d'en face, revancharde, vengeresse. Tout ce qui rit ou se moque du malheur des autres s'inscrit sur les murs. Une façon comme une autre de se croire supérieur, dans la même connerie, le même désespoir. Ou alors : « Fatima B. s'est fait avorter », le genre, là, qui fait d'énormes histoires dans les familles. Des engueulades et puis la cogne, du sang parfois... et les flics. Si une adolescente est souffrante, qu'elle n'aille surtout pas chez le médecin d'en face, ou à l'hôpital du coin, on parlera tout de suite d'avortement. On te balance pour un rien, pour un joint, une baise, une cuite...

Tout le monde s'épie, tout le monde mouscharde et personne, bien entendu, ne sait rien.

Y'a pas de vie privée. Tout s'étale et se renvoie pour contre-attaquer, agresser le voisin.

Madjid traverse le parking jusqu'aux Acacias. C'est l'heure du film ou des variétés à la télévision. 20 h 30. Plus un berger allemand sur la pelouse, là où c'est bien interdit de fouler le gazon. Dupont-Machin est remonté chez lui après avoir arboré son chien bien clinquant, comme un fusil, l'air de dire, un sourire sadique aux lèvres : « Tu peux y venir cambrioler chez moi, quand je suis à l'usine, tu ressortiras pas vivant ! » Presque une invitation !

Chaque fois que Madjid croise un berger allemand et son maître dans la cité, il crache par terre. Il s'ensuit des regards méprisants des deux côtés et chacun continue son chemin. Il suffirait d'un rien, de la moindre étincelle, ce serait l'explosion.

Comme dit Pat, un jour ce sera la guerre entre les parents et les jeunes de la cité, une guerre à mort. Le cauchemar.

Aux Acacias, Madjid va jusqu'au porche central où il voit tous ses copains.

Il y a : Bengston, l'Antillais ; Thierry, surnommé « Pichenette » ; James, Algérien né en France ; Jean-Marc, viré de chez lui par son père et qui loge dans une cave ; Bibiche, Algérien né en France, surnommé « Chopin » parce qu'étant petit, il rêvait de devenir pianiste. Dorénavant il se contente de sa guitare. Il ne rêve plus. Et encore Anita, seule nana de la bande, toujours là dans tous les coups. Bosse pas, ne va plus au lycée. Née de père algérien et de mère française.

Son père, reparti au pays, n'a plus jamais donné de nouvelles. Et enfin Pat, le pote Pat, comme on dit, une masse, une bête baraquée comme un déménageur, rien dans le cigare, tout dans le jean et les baskets, et son tic de remonter la mèche blonde qui lui tombe sur les yeux. Grande gueule de première et dernier de classe.

Madjid serre les mains de ceux qu'il n'a pas vus dans la journée. Certains sont assis sur les premières marches du hall, d'autres adossés aux voitures en stationnement.

Madjid serre la main à Bengston qui lui sort, rigolard :

— Alors, on va chercher son papa ?

Madjid, menaçant :

— Ta mère !

— Ma mère, elle t'emmerde ! répond Bengston.

Bibiche cesse de gratter sa guitare, enlève l'allumette qu'il a entre les dents :

— Arrêtez de gueuler, merde ! je m'entends plus !

Thierry : On a plus le droit de causer, avec Môssieur !

Bibiche : Vous êtes des brêles, vous pigez rien à la musique.

Et il s'arrête de jouer. Il appuie sur un bouton de son magnétophone portatif et le rock surgit.

Madjid n'aime pas qu'on lui cause de son père. Qu'on fasse allusion à quoi que ce soit au sujet de son père le met de mauvaise humeur. Ses potes le savent bien, mais ils ne peuvent s'empêcher de lui balancer des vannes, rien que pour le cham-

brer. Et la chambre là-dessus, Madjid refuse.
Pour changer de conversation, Anita dit en croisant ses bras sur sa poitrine, frileuse :

— Putain de moine, fait pas chaud !

Elle rentre sa petite tête dans les épaules, sa petite tête de fouine sous une épaisse et longue chevelure noire qui lui réchauffe le cou. Elle sourit à Madjid qui vient s'asseoir à côté d'elle. Quand ses lèvres framboise, humides, s'entrouvrent, on voit ses belles dents toutes blanches et on a envie de les caresser avec sa langue. Ses pommettes prennent la couleur d'une dune de sable au sud du pays quand le soleil va piquer un roupillon. Saillantes comme la bosse d'un chameau, aussi douces, avec le duvet en moins, mais c'est déjà beaucoup. Et pour la sauter, Anita, oualou ! Tu peux faire le tour de France, ton vélo volé sur le dos, rien, macache. Elle attend le voyou charmant, qui aime le flipper et Julien Clerc, qui préfère l'autobus à la moto, c'est plus reposant pour rêver. Ce voyou-là qui sortirait d'entre deux tours peintes de toutes les couleurs pour planquer la grisaille du béton, elle l'attend avec tant d'espoir qu'elle en parle à tous les mecs de la bande, et ils ont honte de n'être pas celui-là.

Car ils sentent, ils comprennent que son voyou, elle l'aimera comme une bête, pour rattraper le temps perdu. Les femmes ont le don de refaire le temps perdu sans qu'on s'en aperçoive.

James gémit de son coin, toujours taciturne, toujours à l'écart :

— Putain, c'est vrai ça : où c'est qu'on va aller

28

se foutre cet hiver, maintenant qu'ils ont fermé le club ?

— Tu m'étonnes, qu'ils l'aient fermé, dit Thierry. Les mecs, ils arrivaient avec le joint au bec.

— Les mecs, les mecs ! qui c'est les mecs ! demande Bengston, qui se sent visé. Et toi, t'as jamais fumé un joint ?

— J'ai pas dit ça ! se défend Thierry. Je dis qu'on n'avait qu'à faire gaffe, ils auraient pas fermé la taule.

Pat écrase son mégot de ses grosses santiagos et prend la parole à son tour :

— Après tout qu'est-ce que ça peut leur foutre, un joint ? Ce qu'on veut, c'est un endroit pour se voir, le reste c'est notre problème !

— Toute manière, dit Bengston, les animateurs des clubs, c'est tous des copains aux flics. Tant que tu vas au club pour jouer au ping-pong ou à la belote, y disent rien. Mais si t'as le malheur de proposer quelque chose, y t'écoutent pas. C'est pas prévu dans le programme, qu'ils disent. Et leur programme, il est fait au commissariat, je te le dis, moi.

Il pointe son doigt sur sa poitrine. Quand il s'énerve, Bengston, sa bouche se barre de travers et dessine une superbe grimace. Et il continue :

— Ils font des clubs comme ça, pour nous surveiller, pour te garder devant la téloche, et les mecs là-dedans ils se posent pas de questions. Ils se font chier, mais y disent rien.

Thierry enchaîne :

— Si je rencontre ce fils de pute d'animateur,

29

j'y fais sa fête. C'est lui qu'a fait fermer la taule parce qu'il a trouvé un petit joint de rien du tout. Juste bon à nous balancer des dessins animés, ce con!

— Ben quoi, c'est chouette, les dessins animés! s'exclame Pat.

Thierry, en colère :

— Toi, on t'a rien demandé!

Pat s'avance vers Thierry, le menaçant du doigt.

— Tu veux te faire enfoncer le baigneur, rat de béton?

Thierry fait face, relevant fièrement la tête :

— Arrête ta grande gueule, c'est tout ce que t'as!

Bibiche, agacé, remet une cassette dans son magnéto.

— Vos gueules, merde! Et la zizique alors?

Thierry et Pat reviennent à leur place en se regardant de biais. Bengston se désole auprès de tous :

— Il allait y avoir de la bagarre, et v'la que Chopin fout tout en l'air.

Il grimace en regardant Chopin et lui dit :

— Hein! ma biche?.

Bengston se lève, essuie les fesses de son jean et se met à chanter :

— Qu'est-ce qu'on s'emmerde ici, qu'est-ce qu'on s'emmerde ici, merde ici, merde ici...

Bibiche, le magnéto à l'oreille : « T'as qu'à aller faire un tour, tu casseras pas les couilles! »

A ce moment le locataire d'un appartement du rez-de-chaussée, tout près d'où la bande se

30

trouve, ouvre sa fenêtre et leur dit gentiment, l'air désolé :

— Eh! les gars, parlez doucement, ou alors allez discuter ailleurs, j'ai des gosses qui dorment!

On ne voit que sa tête, à ce père, derrière la fenêtre. Il observe les jeunes, qui ne réagissent pas, qui le regardent sans mot dire, comme gênés. Bengston pouffe et se tape sur la cuisse. Les autres aussi éclatent de rire. le crâne chauve du locataire s'éclipse. La fenêtre se referme.

Thierry fait un bras d'honneur en l'air.

Chopin, qui en loupe pas une, saute sur l'occasion pour ajouter :

— Vous voyez ce qui arrive avec vos grandes gueules!

Bengston repart de plus belle :

— Ben quoi, on a plus le droit de causer dans cette putain de cité, hein?

Il s'avance vers Bibiche, parle en faisant des grands gestes comme un Rital.

— Je fais ce que je veux et dis ce que je veux, moi!

Arrivé près de Bibiche, il lui pique son magnétophone et court se cacher derrière une voiture en stationnement. Bibiche se lève et fonce après Bengston. Ils tournent autour des bagnoles.

Bibiche menace, crie, insulte. Bengston se marre. Il fout la musique à fond, et se met à danser.

— Rends-moi ça, négro! tu sais pas t'en servir, hurle Chopin.

Les autres rigolent. Anita se lève.

31

— Bon, salut, je me casse.

Elle s'en va vers son bâtiment, les mains plaquées dans les poches arrière de son jean.

Bibiche, résigné, se rassoit sur les marches, le poing levé vers Bengston :

— Sale renoi !

En tout cas le renoi, l'appareil à l'oreille, danse au milieu de la chaussée, narguant Bibiche et Bibiche souffle à Pat, près de lui :

— Il est con, ce mec, pas possible !

Bengston cesse de danser et du milieu de la chaussée lance aux copains :

— Bon, je vais vous chanter un truc que je vais enregistrer, hein ! D'accord les mecs ? Okay !

Il manipule l'appareil, et joue avec les touches. Pourtant Bibiche le met en garde :

— Tu le casses, je te casse !

— T'occupe, j'ai le même ! dit Bengston.

Il se fait tard sur la cité, les lumières aux fenêtres commencent à s'éteindre. Et le silence se fait pesant, angoissant. Le froid remonte sur l'échine. Il faut tirer le blouson jusqu'aux fesses.

Bengston n'a pas froid, il se réchauffe en chahutant.

— Ah ! fait-il, je sais ce que je vais enregistrer. Ah ! ah !

Il serre les dents et gonfle le ventre en gémissant. Il pousse sur son ventre.

— Ça va venir, vous impatientez pas, qu'il dit en grimaçant. Bougez pas !

Les autres ne bougent pas.

Madjid rit, Pat l'imite. Thierry hoche la tête, moqueur.

Puis Bengston repart dans son numéro, il serre les dents, des belles dents d'Antillais, pousse encore plus sur son ventre. Il ne bouge pas, concentré, les yeux fermés. Il se met l'appareil aux fesses, fait encore un petit effort, et PROUTT, envoie un gros pet sur le magnéto, puis s'écroule de rire en se tapant sur les cuisses.

Les autres ne se tiennent plus de se marrer, sauf Bibiche, qui se lève et réclame de nouveau son magnéto en hurlant :

— Heureusement qu'il enregistre pas l'odeur, sinon il m'étoufferait.

L'hilarité redouble. Bengston est content de sa farce. Il tient le milieu de la chaussée et ne lâche plus. Il braille à la bétonnade : « Bon, on va se le réécouter, mon pet magistral. L'unique, le vrai, qui proutte mais ne sent rien ! Msieurs dames, écoutez, écoutez ! » et il en appelle à la foule, qu'il salue bien bas avec un regard racoleur.

Le silence se fait. Il appuie sur le bouton, mais silence aussi de ce côté-là.

— Mets-le à fond ! lance Thierry.

— C'est fait, répond l'Antillais.

Et juste à ce moment-là le magnéto émet un proutt considérable, d'où fou rire général. Plié, qu'on est !

Même Bibiche n'y résiste pas, il rigole aussi.

— Quel con ce kebla, tu parles d'un cadeau. Y'a qu'un Noir comme ça dans toute cette banlieue et faut qu'on se le coltine ! Putain ! qu'il se lamente, Chopin.

Le Noir laisse filer la zizique et danse la biguine comme un apache. Il tourne sur la chaussée en brandissant le magnéto à bout de bras comme un trophée.

Et il chante en fermant les yeux.

Jean-Marc et Thierry l'accompagnent en tapant dans leurs mains. Ils improvisent une petite fête. Bibiche, calmé, reprend sa guitare et se mêle au ton.

Et soudain paf! une bouteille s'écrase, tombée du ciel, se fracasse en mille morceaux à deux pas de Bengston, au milieu de la chaussée. Stupeur! Bengston ne bouge plus, le temps de comprendre. Il jette un œil sur les fenêtres du haut et vite fait s'abrite sous le porche avec ses potes. Silence. On s'observe. L'Antillais souffle, comme silicosé. La trouille. Il redonne gentiment le magnéto à Chopin, qui lui dit :

— Ben, mon con, t'as eu chaud. Tu peux prier le dieu des Blacks !

Il se prend sa tête frisée dans ses mains et dit, soulagé, mais encore sous le choc :

— Putain de béton, un mètre de plus et il me cassait la tronche.

Il en tremble encore, en regardant les tessons sur la chaussée.

— Qui est-ce, à votre avis ? demande Thierry.

Bengston l'observe, les yeux grands ouverts :

— Sais pas, j'ai regardé en haut et j'ai vu personne.

Madjid réplique :

— Parce que tu crois qu'on va te prévenir avant ?

34

— C'est pareil que pour le coup de fusil d'il y a deux mois ! dit Pat. Les mecs, y ratent leur coup parce qu'ils ont les jetons de viser !

— Enfoiré ! dit Bengston entre ses dents.

Bibiche sort de sous le porche, descend les marches à reculons en fixant les étages de peur de voir arriver une autre bouteille.

— Fais gaffe ! le prévient Pat. Si ça se trouve, le mec, il a une caisse pleine à répétition.

Bibiche observe les morceaux sur la chaussée et notamment le cul de la bouteille.

Thierry demande :

— C'est Postillon ou Gévéor ?

— Tu m'étonnes, dit Bengston, c'est encore un poivrot qu'a balancé ça !

Bibiche ne répond pas. Il essaie de décoller l'étiquette.

Pat, blagueur :

— Ce coup-ci, ç'a pas l'air d'être du Ricard. Ah ! ah !

— A cette heure-ci, c'est plutôt le digestif ! dit Madjid.

Chopin revient sous le porche avec l'étiquette enfin décollée. A la lueur du néon, il arrive à lire le nom du pinard :

— Pastelvin.

— Comment t'as dit ? demande Bengston.

— Pastelvin ! c'est marqué dessus, tu sais pas lire ou quoi ?

Ils se regardent en s'interrogeant :

— Pastelvin, c'est du luxe, ça, dit Titi — et il rit.

— On va faire le point sur les étages, hein ? reprend l'Antillais.

— En tout cas, dit Titi, ça ne vient ni du rez-de-chaussée ni du premier... Okay ?

A ce moment-là, Jean-Marc sort de son mutisme, lui qui ne dit jamais grand-chose. Il tire un bon coup sur le joint fraîchement roulé et annonce :

— Cherchez pas, c'est mon vieux...

Les autres se retournent sur lui. Titi fronce les sourcils, surpris, et regarde Pat. Jean-Marc ferme les yeux en crachant la fumée.

— T'es sûr de ce que t'avances, c'est bien ton vieux ? demande Titi.

Jean-Marc tend le joint à Bibiche :

— Si je vous le dis ! C'est du pinard qu'il ramène de chez le grand-père de la campagne.

Bengston jure, sort de sa poche une boîte d'allumettes et dit :

— Tu diras à ton paternel que c'est un enculé.

Jean-Marc :

— T'inquiète pas, je le lui ai déjà dit et il m'a lourdé !

Bengston jongle avec la boîte d'allumettes et en appelle aux autres :

— Je vais y cramer sa bagnole, à ton vieux. Y va la trouver en cendre, sa caisse, demain matin !

— C'est pas con, ce que tu dis là, approuve Pat. Je vais avec toi, on va se la donner !

— Je sais pas où elle est garée, mais on la trouvera bien, dit Thierry.

Bibiche redonne le joint à Jean-Marc et lui glisse :

— Tu l'aimes bien, ton darron, toi !

Jean-Marc ne répond pas. Il met délicatement le stick entre ses doigts et le porte à ses lèvres.

— Bon, ben moi je m'arrache, je monte, dit Chopin.

— Aie pas peur, on t'a pas vu, lui répond, moqueur, Bengston.

— Pov'con! grogne Chopin en poussant la porte du hall.

Il va traverser le bâtiment par la cave et ressortira de l'autre côté, ni vu ni connu. Ses potes le savent.

La nuit est chez elle, bien plus pénétrante que nulle part ailleurs. La cité se meurt et on entend les pas du passant qui résonnent comme un tambour perdu. On croit marcher derrière le mur d'un cimetière en rase campagne dans l'obscurité, quand on cherche son chemin dans un village inconnu.

Les garçons s'en vont à la recherche de la voiture à brûler, de parking en parking, comme on traverse un cimetière entre les tombes en faisant valser à coup de santiagos les fleurs et les écriteaux. Ici c'est les rétroviseurs, les pare-chocs et les essuie-glaces qui paient.

Madjid les suit un moment, puis se ravise, il avait presque oublié :

— Faut que j'aille chercher mon père!

Les autres s'en fichent. Leur idée dévastatrice bien ancrée dans le cigare, ils continuent sans faire gaffe à Madjid. Celui-ci s'arrête et fait demi-tour. Pat le rappelle :

— Je te rejoins!

— Okay, fait Madjid.

Il s'en va en sens opposé, les mains enfoncées dans les poches de son blouson. Il en relève le col. Il marche comme un canard qui cherche la sortie de sa cage. Son pantalon en pattes d'elphe flotte au vent en suivant le mouvement. On dirait une armée de voyous à lui tout seul, qui va prendre d'assaut la prochaine tour. Dans le silence du béton retentit le claquement des hauts talons ferrés de ses santiagos.

Il passe plusieurs allées en contournant les bagnoles garées sur les trottoirs. Il sort enfin de la cité et remonte la rue des Compagnons jusqu'au bout, à la limite de Colombes. Au coin, il y a le bistro arabe chez Hamid, il y entre.

C'est l'endroit où les immigrés du quartier — les ouvriers célibataires, comme on les appelle — et même les autres viennent noyer dans la Kronenbourg le mal du pays. Madjid serre quelques mains, et vient s'accouder au zinc. Les dominos claquent sur la table, avec appels d'annonces, les chiffres mal prononcés en français.

Une fumée dense et dansante comme une

ombre chinoise monte au plafond, alourdissant l'atmosphère. L'endroit est mal éclairé et bruyant. Madjid serre la main du barman qu'il connaît et commande une « Kro », puis observe le petit bonhomme âgé debout à côté de lui. Le petit homme tire sur une gauloise qu'il tient entre ses doigts longs et maigres, jaunis par le tabac. Il a les joues creuses et mal rasées. Ses petits yeux noirs, sous d'épais sourcils, se perdent dans le miroir accroché au mur derrière le bar. Ses coudes reposent sur le comptoir humide. Il ne bronche pas. Madjid verse la bière dans le verre en faisant attention qu'elle ne mousse pas trop. Au bout du comptoir, la pute de la maison, une grosse brune au rouge à lèvres arrogant, se fait draguer par un client ivre, qui essaie de finir de la soûler. Le juke-box chante en kabyle la beauté des femmes au pied des montagnes du Djurdjura.

La pute pousse un cri aigu qui fait se retourner toute la salle sur son corsage. Son client lui pelote les nichons en tirant une langue de clébard assoiffé. Il lui met un billet de banque dans son chemisier moulant et échancré, entre les deux seins provocateurs. Elle en rit et frémit, ou fait semblant. Madjid pose une pièce de monnaie sur le zinc et indique au barman que c'est pour sa bière, plus le rouge du petit vieux. Celui-ci finit son verre d'un trait et plonge une main dans la poche de son sombre et long manteau. Il en sort un béret basque qu'il enfonce sur son crâne chauve. Madjid ramasse sa monnaie et se dirige vers la sortie.

Le petit vieux le suit sans rien dire. Ils descendent la rue des Compagnons dans la nuit froide. Le petit vieux marche au milieu de la chaussée d'un pas court et rapide, les mains enfouies dans ses grandes poches. Une voiture derrière eux, tous phares allumés, les surprend.

Madjid prend le petit homme par le bras et le ramène sur le trottoir. La bagnole passe. Le jeune homme et son père se remettent sur la chaussée, les bas-côtés étant encombrés par les voitures. Madjid sort deux cigarettes de son paquet, qu'il allume.

Il en donne une à son père. Le vieux prend la cigarette avec la même éternelle expression dans le regard, un mélange de vide et de lointain. Madjid l'observe un instant, pitié et tendresse montent en lui, l'émeuvent pour son malade de père. Le papa a perdu la raison depuis qu'il est tombé du toit qu'il couvrait. Sur la tête. Il n'a plus sa tête, comme dit sa femme. Elle s'en occupe comme d'un enfant, un de plus. Elle le lave, l'habille, le rase, et lui donne quelques sous pour son paquet de gauloises, son verre de rouge.

— Comme il était bon et bien brave, et pas fainéant avant ce malheur, pas comme toi! qu'elle se lamente à Madjid, la Malika. Ah! si seulement tu étais comme ton père avant son accident!... lui répète-t-elle souvent.

Mais Madjid n'est pas comme son vieux. Déjà de taille, bien plus grand, plus costaud que lui. Il peut soulever son père d'une main comme lui le prenait quand il était petit. Madjid s'en souvient. C'est vrai que son père était chouette, qu'il aimait les enfants. Ses enfants, il les choyait, les

41

pomponnait comme une femme. Et que même le dimanche quand il faisait beau, il les emmenait au champ de courses, Maisons-Laffitte, Auteuil, Enghien. Les mômes aimaient ça. Ils pique-niquaient dans le bois, jouaient au football avant d'aller voir les chevaux. Il fallait les voir partir, ces dimanches-là, chacun et chacune le casse-croûte sous le bras et la gourde en plastique blanche pleine d'eau ou de sirop de menthe, ou de grenadine, accrochée à la ceinture. Le père se mettait en tête de peloton et faisait activer les mômes quand ils s'attardaient devant une vitrine, en regardant sa montre.

C'est que la première course n'attend pas. Et on prenait l'autobus comme d'autres prennent l'avion : le grand voyage. Malika restait à la maison, il faut bien que quelqu'un fasse le ménage, lave, repasse. Enfin elle aimait ces dimanches après-midi où elle se retrouvait seule chez elle.

Le père dorénavant vogue sur une galère qui a paumé sa voile. Et même s'il débarque quelque part, sûr que c'est une île déserte, se dit son fils.

Pat vient à leur rencontre du bout de la rue, les mains dans les poches arrière de son jean. Il marche comme un cow-boy qui va tout casser au saloon. Le trousseau de clefs qui pend à son ceinturon résonne au rythme de ses pas.

— Alors on rentre son papa ? nargue-t-il.

« Ah ! », crie-t-il après sa phrase. Toujours ces « Ah ! » terribles qu'il pousse, le Pat, en se pliant en deux quand il se fiche de quelqu'un. Dans le silence de la nuit, la sirène des pompiers retentit.

42

Madjid regarde Pat. Celui-ci se gratte la tête en grimaçant :

— Ils arrivent toujours à la bourre, ces cons-là !

Madjid prend son père par le bras et dit :

— On change de direction.

Tandis qu'ils contournent la cité par la gauche, le long de l'autoroute, Pat fait des grimaces au père de Madjid. Il marche à reculons. Des pieds de nez, puis il lui tire la langue, va jusqu'à un bras d'honneur, et des plus nets. Le petit vieux dans sa complète léthargie ne réagit pas, comme s'il ne voyait pas.

— Lâche-lui la grappe, dit Madjid, agacé.

— Ben quoi ? j'essaie de le faire rire. Y rigole jamais, ton daron ?

— C'est pas avec tes conneries qu'il va se la fendre !

Et voilà que Pat pique le béret du vieux et s'en va avec. Le père s'arrête net au milieu de la chaussée. Il s'est mis à hurler. Il crie comme un muet :

— Mmmm... Oumm... !

Madjid court après Pat.

— Rends-lui sa couvrante, merde !

Pat, lui, rigole, le béret sur la tête. Le fils revient vers son père qui pousse des cris aigus, la main tendue vers Pat. Il ne bouge pas. Il ne veut plus. Madjid le reprend par le bras pour le faire avancer. Niet. Le vieux veut son béret comme un gamin son jouet. Il tape des pieds.

— Rends-le-lui, putain, quoi ! supplie une nouvelle fois Madjid.

43

Le père hurle toujours, encore, et se met à pleurer. Un gosse.

— Tu vois ce que t'as fait. Il chiale à présent, dit Madjid, en colère cette fois.

« Ah ! » fait Pat, et il revient avec le béret qu'il lance à Madjid. Le vieux se renfonce son couvert sur le crâne et repart. Il ne pleure plus.

— T'es con, des fois, tu sais ! dit Madjid à Pat.

— Oh ! répond Pat, en levant les bras au ciel, si on ne peut plus rigoler maintenant, avec les jeunes !... Pfff...

Ça, c'est sa phrase favorite. Des fois il rajoute : « Sont cons les jeunes, maintenant ! »

Quand ils arrivent dans la cité après avoir évité l'allée des Acacias, police-secours apparaît tous phares agressifs dehors. Les flics se dirigent vers le parking où les pompiers luttent contre les flammes qui jaillissent de la voiture du père à Jean-Marc.

C'est du spectacle, et du gratuit. Les gens sont aux fenêtres, d'autres sont descendus en pyjama, un manteau enfilé en toute hâte. C'est comme un feu d'artifice, ça change un peu de la monotonie du béton ! Le père de Jean-Marc hurle, le poing levé.

« Jeunes cons, ordures, je vous aurai ! » perçoit-on de loin.

Un groupe de locataires est autour de lui, qui l'approuvent et serrent les poings aussi.

Ce n'est plus des bouteilles qu'il va balancer de sa fenêtre, le père à Jean-Marc, il va s'acheter un fusil. Il rêvera de « cartonner » dans le tas. Il en rêve. Ils sont des tas, ici, à en rêver.

44

L'allée des Acacias, vaudra mieux l'éviter quelque temps. La guéguerre jeunes-vieux va repartir de plus belle.

Pat, Madjid et son père se faufilent derrière une haie et rejoignent leurs bâtiments respectifs.

Josette amène son fils Stéphane chez Malika comme tous les matins de semaine. Elle trouve Malika affairée à vêtir ses propres gosses avant le départ pour l'école. Stéphane a grandi ici, puisque Malika fut sa nourrice au cours de ses trois premières années. Elle le demeure, car Josette commence en usine le matin très tôt. C'est Malika qui conduit Stéphane à l'école et qui le ramène le soir. Comme nounou, elle se faisait payer un peu. Maintenant c'est gratuit. D'autant qu'elle croit avoir entendu le mot « chômage » dans la bouche de Josette. Elle n'a pas posé de questions.

Il faut faire déjeuner les petits, l'heure tourne et Stéphane se mêle au chahut. Il joue à d'Artagnan avec les autres. Josette est déjà repartie. Emmitouflée dans un léger imperméable bleu marine, un foulard autour du cou, elle presse le pas entre les rangées de bagnoles. Le jour se lève à peine sur la banlieue ringarde, la nuit fait la grasse matinée.

On appelle ça l'hiver, et le soir elle se couche tôt, déjà fatiguée de l'été.

47

« Chousette », comme l'appelle Malika avec son bel accent, arrive enfin à l'arrêt du bus, qui évidemment vient tout juste de passer. Elle se met sous l'abri et allume une cigarette en jetant un œil à sa montre.

C'est l'heure du travailleur immigré, après le laitier, avant les boueux. Josette a salué deux Africains qui viennent d'arriver et qu'elle voit tous les matins. Ils sont en retard aussi. L'abri-bus agresse de ses néons les yeux tirés des lève-tôt. Josette n'est pas maquillée. Elle ne se fait une petite beauté que très rarement, le jour de la paye entre autres.

Depuis son divorce elle a tendance à se laisser aller. Son fin visage manque de couleur et d'espoir. Ses vingt-huit ans se dressent comme une belle plante bien verte et bien montée, hélas pas entretenue. Voilà l'autobus. Elle sort sa carte orange. Les deux Noirs la laissent monter la première. Elle s'installe à sa place habituelle, au fond à droite, contre la vitre.

L'autobus déchire la nuit banlieusarde, comme à la recherche d'une vérité appelant au jour les citadins. Ce sont les matins de Josette, sa vie de tous les jours, son environnement, avec ce chauffeur qui annonce chaque station, comme un garçon de café demandant une saucisse-frites. Il se retourne, le chauffeur, sur les gonzesses qui montent.

Le bus va son petit bonhomme de chemin, rythme de croisière. La promenade du prolétaire. Josette demande l'arrêt au pont de Clichy. Un léger vent la prend de face, elle baisse la tête et se

48

retourne pour allumer encore une cigarette. Elle longe la Seine par les quais de Levallois.

Le jour se cherche encore. Silhouette recroquevillée, Josette se perd dans l'obscurité des murs d'usines. Elle retrouve quelques collègues en chemin. Elles se serrent la main avec un petit « b'jour » à peine prononcé et pénètrent prestement dans l'usine pour s'engouffrer dans les ateliers, au chaud, devant les machines à café. Les filles, une cinquantaine, ont l'air las, éprouvé, angoissé. Par petits groupes elles discutent à voix basse, comme craintives. Inquiètes qu'on les entende.

Une immense pancarte dressée au milieu de l'atelier annonce :

GRÈVE ILLIMITÉE.
NON AUX LICENCIEMENTS !
USINE OCCUPÉE.

Josette souffle du bout des lèvres sur sa tasse de café. Elle s'est faufilée au milieu d'un groupe de femmes et écoute les commentaires avant la manifestation de ce matin même. Bien alignées sur un immense établi tout au long de l'atelier, les machines à coudre, leur outil de travail, sont recouvertes de plastiques bleu marine qui les protègent de la poussière et de l'humidité.

Des cartons d'étoffes attendent contre le mur les filles qui viendront les éventrer de leurs doigts agiles et fermes. Celles-là ont le droit d'aller pisser en grillant une sèche, trois minutes toutes les deux heures. Faut pas brûler le tissu, interdit de fumer. Et voilà que le patron veut licencier le tiers de la fabrique, crise économique oblige.

Des filles mères pour la plupart, celles qui sont le plus dans le besoin, celles qui font pas grève, c'est celles-là qu'on embauche en priorité, mais qu'on lourde aussi sec à la moindre alerte.

Josette fait partie des licenciables, elle n'a que deux années d'ancienneté, c'est théoriquement une nouvelle, et les nouveaux sont tête de liste pour aller faire la queue à l'agence pour l'emploi.

C'est au collège d'enseignement technique,
l'université du fils-du-pauvre-qui-n'a-pas-eu-de-
chance, que Pat et Madjid se sont liés d'amitié. Ils
se connaissaient déjà depuis belle lurette, mais
n'avaient pas d'atomes crochus avant.

Ils se sont méfiés l'un de l'autre durant des
années, mais en deuxième année de collège ils se
sont serré la main une bonne fois pour toutes.
Plus on est de fous plus on rigole. Mais ces liens
sont terribles. Ce genre d'union est bizarre. C'est
la peur de l'un et de l'autre qui au début prime
dans la liaison, surtout quand on est dans la
même classe.

En cas de bagarre entre les deux, le battu
passera pour un con devant toute la salle, même
s'il reste le deuxième, le challenger du champion.
Alors ça, ni Pat ni Madjid ne le désiraient. Ils
préféraient être à deux pour cogner sur les autres,
les commander avant le prof. C'est une forme de
faiblesse. Ils en étaient conscients. Deux fai-
blesses qui s'unissent n'égalent pas une force,
mais c'est la peur en moins.

A deux on n'est pas plus fort, on a moins les jetons.

Ils furent vite repérés comme deux êtres nuisibles, irrécupérables, pas fréquentables. Pourtant ils ne se gênaient pas pour fréquenter leurs camarades de classe, les récupérer, les associer à leurs coups les plus bas. Ils taxaient déjà les petits copains. Madjid suivait ses cours tant bien que mal en essayant, plutôt mal, de rester au milieu du tableau. Pat, lui, était dernier de classe, mais pas au fond de la salle, là où il y a le chauffage central. Non : devant, à la première table, face au bureau du prof, parce qu'on est moins repéré. C'était sa place et personne n'avait le droit d'y poser les fesses, car il avait, un jour, entre deux cours, percé, sacré Pat ! un trou dans le bureau d'en face pour mater les jambes des professeurs « femelles ». C'étaient ses meilleurs moments de la semaine. Il en faisait tout un plat, de ses séances de voyeur.

« Aujourd'hui, elle avait une culotte bleue, un peu transparente, on voyait la touffe noire à travers », qu'il disait à la récré. Les copains en tiraient une langue !

Si un autre réussissait à se glisser discrètement jusque devant le trou, Pat le laissait se rincer l'œil avant de lui ajuster un maître coup de pied au cul. La tête de l'élève cognait le bureau et la prof se dressait brusquement sur sa chaise. Elle se doutait bien de quelque chose, mais ne disait rien. Elle grondait Pat, si méchant avec ses camarades.

— Il a qu'à pas se foutre dans mes jambes ! se défendait Pat.

L'autre repartait à sa place en se frottant le front et les fesses et jamais la prof ne fit de commentaire à propos du trou. Ça devait certainement l'amuser de faire bander des adolescents. Pendant qu'ils bandent, ils gueulent pas. Quand Pat était de bonne humeur, toute la classe y passait, au trou. Furtivement, discrètement, à quatre pattes, les élèves approchaient au commandement de Pat. Il choisissait l'ordre des passages. Les murmures qui s'ensuivaient éveillaient les soupçons de la prof. Elle écartait encore plus les jambes, mine de rien. L'élève revenait à sa place sur cinq pattes.

Des fois elle se faisait garce, plus salope que de coutume. Elle commençait sa séance de strip-tease, les élèves même pas encore en classe. Ces jours-là, elle tenait absolument à monter l'escalier la première. On la laissait grimper quelques marches et on suivait le pas.

C'était le seul moment où elle avait le silence complet. Elle montait nonchalamment et en se mettant bien contre la rampe pour que même les derniers, les petits, se rincent l'œil, en compensation pour leurs deux heures inintéressantes. Et sa petite culotte dessous sa robe, une merveille, un défi. Une reprise de volée en pleine poire. La lucarne. Toutes les têtes levées comme une seule, et pour tous la même idée, la même envie qui sèche la bouche. Trois étages comme ça sans respirer, le souffle coupé. Un chemin de choix. Les glandes ! Et Pat, le Pat devenait tout petit. On aurait cru un enfant de chœur qui suit le curé, un cierge à la main. Il grimpait mécaniquement les marches, les yeux au ciel, et au bout la Sainte Vierge. Son regard mouillant s'éclaircissait, comme hypnotisé. Tu pouvais le bousculer à ce moment-là, il te balançait pas de baffes. Il était dans son vertige et son horizon se figeait là où le slip coupe l'entrecuisse, là où il y a la petite dune fleurie avec un sillon creux et court. On arrivait déjà en salle, avec plein de rêves et d'espoir dans sa tête et son cartable. Seul Pat continuait le voyage, les yeux perdus dans le trou du bureau.

Ils ne durèrent pas longtemps au collège, Pat et Madjid, mais ils y firent régner leur loi avant d'être renvoyés à leur béton. Ils ne craignaient ni profs ni pions, seul l'ennui les angoissait. Pat passa au conseil de discipline, mais rien n'y fit. Il n'aimait pas l'école, un point c'est tout! Pour tuer le temps, il jouait au dur, et le meilleur moment de la journée, c'était l'heure du déjeuner. La cantine.

Évidemment Pat était chef de table, Madjid devant lui, et six autres autour : c'était une table de huit. Pour les hors-d'œuvre, pas de problème, tous mangeaient leur part. Mais quand Pat avait vraiment faim, une bonne et vieille faim, surtout quand il n'était pas rentré chez lui la veille, il s'en donnait à ventre joie! Au mépris de la tablée! Viande et légumes étaient servis dans le même plat. Pat laissait se servir Madjid qui garnissait copieusement son assiette, puis ramenait le plat vers lui et, pouffant de rire, un rire sadique, préparait un crachat, un de ces molards qu'il va chercher au fin fond de sa gorge en raclant bien

54

sur les côtés, pour l'envoyer en plein milieu du plat. Il s'essuyait les lèvres de la main et faisait passer aux petits camarades. Pensez qu'aucun n'en voulait !

— Bon, vous vous servez ou quoi ? demandait Pat.

Personne ne lui répondait. Madjid ne faisait aucun commentaire, aucun geste : l'habitude aussi. Plutôt envie de vomir, qu'ils avaient, les copains.

Alors Pat reprenait le plat et mangeait à même dedans. Les autres grignotaient un morceau de pain, une main défendante sur le dessert qu'ils avaient pu sauver. Évidemment plus personne ne désirait déjeuner à cette table, mais il fallait bien compléter les places vacantes, sinon pas de service. Et il y avait toujours les « première année » qui ne savaient pas encore se défendre. Ils bouchaient les trous en priant que l'ogre n'ait pas trop faim...

Quel soulagement pour les petits, et pour le collège, quand Pat et Madjid furent virés ! C'était un après-midi en cours de maths, drôle de langage pour eux.

Pat disait souvent fièrement qu'il possédait la plus grosse bite de la classe. Madjid, épuisé d'entendre toujours ce même refrain prétentieux, le mit ce jour-là au défi :

— On va mesurer !

Sous la table, ils se branlent pour bander au maximum. Le prof s'est plongé dans un livre en attendant la fin de l'interro écrite. C'est le calme plat, tout le monde bosse, sauf eux deux.

Pat prend la règle et discrètement prend sa mesure. Puis, à l'oreille de Madjid il annonce :

— Quinze.

Madjid s'étonne, fixe Pat et lui lance :

— Menteur !

— Si, je te le dis !

Madjid mesure son sexe :

— Quatorze et demi.

— Je te bats ! dit fièrement Pat.

— De toute façon, je te crois pas.

— Tu vas voir ! s'insurge Pat en remettant la règle sur son engin.

— Pousse pas trop sur la règle, tu vas te crever le ventre ! dit Madjid.

— Je pousse pas. Tiens, combien ?

Madjid se penche et chiffre :

— Quatorze... quatorze faible.

— Tu vois pas clair, ma parole ! s'inquiète Pat.

Outré, diminué, il se lève, pose sa queue sur la table et gueule carrément :

— Tiens, mesure à la lumière !

Madjid ne bouge pas. Les bras croisés sur sa feuille blanche, il regarde, amusé, le prof qui hurle à Pat : « Ça va pas, non ? Cochon ! Idiot ! Imbécile ! », puis se lève et se dirige vers Pat, rouge de colère, le saisit par le col et le traîne vers la sortie.

— Chez monsieur le directeur, et tout de suite !

Pat se dégage en repoussant le prof et lui crie :

— Je vais te mettre une tête, tu vas voir !

Madjid, mine de rien, referme sa braguette.

— Toi aussi, hurle le prof. Allez, ouste !

— N'aie pas peur, fait Pat au prof : on ne va pas t'enculer !

Ils se retrouvèrent dehors, assis sur les marches de l'escalier d'entrée d'une tour de béton, comme un étranger débarquant dans un pays neuf où tout va très vite. Cet étranger, il lui faut s'adapter au mode de vie, aux exigences, au tempérament des autres pour survivre. Faire semblant de suivre le mouvement, ou alors refuser le système et se mettre à dos la société. Parce que c'est épuisant de courir après une carotte quand, de surcroît, on la sait pourrie depuis lurette.

— On va pas se taper sur la tête, dit Pat. On voit, en attendant, et si on trouve rien, demain on s'en fout.

Le collège, c'est terminé. Pas la peine de rempiler dans un autre. Quand on s'est fait lourder de celui des Marguerites, le dernier des derniers, on se retrouve triquard partout, dans toute la région.

— D'abord, on t'avait prévenu..., qu'ils disent, les gens.

— Et puis je m'en fous, dit Pat.

C'est vrai qu'il s'en fout, avec une petite pointe d'angoisse quand même, dans l'âme.

— Hein, Madj, qu'on s'en tamponne le coquillard ? Ah ! ah !

— Tu m'étonnes ! répond Madjid, pour se donner du courage.

Ils rient en se tapant dans la main. La tape de l'amitié. Unis pour le meilleur et pour le pire. Et puis, que craignent-ils ? Ils n'ont même pas un daron pour leur filer la bonne tannée supposée leur servir de leçon.

Celui de Pat a mis les bouts avec une jeunette de la cité, Marinette. Leur manège était connu, mais personne ne pensait qu'ils iraient jusqu'à se tirer de la zone, main dans la main.

Un matin, il est parti, le père de Pat, comme on va à l'usine, avec son petit sac sur l'épaule et sa casquette sur la tête. On l'attend encore, à c't'heure-ci ! Plus de nouvelles.

Il baisait Marinette, la voisine du troisième, celle qui a trois gosses et un mari routier. Coqueluche, qu'on l'appelle dans la cité, le routier, avec sa tête d'écrevisse de lavabo, comme dit Pat. On ne le voyait qu'en fin de semaine, Coqueluche, à cette époque, avant que sa femme le quitte pour le dab de Pat. Maintenant il est là tous les jours, il a changé de boulot, il bosse à la mairie et il s'occupe lui-même de ses gosses. Marinette a bien quinze ans de moins que son amant. Peut-être bien qu'elle avait le sexe qui commençait à rouiller, avec un mari jamais là.

Ils se sont barrés, les amants, laissant tout tomber sans regrets ni remords, du moment qu'ils s'arrachent du béton et de ses habitudes. Pat était au courant que son père sautait la Marinette. Il en riait, ce con, se vantant que dans sa famille on avait des couilles au cul. Puis lui aussi il avait fait l'amour avec Marinette, il s'en flatte.

Enfin, qui peut se vanter de ne point porter de cornes dans ces pigeonniers d'immeubles ? Il y a l'ennui, les habitudes, le désir d'autre chose pour sortir de routine. Faut bien casser une certaine morosité. Cette grisaillerie qui s'installe et qui étouffe en serrant fort sur le corps petit à petit comme une pieuvre. Elle entoure, tire et monte jusqu'à la gorge.

Dans la médiocrité, faut être le moins médiocre. Sauter la femme du voisin, c'est se croire moins con que lui, puisqu'on lui pique sa bergère. Et plaire, c'est se dire qu'on mérite mieux que ce qu'on a et qu'on est digne d'une autre vie. Les sentiments ? Que dalle ! C'est plutôt fuir le désespoir et chercher à croire en quelque chose par n'importe quel moyen, avec ce qui ressemble à une sécurité sûre : un trou avec du poil autour. Combien sont partis comme ça, fuyant le béton, larguant femme et enfants. Et la belle-mère qui n'a plus que ses mains pour trembler.

Pour respirer un petit coup, qu'ils s'en vont, avec n'importe quel petit cul rond et rose, jeune, qui sent encore le pipi des chiottes de la récré. Ils ne reviennent pas, jamais plus. On ne sait pas si c'est parce qu'ils sont heureux ailleurs ou qu'ils se font encore plus chier, regrettant, mais n'osant pas revenir, de honte.

Peut-être qu'ils reviennent en douce et se planquent derrière une bagnole pour voir leurs gosses à la sortie de l'école. Les mômes sont pâles et tristes, main dans la main, et ils ont grandi. Le fuyard a le cœur pincé. Dans le béton, qu'ils poussent, les enfants. Ils grandissent et lui ressemblent, à ce béton sec et froid. Ils sont secs et froids aussi, durs, apparemment indestructibles, mais il y a aussi des fissures dans le béton. Quand il pleut, on les distingue mieux, c'est comme des larmes qui coulent sur les joues pâles d'un petit à qui on a taxé ses billes et qu'a pas de grand frère pour le défendre.

Ça se lézarde sur la peau, et ça surprend et ça descend comme un fleuve sur une de ces cartes de géographie qu'on essayait de nous faire entrer dans la tête à grands coups de pied au cul, à nous dégoûter des voyages. Qu'est-ce qu'il y a comme fissures dans le béton : sur le cœur, sur le front, déjà tout petit. Ça s'élargit avec le temps, ça pénètre davantage et ça s'étend comme un lac, une déchirure, cicatrice indélébile, jusqu'aux tripes. Et ça ressort dans les moments difficiles, quand le corps et l'âme sont fâchés, ne se tiennent plus la main. Elles reviennent, ces fissures, elles démantèlent, il faut qu'on s'en occupe, sinon ça te bouffe, ça gonfle, ça t'étouffe, l'envie d'exploser, l'envie de crier.

Faut surtout pas chialer, parce que la faiblesse est alors reconnue, citée, criée, répandue. Faut pas pleurer. Faut pas, petit !

Emmagasiner encore et toujours en attendant, avec l'espoir peut-être de se réconcilier avec soi-même et avec la vie. Sinon c'est l'explosion, ça se réveille comme un volcan qui a longtemps ruminé sa vengeance contre tout ce qui lui a été bourré dans la gueule. Il évacue l'énergie somnolente en ses tripes. De bonne elle est devenue mauvaise, dévastatrice, et c'est la violence. Le refus. Le refus de se laisser étouffer. Contre la récupération de soi.

Contre l'autodestruction, le silence, c'est la violence qui prend le dessus et on devient irrécupérable. On ne se remet pas du béton. Il est partout présent, pesant, dans les gestes, dans la voix, dans le langage, jusqu'au fond des yeux, jusqu'au bout des ongles. Sur les bras il se transforme en trèfle à quatre feuilles tatoué en vert bouteille et dédié à sa mère, avec une rose. A jamais. Il suit partout comme une ombre. Même au Pérou, il suivra celui qui est né dedans. Même dans le lit de la plus belle, de la plus riche.

Ça a une odeur aussi, le béton... Celle qui dort au fond de la gorge. Plutôt entre le palais et le commencement de la gorge, dans le petit creux. Pour l'enlever, cette odeur ? Oualou ! Tout a été essayé, toutes les bières, toutes les drogues.

Rien. Elle reste, comme une chenille s'accroche à sa branche. Ceux qui ont essayé par la strangulation y sont restés. Ce petit creux qui dit bien ce qu'il veut dire ne te lâche pas la grappe. Il ne te la lâche que quand le Bon Dieu t'a fait dans ses vendanges.

Ça chante pas, le béton, ça hurle au désespoir comme les loups dans la forêt, les pattes dans la neige, et qui n'ont même plus la force de creuser un trou pour y mourir. Ils attendent comme des cons, voir si quelqu'un viendrait pas leur donner un coup de main. Ils attendent comme les mômes du béton. Ils font peur. On s'écarte de leur territoire. Quand on veut s'occuper d'eux, c'est pour mieux les détruire, proprement. Pour les séparer. En horde ils attaquent. Ils dérangent.

Josette vient prendre son môme chez Malika. Elle arrive plus tard que d'habitude. Stéphane est assis sur les genoux d'Amaria, sur le lit du salon. Dans l'appartement ça sent la *chorba*, la soupe chaude bien relevée qui tue tous les microbes de l'hiver, comme le dit la maîtresse de maison aux gosses qui n'en veulent pas.

Madjid est descendu chercher son père, il croise Josette dans le hall. Ils se saluent, sans s'arrêter. Juste un petit bonsoir et le petit sourire amical.

Malika demande à Josette de rester dîner à la maison.

— De la soupe chaude! elle insiste.

Non, Josette n'a pas le cœur à manger, ni à autre chose.

— Pour le petit, dit Malika.

— Non, je suis fatiguée.

Amaria se lève pour mettre le couvert. Stéphane endosse son manteau et cherche après son cartable.

— Et la grive? demande Malika.

— Toujours en grève ! On a fait une réunion syndicale ce soir, c'est pour ça que je suis venue tard...

Josette s'agenouille devant son gosse, lui boutonne son manteau, lui arrange son cache-nez, puis continue d'une voix lasse :

— Je crois que c'est terminé, maintenant, on est licencié, et c'est tout...

Amaria :

— Toutes ?

— Non, une partie seulement. Les nouvelles embauchées.

— Qu'est-ce que tu vas faire ?

— Chercher du travail, dit Josette en hochant la tête, l'air de dire : ça sera dur de trouver.

Stéphane va embrasser Malika avant de partir. Malika lève le doigt et le prévient :

— Gentil pour ta maman, Chousette fatigui ce soir !

Le gosse s'en fout. Josette sourit. Un sourire triste.

Malika insiste encore pour les garder à dîner. Elle fait comprendre à Josette qu'elle est de la famille. Et qu'elle considère Stéphane comme son fils. Pourquoi ne pas rester ? Josette la croit. Elle sait Malika bonne, généreuse et chaleureuse, elle sait ce qu'elle lui doit, mais ce soir le cœur n'y est pas.

Elle désire être seule, Josette, dans son petit deux pièces, au milieu de la tour, pour familles pas nombreuses. La déprime.

Elle prépare une assiette de crudités avec une tranche de jambon. Stéphane n'a pas faim, il a mangé des gâteaux au chocolat chez Malika. Il a fait ses devoirs avec Mehdi, qui l'aide et lui explique, quand ce n'est pas Amaria. Josette écoute les informations télévisées, le petit s'allonge sur la moquette et joue avec ses voitures miniatures. Il imagine un accident entre deux camions : « Boum », et sa petite main dessine un nuage de poussière...

On parle du chômage à la télé. Josette débarrasse la table, emporte les couverts à la cuisine, dans l'évier. Elle colle son nez à la vitre.

La cité s'endort sur les âmes seules. Elle n'attend rien, Josette. Son corps, son corps perdu, elle lui laisse juste une petite fente d'aération, pour qu'il respire, pour se le garder, se le préserver, pour des nuits encore plus dures, les nuits sans sommeil, parce que la peur, parce que la solitude. Il faut tirer les rideaux, pour cacher cette peur, cette solitude, puis il y a toujours plus seul que soi. Faut se donner du courage.

Le petit joue aux 24 heures du Mans.

La maman va se déshabiller dans la salle de bains. Elle enlève son collant et se passe les mains sur les cuisses comme pour les masser. Sa poitrine dessine deux petites dunes pointues, comme sur les statues du jardin des Tuileries. Elle démêle ses longs cheveux bruns qui tombent, caressent ses rondes épaules. Le peigne trace des sillons fins et brillants en gardant entre ses dents le cheveu récalcitrant.

Au salon, après l'accident, Stéphane fait appel à Police-Secours « Pin pon, pin pon. »

Josette repose le peigne sur la planchette de

faner = to wither

l'armoire de toilette, à côté de la plaquette de pilules contraceptives. Elle prend la plaquette et lit le dernier jour qu'elle en a usé. C'était un mardi. Quand ? Elle ne se souvient plus du mois... Son corps lui apparaît dans le miroir. Elle a l'impression de faner, d'être inutile, inanimée.

Comme elle n'a plus de relations sexuelles, elle a peur que son corps ne réponde plus. Elle passe ses mains sur ses hanches et remonte jusqu'aux seins, puis aux épaules, et remarque qu'elle a la chair de poule. Elle n'a pas eu de rapport depuis qu'elle est divorcée. Elle n'en a jamais ressenti le besoin ou l'envie, sauf une fois, après avoir fêté le mariage d'une collègue.

goose pimple

Elles avaient sablé le champagne, un peu trop pour elle. Le soir, dans son lit, elle avait eu mal au crâne et une envie de faire l'amour. Elle s'était caressée sous les draps.

C'est la dernière fois que son échine a vibré en bas des reins, la dernière fois qu'elle a senti son corps. Elle se souvient de cette chaleur qu'elle s'offrait elle-même, toute seule. Après l'ultime gémissement, évanouie, les bras en croix sur l'oreiller, elle avait sursauté en s'apercevant qu'elle pleurait. Pas des larmes de plaisir, pas ces larmes qui disparaissent après l'orgasme, mais des pleurs de manque, de remords et de solitude. Impression de vide, comme ce soir. Sentiment de faire du surplace dans une vie qui va si vite, qui n'attend pas. Si on ne prend pas le bon wagon, ça sèche le fond du palais. On reste sur le quai, comme un oublié. Avec un lardon dans les bras, c'est dur !

Plus dur encore quand, en plus, le rejeton demande parfois son père. Que lui répondre ? Il a son doigt dans le nez, des petits yeux ronds qui questionnent. Alors faut lui dire...

— Enlève le doigt de ton nez !

Le môme pige et s'en va rejoindre son nuage de jeux.

Elle enfile sa robe de chambre, rejoint Stéphane au salon, fuyant le miroir.

Quand Pat lui met la main sur l'épaule, elle sursaute en se retournant prestement, Solange.

— Je t'ai fait peur ?

— Un peu ; la surprise, quoi ! répond-elle avec son accent parigot à traîner sur un fil de fer rouillé.

Elle plisse des yeux sourcilleux et son visage grimace quand elle cause. Quel âge peut-elle bien avoir ? Vingt-huit ans ? L'alcool l'a séchée, enlaidie. Ses longs cheveux châtains, gras, tombent sur ses épaules comme la crinière d'un cheval qui vient de se rouler dans la boue. Elle est ronde du matin au soir et traîne de bar en bar. Et qui ne l'a pas sautée dans le quartier, la Solange ? *Prostituée*

— C'est pas des bites qu'elle a vues, c'est des kilomètres de nœuds ! qu'il dit, le Pat, quand il parle d'elle.

Elle se fait monter pour un demi-pression ou un litre de Postillon. Son mec est en cabane et pour un bout de temps, un dur. Elle a deux gosses dont s'occupe la belle-mère, une vieille folle qui tire à coups de chevrotines sur tout ce qui bouge

71

devant sa porte, la nuit tombée. Un de ses gosses traîne souvent après son jupon comme un jeune chien, maigrichon et sale. Quand, bien ivre, elle s'écroule au bord du caniveau, c'est lui qui la ramasse. Il met son fil de réglisse entre ses dents et relève sa maman de ses petits bras, sans émotion. Le train-train. Parfois, quand elle a vraiment trop bu, donc bien lourde, et qu'il ne peut pas la relever, il s'assoit contre le mur à côté d'elle, attendant qu'elle finisse de délirer, de vomir. Il attend en regardant les enfants jouer dans le bac à sable.

Ce soir elle tient, tant bien que mal. C'est pas encore la grosse cuite.

— Tu viens avec nous ?

— Où que ça ? Eh ! eh ! dit-elle.

— On va se faire un peu de némo, ça te dit ?

— Alors vous alors !... Hé ! vous manquez pas de culot, hein !

— Alors, tu viens ?

— Okay, je vous suis, mais ce soir je suis pas en forme !

Le môme de Solange suit. Madjid prend son air ennuyé et repousse le petit.

— Tu restes là et tu nous attends ! lui dit-il en lui caressant les cheveux.

L'enfant tend la main comme un mendiant. Madjid appelle Pat. Celui-ci sort une pièce de monnaie qu'il tend au môme.

— Dis merci aux messieurs, qu'elle ordonne à son fils, Solange.

Mais le petit est déjà loin, presque arrivé à la hauteur de la boulangerie.

— C'est un rapide, hein ? dit-elle fièrement. Il ira loin !

— Comme son père, dit Pat.

— Qu'est-ce que tu dis ?

Solange n'apprécie pas.

— Je disais que son père, y courait vite aussi, répond Pat.

— Ah ! bon, je préfère, dit Solange en marchant à côté de ses pompes.

Le temps de renifler un bon coup, elle reprend :

— Ouais, il cognait fort aussi... mon mari...

Le trio s'en va sur la route du port de Gennevilliers, longeant les maraîchers qui vont bientôt déguster l'autoroute.

Et des terrains vagues, et des tas d'ordures, avec un petit vent coquet qui ne dépeigne pas le moindre cheveu. Ils arrivent au campement des Gitans. Il y a l'odeur des pneus brûlés qui squatte les poumons. Ça arrache. Il y a le cuivre encore chaud, à peine sorti du feu entre trois grosses caillasses, que Manitas, le fils gitan, fourre dans une bassine. Il y a les chiens qui se tordent le cou à tirer sur leur chaîne pour mieux aboyer. Le boucan. L'alerte. Le trio est vite repéré. Toute la famille gitane se retourne et dévisage ces intrus.

— Faut surtout pas regarder leurs femmes, dit Pat à l'oreille de Madjid. Faut jouer au passant qui passe et cherche son chemin.

Mais Madjid ne peut s'empêcher d'admirer les femmes des Gitans. Il les trouve belles... Elles sont vraiment belles. Elles sont toujours en technicolor. On dirait un bouquet de fleurs japonaises qui se balade dans un pot oriental. Elles portent

73

des robes longues aux teintes criardes, d'un jaune vif et aveuglant, presque phosphorescent, décorées de roses, un rose outrageant, clinquant, comme un coup sur la tête. Quand elles marchent, les Gitanes, on croirait qu'elles glissent, qu'elles dansent, gracieuses et détendues, sur un tapis roulant. C'est comme les cygnes du lac de Saint-Mandé, on ne voit pas leurs palmes qui s'activent dans le bouillon.

Quand Madjid les observe, il se demande toujours ce que de belles femmes comme elles fichent accrochées à une caravane, une gamelle dégueulasse à la main, dans ces sordides trous de terrain vague. Lui, il les emmènerait, ces belles dames, vers une pâtisserie huppée et leur ferait un lit entre les dragées de toutes les couleurs, les blanches rondes, les bleues ovales et les roses plates. Comme quand on était gosse, léchant la vitrine.

Elles sont toujours fardées un maximum, des bagues à chaque doigt, des bracelets jaunes aux poignets et des boucles d'oreilles arrogantes qui balancent en frôlant les épaules. On voudrait s'y accrocher, pour mieux sentir le parfum de ces dames. Leurs gestes sont indifférents, tout est dans la voix, mais l'émotion ou la lassitude se lisent dans la pierre noire piquée au milieu des grands yeux noirs.

Leurs longs cheveux sont colorés au henné, comme l'horizon au coucher du soleil, couverts d'un foulard vert pistache ou bleu ciel. Et le chewing-gum, l'éternel chewing-gum qu'elles ruminent.

74

Leurs mecs, aux Gitanes, Madjid s'y attarde pas. La plupart du temps, ils sont en bras de chemise. Chemises à carreaux de préférence avec cravate vert bouteille. T'as pas besoin d'aller dans l'Est, quand t'en as vu un, t'as fait le voyage et à l'œil, et ça vaut le coup. Le père gitan, on dirait un videur de boîte de nuit mal fréquentée. La moustache à la Clark Gable et une armoire à glace de bonhomme. Le regard usé par les chemins à suivre, il fume une cigarette que ses doigts graisseux ont mal roulée. Quand la cigarette se fait sèche, il attrape le litron de mauvais pinard qui repose à l'ombre de la vieille 403 Peugeot noire. Il se rince la dalle après avoir chassé la mouche qui se promenait sur le goulot. Il regarde le ciel, le Gitan, assis sur les marches de la caravane, la bouteille sur les genoux, comme sa femme observe dans la boule de cristal.

Madjid a envie de le saluer, rien que pour entendre le son et l'accent de sa voix. Il n'ose pas. Manitas vient à leur rencontre, le torse nu, les mains et le visage noircis par la fumée du plastique. Mains sur les hanches, il les stoppe comme un douanier, il a l'air furieux. Quand il traverse la cité, il se fait tout petit, discret, mais là, dans son campement, il est le maître, il joue au dur.

— Qu'est-ce que vous venez foutre ici ? qu'il gueule.

— Ben, on passe, dit Pat.

— Vous pouvez passer ailleurs, non ?

— Te fâche pas, Manitas, tu nous connais !

— Comment qu'il s'appelle ? demande Solange de sa voix étranglée de femme soûle.

— Manitas, répond Pat.

— Comme le chanteur espagnol ? C'est joli, hé ! hé ! dit-elle en montrant toutes ses dents. Et Madjid lui glisse doucement à l'oreille :

— Non, le chanteur, c'est un Gitan aussi !

— Ouais ! reprend Pat. Avec un prénom comme ça, tu dois t'envoyer toutes les petites Gitanes ?

— Ça va, dit Manitas, faut plus passer par là, c'est tout.

Pat et Madjid se regardent. Leur regard en dit long sur le prochain accueil qu'ils feront à Manitas quand il s'amusera à passer par la cité. Ils lui feront un tapis rouge, à la trace, mais le Gitan n'a pas l'air de comprendre, il menace encore.

— Je vous ai dit de décamper !

— Qu'est-ce que tu nous les broutes ! dit Madjid qui s'énerve. Va cramer ton cuivre et lâche-nous le crachoir !

— Du cuivre ? s'insurge Manitas. Où que c'est que t'as vu du cuivre, toi, petit con, hein ? J'ai pigé, vous venez voir ce qu'on fait. Je le savais !

— Mais non, dit Pat, prenant des airs de gros bonhomme moralisateur. On s'en fout, nous. On va à Gennevilliers.

— Alors, arrachez-vous ! hurle le Gitan en s'écartant, sinon je lâche les chiens !

— T'aimes donc pas tes bêtes ? dit Pat en fixant bien Manitas. Tu vas quand même pas les fatiguer à nous courser ? Sauvage !

Et le trio s'éloigne en pouffant de rire. Doucement : il y a toujours les chiens qui aboient.

Le Gitan retourne à son feu en jurant entre ses
dents. Pas plus haut qu'un tabouret, cet adolescent, mais ce qu'il est teigneux ! Puis il rigole
pas !

Ils longent la vieille ligne de chemin de fer à
l'herbe haute et sauvage, jusqu'au foyer des
travailleurs immigrés. Solange ne cesse de se
plaindre.

— C'est loin encore ? qu'elle demande. J'ai des
cailloux dans les godasses.

Et en plus elle marche sur sa longue robe
indienne froissée.

— On arrive, la rassure Madjid. C'est là, tu
vois, ces baraques en bas, jaunes, derrière la
grue.

Ils dévalent le talus en se tenant aux hautes
herbes sauvages.

Solange descend sur les fesses. C'est des bara-
quements en préfabriqué, plantés sur un terrain
vague, rocailleux et poussiéreux. L'hiver, c'est la
boue qui prend place.

Des travailleurs latins, nord-africains, y logent,
dans cette cité gérée par l'employeur. Ils vivent là
comme des bêtes, à l'écart de la ville, entre les
travaux de l'autoroute, la voie du chemin de fer
et le port de Gennevilliers, dans ce camp de
travail entouré d'un haut grillage.

Madjid se dirige vers la première baraque. Il en
fait le tour. Pas âme qui vive. A la seconde, il

entend du bruit, il fait signe à Solange et à Pat de le rejoindre.

Madjid frappe à la porte de la baraque.

Pat pousse Solange doucement vers cette porte qui s'ouvre sur un homme d'une quarantaine d'années, les joues mal rasées, l'air débarqué précipitamment de Lisbonne.

— Ch'est quoi ? dit-il en dévisageant le trio.

Pat lui sourit en lui montrant Solange :

— Tu vois, dit-il en passant ses doigts dans les cheveux de Solange. Elle te plaît ma sœur ?

Le Portugais, surpris par l'offre, déshabille Solange des yeux. Il ne sait que dire, pris de court. Il se retourne vers l'intérieur de la carrée et appelle :

— Joachim !

C'est un grand rougeaud, les cheveux en épis de blé, portant toute la carte des vignobles de Porto sur les joues.

— Combien ? demande Joachim.

— Cinquante ! répond Pat.

— Tou rigoles, non ? répond le rougeaud.

— Bon, ben salut, mes petits canards, leur dit Solange en faisant une bien basse révérence.

— On va voir à côté, dit Madjid.

Mais le Joachim se ravise :

— Trente !

Solange fonce sur l'occase, elle qui se fait sauter pour un paquet de cigarettes. Pat et Madjid n'ont pas le temps d'intervenir qu'elle entre déjà dans la baraque.

— Okay ! dit-elle. Ça marche, mais alors un coup chacun, j'ai pas que ça à foutre.

78

Les Portugais la suivent.

— Fait sombre chez vous ! qu'elle leur dit.

Elle retire déjà son slip en fixant les photos pornos accrochées entre les lits superposées contre le mur. Un des Portugais sourit, gêné. Elle lui montre sa chatte :

— Ça, c'est du vrai ! qu'elle dit en remontant sa robe. Mais faut payer d'avance.

Les clients se dépêchent de trouver la monnaie et de la poser sur la petite table, au milieu de la chambre.

Le premier demande à Pat et à Madjid de sortir.

Solange veut que l'un d'eux reste, mais c'est refusé. D'ailleurs tous sortent, le petit gros veut baiser seul et dans le noir.

— T'as une petite bite et tu veux pas qu'on la voie, hein ? lui lance Pat, moqueur, avant de sortir.

Le mec ne répond pas.

Ils grillent une sèche à l'extérieur avec le grand Portugais qui s'impatiente.

— Bon, je vais voir dans les autres carrées s'il y a du trèfle, dit Madjid.

Il leur faut bien une heure pour faire le tour de tous les postulants pour une passe. C'est payant, la misère sexuelle des travailleurs immigrés ! En rien de temps, on ramasse une poignée de fric.

Solange est complètement soûle, d'autant qu'elle demande à chaque client de la bière. Un petit coup de toilette dans l'évier et en route vers une nouvelle baraque. Pat tient le chronomètre, cinq minutes par client, pas plus. Sinon il fait

irruption dans la bicoque et donne la lumière.
Rien de tel pour faire débander un taureau. Tout
se passe bien jusqu'à ce qu'un locataire les traite
de tous les noms :

— Maquereaux, petits salauds !

Et Solange, de véroleuse.

— Vendeurs de chaude-pisse, hurle le mec en
les virant du camp, et il menace que la prochaine
fois il préviendra les flics. Le scandale !

« On n'est quand même pas des sauvages ni des
bêtes ! » fut la dernière phrase qu'ils entendirent.
Ils reprirent le chemin du retour en évitant, cette
fois, de traverser le campement forain. Pat parta-
gea le fric en trois. Il marchait doucement en
comptant les billets, plus la monnaie. Solange se
plaignait des reins.

— Tu m'étonnes ! lui dit Pat. Quand tu te fais
casser la rondelle par des gorilles pareils, tu vas
passer la bonne nuit !...

— Tu parles que j'ai rien senti. Au contraire,
ça me donne envie de dégobiller.

— T'as pas pris ton pied avec tous ces mecs ?
demanda Pat, surpris.

Solange s'arrêta, vacilla, sourcilla et répondit :

— Terminé pour moi, ces jouissances ! Il n'y a
que le foutre qui me dégouline entre les cuisses
que je sens.

Du coup la larme lui vint à l'œil. Sa main qui
tenait le fric tomba, ballante, doucement, le long
de son corps, et sa tête se rabaissa, ses cheveux
cachant son visage, et elle dit encore :

— Je sens plus rien, quoi que je fasse, et quand
ça me prend au palpitant, j'ai envie de mourir...

Elle resta plantée au milieu du chemin, pleurnichant.

Madjid, gagné par la sensibilité, lui offrit sa
part d'argent.

Elle refusa. Ennuyé, il ne sut quoi dire.

La môme renifla et repartit dans ses larmes.

Pat soupira, agacé. Les histoires de cœur, il s'en
foutait. Il lui tardait de repartir vers la cité.

Madjid insista pour donner son fric à Solange.

— Tu crois que c'est ça qui va me rendre
heureuse ? dit-elle.

Il lui fourra les biftons dans le corsage.

— Allez ! pleure plus. C'est pour tes gosses.

Pat n'apprécia guère. Il voulait plutôt garder sa
part, mais lui aussi, finalement, offrit son fric à la
môme, puis il se retourna vers Madjid, et
méchamment :

— Tout ça pour rien !

— Ben, quoi ! On va pas la laisser crever,
quand même, non ?

— C'est du cinoche qu'elle nous fait, t'as pas
compris !

Solange releva la tête et leur tendit les bras.
Elle embrassa Pat sur les deux joues. Quand il est
comme ça, Pat, la tête rentrée dans les épaules et
qu'on ne voit plus ses oreilles sous le col de son
blouson, c'est qu'il est pas content. Et il le
montra. Solange ne remarqua rien. Les bisous, il
s'en fiche. Il grimaça en plus, car la petite n'a pas
l'haleine fraîche. Il partit seul, devant, pour bien
montrer à Madjid que, ce coup-ci, ça avait bien
foiré !

Madjid se laissa embrasser.

81

— Merci, dit Solange. Vous êtes gentils, vous, au moins. Quand je pense à tous ces gens qui disent que les jeunes c'est des cons ! Voilà la preuve du contraire. J'oublierai pas.

Pat pouffa de rire. Madjid se laissa embrasser une seconde fois. Elle insista. Rebelote. L'haleine n'était pas fraîche non ! Madjid, ça lui rappela Madeleine.

Madeleine, la petite Bretonne rondouillarde avec les joues roses, qui habitait dans la cité avec ses parents. A quatorze ans déjà, elle avait dépucelé tous les adolescents du quartier. Elle avait une sacrée mauvaise haleine aussi, à étouffer une armée de mouches. Aucun de ses amoureux ne flirtait avec elle, et pourtant elle en eut !

Elle descendait dans la cave, les garçons la suivaient à deux ou à trois, et l'allongeaient sur une caisse.

Paumée dans sa tête, elle se laissait faire, et même que parfois au bout du dernier elle y prenait du plaisir. Les gars faisaient la queue bite à la main en observant le travail de celui qui était dessus. Ils la tournaient, retournaient, lui caressaient les seins, en profitant pour apprendre le sexe féminin. Elle aimait les caresses, Madeleine, ça devait certainement lui manquer chez elle.

Pat, qui en passa par-là aussi avec Madjid, lui reniflait le vagin, l'écoutait en essayant de voir au fond du trou ce qui « peut bien faire jouir les gonzesses ». Il finissait, majestueux :

83

— Ce qu'il y a au-dessus du trou, là (il montrait aux copains), comme les oreilles d'un éléphant, c'est le clitoris.

Madjid riait.

— Qu'est-ce qui te fait marrer ? demanda Pat, outré qu'on se moque de son savoir.

— C'est pas de ce que tu dis que je rigole. Ah ! ah ! C'est le coup de l'éléphant. Tu te souviens à l'école, quand l'instit t'avait demandé le nom d'un animal commençant par la lettre N, t'as répondu un ours. Ah ! ah ! Même que t'as pris une baffe !

Pour pas « payer », Pat avait fait semblant de rire aussi, mais pas de bon cœur.

Le manège avec Madeleine dura longtemps.

Les adolescents tiraient leur crampe en moyenne une fois la semaine et ils étaient un paquet. Jusqu'au jour où Bengston eut le chibre en fleur. Au début ça le démangeait, puis ce fut la douleur, il souffrait le martyre pour pisser. Tout le monde paniqua. Chacun s'enfermait dans les toilettes pour examiner son sexe. Il y eut cinq cas.

— C'est rien, une chaude-lance ! disait Pat. C'est l'amour qui rentre. Et pour te soigner l'infirmière te fend la queue, elle souffle dedans pour virer les microbes ! C'est bandant les lèvres d'une infirmière ! Puis après elle te la recoud. Là, par contre, ça fait un peu mal, mais c'est rien à côté du cancer de la couille gauche...

Et il continuait à saper le moral de ses copains perturbés et angoissés. C'est Bengston qui avait le plus peur.

84

Bengston chercha Madeleine partout en jurant toute la journée.

— Ça t'apprendra à tremper ton biscuit dans un égout, lui disait Thierry, jouant au maître penseur, mais Pat n'apprécia guère.

— Qu'est-ce que t'en sais, Thierry de mes deux, si Mado c'est un trou béant d'égout ? Hein ? Tu l'as jamais sautée, Mado ?

— Si. Mais qu'une fois.

— Ben, heureusement qu'elle est là, Mado ! Avec la tête que t'as tu serais encore puceau !... Peut-être qu'elle pue de la gueule, la Mado, mais elle suce mieux que ta frangine !

Paf ! Thierry encaissa, puis se défendit, mais en restant sur ses gardes, il craignait Pat.

— Ça m'étonnerait que ma sœur baise avec un mec de ton genre !

Pat tira sur sa cigarette, un sourire vengeur au coin de la bouche, puis acheva son pote à la dérive :

— Et même qu'elle avale tout, ta frangine !... Tu lui demanderas si elle a toujours sa petite culotte bleue Petit Bateau.

Ce soir-là, Thierry attendit son adolescente de sœur à la sortie du lycée. Elle reçut la plus forte raclée de sa vie. L'honneur sauf, Thierry revint peinard dans la bande. Et on ne revit pas Madeleine dans la cité. Pour cause : ses parents l'avaient envoyée grandir loin de la sale mentalité des jeunes citadins, à la campagne, chez les grands-parents.

Il était temps, car Balou, un de l'allée des Dahlias, voulait la maquer, la Mado. Il parlait souvent de la mettre sur le trottoir : sûr qu'avec le cul et les nichons qu'elle avait il en tirerait du pognon. Ce Balou-là était un dangereux. D'ailleurs Madjid, Pat et les autres ne le fréquentaient pas. Une nuit, il arriva aux Acacias rond comme une boule de pétanque. La bande était assise comme d'habitude sous le porche quand il déboucha au coin. D'abord ce fut la rigolade, rapport à sa cuite, puis voilà qu'il sort un flingue et tire en l'air. La panique. Et encore un coup vers le ciel. Il se tordait de rire, Balou, pendant que la bande décampait comme athlète devant le starter. Puis il partit, le Balou, tout heureux qu'on s'intéresse enfin à lui. Toutes les fenêtres s'allumaient. Il leva presque les bras en l'air, de triomphe.

Un autre soir, il revint, tout aussi clinquant. A l'époque, la Maison des Jeunes n'avait pas encore fermé ses portes. Les adolescents étaient autour du baby-foot ou de la table de ping-pong quand ils perçurent un klaxon.

Jean-Marc, le premier, mit le nez à la fenêtre et découvrit le spectacle.

Dans l'obscurité, une voiture noire immatriculée on ne sait dans quel département, était garée juste à l'entrée de la cour de la M. J., tous phares allumés. Pat ouvrit grands ses yeux, la bouche au vent comme une sardine, et cracha par terre. La vache ! Putain ! Ouahh ! La bagnole, les mecs !

— C'est Balou, affirmait Jean-Marc. Z'avez vu la caisse ? Quelle surprise !

Une paye qu'on ne l'avait vu, le Balou ! D'où sortait-il ? Il devenait fou, ou quoi ? Toutes les vitres de la voiture empruntée, il les avait tapissées de billets de banque. Des vrais. Que des gros biftons, même sur le pare-brise. Madjid en eut la chair de poule. Pat suait. Ils tournèrent autour de la caisse en plaquant les mains sur les carreaux. Ils riaient. Un rire nerveux et fuyant. Balou, grand seigneur, enfoncé dans son siège. Empaqueté dans un costard de première, un œillet rouge à la boutonnière, le cigare, et un maousse, un manche de lime.

Il joua à fond et jusqu'au bout. Il regardait droit devant lui, souriant, comme un chef de bandits dans les films de cow-boys. *← macho!!*

Les gars tournaient et retournaient tout autour en se tapant dans les mains. C'était bon de fêter la victoire, enfin, d'un ami. Ils en avaient plein la vue. Ce cinoche !

Sur la banquette arrière était une fille aux cheveux blonds et bouclés. Elle tirait sur une sèche longue et fine à bout doré teinté de rouge à lèvres, le regard hagard et lointain, l'air de se demander ce qu'elle fichait au milieu de cette bande de fous. Les fous balançaient la voiture, tout en cognant sur les carreaux pour faire tomber les billets, mais chaque bifton qui lâchait prise, Balou le ramassait, le léchait et le recollait à sa place.

La nana avait le chemisier déboutonné de haut en bas. Pat ne quittait pas des yeux ses petits seins de gamine. Enfoiré de Balou, il avait tout prévu. Dû en rêver nuit et jour, de sa mise en scène réussie.

La fille jeta un œil sur Pat, qui sourit bêtement,

87

comme un primitif devant un miroir. Balou baissa un peu la vitre de son côté, la bande s'approcha. Il ne pipa mot. Il décolla un billet de sur le pare-brise, y mit le feu avec son briquet en or et ralluma son cigare d'un geste lent et bien étudié, pour la montre. Il éteignit le billet en l'écrasant dans sa main, souffla sur la fumée en l'envoyant sur la gueule des mecs pendus à la lucarne, puis balança les restes des cinq cents balles à l'extérieur. Bengston ramassa et tous rirent. Pas Balou.

C'était pas fini. Il se retourna vers la fille, lui fit un geste de l'index de gauche à droite, latéralement, et elle écarta les jambes. Balou refit le même geste, en plus insistant, et elle écarta ses cuisses encore plus. Il changea son cigare de main pour soulever sa jupette fine et la rabattre sur son ventre.

— Mama mia ! s'exclama Pat, émerveillé devant le sexe endormi comme un bébé rose entre les cuisses. Un sexe rasé de femme, comme on en rêvait étant môme. Balou t'es un chef !

Il avait tout prévu, oui, se rappelant nos fantasmes de gamin, ce qu'on se racontait au fond d'une cave. Il nous amenait une poule avec la chatte de nos récrés, preuve que c'était lui donc qui se l'était farcie le premier, cette chatte. Doublés, ils étaient doublés, les mecs ! Bengston en piqua un rire nerveux et Pat effaça la buée d'air chaud qu'il avait dessinée sur la vitre à souffler comme un taureau, pour voir.

Balou jeta son cigare dehors, personne ne le ramassa. Ça l'emmerda un peu, il aurait bien voulu. Mais les gars étaient ailleurs. « Une chatte rasée, putain de moine! », avait l'air de se dire Thierry, en agitant sa main comme s'il venait de se brûler les doigts.

Madjid essaya de piquer un billet par la vitre baissée. Balou lui fit un signe de la tête :

— Essaie!

Il posa son doigt sur un bouton du tableau de bord et réinvita Madjid :

— Hum! fit Madjid. Pas confiance!

Le sourire sadique de Balou en disait long sur ses intentions.

La bande faisait semblant de rire aussi, mais le metteur en scène les inquiétait. Il avait pas l'air net dans sa tête. Un billet se décolla et s'abattit comme une feuille sur le levier de vitesse. Balou le ramassa, le lécha comme un qui bouffe une glace, commença de le recoller sur la vitre, puis, se ravisant, le tendit à Thierry sans le regarder. Thierry dit merci et demanda :

— D'où ce que tu viens, Balou?

Balou réfléchit, son regard frimeur se tendit, se tira :

— Tu veux pas que je ressorte mon flingue, n'est-ce pas? demanda-t-il.

Il mit la main sur son cœur. La bande recula. Il éclata de rire, mit le contact et la bagnole démarra sec, crissant de tous ses pneus.

— N'empêche qu'à la place de la gonzesse, j'aurais les jetons avec un gus pareil! dit Thierry en essuyant le billet avec la manche de son blouson.

— T'es jaloux ou quoi? demanda Madjid.

— Il nous en a mis plein la gueule, le salaud! conclut Pat.

Ils retournèrent au ping-pong, l'esprit vagabond.

On ne le revit plus dans la cité, Balou. Le bruit courait qu'il était maquereau à Barbès, et même que si quelqu'un voulait tirer un coup il aille le voir, c'était gratuit pour les copains. Il faisait des fleurs, on pouvait même choisir sa pute.

— Sacré Balou! dit Madjid en poussant la porte de la M. J.

Il pensait au chemin parcouru par Balou. Une ligne qu'on lui avait tracée bien avant. Il n'avait plus qu'à suivre. On dirait que pour certains êtres tout est prévu d'avance, qu'ils sont devenus ce qu'on a voulu qu'ils soient. Et que ces êtres, que ça leur soit facile ou difficile, ils finissent toujours par foncer dans le panneau, par infortune ou par vengeance. Déjà môme, surpris à taxer ses petits copains, Balou avait été jeté de l'école.

Ce qui fait qu'à treize ans il se retrouvait sur le macadam à apprendre la vie sur le tas. Son père l'avait fourgué à un pâtissier véreux qui le faisait bosser jusqu'à quinze heures par jour. Il rentrait le soir épuisé, après avoir traversé à pied toute la sordide banlieue ouest, son petit paquet de gâteaux sous le bras, pour ses frères et sœurs. Ils étaient neuf gosses. Et leur père, un cafetier, les avait quittés pour vivre avec une minette de comptoir dans une chambre d'hôtel. Il venait les voir occasionnellement, toujours bon père, mais sans lâcher un sou.

La mère n'en pouvait plus de survivre.

On ne le voyait même plus sur le terrain de foot, Balou, tant il était fatigué. Le dimanche, il dormait toute la journée.

Puis, un soir, il en eut marre. Il rentra chez lui, toujours son petit paquet sous le bras, mais avec en prime le tiroir-caisse du pâtissier. Les flics, le pâtissier, le père le cherchèrent partout. Il était à la fête avec ses potes, et c'est lui qui rinçait, le bougre! Ça dura quatre jours, cette fête, puis son père lui mit le grappin dessus. Il le ligota, le fourra dans la baignoire et le roua de coups jusqu'au sang, puis s'en prit à la mère à grands flacs de ceinturon, la mère qui n'avait pas su élever ses gosses. Il envoya Balou en maison de correction, divorça et expédia en Tunisie son ex-épouse vieillissante. Elle n'avait plus que ses larmes pour s'accrocher à ses gosses.

Le vieux se fit envoyer une jeunette du pays, une pauvre fille sortie d'un fond de djebel, et l'épousa.

Elle ne savait pas un mot de français. Elle dut s'occuper de la marmaille, mais pas un des gosses ne parlait un mot d'arabe.

Après plusieurs séjours en maison de correction, Balou revint dans la cité à dix-sept ans. Il se la coula douce quelque temps, peinard, rechargeant ses accus, jusqu'au jour où une de ses sœurs le surprit en train de baiser sa belle-maman. C'était la plus petite des filles et elle hurla, choquée. Balou déchargea sur les draps.

Insatisfaite du vieux, la jeune maman se tapait le fiston. Le père au courant, Balou ne remit plus les pieds chez lui. La belle-maman fut mise dans le premier bateau et les gosses fourgués à l'Assistance.

Son journal sous le bras, plié à la rubrique « offres d'emploi », Josette déambule dans Paris. De métro en métro, de bus en bus, elle se rend à toutes les adresses intéressantes, refoulée chaque fois. La lassitude la prend sur le coup de midi. Elle s'achète un pain au chocolat dans une pâtisserie et le mange sur un banc du boulevard Haussmann. Quelques pigeons l'entourent, attendant qu'elle leur jette des miettes. Ce qu'elle fait. Elle a envie de retirer ses chaussures, mais elle n'ose pas, dans la rue. Ses pieds lui font mal, la prochaine fois elle ne mettra pas de hauts talons, mais il faut être présentable quand on cherche un emploi. Surtout pas de pantalon ! Le chef du personnel, lui, est en général mal fagoté, débraillé, mais cela ne l'empêche pas de détailler les postulants de haut en bas. Il peut même critiquer le physique, l'habillement. Quand c'est par correspondance et qu'il demande une photo, c'est pas pour voir si la nana a une bouche à sucer, c'est pour voir si ce n'est pas une Antillaise avec un nom bien français... Les Antillais, c'est des Français pourtant. Mais à part entière seulement pour voter. Bengston, lui, l'a compris. Il ne se balade qu'avec des fils d'Arabes. Il dit toujours :

— Même si certains politiciens antillais sont des vendus, les Antilles ne sont pas à vendre.

Et il gueule en faisant des bras d'honneur à qui en veut.

Josette reprend le train à la gare Saint-Lazare pour rentrer.

Elle traîne les usines de banlieues tout l'après-midi, sans se décourager. Même les stations d'essence, les grands magasins...

« Faut que je trouve du boulot, faut que je trouve... », se répète-t-elle.

Elle rentre chez elle quand le jour court de l'hiver s'enfuit. Elle reprend Stéphane chez Malika ; en même temps demande une demi-baguette, elle n'a pas pensé à acheter du pain. Malika s'inquiète.

— Ti l'as di l'argent, au moins ?

— Bien sûr, seulement j'ai oublié de passer à la boulangerie. Autrement, j'ai tout ce qu'il faut.

— Riste manger, Chousette !

— Non, faut que j'y aille, j'ai des tas de choses à faire.

Malika n'est pas contente. Josette prend la main de Stéphane et s'en va. Le petit pousse un cri de Tarzan dans le couloir, il a dû l'apprendre à la récré.

Josette et son fils sont à peine rentrés chez eux qu'on sonne à la porte. C'est le père du petit.

94

Josette accueille son ex-mari avec crainte. Elle a oublié encore une fois qu'on était vendredi, jour où le père vient chercher le petit pour le week-end.

L'enfant n'est pas prêt. Il embrasse son père comme s'il rentrait du travail comme avant. Il le tire par la main pour lui montrer son cahier de dessin.

— Ça va ? demande l'ex-mari.

— Oui, ça peut aller, dit Josette.

Il a une trentaine d'années, genre sportif, en blouson grenat et pantalon de velours, les cheveux très courts. Ses traits annoncent un type dur et secret, pas le genre grande gueule.

Josette prépare un sac de vêtements pour Stéphane. Elle se souvient que c'est la Toussaint.

Deux jours sans le gosse, ça va être dur !

Le père prend Stéphane dans ses bras, attrape le sac de voyage.

— Tu viens pas, Mman ?

— Non...

— Pourquoi tu viens pas avec nous ?

— Je peux pas, j'ai du travail.

Le père s'éclipse et appelle l'ascenseur.

Josette s'adosse contre le mur du couloir, ferme les yeux et laisse glisser tout doucement ses mains. Son corps plaqué contre la paroi descend, descend, jusqu'à ce qu'elle se retrouve assise. Sa tête penchée sur ses genoux, ses longs cheveux cachant sa figure, elle renifle, puis se relève brusquement et se précipite dans sa chambre, d'où elle ressort avec un flacon de sirop à la main. Elle se chausse vivement et se rue dans l'escalier de service.

Stéphane monte dans la voiture de son père et s'assied sur la banquette arrière. Devant, il y a une dame. Le petit regarde la rousse chevelure de cette dame. Il se penche, essayant de voir son visage. Elle se retourne et lui sourit. Elle est plus âgée que sa mère et bien maquillée. Stéphane baisse les yeux, intimidé. Le père se met au volant et attache sa ceinture de sécurité. Le petit se lève, se met à pleurer en regardant craintivement la femme, puis s'accroche au cou de son père.

— Qu'est-ce qu'il y a, Steph ? demande le père.

L'enfant pleure et cache son visage dans le dos du père. Josette arrive devant la voiture et fait semblant de ne pas voir la rousse. Elle tend le flacon de sirop côté chauffeur :

— S'il tousse en pleine nuit, tu lui en donnes une cuillerée et tu lui relèves la tête avec un oreiller...

— Maman ! appelle Stéphane.

Josette passe la main à l'intérieur et caresse les joues du petit.

— Qu'est-ce que tu as ? demande sa mère, la gorge serrée.

Il pleure à chaudes larmes, les mains tendues comme un noyé qui s'enfonce, sans prise.

Josette ouvre la portière arrière et s'empare de son fils qu'elle serre fortement contre elle.

Le môme se cache en sa mère, ses bras sont trop petits pour l'entourer comme il voudrait. La voiture démarre...

Le lendemain matin, Pat et Madjid sortent de l'agence pour l'emploi. Déçus.

— Plus la peine de revenir là-dedans, y'a jamais rien pour nous !

— Faut bien pointer !

Les deux amis remontent l'avenue en direction de la gare de Colombes.

— T'as pas une cigarette ? demande Pat en se retournant sur une fille qu'ils croisent.

— La dernière du paquet !

Ils la fument à deux.

— Tiens, dit Pat, je vais aller voir ma mère à son travail, elle aura bien une pièce de dix balles à me filer.

— Tu vas encore te faire engueuler, oui !

— Surtout que ma frangine bosse.

— Ah bon ?

— Ouais. Je sais pas ce qu'elle fout, mais elle bosse.

— C'est ta mère qui doit être contente !

— Tu m'étonnes ! Et puis elle me dit : « Ouais, ta sœur travaille et toi, fainéant, tu te promènes », et patati et patata. Je te les envoie se faire foutre, toutes les deux.

— Et ton père ? T'as des nouvelles ?

— Celui-là, j'sais pas où il est, mais il est bien où il est ! Au moins il fait pas chier !

Ils arrivent à l'usine Chausson à Asnières. Ils passent la grande porte et se dirigent directement vers le réfectoire. C'est une salle immense qui résonne du fracas des couverts que les serveuses alignent soigneusement sur des tables de huit. Madjid reste à la porte, tandis que Pat va chercher sa mère parmi les filles en blouse orange et bonnet blanc.

C'est bientôt l'heure du déjeuner. Slalomant entre les tables, Pat finit par trouver sa mère, bien surprise de le voir là. Elle stoppe le chariot qu'elle poussait. Madjid joue avec son briquet, sourire aux lèvres, sachant que Pat est en train de se faire engueuler par sa mère. C'est presque de la provocation que de venir la voir ici, surtout pour lui soutirer de l'argent. Elle fait plus que son âge, usée par une vie de labeur et de déceptions, le teint blafard, la mise en plis qui fout le camp, heureusement à moitié cachée par le bonnet.

Madjid voit de loin qu'elle n'a pas l'air contente, la pauvre. Elle fait des grands gestes de désolation. Pat insiste, on le voit bien aussi. Puis elle menace, son doigt haut levé, doit dire quelque chose comme : « C'est la dernière fois, t'as qu'à aller travailler ! », et Pat doit répondre, menteur : « Je te jure, maman, je vais m'inscrire à un stage d'électricité ; en plus ils me paieront, c'est ce qu'ils m'ont dit à l'agence de l'emploi.

J'ai même rempli un dossier, j'attends qu'ils me convoquent. »

« Salaud de Pat », pense Madjid. La mère se dirige vers le vestiaire, franchit une porte et disparaît. Pat l'attend. Il se retourne vers Madjid et lui fait un clin d'œil en souriant. Il est à l'autre bout du réfectoire, Madjid, il ne voit pas le clin d'œil, mais il comprend.

La mère revient, met quelque chose dans la main de son fils et le prévient une dernière fois. Pat prend, remercie. Il essaie d'embrasser sa mère mais elle ne veut pas. Il insiste encore, pour rire.

Elle s'en va avec son chariot lourd de vaisselle, sans se retourner.

— Combien qu'elle t'a donné ? demande Madjid.

— Vingt balles.

— Tu vas pouvoir acheter des clopes !

Ils remontent vers la gare de Colombes. Pat entre dans le premier tabac. Madjid l'attend dehors. Quand le blond ressort en ouvrant déjà son paquet de cigarettes, il lui demande :

— On va se faire un métro ?

— Justement, j'y pensais.

Ils foncent prendre le train de Paris. A Saint-Lazare terminus, ils attendent pour descendre du wagon que les employés chargés de recueillir les billets aient quitté leur poste, puis ils s'engouffrent dans le métro. Ils empruntent le passage interdit pour descendre sur le quai au moment où une marée humaine arrive en sens inverse. Ils ont du mal à se frayer un chemin au milieu du troupeau. La grande bousculade. Les temps modernes.

Pat rit entre ses dents.

— Tu trouves ça drôle, toi ? dit Madjid exaspéré, se cramponnant à la rampe.

— Non, répond Pat, je pensais à ce que j'ai dit à ma mère.

— Ah bon ?

— Je lui ai baratiné que j'ai rempli un dossier au bureau de chômage. Ah ! ah !... Chien de menteur que je suis !

— Parce que tu penses qu'elle t'a cru ?

— J'en sais rien.

— Elle peut pas te croire, tu sais pas écrire !

— Déconne pas ! ordonne Pat : il n'aime pas qu'on cause scolarité.

Madjid se souvient que Pat demeura trois années en classe de rattrapage. Lui-même y passa une année.

A l'école des Fleurs, la direction avait créé une section pour enfants analphabètes ou à moitié. On l'appelait classe de rattrapage. Mais bientôt elle devint la classe des fous : ceux qu'on montre du doigt en mimant des grimaces de chimpanzé.

On entassait là toute la mauvaise herbe du béton, tous les futurs locataires de Fleury-Mérogis. C'est Balou et Pat qui battirent les records, ils s'y encroûtèrent trois longues années. Même Raffin, l'instit de cette drôle de classe, lui qui en a vu d'autres ! des fils d'alcoolos, de malades, de putes, de Gitans, d'immigrés, n'en voulait plus, de ces deux-là.

Et il n'y allait pas de main morte, le père

Raffin, pour leur enfoncer le programme dans la tête. A grands coups de règle sur le crâne, qu'il s'y prenait, le Raffin. Oualou! C'est la règle qui cassa. Balou et Pat continuèrent à se mesurer leur bite sous la table, ou à arroser leurs petits camarades de leurs crachats!

Dès qu'un pauvre élève avait du mal à suivre et freinait la classe, le directeur sifflait Raffin. Celui-ci ramenait sa tronche de croque-mort qui vient déjà prendre les mesures. Il saisissait le môme par l'oreille, le contemplait de haut en bas et lui disait : « Les grands, je les tords, les petits je les casse! » Le môme baissait les yeux et Raffin le tirait jusqu'à sa classe et l'asseyait à la première table, face à lui, le fixait de son regard méchant, avec un sourire qui en annonçait long sur ses méthodes.

On lui fourguait tout, à Raffin, les bavards, les voleurs, les bagarreurs, les copieurs, les timbrés, les voyeurs, les fainéants. Il se vantait de les dresser. Mais de Balou et de Pat, il en fut malade, il en tremblait de colère, prêt à exploser comme une bombe, tout rouge, à cogner sur ces mules.

Même l'haleine de Raffin, un mélange d'ail et de pinard, ne les secouait pas. Ils se trouvaient bien en rattrapage, alors à quoi bon tant d'efforts? Ils étaient la risée de l'école, mais je t'en fiche.

Rien de tel pourtant pour foutre les jetons à un élève que de le menacer de Raffin. C'est pire que de l'envoyer se faire voir chez les Grecs. Madjid resta une année dans la section, juste après l'accident de son père, quand il comprit que celui-ci avait paumé dans sa chute toutes ses facultés et ne possédait plus aucune autorité. Il se laissa bercer par les lois de la pesanteur, bien enfoncé dans son banc d'école.

C'est en hiver qu'il fut conduit en rattrapage. La neige sale et grise de banlieue couvrait la cité. Cette même neige qui a fait chuter son père du toit qu'il couvrait.

Raffin, son long et large cache-col de laine autour du cou, toussait déjà. La maladie. Lui et Madjid n'eurent guère que le temps de faire connaissance, car Raffin toussa de plus en plus les jours qui suivirent et il était incapable de se comporter comme à l'accoutumée. Ses gueulantes n'avaient plus le même impact, on ne se pinçait plus le nez. Ses coups ne faisaient plus bander les maso. Il faiblissait. On chuchotait qu'il passerait pas l'hiver, l'instit.

Même quand Balou traduisit le théorème d'Archimède par « le thé au harem d'Archi Ahmed », ce qui souleva une branca d'hilarité, Raffin ne broncha pas. Il ne balança même pas l'épaisse brosse du tableau à travers la figure de Balou. Il séchait, Raffin. Il abandonna sa petite habitude de s'envoyer, dans le dos des élèves, pendant la lecture, un gorgeon de blanc sec qu'il planquait dans son placard au fond de la classe.

Il s'était usé la santé à jouer au chat et à la souris, au dompteur de fauves. C'est que les bêtes qu'on lui menait changeaient tous les ans. La classe vieillissait pas, lui prenait de la bouteille.

Les fauves ne rugissaient plus. Raffin présentait comme une cassure, qui les refroidissait. Ils ne testèrent plus ses colères, il n'avait plus de réflexes. Il devint gentil. Ils ne pensèrent nullement à l'achever.

Un après-midi, Raffin fut pris d'une nouvelle crise de toux. Il n'eut ni le temps ni la force d'aller jusqu'aux toilettes. Il vomit sur l'estrade, caché derrière son bureau, à genoux. On entendit les suffocations qui l'étouffaient. Un silence pesant et froid couvrit la salle, un silence qu'il n'avait pas demandé, d'enterrement. C'est Pat et Balou, les anciens, qui le relevèrent.

Pauvre Raffin, la langue basse, le regard vacillant, de la bave sur sa légendaire blouse grise, et la morve qui lui pendait du nez jusqu'au menton ! Une respiration de moteur Diesel le secouait, le gardait encore en vie. Cet ultime après-midi passé avec Raffin marqua plus d'un élève. On prévint le directeur, qui appela Police-Secours.

Qui aurait cru qu'un jour les flics viendraient chercher Raffin ? C'étaient plutôt les flics qui lui ramenaient ses élèves. Et plus d'une fois.

Pat et Madjid arrivent finalement sur le quai, et ils prennent place sur une banquette. Ils restent là un bon moment à regarder, guettant le sac à main propice ou le portefeuille qui dépasserait d'une poche. Pour eux, c'est un moyen comme un autre de se faire du pognon. Ils n'en sont pas à leur première tentative.

« Se faire un métro » voulait dire dans leur jargon : faire le pickpocket en sous-sol. Puis, quand on est chômeur et pas aidé, on ne regarde pas aux moyens de se payer un sandwich et un paquet de cigarettes. Vivre au jour le jour et se taper le coquillard de ce que pourra être demain ! Tels les animaux.

Voilà qu'un gros type, balaise, la quarantaine, sort d'une voiture stoppant à quai, avec une énorme valise à la main droite. Il sue. Une femme, certainement la sienne, l'accompagne, qui tient un sac de voyage. Sur le quai, le gars s'arrête, sort son mouchoir de sa poche et s'essuie le front. Sa femme l'attend. Il porte un blouson en skaï qui lui arrive à la ceinture, si bien qu'on voit son portefeuille dépassant de la poche arrière de son pantalon. Pat le voit et le montre à Madjid qui aurait plutôt tendance, lui, à regarder les filles.

Le gros suant et sa femme se dirigent vers le couloir de correspondances. Madjid et Pat aussi. La valise semble lourde pour le type, il change souvent de main. Visiblement sa femme a de la peine pour lui. Elle profite qu'il s'arrête pour lui passer un coup de mouchoir sur le front. Madjid et Pat les suivent à distance, marquant le pas quand il faut, faisant mine de regarder les affiches publicitaires sur les murs du couloir.

A une intersection de correspondances, le gros et sa femme prennent la direction Mairie d'Issy. Sur le quai, ils marchent jusqu'au milieu : les premières classes.

Le gros pose sa valise en soupirant. Il sort une nouvelle fois son mouchoir et s'essuie le front, le cou. Il regarde sa montre et dit quelque chose à sa femme, qui répond d'un geste affirmatif de la tête. Pat arrive seul et s'assoit sur la banquette juste derrière le gros.

Le portefeuille est remonté de la poche arrière du gros quand celui-ci s'est baissé pour poser la valise. Madjid arrive à son tour, les mains dans les poches de son blouson. Tranquille, il regarde une pub à quelques mètres de Pat et du gros. Quelques voyageurs patientent aussi.

Il est déjà presque quatorze heures, heure creuse.

La rame montre son nez. Madjid s'avance discrètement derrière le gros. Celui-ci prend sa valise et fait un pas vers le bord du quai. Pat se lève et descend à moitié la fermeture éclair de son blouson.

La rame stoppe, quelques voyageurs descendent. Le gros monte, suivi de sa femme. Il prend la lourde valise à deux mains pour la faire glisser. Madjid monte à son tour, frôlant le plus possible le gros au moment où il se baisse pour reposer son bagage. Madjid en profite pour tirer prestement le portefeuille de sa main gauche et, vite, se retourne contre la portière.

Entre Pat et Madjid, il y a une fille, une belle minette comme Pat les aime, qui s'admire dans la vitre de la portière, plaquant de la main ses longs cheveux. Madjid passe le portefeuille discrètement à Pat sur sa gauche. Celui-ci quitte sa place, les yeux fixés sur le plan de la ligne de métro au-dessus de la portière.

Pat se dégage doucement, mine de rien. Madjid reste où il est, dos tourné au gros. Les portières fermées, la rame prend son élan. Le gros et sa femme consultent le trajet de la ligne. Ils parlent à voix basse. L'homme s'éponge une nouvelle fois le visage.

Madjid regarde le couple reflété dans la vitre. Le gros enfouit son mouchoir humide dans une poche avant de son pantalon. Brusquement il porte la main sur sa poche arrière, du même côté.

Il regarde sa femme, l'air affolé.

— Mon portefeuille !

— Tu ne l'as plus ? Tu es sûr ?

— Non. Regarde dans ton sac.

La dame ouvre son sac, évidemment pour rien. Elle demande :

— Tu ne l'as pas oublié à la maison ?

— Je suis sûr que je l'avais : j'y ai mis mes tickets de métro.

Il regarde par terre au cas où... puis se retourne sur Madjid.

Il le dévisage de haut en bas et sans se gêner : un Arabe !

Il prend l'Arabe par le colbac et l'attire vers lui :

— Mon portefeuille, fumier !

Madjid se fait tout petit, tout tremblant, trouillard. Murmure :

— Ça va pas, non ? je vous ai rien fait, moi.

Et finalement crie :

— Il est fou, ce mec, il est dingue !

Il voit Pat qui se marre, là-bas. Il continue de crier :

— De quel droit, hein ? Je m'en fous, moi, de

ton larfeuille. Mais ça y est : ils voient un Arabe, c'est un voleur !

Le gros le plaque contre la portière et Madjid se laisse fouiller tout en protestant. Le gros fouille bien comme il faut, devant, derrière, le froc et tout.

— Tu veux pas que j'enlève mes pompes aussi ? demande Madjid. Et mon slip, peut-être ?

Le gros se retrouve comme un con. Il s'excuserait presque. Quand ils voient l'Arabe s'avancer vers lui, quelques voyageurs, par peur, reculent.

Madjid, au gros :

— Et maintenant ?

La rame arrive à une nouvelle station, des gens descendent. Madjid aussi, fixant le gros et sa femme avec méchanceté. Pat est sorti par une autre portière et s'en va vers la sortie du quai. Le gros, vexé, glisse quelques mots à sa femme. Madjid, jouant le jeu à fond, l'insulte une dernière fois du quai, et suit Pat.

Pat l'attend en haut des marches. Il sourit. Ils sont à « Madeleine ». Pat sort le larfeuille de sous son blouson, et après avoir jeté un œil autour de lui, pas de flic, fouille. Deux billets de cent francs, pas plus.

— Tu parles d'un fauché ! On ira pas loin, avec ça !

Ils se dirigent vers Strasbourg-Saint-Denis par les grands boulevards. Faubourg Saint-Martin, ils cassent la croûte au bar d'un bistro. Sandwich aux merguez avec harissa pour Madjid et un jambon-beurre pour Pat. Et de la bière. Ensuite, ils flânent le long du Sébasto jusqu'au Châtelet.

107

Ils font un tour rue Saint-Denis pour mater les putes. Pat va même demander le prix à l'une d'elles, montée comme une danseuse qui passe à la télé. Trop cher pour lui. Pat discute le prix avec la fille, puis, montrant Madjid :

— Mon copain, il a une réduction familles nombreuses. Ça marche pas chez vous ?

La fille :

— Allez, barrez-vous, laissez-moi bosser.

— Salope ! dit Pat en continuant son chemin.

La fille ne répond pas. Elle les regarde de travers.

Dès qu'ils voient une belle des plus dénudées, ils vont vers elle. Ils se rincent l'œil pour tuer le temps...

— Ça me donne envie de baiser, dit Pat. J'ai la barre à mine.

— On rentre, dit Madjid, on va se taper Joséphine.

— Okay, mec, avant que son Jules rentre du boulot.

Ils reprennent le métro, puis le train jusqu'à la cité.

Pat monte directement chez la Joséphine en se pressant.

Madjid n'y va pas. Tout compte fait, il préfère rentrer chez lui.

— A tout à l'heure ! dit Pat.

— Ouais, dit Madjid.

Comme l'ascenseur est coincé quelque part, Madjid emprunte l'escalier de service, mais attention à ne pas marcher dans la pisse.

Au troisième, il trouve, assis sur une marche, Farid. Farid lève la tête, le reconnaît et lui sourit — un sourire maladif.

— Alors, le père, qu'est-ce que tu fous là ?

Farid ne répond pas. Les mains croisées sur ses genoux, il regarde droit devant lui.

— Oh ! oh ! appelle Madjid.

Farid ne bronche pas.

— Ç'a pas l'air d'aller, hein, Rustine ?

Toujours pas de réponse. Alors Madjid soulève Rustine par les bras et décide de le ramener chez lui.

Pat sonne à la porte de Joséphine qui lui ouvre, mais ne veut pas qu'il entre.

— Non, Patrick, mon mari ne va pas tarder à rentrer.

— Tu rigoles, dit Pat. Il n'est que quatre heures et demie.

Elle est belle, Joséphine. Ses longs cheveux châtains coiffés en chignon mettent en évidence ses grands yeux noisette. Elle porte une robe sans manches qui laisse apparaître ses rondes épaules.

Elle tient son bébé contre sa poitrine, un bébé de huit mois qui chiale et qu'elle rassure tout en essayant de refermer la porte sur Pat.

Lui ne veut pas sortir, il entre en force.

Un autre enfant de Joséphine, une fille de trois ans, vient à elle et la tire par la robe en répétant : « Maman, maman ! »

Pat referme la porte et embrasse Joséphine dans le cou.

Joséphine se débat : « Patrick, fais pas l'imbécile ! » mais Pat continue à le faire, l'imbécile. Profitant que Joséphine tient son rejeton dans ses bras et ne peut se défendre, il l'embrasse sur la bouche.

Joséphine recule :

— Pas devant les gosses, écoute !

Pat la relâche. Elle s'occupe de sa fille qui la tient toujours par la robe et va vers une chambre. Pat entre au salon et enlève ses chaussures. Il entend Joséphine qui rassure les enfants. Il quitte son jean et Joséphine reparaît sans ses gosses.

— T'aurais pu venir plus tôt !

Pat, pliant son jean : « J'ai pas pu ! »

Elle enlève sa robe légère, révélant des nichons bien dodus, bien fermes, bien blancs, qui sentent le bébé.

Quand elle retire son slip, Pat est déjà allongé sur le canapé, prêt à la prendre. Elle vient sur lui, écartant les cuisses pour s'asseoir sur son ventre.

— Et Madjid ? demande-t-elle.

Il ne répond pas, préférant écraser sa bouche contre la sienne. Il dénoue son chignon, les longs cheveux châtains tombent comme du blé qu'on fauche, cachant le visage.

Madjid ramène Farid chez lui. Devant la porte, il lui dit :

— Tiens-toi droit !

Farid essaie. Sa gueule enfarinée, ses cheveux en bataille dont une longue mèche lui tombe sur les yeux, lui font vraiment une sale mine, une vraie tête de toxico. On peut pas se tromper.

La porte s'ouvre : c'est le grand frère de Farid, une vraie armoire à glace. A la vue de Farid, son torse de déménageur se gonfle de colère sous le maillot de corps italien.

— Où c'est que tu l'as trouvé, cet enfoiré ? demande-t-il à Madjid.

— Dans l'escalier.

Abdallah, c'est comme ça qu'il s'appelle, le monstre, prend son petit frère par le pull-over et le jette dans le couloir. Farid va s'écraser à plat ventre dans le salon. Madjid, surpris, n'a que le temps de crier à la brute :

— Doucement, tu vas le claquer !

— Qu'est-ce que ça peut te foutre ? crie l'autre, prêt à frapper encore.

Madjid va relever Farid à moitié dans le cirage et le conduit vers sa chambre.

— Une bande de cons, que vous êtes ! continue le grand. Vous vous croyez malins à vous défoncer, à faire les cons! Regarde comment il est, lui, maintenant. Hein! t'as vu : une loque.

Dans le salon, une petite vieille arabe, assise les jambes croisées sur un tapis, la tête cachée par un turban et vêtue d'une robe orientale, prie. Ses mains furtives glissent sur les perles d'ivoire d'un chapelet musulman. Elle ne s'est pas occupée de ce qui se passe dans le couloir.

Le grand gueule toujours. Dans sa chambre, Farid péniblement s'allonge, en cachant son visage dans ses mains. Ils entendent Abdallah qui continue de râler, nerveux comme un tigre, juron sur juron, dans l'autre chambre, celle de Naima, la frangine.

Elle n'a que seize ans, et déjà enceinte. La honte de la famille, le malheur. Belle fille, la gamine. Tout le monde dans la cité sait qu'elle est en cloque. Les bruit vont vite. C'est pour ça que l'Abdallah la laisse plus sortir. Il faut cacher la misère.

Elle aurait pu se faire avorter, si elle n'avait pas craint de le dire à sa famille. Elle aurait pris une bonne trempe par le grand frère, mais aujourd'hui elle en serait pas là. C'est pas la première gamine qui avorterait dans le quartier. Elles ne connaissent rien à la contraception et les mecs, ils s'en fichent, eux ils baisent.

— Qui c'est qui va se marier avec toi, maintenant? se plaint sa mère. Hein, dis-moi? Avec un gosse sur les bras, tu trouveras pas, salope! Putain!

Madjid pense à tout ça dans le couloir. En passant, il la voit assise sur son lit, Naima, les mains sur le ventre. Elle ne se peigne plus, elle est pâle, le visage amaigri, tout tiré. On dirait qu'elle n'a plus de larmes pour pleurer devant tant d'insultes, puis les coups de pied dans le ventre que sûrement elle encaisse.

Le soir, la vieille grand-mère lui apporte un bol de soupe, un morceau de pain. Elle mange ça cloîtrée.

Quant au père, il a failli la tuer, un soir qu'il rentrait ivre. Il voulait la jeter par la fenêtre. Elle hurlait, la môme, son cri déchirait le silence du béton. Heureusement la mère empêcha le forfait. Depuis, on ne laisse plus le père voir sa fille, surtout quand il a bu.

Madjid rentre chez lui. Sa mère n'est pas là, c'est l'heure des sorties de bureau, elle fait le ménage. Dans sa chambre, son petit frère Mehdi fait ses devoirs. Tête dans les mains, accoudé à la petite table récupérée par Madjid dans une cave, le môme s'entête sur un livre de calcul.

Des devoirs, il n'en a pas fait beaucoup, Madjid, de son temps d'écolier. Dès la sortie de la classe, il balançait son cartable dans un fossé et surgissait la balle de foot. On organisait le match sur le premier terrain vague, des parties interminables, à vingt et plus, des cartables comme poteaux de but. Ils s'en donnaient, les mômes, comme des bêtes, après la quotidienne captivité. T'avais intérêt à savoir dribbler si tu voulais caresser la balle, avec tant de désirs et d'ardentes jambes qui tournaient autour du ballon. Et pour faire une passe à l'autre bout du petit terrain, fallait la prendre, la baballe, comme on prend les

113

seins d'une fille, avec délicatesse et amour. Avec tous ces gus entre toi et ton partenaire, fallait rudement biaiser.

C'est comme ça que naissent les grands footballeurs ; sur les terrains vagues. Une feinte de corps, un supercontrôle, ça s'apprend pas pour la frime, mais par égoïsme, pour pouvoir se le garder, le ballon, dans la fourmilière. Le dribble aussi. Les grands techniciens du football, ceux qui font lever la foule par leurs gestes glorieux, cherchez pas, ils ont été ce genre de petits égoïstes.

Les devoirs et les leçons venaient après.

A l'époque, Madjid et ses parents habitaient le bidonville de Nanterre, rue de la Folie, le plus grand, le plus cruel des bidonvilles de toute la banlieue parisienne. Des vraies *favellas* brésiliennes, le soleil en moins, sans la musique endiablée pour crier au secours.

Quand il avait fait venir sa femme et son gosse d'Algérie, le père de Madjid ne leur avait pas dit dans ses lettres qu'ils logeraient dans des baraques enfumées et froides. Au vu de ce que c'était, Malika en pleura de misère et Madjid se demanda si c'était pas une blague. Au pays, on ne mangeait pas à sa faim, d'accord, mais on avait une petite maison en pierre, en chaume, un abri propre. Un ventre creux, ça peut se cacher, mais un taudis, tout le monde le voit. Et la dignité, alors ! Malika regrettait son voyage, serrant son petit dans ses bras. Le père disait :

— Ils vont nous reloger convenablement, je suis allé à la mairie !

Des mois, des années passèrent sur le qui-vive, à surveiller le feu.

Il y avait une alerte par semaine, dans ce bidonville. Parfois des feux grandioses et qui duraient des heures. On allait se recoucher au petit matin, quand les pompiers commençaient à bâiller.

Madjid avait sept ans quand, par un matin de novembre, sa maman et lui s'étaient retrouvés sur le quai de la gare d'Austerlitz. Son père devait être là, il n'y était pas. Ils l'attendirent, errant dans la gare, à l'heure de la première presse et du café-crème. Malika avait gardé son voile, perdue entre deux civilisations. Elle fut la curiosité des banlieusards qui allaient pointer au bureau. Elle n'avait jamais quitté son village de l'Est algérien et, d'un seul coup, la voilà d'un seul bond de l'autre côté de la Méditerranée. Tout est grand et démesuré. « Le progrès », qu'elle se dit sous son voile. Son haïk, elle l'avait acheté exprès pour le voyage. C'est son costume de première, et elle découvre qu'ici les femmes n'en portent pas. Dur pour elle ! Enfin, le papa arrive. Madjid ne le reconnaît pas, il était trop jeune quand son père avait émigré. Il se laisse embrasser par le monsieur coiffé d'une chéchia, puisque Malika lui dit que c'est son papa.

Puis le taxi, puis les bidonvilles.

Et des mômes, le môme Madjid en cherche et en trouve tout autour !

— Ne te perds pas, lui disait Malika quand il sortait.

Les enfants arabes le surprennent, ils parlent tous français, dis donc ! Puis ils s'en fichent, les gosses, du bidonville, des décharges d'ordures, de la boue. Il y a même des Blancs, des Bernardo, des Fernando, des Miguel, qui s'amusent dans des cadavres de bagnoles.

Et le terrain de foot ! Il est au bord de la route, rue de la Folie. Les buts sont des grands tonneaux remplis de cailloux. Fait pas chaud, quand même, ici. Le petit a les joues qui prennent des couleurs et les lèvres qui gercent. Personne ne fait attention à lui. Il se promène dans le village, un vrai labyrinthe mais organisé, avec un boucher, un épicier, un café-bar, un restaurant, même un coiffeur. Une boîte aux lettres au bord de la route sert de carton aux tireurs au lance-pierres. Le champion, c'est celui qui met son caillou dans la fente.

Les enfants jouent avec une petite graine d'insouciance dans la misère, dans la boue, sous la fumée dense et épaisse que crachent les cheminées. Ils se débrouillent toujours, les gosses, pour s'amuser, même sur un champ de mines...

Madjid fut inscrit à l'école. Les copains du bidonville, il les reconnut à leurs godasses sales. La boue. C'était pas la peine de cirer ses pompes là-bas, ou alors il fallait être drôlement acrobate ! Dès qu'on avait fait deux pas, on était marqué. Entre le bidonville et la route, il y avait une tirée, on pouvait pas la faire sur la tête.

Dieu ! qu'elle est grande, cette cour de récréation, le premier jour d'école, quand on connaît personne. Il faut prendre ses marques comme sur un terrain de foot, comme plus tard dans la vie. Si on veut s'en sortir pas crevé. Et Madjid est de ceux-là, de ceux qui désirent se battre pour survivre. Pas planqué, lui, à l'arrière dans le troupeau. Devant, sur le front, encore et toujours, même si quelquefois c'est épuisant, parce qu'on se retrouve généralement bien seul. Pour ne pas être seul, faudrait tirer les autres en avant, mais ils sont souvent tellement cons qu'on se décourage. Alors faut y aller seul.

Le soir, quand il rentre, Madjid trouve sa maman assise devant la table de cuisine, à éplucher les pommes de terre. Malika sur une chaise, Madjid n'a pas encore l'habitude. En Algérie, on mangeait par terre, on discutait par terre, et c'était bien. Faut suivre, sinon les voisins...

Elle est malheureuse, la mère, elle ne peut même pas nettoyer les murs, c'est des planches. Ni le sol, la serpillière ne s'y prête pas, c'est de la terre et un coup de balai soulève de la poussière. Elle n'ose pas encore sortir, parce qu'ici les femmes n'ont pas le voile et elle ne se voit pas dans la rue sans haïk. Elle n'ose pas encore. C'est Madjid qui va chercher l'eau au robinet du bidonville, il n'y en a qu'un pour tout le village et l'hiver il est gelé. Il faut dégeler. On emporte du papier journal, des planches, des cartons, des cageots, et on fait un feu autour. En attendant, on discute assis sur un jerrican, on profite du feu.

De temps en temps, quelqu'un manipule la tête

du robinet pour voir si l'eau arrive. Non. Elle se fait prier, la flotte, il faut la réchauffer, attendre le miracle. On pourrait danser autour en implorant les dieux, appeler un sorcier pour souffler sur le feu, les assoiffés en posture de méditation spirituelle.

Pour les H.L.M. avoisinantes, ça fait un beau spectacle, l'eau chaude coule à flot chez eux. On en voit derrière les fenêtres. Madjid a peut-être un camarade de classe qui l'observe de là-haut, dans des chaussons propres et chauds, en pyjama, repu, lavé, avec *Bibi Fricotin* à la main. Il n'ose pas regarder, il se retourne vers le feu.

Le robinet est gelé presque tout l'hiver et il faut le réchauffer deux à trois fois par jour. Quant aux cabinets, c'est un grand trou profond, avec deux planches dessus, le tout dans une petite baraque sans toit.

Malika plana longtemps avant de s'habituer à peu près, de s'acclimater. De temps à autre, les cousins, les cousines, venaient manger à la baraque. Le dimanche après-midi, elle retrouvait ses couleurs parce qu'on parlait du pays. Quand on lui reprochait de ne pas sortir, elle haussait les épaules. A quoi bon ? Il fait si froid dans ce pays, le ciel est toujours si gris. Madjid faisait ses devoirs assis sur son lit, une chaise en guise de bureau, à côté du petit poêle à charbon.

Après les planches du bidonville, le béton.

Allongé sur son lit, Madjid regarde son petit frère ranger ses cahiers.

Les images défilent à toute allure dans sa tête. Il ne veut pas s'y attarder. Il n'a pas le cœur à fouiller dans sa mémoire. La lassitude.

Le petit referme son cartable et quitte la chambre. Madjid se lève aussi en s'étirant. Malika va rentrer de ses ménages, vaut mieux partir, si elle est en colère, il aura droit à la tançante !

Que faire, sinon aller chez Pat ?

C'est Chantal, la grande sœur de Pat, qui lui ouvre.

— Salut ! qu'ils se disent.

Chantal appelle son frère :

— C'est Madjid !

Pat sort de la cuisine en mordant dans une pomme verte.

— T'as vu ta frangine ? dit Madjid. Depuis qu'elle bosse, dis donc, elle fait plus la bise ! Elle est fiérote maintenant, elle crâne !

— Ta gueule, dit Pat, on va encore s'engueuler !

— N'empêche qu'elle a un beau petit cul.

Chantal, de la cuisine :

— Ta gueule, fainéant !

— T'entends, dit Madjid. Non, mais franchement !

— T'es pas marrant, répond Pat.

Madjid continue du même ton blagueur :

— Chantal !

— Ouais.

— Tu vois, j'aurais un beau petit cul comme toi, j'irais pas m'emmerder dans un bureau.

Chantal revient, les mains aux hanches, l'air pas content du tout, et ne le lui mâche pas :

— Tu nous les casses !

Madjid se gratte la tête :

— Bon, ben, d'accord... Hein, Pat, sont cons les jeunes maintenant, savent plus rigoler, pas comme dans le temps.

Pat enfile son blouson et ses santiagos et sur le pas de la porte Madjid s'émerveille encore :

— Ce cul, mon vieux ! Ah ! ces miches !

Quand ils arrivent chez Maggy, il y a toute la bande. Anita est au flipper. A elle seule elle fait un boucan terrible. Elle traite le flipper de tous les noms.

Thierry, Bengston, Jean-Marc et Bibiche sont au baby-foot. Pat et Madjid vont chahuter Anita. Ils posent leurs coudes sur la vitre du flipper et discutent de la pluie et du vent.

— Faites pas les cons, merde, dit Anita, je vois rien, je vais paumer la boule.

Elle grouille comme une puce. Pat lui pelote les fesses, tandis que Madjid lui souffle dans les yeux la fumée de sa cigarette.

— Arrêtez, quoi !

Puis elle s'énerve, secoue brusquement l'appareil qui fait « tilt ».

— Voilà, dit-elle, avec vos conneries !...

Pat s'approche toutes lèvres dehors :

— Je t'aime, Anita, ma poule... hum, un baiser...

Elle recule.

— Tu me rends dingue, dit Pat.

Elle n'apprécie pas, Anita. Elle se réfugie près de Maggy, la patronne, devant la caisse.

Madjid rit et va voir au baby-foot.

Pat a pris Anita par la taille et l'attire contre lui.

Elle se débat, Anita.

— Tu vas la laisser tranquille ! dit Maggy, ou je te fous dehors.

Pat lâche prise.

« Même les vieux savent plus rigoler... Où va-t-on ! » soupire-t-il. Et il lève les bras au ciel.

La porte s'ouvre. C'est Solange, son fils à la traîne. Elle referme la lourde, puis se tient debout à l'entrée et observe de son regard paumé, alcoolisé, avec la bouche qui se tire de travers.

— Le premier qui bouge, dit-elle, il paie mon verre.

Personne ne l'écoute, personne ne bronche.

— Tu parles d'une bande, toi ! Pas un qui lèverait le petit doigt.

Elle va au bar, son fils vers le baby-foot. Elle commande une pression. Maggy refuse de la servir, vu son état.

Solange se plaint à la cantonade :

— Qu'est-ce que j'ai de moins que les autres ?

On ne fait guère attention. Quand Maggy a dit non, c'est pas la peine d'insister. Mais elle insiste, Solange :

— J'ai pas chouravé ta caisse, pourtant. J'ai pas la gale ! Alors ?...

Maggy lui répond gentiment, lui fait ses yeux de bonne maman :

— T'en as assez bu pour aujourd'hui, hein ! Tu vas rentrer chez ta belle-mère et coucher le petit. T'as vu dans quel état il est ? Regarde sa tête s'il est pas fatigué.

Quand on prend Solange par le sentiment, elle se calme. Elle fixe son lardon. Pas si crevé que ça, le môme ! Il a encore du jus, il suit la balle du baby-foot comme un chiot qui essaie d'attraper une mouche.

Noël approche. Malika emmène ses enfants, les trois derniers, à la mairie pour les cadeaux de Noël. Chaque année, la municipalité offre des chaussures aux mômes nécessiteux.

On va prendre le bus. Il fait froid.

Malika s'est mal réveillée ce matin. Fatiguée, alors que la journée commence à peine.

Elle s'est couchée très tard, le père Levesque a encore fait des siennes, il a failli étrangler sa femme ; elle en garde les marques sur le cou. Comme Éric et Fabienne dormaient, ils n'ont pas entendu leur maman se débattre. Elle a mordu Levesque à une main, puis elle s'est mise à hurler. Alors Éric s'est réveillé et a couru chercher Malika qui, heureusement, ne dormait pas encore. Elle a trouvé Levesque à poil, et sa femme tout autant.

— Elle m'a mordu, la salope, hurlait Levesque.

Il était en forme, le bougre ! Impossible à coincer.

— Je vais t'apprendre à respecter ton mari !

125

qu'il criait à sa femme en essayant de l'alpaguer derrière Malika.

Elle avait dû refuser de le sucer jusqu'au bout, l'abruti, mais comment avaler le foutre d'un mec pareil, si repoussant, si ignoble, tellement égoïste ? Comment être disposée à aimer cette viande soûle et méchante ?

Malika imaginait très bien la scène : Levesque demandant sa gâterie favorite ; elle, d'abord réticente, acceptant par peur, le suçant, mais refusant qu'il éjacule dans sa bouche, et Levesque la prenant par le cou, serrant, et elle, alors, qui arrive à le mordre, heureusement !

Levesque ne s'était calmé que tard, mais pas encore endormi, l'affreux !

Sa femme s'était terrée avec les enfants chez Malika. On avait même fait du thé en attendant que le fauve cesse de rugir dans sa cage. Quand, vers deux heures du matin, Madjid était rentré, Malika l'avait envoyé voir si « Missié Levesque » avait enfin baissé pavillon. Oui, il dormait, et sa petite famille avait pu regagner l'appartement, non sans crainte, et dans quel désespoir !...

C'étaient de grosses godasses qu'on donnait, de belles groles d'hiver, de celles qui font bien mal à la récré quand on les reçoit dans le tibia. La mairie était noire de monde...

Dans l'immense salon du rez-de-chaussée, les gosses essayaient devant les mamans soucieuses de la bonne pointure. On rencontrait des voisins, on faisait la causette. Malika se plaisait à exhiber ses enfants clinquant neufs, bien propres, bien élevés.

Ils furent tous contents de leurs pompes, sauf Ounissa, la plus petite, qui ne voulait pas ce genre-là, pas des souliers de garçon. Malika les prit quand même, mais une taille au-dessous, à la pointure de Stéphane, le petit à « Chousette ».

Chousette n'a toujours pas trouvé d'emploi. Elle désespère parfois. Son mari ne lui verse plus la pension alimentaire, elle s'en est plainte à l'assistante sociale, mais il est parti sans laisser d'adresse. Alors, les fêtes de Noël et du jour de l'An, pour Josette, c'est carrément l'angoisse.

Finalement, elle a décidé d'aller avec le petit chez ses parents dans le Loiret, pas loin d'Orléans, où sa mère, c'est sûr, va lui reprocher encore et encore son mariage. Elle entend les réflexions : « On te l'avait bien dit, hein ? Mais t'en fais qu'à ta tête !... »

Elle ne se sent guère un moral à supporter ça, Josette !

Il y aura sa sœur, le jour de l'An, sa frangine Cathy, bien mariée, deux gosses. Le mari a la bonne situation, la belle voiture. Et tout ça sur place, dans le Loiret, toutes les chances ! Elle sent, Josette, l'étau se resserrer, l'espoir, la foi foutre le camp.

Le silence l'oppresse. Pendant les fêtes, on imagine tout le monde heureux, surtout qu'on les voit, ces gens heureux, à la télé...

Stéphane écarquille les yeux sur son tout petit sapin de Noël, ses tout petits cadeaux de Noël ! Il restait si peu d'argent. Faut faire semblant d'être bien. A minuit, le gros baiser au gosse, imiter les autres à la télé, mais parce qu'elle en a envie aussi. Envie, besoin de sentir un peu de chaleur humaine, de se réfugier dans le dernier espoir restant.

Le samedi, la cité montait d'un ton. Ses âmes avaient l'air plus vrai. On descendait en tirant sur un chariot à provisions, détendu, frais après la grasse matinée. En route pour le marché, boutiques, magasins, grandes surfaces. Malard en survêtement de sport bien cintré sur son petit corps rond, promène son berger allemand. Il lui apprend à faire pipi dans le caniveau.

— Assis... debout... hurle Malard.

Et le chien obéit. Malard exulte, gonfle le torse, fier de sa bête devant les passants, et il recommence.

Le soleil cligne de l'œil au béton, ravive le sommet de la tour centrale. Aux fenêtres et balcons, c'est le ballet du balai, le grand nettoyage hebdomadaire. Paillassons, tapis, descentes de lit claquent au vent, vomissent leur poussière, et tant pis pour le voisin du dessous.

A poil à sa fenêtre, Coqueluche, ce type dont l'épouse est partie avec le père de Pat, règle une paire de jumelles sur les balcons alentour, car à moitié nues souvent sont les ménagères.

Au bout du cinquième aller et retour, l'ascenseur se bloque, vu l'affluence. Jurons et insultes résonnent dans l'escalier, mais il y en a aussi qui se saluent, qui se fendent d'une politesse : faites donc, passez ! Passer, des fois, dans une flaque de pisse, et l'on s'excuse en tirant son chariot plein de victuailles, et l'on sourit, gêné, l'air de dire :

« L'habitude, c'est pas grave ! »

La plupart prennent leur voiture pour aller au marché, pourtant guère loin. Dix petites minutes à pied, mais faut faire rouler Titine qui ne bouge pas de la semaine. Elle bouge que ce matin du samedi, puis le dimanche après-midi, pour aller chez la belle-mère.

Ce qui est chouette, c'est le mois d'août : les trois quarts des « citadins » sont partis se faire bronzer le coquillard, en bagnole, laissant la place aux autres pour respirer. Quand ils partent au vert, ils emmènent tout, le frigo, la télé, la lessiveuse, le chien quand ils ne s'en débarrassent pas dans un champ de maïs.

Encaravanés, encampingés, ils pourraient emmener la tour qu'ils l'emmèneraient. Ils partent bourrés pour fêter ça, ils reviennent bourrés d'avoir arrosé l'adieu aux autres campeurs. Y a ceux qui reviendront jamais parce que Fonfonsse fonceur s'est endormi sur le volant. Y en a d'autres qui rentrent avec un membre de l'équipe en moins, il s'est noyé en voulant nager au large pour chier tranquille dans la Grande Bleue.

Ils balancent des cartes postales à toute berzingue où on voit leurs pareils entassés les uns sur les autres, avec mention « il fait beau, on mange bien ». Le père rapporte un coup de soleil sur la tronche, la mère se retrouve en cloque, et les gosses pleins de boutons. L'année prochaine on ira ailleurs.

Les jeunes du béton descendent carrément sur la Côte d'Azur. C'est que quand il s'agit de tirer un larfeuille, vaut mieux que ce soit un gros. Vers Saint-Tropez paraît qu'ils sont mastoc, en croco, en lézard. Même vide, tu pourras toujours le refourguer.

Puis sur la Côte, les nichons sont classes. Les petites caissières de chez Mammouth (celui qui vend du désespoir par paquet de six pour le prix d'un), celles qui se prennent pour des starlettes et jouent à la Neuillylienne ou à la Seizièmoise, ont des nibards plus bandants que les belles-doches de Bretagne. Quand tu tires pas, tu mates.

Tu te fais une petite coupe de cheveux à la Travolta, tu fauches un maillot de bain au marché sans oublier le tube de pommade à bronzer, tu t'allonges sur le sable, et les calots en forme de canne à pêche, tu guettes tous les sacs à main de belle signature, surtout ceux qui sont restés seuls du fait que la donzelle est partie se mouiller les roberts.

Alors y en a qui reviennent tout de suite, vite fait, parce qu'ils ont la flicaille au cul, et d'autres qu'on revoit que six mois, un an après : ils couraient pas assez vite.

Malika préfère, comme tous les immigrés, le marché de Gennevilliers, où l'on compte trois

131

rangées exclusivement de marchands arabes. On se croirait au pays.

Ça sent la menthe fraîche, encore mouillée de rosée, la menthe sauvage. En Algérie on voit des gens parfois qui se baladent avec une feuille de menthe qu'ils portent souvent à leur nez, ça sent bon et ça rafraîchit. Il y a du rassoul, du vrai khôl, du souak (c'est de l'écorce de châtaignier, châtaigne ovale, et non ronde), ce souak que les femmes, après leur bain, mâchent pour s'embellir les gencives, qui prennent alors une couleur hennéique, et il blanchit les dents. Il y a de la *chhiba*, petite plante gris-vert qu'on trempe aussi dans le thé. Oui, toutes les épices, tous les aromates d'Afrique du Nord sont au marché de Gennevilliers.

Quand son mari n'était pas encore tombé sur la tête, Malika achetait tous les samedis une poule vivante. Elle la trimbalait dans son cabas, la tête de la volaille laissée à l'air. Comme elle n'était pas seule dans ce cas, fallait entendre le tintamarre dans l'autobus.

Les Blancs n'apprécient guère, c'est peut-être pour ça qu'ils prennent leur voiture pour aller au marché. Et, en plus, les cousins, ils se causent de bout en bout du bus...

— Hammdoullah !
— Hammdoullah !

et on enfonce la tête de la poule dans le sac, qu'elle arrête de caqueter.

Maintenant que le vieux est malade, il ne sait plus égorger la poule et Malika n'en achète plus. Ou alors il faut aller chez un voisin arabe, un qui connaît la bonne façon.

Car y a la petite prière avant de faire sa fête à l'animal : lui sortir la langue du côté droit du bec, lui diriger la tête vers La Mecque, prière, et hop ! on lui tranche le cou pour qu'elle se vide, la poule, et on la tient bien dans la baignoire, sans quoi elle ferait le tour de l'appartement.

Dans les bidonvilles, on tuait les poules dehors, et puis on les lâchait. Elles faisaient une ultime promenade dans l'allée boueuse et tombaient au milieu des gosses qui leur couraient après.

A midi déjà, le samedi, Levesque est bourré. Après le marché il fait la tournée des bistrots, son panier à la main. Il retrouve Mimile, Dédé, Nénesse, Jacquot et toute la clique et chacun y va de sa tournée de Ricard. On se fait un petit couplé au P.M.U. et : « Remettez nous ça, Mame Marcel !

— Encore une pour oublier !

— Dans ce cas, faut payer de suite ! »

Et ils s'écroulent de rire, ces cons.

Ils chambrent le marchand de tapis, celui qu'a la gueule comme sur les prospectus du Club de Djerba ; d'ailleurs, il sourit tout le temps. Il comprend très bien les allusions racistes que les poivrots lui envoient. Il sourit ; du moment qu'il leur fourgue un de ses tapis, pour lui c'est revanche, puisqu'à tous les coups ils se font baiser, les acheteurs, quand ils achètent.

— Pas de pitrole, pas de client !

— Z'ont qu'à se le siffler, leur fuel, nous on a le Ricard !

— C'est interdit par Allah !

— A la tienne !

Il s'en tape sur le ventre d'avoir trouvé ça, Mimile.

Les gosses sortent de l'école et traversent la cité en chahutant. Pas de cantine le samedi, on mange en famille. L'après-midi pas de classe, ils sont contents. Maintenant qu'ils font leurs quarante heures comme leurs parents prolos, avec en prime des devoirs et des leçons à apprendre en dehors des cours, ils n'ont pas le temps des loisirs et du sport, ou alors faut être drôlement futé. Y'en a bien certains qui prennent le temps de vivre, mais c'est qu'ils l'arrachent aux parents, aux profs. Ils en ont marre d'être saucissonnés. Ce sont les mêmes qui regardent par la fenêtre de la classe pendant que les autres lisent le black-board. Ils jouent à cache-cache derrière les voitures ou se cognent dessus à coups de cartable.

Malika revient avec trois gros pains sous le bras gauche et un sac plein de légumes, de fruits et de viande dans la main droite. Son mari la suit. Il ne sait plus rien faire. Mais suit toujours pour porter un cabas. Il est tout petit à côté d'elle. Il ne fait pas le poids non plus.

Les gosses sont déjà rentrés, ils grignotent du pain sec, des restes de petits gâteaux. Ils boivent l'eau à même le robinet, pas besoin de verre chez les Indiens. A peine les provisions rangées, la mère fait sa toilette spirituelle d'avant-prière. Elle s'enferme dans la salle d'eau et se lave les bras jusqu'aux épaules, l'entrecuisse, le visage une fois, se rince les dents, repasse ses mains sur son visage et murmure « Allah akbar ». Ensuite, dans sa chambre, elle récite la prière à genoux sur une peau de chèvre importée d'Algérie, en direction supposée de La Mecque, et ce quatre fois par jour. Elle cause au bon Dieu, les yeux mi-clos, les mains jointes, elle le supplie pour Madjid, pour Josette, du travail pour ceux qui sont dans la misère, du mieux pour tous ceux qui vivent dans l'angoisse, elle demande force et protection :

— *Allah akbar...*

Et elle se relève péniblement pour aller affronter les humains.

Ils ont faim, les humains, assis autour de la table. Ils attendent la salade de concombres qu'Amaria est en train de préparer. Ils s'impatientent, ils jouent avec les couverts, Malika a sorti une douzaine d'œufs pour sa fameuse omelette aux tomates et à l'ail du samedi midi.

Le plus calme, le plus gentil, c'est le père. On l'assoit sur une chaise devant la table et on lui allume la télé. Il bronche plus. Il est comme le dernier de la famille, le plus petit, le plus jeune. Il regarde défiler les images, sans rien demander de plus. De temps en temps la petite Ounissa se met sur ses genoux et se serre contre lui. Le petit vieux sourit maladroitement et pose sa tête sur celle de sa fille. On ne sait plus ce qui se passe dans sa tête, mais quand même il doit bien sentir qu'il est chez les siens dans cet appartement. Un peu comme un chien, il reconnaît ses maîtres, mais s'il était largué en pleine brousse, il n'en mourrait pas pour autant, il irait avec la première personne qui le sifflerait...

Pour Pat et Madjid le samedi est un jour comme un autre. Sauf le soir quand ils vont au rassemblement.

A l'Alhambra, la séance de minuit est généralement un film porno. Tous les loubards du quartier s'y donnent rencart. La projection se passe dans une ambiance indescriptible. Tout y passe : cris, insultes, applaudissements, l'ouvreuse n'en peut plus de réclamer le silence. D'ailleurs elle se fait traiter de tous les noms, pire que l'héroïne du film... Le patron du ciné, lui, n'intervient plus. Il s'est pris quelques grosses têtes, depuis il entend plus rien... Et ça fume dans la salle, ça crache par terre, on se cause du balcon au premier rang, tranquille...

On s'annonce les nouvelles :

— Eh ! Maxou est béton !

— Oh !...

— Il a fait une bijouterie... Ils l'ont chopé aux Alouettes.

— Il va prendre facile une pige !

137

— James... tu te souviens de James, celui qui boitait ?

— Un blondinet avec des boutons plein la tronche ?

— Ouala ! Eh ben, il s'est planté en moto sur l'autoroute de Pontoise, il allait voir sa gonzesse !

— Dur !

Puis, tout ce petit monde se retrouve au café du coin. Il y a toujours deux bandes rivales qui passent par là, et bagarre au comptoir. Parfois, c'est vraiment horrible, surtout pour le malheureux cogneur qui se retrouve par terre, il se fait relever à coups de santiagos.

A se faire chier, ils se tapent sur le ventre...

Un 14 Juillet, le bal du quartier fut interrompu par une bagarre gigantesque, du jamais vu dans la banlieue, facilement une cinquantaine, à coups de bouteilles, de couteaux, de poings américains. Les flics ne voulaient même plus s'en mêler !...

Elle nous aimait bien, la Maggy, on le lui rendait bien aussi. Elle nous appelait ses petits. Dans son bistrot, restait toujours un peu de chaleur humaine, toujours un pote, une cigarette, une pièce qu'on te tendait. Jamais d'histoires non plus chez Maggy : pour se battre on allait dehors, loin. Pour ne pas la contrarier.

Son fils, Noël, était en taule pour vol. Il faisait partie de la bande, habituellement. Elle nous en voulait pas.

Ce soir-là, il y eut une descente de flics. Pas de panique, on avait l'habitude. Le train-train : fiche de paie, papiers, chômage.

Ceux qui n'avaient pas de fiche de paie et n'étaient plus étudiants avaient droit à une faveur spéciale. C'est-à-dire la plupart. Le flic prenait leur carte et allait dans le car, dehors, appeler le commissariat pour vérifier l'identité, voir s'ils étaient pas recherchés, inscrits sur une fiche quelconque.

Un flic demande ses papiers à Pat, qui refuse. Le flic, furieux, répète :

— Les papiers !

Pat, en buvant sa bière, nonchalant, pour bien montrer aux copains qu'il n'a pas peur, répond au flic :

— Je suis français, moi. Je suis dans mon pays. Tu me prends pour un Arabe, ou quoi ?

— Gardez vos distances, vous n'avez pas à me tutoyer !

Pat pose son verre sur le bar, sûr de lui, et reprend :

— Vous n'avez pas non plus à me demander mes papiers.

— Ça va mal aller, si vous refusez.

Pat, qui n'a pas tellement envie d'aller faire un tour dans le panier à salade, sort sa carte bien abîmée. Le flic la prend du bout des doigts, peur de se salir. Il fait répéter à Pat ses nom et adresse, et lui rend son bien.

Ils embarquèrent quand même deux gars de la cité, deux qui n'avaient pas l'air confiants. Qu'avaient-ils fait ? On ne savait pas.

Les flics repartis, Bibiche sortit de l'intérieur des buts, dans la cage du baby-foot, les quelques grammes de shit qu'il y avait planqués. Maggy, évidemment, n'y vit que du feu.

Pat insulta les flics quand il entendit le car démarrer :

— Enfoirés !

Madjid paya les consommations avant de partir, ce qui lui valut ce commentaire de Thierry :

— Dis donc, t'as été à la pêche aujourd'hui ?

Madjid :

140

— Je t'ai payé ton verre et tu poses des questions ?

Thierry :

— Te fâche pas, c'est pour rire.

Madjid :

— Je préfère.

Ils sortirent ensemble, Madjid, Pat, Bengston et Thierry. Il faisait nuit déjà, et l'air était frais. A peine arrivés à l'entrée de la cité, ils aperçurent Loucif, un Arabe de dix-sept ans, surnommé Loulou, complètement ivre, qui pissait tant bien que mal contre le grillage. Il tenait à peine debout. Ils avancèrent vers lui, bien étonnés de le voir dans un état pareil. Il urinait carrément sur ses santiagos. Eux, derrière, attendaient. Ils attendaient que le Loulou s'aperçoive qu'il avait du monde. Sans même ranger sa bite dans sa braguette, il se tenait au grillage de ses deux mains. Il respirait fort.

Pat dit :

— Heureusement qu'ils ont mis un grillage là !

Les autres sourirent.

Loulou se retourna péniblement. Sa main gauche tenait toujours la grille. Il plissait les yeux. Il observa un moment les mecs, puis les reconnut. Il dit :

— Ah, bande de cons !

Et Bengston, en riant :

— Ferme ton magasin, on voit tes outils.

— Hein ?

— Planque ta bite, précisa Thierry, on va te la couper.

141

Loulou baissa la tête et vit le travail. Alors il rangea ses outils.

— Qu'est-ce qu'il t'arrive, mon con ? demanda Madjid.

Loulou essaya de répondre, fit un effort qui lui remonta à la gorge et vomit d'un seul coup. Les autres reculèrent en riant. Il dégueula contre la grille. Toutes ses tripes. Il s'essuya avec ses manches de blouson et finit par avouer :

— C'est le pinard du père Malard !... Ah ! et... et... il est bon... Ah ! ah !...

Et il arriva à rire avec les autres.

— Dans sa cave, au vieux con... Ah ! ah !...

Les autres l'empoignèrent par le bras et l'emmenèrent.

— On va vérifier si tu dis pas de conneries.

Ils contournèrent le parking et entrèrent dans un hall du bâtiment Coquelicots, Thierry donna la lumière dans le couloir des caves. Ils trouvèrent celle du père Malard la porte grande ouverte. Quelques bouteilles vides jonchaient le sol. Y'en avait cinq caisses, de pinard ! Et du bon ! Ils commencèrent la dégustation au goulot. Loulou riait de les voir faire.

— Mmm... pas dégueulasse ! dit Pat en connaisseur.

Ils planquèrent deux ou trois bouteilles chacun sous leur blouson avant de quitter l'endroit. Pat rota dans le couloir obscur avec un « ah ! » de soulagement, et Thierry prophétisait :

— Je sens qu'on va se la donner, ce soir.

Ils sortirent par l'arrière, se faufilant dans la

142

pénombre jusqu'aux Azalées, où habitaient Pat et Madjid.

Là aussi, ils allèrent aux caves, mais Loulou tenait à peine sur ses jambes, Thierry devait le traîner. Madjid dit aux autres :

— On va chez Rustine.

Dans la cave du fond, ils trouvèrent Rustine, Miloud et Delphine, deux autres Acaciens, en train de fumer un joint.

Bengston :

— Salut les jeunes ! Nous, on ramène le rince-dalle.

Delphine la rousse sursauta de peur. Miloud, le Marocain, tendait déjà la main, mendiant un litron. Pat le lui donna. Ils s'assirent l'un contre l'autre dans le petit réduit et débouchèrent les litres. Thierry roula un autre joint.

Bengston dit :

— C'est le père Malard qui va en faire une gueule, quand il s'apercevra !

Les autres éclatèrent de rire. Madjid estima que c'était bien fait pour sa gueule !

Pat s'était assis à côté de Delphine. Il la prit par l'épaule et l'embrassa sur les joues. Elle avait les yeux fermés, assise sur son nuage, les jambes croisées. Pat lui mit la main aux seins, puis il l'embrassa sur la bouche.

— Tu nous en laisses un peu ? demanda Thierry en allumant le joint.

Delphine mit sa tête dans l'épaule de Pat et continua son voyage. Ils tiraient chacun leur tour sur le joint, délicatement. Le vin aidant, les têtes commencèrent à tourner et le silence se fit. La fumée montait fièrement, longiligne, avant de s'écraser au plafond. Elle remplissait la cave de son odeur, lourde et âcre, qui donnait encore plus soif. Loulou s'endormit contre l'épaule de Miloud.

Moment de méditation et de paix. Au diable l'angoisse, le chômage, le béton. Silence et repos, et un peu de chaleur humaine, comme quand on s'endort fatigué d'une journée trop remplie. Le temps n'a plus d'importance, seul le moment même, le moment présent, compte. Hier, c'est pas de chance, demain, avec un peu de chance ! Et puis merde, le joint plie, y'en a qui tirent trop dessus, à s'en faire péter les poumons. Ils y mettent trop d'énergie, de cette énergie qui s'ennuie avec eux, qu'ils emmagasinent faute de ne point faire ce qu'ils ont vraiment envie de faire, faute de ne pouvoir l'utiliser à bon escient.

Ils étaient bien « emportés », tranquilles, quand une bombe lacrymogène explosa, juste en face, contre le mur du couloir. Panique dans la cave. Tirés brusquement de leur rêve, ils cherchèrent l'issue dans le désarroi total. Delphine hurla de peur. Pat la tenait par la main et la tirait vers la sortie. Thierry et Madjid s'occupèrent de Loucif bourré comme une vache, et de Farid encore dans le cirage et qui toussait.

Ils quittèrent en trombe leur repaire, fuyant le gaz et l'aveuglement. Du couloir des caves, fallait monter quelques marches avant de se retrouver à l'air dans le hall.

C'est là que la milice les attendait.

La milice, c'est un groupe de locataires, souvent des parents exaspérés par les vols de toutes sortes, le bruit, les voitures volées ou brûlées, et qui ont décidé de jouer eux-mêmes les flics. En groupe ils se sentent forts, poussés par leur haine des jeunes, et la peur, cette peur qu'ils se donnent et que leur flanquent les médias. Ils s'arment de nerfs de bœuf, de barres de fer, quand ils descendent à la ratonade. Ce soir-là, ils étaient une dizaine, là, dans le hall, à attendre, à guetter les jeunes asphyxiés par le gaz.

C'est Pat qui déboucha le premier, Delphine derrière. Il s'arrêta net en voyant Finet, le père à Jean-Marc, dont la voiture avait brûlé la veille; Langlois et sa carcasse de boucher; Malard évidemment; Yvon et son berger allemand, et encore bien d'autres Dupont en survêtement, trique et nerf de bœuf dans la pogne.

Thierry, Miloud, Bengston, Madjid apparurent dans l'ordre aux côtés de Pat.

— Montez, allez, quoi! disait le père Finet aux jeunots surpris.

— Je croyais que les jeunes de maintenant avaient peur de rien, poursuivait le Langlois en jonglant avec son nerf de bœuf.

Pat ferma son blouson, prêt. Le gaz leur picotait les yeux, la peur les dessoulait. Thierry nargua le père Malard et Malard frappa dans le vide avec sa trique. Thierry recula et lui dit, avec ironie:

— T'es encore bourré, vieux con!

Bengston enleva son ceinturon qu'il roula autour de son poing droit et avança, en garde. L'odeur du gaz remontait vers le hall; les vieux aussi commençaient à se frotter les yeux et à tousser. Madjid fonça le premier dans le tas. Il fut accueilli par un formidable coup de matraque qu'il dévia du bras. Les autres suivirent en force. Les vieux reculèrent. Le père Langlois prit un coup au bas-ventre et s'écroula. Les jeunes s'enhardirent, plus rapides, plus connaisseurs en la matière. Le berger allemand aboyait, mais n'attaquait pas.

Pat fit fuir deux vieux à lui tout seul. Un vrai tank, le Pat. Quand il réussit à attraper le père Finet, il le poussa si fort contre la porte vitrée que celle-ci se brisa. La bagarre faisait rage. Thierry, qui avait pris un coup de matraque dans le dos, un autre sur l'épaule, s'était replié contre l'ascenseur. Entouré de trois vieux lâchés comme des bêtes, il fut roué de coups, même quand il eut glissé par terre. Madjid se défendait tant bien que mal. Des coups il en reçut, mais il réussit à sortir. Il prit le nerf de bœuf du père Finet qui se tordait de douleur sur l'escalier de l'entrée, suite au coup reçu de Pat, puis revint dans le hall, et c'est au père Langlois qu'il envoya sa première volée, plein dans les reins. Le quadragénaire toucha terre. Delphine s'enfuit par l'escalier de service, poursuivie par le vieux Bonnaud. Miloud, le front en sang, se défendait comme un beau diable, mais c'était trop d'agresseurs et il s'enfuit sous des coups à foison. Bengston fut mis K.O. sous les boîtes aux lettres par un coup de trique au niveau de la nuque. Seuls Madjid et Pat résistaient encore quand les vieux, le travail fini, se décidè-rent à quitter le terrain.

Pat les suivit.

Madjid à genoux, essoufflé, grimaçant, se tenait le bras droit. Miloud et Thierry gisaient à terre. Thierry tenait les mains autour de sa tête, allongé sur le côté, bloquant l'issue de l'ascenseur. On aurait cru qu'il dormait.

Pat revint, en colère. Il cracha par terre. Miloud pleurait, il se plaignait de son ventre. De son arcade gauche ouverte coulait du sang jusque dans son cou. Pat s'enquit de Thierry qui revenait à lui petit à petit. Madjid releva Bengston et le secoua. Sa nuque était en sang, vraiment un sale coup.

— Et Fifine ? Et Farid ? demanda Pat.

Ils allèrent à la cave. Farid était assis sur les marches de l'escalier, dos au mur. Il toussait. Il était resté là tout le temps de la bagarre. Il était toujours dans le cirage. Mais pas de Delphine.

— Merde ! cria Pat.

Il avait compris.

Ils se ruèrent vers l'escalier, le grimpèrent quatre à quatre. Entre le troisième et le quatrième étage ils trouvèrent Fifine. Elle pleurait à chaudes larmes et se tortillait de douleur, allongée sur les marches.

Pat la releva délicatement et la prit dans ses bras.

La même nuit, cinq voitures brûlèrent, le plus beau feu d'artifice jamais vu à la cité des Fleurs. On en parle encore.

Madjid sortit de chez lui de bonne heure ce matin-là; il avait rendez-vous à l'agence pour l'emploi. Sur le palier, les enfants Levesque, Fabienne et son petit frère, attendaient l'ascenseur. Ils allaient à l'école, cartables au dos. La petite Fabienne, qui ressemble tant à Brigitte Fossey dans *Jeux interdits*, n'osait pas lever la tête devant Madjid. Elle avait l'œil droit au beurre noir, comme ne manqueraient pas de lui dire ses camarades à la récré, pour se ficher d'elle. Madjid s'accroupit devant elle et lui prit le visage dans ses mains.

— Qu'est-ce qu'il t'est arrivé? lui demanda-t-il, peiné.

Elle ne répondit pas, honteuse, les larmes aux yeux.

— C'est papa, dit Éric à la place de sa sœur.

L'ascenseur arrivait.

A l'agence, il fut reçu par un de ces mecs qui aiment le travail bâclé. A peine ouvert le dossier de Madjid :

149

— On n'a rien pour vous, mon vieux !

Madjid acquiesça. Le type reprit son travail en remettant ses lunettes sur le front.

— Vous sortez à peine du collège, sans expérience, c'est vraiment dur de vous trouver quelque chose. Et puis il y a priorité aux ouvriers qui ont des enfants à nourrir, un loyer à payer, et...

— J'ai compris ! coupa Madjid.

Sur le pont Cardinet, Madjid est accoudé à la rampe et regarde passer les trains qui vont et viennent de la gare Saint-Lazare. L'après-midi tire à sa fin. De temps à autre, il se retourne et, toujours adossé à la rampe, observe les gens qui traversent.

Le pont Cardinet est un des lieux de rendez-vous d'homosexuels. Madjid attend.

Des pédés, il y en a qui passent, qui le regardent, mais ce n'est pas ce qu'il lui faut. Ils ont l'air fauché, paumé, ceux-là. Ils font l'aller et retour sur le pont, se font leur drague mine de rien. Ils sont une demi-douzaine à tourner en rond, à attendre, les mains dans les poches, leur petit journal sous le bras.

Un nouveau arrive, genre très chic, bon genre, la trentaine, un costume trois pièces impeccable, jeune cadre dynamique, pas un cheveu qui dépasse, sa petite mallette Delsey à la main.

Il passe tout près de Madjid, le frôle du coude et continue sa route. Madjid ne bouge pas, il le suit du regard. L'homo se retourne et sourit. Madjid aussi, mais reste à sa place. Le pédé va jusqu'au bout du pont et se retourne une nouvelle fois. Madjid le fixe, quitte sa place et part en sens inverse, vers le square. L'homo a un moment d'hésitation, puis revient sur ses pas. Madjid marche doucement. Le pédé le suit. Il a trouvé l'aubaine, il presse l'allure.

Quand Madjid pénètre dans le square, l'autre n'est qu'à quelques mètres derrière lui. Le square est désert. Madjid longe une haute haie, marchant sur la pelouse. L'homo suit. Madjid continue sans se retourner, puis Pat sort de la haie, derrière le pédé, et lui balance un coup violent avec l'arête de la main sur la nuque.

L'homo s'écroule en se tenant le visage, recroquevillé sur lui-même. Il grimace. Madjid le soulage de son portefeuille qu'il sort de la poche intérieure de la veste. Ils fichent le camp en vitesse. L'homo reste à terre.

Ils arrivèrent au Chalet du Lac en taxi. A voir la masse de voitures garées autour du dancing, Pat dit à Madjid :

— Je sens que ça va être bon, ce soir !

Le Chalet du Lac est un dancing au bord du bois de Vincennes, près du lac de Saint-Mandé.

Sitôt à l'intérieur, ils se dirigèrent vers le bar.

— Bière.

— Deux bières, siouplaît !

Pat but au goulot en observant la piste. Les lumières tamisées tournaient et changeaient de couleurs au rythme de la musique. Et les femmes, Pat les bouffait des yeux. Il y en avait de toutes les couleurs, de toutes les tailles. Un régal.

Madjid finit sa canette, la posa sur le bar et

151

partit vers la piste de danse. Pat le suivit en poussant un « youpi » terrible ! Il posa sa bouteille sur une table du bord de piste et fit son entrée dans le cercle en se démenant comme un diable. « Stevie Wonder » ne tournait pas assez vite pour lui. Madjid le prit au mot, à qui se défoncera le plus. Ils dansèrent ainsi un bon quart d'heure. Seul, les yeux fermés, seul avec la musique, ne vivre que ce moment présent, être là dans sa peau et bien ! Puis ce furent les slows, la drague. Ils revinrent au bar et reprirent deux autres canettes.

Ils repéraient les filles qui étaient deux par deux. Il y en avait pas des foules, mais il y en avait quand même. Le choix devenait même des plus difficiles : ils n'étaient pas d'accord sur la paire à draguer.

Finalement ils se mirent d'accord pour inviter deux brunes assises à une table devant deux verres vides. Ça tombait bien, elles avaient l'air de s'ennuyer. Pat était branché sur celle de gauche qui avait les cheveux longs. Il le dit à Madjid, qui trouva ça O.K.

— Tu crois que ça baise ?
— J'espère.
— Allez, go.

Pat arriva le premier devant les filles et les salua. Puis il invita à danser celle qui avait les cheveux longs. Elle sourit et se leva. Pat lui prit la main et l'entraîna vers la piste.

L'autre fille, ne voulant pas faire tapisserie devant sa copine, accepta Madjid.

Les deux couples tournaient côte à côte dans le

cercle. Quand leurs regards se croisaient, Madjid et Pat se faisaient un clin d'œil vainqueur. Ils dansèrent encore deux autres slows pour se rassurer que les filles étaient bien consentantes.

— C'est souvent que tu viens ici ? demanda Pat à sa brune.

La fille sourit. Elle savait bien que c'est la façon pour la drague. Une connaisseuse ! Madjid embrassait déjà l'autre dans le cou et remontait petit à petit ses baisers jusqu'au nez. Puis il la fixa et elle lui sourit. Ils s'embrassèrent sur la bouche.

Ils se retrouvèrent au bar avec les filles, à picoler de la bière. Ils passèrent ainsi la soirée. Danser, boire, flirter et rire.

Tard dans la nuit, ils sortirent du dancing, bras dessus, bras dessous. Le temps froid les saisit. Pat serra sa nénette bien fort contre lui avant que les deux couples ne montent dans la voiture, qui justement était à elle. Avant de démarrer, clé au contact, elle demande ironiquement :

— On vous dépose où ?

Pat ne répondit pas, il rit un bon coup. Madjid, tout aussi ennuyé, ne savait que répondre.

Elle reprit :

— Faut qu'on rentre, parce que demain on bosse !

— Nous aussi, on bosse, dit Pat.

— On va pas se quitter comme ça, quand même, dit Madjid.

La voiture démarra, tous phares dehors, dans l'obscurité du bois de Vincennes à cette heure de la nuit.

La brune aux cheveux longs dit à Pat, assis à sa droite :

— On va chez nous, mais faites pas de bruit.

— O.K.

Les filles habitaient un grand studio dans un immeuble tout neuf près de la gare de Lyon.

Avant de faire l'amour à leurs nanas, Pat et Madjid, se croisant dans le coin toilette, se mirent d'accord :

— On commence chacun avec la sienne, dit Pat à l'oreille de Madjid, puis après on change.

— D'accord, dit Madjid en se lavant les outils dans le lavabo.

Ils firent l'amour, lumière éteinte, chaque couple dans son coin. Quelques gémissements et plaintes de plaisir troublèrent le silence.

Le lendemain matin, gare Saint-Lazare, fendant la marée qui se ruait au boulot, Pat dit :

— N'empêche que la mienne baisait mieux que la tienne !

— Normal, dit Madjid, tu l'as prise en deuxième, elle était crevée. Et la tienne, c'est pareil, elle était plus fraîche. Elle valait plus un joint, quand je l'ai prise !

— Merde, sois sport ! dit Pat. La mienne était mieux.

— D'accord, elle était mieux, accorda Madjid.

Ils montèrent dans le train et s'assirent au fond du wagon.

Madjid n'avait pas tellement encaissé les commentaires de Pat. Il relança le débat :

— On demandera à Joséphine qui c'est qui baise le mieux de nous deux !

— O.K., dit Pat.

Ils arrivèrent à la cité vers neuf heures du matin.

Dans le hall du bâtiment, deux mères de famille, une Française, une Algérienne, se traitaient de tous les noms à propos des gosses. La grosse querelle.

— C'est ton fils qui a frappé ma fille !

— C'est pas vrai !

— Il lui a même dit « sale bicot » !

— Il a raison !

— Salope !

— Toi-même !

— Putain !

— Va dans ton pays, si t'es pas contente !

Les gosses tiraient leur mère, chacune par sa robe. Et ils pleuraient.

Une des mères finit par gifler un de ses gosses :

— Veux-tu me lâcher, toi ! Je vais lui cracher à la figure, à cette salope !

Madjid et Pat attendaient devant la porte de l'ascenseur qui ne venait pas, encore bloqué quelque part. Pat frappa la porte d'un grand coup de pied et ça se finit par l'escalier de service.

Les bonnes femmes continuaient à s'engueuler.

Des disputes de ce genre, il y en avait journellement dans ce grand ensemble. C'est la règle dans tous. On n'y faisait même plus attention. La surpopulation s'y prêtait.

Quand Madjid entra chez lui, il fut reçu comme il se doit par sa mère :

— C'est maintenant que tu rentres ? hein, finiant...

Il alla directement vers sa chambre, mais elle le suivit.

— Et li travail ? Ti cherches di travail ?

Il s'allongea sur le lit.

— Finiant, foyou !

Elle parla au Bon Dieu en arabe. Elle se plaignait en arabe. Elle n'en pouvait plus.

Madjid ferma les yeux, essayant de trouver le sommeil.

Il avait l'habitude d'être reçu de cette façon. Et il pensait à autre chose quand sa mère continuait à le tancer, à hurler, à se plaindre de son fils à Allah.

En fin d'après-midi, Pat fut réveillé par la sirène de Police-Secours. Il jura quand, de sa fenêtre, il vit les flics. Ils déposaient délicatement une personne sur une civière, au milieu de la foule de la cité, accourue. Il fit une légère toilette, qui consistait à simplement se raser, puis il descendit.

Il trouva Madjid assis sur les marches du perron, regardant l' « accident ».

— Qu'est-ce qui se passe ? Y m'ont réveillé, ces cons-là !

— C'est Naima, la frangine de Farid, dit Madjid. Tu sais, celle qui sortait plus parce qu'elle était enceinte !

— Ah ! ouais.

— Elle en avait marre de se faire tabasser par la famille, elle s'est jetée par la fenêtre.

— Dur !

— Tu m'étonnes !

157

— Et Farid ?

— Il a eu une crise. Ils l'ont embarqué aussi.

Le car de police démarra. La foule des curieux s'écarta bien docilement pour laisser le passage. La sirène retentit.

— On s'arrache ?

— Ouais ! dit Madjid.

Ils allèrent au bistro, chez Maggy.

— Faut que je voie James, annonça Madjid.

— Pourquoi ?

— Il a trouvé du taf, je vais y demander s'ils embauchent pas dans sa taule.

— Qu'est-ce qu'il fout là-dedans ?

— Il monte des tourne-disques.

Ils s'escrimaient chacun leur tour au flipper.

— T'es sérieux ? demanda Pat.

— Ouais... J'en ai marre de vadrouiller... Puis la vieille qui pleure chaque fois que je rentre.

— Comme tu veux, tu choises ! dit Pat.

James n'arriva qu'en fin de soirée. Il sortait directement du boulot. Il leur expliqua que c'était pas un travail difficile. Il était prêt à les présenter à son chef d'atelier. Ils se donnèrent rendez-vous, lundi à 7 heures du matin, à l'entrée de l'immeuble.

— Vous ferez pas les cons, les mecs, leur a dit James en les quittant. Sinon, je me fais lourder.

Malika repasse quelques chemises sur la table du salon, les enfants sont pris par le film à la télévision, silencieux chacun dans son coin. Même Madjid est là, il n'est pas sorti, dehors il fait froid. Il a rentré son père et n'est pas redescendu.

Le vieux malade est assis par terre jambes croisées sur le tapis, adossé au pied de la table. On ne sait pas s'il comprend le film, mais il regarde l'écran. Il ne le quitte pas des yeux, même si aucune expression ne se lit sur son visage. Madjid est seul à table, accoudé, la tête dans les mains. Il attend minuit, l'heure où sont programmées les filles des Folies-Bergère. A moitié nues, elles danseront le french cancan comme à chaque jour de l'An, puis nous souhaiteront la bonne année. A chaque nouvelle année, Madjid se souhaite de s'en taper une, de ces gonzesses montées sur pilotis comme des échassiers des Landes.

La chorégraphie, les décors, la musique, il s'en fout, mais ces culs, mon pauvre, au sommet de ces jambes interminables !... Il faudrait pouvoir vivre dix mille ans pour les caresser toutes.

Malika les regarde aussi, et de près ! les filles dévergondées de la « tili ». Elle met son fer à repasser de côté et se prosterne devant le poste et repense au temps où elle dansait et chantait aussi. Madjid s'en souvient. Il était môme, il se rappelle sa mère menant la danse dans les mariages de famille en Algérie.

Les femmes d'un côté, derrière le mur en chaume, les hommes de l'autre. Les femmes se mettaient à une vingtaine sur deux rangées, face à face, avançaient et reculaient au rythme du *bendir* que Malika tenait dans ses mains avec grâce et fierté. Ses longs cheveux noirs tressés et cachés sous un foulard dernier cri, elle entonnait la chansonnette que répétaient les autres. Elles chantaient des chansons qui se moquent souvent des hommes comme de vulgaires prétentieux.

Elle était belle, Malika, grande, élancée, elle n'avait à l'époque qu'un enfant, elle était bien jeune. Madjid venait la tirer par la robe en pleurnichant pour qu'elle le prenne dans ses bras. Oualou ! Après la fête ! Il avait de la place pour jouer, on était en pleine campagne dans le Nord-Ouest algérien, chez des paysans qui ne connaissaient pas encore la ville, et s'en fichaient éperdument. Le soleil ne les quittait pas de ses rayons, devait même prendre du plaisir à la fête, car il cognait fort.

Stéphane entre dans l'appartement sans frapper. Malika est surprise de le voir à cette heure-ci et tout seul.

— Ta maman, hein ? demande-t-elle, affolée.

L'enfant ne répond pas, il s'en va chahuter avec Mehdi son grand copain sur le lit du salon. Malika débranche le fer à repasser et demande à Amaria de ranger les fringues dans l'armoire. Elle va enfiler un manteau dans le couloir. Elle se chausse et appelle Madjid, pour lui demander de la suivre. Il ne comprend pas.

— Où vas-tu ? dit-il, étonné.

— C'est pas normal, ce gosse à cette heure-ci et tout seul, répond-elle en arabe. On va voir chez Chousette. Allez fissa !...

Il se lève en grimaçant, plutôt dépité. Amaria s'inquiète. Elle fait dépêcher son frère. Il s'habille et sort derrière sa mère, qui attend l'ascenseur.

La neige grise de banlieue, râpeuse et lourde, a épousé le macadam et planque les voitures sous une déjà épaisse couche. Deux silhouettes traversent la cité, maladroites sur la chaussée glissante. Plus haut, le béton devient livide, se confond avec le ciel gris. Dans les caniveaux, la neige fond vite en boue qui transperce les godasses.

Le bâtiment où habite Josette est entouré d'une pelouse dont on ne voit plus le gazon sous la neige. Les flocons tombent, il ne faut pas en prendre un dans le cou, le frisson. La tête enfouie dans le col de son blouson, Madjid presse le pas, car Malika marche plus vite que lui. Il regarde ses santiagos qui prennent l'eau, sa mère le bouscule :

161

— Vite, monte chez Chousette !

Elle lève les yeux au ciel, vers le balcon de l'appartement de Josette, et crie encore :

— Dépêche-toi !

Madjid aussi lève la tête et comprend l'affolement de sa mère. Josette est sur le balcon, les mains sur la rampe, elle regarde droit devant elle. Malika franchit la petite barrière qui entoure la pelouse, se pointe sous le balcon, et appelle Josette, les bras au ciel.

Madjid escalade quatre à quatre l'escalier de service et arrive essoufflé devant la porte. Fermée.

Malika hurle, brandit les bras vers le balcon, et appelle Chousette à la raison.

Insensible au froid, à la neige, à l'appel de sa voisine, Josette, comme hypnotisée, le regard perdu à l'horizon, ne bouge plus.

Les flocons aveuglent Malika qui avance, recule, appelle, supplie Josette d'ouvrir à Madjid. Quelques voisins, alertés par ses plaintes, ouvrent leur fenêtre et cherchent à qui elle parle.

Les sapins de Noël enguirlandés, couverts de petites bougies électriques qui clignotent à travers les vitres des salons, Josette ne les voit pas. Du noir, le trou noir, le tunnel interminable d'où l'on croit qu'on ne sortira jamais. Elle est dedans et elle s'est fait larguer par la lanterne rouge. Ils l'ont tous laissée là, les mains agrippées à une rampe de balcon. Ses larmes font fondre les flocons qui lui caressent le visage, sa bouche s'ouvre et grimace de désespoir.

Malika hurle, épuisée, marquant la couche de

162

neige de ses pas. Elle ne sait plus que dire, plus où se mettre. Un voisin crie :

— Faut appeler les flics !

Madjid redescend aussi vite qu'il est monté, sans avoir pu enfoncer la porte. Si seulement Jean-Marc était dans le coin, avec son passe, il réussirait peut-être à forcer la lourde.

Revenu avec sa mère, Madjid voit la môme Josette passer une jambe par-dessus la rampe, l'épaule basse, et des bras qui n'ont plus envie de tenir quoi que ce soit. On voit bien qu'elle n'a plus les bras à ça, ni le cœur.

Madjid fonce vers une cabine téléphonique au milieu de la cité, tandis que Malika cause, cause toujours, implore, puis pousse un cri terrible quand Josette enjambe la balustrade.

— Ya ! Chousette, fi pas ça, Chousette, et li Stiphane y va pleurer, y va chercher la maman partout...

La maman se plie sur la rampe, son visage repose à même la rampe, elle doit rien entendre.

La cabine est dévastée, il n'y a plus de combiné, Madjid court vers une autre.

— Je ti li trouve di travail, moi, Chousette, je ti li trouve... à la cantine di l'icole... serveuse, ti seras !... Ya ! Chousette ya Allah a Rabbi...

Malika est à genoux dans la neige. Les voisins se concertent, désarmés.

Les flics, les pompiers, faut téléphoner : personne ne bouge, sauf le gardien de la tour qui arrive en remontant son froc. Il lève la tête, reconnaît Josette et lance aux curieux en soufflant entre ses mains :

— Ah! c'est la môme qui n'a pas payé son loyer depuis deux mois.

Madjid trouve une nouvelle cabine, mais complètement vide, celle-là. Les loubards ont emporté toute la machine pour la désosser tranquillement dans une cave et tirer la monnaie.

Madjid fonce chez lui à toute vitesse, se fichant bien de prendre une gamelle sur la neige.

Malika prie Allah en suppliant la môme Josette de ne pas se jeter...

— Ci une bien place... Chousette... ti tranquille à la cantine, travail pour toujours... et ti seras content, ya Chousette.... si ti pli... Demain Chousette... ji dimande l'embauche pour toi... ci une place propre, i bien piyi... demain!

Elle prie, Malika, sous son manteau devenu blanc, et ses mains tremblantes montent au ciel, et supplient.

Madjid repart de chez lui. Il a pris Stéphane par la taille, il le colle contre sa poitrine. Il repart comme il est venu, à toute vitesse. Le môme tient dans ses mains un jouet, l'éléphant Babar.

Il n'a même pas vu, Madjid, que sur l'écran le french cancan battait son plein, que les guibolles de ces dames volaient haut et en rythme. Il n'a pas entendu les applaudissements des fêtards en nœud pap. Paris c'est une blonde, qu'elles chantaient, les filles. Il n'a pas entendu, il court, Stéphane dans ses bras, sous la neige. Le môme protège son Babar des flocons.

Malika est toujours agenouillée dans la neige, Josette toujours prête à se jeter dans le vide, toute une moitié de son corps à l'extérieur du balcon.

Madjid pose Stéphane à terre et lui montre sa mère. Le môme lève la tête, écarquille les yeux, s'avance pour se faire bien entendre et crie :

— Maman... maman... t'as vu ce qu'il m'a donné Mehdi... Babar... le petit éléphant !

Josette a bougé la tête. Peut-être voit-elle son fils.

— Maman, t'as vu ?... répète Stéphane en brandissant le jouet vers Josette.

— Ci li pitit... crie Malika en direction du balcon. Ton piti...

Josette se laisse glisser doucement de la rampe et retombe sur le balcon. Malika se lève, prend sa tête dans ses mains et de nouveau fond en larmes.

— Allah akbar ! dit-elle.

Et se laisse guider par son fils pour quitter la pelouse blanche.

Madjid se retourne une dernière fois sur Josette, couchée sur le balcon. On n'aperçoit que le genou de sa jambe pliée, sous les flocons qui continuent de tomber. Les rideaux flottent.

Les flics arrivent au bout de l'allée. Malika, Madjid et Stéphane franchissent la petite barrière qui entoure le bâtiment et se dirigent vers le hall d'entrée.

Le concierge discute avec les flics en montrant le balcon où Josette est restée allongée. Malika prend Stéphane dans ses bras et l'emmène à sa mère. Madjid s'allume une gitane, qu'il tient difficilement entre ses doigts gourds. Sa mère pleure, elle marche doucement comme une

165

errante dans la nuit, serrant fortement le petit blond contre elle.

Madjid s'en va vers son bâtiment. Par une fenêtre entrouverte au rez-de-chaussée, il entend la télévision. Une voix chante : « BONNE ANNÉE, BONNE CHANCE. »

C'était une vraie fabrique installée au premier étage d'un vieil immeuble de Courbevoie. Le chef, un petit gros d'une quarantaine d'années, leur donna à chacun une blouse grise et leur expliqua le travail. A l'aide d'un appareil à souder, coller et braser toutes sortes de fils et pièces électriques sur un circuit imprimé, le tout branché sur le parleur du futur tourne-disque. Après, il fallait essayer avec un disque de Claude François. S'il n'y avait pas de son, tout était à recommencer. Ils avaient dix appareils à finir avant midi. On ne les mit pas à un même établi, pour ne pas qu'ils se parlent.

James, du fond de l'atelier, les encourageait. Pat alluma une cigarette et commença son travail, très détendu. Il avait envie de rire. Il se retenait de ne pas pouffer. Il prit l'appareil à souder et le mit en route.

Madjid, au contraire, était très concentré, ne perdait pas une seconde. Il voulait le réussir, son essai. Le salaire n'était pas des plus allé-

167

chants, mais c'était toujours ça de pris, qu'il avait dit à Pat.

Les autres, tous des jeunes, des adolescents pour la plupart, abattaient la besogne comme des dératés. Comme des machines. A la pièce. Pas le temps de se parler, fallait produire. Quand ils allumaient une cigarette, ils tiraient dessus une fois, puis la reposaient sur le bord de l'établi, où elle se consumait toute seule. Ils n'avaient pas le temps d'une seconde bouffée, sinon ils perdaient la cadence.

Pat, visiblement, n'y arrivait pas. Il s'en fichait pas mal. Il observa Madjid, qui avait trouvé le rythme. Il carburait comme un ancien de la taule.

Le chef, qui ne cessait de tourner autour des gars pour les surveiller ou les ravitailler en pièces détachées, se pencha sur Pat, pour bien lui expliquer. Dès qu'il eut le dos tourné, Pat se remit à mater les filles qui travaillaient dans le bureau d'en face. Elles lui souriaient, lui faisaient de petits gestes de la main, mais vite : la peur, elles aussi, de se faire surprendre par le chef.

A dix heures, Madjid finissait son quatrième appareil. Il regarda Pat, désolé de le voir si mal parti.

Pat finit quand même son premier appareil. Il se leva de son tabouret et brancha le tourne-disque à une prise installée sur le bord de l'établi. Il tourna le bouton « marche » et fit pivoter le bras. Rien !

— Sais pas ce qui va pas, dit Pat.

Le chef débrancha l'appareil, l'examina, voulut expliquer quelque chose, mais Pat, écœuré, lui dit tranquillement :

— Je m'en fous.

— Ah bon ! dit le chef. Ben, vous rentrez chez vous, mon vieux !

Pat regarda sa montre.

— Ça fait quand même deux heures que je suis là. Faudrait me les payer !

— Allez au bureau, j'arrive, dit le chef.

Madjid arrêta le boulot quand Pat passa devant lui, direction le bureau. Congédié !

Madjid regarda autour de lui. Ces boîtes de carton superposées par centaines, tout autour de l'atelier, qui cachaient la lumière du jour, et ces jeunes bossant sans lever la tête, sans se parler, aucune communication, et ces chansons qu'on entendait, toujours les mêmes à chaque tourne-disque essayé, ça faisait beaucoup ! Il sortit son paquet de clopes et en alluma une.

Dans le bureau du rez-de-chaussée, le chef dit à la secrétaire, assise derrière sa machine :

— Donnez trente francs à ce monsieur, s'il vous plaît.

La secrétaire s'exécuta. Pat prit les trois pièces de dix balles et sortit sans saluer. Dehors, un discret petit soleil montrait le bout de son nez. Pat se dirigea vers la gare de Courbevoie, les mains dans les poches.

Au bout, alors qu'il allait virer à droite, il entendit siffler. Il se retourna et vit Madjid, qui arrivait en courant. Pat hocha la tête.

— Il t'a jeté aussi ?

— Si tu veux, dit Madjid.

— Viens pas me dire que c'est parce que tu veux pas me laisser tomber que tu t'es cassé !

— J'ai pas dit ça, dit Madjid.

— T'es con, tiens !

Madjid s'arrête, fixe son pote méchamment :

— Ah bon ! C'est moi qui suis con ! Alors que, toi, tu ne sais même pas souder trois fils sur un tourne-disque ?

— De quoi ? Qu'est-ce que tu chantes, grand con ? Écoute bien : ça m'intéresse pas, voilà tout !

— C'est quoi le boulot qui intéresserait Môssieu ?

— Ta gueule... Merde..., cria Pat.

— Okay... fini !

Mais ils ne se parlaient plus. Ils se faisaient la tête.

Ils marchèrent longtemps, passant Courbevoie. Ils traversèrent Colombes. Il faisait un petit soleil printanier qui donnait envie de flâner sur la neige fondante. Ils allaient droit vers le pont d'Argenteuil, et ils ne savaient pas où après. Pat s'arrêta dans une pâtisserie pour des croissants. Puis ils passèrent devant un tennis couvert. Des joueurs, des joueuses, s'affrontaient sur plusieurs courts. Ils entrèrent, bien plus intéressés par les joueuses en mini-jupes blanches que par le jeu.

170

— Des riches, ça! estima Pat.

— Il paraît qu'y a que les riches qui font du tennis. Puis ils mangent pas! L'est déjà midi et ils arrivent encore, ces cons-là, t'as vu?

— Ça fait grossir de bouffer. Faut garder la ligne, pour épater les copines...

— Si les Biafrais savaient ça!

— On devrait le leur écrire, aux mecs qui crèvent de faim, pour qu'y rigolent un peu!

— Y boufferaient la lettre, ces cons-là... De rage.

— T'as vu le cul qu'elle a, l'autre, celle qui vient de louper son smatch?

— Je lui ferais bien sa fête, moi, la vache!

— Et puis y savent même pas jouer!

— C'est pour la frime!

Deux autres couples en tenue, raquettes en main, sortirent d'un vestiaire.

Pat, qui les regardait, réfléchit.

— Si on faisait les vestiaires? suggéra-t-il. Hein?

— Y courent vite, dit Madjid, c'est des sportifs. Pas intérêt à se faire gauler!

— T'occupe... tu vas voir. Doit y en avoir du pognon dans ces vestiaires. Allez, viens!

Discrètement, ils longèrent les haies entourant le gymnase. Quand ils arrivèrent derrière le bâtiment, ils virent, entre la haie et les vestiaires, un petit passage qu'ils empruntèrent. Chaque vestiaire avait sa fenêtre, suffisait de trouver celui où il y avait le plus de vestes accrochées. Ils se mirent d'accord sur un, mais, manque de chance, la fenêtre était verrouillée. Alors Pat ramassa une pierre grosse comme le poing et cassa un carreau. Après le choc, ils attendirent un moment, voir si personne n'avait entendu, mais non, il ne semblait pas. Pat ouvrit en passant sa main à l'intérieur.

— Vas-y, dit-il.

Madjid grimpa sur la rampe, sauta dans le vestiaire et prit soin de mettre une chaise en biais contre la porte pour bloquer l'entrée. Pat sauta à son tour. Ils fouillèrent toutes les poches sans exception.

Ils prirent même le temps de remettre à leur place portefeuilles et porte-monnaie vidés de leurs billets de banque et des grosses pièces. Ils ressortirent comme ils étaient venus.

Avant d'arriver à la grande porte, Pat fit signe à Madjid de stopper. Le gardien des courts traversait l'allée centrale en poussant une brouette. Ils patientèrent jusqu'à ce que l'homme entre dans une petite cabane. Alors ils sortirent, tranquilles, les mains dans les poches.

Dehors, Pat se retourna. Personne derrière, et, hop, ils piquèrent un sprint en remontant vers la gare de Colombes. Ils riaient comme des fous. Ils ne cessèrent de courir qu'arrivés sous le long pont du chemin de fer, entre la gare du Stade et la gare de Colombes.

Pat frappait des deux mains sur ses poches en criant : « Là, il y a le paquet ! »

Essoufflés, ils trouvaient quand même la force de rire. « Eh ! Paris ! tiens-toi bien, v'la les banlieusards ! » criait Madjid.

172

Naturellement, pour claquer le fric, ils montèrent à Paris. Toujours dans le même rade, ils descendirent se manger des merguez-frites au comptoir, avec de la bière, encore de la bière.

L'estomac bien calé, ils allèrent rue Saint-Denis se rincer l'œil sur les putes à moitié nues.

A l'entrée d'un hôtel, il y en avait deux, grandes, toutes colorées, ne portant que le slip sous le manteau de fourrure ouvert. Ils s'y attardèrent, l'eau à la bouche. Une troisième fille était assise derrière, sur les marches de l'hôtel, les jambes écartées. Pat remarqua :

— Dur, dis donc, elle a pas de culotte !

Madjid se pencha pour voir :

— Je vois que dalle !

— C'est pas des cageots !

— Les glandes !

— Mate l'autre là-bas, dit Pat. La négresse sur l'autre trottoir.

— Putain de moine !

— Cette bouche qu'elle a !

— Faut une trique pour la bouger !

— Des grosses lèvres comme ça, s'extasia Pat, qui te font turlutte, tu t'arraches !

— J'ai le baigneur qui veut piquer une tête.

— Ben, va le tremper !

— Je suis pas cap, avoua Madjid.

— T'en as rien à glander des gens ! Tiens, celle d'en face, tu parles d'une cheminée. Oh, ma mère !

— Ça craint.

— Tu m'étonnes !

Ils s'arrêtent devant un bistro.

— Alors, t'y vas ou pas ? demande Pat.

— Je sais pas laquelle.

Pat fit un tour d'horizon.

— Vise celle-là, là-bas. La toute seule avec le chapeau vert.

Seule, en effet, à l'entrée d'un petit hôtel, à une cinquantaine de mètres. On la voyait mal. Elle portait un short noir moulant sous blouson de jean, des bottes à talons hauts.

— Elle a pas l'air dégueu, dit Pat.

— Ouais. Puis y'a pas de mateurs, observa Madjid, pour se donner du courage.

— Vas-y donc, je t'attends au rade.

Madjid traversa la rue, se retourna pour voir s'il y avait du monde. C'était l'après-midi, il y a moins de mateurs que le soir. Mais dans ces moments-là on voudrait être tout seul, bien caché.

Il s'approcha de la pute, toujours presque honteux, mais poussé par l'envie. Elle ne le vit pas arriver. D'ailleurs d'elle on ne voyait que ses grandes jambes qui dépassaient de la porte, et sa main qui se levait quand elle portait sa cigarette à sa bouche. Madjid l'aborda brusquement en avançant d'un pas à l'intérieur du couloir. Puis là, comble de connerie, il s'envoya un super « merde » dans la tête. Il se gratta le crâne et recula d'un pas, les yeux grands ouverts. Tu parles d'une surprise !

La fille c'était Chantal, la sœur de Pat. Bouche bée, elle était devenue toute pâle, ne disait rien. Et lui, encore plus embêté, tout ce qu'il put articuler dans l'étonnement fut :

— M'excuse !

174

Il recula encore un peu, ajoutant :

— Je fais que des conneries !

Chantal au milieu du couloir écrasa sa cigarette par terre, et fit un signe de la main comme
pour lui dire : ne pars pas. Enfin, elle ouvrit la
bouche, mais aucun son ne sortit. Elle hocha la
tête, nettement désemparée.

— Tu... tu ne dis rien... hein ? A personne...

Elle le suppliait. Il recula en disant :

— Non, non, t'en fais pas. Je te le jure.

Elle s'avança vers lui, en continuant de le
prier :

— Tu ne m'as pas vue, hein, Madjid ?

Il la repoussa dans le couloir.

— Sors pas, ton frangin est dehors qui m'attend.

Sa peur redoubla, à Chantal. Elle devint toute
rouge, couvrit même son visage de ses deux
mains.

— Il m'a vue ?

— Non, non, assura Madjid. Et je lui en cause-
rai pas.

Il allait s'en aller quand elle le rappela en
fouillant dans son sac.

— Non, trancha-t-il. Je veux rien.

— Si !

Il était déjà parti. Quel coup sur la tête il venait
de prendre ! Son baigneur ne voulait plus du tout
piquer une tête. Il allait sans se retourner au
bistro où l'attendait Pat.

Pat était au flipper. Il laissa passer la boule,
surpris de voir Madjid si tôt de retour.

— Dis donc, fit-il, on va t'appeler Lucky Luke,

175

ah! ah! Celui qui décharge plus vite que son ombre! Ah, ah! Ben, mon salaud!

Madjid commanda une bière pour ne pas répondre tout de suite.

— Alors?

— J'y suis pas allé, dit Madjid.

— Hein?... Because?...

— J'ai pas osé!

— Ah! ah! t'as encore les chiottes au bout du comptoir à gauche. Ah! ah! comment veux-tu oser : t'as pas de couilles au cul. Ah ah ah!

Ça ne le faisait pas du tout rire, Madjid. Il but une gorgée pour se remettre de ses émotions.

En fin d'après-midi, ils remontèrent sur Belleville se ravitailler en dope. Depuis quelque temps, le commerce se passait dans un parking souterrain. Le dealer arriva sur le coup de six heures, le même avec lequel ils avaient eu affaire la dernière fois, un petit trapu, fringué tout en cuir, barbe et lunettes noires. Ils lui achetèrent deux barrettes, du libanais.

Pat prit soin de vérifier la came, selon la coutume.

Le dealer ne parlait jamais, sauf quand le prix du gramme avait augmenté. Alors il annonçait le nouveau prix. Parfois, il leur donnait un autre lieu de rendez-vous. Chacun prit sa barrette et ils quittèrent le dealer.

La nuit tombait quand ils revinrent dans la cité.

— On va chez Maggy ? demanda Pat.

— Non, je vais rentrer le père, dit Madjid.

Et Pat l'accompagna.

Dans la rue des Compagnons, Madjid s'arrêta pour pisser contre un mur. Avec toute la bière qu'il s'était envoyée l'après-midi, il urinait toutes les demi-heures. Pat en fit autant. Ils étaient tous les deux face au mur, quand une B.M.W. déboucha du coin de la rue à toute allure. Ils se retournèrent. La voiture passa derrière eux, puis freina vingt mètres plus loin. Pat referma sa braguette. La bagnole fit marche arrière jusqu'à eux. Bengston poussa son rire aigu. Assise sur le siège arrière, Anita les invita à monter.

Pat répondit en blaguant et pour se fiche de Madjid :

— On peut pas, il va chercher son père.

Rire collectif dans la voiture.

Madjid, à moitié ivre, rétorqua :

— Ben quoi ! J'ai le droit !

Jean-Marc, qui était au volant, klaxonna. Thierry pointa sa tête de fouine :

— Montez, quoi, on n'a pas que ça à foutre.

— Et puis, merde ! fit Madjid.

C'est comme ça, par dépit, qu'il monta dans cette B.M.W. Pat suivit, évidemment. Le démarrage fit crisser les pneus. Ils empruntèrent l'autoroute de Nanterre à fond la caisse. Pat sortit sa barrette de dope et demanda à Anita de rouler un joint. A la vue de la barrette, Bengston fit un « youpi » de joie, Thierry applaudit.

— Où c'est que tu as eu ça ? demanda Jean-Marc.

— Je te demande, moi, où tu l'as eue, ta tire ?

— C'est à son papa, dit Bengston. Il nous la prête pour la roder.

Et de rire, tous ! Puis Thierry dit :

— Eh, les mecs, j'ai une idée !

— Ouais, ben tu la gardes, ta lampe, dit Anita. La dernière fois que tu nous a branchés, on s'est retrouvés chez les flics !

Thierry répondit que c'était pas une connerie, ce coup-ci.

— Explique toujours, dit Bengston.

— Ce serait d'aller voir la mer.

Les autres se regardèrent, puis Jean-Marc :

— Pourquoi pas !

Anita objecta qu'elle n'avait pas son maillot de bain.

— A poil ! cria Pat. Ah ! ah ! non, mais franchement !

Jean-Marc se retourna vers Madjid :

— T'es d'accord... On va à Deauville ?

— Fous la zizique à fond et ferme ta gueule !
dit Madjid.

— Te fâche pas, je disais ça comme ça. Vu
qu'ils veulent voir la mer, et comme toi tu
préfères voir ton père, je voudrais savoir.

Nouveaux grands rires. Alors Pat frappa sur
l'épaule de Jean-Marc :

— Pousse la soupape !

Anita alluma le joint et le passa à Bengston qui
le réclamait. Madjid ferma les yeux et se laissa
emporter par le sommeil. La voiture à fond sur
l'autoroute doublait tout le monde. Jean-Marc
jouissait :

— Tous derrière ces cons, et pépère devant !
Ah ! ah !

— Et demain matin on va se draguer les
bourgeoises de Deauville ! dit Pat. Ah ! Ah !

— Les vieilles ? demanda Bengston.

— Ouais, les vieilles pleines de kefri !

— Et fifty fifty, hein ?

— Tu peux pas, toi !

— Because ?

— Elles aiment pas les keblas, les bourgeoises !
lui assena Pat.

— Pourquoi ? fit Bengston en se redressant.

Pat, avant de tirer sur le joint :

— Pour baiser, peut-être qu'elles aiment bien
les renoi, mais pas pour sortir !

— Qu'est-ce que t'en sais ? demanda Thierry.

— En été, avec Madjid, dit Pat, on va descendre sur la Côte. Le festival qu'on va se faire !

Il cracha la fumée du joint et expliqua sa
pensée :

— C'est pas compliqué, tu te fous à une ter-
rasse de café, là où qu'elles viennent boire leur
thé. T'en z'yeutes une qu'est pas trop mère Denis,
hein ? Elle te remarque. Paf ! tu y fais un sourire
bébé Cadum, elle mouille sa culotte. Son mari, à
côté d'elle, y te voit, y dit rien. Y s'en fout, c'est
un pèd. C'est tous des pèds, les bourgeois, y vont
se faire casser chez Mme Arthur. Leurs bonnes
femmes, elles s'emmerdent. Tu restes à la ter-
rasse. Tu vois. Tu la mates encore. Elle aussi,
hein. Puis après, qu'est-ce qu'elle fait ? Elle se
lève pour aller aux chiottes, elle prend son petit
sac et tout, puis, quand elle est aux gogs, elle
attrape un bout de papier, elle marque son
numéro de téléphone, puis elle revient. Elle dit à
son mari « on y va ». Paf ! il se lève. Elle le laisse
passer devant, et le suit. Quand elle est à côté de
la table où t'es, elle pose discrètement le papier
avec le numéro. Après ça, le soir, t'as plus qu'à
l'appeler. Elle t'invite dans sa villa planquée sur
une colline derrière une grande grille avec des
arbres tout autour. T'appuies sur un bouton sur
le mur à côté de la lourde, puis t'entends une voix
érotique qui te dit : « Je t'ouvre mon amour. » Tu
bandes déjà ! Tu traverses le jardin, après tu
montes l'escalier. Elle t'ouvre la porte. La salope,
elle a une robe de chambre blanche, blanche
transparente. Elle te conduit jusqu'au fauteuil en
te prenant par la main. Mine de rien, tu mates ses
fesses toutes blanches, parce que quand elle
bronze, elle garde son slip. Tu t'assois dans le
fauteuil, elle te débarrasse de ta veste. Puis elle te
dit : « Whisky ? Champagne ? » Elle remplit ton

verre. Elle lève le sien en te fixant avec ses yeux vicieux : « Santé, santé. » Elle repose son verre et elle te présente la boîte à cigares, et t'en prends un, elle te l'allume. Tu tires une bouffée et tu te laisses retomber dans le fauteuil. Tu fermes les yeux et tu sens ses doigts qui t'ouvrent ta braguette, et c'est parti mon kiki !

» T'y fais sa fête. Pas comme les bourgeois, avec des pincettes. Non, comme un prolo, tu la crèves jusqu'à ce qu'elle tombe. Comme ça elle te rappelle. Après elle te file une liasse de biftons, qu'elle te met dans la poche. Après, tu reviens la voir souvent, elle te présente sa fille, sa mère, sa sœur, tu t'en fous, pas de quartier, pas de chichis, tu te les envoies toutes. Pendant que le mari, y fait le zouave sur son yacht.

Jean-Marc dit :

— Avec tes histoires à la con, du coup t'as fait dormir Madjid !

— Lui, il peut dormir, dit Pat, je lui ai déjà raconté.

— T'as déjà sauté une bourgeoise ? questionne Thierry.

— Non, mais ça va venir. Je te dis qu'on va descendre sur la Côte avec Madjid, cette année.

— Je serai jamais riche, moi, soupire Anita, si tous les bourgeois c'est des pèds.

— T'as pas le pot, c'est tout, dit Pat. Y peuvent pas et courir les gonzesses et compter leur pognon. Pas possible !

Ils arrivèrent au bord de la mer en pleine nuit. Un vent léger soufflait sur la plage. Ils laissèrent la voiture sur la route et coururent vers l'eau en chahutant. Madjid était à la traîne, il les rejoignit au bord de l'eau en marchant. Il avait pas le moral. Ils se poussaient les uns les autres vers les petites vagues qui arrivaient.

— On se baigne ? proposa Pat.

— Trop froide ! dit Thierry.

— Je vais à la voiture, j'ai froid ! dit Anita.

Jean-Marc la suivit.

Pat respira un bon coup, poitrine gonflée. Il sourit à Madjid et dit :

— Ça dessoûle, hein ?

Madjid fixait l'horizon sombre, cheveux au vent, mains dans les poches. Il était mal à l'aise, comme quand on s'ennuie.

Ils revinrent tous dans la voiture.

— Hein qu'on est mieux au chaud ? ronronna Anita.

— Tu m'étonnes ! dit Bengston.

Quand Madjid monta dans la voiture, Pat vit bien qu'il n'était pas dans son assiette.

— Qu'est-ce que t'as, le père ? demanda-t-il.

— Rien, ça va, dit Madjid en se forçant.

— Madone ! T'as une de ces tronches !

La voiture repartit sur un chemin rocailleux, les phares déchirant l'obscurité de la campagne endormie.

La fatigue les gagnait peu à peu. Sauf Pat et Jean-Marc. Heureusement, c'est Jean-Marc qui conduisait. Anita bâilla.

— Holà ! ça roupille là-dedans ? gueula Pat en regardant autour de lui.

Il tapa sur l'épaule de Thierry.

— Mais non, je dors pas, dit Thierry. La preuve, regarde : on va croiser une bagnole, je vois de la lumière qui bouge. Là, tiens, après le virage. Fais gaffe Jean-Marc !

La B.M.W. roulait doucement, la visibilité n'étant pas bonne. Madjid dormait à moitié, il n'écoutait plus, il ne bougeait plus, il voulait dormir. Rien que ça, dormir !

— Merde, les gendarmes !

Jean-Marc les avait vus le premier. Les autres se redressèrent. Une Estafette de la gendarmerie se pointait en face, bien reconnaissable à son avertisseur lumineux bleu.

— Continue, t'arrête pas, ordonna Pat. Fais mine de rien. S'ils bloquent la route, sauve qui peut !

Il réveilla Madjid et lui montra ce qui arrivait devant eux. Madjid leva la tête, fixa l'Estafette qui brusquement s'arrêta en plein milieu de la chaussée, et il vit un gendarme descendre.

Jean-Marc freina et cria :

— On s'arrache !

Ils se ruèrent hors de la voiture et s'enfuirent à travers champs. Avant de partir, Pat avait hurlé à Madjid qui visiblement ne voulait pas quitter son siège : « Dépêche-toi, putain ! »

Madjid ne bougeait pas. Il regardait droit

devant lui, les yeux mi-clos, las, dégoûté, fatigué.

Alors, Pat partit en courant derrière les autres. Un gendarme prit les fuyards en chasse, mais n'insista pas trop longtemps. Il revint essoufflé.

Le brigadier se pencha à l'intérieur de la B.M.W. Il observa longuement Madjid et lui dit de sortir. Madjid obéit sans un mot. La tête baissée, il prit place dans l'Estafette.

— Avec celui-là, on aura la bande, dit le brigadier en regardant du côté où Pat et les autres avaient fui.

L'Estafette démarra, suivie de la B.M.W. conduite par un gendarme.

Le brigadier-chef se retourna vers Madjid qui portait maintenant des menottes, et ils avaient fixé ces menottes à la barre du siège.

— Toi et tes copains, vous venez d'où ?

Madjid ne répondit pas. Il laissa sa tête basculer derrière lui, et il ferma les yeux.

Le brigadier n'insista pas.

L'Estafette roula jusqu'à un carrefour éclairé, bien qu'en rase campagne.

A ce carrefour, ils virent Pat assis sur une borne. Il se leva quand le clignotant bleu eut commencé de le balayer. Il tirait sur une cigarette. Il fit signe à l'Estafette de s'arrêter, comme on le fait à un autobus.

— Qui c'est, celui-là ? dit le brigadier.

Pat écrasa sa cigarette sur le gravier et monta dans l'Estafette.

— J'étais avec lui, dit-il en montrant Madjid.
Il s'assit en face de son ami. Madjid dormait. Pat le regardait. L'Estafette roulait dans la nuit.

Impression Novoprint
á Barcelone, le 2 mars 2007
Dépôt légal: mars 2007
Premier dépôt légal dans la collection: mai 1988

ISBN 978-2-07-038041-1./Imprimé en Espagne.